CATASTROPHIC FAILURE

Catastrophic Failure

*Blindfolding America
In the Face of Jihad*

Stephen Coughlin

Center for Security Policy Press
Washington, D.C.

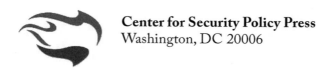

Center for Security Policy Press
Washington, DC 20006

CATASTROPHIC FAILURE
Copyright © 2015 by Stephen Coughlin

Cover design by David Reaboi

Coughlin, Stephen
  Catastrophic Failure

ISBN-13: 978-1511617505

Library of Congress Control Number: 2015905620
CreateSpace Independent Publishing Platform
North Charleston, SC

May 2015

CONTENTS

Acknowledgments. 9

Introduction 11

PART I: The One Organizing Principle. 25

PART II: The Red Pill 65

PART III: The Islamic Movement and its Awakening. 149

PART IV: Organization of the Islamic Caliphate 219

PART V: Days of Rage. 263

PART VI: Blasphemy and Deterrent Punishment
          in America. 301

PART VII: Catastrophic Failures 335

PART VIII: Our Ignorance 443

PART IX: The Duty to Know 485

PART X: Conclusion 507

PART XI: Appendix One. 511

PART XII: Appendix Two 575

About the Author 599

Notes. 601

Index 747

Acknowledgments

By 2009, the "Red Pill" briefings I had been giving for some time had gained a degree of notoriety. Christine Brim, Vice President of the Center for Security Policy (CSP), approached me and asked if I'd be interested in transforming my briefings to book form. I did not have to ponder the question for long. We got started soon thereafter, with CSP recording my briefings, transcribing them, and then embedding the proper source citations. That thankless job went to Ned May. Then Clare Lopez took the lead in preparing an early draft. Around that time, the War on Terror was beginning to take new turns, and my briefings evolved to account for the rapidly unfolding events. Our nation's response (or lack thereof) to the terror threat also opened up new lines of analysis that were added to my briefings. As a result, the initial draft of the book was quickly rendered OBE – overcome by events. But by the summer of 2014, thanks to the editorial assistance of Marilyn Stern, the project was back in full swing.

While the manuscript faithfully reflected the material as I briefed it in my various presentations, it became clear that if published in that form, there would be substantial overlap, as individual briefings often keyed off points common to all of them. David Reaboi and Kyle Shideler recommended a more systematic approach, then undertook the painstaking effort of bringing this about. (Thanks also to David Reaboi for the book's cover design.) There is also Lauren Wilson, who patiently undertook the task of reviewing and editing the new manuscript so informed readers could hope to get their hands around it. Thanks also to Adam Savit, CSP's ace production coordinator, whose assistance with the final review and preparation for publication is greatly appreciated. With the final review – and there has been considerable effort in keeping it up-to-date – the book is once again ready to go.

In a continuous effort to stay true to what was originally briefed while also remaining current to today's events, it often happened that close friends and associates would send me articles that made this effort much easier than it could have been. Patrick Poole stands out in this regard for his ongoing prescient ability to drop a data point in my inbox at the very time I was covering that issue.

Special thanks also to Connie Hair, whose support in dark times has always shown the light ahead.

Finally, I would like to thank Frank Gaffney, president of CSP, for his patience and sponsorship in getting this book out. Thanks also to the staff and interns at CSP for their back-room support.

Stephen Coughlin
May 2015

Introduction

What constitutes the bulwark of our own liberty and independence? It is not our frowning battlements, our bristling sea coasts, our army and our navy. These are not our reliance against tyranny. All of those may be turned against us without making us weaker for the struggle. Our reliance is in the love of liberty which God has planted in our bosoms. Our defense is in the spirit which prizes liberty as the heritage of all men, in all lands everywhere. Destroy this spirit and you have planted the seeds of despotism at your own doors. Familiarize yourselves with the chains of bondage and you prepare your own limbs to wear them. Accustomed to trample on the rights of others, you have lost the genius of your own independence and become the fit subjects of the first cunning tyrant who rises among you.

Abraham Lincoln
Speech at Edwardsville, Illinois
September 13, 1858

Why Me?

I did not set out in life to be a student of jihad and Islamic-based terrorism. In the fall of 2001, I was a reserve officer in the United States Army, called to active duty from the private sector due to the events of September 11. My posting was to the Joint Chiefs of Staff Intelligence Directorate (JS-J2). As I watched America respond to events across the world, I noticed with alarm that decision-making seemed to be increasingly less focused on the threat as it presented itself and more on the narratives that reduced the threat to a nameless abstraction.

As a mobilized officer brought into the heart of the strategic intelligence world, I knew there would be a large learning curve involved in formulating the threat doctrine of an enemy that had brought down the Twin Towers in the name of Islam and according to Islamic law.

I made a point of going to the source. I found actual books of Islamic law. I read them and found they could be mapped, with repeatable precision, to the stated doctrines and information that groups like al-Qaeda and the Muslim Brotherhood disclosed about themselves and used when speaking to each other. My analysis helped me develop a threat doctrine, an understanding of the enemy as he understands himself unconstrained by the influences of the environment – Sun Tzu's "Know your enemy." That threat analysis was in line with all the standard doctrines on threat development I had been taught when I learned to do intelligence analysis. Because the declared enemy stated that his fighting doctrine was based on the Islamic law of jihad, Islamic law had to be incorporated into any competent threat analysis. When assessing al-Qaeda in light of the jihad doctrines that the group's members actually cite, I came to realize that such doctrines did exist, they are generally cited properly, and that al-Qaeda made plausible claims to be actually following those doctrines. In legal parlance, al-Qaeda's claims to be operating in accordance with mainstream Islamic law could at least survive summary judgment. By the same token, any analysis of al-Qaeda that failed to account for such a self-disclosed component of an identified threat doctrine could not be competent. I assumed everyone with whom I worked in the intelligence directorate was aware of the most basic aspects of intelligence, such as threat identification.

I was wrong. I had entered the Intelligence Directorate adhering to the traditional methods of analysis. Soon, however, I discovered that within the division there seemed to be a preference for political correctness over accuracy and for models that were generated not by what the enemy said he was, but on what academics and "cultural advisors" said the enemy needed to be, based on contrived social science theories.

It seemed the enemy was aware of this as well. Forces hostile to the United States in the War on Terror appeared to have successfully calculated that they could win the war by convincing our national security leaders of the immorality of studying and knowing the enemy. It is not our fault that the threat we face identifies its doctrine along Islamic lines, but it is our fault that we refuse to look at that doctrine simply because our enemy wishes to blind us to its strategic design.

Some time ago, I had an opportunity to analyze the Muslim Brotherhood in North America's strategic documents, which were entered into evidence in a federal terrorism trial. In those documents, the Muslim Brotherhood explicitly states its designs for "civilization-jihad" and its intent to sabotage America by getting us to do the job for them. This doctrine of subversion could likewise be mapped to mainstream Islamic law. Individuals and organizations named in the Brotherhood's documents were shown in the government's investigative files, surveillance photos, audio recordings, and wiretaps to have been aligned with or members of the Muslim Brotherhood. But while the government was identifying many of these people and entities as providing material support to terrorism in a federal court, it was also seeking out those same people as cultural experts, "moderates," and community outreach partners.

As early as 2003, I began putting together briefings that easily outperformed competing explanations for the enemy's doctrinal motivations. My briefings have always spoken to verifiable and authoritative facts. Others, however, were based on social science modeling and depended on dubious academic constructs—which, of course, were needed to satisfy the overriding requirement that we avoid associating the war we were fighting with the very Islamic concepts that the enemy self identified as the justification and basis for their actions.

Before demobilizing from the Joint Staff in 2004, I wrote a forecast of adverse events that would occur because of our refusal to undertake evidentiary threat analysis. Eighteen months later, while standing on a Metro platform in downtown Washington, D.C., I happened to run into the senior civilian in the Joint Staff Intelligence Directorate, retired Marine Corps Colonel David Kiffer. He told me he was impressed by my briefs, particularly by how the presentations accurately frame emerging events to that day.

When asked how I could identify emerging threats with such precision, I explained that there is no crystal ball. It's just that al-Qaeda, the Taliban, the Muslim Brotherhood, and others have knowable threat doctrines. Forecasting is as simple as mapping their stated objectives to the doctrines they follow in conjunction with their known capabilities. At the core of those doctrines, of course, was Islamic law.

As a retired Marine Corps officer, the senior civilian intelligence officer understood my concern for the lack of basic analysis. He asked me to come to the Pentagon and brief the Flag and General officers on the J2 Staff. I accepted the offer but insisted that I be able to present what I believed to be the central problem in the War on Terror. He agreed, so I put a briefing together and spoke at the Pentagon around Christmastime in 2005. The briefing culminated in a slide that raised two central questions:

> Can overdependence on "moderates" to explain non-Western motivations and beliefs lead us to (overly) depend on them for the decisions we make?

> Is there a point where the outsourcing of an understanding of events leads to the outsourcing of the decision-making associated with those events?

Underlying both questions was my concern that decisions central to the warfighting effort are based solely on the inputs of experts on subjects that the decision-makers themselves do not understand. When such a practice becomes chronic, actual decision-making shifts from those responsible for making decisions to the experts they rely on for information. It is a subversion of both the decision-making and the warfighting processes.

At the Pentagon, after I had expressed my opinion on these issues directly, I was asked to join the Intelligence Directorate as a full-time consultant. Since then, while I repackaged my presentations and restated them in many ways with greater demonstrated foreseeability, the central issue has remained the same: Senior leaders remain profoundly unaware of the Islamic doctrines that frame the War on Terror. Tragically, not knowing these doctrines kills Americans and undermines our security.

By late summer 2006, the presentations I put together were in high demand at the Pentagon and throughout the law enforcement and national security communities. Word spread to the legislative branch as well, and I was soon briefing members of Congress and their staffs. The core presentation—the presentation which mirrored Nidal Hasan's—came to be called The Red Pill Brief. It earned this nickname thanks to its ability to shift the audience's understanding of the nature of the threat in the War on Terror in ways that—like the "Red Pill" given to Keanu Reeves's character in the science-fiction movie *The Matrix*—enabled them to see the enemy in the War on Terror as it really is. And it gave them an understanding that ensured they would never go back to the false "virtual reality" constructed by outside advisors and enforced by our seniors.

At the core of The Red Pill was an evolving analysis of the relationship between the Islamic legal doctrine of abrogation and a Muslim Brotherhood strategic doctrine based on a book called *Milestones* by Muslim Brother and Islamic thinker Sayyid Qutb. Those who attended these presentations left with the realization that there is no understanding Islamic terrorism and jihad without understanding the *Milestones* doctrine; similarly, there is no understanding the *Milestones* doctrine if one doesn't understand that it seamlessly merges with Islamic law through the doctrine of abrogation. To demonstrate that this concept is based on authoritative shariah and not personal opinion—and to underscore the lethal consequences of ignoring it—after the Fort Hood attack, I superimposed MAJ Hasan's slides over my own on the same point to show how closely they mirrored each other.

Gradually, the material I covered expanded to include a little-known international organization known (at that time) as the Organization of Islamic Conference, made up of all the self-defined Islamic states, including those claiming to be our coalition allies. Here was an organization that considers itself the arbiter and authority for all Muslims on matters ranging from what constitutes international human rights to defining terrorism. This organization, which was unknown to most of the senior officials I briefed, was asserting its right to claim to be the arbiter of what could or could not be said about Islam by non-Muslims in the non-Muslim world in an effort to stifle what has come to be known as "Islamophobia." Further, their declarations and programs, like those of al-Qaeda and the Muslim Brotherhood, could be understood by examination through the lens of Islamic law. What I discovered was an organization for whom "human rights" meant Islamic law, and for whom "terrorism" did not necessarily mean the jihadis we were fighting. I also discovered that when the Organization of Islamic Conference echoed Islamic legal pronouncements that called for violence against non-Muslims, typically in regard to statements about Islam, these calls to violence were answered by Days of Rage.

During my time at the Pentagon, I explained that there has been a purposeful ratcheting down of analytical standards in this war, to the point where they ceased to meet minimum standards of professionalism. From the beginning, my briefings reflected a preference for factual analysis that maps to evidentiary data; events are explained in plain terms and within the context of the picture that emerges from such analysis. I disfavored a reliance on academic and overwrought intellectual constructs that, while creating the illusion of scientific methodology, only mask what are otherwise incoherent ideations. One need only watch a competent joint staff officer have to defer to an anthropologist or "cultural expert" on mission-critical concerns to understand how this works. Scientism is the Gnosticism of our time.

The more popular my briefings became with military officers and special agents directly engaged in the War on Terror, the more senior leadership resisted them. Sensing that these briefings could at some point be banned in the national security space, the Center for Security Policy approached and asked if I would convert my briefings to book form. I agreed.

Unfortunately, my concern about a future banning has proven just as legitimate as my other forecasts. Much of the information presented in my briefings, and which is available to readers of this book, is no longer welcome in the Departments of Defense, Justice, and Homeland Security, or within the Intelligence Community. Professional analysts and trainers in counterterrorism, intelligence, and asymmetrical warfare have had their slides edited or censored, their names maligned, and, in some cases, their jobs threatened. Even elected officials, the members of Congress whom I briefed, have been aggressively criticized by the media and by their fellow legislators for discussing issues related to the Muslim Brotherhood and Islamic law.

Ignorance Kills

This book is based on briefings that have explained the current situation while forecasting future activity accurately enough to provide warning. Importantly, all of it is based on open source information. While this analysis has consistently outperformed the prevailing paradigm, national security decision-makers have nonetheless ignored, disfavored, or even prohibited it.

Ignorance kills. In war, ignorance brings defeat, especially for those who are sworn to support and defend us. While ignorance is not a crime for the average person, it *is* for professionals concerning subject matter that is the object of their professions. Why shouldn't this hold true for national security professionals? For them, one requirement is that they know the enemy by undertaking real threat identification of entities that constitute actual threats to the Constitution and people of the United States.

None of this is complicated; it is, in fact, quite simple.

The time has come to present this case to the American people. I hope to offer to the reader the same quality of information and analysis that has been presented to national security professionals and which has been studiously ignored. I will provide the necessary citations to Islamic law, both historical and contemporary, from books written in English for Muslim consumers of Islamic law (also called shariah), and will explain the key principles for interpreting these laws, particularly as they relate to non-Muslims and jihad. We will go through, in detail, the Islamic legal concept of abrogation and how it impacts the actions of Muslims who have chosen to wage jihad. We will examine the impact of Islamic scholar and Muslim Brotherhood ideologue Sayyid Qutb, and how his understanding of abrogation led to what I call "The Milestone Process," which guides the performance of jihad for our enemies in the War on Terror. We will discuss what is called the "Islamic Movement" and how the Muslim Brotherhood, Hamas, al-Qaeda, the Taliban, and other groups oriented on the Milestone Process view themselves as unified by varying degrees against us. We'll examine the Organization of the Islamic Cooperation and see how their understanding of themselves as a kind of "Proto-Caliphate" may be accurate, even though our decision-makers don't even know they exist.

With this understanding of the rules and the players achieved, we'll discuss how each of these groups works in accordance with Islamic law as they understand it, to the great detriment of those who fail to recognize the threat they pose. We'll examine the postmodern world of American national security policymaking, where fidelity to political correctness, the need for "balance," and standards that put assumptions and social science theories before facts have left us dangerously exposed.

And we will examine how our failure to understand these factors has repeatedly led to tragedy and real loss of life, leaving America vulnerable to those who wish to destroy us.

I hope to show that returning to traditional standards of threat analysis—bolstered by common-sense professional standards and grounded in the obligations we have to support and defend the Constitution—will enable us once again to know our enemies and develop methods to defeat them.

What I Learned In Egypt

When traveling in Egypt with Patrick Poole, a colleague in counterterror analysis, in the spring of 2014, we spent a good deal of time with Egyptian Muslims unaffiliated with the government. It became apparent that they shared our view that the Muslim Brotherhood is not a moderate alternative to more radical groups like al-Qaeda, but rather the gateway entity from which these "radical" groups spring and gain momentum. Far from "moderate," the Brotherhood is the most dangerous player in the War on Terror—not least because of its demonstrated ability to penetrate and subvert.

This led to probing questions about how the United States, as far back as the Bush administration (in the War on Terror), could have fallen so easily under the sway of the Brotherhood's counsel. Since America is the world's only superpower, so their thinking went, there must be some intent, some master plan, behind the administration's actions. They supported their view by reference to the active role the U.S. has played since 2010 in toppling what were, to that point, friendly Arab governments when adopting new policies that systematically favored the Brotherhood and al-Qaeda. Our Egyptian hosts provided substantive observations to support their concerns and asked us to explain America's actions.

At first, our answers were met with skepticism. Over the following weeks, however, they began to take hold. Not making any claims about average Muslims living in the United States, we nonetheless pointed out that the public face of Islam in America is framed by the Muslim Brotherhood and that, in effect, Islam in America takes the form favored by the Brotherhood. Once the Egyptians realized we were serious, it became increasingly less difficult to convince them that the Muslim Brotherhood in America dominates—whether it's about who gets to visit the White House, represents Islam in interfaith activities, or provides the Islamic perspective on evening programming.

The strength of the Brotherhood's position in America initially surprised the Egyptians, but once we were able to identify leaders, doctrines, and court documents that they were in a position to confirm, their skepticism transitioned to disbelief. "How could America be taken in by these people?" In the main, the answer is that a postmodern form of relativism has rendered America incapable of recognizing existential epistemic threats and hence made it defenseless in the face of them. A collapse of critical thinking has left America disarmed in the war of ideas. We noted that American reporting on events in Egypt often comes from reporters who are nested with Muslim Brothers. (The Egyptians were painfully aware of this last point.)

It did not take long for us to agree that, while groups like al-Qaeda or Islamic Jihad may be more violent and more immediately dangerous, groups like the Muslim Brotherhood are far more dangerous in the long term. It is the Brotherhood that manages the ocean in which fish like al-Qaeda swim. In the Arab world, it's not just the Egyptians who have become aware of this. In November 2014, the UAE Cabinet published a list of terrorist organizations that makes no distinction between groups like ISIS, al-Qaeda, Boko Haram, the Haqqani Network, Lashkar-e-Taiba, and Abu Sayyaf on one hand and the Muslim Brotherhood (including Qaradawi's Association of Muslim Scholars [IAMS or IUMS]), the Muslim American Society (MAS), and the Council on American Islamic Relations (CAIR) – America's Hamas presence[1] – on the other.

The UAE identified two affiliated entities of the American Muslim Brotherhood, but the *Explanatory Memorandum: On the General Strategic Goal for the Group*, written by Mohamed Akram in 1991, also lists other American affiliates, such as the Muslim Student Association (MSA), Islamic Society of North America (ISNA), the North American Islamic Trust (NAIT), and the International Institute of Islamic Thought (IIIT).[2] The Muslim Public Affairs Council (MPAC) is also included because prominent Muslim Brotherhood leaders formed it out of the Islamic Center of Southern California[3] and because it closely associates with Brotherhood organizations like ISNA and CAIR in public forums.[4]

Domestically and internationally, two camps exist in the War on Terror: one believes that the Muslim Brotherhood is the "moderate" alternative to "extremist" groups like al-Qaeda and that the Free Syrian Army really is an alternative to Jabhat al Nusra or ISIS. The other believes that the Brotherhood is the most dangerous of the groups because of its seductive claims of moderation. One side is surprised every time the war material and training we provide to our "moderate" friends end up in the service of "extremists," while the other side is surprised only at how often the first is surprised by what has become so predictable. America cast its lot with the "moderate" paradigm, and the Brotherhood made sure to fill that space. America has yet to recover from that decision, even as Arab states are criminalizing the Brotherhood and casting them out of their countries. Egyptian President Abdel Fattah al-Sisi is well aware of the stakes. In a speech at al-Azhar on January 1, 2015, he identifies the role of shariah in the crisis:

> It's inconceivable that the thinking that we hold most sacred should cause the entire *umma* [Islamic world] to be a source of anxiety, danger, killing and destruction for the rest of the world. Impossible! … That thinking — I am not saying "religion" but "thinking" — that corpus of texts and ideas that we have sacralized over the years, to the point that departing from them has become almost impossible, is antagonizing the entire world. It's antagonizing the entire world![5]

… recognizes the consequences of this world view:

> Is it possible that 1.6 billion people (Muslims worldwide) should want to kill the rest of the world's population — that is, 7 billion people — so that they themselves may live? Impossible.[6]

… holds the Imams responsible for the destruction they are causing to the Muslim world:

> I am saying these words here at Al Azhar, before this assembly of scholars and ulema — Allah Almighty be witness to your truth on Judgment Day concerning that which I'm talking about now. … You, imams, are responsible before Allah. The entire world, I say it again, the entire world is waiting for your next move … because this *umma* is being torn, it is being destroyed, it is being lost — and it is being lost by our own hands.[7]

… and calls for "religious revolution"[8] to change it. Correctly interpreted or not, Sisi recognizes that shariah is the heart of the issue; that jihadi-based terror is the consequence of that "sacralized corpus of texts," not the drivers of it. There are compelling reasons to think President Sisi is serious about taking on this issue at a time when the Arab Muslim world may be turning in that direction. Muslim leaders like Sisi should be our natural allies, as their emergence signals the prospect of a genuine meeting of the minds. The stakes are high. The very next day, fully decked in garments indicating his Al-Azhar pedigree, virulent anti-Semite,[9] Muslim Brother and member of Morsi's Ministry of Religious Endowment appeared[10] on *Mekameleen TV*[11] to attack the Sisi initiative, going so far as calling him an apostate and his speech kufr.[12] This would be the same Al-Azhar that, in reference to ISIS, twice declared (in December 2014 and then again in January 2015) that "no believer can be declared an apostate."[13] As the book will explain, when claims of apostasy and kufr are directed against a person, that person's right to live is being seriously challenged. Yet it seems that our national leaders have chosen to back the likes of the Brotherhood, Morsi, and Qawi.

Both friend and foe in the Arab world know who advises our senior leaders on terrorism. Mohamed Elibiary, former senior Homeland Security Advisor and member of the Department of Homeland Security's Security Council, was unconcerned by the UAE designations. Elibiary, who is also founder and president of the Freedom and Justice Foundation[14/15] and Committee Chairman[16] and Board Member[17] of the Dallas-Fort Worth chapter of CAIR, immediately condemned the designation of CAIR and MAS[18] as terrorist organizations and assured his Twitter followers, based on his inside knowledge, that the United States counterterror community would ignore the UAE action.[19] Given the current political climate, Elibiary may be right, which further proves the need to expose the threat posed by the Muslim Brotherhood.

While the threat is more apparent in countries like Egypt, the Brotherhood is a threat to America, as well. On this we agreed, complete with common reference points and a shared site picture.

MAJ Nidal Hasan

As part of his medical rounds at Walter Reed National Medical Center, Army psychiatrist MAJ Nidal Malik Hasan wanted to do his colleagues a service. Using PowerPoint slides and handouts, Hasan expounded on the concepts of murder, jihad, and justice in Islamic law, focusing especially on the doctrine of abrogation (see discussion in Part II, "The Red Pill"). In his presentation, "The Koranic Worldview as it Relates to Muslims in the US Military," which he delivered multiple times, Hasan declared his hostility to his fellow officers, announced his status as a jihadi, and stated the reasons and conditions for why he would soon commit multiple homicides.

During the course of these presentations, the scores of attendees in the military had no idea that they were listening to a self-proclaimed "soldier of Allah" announce his intention to betray both the military and the nation he had sworn to serve. Finally, on November 5, 2009, Hasan attacked the military base in Fort Hood, Texas, where he was stationed. Dressed in uniform, he killed over thirteen of his fellow servicemen and civilians and wounded thirty more after shouting, "Allahu Akbar."

Like nearly everyone else in America, I watched news of the carnage on television. It was an outrage. A few days later, I started receiving phone calls from FBI agents. *The Washington Post* had published the complete series of slides from Hasan's presentations, and it was making its way through the rest of the media. The agents had just seen the slides; their voices were full of disbelief as several of them asked me the same questions.

"Did you know Nidal Hasan? Had he attended any of your briefings? Did he see your material on abrogation?—Because his slides were almost exactly like yours; you both even used the same quotes from the Qur'an."

Of course, I had never met Hasan.

The slides on terrorism they were referring to were from briefings I had created years earlier for use in the Department of Defense, the FBI, and other government agencies. Well before Hasan's Fort Hood attack in 2009, I was giving briefings at the Pentagon on the underlying rationale that orients some Muslims to jihad, defined by some as holy war. That rationale was based on the nexus between the Islamic concept of abrogation and the Islamic legal basis for jihad, which will be discussed in depth later in the book.

Hasan had never attended any of my presentations on abrogation or jihad. Yet with uncommon specificity, my briefings mapped with the briefing given by Nidal Hasan.

How was this possible?

It was possible because neither MAJ Hasan nor I was merely giving a personal opinion on what the Qur'an says about abrogation and Islamic legal obligations to engage in jihad. I was not providing mere conjecture about what may motivate adherents; my presentations anticipated Hasan's because they were based on the same sources—a clear reading of the same Islamic law—rather than relying on sociological or other soft-science explanations. In other words, my briefings on abrogation and jihad for the Department of Defense provided actual indicators and warning of a real threat to the leaders that needed it most. Tragically, those warnings went unheeded. They still are.

Banned by the White House

In October 2011, elements of the American Muslim Brotherhood wrote the White House demanding an embargo or discontinuation of information and materials relating to Islamic-based terrorism—even insisting on firings, "re-training," and "purges"[20] of officers, analysts, special agents, and decision-makers who created or made such materials available. The letter was drafted by Farhana Khera, President and Executive Director of Muslim Advocates, and addressed to John Brennan, then Assistant to the President for Homeland Security and Counterterrorism (now Director of the CIA). Days later, Brennan responded by agreeing on the necessity for the "White House [to] immediately create an interagency task force to address the problem"[21] by removing personnel and products that the Muslim Brotherhood deemed "biased, false, and highly offensive."[22]

Brennan answered the Brotherhood's demands by referencing the Obama administration's Countering Violent Extremism (CVE) narrative: "We share your sense of concern over these recent unfortunate incidents, and are moving forward to ensure problems are addressed with a keen sense of urgency."[23]

Talks between the administration and the Brotherhood took place at high levels, with the Director of the FBI going so far as to meet with the Brotherhood in February 2012[24] against the expressed directives of Congress.[25] More alarming, however, is that the FBI then proceeded to undertake the very purging of documents that the Brotherhood had demanded.[26] The Department of Defense followed shortly thereafter with a Soviet-style purge of individuals along with disciplinary actions and re-education.[27]

Not only did the Secretary of State endorse such curbs on speech,[28] the Assistant Attorney General seemed eager to enforce them. As with the Muslim

Brotherhood, the Organization of Islamic Cooperation (OIC)—and, through it, our Middle Eastern allies—also seek to embargo all unsanctioned discussions of Islam as a matter of international law.[29] Though such a law would constitute a serious assault on the First Amendment, our Secretary of State met with the General Secretary of the OIC in July 2011 and personally committed the State Department's best efforts to secure the passage of a law restricting such speech; she even agreed to intimidate American citizens through "peer pressure and shaming" should they choose to exercise their First Amendment rights of free speech to express repeatable relevant facts.[30] When asked by the Chairman of the House Subcommittee on the Constitution to affirm that the administration would "never entertain or advance a proposal that criminalizes speech against any religion," the Assistant Attorney General, Tom Perez, refused to answer.[31] Shouldn't this be cause for concern? When the Assistant Attorney General refuses to answer such a question, things bode ill for the integrity of the First Amendment and add credence to President Obama's warning at the UN General Assembly that "the future must not belong to those who slander the prophet of Islam."[32] All these issues left unaddressed in the introduction will be explained in the body of the book, which will shed much-needed light on what I believe is the most serious threat of our time.

'Core Values'

How bad can it get? The very information that senior leaders sought to purge from analysis and censor from discussion is the same information that has repeatedly provided indicators and warning of threat activity when presented in national security forums. It is the same information that Pentagon Spokesperson U.S. Navy Captain John Kirby designated as "warped" in May 2012, when he appeared with known Muslim Brotherhood operatives on Al-Jazeera, a foreign television station known to be friendly to the Brotherhood and unfriendly to U.S. interests:

> The concern here is not so much that we would be spinning down and creating a cadre of individuals with these **warped views** but that it's not in keeping, frankly, this material is not in keeping with our **core values** and is not in keeping with **the strategy that we know we're out there executing**.[33/1]

Is it a "core value" to deride fellow Americans when speaking in uniform and representing the United States on foreign broadcasts known to be close to the Muslim Brotherhood? Isn't commitment to the truth as demonstrated by factual analysis supposed to be a "core value"? What of sensitivity to constitutional concepts like "free speech" and "due process"? Those in the national security establishment who had their work products purged—including brief-

1 It is worth noting that *Al-Jazeera* blocks the video of this news story in the United States, even though it is available on both the *Al-Jazeera* website and its YouTube account abroad.

ings, counterterror analysis, threat assessments, and special agent reports—were given no notice, no opportunity, and no due process to defend themselves against unnamed censors. The FBI used these censors to make the determination, shielded them from public disclosure, and were then held entirely unaccountable for the decisions they made and the manner in which they made them. The suppressed were not even given the Fourth Amendment right to confront their accusers.

Warped? Kirby assaulted the reputation of American citizens in a news story that was in support of a Muslim Brotherhood initiative that is overtly hostile to U.S. free speech standards. Getting Captain Kirby to trash Americans on *Al-Jazeera* may be an example of what the Muslim Brotherhood said is its preferred method of destroying America—"civilizational jihad by our hands."[34] The Office of Civil Rights and Civil Liberties in the Department of Homeland Security—part of the same counterterrorism leadership that seeks to criminalize relevant factual analysis—provides this training guidance to national security analysts, special agents, and decision-makers:

> Don't use training that equates radical thought, religious expression, freedom to protest, or other constitutionally protected activity, with criminal activity. One can have radical thoughts/ideas, including disliking the U.S. government, without being violent; for example, trainers who equate the desire for Shari'a law with criminal activity violate basic tenets of the First Amendment.[35]

With Captain Kirby's use of talking points such as "core values" and "warped" comes the sad realization that one must be on guard for the Alinskyist repurposing of valued terms and phrases to a different purpose. This book is designed to be a competing analysis of the strategy Captain Kirby said he "knows we're out there executing."[36] He attacks the integrity of fellow U.S. military officers and American citizens on a network owned by an OIC Member State in a story scripted by the Muslim Brotherhood. He speaks proudly of the strategy "we're out there executing." But just whose strategy is it, and who benefits from it? This book attempts to piece together exactly what strategy we are out there executing. What becomes clear is that the "strategy we're out their executing" may not be *our* strategy. It will be left to the reader to decide whose approach to the crisis reflects America's "core values" and which is "warped."

A Note

When one speaks of the Putin government and later refers to it as "the Russians," or speaks of the Conservative government in the U.K. and then later refers to "the English," or speaks of the Vatican and then later refers to "Catholics," no one challenges this convention by saying, "You're painting with too broad a brush. You can't speak about all Russians when you mean Putin (or the Conservatives or Catholics). You're engaging in generalities, stereotypes, and over-simplifications." Yet when one speaks about organizations like the Muslim Brotherhood or al-Qaeda and then later refers back to them as Muslims, it is often used as a semantic opening to make non-substantive challenges.

When analyzing terrorism undertaken by individuals and groups claiming to be Muslim and claiming to be acting according to Islamic doctrines, it is necessary to identify both the individuals and the motivations in order to develop a coherent threat analysis. Early in such an assessment, it doesn't matter whether the terrorists' "version" of Islam is in some higher sense true. What matters is that it is the "version" they accept when choosing to engage in acts of terrorism. Threat assessments that fail to account for such expressed motivations are defective. This book limits the discussion of Islam to the elements needed to analyze the threat motivations of those claiming it as the basis for their actions. In this book, Islam is assessed in the context of its use by the individuals and organizations under discussion. In most instances, such usage is limited to the organizations identified above or included in the more extensive lists provided by the UAE Cabinet and Akram's *Explanatory Memorandum*.

And Finally

This book was written with conflicting expectations. On the one hand, I hope people will read it, do some fact-checking, hold their elected officials and national security leaders responsible, and demand an accounting. But there is also the sobering thought that, like some Old Testament prophets, I may have to be content with knowing that I provided valid indicators and warning of the disastrous path we are on; that at some future date, when people look back to figure out what went wrong, they will realize that warning of catastrophic failure was timely and accurately provided—and ignored. Sometimes things must break before they can be put back together. The problem is that when things fall apart, there is no guarantee that they *can* be put back together.

> *The dogmas of the quiet past, are inadequate to the stormy present. The occasion is piled high with difficulty, and we must rise – with the occasion. As our case is new, so we must think anew, and act anew. We must disenthrall ourselves, and then we shall save our country. ... We shall nobly save, or meanly lose, the last best hope on earth.*

Abraham Lincoln
Annual Message to Congress
Washington, D.C.
December, 1862

The One Organizing Principle

Truth does not become more true by virtue of the fact that the entire world agrees with it, not less so even if the whole world disagrees with it.

Maimonides
Moreh Nevvichim, 2:15

On September 23, 2012, President Barack Obama made the following observation about the Middle East:

> I was certain and continue to be pretty certain that there are going to be bumps in the road because, in a lot of these places, the one organizing principle has been Islam, the one part of society that hasn't been completely controlled by the government.[1]

This book is written because I agree with the president's statement – so much so that I believe not to recognize this "one organizing principle" is to lack any coherent understanding of the issues and decision-making arising out of that part of the world. Because this was true long before the start of the War on Terror, the refusal to account for the doctrinal elements of Islam in our national security analyses constitutes professional malpractice that reduces our strategic comprehension to incoherence.

The cost of not understanding the enemy has been high, and it is getting higher every day. This strategic incoherence in the War on Terror will increasingly be measured by news stories that reveal senior leaders' inability to answer basic questions about the nature of the enemy and his environment. It will also manifest itself in official responses to terrorist attacks that become progressively less reality-based. As the American people grow more outraged, those professionally and constitutionally tasked with keeping them safe continue to lack awareness, understanding, and even professional curiosity about the doctrines that drive enemy action.

For these enemies, the implementation of Islamic law—*shariah*—as the governing law of the land is the objective. This is true not only for jihadi groups like al-Qaeda, but also for dawah organizations such as the Muslim Brotherhood and ummah entities[1] like the Organization of the Islamic Cooperation (OIC),[2] a transnational body that makes reasonable claims to represent the ummah, or the entire Muslim world.[3]

The catastrophic failure of American strategy in the War on Terror is the refusal to contend with the convergence of these three forces (jihadi, dawah, and ummah), which, as this book will explain, interact to our great detriment.

Self-identified jihadi entities—al-Qaeda, Hamas, and others—claim shariah as their "organizing principle." As Osama bin Laden stated it in 2002:

> Muslims, and especially the learned among them, should spread *Shari'a* law to the world—that and nothing else. Not laws under the "umbrella of justice, morality, and rights" as understood by the masses. No, the *Shari'a* of Islam is the foundation. ... In fact, Muslims are obligated to raid the lands of the infidels, occupy them, and exchange their system of governance for an Islamic system, barring any practice that contradicts *Shari'a* from being publicly voiced among the people, as was the case in the dawn of Islam. ... They say that our *Shari'a* does not impose our particular beliefs upon others; this is a false assertion. For it is, in fact, part of our religion to impose our particular beliefs upon others. ... Thus whoever refuses the principle of terror[ism] against the enemy also refuses the commandment of Allah the Exalted, the Most High, and His Shari'a.[4]

> And we also stress to honest Muslims that, in the midst of such momentous events and in this heated atmosphere, they must move, incite, and mobilize the Muslim *umma* to liberate itself from being enthralled to these unjust and apostate ruling regimes, who themselves are enslaved to America, and to establish the *Shari'a* of Allah on earth.[5]

---

1   As will be discussed in greater detail in Part II, while dawah is often defined as the "invitation" or "call to Islam," the meaning and purpose of dawah is more extensive and closely related to doctrines of jihad. Ummah entities will be discussed in Part IV.

Meanwhile, the Muslim Brotherhood, an international organization best understood as a dawah entity, has the same goal. Its founding branch in Egypt describes its mission this way:

> The Muslim Brotherhood is an international Muslim Body, which seeks to establish Allah's law in the land by achieving the spiritual goals of Islam and the true religion …
>
> E. The need to work on establishing the Islamic State … Defend the (Islamic) nation against the internal enemies …[6]

In America, Brotherhood-linked groups and individuals have dedicated themselves to the same purpose—installing shariah as the law of the land worldwide, culminating in an "Islamic state," or Caliphate, governed by Islamic law. As the Brotherhood described its objective in its 1991 *Explanatory Memorandum:*

> The general strategic goal of the Group in America … is the "Enablement of Islam in North America, meaning: establishing an effective and stable Islamic Movement led by the Muslim Brotherhood which adopts Muslims' causes domestically and globally, and which works to expand the observant Muslim base, aims at unifying and directing Muslims' efforts, presents a civilization alternative, and supports the global Islamic State wherever it is."[7]

Most are unaware that the implementation of Islamic law is a declared policy objective of all self-described Islamic states—including, of course, America's allies in the Middle East, our Coalition Partners in Afghanistan and Iraq. In 1981, as Member States of the OIC, they declared:

> Strict adherence to Islam and to Islamic principles and values as a way of life constitutes the highest protection for Muslims against the dangers that confront them. Islam is the only path that can lead them to strength, dignity, prosperity, and a better future. Islam is the pledge and guarantee of the authenticity of the *ummah* safeguarding it from the tyrannical onrush of materialism.[8]

More than a decade into the War on Terror, we should have a common understanding of the common objectives of jihadi, dawah, and ummah forces in the Islamic world, as their self-declared "organizing principle" also serves as their single unifying and governing principle. As this book will make clear, such unity of purpose is ubiquitous throughout the published doctrine of the self-described Islamic Movement. This information is simply too important to ignore or pre-emptively embargo. We can succeed only by honestly assessing it.

Not only is there an absence of functional knowledge of Islamic law in America's halls of power, our national security leaders have taken active measures to suppress both analysis and discussion[9] of the topic, under threat of harsh sanctions.[10] As the former Supreme Court Justice, former Chief U.S. Prosecutor at Nuremberg, and former U.S. Attorney General Robert Jackson stated in 1955, Islamic law is incompatible with our constitutional system:

> In any broad sense, Islamic law offers the American lawyer a study in dramatic contrasts. Even casual acquaintance and superficial knowledge—all that most of us at bench or bar will be able to acquire—reveal that its striking features relative to our law are not likenesses but inconsistencies, not similarities but contrarieties. In its source, its scope and its sanctions, the law of the Middle East is the antithesis of Western law.[11]

As Justice Jackson recognized, Islamic law is antithetical to American legal principles but still worth knowing. Shariah, **as understood by terrorists, agents of influence, and even some state actors**, is what Muslim Brotherhood–linked groups and individuals seek to implement in America. As such, it should necessarily be classified as foreign law, and yet these are precisely the groups that our national security leaders turn to for awareness, assistance, and support in prosecuting the War on Terror.

Consequently, there is no analysis of (1) what constitutes the governing law of much of the Islamic world, (2) the law that drives organizations like the Brotherhood to explicitly state that their mission is to subvert America, and (3) the law that rightly or wrongly interpreted leads al-Qaeda to openly proclaim its right to kill Americans. As will be seen, the very information senior leaders seek to purge from analysis and censor from discussion has repeatedly demonstrated an ability to provide indicators and warning of threat activity when presented in national security forums.

Is it possible to have a strategy to defeat an enemy without knowing its most significant—to use Obama's phrase—"organizing principle"? Can you defeat an enemy if you have convinced yourself you aren't permitted to know what animates it? In such a situation, it should be obvious that the enemy has gotten the upper hand. These are not just academic questions. Decision-makers, legislators, officers, analysts and special agents who cannot articulate their war strategy may be subject to an enemy information campaign that, in effect, executes someone else's strategy.

In this book, recognized Islamic sources will be properly cited to support the points being made. As a non-Muslim, I cannot practice Islamic law. As a trained intelligence officer and attorney, however, I can analyze sources that are recognized by the Islamic community as shariah. The purpose is not to reach an understanding of the "true" nature of Islam, but to understand the nature of the threat that faces us. There are enemies killing Americans, and it is crucial to listen to them and know why they are doing so. This enemy says he is fighting jihad. This enemy says that Islamic law serves as the doctrinal driver to jihad. To deny this reality is to engage in a level of reality dislocation that the mental health field calls "dissociation."

While the following explanations may present a true and valid understanding of Islamic law, such a determination is, in many respects, immaterial to the question of what constitutes the enemy's stated threat doctrine. This book demonstrates that certain doctrines drive the decision-making of some Muslims—regardless of whether other Muslims think those doctrines are right, wrong, or misapplied. Because shariah constitutes an identified element of the threat doctrine, there is no requirement to determine the validity of its use before considering its inclusion, only a factual determination that the enemy states his reliance on it.

Indeed, it is not possible to understand the nature of the threat unless one understands Islamic law, because the people who are killing us say they rely on it. Even if they are wrong in their interpretation of Islamic law, they still justify their actions by reference to Islamic law. If they are in error, at a later phase of analysis we will be required to determine *where* they are in error in order to devise courses of action to counter them. Regardless of whether shariah serves as a doctrinal driver in the War on Terror, or whether jihadis are correct in their assessment, one thing is certain: the actual content of Islamic law is an issue of fact to be determined by dispassionate analysis. Only then can the findings of that analysis produce a fact-driven understanding of the threat. We cannot defeat a threat we refuse to define.

A particularly contentious issue in the American media is the true status and nature of holy war in Islam. *The Muqaddimah*, Ibn Khaldun's iconic 1377 work of Islamic history and sociology, describes the concept this way:

> The secret of it lay in the willingness of the Muslims to die in the holy war against their enemies because of their feeling that they had the right religious insight and in the corresponding fear and defeatism that Allah put into the hearts of their enemies … **in the Muslim community, the holy war is a religious duty because of the universalism of the Muslim mission and the obligation to convert everybody to Islam either by persuasion or by force**.[12]

Even if Khaldun was wrong, there are still a lot of people trying to kill us who read what Khaldun wrote and believe it is true precisely because it is written and available in Islamic bookstores. Because Khaldun's status as an Islamic jurist and thinker is well established, the assumption going in should be that his commentaries likely are considered valid by both Islamic scholars and ordinary Muslims. Of course, there is the Ibn Khaldun Chair of Islamic Studies at American University in Washington, D.C.[13]

From a threat analysis perspective, the fact that our enemies think it is true when they act upon it makes it the basis for their doctrinal understanding. Because of this, a sound doctrine on threat development requires national security professionals to account for it.

Consider what happens when the typical suicide operation occurs: We see the farewell video of the martyr giving his reasons for carrying out the attack. He is neither white-knuckled nor perspiring. He is calm and very collected. He is a man who has made a decision to die for what he believes in, a decision that—given his worldview—could reasonably be described as rational. Any threat doctrine capable of motivating people to undertake such actions has demonstrated a capacity to inspire intense commitment. Anyone who mocks this commitment or looks down on those able to inspire it is seriously underestimating the nature of the threat, as well as the capability and doctrine of its "soldiers."

The suicide attack occurs; we watch the carnage on the news. Later, news reports carry images of an entire town celebrating the suicide bomber's becoming a shahid, often translated as martyr. But this is usually only half the story. What happens next is that the reporter will interview a terrorism expert in a book-lined office on a college campus or consult a senior U.S. government official in Washington and then tell viewers that what they just saw—and what Americans have seen for more than a decade—is not real, has nothing to do with Islam, and is too complicated to explain.

Again, the people killing us claim they do so to wage jihad in the cause of Allah, to impose Islamic law and reestablish the Caliphate. It is an unalterable fact that nearly all "violent extremists" with whom the United States is presently engaged in military operations make that very claim. Shahids define Islam as the basis for their motivation before carrying out their attack. This is true regardless of whether their understanding of Islam is correct and regardless of what percentage of Muslims globally agrees or disagrees with that doctrine.

"Jihad in the cause of Allah" is what the enemy claims it is doing, to the exclusion of all other reasons, including "underlying causes" such as economic deprivation. The enemy doesn't just make this claim. What the jihadis say they will do tracks *exactly* with what they do.

Extremists and the Mainstream

Conventional wisdom is often neither correct nor wise. Most of our analysts, when assessing the ideological contours of the War on Terror, emphasize the need to cleave the radicals from the mainstream. This has become an archetypal model that has informed our strategy for dealing with Islamic terrorists and the Muslim world. In the absence of analysis, however, following this model simply converts an assumption into a conclusion.

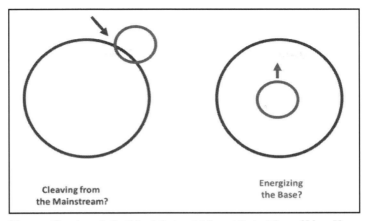

The prevailing theory is that Islamic "extremists" are at the periphery of Islam. Hence, all that is needed is to cleave the radicals from the mainstream (left). But if Islamic doctrines we brand "extreme" are at the center of Islamic law, then our messaging designed to cleave from the mainstream could end up energizing the base (right).

The conventional wisdom that has driven the United States' thinking from the beginning of the War on Terror is best reflected in the "Cleaving from the Mainstream" image above. The large circle on the left represents the Islamic world. The small circle at the periphery contains "extremist" Islamic "ideology." Even if there is some overlap with the main body of Islam, so the thinking goes, the extremists manipulate it to advance extremist agendas that are, at best, on the periphery of Islam and not representative of either the mainstream population or genuine Islamic doctrines. Hence, if we could just cleave the radicals from the mainstream, Islam would revert to its peaceful status.

But what if the "extremist ideologies" we positioned at the periphery of Islam actually reflect core Islamic legal doctrines understood to be central to Islam? Short of that, what if "extremists" could at least make plausible claims that this is true? If true, it would suggest that our assumptions about Islam are not only wrong but also counterfactual. Of course, whether such doctrines are on the periphery or at the center is an issue of fact that can be resolved only by direct inspection of Islam and shariah. Getting this wrong would seriously disrupt all information campaigns. If the conclusory assumptions driving a messaging campaign are erroneous, the message will be as well.

What if Western leaders were convinced that Salafi jihadi Islam represents a strain that is distinct and separate from the mainstream, and our messaging simply assumed this to be true? In such a case, the things we would say in order to cleave the radicals from the mainstream would have the effect of energizing the base.

The ability to generate predictive models of "extremist" behavior requires an actual understanding of the enemy's stated doctrine. As shariah is not a severable element of Islam, it cannot be left out of the analytical process. When explaining jihadi motivations without reference to its defining doctrines, national security analysts and decision-makers end up projecting Western philosophy, jurisprudence, and cultural preferences onto clearly non-Western systems; almost without exception, this leads to erroneous conclusions and strategic failure.

At the Islamic Bookstore

The following quote is somewhat incendiary:

> Priests in their churches, unlike recluse worshipping monks, should, of course, be killed without any exception. Malik in the 'Utbiyya included nuns along with monks, and said that they deserved killing even more. (*The Sign of the Sword*, Shaykh 'Abdabqadic ad Murabit[14])

Where did this passage come from? A radical mosque in the Middle East? An al-Qaeda stronghold? Maybe a text from the medieval era?

No, it's from a book sold at the Halalco Supermarket in Falls Church, Virginia—near the dar al-Hijrah Mosque. It should concern us that this type of material is readily available on bookshelves in far too many Islamic bookstores, even in the United States.

Many Middle East or Islamic studies experts often assert that it's impossible to understand the true nature or meaning of Islam without understanding classical Arabic. That may or may not be true. This reasoning is legitimate in describing how, for example, certain turns of phrase or word choices in the text add shades of meaning. However, translations exist to provide—as clearly as possible—just this kind of elucidation.

Claims about the impenetrability of understanding Islam without a grounding in classical Arabic ultimately fail when faced with the reality that roughly *80 percent of the Muslim world does not speak Arabic.* A very high percentage of them do, however, speak English. The three countries with the largest Muslim population – India, Indonesia, and Pakistan – have English as an official language. Thus it should come as no surprise that English is a major publishing language for Islam and has been for a long time.

Of course, a Muslim bookstore will have many books written in both Arabic and English. Typically, things written for the benefit of non-Muslim visitors looking for introductory guides on Islamic practice are placed conspicuously toward the front of the store.

But if you go to an Islamic bookstore, don't limit yourself to those books at the front—those designed to teach what you are allowed to know about Islam. Check out the other English-language books toward the back, on the shelves lined with volumes of educational material for practicing Muslims who turn to such publications as sources for their own understanding of Islam.

The intention of shariah authorities today is to limit the knowledge of non-Muslims to what they are allowed to know about Islam. If we read the books which the enemy declares are the basis of his intentions, we will better understand the nature of the threat. Because the enemy knows he lacks the kinetic ability to defeat us in battle, it is of utmost importance that he prevent us from properly defining him. The primary objective of the enemy in the War on Terror is to keep us from understanding his threat doctrine by keeping us from looking at the fact of Islamic law—"the one organizing principle"—that he, in fact, states is the driver of his threat doctrine. Once we understand his threat doctrine, the game is up. This is true even if he is wrong in his interpretation of Islam and shariah.

The United States is currently fighting this war according to the Barnes and Noble Standard. That is, every insight into the enemy's threat drivers derives from sources no deeper than an introductory book from Barnes and Noble. This sort of superficial examination is not how we gain an understanding of a threat. Instead, we should be mapping his doctrinal writings against Islamic law as understood by both jihadis and the larger Islamic community.

Think of it this way: You are lying on the operating table, and the brain surgeon is about to put you under. Suddenly you say, "Doctor, are you confident you can do the surgery?" The doctor replies, "Yes. As a matter of fact, I just went to Barnes and Noble yesterday and got this cool book on neurosurgery. I also watched a show on the Discovery Channel last night. If that doesn't work, I can call my friend, who's going to tell me everything he thinks I should know about brain surgery."

In such a circumstance, your response could well be, "Doctor, as a professional, you're required to know everything that a brain surgeon is supposed to know before doing brain surgery. And you are making your decisions based on a Discovery Channel show and a book you bought at Barnes and Noble? You're supposed to be doing your surgery based on all those books with titles I can't pronounce and with words I don't understand! Because that's what makes you the professional and me the guy who reads about brain surgery from books sold at Barnes and Noble and programs on Discovery. Are you telling me you haven't been trained?" You might feel compelled to yell, "Stop! You're not cracking my head open. You would kill me!" That's the Barnes and Noble Standard.

In a debate on these topics, disagreement is perfectly acceptable. But for disagreement to be reasonable, one's analysis should show some familiarity with primary sources that are recognized within the Muslim community as authoritative. According to the postmodern view, because there are no facts, there is no truth; everything is a matter of interpretation. Raising such postmodern objections to factual analysis lacks a professional basis.

Rather than the Barnes and Noble Standard, decision-making analysis should be held to a professional one. To meet this standard, an expert must read materials written by Muslims who are recognized in the Islamic community as authorities in the subjects they are discussing when writing for a Muslim audience.

The Dexter Standard

In the fall 2011 season of the Showtime series *Dexter*, the plot revolved around a serial killer who acted in furtherance of an End-Times scenario based on his understanding of the New Testament's *Book of Revelation*. As a foil for the serial killer's idiosyncratic beliefs is a former gang leader, now a practicing Christian, who comes to faith while in prison. One suspects that a principal role of the Christian convert was to set apart the serial killer from mainstream Christianity.

This is important because, early in the series, the homicide detectives realize that the killer's predation is based on his understanding of *Revelation*, even as they also understand that his views are warped. As errant as the killer's perceptions of the book are, because *Revelation* clearly serves as a key to his state of mind and a roadmap of his plan of action, the inspectors keep copies of it close by as an analytical tool and ready reference.

Nobody questioned the necessity of this activity, even though a number of the inspectors relying on the text were either nominally religious or non-believers. There was never a suggestion that only Christian inspectors were qualified to carry on the investigation. In fact, their subjective religious beliefs were not held to be relevant to their qualifications as investigators. What qualified them was not their prowess in theology but their skills as homicide detectives. Of course, this last point is so self-evident that the issue never became a topic of debate in the program. The necessity of looking at *Revelation* to generate leads and situational awareness to catch the serial killer was manifestly obvious.

In the War on Terror, there should be no controversy over the need to look to the self-identified doctrinal drivers of a self-identified theat. This book simply argues for the same latitude when following the evidence granted to ordinary homicide detectives, albeit in a television drama. After all, there would be no question as to the serious malpractice of those detectives if, knowing the relevance of the *Book of Revelation* – and knowing that people were being killed because of it – they nevertheless chose to ignore it.

Sources of Sunni Islamic Law

Many assume the Qur'an to be the equivalent of the Bible. It is not; the closest Western equivalent would be the Ten Commandments. Like the Ten Commandments, which were given to Moses by God, the Qur'an was directly revealed by Allah. In Islamic parlance, the Qur'an is the "Uncreated Word of Allah," meaning it has existed from the beginning of time. It's logical, then, for Muslims to consider its dictates to be both divine and outside of time. An attempt to place the Qur'an in the context of a certain historical period could lead to the argument that the text and message are tied to a particular time and place and, hence, could become obsolete. This cannot be, because, for believing Muslims, both Allah and his message are eternal; to assert such a thing could raise issues of blasphemy.

The Qur'an asserts itself as the pinnacle of Islam and serves as the basis for Islamic law with verses like:

> Nothing have we omitted from the Book. (Qur'an 6:38)

> And We have sent down to thee, a Book explaining all things. (Qur'an 16:89)

> Whatever the Messenger gives you, then take it and whatever he prohibits you, then stay away from it. (Qur'an 59:7)

Putting the body of Islamic law beyond the reach of man reflects the sacred nature of its primary sources, the Qur'an and hadith. Both sources represent a form of binding ordinance when used to support issues of Islamic law. A third source of law, scholarly consensus (ijma), represents the unanimous acceptance of laws immediately derived from the Qur'an and hadith, and it too operates beyond the reach of what we might consider judicial review.

Indian Islamic jurist Asaf A.A. Fyzee explains the three primary sources of Islamic law:

> **The Koran according to this theory is the first source of law.** Its importance is religious and spiritual, no less than legal, as it is, in Muslim belief, the Word of Allah. When a verse of the Koran is cited, the Muslim authors say: 'Allah says, Mighty and Glorious is He' or 'Says Allah, the Blessed and Exalted'. It is for this reason that the verses of the Koran (*ayat*), although only a few of them deal specifically with legal questions, are held to be of paramount authority. In interpreting the Koranic verses, one important principle has to be observed. *Some verses are deemed to be the abrogating (nasikh) verses and some to be the abrogated (mansukh) ones. Generally speaking the earlier verses are deemed to be repealed by the latter ones.* The textbooks on Islamic law give a good deal of attention to problems of interpretation and discuss exhaustively the question of how the rule of law is to be deduced when several Koranic verses deal with the same or a similar problem, or when one verse affects another, directly

or indirectly.

The second source of law is the *sunna*, the practice of the Prophet. The word *sunna* was used in pre-Islamic times for an ancient and continuous usage, well established in the community (*sunnat al-umma*); later, the term was applied to the practice of the Prophet (*sunna al-nabi*). The word *sunna* must be distinguished from the word hadith, for a promiscuous use of the two terms leads sometimes to confusion of thought. Hadith is the story of a particular occurrence; *sunna*, the rule of law deduced from it is the 'practice' of the Prophet, his model behavior. The two sources, Koran and *sunna*, are often called *nass* (binding ordinance) and represent direct and indirect revelation.

The third source of law is *ijma*, consensus of opinion among the learned of the community. Although the Muslim legists give it the third place in descending order, ***modern critics consider it to be the most important element in Islamic law***, and an examination of the corpus of the *fiqh* reveals that a major portion of the law consists of the concurrent opinions of scholars on legal questions.[15]

Professor Mohammad Kamali emphasizes this point in his treatise *Principles of Islamic Jurisprudence*. In Chapter 2, titled "The First Source of Shari'ah: The Qur'an," he writes:

Being the verbal noun of the root word *qara'a* (to read), 'Qur'an' literally means 'reading' or 'recitation'. It may be defined as 'the book containing the speech of God revealed to the Prophet Muhammad in Arabic and transmitted to us by continuous testimony, or *tawatur*.' It is proof of the prophesy of Muhammad, the most authoritative for Muslims, and the first source of the *Shari'ah*. The *'ulama'* are unanimous [meaning there is scholarly consensus] on this, and some even say that it is the only source and that all other sources are explanatory to the Qur'an. The salient attributes of the Qur'an that are indicated in this definition may be summarized as five: it is revealed exclusively to the Prophet Muhammad; it was put into writing; it is all *mutawatir*; it is the inimitable speech of God; and it is recited in *salah*. The revelation of the Qur'an began with sura al-Alaq (96:1) starting with the words, 'Read the name of your Lord' and ending with the *ayah* in sura al-Mad'idah (5:3): 'Today I have perfected your religion for you and completed my favor toward you, and chosen Islam as your religion.'[16]

Kamali's explanation reflects both the classical and exclusive understanding of the status of the Qur'an in Islamic law. From Muhammad ibn Idris al-Shafi'i's classic treatise *The Risala*, for example, we have the following:

> Included in what I have stated concerning God's command to His creatures ordering obedience to the Apostle and specifying the place it has in religion, is a proof of the precise definition of the duties stated in the Qur'an, which consists of the following categories:
>
> The first category is what the Book has laid down with such clarity that nothing further—in addition to revelation (*tanzil*)—was needed.
>
> The second category consists in what is clearly stated in the obligation imposed by God ordering obedience to the Prophet. The Apostle in his turn precisely stated on the authority of God what the duties are, upon whom they are binding, and in what circumstances some of them are required or not required, and when they are binding.
>
> The third category consists in what God has specified only in the Sunna of His Prophet, in the absence of a textual legislation in the Book.[17]

The Risala ("Letter") was written in the early ninth century and is both seminal and authoritative owing to the status of its author.[18] As both a mujtahid and founder of the third of the four formally recognized schools of Sunni Islamic law, Imam Shafi'i's status in Islamic jurisprudence is particularly high. *Reliance of the Traveller: A Classic Manual of Islamic Law* (or *'Umdat al-Salik*)—a 14th-century classic text from the Shafi'ite school by Al-Misri,[19] in print in America—likewise reflects this view as a contemporary American statement on the status of the Qur'an in shariah:

> The Prophet (Allah bless him and give him Peace) said, "None of you believe until his inclinations conform to what I have brought." This means that **a person must examine his acts in light of the Koran and sunna, suspending his own inclinations and following what the Prophet** (Allah bless him and give him peace) **has brought**. The hadith resembles the word of Allah Most High, "When Allah and His messenger have decided a matter, no believer, male or female, has

a choice in the affair." (Koran 33:36)[20]

Because the proper meaning of the Qur'an is intended to bring with it the force of law, Muslims are not allowed to explain verses of the Qur'an based on their own opinion but rather are required to "check as to how it has been understood by the scholars of Sacred Law and men of wisdom who came before."[21] The primary status of the Qur'an, including its relative hierarchy, is best explained by hadith from Nisa'i, in which Mohammed raises this point:

The Prophet asked: 'How will you judge the cases that come to you? He replied: 'I will judge according to the Book of Allah'. 'But if you do not get anything there, what will you do?', the Prophet (sws) asked. He said: 'I will refer to the Sunnah of the Prophet (sws)'. 'But if you do not get it even there, what will you do?', the Prophet (sws) asked again. He replied: "I will exercise my judgement [sic].' Hearing this, the Prophet (sws) patted Mu'adh (rta) on the shoulder and said: 'Praise be to Allah who has guided the Messenger of His Messenger to what pleases His Messenger'. (Nisa'i: No. 1327)

The Hadith: Strong and Weak

In Islam, the rough equivalent to the Bible would be the hadith, which are the sayings and the acts of Mohammed, Islam's Prophet, as recorded by his contemporaries. Because Islamic scholars and believers consider him *al-Insān al-Kāmil*, or "the perfect man," Mohammed's deeds and sayings have the utmost bearing on Islamic law and practice. When these generate a directive applicable to Muslims, that directive is called sunnah. When people refer to the hadith, they usually mean the sunnah of the hadith. And when they say sunnah, they are referring to a specific point of law that has emerged from a hadith. In *Shari'ah: The Islamic Law*, 'Abdur Rahman Doi explains the origins of these crucial components of Islam:

> Individuals associated with Mohammed in his lifetime were called "companions." Among the numerous companions, the seven most prolific commentators on his life were Abu Hurrairah 'Abdur Rahman bin Sakhar Dasi (5,374 hadith), Abdullah bin Umar bin Khattab (2,630), Anas bin Malik (2,286), Aisha (2,210), Abdullah bin Abbas (1,660), Jabir bin Abdullah Ahsan (1,540), and Sa'ad bin Malik Abu Saeed Khudhri (1,540). The compiled hadith of these companions did not survive in their original creations but were passed down and collected by numerous hadith collectors of varying quality and repute.[22]

Shortly after Mohammed's death, more hadith emerged about his sayings than could have reasonably been produced. To resolve the problem, Islamic authorities instituted various disciplines to both validate the hadith and establish its authority based on, among other things, its chain of transmission. At one extreme, a hadith might be confirmed by four different witnesses, and thus would be considered a reliable account of what happened. At the other extreme, there might be a single witness who was considered unreliable.

Using this process, Islamic scholars created a hierarchy. The gold standard for hadith—the highest authority—was designated as mutawatir hadith, or strong hadith.[23] The weakest form that was still admissible was something called da'if hadith.[24] Hadith lower than da'if[25] is known as false hadith, which can never be used as a reference in Islamic law.[26] As a general proposition, da'if hadith cannot be used to challenge strong hadith.[27] Muslims can be obligated to follow hadith designated as mutawatir under pain of apostasy.[28] This is followed by hadith designated as "well authenticated," or sahih. It is also obligatory for Muslims to believe in sahih hadith, but failing to do so falls short of the charge of unbelief.[29]

Because so many people were assembling hadith, Islamic scholars instituted quality standards to qualify and validate hadith and determined that a particular group of collectors stood out for the quality of their hadith collections. They are known as the "Sacred Six" (the Sahih Sittah), and they are ranked in order.[30] The most authoritative hadith collector was named Bukhari; another man, known as Muslim, was the second most authoritative collector.[31] In full precedent order, the six "correct" collections of the Sunni, also called the "Six Canonical Collections" (the *Sahih Sittah*), are the works of **Bukhari, Muslim**, Abu Dawud, Tirmidhi, Ibn Maja and Nasa'i.[32]

Hence, if a story concerning Mohammed is related through one of the six "correct" collections and it reliably cites one of the seven companions, **a presumption emerges, verging on irrebuttable, that the texts cited are accurate for the points being made—as matters of both Islamic theology and law.** Because those accounts are presumed reliable, the *Sunna* arising from them cannot be construed to contradict the Qur'an but rather are to be understood as doctrinally authoritative explanations of the Quranic verses they support: "*Whatever the Messenger gives you, then take it and whatever he prohibits you, then stay away from it.*" (Qur'an 59:7)[33]

As recently as August 2014, the Mufti of Egypt upheld the authoritative status of Bukhari.[34] If you are reading a hadith collected by Bukhari, Muslim, or another of the "Sacred Six" collectors—and the chain of transmission has been established as mutawatir or sahih—then it has been designated as authoritative on the issue it addresses. Such hadith would be on a par with the Gospels of the New Testament, which reflect what the apostles said they heard Jesus Christ say or do (i.e., indirect divine revelation). When a sacred rule—in this case, an indirect divine revelation drawn from the sayings or acts of Mohammed—is used to support a statement from the Qur'an (direct divine revelation), it will often reflect or support the final word on the issue. In addition, as Doi made clear, a hadith can never be interpreted in such a way that it contradicts the Qur'an. It is always understood to reinforce a point in the Qur'an when there is overlap.

Being aware of these distinctions on the nature and quality of hadith is crucial when reading Islamic law. For example, much hadith on the requirements to fight jihad—understood as "warfare against non-Muslims to establish the religion"—falls in the mutawatir or sahih category. Those speaking of the peaceful "greater jihad" are qualified as either da'if or false.

The top two levels of Islamic law are divine revelation – directly through the Qur'an – and indirect though properly qualified hadith. This distinction is important, because the Qur'an is believed to have been revealed over a 22-year period, as the Islamic community developed methods of dealing with new circumstances throughout the period of revelation.[35]

Macros Packed with Meaning

Imran Ahsan Khan Nyazee, who translated *Al-Hidayah*—a classical manual of Hanafi Islamic law from the 12th century—received an advanced legal degree in American law from the University of Michigan.[36] When he explains Islamic law, he uses terminology that he knows Americans will understand. I like reading his material; he knows how to make Islamic legal concepts comprehensible.

Nyazee highlights certain important facts about Islamic law. For example, he makes clear that, when reading the Qur'an, one is not allowed simply to *read* it. There are rules about what it says, about what certain words and phrases mean. There are terms in Islamic law that contain specific, embedded meanings. Nyazee talks about codification as it applies to Islamic texts:

> When we use the word code with reference to Islamic legal texts, we obviously do not mean a statute enforced with the authority of the state. Codification with reference to Islamic schools means the attempt to bring uniformity into the law out of a mass of available rulings.[37]

In my book, the words "doctrine" and "Islamic law" are used in the same sense described by Nyazee. Shariah is just a bit broader in its understanding than what we would consider law. Nyazee goes on to say that

> [t]his book [*Al-Hidaya*] contains a huge amount of "coded" information. We use the term coded here to mean what people in the computer world would mean. Within this information are "macros"—short statements that pack within them pages of information. **The macro needs to be preprocessed before the code can reveal its entire meaning**.[38]

Nyazee does not mean there is a secret language. He is using the word "coded" in a way that an American lawyer would understand—or a computer programmer, which is why he uses a programming metaphor. He means there are certain words or phrases that are terms of art, or codified legal terms. Just as a non-lawyer can't pick up a copy of the U.S. Code and make sense of it, so a non-Muslim cannot just pick up a book of Islamic law and decide for himself what it means.

For example, when American law describes who is and who is not a legal person, it uses the phrase "U.S. person." Anyone writing a legal brief based on his own personal understanding of what "U.S. person" means would be making a big mistake. The phrase "U.S. person" means only what the U.S. Code says it means, to the exclusion of other possible definitions. Nyazee is saying the same thing about Islamic law: there are certain terms that may appear to be generic but have actually been given concrete definitions in advance. Such terms are packed with a preset amount of known information. Entire books have been written about what some of these terms and phrases mean.

Scholarly Consensus

One often hears that there are no absolute rules in Islam, that there are thousands of different interpretations of Islamic law—or shariah—on any given position. Of course, this narrative has the intended effect of discouraging decision-makers and analysts from analyzing Islamic law by convincing them (erroneously) that there is no purpose to reading it at all. With this decision comes the total suspension of real threat analysis.

As with all major legal systems, Islam has developed its own rules of interpretation that range from elective to required. Some rules become so fixed in doctrine—hardwired even—that interpreting a text without reference to its associated rule in Islamic law becomes impermissible. These mandatory rules have a powerful influence on the interpretation and meaning of the Qur'an and hadith, especially as they relate to the topic of jihad. Textual analysis with or without reference to these doctrines can create dramatically different understandings of Islamic law.

Scholarly consensus, or ijma, holds that there are fixed rules in Islamic law that are not subject to change. In Islamic law, phrases like "all the scholars agree" or "there is no disagreement among the scholars" are examples of coded language that signal the rule of scholarly consensus is being asserted.

Scholarly consensus exists when there is agreement among all the scholars who were mujtahids in a given period on a single matter or event.[39] Consensus on a given rule has dramatic consequences because it reflects a finding that has become a permanently fixed element of Islamic law; once a ruling is fixed, one is obliged to obey it and acts unlawfully if he disobeys it. When a point of law rises to the level of scholarly consensus, it becomes a part of the "fixed" inner sphere of Islamic law.

Authority for the primacy of scholarly consensus can be found in the sayings of Mohammed as relied on in shariah, such as:

§ bˇ,ˆ A second evidentiary aspect is that a ruling **agreed upon by all the *mujtahids* in the Islamic Community** (*Umma*) is in fact the ruling of the Community, represented by its *mujtahids*, and there are many hadiths that have come from the Prophet (Allah bless him and give him peace), as well as quotes from the Companions, which indicate that the Community is divinely protected from error, including his saying (Allah bless him and give him peace).

"My Community shall not agree on an error."

"Allah is not wont to make my Community concur on misguidance."

"That which the Muslims consider good, Allah considers good."[40]

Nyazee affirms the continuing status ijma enjoys in Islamic law to this day:

The majority of the jurists agreed upon the rule that **explicit *ijma* is a definitive source and it is obligatory to act upon it; its opposition is prohibited.** Thus, if explicit *ijma* occurs on an issue and is published, then, the *hukm* (rule) upon which agreement is found stands established definitively (*qat'an*) and it is not permitted to oppose it. Further, **the issue that has been settled through such *ijma* can no longer be opened up again** and be subjected to *ijtihad*.[41]

This is why mujtahids cannot contradict scholarly consensus from earlier periods. Once a doctrine has been established as a matter of scholarly consensus, it can never be changed. *Reliance of the Traveller* confirms the current status of scholarly consensus in Islam law:

§ b7.2 **When the ... necessary integrals of consensus exist, the ruling agreed upon is an authoritative part of Sacred Law that is obligatory to obey and not lawful to disobey.** Nor can *mujtahids* of a succeeding era make the thing an object of new *ijtihad*, because the ruling on it, verified by scholarly consensus, is **an absolute ruling which does not admit of being contravened or annulled.**[42]

Quranic authority for consensus is found in such verses as:

Whoever controverts the Messenger after guidance has become clear to him and follows other than the believers' way,

We shall give him over to what he has turned to and roast him in hell, and how evil an outcome. (Qur'an 4:115)

Oh you who believe, obey Allah and obey the Prophet and those in authority among you. (Qur'an 4:59)

In Islamic parlance, the terms "scholar" and "scholarship" have meanings that extend beyond conventional Western scholastic understanding. As a translated Islamic term of art, "scholar" means "one qualified to issue legal opinions" when the scholar is a mujtahid.[43] Islamic law requires that those not qualified to issue expert legal opinion (ijtihad) follow qualified scholarship (taqlid) on matters of law.[44] In stating the requirement, *Reliance* references Mohammed Sa'id Buti, who relied on Quranic verse 16:43 for authority:

> b2.0. THE KORANIC EVIDENCE FOR FOLLOW-ING SCHOLARS—at b2.1 (Muhammad Sa'id Buti:) The first aspect of it is the work of Allah the Majestic, "*Ask those who recall if you know not.*" (Qur'an 16:43) By **consensus of all the scholars** (*ijma*), this verse is an imperative for someone who does not know a ruling in Sacred Law or the evidence for it to follow someone who does. **Virtually all scholars** of fundamental Islamic law have made this verse their principle evidence that it is obligatory for the ordinary person to follow the scholar who is a *mujtahid*.[45]

In this context, a "scholar" is a person of real stature with actual authority to compel. Given the precise nature of the term "scholar," its generic use in discussions on Islamic law and doctrine can lead to ambiguity. When using the term indiscriminately to refer to both contemporary academicians and Islamic authorities in the same conversation, the imputed equivalency—even when unintended—is erroneous and misleading.

As just stated, Muslims who are not formally trained are required to follow the orders of a recognized leader. It also means that such a Muslim is, likewise, not allowed to formulate his own opinions on Islamic matters. If a mujtahid is proven to be wrong in a fatwa, he may be disciplined, possibly severely. But the Muslim who, in good faith, follows that erroneous fatwa may still escape punishment. The oft-cited explanation for why many Muslims act as jihadis—because they are only following what their imams have told them—may well be true, and in that case, their jihadist actions will be deemed valid according to Islamic law.

Rules of Interpretation

Arguments in Islamic law that are grounded in scholarly consensus can take on a status approaching irrefutable. This is what Albert Hourani, author of *A His-*

tory of the Arab Peoples, meant when he wrote: "[W]hen there was general agreement as a result of an exercise of reason, then this consensus (ijma) would be regarded as having the status of certain and unquestionable truth."[46] Regarding the relevant authority for establishing scholarly consensus, orthodox Islamic law only recognizes rulings from the four doctrinal Sunni schools of Islamic law (Hanafi, Maliki, Shafi'i, and Hanbali). For purposes of establishing scholarly consensus, it is unlawful to follow the rulings from other schools.[47] Thus, "moderates" who are neither Islamic jurists nor formally aligned with one of the four schools lack standing to argue for new rulings in shariah.

When scholarly consensus exists on a point of Islamic law, a number of things follow. First, as a matter of law, arguments that challenge positions of scholarly consensus cannot themselves be based on Islamic law or doctrine. The legal proofs in the Qur'an and hadith for the doctrine of scholarly consensus are firmly established and agreed upon (as a matter of that same consensus), as are the harsh consequences for those who choose not to conform to them.[48] Further, scholarly consensus is not limited to the ossified interpretations of medieval scholars, as "moderates" often assert. In a modern legal treatise on scholarly consensus, *The Doctrine of Ijma in Islam: A Study of the Judicial Principle of Consensus*, Ahmad Hasan gives a thorough explanation of how Islamic law accounts for the status it affords scholarly consensus. When reading Hasan's explanation, it is crucial to remember that this is the perspective of a Muslim who believes in the fixed nature of the underlying sacred law.

> Now if *ijma* runs contrary to the revealed text, such an *ijma* would be erroneous. But *ijma* of the community can never be erroneous. Hence it cannot be abrogated by the Qur'an or the Sunnah. Similarly, it cannot be repealed by a subsequent *ijma* because the latter is either based on an evidence contrary to the evidence of the former or it has no evidence. If the subsequent *ijma* is not based on evidence, it would be erroneous. But that would be impossible. If it is based on some evidence, that evidence would either be a text of the Qur'an or the Sunnah, or it would be an analogy. The evidence cannot be a text of the Qur'an or the Sunnah because it precedes ijma. Now if *ijma* contradicts the text, it is impossible. The evidence cannot be an analogy because it requires an original basis. The original basis would again be a clear injunction from the Qur'an or the Sunnah or that would be an *ijma* or *qiyas* (analogy). In the case of *ijma*, it again requires supporting evidence from the Qur'an or the Sunnah or analogical extension. In both cases, an original basis is again required, and the reasoning goes on as infinitum. ...
> **Hence, the abrogation of *ijma* by any other authority is not**

allowed. Conversely, *ijma* cannot abrogate any rule of law based on the Qur'an, *Sunnah, ijma,* or *qiyas.* **Hence the injunctions enunciated in the Qur'an on the rules ordained by the Prophet could only be repealed in his lifetime,** and not by **ijma** after him. This view is agreed upon by the scholars in general. Further, no rule of law can be repealed by *ijma* during the time of the Prophet, for the *ijma* established in his time must have his approval. **If he abrogates a rule expressly, his statement will count and not the *ijma*.** Hence *ijma* in his time carries no value.[49]

Note that Hasan's explanation reveals the close relationship between scholarly consensus and abrogation. Though Islamic scholars still retain some latitude to reason to a conclusion (ijtihad) by applying Islamic law to particular new fact patterns or ethical situations in the flexible sphere of law, the days of "absolute ijtihad" on doctrinal issues of Islam in the fixed sphere have—since the days of Malik, Hanafi, Shafi'i, and Hanbal—effectively passed. Furthermore, attempts at ijtihad are barred where there is existing consensus. As a practical matter, this constrains new scholarly consensus that, in any event, can never serve as a basis to overrule legal positions where ijma has already been established.[50]

This leads to another general rule: when an "extremist" position is shown to be grounded in consensus, the presumption must be—barring an equally weighted argument to the contrary—that the extremist is correct in his assessment of Islamic law. Of course, it necessarily follows that his position, by definition, is not "extreme."

According to Islamic law, the status of scholarly consensus is not elective. When stating, "there is no disagreement among the scholars," *Reliance* is asserting that Islamic scholars consider the issue to have been authoritatively and permanently settled.[51] While some assert that there are no "absolute rules" in Islam, as we have seen, shariah considers it apostasy to violate such consensus. In the section of *Reliance* titled "Acts that Constitute Apostasy," we find that violating consensus is equated with leaving Islam itself.

Among the things that entail apostasy from Islam:

> (7) **To deny any verse of the Koran or anything which by scholarly consensus** . . . belongs to it, or to add a verse that does belong to it;

> (14) To deny the obligatory character of **something which by the consensus of Muslims . . . is a part of Islam.** [52]

In other words, if scholarly consensus on a point of Islamic law has been established, breaking from it runs the risk of apostasy.

Accounting for Consensus in Threat Analysis

A professional approach to intelligence in the War on Terror should account for the enemy's threat doctrine. It should quickly identify the Islamic doctrine of scholarly consensus and realize that it establishes certain absolute rules that can be used to assess the relative strength of "extremist" claims when compared to those of the "moderates." When "extremists" claim that scholarly consensus supports their position, an analyst need only determine whether the claim of ijma was properly asserted. For example, while conventional wisdom holds that those calling for a return of the Caliphate project utopian visions exhibiting "extremist" tendencies, a cursory review of shariah reveals that

> the investiture of someone from the Islamic community (*Umma*) able to fulfill the duties **of the Caliphate is obligatory by scholarly consensus.**[53]

Once scholarly consensus is established, the "extremist" should be understood to be unequivocally correct as a matter of law. As part of an ongoing intelligence collection cycle, a list of Islamic rules that reflect scholarly consensus could be assembled for quick reference; the ability to rapidly assess claims of scholarly consensus would help analysts gauge the relative strength of the enemy's threat doctrine.

As a list of rules on which there is scholarly consensus in Islamic law is assembled, some patterns will emerge. For example, analysts and policymakers will quickly notice that, rather than being an inconsequential cultural formality, the shariah supremacy clauses in both the Afghan and Iraqi constitutions specifically subordinate those governing instruments to Islam's absolute rules.

Those unaware of the legal doctrine are not likely to recognize it, even when it is boldly declared in an argument. Arguments from a so-called "extremist" that successfully claim consensus are made strong because of it. Once recognized, it becomes clear that reference is made to ijma on a regular basis. What follows is a series of citations of relevance to the national security domain that assert scholarly consensus. These examples—and many more—should be the subject of analysis by national security and counterterror professionals. Emphasis has been added to passages that describe scholarly consensus as a basis for jihadists' actions.

The Declaration of Jihad against Jews and Crusaders World Islamic Front Statement, better known as the 1998 Osama bin Laden "Fatwa":

> All these crimes and sins committed by the Americans are a clear declaration of war on Allah, his messenger, and Muslims. **And ulema have throughout Islamic history unanimously agreed** that the jihad is an individual duty if the

enemy destroys the Muslim countries. This was revealed by Imam Bin-Qadamah in "Al-Mughni," Imam al-Kisa'i in "Al-Bada'i," al-Qurtubi in his interpretation, and the shaykh of al-Islam in his books, where he said: "As for the fighting to repulse [an enemy], it is aimed at defending sanctity and religion, **and it is a duty as agreed by the ulema.** Nothing is more sacred than belief except repulsing an enemy who is attacking religion and life."[54]

From al-Qaeda in Iraq in 2005, now ISIS, Al-Zarqawi Group's First Legal Council Statement Condemning Aiding 'Polytheists,' Participating in Writing the Iraqi Constitution—from one page alone:

> As for obstacles that prevent ruling with Islamic laws ... the **scholars have agreed** upon and approved only 10.

> Those who seek mediums [idols or a person] between them and God who they ask to intercede on their behalf and have committed blasphemy **as agreed upon among scholars.**

> Those who do not curse the polytheists or those who associate with God ahs [sic] some doubts about their blasphemy or attempted to correct them have committed blasphemy **as agreed upon among the scholars.**

> Those who abhor any teachings of the Prophet, may God's peace and prayers be upon him, even if they follow it, have committed blasphemy, **as agreed upon among the scholars.**[55]

From televised comments by Muslim Brotherhood leader Yusuf al-Qaradawi in 2006:

> **All the schools of Islamic jurisprudence—the Sunni, the Shi'ite ... and all the ancient and modern schools of jurisprudence—agree** that any invader, who occupies even an inch of land of the Muslims, must face resistance.[56]

Al-Azhar Mufti Dr. 'Imad Mustafa's fatwa, published by the Muslim Brotherhood's *IslamOnline* on 8 January 2011, in support of defensive jihad in advance of activities associated with the "Arab Spring":

> Fighting against non-Muslims is what is known in Islamic jurisprudence as Jihad in the path of God. Jihad is a prescribed duty in cases of aggression from the infidels against

Muslims, for we must resist them, make jihad against them, and defend against them. This is according to the text of the Qur'an, for Almighty God has said: "Fight in the way of Allah those who fight you but do not transgress. Indeed. Allah does not like transgressors" (Qur'an 2:190). This type of jihad is known as defensive jihad, **and it is a duty agreed to by all Islamic scholars and all who are wise**, and is endorsed in our day by recognized international charters. However, the occupier and his associates have come to label this "terrorism."[57]

Majid Khadduri, in the *Islamic Law of Nations*:

> **"No essential difference among leading jurists is to be found** on this fundamental duty, whether in orthodox or heterodox doctrine."[58]

Relating back to the discussion on Bukhari, on the back cover of the multi-volume collection of *Sahih Al-Bukhari* to establish the authority of Bukhari's hadith collection:

> **"All Muslim scholars are agreed** that Sahih Al-Bukhari is the most authentic and reliable book after the Book of Allah."[59]

Often, in Islamic texts (or declarations, fatwas, or other legal instruments emerging from Islamic jurisprudence), a form of "universal agreement" will be used. While it does not mention the scholars themselves, this construction should also be understood to reflect the doctrine of ijma. For example, Chapter X of the Organization of Islamic Cooperation's Charter declares the universal agreement within the OIC that "human rights" is shariah. From the 2008 OIC Charter:

> The Independent Permanent Commission on Human Rights shall promote the civil, political, social and economic rights enshrined in the organisation's covenants and declarations and in **universally agreed** human rights instruments, in conformity with Islamic values. [60]

The following was issued by the OIC in the October 12, 2006, press release "Points of Clarification on the Initiative to Spare the Blood of Muslims in Iraq," associated with the upcoming conference in Mecca, Saudi Arabia, that promulgated the "Mecca Declaration." The press release authors took some effort to frame the OIC Declaration in the language of **scholarly consensus**:

> Its objective is to put an end to the sectarian infighting and its religious background is founded on a unified Islamic per-

ception, on the texts of the holy Qur'an, its public rulings, the tradition of the Prophet, and **the common agreement** of the Islamic Ummah with all its sects and affiliations, both Shia and Sunna—**They are all agreed, without any shadow of doubt** …

These are all general principles, which are the subject of common agreement among all Muslims without exception.

This initiative is founded on a mechanism that calls for this **"Makkah Document" to be given the broadest possible circulation, to be endorsed and confirmed publicly by all religious bodies and references** …[61]

Fixed and Flexible Spheres

The primary and secondary sources of Islamic law—the Qur'an and authoritative (mutawatir) hadith—are considered the products of divine revelation. For believing Muslims who adhere to Islamic law, they cannot be overruled or changed. In the introduction to *Reliance of the Traveller*, translator Nuh Ha Mim Keller notes that "the four *Sunni* schools of Islamic law, Hanafi, Maliki, Shafi'i, and Hanbali are identical in approximately 75 percent of their legal conclusions."[62]

In establishing the line separating the permanent body of law from that which is amendable, Imran Khan Nyazee's "Fixed and Flexible Spheres" metaphor explains the bifurcation of Islamic law into two spheres—the permanently fixed and the mutably flexible:

> The two spheres of the law, which we may, for the sake of convenience call the "fixed" and the "flexible" spheres, are linked to each other through an organic relationship. They are not mutually dependent. In fact, it is the flexible sphere that is dependent on the fixed and unchangeable sphere, and may be said to revolve around it, changing its complexion in each age. The relationship is best described through our example of a tree. The fixed part is firmly planted in the ground, while the changing part is like the branches that spread out and keep changing their shape and appearance in different times and seasons.[63]

This duality in shariah reflects competing requirements to conform to an eternal body of law while remaining relevant to the times and cultures in which

Islam is practiced. As Nyazee elaborates:

> The word evolution when used with Islamic law is likely to evoke different reactions. Those who feel that the *shari'ah* was laid down once and for all may reject the idea of evolution in Islamic law. Their objections are partly justified. But, as Islamic law is meant to apply to every aspect of a Muslim's life in all ages, it follows that it has to evolve and grow like any other legal system so that it may be able to cater to the demands of the changing times. That is exactly what it does and is designed to do. The shari'ah may be fixed and immutable at its central core, as is claimed by some, but is not so in its extensions. . . . **The laws in the Qur'an and the Sunnah of the Prophet, it is true, have been determined and fixed for all times to come.** These comprise the core legal concepts, the genetic code, so to say. As Muhammad was the last of the prophets, **there is no chance of mutation in these laws.** Calls for *ijtihad* [reassessment] in the present age, if they are meant to alter such fixed laws, are futile and unnecessary.[64]

Nyazee's analogy to genetic coding seems reasonable. No matter how hard Islamic reformers, national security analysts, or pundits wish for a "reformation" that would leave behind the Islamic law that non-Muslims consider objectionable, the genetic coding (in the form of Islamic doctrine) will force a reversion to the Islamic legal norm. With the Qur'an and sunnah representing the "fixed" inner sphere of Islamic law, the two spheres are not equally weighted. This inner sphere represents the rights of Allah or of individuals who are fixed in the Qur'an, hadith [or consensus] that cannot be modified, amended, or suspended.[65] For this reason, this inner sphere really is like genetic coding, and it controls the larger body of Islamic law in both spheres. It does this through a series of functions that reflect its controlling authority or, as Nyazee describes them, "boundaries":

> The first function [of the fixed inner sphere] is to provide the basic law on which the foundations of Muslim society are laid.

> It lays down the limits or outer boundaries within which the flexible part is to be developed or evolved. These boundaries are never to be crossed. ... **All laws laid down as boundaries shall forever remain unaltered and fixed.** The flexible or changing law will have to grow and develop within these boundaries, but will never be able to affect or alter the nature of the fixed law.

> Another function of the fixed part is that it furnishes the
> principles of Islamic law. ... The sources for the principles
> of Islamic law are the Qur'an and the *Sunnah*. These princi-
> ples may be explicitly stated in the sources or may be derived
> from them and then unanimously accepted through consen-
> sus (*ijma*), which is a judicial function.[66]

Therefore, when citing laws that are known to be fixed in the Qur'an and hadith or which represent scholarly consensus (ijma), one must presume—as a matter
of law—that the fixed law represents either the exclusive or ultimate position in
shariah. This position, then, can preempt all lesser understandings of the same
concept. When accurately assessed in the inner sphere, shariah overcomes nearly all "moderate" narratives—especially the popular misconception that there are
thousands of different interpretations on any given point of Islamic law. Understood this way, competing narratives that cannot substantiate their claims should
be disfavored in national security analysis.

This gives rise to a firm rule of interpretation: If a position reflects consensus,
hadith, or the Qur'an, competing interpretations of Islamic law offered in the interest of balance must demonstrate their validity at the same level of law at which
consensus is asserted. Specifically excluded from the debate are interpretations
that cannot establish a nexus to the fixed law. Far too often, such interpretations
reflect only the aspirational ideals of self-described Islamic moderates who con-
fuse the law *as it is* with the law *as they would like it to be*. Analysis based on this
kind of aspirational moderation corrupts the analytical processes, is misleading,
and ultimately constitutes malpractice.

It is through the fixed sphere metaphor that another hard rule emerges: At
no time can a theory of law that relies solely on the flexible ever be used to defeat
a doctrine grounded in the fixed. Self-described moderates or Islamic cultural
advisors who proffer flexible arguments against fixed doctrines without disclosing
their structural weakness create an assumption of malleability in shariah where
none exists. This assumption causes analysts and decision-makers to miscalculate.

Islamic law does not appear to provide a legal basis for new interpretations of
law capable of overwriting existing rules where scholarly consensus exists. Contemporary scholar Ahmad Hasan cites Abu Dawud—one of the "sacred six" hadith authorities—to remind Muslim jurists of the dangers of violating scholarly
consensus:

> The following tradition emphasizes obedience to the first
> four Caliphs: "I [Mohammed] advise you to fear Allah and
> to obey the leader, even if he is a negro slave. One who sur-
> vives me shall see profound disagreement. You should then
> follow my Sunnah and the Sunnah of the rightly-guided
> Caliphs. Hold fast to it and follow it to the last letter. You

should desist from following new practices, because every new practice is innovation (heresy) and every innovation is error."[67]

From an authoritative voice such as Abu Dawud, the strength of the Salafi view emerges. When Hasan makes reference to "innovation" as heresy, he is referring to the Islamic concept of bid'a ("innovation"). Whereas scholarly consensus is concerned with the concept of doctrinal belief, bid'a serves as the other bookend, excluding new ideas that conflict with established principles.[68] 'Abdur Rahman I. Doi, in his treatise *Shari'ah: The Islamic Law*, asserts scholarly consensus on the concept of bid'a.[69] It stems from the doctrine that the message (deen) of Islam "is totally complete, there being no need to add to it, just as it is not permitted to take anything away from it."[70] If the sunnah points to "the right path," bid'a indicates the wrong.[71] For this reason, when arguments run afoul of hadith or established scholarly consensus, they become vulnerable to accusations of bid'a, even when such accusations come from groups we prefer to classify as "extreme." From Muhammad Al-Uthaymeen's treatise *Bidah: The Unique Nature of the Perfection Found in Islaam and the Grave Danger of Innovating It*, under the header "The Sharp Sword against the People of Innovation," we find:

> So for everything that is used to claim that there exists a good *bid'ah*, then the answer for it is all the above. Thus there can be no room for the People of Innovation to claim that their innovations are good while we have in our hand the sharp sword that Allaah's Messenger gave us—i.e., his saying that "*... every innovation leads astray.*" Indeed, this sharp sword was forged in the steel-works of Prophethood and Messengership. It was not forged in some second rate iron-mill, rather in the steel-works of the Prophet and he forged it so eloquently, that anyone who has the likes of this sharp sword in his hand would never be dumb-founded by someone claiming that bid'ah is good, for the Messenger of Allaah said that, "**... every bid'ah leads astray.**"[72]

Quranic support for the concept of bid'a comes from such verses as:

> This day have I perfected your religion for you, completed My favour upon you and have chosen for you Islam as your religion. (5:3)

> Nothing have we omitted from the Book. (6:38)

> And We have sent down to thee, a Book explaining all things. (16:89)

> So take what the Messenger assigns to you, and deny your-
> selves that which he withholds from you. And fear Allah; for
> Allah is strict in Punishment. (59:7)

Bid'a is not just an archaic doctrine; jihadis today often use it to challenge
the legitimacy of non-jihadi Muslims and "moderate" Muslim governments. For
example, through bid'a, accusations of takfirism are leveled against those who seek
to govern through democratic processes. Takfirism is a contentious doctrine principally formulated by Ibn Taymiya, a 13th-century Hanbali imam.[73] While iconic
in Hanbali circles,[74] Taymiya is disfavored in the larger Sunni community.[75] Just
as takfirism rises out of the Hanbali School, Muhammad bin Abdul Wahhab's
concepts, often referred to as Wahhabism,[76] spring from Taymiyan Hanbalism.[77]
Accusations of takfirism directly challenge the quality of a Muslim's belief. Because claims of being kufr[78]—a capital offense—are subsumed in the charge of
takfirism, the accusation is severe. In *Ruling by Other than What Allah Revealed:
The Fundamentals of Takfir*, Khalid bin Muhammad al-'Anbari explains the basis
of takfirism as a knowing act of disobedience to Allah:

> [Takfirism is when a person] is aware of all that Allah and
> His Messenger informed him, and he trusts that all which the
> believers accept is true, but he dislikes it and it angers him,
> and he is dissatisfied, so that he does not act in accordance
> with it, nor desire to. He says, 'I do not endorse, nor honor
> this.' Thereby detesting the truth and being disgusted with it
> … and labeling such a disbeliever is well known by necessi-
> ty in the religion of Islam, and the Qur'an cites the example
> of this category of *takfir*. … This is the example of Iblis [the
> Devil] and whoever follows his path. So, from this, the dis-
> tinction between the different types of disobedience is clear. If
> he believes that an act is obligatory for him, and he wants to
> do it, but his desires and weaknesses prevent him from acting
> accordingly, then he comes with faith in the truthfulness and
> submission and the willingness to comply, yet his saying that
> does not cause him to fulfill the act.[79]

Stating there is scholarly consensus that some forms of bid'a "amount to kufr
that removes the practitioner from Islam,"[80] 'Anbar then argues that "one who
innovates in religion, and one who legislates by man made laws are the same, there
is no difference between them"[81] 'Anbari then concludes that:

> the truth which cannot be denied is that the status of the
> one who judges with other than what the Lord of the worlds
> revealed is the same as the status of the one who innovates in
> the religion. Both of them legislate what Allah did not permit,
> competing with Allah over one of His attributes, attempting

to finish something for Him, by what they utter or believe. So the consensus among the *Ahl as-Sunnah* that the details of the ruling that applies to those who do these crimes, without a doubt, also apply to the one who judges by other than what Allah revealed. ...[82]

Shariah doctrines like ijma and bid'a are far from irrelevant. Given the status shariah affords scholarly consensus and, to a lesser degree, unlawful innovation (bid'a), those advocating innovative views under Islamic law should be under some obligation to disclose the inherent weakness of these views when used to challenge established doctrines. In the decade following 9/11, there have been many examples of innovation in shariah and Islamic jurisprudence, asserted or hypothesized by pundits, analysts, politicians, and Western cultural experts. ("What Islam needs is a reformation!") Some of these are little more than vaporous suggestions or fantasies about changing settled Islamic law on, for example, jihad or apostasy.

Bona fide Islamic authorities will recognize these innovations as bid'a. When those Islamic authorities (not to mention self-described "moderates") remain silent concerning arguments understood to be false, we must ask: Why? As will be explained, when such ersatz arguments are directed primarily at Western audiences and not toward the Muslim world at large, no harm is committed. The situation is entirely different, however, when those same arguments are directed at the Islamic population.

Scholarly consensus cannot be denied. The goal of narratives like "there are thousands of different interpretations of Islamic law" is to block analysis on the doctrine of scholarly consensus by insisting that it does not even need to be discussed. But if shariah is the standard by which Islam is to be measured, such a position is not sustainable.

The 'Law of the Land'

A crucial characteristic of Islamic law is that it is supposed to be the "law of the land." Contrary to popular belief, "radical" or "extremist" Muslims almost never say, "I fight jihad to gain converts to Islam." When they talk about bringing Islam to the world, they are usually referring to *Islamic law*. In fact, nearly without exception, when jihadis communicate their intentions to their enemies or to fellow Muslims, they claim that their mission is to implement the Islamic deen (law) and re-establish the Caliphate. They do not talk about religion.

Everyone who has spent time researching Islam has heard the statement: *Islam is not just a religion, but a complete way of life governed by Islamic law, which comes from Allah, who is alone sovereign.* This is not just an aphorism, but rather it states the hierarchical elements of Islam. If you are a public official charged with protecting our national security, shouldn't you be required to understand Islam as it understands itself if the enemies we fight orient and communicate in that language? Let's look at these basic components of Islam.

"Not just a religion" indicates that the theology of Islam is subordinate to the law of Islam. While the personal religious elements of Islam are—and ought to be—protected by the First Amendment, to the extent that "governed by Islamic law" means Islam should be the "law of the land," Islam's ambitions might conflict with Article VI of the U.S. Constitution. In stipulating that the Constitution "shall be the **supreme** law of the land," Article VI establishes that no higher authority or system of government can supersede its influence.

Both classical and modern views of Islamic law stress the aspirational desire of its adherents to impose it as a governing system. Islamic law addresses human behavior comprehensively, from private religious practice to politics as originally understood—that is, as a system governing the affairs between citizens of a polity. Analysis should be limited to those non-religious practices based in Islamic legal requirements that necessarily bring them into conflict with Article VI. Strictly religious practices as historically understood in the West should not serve as a basis for subjecting Muslims to discrimination. Our way of life is not threatened by a religion. It is threatened by those claiming a body of law that asserts jurisdiction over non-Muslims that is explicitly antithetical to our own Constitution and democratic principles.

Hence, it is important to understand the claim that Islam is a way of life "governed by Islamic law." If Islamic law really does make a claim to being the "law of the land," then we must remember that we took oaths to support and defend the Constitution against the unlawful imposition of foreign law in the United States. Certainly "violent extremists" declare that Islamic law is, or should be, the "law of the land." But are they right? When considering this question, we should remember that the proper answer is based on issues of fact, not opinion.

If we followed our own threat doctrine, we would only orient on the facts of the enemy's stated threat doctrine, not on presuppositions about what we think it means to us. The jihadis do not say they fight to impose Islamic *theology* on non-Muslims; they say they undertake the mission of jihad in the cause of Allah to implement shariah. The constitutional oath requires us to "support and defend against all enemies," and it makes no exception for those who fight us for a "religious" purpose. We do not hesitate to monitor extreme groups such as the Ku Klux Klan and other outliers of other religious communities that articulate a threat.

To get a sense for how shariah characterizes itself as a body of law governing man and society, consider the views of some moderate Islamic jurists from reasonably moderate jurisdictions. Note that the books cited do not have "theology" or "religion" in the title, but rather "law" and "jurisprudence" in jurisdictions that recognize shariah as law. Indian Islamic jurist Asaf A.A. Fyzee, writing in *Outlines of Muhammadan Law*, maintains that:

The Koran according to this theory is the first source of law.
...It is for this reason that the verses of the Koran (ayat),
although only a few of them deal specifically with legal questions, are held to be of paramount authority.[83]

By establishing the supremacy of shariah, 'Abdur Rahman Doi, Malaysian
jurist and author of *Shari'ah: The Islamic Law*, denies a substantive role for democracy in Islamic law. As the outlines of the Islamic governing system emerge from
Allah, individuals and governments may "enjoy a derivative rule-making power,"
as long as it doesn't contradict the shariah. He writes:

In the Shari'ah, there is an explicit emphasis on the fact that
Allah is the Lawgiver and the whole Ummah, the nation of
Islam, is merely His trustee. **It is because of this principle
that the Ummah enjoys a derivative rule-making power**
and not an absolute law-creating prerogative. The Islamic
State, like the whole of what one might call Islamic political psychology, views the Dar al-Islam (Abode of Islam) as
one vast homogeneous commonwealth of people who have
a common ideology in all matters both spiritual and tem-
poral. The entire Muslim Ummah lives under the Shari'ah
to which every member has to submit, with sovereignty belonging to Allah alone.[84]

The Holy Qur'an has warned those who fail to apply the
Shari'ah in the following strong words:

"And if any fail to judge by the light of what Allah has revealed, they are not better than those who rebel." (5:50) "And
if any fail to judge by the light of what Allah has revealed,
they are no better than wrong-doers." (5:48) "And if any fail
to judge by the light of what Allah has revealed, they are no
better than unbelievers." (5:47)[85]

After these Qur'anic references, Doi continues:

As we noted before, the Shari'ah was not revealed for limited
application for a specific age. It will suit every age and time.
It will remain valid and shall continue to be, till the end of
this life on earth. Its injunctions were coined in such a manner that they are not affected by the lapse of time. **They do
not become obsolete, nor do their general principles and
basic theories need to be changed or renovated.**[86]

Mohammad Hashim Kamali, a professor of law at the International Islamic

University of Malaysia, says in *Principles of Islamic Jurisprudence*:

> **Sovereignty in Islam is the prerogative of Almighty Allah alone.** He is the absolute arbiter of values and it is His will that determines good and evil, right and wrong. [87]

Kamali's next statement reflects a rejection of democratic principles that is in line with Doi's reasoning:

> It is neither the will of the ruler **nor of any assembly of men, nor even the community as a whole,** that determines the values and the laws which uphold those values. ...The sovereignty of the people, if the use of the word 'sovereignty' is appropriate at all, is a delegated, or executive, sovereignty ... only. [88]

These jurists are not members of al-Qaeda. They did not publish their treatises in so-called "radicalized" countries. And yet they state—in unambiguous terms—that Islamic law is the law of the land.

Imran Ahsan Khan Nyazee is a Pakistani associate professor of Islamic law in Islamabad. In his treatise *Theories of Islamic Law: The Methodology of Ijtihad* , Nyazee states: [89]

> Islam, it is generally acknowledged, is a "complete way of life" and at the core of this code is the law of Islam.

He goes on to describe a concept demonstrating that Islamic law rejects democratic principles:

> No other sovereign or authority is acceptable to the Muslim, unless it guarantees the application of these laws in their entirety. **Any other legal system, howsoever attractive it may appear on the surface, is alien for Muslims and is not likely to succeed in the solution of their problems; it would be doomed from the start. ... A comprehensive application of these laws,** which flow directly or indirectly from the decrees (*ahkam*) of Allah, would mean that they **should regulate every area of life,** from politics to private transactions, from criminal justice to the laws of traffic, from ritual to international law, and from the laws of taxation and finance to embezzlement and white collar crimes.[90]

This is a clear assertion that Islamic law requires the regulation of *everything*. It also says that "no other sovereign or authority is acceptable to the Muslim, unless it guarantees the application of these laws in their entirety."

What about Islamic authorities in the United States? Surely they would not take the same hard line as some of the foreign imams from the Middle East. What about an imam with a reputation for peace and healing? In his treatise *Islam: A Sacred Law*, Feisal Abdul Rauf, the lead advocate for the Ground Zero Mosque in New York City, establishes the types of things governed by Islamic law.

> But justice and equity, and the concepts of right and wrong, can only be an extension of an attachment to God and abiding by His dictates. And since a *Shari'ah* is understood as a law with God at its center, it is not possible in principle to limit the *Shari'ah* to some aspect of human life and leave out others. ...
>
> And in reading a typical compendium on Islamic law, you will notice that, having discussed the list of credal (sic) and specifically religious ritual topics given above, it goes on to deal with family or personal law (i.e., marriage, divorce, paternity, guardianship and succession and inheritance), then with the law of contracts, or civil wrongs and criminal law; followed by the law of evidence and procedure, and with a multitude of other subjects, to a degree of detail that it covers even the rules of social etiquette, called *adab*. Even "Emily Post" issues are under the umbrella of the *Shari'ah*. The ***Shari'ah* thus covers every field of law—public and private, national and international**—together with enormous amounts of material that Westerners would not regard as law at all, because the basis of *Shari'ah* is the worship and obedience to, God through good works and moral behavior. Following the Sacred Law thus defines the Muslim's belief in God. [91]

Accepting the current necessity of having to rely on the U.S. court system, Minneapolis Imam Walid bin Idris bin 'Abd Al-'Aziz Al-Manisi, as a member of the "Permanent Fatwa Committee" of the Assembly of Muslim Jurists of America (AMJA), wrote a legal analysis in Arabic concerning the posture that American Muslims should take with regard to the courts in which they operate, including officers of the court—attorneys and judges.[92] Titled "Judicial Work Outside the Lands of Islam—What Is Permitted and What Is Forbidden" and published by AMJA in 2007, al-Manisi's legal monograph stated that Muslims who are appointed judges in American courts should judge according to shariah while always hating "man-made" law:

> That he understand the Shari'a in such a manner as to be able to rule by it in every case brought before him, or at least

as close as he's able to from the cases brought before him. He also must in his heart hate the man-made law.[93]

Hatred of man-made law is hatred of the American legal system. The AMJA imam continued by relying on Sheikh Salih bin 'Abd-al-'Aziz al-Shaykh to point out that even though necessity may require one to use a *kufar* court (*kufar* is a derogatory term meaning "infidel" / "unbeliever"), one must nevertheless always remain hostile to that forum:

> Shaykh Salih bin 'Abd-al-'Aziz Al al-Shaykh explained that this means:

> It is required for a Muslim to be hostile to courts which rule by man-made law, and to dislike them.

> If you were wronged and you demand your rights which are guaranteed by the Shari'a, and you have no other recourse but to go to the man-made courts, **and you have hatred in your heart for the courts,** you are permitted to do so.

> Some scholars say "**with hatred for the courts,**" but there is no validity for the hatred. It is permitted for him to reclaim his right without hatred.

Al-Manisi then recapped Islamic scholarship on the use of *kufar* courts:

> To summarize the words of the scholars, it is permitted to seek recourse in man-made courts if the following three conditions are present:

> 1. You are unable to reclaim your rights in any other way, because your adversary refuses to refer the case to the Shari'a, or he refuses to execute the ruling of the Shari'a.

> 2. You do not take more than the rights guaranteed by the Shari'a; for if they ruled that you should receive more than your rights under the Shari'a, you do not take more than what you're entitled to by the Shari'a from your adversary.

> 3. **At the time that you go to the court, you feel hatred for it in your heart.** Without these three conditions present, it is forbidden to refer judgment to man-made courts. He who does so is in danger of **apostatizing** from Islam, Allah forbid(s).[94]

It should be noted that the English name of the group, "Assembly of Muslim Jurists of America," is not a direct translation of its Arabic name. The Arabic designation is *M'juma Fuqaha Shariah Amrikia* and translates as "The Association (Group) of Legal Specialists in *Shari'a* Law in America." This means that AMJA's role in America is to covertly implement shariah law within the American legal system. At what point does covert fidelity to one legal system while working in another begin to represent a profound contempt of court—a miscarriage of justice—and subversion? Not to be overlooked, al-Manisi wrote his analysis for the benefit of American Muslims who are already members of an American bar, and he states that the only legitimate law is shariah, citing non-American foreign jurists for authority. Imam Manisi cites the Saudi Minister in his legal brief as an authority for the proper practice of law for American judges who are Muslim. This should cause some concern.

It would also be easier to downplay all of this were it not for the fact that the document appears to have currency within the American Islamic community. AMJA is an association of American Muslim jurists, with prominent members and experts[95] among its cadre and a senior leadership with exceptionally elite shariah pedigrees.[96] The Minneapolis imam's legal analysis advocates that Muslims who are judges in American courts should render decisions according to Islamic law. This is certainly the stated goal of the Muslim Brotherhood. Finally, there is Manisi's repeated use of the term *dar al-Kufar* ("the land [house] of the infidel") to refer to America, effectively endorsing America's status as the object of jihad.

Some of the best resources for Western analysts seeking to understand what the Qur'an and shariah mean to Muslims are textbooks designed to instruct Muslim students in their own way of life. A wealth of middle-school instructional material—all written in English—is available in the United States for anyone interested in learning more about Islam. A good example is the school textbook *What Islam Is All About,* by Yahiya Emerick. This is what is taught to American Muslims at the seventh-grade level:

> Muslims know that Allah is the Supreme Being in the universe; therefore, His laws and commandments must form the basis for all human affairs.[97]

While that statement might be relatively uncontroversial, what about this one?

> **The basis of the legal and political system is the Shari'ah of Allah.** Its main sources are the Qur'an and Sunnah. **Muslims dream of establishing the power of Islam in the world.**[98]

It seems Emerick is saying Muslims dream of establishing the power of Islamic law in the world. In fact, he tells us explicitly:

> The law of the land is the Shari'ah of Allah.[99]

The idea that Islamic law is the law of the land is not just something taught in rarified treatises or remote madrassas; it is taught in the United States—today—as a part of children's instruction. Of course, if Islamic school texts teach that shariah is the law of the land, it necessarily means that American Muslim children are taught that the Constitution is *not* the law of the land.

There is ample evidence that mainstream Islamic law considers itself to be the law of the land. For the extreme skeptic, there is dispositive proof that an American Muslim, in reading books on Islamic law in English, could reasonably believe this to be the case, even if those books incorrectly describe the status of Islam. Because these books—as well as the recognized experts who wrote them—are authoritative within the Muslim community, analysis of threats associated with Islamic legal motivations must account for them.

With regard to the claim that, according to Islamic texts, Islamic law should be the law of the land, a burden of proof has been met. It is supported by numerous authorities from moderate Muslim countries and by a well-established American imam's treatise on Islamic law, and it is even recognized as a part of children's instruction in the United States.

To overcome the burden these facts present—or, more accurately, to create the illusion that it has been overcome—the national security community has extended its source selection into the counterfactual domain. In other words, it introduces doctrinally incorrect or vague hypotheses about Islam to create the requisite "balance" that provides cover for the adoption of competing positions in deliberate decision-making and policy circles. Un-sourced claims based on cultural advisors' articulation of their own "personal Islam" are then weighted as strongly as real evidence. In a court of law, this would be called hearsay. Absent any facts to support such competing narratives, the ensuing "balance" facilitates a misrepresentation of knowable facts.

Constitutions and Islamic States

Thus far, we have seen from Islamic legal sources, including professors and experts who write treatises and educational materials on Islamic law, that Islamic law is understood to be the law of the land. If that fails to be convincing, remember that the constitutions of the Arab world and, indeed, in most of the Muslim world, likewise regard Islamic law as the law of the land.

Some may think the world's only Islamic Republics are Pakistan and Iran. That is not so. Add Afghanistan and Iraq to the list, because we designated them as such even before ISIS began making its move. The constitutions drafted by the U.S. State Department for Afghanistan and Iraq expressly establish both countries as Islamic Republics. Both constitutions are expressly subordinated to Islamic law and, as written, nullify the democratic principles we claim to be fighting to establish. In real terms, this means al-Qaeda's long-term objectives were met at the expense of America's by the constitutions we wrote. From the Constitution of Iraq:

> Section One, Article 2: **First:** Islam is the official religion of
> the State and it is a basic source of legislation: (a) No law can
> be passed that contradicts **the undisputed rules of Islam.** [100]

Overseeing the production of a constitution with this language constitutes unrecoverable error that made either Iranian hegemony or the rise of ISIS – or both – inevitable, and I briefed this as early as 2003. Self-described Muslim moderates and cultural experts tell us there are no "undisputed rules of Islam." If they are right, we can wink and allow this language of deference to "undisputed rules" in their constitutions, knowing it reflects little more than an aspirational gesture. But what of those who demanded it be included out of a sincere desire to see those "undisputed rules" govern their country? What of those who make the same demands and become suicide bombers? They really believe there are "undisputed rules" in Islam—and we established those rules as "the law of the land."

We did the same in the Constitution of Afghanistan:

> [Article 2, Religions] (1) The religion of the state of the Islamic Republic of Afghanistan is the sacred religion of Islam.

> [Article 3, Law and Religion] **In Afghanistan, no law can be contrary to the beliefs and provisions of the sacred religion of Islam.** [101]

What of the constitutions of other Muslim countries? They include deference to shariah as well. To begin with, take a look at Syria:

> [Article 3, Section 2, Islam] of the Syrian Constitution: **Islamic jurisprudence is a main source of legislation.**[102]

Then there is Jordan:

> [Chapter 1, Article 2] Islam is the religion of the State and Arabic is its official language.

> [Chapter 1, Article 106] The Shari'a Courts shall in the exercise of their jurisdiction **apply the provisions of the Shari'a law.**[103]

Saudi Arabia:

> [Chapter 1, Article 7] Government in Saudi Arabia derives power from the Holy Qur'an and the Prophet's tradition[104]

Even before a new constitution was approved in Egypt, even during the Mubarak regime, Islam's basis as the source of law was assured:

> [Part 1, Article 2] **Islamic jurisprudence is the principal source of legislation.** [105]

The American-sponsored constitutions of Afghanistan and Iraq, along with those of Jordan, Saudi Arabia, Egypt, and Syria, all name shariah as the primary basis of law. In anticipation of the Muslim Brotherhood's brief ascent to power in Egypt, a referendum revealed that 77 percent of Egyptians called for the retention of the constitutional language making shariah the basis of law in Egypt.[106] Remembering that at least 12 percent of Egypt is Coptic Christian, this puts the referendum at a number approaching 90 percent of Egyptian Muslims who voted. That is far from our unprofessional yet widely cited estimate that only 10 percent of the Muslim population agreed with the Islamic law that al-Qaeda and the Muslim Brotherhood seeks to implement.

Skeptics might argue that these countries do not really follow Islamic law. And that may be true. Indeed, when we hear Muslim "violent extremists" accuse their governments and their leaders of violating their own constitutions by not following Islamic law, they may be "radically" correct.

Looking at the constitutions of much of the Muslim world, Nyazee seems to be correct in saying no other sovereign or authority is acceptable to a great many Muslims unless it guarantees the application of Islamic law in its entirety. That's what we gave Iraq and Afghanistan. But if both of those constitutions are subordinated to the whole of Islamic law, then wherever the rights and freedoms articulated in the constitutions conflict with Islamic law, shariah must prevail.

Even if only for the purpose of due diligence, when we analyze countries that officially subordinate their constitutions to shariah, our analysis should be required to account for shariah as the law of the land. After all, their constitutions explicitly state it is the law of the land. Failure to take this relevant fact into account degrades the integrity of our intelligence analysis, undermining the production of the enemy's most likely and most dangerous courses of action. Not to account for it at all—or, worse, to erect barriers to even recognizing its existence—is to deny ourselves vital information that should be supporting critical decision-making. This is not to say that every Muslim country that recognizes a role for shariah in its governance promotes terrorism. Threat analysis is concerned only with those countries, organizations, and individuals that actually promote, facilitate, or engage in such activities. Likewise, it is also concerned only with Islamic-based doctrines in so far as they support a threat doctrine, regardless of whether those doctrines are correctly or incorrectly characterized by those acting in furtherance of them.

One is hard put to explain the attitude among our military and government leaders toward efforts to explore the forces that motivate our enemies' actions. If President Obama is correct that Islam has been the "one organizing principle" in the Muslim world, why would the national security apparatus punish those who seek to understand it?

The Red Pill

Once satisfying personal needs and making a private profit are considered important and legitimate motives [of war], subversion, treachery and shifting allegiances by individuals and entire units will become as commonplace as they have often been in the past. To quote Philip II, father of Alexander the Great: where an army cannot pass, a donkey laden with gold often will. Such is likely to be the stuff of which future strategy is made.

Judging by the experience of the last two decades, the visions of long-range, computerized, high-tech warfare so dear to the military-industrial complex will never come to pass. Armed conflict will be waged by men on earth, not robots in space. It will have more in common with the struggles of primitive tribes than with large-scale conventional war of the kind that the world may have seen.

Martin Van Creveld
The Transformation of War, 1991[1]

Within the U.S. national security community, as well as among the general public, there is a hunger to understand who are America's enemies in the War on Terror, why they targeted us on 9/11, and why they continue to do so with vehemence. Many books have been written on the subject. But there is a growing sense among the American public, and certainly among some elements of the intelligence and law enforcement communities, that the available explanations do not "add up." And while many analysts have been briefed on aspects of Islam referenced by al-Qaeda and Islamic thinkers like Muslim Brotherhood theorist Sayyid Qutb—who was named in the 9/11 Commission report—there is no over-arching explanation that satisfies.

In 2005, I began to lecture on Sayyid Qutb and his *Milestones* as the central basis for understanding the operational aspects of Islamic terrorism. Far from being obviously "radical" and isolated from the mainstream, Qutb's position—his process of re-establishing Islamic governance, which has been adopted by our terrorist enemies and, at one point, by the elected Government of Egypt—makes genuine claims to being substantively aligned with mainstream Islamic law from which it draws its authority. This alignment comes through a doctrine of Islamic law known as abrogation, which asserts that Qur'an verses revealed later in time supersede those come earlier. (The concept will be dealt with in greater detail shortly.) By understanding abrogation, we can understand terrorism's nexus to shariah on issues that affect America, namely jihad and the laws regarding Muslim interactions with non-Muslims. We can also understand the process, laid down by Qutb, by which Islamic groups intend to institute these laws.

Recognition of the relationship between shariah and Brotherhood doctrine opens up a new way to understand our self-identified enemy, a way that has proven its ability to interpret enemy strategic communications and to predict threat behavior. It has had a transformative effect on how those who have been briefed on the topic now understand the enemy – so much so that some took to calling it "The Red Pill Brief."

The reference is to the popular 1999 science fiction movie *The Matrix*, in which the hero is given the option of taking a red pill that will enable him to see the world as it truly is. He is warned, however, that if he takes the pill, he can never return to the computer-generated reality to which he is accustomed, made necessary by the requirement to hide the malevolent nature of the world in which he actually lives.

Understanding the law of abrogation and its effects on the Islamic concept of jihad has a similar effect. If properly understood, you may come to see the War on Terror in an entirely different light. You will also see that many of the explanations we've been given are not only fantasy but, as in *The Matrix*, propagated by the very forces we are fighting in order to neutralize our ability to defend ourselves and defeat them.

Abrogation

Imagine that over the weekend, al-Qaeda leader Ayman al-Zawahiri gives a speech. In it, he asks his fellow Muslims, "Why are some of you siding with the Americans? They are a bunch of Crusaders and Zionists; they are a bunch of Christians and Jews. Islamic law clearly states that you are not allowed to take them as friends."

At the White House, the State Department, and the Pentagon, policymakers and analysts salivate over an opportunity to isolate the extremists from mainstream Muslims. Afraid of an al-Qaeda propaganda coup, the U.S. government spends a few million dollars over the next few days in an earnest public diplomacy campaign targeting the Muslim community in that part of the world. "Al-Qaeda is engaging in hate speech," our narrative maintains. "They are distorting the true, peaceful message of Islam." Buoyed by self-described moderate cultural advisors from Islamic organizations, our best and brightest confidently attack Zawahiri's argument, pointing out that "Islam, in fact, reveres Christians and Jews as People of the Book."

Soon, our message is disseminated with all the resources afforded to us by our status as a media and social media superpower. Translated quickly into Arabic, Pashto, Farsi, and Urdu, our message is primed for discussion at the upcoming Friday sermons across the Islamic world. We wait expectantly, ready to hear imams call out both Zawahiri and al-Qaeda for their hate speech. But there's silence.

What happened? Regardless of the money and energy we spent on public diplomacy, the Islamic world understood Zawahiri's statement as being *doctrinally correct* based on the concept of abrogation. Our leaders' failure to grasp this concept is why this type of messaging not only doesn't work—it actually gives an advantage to our foes.

More than any other aspect of shariah, the Islamic doctrine of abrogation provides the key to unlocking the jihadi meta-narrative. Briefing on abrogation is controversial because it explains the alignment of Islamic law with Muslim Brotherhood doctrines that groups like al-Qaeda also follow -- and because the material can be presented in a non-speculative manner. In fact, within the national security space, cultural experts and self-described moderates demand policymakers remain ignorant of the power and implications of abrogation, going so far as insisting the concept doesn't exist at all. I have been asked not to brief it. But awareness of how it works brings clarity to what the Intelligence Community has stubbornly refused to understand and can allow analysts to generate indicators of future intent that give decision-makers the ability to make informed decisions. Based on these insights, forecasts of the strategic posture of the Islamic Movement have proven to be productive and stable.

To explain this in a substantive manner, we must go where our moderates and cultural experts tell us not to go: to the Qur'an. We will look at a few verses and provide some explanation of their meaning based on recognized Islamic sources. This deep dive into Islamic doctrine will set up our future understanding of arguments that can be understood only when assessed in light of shariah.

During the course of the discussion, the focus will be on several classic texts of Islamic law. The first, from the Shafi'ite school, is *Reliance of the Traveller*, or the *'Umdat al-Salik*, by Al-Misri. It was written in the 14th century and later translated and annotated by Nuh Ha Mim Keller. The second is the *Al-Hidayah by al-Marghinani,* which came out of the 12th century and reflects classic Hanafi Islamic law.[2] Third is the classic Islamic treatise *Shaybani's Siyar*—available to us today in Professor Majid Khadduri's translation, *The Islamic Law of Nations*—the oldest extant text of Islamic law on warfare.[3] Fourth is *The Distinguished Jurist's Primer,* by Ibn Rushd, a classic Maliki text first published in the 12th century.[4] Ibn Rushd was a *qadi,* or Islamic law judge, in the Cordoban court in Andalus (now Spain). He is better known by the *nom de plume* "Averroës" in the West. Other useful classical texts include *Tafsir Ibn Kathir* and others with recognized status in the Islamic world.[5]

Reliance recognizes the dangers associated with personal interpretation of the Qur'an. It cites Mohammed's warning that "whoever speaks of the Book of Allah from his own opinion is in error."[6] *Reliance* restates this concern again later:

> Never explain the Holy Koran by your own opinion, but check to see how it has been understood by the scholars of Sacred Law and men of wisdom who came before you. If you comprehend something else by it and what you have understood contradicts the Sacred Law, forsake your wretched opinion and fling it against the wall.[7]

As explained in *Tafsir al-Jalalayn,* a classic 15th century tafsir commentary, "in order to gain access to this precious knowledge [of the Qur'an] and to the wisdom in engenders, it is necessary to refer to a *tafsir* or commentary that is based on authoritative transmitted knowledge and is free from the subjective speculation that characterizes certain more recent commentaries."[8] A tafsir is "a commentary of explanations of the meaning of the Qur'an."[9] As *Reliance* states, "the Koran and hadith commentaries are of tremendous importance to teachers, speakers, and translators who are preparing materials to present to Muslim audiences."[10] Recognizing that it is difficult for non-Arabic-speaking Muslims to get to the meaning of the Qur'an, *Tafsir al-Jalalayn* notes:

> Those that are well-versed in classical Arabic can refer to any of the standard *tafsirs* they may find. But what of the Muslim whose mother tongue is not Arabic? How can he or she begin to approach the meaning of the Qur'an without being daunted at the outset? How can the seeker's hunger for knowledge be both satisfied and further stimulated without risk of either an overdose or indigestion? The answer is to refer to a reliable translation of the text, and also a reliable translation of at least one authoritative commentary.[11]

To fill the need for reliable translations of authoritative commentary, this book relies primarily on *Tafsir Ibn Kathir,* with some support from *Tafsir al-Jalalayn.* Of *Tafsir Ibn Kathir,* Darussalam, the Saudi publisher states:

> Since the Qur'an is the primary source of Islamic teachings, the correct understanding of the Qur'an is necessary for ev-

ery Muslim. The *Tafsir of Ibn Kathir* is the most renowned and accepted explanation of the Qur'an in the entire world.[12]

Regarding Tafsir *al-Jalalayn*:

> There have been a number of standard classical *tafsirs* that have stood the test of time, such as ... Ibn Kathir. Among the briefest and most easily accessible is *Tafsir al-Jalalayn*, which ever since its completion more than half a millennium ago has been considered the essential first text in the study of the meaning of the Qur'an by teachers and students throughout the Islamic world.[13]

Modern texts are also appropriate to this discussion if they are credible reflections of authoritative Islamic law or doctrine. The *Quranic Concept of War*, written in 1979 by Pakistani Brigadier General S. K. Malik,[14] was praised by the country's future president, Zia ul Haq, then serving as the Army Chief of Staff. Significantly, Haq declared the book to be Pakistani war doctrine.15 Closer to home, we find a top-selling school text for American Muslim children, Yahiya Emerick's *What Islam Is All About*. This text has also been approved for use in federal penitentiaries.[16] Another focus of our study is a monograph by Imran Ahsan Khan Nyazee on *The Methodology of Ijtihad*, or the roots of Islamic law.[17]

Everything you are about to read has been briefed at all levels of the Department of Defense since 2005, much of it since 2003. If you are unfamiliar with the concepts that follow—or are unfamiliar with these or similar Islamic doctrinal texts—you cannot understand the jihadi narrative and, hence, cannot not understand the nature of the threat in what has been called, for better or for worse, the War on Terror. If you have responsibilities in the War on Terror, and you have never heard of these terms, it is prima facie evidence of never having researched the basis of the enemy's stated threat doctrine. I recommended an entire year of study for these topics because of the depth of research required: one hour to learn it, and the rest of the year to come to terms with the fact that that's what it means, it's so straightforward—yet so wildly unknown—and of such great consequence not only in itself but because of its impact on our downstream understanding of current and future events.

How Abrogation Works

Over the time of revelation in the period of the Prophet Mohammed, contradictions in what was revealed to him became apparent. For example, while both of the following Quranic verses deal with the same subject matter—relations between Muslims and non-Muslims—their meanings could not be more different.

Let there be no compulsion in religion: Truth stands out clear from error: whoever rejects evil and believes in Allah hath grasped the most trustworthy handhold. (Qur'an 2:256)

Whoever seeks a religion other than Islam will never have it accepted of him, and he will be of those who have truly failed in the hereafter. (Qur'an 3:85)

Because of these apparent contradictions, Islamic scholars and ordinary believers expended some effort to ensure they follow Allah's commandments correctly. As the Muslim Brotherhood argues, the process by which these messages are reconciled within shariah is the one dictated by the Qur'an itself: abrogation.

No fewer than three different citations from the Qur'an find Allah explaining that he reveals directives in stages; with each advance to a new stage, he abrogates, or controls directives associated with earlier stages. Nyazee describes abrogation in *Islamic Jurisprudence* by establishing the doctrine as revealed through direct divine revelation in the period of Mohammed:

> The law was laid down in the period of the Prophet (peace be unto him) **gradually and in stages**. The aim was to bring a society steeped in immorality to observe the highest standards of morality. This could not be done abruptly. It was done in stages, and doing so **necessitated repeal and abrogation of certain laws.**[18]

He continues, explaining abrogation using its legal meanings in Arabic terms:

> The literal meaning of *naskh* is canceling or transferring. In its technical sense it is used to mean the "lifting (*raf'*) of a legal rule through a legal evidence of a later date." The abrogating text or evidence is called *nasikh*, while the repealed rule is called the *mansukh*.[19]

As the Brotherhood insists, abrogation is central to understanding what Allah prescribes for those who follow His message; in fact, there can be no coherent understanding of Islam, its law or its religious teachings, without it. This is so obvious that cultural experts or self-described moderates who fail to account for the doctrine of abrogation should be considered suspect.

Because the Qur'an—the basis for Islamic law—was revealed "gradually and in stages," the chronologically later verses are always considered to reflect the more binding points of Islamic law. In other words, we should expect that verses revealed later overrule or control what was revealed earlier. Fyzee remarks in *Outlines of Muhammadan Law*:

> The Qur'an according to this theory is the first source of law.

... It is for this reason that the verse of the Qur'an (*ayat*), although only a few of them deal specifically with legal questions, are held to be of paramount authority. **In interpreting the Quranic verses, one important principle has to be observed. Some verses are deemed to be the abrogating (*nasikh*) verses and some to be the abrogated (*mansukh*) ones. Generally speaking the earlier verses are deemed to be repealed by the later ones.**[20]

Tafsir Al-Jalalayn is an authoritative commentary on the Qur'an. It can serve as a powerful indicator that there is no genuine controversy concerning the status of abrogation within the Islamic community. In the section below, the words in bold are Quranic citations and those in normal font represent *Al-Jalalayn's* interlinear tafsir explanation.

Verse 17:106. **We have divided up the Qur'an**—meaning "We have sent it down in parts over the course of twenty or twenty-three years"—**so you may recite it to mankind at intervals**—slowly and deliberately over time so that they may understand it—**and we have sent it down little by little**—in to their best interests.

Verse 16:101. **If We replace one ayat with another one**, by abrogating it and replacing it with another, in mankind's best interests—**and Allah knows best what He is sending down**—they (the unbelievers) say to the Prophet, may Allah bless him and grant him peace, '**You are just inventing this** and are lying, making it up!' **No indeed! Most of them have no knowledge** of the reality of the Qur'an and the benefit of abrogation.

Verse 2:106. When the unbelievers attacked the possibility of abrogation and said, "Muhammad commands his companions to do something one day and forbids them it the next," this was revealed. **Whenever We abrogate** (read as *nansahk* and *nunsikh*) **an ayat** by changing the judgement (sic) it contains, in expression or in recitation **or cause it to be forgotten**, meaning We hold it back and do not send down its decrees and remove its recitation, or keep it in the Preserved Tablet, **We bring one better than it** and more beneficial for people in that it is easier or has a greater reward **or equal to it** in respect of obligation and reward. **Do you not know that Allah has power over all things**, meaning He can alter, change or affirm as He likes?[21]

Verses 16:101 and 2:106 were the same selected by Fort Hood shooter Nidal Hasan in slide 17 of his presentation, "The Koranic Worldview as it Relates to Muslims in the U.S. Military." Unsurprisingly, he titled that slide "Rule of Abrogation."[22]

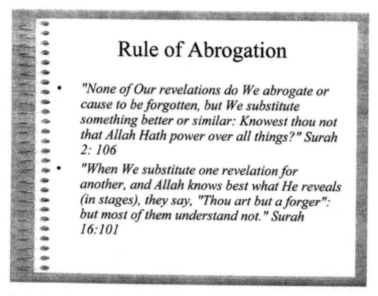

In his slide presentation, Fort Hood shooter MAJ Nidal Malik Hasan accurately cites Surahs 16:101 and 2:106 to explain the Islamic concept of abrogation. Its reference in the Qur'an means that abrogation is understood as the revealed word of Allah

When reading Verse 16:101, imagine that you are in 7th-century Arabia. Mohammed is receiving a revelation, and the new revelation seems to contradict an earlier revelation. A critic of the prophet stands up and says, "But Mohammed, you're making this stuff up!" This must have caused some controversy—so much so that a revelation arose that was both an admonition and a warning to those who questioned Mohammed's sincerity. A paraphrase of Verse 16:101 demonstrates how it affirmed Mohammed's authority by affirming progressive revelation: "When I, Allah, substitute one revelation for another, I know what I am doing. How dare you accuse Mohammed of falsifying my revelations! You don't understand!" Yes, the status of abrogation was resolved in the period of the Prophet by no less an authority than Allah, as recorded in the Qur'an. In a commentary of Verse 16:101 in *The Meaning of the Holy Qur'an*, Yusuf Ali explains how Islamic scholars deal with charges of "forgery" arising from abrogation, from Mohammed's time to the present day:

The **doctrine of progressive revelation** from age to age and time to time does not mean that Allah's fundamental Law changes. It is not fair to charge a Prophet of Allah with forgery because the Message, as revealed to him, is in a different form than revealed before, when the core of the Truth is the same, for it comes from Allah.[23]

Well-meaning Christians and Jews who take their biblical studies seriously often transpose their notions of progressive revelation to the Islamic one. In so doing, they arrive at mistaken understandings that nonetheless make sense to them. Similarities between Judeo-Christian and Islamic concepts are superficial, often beginning and ending with the use of a term they have in common. When talking about Islamic concepts of progressive revelation, it is only the Islamic concept of progressive revelation that centers on the rule of abrogation.

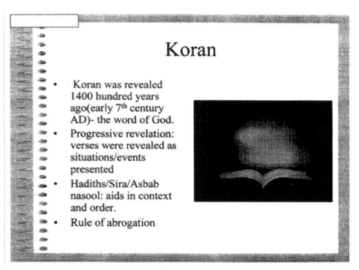

In this slide, Hasan is describing progressive revelation in the Islamic context. It is a mistake to interpret Islamic law through preconceived notions of what certain terms mean in a Western context.

In slide 16 of his presentation, titled "Koran," Hasan affirms this Islamic concept of progressive revelation that centers on the "Rule of Abrogation":

> Progressive Revelation: verses were revealed as situation/ events presented.[24]

Deciphering Allah's definitive view of a given verse is made slightly more difficult by the Qur'an's organization, as it is arranged not chronologically but by the length of the surahs, or chapters. When the scholars compiled the Qur'an, they put an introductory surah first, but after that the Qur'an was ordered by the size of the surahs, from the longest to the shortest. The first surah in the Qur'an is very brief and serves as an introduction. After that, Surah 2 (at around 105 pages) is the longest in the Qur'an. Surah 3 is the second-longest, Surah 4 is the third longest, and so on.

Chronologically, the Qur'an is divided into the Meccan and Medinan periods. Some scholars break the Meccan period down further into early, middle, and late periods. Surah 2 is generally understood to be the first surah of the later Medina period. Surah 9 is understood to be the last chapter to speak on the issue of jihad, and Surah 5 is the final word on relations with non-Muslims. It should be noted that while there is some disagreement among Islamic authorities on the specific ordering of some surahs, there is agreement on the relative ordering as it relates to this discussion.

As noted, the four main schools of Sunni Islamic law are in general agreement on most aspects of Islamic law. A single Muslim jurist does not read Islamic law and decide for himself what is or is not abrogated. These issues have already been decided. If he follows Hanafi, Maliki, Shafi'ite, or Hanbali schools of Islamic jurisprudence, he will refer to his school's books on abrogating (nasikh) and abrogated (mansukh) texts. No one can become an Islamic jurist until he knows the abrogating and abrogated texts by heart; they are that important.[25]

Looking at the entire body of the Qur'an, there are far more surahs associated with the Meccan period than with the Medinan period. Yet in size, Surahs 2, 3, 4, 5, 8, and 9 are among the largest surahs in the Qur'an, and they are all from the Medinan period. Surahs 109, 112, 113, and 114—from the Meccan period— occupy less than a page. In other words, the number of surahs does not reflect either the relative size or authority of the Meccan verses when compared to the Medinan.

Islamic law is substantially derived from the Medinan period, so a rule of law emerging from the Medinan period, through abrogation, controls or overrules anything on the same subject from the Meccan period. Similarly, the later Medinan writings control or overrule the earlier. MAJ Nidal Hasan pointed out this distinction between Medinan and Meccan verses in his slide 35, "Jihad-rule of Abrogation," where he associates the concept of abrogation with the obligation to build up power to engage in offensive jihad.

> ## Example: Jihad-rule of Abrogation
>
> - In Mecca Muslims were not permitted to defend themselves/fight. There only job was to deliver the message (peaceful verses)
> - Emigration to Medina: self defense was allowed
> - Then offensive fighting was allowed
> - Later verses abrogated former ie: peaceful verses no longer apply
> - Indeed at one point Islamic empire spanned form Morocco/Spain to the Border of India/China.

Hasan notes the next stage, in which offensive fighting was permitted, and then states, "Later verses abrogated former ie: peaceful verses no longer apply."[26] There is no question that abrogation played a substantive role in forming Hasan's orientation to both Islamic law and to jihad.

Abrogation and Threat Analysis

Later in the book, we will examine how Islamic law answers questions that are crucial in defining the enemy threat doctrine. These will include the legal definition of jihad, clarity on relations with non-Muslims, and the meaning of terrorism, blasphemy, and other concepts. In order to understand the Islamic legal basis for these issues and their subsequent resolution by scholars in shariah, we must understand the abrogating effects of certain doctrinally important verses in the Qur'an. Only then can we understand how to forge ahead in the War on Terror.

Decision-makers and analysts who examine the entire body of the Qur'an from a threat analysis perspective, as opposed to a personal spiritual pursuit, will see it is not oriented on Islamic law; the Qur'an is *weighted*, just as our legal system is weighted, to recognize the most recent precedent. Consequently, in Islamic law, precedence is established by the final revelations as revealed to Mohammed.

For example, whenever self-described Islamic moderates are forced to concede that there is such a thing as jihadi warfare, they will quote Surah 2 (with some support from Surah 8) and insist on a "defensive" reading of jihad. Mohammed's initial jihads were mentioned in Surah 2, and they were indeed more defensive.

Let there be no compulsion in religion: Truth stands out clear from error: whoever rejects evil and believes in Allah hath grasped the most trustworthy handhold. (Qur'an 2:256)

Many Westerners have heard this, and its meaning is pretty clear. But what most people do not hear is the Qur'an's treatment of the same issue in Surah 3. Because Surah 3 follows Surah 2 chronologically, Surah 3 *abrogates, or controls,* Surah 2. The revision states Allah's proclamation that those who fail to convert will go to Hell.

> **Whoever seeks a religion other than Islam will never have it accepted of him**, and he will be of those who have truly failed in the hereafter. (Qur'an 3:85)

Equally important, the Qur'an states in Surah 5 that Muslims cannot be friends with Jews and Christians:

> Oh ye who believe! **Take not the Jews and the Christians for your friends and protectors**; they are but friends and protectors to each other. And he amongst you that turns to them for friendship is of them. **Verily Allah guideth not the unjust**. (Qur'an 5:51)

The Qur'an describes Jews and Christians, as well as those Muslims who take them as friends, as "the unjust." It's crucial to remember that Surah 5 reflects a divine command from Allah, who is infallible. This means that Surah 2 is abrogated by Surah 3, and Surah 3 facilitates Surah 5. In other words, Verse 5:51 reflects the end-state understanding of how an informed Muslim is to regard Christians and Jews.

So who is right about the jihad-sanctioning verses of the Qur'an: the moderates or the "extremists"? Once we understand how abrogation works, maybe the better question is this: Which is right – the "moderates" or the Qur'an? If the concept of abrogation is valid, the "extremist" who "cherry-picks" from the chronological (or abrogating) end of the Qur'an *would be extremely correct*—especially when arguing against a moderate counterpart who relies on the abrogated text or, more often, simply counterclaims in exasperating tones that "that's not my Islam"—at which point all discussion is supposed to stop.

This brings us back to our earlier thought experiment on "cleaving from the mainstream" versus "energizing the base." As told in our hypothetical example, we spent millions on an information campaign to prove that Ayman al-Zawahiri was a hater. After all, he said no Muslim should be friends with the Americans, who are a bunch of Zionists and Crusaders. We mobilized an information campaign to get the word out, and now it's time for the Friday prayers; we are waiting for the imams to condemn Zawahiri. But to our real shock, even the moderates support what the al-Qaeda leader said. How could they do that? What went wrong?

In response, our analysts and decision-makers say, "Those imams must be extremists as well, and we just never knew. They've been—get ready—*radicalized*."

Unfortunately, those imams who were trying to work with us could only say something like this: "There are any number of things that you, as the United States, could do that we would support—directly or indirectly—because there are reasons we don't like Al-Qaeda, reasons that have nothing to do with whether we like you. But when you accuse Ayman al-Zawahiri of engaging in hate speech when he says not to befriend Americans because they are Jews and Christians—when you call that 'hate speech'—you have effectively said that Allah engages in hate speech. And that, we cannot have. Remember Verse 5:51, above. So to our great detriment, you put us in the position of having to support al-Qaeda and its message when we would have preferred not to raise the divine command at all."

So the question must be asked: Judging the results of our efforts, when we organize education campaigns to delegitimize people like Zawahiri, are we cleaving him from the mainstream or energizing the base? Clearly we not only did not cleave the "radicals" from the mainstream – *we energized their base.*

When we undertake an information campaign, how many times do we actually cleave radicals from the mainstream? And how many times do we end up energizing their base?

We can assume that a conversation among top al-Qaeda leadership runs something like this:

"How much are we budgeting for this next propaganda campaign?"

"Our information says millions."

"Wait a minute—isn't that how much the *Americans* are spending on their campaign?"

"Yes, that's right. So that's how much *we're* getting them to spend on it. We got the Americans to do it because we couldn't do it ourselves. We didn't have the money."

In a nutshell, this has been the story of the War on Terror.

The Brotherhood calls this "civilization jihad by our hands." And it's working. They can rely on us to do precisely the wrong thing almost every time because we will not look at Islam on its own terms. Those who say they fight jihad in the cause of Allah *think we don't know what we are doing. And they're right.*

Imagine once again: A member of the Muslim Brotherhood comes to us with offers of help and says, "Zawahiri's statement against Jews and Christians is 'hate speech.' You should come up with a message campaign." All of the "moderates" and cultural experts in America's national security space agree, pushing that same message. Did they help us, or did they help us to energize the jihadi base?

You might be skeptical and say, "You tell me the surahs in the Qur'an are ordered in a certain way, and that the order makes a difference. But maybe this isn't true for all Muslims at all times." And you might be right. Remember, I do not have to *prove* this is "true Islam"; I simply have to prove that most of the Muslim world, or a large portion of that world—or maybe just the "extremists"—believes it is true. For it to count as a valid part of the threat doctrine, I only have to prove there are some who think it is true and are trying to kill us for that reason. I just cited books credibly purporting to be Islamic law validating the doctrine of abrogation. I also cited MAJ Hasan's declaration of jihad based on that same doctrine of abrogation as the basis for his murder spree at Fort Hood. Clearly, a burden of proof has been met.

Why is it important? Because if the Doctrine of Abrogation in Islamic law is valid as stated, it means that what was said later overrules what was said earlier. More importantly, *it means that the radicals may be radically correct, thus raising the real possibility of there being little chance of a genuine moderate counter argument.* With the promising exception of recent developments in Egypt aside, there has been little in the way of a moderate, doctrine-based alternative able to provide any real hope.

Abrogation cripples the "moderate" narrative, which holds that there are thousands of different interpretations of Islam and that one has to read the entire body of the Qur'an to grasp its true meaning.

The House of War

Islamic law recognizes a division between two distinct societies. One is the dar al-Islam, the "house of Islam" and peace. The other one is the dar al-harb, the "house of war," or the "house of the sword." Dar al-harb is the world of the infidel and the region of perpetual warfare.

Barring any treaty, anyone who comes from the dar al-harb has the status under Islamic law of harbi. According to three different sources on Islamic law—*Shaybani's Siyar: The Islamic Law of Nations* by Majid Khadduri,[27] *Al-Hidayah*,[28] and Ibn Rushd's *The Distinguished Jurist's Primer*[29]—the word harbi means "enemy." As a country not governed by Islamic law, the United States resides in the dar al-harb, so we Americans are harbi. Sadly, getting this information really is as simple as looking in the glossary of these three classic treatises.

To elaborate on these concepts, let's look at two sources. The first is Majid Khadduri, a professor at Johns Hopkins University.[30] He wrote *War and Peace in the Law of Islam* (1955)[31] and published his translation of the classic 8th-century treatise *Shaybani's Siyar* (1966). The *Siyar* is among the oldest treatments on international relations and the law of war in Islamic law.

Drawing from the *Siyar*, Khadduri defines harbi as "a person belonging to the territory of war, equivalent to an alien in modern terminology, but may be regarded as an enemy as well since he was also in a state of war with the Muslims." In

War and Peace in the Law of Islam, Khadduri writes:

> It follows that the existence of a *dar al-Harb* is ultimately outlawed under the Islamic jural order; that the *dar al-Islam* is permanently under jihad obligation until the *dar al-Harb* is reduced to non-existence; and that any community accepting certain disabilities must submit to Islamic rule and reside in the *dar al-Islam* or be bound as clients to the Muslim community. The universality of Islam, in its all-embracing creed, is imposed on the believers as a continuous process of warfare, psychological and political if not strictly military.[32]

Even when a fighting jihad is not underway, however, a "continuous process of warfare" is waged at the psychological and political levels. Khadduri states this as a matter of doctrine—because the "*dar al-harb* is ultimately outlawed under the Islamic jural order; ... the *dar al-Islam* is permanently under jihad obligation until the *dar al-harb* is reduced to non-existence." *Reliance of the Traveller* confirms this:

> o4.17 There is no indemnity obligatory for **killing a non-Muslim at war with Muslims** (*harbi*), someone who has left Islam, someone sentenced to death by stoning for adultery by virtue of having been convicted in court, or those it is obligatory to kill by military action such as a band of highwaymen.[33]

As stated by Shaybani, affirmed by Khadduri, and confirmed by the *Reliance of the Traveller*, the term harbi retains its legal status in Islamic law. Since published shariah holds that the dar al-Islam is in an ongoing state of war with the dar al-harb, the legal theory indicates that all non-Muslims not a part of the dar al-Islam (and not under treaty) are classified as harbi. Understood in this way—at least as a matter of published doctrine—Islam is always at war with the dar al-harb, even if the dar al-harb doesn't believe it's at war with the dar al-Islam.

Truces

Having noted that classic Islamic jurisprudence views harbi as legitimate enemies, barring a treaty, it's worth examining what Islamic law has to say on the subject of truces. In his work Ijtihad, Nyazee finds:

> That **the aggressive propagation of Islam and the activity of jihad can be suspended** with or without necessity in the opinion of some jurists, **but it is only a transitory phase**, for which some jurists fix a specified period, while others do not.

That Professor W. Montgomery Watt maintains that the expansion of Muhammad's city-state into an empire raised the expectation that the Islamic empire would ultimately include the whole human race. We would agree with Professor Watt on this point with a slight qualification. The idea that Islam (not the Islamic Empire) would ultimately include the whole human race is not based on early conquests alone, **but is an acknowledged goal of the Muslim community**, and it arises from the texts of the Qur'an as well as the *Sunnah*, as quoted by ibn Rushd above. **According to such reasoning, the Muslim community may be considered to be passing through a period of truce. In its present state of weakness, there is nothing much it can do about it.**

Will this community annul this truce, if tomorrow, it were to gain its strength? Perhaps, this is what Watt has in mind when he says that that intentions of ultimate world domination are not so much a cause of worry for the non-Muslim states as are the treaties signed by the Muslim states, for **"the division of the world into the sphere of Islam and the sphere of war" is by no means a thing of the past**. In so far as traditional Islam grows in strength it could come into the forefront of world politics.

Relying on Qur'an Verse 47:35 for its authority (**"So do not be fainthearted and call for peace, when it is you who are the uppermost"**), Islamic law states that maintaining a peaceful status quo is no basis for a truce when the situation favors Islamic success in jihad. When Nyazee affirms that the "Muslim community may be considered to be passing through a period of truce" and then associates it with Islam's "present state of weakness,"[34] he faithfully reflects the legal standard that truces with the dar al-harb are defensive, time limited, and inappropriate once Islam reclaims its strength.[35]

Nyazee also recognizes the classic 8th-century Islamic division of the world into two spheres, the dar al-Islam and the dar al-harb, a distinction first established by Abu Hanifa as recorded by Muhammad ibn al-Hasan al-Shaybani in his *Siyar*.[36] The translator of the *Siyar*, Majid Khadduri, confirms Nyazee's restatement of the law that Muslim rulers can resort to peace treaties only out of necessity:

> Muslim authorities concluded peace treaties with the enemy **only when it was to the advantage of Islam, whether because it found itself in a state of temporary weakness** following a military defeat or because of engagement in war

in another area.[37]

Finally, this rule is reflected in contemporary treatments of Islamic law. *Reliance of the Traveller* states that:

> Interests that justify making a truce are such things as **Muslim weakness because of lack of numbers or material**, or the hope of an enemy becoming Muslim.[38]

In fact, truces are disfavored "because [they] entail the nonperformance of jihad."[39] Nyazee's comment that "some jurists fix a specified period" for truces is also reflected in *Reliance,* which notes:

> If the Muslims are weak, a truce may be made for ten years if necessary, for the Prophet (Allah bless him and grant him Peace) made a truce with Quraysh for that long, as it related by Abu Dawud. It is not permissible to stipulate longer than that, save by means of new truces, each of which does not exceed ten years. [40]

The reference to Mohammed's treaty with the Quraysh refers to what is called the Treaty of Hudaybiyyah. As *Reliance* recounts, the Prophet Mohammed concluded a truce with the Quraysh tribe that ruled Mecca in order to permit him and his followers to pilgrimage there. The truce was to last for a period of ten years and had other stipulations, including that members of the Quraysh who attempted to join Mohammed and the Muslims would be returned to Mecca. Before the ten-year period was up, however, Mohammed received a revelation saying that a Muslim woman who had left Mecca should not be returned. Thus the treaty was broken, and violence between the Muslims and the Quraysh continued.[41]

Even in modern times, it remains common for Muslims to refer to a proposed peace treaty or peace talks as hudna (a ten-year truce), and to cite the Treaty of Hudabiyyah as their example. Perhaps the most well-known exponent of this practice was former Palestinian Liberation Organization (PLO) leader Yasser Arafat.

After signing the Oslo Accords with Israel in 1993, Arafat assured supporters in Johannesburg, South Africa, that his position on Israel's destruction had not softened. While mouthing words of peace in English to his American and Israeli interlocutors, Arafat maintained in Arabic that his commitment to peace was intended only to further the "jihad to liberate Jerusalem."[42]

> This agreement, I am not considering it more than the agreement which had been signed between our Prophet Muhammad and Quraish, and you remember the Caliph Omar had refused this agreement and considered it 'Sulha Dania' [a de-

spicable truce]. But Muhammad had accepted it and we are accepting now this [Oslo] peace accord.[43]

The template has continued to the present day with Arafat's successors in the Palestinian Authority (PA). In a 2013 speech, Mahmoud al-Habbash, the PA's Minister of Religious Affairs, used the same Quranic example to illustrate the group's position on negotiations with Israel. Like Arafat, al-Habbash referenced the Treaty of Hudabiyyah, emphasizing that it led to the eventual defeat of Mohammed's hated enemies. He contrasted the willingness of the PLO and the PA to engage in this kind of subterfuge with the position of Hamas, which has traditionally rejected the tactic:

> The Palestinian leadership's sense of responsibility towards its nation made it take political steps about 20 years ago [by signing the Oslo Accords with Israel]. ... All this never would have happened through Hamas' impulsive adventure, but only through the wisdom of the leadership, conscious action, consideration, and **walking the right path**, which leads to achievement, exactly like the Prophet [Muhammad] did in the Treaty of Hudaybiyyah, even though some opposed it. ...
>
> The hearts of the Prophet's companions burned with anger and fury. The Prophet said: 'I'm the Messenger of Allah and I will not disobey Him.' This is not disobedience; it is politics. This is crisis management, situation management, conflict management. ... Allah called this treaty a clear victory. ... Omar ibn Al-Khattab said: 'Messenger of Allah, is this a victory? Is this logical? Is this victory? We are giving up and going back, and not entering Mecca. Is that a victory?' The Prophet said: 'Yes, it is a victory.' In less than two years, the Prophet returned and based on this treaty, he conquered Mecca. **This is the example, this is the model.**"[44]

In Islamic parlance, there is no mistaking Habbash's point. American officials responsible for negotiations with entities that say they are guided by Islamic law, not to mention mainstream reporting, must be aware of Islamic narratives that define the meaning and limits of peace. Failure to understand this in the diplomatic arena constitutes a form of malpractice. Similarly, reporting in the absence of such awareness has the effect of reducing news to propaganda. As Appendix 1: Interfaith Outreach attests, this negligent lack of understanding extends to those engaged in interfaith dialogue as well.

Jihad

When briefing the national security and intelligence communities on the Islamic doctrinal elements of jihad, it became clear to me that, on some level, nearly everyone has a basic understanding of what it is. That understanding—while being largely correct—is almost precisely what the bureaucratic narrative tells us it isn't. Public discourse on jihad has been effectively subordinated to converging narratives that suppress any informed discussion on the subject. While some doctrines on jihad comprise only a portion of the larger threat doctrine, they may be both less obvious and more dangerous.

Analysis that successfully grounds itself in published Islamic law preempts lesser constructions that compete with it. Because, for believing Muslims, Islam is a complete way of life governed by Islamic law, the legal definition of jihad will be used in this analysis. Because Islamic law comes from Allah "who is alone sovereign," the legal definition should be the controlling definition. If the two previous points end up being true and valid, the doctrine that "extremists" say they rely on when seeking to impose it through jihad would qualify as validated.

In the Islamic world today, martyrdom operations against non-Muslims enjoy considerable support because they draw their authority from foundational sources of Islamic law. From Mohammed's example, as related in authoritative Sunna from the hadith collections of both Bukhari and Muslim:

> Narrated Abu Huraira: I heard Allah's Apostle saying, "The example of a Mujahid in Allah's Cause—and Allah knows better who really strives in His Cause—is like a person who fasts and prays continuously. Allah guarantees that He will admit the Mujahid in His Cause into Paradise if he is killed, otherwise He will return him to his home safely with rewards and war booty." (*Sahih Bukhari*, Volume 4, Book 52, Number 46)[45]

> It has been reported on the authority of Jabir that a man said: Messenger of Allah, where shall I be if I am killed? He replied: In Paradise. The man threw away the dates he had in his hand and fought until he was killed (i.e. he did not wait until he could finish the dates). (*Sahih Muslim*, Book 20, Number 4678)[46]

And also from the Qur'an itself:

> And if ye are slain, or die, in the way of Allah, forgiveness and mercy from Allah are far better than all they could amass. (Qur'an 3:157)

Let those fight in the cause of Allah Who sell the life of this world for the hereafter. To him who fighteth in the cause of Allah, whether he is slain or gets victory—Soon shall We give him a reward of great value. (Qur'an 4:74)

Allah hath purchased of the believers their persons and their goods; for theirs (in return) is the garden (of Paradise): they fight in His cause, and slay and are slain: a promise binding on Him in truth, through the Law, the Gospel, and the Qur'an: and who is more faithful to his covenant than Allah? then rejoice in the bargain which ye have concluded: that is the achievement supreme. (Qur'an 9:111)

These sources suggest that a thorough threat analysis may not be able to rely on classical authorities to constrain enemy operations that center on martyrdom operations. This may also explain why "moderates" are typically silent on those same authorities. From early authorities to contemporary jurists, there is a consistent pattern regarding the legal status of jihad that warrants a closer comparison of jihad's current status in Islamic law to that of the classical and historic.

This analysis will start with a contemporary Hanafi Islamic legal explanation of jihad to provide a baseline understanding of the subject. The focus will then shift to more traditional concepts, as explained by foundational authorities like Imam al-Shafi'i and Imam Malik ibn Anas, both founders of doctrinal schools within Sunni Islamic law. From there, a review of shariah on jihad will demonstrate both continuity and consensus through time. The goal is to identify broadly accepted doctrines that are reasonably fixed in the inner sphere of Islamic law.

Analyzing Islamic Law on Jihad

Al-Misri's *Reliance of the Traveller* dedicates seven pages to jihad. Our discussion of jihad will concern itself with its controlling legal definition, as explained in Section o9.0 "Jihad," cited in its entirety below:

Book O: "Justice," at o9.0: "Jihad"

Jihad means to wage war against non-Muslims, and is etymologically derived from the word *mujahada*, signifying warfare to establish the religion. And it is the lesser jihad. As for the greater jihad, it is spiritual warfare against the lower self (*nafs*), which is why the Prophet (Allah bless him and give him peace) said as he was returning from jihad, "We have returned from the lesser jihad to the greater jihad."

The scriptural basis for jihad, **prior to scholarly consensus** (def: b7) is such Quranic verses as: (1) "Fighting is prescribed for you" (2:216); (2) "Slay them wherever you find them" (4:89); (3) "Fight the idolaters utterly" (9:36) and such hadiths as the one related by Bukhari and Muslim that the Prophet (Allah bless him and give him peace) said:

"I have been commanded to fight people until they testify that there is no god but Allah and that Muhammad is the Messenger of Allah, and perform the prayer, and pay the zakat. If they say it, they have saved their blood and possessions from me, except for the rights of Islam over them. And their final reckoning is with Allah"

and the hadith report by Muslim, "To go forth in the morning or evening to fight in the path of Allah is better than the whole world and everything in it."

Details concerning jihad are found in the accounts of the military expeditions of the Prophet (Allah bless him and give him peace), including his own martial forays and those on which he dispatched others. The former consists of the ones he personally attended, some twenty-seven (others say twenty-nine) of them. He fought in eight of them, and killed only one person with his noble hand, Ubayy ibn Kalaf, at the battle of Uhud. On the latter expeditions he sent others to fight, himself remaining at Medina, and these were forty-seven in number).[47]

The first observation is that the "Law of Jihad" is classified as a subset of "Justice," indicating its close association with Islamic concepts of justice. The rendered definition of jihad is particularly strong; it starts with an assertion of scholarly consensus, followed by Quranic support, which is, in turn, backed by strong (sahih) hadith. From the very beginning, Islamic law "fixes" jihad in the inner sphere of Islamic law. As *Reliance* uses a statutory schema, this analysis will apply statutory construction methodology to explain its language.[48]

The section on jihad begins with a one-sentence definition: "Jihad means to wage war against non-Muslims, and is etymologically derived from the word *mujahada*, signifying warfare to establish the religion."[49] Arab linguists and native-speaking Arabs do not agree on that etymology. But *Reliance* is an approved treatment of Islamic law, not a linguistics manual.

When a term of art is assigned a statutory definition, its meaning is controlled by the statutory definition to the exclusion of other meanings. Applying this principle to *Reliance*, "jihad" means "to wage war against non-Muslims." In addition, where the legal association of that term with the word "mujahada" means "to wage war against non-Muslims," it should be associated with "warfare to establish the religion." Thus, the legal definition of jihad—that is, according to Islamic law, or shariah—is "to wage war against non-Muslims to establish the religion."[50]

Greater and Lesser Jihads

To further fix jihad's meaning and usage according to Islamic law, the next two sentences in *Reliance* rely on what, in legal terminology, are known as Terms of Inclusion and Exclusion. The passage begins: "And, it is the lesser jihad."[51]

This sentence is a term of inclusion, positively associating the concept of "the lesser jihad" with the legal definition of jihad as "war against non-Muslims to establish the religion." In other words, the term of inclusion should be understood to suggest: *As for the legal definition of jihad, its meaning is the same as the "lesser jihad."* That is, the legal definition of jihad is the same as the "lesser jihad" when that term is used in normal discourse concerning the "lesser and greater jihad."

In statutory usage, terms of inclusion are generally used in conjunction with terms of exclusion. Whereas a term of inclusion positively associates a defined term with a concept, a term of exclusion excludes concepts that are not a part of the term's definition. The third sentence in the legal definition of jihad from *Reliance* is a term of exclusion:

> As for the greater jihad, it is spiritual warfare against the lower self (*nafs*), which is why the Prophet (Allah bless him and give him peace) said as he was returning from jihad, "We have returned from the lesser jihad to the greater jihad."[52]

This sentence disassociates the concept of "greater jihad" from the legal definition of jihad. Jihad in the second sentence means the lesser jihad; the greater jihad is something else: "spiritual warfare against the lower self." Hence, this exclusionary statement should be read to mean, "The greater jihad is not the same as the statutory meaning of jihad; rather, it is spiritual warfare against the lower self."

From there, *Reliance* transitions to a reference of Mohammed's saying, "We have returned from the lesser jihad to the greater jihad." Most remarkable is what's missing: While the other five referenced sources are both identified and cited—three to the Qur'an and two to hadith collections of Bukhari and Muslim—Mohammed's reference to "lesser" and "greater" jihads is neither identified as hadith nor attributed to an authority. In legal parlance, a reference has authority only when it is (1) cited (2) to an authority. This means that the *Reliance*'s "greater" jihad statement is not offered as authority; in fact, it is not even recognized as hadith when used in this instance. This is because the definition of jihad rendered in *Reliance* must reflect the consensus position in Islamic law. It cannot incorporate concepts that do not meet minimum consensus standards.

Having established the primacy of the legal definition of the "lesser" jihad in Islamic law, let's examine the concept's doctrinal underpinning. In his *tafsir*, ibn Kathir explains Qur'an Verse 9:5, confirming the "warfare to establish the religion" aspect of jihad stated in *Reliance*. From ibn Kathir:

> But when the forbidden months are past, then fight and slay the pagans wherever ye find them, and seize them and beleaguer them, and lie in wait for them in every stratagem of war; but if they repent, and establish regular prayers and practice regular charity, then open the way for them. (Qur'an 9:5)

> Mujahid, 'Amr bin Shu'ayb, Muhammad bin Ishaq, Qatadah, As-Suddi and 'Abdur-Rahman bin Zayd Aslam said that the four months mentioned in this *Ayah* are the four months grace period mentioned in earlier *Ayah*, **"So travel freely for four months throughout the land."**

> Allah said next, **"So when the Sacred Months have passed ..."** meaning, 'Upon the end of the four months during which We prohibited you from fighting the idolaters, and which is the grace period We gave them, then fight and kill the idolaters wherever you may find them.' Allah's statement next, **"then fight the *Mushrikin* wherever you find them,"** means, on the earth in general, except for the Sacred Area, for Allah said, **"And fight not with them at Al-Masjid Al-Haram, unless they fight you there. But if they attack you, then fight them"** [2:191].

> Allah said there, "And capture them," executing some and keeping some as prisoners, "and besiege them, and lie in wait for them in each and every ambush," do not wait until you find them. Rather, seek and besiege them in their areas and forts, gather intelligence about them in the various roads and fairways so that what is made wide looks ever smaller to them. This way, they have no choice, but to die or embrace Islam.[53]

Ibn Kathir's parsing analysis of Verse 9:5 leads to the (not so) surprising conclusion that the consensus of Islamic scholars has established that the verse means exactly what it says. That is, the scholarly consensus view coincides with the "extremist" narrative. While Ibn Kathir's commentary on this verse may seem "extreme" to non-believers, his writings are recommended to Muslim students in this country; they are told that Ibn Kathir is one of the four most important historians on the life of Mohammed.[54] His interpretation of Verse 9:5 carries weight—not simply because of his established reputation in Islamic scholarship, but because it accurately captures what appears to be the consensus view.

The shariah definition of jihad is based on authority from the Qur'an, sahih hadith, and scholarly consensus. Those three sources of sacred authority fix the legal definition of jihad in the inner sphere of Islamic law so securely that self-described moderates have yet to displace it.

Reliance's treatment of the greater jihad reflects an ongoing controversy. Some recognize the statement "We have returned from the lesser jihad to the greater jihad" as hadith, though they concede that it only qualifies as the weakest form of hadith (da'if). Other authorities, however, reject its status as hadith entirely; in their view, it is false hadith. Islamic law does not allow weak hadith to challenge doctrines grounded in the Qur'an, strong (mutawatir) hadith, and scholarly consensus. Because the reference to the "greater jihad" is not based on cited authority, jurists who reject statements like the one above as hadith also insist that, if used in published shariah, it should be done only as an example of its usage without any implication of status or authority.[55] Because references to the greater jihad have no authority, *Reliance* states the greater jihad verse without citing it.

For the same reason that Nyazee was compelled to reject popular notions of jihad in favor of the traditional view, an Islamic text like *Reliance* must exclude the "greater jihad" from the body of Islamic law on jihad. In fact, except for raising the issue in order to rule it out, Islamic law is virtually silent on the greater jihad. Competent threat analysis should recognize discussions of the greater jihad as irrelevant distractions that interfere with our understanding of the actual threat doctrine.

Teaching doctrinal concepts of jihad to non-Muslim American students has both practical and procedural limitations, but these concepts are taught to contemporary seventh-grade Muslims in ways that are consistent with the legal definition. The following statements and supporting Qur'an verses are from the widely used text *What Islam Is All About*, which is provided to American junior-high-aged Muslim students. Notice the parallels to the treatment of jihad in *Reliance*:

> **If we were called upon to participate in a true Jihad, declared by our chosen leader, then we must give our all in the effort.** (3:142-143) Allah has promised that those who struggle (make Jihad) with strength, property and lives will be rewarded with the highest rank near to Him. (9:20 & 3:195 & 49:15)[56]

> "Did ye think that ye would enter Heaven without Allah testing those of you who fought hard in His Cause and remained steadfast?" (Qur'an 3:142)

"Those who believe, and **suffer exile and strive with might and main, in Allah's cause, with their goods and their persons,** have the highest rank in the sight of Allah: They are the people who will achieve salvation." (Qur'an 9:20)

"Only those are Believers who have believed in Allah and His Messenger, and have never since doubted, but **have striven with their belongings and their persons** in the Cause of Allah: Such are the sincere ones." (Qur'an 49:15)

Today there is a contentious debate over whether jihad means "holy war," but historic Islamic authorities accepted this definition. For example, ibn Khaldun, the 14th-century North African Maliki qadi (judge), maintained that faith was a factor in the military prowess of Muslims in battle. He wrote, "The secret of it lay in the willingness of the Muslims to die in the holy war against their enemies because of their feeling that they had the right religious insight."[57] Beyond associating holy war with jihad, ibn Khaldun asserted that holy war is a duty in a way that suggests it may be the consensus view:

> In the Muslim community, the holy war is a religious duty, because of the universalism of the Muslim mission and the obligation to convert everybody to Islam either by persuasion or by force. Therefore, caliphate and royal authority are united in Islam, so that the person in charge can devote the available strength to both of them [religion and politics] at the same time. The other religious groups did not have a universal mission, and the *holy war* was not a religious duty for them, save only for purposes of defense. ... Among them, royal authority comes to those who have it, by accident and in some way that has nothing to do with religion. It comes to them as the necessary result of group feeling, which by its very nature seeks to obtain royal authority, as we have mentioned before, and not because they are under obligation to gain power over other nations, as is the case with Islam. They are merely required to establish their religion among their own people.[58]

Khaldun corroborated ibn Kathir's treatment of the same issue. The interlocking, reinforcing nature of Islamic law becomes evident.

Non-kinetic Jihad

A detailed description of the individual duty of jihad was promulgated in a fatwa[1/59] from the Seat of the Caliphate of the Ottoman Empire in 1915.[60] That fatwa called for global jihad. Because it was issued from the Seat of the Caliphate, analysts should presume it was an authoritative document, accurately stating the requirements of jihad in a manner intended to carry the force of law. The fatwa listed the various types of jihad and the requirements associated with them—including those associated with psychological and political warfare. This section will rely on this fatwa to explain a few of the non-kinetic (non-violent) elements of jihad.

The three forms of non-kinetic jihad raised by the 1915 Fatwa are the War of the Heart, the War of the Tongue and Pen, and the Individual Jihad. While the Individual Jihad includes killing, it is grouped with non-violent forms because it generally occurs in support of submission campaigns conducted in all phases of jihad, kinetic and non-kinetic, as well as in the dawah (preparation) phase.

In the 1915 Fatwa, the Caliphate explained the War of the Heart as follows:

> The heart-war—and that is the lowest form of the war. And it is that the Muslim should believe in his heart that the infidels are enemies to him and to his religion, and that he should desire their disappearance and the destruction of their power. And no Muslim can be imagined who is not under obligation to this degree of the war. Verily all the people of the Faith are under obligation to this amount without any question whatever, in whatever place they may be and in whatsoever condition they may be found.[61]

The language of the War of the Heart reflects the continuous nature of jihad noted earlier by Khadduri. Even for those unable to engage in jihad, permanent hostility to non-believers is a requirement. Hence, "people of Faith" are obligated to see non-Muslims as "enemies to him and his religion." Comments like "the Muslim should believe in his heart that the infidels are enemies to him and to his religion, and ... he should desire their disappearance and the destruction of their

---

1   *Al-Hidayah* defines fatwa (plural fatawa) as "a legal ruling issued by the jurist." (Marghinani, *Al-Hidaya: The Guidance*, 621.) *Reliance of the Traveller* identifies fatwa as a formal legal opinion and identifies formal legal opinions as fatawa. (Keller, *Reliance of the Traveller*, 1152, 1154). *Reliance of the Traveller* states that it is unlawful to accept formal legal opinions from any other than one of the four Sunni schools [Hanafi, Maliki, Shafi'ite, or Hanbali] (b7.6)[a] and unlawful for opinions (fatawa) to contradict ijma - scholarly consensus (b7.2).[b] Fatawa can only be issued by a person qualified to issue expert opinions [mujtahids - already discussed, muftis, and qadis] (b1.2).[c] Among the qualifications required to issue formal legal rulings is the knowledge of ijma – scholarly consensus as well as knowing the abrogating and abrogated verses of the Qur'an (o22.1(d)).[d]

power" are difficult to misconstrue. They also reflect the requirement to fight jihad in some capacity until the world comes under Islamic rule.

The 1915 Fatwa's discussion of the War of the Tongue and Pen explains the critical role communications play in jihad. Speech war integrates strategic communication, information operations, public affairs, and public diplomacy into one overall warfighting doctrine:

> The war of speech, **and that may be with the tongue and the pen**, and that in the condition of some of the Islamic kingdoms before this date. This applies in times like those of the Muslims of Caucasia which were before in a condition which did not admit of there being under obligations to do more than the war of speech, because their condition did not aid them to do more than this. And if there does not exist an excuse which permits contentment with the heart-war, **the war of speech is strictly enjoined upon all Muslims, and it is the duty of the masters of the pen to dissipate the darkness of the infidels and of infidelity with their pens, and the people of eloquence with their tongues; and the war of speech today is a duty decreed on the Islamic world in its entirety.** No one is excepted from it, not even the Muslims who dwell in the interior of the land of Russia. But this kind of war is strictly enjoined upon all of them.[62]

Strategic communications is integral to jihadi concepts of warfare, and has been so from the beginning. Note how communications is embedded within the very meaning of jihad. When a fatwa is issued, authority is delegated to communications experts, i.e., "masters of the pen and people of eloquence with their tongue." As stated, the War of the Tongue and Pen furthers jihad as war. The citation on the Wars of the Heart and of the Tongue and Pen shows that the level of one's commitment to the jihad is based on his or her capabilities: one is required to fight to one's ability. This is not a concept original to shariah; it is in keeping with Islamic law on jihad not to fight beyond one's ability. As the Qur'an states: "So fear Allah as far as you are able" (Qur'an 64:16). For those communications experts explicitly enjoined, however, the duty is obligatory.

As opposed to calls for kinetic jihad, the War of the Tongue and Pen often presents itself in cloyingly friendly terms. It can take the form of offered assistance—i.e., as an opportunity to disinform—which then encourages national security leaders to depend on outside advice rather than conduct real threat analysis. Such assistance should be assessed in light of our awareness that Wars of the Tongue and Pen are forms of jihad that are doctrinally tied to the "continuous process of warfare" that, in Islamic legal theory, is ever-present. This awareness would also help us better understand the mission of the Muslim Brotherhood in

America.

Most of today's analysts and decision-makers ignore the relationship between jihad and the War of the Tongue and Pen, regarding it more as a rhetorical flourish. One example is Maulana Muhammad Ali's monograph *A Manual of Hadith*, in which he introduces himself as a "soldier in the literary service of Islam."[63]

This concepts of jihad expressed in the 1915 Fatwa cannot be discounted as a vestige of the Ottoman era, for the Muslim Brotherhood in America recognizes its status. The Islamic Society of North America (ISNA) is among the leading Muslim Brotherhood front groups in America[64] and publishes *Islamic Horizons*, a Brotherhood-identified periodical.[65] In a 1986 article in *Islamic Horizons* titled "Jihad is Imperative to Muslims," Mohammad Fadel provided an explanation of jihad that followed the same lines as the Caliphate in the 1915 Fatwa:

> The lesser jihad, then, is the actual military/political struggle. The lesser jihad, however, is not only limited to physical fighting; rather, it is divided into three levels – jihad of the heart, jihad of the tongue, and, finally, jihad of the sword.[66]

Fadel declared jihad to be "a duty for all able Muslims, whether it is with the heart, tongue, or through fighting."[67] He also stressed that the principal form of jihad for Muslim Brothers in America is that of the tongue:

> How does this affect us in America? *Alhumdulillah*, we enjoy freedoms in the United States which permit us to practice jihad of the tongue to our utmost ability. Because we have this freedom, it is our responsibility to take advantage of this freedom for the cause of justice in the world. In general, one can speak out on any just cause and that is jihad.[68]

As will be discussed shortly, the primary mission of the Brotherhood in America has been dawah in preparation of jihad.[69] Since 1986, ISNA has been using American freedoms to subvert those same freedoms through a recognized form of jihad calibrated to the early preparatory stages of operation.[70] Fadel explains the importance of jihad by reference to Qur'an Verses 3:169–171, which emphasize the rewards of jihad, including the guarantee of Paradise if killed while waging it:

> "Think not of those who are slain in Allah's way as dead. Nay, they live, finding that with their Lord they have provision: Jubilant (are they) because of that which Allah hath bestowed upon them of his bounty, rejoicing for the sake of those left behind: that there shall no fear come upon them, neither shall they grieve. They rejoice because of favour from Allah and kindness, and that Allah wasteth not the wages of the believ-

ers." – lmran vs. 169-7 1 (Yusuf Ali Trans.)[71]

Fadel then relies on Verse 4:95 to remind readers that believers who participate in jihad are superior to those who do not:

> "Those of the believers who sit still, other than those who have
> a (disabling) hurt, are not on equality with those who strive in
> the way of Allah with their wealth and lives. Allah hath con-
> ferred on those who strive with their wealth and lives a rank
> above the sedentary. Unto each Allah hath promised good,
> but He hath bestowed on those who strive a great reward
> above the sedentary." – Al-Nisa'a. v. 95 (Yusuf Ali Trans.)[72]

And finally, Fadel explains that Islam places such an emphasis on jihad because Verse 3:110 calls on Muslims to enforce what is right and forbid what is wrong:

> "You are the best community that hath been raised up for
> mankind. Ye enjoin right and forbid indecency; and ye believe
> in Allah." – lmran. v. 110 (Yusuf Ali Trans.)[73]

As Fadel explained, "it is clear that without enjoining the right and forbidding the evil, Muslims would not be the best community. Without jihad, then, Muslims cannot be the best community because Jihad is the enjoining of the right and the prohibition of the wrong."[74] It should be noted that the verse following 3:110 confirms the jihadi nature of the mission by making it clear that resistance should be anticipated but will be easily overcome.

> They will do you no harm, barring a trifling annoyance; if they
> come out to fight you, they will show you their backs, and no
> help shall they get. (Yusuf Ali, Qur'an 3:111)

The Brotherhood understands jihad of the tongue to be a recognized form of jihad alongside the jihads of the heart and of the sword, defined in terms of military and political struggle that has historic and classical roots that affirm the statements of the 1915 Fatwa promulgated from the Seat of the Caliphate. As such, in the 1980s, the Brotherhood in America viewed its primary mission as that of jihad in the form of speech war.

Finally, the Individual Jihad involves direct personal action, including targeted acts of assassination and murder that may include indiscriminate acts of violence where non-Muslims are concerned:

> First the individual Jihad, and it consists of the individual
> personal deed, and it may be by the use of cutting, killing
> instruments like the Jihad of the late Wurdanee who killed

with his "musdis" Peter Galy Pasha the infidel, the English
governor, and like the slaying of the chief of the English Police in India by one of our brothers there, **and like the killing
of one of the officials arriving from Mecca by Abi Busir
(May Allah be pleased with him) in the age of the Prophet
(May Allah be gracious to Him and give Him peace!) and
in like manner a similar thing took place when the Prophet (May Allah be gracious to Him and give Him peace!)
commanded Abdullah the son of Atik that he and four of
his companions should go to kill Abi Rafi, the chief of the
Jews of Khaibar.** ... O Lord, what is incumbent upon the
Muslims today also, if there be found in the Islamic world
those who fight like this fight? What will be the event if
there shall go out from them some of the deliverers, and kill
one of those who belong to the Triple Entente of the infidels
who are known by their hostility to Islam, and **so purify the
face of the earth from his existence.** O Allah, O our Lord,
be a helper to us and cause the spirit to the jihad to live in
our souls![75]

The 1915 Fatwa provides examples that link contemporary assassinations of
British colonial officials to specific examples of Mohammed's deeds from sahih
hadith. That connection is necessary to fix the current requirements within the
inner sphere of Islamic law. For example, the killing of Abu-Rafi'—known as the
"chief of the Jews of Khaibar"—can be found in the Sahih Bukhari collection:

Al-Bara bin Azib said, "Allah's Apostle sent a group of Ansari men to kill Abu-Rafi'. One of them set out and entered
their (i.e., the enemies') fort. That man said, 'I hid myself ...
and came upon Abu Rafi' and said, 'O Abu Rafi'.' When he
replied me, I proceeded towards the voice and hit him. He
shouted and I came out to come back, pretending to be a
helper. I said, 'O Abu Rafi',' changing the tone of my voice.
... I asked him, 'What happened to you?' He said, 'I don't
know who came to me and hit me.' Then I drove my sword
into his belly and pushed it forcibly till it touched the bone.
Then I came out, filled with puzzlement and went towards
a ladder of theirs in order to get down but I fell down and
sprained my foot. I came to my companions and said, 'I will
not leave till I hear the wailing of the women.' So, I did not
leave till I heard the women bewailing Abu Rafi', the merchant of Hijaz. Then I got up, feeling no ailment, (and we
proceeded) till we came upon the Prophet and informed
him." (Bukhari 4:264)

With exhortations to "purify the face of the earth from … existence," Individual Jihad as explained in the 1915 Fatwa calls for high-volume acts of individual jihad, like the Boston Marathon and the Fort Hood attacks multiplied many times over. (Times, and maybe phases of operation, have changed since the 1980s.) It could take on genocidal proportions, like the Armenian genocide at the time of the Ottoman-era fatwa, the last decade's slaughter of Christians in Darfur, or with ISIS today in Iraq. These high-volume acts of terror are difficult to template and impossible to predict if one adopts a policy of official ignorance with regard to their doctrinal basis. Trainees at Taliban and al-Qaeda camps should be assessed with an eye toward the requirements associated with Individual Jihad. Since at least 2010, Individual Jihad has become the expressed tactic of choice for al-Qaeda operatives in the West, as stated in the glossy English-language al-Qaeda periodical *Inspire Magazine*.[76] (ISIS is a branch of al-Qaeda that originated out of Iraq.[77])

The Modern Legal Classification of Jihad

In his book *Theories of Islamic Law: The Methodology of Ijtihad*, Imran Ahsan Khan Nyazee discusses how the methodology of ijtihad can be used to extend Islamic law as the basis for all law in a Muslim state.[78] As a Hanafi[79] jurist and Pakistani law professor, Nyazee relies on a methodology developed by Abu Hamid Muhammad al-Ghazali—a pre-eminent 11th-century Shafi'i (and Sufi) authority—to develop concepts of ijtihad tailored to meet the daily needs of governance in a contemporary Islamic society under Hanafi Islamic law.[80] *Theories of Islamic Law* is a serious legal treatise that states the role of jihad in Islamic governance:

> What are the goals of the Muslim community? The moment the *maqasid* are viewed as the goals of the Muslim community, the interest of *Din* moves up and represents its external goals. The positive aspect of this interest conveys a single goal: to spread the message of Islam in the whole world. **The instrument utilized for attaining this goal is *da'wah* in conjunction with jihad.** There are numerous opinions on the meaning and role of jihad in the modern age. **These however, are not relevant for the present study as we are looking for the traditional point of view. What is relevant is the opinion of the jurists, and hence the law on this point.**[81]

While noting the irrelevance of non-legal characterizations of jihad, Nyazee explains that Islamic law controls the term's definition. When deferring to "traditional points of view," Nyazee is not referring to a view from the misty past but rather to the hadith. Nor does he entertain frivolous discussions of jihad that operate outside the doctrinal footprint of shariah. When a legal term adopts a strict definition or mandatory rule of construction, the jurist must apply it. Where such definitions and rules exist—as in any legal system—Islamic law requires Muslim jurists to confine their discussions of terms to their legal framework.

Answering the question "Why wage war?" in his treatise on Islamic law, 12th-century Andalusian qadi ibn Rushd relied on Verse 9:29 to state that the requirement of jihad in shariah reflects scholarly consensus:

> Why wage war? The Muslim jurists agree that the purpose of fighting the People of the Book, excluding the (Qurayshite) People of the Book and the Christian Arabs, is one of two things: it is either for the conversion to Islam or the payment of the *jizya*. The payment of the *jizya* is because of the words of the Exalted, "Fight against such as those who have been given the Scripture as believe not in Allah or the Last Day, and forbid not that which Allah and His Messenger hath forbidden, and follow not the religion of truth, until they pay the tribute readily being brought low."[82]

Ibn Rushd also confirmed the scholarly consensus on jizya. The Muslim jurists, he pointed out, were in agreement regarding the non-Muslim tax that is to be "imposed" on those "non-Arab People of the Book" who are male, have reached puberty, and are not slaves.[83] Nyazee also makes this point in *The Methodology of Ijtihad*. Relying on ibn Rushd's "Why wage war?" discussion, Nyazee confirms the Quranic basis for the requirement of jihad today.[84] From this, Nyazee concludes there is still scholarly consensus on the requirements of jihad:

> **This leaves no doubt that the primary goal of the Muslim community, in the eyes of its jurists,** is to spread the word of Allah through jihad, and the option of poll tax is to be exercised only after subjugation.[85]

When writing that there is "no doubt ... in the eyes of the jurists," Nyazee confirms that scholarly consensus remains a doctrinal point of Islamic law. Because the legal definition of jihad is the controlling definition in Islam, this has far-reaching consequences for the status of jihad regarding relations between Muslims and non-Muslims.

Limiting his analysis of jihad to the fixed elements of Islamic law, Nyazee finds:

> that **the aggressive propagation of Islam and the activity of jihad can be suspended** with or without necessity in the opinion of some jurists, **but it is only a transitory phase,** for which some jurists fix a specified period, while others do not.

That Professor W. Montgomery Watt maintains that the expansion of Muhammad's city-state into an empire raised the expectation that the Islamic empire would ultimately include the whole human race. We would agree with Professor Watt on this point with a slight qualification. The idea that Islam (not the Islamic Empire) would ultimately include the whole human race is not based on early conquests alone, **but is an acknowledged goal of the Muslim community**, and it arises from the texts of the Qur'an as well as the *Sunnah*, as quoted by ibn Rushd above. **According to such reasoning, the Muslim community may be considered to be passing through a period of truce. In its present state of weakness, there is nothing much it can do about it.**

The Hanbali School on Jihad

When jihadi-based terrorism occurs, "extremists" are accused of manipulating mainstream traditions. This behavior is often based, it is alleged, on the mistreatment or mistranslation of texts, usually by Hanbalis, Saudis, Salafis, jihadis, or Wahhabis. Although popular, there is less to the "but for Wahhabism" argument than is assumed. Because this book seeks the broader consensus view, it will rely on Islamic authorities and authoritative sources whose writings on jihad are broadly accepted within the four orthodox schools of Sunni Islamic law—the Hanafi, Maliki, Shafi'i, and Hanbali.

While reference to Hanbali authorities may be made to round out representation of the four doctrinal schools, for several reasons this book will not rely on Hanbali law to establish the doctrinal authority of any point of law:

First, there is a powerful tendency to blame Islamic-based terrorism almost exclusively on Wahhabism. Wahhabism, it should be noted, is a view of Islam that arises out of the Taymiyan tradition of Hanbali law. But "extremist" literature from Wahhabi groups, such as al-Qaeda, reveals that they rely on authorities from all the schools to demonstrate the mainstream basis of the positions they take on the duty of jihad. Hence, extremists rely on recognized authorities from outside the Hanbali school not only because these authorities have status within the broader Islamic community, but also because, by using them, the extremists can genuinely demonstrate that jihad—as they define it—actually is a requirement of Islam for all Muslims.

Second, when Islamic influence on terrorist attacks becomes too obvious to deny, there is a tendency to attribute the driving motivations to Wahhabism, which, by implication, places it outside the mainstream of Islamic thought. For example:

El Fadl states that "fanatic groups derive their ideological premises from the intolerant Puritanism of the *Wahhabi* and *Salafi* creeds."[86]

Esposito says that "They contribute to a worldview that is anti-reformist at best or one that promotes a militant exclusivist Islam and vision of the world. The spread of *Wahhabi* or *Salafi* Islam is a reflection of this problem."[87]

Stephen Schwartz, a convert to Islam, said in the introduction to his book *The Two Faces of Islam: Saudi Fundamentalism and its Role in Terrorism*: "Despite the proliferation of terrorist groups with diverse sounding names and backers, the real source of our problem is the perversion of Islamic teachings by the fascistic *Wahhabi* cult that resides at the heart of the Saudi establishment, our putative friends in the region."[88]

The fallback defense has been to focus the blame for Islamic-based terrorism on Wahhabism, Hanbali law, and Saudi Arabia. Because Saudi Arabia governs along Hanbali lines[89] and recognizes Muhammad bin Abdul Wahhab as a defining Hanbali legal authority,[90] there is good reason to equate Wahhabism with Hanbali law. Despite such attacks on the Hanbali school, its status as one of the four *bona fide* doctrinal schools of Sacred Islamic law remains both unchanged and unchallenged. Hence, without excusing Wahhabism, it is also important to show there is a clear doctrinal basis for jihad on which all doctrinal schools agree.

By not relying on Hanbali authorities, it can be shown that mainstream Sunni shariah supports the concepts of jihad popularly associated only with Wahhabism or Islamic "extremism," and this can be done without having to redefine, misrepresent, or misinterpret mainstream Sunni Islamic law. As this book seeks to demonstrate, the Muslim Brotherhood sets the dominant narrative in the dawah/jihadi domains, and neither they nor the Deobandis are Hanbalis.

Lastly, the Hanbali is the smallest and most recently founded of the four doctrinal schools. Although it is named for Imam Ahmad bin Hanbal[91] (780–855 AD), he focused mainly on the systematic study of hadith. It was Hanbal's students who collected his thoughts on law and legal theory and transformed them into a coherent set of legal doctrines that distinguished it as a school.[92] Central to the Hanbali methodology is an emphasis on the supremacy of Islamic primary texts in legal analysis as well as a skeptical view of human reasoning, especially qiyas (a form of deductive analogy in Islamic jurisprudence), in the production of legal opinions.[93] Because Hanbali legal theory holds that jurists should base their opinions primarily on direct reference to the primary texts (the Qur'an and hadith) while minimizing human reasoning, there seems to be an institutionalized preference toward devaluing the precedential value of those opinions. Inherent in this view has been a preference to de-emphasize the value of any particular legal opinion outside its specific application, or so it would seem. This may explain the relative lack of availability of Hanbali opinions compared to those from the other schools.

The Hanafi School on Jihad

With the exception of *Reliance of the Traveller*, which is Shafi'ite, this book relies most heavily on Hanafi sources. Hanafi shariah is the most broadly practiced in terms of the number of people and extent of territory under its jurisdiction, which includes Iraq, Afghanistan, Turkey, Pakistan, India, and Indonesia. Established by Abu Hanifa in the 8th century, Hanafi law is also the oldest of the Islamic schools and the first of the four doctrinal schools. Hanafi Islamic law recognizes jihad as a requirement of Islam in precisely the way "extremists" today claim it does. As with Suleyman Ahmad's (Stephen Schwartz) *The Two Faces of Islam*, the conventional wisdom has been that "extremists" abuse jihad by straining Islamic law to arrive at concepts that permit terrorism yet are outside the scope of mainstream Islamic tradition and doctrine.[94] This is simply not borne out by the evidence.

Hanafi law recognizes jihad through a series of primary rules (hukm taklifi)[95] that create obligations that, in turn, impose duties. These primary rules are based on a series of rights. Hanafi law recognizes three basic sets of rights, as well as a fourth composite set: (1) the rights of Allah, (2) the rights of the individual, (3) the rights of individuals collectively (or of the state), and (4) a composite set of rights of Allah lying side by side with the individual—with the two cases of predominance of one or the other. From a hierarchical perspective, the rights of Allah (haqq Allah) take primacy of position.[96]

In the 11th century, the pre-eminent Hanafi imam, mujtahid, and qadi (judge) al-Sarakhsi explained the four categories and described how the rules (ahkam) in each category are further subdivided into a series of rights.[97] Regarding the rights of Allah, eight were identified in priority order, with the first two being the "right of Pure Worship" and the "right of Pure Punishment."

> PURE WORSHIP. The first of these is belief in Allah, or *iman*.
> The second is prayer. The third is *zakah*. The fourth is fasting
> (*sawm*). The fifth is *hajj*. **The sixth is jihad**.

> PURE PUNISHMENT. These are the *hudud* penalties that have
> been instituted as deterrents, as a pure right of Allah.[98]

As indicated, jihad holds a prominent status in Hanafi law as a right of Allah that is the sixth right of Pure Worship. Hence:

> Jihad belongs to that group of rules having the highest clas-
> sification of rights – the rights of Allah.

> Among the rights of Allah, it belongs to the highest classifi-
> cation of rights -- a "Right of Pure Worship."

> As a Right of Pure Worship, jihad is number six in the or-
> dering – following only the Five Pillars of Islam – and of a
> kind with them.

A principle characteristic of the rights of Allah is that they concern Allah's absolute sovereign status. Shariah's status as part of Allah's most perfect justice is the basis for "extremist" claims that democratic forms of governance are incompatible with Islam that give rise to al-Qaeda claims of takfirism (as discussed earlier) and Muslim Brotherhood claims of jahiliyyah (as will be discussed shortly). The divine status of the "rights of Allah" carries substantive weight inside the Muslim community. In his treatise *The Neglected Duty*, Muslim Brother Muhammad 'Abd al-Salam Faraj – who eventually was executed for his participation in the assassination of Anwar Sadat – went so far as describe jihad as one of the Pillars of Islam:

> Whoever really wants to be occupied with the highest de-
> grees of obedience and wants to reach the peak of devotion
> must commit himself to jihad for the cause of Allah, without,
> however, neglecting the other (prescribed) pillars of Islam. [99]

Faraj's characterization of jihad as a pillar of Islam is procedurally accurate if not technically correct.[100] Unlike laws coming from man or government, a rule (hukm) qualified with the term *shar'i* means it belongs to Islamic law and is understood to be a communication from Allah through a demand, option, or declaration relating to the acts of his subjects.[101] Hence, when Allah places an obligation on believers, it becomes hukm shar'i. Because they are hukm shar'i, rights of Allah create binding obligations. In other words, jihad is hukm shar'i – a communication from Allah that creates an obligation on man. Because man cannot overrule a communication from Allah, man can never overrule the obligation of jihad.

> The first point to notice about this definition is that (*shari'a*)
> *hukm* or a rule of law is a communication from Allah. This
> means that it is not treated merely as a command. It also
> means that a communication from anyone else cannot be
> considered as a *hukm*, be he a ruler or someone else.[102]

The same theories of Islamic law that designate Allah as the exclusive law-giver also define jihad as a right of Allah that is a right of Pure Worship, creating obligations for all Muslims. For Hanafi jurists, then, jihad is fixed in the inner sphere as a non-optional rule of Islam. Elements of the rule of Islamic law (hukm shar'i) interact with each other to give rise to liabilities and obligations to obey laws that are divinely created and, hence, immutable.

Four elements of the rule of law come together in the Islamic legal system: the Lawgiver (Hakim), the relevant law (hukm), the act to which the legal rule is related, and the subject who performs the act and who is under an obligation to conform.[103] As it relates to jihad: (1) The lawgiver, Allah, (2) creates the requirement of jihad (3) in order that jihad be undertaken (4) by the Muslim community, joint and severable, (5) when under a legal obligation to do so. If "extremists" like Faraj, in *The Neglected Duty,* can establish jihad as an obligation that is a right of Allah, then they can assert that its non-performance is, as a matter of law, a *neglected duty.*

This legal explanation for the duty of jihad is taught to contemporary American Muslim students. When teaching that jihad is a duty of Islam arising out of a direct command from Allah, Emerick (in the seventh-grade text *What Islam is All About)* is simply teaching established doctrines.

> There are seven main beliefs, five main practices and three main duties to Islam. ... The three duties are extra things which Muslims do based on the commandments of Allah in the Qur'an. They are: 1) *Da'wah*, (Calling others to Islam) 2) Jihad (Striving in Allah's Cause) and finally, 3) Encouraging the good while forbidding wrong. (3:110)[104]

> If a real jihad was declared, then we, as Muslims, must obey and follow the rules of Islam in our conduct. (9:38-41)[105]

Majid Khadduri, an Iraqi-born academic and the founder of the Nitze School of Advanced International Studies at Johns Hopkins University, reconciles the earlier discussion on the temporary nature of truces with the current discussion on the duty to conduct jihad:

> Peace does not supersede the state of war, for the jihad is a legal duty prescribed by the law; peace means the grant of security or protection to non-Muslims for certain specified purposes, and the achievement of them brings the grant of peace to an end.[106]

Nyazee's monograph *Methodology of Ijtihad* explores the ways ijtihad can be used to apply Islamic law to all aspects of modern Islamic society. His conclusion that the rights of Allah[107] are beyond the scope of ijtihad poses a problem for "moderates" who claim ijtihad as a tool to modify jihad's status.[108] Because the rights of Allah are a part of the fixed inner sphere of Islamic law, jihad is beyond the reasoning of man and therefore substantially outside the scope of ijtihad.[109] The general rule on ijtihad is that it can be used to "reason to a conclusion" in the flexible realm of man-made law[110] but not in the fixed sphere, which is the province of Allah.[111] To do so would put the reasoning of man before the "rights of Allah," and this is impermissible. In fact, putting the reasoning of man ahead of the "rights of Allah" is shirk, as will be discussed shortly.

When "extremists" properly cite shariah on jihad, they are referencing a body of law that is beyond the jurisdiction of man and thus outside the scope of ijtihad. This is all the more true when the authority of scholarly consensus can be brought to bear on an issue. This must be remembered when assessing the validity of self-described moderates who claim that ijtihad can counter the juristic claims of the jihadis.

The Shafi'i School on Jihad

Indicating consensus among the scholars on the concept of jihad,[112] Nyazee stressed that genuine analysis must be grounded on established legal norms that draw their authority from tradition. Shafi'i, the scholar on which a school of Islamic jurisprudence is based, was among the early authorities to establish a firm legal basis for jihad in the Qur'an and hadith. As noted in *Reliance*:

> His *al-Risala* [*The Letter*] was the first work in the history of mankind to investigate the theory and practical bases of jurisprudence. **In Koranic exegesis, he was the first to formulate the principles of the science of which verses abrogate others and which are abrogated (*'ilm al-nasikh wa al-mansukh*).** ... He [Shafi'i] paved the way for the enormous importance attached by subsequent generations of Muslims to the study of prophetic hadith, as reflected in the fact that most of the Imams in the field were of his school, including Bukhari, Muslim, Abu Dawud ... and others.[113]

What Nyazee, a 21st-century Hanafi legal scholar, calls an "obligation," the 9th-century mujtahid referred to as a "duty." In his classic legal treatise *Risala*, Shafi'i discussed the status of jihad in a chapter titled "On Legal Knowledge."[114] Here, he offered a basic legal proposition that a legal duty arises when one gains knowledge of it. Using jihad as the example, Shafi'i explained that, where legal knowledge of jihad exists, that knowledge creates a specific duty that must be obeyed. This line of reasoning has consequences for the Individual Jihadi who, while maybe not a formal member of a "radicalized" group like al-Qaeda, nevertheless hears a specific call to jihad and agrees with it, thus creating a duty that compels him to act. Short of establishing a pattern of behavior, and while it may never meet an evidentiary standard, the lone jihadi's decision to act in conformance with an "extremist" group's declaration is what establishes group association. Shafi'i constructed his argument exclusively from legal principles arising from the Qur'an and hadith. Hence, his discussion begins with the general statement that Allah created a legal duty, followed by a string of citations, first to the Qur'an to affirm the duty's direct divine basis and then to hadith citations that established that Mohammed understood the nature of the duty created:

> 40. Shafi'i replied: God has imposed the duty of jihad as laid down in His Book and uttered by His Prophet's tongue. He stressed the calling of men to fulfill the jihad duty as follows: **God had bought from the believers their selves and their possessions against the gift of Paradise. They fight in the way of God; they kill, and are killed; that is a promise binding upon God in the Torah and Gospel and the Qur'an; and who fulfills his covenant better than God? So rejoice in the bargain you have made with Him. That is the mighty triumph.** [Q. IX, 112]

> And He said:

> Fight polytheists totally as they fight you totally; and know that God is with the Godfearing. [Q. IX, 36]

> And He said: Slay the polytheists wherever you find them, and take them and confine them, and lie in ambush for them everywhere. But if they repent and perform the prayer and pay the zakat, then set them free. God is All-forgiving, All-compassionate. [Q. IX, 5]

> And He said:

> Fight those who do not believe in God nor in the Last Day, who do not forbid what God and His Apostle have made forbidden, and who do not practice the religion of truth, of those who have been given the Book, until they pay the jizya out of hand and have been humbled. [Q. IX, 29]

> 41. 'Abd al-'Aziz b. Muhammad al-Darawardi told us from Muhammad b. 'Amr b. 'Alqama from Abu Salama [b. 'Abd al-Rahman] from Abu Hurayra, who said the Apostle of God said:

> I shall continue to fight the unbelievers until they say: 'There

is no God but God,' if they make this pronouncement they shall be secured in their blood and property, unless taken for its price, and their reward shall be given by God.

And God, glorified be His praise, said:

O believers, what is the matter with you, that when it is said to you: 'Go forth in the way of God,' you sink down to the ground? Are you so content with this present life as to neglect the Hereafter? The enjoyment of this life is little in comparison with the Hereafter. If you do not go forth, He will inflict upon you a painful punishment, and instead of you He will substitute another people; and you will not hurt Him at all, for God is powerful over everything. [Q. IX, 38–39]

And He said:

Go forth, light and heavy! Struggle in God's way with your possessions and yourselves! That is better for you, did you but know. [Q. IX, 41][115]

Grounding his authority in the Qur'an, Shafi'i relied exclusively on verses from Surah 9, thereby recognizing its pre-eminent status on issues of jihad and, by implication, the doctrine of abrogation. By establishing jihad as a duty arising out of the Qur'an, Shafi'i fixed it in the inner sphere of classical Islamic law in just the way Nyazee, the modern Hanafi jurist, explained.

Shafi'i relied on Qur'an verses that take a particularly aggressive posture on jihad: "Slay the polytheists where you find them," "lie in ambush for them everywhere," "Fight those who do not believe in Allah nor in the Last Day," etc. The interaction between Verse 9:29 and the cited hadith reveals Mohammed's understanding that if one has knowledge of the requirement from Allah to "Fight those who do not believe," that person then has a duty "to continue to fight the unbelievers until [the world has been brought under the control of Islam]." Because Mohammed said that jihad is to continue until the world submits to Islam, jihad remains a duty for all Muslims until then.[116]

The aggressive tone of jihad found in Shafi'i's selection of hadith is reflected by other sahih hadith, as well. From Bukhari:

Muhammad said, "Know that Paradise is under the shade of swords." (Bukhari 4:73)

Umair said, "Um Haram informed us that she heard the

Prophet saying, 'Paradise is granted to the first batch of my followers who will undertake a naval expedition.' Um Haram added, 'I said, O Allah's Apostle! Will I be amongst them?' He replied, 'You are amongst them.' The Prophet then said, 'The first army amongst my followers who will invade Caesar's city will be forgiven their sins.' I asked, 'Will I be one of them, O Allah's Apostle?' He replied in the negative." (Bukhari 4:175)

Muhammad said, "The hour will not be established until you fight with the Turks; people with small eyes, red faces, and flat noses. Their faces will look like shields coated with leather. The hour will not be established till you fight with people whose shoes are made of hair." (Bukhari 4:179)

Additionally, Shafi'i used Verse 9:38 to remind Muslims of the obligatory nature of jihad:

O believers, what is the matter with you, that when it is said to you: 'Go forth in the way of God,' you sink down to the ground? (Qur'an 9:38)

There are serious and powerful consequences that come from establishing jihad as a divinely mandated legal duty. Arguably, if "extremists" succeed at establishing the *bona fides* of the duty of jihad, they can take steps to enforce compliance in the Muslim community at large.

Fighting is prescribed for you, and ye dislike it. But it is possible that ye dislike a thing which is good for you, and that ye love a thing which is bad for you. But Allah knoweth, and ye know not. (Qur'an 2:216)

Once the duty is established, the subjective understanding of individual believers becomes less relevant, for they can be subordinated to the objective requirements of the law. This includes the inputs of self-described "moderates" and "reformers" whose narratives fail to meet such requirements. Individual and communal obligations associated with jihad apply to "all able bodied believers, exempting no-one".[117]

Shafi'i equated these individual requirements to the individual requirement to pray, do the *hajj*, and pay the *zakat*. In other words, just like the Egyptian Muslim Brother Faraj and other contemporary Hanafi jurists, he positioned the obligation of jihad at parity with the Five Pillars. In fact, those fighting in jihad are promised a higher status in paradise due to the high esteem in which they are held in the Qur'an. Communal failure to supply mujahids for jihad brings harsh consequences. From the *Risala*:

42. Shafi'i said: These communications mean that the **jihad, and rising up in arms in particular, is obligatory for all able-bodied believers, exempting no one,** just as prayer, pilgrimage and payment of alms are performed, and no person is permitted to perform the duty of another, since performance by one will not fulfill the duty of another.

They may also mean that the duty of jihad is a collective (*kifaya*) duty different from that of prayer: Those who perform it in the war against the polytheists will fulfill the duty and receive the supererogatory merit, thereby preventing those who have stayed behind from falling into error.

But God has not put the two categories of men on an equal footing, for He said: "Such believers who sit at home—unless they have an injury—are not the equals of those who fight in the path of God with their possessions and their selves. **God has given precedence to those who fight with their possessions and their selves over those who sit at home**. God has promised the best of things to both, and **He has preferred those who fight over those who sit at home by granting them a mighty reward.**" [Q. IV, 97][118]

If all men failed to perform the duty so that no able-bodied man went forth to battle, all, I am afraid, would fall into error (although I am certain that this would never happen) in accordance with [Allah's] saying: "**If you do not go forth, He will inflict upon you a painful punishment.**" [Q. IX, 39][119]

The Maliki School on Jihad

Shafi'i's position on jihad represents the majority view among early authorities—including the founders of the other three doctrinal schools. Imam Malik ibn Anas,[120] founder of the second doctrinal school of Islamic law, which bears his name, wrote that jihadis have the highest rank among believers;[121] that Mohammed himself stated a preference for martyrs and martyrdom in jihad;[122] that martyrdom is valued in itself;[123] and that offensive jihad was waged against towns that were subsequently *destroyed* when the inhabitants refused the dawah call to convert—under compulsion—to Islam:

Yahya related to me from Malik from Humayd at-Tawil from Anas ibn Malik that the Messenger of Allah, may Allah bless him and grant him peace, went out to Khaybar, he arrived there at night, and when he came upon a people by night, he did not attack until morning. In the morning, the Jews came out with their spades and baskets. When they saw him, they said, "Muhammad! By Allah, Muhammad and his army!" The Messenger of Allah, may Allah bless him and grant him peace, said, "Allah is greater! Khaybar is destroyed. **When we come to a people, it is an evil morning for those who have been warned.**"[124]

Malik's warning in the passage above is the invitation to join Islam given prior to the initiation of hostilities.[125] Also in the *Muwatta*,[126] Mohammed confirms that seeking martyrdom in its own right is an exceptionally praiseworthy undertaking.[127]

Contemporary arguments that modern-day martyrdom operations violate Islamic concepts of intent (niyah) are unable to displace Islamic commentaries based on authoritative hadith that "extremists" use to legitimize their claims.[128] On martyrdom, Malik's 8th-century statement of law resonates among modern-day Hanafi jurists. Pakistani Maulana Muhammad Ali, in his 1941 *Manual of Hadith*, relied on Bukhari for his comment that "the Holy Prophet's own soul yearned after martyrdom in defense of the truth and if possible, to come back to life and die again defending the Truth, and such should, therefore, be the desire of every Muslim."[129] Ali grounded his position in hadith from Bukhari:

Abu Hurairah said, I heard the Prophet, peace and blessings of Allah be on him, say: "By Him in Whose hand is my soul, were it not that there are men among the believers who cannot bear to remain behind me—and I do not find that on which to carry them—I would not remain behind an army that fights in the way of Allah; and by Him in Whose hand is my soul, **I love that I should be killed in the way of Allah then brought to life, then killed again then brought back to life, then killed again then brought to life, then killed again.**" (Bukhari 56:7)[130]

Jihad and Threat Analysis

We opened this discussion with Nyazee's contemporary characterization of jihad as expressed by Hanafi law. Looking backward, then, we sampled the classical formulations from Shafi'i and Malik ibn Anas, two towering icons of Islamic jurisprudence (reflecting the Shafi'ite and Maliki schools of law). We then compared those views to the formal codification of the law of jihad as stated in *Reliance of the Traveller*, an Islamic legal text found ubiquitously in Islamic bookstores and Islamic events in America today. From this analysis, a consistent picture emerges that unambiguously identifies jihad as a "right of Allah," creating a duty on man that is defined as "warfare against non-Muslims to establish the religion." This conforms to the consensus position of Islamic scholarship on the issue as well as the end-state conceptualization of jihad resulting from the application of the doctrine of abrogation.

If national security decision-making does not account for the legal, doctrinal, and historical fact of jihad when undertaking threat analysis, it is more than just incomplete. It is malpractice. A burden of proof has been met. Unless competing analyses can meet this burden, analysis and decision-making that posits a definition of jihad that is opposed to the one generated by an investigation into Islamic law—its foundations and centuries of rigorous Islamic scholarship—it should be considered suspect if not outright disinformation. This is true regardless of its proponents' awareness. Without a focus on the doctrinal threat drivers of the enemy, we leave "extremists" unchallenged in the Islamic domain, communicating doctrines of jihad to receptive audiences. As "extremists" expand on the requirements of jihad for committed Muslims, it must be assumed that the population will develop a deeper regard for those duties as their awareness increases. Conceding the information battle space to the threat leaves the national security community in a continuous state of strategic incomprehension.

Because "extremists" overtly rely on the legal definition of jihad to demonstrate the legitimacy of their cause when justifying attacks against the United States, its citizens and its allies, it is this form of jihad that must be incorporated into the doctrinal phase of any competent threat analysis. This remains true even when our Islamic advisers ask us to accept, at face value, that "there are thousands of different interpretations of Islamic law." *Even if there are many interpretations, it would still not exclude the one interpretation of Islamic law that Islamic terrorists rely on to attack non-Muslims.*

It is mystifying how often one hears this "many interpretations" claim associated with the summary dismissal of genuine analysis of shariah. This statement is typically used in one of two situations: first, when there is an accurate assessment of shariah that does not fit with the preferred narrative but against which there is no effective response; second, when designated experts are consistently wrong in their analysis and are searching for an excuse or some basis to relieve themselves of responsibility.

As the thinking goes, if there are a thousand different interpretations of any statement of Islamic law, one only has to be right once every 999 times to remain statistically valid. Even accepting such an absurd standard, real threat analysis is not concerned with the 999 times Islamic law *doesn't* constitute a threat, but rather with the one time that it does—even if that understanding of shariah is a minority view, an outlier, or even erroneous. The narrative of "infinite shariah possibilities" continues to mire the national security community in extraneous issues at the expense of actual threat identification.

Another common narrative obscures the threat doctrine by erecting a politically correct barrier to the study of shariah: "These assessments of jihad are inaccurate and defame the true nature of Islam." Couched in terms of inaccuracy, this narrative recognizes the analyst or decision-maker's aversion to being wrong. Typically, accusations of ignorance are simply asserted, often with a calculated emotional affect.

Even if it turns out that all the Islamic authorities are wrong and that, for example, jihad does not mean holy war, it would still be true that "extremists" misrepresent jihad along those lines when motivating otherwise faithful Muslims to wage jihad against America. For the threat doctrine to be valid, all that is needed is a doctrine that relies on such a view to justify itself and to motivate adherents to subvert, destabilize, and kill.

Non-Muslims in the Islamic State

The requirements of jihad neither begin nor end with the kinetic aspects of warfare. As we have seen, Islamic law divides the world into two states, dar-al-Islam and dar-al-harb, with jihad being an unabrogable obligation for Muslims until the dar-al-harb is eliminated and the People of the Book "pay the jizya with willing submission, and feel themselves subdued" (Qur'an 9:29). Because Verse 9:29 sets the standard for jihad against People of the Book and their subsequent submission, we can look to *Tasfir Ibn Kathir* for an explanation of how the submission requirement governs Muslim relations with non-Muslims.

The Islamic concept of submission flows from the law of jihad. While Qur'an Verse 9:29 permits People of the Book, should they choose not to convert, to "submit and feel themselves subdued" rather than be executed, they are given the option of servitude **only after** they have submitted: [131]

> It is not fitting for a Prophet that he should have prisoners of
> war until he has thoroughly subdued the land. (Qur'an 8:67)

Once subdued, non-Muslim subjects of the Islamic State can then be afforded certain "protections" that include onerous restrictions calculated to institutionalize their status as a submitted population. While *Reliance* describes the legal status and rights of submitted People of the Book, Majid Khadduri explains the close relationship between jihad, the division of the world into the dar al-Islam and the dar al-harb, and submission:

> Thus the jihad may be regarded as Islam's instrument for
> carrying out its ultimate objective by turning all people into
> believers, if not in the Prophethood of Muhammad (as in
> the case of the *dhimmis*), at least in the belief of Allah. The
> Prophet Muhammad is reported to have declared "some of

my people will continue to fight victoriously for the sake of the truth until the last one of them will combat the anti-Christ." **Until that moment is reached the jihad, in one form or another will remain as a permanent obligation upon the entire Muslim community. It follows that the existence of a *dar al-harb* is ultimately outlawed under the Islamic jural order; that the *dar al-Islam* is permanently under jihad obligation until the *dar al-harb* is reduced to non-existence; and that any community accepting certain disabilities—must submit to Islamic rule and reside in the *dar al-Islam* or be bound as clients to the Muslim community.** The universality of Islam, in its all embracing creed, is imposed on the believers as a continuous process of warfare, *psychological* and *political* if not strictly military.[132]

This concept is by no means just a historical curiosity. As recently as November 2012, Brotherhood-linked Imam Abdallah bin Mahfudh ibn Bayyah debated the proper classification of non-Muslims in the contemporary world along the dar al Islam/dar al harb axis.[133] Bin Bayyah is a senior imam and shaykh residing in Egypt. He is also associated with the International Union of Muslim Scholars (IUMS), an organization founded by the Brotherhood's chief jurist, Yusuf al-Qaradawi. When Qaradawi issued the fatwa encouraging Muslims to kill all Americans in Iraq in 2004, bin Bayyah was the Deputy President of Muslim Scholars.[134/135] He is also a member of both the Counsel of Jurists attached to the Organization of Islamic Cooperation and of the European Research & Fatwa Council in Ireland.[136]

Special attention should be given to Khadduri's comment that jihad is "a continuous process of warfare, **psychological and political if not strictly military**."[137] This reflects his understanding that Islamic concepts of warfare go beyond the kinetic—that jihad as "warfare to establish the religion" encompasses the entire spectrum of warfare, including the psychological, political and spiritual.

Khadduri made similar comments in his translator's introduction to the 9th-century legal work of Muhammad ibn al-Hasan al-Shaybani, author of *The Islamic Law of Nations: Shaybani's Siyar*, the earliest writing of Islamic law to discuss the legal concept of jihad and submission.[138] From Shaybani:

And the Apostle said: "Fight in the name of Allah and in the "path of Allah [i.e., the truth]. Combat only those who disbelieve in Allah. Whenever you meet your polytheist enemies, invite them first to adopt Islam. It they do so, accept it, and let them alone. You should then invite them to move from their territory to the territory of the émigrés Madina. If they do so, accept it and let them alone. Otherwise, they should be informed that they would be treated like the Muslim nomads (Bedouins) who take no part in the war in that they are subjects of Allah's orders as other Muslims, but they will receive no share in either the *ghanima* (spoils of war) or in the fat. If they refuse to accept Islam, then call upon them to pay the *jizya* (poll tax); if they do, accept it and leave them alone. If you besiege the inhabitants of a fortress of a town and they try to get you to let them surrender on the basis of Allah's judgment, do not do so, since you do not know what Allah's judgment is, but make them surrender to your judgment and then decide their case according to your own view."[139]

Ibn Kathir explains the conditions of submission by reference to the Pact of Umar, which was the treaty governing the submission of Syrian Christians to Umar, the second of the four Rightly Guided Caliphs (634–644 AD). As we proceed through the Pact of Umar, it would be good to do so with an eye toward what ISIS is imposing on "People of the Book" today. Because it is embedded in an authoritative tafsir as the explanation of the Quranic verse, the reader should be on notice that the Pact may be authoritative on the treatment of submitted People of the Book. Certainly, when analyzing Verse 9:29, that position should receive consideration. In fact, the Pact of Umar established the precedent for setting the conditions of "tolerance" of non-Muslims under Islamic law: submission that ensures continuous humiliation, degradation, and disgrace. Under the header "Paying the *Jizyah* is a Sign of *Kufr* and Disgrace," ibn Kathir explained that the meaning of submission according to Verse 9:29 is answered by the Pact:

> This is why the Leader of the faithful 'Umar bin Al-Khattab, may Allah be pleased with him, demanded his well-known conditions be met by the Christians, **these conditions that ensured their continued humiliation, degradation and disgrace.** The scholars of Hadith narrated from 'Abdur-Rahman bin Ghanm Al-Ash'ari that he said, "I recorded for 'Umar bin Al-Khattab, may Allah be pleased with him, the terms of the treaty of peace he conducted with the Christians of Ash-Sham: 'In the Name of Allah, Most Gracious, Most Merciful. This is a document to the servant of Allah 'Umar, the Leader of the faithful, from the Christians of such and such city:
>
> "When you (Muslims) came to us we requested safety for ourselves, children, property and followers of our religion. We made a condition on ourselves that we will neither erect in our areas a monastery, church, or a sanctuary for a monk,

nor restore any place of worship that needs restoration nor use any of them for the purpose of enmity against Muslims. We will not prevent any Muslim from resting in our churches whether they come by day or night, and we will open the doors (of our houses of worship) for the wayfarer and passerby. Those Muslims who come as guests, will enjoy boarding and food for three days. We will not allow a spy against Muslims into our churches and homes or hide deceit (or betrayal) against Muslims. **We will not teach our children the Qur'an, publicize practices of *Shirk*, invite anyone to *Shirk* or prevent any of our fellows from embracing Islam, if they choose to do so.** We will respect Muslims."[140]

Shirk, it should be noted, is the worst crime in shariah and among the most unforgivable. In *Reliance of the Traveller*, in the section on "Enormities", shirk is listed as the first in a list of Enormities:

p1.0 Ascribing Associates to Allah Most High (*SHIRK*) –

p1.1 Ascribing associates to Allah Most High means to hold that Allah has an equal, whereas He has created you, and to worship another with Him, whether it be stone, human, sun, moon, prophet, sheikh, jinn, star angel, or other.

p1.2 Allah Most High says:

> (1) "Allah does not forgive that any should be associated with Him, but forgives what is other than that to whomever He wills" (Koran 4:48)

> (2) "Surely, whoever ascribes associates to Allah, Allah has forbidden him paradise, and his refuge is hell" (Koran 5:72)

> (3) "Of a certainty, worshipping others with Allah is a tremendous injustice" (Koran 31:13)

p1.3 The Koranic verses concerning this are very numerous, it being absolutely certain that whoever ascribes associates to Allah and dies in such a state is one of hell's inhabitants, just as whoever believes in Allah and dies as a believer is one of the inhabitants of paradise, even if he should be punished first."[141]

Shirk is apostasy. *Reliance* reinforces the apostasy involved in shirk when stating that it is apostasy "(3) to speak words that imply unbelief such as 'Allah is the third of three'" ... The punishment for apostasy is severe:

> "When a person who has reached puberty and is sane volun-
> tarily apostatizes from Islam, he deserves to be killed."[142]

Dhimmitude

It is from the Pact of Umar that the laws of *Dhimmitude* emerge—as mandated by Verse 9:29. The rules, established in the ancient language of the Pact of
Umar, appear to remain in effect in modern Islamic law. Not surprisingly, *Reliance
of the Traveller* confirms ibn Kathir:

> Such non-Muslim subjects are obliged to comply with the
> Islamic rules that pertain to safety and indemnity of life, rep-
> utation, and property. In addition they:
>
> (2) are distinguished from Muslims in dress by wearing a
> wide cloth belt (zunnar);
>
> (3) are not greeted with "*as-Salamu 'alaykum*";
>
> (4) must keep to the side of the street;
>
> (5) may not build higher than or as high as the Muslims'
> buildings, though if they acquire a tall house, it is not razed;
>
> (6) **are forbidden to openly display** wine or pork, to ring
> church bells or **display crosses, recite** the **Torah** or **Evangel
> aloud**, or make public display of their funerals and feast days;
>
> (7) and are forbidden to build new churches.[143]

This analysis demonstrates established Islamic law on the treatment of
non-Muslims under Muslim rule. Because research verifies that this information
has remained consistent from its inception to modern times, it should not be
considered controversial from a doctrinal perspective within mainstream Islamic
law. Rather, it reflects settled concepts of Islamic doctrine in support of real Islamic principles, applicable at all times and in all places. Published in English in
the United States, *Reliance* sets the standard and the consequences for American
"People of the Book" should the conditions to implement this law come to pass.

The doctrine of *dhimmitude* demanded by the Pact of Umar has real-world
consequences. When the Muslim Brotherhood controlled Egypt, Islamic law
built upon the Pact was enforced against Coptic Christians. Violations of clearly

established and articulated Islamic law carry real consequences. Section o11.5(6) from *Reliance of the Traveller* declares that "Non-Muslims ... are forbidden to openly display ... crosses." This prohibition on non-Islamic religious expression should be remembered when reading news like this:

> In mid-October 2011 Egyptian media published news of an altercation between Muslim and Christian students over a classroom seat at a school in Mallawi, Minya Province. The altercation lead to the murder of a Christian student. The media portrayed the incident as non-sectarian. However, Copts Without Borders, a Coptic news website, refuted this version and was first to report that **the Christian student was murdered because he was wearing a crucifix.**[144]

Because 77 percent of Egyptians voting in the first referendum in March 2011 voted to retain shariah in the Egyptian Constitution, Copts were indeed guilty of the offense they are accused of committing while the Brotherhood enforced shariah. Refusing to comply with the terms of dhimmitude constitutes a crime against what is considered the law of the land.[145] It is similarly enforced against Christians in Syria, Nigeria, Sudan, and now, as imposed by ISIS in July 2014, in parts of Iraq.

Non-Muslims in the Middle East are finding they have to act according to shariah as classically understood. We, as Americans, have to ask ourselves if we want to have anything to do with such a turn of events, either by supporting it over there or letting it creep in here. For example, is the Catholic University of America in Washington, D.C., in violation of the rights of its Muslim students because it places crucifixes in its rooms?[146] The answer, clearly, is yes—under Islamic law. As will be discussed later, it is important that the opposition to crosses was framed in terms of human rights even as it represents an attempt to enforce Islamic legal prohibitions against the display of crucifixes. Back to *Reliance of the Traveller*, Book O "Justice," section 11:

> o11.10 The agreement is also violated with respect to the offender alone if the state has stipulated that any of the following things break it, and one of the subjects does so anyway, though if the state has not stipulated that these break the agreement, then they do not; namely, if one of the subject people:
>
> (2) conceals spies of hostile forces;
>
> (3) leads a Muslim away from Islam;

(4) kills a Muslim;

(5) or mentions something impermissible about Allah, the Prophet (Allah bless him and give him peace), or Islam.[147]

A non-Muslim can be made subject to Islamic law, and this includes the prohibition of making comments critical of Islam, the Qur'an, or Mohammed. Let's return to that portion of the Pact of Umar cited by ibn Kathir to explain Verse 9:29. It says that non-Muslims "will not teach [their] children the Qur'an." This seems to mean that non-Muslims cannot express an independent understanding of Islam, as they cannot pass on their own concerns about Islam to their children. This is important because, as the Pact of Umar establishes (specifically in the statement "We will not teach our children the Qur'an"), even an entirely accurate understanding of Islam and Islamic law is "impermissible" knowledge. This is relevant when considering the Islamic concept of Slander and current efforts to prevent non-Muslims from discussing Islam.

Let us continue with the terms of submission from *Tafsir ibn Kathir's* treatment of Qur'an Verse 9:29 with respect to the Christian leaders' compact of submission to the Muslims:

> We will not teach our children the Qur'an, publicize practices of Shirk, invite anyone to Shirk or prevent any of our fellows from embracing Islam, if they choose to do so. We will respect Muslims, move from the places we sit in if they choose to sit in them. We will not imitate their clothing, caps, turbans, sandals, hairstyles, speech, nicknames and title names, or ride on saddles, hang swords on the shoulders, collect weapons of any kind or carry these weapons. We will not encrypt our stamps in Arabic, or sell liquor. We will have the front of our hair cut, wear our customary clothes wherever we are, wear belts around our waist, refrain from erecting crosses on the outside of our churches and demonstrating them and our books in public in Muslim fairways and markets. We will not sound the bells in our churches, except discretely, or raise our voices while reciting our holy books inside our churches in the presence of Muslims, nor raise our voices (with prayer) at our funerals, or light torches in funeral processions in the fairways of Muslims, or their markets. We will not bury our dead next to Muslim dead, or buy servants who were captured by Muslims. We will be guides for Muslims and refrain from breaching their privacy in their homes.' When I gave this document to `Umar, he added to it, 'We will not beat

any Muslim. These are the conditions …'"[148]

This language mirrors what was affirmed in *Reliance*. In societies governed by Islamic law, activities associated with Ibn Kathir and *Reliance* § o11.5 continue to play themselves out. Looking at the two legal texts and the plight of Christians in Egypt, Syria, Iraq and Nigeria, we can see the real effects of Islamic law of submission.

The 'Good News' of Humiliation

The humiliation standard of Qur'an Verse 9:29 was anticipated in earlier verses—for example, Verses 3:111 and 3:112:

> They will do you no harm, barring a trifling annoyance; if they come out to fight you, they will show you their backs, and no help shall they get. (Qur'an 3:111)

> Shame is pitched over them (Like a tent) wherever they are found, except when under a covenant (of protection) from Allah and from men; they draw on themselves wrath from Allah, and pitched over them is (the tent of) destitution. This because they rejected the Signs of Allah, and slew the prophets in defiance of right; this because they rebelled and transgressed beyond bounds. (Qur'an 3:112)

The "they" in Verse 3:111 are the People of the Book. In ibn Kathir's explanation, much of the treatment of Verse 3:111 falls under the heading "The Good News that Muslims will Dominate the People of the Book."[149] Given that the "Good News" is a known synonym for the gospels of the New Testament,[150] it must be pointed out that the editorial staff of Darussalam wrote the heading as a gratuitous slap at Christians. Still, it is important to note, especially given all the choreographed rage regarding Qur'an abuses of late, that "tolerance" regarding the People of the Book is a one-way street. Ibn Kathir explains the meaning of Verse 3:112:

> Allah said next, "Indignity is put over them wherever they may be, except when under a covenant of protection from Allah, and a covenant from men;" **meaning, Allah has placed humiliation and disgrace on them wherever they may be, and they will never be safe**, "except when under a covenant from Allah," **under the *Dhimmah* (covenant of protection) from Allah that requires them to pay the *Ji-zyah* (tax, to Muslims,) [sic] and makes them subservient to Islamic Law.** "And a covenant from men;" meaning, cov-

enant from men, such as pledges of protection and safety offered to them by Muslim men and women, and even a slave,
according to one of the sayings of the scholars. Ibn 'Abbas
said that, "except when under a covenant from Allah, and
a covenant from men;" [sic] refers to a covenant of protection from Allah and a pledge of safety from people. Similar
was said by Mujahid, 'Ikrimah, 'Ata', Ad-Dahhak, Al-Hasan,
Qatadah, As-Suddi and Ar-Rabi' bin Anas. **Allah's statement, "they have drawn on themselves the wrath of Allah,"
means, they earned Allah's anger, which they deserved,
"and destitution is put over them," meaning they deserve
it by decree and legislatively.**[151]

While the verse is reasonably clear, Ibn Kathir's explanation removes any
doubt. Because the People of the Book incurred the wrath of Allah, they may
be treated with indignity—except under a Muslim's covenant of protection. This
confirms the shariah concept of tolerance relegating those being "tolerated" to the
status of second-class citizens.

Ibn Kathir's language about the status of Christians and Jews resonates in
today's news. For example, regarding the killing of Coptic Christians, in October
2011 Imam Yasir al-Bahrani boldly commented on the al-Rahma Satellite Channel in Cairo that:

> Copts are infidels towards Allah, Glory be unto Him, as
> found in the Holy Qur'an, Allah's curse upon them. Do we
> apologize for the Qur'an and pervert what is found in it so
> we can please them? [152]

Hence, ISIS leader Al-Baghdadi was on firm ground on July 18, 2014, when
providing the dawah notice to the Christians of Mosul to "choose one of these:
Islam, the sword, al-Jiziya (sic) (tax) or till Saturday to flee."[153] In fact, Baghdadi
laid down the same conditions enumerated in Verse 9:29.

Prisoners of War

As part of the humiliation of People of the Book, the leader of Ash Sham
was forced to write his own degrading terms of submission in the Pact of Umar.
Ibn Kathir continues his explanation of Qur'an Verse 9:29 by quoting from the
pact itself:

> **These are the conditions** ... that we set against ourselves
> and followers of our religion in return for safety and pro-
> tection. If we break any of these promises that we set for
> your benefit against ourselves, then our **Dhimmah** (promise

of protection) is broken and you are allowed to do with us what you are allowed of **people of defiance and rebellion**.[154]

What is meant by the statement that if the Pact "is broken you are allowed to do with us what you are allowed of people of defiance and rebellion"? *Reliance of the Traveller*, in the section titled "Non-Muslim Subjects of the Islamic State," can shed some light on this:

> When a subject's agreement with the state has been violated, the caliph chooses between the four alternatives mentioned above in connection with prisoners of war (see o9.14).[155]

This means that when the dhimma pact is violated, the non-Muslim reverts to prisoner-of-war status. Islamic law of submission in *Reliance* is quite telling for our purposes. Starting with § o١١,٩, followed by § o١١,١٠, we read that:

> If non-Muslim subjects of the Islamic state refuse to con-form to the rules of Islam, or to pay the non-Muslim poll tax, then their agreement with the state has been violated though if only one of them disobeys, it concerns him alone.[156]

> The agreement is also violated with respect to the offend-er alone if the state has stipulated that any of the follow-ing things break it, and one of the subjects does so anyway, though if the state has not stipulated that these break the agreement, then they do not; namely, if one of the subject people: leads a Muslim away from Islam; **or mentions some-thing impermissible about Allah**, the **Prophet**, or **Islam**.[157]

Defamation, according to Islamic criteria, creates a specifically enumerated basis for losing dhimma status. As we will see when discussing slander, a non-Mus-lim can be punished for defamation of Islam in classic Islamic law. Indeed, the punishment for this crime seems severe, given that the loss of the dhimma com-pact causes a reversion to prisoner-of-war status. So what does § o11.11 mean by "the caliph chooses between the four alternatives mentioned above in connection with prisoners of war (see § o9.14)"?[158] The best way to answer this question is to look at the referenced section, § o9.14, which deals with the law of jihad:

> When an adult male is taken captive, the caliph considers the interests of Islam and the Muslims and decides between the prisoner's **death, slavery, release without paying any-thing,** or **ransoming** himself in exchange for money or for a Muslim captive held by the enemy.[159]

To reiterate, according to Islamic law, a tolerated dhimmi is actually a pris-oner of war in a state of abeyance. This is what the Chief of the Christians of

Ash Sham meant in the pact to Umar when he said, "If we break any of these promises that we set for your benefit against ourselves, then … you are allowed to do with us what you are allowed of people of defiance and rebellion."[160] For example, non-Muslims are, as a class, subject to Islamic blasphemy laws. Hence, a dhimmi who defames Islam can be reverted to prisoner-of-war status and put to death. Mohammad Kamali, in his *Freedom and Expression in Islam*, recounts Shafi'i's position:

> In yet another report, Imam al-Shafi'i is said to have held that the protected status of the *dhimmi* terminates when he commits blasphemy and that, consequently, he becomes an enemy of war (*harbi*), in which case the head of state is within his rights to punish him as such. Imam al-Shafi'i adds that in this matter the head of state has discretionary powers similar to he has with regard to prisoners of war, that is, over whether to kill the offender or ask for ransom, and over whether or not to expropriate his property.[161]

As we will see, the penalty for defamation of Islam has always included death.

Islam and the Abrogation of Judaism and Christianity

The following comes from a first-grade textbook for a class on Islam in Saudi Arabia, but it could just as easily have come from Pakistan, Kuwait, Northern Africa, or a mosque in Falls Church, Virginia.

> The foundation of Islam is the profession of faith that there is no deity other than God and Muhammad is God's Prophet. Every religion other than Islam is false. [162]

Why? As stated in the Qur'an:

> Allah said, "If anyone desires a religion other than Islam (submission to Allah), never will it be accepted of him; and in the Hereafter He will be in the ranks of those who have lost (All spiritual good)." (Qur'an 3:85) [163]

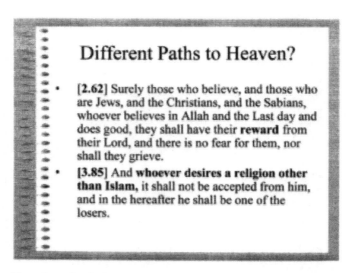

Hasan knew that Qur'an Verse 3:85 abrogated Verse 2:62. Therefore, the question "Different Paths to Heaven?" in his slide presentation is rhetorical, as Allah has definitively spoken on the matter.

Reliance affirms the abrogation of previously revealed religions by citing sahih hadith when Mohammed said:

> "By Him in whose hand is the soul of Muhammad, any person of this community, any Jew, or any Christian who hears of me and dies without believing in what I have been sent with will be an inhabitant of hell."... This is a rigorously authenticated (*sahih*) hadith that was recorded by Muslim.[164]

Now that we understand the mechanism by which Islamic law draws from the structure of the Qur'an, the excerpts from the Islamic textbook makes sense. We have seen published Islamic law relying on a recognized authority, citing authoritative hadith, which validates the plain reading of Qur'an verse 3:85. The first-grade text stands affirmed.

You might protest, however, that Qur'an 2:62 reads:

> Surely those who believe, those of Jewry, the Christians, and the Sabaeans—whoever has faith in Allah and the Last Day, and works righteousness, their wage awaits them with their Lord, and no fear shall be upon them, and neither shall they sorrow. [165]

As explained in *Reliance*, relying on Ibn Kathir, the Qur'an does indeed say this. However:

> The faith of the Jews was that of whoever adhered to the Torah and the sunna of Moses ... until the coming of Jesus. When Jesus came, **whoever held fast to the Torah and the sunna of Moses without giving them up and following Jesus was lost.**[166]

In other words, once Jesus (the Muslim prophet 'Isa, *not* the Jesus as defined in the New Testament) came, the laws of Moses (who was also a Muslim prophet and *not* the Moses as defined in the Torah) were abrogated. It continues:

> The *faith* of the Christians was that whoever adhered to the Evangel [the New Testament] and precepts of Jesus, their faith was valid and acceptable **until the coming of Muhammad. ...** [T]hose of them who did not then follow Muhammad and give up the sunna of Jesus and the Evangel were lost.[167]

Reliance goes on to say that "the foregoing is not contradicted by the hadith relating to the verse"[168] because it "was followed by Allah revealing" Qur'an Verse 3:85.[169] In other words, Verse 3:85 abrogated Verse 2:62, and Islamic law confirms this. These verses were displayed in Army shooter Hasan's PowerPoint under the heading "Different Paths to Heaven?" in which he explained the Islamic law by which Christianity and Judaism were abrogated religions.[170]

The status of non-Muslim People of the Book, Jews and Christians, has not changed. In January 2012, bin Bayyah published a statement on the status of Jews and Christians based on a question presented to him seeking shariah clarification.[171] In June 2013, he visited the White House to assist our leaders in developing a "moderate" position by working with the Brotherhood to isolate al-Qaeda. Bin Bayyah's statement on the status of Jews and Christians is fully in line with classical Islamic law. Its reiteration in 2012 was used to frame the planned treatment of Christians in the Arab world at a time when the Muslim Brotherhood was engaging in violent persecution and brutality toward Copts in Egypt (and ISIS was setting its sights on Eastern Rite Catholics and Orthodox Christians):

> *My question is:* What is the ruling of Mushriks or the people of the book who receive the message of Islam but do not join Islam? And what is the ruling of those who do not receive the message of Islam? Similarly, what is the ruling of Christians who admit Allah is One but follow the religion of 'Isa (Jesus, peace be upon him)? Will they be among the dwellers of Paradise or the denizens of Hell? Enlighten us, may Allah

reward you with good!

Allah, Glorified be He, says: "And whoever seeks a religion other than Islam, it will never be accepted of him, and in the Hereafter he will be one of the losers." (Al-`Imran, 3:85) The Prophet (peace be upon him) stressed the same ruling by saying that any Jew or Christian who heard about him and did not follow him would be among the denizens of Hell. This is related by Muslim (153) on the authority of Abu Hurairah (may Allah be pleased with him). Anyone who receives the message of Islam and does not enter Islam will not be saved from the punishment of Allah; he will enter the Hell. Allah, Praised be He, says: "… this Qur'an has been revealed to me that I may therewith warn you and whomsoever it may reach." (Al-An`am, 6:19) The message of Prophet Muhammad (peace be upon him) **nullifies all previous messages**, for he is the final Messenger and his message prevails over all messages. That is what we believe.[172]

Convert or die.

From our understanding of the abrogation of Judaism and Christianity under Islamic law, we can now see the basis for Surah 9, known as the "surah of the sword," and the fifth verse, the "verse of the sword":

Fight and slay the unbelievers wherever ye find them, and lie in wait for them in every stratagem of war. But if they repent, and establish regular prayers and practice regular charity, then open the way for them; for Allah is Oft-forgiving, Most Merciful. (Qur'an 9:5)

Yet we are often told that there is no concept of holy war in Islam. How, then, do we interpret "every stratagem of war" directed at unbelievers—unless, of course, they convert?

Convert or submit.

Regarding the People of the Book, the surah states:

Fight those who believe not in Allah nor the Last Day, nor hold that forbidden which hath been forbidden by Allah and His Apostle, nor acknowledge the religion of truth, **even if they are of the people of the Book, until they pay the jizya with willing submission, and feel themselves subdued.** (Qur'an 9:29)

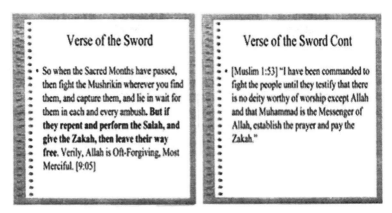

Slides in Hasan's presentation quote the "Verse of the Sword" from the Qur'an along with supporting hadith.

MAJ Hasan incorporated these same verses into his presentation under the heading "Verse of the Sword." His understanding of Christianity and Judaism as abrogated religions becomes relevant once one considers the high probability that many of his Fort Hood victims were likely self-identified as Christians—People of the Book "who believe not in Allah nor the Last Day, nor hold that forbidden which hath been forbidden"—and, therefore, should be fought. As noted, the terms of submission identified in Verse 9:29 are the ones ISIS leader Al-Baghdadi followed to the letter in July 2014 when stating terms to the Christians of Mosul: "[C]hoose one of these: Islam, the sword, al-Jiziya (sic) (tax) or till Saturday to flee."[173]

Apes, Pigs, and End Times

It is not uncommon to occasionally hear news reports about offensive materials in the schoolbooks of Islamic states. One in particular, referring to Jews as "apes" and Christians as "pigs," is particularly widespread. Consider these excerpts from eighth-grade school textbooks published by the Ministry of Education in Saudi Arabia:

> The Prophet made it known that polytheism occurs in this nation just as it occurred in earlier nations, and it occurred as he said.[174]

The text goes on to quote Verse 5:60:

2. God said: "Say: 'Shall I point out to you something much worse than this, (as judged) by the treatment it received from Allah? those who incurred the curse of Allah and His wrath, those of whom some He transformed into apes and swine, those who worshipped evil.'" (Qur'an 5:60) [175]

In a section on word definitions, the text explained that,

They are the people of the Sabbath, whose young people God turned into apes, and whose old people God turned into swine to punish them.[(7)] [176]

And, in the text, the original footnote #7 is:

As cited in Ibn Abbas: The apes are Jews, the people of the Sabbath; while the swine are Christians, the infidels of the communion of Jesus.[177]

People may wonder why this apparently "extremist" view of Jews and Christians as apes and pigs is so common in Islamic teaching materials, but it is quite simple. According to Verse 5:60, Allah *did* turn people who worshipped evil into apes and swine, and those evil-worshippers are understood by Islamic sources to have been the Jews and Christians. It's not surprising that Western calls for the removal of such "offensive" material go unheeded. After all, how could Saudi Arabian schools, or other schools operating in countries beholden to Islamic law, accept that the Qur'an is offensive?

Another notorious and often-referenced "extremist" passage relating to non-Muslims appears in Article Seven of the Hamas Covenant:

"The Day of Judgment will not come about until the Moslems fight the Jews (kill the Jews), when the Jew will hide behind stones and trees. The stones and trees will say O Moslem, O Abdulla, there is a Jew behind me, come and kill him. Only the Gharkad tree (evidently a certain kind of tree) would not do that because it is one of the trees of the Jews." (Related by Bukhari and Moslem)[178]

Because this Article is used by Hamas (whose full name is the Islamic Resistance Movement), a designated foreign terrorist organization, it is routinely treated as the ravings of "extremists." But the reference to Bukhari and Muslim indicates that Hamas is citing an authentic hadith. The same language is taught to ninth graders in instruction on hadith, as a recent Saudi school text teaches:

When God sent his Prophet Muhammad, **He abrogated with his law all other laws** and He commanded all people, including the people of the book, to believe him and to follow him. The people of the book should have been the first to believe him because they find him in their scriptures.

The clash between this Muslim nation and the Jews and Christians has endured, and it will continue as long as God wills. In this hadith, Muhammad gives us an example of the battle between the Muslims and the Jews.[179]

The above passage narrates Abu Hurayrah as recorded by Bukhari and Muslim, who are the two most authoritative hadith scholars for the following:

Narrated by Abu Hurayrah: The Prophet said, "**The hour of judgment will not come until the Muslims fight the Jews and kill them.** It will not come until the Jew hides behind rocks and trees. It will not come until the rocks or the trees say, 'O Muslim! O servant of God! There is a Jew behind me. Come and kill him. Except for the gharqad, which is a tree of the Jews.'"[180]

This last citation constitutes sahih hadith—indirect divine revelation—establishing the murder of the Jews at the End of Days as a prerequisite duty for Muslims before they can enter paradise. Yet, if one brings this up in polite interfaith "dialogue," it is dismissed as a misrepresentation of Islam. Unfortunately, this seems to reflect the view of the Vatican. In a televised speech in late November 2014 at Turkish President Erdogan's official residence in Ankara, Pope Francis attributed persecution of Christians, non-Sunni Muslims, and others to "fanaticism and fundamentalism, as well as irrational fears, which foster misunderstanding and discrimination." Such fanaticism and fundamentalism, he said, "need to be countered by the solidarity of all believers."[181]

A burden of proof has been met capable of supporting a presumption of correctness. The quotes from Bukhari and Muslim are both real and authoritative; they are used to sacralize the genocidal objectives of Hamas. If properly asserted, a standard is established that must be rebutted as part of any counterclaim that such shariah-based arguments are incorrect. When accusations of prejudicial misinterpretation are made, therefore, they should not be allowed to be simply asserted but rather should be made to meet the burden as a condition of offering their claim.

Both Hamas and the textbook authors seem to have it right. What Hamas declares as its aspiration—to fulfill laws that call for the killing of all Jews, no matter how long it should take—is what is taught to ninth-graders in Saudi Arabia. There is no reason to think it is not taught to ninth-graders in other Muslim jurisdictions as well. Bukhari and Muslim *did* authentically record it, and the Ministry of Education included citations so anyone could look it up.

There is a Christian corollary to the killing of the Jews. Ibn Kathir explains:

> While delivering the good news to His believing servants that victory and dominance will be theirs against the disbelieving, atheistic People of the Scriptures, Allah then said,

> They will do you no harm, barring a trifling annoyance; and if they fight against you, they will show you their backs, and they will not be helped. (3:111)

> This is what occurred, for at the battle of Khaybar, Allah brought humiliation and disgrace to the Jews. Before that, the Jews in Al-Madinah, the tribes of Qaynuqa`, Nadir and Qurayzah, were also humiliated by Allah. Such was the case with the Christians in the area of Ash-Sham later on, when the Companions defeated them in many battles and took over the leadership of Ash-Sham forever. There shall always be a group of Muslims in Ash-Sham area until `Isa, son of Maryam, descends while they are like this on the truth, apparent and victorious. `Isa will at that time rule according to the Law of Muhammad, break the cross, kill the swine, banish the Jizyah and only accept Islam from the people.[182]

You'll recognize the reference to Jews as swine to be killed. Ibn Kathir is saying that the People of the Scriptures (Jews and Christians) are unbelievers. Referencing the Pact of Umar, the commentary concerns the End of Days when Jesus returns to condemn all Jews and Christians to hell for failing to convert to Islam. This eschatological understanding is not the outlier in Islamic jurisprudence that some would like to think. *Reliance*, Book O "Justice," 9 "Jihad," at § o9.8 suggests the same End of Days scenario:

> the time and place for which is before the final descent of Jesus (upon whom be peace). After his final coming, nothing but Islam will be accepted from them, for taking the poll tax is only effective until Jesus' descent, which is the divinely revealed law of Muhammad. The coming of Jesus does not entail a separate divinely revealed law, for he will rule by the law of Muhammad. As for the Prophet's saying,

> "I am the last, there will be no prophet after me,"

> this does not contradict the final coming of Jesus, since he will not rule according to the Evangel, but as a follower of our Prophet.[183]

Offensive Islam If the Future

- Al-Bukhaari (2222) and Muslim (155) : The Messenger of Allah (SAWS) said: "By the One in Whose hand is my soul, soon the son of Maryam will descend among you as a just judge. He will break the cross, kill the pigs and abolish the jizyah, and money will become abundant until no one will accept it."

MAJ Hasan quotes authoritative End Times hadith from Bukhari and Muslim in which Jesus returns to kill the pigs (meaning Christians). Hasan presented this brief in a room full of military members who were at least nominally Christians, and yet none realized the threat.

Reliance § o9.8 relies on Qur'an Verse 9:29 for its authority. It should come as no surprise that Fort Hood terrorist MAJ Nidal Hasan also noted the true status of Jesus at the End of Days when giving his fellow officers a briefing in which he stated his declaration of jihad. In fact, Hasan cited the two most authoritative hadith collections, Bukhari at 2222 and Muslim at 155, to make his point:

> Al-Bukhari and Muslim said, the messenger of Allah said, quote, by the one in whose hand is my soul, soon the son of Miriam will descend upon you as a just judge. He will break the cross and kill the pigs and abolish the jizyah and money will become abundant till no one will accept it.[184]

Dawah – Preparation for jihad

Throughout this book, Islamic concepts that are regarded as conventional wisdom in the national security space—as well as in much of the mainstream media and in political discourse—meet the reality of authoritative published law. In many of the instances chronicled in the text, the misunderstanding of an Islamic point of law or term of art stems from an erroneous mirror-imaging of a what might appear to be a similar concept in Christianity or Judaism.

Nowhere has the lexical mirror-imaging been more inappropriate than when, in late January 2015, Pentagon Spokesman Rear Admiral John Kirby said, "Look, we know they [ISIS] have a fairly evangelistic view, particularly ISIL; they do want to spread this radical ideology."[185] An evangelist is "one of the four authors to whom is ascribed the writing of the Gospels" and, by extension, "one who works actively to spread and promote the Christian faith."[186] The term evangelist comes from the Latin evangelium, which means gospel. Gospel comes from the Anglo-Saxon "god-spell, "good tidings," or "good news."[187] ISIS is engaged in the mass persecution and killing of people who believe in the evangelium. There is a trend to demonizing Christian terms in the process of misusing them to explain Islamic realities, making those terms generally applicable and ensuring that they carry a negative connotation. In the process of developing these terms, it should not be overlooked that over time the lexicon becomes much better suited for use against Christians. Among the strategic communications savvy, it was not lost on anyone that Kirby's use of the term "evangelistic" came three days after Mohamed Elibiary, under the Twitter handle "TX Muslim Republican," launched an anti-Christian tirade promoting the terms "christianists" and "evangelicals."[188]

While the general public may be forgiven for missing the point, individuals tasked with keeping the nation safe are responsible for holding themselves to a higher, more rigorous analytical standard. As will be explained, that standard is one of professionalism. Professionals executing national or homeland security policy at every level have an obligation to investigate verifiable facts and to do the due diligence required when assessing comparative religious or legal doctrines that may have a bearing on the War on Terror.

Few concepts are as open to such deceptive mirror-imaging as *dawah*, as many national security analysts and decision-makers are familiar with proselytizing in Christianity. Often defined as the "invitation" or "call to Islam," the meaning and purpose of dawah is more extensive—and closely associated with jihad. In fact, much of what is popularly called "stealth jihad" are actions taken in preparation for jihad in the dawah phase of operations.

While military language like "phases of operation" may seem out of place for actions that don't extend beyond proselytizing, a more complete understanding of dawah as the Muslim Brotherhood uses the term will demonstrate that the military analogy is not wholly inappropriate. "Phases of operation" begin in the preparation stage—dawah—and transition to actions on the objective in the execution stage: jihad.

A classic statement on the relationship between dawah and jihad can be found in Malik Ibn Anas's 8th-century hadith collection, the *Muwatta*, citing Mohammed himself:

> Yahya related to me ... that the Messenger of Allah, may Allah bless him and grant him peace, went out to Khaybar, he arrived there at night, and when he came upon a people by night, he did not attack until morning. In the morning, the Jews came out with their spades and baskets. When they saw him, they said, "Muhammad! By Allah, Muhammad and his army!" The Messenger of Allah, may Allah bless him and grant him peace, said, "Allah is greater! Khaybar is destroyed. **When we come to a people, it is an evil morning for those who have been warned.**"[189]

This hadith is also recorded in Bukhari.[190] In its purest form, the dawah message would come before the attack—in what Pakistani Brigadier S.K. Malik calls the preparation stage. If the army arrived in the evening, the dawah message was issued one last time. In the morning, if the encamped army heard the call to prayer, the issue was resolved. If not, "it is an evil morning for those who have been warned."

We can also find continuity with the classic understanding of dawah, repackaged in facially neutral terms, in today's narratives. In Nyazee's *Methodology of Ijtihad*, we are told the objective of Islam remains unchanged: "to spread the message of Islam in the whole world." These goals are to be accomplished through dawah and jihad. While it is hoped that non-Muslims will embrace Islam when invited, it will be "an evil morning indeed for those who have been warned" and rejected the call:

> What are the goals of the Muslim community? ... The positive aspect of this interest conveys a single goal: to spread the message of Islam in the whole world. **The instrument utilized for attaining this goal is *da'wah* in conjunction with *jihad*.** There are numerous opinions on the meaning and role of *jihad* in the modern age. These however, are not relevant for the present study as we are looking for the traditional point of view. What is relevant is the opinion of the jurists, and hence the law on this point.[191]

> Will this community annul this truce, if tomorrow, it were to gain its strength? ... In so far as traditional Islam grows in strength it could come into the forefront of world politics. ... It is to be hoped that in this modern world, where religion has been given a back seat in the general scheme of things and where other problems will continue to maintain the truce and agreements in a spirit of cooperation and **focus more on the institution of *da'wah* (invitation) than on the**

instrument of *jihad* (holy war), especially when there are legal opinions supporting truce.[192]

The Islamic community remains in the preparation stage while still "gain[ing] its strength." As that strength builds, so will the dawah initiatives. Later, we will examine how the Organization of Islamic Cooperation's Ten Year Programme of Action builds momentum in a parallel way to deprive American citizens, among others, of their civil liberties. Discussions on dawah that do not account for the supporting role it plays for jihad should be understood to be defective—often purposefully so.

In his instructional text *What Islam is All About*, Yahiya Emerick explains to seventh-grade American Muslims that dawah is designated as one of the "Three Duties of Islam":

> The three duties are extra things which Muslims do based on commandments of Allah in the Qur'an. They are: 1) *Da'wah* (Calling others to Islam), 2) *Jihad* (Striving in Allah's Cause), and finally 3) **Encouraging the good while forbidding the wrong**. (3:110)[193]

> "*Dawah* means to call others. A person who is giving the *Dawah* to others, or telling them about Islam, is termed a *Da'i*, or Caller."[194]

The "3:110" following the explanation above refers to Qur'an Verse 3:110: "Ye are the best of peoples, evolved for mankind, **enjoining what is right, forbidding what is wrong**, and believing in Allah. If only the People of the Book had faith, it were best for them: among them are some who have faith, but **most of them are perverted transgressors**." This verse, as noted, separates Muslims from the Jews and Christians, or People of the Book.

As the verse indicates, a relationship exists between dawah, jihad, and what it calls "encouraging good and forbidding wrong." Justifying its place in Islamic law through scholarly consensus, *Reliance of the Traveller* develops the relationship between the three duties in Book A "Sacred Knowledge," starting with Part a1.0 "The Knowledge of Good and Bad":

> There is **no disagreement among the scholars** of Muslims that the source of legal rulings for all the acts of those who are morally responsible is Allah Most Glorious[195]

> The mind is unable to know the rule of Allah about the acts of those morally responsible except by means of His messengers and inspired books. Some minds find certain acts

good, others find them bad. So it cannot be said that an act which the mind deems good is therefore good in the eyes of Allah …"[196]

"The *good* of acts of those morally responsible is what the lawgiver (syn. Allah or His messenger) has indicated is good by permitting it or asking it be done. And the *bad* is what the Lawgiver has indicated is bad by asking it not be done. The good is not what reason considers good, nor the bad what reason considers bad. The measure of good and bad, according to the school of thought, is the Sacred Law, not reason"[197]

"A person is not morally obligated by Allah to do or refrain from anything unless the invitation of a prophet and what Allah has legislated have reached him. No one is rewarded for doing something or punished for refraining from or doing something until he knows by means of Allah's messengers what he is obliged to do or obliged to refrain from. … By the word of Allah Most High, 'We do not punish until We send a messenger' (Koran 17:15)."[198]

This passage holds three crucial principles in Islamic doctrine and establishes them with scholarly consensus: (1) one can only know what is right and wrong through what was revealed by a Messenger; (2) reason does not serve as a basis for making such determinations; and (3) persons are not held accountable for what they do until they receive a proper call to Islam. Closer to home, American Muslim Brotherhood activist and thinker Shamim Siddiqi, in his *Methodology of Dawah Ilallah in American Perspective*, makes it clear that only shariah serves as the basis for determining what is right and wrong:

"Call unto Allah" means surrender to Allah Who is the Creator, the Lawgiver and the Sustainer. It means to accept His authority in its totality in every walk of life. It advocates that sovereignty belongs to Allah alone and denies all authorities besides Him. … **Only Allah-given laws are to be accepted, practiced and implemented in an individual's life and established in the society where the Muslims live**. A joint and concerted effort of all Muslims in that direction is the direct sequence of call unto Allah. **Surrendering to His authority and making His *Deen* dominant are the culminating points of the call unto Allah.**[199]

In addition to the duty of knowing the relationship of right and wrong to dawah and acceptance of Islam, there is an additional, parallel role for dawah. To understand the strategic importance of the call to Islam, one must understand the role it plays in initiating jihad. In keeping with the Quranic proscription just noted, that "We do not punish until We Send a Messenger," in Book O "Justice," Part 9 "Jihad," in the section "Objectives of Jihad," *Reliance* makes clear that the dawah message must precede jihad:

> "The Caliph makes war upon Jews, Christians, and Zoroastrians **provided he has first invited them to enter Islam** in faith and practice, and if they will not, then invited them to enter the social order of Islam by paying the non-Muslim poll tax (*jizya*).[200]

The explanation in *Reliance* conforms to what was stated in the sacralized first biography of Mohammed, *Sirat Rasul Allah* by Muhammad ibn Ishaq (d. 767 or 761). As translated by Alfred Guillaume:

> Then the apostle sent Khalid b. al-Walid in the month of Rabi u l-Akhir or Jumadal'l-Ula in the year ten to the B. al-Harith b. Ka'b in Najarn, **and ordered him to invite them to Islam three days before he attacked them**. If they accepted then he was to accept it from them, and if they declined he was to fight them. So Khalid set out and came to them, and sent out riders in all directions inviting the people to Islam, saying, "If you accept Islam you will be safe." So the men accepted Islam as they were invited.[201]

Isn't this the form ISIS has followed in Iraq and Syria since 2014?[202] One gets a sense of the relationship that exists between dawah and jihad in assessing the benefit of heeding the call to Islam. This is made clearer in the annotation to Qur'an Verse 9:5 in *Interpretations of the Meanings of the Noble Qur'an*:

> Then when the Sacred Months (the 1st, 7th, 11th, and 12th months of the Islamic calendar) have passed, then kill the *Mushrikun* (see V. 2:105) wherever you find them, and capture them and besiege them, and lie in wait for them in every ambush. But if they repent [by rejecting *Shirk* (polytheism) and accept Islamic Monotheism] and perform *As-Salat* (*Iqamat-as-Salat*), and give *Zakat*, then leave their way free. Verily, Allah is Oft-Forgiving, Most Merciful.[(1)]
>
> (1) b) Narrated Abu Hurairah: When the Prophet died and Abu Bakr became his successor and some of the Arabs reverted to disbelief, 'Umar said, "O Abu Bakr! How can you

fight these people although Allah's Messenger said, "I have been ordered to fight the people till they say: *La ilaha illallah* (none has the right to be worshipped but Allah), and whoever said *La ilaha illallah* will save his property and his life from me, unless (he does something for which he receives legal punishment) justly, and his account will be with Allah?[203]

'Dislocation of Faith'

The Islamic way of war places substantial effort on the preparation stage, the object of which is to induce a collapse of faith in the cultural, political, and religious institutions underpinning the target. A very clear example of this doctrine is Pakistani Brigadier General S.K. Malik's *The Quranic Concept of War*. In the forward to the treatise, then-General M. Zia ul-Haq, Chief of Staff of the Pakistani army, wrote of its doctrinal relevance to Pakistan.[204] When ul-Haq later became President, he designated Pakistan an Islamic Republic. The book's introduction was written by Brohi, a man who would later become the Advocate General of Pakistan. He declared *The Quranic Concept of War* a "Restatement" of Islamic principles of war.[205] Lawyers should take heed of what Brohi meant when declaring Brigadier Malik's monograph a "Restatement" (of the law of jihad).

If a Muslim general in a Muslim country writes a book titled *The Quranic Concept of War*, he is asserting that there is a form of warfare that comes from the Qur'an. Because the Qur'an is considered the "Uncreated Word" of Allah, the assertion of there being a Quranic concept of war strongly suggests that such a form exists. Hence, the fact that the Muslim Brigadier was allowed to title the monograph as he did when working for a Muslim Chief of Staff of the Army in a Muslim country suggests its status was accepted the moment the title was approved.

In the *Quranic Concept of War*, Malik emphasized the importance of laying the groundwork for successful military operations. He explained this preparatory stage as a "dislocation of faith" in the target nation's sense of security and in the capability of its leaders to defend its territory. The inability of the target population's leadership to protect its citizens in the face of a terror campaign signals the beginning of kinetic operations in earnest. At some point, dawah transitions to jihad.

> The Quranic strategy comes into to play from the preparation stage, and aims at imposing a direct decision upon the enemy. Other things remaining the same, our preparation for war is the true index of our performance during war. We must aim at creating a wholesome respect for our *Cause* and our will and determination to attain it, in the minds of the enemies, well before facing them on the field of battle. So spirited, zealous, complete and thorough should be our

preparation for war that we should enter upon the 'war of muscles' having already won the 'war of will'. Only a strategy that aims at striking terror into the hearts of the enemies from the preparation stage can produce direct results and turn Liddell Hart's dream into a reality.[206]

To instill terror into the hearts of the enemy is essential in the ultimate analysis to **dislocate his faith**. An invincible faith is immune to terror. A weak faith offers inroads to terror.[207]

Malik's preparation stage concerns those actions taken in the dawah phase in anticipation of jihad. In the early phases of dawah, one should expect to see an emphasis on penetration and subversion campaigns directed at cultural, political, media, and religious institutions. Actions taken in the early dawah phase aimed at compromising a community's core beliefs will substantially contribute to the sense of hopelessness that magnifies the effects of terror when the final call to Islam is made—at a time and place calculated to induce mass conversion or submission.

It is psychological demoralization and political subversion, or, as Malik puts it, a "war of will." While this form of warfare is stated as a general proposition, it also reflects the more prudent approach when fighting a militarily superior enemy—such as the United States. He is admonishing, in effect, that a fighting war—his "war of muscle"—should not begin until its been assessed that the enemy has been demoralized. On this point, is America's current mood in the War on Terror beginning to reflect this outcome?

Malik's articulation of Quranic warfare doctrine makes sense in its original context, the Arabian Desert in the time of Mohammed. Jihadis were Bedouins; their forces were distributed, and they did not have large numbers when they attacked. Because the desert made siege operations unforgiving, Mohammed's army valued the strategic necessity of psychological warfare. When they raided a town, they wanted the townspeople to be so terrified and demoralized that they would quickly surrender.

So what is behind the Pakistani Brigadier's comment that "the Quranic strategy comes into play from the preparation stage, and aims at imposing a direct decision upon the enemy?"[208] Malik builds his argument by referencing four Quranic verses that form the basis of his Quranic concept of war. He begins by reference to three verses cited in rapid succession:

'I am with you: give firmness to the Believers: I will **instill terror into the hearts** of the Unbelievers." (Anfal: 12)[209]

Soon shall We **cast terror into the hearts** of the Unbelievers. (Al-i-Imran: 151)[210]

> And those of the people of the Book who aided them, Allah did take them down from their strongholds and **cast terror into their hearts**, (so that) some ye slew, and some ye made prisoners. And He made you heirs of their lands, their houses, and their goods, and of a land which ye had not frequented (before). And Allah has power over all things. (Ahzab: 26–27)[211]

A close inspection of those verses indicates a common focus on terror, reflecting Malik's view that when Allah wishes to impose His will upon His enemies, He chooses to do so by "**casting terror in their hearts**." So how are Muslims supposed to wage war? Malik asks and answers his own question. "But, what strategy does He [Allah] prescribe for the Believers to enforce their decision upon their foes?"[212]

> "Let not the Unbelievers think," God commands us directly and pointedly, "that they can get the better of the Godly: they will never frustrate them. Against them make ready your strength to the utmost of your power, including steeds of war, **to strike terror into the hearts of the enemies** of Allah and your enemies, and others besides, whom ye may not know, but whom Allah doth know." (Anfal: 59–60)[213]

For Malik, victory in the preparation stage comes in the form of political subversion and psychological demoralization through the calculated application of terror. The objective of jihad, he points out, is the destruction of faith: "To instill terror into the hearts of the enemy it is essential in the ultimate analysis to dislocate his faith. An invincible faith is immune to terror. A weak faith offers inroads to terror."[214] In this effort, he insists that such destruction be complete:

> Terror cannot be struck into the hearts of an army by merely cutting its lines of communication or depriving it of its routes to withdraw. It is basically related to the strength or weakness of the human soul. It can be instilled only if the opponent's faith is destroyed.[215]

The object of jihad is the destruction of faith; when directed at America, it aims to destroy our faith in our God, our government, our legal system, our leadership, and our society. Jihad is primarily understood in terms of spiritual warfare. This happens to be a form of warfare that the Pentagon is not disposed to recognize and allocates no requirements to resist. It is in this context that we should also understand interfaith activities. Bishops, ministers, and rabbis blindly addicted to interfaith dialogue should consider whether their actions contribute to the defense of their respective faiths or to their destruction. Once demoralized, we become the object of increasingly intense forms of dawah meant to convert us or to cause us to submit. These dawah efforts will contrast with the alternative path, that of jihad. Malik makes it clear how far he is willing to go in this venture, stating plainly:

This rule is fully applicable to nuclear as well as conventional wars.[216]

If Malik is right, instead of asking "Why do they hate us?" when al-Qaeda struck America on 9/11, we should have asked ourselves, "What are we missing that we still refuse to see?"

The Preparation Stage

Even if al-Qaeda is wrong in its interpretation of Islamic law, prior to its attacks on the United States the group still considered itself a part of the jihadi wing of the dar al-Islam. In that capacity, it concluded that an attack would deliver a dawah message to the heart of the dar al-harb. Al-Qaeda—and the Islamic Movement more broadly—expected that the Ummah, the Muslim community, across the globe would recognize this message and would, at least tacitly, conform. While the jury is still out on al-Qaeda's estimation, it was a judgment based on the group's understanding of Islamic law.

If Khadduri and Malik are correct, the preparation stage in anticipation for all-out kinetic war would look very much like what we've experienced since 9/11—complete with state actor deniability of the events that define our time. At least one country's Army Chief of Staff said that S.K. Malik's concepts merited adoption, and a senior jurist designated Quranic jihad against the dar al-harb a "Restatement" of classically understood Islamic law. Khadduri and Malik's reasoning would make some aspects of kinetic war a viable option for all shariah states in all phases of operation. Hence, dawah is better understood as a pre-violent rather than a non-violent phase.

9/11 was not the tooth of the tiger. It was the *tail*. As long as we believe we are fighting only the jihad wing of radical Islam—the one that carried out the attacks on the World Trade Center and the Pentagon—we fail to understand that there had to be *at least* the perception of consensus in the Muslim world that open warfare in the heart of infidel lands is condoned by Islamic law. Battle preparation must have progressed to the point where this kind of action was thinkable.

The Milestones Process

By now, readers should realize they cannot understand what drives the enemy if they do not understand abrogation. Portions of the Qur'an revealed later in the book have a disproportionate effect on how Islam and its laws are understood. This is true as a matter of published Islamic law. In fact, in certain instances, the "radical" interpretations end up being the *only* interpretations. Furthermore, regardless of whether abrogation is broadly accepted within the Muslim community, we still cannot understand "extremist" Islam without understanding abrogation. But if abrogation is valid as law, and if violent jihadi verses abrogate non-violent verses, then why are not all Islamic entities engaged in violent jihad at all times?

The reason is that the threat doctrine based on abrogation orients the Islamic world through what we will call the *Milestones Process*. The conceptual framework underlying the Milestones Process forms both the doctrinal foundation of the threat doctrine and the mechanisms that drive decision-making.

Muslim Brotherhood strategist Sayyid Qutb wrote *Milestones* in 1966 while awaiting execution in an Egyptian prison.[217] Drawing from his popular tafsir, *In the Shade of the Qur'an,* Qutb's overriding concern was to call the modern Muslim world—1960s Egypt and, more generally, the entire Arab and Muslim world—to return to the true faith.

For Qutb, this was not an abstract issue. His question was how to restore Islam to a generation of 20th-century Muslims who had backslid into unbelief. The term Qutb used for this condition was *jahiliyyah* (or "the state of ignorance of the Guidance from God"), a reference to the time before Quranic revelation.[218] While the word occurs in the Qur'an four times, its broad contemporary usage is most associated with Qutb's reintroduction of the term in *Milestones*. He associated the current state of ignorance (jahiliyyah) with the "primitive savagery of pre-Islamic days,"[219] which revealed "the utter bleakness of the Muslim predicament" in modern times and served as "an epistemological device for rejecting all allegiances other than Islam."[220] Qutb was critiquing the absence of Allah's law, shariah, as governing law in the modern Islamic world. From *Milestones*:

> If we look at the sources and foundations of modern ways of living, it becomes clear that the whole world is steeped in *Jahiliyyah*, and all the marvelous material comforts and high-level inventions do not diminish this ignorance. This *Jahiliyyah* is based on rebellion against Allah's sovereignty on earth. **It transfers to man one of the greatest attributes of Allah, namely sovereignty, and makes some men lords over others**. It is now not in that simple and primitive form of the ancient *Jahiliyyah*, but takes the form of claiming that **the right to create values, to legislate rules of collective behavior** (sic), and to choose any way of life rests with men, without regard to **what Allah Almighty has prescribed**. The result of this **rebellion against the authority of Allah** is the oppression of His creatures.[221]

In *Islamic Movement: Problems and Perspective*, published by American Trust Publications, Fathi Yakan confirmed that jahiliyyah "applies to all non-Islamic cultures and influences, including modern secular society"[222] and then declared that "Islam is a call to revolution, revolution against the manifestion (sic) of jahiliyyah life in all shapes and forms. It is a revolution against the jahiliyyah traditions, and a revolution against jahiliyyah laws and legislation."[223] In *To Be a Muslim*, published in America by the ISNA publishing house American Trust Publications, Yakan went on to say that "the responsibilities and duties to work for Islam are too big a load for one person, because the goal is to obliterate jahiliyyah (evil ways and systems of thought and life) down to their roots and replace it with the truth of Divine Revelation."[224] This bodes ill for American culture and governance. In *Milestones*, Sayyid Qutb associates jahiliyyah with shirk:

> This association with God has been either in belief and worship, or in accepting the sovereignty of others besides God. Both of these aspects are *Shirk* in the sense that they take human beings away from the religion of God, which was brought by the Prophets. After each Prophet, there was a period during which people understood this religion, but then gradually later generations forgot it and returned to *Jahiliyyah*. They started again on the way of *Shirk*, sometimes in their belief and worship and sometimes in their submission to the authority of others, and sometimes in both.[225]

The relationship between the Islamic doctrine of shirk and the Muslim Brotherhood concept of jahiliyyah has important consequences for the role the Brotherhood sees itself playing in the United States.

As Nyazee indicated in the discussion on abrogation, when Allah began the period of revelations to Mohammed, the Arabs were in such a state of immorality that Allah chose to reveal his message progressively; thus, once the people reached a certain stage of understanding, the message would change to reflect the evolved and evolving circumstances. Once a new stage was reached, new revelations would then overrule the revelations from previous stages. This process enabled Muslims to build Allah's desired end-state "gradually and in stages." Of course, because abrogation is a foundational concept in Islamic law grounded in the Qur'an, Qutb was aware of the process:

> The Qur'an did not come down all at once; rather it came down according to the needs of the Islamic society in facing new problems, according to the growth of ideas and concepts, according to the progress of general social life, and according to new challenges faced by the Muslim community in its practical life.[226]

Qutb's solution to the problem was to encourage the current generation of Muslims to emulate the first generation of Muslims, those to whom Allah revealed His message—"gradually and in stages." He proposed mapping the stages of Quranic revelation, as they reached full implementation of Islamic law, for today's Muslims to follow. Each stage continued until the community of Muslims had reached a "milestone" or, as sometimes translated, a "signpost along the road." Since Allah had already revealed the stages in the Qur'an, the path was preordained. Qutb wrote:

> The milestones will necessarily be determined by the light of **the first source of this faith the Holy Qur'an**—and from its basic teachings, and from **the concept which it created** in the minds of the first group of Muslims, those whom God raised to fulfill (sic) His will, those who once changed the course of human history in the direction ordained by God. **Only in the light of this explanation can we understand those verses of the Holy Qur'an which are concerned with the various stages of this movement. In reading these verses, we should always keep in mind that one of their meanings is related to the particular stages of the development of Islam,** while there is another general meaning which is related to the unchangeable and eternal message of Islam. We should not confuse these two aspects.[227]

As Qutb's thinking went, if this is how Allah led the first generation, could there be any better way for today's generation? This is the Milestones Process. Of course, it is directly aligned with the Islamic concept of progressive revelation, the doctrine of abrogation. From the Islamic perspective, Qutb's reasoning is powerful and persuasive. *Milestones* established the doctrinal baseline that permits synchronization both within the Muslim Brotherhood as well as across the entire Salafi jihadi spectrum—including al-Qaeda and ISIS.

Because the main focus on the Muslim Brotherhood in this book is on activities directed at the United States and the West, it should be noted that its main effort is still the restoration of the Muslim world. This is certainly true with regard to the jahiliyyah narrative. For this reason, a few observations are warranted before moving on. As Qutb argues in *Milestones*, the Muslim world has regressed to a state of jahiliyyah because it is in rebellion:

> If we look at the sources and foundations of modern ways of living, it becomes clear that the whole world is steeped in *Jahiliyyah*, and all the marvelous material comforts and high-level inventions do not diminish this ignorance. This *Jahiliyyah* is based on rebellion against Allah's sovereignty on earth. It transfers to man one of the greatest attributes of Allah, namely sovereignty, and makes some men lords over others. It is now not in that simple and primitive form of the ancient *Jahiliyyah*, but takes the form of claiming that the right to create values, to legislate rules of collective behavior, and to choose any way of life rests with men, without regard to what Allah Almighty has prescribed. The result of this rebellion against the authority of Allah is the oppression of His creatures.[228]

We must also free ourselves from the clutches of Jahili society, Jahili concepts, Jahili traditions and *Jahili* leadership. Our
mission is not to compromise with the practices of Jahili society, nor can we be loyal to it. *Jahili* society, because of its Jahili
characteristics, is not worthy to be compromised with. Our
aim is first to change ourselves so that we may later change
the society. Our foremost objective is to change the practices of this society. Our aim is to change the *Jahili* system at
its very roots, this system which is fundamentally at variance
with Islam and which, with the help of force and oppression,
is keeping us from living the sort of life which is demanded
by our Creator.[229]

In this context, the similarities between Qutb's association of shirk with jahiliyyah and 'Anbari's earlier association of bid'a with takfirism (in Part 1) are
noteworthy. Compare Qutb's belief in *Milestones*—that because jahiliyyah arises out of shirk, it renders democratic governments unacceptable—with 'Anbari's
statement on takfirism in *Fundamentals of Takfir*.

From Qutb:

This *Jahiliyyah* is based on rebellion against Allah's sovereignty on earth. It transfers to man one of the greatest attributes
of Allah, namely sovereignty, and makes some men lords over
others.[230]

This is the basic difference between the concept of life taught
by God and man-made theories, and hence it is impossible to
gather them together under one system. It is fruitless to try to
construct a system of life which is half-Islam and half-*Jahiliyyah*. God does not forgive any association with His person,
and He does not accept any association with His revealed way
of life. Both are equally *Shirk* in the sight of God, as both are
the product of the same mentality.[231]

From 'Anbari:

What the modern people say about those who judge by man-
made law is what our scholars of the past have said about the
innovator, but the difference between the modern people and
the scholars of the past is that the modern people issue *takfir*
without any differentiation. As for those firmly grounded in
knowledge from the past, then they divide innovation into
two types, the innovation that warrants *takfir*, and innova-

tion that does not, and *Ahl as-Sunnah* have agreed on this categorization, and the *shari'ah* does not allow distinguishing between two of the same thing, and making different things the same. So the innovator and the one who judges with other than what Allah revealed are two of a kind, and the judgement (sic) for them is the same, there is no difference at all.[232]

While governing according to man-made law is a form of bid'a (innovation) that rises to takfir, jahiliyyah is the resulting state of that activity. In both, the central offense is shirk, the only difference being that takfirism is limited to Muslims. In many respects, the Brotherhood's jahiliyyah narrative parallels the Wahhabi's on takfirism. In an April 2014 interview in Cairo, this observation was brought to the attention of Nabil Na'eem, founding member of the Egyptian Islamic Jihad (EIJ) and former close associate of Ayman al-Zawahiri. Na'eem has since renounced violence.[233] In his view, the jahiliyyah narrative Sayyid Qutb outlined in Egypt was fully developed by his brother Muhammad upon fleeing to Saudi Arabia. In reference to Muhammad Qutb's 1980 book *Jahiliyya of the Twentieth Century*,[234] Na'eem said takfirism was imported into the larger Sunni community masked in the jahiliyyah narrative. To highlight the Wahhabi nature of takfirism, Na'eem emphasized that Muhammad Qutb's work product was formulated in Saudi Arabia, while Muhammad lived there as a refugee academic.

When listening to discussions on terrorism in the Muslim world, much of the focus centers on underlying claims of takfirism because Muslims and Muslim states that are the target of takfiri claims tend to become the objects of jihad for much the same reasons as non-Muslims. Voices and actions that seem intent on pushing back on the takfiri and jahiliyyah narratives should be deemed more likely to be allies in the fight against terrorism.

Doctrines of jahiliyyah and takfirism aside, shariah nevertheless still seems to heavily disfavor governing systems that operate outside the limits of shariah owing to issues of shirk. As Malaysian jurist Professor Doi said in his treatise *Shari'ah: The Islamic Law*:

> But the fundamental principles on which rests the Islamic legal system is that the laws of Islam are not passed in a heated assembly by men who ardently desire the legislation in their interests against men who oppose it in their interest. ... The difference between other legal systems and the Shari'ah is that under the Shari'ah its fountainhead is the Qur'an and Sunnah. ... The Qur'an and Sunnah are the gifts given to the entire *Ummah*. Therefore the *Ummah* as a whole is collectively responsible for the administration of Justice. This is the reason why any legislative or consultative assembly in any Muslim land has no power of encroachment on any legal

right of the members of the *Ummah* and those who live with them in peaceful co-existence.[235]

The Vanguard

Sayyid Qutb lived in Egypt in the 1950s and '60s, when the Soviet Union was the major influence. He and his intellectual cohort read Soviet materials and were impressed with the Soviet system's effectiveness, but not because they liked communism. A glancing influence of Leninism may be detected early in *Milestones*, when Qutb speaks of "the vanguard of the believer." Just as Lenin described a "correlation of forces" ("when the correlation of forces is right, you will strike"), Qutb said that when a Muslim reaches the proper milestone, he must transition to the next phase of revelation.

Lenin's vanguard was the Bolshevik party. Qutb's was the Muslim Brotherhood. Because certain operational requirements are associated with later stages of revelation, following the Milestones Process entails a disciplined but tactically flexible approach. As we will soon see, Qutb's proscriptions in *Milestones* have taken on doctrinal meaning for the Brotherhood, including in the United States. He writes:

> It is necessary that **there should be a vanguard which sets out with this determination** and then keeps walking on the path, marching through the vast ocean of *Jahiliyyah* which has encompassed the entire world. During its course, it should keep itself somewhat aloof from this all-encompassing *Jahiliyyah* and should also keep some ties with it. **It is necessary that this vanguard should know the landmarks and the milestones of the road toward this goal so that they may recognize the starting place, the nature, the responsibilities and the ultimate purpose of this long journey.** Not only this, but they ought to be aware of their position vis-à-vis this *Jahiliyyah*, which has struck its stakes throughout the earth: when to cooperate with others and when to separate from them: what characteristics and qualities they should cultivate, and with what characteristics and qualities the *Jahiliyyah* immediately surrounding them is armed; **how to address the people of *Jahiliyyah* in the language of Islam, and what topics and problems ought to be discussed**; and where and how to obtain guidance in all these matters.[236]

The Brotherhood is mindful to ensure that its capabilities retain their connection to the respective period of revelation. As Qutb explained, it is pointless to provide resources that the Muslim community lacks the capacity to put in motion; he also warned of the risks of operationalizing a capability prematurely:

> The second aspect of the religion is that it is a practical move-
> ment which progresses stage by stage, and **at every stage it
> provides resources according to the practical needs of the
> situation and prepares the ground for the next one**. It does
> not face practical problems with abstract theories, **nor does
> it confront various stages with unchangeable means**.[237]

Based, as it is, on the Islamic doctrine of abrogation, Qutb was clear about what the end-stage of the Milestones Process would entail:

> Wherever an Islamic community exists which is a concrete
> example of the Divinely-ordained system of life [i.e., once it
> has gotten to the top of the milestones], **it has a God-given
> right to step forward and take control of the political au-
> thority so that it may establish the Divine system on earth,**
> while it leaves the matter of belief to individual conscience.

> When God restrained Muslims from Jihaad for a certain
> period, it was a question of strategy rather than of princi-
> ple; this was a matter pertaining to the requirements of the
> movement and not to belief.

> Only in the light of this explanation can we understand
> those verses of the Holy Qur'an which are **concerned with
> the various stages of this movement**.[238]

For the Islamic Movement that would soon be based around Qutb's strategy, these stages are eventually to build to an all-out confrontation with the non-Muslim world, the dar al-harb. For this reason, there is no understanding the "extremist" narrative without understanding the Milestones Process. And there is no understanding that process without recognizing that it is a direct inject into core Islamic law through the Quranic doctrine of abrogation. Readers who fail to understand any of this will fail to understand *all* of it. This relationship helps to explain the intense effort of the Muslim Brotherhood and entities like the Organization of the Islamic Cooperation to shut down all discussion of this concept.

Message Continuity from 1966 to Today

After 9/11, *Milestones* was recognized as a capstone document to violent jihadist groups like al-Qaeda. For a time, Qutb's name seemed poised to become nearly as famous in the West as it is in the Muslim world. Analysis in the mainstream press, however, continues to completely miss the Milestones Process.

Instead, analysts stressed Qutb's connection to takfirism. Rather than deal with the underlying threat doctrine as operationalized by the Brotherhood, national security experts, self-described moderates, and pundits busied themselves with procedural questions, such as whether jihadi leaders had the standing to accuse other Muslims of takfir or apostasy. As a tactical consideration, this line of inquiry misses the larger strategic importance of Qutb and the Milestones Process.

Recognizing the Milestones Process allows an analyst to make assessments and predictions based on the posture of the Islamic Movement at a given moment. Similarly, an individual or group's fidelity to the Process is indicated in the use of terminology arising out of the *Milestones* narrative.

For the Brotherhood, it is unsurprising that there has been substantial continuity of *Milestone*'s messaging over time. It provides a common reference and strategic direction to the group. In 2011, a half-century after Qutb, an Egyptian Brotherhood leader conveyed the same idea in *Ikhwanonline* when discussing future courses of action in Egypt. Note the similarities between this narrative—including Qur'an Verse 17:106—and that of *Milestones,* as already discussed:

> *Gradual Action Does Not Impose Islam at Once—But Rather Step by Step.* There is no other way but gradual action, preparing the [people's] souls and setting an example, so that faith will enter their hearts. ... Gradual action does not impose Islam at once, but rather **step by step, in order to facilitate understanding, studying, acceptance, and submission.**

> Allah the Exalted said: "And those who disbelieve say, Why was the Koran not revealed to him [i.e., to the Prophet] all at once? So that We may strengthen thereby your heart" [Koran 25:32].

> The Koran was sent down in parts over 23 years, according to the events, the circumstances, and the laws that these circumstances entailed, and **in order to strengthen [people's] hearts** and make it easier [for them] to memorize and understand the Koran. And this verse is the ultimate proof:

> "And it is a Koran which We have revealed in portions so that you may read it to the people by slow degrees ..." [Koran 17:106].

> The Prophet, peace be upon him, acted in a gradual manner, **by first preparing the people, and then [preparing] family, society, state, and finally the caliphate. ...** This gradual method is also employed in the Koran itself with respect to

the prohibition on drinking wine. ... It was also employed in presenting the duties of Islam. ... First, there were two prayers—at noon and in the evening—and after people grew accustomed to them, Allah ordered five prayers during the day and night ...

At the [Muslim Brotherhood's] fifth conference, [the movement's founder,] Imam [Hassan] **Al-Banna, spoke about gradual action and reliance on education, and clarified the stages [of implementing the Shari'a].** They [i.e., the movement's founding members] believed that *da'wa* must come in phases:

"The phase of reading, learning the idea, and delivering it to the public; the phase of forming [the idea]; and the phase of implementation, work and results. At that same conference, Al-Banna said, addressing the hasty: 'Listen to what I say in a loud, resounding voice: This way of yours, whose phases are written and whose boundaries are defined, is long, but there is no alternative [way]. **I am not with those who want to pick the fruit before it has ripened. Those who wait patiently for the seed to sprout, the tree to grow, the fruit to ripen, and the harvest to arrive—their reward will be with Allah**. ... May that be the payment of those who do good.'"[239]

In 2012, Sunni scholar and chief Muslim Brotherhood jurist Sheikh Yusuf al-Qaradawi used *Milestones* vocabulary when discussing the strategic implementation of Islamic law in then-Brotherhood-controlled Egypt:

I think the *shari'a* should be implemented gradually. **This is a law of the *shari'a* and a law of nature. ... We should do things gradually. We should prepare the people, teach them.** People have to learn. We have to make an effort to teach people the truth about Islam. ... People do not understand the *shari'a* properly. We have to teach people the laws of the *shari'a* and explain them, before anything else. I think that in the first five years, there should be no chopping off of hands. This period should be dedicated to teaching things. **A transitional phase.** ... This should be a period in which we teach people the true laws of the *shari'a*.[240]

Jailed Brotherhood General Guide Muhammad Badi hit many of Qutb's key points almost verbatim in a 2011 article for *Ikhwanonline*:

[Our] Long-Term Goal ... Involves Changing and Transforming All the Exiting Conditions, So that the Islamic State and the Law of the Koran May Live Again. In our modern age, the Muslim Brotherhood launched its call to Islam **in attempt to guide the nation and reawaken it, so as to bring it back to its former] status and to its mission after a long period of backwardness and lethargy.** At the Sixth Muslim Brotherhood Congress, Muslim Brotherhood founder Hassan Al-Bana [sic], defined two goals for our blessed organization:

"... One is an immediate goal, which becomes evident and yields fruits as soon as a person joins the Brotherhood. It starts with purifying the soul, amending behavior, and preparing the spirit, the mind and the body for a long struggle. ... **The second goal is a long-term goal, which requires utilizing opportunities, waiting for the right time, making preparations and planning in advance. It entails a total reform of all domains of life,** in which all the nation's forces should participate, and also involves changing and transforming all the exiting conditions, so that the Islamic state and the law of the Koran may live again."

Al-Bana set out the stages and detailed the means by which this great goal might be achieved, starting by reforming the individual, followed by building the family, the society and the government, and then the rightly guided Caliphate, and finally achieving mastership of the world—a mastership of guidance, instruction, truth and justice. Al-Bana explained that all these purposes and goals, having been defined and clarified, must be realized through earnest, persistent and gradual effort, through unity of ranks not division, by persuasion, not coercion, and by love, not by force. We must be steadfast in our course, no matter obstacles, hardships, traps or conspiracies we encounter.[241]

Through time, fidelity to the *Milestones* narrative has been consistent—including within the Muslim Brotherhood in America. Its secret strategy document restates Qutb's message and includes a common emphasis on development in stages, as stated in Qur'an Verse 17:106 in the 1991 *Explanatory Memorandum*:

The writer of the memorandum believes that understanding and comprehending the historical stages of the Islamic activism which was led and being led by the Muslim Brotherhood in this continent is a very important key in working towards settlement, through which the Group observes its march, the direction of its movement and the curves and turns of its road. [*Note*: the *Explanatory Memorandum* associates "settlement" with "civilization jihad"][242]

It should come as no surprise, too, that modern Brotherhood intellectuals often speak in terms consistent with the Milestones Process. Tariq Ramadan—grandson of Brotherhood founder Hassan al-Banna—described it explicitly in his 1997 book *To Be a European Muslim*:

> This is the path of wisdom that Revelation taught us: during the 23 years of successive Revelations, **many prohibitions and obligations were revealed step by step** in order both to make the new rulings easily attainable and to uplift Muslims' hearts and intelligence towards a deeper respect and a more profound spirituality.[243]

The Islamic Movement and Its Awakening

I say to you: that we are in a battle, and that more than half of this battle is taking place in the battlefield of the media. And that we are in a media battle in a race for the hearts and minds of our Ummah. And that however far our capabilities reach, they will never be equal to one thousandth of the capabilities of the Kingdom of Satan that is waging war on us.

Eaman al-Zawahiri, "Al-Zawahiri Letter to
Abu Musab al-Zarqawi"
(The Zarqawi Network that went by the name
Al-Qaeda in Iraq is today ISIS)
July 9, 2005

We should all be very careful not to be colonized by something which is coming from this consumerist society. … It should be us with our understanding of Islam, our principles, colonizing positively the United States of America.

Tariq Ramadan
Grandson of Hassan al-Banna
(Founder of the Muslim Brotherhood)
ICNA Conference, Dallas, Texas, June 2012[1]

From the Philippines, Indonesia, and Malaysia to Northern Africa, Egypt, and Saudi Arabia; from Pakistan, Iraq, and Chechnya to Northern Virginia, the messaging is the same. Sayid Qutb's Milestones Process operationalizes the doctrine of abrogation for the Islamic Movement, creating a path for implementing shariah in stages. It was modeled after Allah's progressive revelations to Mohammed in the period of the first generation of Muslims. *Milestones* forms a strategic understanding of the Islamic Movement, facilitating a common reference point around which disparate "violent extremist" groups can coalesce. As we have seen, the end-state conception of relations between the Islamic world and the infidel residing in the dar al-harb is jihad, until non-Muslim jurisdictions are "ultimately outlawed."[2]

Qutb's status is iconic. Because he contributed the operational framework for what would become the Islamic Movement, he is sometimes considered a progenitor of al-Qaeda and other jihadist groups. It is crucial to understand that many "violent extremist" are well-versed in Qutb's *Milestones*. Alarmingly, the text is part of formal instruction in the Tarbiyah Guide that the Islamic Circle of North America (ICNA) uses to train teenagers in its American Islamic Centers.[3]

The Milestones Process is about building an Islamic Movement based on Islamic principles. The end goal of that process is a movement capable of engaging in jihad. In *Milestones*, Qutb discusses Islam and the role of jihad:

> Since the objective of the message of Islam is a decisive declaration of man's freedom, not merely on the philosophical plane but also in the actual conditions of life, it must employ *Jihaad*. ... The reasons for *Jihaad* which have been described in the above verses are these; **to establish God's authority in the earth; to arrange human affairs according to the true guidance provided by God; to abolish all the Satanic forces and Satanic systems of life; and to end the lordship of one man over others** since all men are creatures of God and no one has the authority to make them his servants or to make arbitrary laws for them.[4]

After Qutb's execution in 1966, his works transcended Egyptian politics and became the strategic pivot point in the Islamic Movement. The Muslim Brotherhood, of which Qutb was a member, served as the most important facet of that movement, with its members and leadership providing the "vanguard."

The Muslim Brotherhood

In 1924, the first President of the newly formed Turkish Republic, Mustafa Kemal Atatürk, abolished the institution of the Ottoman Caliphate, replacing it with a parliamentary system.[5] Almost immediately, efforts to reestablish the caliphate, a governing system mandated by Islamic law, began throughout the Muslim world. The General Caliphate Conference was held in Cairo in 1926, and it quickly devolved into a forum for theoretical and political disagreement about who would select the head of state. Scholar Nibras Kazimi notes that:

> It drew together notables and scholars from the Levant, the Maghreb, Iraq, and the Arabian Peninsula, together with representatives from far-flung Muslim communities in such places as South Africa and Poland. However, the important factions in the Indian subcontinent that had sought a reinvigorated caliphate decided to boycott the proceedings, partly over fears that Egypt's [King] Fuad would try to steer the delegates towards declaring him caliph. The Congress formed two committees **to ponder classical and modern questions pertaining to the caliphate**. The first, which **studied the doctrinal underpinning of the caliphate, was composed of three scholars representing each of the three dominant Sunni schools** (Hanafi, Shafi'i, and Maliki) with a single Hanbali scholar accorded a lesser observer status among them. Al-Zawahiri [grandfather of the al-Qaeda leader] was chosen as the head of Shafi'i group, as well as the speaker for the committee.[6]

The failure of this prominent group—consisting of most of the region's heads of state and renowned Islamic scholars—to come to an agreement about a future caliphate disappointed and frustrated many in the Muslim world. This was especially true in Egypt, where many looked forward to the prestige of situating the caliphate in Cairo for the first time since the end of the Shia Fatimid Caliphate in the 12th century.[7]

Two years later, in 1928, a schoolteacher named Hassan al-Banna founded the Muslim Brotherhood (or *al-Ikhwan al-Muslimin*) in the port town of Ismailia, Egypt. The fall of the caliphate was, for him, a calamity that highlighted how far the Islamic world had strayed from the true message and governing system of Islam. Like Qutb after him, al-Banna recognized that Islamic law—in its logical fulfillment—does not allow for truly Western democratic forms of governance.

Al-Banna took an oath to Allah, with his followers in Ismailia, to be "troops for the message of Islam." Noting that they were "brothers in the service of Islam," he named his group the Muslim Brothers. The group quickly established itself, acquiring buildings, land, and secretarial staff. At the Fifth Annual Conference in 1939, the Brotherhood formally established itself along the following principles:

> (1) Islam as a total system, complete unto itself, and the final arbiter of life in all categories; (2) an Islam formulated from

and based on its two primary sources, the revelation in the Qur'an and the wisdom of the Prophet in the Sunna; and (3) an Islam applicable to all times and all places."[8]

For Imam Hassan Al Banna, "the Muslim Brotherhood are a Salafi [looking to the early practice of Islam] call, a Sunni [following the steps of the Prophet], a Sufi fact, a political body, a sports band, a cultural and scientific association, an economic company, and a social idea."[9] It should not be a surprise that, from its founding, the Brotherhood has been dedicated to the centrality of violent jihad according to Islamic law. The motto al-Banna created for the Brotherhood has become an identifiable rallying cry:

> Allah is our objective, the Prophet is our leader, the Qur'an is our law, Jihad is our way, dying in the way of Allah is our highest hope.[10]

Brotherhood chief jurist Yusuf al-Qaradawi praised al-Banna for committing his group to "awaken[ing jihad] afresh before the public." Qaradawi is among the elites in contemporary Islamic intellectual and jurisprudential circles. He obtained his doctorate in shariah from the prestigious al-Azhar University, has written numerous books on Islamic law, and has been influential as a television personality on his Al-Jazeera program "Shariah and Life," which reaches an estimated 30 million across the globe.[11] On one of his programs, Qaradawi made the following observation:

> When the movement of [the Muslim Brotherhood] came into existence **it breathed new life in the carcass of [jihad] and awakened it afresh before the public**. They gave it due place in their treaties, books and newspapers; stressed upon its importance and necessity in their lectures, meetings and songs, and manifested its superiority and its fruits upon individual and collective life. …
>
> In order to **impress the meaning and implication of Jihad** they adopted many methods. … One of the chapters of the holy Quran which was expected to be memorized by the Ikhwans [Muslim Brothers] is sura *Infal*, **so that the meaning of Jihad, of which Muslims were ignorant for a long period, may penetrate deeply in their minds**.[12]

Today, Qaradawi is a revered leader and lead jurist of the Muslim Brotherhood. When making pronouncements such as these he is, in many respects, the voice of the Brotherhood internationally. An entire chapter could be written on both Qaradawi and al-Banna's deep-seated doctrinal hostility to the West that narrows in on the need for jihad. On another occasion, Qaradawi explained the relationship of Islam to warfare:

> We do not disassociate Islam from war. On the contrary, dis-
> associating Islam from war is the reason for our defeat. We
> are fighting in the name of Islam. Religion must lead to war.
> This is the only way we can win.[13]

In his treatise on jihad, al-Banna begins by admonishing Muslims with reference to Qur'an Verse 2:216: "Fighting is obligatory to you, much as you dislike
it."[14] He further informs them that "If you should die or be slain in the cause of
Allah, his mercy will surely be better than all the riches you amass" (Qur'an 3:158).
To remove any doubt about the nature of the Brotherhood's conception of jihad,
al-Banna explained, "**It is the nature of Islam to dominate, not to be dominated, to impose its law on all nations and to extend its power to the entire plan-
et.**"[15] As this discussion of the Brotherhood continues, it is important to bear in
mind that from the beginning, the Brotherhood vision statement has been hostile,
specifically political, and not theological. Note the similarity to the explanation
offered by Washington-based academic Majid Khadduri in *War and Peace in the
Law of Islam*:

> It follows that **the existence of a *dar al-Harb* is ultimately
> outlawed under the Islamic jural order; that the *dar al-Is-
> lam* is permanently under jihad obligation until the *dar al-
> Harb* is reduced to non-existence.**[16]

Al-Banna also had an expansive view of dawah. His Muslim Brotherhood
would be the opposite of the failed 1926 General Caliphate Conference, with
its renowned attendees. As his aim was to change Muslim societies (beginning
with his native Egypt), he realized that victories in the academic, intellectual, or
political spheres were no substitute for creating long-term grassroots movements.

In the 1970s, Qaradawi wrote a book outlining the group's pedagogical meth-
od. Its title, *Islamic Education and Hassan al-Banna*, indicates the debt the Islamic
Movement owes to al-Banna's concepts of imposing an Islamic political order. As
Qaradawi explained,

> The greatest responsibility of [the Muslim Brotherhood] is
> to train [the] Muslim, because he is **the foundation stone
> of revolution**. He is the axis of welfare and rectification of
> deeds, without which, **the establishment of Islamic society**
> or the **enforcement of Islamic laws** or **establishment of
> government** cannot be imagined.[17]

In other words, the Brotherhood understood from the beginning that only by
making society more amenable to the Quranic message would that "foundation
stone of revolution" reap dividends in the re-establishment of shariah as governing

law. Under Banna's leadership, the Muslim Brotherhood would become an exemplar for what would later be known as local "community organizing." He preached not only in mosques but also in community spaces, such as coffee shops. The group began creating the basic infrastructure of social services that soon won the loyalty of hundreds of thousands of Egyptians.

At the same time, al-Banna appropriated the Sufi organizational methods he learned in his youth to create an insurgent force.[18] Outside of the top leadership level (the Shura Council), the Brotherhood is concentrated in close decentralized units ("study circles" and 'Usar groups) along what it calls "Three Parallel Lines," which engender fierce loyalty that reinforces conformity. The Muslim Brotherhood is so confident that American national security analysts and policymakers are unaware of the threat that they openly describe the components of the group's "Structure and Spread" on their English-language website, Ikhwanweb. The "Three Parallel Lines":

> **The system of study circles to achieve knowledge line.** ...
> This system achieves "Knowledge" which is the first pillar
> of dawah along with the principle of publicity in calling for
> Islam and Islamism. Mosque is the natural target for establishing such circles.

> **The system of 'Usar al-Takween (The smallest units in the
> preparation stage) to achieve the line of Tarbiah (training).**
> ... While the study circles system aims at strengthening general attachment to Islam, the objective of 'Usar system is to
> achieve special attachment to Islam and stimulating all powers, consequently there are two forms of 'Usar:

> (1) 'Usar al-Takween entrusted with **preparing and
> cultivating MB members**; and ...[19]

Finally, Ikhwanweb lists the 'Usar al-Amal groups—clandestine paramilitary or terrorist units formed "to achieve the line of jihad"—sometimes known as the Brotherhood's "secret cells"[20] or "secret apparatus."

> (2) 'Usar al-'amal entrusted with **stimulating one's powers
> in the continuous daily work for implementing Islam entirely or partially.** ... The system of 'Usar al-'amal (Action
> Unit) to **achieve the line of jihad.**[21]

From Brotherhood sources on an official Brotherhood portal, we are put on notice that if a mosque is under Brotherhood control, there is reason to presume that it is engaged in such activities. At least as early as 1942, successive Egyptian governments recognized the inherently subversive nature of the Brotherhood and its Milestones Process as a threat to the status quo political order. Its embrace of jihad included the 1948 murder of a judge that sent several of its members to prison for their part in an anti-government conspiracy.[22] In response, the group was officially dismantled under orders from then–Egyptian Prime Minister Mahmud Fahmi al-Nuqrashi, who was assassinated by the Brotherhood before the year was out. The bloodletting continued, and Hassan al-Banna was killed early in 1949. In an interesting sidebar, it wasn't until January 27, 2015, that the Brotherhood publicly acknowledged its use of secret cells for terrorist activities. In a declaration on *Ikhwanonline* announcing the transition to the next stage of operations—jihad (think Milestones Process)—the Brotherhood acknowledged that the second general guide, Hassan al-Hudaybi, used the secret apparatus to engage in terror campaigns:

> The founding Imam, Hassan Al Banna, established the "Brotherhood Scouts" which represented fitness/discipline and the "Secret Apparatus" which represented the most significant facet of the brotherhood's power. The Imam also formed the "Jihad Brigades" which were deployed to combat the Jews in Palestine while the second Imam, Hodaiby, reinstated the "Secret Apparatus" to lead a war of attrition against the British occupiers in Egypt.[23]

When cracking down on the secretive group in the later 1960s, Egyptian security forces were said to have encountered copies of Qutb's *Milestones* at the home of every Muslim Brother.[24] The authorities considered the presence of the book "evidence they were preparing a coup."

The Islamic Movement

While the term "Islamic Movement" is closely associated with the Muslim Brotherhood and a 1991 document called "Explanatory Memorandum: On the General Strategic Goal for the Group in North America," written by Palestine Committee member Mohamed Akram, it has a much larger scope of meaning. In the 1994 "for subscribers only" pamphlet *The West in the Eyes of the Egyptian Islamic Movement,* Ibrahim Ghanem said that the Islamic Movement is an integrated system[25] that includes both "reformist" and "revolutionary" components—by which was meant both the dawah and jihadi elements—one led by the Muslim Brotherhood and the other by the Jihad Group and the Islamic Group.[26] Jihad is an obligation for all participants in the Islamic Movement, including those in the Brotherhood. Fathi Yakan, in his 1990 *To be a Muslim*, relied on Brotherhood founder Hassan al-Banna to establish this point: "Imam Hassan al Banna outlined .... responsibilities of the Islamic Movement" that include "regularly making the intention to go on jihad with the ambition to die as a martyr." Banna went on to say that "you should be ready for this right now, even though its time may not have come yet."[27] As Yakan explained:

> Muslims in an Islamic Movement are the true servants of Al-
> lah and their obedience is only to Allah, the Almighty, in all
> matters of life. It encompasses not only religious affairs but
> also worldly affairs. This is because Islam teaches its followers
> that there is no segregation or separation between religion
> and worldly affairs. Islam rejects the idea of secularism which
> is based on separation of religion and state in accordance with
> the superficial understanding of the supposed statement of
> the Prophet Jesus, peace be upon him, - Render unto Cae-
> sar what is Caesar's and unto God what is God's, which is
> translated into the idea that religion is for God (Allah) and
> the state is for everyone. The servitude of man means that
> he must reject all manmade philosophies and systems that by
> nature lead mankind to submit to the false gods of material-
> ism. Islam rejects totally all of these paradigms, systems and
> methods because:
>
> 1) It is clear that they transgress against Allah's rights and
> rules. Allah, the Almighty, says: "The Command Rests with
> none but Allah." [Qur'an 6:57]
>
> 2) All such man-made concepts and practices cause weakness
> and failure. Therefore they are unable to bring out the true
> nature of mankind in the trials of life. Allah, the Almighty,
> says: "Is then He Who creates like one that creates not? Will
> you not receive admonition?" [Qur'an 16:17][28]

In *The Priorities of the Islamic Movement in the Coming Phase*, first published
in 1990, "Shaykh" Yusuf Al-Qaradawi delved deeper into the qualities of those in
the Islamic Movement:

> The core of this self-motivation is the unrest and tension that
> a Muslim feels inside himself when he becomes conscious of
> the Islamic Awakening. He feels a turmoil deep inside him
> resulting from the contradiction between his faith, on the one
> hand, and the reality of the state of the *Ummah* on the other.
> Upon this realization he launches himself into action, driven
> by his love for his *Din*, his faith in Allah and His Messenger,
> his faith in the Quran and the Muslim *Ummah*, his realiza-
> tion of his own weakness as well as those around him, and his
> keenness in fulfilling his duties and contributing to the revival
> of the neglected *fara'id*, which include obligations like imple-

menting the *Shari'ah* of Allah, unifying the Muslim *Ummah*, supporting the friends of Allah and fighting the entrenched enemies of Allah, liberating Muslim lands from all aggression and non-Muslim control, re-establish the *khilafah* (sic), renewing the obligation of *da'wah*, enjoining the *ma'ruf* [good] and forbidding the *munkar* [evil] and fulfilling the obligation of *jihad*, whether by action, word or by the heart [the later being the weakest level of *iman*]. He strives for all of this so that the word of Allah reigns supreme in all spheres of life.[29]

Note how the very title of Qaradawi's book speaks to the Milestones Process. For Qaradawi, a member of the Islamic Movement is any Muslim who is self-motivated to (1) engage in dawah ("renewing the obligation to spread the call of Islam"), (2) work to establish shariah ("Enjoin what is right and forbid what is wrong"), and (3) engage in jihad ("strive in Allah's cause by deed, by word, or by the heart"). This is not to say that the Islamic Movement is an individual rather than a collective effort, or that it is disorganized. Qaradawi warns against any misunderstandings in that regard:

> The sheer state of affairs is an inextricable reality that fruitful work must be done collectively. It takes two hands to clap, and one is weak by himself but is rendered strong by his fellows. Great achievements are made through concerted efforts, and decisive battles are won only through the unity of hands, as the Quran says, *Indeed, Allah loves those who fight in His cause in ranks as if they were a solid structure* [Qur'an, 61:4].

> Collective work should be organized and based on a responsible leadership, a solid foundations and clear conceptions that define the relationships between the leadership and the grassroots efforts, all according to the fundamentals of obligatory *shura* [consultation] and obedience. ... Islam recognizes no collective work that does not have a system.[30]

In *To Be a Muslim*, Yakan said,

> The **Islamic Movement**: Its Task, Characteristics and Tools - The duty of the **Islamic movement** is to help people submit to Allah as individuals and groups by working for the establishment of an Islamic community deriving its rules and teachings from the book of Allah and His Prophets' sunnah.[31]

> In declaring that jihad is a duty, Yakan further asserts that it includes the complete rejection of every aspect of the Western

way of life—from capitalism, to socialism, to postmodernism, to faith—and that it has a Quranic basis:

The Islamic Movement is rooted in some basic principles, namely, that:

> 1) Islamic teachings and rules are comprehensive and designed by Allah to govern the affairs of man at all levels of community, from the family to the whole of the human race.
>
> 2) The fundamental theme of Islam throughout history has been "there is no god but Allah," which means, that Allah alone is Divine and Sovereign.
>
> 3) Islam alone can provide the power for Muslims to liberate oppressed peoples from the control of those who worship the false gods of modernist and postmodernist cultures, namely, from *taghut*, so that these false gods will no longer be in a position to persecute or put obstacles in the way of sincere people and so all religion will be exclusively for Allah.
>
> 4) The adoption and adaptation of capitalist, socialist, communist or other manmade systems, either in whole or in part, constitutes a denial of Islam and disbelief in Allah the Lord of the worlds. Such adoption and adaptation diverts Muslims into unguided, haphazard, and wasteful efforts. Allah, the Almighty, has said:
>
> > If anyone desires a religion other than Islam (submission to Allah), never will it be accepted of him and in the hereafter he will be in the ranks of those who have lost (all spiritual good). [Qur'an 3:85][32]

In keeping with the Milestones Process, Yakan associates the duties of the Islamic Movement in this age to those in the period of the Prophet, emphasizing that these duties include jihad:

> Muslims should realize that their self-value derives only from Islam, without which they are like animals or worse. They must know however, that true honor can never be achieved

unless they continue actively to involve themselves in the Islamic Movement. Those who remain in isolation will be in the Hellfire. Those who join in the Islamic Movement are joining themselves with an honorable people. They are the enlightened, the "prophets" and the "martyrs" on whom Allah, the Almighty, bestows his blessings. How fortunate they are![33]

Our predecessors in faith heard the call to Allah, so they believed, and we pray that Allah will make this faith beloved to us as it was to them because this love of Allah and Islam is our faith. Our faith is our greatest strength and our most powerful tool; it is also the source of the second most powerful instrument of the Islamic movement, which is *jihad. The companions of the Prophet (s) knew that Islam prevails only through the sacrifice of self and wealth in jihad,* and they were right. They heard the call of Allah."[34]

Reaching further back to 1981, in the work *Islamic Movement in the West,* Khurram Murad[35] attributes the rise of the term "Islamic Movement" to both the Pakistani Jamaat-e-Islami and the Egyptian Muslim Brotherhood.[36] Saying that the first Islamic Movement can be found in the life events of the Prophet, Murad asks, "What is an Islamic Movement?" and then answers that:

its prevalent usage, in theory and practice, seems to embody certain common elements which are likely to be best expressed if we define the Islamic movement as 'an organized struggle to change the existing society into an Islamic society based on the Qur'an and Sunna and make Islam, which is a code for entire life, supreme and dominant, especially in socio-political spheres'.[37]

Because "the Islamic movement is inherent in the very nature of Islam—in its very purpose and core," Murad distinguishes it from other Islamic activities by emphasizing "the four elements of total change, the supremacy of Islam, the socio-political aspects and the organized struggle."[38] Likewise, in his 1992 work, *The Priorities of the Islamic Movement in the Coming Phase,* Brotherhood chief jurist "Shaykh" Qaradawi asked and answered the same question on the Islamic Movement:

Definition of the Islamic Movement?

By *Islamic Movement* I mean that organised and collective work that is undertaken by the people, to restore Islam **to the leadership of society** and to **the helm of**

life.

Before being anything else, the Islamic Movement is work – persistent and industrious work, not just words to be said, speeches and lectures to be delivered, or books and articles to be written. All of these are indeed required but they are merely parts of a movement, not the movement itself. Allah the Almighty says, *And say [O Muhammad] Work! Allah will see your deeds, as will His Messenger and the believers.*" (Quran 9:105)

The Islamic Movement is a work performed by the masses based on motivation and personal conviction. It is work performed out of faith and for nothing other than the sake of Allah, with the hope of being rewarded by Him and not by people.[39]

Qaradawi makes clear that the Islamic Movement is all the work being done by Muslims to restore an Islamic society. His fidelity to the Milestones Process is readily apparent, even from the book title's reference to "the coming phase." In *To be a Muslim*, Yakan again relied on Hassan al-Banna to emphasize that the mission of the Islamic Movement is universal and includes the demand to transition to the offensive and penetrate deep into the West:

> Hassan Al-Banna summarized the **Islamic movement**'s general task of universal outreach as follows:
>
>> Our task in general is to stand against the flood of modernist civilization overflowing from the swamp of materialistic and sinful desires. This flood has swept the Muslim nation away from the Prophet's leadership and Qur'anic guidance and deprived the world of its guiding light. Western secularism moved into a Muslim world already estranged from its Qur'anic roots, and delayed its advancement for centuries, and will continue to do so until we drive it from our lands. Moreover, we will not stop at this point, but will pursue this evil force to its own lands, **invade its Western heartland**, and struggle to overcome it until all the world shouts by the name of the Prophet and the teachings of Islam spread throughout the world. Only then will Muslims achieve their fundamental goal, and there will be no more "persecution" and all religion will be exclusively for Al-

lah. "With Allah is the decision, in the past and in the future: on that day shall the believers rejoice." [Qur'an 30:4][40]

Anticipating the Explanatory Memorandum's call for a "Civilization-Jihadist Process" that "is a kind of grand Jihad in eliminating and destroying the Western civilization .... so that it is eliminated and Allah's religion is made victorious over all other religions,"[41] Yakan concludes that this process must be complete and systematic:

> Fundamental transformation of society requires actions that can change it at its very roots. The Islamic Movement therefore must reject every cosmetic act or process of putting bandaids on the wounds of the fundamentally flawed societies of materialism. The Islamic Movement must reject un-Islamic methods and refuse to coexist with any man-made ideologies.[42]

Yakan's reasoning is consistent with general Brotherhood principles. Returning to an established meme, fundamental transformation is necessary because Western civilization is in a state of *jahiliyyah*, which requires jihad to root it out where the failure to undertake this mission is evidence that the Islamic community is in its own state of jahiliyyah:

> Jihad is a continuous struggle that will last till the Day of Judgement (sic). Failure to engage in jihad or to have no intention for it is a sure sign of *jahiliyyah*, as the Prophet (s), said: Those who die and never went to war (in the cause of Allah), nor had the intention of doing so, will die as in the state of *jahiliyyah* (ignorance).[43]

The Muslim Brotherhood views itself as being among the leadership elements of the Islamic Movement globally, including in the United States. Among the world's foremost and most established groups dedicated to what some have called "Islamism" or "political Islam," the Brotherhood makes solid claims to the Movement's leadership. The Brotherhood's 1991 Explanatory Memorandum, addressing the "general strategic goal of the Group in America," opens by noting that the document had been approved by its Shura Council.

> [This memorandum] was approved by the Shura Council and the Organizational Conference for the year [1987] is 'Enablement of Islam in North America, meaning: establishing an effective and a stable Islamic Movement led by the Muslim Brotherhood.'[44]

In 1994 in Egypt, Ibrahim Ghanem confirmed that the Islamic Movement has a universal mission that is doctrinally based and includes the West.[45] In line with the Explanatory Memorandum mission, Ghanem said:

> An analysis of … the document and the writings of the Egyptian Islamic movement … proves that the West in the movement's view **is the object of action**, the field of effort, and the place of spreading the call as well as Jihad to free the world of corruption so that the word of God will be uppermost and there prevail justice and faith in God altogether and everywhere.[46]

Not only is there symmetry between the mission statement in the Explanatory Memorandum and contemporary Brotherhood literature, the Memorandum also reflects an organic application and continuation of the Western strategy laid out by Yusuf Nada in 1982 in the strategy document titled "Toward a Worldwide Strategy for Islamic Polity," more commonly known as "The Project" document.[47] The term Islamic Movement indicates that a group of individuals or organizations is operating in accordance with the Milestones Process. In the Arab world and in the West, there is a high probability of Brotherhood alignment and leadership along the lines established in the Explanatory Memorandum.

Those struggling with the idea that a seemingly generic term like Islamic Movement is actually a recognized term of art with a set understanding may want to check out the books and pamphlets used in this section that were written around the time Akram promulgated the Explanatory Memorandum. They could start with Fathi Yakan's 1984 Brotherhood monograph *Islamic Movement: Problems and Perspectives*, also published under the ISNA label, American Trust Publications.[48] Written seven years before the Explanatory Memorandum, Yakan's *Islamic Movement* affirmed Qutb's concern regarding jahiliyyah.[49] It also affirmed Qaradawi's view that the Islamic Movement mission is to root out jahiliyyah[50] by all means,[51] including jihad[52] (defined as "holy war"[53]); that members should be trained as "warriors not philosophers";[54] that the Movement follow the Milestones Process[55] (that relates back to the first generation)[56]; and that the Muslim Brotherhood should be seen as the natural leader of this Movement.[57]

At all times, Brotherhood messaging on the Islamic Movement has been consistent, clear, and precise. So, too, is the Explanatory Memorandum when read in light of the bountiful Brotherhood literature of the time. As will be discussed in further detail later, "Islamic Movement" is among the terms the leadership in the national security and law enforcement communities disfavor for use in work product.

Hamas and the Islamic Movement

In some cases, the term Islamic Movement is used interchangeably with the Muslim Brotherhood. For example, it appears in the Covenant of the "Islamic Resistance Movement," better known as Hamas:

> Article One: The Islamic Resistance Movement:
>
> The Movement's programme is Islam …
>
> The Islamic Resistance Movement's Relation With the Moslem Brotherhood Group
>
> Article Two: The Islamic Resistance Movement is one of the wings of Moslem Brotherhood in Palestine. **Moslem Brotherhood Movement is a universal organization** which constitutes the largest Islamic movement in modern times. It is characterized by its deep understanding, accurate comprehension, and its complete embrace of all Islamic concepts of all aspects of life.[58]

"The Islamic Resistance Movement": Capital "I," capital "M," with "Resistance" in the middle. As the Covenant makes clear, it is "universal," which means the policies of Hamas are of a kind with the policies of the parent organization, the International Muslim Brotherhood.

Not only does Hamas officially hold itself out to the public as being the Brotherhood, ample documentation of the fact is readily available on the Internet. A quick Google search reveals any number of websites in English that confirm the relationship, including the English-language versions of both Ikhwanweb (which self-identifies as "the Muslim Brotherhood's Official English Language Website") and IslamOnline, a Brotherhood-linked fatwa-publishing website under the control of Yusuf al-Qaradawi.

Hamas leader Ismail Haniyeh openly identified Hamas as the "jihadi movement of the Brotherhood with a Palestinian face," referring in 2011 to the Muslim Brotherhood's Cairo Headquarters as "Brotherhood Central."[59]

While Hamas's official documents make its Brotherhood affiliation clear, analysts in and out of the U.S. government struggle to find ways to separate Hamas from the Muslim Brotherhood. Why is our focus on the shell entity, when we should be focusing on the entire body? If any more evidence is needed, compare the slogans of the Islamic Resistance Movement (a.k.a. Hamas) and the Muslim Brotherhood.

The Islamic Resistance Movement's motto:

Allah is its target, the Prophet is its model, the Qur'an its constitution: Jihad is its path and death for the sake of Allah is the loftiest of its wishes.[60]

The Muslim Brotherhood motto:

Allah is our objective. The Prophet is our leader. The Qur'an is our law. Jihad is our way. Dying in the way of Allah is our highest hope. [61]

The Brotherhood in North America

In November 2008, the directors of America's largest Islamic charity, the Holy Land Foundation (HLF), were convicted on multiple charges of terrorism financing.[62] The jury found the defendants—Mufid Abdulqader, Shukri Abu-Baker, Ghassan Elashi, Mohamed El-Mezain, and Abdelrahman Odeh—guilty of an elaborate money-laundering scheme directed by the Muslim Brotherhood in the United States to finance the designated terrorist group Hamas, the Palestinian branch of the Brotherhood. Much of what is known today about the nature of the Brotherhood's operations in America is based on documents that became publicly available after being introduced as evidence in the Holy Land Foundation trial.

In their original trial brief, the federal prosecutors explained how the HLF had raised funds from the United States for Hamas operations, including dawah:

Through this grass-roots approach, (known as da-wa—"preaching" or "calling"), Hamas achieves a number of goals. Among other perceived benefits, it (1) **assures popular support** for the movement, and through its popular support improves its ability to compete with opposing political factions; (2) provides **a base from which to indoctrinate** and recruit future activists, including military recruits, to carry out suicide bombings and other terrorist acts; (3) **provides a benign cover** through which millions of dollars can be transferred from overseas into Hamas operated or controlled institutions; and (4) since money is fungible, the overseas support for the *dawa* frees resources that can then be devoted to terrorist activity.

In order to raise the requisite funds to support its operations, including its social support network, Hamas looked outside of the Palestinian areas, to individuals, organizations and foreign governments sympathetic to its mission, including the United States.[63]

The chief organ for Muslim Brotherhood work related to the Palestinian cause in the United States was the Palestine Committee. Palestine Committees were established in "Arab, the Islamic, and Western nations" at the direction of the Muslim Brotherhood Guidance Office and Shura Council of the International (Muslim Brotherhood) Movement. As noted in an October 1992 internal memo produced in the Holy Land Foundation trial, the committees were formed in direct response to "the blessed Intifada and the spread of the spirit of Jihad." Their function was "to make the Palestinian cause victorious and to support it with what it needs of media, money, men and all of that."[64] The memo goes on to say that the Palestine Committee in North America is responsible for "supervising" the Occupied Land Fund (which would become the Holy Land Foundation) as well as the Islamic Association for Palestine (IAP) and the United Association for Studies and Research (UASR), two other key organizations for Hamas's operations in the United States.

At the time of the HLF investigation, the Brotherhood's Palestine Committee was led by Mousa Abu Marzook, a member of Hamas and a special designated global terrorist.[65] According to the Internal Revenue Service, Marzook provided $210,000 for the Foundation[66] in what was described as "seed money."[67] During the trial, the government demonstrated that Marzook repeatedly provided payments of tens of thousands of dollars to Palestine Committee organizations, including HLF, while at the same time being registered as an unemployed student.[68] Far from being a fringe player, Abu Marzook remains a high-ranking Hamas leader, serving as the Deputy Chairman of the terror group's political bureau.

According to the Justice Department, HLF's purpose was:

> to subsidize Hamas' vital social recruitment and rewards program designed to win the hearts and minds of the Palestinian population and solidify loyalty to Hamas. In order for Hamas to achieve its ultimate, charter-stated goal of annihilating Israel, it had to win the broad support of the Palestinian population. The defendant HLF set out to do just that.[69]

The Islamic Association for Palestine was incorporated by, among others, HLF defendant Ghassan Elashi to serve the Palestine Committee as a propaganda and publication facility. An internal committee document the government produced at trial clearly stated the IAP's Brotherhood and Hamas connections. It reads, in part:

> **In 1981, the Ikhwan founded the Islamic Association of Palestine to serve the cause of Palestine on the political and media fronts.** The Association has absorbed most of the Ikhwan's Palestinian energy at the leadership and the grass-roots levels in addition to some of the brothers from the oth-

er countries. Attention was given to the Arab new arrivals, immigrants and citizens in general, while focusing on the Palestinians in particular. **The Association's work has developed a great deal since its inception, particularly with the formation of the Palestine Committee, the beginning of the Intifada at the end of 1987 and the proclamation of the Hamas Movement.**[70]

The IAP received $757,864 directly from accounts in Abu Marzook's name over a period of seven years.[71] Similarly, the United Association for Studies and Research (UASR) served as an ideological and research organ designed to pass Hamas communiqués to its operatives in the United States.[72] The UASR also received funds directly from Marzook, receiving $286,272.49 in 1992 alone.[73] Like IAP, UASR was an organization under the direct control of the Palestine Committee and, therefore, of the Brotherhood and Hamas.

Throughout the Holy Land trial, the prosecution was able to show – through evidence that included a series of recorded conversations of Palestine Committee member and suspected Hamas activist Abdelhaleem Ashqar – that Marzook's Palestine Committee had direct control over issues of Hamas fundraising in the United States. In the tape, Ashqar complained that the Palestine Committee had ruled in favor of the HLF over Ashqar's own Al Aqsa Educational Fund in a fundraising dispute. The disagreement involved which organization would receive funds to be raised during a U.S. tour by West Bank Hamas leader Sheikh Jamal Hamami.[74] Marzook was directly involved in resolving the dispute, including sending a letter to Ashqar on the matter.[75]

In October 1993, a group of individuals associated with the Palestine Committee and associated organizations, including several of the HLF defendants, met in Philadelphia to prepare a response to the signing of the Oslo Accords by the Palestinian Liberation Organization and Israel. The central issue for discussion was the plan for continued efforts at fundraising and propagandizing for Hamas, as it was increasingly becoming recognized as a terrorist organization.[76]

During the course of that meeting, HLF defendant Shukri Abu Baker warned the attendees against using the name "Hamas," instructing them instead to use the term "Sister Samah" – Hamas spelled backwards.[77] In a later conversation between Asqhar and Abu Baker, the "Samah" terminology was again used, as the two men attempted to establish the *bona fides* of a Hamas contact from Jericho in the disputed territories.[78] The HLF defendants had not always been so careful, however. In one video played by the prosecution for the jury, HLF defendant Mufid Abdulqader declared, "I am Hamas and I'm going to kill Jews," in a skit performed prior to the Philadelphia conference at an Islamic Association for Palestine event.[79]

During the trial, federal prosecutors proved not only that the Holy Land Foundation had been established in order to fundraise for Hamas, but that they had successfully done so, distributing funds to a variety of Hamas-controlled charities in the disputed territories. As noted in the government's trial brief:

> Between 1995 and December 2001, the defendant HLF delivered hundreds of thousands of dollars into the West Bank and Gaza to construct schools, medical clinics, libraries and other community-based facilities, in addition to individuals and families of individuals arrested, detained or injured during violent confrontations with Israel. This aid continued to be distributed through **an insular network of charity committees controlled by Hamas**, including many of the same committees identified as "ours" in the 1993 Philadelphia Conference.[80]

The government successfully proved during the Holy Land Foundation trial that the Palestine Committee was established at the instruction of the Muslim Brotherhood for the explicit purpose of supporting Hamas.

The Brotherhood's Co-conspirators

These Hamas front groups are by no means the only organizations that have been recognized as having some degree of affiliation with the Brotherhood. Indeed, the U.S. government submitted a list of 306 "co-conspirators or joint-venturers," individuals or organizations that were linked to Hamas, the Brotherhood, and the Palestine Committee, based on the evidence produced at trial. Among those organizations are many of the most important Islamic organizations in the United States.

Some of the evidence in the trial was produced from an FBI raid at the house of a man named Ismail Elbarasse. Maryland State Troopers searched Elbarasse's home after they noticed him videotaping the structural supports of the Chesapeake Bay Bridge while driving along the bridge with his wife. He was discovered to have a material witness warrant in his name out of Chicago for a terrorism finance trial involving Abu Marzook.[81] A subsequent search of the subbasement of his Annandale, Virginia, home uncovered a treasure trove of files understood to be the archival documents of the Muslim Brotherhood in North America. Elbarasse was a member of the Palestine Committee.

Contained within the archive was the Explanatory Memorandum, which was entered as a key piece of evidence for the Holy Land trial.[82] Even more than providing evidence of the Brotherhood's existence in America, the Explanatory Memorandum evinces the goals and methods of the group's operations. It is a direct glimpse into how the Brotherhood's leadership understands its mission in the United States—not for the benefit of outsiders, but when speaking among themselves.

The Explanatory Memorandum contained a list of 29 groups or organizations that Akram describes as "our [the Brotherhood's] organizations and the organizations of our friends."[83] In his July 2009 Memorandum Opinion Order, Federal Judge Jorge Solis expressly identified the 29 organizations listed in the Explanatory Memorandum along with the Brotherhood's mission statement in that same document – "as a kind of grand Jihad in eliminating and destroying the Western civilization from within and sabotaging its miserable house by their hands and the hands of the believers so that it is eliminated" – as a principled basis for his opinion order.[84] The Holy Land Foundation case survived two appellate court appeals.[85]

Because of the judge's ruling, and because of the ease with which Akram presents the information, the list of "our organizations and the organizations of our friends" has become a way to quickly and dispositively bring an audience to a degree of certitude concerning the scope of Brotherhood operations in the United States. Thus, an erroneous impression has formed that the evidence connecting these organizations to the Muslim Brotherhood is threadbare outside of what was disclosed in the Explanatory Memorandum. Also, while the list identifies Brotherhood membership or affiliation, the Explanatory Memorandum does not elaborate on the specific role each organization plays, making it difficult to rely solely upon this document to establish an organization's level of involvement in the Islamic Movement – or so the argument goes. For these reasons, as this book examines organizations with links to the Brotherhood and the Palestine Committee, it will show what connections exist across multiple documents and associations—alongside but independent of the Explanatory Memorandum—in order to demonstrate there is a significant body of overlapping evidence that supports claims of Brotherhood affiliation. With the discussion of the Islamic Movement, it has already been established that the language of the Explanatory Memorandum reflects the Brotherhood thinking of the time.

Let's examine three vitally important organizations, all listed by the Justice Department as unindicted co-conspirators in the Holy Land trial: the Council on American Islamic Relations (CAIR), the Islamic Society of North America (ISNA), and the North American Islamic Trust (NAIT). Although these groups protested being named as unindicted co-conspirators, the court declined to strike them from the list. After an appeal, Judge Solis emphasized that the government had provided "sufficiency of evidence to show their association with HLF, IAP, and Hamas," proving also "by a preponderance of evidence that a conspiracy existed":

> The Muslim Brotherhood supervised the creation of the "Palestine Committee," which was put in charge of other organizations, such as HLF, IAP, UASR, and ISNA. (See Gov't Ex. 3-15 (Elbarasse Search 5) at 14). The July 30, 1994, "Meeting Agenda for the Palestine Committee" lists

IAP, HLF, UASR and CAIR as working organizations for the Palestine Committee.[86]

In 1994, two years after the Brotherhood's Explanatory Memorandum was written, three members of Marzook's Islamic Association of Palestine—Omar Ahmad, Nihad Awad, and Rafeeq Jaber—founded the Council on American Islamic Relations. In explaining its reasoning for including CAIR among the unindicted co-conspirators, the Justice Department included Ahmad's involvement in mediating the dispute, mentioned earlier, between Ashqar and the HLF over Hamas fundraising.[87]

Additionally, as members of the Palestine Committee, both Ahmad[88] and Nihad Awad[89] were present at the 1993 Hamas conference in Philadelphia that featured discussion about "Sister Samah" in code.[90] At that gathering, Ahmad presented his view on the need for a media and political organization that could lobby in Washington:

> Also, forming a lobby for the decision-makers abroad. This is also a very important thing. It is a long-term goal. This can be achieved through our popular, political, financial and media strength in America. I mean, when we are strong like I said in the beginning, [it] can be a means for pressure on them but if we are weak and we don't have an Islamic community, we don't have influence over the Congress or the organizations such as the ADC. ... UI [unintelligible] and others people won't pay attention to us. This will also bolster our position in America with the U.S. Administration and other media and political organizations.[91]

Perhaps ironically, Omar Ahmad would go on to recognize the difficulty of creating his new political and media organization with individuals tied to the Palestine Committee (and, through it, to Hamas). In response to a question about the legal danger the IAP was exposed to and whether it would be easier to register a new organization to perform media tasks, Ahmad pointed out that registering an organization would be simple. However:

> *Ahmad:* The problem is where? We don't have available people to work in the existing organization. Where do we go to find these people? Like I told you, go ahead start a new organization but **you won't be able to find new faces**. Do we have hidden faces we now bring up to light? We have what we have. I mean, we don't really have available people whom we could dedicate for the work we want to hide. We don't have available people to work right now. This is one. The idea which we can discuss in more details is whether we should

drop our Islamic identity or keep it.

Unidentified Male 1: Yes.

Unidentified Male 2: Let us discuss this point after **we listen to brother Nihad regarding the issue of political and media** address and how it should be for the American people for members of the Islamic and Arabic community, and **how do we handle our issues with the brothers**.[92]

FBI Agent Lara Burns would testify at trial that the "Nihad" referred to is Nihad Awad, a founder and current Executive Director of CAIR.[93] At the Philadelphia meeting, Awad presented more detail on the need to perform media tasks on behalf of the Islamic Association for Palestine:

> People contact us [asking] "What is the view of the [Islamic] Association [for Palestine] so that we can adopt it with the media outlets? Issue statements for us, positions," or it could be that they want information. "What do you say? Why don't you hold a press conference, a statement ..." All of these are things the [Islamic] Association [for Palestine] is trying to make available. ... [We are] supplying lecturers and speakers with academic materials and information to facilitate their job. Many of the brothers now would like to give a lecture either to the communities or to the universities but they don't have information. We will try to group it and give it to them, God's willing.[94]

Awad also discussed the issue of recruiting fresh faces, which Omar Ahmad had mentioned earlier:

> For instance, we have about 20 brothers, maybe only brother Nihad or Ghassan who work in media. But it could be that none of us perform that [media] role when he expresses the view of the [Islamic] Association [for Palestine] and the Islamic view to the media outlets. In order to achieve this level of awareness, I have four points I mentioned; the first thing is training and qualifying individuals in the branches and the communities on media activism through holding special courses on media. Also, we could have internships for students, either in institutions or universities.[95]

There is no reason to believe that the organization proposed by Omar Ahmad and Nihad Awad was a mere flight of fancy. Documents acquired by the federal government in the Elbarasse search suggest that as early as 1991, the Brotherhood had been considering creating a political organization that would fulfill a role comparable to CAIR.[96] According to an April 1991 internal Brotherhood memorandum:

> **5- Issues relating to political work and foreign relations**:
> (It is a committee which operates through the Association for now. It is hoped that it will become an official organization for political work and its headquarters will be in Washington, God's willing. It represents the political aspect to support the cause politically on the American front).[97]

Following the Philadelphia meeting, CAIR appeared alongside other Palestine Committee Organizations in a July 1994 Meeting Agenda. That document, also entered into evidence during the Holy Land trial, identified the groups as the Committee's "working organizations."[98] It places CAIR in the same organizational category as IAP, HLF, and UASR, which are the three organs of the Palestine Committee of the Brotherhood in the United States. In other words, there is reason to know that CAIR is an organization that was conceived, planned, founded, and controlled by the Muslim Brotherhood's Palestinian branch, Hamas.

The FBI and the Justice Department have known since at least the 2008 Holy Land trial that CAIR is linked to a designated terrorist organization, and that it was founded in order to generate disinformation and advance the cause of Hamas in the United States. Yet even after Congressional orders to cut ties with the Brotherhood-linked group, the FBI remains CAIR's "partner."[99]

There is also enough evidence to establish that the Islamic Society of North America (ISNA) and the North American Islamic Trust (NAIT) are organizations with close connections to the Brotherhood. According to internal documents provided by federal prosecutors in the Holy Land trial, ISNA was founded in 1982 by members of the Muslim Students Union (also called the Muslim Students Association). Recent immigrants from the Middle East with Brotherhood connections in their home countries founded that group in 1962.[100] ISNA soon established its home office in Plainfield, Indiana.

In another document found in the Brotherhood's American archives, ISNA is described as one of the "apparatuses" of the Brotherhood.[101] The group was designated as being the "nucleus for the Islamic Movement in North America."[102]

While prosecuting the Brotherhood's massive terror-funding scheme on behalf of Hamas, the Justice Department pieced together a web of financially connected individuals and organizations involved in the plot. For example, ISNA had a joint bank account with NAIT and the Occupied Land Fund, the group that would become the Holy Land Foundation. NAIT remains a recognized affiliate of ISNA that:

> supports and provides services to ISNA, MSA (The Muslim Students Association), their affiliates, and other Islamic centers and institutions. The President of ISNA is an ex-officio member of the Board of Trustees of NAIT.[103]

From that shared bank account, hundreds of thousands of dollars were transferred to Hamas leader Abu Marzook and other Hamas-linked entities, as Judge Solis noted when denying ISNA's motion to strike its name from the list of HLF unindicted co-conspirators.[104] Leaders of ISNA with connections to terrorism include Sami-Al-Arian, convicted Palestinian Islamic Jihad organizer and former ISNA board member,[105] and Abduraham Almoudi, jailed al-Qaeda financier and former head of ISNA's Political Action Committee.[106] Additionally, numerous ISNA leaders were associated with the Quranic Literacy Institute of Chicago (QLI). Named as an unindicted co-conspirator in the Holy Land trial, QLI was also listed as one of the Muslim Brotherhood's organizations "or the organizations of our friends" in the Explanatory Memorandum.

Additional information about QLI's involvement in financing Hamas arose from the evidence presented in the Boim civil trial, where the parents of David Boim—a 17-year-old New Yorker killed in a Hamas terrorist attack in the West Bank—filed a lawsuit against those fundraising for terrorist groups in the United States. At the time of the trial, in 2004, the contours of the Brotherhood's American network had not been mapped to the extent it would be later. Regardless, the jury found enough evidence that QLI, the Holy Land Foundation, and the Islamic Association for Palestine and associated IAP organizations provided support and contributions to Hamas.[107] That decision was ultimately upheld on appeal.[108]

Among the ISNA leaders with QLI ties was Ahmad Zaki Hammad, who served as ISNA President from 1986 to 1991.[109] According to bank account information presented in the Boim case, Zaki played a role in a QLI land deal that was likely involved in Hamas funding and directly transmitted funds to Hamas operative Muhammad Salah.[110] Salah was subsequently convicted in Israel for financing the terrorist group and, in the U.S., of perjury regarding his Hamas ties.[111] Other QLI associates with ISNA connections who are known members of the Brotherhood include Jamal Badawi, a former ISNA board member, and Bassem Osman, the former director and current board member of ISNA-affiliate NAIT.[112]

While not connected to QLI directly, Muzzamil Siddiqi, a former ISNA president and chairman of the ISNA-affiliate the Fiqh Council of North America,[113] remains an ISNA executive board member.[114] Siddiqi, Badawi, and Osman were all listed as members of the Muslim Brotherhood Shura Council in Holy Land trial documents.[115]

Civilization Jihad

Having established that the Brotherhood exists in the United States, the proper course of action should be to examine the available documents to determine the threat doctrine that forms the basis of their operations and decision-making. As mentioned, the Explanatory Memorandum provides a great deal of insight into the purpose and methods of the group in America.

While some have attempted to dismiss the Explanatory Memorandum as the disconnected ideations of an old man, it is important to remember that Mohamed Akram was a member of both the Brotherhood's Shura Council and of the Palestine Committee, giving him a position of some note within the group's secret North American network. In fact, there is reason to think that the Explanatory Memorandum, dated May 22, 1991, was written in anticipation of a major Brotherhood conference to be held less than one month later in Herndon, Virginia, where the International Institute of Islamic Thought (IIIT) is headquartered. Found in the Investigative Project on Terrorism (IPT) archives is a brochure for the book *The Islamic Movement in Light of International Developments and the Gulf Crisis*. The book is a compilation of materials from the joint UASR- and IIIT-sponsored conference held from July 19 to 21, 1991.[116] Even though the conference was held in the United States and the book was published in the United States, both the book and the brochure were published in Arabic.

Akram is listed as a "Participant in the Conference" along with more than a few names that are still prominent today - including a few who are discussed in this book. Alongside the names of the participants is the name of the country they represent. The list is a veritable who's who of the Muslim Brotherhood in America that includes Dr. Taha Jaber al Alwani (Iraq), Dr. Jamal al Barzinji (Iraq), Mr. Louay Safi (Syria), Mr. Moussa Abu Marzook (Palestine), Mr. Kamal al Helbawi (Egypt), Dr. Sayyid Muhammad Said (Kashmir), Mr. Yusuf Talal [Delorenzo] (America), Mr. Zayyad Hamdan (Palestine), Mr. Muhammad Tontanji (Iraq), Mr. Ahmed Taha al Alwani (Iraq), and Mr. Abdel Rahman al Alamoudi.[117] Also on the list are individuals who are less well known today but were nevertheless important figures.[118]

The brochure identified Akram as speaking on "The Future Directions of the Modern Islamist Movement within Sight of the 21st Century." It also identified Sami al Arian as speaking on "Tools of the Islamist Movement in Crises: Evaluation and Future Viewpoint," Louay Safi as speaking on "The Islamist Movement and the Gulf Crisis," Mousa Abu Marzook on "Towards a Rightly Guided approach in Review and Reform," and mentioned Taha Jaber al Alwani's organizing role when leading the "Review and Summary of the Realities of the Conference and its Most Important Proposals." Clearly, the focus of the Brotherhood conference was on the Islamic Movement as ubiquitously discussed in the Brotherhood literature of the time that the Explanatory Memorandum was designed to implement.[119]

The information in the brochure is confirmed by another document, titled "D. UASR's Gulf War Conference in June 91."[120] The document provides additional detail including that Akram was a session leader on June 20, 1991. The fragment also identifies Alwani, al Amoudi, al Arian, and Barzinji as session leaders.[121]

These documents establish Akram's presence at the center of the power elite of the Muslim Brotherhood in America at the time the Explanatory Memorandum was published. It is difficult to marginalize Akram's work, especially if it can also be shown that (1) the Memorandum aligns with the Milestones Process and other doctrinal writings important to the Brotherhood globally, and (2) if subsequent investigation leads to the conclusion that the recommendations of the 1991 document were indeed carried out.

On the Explanatory Memorandum itself, Akram wrote that his work is derived from the Brotherhood's "general strategic goal," as approved by its Shura Council and Organizational Conference in 1987. That goal, as Akram describes it, is to establish the "**the Islamic Movement led by Muslim Brotherhood**" in the United States. The Memorandum evinces hostile intent. In sweeping and ominous terms, the document details the group's mission and strategy:

> The Movement must plan and struggle to obtain "the keys" and the tools **of this process** in carry [sic] out this grand mission as a "**Civilization Jihadist**" responsibility which lies on the shoulders of Muslims and—on top of them—**the Muslim Brotherhood in this country**.[122]

When the Memorandum refers to "this country," it means the United States. It continues:

> **The process of settlement is a "Civilization-Jihadist Process"** with all the means. The Ikhwan [Muslim Brotherhood] must understand that their work in America is **a kind of grand Jihad in eliminating and destroying the Western civilization from within and "sabotaging" its miserable house by their hands and the hands of the believers** so that it is eliminated and Allah's religion is made victorious over all other religions. ... It is a Muslim's destiny to perform Jihad and work wherever he is ...[123]

In other words, the Muslim Brotherhood's goal in the United States is jihad; it is understood in a manner comparable to that prescribed by Brigadier Malik in his explanation of the preparation stage. In 1984, Fathi Yakan likewise suggested this in *Islamic Movement* when explaining that the Muslim Brotherhood movement "is also a *jihad* **movement** because it campaigns for the preparation for *jihad* by all means. That is because truth should have the power to protect itself so that the *da'wah* will be able to face challenges and overcome problems."[124] In this stage, the primary lines of operation for the Brotherhood are directed towards subverting Western institutions in order to "sabotage" their "miserable house"; or, as Brigadier Malik described it, to create a "dislocation of faith" in the target civilization. This is achieved, "from within" and "by their hands"—meaning, by American, or non-Muslim, hands—through a process of infiltration and subversion. In other words, if the Brotherhood's strategy is allowed to unfold as envisioned, most of the actions that ensure their success will be carried out by Americans against Americans. The Brotherhood understands this to be a civilizational clash between Islam and the West. As Brotherhood founder Hassan al Banna put it:

> The Holy Quran makes of the Muslims stewards of the un-aware humanity and gives them the right of control and sway over the world in the service of this nobles [sic] stewardship. Thus, this is our affair not that of the West and of the civilization of Islam not the civilization of materialism.[125]

The Explanatory Memorandum made clear that early Brotherhood lines of operation begin with efforts to penetrate U.S. institutions, so that downstream subversion efforts can be supported from within. There is every reason to believe that this has occurred.

The same FBI that discovered the Explanatory Memorandum—amid some 75 boxes of Brotherhood archival material in the home of Palestine Committee member Ismail Elbarasse—has sustained a series of close associations with some of the very organizations the Holy Land trial evidence indicates are associated with the Islamic Movement. Chief among these group are CAIR and ISNA.

The Brotherhood is able to conduct its penetration activities successfully in part because it proceeds in a manner consistent with Palestine Committee member and CAIR founder Omar Ahmad's requirement to send two messages in the same communication, "one to the Americans and one to the Muslims." From the HLF court transcript of the FBI's wiretap of the 1993 Hamas meeting in Philadelphia:

> I believe that our problem is that we stopped working underground. We will recognize the source of any message which comes out of us. I mean, if a message is publicized, we will know. … [T]he media person among us will recognize that you send two messages; **one to the Americans and one to the Muslims**. If they found out who said that—even four years later—it will cause a discredit to the Foundation as far as the Muslims are concerned as they say "Look, he used to tell us about Islam and that is a cause and stuff while he, at the same time, is shooting elsewhere."[126]

The same FBI that undertakes outreach with CAIR also caught Ahmad's comments in this wiretap. Because America's Brotherhood-linked institutions make many of their publications available through normal book-publishing distribution, they know that non-Muslims will be able to read their materials. Ahmad's recorded statement should put readers on notice: What they read from a media outlet associated with the Muslim Brotherhood can often contain an understood secondary meaning.

Ahmad is describing a form of coded language that is considerably more sophisticated than "Sister Samah" (Hamas spelled backwards). Because he is a Muslim Brother well-versed in shariah, it is reasonable to think he is templating Nyazee's notion of coded language against the Milestones Process that is itself anchored in Islamic law.[127] By framing its communications to American Muslims along these lines—that is, to the approximate path of Quranic progressive revelation—the Brotherhood could indeed "send two messages" containing two different messages.

Symbol of the Muslim Brotherhood

A recent example of the two-message strategy came in early 2015, when the Muslim Brotherhood's Arabic language news service communicated one message while its English language service communicated another. On January 27, 2015, the Brotherhood's Arabic language *Ikhwanonline* posted a message addressed to "Revolutionary Brother, Revolutionary Sister" reminding the faithful of the Brotherhood's crossed-swords logo (as shown above) and slogan, "The voice of truth, power, and freedom." It goes on to explain that "Every aspect of this slogan signifies power. 'Truth' needs 'Power' to protect it while 'Freedom' is not granted but seized through 'Power.'"[128] The communiqué concluded by declaring the Brotherhood's commitment to the use of brute force in a prolonged jihad demanding the martyrdom of many:

"The Muslim Brothers shall resort to the necessary brutal and blunt force as the only alternative, remaining confident that they have satisfied the prerequisites of faith and unity." We are entering a new phase where we summon all our strength and the principles of Jihad, where we prepare ourselves, our spouses, children, and our allies for a prolonged Jihad, seeking the honor of Shahidah (martyrdom).[129]

The communiqué was issued days after Georgetown funded[130] senior Egyptian Brothers to fly to Washington to meet with State Department officials[131] and a day after 40 people were killed in Sinai by terrorist attacks[132] that the Egyptian Government blamed on the Brotherhood.[133] The next day, January 30, the "Leadership of the Youth Revolution" posted Statement No. 7 on the *Facebook* page "Lovers of Ikhwan" warning that all:

Foreign nationals are to leave Egypt by February 11, 2015;

Foreign companies are to withdraw their business licenses by February 20;

Foreign nationals and diplomatic staff of the embassies are to be out of the country by February 20; and

Tourists are to cancel their travel to Egypt and leave the country.[134]

The same day, the English language *Ikhwanweb* published "Egypt Muslim Brotherhood Reiterates Commitment to Non-Violence"[135] that contradicted the Arabic:

From the first days of its inception, the Muslim Brotherhood set its stance against violence and terrorism as one of its essential constants. ... Those who belong to the Muslim Brotherhood must adopt its peaceful approach and path of non-violent action; but if they call for a different line of action or chart for themselves an approach different from the group's announced approach, they no longer belong in the Brotherhood, and the group no longer accepts them, no matter what they do or say.[136]

The Duty to Lie

This two-message approach is more than the opinion of one Brotherhood operative. It has, like all Islamic Movement doctrine, a basis in shariah. Some readers may be familiar with the concept of taqiyya, generally described as "lying for the sake of Islam." Taqiyya's importance as a doctrine has been over-emphasized, as its very definition bespeaks a tactical response to a current threat. The following definition is taken from William Gawthrop's briefing, *Islam's Tools of Penetration*:

> Al-Taqiyya—a concept based on Quran 3:28 and 16:106 as well as hadith, *tafsir* literature and judicial commentaries that permit and encourage precautionary dissimulation as a means for hiding true faith in times of persecution or deception when penetrating the enemy camp.

> "Concealing or disguising one's beliefs, convictions, ideas, feelings, opinions, and/or strategies at a time of eminent danger, whether now or later in time, to save oneself from physical and/or mental injury."

> Taqiyya has been used by Muslims since the 7th century to confuse and split the "enemy."

> One result **is the ability to maintain two messages, one to the faithful while obfuscation and denial is sent—and accepted—to the non-Muslim audience**[137]

Notice how closely that definition fits with the words of Holy Land unindicted co-conspirator Omar Ahmad.[138] Gawthrop was briefing the importance of these dual messages to law enforcement and military audiences long before the 2008 Holy Land trial and release of the Ahmad recording proved him right.

While originally formulated to explain the disguising of Shi'ites to protect themselves from Sunni persecution, the role of taqiyya expanded over time to include acts of deception when penetrating an enemy camp. There is ample evidence of this practice and to its being referred to as taqiyya.

While the term "taqiyya" is commonly known, the Qur'an provides a more substantial doctrinal basis for the duty to misrepresent. For example, the phrase from Verse 3:28 "unless you indeed fear a danger from them" is explained by Ibn Kathir to mean that "**believers are allowed to show friendship outwardly, but never inwardly**" to disbelievers. Ibn Kathir further clarified the verse by referring to Bukhari: "We smile in the face of some people although our hearts curse them."[139] This practice goes beyond Shi'ite tradition; it is grounded in the Qur'an and expressed in Sunni Islamic legal terms.

Reliance of the Traveller also addresses the issue of lying, citing the iconic jurist Imam Abu Hamid Ghazali:

> This is an explicit statement that **lying is sometimes permis-**

sible for a given interest. …When it is possible to achieve such an aim by lying but not by telling the truth, it is permissible to lie if attaining the goal is permissible (N: i.e., when the purpose of lying is to circumvent someone who is preventing one from doing something permissible) and **obligatory to lie if the goal is obligatory**.[140]

In Islamic law, an obligation to lie exists if it is the only way to achieve an obligatory goal in Islam. As noted, this becomes a *duty* to lie in some circumstances. *Reliance* further illustrates that for religious considerations, when possible, it is better to mislead than to lie:

> But it is more precautionary in all such cases to employ words that give a misleading impression, meaning to intend by one's words something this is literally true, in respect to which one is not lying, while **the outward purport of the words deceives the hearer**.[141]

Again, it is difficult to avoid making the comparison to Omar Ahmad's two-message statement. In the same section, *Reliance* outlines other rules on deception:

> Giving directions to someone who wants to do wrong. …
>
> It is not permissible to give directions and the like to someone intending to perpetrate a sin, because it is helping another to commit disobedience. [§ r7.0, r7.1][142]

Helping someone can violate Islamic law, and *Reliance* provides examples of when assistance is impermissible:

> Giving directions to wrongdoers includes: (1) showing the way to policemen and tyrants when they are going to commit injustice and corruption." [§r7.1 (1)][143]

Of course, on the basis of Islamic law, a "tyrant" can be anyone not governing according to Islamic law. This is not a theoretical issue. Hearings in both houses of Congress raised questions concerning Brotherhood-linked Islamic entities that directed Muslims not to work with American law enforcement, such as the FBI.[144/ 145] Why? Because they are following Islamic law.

This CAIR flyer became the topic of testimony when House Homeland Security Committee Chairman Rep. Peter King raised it during a hearing on March 10, 2011. Of course, by "building a wall of resistance" from the FBI, CAIR is simply enforcing Islamic law.

Here is another example right out of Islamic law:

> *Lying.* Primary texts from the Sunna say it is unlawful to lie … because of the scholarly consensus of the community that it is prohibited. [§§r8.0, r8.1][146]

But there is an exception:

> Our only concern here being to explain the exceptions to what is considered lying.[147]

So the following is not lying, it is the exception to the rule of lying. As the Prophet said, as stated in §r8.2:

> He who settles disagreements between people to bring about good or says something commendable is not a liar.[148]

Reliance continues by citing another saying of Mohammed based on both Bukhari and Muslim:

> I did not hear him permit untruth in anything people say, except for three things: war, settling disagreements, and a man talking with his wife or she with him (in smoothing over differences).[149]

Outside of those three areas, there is not much left to lie about. *Reliance of the Traveller* §r10.3 makes a distinction between lying and "giving a misleading impression":

> Scholars say that there is no harm in giving a misleading impression if required by an interest countenanced by Sacred Law.[150]

As we can see, Islamic law permits its adherents to utter knowingly misleading and even untruthful statements—if doing so accomplishes a purpose countenanced by sacred law. This is not an argument about whom one should trust or not trust, nor is it an accusation that Muslims are, as a class, liars. In official and professional interactions, however, one should be aware of the relevant Islamic law and take it into account when dealing with self-identified members of an Islamic Movement that declares its reliance on Islamic Law as stated here. It would be malpractice not to account for the fact that one may be interacting with someone who may rightfully feel obligated to mislead. In the earlier phases of the threat analysis process, it is less important to prove whether this is an accurate construction of Islamic law than to demonstrate that such material is abundantly available in the American Islamic stream of commerce and that Muslims can and do rely on it when formulating their world views. It's valid because it's there.

For those still holding on to the idea that the duty to mislead is primarily an outgrowth of Shi'ite tradition and therefore should not be used to support broader analytical efforts, read what Mohammed said, as quoted by Bukhari:

> He who makes peace between the people by inventing good information or saying good things, is not a liar. (Bukhari vol.3:857 p.533)

> And also: Muhammad said, "War is deceit." (Bukhari 4:267 and 269)

"War is deceit." Because Americans are understood to reside in the dar al-harb—as inhabitants of the territory of war—the United States represents the pre-eminent harbi power. Being designated as such, this country can lawfully be made the object of jihad. According to this Islamic legal theory, all believing Muslims, Sunni or Shi'ite, are at war with the dar al-harb. Thus, the "war is deceit"

hadith would be in effect, and lying to Americans in furtherance of the obligatory duty of jihad would not only be permissible, in some circumstances it could be designated an affirmative duty.

Deception campaigns become an intrinsic part of Quranic warfare in what Pakistani Brigadier Malik termed the "preparation stage." From the perspective of the Islamic Movement, it is a line of operation that shariah requires. This is also what the Seat of the Caliphate meant by a "speech war" that is "strictly enjoined upon all Muslims" when discussing the War of the Tongue and the Pen in the 1915 Fatwa calling for global jihad.[151]

Influence Operations

A major effort in the Brotherhood's deception campaign is to engage in what might be called a "lexicon jihad." The objective is to cause Western institutions to deceive themselves through penetration and subversion. This is the operational combination of the "sabotaging" by "their hands" and promoting the two-message approach. The "Civilization Jihad ... by our hands" aspect of the objective is to get America's leaders to agree to enforce a hostile vocabulary—one that denies decision-makers, analysts, and law enforcement the ability to define Islamic-based terrorism with reference to the Islamic identity and Islamic doctrines that drive those activities that President Obama understands to be "the one organizing principle."[152] The intended effect of manipulating our leaders into undermining doctrinal template development is to destroy a coherent threat assessment. One cannot engage what one is not permitted to define.

By controlling the language that decision-makers and analysts use (remember: "one message for the Americans"), the Brotherhood not only controls what they think and say about the threat but also gains control of the decision-making associated with the threat itself. Such a relationship predictably, over time, will create a dependency on Brotherhood-linked representatives within the Muslim community. This, in turn, keeps the United States from achieving its strategic objectives. It also places a barrier between leaders and Muslims who really do reject terrorism and actually are committed to a peaceful resolution of differences.

An emerging consequence will be the public's increasing awareness of their government's national security incompetence that leads to an inability to defeat its enemies. Citizens will lack confidence in a leadership that is unable to speak about or define a self-identified enemy. The Islamic Movement's campaign of subversion will thus achieve the objective of jihad—the destruction of the enemy's faith in itself.

In order to realize this outcome, the Movement must first gain control of the language. When it comes to the establishment of "language dominance" in the War on Terror, few Muslim thinkers have played as significant a role as Louay Safi.

Safi was the Executive Director of the IIIT, a think-tank associated with the Brotherhood that was established in 1978. Ian Johnson's *Mosque in Munich* traces efforts by Egyptian Brotherhood exiles to establish the organization following a strategy session in Lugano, Switzerland.[153] In addition to prominent members of the secretive Islamist organization, Brotherhood chief jurist Yusuf al-Qaradawi was also present. The then–newly created IIIT was created to maintain doctrinal clarity of the Brotherhood's message from its initial home base near Temple University in Philadelphia, where Muslim Brother Ismail Faruqi was teaching at the time. (Some of his writings on the Islamic Movement have already been referenced.) In later years, IIIT would move its headquarters to the Herndon, Virginia, complex that houses other Brotherhood-affiliated groups. It should not come as a surprise that IIIT certified *Reliance of the Travelle*r as an authoritative translation of shariah.

Numerous employees and associates of IIIT have been convicted of financing terrorist abroad, including Palestinian Islamic Jihad leader Sami-al-Arian. Jamal Barzinji, IIIT's founder, has extensive Brotherhood associations; he is a member of CAIR and IIIT, and he is also associated with the Amana Trust, the American Muslim Council, CSID, IIFTIHAR, Mar-Jac Investments, Mena Investments, Reston Investments, the SAAR Foundation, and the SAFA Trust.[154] The U.S. government raided his home and offices during the Green Quest operation, a post-9/11 terrorism finance investigation.[155]

Safi served as IIIT's Executive Director and Director of Research from 1999 to 2003, followed by many years in leadership with ISNA. He then became a "Common Word Fellow" at Georgetown University's Prince al-Waleed bin Talal Center for Muslim-Christian Understanding[156] and served as Chairman of the Syrian American Committee, in which capacity he has testified before the Tom Lantos Commission on Human Rights of the House of Representatives.[157]

Alarmingly, Safi was briefing soldiers at Fort Hood—even after the Nidal Hasan shootings—on issues relating to Islam and terrorism. Following the outbreak of civil war in Syria, he also serves as the political director of the Syrian National Council,[158] an organization known to be dominated by the Muslim Brotherhood.[159]

In 2001, just before the advent of the War on Terror, Safi authored *Peace and the Limits of War: Transcending Classical Conception of Jihad*. The slim volume was published under the aegis of the IIIT. On the subject of jihad as "holy war," Professor Safi wrote the following:

> The advocates of jihad as holy war constitute today a tiny minority of intellectuals in both Muslim societies and the West. **Western scholars, who accept *jihad* as a holy war, feed on the position of radical Muslim ideologues.**[160]

In the benign language of academia, Safi indicated that when confronting

Muslims who are terrorists—who refer to themselves as jihadis or mujahedeen—Americans should not identify them as Muslim terrorists fighting jihad. That identification, he argued, would validate their claims and give them the legitimacy they crave. Safi wrote that those "who accept jihad as a holy war feed on the position of radical Muslim ideologues." But isn't this exactly what competent threat analysis should do as part of any threat assessment? If "violent Islamist extremism" is the enemy's ideology, the mission of an analyst or decision-maker is to orient on that ideology. It is among Sun Tzu's principle rules of war that one should "know thy enemy."

Of course, in one sense, Safi is correct. If American national security and counterterror analysts had acknowledged jihadis by the name they self-identify with, and analyzed them according to the doctrines they claimed to fight in furtherance of, they could have validated (or invalidated) those claims as part of their analysis. Having found their claims of jihad as genuine, we could have then targeted them, kinetically or non-kinetically, based on generating most-likely and most-dangerous enemy courses of action (E-COAs). But we did not, and this is where the War on Terror was lost.

We should consider Safi's claim that jihadi ideologies crave legitimacy to be a calculated exploitation of our arrogance; at no time does an enemy need *us* to legitimize *them*. The legitimacy the enemy seeks comes from two sources: their perceived successes against us, and the perceived fidelity of their doctrines to Islamic law. An enemy must be defeated to be delegitimized. Safi continued:

> Given the fact that radical interpretations of Islam have had a disproportionate influence on the way Islam's position regarding peace and war is perceived and understood, I intend to focus my discussion on rebutting the propositions **of the classical doctrine of jihad embraced by radical Muslims**.[161]

How smooth. Restated, Americans must not identify the enemy as acting on a classical understanding of jihad—even though that understanding is, by Safi's own admission, accurate. "Radical Muslims," as Safi brands them, are entirely within the mainstream of classical shariah. Read closely, Safi is actually saying that the "radical" interpretation is doctrinally aligned with the "classical" and is, therefore, correct.

For intelligence purposes, it is critical that no constraints be placed on the analysts tasked to analyze threat doctrine as "classically" understood. If the doctrinal template is wrong—or if we convince ourselves that it is not even required—the entire decision-making process will be compromised. Considering Safi's close association with Islamic Movement and Brotherhood entities, it is likely this was the objective.

We continue to see evidence that the admonishments by Safi and other Islamic Movement–aligned thinkers not to call the enemy by his name was received and internalized by U.S. leadership. The Department of Homeland Security's 2008 report "Terminology to Define the Terrorists: Recommendations from American Muslims" emphasized the need not to validate the terrorists' message.[162] DHS adopted Safi-style talking points as official policy. So, too, has the Department of Defense. In December 2011, Assistant Secretary of Defense Paul Stockton expressed the very same thinking in testimony to a joint congressional hearing on domestic terrorism:

> Al Qaeda would love to convince Muslims around the world that the United States is at war with Islam. . . . That is a prime propaganda tool. And **I'm not going to aid and abet that effort to advance their propaganda goals.** . . . Sir, with great respect; I don't believe it's helpful to frame our adversary as 'Islamic' with any set of qualifiers that we might add, because we are not at war with Islam.[163]

In the same work in which Safi urges American national security leadership to ignore the enemy's doctrinal orientation, he positions himself—and, more generally, the Islamic Movement in America —on the Milestones Process. From *Peace and the Limits of War*:

> Thus, it is up to the Muslim leadership to assess the situation and weigh the circumstances as well as the capacity of the Muslim community before deciding the appropriate type of jihad. **As one stage, Muslims may find that jihad, through persuasion or peaceful resistance, is the best and most effective** method to achieve just peace, **as was the case during the Makkan period**. At another stage, fortification and defensive tactics may be the best way to achieve these objectives, as was the case of the Battle of al Khadaq. **At yet a third stage, the Muslim leadership may decide that all-out war is the most appropriate measure** to bring about a just peace, as was the case during the war against the Arab apostates.[164]

This is a perfect example of the two-message approach that CAIR's Ahmad advocated. Those in the Islamic Movement have reason to be confident that their deception will not be detected. Entities like the Brotherhood and their affiliated organizations have two purposes, both based on dawah. While they are engaged in "sabotaging" and "dislocating the faith" of the Americans, they also have an obligation to build up an Islamic society in America that operates in accordance with classical Islamic law as understood by the Brotherhood and proceeds along the Milestones path.

The Islamic Society and the 'Process of Settlement'

"Islamic Society" is a term of art within the Islamic Movement that has a history and strategic significance. In Paragraph 17, the Explanatory Memorandum describes the proliferation of local Brotherhood-linked "Islamic Centers":

> [T]his is in order for the **Islamic center** to turn—in action not in words—into a seed 'for a small **Islamic society**' which is a reflection and a mirror to our central organizations.[165]

As the paragraph's heading states, "the role and nature of work of 'the Islamic Center' in every city" is to "achieve the goal of the process of settlement," which includes "supplying the battalions."[166] The word "battalion" itself carries with it a significant connotation for the Brotherhood. From the English-language Brotherhood website, Ikhwanweb:

> The Brotherhood's General Guide, Hassan al-Banna, felt that the Society was not ready to engage in military campaigns, and that those who wished to do so "might take the wrong course and miss the target". He advocated a more cautious, longer-term plan of forming **groups of particularly dedicated members, called "Battalions"**, who would receive rigorous spiritual and physical training; once their numbers were sufficient, Banna felt, the Battalions **would be prepared to engage in warfare**.[167]

An *al-Akbar* story about the Brotherhood's current operations in Syria clarifies the meaning of "battalion":

> Today, things are quite different. **All armed groups whose names begin with the word "liwaa," meaning battalion, are affiliated with the Muslim Brotherhood**, most notably Liwaa al-Islam, Liwaa al-Ridwan, and Liwaa Ahfad al-Rasoul. These groups are mainly present in the eastern Ghouta. ...
>
> Brotherhood operatives who met with Al-Akhbar seemed to all have strict orders not to disclose information about the size of the political wing and where it is active. The answer we received from most everyone being: "**The battalions represent the military wing**, while the political wing works on supporting the revolution from outside Syria."[168]

Paragraph 17 concludes with the crucial observation that Islamic Centers today serve the same role as mosques in the first generation in Medina, which were used to stage kinetic jihad operations.[169] As a result, where this term of art is employed, it serves as an indicator of a corresponding probability that mosques with "Islamic Society" or "Islamic Center" in their names may be affiliated with the Muslim Brotherhood.

Recall that the Explanatory Memorandum describes the Brotherhood's "process of settlement" as "civilization jihad." This means that the objective of these Brotherhood-affiliated facilities—including its "battalions"—"in America is a kind of grand Jihad in eliminating and destroying the Western civilization from within and 'sabotaging' [America's] miserable house by their hands and the hands of the believers so that it is eliminated."[170]

The Explanatory Memorandum's tie-in to the Brotherhood extends beyond al-Banna's emphasis on the necessity of battalions and includes an emphasis on al-Banna himself. When the Brotherhood declared that "the Muslim Brothers shall resort to the necessary brutal and blunt force as the only alternative, remaining confident that they have satisfied the prerequisites of faith and unity"[171] in its January 27, 2015, declaration on Ikhwanonline, it relied on Imam Banna; citing him no fewer than 5 times. In the same way, Paragraph 20 of the Explanatory Memorandum recognized "Imam martyr Hasan al-Banna's" role in helping the Brothers' "understanding of [the] importance of the 'Organizational' shift in [their] movement work, and doing jihad in order to achieve it in the real world with what serves the process of settlement":

> The reason this paragraph was delayed is to stress its utmost importance as it constitutes the heart and the core of this memorandum. It also constitutes the practical aspect and the true measure of our success or failure in our march towards settlement. … And this was done by the pioneer of the contemporary Islamic Dawa', **Imam martyr Hasan al-Banna, may God** have mercy on him, when he and his brothers felt the need to "re-establish" Islam and its movement anew, leading him to establish organizations with all their kinds.[172]

Stepping back in time from the 1991 Explanatory Memorandum, "Toward a Worldwide Strategy for Islamic Policy (Worldwide Strategy)" is a 1982 document that was seized in November 2001 during a raid on Brotherhood leader Yusuf Nada's home in Lugano, Switzerland. It laid out the Muslim Brotherhood's policy objective:

> "This report presents a global vision of a worldwide strategy for Islamic policy [or "political Islam"]." What is the "Worldwide Strategy"? *Ikhwan* members are "**to dedicate ourselves to the establishment of an Islamic state**, in parallel with **gradual efforts aimed at gaining control of local power centers through institutional action**" [in furtherance of] "establish(ing) an Islamic power [government] on the

earth."[173]

The document described that the Brotherhood's goal is "to construct **a permanent force of the Islamic dawa [sic] and support movements engaged in jihad** across the Muslim world, to varying degrees and insofar as possible."[174] By now, this should sound familiar. Because Brotherhood members are few in number and their presence tenuous early in the preparation stages, there is a need for cover. Hence, the Brotherhood "accepts the principle of temporary cooperation" but "without ... having to form alliances." In keeping with the one-way nature of Brotherhood bridge-building projects, cooperative efforts may not be based on mutuality, trust, or amity. The goal, as described in the Worldwide Strategy:

> To accept the principle of temporary cooperation between Islamic movements and nationalist movements in the broad sphere and on common ground such as the struggle against colonialism, preaching and the Jewish state, without however having to form alliances. This will require, on the other hand, **limited contacts between certain leaders, on a case by case basis, as long as these contacts do not violate the [Shari'a] law.** Nevertheless, one must not give them allegiance or take them into confidence, bearing in mind that the Islamic Movement must be the origin of the initiatives and orientations taken.[175]

In other words, while necessity requires establishing such relationships, they are to be for limited purposes and based on cooperation, not trust. As Fathi Yakan explains:

> This does not mean, however, that the **Islamic Movement** should reveal all its strategies, plans, and organization, because this would be foolhardy and put the movement and its members in danger. The slogan should be, "Work in public but organize in secret" which accords with the Prophet saying. "Seek secrecy in what you do", and "War is dissimulation."[176]

Why dissimulation? Because "the Islamic Movement must reject un-Islamic methods and refuse to coexist with any man-made ideologies."[177] Until the earlier stages build capacity to engage in more confrontational dawah, the Brotherhood will seek to avoid open confrontation.

> But we should not look for confrontation with our adversaries, at the local or the global scale, which would be disproportionate and could lead to attacks against the dawa [sic] or its disciples. **a- Elements:** To avoid the Movement hurting itself with major confrontations, which could encourage its

adversaries to give it a fatal blow.[178]

From these "Islamic societies" and "local power centers," the Brotherhood and its affiliates move forward through the Milestones Process, establishing alliances with local and national leaders to protect themselves from scrutiny and further their interests as they proceed in dawah, leading up to an inevitable jihad confrontation.

Dawah in America

The Muslim Brotherhood entities in America were established to advance the causes of the Islamic Movement against the non-Muslim population, including the government, media, businesses, religious communities, and educational institutions. In addition to serving as advisors on a wide range of issues affecting Muslims, the Brotherhood groups have another agenda.

Organizations and individuals originating from the Brotherhood do not define successful outreach the way other lobbying or special interest groups might. For the Brotherhood, outreach is focused on two objectives: (1) inviting everyone to Islam and (2) subverting those who choose to remain infidels. In other words, dawah.

HAMAS STRUCTURE

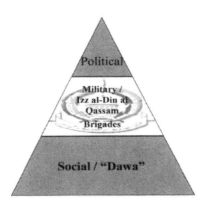

The relationship between dawah and jihad is evident in an image depicting the structure of Hamas. This graphic was admitted into evidence in the Holy Land Foundation trial.[179]

Because the Brotherhood's approach to dawah is based on Islamic doctrine, the group considers it to be prescribed by Allah. The following section will detail the method of one of America's leading early theorists in dawah.

Siddiqi, Jamaat-e-Islami, and the Islamic Circle

Few of America's Islamic intellectuals have been as forthright about the mission of dawah from a Milestones perspective as Shamim Siddiqi. The biographical sketch on his website confirms his affiliation with the larger Islamic Movement, encompassing both the Brotherhood and an organization that could be considered its Pakistani cousin, Jamaat-e-Islami, the same organization with which Khurram Murad was affiliated. Even without looking at Siddiqi's writings, a reader educated in the history of the Islamic Movement should find enough evidence of his ideological commitment to place him squarely in the Islamic Movement camp.

> The author was born in India in July 1928, migrated to East Pakistan in 1950, completed his BA and B. Com. from Dacca University, **joined Jamaat-e-Islami Pakistan in December 1952, became its Rukn [Member]** in September 1955, migrated to the USA in October 1976, **started an Islamic Movement** here in the name of "**The Forum for Islamic Work**" in cooperation with **other movement oriented brothers** in 1977-78, **joined ICNA** in 1995, was **the Chairman of its Dawah and Publication Departments** till October 2001 ...[180]

Siddiqi's affiliations and leadership positions with Islamic Movement groups over the course of more than half a century establish him as a senior member of the Brotherhood's infrastructure in the West. For an analyst or policymaker in the War on Terror, establishing Siddiqi within the Islamic Movement globally should be straightforward. From the biography above, several common-sense assumptions can be made concerning his orientation. Likewise, Siddiqi's continued affiliation with these groups should establish a reasonable expectation that his views reflect those of his employers.

While in his twenties, Siddiqi joined the radical separatist group Jamaat-e-Islami shortly after the partition of the subcontinent and the founding of Pakistan in 1948. The histories of Jamaat-e-Islami and the Muslim Brotherhood, two Sunni Islamic groups, run in parallel. While their missions—the Islamization of society—are identical, the Brotherhood's intellectual tradition made it more influential in the West. Jamaat-e-Islami's founder, Abul A'la Maududi, was a contemporary of Qutb's who was even more influenced by Bolshevism, Trotskyism, and "perpetual revolution" than was his Brotherhood counterpart. They recognized in each other both a common goal and the Quranic foundation on which to base their approaches. Qutb even excerpted large portions of Maududi's speech "Jihad in Islam" for use in the exposition in Surah 8 of his tasfir *In the Shade of the Qur'an.*[181]

In "Jihad in Islam," Maududi ridiculed what he called "revisionist" thinkers in the 19th and early 20th centuries who interpreted jihad as merely "defensive." Referring to Islam as a process of "destruction and reconstruction, revolution and reform," his narrative put Bolshevik memes in an Islamic context that was, nevertheless, grounded in mainstream Islamic law:

> Islam is not merely a religious creed or compound name for a few forms of worship, but **a comprehensive system which envisages to annihilate all tyrannical and evil systems in the world** and **enforces its own programme of reform** which it deems best for the well-being of mankind. Islam addresses its call for effecting **this programme of destruction and reconstruction, revolution and reform** not just to one nation or a group of people, but to all humanity. **Islam itself calls upon all the classes which oppress and exploit the people unlawfully,** its call is addressed even to the kings and the noblemen to affirm faith in Islam and bind themselves to **remain within the lawful limits** enjoined upon them by their Lord.[182]

Maududi's thoughts on jihad were doctrinal for the Jamaat-e-Islami party that accepted Shamim Siddiqi as an oath-taking member in the early 1950s:

> It must be evident to you from this discussion that **the objective of the Islamic 'Jihad' is to eliminate the rule of an un-Islamic system and establish in its stead an Islamic system of state rule.** Islam does not intend to confine this revolution to a single state or a few countries; **the aim of Islam is to bring about a universal revolution.** Although in the initial **stages it is incumbent upon members of the party of Islam to carry out a revolution** in the State system of the countries to which they belong, but their **ultimate objective is no other than to effect a world revolution.** No **revolutionary ideology** which champions the principles of the welfare of humanity as a whole instead of upholding national interests, can restrict its aims and objectives to the limits of a country or a nation. **The goal of such an all-embracing doctrine is naturally bound to be world revolution.**[183]

While his vocabulary may be from Qutb, Maududi's message is essentially the same. Indeed, some of Maududi's "revolutionary" language on jahiliyyah found its way into *Milestones*,[184] creating a cross-continental bridge between Pakistani and Egyptian jihadi groups that would be codified nearly a half-century later in North America with the alliance between the Jamaat-e-Islami-influenced Islamic Circle of North America (ICNA) and groups established by the Brotherhood.

ICNA was established in 1968 by Jamaat-e-Islami from Pakistan, Bangladesh, and elsewhere in South Asia, and it primarily focused its efforts on "education and personal/spiritual development" in those immigrant communities.[185] By the time Shamim Siddiqi arrived in the United States in late 1976, he had been a member of Jamaat-e-Islami for two decades. His biography claims he "started an Islamic Movement [in America] in the name of 'The Forum for Islamic Work' in cooperation with other movement oriented brothers in 1977-78"—at precisely the time ICNA changed its focus to Siddiqi's central preoccupation, dawah:

> *ICNA 1977-Present:* **Objectives of this movement were re-defined**. It was declared by the resolution of its members that **this movement is to work to do Iqamat-ad-Deen in North America**. A new, detailed constitution was published. English was adapted as the official medium of communication. **ICNA established its own forums for dawah work at the local, regional, and national level**. It established vital **institutions at the national level** for support of its dawah activities.[186]

For a disciple of Maududi's like Siddiqi, he would, upon arrival in the United States in the late 1970s, have quickly become acquainted with the Brotherhood's then-emerging network in America. Sharing the Brothers' commitment to dawah, Siddiqi was well placed to play a role in this Islamist alliance. The Brotherhood's 1991 Explanatory Memorandum points to:

> **[t]he positive development with the brothers in the Islamic Circle in an attempt to reach a unity of merger** ... **We have the seed for a "comprehensive Dawa' educational" organization**: We have the Dawa' section in ISNA. ... What encourages us to do that—in addition to the aforementioned—is that we possess "seeds" for each organization from the organization we call for ... [187]

It should not be surprising that the message is consistent over time. ICNA's private 2010 *Member's Hand Book* describes the organization's mission. Nor is it surprising that the group's goals mesh with the Brotherhood's:

> The Islamic Circle of North America is an Islamic Jama'ah, **an organization struggling towards Iqamat-ad-Deen** [the system of Islamic law] **in this land**. ... [ICNA's members] have the unique opportunity to achieve ... these objectives

through **an organized struggle, a national Islamic movement** like ICNA.

> **"Islamic movement"** is the term used for that organized and collective effort **waged to establish Al-Islam in its complete form in all aspects of life**. Its ultimate objective is to achieve the pleasure of our Creator Allah and success in the hereafter through struggle for Iqamat-ad-Deen. **Islamic movements are active in various parts of the world to achieve the same objectives**. It is our obligation as Muslims to engage in the same noble cause here in North America.[188]

The passages are laced with Islamic terms of art that should now be familiar, including emphasis on implementing Islam in "its complete form in all aspects of life." The final stage in the *Hand Book*'s entry, "Levels of the Islamic Movement," defines ICNA's goal on a "Global Level":

> Wherever the Islamic movement succeeds to establish true Islamic society, they will form coalition and alliances. This will lead to the unity of the Ummah and **towards the establishment of the Khilafah** [Caliphate].[189]

ICNA's links to jihadist violence in Pakistan and Bangladesh go beyond the rhetorical. In late 2013, the group's former Secretary General, Ashrafuzzaman Khan, was convicted for war crimes in Bangladesh on eleven charges related to the kidnapping and murder of eighteen "top professors, journalists and doctors" in 1971.[190] Khan, who was also active in ICNA's North American Imam's Federation, was considered "chief executor" of the Jamaat-e-Islami killing squad responsible for the murders.[191]

Siddiqi's views are alarming, especially given his position as a major intellectual force behind dawah in America—as well as directing the financial and infrastructure support of some of the largest Muslim organizations in the country. His positions are not limited to the imposition of Islamic law in America. On his website and in a recent re-packaging of the original 1989 *Methodology of Dawah*, Siddiqi brings the reader up to date with his thoughts on the War on Terror, including a defense of the Taliban and the suggestion that the 9/11 attacks came from elsewhere.

> [The Taliban] tactfully disarmed the people, **brought peace to the war stricken country and established the rule of Shariyah within their domain**. The anti-Islam Western hegemony could not like **the building of an Islamic state** in Afghanistan with the help of Pakistan, SA and Gulf Emirates. They were bent upon to find excuses and they got it in

the name of Osama Bin Laden who was their own creation.

> A very tragic drama of **September 11 was staged** and imme-
> diately **it was pinpointed towards Bin laden, Mullah Omar
> and Taliban as the culprits** without the least ascertaining
> the a [sic] facts and looking elsewhere who were and are the
> greatest beneficiaries of this tragedy. It is the worst case of
> blind mockery and travesty [sic] of facts.[192]

Siddiqi has written that Jews "stand condemned in the sight of Allah till
doomsday." Elsewhere, in a post titled "The Haunting Image of Bin Laden," Siddiqi praised a conspiracy that Jews were alerted prior to the 2001 attack on the
World Trade Center; unsurprisingly, he darkly hinted that "a lot of stories … are
lying hidden behind the camouflaging [of] the White House."[193] As of 2009, Siddiqi still clung to the assertion that al-Qaeda was not responsible for the attacks.

> [T]he misconstrued tragedy of 9/11 that America is pursu-
> ing blindly against Muslims around the world without as-
> certaining for the least through any judicial process: **WHO
> DID IT & WHY? The entire war against terrorism is false
> and concocted. It is nothing but a total war against Islam
> and its values.**[194]

Throughout *Methodology of Dawah,* the author's references to the goal of installing Islamic law in America are boldly stated. In two sentences, Siddiqi explains how he proposes to do this, and to what end:

> I will discuss the entire process of Dawah Ilallah [dawah in
> the path of Allah] from the beginning to its end in this book.
> I will attempt to pinpoint **its important stages through
> which it passes,** and **the culminating point when Allah's
> Deen becomes dominant**.[195]

In Islamic usage, the word "deen" connotes more than its direct translation,
"religion." It more closely resembles the act of adherence to shariah, or Islamic law.
In *Methodology of Dawah,* Siddiqi makes a point to define deen in contradiction to
Christian or Jewish conceptions of secular systems of government, writing that it
is "not religion as it is understood in the West." In his 2012 book *Calling Humanity*, Siddiqi was more direct:

> Islam is a Deen – a system of life and not a religion as Juda-
> ism and Christianity are or have become. Islam covers and
> governs the entire spectrum of human life from birth to death
> and from cradle to grave both at individual and collective lev-
> els. Equally, Islam is a Movement at the same time.[196]

When the Islamic Movement or its representatives in America use phrases like "when Allah's Deen becomes dominant," they are referring to the ascent not just of shariah over Judaism and Christianity, but also of Islamic law over the Constitution. In case it is not clear, Siddiqi is even more explicit.

> **Jihad in the way of Allah (SWT) is a struggle, a force, a challenge and a determined effort to make Allah's Deen dominant on earth.** This is the only way open to us now. **Dawah to individuals is only the first and primary step** in that direction. **It will end only when Allah's Deen is established in the four corners of the world.**[197]

In that second passage, Siddiqi is (1) acknowledging the goal of jihad according to authoritative jurisprudence: the imposition of Islamic law; (2) aligning himself with progressive revelation methodology as expressed in the Milestones Process by reference to "steps," or stages; and (3) reaffirming that jihad will continue until all non-Muslim territories are governed by Islamic law.

It's easy for the gravity of these statements to slip by unnoticed, but it deserves additional emphasis. In a guide to gaining converts in America, a strong voice from the Islamic community fixed his ideology to that of the Muslim Brotherhood and described the imposition of Islamic law as his goal, or "culminating point." Then, he wrote several books on the subject in English, describing exactly how the program is to be implemented. Finally, he made the books and other training materials freely available on his website. In other words, this information is not classified; like everything else in this book, it's hiding in plain sight. National security professionals in the War on Terror are on notice that this body of information exists, and it drives threat decision-making.

Further into *Methodology of Dawah*, Siddiqi again stresses the importance of Islamic law as the goal in America and, indeed, any non-Muslim society. Conversion to the religion of Islam is not synonymous with dawah, he writes; it is not "an end by itself." That end, again, is "the greatest objective of Muslims' lives":

> More often than not the Da'ee [the facilitator of dawah] seems contented if a non-Muslim accepts Islam as his faith. He (Da'ee) thanks God that the job is done or the objective is fulfilled. If a Da'ee stops here, the Dawah becomes an end by itself. **If it is not extended and pursued to the ultimate goal, i.e. to establish Allah's Deen** [Islamic law], **the job of a Da'ee is incomplete.** If his effort and that of those who enter into the fold of Islam are not **channelized in a planned and determined way to accomplish the greatest objective of Muslims' lives**, it may become very difficult then to remain even as Muslims in the midst of Batil. **A Muslim has to put**

all that he has either to change the society into an Islamic society or state or be perished for it. A Muslim has no other choice.[198]

Connecting the stages of installing Islamic law to the Qur'an and the first generation of Muslims, Siddiqi mirrors Qutb by opening *Methodology of Dawah* with a history of Mohammed's efforts to spread the message of Islam.

> The struggle of a Da'ee [one that 'calls' to Islam] must continue up to that stage. This will be possible only when the entire process and **the milestones of different stages of Dawah are clearly understood and kept in the forefront.** The policies to be evolved, the program to be chalked out and the efforts to be sustained, **all should lead to the same goal. It will create cohesiveness in the Islamic Movement and one stage will lead to the next stage automatically.**[199]

With his choice of language, Siddiqi is telling us that he aligned himself with progressive revelation. Note the similarities to Qutb:

> The Qur'an did not come down all at once; rather it came down **according to the needs of the Islamic society** in facing new problems.[200]

And consonant with Islamic law, *Methodology of Dawah* stresses the importance of Mohammed's conquests in the final stage of the "call to Islam."

> There **Muslims concentrate, gain strength and then root out the Batil** [forces of falsehood, i.e., non-Muslims] **with force.** Allah's help comes from all directions and **His Deen becomes dominant.** This is Allah's tradition. **It is laid down in the Qur'an** in dealing with the fate of different people of different Prophets.[201]

The **"ideology of Islam,"** Siddiqi writes in *Methodology of Dawah*, must **"prevail over the mental horizon of the American people."**[202] He explains the plan for America in the later stages by reference to the first generation of Muslims at the time of Mohammed:

> The Islamic Movement was at its zenith at that time. ...The idolaters were finally warned to accept Islam or be ready to fight. *Shirk* was totally routed out from the Arabian Peninsula. ... **Muslims were vehemently exhorted to fight in the way of Allah (SWT) with life and wealth. The people of the Scriptures were warned either to accept Islam or pay *Jizyah* and live a life of second class citizen under**

the bounds and bounties of Islamic State. The game of the hypocrites was smashed. Their mosque, which they built in the vicinity of *Madinah* for hatching conspiracies against the emerging Islamic State was demolished. There was no power in Arabian Peninsula to challenge Islam. **All stood annihilated and humiliated. Only the *Deen* of Allah was in a dominant position.**[203]

Before dismissing Siddiqi's comment as a rant, remember that it simply paraphrases Qur'an Verse 9:29:

Fight those who believe not in Allah nor the Last Day, nor hold that forbidden which hath been forbidden by Allah and His Apostle, nor acknowledge the religion of truth, even if they are of the people of the Book, **until they pay the *jizya* with willing submission, and feel themselves subdued.**

This is straight from the Qur'an. Since it was revealed in Surah 9, it abrogates any earlier revelations on the same topic and is the final word on how Muslims must treat non-Muslims in an Islamic Society. This is certainly what Qutb meant when saying that:

[w]herever an Islamic community exists which is a concrete example of the Divinely-ordained system of life [i.e., once it has gotten to the top of the milestones], **it has a God-given right to step forward and take control of the political authority** so that it may establish the Divine system on earth, while it leaves the matter of belief to individual conscience.[204]

For an example of how this strategy can play itself out, one need look no further than the recent activities in Nigeria, Syria, and Iraq in what has become a relentless and ruthless application of Verse 9:29.

Methodology of Dawah, or the 'Radicalization Process'

In the War on Terror, every analyst has a theory about what is called, euphemistically, the "Radicalization Process." An unclassified internal guide published by the Pentagon's Defense Human Resources Activity (DHRA) quotes a definition of the process by RAND Corporation's Brian Jenkins: "**adopting for oneself or inculcating in others a commitment not only to a system of [radical] beliefs, but to their imposition on the rest of society.**"[205] The Radicalization Process is often thought of as a series of steps, culminating in violent action or efforts to "impose [those radical beliefs] on the rest of society." In the next paragraph, the unsigned DHRA article admits that, as far as they are concerned:

> [t]he exact nature of this process is still poorly understood.
> Researchers have developed a number of different theories
> and conceptual models that seek to explain the process by
> which an individual becomes radicalized, but these theories
> have not been empirically tested.[206]

A hallmark of the modern bureaucratic state is an overriding need to become lost in processes that are understood to be incomprehensible and then losing oneself in the incomprehension. It's the Gnosticism of our time. Rather than focus on "a number of different theories and conceptual models," analysts and decision-makers would do well to purchase a copy of Siddiqi's *Methodology of Dawah* from an Islamic bookstore or at any number of community events co-sponsored or attended by U.S. government entities and personages. Few other books address the "exact nature" of "radicalization" in America so operationally. Even Siddiqi's dedication fits the Pentagon's definition:

> I dedicate this book to those da'ees who are struggling and
> waiting to lay down their lives for establish[ing] God's
> Kingdom on Earth.[207]

Doesn't the dedication say it all? Siddiqi also picks up on the jahiliyyah narrative. As he explains, American society is a pre-Islamic "society of ignorance" in a state of jahiliyyah. Through the slow adoption of Islamic Movement narrative, it was natural for Siddiqi to come to Qutb's understanding of the Milestones Process, "in conformity with the process laid down by Prophet Muhammad":

> In a nutshell, American society resembles the society of
> ignorance (Jahiliyah) where Prophet Muhammad (PBUH)
> was appointed as Messenger of Allah to call the people to
> the fold of their Creator. We can term America as a society
> of modern Ignorance (Jadid Jahiliyah) with slight variations
> here and there. When this society and its condition are prac-
> tically the same as that of the Prophet's (S) time, the basic
> principle for the presentation of Dawah Ilallah should
> naturally be the same.[208]

Given the Islamic Movement meme, the only conclusion that can be reached is that America is to become the object of an aggressive dawah campaign in preparation for jihad. Outlined in *Methodology of Dawah*, Siddiqi's procedure for bringing Americans to Islam aims to "personalize" the Milestones Process. Just as the Qur'an describes the sequence of progressive revelation—and Qutb emphasized the Islamic Movement's tactical transition from one "milestone" to the next—Siddiqi proposed using this blueprint for individuals' immersion into Islam in America. Or, in his own words: "I have laid down the order of priority in **presenting Islam in stages ...**"

A dawah strategy pegged to the Milestones Process would mean that individuals would be introduced to Islam in the same way it was originally disclosed to the first generations of Muslims, with progressive revelations gradually replacing earlier ones. *Methodology of Dawah* describes in detail how new American converts to Islam are to be inculcated, initially to a form of Islam that reflects the non-confrontational Early Meccan period of Quranic revelation. He calls it Islam in a "concocted or abbreviated form." Following the model, Siddiqi argued against presenting a view of Islam that prospective converts would be unprepared to cope with, given their relative lack of commitment. Siddiqi described how to maintain discipline when presenting Islam to non-Muslim potential converts:

> The concept of Tawheed (Oneness of God) is explained to them **in academic fashion without telling what this** Kalimah[1/209] **demands from a Muslim.** Aqidah[2/210] is **explained without giving the details of the impact** of Iman Billah[3/211] and Iman Bil-Akhirah,[4/212] and **without telling what revolution it must bring in the life of an individual and the society in which he lives.**
>
> Some rituals of religion and traditions of the Muslim Community are explained. **A short account of the Prophet's (PBUH) life is presented, without the revolutionary aspect.** When Islam is acceptable to the new entrants in this **concocted or abbreviated form**, the ceremony of Shahadah is performed with great reverence. A non-Muslim thus becomes a Muslim, obedient to Allah (SWT) alone. **The revolutionary aspect of Islam is rarely brought before the new converts,** as in most of the cases the Da'ee (caller) himself is not conversant with it.[213]

"The revolutionary aspect of Islam," Siddiqi wrote, "is rarely brought before the new converts." Even after an American becomes a Muslim, his religious and

---

1   Kalimah – "The words," generally in reference to the Kalimah Shahadah: "La Ilaha Illallah, Muhammadun Rasulullah" [*There is no diety except Allah and Muhammad is the messenger of Allah*]. Shamim Siddiqi, *Looking for the Book of Wisdom*, 47.
2   Aqidah - The correct Islamic creed as outlined in the classical books. According to the scholars of Islam is: The firm creed that one's heart is fixed upon without any wavering or doubt. It excludes any supposition, doubt or suspicion. From *Salafipublications*.
3   Imam Billah – Faith in Allah. *The Dawah Program*, Shamim Siddiqi, 53.
4   Iman Bil-Akhirah – Faith or belief in the Hereafter. *Ummah Reflections / Islamic Da'wa Center*. Also - Akhirah: The Day of Resurrection/Judgment when every human being will face his/her Lord and will be accountable to Him for all his/her actions and deeds on earth – will be rewarded with eternal bliss of paradise if he/she has obeyed Him all through or will be thrown in the eternal ditch of fire if disobeyed Him throughout. Shamim Siddiqi, *Calling Humanity*, 244.

doctrinal training (tarabiya) may be strictly circumscribed, as information about the later, more "revolutionary" incarnations of Islam are hidden from him.

The strategy has effectively found its way into the treatment Islam is given in introductory survey courses at American colleges and universities. For example, in keeping with the Milestones requirement to bring a community in at the early stages of revelation and rely on a vanguard to transition the membership through the milestones, a popular college survey text titled *Approaching the Qur'an*, translated by Michael Sells, presents an image of Islam that focuses exclusively on "a careful selection of the earliest 'suras' [chapters]" that excludes what Siddiqi referred to as the more "revolutionary aspects" of the faith. In keeping with Siddiqi's 1989 requirement, the course book provides a "concocted and abbreviated form" of Islam that withholds the "revolutionary aspect" for a later time.

From a Western perspective, coaxing someone to enter into a commitment— even a non-monetary one—on false pretenses constitutes a kind of fraud. In the context of converting individuals to Islam under the Brotherhood regime, it is dishonest to convert someone to a belief system or religion without telling him or her what is involved. If you want to convert to Catholicism, Protestantism, or Judaism—or if you want to take an oath to enlist in the Army—you must do so with full awareness and without mental reservation.

In the Islamic context described by the Milestones Process, however, the concept of fraud is not applicable; Muslims beholden to the Process see progressive revelation as an integral part of Islam. In addition to being doctrinally correct, the Process is consistent with bringing new converts to a fuller understanding of Islam in stages, just as with the first generation of Muslims. Recall that, in the discussion on abrogation, Allah's revelations to Mohammed were questioned in the Qur'an by the first generation. This prompted a dismissive response from Allah and Mohammed that nevertheless established the practice as a doctrinal element of Islam. "When We substitute one revelation for another, and Allah knows best what He reveals, they say, 'Thou art but a forger': but most of them understand not" (Qur'an 16:101–103).

This does not mean, of course, that analysts, decision-makers, or ordinary citizens should not make ethical judgments concerning Islamic doctrine; in fact, it is imperative for non-Muslims to assess the Islamic rationale of abrogation, dawah, and other concepts in light of America's core values. However, the Islamic Movement understanding of these concepts remains foundational for many Muslims worldwide, including our enemies in the War on Terror. For this reason, Siddiqi and others who implement this dawah strategy in America approach it with the utmost sincerity. This chasm cannot be bridged.

Remember: there were the early, middle, and late Meccan periods before the Medinan period. In the Islamic context, there is no dishonesty in converting someone to Islam by insisting there is no such thing as jihad; it did not become a part of Islam until the Medinan period. Hence, until a convert's journey along the

Milestones Process brings him to the Medinan stage of development, there is for him or her no jihad.

Gradually, and in stages, trained da'ee oversee the new convert's personal journey through the "milestones" culminating in what Siddiqi called the "final stage," when Islamic law will govern the United States. Given the infancy of Islam's status in America, Siddiqi observed that even among those da'ee who are converting new members, many have yet to progress far enough to grasp Islam's full transformational aspects.

By following Siddiqi's prescriptions, a literal reading of the stages corresponding to Mohammed's revelations suggests that a new convert should become a committed Islamist in less than 23 years. During that period, the initiate faces a series of events—milestones—that increasingly isolates him or her from the rest of society. The structured process in which this takes place was perfected 1,400 years ago.

As Chairman of ICNA's Dawah and Publication Departments, Siddiqi was in a position to implement his methodology on a wide scale. In late 2009, Pakistani authorities arrested five young Americans—Ramy Zamzam (22), Umer Farooq Chaudhry (25), Ahmed Minni (20), Aman Hassan Yemer (18), and Waqar Hussain Khan (22). The Pakistani police report said the five men "were of the opinion that a Jihad must be waged against the infidels for the atrocities committed by them against Muslims around the world."[214]

One of the suspects rejected the claim that he and the others were terrorists, telling reporters that "we are jihadists, and jihad is not terrorism." As will be discussed, this is not an empty claim. When hearing very earnest-sounding assertions from Brotherhood members that Islam condemns all forms of terrorism, it is important to keep this distinction in mind:

> **The men apparently knew each other from the Islamic Circle of North America** (ICNA) mosque and center in Alexandria, Virginia. They also reportedly participated in a youth group, the **Young Muslims of Virginia, which is affiliated with the ICNA center**. Zamzam has also reportedly **served as the council president for the Muslim Student Association** (MSA) of Washington, D.C.[215]

The American students:

> allegedly took separate flights from the U.S. and entered Pakistan with valid American passports and Pakistani visas on November 30-December 1, 2009. They reportedly traveled to Hyderabad to attend an Islamic seminary run by Jaish-e-Mohammed (JEM), a Pakistan-based terrorist group that carries out terrorist operations against Indian

interests, installations of the secular Pakistan government, sectarian minorities and civilians.

As Siddiqi and his disciples train young Muslims and converts in America, an authentic "Radicalization Process" is occurring under the noses of our national security leadership and is not, as the internal Pentagon guide put it, "poorly understood."

Modern Jihad

On September 11, 2001, elements associated with al-Qaeda attacked the United States. Since then, discussions about the more physical aspects of terrorism are almost exclusively stated in terms of al-Qaeda and Associated Movements (AQAM). Al-Qaeda is a very dangerous jihadi organization. As it relates to the United States, there is good reason to focus kinetic operations against it. But because even al-Qaeda believes the war will play itself out primarily in the information battlespace, in a certain sense, al-Qaeda could better be understood as a strategic distraction.

Jihad is the line of operation farthest from the Islamic base, since the jihad function, defined in kinetic terms, occurs in the later stages of the process, after the subject population has been optimally subverted and demoralized through dawah. Ayman Zawahiri said that most of the war is to be waged in the information battlespace. Pakistani Brigadier S. K. Malik stated that the war of muscle does not begin until after the war of wills has been won. Majid Khadduri explained that kinetic jihad occurs only when the possibility of success exists, whereas the psychological and political battles are permanent obligations.

Because al-Qaeda is committed to Islamic law, its members follow what they reasonably believe to be Islamic law along the functional lines of a jihad entity. This makes the group predictable, but it also means that al-Qaeda, correctly or not, must have assessed that the situation was ripe for jihad when they struck on 9/11; they believed that the dawah mission had sufficiently advanced and the Ummah was permissive of such activity. Because the "kinetic" jihad is understood to be a culminating event, analysts who consider the threat strictly in terms of al-Qaeda will fail to assess, or will overlook, the main effort of "Civilization Jihad"—ideological subversion in the dawah phase.

"Al-Qaeda" is not the group's official name. This informal title is derived from the group's internal documents, in which it refers to itself as "Qaeda al-Jihad," or "the base of jihad." The official name is the World Islamic Front for Fighting Jews and Crusaders, a moniker that conveys a great deal more information.[216] Crusaders are Western non-Muslims who are not Jewish and who resist dawah and jihad. As Indians have increasingly come under al-Qaeda's focus, the "Hind" [referring to Hindus] has been added to the group's name in some Internet postings. One cannot properly understand the World Islamic Front as the overtly jihadi element of Islam in the political domain without identifying the Muslim Brotherhood as the dawah element in that same domain.

The Muslim Brotherhood oscillates between dawah and jihad in its mission to re-establish the caliphate and impose Islamic law globally.[217] Many modern terrorist groups, including al-Qaeda, Egyptian Islamic Jihad, Hamas, and Palestinian Islamic Jihad, are offshoots of the Brotherhood. Most of the leading Islamic organizations in America are, in fact, either affiliates or front groups of the Muslim Brotherhood or otherwise identify with the Islamic Movement they lead.

The Muslim Brotherhood is by no means the only part of the Islamic Movement that adheres to the Milestones Process. As already discussed, any organization or individual oriented to the Milestones Process is necessarily jihadist, believing in jihad to overthrow—and eventually outlaw—non-Islamic jurisdictions. These teachings were not lost on the larger Islamic Movement. Just three months after 9/11, Ayman al-Zawahiri, the number two of al-Qaeda, wrote *Knights Under the Prophet's Banner* to explain early al-Qaeda doctrinal and strategic formation. In the book, he emphasized the importance of Qutb's strategic vision:

> Sayyid Qutb's call for loyalty to God's oneness and to acknowledge God's sole authority and sovereignty was **the spark that ignited the Islamic revolution against the enemies of Islam at home and abroad**. The bloody chapters of this revolution continue to unfold day after day.[218]

As Zawahiri's praise for Qutb suggests, al-Qaeda's embrace of the process likewise extends to its operational planning. The Milestones Process warns against the harsh enforcement of shariah before the dawah stage, in which the population is first educated on the requirements of Islamic law. Zawahiri's infamous 2005 "Zarqawi Letter" warned Abu Musab Zarqawi against using excessive brutality in Iraq:

> Therefore, the mujahed movement must avoid any action that the masses do not understand or approve, if there is no contravention of Sharia in such avoidance, and as long as there are other options to resort to, meaning we must not throw the masses—scant in knowledge—into the sea before we teach them to swim, relying for guidance on the saying of the Prophet to Umar bin al-Khattab lest the people should say that Mohammed used to kill his Companions.[219]

The leader of al-Qaeda in the Maghreb, Abdelmalek Droukdel, commented in his 2013 "Mali Playbook":

> One of the wrong policies that we think you carried out is the extreme speed with which you applied Shariah, not tak-

ing into consideration the gradual evolution that should be applied in an environment that is ignorant of religion, and a people which hasn't applied Shariah in centuries. And our previous experience proved that applying Shariah this way, without taking the environment into consideration will lead to people rejecting the religion, and engender hatred toward the Mujahideen, and will consequently lead to the failure of our experiment. So in the first stage, we should have focused on preparing the terrain to apply Shariah, to spread dawa, and to talk and preach to people in order to convince them and educate them.[220]

Our leaders have a responsibility to know that the Muslim Brotherhood and al-Qaeda agree on abrogation, the Milestones Process, and the role of Islamic law and conform their strategies to that end.

On September 13, 2012, Zawahiri—who had replaced Osama bin Laden as the leader of al-Qaeda—released a 35-minute audio recording echoing these foundational Muslim Brotherhood precepts. He took the opportunity on the eleventh anniversary of 9/11 to reject secularism and the modern nation state, noting that Islam is a nation undivided by nationalities that believes in unity of Muslim lands and has a God-given right to reclaim its entire historical territory.

We should labor to establish a state that follows a godly path, which will renounce secularism and the rule by the whims of the majority, a state that will believe in brotherhood among Muslims, and will not distinguish among them according to their nationality, in the service of their enemies, a state that will believe in the unity of Muslim lands, and will do away with the borders of national states, which were delineated on our soil by the leaders of colonialism, and later, in our minds and hearts by the secular curricula.

This mujahid Muslim state will consider one of its most important duties to be the liberation of every inch of Muslim land, from the Caucasus to Zanzibar, from Afghanistan and Kashmir to East Timor and the Philippines, and from East Turkestan to Andalusia [Spain].[221]

The "liberation" of these lands from the oppressors of Muslims, he continued, is a "duty incumbent upon each and every Muslim, just like every Muslim in Palestine must labor to liberate every inch of occupied Muslim land." Zawahiri, moreover, like Hasan al-Banna, addressed "the peoples of the Islamic and Arab nation" and admonished them to:

purify their countries of the corrupt and corrupting rulers. They should topple the western proxies in our countries, and especially the Saud clan and the Gulf sheiks in the Arabian peninsula, as well as the sons of France in the Maghreb.

Zawahiri himself joined the Muslim Brotherhood when he was 14, and although he later abandoned the organization, he never abandoned its founding philosophy.[222] Lest there be any doubt as to al-Qaeda's foundational connection to the Brotherhood and its ideological commitments, Zawahiri in September 2012 specifically called for the release of all "our prisoners ... and first and foremost Omar Abd al-Rahman," the blind Brotherhood sheik convicted and sentenced to life imprisonment for plotting to destroy simultaneously several New York City landmarks.[223] They are "brothers," and as to who should govern the world, and how, they are of one mind.

Moreover, Zawahiri quotes Qutb at length on the evils of democracy. In "Sharia and Democracy," which first appeared in his 1991 book on the Muslim Brotherhood *The Bitter Harvest: The [Muslim] Brotherhood in Sixty Years*, Zawahiri cites Qutb's book *In the Shade of the Qur'an*:

> Sovereignty is the most exclusive prerogative of godhood. Therefore, whoever legislates to a people assumes a divine role among them and exercises its privileges. Men become his slaves, not the slaves of Allah; they accept his religion, not the religion of Allah. ... This issue is extremely critical for the faith, for it is an issue concerning godhood and worship [i.e., the relationship between man and Allah], an issue concerning freedom and equality, an issue regarding the very liberation of man—nay, the very coming into being of man! And thus, due to all of this, it is an issue of infidelity or faith, an issue of jahiliyya or Islam.

> Nor is jahiliyya merely a historical period, but rather it is a condition that comes into existence every time its prerequisites are established or organized. Its ultimate goal is to return justice and legislation back to the whims of nations.[224]

In the same 1991 essay, Zawahiri later cites Qutb again to reiterate the point that Islam can never accept man-made governance. Zawahiri relies on Qutb's use and explanation of Qur'an 3:64, "Let us not take others for lords in place of Allah" to make his point:

> This universe, in its entirety, shall never maintain order nor possess a sound countenance, unless it has but one god to order it: 'If there were, in the heavens and the earth, other gods

besides Allah, there would have been chaos in both!' [21:22]
The prerogatives of godhood in respect to mankind are: to be
obeyed by the slaves [mankind]; to give them laws to govern
their lives; and to balance their lives. Whoever, then claims
any one of these for himself [also] claims the most exclusive
rights of godhood for himself. He sets himself up as a god
among the people, in place of Allah. No worse corruption
befalls the earth as when gods multiply in this manner—
when slaves become enslaved to other slaves; when one of
the slaves claims he personally has the right to be obeyed
by the slaves; that he personally has the right to legislate for
them; that likewise he personally possesses the right to establish values and standards. This is a call for godhood, no
less than was spoken by Pharaoh.[225]

In parallel to the thinking of al-Banna, which allows no peace outside the
banner of Islam, Osama bin Laden wrote in an essay titled "Moderate Islam is a
Prostration to the West":

[O]ur talks with the infidel West and our conflict with them
ultimately revolve around one issue—one that demands
our total support, with power and determination, with one
voice—and it is: Does Islam or does it not, force people by
the power of the sword to submit to its authority corporeally
if not spiritually? Yes. There are only three choices in Islam:
either willing submission; or payment of the jizya [annual
head tax for non-Muslims ostensibly to buy them protection
but offering little], through physical though not spiritual,
submission to the authority of Islam; or the sword—for it is
not right to let him [an infidel] live. The matter is summed
up for every person alive: Either submit, or live under the
suzerainty of Islam, or die. And it behooves [Muslim and
Saudi leaders] to clarify this matter to the West—otherwise they will be like those who believe in part of the book
while rejecting the rest. But instead they concoct something
that has no connection to the struggle, dressing it up and
presenting it as Islam. Yet the verse does not support what
they wish and mean regarding this matter. The West avenges
itself against Islam for giving infidels three options: Islam,
jizya, or the sword. Now then, you intellectuals: Are these
options a part of the faith or not? This is what the debates
truly revolve around—so stop evading and dissembling the
truth with lies![226]

Abdullah Azzam

Abdullah Azzam is another prominent member of the Muslim Brotherhood. His book *Come Join the Caravan*[227] was written to mobilize mujahedeen to fight against the Soviets in Afghanistan. For all practical purposes, he was the real founder of what we now call al-Qaeda.

As the leader of the mujahedeen and founder of al-Qaeda, Azzam is, according to current official U.S. policy, a "violent extremist" who has taken Islam completely out of context. For this reason, Assistant Secretary of Defense Stockton would demand that we not associate Azzam with Islam and suppress our analysis of him and his doctrines. But is this really true? If so, is it obviously true?

A review of Azzam's curriculum vitae makes such assertions hardly obvious. Azzam joined the Muslim Brotherhood at an early age, went to Khadorri College, and received a degree in shariah at Damascus University. More important, he obtained his master's degree in shariah and, in 1973, a Ph.D. in the Principles of Islamic Jurisprudence (*Usool ul-Fiqh*) from al-Azhar,[228] which is easily the most prestigious and elite center of Sunni Islamic thinking in the world. Being credentialed by an al-Azhar Ph.D. establishes Azzam as an Islamic elite. Thus, simply asserting the mantra that Azzam is a violent extremist who misrepresents Islam and takes it out of context should be challenged and fact-checked—if for no other reason than simple due diligence.

Our "violent extremism" models encourage us to envision Azzam (whose protégé was Osama bin Laden) as an incoherent, ranting, half-educated Salafist who has no idea what he is talking about. But this is clearly not an accurate picture. Similarly, Zawahiri's grandfather was the grand imam of al-Azhar, and his uncle was the Arab League's first secretary general.[229] So, the next time you hear a senior policy type say that someone like Azzam or Zawahiri understands Islam out of context, ask him to justify that view in a factual manner. It is likely that the response will resemble the following conditioned response: "He's taken Islam out of context because he's a 'violent extremist'. He is violent because he has extreme ideas, his extreme ideas permit him to resort to violence, and his violence makes his views extreme; therefore, he is a violent extremist." Such responses conform to narratives that are circular, sustained without factual support, and infantile.

At al-Azhar, Azzam met key students of Qutb, including Omar Abdel-Rahman (the "Blind Sheikh") and Zawahiri. He went on to teach at King Abdul-Aziz University in Saudi Arabia, where bin Laden was his student.[230] In the Muslim world, Azzam had *bona fides* as a thinker and was a giant among his peers on issues relating to shariah.

So, when Azzam says what he says, is he really distorting Islam? Are these the words of a raving madman?

Allah has preferred in grades those who fight with their pos-

sessions and their lives, over those who sit back. And to all
of them has Allah promised good (Paradise). But Allah has
favoured the Mujahideen over those who sit at home by a
tremendous reward, by higher grades from him, and with
Forgiveness and Mercy.[231]

This seems to say that people who fight jihad are more favored by Allah than
people who do not. Is this a distortion of Islam's teachings? Let's compare it to
Qur'an Verse 4:95:

Not equal are those believers who sit at home and receive
no hurt, and those who strive and fight in the cause of Allah with their goods and their persons. Allah hath granted a
grade higher to those who strive and fight with their goods
and persons than to those who sit at home. Unto all in Faith
Hath Allah promised good: But those who strive and fight
Hath He distinguished above those who sit (at home) by a
special reward.[232]

Of course, Azzam simply paraphrased the Qur'an. In fact, *he got it exactly
right*. So, if someone were to accuse Azzam of taking Islam out of context with his
last statement, barring a valid competing explanation of the verse, wouldn't it come
close to saying that Allah did, as well?

There is no gap between what Azzam says and what traditional Quranic
scholars say because he was, in his own right, a *bona fide* scholar. His words are
aligned with the commonly understood meaning of shariah. Given Azzam's mastery of Islamic law, barring a substantive refutation by a competent imam qualified
to offer such counterargument—or in some other evidentiary manner—accusations of "extremism" should not be permitted to be simply asserted. The next time
you hear someone say they think a jihadi leader has taken Islam out of context,
remind him or her that there should be a determination of fact to support that
position.

On the question of a substantive refutation by a competent imam qualified
to make such arguments, founder and former member of the Egyptian Islamic
Jihad Nabil Na'eem is in the later stages of gaining approval from al-Azhar for his
refutation of the prevailing shariah narrative.[233]

We Westerners seem to think we sit on a perch of higher awareness with a
godlike vantage point that provides a transcendent understanding of non-Western
cultures and beliefs. From there, we utter ill-considered statements about what
Islam is or is not. These utterances, however, reflect only the illusion of knowledge
where none exists. Our lack of knowledge is especially exposed when we speak to
populations that know exactly what they believe (or don't believe but fear terribly).
When Muslims—either those steeped in Islamic cultures or educated in Islamic

law—hear such utterances, they can only conclude that we are profoundly ignorant on one of the most pressing issues of our time and, hence, are undeserving of respect.

Convergence: The Arab Spring, or the Islamic Awakening

Because they orient on Islamic law, dawah entities (like the Muslim Brotherhood) and jihadi entities (like Al-Qaeda) hold themselves to Islamic law on abrogation and, through it, progressive revelation and the Milestones Process. If each entity analyzes events through the same decision support process, we can reasonably expect that they will draw roughly analogous views as to the appropriate course of action for their entities at a given stage in a given situation and will recognize the orientation of other entities following that process as well. They will use comparable sets of criteria to determine which stage (milestone) their part of the Islamic Movement is in. This may be the case even when their representatives do not coordinate among themselves.

Since the purpose of dawah is to lay the groundwork for jihad, as the Milestones Process progresses, dawah entities like the Brotherhood will themselves eventually transition to jihad, seamlessly converging with jihadist groups such as al-Qaeda—until both are predominantly engaged in jihad. We have seen this in places like Syria over the past few years.

Lacking an understanding grounded in Islamic law, and specifically the law of abrogation and the Milestones Process, most observers fail to internalize the significance of key statements and reports as they relate to the Islamic Movement and its role in the Arab Spring. Reporting has instead focused on a supposedly unpredictable outbreak of revolts, led by secular youth, where al-Qaeda and the Muslim Brotherhood are characterized as merely hijacking or exploiting the disorder. Unsurprisingly, this analysis has been unsuccessful at explaining why elements of the Islamic Movement routinely emerge as the primary beneficiaries.

What follows is a different reading of events, a timeline of key messages of the Arab Spring, interpreted through the prism of the stated threat doctrine of the Islamic Movement, specifically the Muslim Brotherhood and Al-Qaeda.

In June 2009, President Obama delivered a major address before an audience at Cairo University in Egypt that was billed as an address to the Muslim world regarding a change in relations with the United States. Two parts of the speech were immediately significant, even before considering the text itself. The first was the implicit recognition of the entirety of the Muslim world—the Ummah, about which more will be said later—as a real entity with which the United States must contend, rather than viewing diplomatic relations as being between nation states, some of which happen to be majority Muslim. Second was the insistence by the Obama administration that members of the Muslim Brotherhood—an organization that was formally banned in Egypt—be permitted to attend the speech, establishing that, as far as the United States was concerned, the Brothers were a legitimate political entity.[234] Within the text of the speech itself, Obama conveyed a series of messages that, leaving aside intention, would have been highly suggestive to the entities of the Islamic Movement that the time was right for entering a new stage of the Milestones.

In Cairo, President Obama took a conciliatory tone. For example, he referenced the 1796 Treaty of Tripoli, which he described as the first "recognition" of the United States. As part of the treaty, the Bey of Morocco agreed to allow free passage for American shipping in exchange for a one-time payment of gold and goods.[235] President Obama quoted a line from the treaty: "The United States has in itself no character of enmity against the laws, religion or tranquility of Muslims"—the 1796 version of "the United States is not at war with Islam."[236] However, despite the payment of "forty thousand Spanish dollars—thirteen watches of gold, silver & pinsbach—five rings, of which three of diamonds, one of saphire and one with a watch in it, One hundred & forty piques of cloth, and four caftans of brocade,"[237] the Bey of Morocco later abrogated the treaty and renewed attacks on American shipping, leading to a series of conflicts known as the Barbary wars. Knowingly or not, President Obama was pointing out that the United States had once before negotiated in good faith and been treated with contempt and duplicity.

Additionally, President Obama's statement that he had a responsibility "to fight against negative stereotypes of Islam wherever they appear" is reminiscent of the Islamic law of dhimmitude, which prohibits mentioning "**something impermissible about Allah, the Prophet** (Allah bless him and give him peace), **or Islam.**"[238] Further, Obama noted that this responsibility derived from his position as President of the United States, suggesting there would be government sanction against such "impermissible" stereotypes.

President Obama also ensured there would be no hindrance of Muslims' right to give zakat, an obligatory Islamic tax—a curious statement since there are no limitations on Muslims giving to recognized charitable organizations in the United States. That is, no limitations unless one considers material support for terror laws to be a hindrance, as the Muslim Brotherhood–affiliated individuals and organizations named in the Holy Land Foundation terror finance trial most certainly would. As former federal prosecutor Andrew McCarthy noted:

> The purpose of these laws is obvious, as has been the stepped-up effort to use them since 9/11. If we are going to prevent terrorist strikes from happening, rather than content ourselves with prosecuting any surviving terrorists after our fellow citizens have been murdered and maimed, we have to identify cells and choke off their resources before attacks can be planned and executed. Thus, a donor who gives to an organization, including an ostensible charity, that he knows to

have been formally designated as a terrorist entity under U.S. law, or that he knows facilitates terrorist activity, is liable.

That shouldn't be a problem, should it?[239]

In his comments regarding democracy, President Obama signaled that the United States had no opposition to governance based on Islamic law, provided the officials were elected democratically. For the Muslim Brothers in the Cairo University audience, the president's statement that "America respects the right of all peaceful and law-abiding voices to be heard around the world, *even if we disagree with them*" must have seemed directed at them. An examination of subsequent Al-Qaeda and Muslim Brotherhood messages suggests that this conclusion was reached, as the Islamic Movement began to orient toward a more aggressive posture.

As far back as July 2010, the Muslim Brotherhood's involvement in Middle East events was beginning to escalate. Ignorant of the doctrines that animate groups like the Muslim Brotherhood and al-Qaeda, American national security and diplomatic leadership was caught unaware. The plan for deposing Egyptian president Hosni Mubarak in February 2011 began to take shape from June through October 2010. The following timeline illustrates the cascade of events that presaged the rise of the Brotherhood to power across the Middle East in the early months of 2011.

This timeline tracks events in the Middle East against al-Qaeda and Muslim Brotherhood pronouncements and activities that contrast with the prevailing meme that such activities were part of a broad-based democratic movement (the "Arab Spring").

In July 2010, al-Qaeda published the first issue of its online magazine, *Inspire*, announcing a new strategy. It echoed the rhetoric of the Brotherhood while upping the ante: al-Qaeda used doctrinal language embedded in terms of art along the common Milestones narrative, telling the Middle East to prepare its populations to transition to a new stage. Al-Qaeda and the Muslim Brotherhood—always aligned through the common objectives of implementing shariah law and re-establishing the caliphate—appeared to be coming into synchrony:

> This Islamic Magazine is geared towards making the Muslim a *mujāhid* in Allah's path. Our intent is to give the most accurate presentation of Islam as followed by the *Ṣalaf as-Ṣālih*. Our concern for the *ummah* is worldwide and thus we try to touch upon all major issues while giving attention to the events unfolding in the Arabian Peninsula as we witness it on the ground. ... Jihad has been deconstructed in our age and thus its revival in comprehension and endeavor is of utmost importance for the Caliphate's manifestation.[240]

It is worth noting that the first issue of al-Qaeda's magazine never mentions Wahhab or Wahhabism. Recognizing that the tactic of military confrontation with the United States and the larger Western world failed to accomplish their objectives, al-Qaeda leadership decided that a change in tactics was in order:

> Our secret organizations were militarily defeated in all the confrontations. Yes, we won many of the battles, but we lost the war in all the [jihadi] experiences and confrontations. I do not spend time on discussions with the obstinate, for reality is the greatest witness.[241]

> The times have changed, and we must design a method of confrontation, which is in accordance with the standards of the present time.[242]

Communicating through the medium of its English-language Internet magazine, al-Qaeda declared that the Meccan period centering on dawah-centric strategies was coming to an end; it was time to move to the Medinan stage. Just as the Qur'an was revealed to Mohammed over time—beginning with the non-confrontational Meccan era revelations and transitioning to the more violent "jihad" revelations after the *hijra* in the Medinan period—so al-Qaeda urged Muslims, and specifically the Muslim Brotherhood, to transition from the pre-violent dawah phase to a more aggressive dawah message in anticipation of jihad:

> Some of them believe we are in the Makkan stage and have therefore set for themselves programs that are limited according to the rules of Makkah.[243]

A clearer articulation of the Milestones Process and the rule of abrogation can hardly be found. The language was specific and explicit: al-Qaeda is telling the Muslim Brotherhood and related Salafi entities to get with the program.

There are indicators that the timing of this change was anything but coincidental. In 2005, a *Der Spiegel* article discussed a book written by a Jordanian journalist with ties to Al-Qaeda—including that he spent time in prison with Iraqi Al-Qaeda leader Zarqawi—that laid out Al-Qaeda's strategic objectives broken into operational phases:

> The Fourth Phase Between 2010 and 2013, Hussein writes that al-Qaida will aim to bring about the collapse of the hated Arabic governments. The estimate is that "the creeping loss of the regimes' power will lead to a steady growth in strength within al-Qaida." At the same time attacks will be carried out against oil suppliers and the US economy will be targeted using cyber terrorism.

> The Fifth Phase This will be the point at which an Islamic state, or caliphate, can be declared. The plan is that by this time, between 2013 and 2016, Western influence in the Islamic world will be so reduced and Israel weakened so much, that resistance will not be feared. Al-Qaida hopes that by then the Islamic state will be able to bring about a new world order.[244]

Recall that national security analysts keep telling us that al-Qaeda is "on the ropes." Looking at the al-Qaeda phases of operation, and possibly running in parallel with it, the Brotherhood began to pick up the pace in a manner that seemed responsive to al-Qaeda's call, as it oriented on Arab regimes. I say "seemed responsive" because Mohamed Badie's election to the General Guide of the Muslim Brotherhood in January 2010 was already understood to reflect a shift to the more militant wing of the Brotherhood. In October 2010, Badi issued a declaration titled "Islam in the Face of Injustice and Tyranny." It "called on the Muslim nation to unite against the enemies who are plotting against it" and to "understand that change and reform cannot be achieved without the ultimate sacrifice."[245] Badie's declaration represented a course change that brought the Muslim Brotherhood and al-Qaeda into tighter alignment. At the time, my colleagues and I realized the significance of Badie's statement.

Then, in the first week of January 2011, the Qaradawi-run *IslamOnline* published a fatwa by a prominent Islamic legal scholar from al-Azhar University, Dr. 'Imad Mustafa. Owing to al-Azhar's status, Mustafa's statement was not only ominous because of what he said, but also because it was released to the Muslim world though *IslamOnline*—thus suggesting Muslim Brotherhood vetting.

Mustafa stated that "jihad is a prescribed duty in cases of aggression from infidels against Muslims, for we must resist them [and] make jihad against them."[246] He continued, "This type of jihad is known as defensive jihad, and it is a duty agreed to by all Islamic scholars and all who are wise, and is endorsed in our day by recognized international charters."[247]

Note the reference to defensive jihad as "*a duty agreed to by all Islamic scholars.*" Mustafa is asserting scholarly consensus (ijma). In an obvious reference to the United States and its Middle Eastern partners, Mustafa noted that "the occupier and his associates have come to label this 'terrorism.' "[248] Dr. Mustafa went on to say, "Offensive jihad is permitted in order to secure Islam's borders, to extend God's religion to people in cases where the governments do not allow it, such as the Pharaoh did with the children of Israel, and to remove every religion but Islam from the Arabian peninsula, and to save the captive and weak."

Clearly, Mustafa's comments are in line with Badie's October statement calling on the Muslim nation to unite against the enemies who are plotting against it.[249] The reference to the pharaoh is worth noting as well. It is a term used, especially by the Brotherhood and its affiliates, against rulers seen as insufficiently Islamic, and Mubarak was (and still is) frequently referred to in both Arab and Western press as a Pharaoh.

By November 2010, this "timeline" of events was developed into a full presentation that was briefed from senior service schools to elements of the Intelligence Community, the FBI, and Capitol Hill, among others. At the time, my colleagues and I communicated the significance of Badie's statement to members of Congress and the Intelligence Community but were often met with perplexed looks. Members of Congress seemed to understand the Brotherhood's dramatic change in strategic posture, but, without grounding in the doctrinal elements of the threat, the national security leadership evinced little more than that look of concern that seeks to mask confusion.

All the evidence pointed to the Islamic Movement converging on the point that transitions to the Medinan stage in the Milestones Process. Yet not only did American national security professionals miss the cues leading to the toppling of Mubarak, the Obama administration supported this outcome, beginning on the last day of January, 2011.[250] That same day, administration officials made it clear that they supported "a role" for the Muslim Brotherhood, with White House Spokesman Robert Gibbs saying that the new Egyptian government had to "include a whole host of important non-secular actors that give Egypt a strong chance to continue to be [a] stable and reliable partner."[251] Mubarak was forced to resign from office eleven days later.[252]

On February 18, 2011, the Muslim Brotherhood held its victory rally in Tahrir Square, where a massive crowd came out to hear Yusuf Al-Qaradawi, flown in from Qatar, preach a Friday sermon—for the first time since he had been exiled under Nasser[253]—to a crowd of well over a million people.[254] Qaradawi's public appearance was a strong indicator that the Muslim Brotherhood intended to publicly step forward as the leader of the "revolution." Four days after Qaradawi's appearance, the Brotherhood announced the formation of its own political party, the Freedom and Justice Party.[255]

When the smoke cleared and the Brotherhood was consolidating its power, the Brothers could admit, as Muslim Brotherhood leader Essam El-Erian did on Arabic television, that the young social-media revolutionaries who had initiated the recent events had Brotherhood ties.[256] In a separate interview that July, responding to questions regarding the Muslim Brotherhood's perceived absence in the Tahrir Square protests, El-Erian said, "Look, Sir, when the history of this revolution is written, everything will be clear. We are not going to say anything about our role in the revolution. Let the others say what they want."[257] The U.S. missed everything but what the Muslim Brotherhood wanted it to see. The lack of awareness continued as the U.S. State Department provided election training to Islamist parties, including the Freedom and Justice Party,[258] and media outlets were surprised by a Muslim Brotherhood electoral victory,[259] after having filed numerous reports about how support for the Ikhwan was "fading" or "plunging."[260] Yet those who understood the situation knew the Brotherhood's electoral victory was all but certain from the beginning.[261]

As the "Arab Spring" progressed, this pattern would repeat itself. On February 25, 2011, Qaradawi called for the assassination of Libyan dictator Muammar Qaddafi.[262] The U.S. supported coalition forces, acting in defense of the rebels, launched airstrikes against Qaddafi beginning March 19.[263] On March 25, 2011, CNN reported that an "energized" Muslim Brotherhood, which included Muslim Brothers coming from Islamic organizations in the West, had their "eye on the prize" of Libya. A Libyan Muslim Brother identified as Hresha who was interviewed for the CNN piece had a particularly insightful comment, informing viewers, "We've been working secretly till this moment."[264] Hresha—and the rest of the Muslim Brotherhood for that matter—recognized the need for secrecy had passed.

Also on March 25th, the British newspaper *The Telegraph* reported that a major Libyan rebel, Adel-Hakim Al-Hadisi, had al-Qaeda ties. Hadisi fought and was captured by coalition forces in Afghanistan, and he also recruited jihadis for fighting in Iraq. The organization that Hadisi belonged to, the Libyan Islamic Fighting Group (LIFG), was the second largest source of foreign jihadis in Iraq after Saudi Arabia.[265] On October 21, 2011, a U.S. drone identified a convoy of Libyan loyalists fleeing Qaddafi's hometown of Sirte. A NATO airstrike followed, and Libyan rebels swarmed in to capture and execute Qaddafi—just as called for by Qaradawi.

The next day, NATO announced its combat mission completed.[266] Thirteen days later, a black flag with the shahada, the Islamic declaration of faith, was photographed flying from the courthouse of Benghazi, the place where the Libyan rebellion originated.[267] Referred to in the news report as the "Al-Qaeda flag," it has been flown routinely by jihadis and is now associated with al-Qaeda, ISIS, and related entities. Unlike in Egypt, the Muslim Brotherhood in Libya's Justice and Construction party did not collect an outright victory in Libya's first election.[268] However, its power is steadily growing as it takes advantage of continued disorder.[269]

Running concurrently with the coup in Libya was the uprising in Syria. By July 12, 2011, despite earlier comments from then-Secretary of State Hillary Clinton that Assad lacked legitimacy,[270] Muslim Brotherhood affiliates in the United States were clearly dissatisfied by America's lack of speed in supporting Assad's ouster. In a hearing of the Tom Lantos Human Rights Commission, two individuals who spoke of the urgency for action in Syria had some connection to organizations with Muslim Brotherhood affiliations.

One was Radwan Ziadeh of the Center for the Study of Islam and Democracy (CSID). The Center was created and founded by members of the American Muslim Council, an organization established by self-confessed Muslim Brother and Al-Qaeda financier Abdurrahman Almoudi. CSID has been noted for having a number of known Muslim Brotherhood affiliates on its Board of Directors, including Jamal Barzinji, founder of the International Institute for Islamic Thought (IIIT), and Dr. Taha Jaber Al-Alwani of IIIT and the Fiqh Council of North America (part of ISNA). Daniel Pipes, a scholar of Islamism, warned of the "extremist nature of CSID itself" and called it "part of the militant Islamist lobby."[271] CSID's Tunisia branch was involved in election training in Tunisia,[272] where the Brotherhood-affiliated Ennahda Party's Rached Ghannouchi triumphed in parliamentary elections.[273] Ghannouchi was then brought to the United States to speak at a joint ISNA/CSID presentation on the Arab Spring.[274]

Before the Human Rights Commission, Ziadeh complained that the Obama administration had been slow to act in Syria just as it had in Egypt and Libya:

> President Obama, he made statements pushing for immediate transition in Egypt in several public remarks or speeches on Libya, but in Syria the rhetoric was actually a little bit slowly [sic], and this is why we need President Obama to make a speech on that to encourage more leaders on the international community to have the same position.[275]

Joining Ziadeh was Louay Safi, who identified himself as a Georgetown Common Word fellow but not as having been Executive Director for the Muslim Brotherhood-linked IIIT. Interestingly, both Ziadeh[276] and Safi[277] would go on to join the Syrian National Council, the political opposition coalition for the Syrian rebels that is dominated by the Muslim Brotherhood.[278]

On August 18, 2011, President Obama formally called for Assad's ouster.[279] By January 2012, arms—paid for by Qatar and Saudi Arabia but facilitated by U.S. intelligence—began to flow into Syria through Turkey and Jordan.[280] By May

2012, mainstream media outlets were covering the dominant role played by the Muslim Brotherhood within the Syrian Opposition.[281] In July, al-Qaeda elements were reported among the opposition. December 2012 featured a flurry of activity with the establishment of a unified military command, dominated by Muslim Brotherhood and related groups.[282] More evidence of Al-Qaeda/Muslim Brotherhood convergence became clear when the U.S. took steps to declare the al-Qaeda group Jabhat al-Nusra a terrorist organization. From a December 2012 *Reuters* news story:

> The decision to blacklist al-Nusra, an important fighting force in the uprising, has already triggered criticism from the powerful Syrian Muslim Brotherhood. A senior Brotherhood official said it was wrong and hasty. "They are seen as (a group that) can be relied on to defend the country and the civilians against the regular army and Assad's gangs," Brotherhood deputy leader Farouq Tayfour told Reuters on Tuesday.[283]

Even as 29 opposition groups declared, "We are all Jabhat al-Nusra," the U.S. still proceeded to support the organization of a "supreme military council" dominated by the Muslim Brotherhood and Salafi rebel units as its primary point of contact for Western support.[284] Recognizing that Jabhat al-Nusra (the al-Nusrah Front) operated on behalf of the Islamic State of Iraq and the Levant (ISIS),[285] the U.S. State Department formally designated the Nusrah Front a terrorist organization by placing it on the Foreign Terrorist Organization (FTO) list in May 2014.[286] Formerly Al-Qaeda in Iraq, ISIS had been on the FTO since 2004.[287]

In March 2013, the Syrian National Coalition elected to the position of Interim Prime Minister[288] Texas resident Ghassan Hitto, who has ties to Muslim Brotherhood affiliates NAIT,[289] CAIR, and the Muslim American Society.[290] On June 2, Brotherhood spiritual leader Yusuf Qaradawi formally declared jihad in Syria and asked for foreign fighters to enter Syria in order to fight Assad and Hezbollah. Speaking in terms of legal obligation, Qaradawi said, "Every Muslim trained to fight and capable of doing that (must) make himself available."[291] Less than two weeks later, Qaradawi's second-in-command of the International Union of Muslim Scholars (IUMS), Bin Bayyah, met with White House Officials[292] to lobby for additional support for Syrian rebels.[293]

As the Syrian civil war rages on, stories continue to accumulate regarding the imposition of shariah law in Syria, both by al-Qaeda forces[294] and the Brotherhood.[295] And yet, U.S. leaders insist that the Syrian rebels aren't jihadis fighting to impose Islamic law, denying clear evidence to the contrary.[296]

Organization of
The Islamic Caliphate

Political war is the use of political means to compel an opponent to do one's will, political being understood to describe purposeful intercourse between peoples and governments affecting national survival and relative advantage. Political war may be combined with violence, economic pressure, subversion, and diplomacy, but its chief aspect is the use of words, images, and ideas, commonly known, according to context, as propaganda and psychological warfare.

Those interested in conducting aggressive political warfare will find their activities facilitated by popular ignorance or uncertainty regarding their operations.

Political will is at the heart of all serious forms of conflict. Often obscure, usually complex in origin, always sensitive to investigation, political will can nevertheless be reduced to two elements: a vision of the world, and a set of assumptions as to the actor's role in it.

On balance, a large multinational empire still seems to require some form of potent ideological adhesive to hold it together. To dissolve that adhesive is a task of political warfare.

Paul A. Smith, Jr.
On Political War
National Defense University Press, 1989

Among the most surprising — and disappointing — aspects of the national security and law enforcement communities is their chronic lack of awareness of the key players on the other side. I can brief an auditorium full of officers, ask them about the Organization of Islamic Cooperation, and see blank faces. Often when I ask the audience "what OIC stands for," the most common answer is "Officer in Charge." Today, fourteen years into the War on Terror, policy makers, decision-makers, and analysts remain fundamentally unaware of both essential published doctrines and key individual players. Our senior leadership has become a self-cleaning *tabula rasa*.

Possibly as a result of the Arab world's humiliating defeat in the 1967 War, or maybe as an effort to initiate a Pan-Islamic movement in the wake of failed attempts at Pan-Arabism, or both, the Organization of the Islamic Conference (OIC) was created in 1969. Its charter emphasized the goal of "revitalizing Islam's pioneering role in the world."[1]

In the eyes of many Islamic intellectuals, the West presents the world with a false choice between the crass materialism of capitalism and the human-less materialism of communism. For many in the Islamic Movement, the choice is between two equally distasteful strands of jahiliyyah. While the 22-state Arab League, formed in 1945, represents only Arab countries at the head-of-state level, the OIC provides an opportunity for its Member States to concentrate on a political organization organized along shariah lines. This group includes Sunni and Shia states and does not limit its membership to Arab states. Alongside Member States, the OIC also allows countries with sizable minority Muslim populations to participate in OIC activities as Observers. As such, the OIC can and does genuinely hold out to the public that it represents the Muslim world.

The Ummah

Renamed the Organization of the Islamic Cooperation in 2011, the OIC is an inter-governmental body comprised of all Muslim states.[2] By its own reckoning, the OIC is composed of real state actors, using real state power to implement real (and expressed) state action in furtherance of real (and expressed) state objectives. It is a political body wielding political power at the supra-national level.

The OIC purports to represent the entire Islamic world and self-identifies as the "Ummah," the global Islamic community:

> The Organization of the Islamic Co-operation (OIC) is the second largest inter-governmental organization after the United Nations which has membership of 57 states spread over four continents. **The Organization is the collective voice of the Muslim world** and ensuring to safeguard and protect the interests of the Muslim world ...[3]

This seems to be a fairly pretentious claim. What kind of organization would presume to speak for the entire Muslim world? The OIC Charter explains the organization's structure as follows:

> Article 6. The Islamic Summit is composed of Kings and Heads of State and Government of Member States and is the supreme authority of the Organisation. It convenes once every three years to deliberate, take policy decisions and provide guidance on all issues pertaining to the realization of the objectives and consider other issues of concern to the Member States and **the Ummah**.[4]

Because OIC Islamic Summits are "composed of Kings and Heads of State and Governments of Member States and is the supreme authority of the Organization," the ummah takes on a specifically political character as a part of the governing authority of a political entity.[5] OIC summits are composed of heads of state, which means the OIC has the potential to be an extremely powerful and influential body. Moreover, as an intergovernmental organization that meets at the head-of-state level, it resembles a governing authority with actual state-actor-like power. Additionally:

> The **Council of Foreign Ministers**, which meets once a year, considers the means for the implementation of the general policy of the Organization by, inter alia:
>
> (a) Adopting decisions and resolutions on matters of common interest in the implementation of the objectives and the general policy of the Organization;
>
> (b) Reviewing progress of the implementation of the decisions and resolutions adopted at the previous Summits and Councils of Foreign Ministers;

OIC Member States' heads of state meet every three years (or more often, if a special session is required). The Council of Foreign Ministers meets once a year to "consider the means for implementation of the general policy of the organization." The purpose of the Islamic Summit is "to deliberate, take [sic] policy decisions and provide guidance on all issues pertaining to the realization of the objectives and consider other issues of concern to the Member States and the Ummah."[6] This is the execution of real executive power. Chapter V, Council of Foreign Ministers, Article 10, Section 3:

> The Council of Foreign Ministers may recommend convening other sectorial Ministerial meetings to deal with the **specific issues of concern to the *Ummah***.[7]

The Secretary General also says the OIC represents the Ummah. In his speech at the 35th Session of the Council of Foreign Ministers[8] in June 2008, OIC Secretary-General Ekmeleddin Ihsanoglu said:

> In one word, we have managed to affirm our presence and draw attention to the fact that the OIC is considered an international organisation worthy of representing the **collective will and concerns of the *Ummah*** on the global level.[9]

This entity — which purports to speak for the ummah — makes claims based on the fact that it is comprised of the heads of state of all the Muslim countries. This is an entirely defensible claim. What's alarming, given this reality, is our national security leadership's systemic lack of awareness of the OIC. Arguably, when meeting at the summit level, the OIC really *does* represent the entire Muslim world and, hence, really is the Ummah.

But that means the "ummah" is not the utopian religious concept as described to Westerners when told not to use the term. Invariably, when analysts speak of the ummah, they say, "The Islamic world has this *utopian* view of an ummah." The very way we talk about it is dismissive. In the Western schema, there is no comparable entity to the ummah. Hence, because it is not real to us, we discuss it as if it is not real to Islam. For the Muslim world, however, the concept of the ummah is very real and, as the OIC makes clear, exists as an immediately present political and governing reality.

Historian and OIC critic Bat Ye'or described the organization this way:

> The OIC has a unique structure among nations and human societies. The Vatican and the various churches are de facto devoid of political power, even if they take part in politics, because in Christianity, as in Judaism, the religious and political functions have to be separated. Asian religions, too, do not represent systems that bring together religion, strategy, politics, and law within a single organizational structure.[10]

If the OIC is what it purports to be, how is it possible for our leaders to conduct competent foreign policy — especially in the Middle East — without having a functional understanding of this entity and the role it plays? On the bright side, the unawareness facilitated by our decision not to know such entities has caused a bump in employment among anthropologists, psychologists, sociologists, and other related soft-science practitioners who promise value-neutral (safe) rationales in place of real threat analysis based on actual identification of the real players. Once the choice was made to enforce the decision not to know either the enemy or his environment, our national security policymakers were left with manufacturing and enforcing bureau-academic narratives, while at the same time hoping that the shoe wouldn't drop on their watch. At some point, however, the shoe will drop. The

OIC is the 800-pound gorilla in the room that people work very hard not to see.

How does one competently analyze the foreign policy of a country such as, for example, Turkey — a member of both NATO and the OIC — or Iraq or Afghanistan without taking into account the rules they have formally agreed to follow as Member States of the OIC? Shouldn't at least some group of analysts (themselves not subject to any conflicts of interest or claims arising out of the OIC or the Islamic Movement) be charged with mapping the policies and activities of OIC Member States to the policies and activities they have, in fact, committed to follow at the Member State head-of-state level?

As this book will argue, the three Islamic entities that we confront – the ummah, the dawah, and the jihadi – are openly committed to re-implementing shariah within the ummah. Within the context of Islamic law and the Muslim ummah, this culminates in the re-establishment of the caliphate.

According to Islamic law, the caliphate is supposed to govern the ummah. *Reliance of the Traveller* states this explicitly: "**[T]he investiture of someone from the Islamic Community (Umma) able to fulfill the duties of the caliphate is obligatory by scholarly consensus.**"[11] **By emphasizing that the establishment of the caliphate is "obligatory by scholarly consensus,"**[12] *Reliance* **is stating that the requirement for a caliphate is non-negotiable and absolute.** *Reliance* **was certified by the same Muslim Brotherhood entities to which our federal, state, and local leaders conduct outreach. Hence, we know they are beholden to this claim.**

Already claiming to represent the Ummah, Ihsanoglu said the OIC serves the role of the caliphate.[13]

The Muslim Brotherhood agrees with both the OIC's construction and the OIC's political role in it. As explained back in 1988 in the International Institute of Islamic Thought (IIIT) book *OIC: The Organization of the Islamic Conference, an Introduction to an Islamic Political Institution*, the Brotherhood understands the ummah to be a Quranic construct formally subordinated to Islamic law.[14] Noting that "traditionally the ummah has been understood as an ideological community based on Islamic shari'ah," the Muslim Brotherhood, through the IIIT, has recognized since 1988 that "the OIC reflect[s] the fact that the Islamic ummah has not ceased to be a shariah-based community."[15] In fact, cooperation among individual Islamic states within the OIC is specifically "based on the Islamic concept of ummah."[16] The American Muslim Brotherhood also recognizes the Ummah, that it is based on shariah, and that the OIC is its head.

If the caliphate is re-established, is it unreasonable to think it could arise out of an entity like the OIC? Caliphate is another term national security analysts are told not to use, as it, too, is considered a "utopian" religious concept. Like ummah, the term "caliphate" appears with some frequency in OIC forums. In 2010, OIC Secretary-General Ihsanoglu said the Organization "provides for Muslims today the same religious solidarity and unity which those in the past found in the Islamic caliphate."[17] Mohamed Elibiary, Senior Homeland Security Advisor with close Brotherhood associations, took the same view in June 2014 when saying on Twitter that the caliphate is inevitable and that the only question was "whether we [will] support the EU like Muslim Union vision or not." To buttress his point, Elibiary noted that President Bush created the position of OIC Special Envoy and President Obama removed "discriminatory engagement policy towards the Muslim Brotherhood."[18]

We could call the OIC the "proto-caliphate" encompassing the Muslim ummah. Yet, despite all the evidence that is readily available, some argue the organization doesn't even exist.

That our national security elites could be talked into precluding the use of the only language capable of providing the requisite strategic awareness underlying such terms points to a dangerous level of uninformed gullibility. Ignoring key terms that are strategically relevant, such as "ummah" and "caliphate," is not just ignorant — it's policy.

This discussion serves several important purposes: informing the reader that the OIC (a) actually exists as a governing entity, (b) identifies itself as the Muslim Ummah, (c) sees its emerging role as that of the historical caliphate, (d) executes its mission at the leadership level of the Islamic world, and (e) exists to implement governing principles that orient on Islamic law internationally. The OIC's capacity to execute declarations and conventions at the UN — such as the Cairo Declaration and the 1999 OIC Convention Combating International Terrorism[19] — confirms its status as a state actor and is emblematic of its skill in affecting its strategic vision on the international stage while remaining hidden in plain sight.

The next few chapters will look at critical issues in Islamic law — including shariah concepts of human rights and free expression, as well as the doctrinal view of terrorism in Islam — through the lens of the OIC's stated intention of imposing them on non-Muslim jurisdictions.

Human Rights in Islam

In the United States, the concept of human rights is roughly synonymous with the rights enumerated in the U.S. Constitution. These rights were given international expression in the first half of the 1948 Universal Declaration of Human Rights, the drafting of which Eleanor Roosevelt oversaw through World War II. The first half of the Universal Declaration was an attempt to internationalize the rights that Americans enjoy under the Constitution.

This international extension of rights harmonized with existing political systems in Canada, Australia, and Europe; despite some cultural and language differences, the effort resonated in Latin America and India, as well. But the Declaration has not been a good fit in other parts of the world — and is especially at variance with the laws and traditions of Muslim cultures.

While this book's main focus is on Sunni Islam, an occasional detour into Shi'a Islam with regard to the OIC is instructive. Concerning the Universal Declaration of Human Rights, Sa'id Raja'i-Khorassani, the permanent delegate to the UN from the Islamic Republic of Iran, said this in 1985:

> The very concept of human rights was "a Judeo-Christian invention" and inadmissible in Islam. ... According to Ayatollah Khomeini, one of the Shah's "most despicable sins" was the fact that Iran was one of the original group of nations that drafted and approved the Universal Declaration of Human Rights.[20]

Arguments about the universality of Western principles of human rights aside, what Khorassani said is essentially true, and it is important to understand why. While it's not a religious document, the principles enshrined in the Declaration of Human Rights were the natural outgrowth of specific philosophical concepts in the Western religious tradition. In fact, the concepts of human rights as expressed in the first half of the 1948 Declaration reflect a secularized restatement of human rights constructed upon Judeo-Christian traditions, most importantly that man was created in the image of God. This principle was expressed in the first chapter of Genesis,[1] the first book of the Torah. If all men are equal in the image of God, it reasons that all men are equal in the eyes of God as well. From an American perspective, this concept took on explicit meaning in the Declaration of Independence, where "inalienable rights" are those that are "endowed by their creator."[21]

The Torah holds that man was created in the image of God, and Jews and Christians share   this belief. Islam categorically disagrees. For Muslims, Allah is completely "other."[22] For example, from *Reliance of the Traveller*, we find:

> **W8.0 Allah is Exalted above Needing Space or Time.**
> W8.1 Muhammad Hamid: What is obligatory for a human being to know is that Allah the Creator, glory to Him, is absolutely free of need (*al-Ghani*) of anything He has created, and free of need for the heavens and or the earth. His is transcendently beyond "being in the sky" or "being on earth"

---

1   Then God said, "Let us make man in our image, after our likeness; and let them have dominion over the fish of the sea, and over the birds of the air, and over the cattle, and over all the earth, and over every creeping thing that creeps upon the earth." So God created man in his own image, in the image of God he created him; male and female he created them. (Genesis 1:26-27)

in the manner that things are in things, created beings in created beings, or things in circumstances are encompassed by their circumstances, for it is He who **"There is nothing whatsoever like unto Him,** and He is the All-hearing, the All-seeing" (Koran 42:11), and, "He did not give birth, nor was He born, and there is none who is His equal" (Koran 112:3–4). Aside from all the proofs from the Koran and sunna, the rational evidence is decisive that Allah Most High **is absolutely beyond any resemblance to created things,** in His entity, attributes, and acts.[23]

Notions of human rights that arise from the view of "man in the image of Allah" is necessarily unacceptable to Muslims. At least in part, OIC efforts to draft the Cairo Declaration on Human Rights in Islam stem from Iranian diplomat Raja'i-Khorassani's charge. If this is true, it means there is no basis for a shared notion of "human rights" between Jews and Christians and the Muslim community. As it stands, a shared understanding of human rights does not survive the first chapter of Genesis. When Muslims like Khorassani tell us that such language cannot legally be used under Islamic law, their reasoning is sound.

The crippling problem for us is that, because we believe that our conception of human rights is universal, we tend to believe that this view is universally held. It is not. It has always surprised me how many inside our national security community take for granted that people from non-Western cultures want to enjoy the same rights and freedoms Americans do as a conclusory assumption not worth examining. The lopsided 2011 referendum in Egypt placing shariah at the center of all legislation indicates that this is simply not true. It is imperative that we take other concepts of human rights seriously, if only to acknowledge that they exist and should influence our understanding of the true nature of events.

Entertaining assumptions and presuppositions in our planning processes that Islamic entities hold the same views on human rights — thinking Blue when analyzing Red — is dangerous because it blinds us to hostile doctrines driving hostile intent. If we assume from the start that everybody thinks like we do, we become victims of our own groupthink. "What would I do if I were in their shoes?" becomes the proxy for what the threat might actually do when in fact there is actual notice of what that threat will do. If an enemy figures this out, all it has to do is make our assessments self-referencing by placing a mirror in front of us.

So, how does the Muslim world understand human rights? Enter the Cairo Declaration.

The Cairo Declaration

The Cairo Declaration on Human Rights in Islam is a formal legal instrument promulgated on behalf of OIC Member States in 1990. It was formally served to the United Nations in 1993.[24] In June 2000, OIC Member States agreed to support the Cairo Declaration, and the order was issued to start drawing up covenants and conventions.[25] The document controls OIC policy on human rights, as was explicitly stated at the Islamic Conference of Foreign Ministers in Bamako, Mali, in June 2001:[26]

> (a) The Group of Experts reaffirms the status of the Cairo Declaration on Human Rights in Islam as **the frame of reference and the basis for the formulation of the positions of Member States regarding issues related to human rights** and stresses the need to achieve coordination and cooperation between Member States in international forums and conferences related to human rights.

The Cairo Declaration lays down a clearly stated, coherent, and fairly strict set of articles that define human rights in Islam. For OIC member states, *human rights are defined as shariah.* For parties to the Declaration, there is no right that can contravene or lie outside of shariah. For the purpose of this analysis, all one really needs to know are the two final articles of the Cairo Declaration, Articles 24 and 25:

> ARTICLE 24: **All the rights and freedoms** stipulated in this Declaration **are subject to the Islamic Shari'ah**.

> ARTICLE 25: The Islamic Shari'ah is **the only source of reference for the explanation or clarification** of any of the articles of this Declaration.[27]

Article 24 provides the term of inclusion — "when we say human rights we mean shariah" — while Article 25 contains the terms of exclusion — "when we say human rights we mean nothing but shariah." As will be discussed in greater detail later, whenever an issue of human rights arises with regard to the Muslim world, we are on notice: It must be examined in light of what *shariah* prescribes. In the event that two competing understandings arise, the Cairo Declaration establishes that the shariah understanding of human rights should take precedence when dealing with Muslim countries and Islamic entities.

The strategy behind the Cairo Declaration was well considered. OIC Member States could exempt themselves from parts of the Universal Declaration by reference to the Cairo Declaration where conflict existed. In allowing such exemptions, the illusion of a global human rights consensus was maintained.

By excepting *to* Cairo Declaration articles when excepting *from* Universal Declaration articles, the OIC exceptions swallowed the Universal Declaration's rules. In effect, the Cairo Declaration established itself as a parallel international human rights regime. By remaining parties to the Universal Declaration, OIC

Member States can hold non-Member States accountable to Western human rights standards without having to be held to them. In addition, OIC Member States that are parties to the Universal Declaration can make global appeals in the name of human rights even though they have effectively opted out of its most important provisions. Parties to the Cairo Declaration agree to follow the Universal Declaration of Human Rights only insofar as it does not contradict the Cairo Declaration. Simply stated, the Cairo Declaration takes precedence over the Universal Declaration of Human Rights.

The consequences of the Cairo Declaration are enormous. Given the legal fact of shariah's place in the writings of Islamic jurists and the constitutions in much of the Muslim world, on what factual basis does one maintain that shariah is *not* the law of the land for Muslims? On what professional basis does one justify reliance on analytical products that make no attempt to account for the enumerated role played by shariah in the actual governing of Muslims (and non-Muslims in Muslim lands)? Between the belt of the national constitutions and the suspenders of the Cairo Declaration, analytical products that do not account for the actual legal and policy consequences of shariah in Muslim States and Islamic entities should be assessed as defective as a matter of law. Of course, competent analysis requires familiarity with the very Islamic law that the current national security paradigm places off-limits. The national security apparatus is unaware of the official status of shariah in the Muslim world — and even if it were aware, it currently lacks the ability to perform adequate shariah analysis.

The Muslim Brotherhood says it seeks to implement shariah and re-establish the caliphate. The constitutions of Muslim countries say they rely on shariah as the basis of their law, which means that citizens of those countries are under obligation to observe it regardless of whether they personally accept it. By treaty, shariah is also imported into the legal frameworks of those countries by reference to such agreements, especially as Member States to the OIC. It is a fact that Muslim countries orient to shariah as the law of the land. The only question is the level of commitment and fidelity.

For analytical purposes, since published Islamic law teaches that Islamic law is the law of the land — and the leadership enforces it — Islamic law has to be assessed as if it really were the law of the land. When such an analysis is undertaken in the context of the U.S. Constitution or other laws of this country, shariah should be assessed as *foreign* law. It should not be assessed as ecclesiastical law, analogous to Jewish halacha or Catholic canon law. Shariah states that where it operates, it does so in supersession of all other law. As used here, to supersede is to abrogate.

For OIC Member States that are parties to the Cairo Declaration, Islamic law is the sole criteria by which human rights are to be measured. Because the Cairo Declaration was served as a legal instrument at the United Nations, analysis of OIC Member State policy positions must take this into account if for no other reason than to satisfy due diligence requirements. This includes adversary nations like Iran and the Sudan, as well as Islamic States with which this country has comparatively warmer relations, such as Saudi Arabia, Qatar, and Pakistan.

When analyzing statements from the OIC, its Member States, or entities reasonably beholden to the OIC, communications concerning human rights *must* be read with the presumption that the provisions laid down in Articles 24 and 25 are in effect. This can be reduced to a single statement to guide us in our analysis, which I will call the "24/25 Rule":

> THE 24/25 RULE FOR ANALYSIS. **Human Rights are defined as shariah law for the purpose of any analysis involving the OIC, a Member State, or initiatives reasonably arising from either — including all entities claiming Islamic law as the basis of law, including all elements of the Islamic Movement, the Muslim Brotherhood, and al-Qaeda.**

When the subject matter of an analysis concerns "rights and freedoms" or associated defined concepts that arise out of the Cairo Declaration, those "rights and freedoms" can be assessed *only* in terms of what Islamic law permits them to mean, where Islamic law is the *only* criterion by which a determination can be made in the event of any dispute requiring resolution.

The standard of review is strict because the Cairo Declaration makes it so; Articles 24 and 25 impose a strict construction standard. From the perspective of intelligence analysis, a benefit of following the Rule arises: When analyzing entities that purport to fight America in furtherance of Islamic law, analysis that accounts for the 24/25 Rule will help facilitate the production of valid most likely and most dangerous enemy courses of action (E-COAs). Hence, the intelligence corollary to the Rule: **Analysis undertaken on subject matter where the 24/25 Rule applies and yet *is not* considered should be regarded as suspect for failure to meet explicitly stated minimum analytical thresholds.**

As with the Cairo Declaration, nowhere is the application of the 24/25 Rule more important than when analyzing documents or policies arising out of the OIC, its Member States, or entities reasonably obligated to follow its directives. The implications of the Rule influence perceptions that drive our policies, whether we know it or not. For example, when an American discusses human rights with an OIC delegate, it matters whether the American is unaware that the delegate believes human rights to mean shariah.

It stands to reason that those who don't know the OIC exists would not know that a formally served legal instrument on counterterrorism was delivered under its name to the UN on behalf of its Member States in 1999. The OIC enjoys official UN status, as reflected by its official UN letterhead, which reads: "Permanent Observer Mission to the United Nations in New York."[28] The "Convention of the

Organization of the Islamic Conference on Combating International Terrorism (1999-1420h)"[29] states twice that OIC constructions with regard to terrorism are strictly controlled by shariah:

> Pursuant **to the tenets of the tolerant Islamic Sharia** which reject all forms of violence and terrorism, and in particular specially those based on extremism and call for protection of human rights, which provisions are paralleled by the principles and rules of international law founded on cooperation between peoples for the establishment of peace;

> Abiding by the lofty, moral and religious principles **particularly the provisions of the Islamic Sharia** as well as the human heritage of the Islamic Ummah.[30]

Applying the 24/25 Rule to the Convention indicates that the OIC's treatment of terrorism is explicitly controlled by shariah. In this case, all OIC and OIC Member State pronouncements on terrorism should be read with a mandatory interpretation that accounts for what is meant by those pronouncements if they were actually controlled by shariah — because those same Member States explicitly agreed that this would be the case when becoming parties to the Convention. Because there is formal notice that the OIC and its Member States understand terrorism in exclusively shariah terms, ignoring this in analysis should constitute negligence.

There is no point reading the rest of the "Combating International Terrorism" instrument as though it relates to Western concepts of terrorism. This leads to a preliminary finding: There can be no awareness of an OIC Member State's true position on terrorism until our national security leadership undertakes a directed analysis of what constitutes terrorism in Islamic law. Furthermore, it should be understood that this knowledge gap blinds us to potential competing understandings of the relationships between the OIC, the Islamic Movement, the Muslim Brotherhood, and al-Qaeda.

Terrorism, or 'Killing Without Right'

In May 2008, "thousands of Islamic clerics and madrassa teachers from across India" met in New Delhi for an Anti-Terrorism and Global Peace Conference to issue a fatwa, heralded as the "world's first unequivocal fatwa against Islamic terror."[31] According to a media report, the group "not only declared terror activities to be anti-Islam, but also involved top clerics in **defining terrorism in the light of the Quran and shari'a**." The fatwa stated:

> Islam Has Come to Wipe Out All Kinds of Terrorism and to Spread ... Global Peace. ... Islam is a religion of peace and

security. In its eyes, on any part over the surface of the earth, **spreading mischief, rioting, breach of peace, bloodshed, killing of innocent persons** and **plundering** are the most inhuman crimes."[32]

These scholars quite reasonably based their "peace and terror" fatwa on sharia. How could an Islamic legal ruling be based on anything else? This necessarily means that a competent analysis of the statement would have to account for Islamic law's influence on the fatwa. The corollary is likewise valid: Analytical products that fail to account for Islamic law's influence will also fail precisely because they fail to account for an expressly stated influence. Understood in light of the 24/25 Rule, the real question is whether it is reasonable to accept analysis of Islamic pronouncements that do not account for Islamic law.

While the group meeting in New Delhi did not condemn terrorism as commonly perceived in the West, it did stake out a doctrinal position that is in line with similar statements from other players in the Muslim community: It defined terrorism as the "killing of a Muslim without right."

A review of OIC conferences reveals a consistency in the language and tone of the organization toward the issue of peace reaching as far back as 1995.[33] A review of two post-9/11 Foreign Ministers conferences provides additional detail to the OIC's position on terrorism. One such conference, the Thirtieth Session of the Islamic Conference of Foreign Ministers (Session of Unity and Dignity), was held in Tehran in 2003 and the other, the Thirty-First Session of the Islamic Conference of Foreign Ministers (Session of the Progress and Global Harmony), in Istanbul in 2004. Both the Tehran and Istanbul documents state their alignment with Islamic law:

> Committed to **the moral and human principles that the OIC Member States believe in**, and **inspired by their sublime and tolerant religion** and by their heritage and tradition which call for the rejection of all forms of injustice, aggression, and intolerance ...[34]

In keeping with the 24/25 Rule, both documents also emphasize the role of human rights, especially as they relate to the Islamic definition of human rights:

> Recalling the noble motives and objectives of the glorious religion of Islam, which emphasizes the importance of **human rights**; and mindful of the **universality and integral nature of Islamic laws on human rights** and the prominent place of Man ...[35]

In both 2003 and 2004 conferences, the OIC "strongly condemned terrorism in all its forms and manifestations including state terrorism directed against all

States and peoples."[36] Using identical language, the OIC asserted in both the Tehran and Istanbul documents that Islam is innocent of all killing that is forbidden by Islam:

> Asserts that Islam is innocent of **all forms of terrorism which involve the murder of innocent people whose killing is forbidden by Islam**, and rejects any attempts to link Islam and Muslims to terrorism because the latter has no relation whatsoever with religions, civilizations or nationalities.[37]

A closer look at the language reveals that the OIC definition of terrorism does not include violent activities conducted in the name of jihad. It also reveals that the definition of "innocent people" is tied to Islamic concepts of innocence. Given the mission to bring peace through jihad, this concept of terrorism does not violate the Islamic aim of "global peace in light of shari'a," because the Islamic Movement holds that global peace occurs when the entire world has been brought under shariah[38] and, hence, that jihad has been made lawful to achieve this end. [39]

To develop an understanding of terrorism within an Islamic context, it becomes necessary to identify a functional definition not only of terrorism but also of *innocence*. Fort Hood jihadist U.S. Army MAJ Nidal Hasan explained this when briefing fellow officers about the conditions under which he would strike out in jihad against them.[40] As he described in Slide 12 of his briefing ("The Koranic World View as it Relates to Muslims in the U.S. Military"), the Islamic notion of terrorism is Quranic: The killing of the innocent is associated with the killing of a Muslim without right.

> [4:93] And whoever **kills a believer intentionally**, his punishment is hell; he shall abide in it, and Allah will send His wrath on him and curse him and prepare for him a painful chastisement.

> [17:33] And **do not kill anyone whose killing Allah has forbidden, except for a just cause** ...[41]

To better appreciate Hasan's point, a review of an authoritative Qur'an commentator is in order. Ibn Kathir is such a commentator, and he explained that the language in Verse 4:93 stating "**whoever kills a believer intentionally**" identifies such an act as among the most serious offenses in shariah:

> This *Ayah* carries a stern warning for those who commit so grave a sin that it is mentioned along with *Shirk* in several *Ayat* of Allah's Book. For instance, in *Surat Al-Furqan*, Allah said, "And those who invoke not any other god along with

Allah, nor **kill such person as Allah has forbidden, except of just cause.**"[42]

Hasan was facing possible deployment to Iraq or Afghanistan. He believed that while there, he would be put in a situation where he could be forced to violate this clear Quranic proscription. Regarding Qur'an Verse 17:33, the other verse Hasan relied on, Ibn Kathir explained, under the header "Prohibition of Unlawful Killing," that:

> Allah forbids killing with no legitimate reason. It was report-ed in the Two *Sahihs* that the Messenger of Allah said: "The Blood of a Muslim who bears witness to *la ilaha illallah* and that Muhammad is the Messenger of Allah, is not permis-sible to be shed except in three cases: a soul for a soul (i.e., in the case of **murder**), **an adulterer** who is married, and **a person who leaves his religion** and deserts the *Jama'ah.*"[43]

Ibn Kathir undertakes a supporting parallel treatment of "killing without right" in his treatment of Verses 5:32 and 5:33:

> On that account: We ordained for the Children of Israel that if any one slew a person — unless it be for murder or for spreading mischief in the land — it would be as if he slew the whole people: and if any one saved a life, it would be as if he saved the life of the whole people. Then although there came to them our messengers with clear signs, yet, even af-ter that, many of them continued to commit excesses in the land. (Quran 5:32)

> The punishment of those who wage war against Allah and His Messenger, and strive with might and main for mischief through the land is: execution, or crucifixion, or the cutting off of hands and feet from opposite sides, or exile from the land: that is their disgrace in this world, and a heavy punish-ment is theirs in the Hereafter; [44] (Quran 5:33)

The Quranic reference to the "children of Israel" in Verse 5:32 parallels the *Mishnah Sanhedrin* in its treatment[2] of Cain and Abel from the Fourth Chapter of

---

2 **From Chapter 4, Mishnah Sanhedrin:** Know that capital cases are not like monetary ones. In monetary cases, (a false witness) can return the money and achieve atonement. But in capital cases, the blood of (the victim) and all his future offspring hang upon you until the end of time. **For thus we find in regard to Cain, who killed his brother, "The bloods of your brother scream out!" (Genesis 4:10)** – the verse does not say blood of your brother, but bloods of your brother, because it was his blood and also the blood of his future offspring (screaming out)! [Another explanation of the verse: for his blood was splattered over the trees and rocks (i.e., there was more than one pool of blood).] (The judges'

Genesis.[3] Certain portions of Verse 5:32 are frequently cited in Brotherhood narratives, but rarely in full and almost never in the context of its necessary association with Verse 5:33. After stating the verse, Ibn Kathir provides a section-by-section commentary of 5:32,[45] explaining that the prohibition on killing pertains only to innocent Muslims — *innocent* because the "murder" in Verse 5:32 ("unless it be for murder or for spreading mischief in the land") concerns killing without right, and *Muslim* because the clause "it would be as if he killed all mankind" is explained to mean, "He who allows himself to shed the blood of a Muslim is like he who allows shedding the blood of all people." Ibn Kathir further explains the prohibition as being against one who "kills a believing soul." This explanation restricts the meaning of "person" in Verse 5:32 to Muslims who have neither killed without right nor "spread mischief in the land."

From Verse 17:33, Ibn Kathir tells us that the blood of a Muslim is not to be shed unless for murder, adultery, or apostasy. From Verse 5:32, the rule confirms the proscription against murder and is extended to include "spread[ing] mischief in the land." The restrictive definition of "person" in Verse 5:32 is silent on the slaying of non-Muslims. *Reliance of the Traveller* confirms Ibn Kathir's treatment. An entire section in *Reliance* is dedicated to the question of who can and cannot be killed with cause. Under the heading, "Who is Subject to Retaliation for Injurious Crimes," we find in §o¹˙ that:

> Injurious crimes include not only those committed with injurious weapons, but those inflicted otherwise as well. Such as with sorcery. **Killing without right is, after unbelief, one of the very worst enormities,** as Shafi'i explicitly states in Muzani's The Epitome.

> The Prophet (Allah bless him and give him peace) said: "**The blood of a Muslim man** who testifies that there is no god but Allah and that I am the Messenger of Allah **is not lawful to**

---

speech continues:) "**It was for this reason that man was first created as one person (viz. Adam), to teach you that anyone who destroys a life (some editions: from Israel) is considered by Scripture to have destroyed an entire world; any any [sic] who saves a life (some editions: from Israel) is as if he saved an entire world.**" [And also, to promote peace among the creations, that no man would say to his friend, "My ancestors are greater than yours." (Mishnah Sanhedrin 4:5, *Sepharia - A Living Library of Jewish Texts*, undated, URL: http://www.sefaria.org/Mishnah_Sanhedrin.4.5)nhedrin

3   **From Chapter 4, Genesis:** If you do well, will you not be accepted? And if you do not do well, sin is couching at thedoor; its desire is for you, but you must master it." Cain said to Abel his brother, "Let us go out to the field." And when they were in the field, Cain rose up against his brother Abel, and killed him. Then the LORD said to Cain, "Where is Abel your brother?" He said, "I do not know; am I my brother's keeper?" And the LORD said, "What have you done? **The voice of your brother's blood is crying to me from the ground**. (Genesis 4:7-10)

**shed unless he be one of three: a married adulterer, some-
one killed in retaliation for killing another, or someone
who abandons his religion and the Muslim community."**

And in another hadith,

"The killing of a believer is more heinous in Allah's sight that
[sic] doing away with all this world."

Allah Most High Says:

"… and not to slay the soul that Allah has forbidden, except
with right" (Koran 6:151),

and,

"Oh you who believe, retaliation is prescribed for you regarding the slain …" (Koran 2:178)[46]

As stated, the parsing of this the law relies on Shafi'i, the iconic founder of
the third doctrinal school of Islamic law, for its authority. *Reliance*'s codification
of "killing without right" as "among the worst enormities" mirrors the case MAJ
Hasan made in his presentation. Section o1.0 concludes by relying on Verse 2:178
to remind readers of the obligatory nature of retaliation. On retaliation, Section
o1.1 continues:

Retaliation is obligatory if the person entitled wishes to take
it against anyone who kills a human being purely intentionally **and without right**. Intentionally is a first restriction and
excludes killing someone through an honest mistake, while
purely excludes a mistake made in a deliberate injury, and
without right excludes cases of justifiable homicide such as
lawful retaliation.[47]

Because the meaning of "person" is left open in §o1.1, to avoid confusion regarding the obligation, the next section states those classes of people that cannot
be made the object of retaliation. While the entire list is revealing, of immediate
importance is §o1.2(2): "The following are not subject to retaliation: (2) a Muslim
for killing a non-Muslim."[48]

If the "killing without right" analysis is sustained, then the Islamic definition
of terrorism is limited to the killing of Muslims without right. Conversely, because
the language is silent on the killing of non-Muslims in any status, *the killing of
non-Muslims by Muslims does not meet the legal threshold to qualify as Islamic terrorism*. Because Hasan's argument was based on Islamic doctrines that do not con-

sider the killing of non-Muslims as terrorism, he had a basis for thinking his acts at Fort Hood were not terrorism. Having declared jihad, Hasan understood that his acts did not qualify as terrorism under Islamic law. This explains why groups like the Muslim Brotherhood refuse to call Hasan's act at Fort Hood terrorism.

When the 2003 Tehran Resolution announced that the OIC "strongly condemned terrorism in all its forms and manifestations including state terrorism directed against all States and peoples," Islamic law controlled its scope and meaning. This was made explicit in the annual Foreign Ministers conferences in both 2003 (Tehran) and 2004 (Istanbul):

> Islam is innocent of **all forms of terrorism** which involve the murder of innocent people **whose killing is forbidden by Islam,** and rejects any attempts to link Islam and Muslims to terrorism because the latter has no relation whatsoever with religions, civilizations or nationalities.[49/50]

OIC language expressly limits the condemnation of terrorism to those "forms of terrorism" that have been "forbidden by Islam." Because the language is silent on those forms of terrorism that have not been "forbidden by Islam," the OIC is silent on acts of terrorism inflicted by jihadis on infidels globally. This leaves only those forms of terrorism forbidden by Islam that constitute the killing without right. It is with this terrorism construct that the OIC resolution on terrorism is to be understood:

> [OIC Conference of Foreign Ministers] strongly condemns the perpetrators of terrorist crimes, who pretend to act in the name of Islam or under any other pretext.[51/52]

The OIC's treatment on terrorism states the ummah standard. A sampling of recent statements from Islamic entities regarding terrorism demonstrates a broad adherence to the terrorism standard established in the analysis of "killing without right" (the "killing without right" standard). The OIC's condemnation of terrorism expresses the same concern raised in MAJ Hasan's briefings at Walter Reed and the Pentagon when citing Qur'an Verse 17:33 ("And do not kill anyone whose killing Allah has forbidden except for a just cause") to warn that "Muslim Soldiers should not serve in any capacity that renders them at risk to hurting/killing believers unjustly." From the perspective of the "killing without right" standard, the OIC's condemnation is genuine and consistent with its assertion that "Islam is innocent of all forms of terrorism which involve the murder of innocent people whose killing is forbidden by Islam, and rejects any attempts to link Islam and Muslims to terrorism." For the OIC, jihad is not terrorism.

Returning to the 2003 and 2004 OIC Foreign Ministers Conferences in Tehran and Istanbul, the twice-ratified resolution on terrorism should be analyzed according to the 24/25 Rule in light of the "killing without right" standard's characterization of terrorism. When assessed this way, OIC Member States' official statements take on a harsh complexion with regard to the United States. Because U.S. Forces fought and killed Iraqis who had not apostatized, committed adultery, or killed a fellow Muslim without right, their actions satisfied the "killing without right" standard, thus qualifying U.S. action as terrorism under the criteria expressed by the OIC:

> **Reaffirming** the determination to combat terrorist acts in all their forms and manifestations, **including those where States are directly or indirectly involved**;

> **Reiterating** the commitment to **combat terrorism in all its forms and manifestations**, to eliminate the objectives and causes of terrorism directed against the life and property of innocent people and the sovereignty, territorial integrity, stability, and security of States, and to uphold the provisions of the OIC Convention on Combating International Terrorism, which reaffirm this commitment;

> **Strongly condemning** terrorism in all its forms and manifestations **including state terrorism directed against all States and peoples.**[53/54]

For the OIC, because the U.S. forces were occupying Muslim lands, resistance was not only permitted — it was encouraged.

> Reaffirming the **fundamental and legitimate right of all peoples struggling under the yoke of colonialist and racist regimes** as well as under foreign occupation **to resist occupation** and achieve self-determination, and particularly the struggle of national liberation movements. [55/56]

OIC statements on terrorism are hostile when understood in light of shari-ah. However, the OIC position on terrorism does not conflict with MAJ Hasan's claims. In fact, while stated in the facially neutral language of diplomacy, the OIC position on terrorism is strikingly similar to the 1998 fatwa "Jihad against Jews and Christians," better known as the '98 Bin Laden Fatwa put out by the World Islamic Front (al-Qaeda):

> All these crimes and sins committed by the Americans are a clear declaration of war on Allah, his messenger, and Muslims. And ulema have throughout Islamic history unanimously agreed that the jihad is an individual duty if the enemy destroys the Muslim countries. This was revealed by Imam Bin-Qadamah in "Al- Mughni," Imam al-Kisa'i in

"Al-Bada'i," al-Qurtubi in his interpretation, and the shaykh of al-Islam in his books, where he said: "As for the fighting to repulse [an enemy], it is aimed at defending sanctity and religion, and it is a duty as agreed [by the ulema]. Nothing is more sacred than belief except repulsing an enemy who is attacking religion and life."

On that basis, and in compliance with Allah's order, we issue the following fatwa to all Muslims:

> The ruling to kill the Americans and their allies — civilians and military — is an individual duty for every Muslim who can do it in any country in which it is possible to do it, in order to liberate the al-Aqsa Mosque and the holy mosque [Mecca] from their grip, and in order for their armies to move out of all the lands of Islam, defeated and unable to threaten any Muslim. This is in accordance with the words of Almighty Allah, "and fight the pagans all together as they fight you all together," and "fight them until there is no more tumult or oppression, and there prevail justice and faith in Allah."[57]

If *Reliance of the Traveller*, the text of Sacred Islamic law that was approved by both Al-Azhar,[58] the OIC and the American Muslim Brotherhood,[59] is valid — and there is no reason to think that it isn't — then the OIC and al-Qaeda positions are in line with each other precisely because they both reflect the shariah standard that they claim to follow. From *Reliance*:

> Jihad is also personally obligatory for everyone able to perform it, male or female, old or young when the enemy has surrounded the Muslims on every side, having entered our territory, even if the land consists of ruins, wilderness, or mountains, for non-Muslim forces entering Muslim lands is a weighty matter that cannot be ignored, but must be met with effort and struggle to repel them by every possible means.[60]

The OIC, the Muslim Brotherhood, and al-Qaeda are all on record as communicating the same posture. The OIC has been on record for some time as accepting the obligatory nature of jihad, and it denies any responsibility for the form of terrorism the U.S. has identified as global. Under the Islamic construct, the OIC, the Islamic Movement, the Muslim Brotherhood, and al-Qaeda are converged and apparently correct. That our leaders, decision-makers and analysts have been unaware of this is irresponsible, negligent, and disastrous. Before moving off this point, recall the two questions raised in the Introduction that were put before

Joint Staff Intelligence admirals and generals in the brief I presented in late 2005:

> Can overdependence on "moderates" to explain non-Western motivations and beliefs lead us to (overly) depend on these people for the decisions we make?

> Is there a point where the outsourcing of an understanding of events leads to the outsourcing of the decision-making associated with those same events?

It is the juxtaposition of these questions with our newfound understanding of human rights and terrorism that prompts a critical examination of positions taken by former White House Counterterrorism Strategist Quintan Wiktorowicz – contrasting his recognition of the lethal effectiveness of ISIS's threat doctrine with the ridiculous First Amendment theory he relies on to undermine the Article VI of the U.S. Constitution duty to support and defend when barring appropriate threat analysis; and the follow-on requirement to outsource critical intelligence requirements to third-party state actors beholden to the shariah standards discussed here. As he expressed it:

> While the government has tried to counter terrorist propaganda, it cannot directly address the warped religious interpretations of groups like ISIL because of the constitutional separation of church and state.

> U.S. officials are prohibited from engaging in debates about Islam, and as a result will need to rely on partners in the Muslim world for this part of the ideological struggle.[61]

If Wiktorowicz holds true to his own worldview, how could he know whether ISIS's interpretations of Islam are "warped"? More ominously, if what Wiktorowicz said on the prohibition and subsequent outsourcing of intelligence requirements is true, then the duty to support and defend the Constitution has been subordinated to third-party state actors and the information they choose to provide in light of shariah considerations. If true, it would effectively subordinate our national security to shariah. Is this part of the strategy Captain Kirby knows "we're out there executing"?[62]

The Muslim Brotherhood on Terrorism

We have already encountered Sheikh Yusuf al-Qaradawi, the chief jurist of the Muslim Brotherhood. Prior to becoming famous in the Arab world for his television show, Al Jazeera's *Shariah and Life*, Qaradawi attended the elite al-Ahzar University in Cairo. He serves on various shariah-compliant finance boards for multinational banks and Gulf-based corporations. In addition, Qaradawi has been denied a visa to travel into the United States since 1999 for his associations with terrorism.[63] In comments made in September 2007, Qaradawi emphasized the need to contain extremist activities so that they serve and do not put at risk the interests of the ummah:

> Responding to host 'Uthman 'Uthman's question of how Islam can be protected from **takfir sedition**, Qaradawi advised that in order to protect the Ummah (Islamic nation), **Muslims must "renounce fanaticism and extremism,"** which he asserted had been responsible for destroying it in the past. He called upon Muslims to adopt a **"moderate approach"** so that they may **properly understand and correctly abide by the tenets of Islam.**[64]

Qaradawi walks a fine line when attacking takfirism. When speaking of protecting Islam from "takfir sedition," he is accusing al-Qaeda of killing fellow Muslims without right. The doctrine of takfirism is a central source of tension between more mainstream Sunni Salafis and Wahhabis — the Muslim Brotherhood and al-Qaeda — because it concerns the killing of Muslims in contravention of the norms established in Verse 5:32. It is the same tension we see with ISIS and the rest of the Sunni community today. By calling it "takfir sedition," Qaradawi is warning Wahhabi-based jihadis that their activities transgress the limits of Islam — and that, therefore, they are engaging in "fanaticism and extremism" when killing innocent Muslims.

By associating "takfir" with "fanaticism and extremism," Qaradawi further aligned his accusation with classical language that focuses on the interplay between Verses 5:32 and 5:33 prohibiting the killing of Muslims without right. When he spoke of "protecting the Ummah" in accusing Wahhabi jihadis of bringing "mischief to the land," Qaradawi associated their actions with crimes that trigger the Verse 5:33 requirement that "punishment of those who … strive with might and main for mischief through the land is: execution, or crucifixion, or the cutting off of hands and feet from opposite sides, or exile from the land." In the same communication, however, Qaradawi also opened the door to reconciliation if al-Qaeda "renounced" its "fanaticism and extremism" — i.e., its Wahhabi takfirism. The fault line underlying this tension revealed itself as recently as the exchange between ISIS and the Brotherhood on June 28, 2014, when ISIS declared the caliphate and its leadership of it in "This is the Promise of Allah — English Declaration of the Khaliphate."[65] In that declaration, ISIS took a swipe at the Brotherhood (and possibly the OIC as well), going so far as to imply takfirism.[66] This prompted Qaradawi, in his capacity as chief Brotherhood jurist and head of the International Union of Muslim Scholars (IUMS), to declare the new caliphate "void under sharia"[67] and "lacking any realistic or legitimate standards."[68]

While Qaradawi may have to strike a balance with Muslim entities that violate the "killing without right" standard, he is under a significantly reduced obligation to do so with respect to non-Muslims. At the Egyptian Journalist Union in Cairo in 2004, Qaradawi stated:

> All of the Americans in Iraq are combatants, there is no difference between civilians and soldiers, and one should fight them, since the American civilians came to Iraq in order to serve the occupation. **The abduction and killing of Americans in Iraq is an obligation** so as to cause them to leave Iraq immediately.[69]

It is important to understand Qaradawi's statements in the context of the overall narrative. For Qaradawi and the Brotherhood, when the objects of violence are non-Muslims in Muslim lands, the commitment to jihad remains unchanged and obligatory. This is not just the position of the Brotherhood. Al-Azhar lined up in support of Qaradawi's position, with statements released from Dr. Abd al-Mu'ti Bayyoumi, former Dean of the Faculty of Religious Fundamentals; Dr. Salih Zaydan, Al-Azhar lecturer; Sheikh Mansur Al-Rifa'i Ubeid, former Undersecretary of the Department of Religious Endowments; Dr. Abd Al-Azim Al-Muta'ani, Al-Azhar lecturer and former member of the Supreme Committee for Islamic Affairs in Cairo; and Dr. Abd Al-Sabour Shahin.[70] Qaradawi may be right: When non-Muslim forces enter Muslim lands, jihad is obligatory. And remember, jihad is not terrorism.

We can look to the Brotherhood for further proof of this concept. Mohammed Mahdi Akef was the General Guide of the Brotherhood from 2004 to 2010. In a 2006 Al-Jazeera interview, he made the following comment about jihad:

> I fear that blood will be shed for no price. I want blood that is shed for a price. ... This American Satan claims to be a messenger of divine guidance. ... I go back to the issue of Jihad. **Jihad is an individual duty incumbent upon every Muslim,** male and female, if any inch of the land of Islam and the Muslims is occupied.[71]

Akef's comment mirrors Qaradawi's 2007 statement on the duty of jihad, and it was because of language like this that a warrant was issued for Qaradawi in November 2014 for "incitement and assistance to commit intentional murder." The warrant was not issued by the United States, but rather by Interpol on behalf of the judicial authorities of Egypt for prosecution, with the full charge being "agreement, incitement and assistance to commit intentional murder, helping the prisoners to escape, arson, vandalism and theft."[72] However, Akef and Qaradawi's statements accurately reflect the Islamic legal requirement, as stated in *Reliance*:

Jihad is also personally obligatory for everyone able to perform it ... when the enemy has surrounded the Muslims on every side ... that ... must be met with effort and struggle to repel them by every possible means.[73]

If Islamic law is the criterion, both Qaradawi and Akef are correct when calling for mandatory jihad against American forces inside Muslim lands. In a later interview, Akef shared both Qaradawi's conditional approval of and concern about supporting jihadi groups like al-Qaeda. In 2008, remembering that Qaradawi raised the specter of reconciliation if groups "renounced fanaticism and extremism" in 2004, the Brotherhood's General Guide accepted Osama bin Laden as a member of the fold when designating him a holy warrior:

> *Interviewer:* As we talk about resistance and Jihad, do you consider Usama Bin Laden a terrorist or an Islamic Mujahid?
>
> *Akef:* **Most certainly he is a Mujahid.** I do not doubt his sincerity in resisting occupation for the sake of God Almighty.[74]

When bin Laden and al-Qaeda are "resisting occupation" — that is, fighting non-Muslim forces in Muslim lands as required by Islamic law, as when fighting and killing Americans — they are jihadis. Further questioning indicated that Akef (and, hence, the Brotherhood) makes the same distinctions with respect to terrorism as Qaradawi, which makes Akef's support of bin Laden as a mujahid conditional.

> *Interviewer:* Then, do you support the activities of Al-Qa'ida, and to what extent?
>
> *Akef:* **Yes, I support its activities against the occupier, but not against the people.**

Brotherhood guidance is simple and clear: If al-Qaeda limits its terrorism to non-Muslims, they will be forgiven and welcomed as heroes. If they kill without right, they will be condemned. Both Qaradawi and Akef define terrorism in ways that conform to shariah, support al-Qaeda in its jihad mission, and are doctrinally hostile to the United States.

If this is the position of the Brotherhood's chief jurist and general guide, it has consequences for Brotherhood-associated groups in America. The Fiqh Council of North America (FCNA) is an element of the Islamic Society of North America (ISNA) charged with the specific responsibility of clarifying Islamic law.[75] A review of its position on terrorism demonstrates it is in line with both the Muslim Brotherhood leadership and the "killing without right" standard. To see this, one must parse FCNA's statements and interpret them according to shariah.

Imam Yahya Hendi, in his capacity as a FCNA council member, issued a fatwa condemning terrorism on behalf of the group and, by extension, the Muslim Brotherhood of North America. Hendi, who serves as Muslim Chaplain at Georgetown University,[76] began his fatwa by identifying Islamic law as the authority, and then used language that followed Islamic form:

> The Fiqh, Jurisprudence, Council of North America (FCNA) wishes to address the issue of terrorism and how it is viewed in the Islamic legal and ethical system:
>
> **Islamic law has consistently condemned terrorism and extremism** in all forms and under all circumstances, and we reiterate this unequivocal position. Islam strictly condemns religious extremism and **the use of violence against innocent lives**.
>
> There is no justification in Islamic Law and ethics for extremism or terrorism. **Targeting civilians'** lives and property through suicide bombings or any other method of attack is haram — prohibited in Islam — and those who commit these acts are violators of the teachings of Islam and Shari'ah law, and therefore, **are not seen as "martyrs."**
>
> The Qur'an, Islam's Holy Scripture, states: "Whoever kills a person unjustly, it is as though he has killed all mankind. And whoever saves a life, it is as though he had saved all mankind." (**Qur'an, 5:32**) Recent killings are not justified and not condoned either by FCNA or Islam. **Attacks on civilians are not condoned by Islamic law** and are seen as Haram.[77]

Hendi "condemned terrorism and extremism" that is "against innocent lives." But then he qualified the condemnation to what is "prohibited in Islam" and further clarified it by stating that such acts violate Islamic law. By stating that those who violate Islamic law will not be seen as martyrs, Hendi indicated the fatwa was directed at Muslims who kill without right when engaging in suicide operations against fellow Muslims. He ratified the position by specific reference to Qur'an Verse 5:32, thus contextualizing the terms "civilians" and "innocent lives" with the 5:32 definition of unjust killing as the killing of a Muslim without right. While Hendi's fatwa is not misleading, it does mislead.

If the "killing without right" standard holds up in some authoritative capacity, one would expect to see some downstream consequences in the form of follow-on doctrines reflecting the natural consequence of such a rule. The Muslim community's position on suicide bombings is one such example. Not only has much of the Islamic world been aware of the distinction between "suicide bombing" and "martyrdom operations," authoritative voices on shariah played a key role in defining the difference between the two.

In June 2002, the Muslim American Society (MAS) published Sheikh Faysal Mawlawi's "Fatwa Questions about Palestine" in its monthly journal, *American Muslim*. Mawlawi is the Vice President of the European Council for Fatwa and Research (ECFR), a Dublin-based entity that disseminates Brotherhood-approved fatwas.[78] The president and founder of the ECFR is Qaradawi. Mawlawi explained in his fatwa that while martyrdom operations are justified, suicide bombings are not. Understanding the distinction between the two presupposes an existing understanding of the "killing without right" standard. Blowing oneself up to kill non-Muslims — especially non-Muslim forces — makes the activity a jihad and the actor a shaheed (martyr) if killed. Blowing oneself up to kill only Muslims equates to murder, and the actor is guilty of both murder and suicide. As Mawlawi wrote:

> **Martyr operations are not suicide** and should not be deemed as unjustifiable means of endangering one's life. Allah says in the Glorious Qur'an: "And spend of your substance in the cause of Allah, and make not your own hands contribute to (your) destruction: but do good: for Allah loveth those who do good." (Al-Baqara: 195)

> Prophet Muhammad strictly forbade suicide and made it clear that anyone who commits suicide would be cast into hell. But in such case, suicide means a man's killing himself without any lawfully accepted reason or killing himself to escape pain or social problems.

> **On the other hand, in martyr operations, the Muslim sacrifices his own life for the sake of performing a religious duty which is Jihad against the enemy as scholars say.** Accordingly, a Muslim's intention when committing suicide is certainly different from his intention **when performing a military operation and dying in the Cause of Almighty Allah**. This means that martyr operations are totally different from the forbidden suicide.[79]

It is only by understanding the "killing without right" standard that Mawlawi's fatwa makes sense. The "killing without right" criteria also establish a clear, bright-line standard from the perspective of Islamic law. For those who missed the fatwa's original 2002 publication in *American Muslim*, it was republished verbatim in 2007 in answer to a question put to IslamOnline's "Fatwa Bank" concerning the licit and illicit nature of martyrdom operations and suicide bombing. Mawlawi was the Brotherhood imam designated to answer it. Of particular interest, IslamOnline further bolstered the argument by favorably citing a January 2003 Resolution of the Islamic Fiqh Academy:

> 2. Terrorism equals illegal aggression, terror, threatening both in material and abstract forms which is practiced by states, groups or individuals against man, his religion, soul, honor, intellect or his property via all means, among **which is the spread of corruption on earth**.

> 3. The Islamic Fiqh Academy stresses that martyr operations are a form of Jihad, and carrying out those operations is **a legitimate right that has nothing to do with terrorism or suicide. Those operations become obligatory** when they become the only way to stop the aggression of the enemy, defeat it, and grievously damage its power.

> 4. The Islamic Fiqh Council asserts that jihad and martyr operations done to defend the Islamic creed, dignity, freedom and the sovereignty of states **is not considered terrorism but a basic form of necessary defense for legitimate rights**. Thus the oppressed peoples who are subjected to occupation have the right to seek their freedom via all means possible.

> In light of the above, there is no change concerning the Islamic ruling regarding martyr operations as such operations are considered true jihad in the Cause of Allah.[80]

The Islamic Fiqh Academy is neither a Brotherhood nor an al-Qaeda entity. The Academy's resolution is in line both with published Islamic law on the obligatory requirement of jihad and with Bin Laden's expression of it.[81] In fact, as noted, the statement is essentially a reiteration of *Reliance* at §o9.3. The Islamic Fiqh Academy is designated by the OIC as its authoritative shariah body. As a subsidiary organ of the OIC, the Academy's role is to ensure that OIC Member States conform their decisions Islamic law.

> *Objectives:* To achieve the theoretical and practical unity of the Islamic Ummah by striving to have Man conform his conduct to the principles of the Islamic Shari'a at the individual, social as well as international levels. To strengthen the link of the Muslim community with the Islamic faith. To

draw inspiration from the Islamic Shari'a, to study contemporary problems from the Shari'a point of view and to try to find the solutions in conformity with the Shari'a through an authentic interpretation of its content.[82]

In early 2003, on behalf of all OIC Member States and in advance of the U.S. invasion of Iraq, the Islamic Fiqh Academy issued its resolution ratifying the obligatory nature of jihad. Representing all Muslim countries at the Member State level, the Islamic Fiqh Academy not only endorsed the universal position on martyrdom operations, it also publicly expressed its Member States' concurrence. In this way, clear public notice was given to the entire non-Muslim world. This issue is not going away. As recently as August 2014, in a true example of convergence, Sheik Muhammad al-Suhaybani, imam of the prestigious Prophet's Mosque in Medina, Saudi Arabia, publically endorsed the killing of Americans (as Christians) in language that mapped to shariah (*Reliance* o9.3), was indistinguishable from the OIC declarations listed above, from the Brotherhood leadership's - Chief Jurist (Qaradawi) and General Guide (Badi), and from bin Laden's 1998 fatwa:

> All the pure blood that has been shed in Iraq for decades against whom are they waging Jihad? They are waging Jihad against the Christian American presence in Iraq. In Somalia and Afghanistan — is it not jihad? Are they not God-fearing? You (Arab rulers) have been remiss and neglectful, so you should have kept your mouths shut. Under these circumstances, you should have kept silent and feared Allah. Instead of that, they accuse the *mujahideen* of being kharijites ... Why? Did they rebel against the Emir of the Believers? No, they rebelled against infidels who invaded their countries. We pray for Allah to guide those (critics), so that they stop criticizing the mujahideen. If they do not pray for their success, they should at least stop criticizing them. In general, I consider them to be mujahideen for the sake of Allah, who are driving out the infidels who invaded their lands.[83]

This strongly suggests that the Muslim world is aware of and accepts the distinction between shaheed and suicide bomber that likewise presupposes the "killing without right" standard. On convergence, the Brotherhood, which had relied on an OIC resolution to justify its position on the obligatory nature of jihad, then conditionally endorsed al-Qaeda for undertaking operations in an effort that all parties agreed was lawful when not engaged in the killing without right.

In June 2010, the Muslim Public Affairs Council (MPAC) sent a letter to then-Senator Joseph Lieberman demanding a change in terminology in the War on Terror. Founded by Brotherhood members, MPAC is a part of the Islamic Movement. In the letter to Lieberman, MPAC president Salam Al-Marayati made it clear that the Council's opposition to Osama bin Laden was based on al-Qaeda's killing of Muslims without right:

> Rather, avoiding religious terminology in America's efforts to counter violent extremism makes strategic sense. It denies Al-Qaeda and its affiliates the religious legitimacy they severely lack and so desperately seek. For years, Muslim public opinion has decisively turned against Bin Ladin, Al-Qaeda and other terrorist groups **because of the immoral, unethical** and gruesome tactics they employ and because **the vast majority of their victims have been other Muslims.**[84]

As far back as 2003, MPAC expressed its reliance on the "killing without right" standard; the immorality stems from the killing of innocent Muslims. In its "Review of US Counterterrorism Policy: American Muslim Critique & Recommendations," MPAC maintained that:

> Like other religions, Islam sanctifies life and **forbids arbitrary killing**. On this the Quran is rather explicit: "… whosoever killeth a human being for other than manslaughter or corruption in the earth, it shall be as if he had killed all mankind, and whoso saveth the life of one, it shall be as if he had saved the life of all mankind." [**Quran, 5:32**][85]

When MPAC told Senator Lieberman that its objection to al-Qaeda is based on its violation of Islam's rules on "arbitrary killing," they were being consistent. The reference to "immoral, unethical and gruesome tactics" was in regard to tactics that violate Islamic law because they bring "mischief" to the land or, as the Islamic Fiqh Council Resolution's second point stated, they "**spread corruption on earth.**"[86] MPAC accepts the "killing without right" standard. It uses language that, although facially neutral and seems broadly applicable when viewed through a Western lens, should cause great concern when understood in terms of its known shariah influence.

There is powerful notice that this concept of terrorism reflects the universally recognized and understood standard within the Muslim world. When OIC foreign ministers, MPAC, Qaradawi, and others "reject any attempts to link Islam and Muslims to terrorism," it is possible that the ummah is correctly condemning linkages between Islam and terrorism, as defined in Islamic law, while nonetheless providing silent yet formal approval to what the non-Muslim world — especially the United States — defines as terrorism.

If this is true, and of course it is, the consequences of refusing to understand it has been severe. Being unfamiliar with Islamic law means being unaware of much of the Muslim world's actual position on terrorism as it immediately affects the United States.

Slander and Free Expression

Because the Islamic world defines human rights as shariah, understanding the OIC on its own terms (which is to say, according to Islamic law) requires a dispassionate investigation into shariah. As with the shariah definition of terrorism, there is another concept where Islamic and Western notions differ: freedom of speech.

Free expression is the bedrock freedom on which Western concepts of human rights are based. Advocates of liberty have historically understood free expression to be a definitional characteristic of open societies. In the United States, the initial amendment of the Constitution indicates the primacy of free expression. The framers of the Universal Declaration of Human Rights — understanding that free expression is linked with freedom of thought and conscience — mirrored the First Amendment's intent in Article 19:

> Everyone has the right to freedom of opinion and expression; this right includes freedom to hold opinions without interference and to **seek, receive and impart information and ideas** through any media and regardless of frontiers.[87]

The Cairo Declaration addresses free expression in its Article 22, using language that parallels that of the Universal Declaration:

> (a) Everyone shall have the right to express his opinion freely **in such manner as would not be contrary to the principles of the Shari'ah.**

> (b) Everyone shall have the right to advocate what is right, and propagate what is good, and warn against what is wrong and evil according to the **norms of Islamic Shari'ah.**

For those unmindful of shariah influence, the Cairo Declaration's facially neutral expression of freedom of expression does not appear to conflict with the Universal Declaration in any serious way. An analysis of what is forbidden under shariah will illustrate that this is not the case. To understand the extent of free expression in a society, it is necessary to understand the limits placed on that expression. To find those limits in Islamic societies, look to shariah as it relates to *defamation*, which includes Islamic notions of slander, talebearing, blasphemy, and, in certain instances, lying. From *Reliance of the Traveller*:

> Slander and talebearing are two of the ugliest and most frequently met with qualities among men, few people being safe from them. I have begun with them because of the widespread need to warn people of them. ... *Slander* **(ghiba) means to mention anything concerning a person that he**

would dislike.[88]

As for talebearing ... it consists of **quoting someone's words to another in a way that worsens relations between them**.[89]

According to this definition, to slander someone is to say something about a person that he would dislike. This is not the Western understanding of slander. In the American (and broader Western) understanding, slander is a defamatory statement expressed in transitory form, usually speech,[90] while libel is a defamatory statement expressed in a fixed medium — usually writing but also in pictures, signs, or electronic broadcast.[91] In this discussion, the terms "slander" and "defamation" will be used interchangeably. Both concern defamatory expressions understood to involve the "act of harming the reputation of another by making **a false statement** to a third person." Falsity is important to U.S. legal claims of defamation, so much so that "if the alleged defamation involves a matter of public concern, the plaintiff is *constitutionally required to prove both the statement's falsity* and the defendant's fault."[92]

In other words, defamation in America requires the defaming statement to be false for defamation to exist. If someone accused of defamation can prove that his statements are true, he will normally defeat any defamation claim. As will be shown, this is not necessarily true with Islamic notions of slander, libel, and defamation.

r2.6 The Prophet (Allah bless him and give him peace) said: (1) "The talebearer will not enter paradise." (2) "Do you know what slander is?" They answered, "Allah and His Messenger know best." He said, "It is to mention of your brother that which he would dislike." Someone asked, "What if he is as I say?" And he replied, "If he is as you say, you have slandered him, and if not, you have calumniated him." (3) "The Muslim is the brother of the Muslim. He does not betray him, lie to him, or hang back from coming to his aid. All of the Muslim is inviolable to his fellow Muslim. [93]

Under the shariah slander regime, someone can be guilty of slander even if what is said is true. Getting more specific, from *Reliance*:

In fact, **talebearing** is not limited to that, but rather **consists of revealing anything whose disclosure is resented**. ... The reality of talebearing lies in **divulging a secret,** in revealing something confidential whose disclosure is resented. **A person should not speak of anything he notices about people besides that which benefits a Muslim**.[94]

Slander in Islamic law does not necessarily concern questions of truth or falsity but rather the inviolability of Muslims and, by extension, the Qur'an, Islam, and its Prophet. Slander is saying something disfavored by Islam. As will be discussed in greater detail, this helps to explain the severe punishment associated with violating the compact of submission, as stated earlier in o11.10 (5), by "mention[ing] something impermissible about Allah, the Prophet, or Islam."[95] When someone from the Islamic world levels an accusation of defamation, it is important to recognize the possibility that the accusation could be based on an entirely different understanding of the word. There are, however, six reasons for permitting slander, only one of which we will review. From "Permissible Slander," in *Reliance*:

> Slander, though unlawful, is sometimes permissible for a lawful purpose ... the legitimating factor being that there is **some aim countenanced by sacred law that is unattainable by other means.**[96]

This means that when an issue favored by shariah cannot be advanced honestly, then defaming an opponent or his issue becomes permissible. This can take the form of accusing someone of defaming Islam or, as has become the narrative, of Islamophobia. When governing entities in America — the U.S. State Department, Justice Department, or DHS, for example — take action against a person because an Islamic entity has charged him with slander or defamation, they run the risk of attacking a citizen for what he had a right to say, if what he said was true.

Aside from *Reliance of the Traveller*, Professor Hashim Kamali's *Freedom of Expression in Islam* (1997) details the current state of Islamic law on defamation.[97] It is a contemporary treatise on freedom of expression in Islam from the perspective of a moderate Muslim professor from a moderate Muslim country. Kamali is a professor of law at the International Islamic University in Malaysia, where he teaches Islamic law and jurisprudence. His career outside academia was that of a jurist, not a theologian. **The distinction is important because this book focuses on law and legal analysis, not theology and hermeneutics.** After discussing the similarity between Islamic notions of blasphemy, apostasy, disbelief, and heresy, Professor Kamali establishes the basic criteria for blasphemy:

> The principal offense of blasphemy in Islam, which I shall address in the following pages, is the reviling of God and the Prophet Muhammad, and a contemptuous rejection of their injunctions. The *'ulama'* of the various schools have expounded on the words, acts and expressions which amount to a renunciation of the faith. These include insults to God Most High and the Prophet, irreverent and contemptuous statements that outrage the religious sensibilities of believers, acts such as throwing the Holy Qur'an on a heap of rubbish, giving the lie to the fundamentals of law and religion, and so on. These have all been identified as words and acts

that at one and the same time amount to apostasy, disbelief, heresy, and blasphemy.[98]

Kamali then explains that shariah notions of blasphemy are likewise applicable to non-Muslims:

> THE BLASPHEMY ON A NON-MUSLIM. There are three possible situations where a non-Muslim may be involved in blasphemy against Islam:
>
> When a non-Muslim professes an article of his own faith which happens to contradict the Islamic creed, such as when a Christian states that Jesus is the son of God. However, this is, from the viewpoint of Islam, a simple variety of disbelief rather than actual blasphemy.
>
> When a non-Muslim says something which although part of his belief, is said in an offensive manner. An example of this is the incident which occurred after the call to prayer, when a Jew addressed the muezzin with the words 'you lied'. **The case here is similar to any involving a non-Muslim scorning an article of the Muslim faith or any of the injunctions of God that are contained in the Qur'an. In this case, if the non-Muslim is a *dhimmi*, he loses his protected status and becomes liable to punishment**.
>
> When the insult in question is not a part of the faith of its perpetrator, and consists of something which is equally forbidden in his own religion. No distinction is made, in regard to this type of blasphemy, between Muslims and non-Muslims, as anyone who reviles God commits a blasphemous offence, regardless of his or her religious denomination.[99]

Because Professor Kamali wrote his treatise to discuss the current state of freedom of expression in the Muslim world from a legal perspective, he included a survey on the status of freedom of expression laws in a number of Muslims countries in an appendix. This indicates that Muslim countries currently recognize the legal status of such laws and have codified them in their law:

> In Appendix IV, which appears at the end of this volume, I have presented a brief account of the law of blasphemy in Malaysia, Indonesia, Pakistan and Egypt. A section has also been devoted in Appendix V, to Salmon Rushdie's novel, *The Satanic Verses*, where I have reviewed some of the opinions and responses proffered by contemporary jurists and commentators.[100]

It is a relevant fact that Islamic law of defamation exists as law in Muslim jurisdictions. *Reliance* makes clear that it can be applied to non-Muslims in theory, and Kamali explains that it is to be imposed as a matter of fact. With regard to blasphemy or defamation of Islam in a modern context, Kamali was explicit:

> I begin my presentation here with a general statement that **classical Islamic law penalizes both blasphemy and apostasy with death** — the juristic manuals of *fiqh* across the *madhahib* leave one in little doubt that this is the stand of the law. Yet, despite **the remarkable consistency** that one finds on this point, the issue of punishment by death for apostasy is controversial.[101]

Kamali states that defamation against Islam by a Muslim is a form of blasphemy that is considered apostasy. Once a Muslim has slandered or blasphemed, he may be considered outside of the Muslim community. Unless retracted, this carries potentially severe penalties that can rise to the level of a capital offense. From *Reliance of the Traveller*'s treatment of acts considered apostasy:

> Among the things that entail **apostasy from Islam** ... are: ...
>
> (4) to revile Allah or his messenger ...
>
> (5) to deny the existence of Allah ...
>
> (6) to be sarcastic about Allah's name ...
>
> (15) to hold that any of Allah's messengers or prophets are liars, or to deny their being sent ...
>
> (16) to revile the religion of Islam ...
>
> (19) to be sarcastic about any ruling of the sacred law ...
>
> (20) or to deny that Allah intended the prophet's message ... to be the religion followed by the entire world ...[102]

When writing that this "leave[s] one little doubt that this is the stand of the law," Kamali is describing the consensus view of Islamic law *today*. *Reliance* confirms it. Kamali makes it very clear that Islamic law understands the punishment for blasphemy to be death, and, despite the fact that people don't always like it, the controversy exists precisely because it is settled law. In fact, Kamali explains that there is no controversy in the statement of the law itself.

If defamation or blasphemy is considered apostasy from Islam that warrants death for a Muslim, what is the penalty for non-Muslims who slander or blaspheme against Islam or Mohammed? To start with, it is worth examining what happens to dhimmis, or those who have submitted to Islamic rule by becoming non-Muslim subjects of the Muslim state. Once again, *Reliance of the Traveller* states:

> **The agreement** [with the dhimmi] **is also violated** ... if one of the subject people ... (5) **mentions something impermissible** about Allah, the Prophet, or Islam.[103]

Reliance continues:

> When a subject's agreement with the state has been violated, the Caliph chooses between the four alternatives mentioned above in connection with prisoners of war (o9.14)[104]

For submitted non-Muslims, Islamic slander is a serious crime, comparable to apostasy. In a sense, slander is the offense of blasphemy applied to non-Muslims. Once again, we revisit §o9.14 to recall that dhimmi status is that of a prisoner of war in a state of abeyance. The importance of this review is that it shows how this concept is put in motion in the service of enforcing defamation. If the non-Muslim breaches the dhimmi compact, he reverts to the status of a prisoner of war.[105] A **dhimmi is less than a second-class citizen; his status in law is that of a prisoner of war in a state of abeyance**. The text from §o٩,١٤ of *Reliance* is concerned with the "Rules of Warfare":

> When an adult male is taken captive [the women and children are made slaves], the Caliph ... **considers the interests ... of Islam and the Muslims** ... and decides between the prisoner's death, slavery, release without paying anything, or ransoming himself in exchange for money or for a Muslim captive held by the enemy.[106]

This is a concern. When some Muslims accuse non-Muslims of defamation or "hurt feelings," they are making an accusation that establishes the right to kill.

Aside from *Reliance* and *Freedom of Expression in Islam*, there is additional support for this understanding of slander, defamation, and blasphemy from classical Islamic texts. My briefings often contain information that is not much more difficult than what would be taught to a seventh-grader. To ensure this, I rely on three books that are recommended to seventh-graders by Yahiya Emerick in *What Islam is All About:*[107] *Tafsir Ibn Kathir*, a recognized official translation,[108] which we've already heard from; *Kitab Al-Tabaqat Al-Kabir*, by Ibn Sa'ad, translated by S. Moinul Haq;[109] and *The Life of Muhammad*, a sacralized biography translated from Ibn Ishaq's *Sirat Rasul-Allah*, by A. Guillaume.[110] Ibn Sa'ad's book relates the following event:

> Asma was the wife of Yazid Ibn Zayd Ibn Hisn al-Khatmi. She used to revile Islam, offend the prophet and instigate

the people against him. She composed verses. Umayr Ibn Adi came to her in the night and entered her house. Her children were sleeping around her. There was one whom she was suckling. He searched her with his hand because he was blind, and separated the child from her. He thrust his sword in her chest till it pierced up to her back. Then he offered the morning prayers with the prophet at al-Medina. The apostle of Allah said to him: "Have you slain the daughter of Marwan?" He said: "Yes. Is there something more for me to do?" (Vol. 2, p. 31)[111]

Ishaq corroborates this account:

When the apostle heard what she had said, he said, "Who will rid me of [Asma bint] Marwan's daughter?" Umayr b. Adiy al-Khatmi who was with him heard him, and that very night he went to her house and killed her. In the morning he came to the apostle and told him what he had done and he [Mohammed] said, "You have helped God and His apostle, O Umayr." When he asked if he would have to bear any evil consequences the apostle said, "Two goats will not butt their heads about her," so Umayr went back to his people.[112]

The next paragraph says:

The day after Bint Marwan was killed the men of Banu Khatma became Muslims because they feared for their lives.[113]

Ibn Sa'ad and Ibn Ishaq's works are used ubiquitously as part of Islamic instruction. Both works date to the earliest periods of Islam and are recognized as Islamic classics that serve as a basis for instruction as early as the seventh grade for American Muslim children. They also fully support the juristic concepts of Islamic slander. The lesson here is that non-Muslims are subject to Islamic slander laws and have been from the beginning of Islam — and the penalty has, from the beginning, included death à la bint Marwan. This is known and taught in the Islamic community, even in America, and it confirms what Kamali said about the penalty for non-Muslims when they "blaspheme" today. When being briefed on this material, senior national security decision-makers often ask, "I understand what you're trying to say, but how do you know it's true?"

"Sir, there are people, even cute little children, who make posters that say, 'Kill those who defame Islam,' and hold them up in public places."

"Ha, ha, ha! That's really funny. But seriously, how do you know it's actually true?"

"No, sir, there really are people who make posters that say, 'Exterminate those who slander Islam,' and 'Massacre those who insult Islam.' They stand in public places holding them up, providing actual NOTICE (legally understood) to their non-Muslim neighbors of the rules of slander in shariah — so that those rules can be fairly enforced against them. They're not allowed to enforce laws that they know the people do not know. Because there is real intent to enforce Islamic slander laws, there is likewise a real effort to put non-Muslims on NOTICE, as well."

"What Islam is All About" is the leading English text for 7th-grade-level instruction. Page 15 lists what the author considers the most authoritative sources on the life of Muhammad; those are the sources for this book.

As will be discussed later in greater detail, the Muslim world erupted for days in 2006 to protest a Danish magazine's publication of cartoons mocking the Prophet Mohammed. In the West, there was implicit recognition of the differences between Islamic and Western slander, defamation, and free expression. Many publications earnestly attempted to stand up for Western freedoms by republishing the cartoons. One American bookstore chain was fearful enough of the consequences of that type of activity to take action.

"For us, the safety and security of our customers and employees is a top priority, and we believe that carrying this issue [of

a magazine] could challenge that priority," said Beth Bingham, a spokeswoman for the Borders Group.[114]

As with most in the West, Borders executives were aware that people die
when things are "deemed insulting to Islam," even though they also generally insist that it has nothing to do with Islam. Nothing has changed since this Borders
pronouncement in the flush of the initial Cartoon Crisis in 2006. Shouting, "Allahu akbar" and "We have avenged the Prophet Muhammad; we have killed *Charlie
Hebdo*," armed jihadis claiming al-Qaeda affiliation stormed the Paris offices of
the newspaper *Charlie Hebdo* on January 7, 2015, killing 12 people, including the
cartoonists, editorial staff, and police.[115] It may be that those seeking to impose
shariah slander standards are aware that our law enforcement and constitutional
guardians have averted their eyes from this issue. At some level, everybody knows
that insulting Islam is a capital offense, and they know people have been hurt
or killed for it. The disassociation these intimidation campaigns are designed to
induce is remarkable. Commenting on the *Hebdo* killings that morning on MSN-
BC's *Morning Joe*, Howard Dean, former Vermont Governor and past Chairman
of the Democratic National Committee, felt compelled to claim counterfactually
and in the face of the obvious that the killings had nothing to do with Islam:

> You know, this is a chronic problem. I stopped calling these
> people Muslim terrorists. They're about as Muslim as I am. I
> mean, they have no respect for anybody else's life, that's not
> what the Koran says.[116]

*A newspaper's publicaion
of cartoons lampooning
Islam's Prophet, Muham-
mad, ignited a storm of
protests throughout the
Muslim world.*

The conditioning of such responses early in the preparation stage is an indicator of success in the dawah mission. Understood this way, Kamali's *Freedom of
Expression in Islam* and similar writings should be understood as instruments for

use in the initial sculpting phase (the preparation phase) of the future information battle space.

On blasphemy and defamation in Islam, we have seen ancient Islamic doctrines link up with contemporary shariah treatments of those same laws. The results are real and play out daily in the news. In fact, the Islamic understanding of slander, defamation, and talebearing end up being not only fundamentally different from Western notions but overtly hostile to the very notion of free speech. One need only review Kamali's discussion of freedom of expression to understand it is a fully grounded and well-understood legal concept in shariah. A central question of this book is how long we will continue to see such slander campaigns as being divorced from the OIC's Ten Year Program of Action. The effectiveness of this campaign will be measured by the degree to which Islamic speech laws are able to overwrite our protected speech as a de facto enforced speech code that effectively abrogates the First Amendment rights of Americans in the United States.

Non-Muslims, especially those with national security responsibilities, should know that because Islamic notions of slander are not analogous to Western notions of the same, an understanding of the one does not necessarily imply knowledge of the other. The inability to articulate these competing standards meaningfully in our analytical processes — either because we don't know them or because communication of them has been restricted — is negligence.

When accusations based on Islamic notions of slander, talebearing, and defamation — or Islamophobia — include either *true statements whose disclosure is resented or true sayings that do not benefit a Muslim or Islam*, then enforcement of this standard in normal discourse has the intended effect of suppressing otherwise protected speech. This is a recurring problem, as there are active measures in place to suppress discussions of Islam both in everyday discourse and as a part of the debate that drives national security analytical processes. The only people who are allowed to tell us about Islam are self-described moderate Muslims and cultural experts (or their approved proxies). Those presenting material similar to what you're reading in this book necessarily run afoul of Islamic concepts of slander — not always because they're wrong, but rather precisely because they are right. Enforcement of Islamic speech codes in national security analytical spaces suppresses relevant facts, rendering us unable to develop valid threat profiles. This leaves us powerless to defend against them. Yet, as former White House Counterterrorism Strategist Wiktorowicz made clear, the national security community is prohibited from engaging in such a discussion. [117] The enforcement of such a shariah standard constitutes a direct challenge to the First Amendment and a clear and present danger to the Republic.

When national security professionals bow to accusations of slander or defamation that meet the criteria under shariah but not under the Western understanding of those terms, they have, in effect, submitted to and are enforcing Islamic notions of defamation against U.S. standards of free speech and professional analysis. In such scenarios, otherwise protected speech is abridged and otherwise factual work product is suppressed. Properly understood, this should be unlawful.

As an operational matter, the relevant question is whether the information requirements of the United States in the War on Terror have been subordinated to what Islamic law allows us to know. Has conformance to Islamic information requirements put us in violation of our professional canons concerning the duty to know? And does that failure likewise put national security professionals in violation of their constitutional oaths to "support and defend"?

Let's Pause for a Moment. We have just learned of the OIC and that it represents the Islamic countries at the head-of-state level. We also learned that the OIC, by applying the 24/25 Rule to its facially neutral pronouncements, defines human rights as shariah, excludes acts of jihadi terrorism from its definition of terrorism, accepts the "killing without right" standard, and agrees on the duty of jihad when non-Muslims enter Muslim lands. From Part I, we learned that Muslim Brotherhood front groups which the national security community relies on for guidance and information certified *Reliance of the Traveller*,[118] a text of shariah that upholds those same views. From Part III, we know that *Reliance* also upholds the obligatory duty to lie[119] and that CAIR, the Hamas/Muslim Brotherhood front group, is actively engaged in the production of "two messages; one to the Americans and one to the Muslims."[120]

It is in this context that we should understand Wiktorowicz's concern:

> Not enough resources are being devoted to the counter-ideol-
> ogy component of the administration's strategy. The long war
> is the war against violent ideologies and there hasn't been the
> resource investment since 9/11.[121]

The former counterterror strategist goes on to say that "as a result of this and other factors, we're seeing the reincarnation of al Qaeda as ISIL in Iraq and Syria."[122] In other words, Wiktorowicz attributes the rise of al-Qaeda to our failure to counter the very ideology he says the counterterror community is prohibited from discussing on the ridiculous claim that such analysis violates the First Amendment. How does one allocate resources to counter an ideology that one is not allowed to discuss? As important, what staff judge advocate (SJA) would allow such a novel First Amendment doctrine, tailored to limit the constitutional duty to support and defend, to influence national security decision support processes? For Wiktorowicz, the solution is obvious: the Obama administration works with partners in the Muslim world "who can push back against the ideology."[123]

Not only have we outsourced our understanding of the critical information requirements that support warfighting decisions, it can be demonstrated in a factual manner that they have been outsourced to third parties who have actual hostile intent toward the United States and the American way of life. Because due diligence and quality assurance evaluations of our "partners'" counter-ideology efforts are effectively barred, it necessarily means that such efforts must be blindly accepted. This is actual submission of our national security interests to Islamic requirements that run contrary to those interests. While this analysis is far from being finished, enough information has been provided that, unless disproved or rebutted,[124] already establishes an analytical presumption[125] that should prevail unless contradicted or overcome by competing evidence.[126] The presumption, simply stated, holds that the strategy driving the War on Terror has been compromised and reduced to incoherence, and that the duty to support and defend has been eclipsed.

For those quick to cry bias and point out that Wiktorowicz is from the Obama administration, it must be noted that my concerns on the outsourcing of our decision-support awareness were first raised in 2005 under the Bush administration.

A First Pass at Defamation of Religions

The OIC's agenda on Islamic slander was not unique to the 1990s. The OIC outlined its objectives in September 1969, when Saudi Arabia first convened all the Muslim nations to unify "the struggle for Islam"[127] and temporarily established its headquarters in Jeddah, "pending the liberation of Jerusalem."[128] What follows is a brief history of the evolution of the defamation agenda through 2005.

In 1999, the OIC began to implement its agenda to curb free expression at the United Nations in a concerted effort to impose Islamic blasphemy laws on the world. Of course, attempts to silence criticism of Islam and Mohammed were not stated in so forward or threatening a manner. Rather, the OIC initiated blanket condemnations for any commentary or action deemed by its members to constitute "defamation" of Islam. The OIC introduced "defamation" resolutions at the UN every year from 1999 through 2010. In 2011, the OIC made no such resolution.[129]

The efforts began in September 1999 with a request from the Jordanian foreign minister,[130] Abdulilah M. al-Khatib, that the UN General Assembly assure that the international community:

> use dialogue to combat dangerous discriminatory practices, which we see today, such as Islamophobia. Islam is being subjected to a severe and unjustified attack, which attempts, intentionally or unintentionally, to establish a linkage between Islam and those extremist and terrorist movements that hurt Islam and Muslims by using religion as a tool. Discrimination and arbitrary practices against Muslim populations in various countries are only a result of extremist thinking, far removed from the principles of civilized behaviour and humanity. The international community must consider how to confront this phenomenon of Islamophobia in order

to prevent its proliferation."[131]

Since terrorists themselves often associate their actions with Islam, and in doing so violate human rights, the Jordanian foreign minister seemed to suggest that criticism of Islam amounted to defamation.

Also in 1999, Pakistan introduced at the UN Commission on Human Rights a "defamation of religion" resolution, with Islam as the only religion identified that could be defamed. It was adopted in April of that year, without a vote.[132] In it, the OIC specifically referred to its November 1998 position paper, presented in Geneva, "Enriching the Universality of Human Rights: Islamic Perspectives on the Universal Declaration of Human Rights." That document called upon governments globally to:

> counter intolerance and related violence based on religion or belief, including practices of discrimination against women and including desecration of religious sites, recognizing that every individual has the right to freedom of thought, conscience, expression and religion.[133]

Further, it expressed "deep concern":

> that Islam is frequently and wrongly associated with human rights violations and with terrorism [and over any use of] ... print, audio-visual or electronic media or any other means ... to incite acts of violence, xenophobia or related intolerance and discrimination towards Islam [and in preparation for the year of Dialogue of the Nations].

> Urges all states ... to take all appropriate measures to combat hatred, discrimination, intolerance and acts of violence, intimidation and coercion motivated by religious intolerance, including attacks on religious places, and to encourage understanding, tolerance and respect in matters relating to freedom of religion or belief.[134]

From the beginning of this OIC initiative, one can see how Islamic speech law was masked in the Islamophobia narrative so as to fit seamlessly into the multicultural narrative. In 2000, the Human Rights Commission struck a compromise, agreeing to combat "defamation of religions" by focusing on religious discrimination rather than issues concerning religious freedom. While India and the European Union both objected that the focus even in that regard was directed at only one religion, namely Islam, the Commission was distracted from promotiong religious freedom generally and freedom of all beliefs. But given an informal understanding that the issue would not be raised again, they nevertheless approved the resolution and allowed its adoption without a vote.

When the OIC broke its promise not to raise the issue in 2001, Western nations for the first time actively objected to yet another "defamation" resolution, which Pakistan introduced by equating Islamophobia with a contemporary form of racism. Belgium even complained that a General Assembly effort to halt crimes against women in the name of "honor" was considered defamation of religion.[135] But the April 18, 2001 resolution passed anyway, by 28 to 15, with 9 abstaining. This occured while preparations were underway for the notorious September 2001 UN Conference in Durban "against Racism, Racial Discrimination, Xenophobia and Related Intolerance," where disturbing sterotyping of religions, meaning Islam, led to the claim of "deep concern that Islam is frequently and wrongly associated with human rights violations and with terrorism." It also claimed that "defamation of religions" causes both social disharmony and human rights violations.[136]

Next, the OIC enlisted the aid of the Special Rapporteur on Racism, Racial Discrimination, Xenophobia, and Related Intolerance, Senegal jurist Doudou Diène, who, while serving from 2002 through 2008, published numerous reports, devoid of evidence, equating any complaint of Islamic extremism with racism against Muslims.[137]

In 2002, the UN Human Rights Commission voted yet again on a resolution called "Combating defamation of religion." This resolution won 30 approvals, against 15 opposing, with 8 abstentions.[138] The Commission produced a similar result in 2003.[139]

In April 2004, the Human Rights Commission adopted yet another resolution "combating defamation of religions,"[140] also by a rather wide margin, expressing "deep concern" over:

> negative stereotyping of religions and manifestations of intolerance in some regions of the world, and the **frequent and wrong association of Islam with human rights violations and terrorism** ... [and over] **intensification of the campaign of defamation** of religions and the ethnic and religious profiling of Muslim minorities [after 9/11].[141]

In all, the OIC and its Member States pushed seven "defamation of religion" resolutions at the UN Human Rights Commission every April from 1999 through 2005.[142] Still, as much as they attempted to silence criticism of Islam, they were unable to advance the agenda in the non-Muslim world where it mattered the most. Beneath the surface of the OIC's multicultural posturing, one can see the secondary meaning associated with Islamic notions of human rights and defamation.

Days of Rage

The soundest strategy in war is to postpone operations until the moral disintegration of the enemy renders the delivery of the mortal blow both possible and easy.

V. I. Lenin
Russian Revolutionary Leader

The OIC wasted little time initiating its Ten-Year Programme to "combat Islamophobia" after it was ratified in late 2005. It began with a full-blown information campaign directed at a set of cartoons. On September 30, 2005, the Danish newspaper *Jyllands-Posten* published a series of unflattering cartoons depicting the Prophet Mohammed.[1] Outrage in the Muslim world quickly intensified, creating what has been called the Danish Cartoon Crisis.

On the heels of the OIC's announcement of its Ten-Year Programme, which called for legislation and punishment for violations of Islamic law on slander and blasphemy, I noticed the addition of new players, an acceleration and intensification of provocative events, and an echo-chamber pointing in a single, unified direction. Something big was happening, and I could see the gathering storm. In January 2006, I sent emails to the Office of the Secretary of Defense, the Joint Chiefs of Staff, and the Special Operations Command warning of what was unfolding and explaining its seriousness. Nobody took the message seriously.

By mid-February, the Muslim world had worked itself into such a convulsive rage that the Cartoon Crisis gained intense media attention. I was asked in early March to brief Special Operations Command's (SOCOM) Strategic Communication Synchronization Conference on the matter. Recalling the January e-mail, they asked me to explain how I was able to warn them of these events by identifying and forecasting them with such precision before they occurred. The briefing brought the conference to a standstill.

The calculated manufacture of outrage is among the principle lines of operation that the OIC uses to implement its Ten-Year Programme of Action. The Cartoon Crisis was the prototype event in a campaign toward implementing Islamic principles of slander, giving rise to talking points and demands that have remained consistent through similar incidents. The rhetoric surrounding these events is identical and will be described and analyzed in detail in the following pages. The challenge is to identify elements of messaging that find their way into what should be recognized as a sustained strategic communications and information operations campaign.

During the Cartoon Crisis, I began to recognize a convergence among the ummah, dawah, and jihadi elements within the Islamic domain. This convergence centered clearly on the Islamic law of slander and the effort to implement it globally. Dawah, jihad, and ummah entities worked together to move the ball forward, with each element concentrating on its own principal function, from the nation-states and the supra-national OIC (the ummah) managing the meta-narrative, to the Muslim Brotherhood's Days of Rage as instigators (representing dawah), to the actual rioters infusing terror into the process (jihad). In these Programme of Action campaigns, it is important to note that groups like al-Qaeda are only peripherally involved.

Throughout the contours of this convergence, there is a place for all three components of the Islamic Movement. The ummah entities identify the offense and establish the narrative, dawah entities demand compliance, and jihadis—in this scenario, the incited mob—exact violence. For example, when Pope Benedict gave his lecture at a rarified Regensburg seminar, the ummah—represented by the OIC and leaders of its Member States—used the opportunity to attack him by calling his statements an outrage. Dawah entities around the world amplified the message to incite Muslim groups to elevated levels of anger, agitating for a Day of Rage (tacitly sanctioned by the ummah) and thus creating a permissive environment for jihadi violence—targeted rioting and murder. Yet no one is interested in pulling out their flowcharts and block diagram programs to connect these dots. Here is how the script unfolds:

1   *Ummah:* The OIC's Islamophobia Observatory presents material from real-time, so-called Islamophobic incidents, also known as infractions against Islamic law prohibiting slander.

1   *Ummah:* A suitable "crisis event" is chosen from this material—or manufactured outright—at the nation-state or OIC level. These events are always expressions of speech that, while violating Islamic notions of slander, have always been considered protected speech by the U.S. Constitution. A recognized narrative energizes the process and targets an offender.

1   *Dawah/Jihad:* The Muslim Brotherhood or other dawah entities use new and traditional media to foment outrage calculated to incite violence, called Days of Rage. These are quickly followed by bursts of violence targeting the interests of the offending non-Muslim party or state.

1   *Ummah/Dawah:* An echo chamber of governmental, NGO, and Brotherhood entities amplify outrage and (a) demand apologies from the offending nation-state, now intimidated; (b) use the opportunity to once again promote legislative solutions to curb blasphemy or slander against Islam; and (c) offer to play the "good cop" to avoid the actions of the "bad cops."

The dynamics of this convergence do not necessarily indicate—and do not require—a formal chain of command and control authority. Enforcement comes from the functional roles each entity plays based on the line of operation it holds and its orientation to Islamic law.

When the OIC made "Defamation of Islam" its standard, the punishment for transgressing that standard became enforceable by the Islamic Movement's dawah and jihadi entities. And, because the penalty for this crime according to shariah can be death, it becomes permissive for jihadi entities to take action. Stated differently, the OIC's decision to declare the slander standard establishes a permissive environment. Given the functional orientation of dawah entities, they would see their role as enforcing that standard by warning non-Muslims when a given event constitutes slander (according to Islamic norms). If the dawah condition goes unmet, a jihadi entity's functional orientation to Islamic law would require that action be taken.

Even as there may be no formal chain of command by Western estimations, there exists an efficient form of command and control that is determined by the requirements set by shariah and the functional roles of the players. It is difficult to recognize the relationship without understanding the discipline-enforcing role that shariah brings to Islamic entities expressly acting in subordination to its rules.

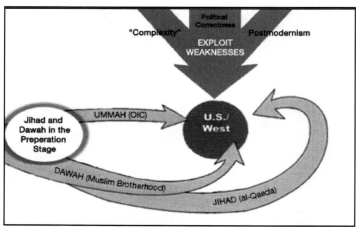

This graphic illustrates how a target group (the U.S./West, in this example) will experience multiple lines of operation against it simultaneously.

The following list shows significant events stemming from the ratification of the OIC's Ten-Year Programme of Action in December 2005. Notice the addition in 2009 of an important new category, Western Action, which refers to actual Western legal support for enforcing an action.

2005 Ten-Year Programme of Action ratified

2006 *Day of Rage:* Danish Cartoon Crisis
      Day of Rage: Pope Benedict's Regensburg Speech

2007 *Day of Rage:* Knighting of Salman Rushdie
      Warning: Pakistani demands on Rushdie and UK

2008 *Warning:* OIC targets Geert Wilders, presses for criminal prosecution

2009 *Western Action:* Geert Wilders charged with hate speech by Dutch court
      Western Action: U.S. co-sponsors UN Resolution on Defamation of Religions with OIC

2010 *Western Action:* U.S. government pressures Florida man for Qur'an burning

2011 *Day of Rage:* Qur'an burning in Afghanistan
      Western Action: U.S. Secretary of State makes Joint Remarks with OIC General Secretary

2012 *Day of Rage:* Riots around the Middle East in response to *Innocence of Muslims* film
      Western Action: U.S. jails *Innocence of Muslims* filmmaker

2015 *Escalation / Execution / Year ten of Ten-Year Programme of Action – Charlie Hebdo executions.*

If the goal of the Islamic Movement and the OIC is to institute Islamic law—beginning with its notions of slander—in non-Muslim jurisdictions, this carefully orchestrated drama is incomplete without recognizing some corroboration from the target population, represented above as Western Action. With feckless Western leaders responding as the Days of Rage intended, we can add the final element to the dynamics of convergence:

1   *Dhimmi:* Representatives of non-Muslim states, whether fearful of violent retribution or ideologically over-committed to "hate crime" curbs on free expression, apologize to the gravely offended among those in the Muslim community whose job it is to be outraged. Their actions usually range from (a) statements of condemnation of the offending speech that frame Muslim violence as the natural response to (b) promises to advance OIC treaties that circumvent the plain meaning of the First Amendment. After the Benghazi attack of 2012, an outrageous new milestone was reached in the non-Muslim world, including (c) criminal punishment and even prison time to appease Muslim demands for what was otherwise protected speech.

The "dhimmi" label seems appropriate. Regardless of how non-Muslim leaders in the West justify the actions they take—from tangible fear of violence to multicultural or "hate crime" rationales—by caving to shariah curbs on free expression, our representatives are, in fact, bringing their populations under the sway of shariah. Kamali, in *Freedom of Expression in Islam*, records a traditional Islamic position on dhimmitude that captures this dynamic:

Imam al-Shafi'i is said to have held that the protected status of the *dhimmi* terminates when he commits blasphemy and that, consequently, he becomes an enemy of war (*harbi*), in which case the head of state is within his rights to punish him as such. Imam al-Shafi'i adds that in this matter the head of state has discretionary powers similar to he has with regard to prisoners of war, that is, over whether to kill the offender or ask for ransom, and over whether or not to expropriate his property.[2]

While our leaders choose to remain unaware of the consequences of their actions, they are nevertheless operating under degraded norms of free expression and imposing them on the population. Understood this way, the supra-national campaign to stamp out Islamophobia actually represents a purposeful, directed hostile foreign assault on First Amendment free expression standards.

The Ten-Year Programme came in the wake of the OIC's failed efforts to criminalize blasphemy on an international level. Since 2006, the OIC has harnessed the power of disparate elements of the Islamic community to this single purpose. The chapters that follow describe how the pieces fit together.

Islamophobia

Both Islamic law and the intent to enforce it are real. Islamic principles of free expression—based on Islamic jurisprudence on slander, defamation, talebearing, and blasphemy—differ greatly from Western, or at least non-Muslim, conceptions of this fundamental human right. As we have seen in the case of slander, shariah also applies to the behavior of non-Muslims, both as non-Muslim subjects of the Islamic state and in jurisdictions in the dar al-harb. Given the imperative to spread shariah as the law of the land, it is only natural that an entity capable of such an effort throughout "the four corners of the world" engages in a campaign to do so.[3] As an organization that makes plausible claims to represent the Muslim Ummah, the OIC is well situated to embark on a campaign to impose Islamic legal standards globally, beginning with the subordination of free expression to Islamic law.

The framers of the Cairo Declaration made a point of defining human rights *as* shariah. In the Islamic context, this is a valid equation. Yet the OIC's use of the term "human rights" is also an indication that it understands the importance the West places on this language in global forums. This is not completely an issue of subterfuge. Today, many Islamic thinkers have so thoroughly assimilated the terminology of Western trans-national forums and high-level bureaucratic conferences that, in some elite circles, representatives of the Muslim world understand their own worldview as comfortably sitting in Western postmodernism narratives. Before he was a leading Middle Eastern studies expert, Edward Said was in the vanguard of literary deconstructionism. In a sense, Islamophobia is simply deconstructionism applied. Islamic law enters into the Western world through the diversity-friendly Islamophobia construct.

The term "Islamophobia" emerges from the chain of "phobias" that left-leaning minority-rights groups affix as clinical-sounding descriptors to critics of their agendas. Islamophobia is not descriptive, however, for it is purposefully imprecise; it is used chiefly as a blunt rhetorical object, impugning the motives and mental state of those at whom it is hurled. The construction "-phobia" nearly always suggests an irrational or unfounded fear that is linked to a mental pathology. The Mayo Clinic defines it as "an overwhelming and **unreasonable fear** of an object or situation **that poses little real danger.**"[4]

Abdur-Rahman Muhammad, a "former radical Islamist," said that the Brotherhood-associated International Institute for Islamic Thought (IIIT) developed the concept of Islamophobia, as it is currently used, in the 1980s to "emulate the homosexual activists who used the term 'homophobia' to great effect." The group meeting at IIIT, he said, "saw 'Islamophobia' as a way to 'beat up their critics.' "[5] The OIC has taken control of the term's usage and retains control of its application for use in hostile information campaigns. The term Islamophobia has become, in effect, a brand that is managed by the OIC. When we see the word Islamophobia we should instantly be aware that it represents an OIC campaign package that seeks its implementation internationally as well as in America, with support from the Brotherhood through front groups that, as the Explanatory Memorandum says, "adopt Muslims' causes domestically and globally ... and support the global Islamic State wherever it is."[6]

In the non-Muslim world, Islamophobia has also been closely associated with the efforts of a left-leaning independent research and social policy agency since the mid-1990s called the Runnymede Trust. Founded in London in 1968 as a think tank dedicated to domestic race relations, the group eventually shifted its focus from combatting anti-Semitism to researching and advocating for the increasing population of Muslims in Britain. In 1996, it formed the Commission on British Muslims and Islamophobia and in the following year published *Islamophobia: A Challenge for Us All*.

Conflating ideological elements with racial matters, *Islamophobia: A Challenge for Us All* set the tone for pseudo-analysis in the decades to come. The OIC, in its Third OIC Observatory Report (2010),[7] favorably relied on *Islamophobia: A Challenge for Us All*, going so far as to link to a brochure that prominently displays the notorious "closed view/open view" Islamophobia matrix.[8] The book argues that "Islamophobia refers to unfounded hostility towards Islam," which it claims leads to "hostility in unfair discrimination against Muslim individuals and communities and to the exclusion of Muslims from mainstream political and social life."[9] While the book reflects the political activism of the Runnymede Trust, it also resembles an information campaign to impose a narrative by favoring "open views" that reflect diversity and multicultural standards over targeted "closed views" that were to be — and still are — disfavored. In Runnymede's simplistic but effective paradigm, everyone is supposed to be "open" and should be made to feel isolated and looked down upon when "closed." Throughout the paper, "closed views" of Islam are contrasted with "open views" along a very suspect and subjective axis. For example,

> *Closed View:* Islam is seen as a single monolithic bloc, static and **unresponsive to new realities**.

> *Open View:* Islam seen as **diverse and progressive**, with internal differences, debates and development.

In chameleon-like fashion, Runnymede casts Islamophobia as the modern equivalent of anti-Semitism.[10] It also provides a disparaging definition of Christians in an effort to genericize the term "fundamentalism," assigning the term a negative connotation.[11] One suspects that Runnymede would harshly criticize this approach as a form of Islamophobia if it were directed at an Islamic practice as opposed to a Christian one.

Of course, Runnymede recognizes that "Islamophobia" lacks a coherent definition and that its associated narratives are hostile; it's inherent in the design. To deflect these criticisms, *Islamophobia: A Challenge for Us All* places these concerns in the mouths of its critics so that it can acknowledge these truths while at the same time dismissing them. From the mouth of the "critic," what we really have is the mission statement of the Islamophobia initiative back in 1997:

> The term [Islamophobia] is not, admittedly, ideal. Critics of it consider that its use panders to what they call political correctness, that it stifles legitimate criticism of Islam, and that it demonises [sic] and stigmatizes anyone who wished to engage in such criticism.[12]

Watching the interplay between left-leaning groups like Runnymede Trust and the OIC (or the Brotherhood), it's important not to lose sight of the fact that Islamic scholars have established the knowability of Islamic law based on the unchanging revelation of the Qur'an, the hadith, and scholarly consensus. Describing the "fixed inner sphere" of Islamic law as "diverse and progressive"—meaning, presumably, that no system exists for enforcing the stability of the doctrine over time—is incorrect. While there are variations across the schools of Islamic jurisprudence, the range of possible legal opinions is circumscribed and does not affect those aspects of shariah that are relevant to national security, such as jihad and the relations between Muslims and non-Muslims.

Starting with its first report on the subject in 1996, the OIC has relied on the Runnymede Trust for its application of Islamophobia. Still, Runnymede's calculated ambiguity about the term's precise meaning persists. At a September 2013 meeting of the Organization for Security and Co-operation in Europe (OSCE) in Warsaw, former Runnymede staffer Robin Richardson—author of *Guidelines for Educators on Countering Intolerance and Discrimination against Muslims: Addressing Islamophobia through Education*—conceded again that, in regard to the word Islamophobia, "terminology is important and we've got the wrong terminology. ... I'm not ashamed that our language isn't good enough."[13]

Lost in its own ideology, or perhaps because of it, Runnymede is in the position, as we have seen with its tortured use of "open" and "closed" views, of trying to maintain a postmodern narrative that supports the OIC's Islamophobia initiative. It is through the scientism of groups like Runnymede that the -phobia construction is able to mask shariah initiatives that seek to criminalize not just expression, but also thought, in postmodern terms. To accomplish this, the OIC expanded the definition of the postmodern use of terms like racism. In November 2007, OIC Secretary General Ekmeleddin Ihsanoglu decried:

> **defamatory** campaigns that seek to incite a particular civilization against another, thereby inflaming violence, hatred and extremism, and ultimately leading to terrorism.

> As reiterated by the OIC, the international community must counter **campaigns of calumny against Islam** and Muslims to prevent the spread of Islamophobia which attempts to cause a rift between civilizations, a situation that has become **a new form of racial discrimination**.[14]

By casting Islamophobia as a new form of racism, the OIC masks Islamic submission campaigns in narratives calculated to appeal to politically correct audiences. Runnymede serves this purpose. The goal is to criminalize Islamic notions of slander in non-Muslim jurisdictions. Furthermore, according to the OIC, defamation "seeks to incite a particular civilization against another" — the so-called "rift between civilizations." In this language, one begins to see the shifting of responsibility for acts of violence from the perpetrator to the victim. The word "calumny" used here must be understood as it is defined in Islamic law. The insistence that "the international community must counter campaigns of calumny against Islam and Muslims" constitutes a state-sponsored demand that non-Muslim jurisdictions implement shariah doctrines of slander against its non-Muslim citizens.

Consider the final communiqué of the Third Extraordinary Session of the Islamic Summit Conference in 2005. Remember, because it was a summit, it consisted of the heads of state of the OIC Member States. From Section II, "In the Political Field":

> The Conference underlined the need to collectively endeavor to reflect the noble Islamic values, counter Islamophobia, **defamation of Islam** and its values and desecration of Islamic holy sites, and to effectively coordinate with States as well as **regional** and **international** institutions and organizations to **urge them to criminalize this phenomenon as a form of racism**.[15]

That expansive definition of racism—"based on discrimination **and disparagement** on a cultural, rather than biological basis"—was on display at the 2001 Conference of Foreign Ministers in Bamako, Mali. From a section titled "Contemporary Forms of Racism":

> Contemporary forms of racism are based on discrimination

and disparagement on **a cultural, rather than biological basis**. In this content, the increasing trend of Islamophobia, as a distinct form of xenophobia in non-Muslim societies is very alarming.[16]

The term "disparagement" is an indicator that the OIC understands criticism of Islam as a "contemporary form of racism." As we have seen in *Reliance*, the Islamic view of disparagement is essentially defined as slander when it comes to things related to Islam or Muslims. In this case, the relevant language on talebearing is worth reviewing: "A person should not speak of anything he notices about people besides that which benefits a Muslim …"[17]

Note that "racism" as defined by the OIC falls under the category "Contemporary Forms of Racism"—which does not comport with standard notions of racism because it has nothing to do with biology or race. The next paragraph makes it clear that the desired outcome is the "elimination" of such "disparagement," i.e., speech:

> The Committee for the Elimination of Racial Discrimination and the Commission on **Human Rights** along with its subsidiary bodies and mechanisms, **have an important guiding role in the elimination of the contemporary forms of racism. All governments should cooperate fully** with the Committee and the Special Rapporteur on the Contemporary Forms of Racism, Racial Discrimination, Xenophobia and Related Intolerance with the view to enabling them to fulfill their mandates and to examine the incidents of **contemporary forms of racism, more specifically discrimination based on religion, including against Islam** and Muslims.[18]

So "contemporary forms" of racial discrimination are actually based on something else entirely. Obviously, this is not the racism that United States Code was written to enforce. The 2001 OIC Bamako document continues:

> The World Conference considers that the **defamation of an individual's religion** provides the basis of, legitimises [sic] and inevitably leads to the **manifestation of racism, including in their structural forms,** such as **Islamophobia** against the adherents of that religion. Furthermore, the **defamation of religions**, including its denial is a primary source of both **the persistence and mutation of racism**. UN organs and specialized agencies should therefore strengthen their collective efforts together with the relevant intergovernmental organizations, such as the OIC, to implement programmes

and **undertake initiatives to combat the defamation of religions and manifestations of this in any form.**[19]

The OIC's alarming description of Islamophobia as "a contemporary form of racism" is echoed by others in the Islamic community. Turkish Ambassador Ömür Orhun, former Personal Representative to the OSCE, currently serves as Adviser of the Secretary General of the OIC on "Combating Discrimination and Promoting Human Rights." In 2011, Orhun authored a paper titled "Challenges Facing Muslims in Europe." It was subsequently endorsed by the OIC and posted on its website in English. Just like Runnymede, Orhun spoke of the lack of a commonly agreed-upon definition of Islamophobia just before providing the OIC's more expansive (and official) one:

> Islamophobia needs but lacks a commonly agreed definition. It has often been defined as "fear or suspicion of Islam, Muslims, and matters pertaining to them." **I think that this is a rather narrow definition.** I prefer to base my definition on the following concepts:

> "Islamophobia is **a contemporary form of racism** and xenophobia motivated by unfounded fear, mistrust and hatred of Muslims and Islam. Islamophobia is also manifested through intolerance, discrimination and **adverse public discourse against** Muslims and **Islam.** Differentiating from classical racism and xenophobia, Islamophobia is mainly based on radicalization [sic] of Islam and its followers."[20]

Underneath the purported lack of a "commonly agreed definition" of Islamophobia, there invariably rests a very concrete definition that is explicitly based on OIC constructs. At this point, it makes sense to apply the 24/25 Rule: Since the OIC has made clear that "Shari'ah is the only source of reference for … explanation or clarification" on matters of human rights, it can only point to Islamic standards of slander and punishment. Because so few understand the interplay between the postmodern narrative and shariah, predominantly non-Muslim international bodies have allowed their discussion on Islam to be controlled by entities that define human rights according to shariah and, in the process, have implemented those standards. For the OIC:

Defamation = Racism = Defamation of Religions = Islamophobia

At the center of this process is the left/Islamist alliance. Allowing left-leaning multicultural organizations like Runnymede to take point in the development and implementation of Islamophobia narratives in Western venues introduces a measure of ambiguity that provides ummah entities like the OIC with room to maneuver. In many respects, the Runnymede relationship perfectly reflects the thinking behind the 1982 Muslim Brotherhood document, seized in Lugano, Switzerland, that holds that, in order for "gradual efforts aimed at gaining control of local centers through institutional action in furtherance of establishing an Islamic power [government] on earth"[21] to succeed, they must "avoid the Movement hurting itself with major confrontation"[22] early on. They do this by resorting to the "principle of temporary cooperation" through "limited contacts between certain leaders, on a case-by-case basis, as long as these contacts do not violate the [shariah] law"—but they "must not give them allegiance or take them into confidence."[23] For the OIC, Runnymede is a tool to be used for a purpose, then disposed of when no longer needed.

An example of how this ambiguity creates room for maneuvering arose at that same 2013 OSCE Conference in Warsaw. As noted, original Runnymede staffer Robin Richardson acknowledged that the group's definition of Islamophobia was seriously defective. Seeing that the Islamophobia narrative was under direct public assault in an international forum, Umut Topçuoğlu, Counselor to the Permanent OSCE Delegation of Turkey, played on the ambiguity by seemingly distancing the Islamophobia discussion from the OIC's while suggesting a retreat from the Islamophobia definition:

> You, Sir, mentioned that the Turkish delegation provided a definition of Islamophobia which came from the Organization of Islamic Cooperation [that] my delegation provided in some previous sessions or meetings on tolerance and non-discrimination [that] was formulated by a retired Turkish ambassador, Mr. Ömür Orhun. ... But the point is that the definition was formulated by someone who has deep experience in these affairs and who actually worked within the OSCE in these affairs, so I think saying it's an OIC definition is really sort of distorting the facts.[24]

Yet even with all the contrived confusion, Counselor Topçuoğlu could not help but tip his hat to the real status of Islamophobia when, a few days later, he said:

> One other thing I wanted to mention is I keep hearing "the official definition brought by the Turkish Delegation, the official definition of the Turkish Delegation," now, the definition you're referring to ... of course there is no official agreement among the OSCE States ... as long as you go on saying "the official definition by Turkey, the official definition by Turkey," well, I mean, you're doing our advertising, maybe it'll become the official definition.[25]

Because Turkey is an OIC Member State and Ambassador Orhun represented Turkey at both the OSCE and the OIC, the 24/25 Rule demands that analysts understand that Orhun's treatment of Islamophobia is consistent not only with regard to the OIC's definition of Islamophobia but also with Turkey's treatment of Islamophobia in such international forums as the OSCE. (For a more detailed discussion on how the OIC interoperates with left-leaning groups like Runnymede in international forums, Appendix 2 "The OSCE" is a case study that provides greater detail on the events of that forum.)

Islamophobia provides the OIC with a linguistic mechanism to advance its contention that any criticism of Islamic doctrine, Islam's leading figures, and Islamic practices—however barbaric or true—constitutes a hate crime, "defamation of Islam," based on a new form of racism.

As we will soon see, Islamophobia is immediately associated with an OIC initiative to criminalize the speech of non-Muslims in non-Muslim jurisdictions through the auspices of the United Nations. Since at least 2005, we have been on formal notice that the term Islamophobia is under the active control of state actor foreign powers. As a foreign instrument that seeks enforcement through extralegal means over the First Amendment, the OIC's campaign should be understood to be hostile, as should all activities that facilitate it. As Josef Pieper warned, once a foreign power controls a country's speech, it will ultimately control its thought.

The Islamophobia Observatory and Its Targets

As mandated by the Ten Year Programme of Action in December 2005, the OIC called for the creation of an "Islamophobia Observatory," charged with monitoring and reporting all issues of Islamophobia on an annual basis.[26] It is essentially a state-sponsored collection effort targeting non-Muslims living in non-Muslim jurisdictions, including the United States, for the purpose of intimidation and attacking their free speech rights. Ihsanoglu expressed satisfaction with the "daily, 24-hour documentation of every single occurrence" of Islamophobic speech.[27] The Observatory, together with its reports, is a documentation process in furtherance of creating pretexts to launch multi-tiered information campaigns.

The Islamophobia Observatory represents the OIC's capability to determine whether countries like the United States are in compliance with OIC requirements to enforce the Islamic law of slander (thus undermining the integrity of the First Amendment). This is important because, in order to enforce OIC-directed law in foreign jurisdictions, it has to be able to develop accurate assessment tools to measure a country's conformance to its standard.

By May 2006, the Middle-Eastern press announced the formation of the Islamophobia Observatory in Jeddah, Saudi Arabia. At the Senior Officials' Preparatory Meeting to the 33rd Session of the Islamic Conference of Foreign Ministers (i.e., a meeting of real state actors), OIC Secretary General Ihsanoglu said the aim of the Observatory was "to tackle the issue of Islamophobia head on."[28]

The OIC's annual *Observatory Reports on Islamophobia* purports to offer "a comprehensive picture of Islamophobia as it exists mainly in contemporary Western societies."[29] The first *Observatory Report* was released in March 2008,[30] the second in May 2009,[31] the third in May 2010,[32] and the most recent in June 2014.[33]

The OIC's Islamophobia Observatory has been issuing Islamophobia Reports on a regular basis since its creation. Properly understood, the Observatory's mission represents a collection effort by a foreign state actor directed against, among others, American citizens inside the United States when exercising their constitutionally protected speech. It is a hostile act. The titles of the *Observatory Reports* indicate that they are presented to OIC foreign ministers in council, which demonstrates that the reports reflect state action. For example: *Seventh OIC Observatory Report on Islamophobia October 2013–April 2014*, Presented to the 41st Council of Foreign Ministers, Jeddah, Kingdom of Saudi Arabia, 18–19 June 2014.[34]

Respect for All Religions, so Long as they are all Islam

Let's re-examine the first passage from the Ten-Year Programme of Action. The first item under the heading "Combating Islamophobia" says:

> Emphasize the responsibility of the international community, including all governments, to **ensure respect for all religions** and combat their defamation.[35]

"Ensure respect for all religions"? This sounds good. It seems inclusive, both interfaith and multicultural; it is something all of us can support. But remember the requirement to follow the 24/25 Rule. Per the Cairo Declaration, because the OIC definition of "human rights" is shariah, we must consider the statement "ensure respect for all religions and combat their defamation" in light of Islamic law to understand what the OIC means. That this statement is located in a section titled "Combating Islamophobia" should serve as an indicator.

To start, Islamic law does not allow for the actual recognition of other religions. The Qur'an—and Islamic law—recognizes *only Islam*. Surah 3 tells us that:

> Allah said, "If anyone desires a religion other than Islam (submission to Allah), [418] **never will it be accepted of him**; and in the Hereafter He will be in the ranks of those who have lost All spiritual good." (Qur'an 3:85)

Translator Yusuf Ali footnotes this passage with commentary #418:

> The Muslim position is clear. The Muslim does not claim to have a religion peculiar to himself. **Islam is not a sect or an**

ethnic religion. In its view all Religion is one, for the Truth is one. It was the religion preached by all the earlier Prophets. It was the truth taught by all the inspired Books. In essence it amounts to a consciousness of the Will and Plan of Allah and a joyful submission to that Will and Plan. **If anyone wants a religion other than that, he is false to his own nature, as he is false to Allah's Will and Plan.** Such a one cannot expect guidance, for he has deliberately renounced guidance.

If the Qur'an—the basis of all Islamic law—tells us that any religion other than Islam is "false," what does the OIC mean when it proposes, "to ensure respect for all religions and combat their defamation"? Further, in light of the 24/25 Rule, what can the OIC consider as other religions? In the section titled "Abrogation of Previously Revealed Religions," *Reliance* relies on hadith to shed some light on this question. In a rigorously authenticated hadith from *Sahih Muslim*, it says:

> By Him in whose hand is the soul of Muhammad (pbuh), any person of this Community, **any Jew, or any Christian who hears me and dies without believing** in what I have been sent with **will be an inhabitant of hell.**[36]

What does "defamation of religion" consist of? If published Islamic law is the criterion, then Book W, Section 4, "The Finality of the Prophet's Message," in *Reliance* tells us that "**Islam is the final religion** that Allah Most High will never lessen or abrogate until the Last Day."[37] For our purposes, the most important part is in paragraph 2 of Section 4:

> (2) **Previously revealed religions were valid in their own eras,** as is attested to by many verses in the Holy Koran, **but were abrogated by the universal message of Islam,** as is equally attested to by many verses of the Koran. Both points are worthy of attention from English-speaking Muslims, who are occasionally exposed to erroneous theories advanced by some teachers and Koran translators **affirming these religions' validity but denying or not mentioning their abrogation,** or that it is **unbelief (kufr)** to hold that the remnant cults now bearing the names of formerly valid religions, such as "Christianity" or "Judaism," are acceptable to Allah Most High after He sent the final Messenger (Allah bless him and give him peace) to the entire world. This is a matter over which there is **no disagreement among the scholars** ...[38]

Firmly stated here, the message becomes even more powerful when understood in light of the shariah we've already covered. Given that "denying or not mentioning" the abrogation of the other religions is described as "unbelief (*kufr*)," this rule tells us that anyone who thinks Christianity or Judaism is acceptable is subject to accusations of apostasy. When Section 4.1(2) is parsed with a proper application of the 24/25 Rule, the statement is boldly dispositive on three important points: (1) that all other religions have been abrogated; (2) that it is apostasy to believe otherwise; and (3) that this is a universally held doctrine within the Sunni world because there is consensus among the scholars—ijma. This explains the statement that "it is unbelief (*kufr*) to hold that the remnant cults," such as Judaism or Christianity, are "acceptable." What does *Reliance* mean by "unbelief"? In the chapter on "Apostasy from Islam"[39] in Book O, "Justice," Section 8, "Apostasy from Islam," we read that:

> Leaving Islam is the ugliest form of unbelief and the worst.
> (o8.0) **Whoever Voluntarily Leaves Islam Is Killed**. When a person who has reached puberty and is sane voluntarily apostatizes from Islam, **he deserves to be killed**. (o8.1)[40]

This principle in Islamic law is neither obscure nor outdated. As of 2006, first-grade students in Saudi Arabia are taught that "Every religion other than Islam is false."[41] When stating this position, the text specifically relies on the Qur'an verse we already encountered, Verse 3:85:

> God said, "If anyone desires a religion other than Islam (submission to Allah), never will it be accepted of him; and in the Hereafter He will be in the ranks of those who have lost All spiritual good." (Qur'an 3:85)

Published Islamic law, relying on recognized authority that cites authoritative hadith, validates the plain reading of Qur'an 3:85. That verse establishes the set of all religions recognized as valid by Islam as limited to Islam alone. This knowledge should influence our understanding of phrases like "respect for all religions" in a section on "Combating Islamophobia" when used by an entity that speaks for the Ummah (which the OIC emphatically says it does). When an entity that is explicitly beholden to Islamic law speaks of "defamation of religion," it means defamation of Islam and *only* Islam. Read with this understanding of what constitutes religion, the 2012 statement of a Turkish minister that "Christianity has ceased to be a religion but has become a culture of its own"[42] not only doesn't seem ridiculous, it actually makes sense.

When assessing the meaning of OIC statements, legal documents, and resolutions, it is crucial to use Islamic definitions of terms when they arise. The 24/25 Rule must be applied. Considering shariah on the subject of religions other than Islam, we now know what the OIC means by "respect for other religions." Following published Islamic law, the OIC simply does not recognize the legitimacy of other religions, specifically Judaism and Christianity. Such manipulation of terms and concepts with known dual meanings when dealing with non-Muslim audiences is perfectly in keeping with *Reliance*'s admonition "to employ words that give a misleading impression, meaning to intend by one's words something that is literally true, in respect to which one is not lying, while the outward purport of the words deceives the hearer."[43]

Days of Rage

The Danish Cartoon Crisis erupted in September 2005 after the Danish newspaper *Jyllands-Posten* published a series of 12 caricatures that depicted the Prophet Mohammed. Commissioned as part of the paper's editorial campaign to highlight the debate about criticism of Islam and self-censorship in Denmark, the images included the now-famous caricature of Mohammed with a bomb-shaped turban; another poked fun at the Islamic promise of 72 virgins awaiting the faithful who die in jihad. Diplomatic protests from Islamic countries and death threats from Muslims who believe Islam forbids the depiction of Mohammed began within days of the cartoons' publication. Months later, in February 2006, widespread violent protests broke out across the Muslim world after a delegation of Danish imams[44] toured Muslim capitals in an effort to stir up outrage.[45]

Days of Rage are calculated spasms of anger in the Muslim Street; they are violent protests where people have been killed. These events are intended to induce fear and extract groveling apologies, and they operate on the same principle as spousal abuse: The abusers threaten a population that, if they say what the abusers say is not permitted, hostile action will be taken and innocent people will be terrorized, hurt, and maybe even killed. The resulting violence is always the victim's fault. "Stop me before I kill again."

The Islamophobia/Day of Rage narrative was set. On January 29, 2006, *Arab News* reported that the General Secretary of the OIC had put the West on notice for violations of Islamic law, using the phrase, "the civilized **boundaries** of freedom."

> The **OIC represents fifty-seven countries** and Ihsanoglu said the Muslim world expected an apology. It is legitimate—it is the **legitimate expectation of 1.3 billion Muslims** that perpetrators of blasphemy who have **transgressed the civilized boundaries of freedom** redress the situation by extending an **unqualified apology**,[46]

That same day, the *Bahrain Tribune Daily* also quoted Ihsanoglu's bellicose comments on the cartoons:

> The angry reaction in the Muslim world … is mainly due to the premeditated and deliberate attack on the revered person

of the prophet, whose holy position, message and teachings were maliciously and calculatingly sacrilege by the so called defenders of freedom.[47]

It can reasonably be said that Ihsanoglu, as the Secretary General of the OIC, speaks for the organization's 57 Member States—several of which are considered allies in the War on Terror. As other examples are provided, please note the use of the term "unqualified apology," as this term conveys the sense of an ultimatum. Pakistani Prime Minister Nawaz went even further:

> The exiled former prime minister said the Muslim fury could spread further if the advocates of so-called freedom of expression failed to offer unconditional apology. He said **the culprits must be punished** and the **civilized countries must enact clear legislation** to check such incidents in the future. Nawaz said the UN Charter of universal ethical principles and even the Constitution of Denmark did not permit **hurting the feelings** of the people of other faiths.[48]

From the *Turkish Daily News*, we have the following comments from Tayyip Erdogan, then the widely touted "moderate" Prime Minister of Turkey:

> Turkish Prime Minister Erdogan, in a letter to world leaders, warns of "a dangerous escalation in tension over the publication of the caricatures of the Prophet Mohammed in European newspapers that is **threatening global peace and stability**." He said in his letter that **"Muslims could not be expected to tolerate** their Prophet being insulted in a manner that goes well beyond limits of criticism and said, "No culture has the right to insult sensitivities of another culture."[49]

The Chairman of the Saudi Foreign Affairs Committee in the Majlis al Shura (Consultative Council), Dr. Bandar al Ayban, told the Arabic London daily *Asharq Al-Awsat* that:

> [the Saudi government] **does not accept anything that harms Islam and the Prophet** or that destroys the friendly relations that link the Muslim world and the West, **under any pretext**.[50]

Mohammad Hamdan, the head of Norway's Supreme Islamic Council, gave voice to some rather threatening language in the Muslim Brotherhood-affiliated IslamOnline. The "grave consequences" comment made the threat explicit.

> The SIC condemns in the strongest possible terms the pub-

lishing of such offensive cartoons. These caricatures do no good for Muslims, Christians or even atheists, but will only shake that national unity to its foundation. **Editors should not take free speech as an excuse** to insult a certain religion; otherwise **they risk an extremist response** from the offended, which **carries grave consequences**.[51]

As the Cartoon Crisis continued to escalate, *Arab News* reported on the words of Saudi Sheikh Ali al-Hudaify, Imam of the Prophet's Mosque in Medina:

> He said many people in the past had tried to defame the Prophet: "They were thrown in the dustbin of history and nobody remembers them."[52]

None of these citations came from al-Qaeda or al-Qaeda-like jihadi groups. Indeed, the sentiments expressed were mainstream state actors in the ummah. Also note that the threatening language emanating from state actors is strikingly similar to that of non-state actors like the Muslim Brotherhood.

Not every article that uses the Day of Rage narrative explicitly calls for this kind of protest; these events usually come in clusters, and only a few authoritative Islamic figures have the stature within the ummah to make credible and influential headlines pronouncing it. The Muslim Brotherhood's chief jurist, Yusuf al-Qaradawi is one such figure.

As noted earlier, Qaradawi is not only the chief jurist of the Muslim Brotherhood, he is also the president and founder of both the European Council for Fatwa and Research and the International Association of Muslim Scholars. By inciting Muslims to "rage for the sake of Allah" on February 3, 2006, in connection with the Cartoon Crisis, Qaradawi defined what would soon become recurring Days of Rage.

> **"The nation must rage in anger.** It is told that Imam Al-Shafi'i said: 'Whoever was angered and did not rage is a jackass.' We are not a nation of jackasses. We are not jackasses for riding, but lions that roar. We are lions that zealously protect their dens, and avenge affronts to their sanctities. We are not a nation of jackasses. **We are a nation that should rage for the sake of Allah,** His Prophet, and His book. We are the nation of Muhammad, and we must never accept the degradation of our religion.... **"We must rage, and show our rage to the world ..."**[53]

Even *Asharq al-Aswat* acknowledged the role of the Muslim Brotherhood in organizing the Days of Rage (through Al Jazeera) associated with the Cartoon Crisis.

> "The Muslim Fury," one newspaper headline screamed the other day. "The rage of Islam sweeps Europe," said another. "The clash of civilizations is coming," warned one commentator. As you might have guessed, all that refers to the row provoked by the publication of cartoons of the Prophet Muhammad in a Danish newspaper four months ago. ... The "rage machine" was set in motion when the Muslim Brotherhood, which is a political and not a religious organization, called on its sympathizers in the Middle East and Europe to take the field. A "fatwa" was issued by Yussuf al-Qaradawi, a Brotherhood sheikh with a program on the *Al Jazeera* television channel that is owned by the Emir of Qatar.[54]

Let's take this apart. Qaradawi has one of the Sunni Muslim world's most popular television shows, with an estimated audience in the tens of millions. He not only calls for a Day of Rage, he issues a fatwa sanctioning it under Islamic law. Al Jazeera broadcasts across the entire Muslim world. Hence, not only does formal Muslim leadership in the form of heads of state legitimize the Days of Rage, the position is reinforced by the Brotherhood. For Qaradawi's fatwa to be broadcast, state actors had to permit it to be aired. From the beginning, the ummah and dawah entities were converged on the Islamophobia narrative.

Like the OIC itself, Days of Rage are not limited to the Sunni Muslim world. The *Bahrain Tribune* reported the Iranian president's praise for the violent protests on state radio.

> A leading Iranian scholar yesterday praised Muslims' "**holy rage**" against the publication of the Prophet Mohammed (peace be upon him) cartoons and accused the US of backing insults to Islam. The caricatures are at the heart of an international row that has seen angry and increasingly violent protests across the Muslim world, where any depiction of the Prophet is considered blasphemous. "Thank Allah the Islamic nation has shown itself well, it is a holy rage," Hojatoleslam Ahmad Khatami said in his Friday prayers sermon, carried live on state radio. ... Khatami urged Muslims to "**press on with your holy rage until you make them regret.**"[55]

The Shia Iranian president sounds just like Salafi Sunni Qaradawi. This is the **real** language of deliberate incitement. These are threats of real violence made by state actors against the citizens of a non-Muslim state actor for lawful actions taken within its jurisdiction.

As the Islamic world became increasingly incited to anger by the cartoons, violent riots broke out in Muslim communities across Africa, the Middle East, and as far east as Indonesia. The protests lasted for weeks and resulted in the deaths of more than two hundred people.[56] The Danish embassy in Damascus was burned down.[57] The number-two man of al-Qaeda, Ayman al-Zawahiri, broadcasted a call for Muslims to boycott Denmark, Norway, France, Germany, and others he claimed had "insulted the Prophet Mohammed."[58]

The campaigns incorporated physical intimidation, including direct threats of violence against individual "offenders," and Days of Rage calculated to intimidate leadership. On January 30, the OIC and the Arab League jointly called for a UN resolution and even suggested sanctions.[59] As the OIC is an inter-governmental organization, the Ten-Year Programme constitutes state action directed against people living in non-Muslim jurisdictions. It is in this context that one should recognize that Ihsanoglu had no problem manufacturing mob rage as a means to directly assault freedom of expression. Days of Rage have been the enforcement mechanism of the Ten-Year Programme since January 2006. As Ihsanoglu said:

> I do not blame the people who demonstrate but rather I blame those who motivate these people, and as I said, we have extremists on this side and there are extremists on the other side, and it is required of us that we follow the voice of sound mind in dealing with these people … the most important point here is that we have succeeded in the period since 2005 (the publishing of the Danish cartoons) succeeded internationally in that we issued reports from the Human Rights Council of the UN on how to deal with such issues …[60]

Turning a treaty on its head (and getting away with it), those driving the Day of Rage campaigns are guilty of the very "advocacy of national, racial or religious hatred that constitutes incitement to discrimination, hostility or violence" that the International Covenant on Civil and Political Rights actually "prohibits by law."[61]

The fear generated by this overt intimidation had its intended effect: capitulation and compliance with Islamic law on slander and blasphemy. The repercussions continued long after the initial publication of the cartoons, including a 2010 assassination attempt against Kurt Westergaard, the Danish artist who created the cartoons. Armed with an axe and a knife, a Somali Muslim man with possible connections to al-Qaeda broke into Westergaard's home on New Year's Day 2010 with intent to kill.[62] In March 2008, protests broke out anew after several Danish newspapers reprinted the cartoons following the arrest of several suspects who were accused of plotting another assassination attempt against Westergaard.[63] Westergaard survived. Prominent French cartoonists and editors at the *Charlie Hebdo* magazine were not so fortunate. On January 7, 2015, they were murdered when terrorists raided their offices for the specific purpose of "avenging the Prophet Mohammad."[64]

In the 2009 book about the Cartoon Crisis called *The Cartoons That Shook the World*, Danish-born author Jytte Klausen, a professor of politics at Brandeis

University, accepted Yale University Press's decision not to publish the cartoons.[65] To its credit, Denmark held firm in support of a free press. For Yale, on the other hand, cries for academic freedom ring increasingly hollow.

Days of Rage are coordinated information campaigns that operate at the leadership level. Besides the "unqualified apology" meme, other talking points emerged from the Cartoon Crisis that are worth reviewing, starting with "hurt feelings."

'Hurt Feelings' of a Billion Muslims

In the midst of the Cartoon Crisis, the rhetoric of "hurt feelings" crept into many statements of outrage from Muslims worldwide. The expression is not just used in sanctioned Days of Rage narratives; it has become a steady part of the rhetoric of Islamic grievance and usually indicates that one is being accused of violating Islamic slander laws. Beginning in December 2005, the *Arab News* reported:

> "Those cartoons are very offensive to every Muslim feeling, and to Islam as a religion," said Abdel Moeti Baoumi, a theology professor at Al-Azhar University in Cairo. "Do you expect Muslims to remain silent or rise and defend their religion?"[66]

From an editorial in the *Pakistani Observer*, the "hurt feelings" meme was advanced in conjunction with an ominous threat that "no Muslim can bear with such acts of provocation," acts which can only be off-set by the oft-demanded "unqualified apology":

> The **religious sentiments of Muslims the world over have been hurt** as a result of the publication of blasphemous cartoons in newspapers in Denmark and some other European countries. The ongoing protest demonstrations and violent incidents is an **unambiguous proof of the fact that no Muslim can bear with such acts of provocation. ...** These newspapers should tender **unqualified apology** to the Muslims to defuse the tension that has gripped the whole world.[67]

Another missive, in Karachi's *The News*, spoke of "hurt feelings," with a similarly threatening tone:

> It says over **1.5 billion Muslims** are followers of the prophet Muhammad and **their sentiments were hurt** by the publication of the cartoons. They demanded that the Pakistan government to sever diplomatic ties with the European countries.[68]

It is possible that the phrase "hurt feelings" reflects an Islamic term of art that conveys a harsher point that is lost in translation. There seems to be something more being communicated than mere "hurt feelings." The phrase is used as preparatory language in anticipation of intensified activity—in the event that groveling apologies are not forthcoming.

The "hurt feelings" narrative has been employed since the Cartoon Crisis. The attack on Pope Benedict's speech at Regensburg in September 2006 provides another example:

> Mimi Daher, a Muslim woman working in the ABC Jerusalem bureau, explained that the Grand Mufti in Jerusalem reflected this cultural mindset today when he said, "Muslims have to express their anger. Was the pope expecting Muslims to clap their hands to him while **hurting their faith and prophet**? Of course not. We call on Muslims throughout the world to react in a disciplined manner, according to our Islamic faith." As Gerges reminded me, when the cleric al-Qaradawi called for **a day of rage** …[69]

The U.S. Conference of Catholic Bishops conducts outreach to the Muslim Brotherhood, the very organization that Qaradawi leads. The language of "hurt feelings" was invoked again in January 2011 when Pope Benedict raised concerns about the Pakistani blasphemy laws that served as the rationale for assassinating a Christian Pakistani governor.

> The pope has given a statement today that has not only **offended the 180 million Muslims** in Pakistan, it has also **hurt the sentiments of the entire Islamic world**," said Hafiz Hussain Ahmed, a senior leader of Jamiat-e-Ulema-e-Islam.[70]

From the very beginning, those on the receiving end of Day of Rage campaigns—those in the West exercising their free expression—are routinely met with a phrase that paralyzes reason: "There are more than 1.x billion Muslims, and we just want to live in peace (unless …)"[71]

For example, on January 13, 2006, the *Arab News* quoted Dr. Abdullah al-Turki, Secretary General of the Muslim World League, who "warned of the negative consequences if the Danes did not conform to the demand to apologize by stating that 'such incidents anger over **1.5 billion Muslims who want to live in peace and harmony** over the world.'"[72]

This is the language of intimidation, similar to the language endured by women with battered wife syndrome. "You hurt my feelings. I'm bigger than you. It is your fault if I beat you up." Like a global battered wife, the non-Muslim world is supposed to submit under threat of actual violence that will be forthcoming.

Intimidation by numbers also serves a secondary purpose. For the postmodern West, the sheer number of those that clamor for prohibitions on insulting Islam is enough to coerce them into thinking that world peace cannot be achieved without the cooperation of that billion-plus. Down this road, free speech will be put to a popular vote and denied as a universal right. After all, if our most fundamental freedoms are simply a custom or preference—and ones that prevent us from living in harmony with 1.x billion of our fellow human beings—is it really that important?

Remember the words of the head of the OIC, taking note of the buzz phrases:

> It is the legitimate expectation of **1.3 billion Muslims** that **perpetrators of blasphemy** who have **transgressed the civilized boundaries** of freedom redress the situation by extending an **unqualified apology**.[73]

"Legitimate"? The OIC is stating what constitutes "civilized" behavior in the context of "free speech" in reference to Western jurisdictions. From *The News* (Karachi) on February 11, 2006:

> It said **over 1.5 billion Muslims** are followers of the Prophet Muhammad (SAW) and **their sentiments were hurt** by the publication of the cartoons. They demanded the Pakistan Government to sever diplomatic ties with these European countries.[74]

The OIC continues this "hurt feeling/1.x billion Muslims" narrative to this day. The Sixth OIC Observatory Report on Islamophobia, issued in December 2013, reported that the OIC had issued a resolution in November 2012 "condemning in the strongest possible terms the reprehensible release of the film 'Innocence of Muslims' on *YouTube* as a deliberate act of incitement to hatred that has **deeply offended more than a 1.5 billion Muslims** and all peoples of conscience around the world."[75] The report also noted a June 2013 speech that OIC General Secretary Ihsanoglu gave to UN diplomats in Geneva, Switzerland, on the "**alarming increase in Islamophobic incidents** like the Utoya massacre in Norway, the burning of Qurans by the Florida Pastor and release of the reprehensible trailer on *YouTube* [that] **continue to hurt the religious sentiments of over 1.5 billion Muslims**." He added, "the political leadership of OIC Member States has been calling for immediate remedial action."[76] From his comments, it is evident Ihsanoglu recognized that state action was taken to demand punishment where, in two instances, Days of Rage occurred.

Because the "1.x billion Muslims" is an OIC talking point, attention should be given whenever senior U.S. national security leaders make reference to it. When this happens, notice how the phrase carries a sense of futility and defeat, like when the general says, "There are 1.x billion Muslims. … What do you expect us to do?"

Watch for it. The next time you hear a national security decision-maker start a sentence with "There are 1.x billion Muslims," the next thing coming out of his or her mouth will be defeatist. This talking point was constructed to convey defeat to those willing to be intimidated. When our senior leaders say it, they are already beaten in their own minds.

The Pope and *The Satanic Verses*

On September 12, 2006, Pope Benedict XVI—who was once a professor and vice rector at the University of Regensburg, Germany—delivered a speech to a group of scholars that came to be known as his Regensburg Address. Entitled "Faith, Reason, and the University: Memories and Reflections," the text was an erudite reflection on the role of reason rather than violence in the inspiration of faith. The speech sparked a violent reaction from the Muslim world because of a reference to the words of the 14th-century Byzantine emperor Manuel II Paleologus.[77] Benedict quoted the emperor, speaking at a time when Constantinople was under siege from rampaging Islamic armies, as saying, "Show me just what Mohammed brought that was new, and there you will find things only evil and inhuman, such as his command to spread by the sword the faith he preached."[78]

Pope Benedict XVI was accused of slandering Islam. As noted, the Muslim Brotherhood—through its most prominent spokesman, Qaradawi—condemned him and called for a Day of Rage.

> Consistent with the cartoon crisis earlier, subsequent to Pope Benedict's remarks concerning Islam on 12 September 2006, Muslim Brotherhood scholar Yusuf al-Qaradawi called for "*Yaum al-Ghadab*"—a Day of Rage, that led to a weekend of riots and killing that included shooting a nun in the back.[79]

Again, this is the same Muslim Brotherhood that the U.S. Conference of Catholic Bishops (USCCB) conducts its outreach to the Muslim community. Soon, representatives of both dawah and ummah entities joined Qaradawi in publically inciting the Islamic world to violence. On September 31, 2006, *Pravda* reported:

> Haken al-Mutairi, Secretary General of Kuwait's Umma party asked Pope Benedict to immediately apologize "to the Muslim world for his calumnies against the Prophet Muhammed and Islam." The remarks have also drawn fire from Turkey's highest religious authority, reported Agence France-Presse. "The remarks reflect the hatred in his heart. It is a statement full of enmity and grudge," Ali Bardakoglu, the head of Turkey's religious affairs directorate said.[80]

Some of the harshest condemnation of the Pope's remarks came from Sa- lih Kapusuz, deputy leader of the ruling Turkish Justice and Development Party (AKP), who said Benedict would go down in history "in the same category ... as [Benito] Mussolini and [Adolf] Hitler," adding that Benedict's comments were a deliberate attempt to "revive the mentality of the Crusades."[81] Muslim leaders in Iran, Kuwait, Morocco, and Pakistan also condemned the Pope's remarks, de- manding an apology and clarification. In Iran, Ahmad Khatami, a hardline cleric in Qom, warned, "If the Pope does not apologize, Muslims' anger will continue until he becomes remorseful."[82] This issue is still unresolved. As recently as March 2012, Al-Jazeera unsuccessfully tried to get the Vatican to step back from Pope Benedict's Regensburg comment.[83]

A surge of violence erupted across the Muslim world and jihadi entities sprang to action, with Catholic communities in Africa and the Middle East bear- ing the brunt of the Days of Rage. A seventy-year-old Italian nun was shot four times in the back at the school where she worked in Mogadishu, Somalia; she later died in the hospital. Multiple churches in the West Bank were attacked with firebombs and burned.[84]

The effort to trample Western free speech on the topic of Islam is not just directed against governing entities; through skillful manipulation of the "inter- faith dialogue" narrative, it also targets religious non-Muslims who are encour- aged to view their Islamic interlocutors through the lens of their own religious worldviews. Institutional leadership of the Muslim world later responded to the Pope's Regensburg address with an initial 2006 "Open Letter" to Benedict that was signed by thirty-eight shariah scholars.[85]

For many in the non-Muslim world, the global furor over Salman Rush- die's fourth novel, *The Satanic Verses*, was their first exposure to the limits of free expression in Islam. His story should have served as the canary in the coalmine. Rushdie's 1988 book was a work of fiction that featured Mohammad abandon- ing monotheism to appeal to three goddesses worshipped in pre-Islamic Mecca. Rushdie, a UK citizen from India, used Al-Tabari as the source for his work of fiction,[86] winning numerous awards for *The Satanic Verses* worldwide.

Rushdie's book was offensive to Islam in a way that non-Muslims might find difficult to understand. Rather than disrespectfully mocking, lampooning, or criti- cizing Mohammed, the book depicted the Prophet in a way that would undermine the doctrinal validity of Islam's core teachings. For this reason, it clearly violated Islamic law. As an apostate, Rushdie had no standing in the Muslim world. On February 14, 1989, Iran's Supreme Leader, Ayatollah Ruhollah Khomeini, issued a short fatwa condemning Rushdie to death, along with anyone involved with the book's publication:

> The author of *The Satanic Verses*, a text written, edited, and published **against Islam, against the Prophet** of Islam, and

against the Koran, along with all the editors and publishers aware of its contents, are condemned to capital punishment. I call on all valiant Muslims wherever they may be in the world to execute this sentence without delay, **so that no one henceforth will dare insult the sacred beliefs of the Muslims.**[87]

The songwriter Cat Stevens (now Yusuf Islam), a convert to Islam, endorsed the Iranian fatwa in a speech in London during the controversy. Asked about Khomeini's pronouncement urging Rushdie's execution, Stevens answered that, "He must be killed. The Qur'an makes it clear—if someone defames the Prophet, then he must die."[88] Khomeini's fatwa served as a declaration of the worldwide violence that followed. While the moniker "Days of Rage" had yet to be used by Qaradawi, the carnage was the same. Tens of thousands protested violently in the Islamic world; thousands were injured and scores were killed.[89] Furious protests began in Muslim countries and made their way into non-Muslim countries. Stores that sold copies of *The Satanic Verses* were targeted and threatened; several were firebombed, including the offices of a community newspaper in New York that published an editorial supporting the right to publish and read the book.[90]

Prior to most of the worldwide outrage, the London-based Islamic weekly *Impact International* carried an editorial about *The Satanic Verses* signed by its then-publisher, Hashir Faruqi.[91] The piece was intended to amplify a campaign by the Muslim community in England led by the UK Action Committee on Islamic Affairs (ACIA), an umbrella group of Brotherhood-linked organizations. Faruqi's editorial echoed the ACIA's list of three demands directed at Penguin, Rushdie's publisher. Run under the title "Publishing Sacrilege is Not Acceptable," the piece is representative of more than just the efforts of a local pressure group; the rhetoric employed by Faruqi demonstrates the continuity of message from 1989 to today.

> Muslim organisations in Britain are, therefore, asking Penguin: (1) To withdraw and pulp all the copies of The Satanic Verses and to undertake not to reprint it in the future. (2) **To offer unqualified public apology to the World Muslim community.** (3) To pay damages equal to the returns received from the copies already sold in Britain and abroad.
>
> Failing which they are asking Muslim authorities to freeze all Penguin and Viking business in their jurisdictions and to exempt from copyright law such titles as may be needed for educational purposes. The book should be banned in any case, **but banning is meaningless unless it is accompanied by deterrent measures.**[92]

The piece quotes the then-secretary general of the OIC, illustrating the group's shariah-based agenda on blasphemy long before the Ten-Year Programme.

> **These demands have been supported by the Secretary General of the 46-nation Organisation of the Islamic Conference** (OIC), Syed Sharifuddin Piozada, who has called upon member states to "**take strong measures to ensure that this book is withdrawn from circulation by its publisher immediately and its copies are destroyed**" and "**the blasphemous book and its author must be banned from entry into all Islamic countries.**"

> Perhaps it would be more salutary if the author is allowed **to enter into Islamic jurisdiction and be prosecuted under relevant law**.[93]

The "relevant law" is clearly the Islamic legal prohibition against slander and blasphemy. For the OIC Secretary General, it wasn't an issue that requires clarification, nor did he seem to believe that, in any case, Rushdie would emerge from such a prosecution as anything but guilty. Prefacing the remark with "perhaps it would be more salutary," Faruqi indicated that the proper way of doing things is according to a known legal standard. Finally, he concluded by bemoaning the refusal of then-Prime Minister Margaret Thatcher to ban *The Satanic Verses*: "Definitely [the UK government does] not seem to be willing to think much of the **deeply hurt feelings within the Muslim community.**"[94]

There is a bloody history for those associated with *Satanic Verses*' translation. For example, Japanese scholar Hitoshi Igarashi was stabbed to death in July 1991 for translating the book; Italian translator Ettore Caprioli was wounded by a knife attack that same month; in July 1993, Turkish publisher Aziz Nesin printed extracts from the book and was cornered in a hotel by rioters, who then set fire to the building and killed thirty-seven people, though Nesin escaped; and Norwegian translator William Nygaard was shot three times and seriously wounded in October 1993.[95]

This brings us to the summer of 2007. After it was announced that Rushdie was to be knighted by Queen Elizabeth II for his work in literature, the global Islamic protests began afresh. This time, the OIC's Ten-Year Programme was in place to amplify the disparate efforts. Almost immediately, the intimidation began as the author was burned in effigy or protested against in Malaysia, Kuwait, Afghanistan, India, Iraq, Egypt, Pakistan, and elsewhere. In Egypt, the Parliamentary speaker condemned the government in London, describing its supposed misdeed as worse than the traumatic offenses that launched the Cartoon Crisis. "To honor someone who has offended the Muslim religion," he said, "is a bigger error still than the publication of caricatures attacking the Prophet Mohammed."[96] Hundreds in Pakistan's capital city of Islamabad chanted, "Our struggle will continue until Salman Rushdie is killed!"[97] At the same protest, Fazalur Rehman, a Taliban-supporting Islamic cleric and leader of the opposition in Pakistan's parliament, demanded that Britain "withdraw the knighthood and hand Rushdie to Pakistan to be **punished under Islamic laws.**"[98]

Perhaps no country was as aggressive on the world stage in response to the Rushdie knighthood as Pakistan. The Pakistani Foreign Ministry summoned the British High Commissioner in Islamabad.

> Salman Rushdie has been a controversial figure who is known less for his literary contribution and more for **his offensive and insulting writing** which **deeply hurts the sentiments of Muslims** all over the world. Conferment of a knighthood on Salman Rushdie shows **an utter lack of sensitivity** on the part of the British government.[99]

In addition to using many now-familiar OIC talking points associated with the Days of Rage campaigns, the Pakistanis upped the ante by framing their complaint in the language of international law. At the same meeting, the Foreign Ministry alerted the British of their potential violation of UN Security Council Resolution 1624, meant to "enhance dialogue and broaden understanding … [to prevent] **the indiscriminate targeting of religions** and cultures."[100] Note that almost no daylight exists between the OIC's messaging and that of its Member States.

The comments of Pakistan's Religious Affairs Minister were even more startling than the Foreign Ministry's. It made news around the world. As the *Washington Times* reported:

> Pakistan yesterday condemned Britain's award of a knighthood to author Salman Rushdie, and a **Cabinet minister said the honor provided a justification for suicide attacks.** "This is an occasion for the world's 1.5 billion Muslims to look at the seriousness of this decision," Mohammed Ijaz ul-Haq, religious affairs minister, said in parliament. "**The West is accusing Muslims of extremism and terrorism. If someone exploded a bomb on his body, he would be right to do so unless the British government apologizes** and withdraws the 'sir' title," Mr. ul-Haq said. … "The 'sir' title from Britain for blasphemer Salman Rushdie has **hurt the sentiments of the Muslims across the world**."[101]

It may sound strange that on the one hand the Pakistani Religious Affairs Minister Mohammed Ijaz ul-Haq calls for suicide attacks, and on the other he takes exception to accusations of "terrorism and extremism." To Westerners, it seems like just another rant or, worse, an example of cognitive dissonance at some pathological level. But is that really the case? With the information we have discussed on Islamic law of slander and terrorism, you may recognize that ul-Haq is making a specific series of rational statements that conform to shariah. Let's break it down:

1   A Pakistani cabinet minister in parliament said the knighthood awarded to Salman Rushdie provided a justification for suicide attacks. *Warning and formal notice is issued.*

2   Mohammed Ijaz ul-Haq is the Pakistani Religious Affairs Minister. In an Islamic Republic, the Religious Affairs Minister holds a powerful position. Moreover, he is the son of Zia ul-Haq, the country's president from 1978 until his death in 1988.[102] This means that a very powerful cabinet minister in Pakistan's parliament, who is part of a very powerful family, said that England's action provides a justification for suicide attacks. *The "fatwa" is issued by a minister with authority in parliament.*

3   To the charge that the West is accusing Muslims of extremism and terrorism, ul-Haq responds that a Muslim undertaking a suicide mission is "right to do so" and that it is not terrorism because it does not involve the killing of Muslims without right. *As was demonstrated in the discussion on Abrogation and later concerning the OIC, terrorism is defined strictly according to Islamic law. If Muslims are not targeted, strictly speaking, there may be no terrorism.*

4   The Pakistanis argued that a suicide mission in this case would not be extremism because notice was provided and time allotted for the knighthood to be withdrawn. *Because there was warning, it cannot be considered extreme.*

Because ul-Haq gave the UK notice, if the British authorities were to fail to comply with this demand, after a decent interval, action was justified. That is what happened. The British did not rescind Rushdie's Knighthood. Days later, Pakistani doctors in the UK loaded their upscale Mercedes with explosives, ready to commit acts of murder in downtown London. At the same time, a Pakistani medical school student in northern England tried to blow up a vehicle at the Glasgow airport.[103] Thankfully, they were apprehended.

There may have been no operational link between the Pakistani minister and the Pakistanis apprehended in the UK ready to unleash kinetic violence. An ummah element spoke, and jihadi elements agreed and therefore responded. No conspiracy was necessary, aside from a common understanding of shariah by those who agreed with a ruling that created a duty to act. So was an order issued, and was it carried out? Yes and yes. A call for action was issued by a person holding

state power. It was quite specific, with specific qualifications and specific consequences. There was nothing incoherent about it. And it was not al-Qaeda, the
Taliban, or the Muslim Brotherhood. Rather, it was a Coalition Partner. As discussed in Part II, this activity conforms to the Islamic concept of individual jihad
that the 1915 Ottoman Fatwa prescribed for the killing of Christians[104] and that
al-Qaeda said would be its preferred form of jihad moving forward in 2010.[105] It
is also what Homeland Security Secretary Jeh Johnson, designated as "lone wolf"
terrorism when characterizing the terror attacks on the *Charlie Hebdo* newspaper
in Paris on January 7, 2015. Using the dissociative narrative that delinks Islam
from jihadi actors, Johnson also said:

> "[These are] actors who may lurk within our society, that
> could strike with little notice, commit an act of violence be-
> cause they have been inspired by things they have seen on the
> internet, social media, in literature, without accepting a direct
> order … from a terrorist organization."[106]

There is a price to pay for adopting analytical processes that disassociate
clearly associated events. Returning to the Rushdie knighting, were those apprehended in the UK poor madrassa children given rucksacks and told to run from
Pakistan to the UK and blow themselves up because of issues of economic deprivation? No! But that is one of the preferred narratives we use to control our understanding of jihadi events. As our national security decision-makers fixate on theoretical models to define the enemy, they are consistently left with conclusions that
do not solve. Models that explain terrorist events through the lens of economic
deprivation insist that all terrorism is a product of economic circumstances, which
turns our focus on destitute and manipulated madrassa children. Of course, what
is taught in Pakistani madrassas is also taught in all Pakistani schools, including
the most prestigious, as part of the mandatory curriculum. As Federal Minister
of Education (and retired Pakistani Lt. General) Javed Ashraf Qazi stated, "jihad
will stay in the text books because it is an integral part of Islamic teachings and
Muslim beliefs.[107]

Fidelity to narratives provides the façade behind which the national security
community finds cover for its refusal to undertake fact-based threat development.
As we will see, it does this in furtherance of its aversion to slandering Islam. When
doing so, it conforms to Islamic law.

Geert Wilders on Trial

As we are beginning to see, the OIC seeks to assist the implementation of
its Ten-Year Programme of Action by manufacturing events in order to shock
and intimidate. The trial of Geert Wilders in the Netherlands is an example of
a high-profile attempt to impose Islamic speech standards on a high-profile
non-Muslim in a non-Muslim jurisdiction through the judicial offices of that

country's legal system. "By their hands!"

With an increase in immigration from Islamic countries and a high immigrant birth rate, the religious and cultural demographics of Holland are changing rapidly. An embrace of multiculturalism has, in the country's largest cities, empowered a Muslim minority that resists integration with Dutch society. This includes embracing Islamic law. Consequently, the Netherlands has experienced a spate of shariah-based assassinations, beginning with the openly homosexual Dutch politician and critic of Islamic immigration Pim Fortuyn in 2004.[108]

That same year, director Theo van Gogh collaborated with then-politician and former Muslim Ayaan Hirsi Ali on *Submission*, a short film criticizing Islamic doctrine and the treatment of women under shariah.[109] After the release of that film, Van Gogh was murdered on the street in broad daylight by a young Muslim. His crime was defaming Islam.[110] The assassin—calling himself the "Emir of the Muhajideen"—left two long letters, filled with Quranic verses and death threats addressed to the film's co-producer, Hirsi Ali.

> Since your appearance in the Dutch political arena you have been constantly busy criticizing Muslims and terrorizing Islam with your statements. ... With these hostilities you have unleashed a boomerang effect and you know that it is only a question of time until this boomerang will seal your fate. ... Islam will be victorious through the blood of the martyrs. They will spread its light in every dark corner of this earth and it will drive evil with the sword if necessary back into its dark hole.[111]

Shortly thereafter, Hirsi Ali moved to the United States, and she is still not safe in the Netherlands.[112] Even though she was an elected political figure in her adopted European country, she was told to fend for herself, as the local police could not protect her from potential Muslim assassins in the Netherlands.

On Ali's arrival in America, CAIR's communications director Ibrahim Hooper told reporters, "we believe that [Ayaan Hirsi Ali] will bring an increase to the level of anti-Muslim bias in this country that we saw her bring to the situation in Europe."[113] Hooper's condemnation can be understood as support of the view that Ali had violated Islamic law. When Muslim Brotherhood entities accuse someone of slander, there is reason to view the accusation as a threat against her safety, if not her life.

Van Gogh's assassin sent another threatening letter, in addition to one to Hirsi Ali. The second letter was addressed to Dutch politician Geert Wilders. "You must know Wilders," he wrote, "that Allah has sent the Messenger Mohammed (vzmh) with the Qur'an to warn you and your kind about **the consequences of your repugnant actions**."[114] Like Hirsi Ali, Wilders was being warned of the consequence of violating Islamic law. Following Van Gogh's murder, both politicians implemented around-the-clock personal security that has continued for nearly a decade.[115]

Geert Wilders is a Member of Parliament from the Netherlands and the founder and leader of one of the country's largest political parties, the Party For Freedom.[116] In 2007, Dutch intelligence and security officials reportedly demanded that Wilders "tone down" his rhetoric with regard to Islam. He refused.[117] In 2008, he told a hostile interviewer at *The Guardian*, "I have a problem with Islamic tradition, culture, ideology. Not with Muslim people."[118]

In 2008, Wilders released a short film called *Fitna*, named after the Quranic concept that describes the type of internal upheaval that upsets the well-being of the ummah. In terms of content, *Fitna* is a criticism of Islamic doctrine in pastiche form; Quranic exhortations to violence are interspersed with newspaper clippings and graphic video of bloodshed committed by Muslims in the name of Islam.

> "It's like a walk through the Koran," [Wilders] explains in a sterile conference room in the Dutch parliament in The Hague, security chaps hovering outside. "My intention is to show the real face of Islam. I see it as a threat. I'm trying to use images to show that what's written in the Koran is giving incentives to people all over the world. On a daily basis Moroccan youths are beating up homosexuals on the streets of Amsterdam."[119]

Even before the release of *Fitna*, prominent far-leftist Doekle Terpstra took to *De Telegraaf*, the largest paper in the Netherlands, and agitated against Wilders. "Geert Wilders is evil," he pronounced, "and evil has to be stopped."[120] Following this exhortation, death threats against Wilders intensified.[121] A coalition of radical leftist and Muslim groups soon demanded criminal prosecution of the filmmaker, littering the Dutch legal system with lawsuits and complaints. One Danish imam sought 55,000 Euros from Wilders to compensate for what he referred to as his "hurt feelings."[122]

At first, Dutch prosecutors conceded that, while "offensive," Wilder's "comments can be made in a political debate."[123] By the next year, however, the Dutch government bowed to pressure from Islamic groups. After the prosecutors decided not to pursue Wilders, the Dutch court that would hear his case demanded his prosecution. They ordered him to stand trial for "inciting hatred" in his public statements and for making *Fitna*: "In a democratic system, hate speech is considered so serious that it is in the general interest to draw a clear line."[124] Note how closely this language maps to the OIC narrative. He was charged with, "**insulting** as well [as] substantially **harm[ing] the religious esteem** of the Islamic worshippers."[125] The bias of the judges was so brazen that, in October 2010, "an appeals panel at the Amsterdam District Court … ordered judges in the trial of

MP Geert Wilders to step down, agreeing with Wilders' lawyers that the judges were biased."[126] In 2011, the Institute for Multicultural Affairs (FORUM) looked back on the case and summarized the appeals court's rationale:

> the appeals court was of the opinion that the majority of the comments were defamatory, as they **attacked the essential religious dignity** of Muslims. According to the court of appeal, **by attacking the symbols of Islam, Wilders in fact harmed Muslims themselves.**[127]

How biased were the judges? Wilders' first selection of expert witnesses—slated to include Theo van Gogh's assassin—intended to show that the statements of Islamic doctrine and quotes from the Qur'an he was being tried for expressing were true as a matter of fact and a matter of Islamic law. The court denied Wilders his witnesses.

> "It is irrelevant whether Wilder's witnesses might prove Wilders' observations to be correct," the [Dutch Public Prosecution] stated, "what's relevant is that **his observations are illegal.**"[128]

For such a ruling to come out of a Western court is shocking. It not only constitutes an assault on the truth, but also an assault on thought itself. Remember, Western notions of slander hold that being correct about something is a defense against liability. The new standard on Islamophobia sees this principle eviscerated. When disallowing Wilder's panel of experts, the judges essentially stipulated to the factual basis of his claims while asserting that they were nevertheless "illegal." *PressTV*, the Iranian government's news agency, likewise reported on the Dutch prosecution's harsh posture to free speech arising out of the same issue:

> But prosecutor Birgit van Roessel said that "expressing his opinion in the media or through other channels is not part of an MP's duties."[129]

What would a Member of Congress think if told that "expressing his opinions" through media outlets was not a part of his or her congressional duty? The Dutch court was forcing the prosecution of a man for saying something it knew to be true. While this seems alien from a Western legal perspective, it does align the Dutch court with the OIC position on Islamophobia, which is designed to enforce Islamic laws of slander at the expense of the free speech rights of Dutch citizens. This is not limited to the Netherlands. In April 2014, a British politician was arrested for "religious or racial harassment" in Hampshire when a member of the public took offense at his quoting Winston Churchill.[130]

Can quoting Islamic law in a critical but accurate manner qualify as slander? Returning to Book R, "Holding One's Tongue," in *Reliance of the Traveller*, we learn the following:

> ... **quoting someone's words to another in a way that worsens relations between them**. ... The above define slander and talebearing. As for the ruling on them, it is that they are unlawful, by the consensus ... of Muslims.[131]

We have already learned that scholarly consensus on a point of law means that the Sunni community recognizes this concept as being fixed in law and not subject to change. The clause that merits our attention now is this:

> (3) The Muslim is the brother of the Muslim. He does not betray him, lie to him, or hang back from coming to his aid. **All of the Muslim is inviolable to his fellow Muslim: his reputation**, his property, his blood. (r2.6)

This tells us that the Islamic concept of slander is at least in part specifically oriented toward Islam and Islamic identity; it concerns who is allowed to participate in that discussion and who is not. This is a different understanding of slander from ours in the West. Analyzing defamation in the context of shariah is important, because the OIC says its mission is to "[p]rotect and defend the true image of Islam and to combat defamation of Islam." Our reading of Islamic law tells us what is meant by defamation when the OIC makes such a claim. As defined in shariah and stated by the OIC, it is entirely possible that someone can say something that is entirely true about Islam *but that does not benefit Islam*. In such a case, that person would still be guilty under Islamic concepts of defamation and subject to potentially severe punishment.

In his speech at the 35th Session of the Council of Foreign Ministers of the OIC in June 2008, Secretary General Ihsanoglu described how Wilders' film *Fitna* related to free speech. He acknowledged that the film was purposefully used to target known "freedom of expression" standards:

> They have also started to look seriously into the question **of freedom of expression from the perspective of its inherent responsibility**, which should not be overlooked. [132]

What is the "inherent responsibility" of free expression as understood according to the 24/25 Rule? The "inherent responsibility" is Islamic notions of slander and blasphemy. When the OIC, its Member States, or subordinate elements speak of "freedom of expression," the term is exclusively controlled by the Cairo Declaration, which in turn ratifies Islamic law. The Cairo Declaration allows only for "freedom of expression" that is *not* "contrary to the principles of shariah." This necessarily holds true for the OIC and its Member States, as well.

When the Secretary General of the OIC talks about targeting *Fitna*, he is speaking on behalf of the heads of state of the 57 Member States. Ihsanoglu's statement was intended to bring the full weight of the Muslim world against Geert Wilders through the best efforts of his own country's court system.

It took until June 2011 for Wilders' trial to result in acquittal.[133] Why? Because (Islamic sensitivities notwithstanding) it was obvious that Wilders' statements were true. Even so, Dutch citizens are now on notice that their courts believe they are under some obligation to enforce Islamic speech standards against them. This is true even if the prosecutors themselves aren't aware of it.

The OIC wasted little time in voicing its displeasure with the trial's outcome. Through the Iranian government's news outlet, *Press TV*, Ihsanoglu and the OIC Foreign Minister openly demanded conformance to OIC requirements. After all, it does no good to force a show trial only to lose. The OIC denounced the outcome of the case, blaming a number of Dutch politicians for supporting Islamophobia. The article went on to quote the OIC Foreign Minister:

> Repeated cases of insult to individuals or their beliefs by people, organizations or radical groups, especially when supported by governments, are **unacceptable and cause a grave concern**.

What is the "grave concern"? Is this a threat of violence?

> **Wilders has taken a dangerous path**, endangering the peace and harmony of civilizations by spreading hate against Islam and Muslims in his own country as well as in other European countries. ...
>
> Insult to Islam and to the honored Prophet of Islam Hasrat Muhammad (PBUH), has reached a stage that can no longer be tolerated under any pretext including freedom of speech.[134]

There is a not-so-thinly veiled threat here. Indeed, it is a threat on top of a demand. The OIC Secretary General was telling the Dutch that the ruling was unacceptable and that they must take action—or else. Of course, under normal circumstances, Wilders would never have been prosecuted in the first place. His acquittal in Amsterdam was significant, not just for the victory of free speech principles over the OIC's Islamophobia agenda; it was also a demonstration of the encroachment and manipulation of traditional Dutch notions of tolerance by a vocal minority of immigrants. This vocal minority was heavily supported in its effort, from abroad by the OIC and in the Netherlands by the far-left. The very language of the prosecution echoes the OIC narrative. The Geert Wilders case should be understood to be a part of the OIC's attempt to implement its Ten Year Programme of Action. As a postscript, as of October 2014, Dutch prosecutors yet again opened an investigation on Wilders.[135]

All the examples in Part V of this book bespeak an active, hostile information campaign designed to subordinate and subvert Western free speech rights to Islamic law of slander through intimidation and violence lead by state actors. The trial of Geert Wilders was the first test case for the criminal prosecution of individuals in non-Muslim countries for reasons of shariah. Recall the words of OIC Secretary General Ekmeleddin Ihsanoglu on the issue in June 2008:

> In confronting the Danish cartoons and the Dutch film "Fitna," we sent a clear message to the West regarding **the red lines that should not be crossed.** As we speak, the official West and its public opinion are all now well-aware of the sensitivities of these issues. They have also started to look seriously into the question of freedom of expression from the perspective of its inherent responsibility, which should not be overlooked.[136]

Blasphemy and Deterrent Punishment in America

Well, I suppose I see a different world than you do, and the truth is that what I see frightens me. I'm frightened because our enemies are no longer known to us. They do not exist on a map. They aren't nations. They are individuals. And look around you, who do you fear? Can you see a face, a uniform, a flag? No! Our world is not more transparent now, it's more opaque! The shadows—that's where we must do battle. So before you declare us irrelevant, ask yourselves—how safe do you feel?

M

Addressing a Parliamentary Committee
Skyfall (2012)

By masking laws prohibiting Islamic concepts of slander and defamation in the language of diversity, tolerance, and multiculturalism, the OIC is succeeding at applying Islamic law to non-Muslim jurisdictions. As this book documents, the desire to install shariah as governing law has its roots in Islamic doctrine through the centuries, from Quranic mandates to modern jurisprudence. Similarly, the OIC has been demanding that the United Nations pass laws making blasphemy and "defamation of religions" a punishable crime internationally since 1999. The OIC considers criminalization of the criticism of Islam a key milestone and works relentlessly through the United Nations—as well as through bilateral and multilateral relationships, conferences, and "interfaith dialogue"—to achieve this end.

Things began to change in December 2005, when the OIC resolved to assemble capability and infrastructure to leverage all aspects of the information domain to the objective of making Islamic speech codes an enforceable international legal standard. At its Third Extraordinary Session in Mecca, the OIC approved its

"Ten-Year Programme of Action to Meet Challenges Facing the Muslim Ummah in the 21st Century." The most chilling aspect of this plan came under the heading "Combatting Islamophobia." The Ten-Year Programme described the OIC's goal candidly:

> Emphasize **the responsibility of** the international community, including **all governments**, to **ensure respect** for all religions and **combat their defamation**.
>
> Endeavor to have the United Nations adopt an international resolution to **counter Islamophobia** and to call upon all states to **enact laws to counter it**, including **deterrent punishment**.[1]

What is "**deterrent punishment**"? The OIC is demanding that the United Nations, the European Union, the United States and all other non-Muslim countries pass laws criminalizing Islamophobia. This is a direct extraterritorial demand that non-Muslim jurisdictions submit to Islamic law and implement shariah-based punishment over time. In other words, the OIC is set on making it an enforceable crime for non-Muslim people anywhere in the world—including the United States—to say anything about Islam that Islam does not permit.

UN Human Rights Commission Resolution 16/18 is the leading edge of the OIC's Ten-Year Programme. It is buttressed by Days of Rage campaigns that the OIC has been stage-managing since its passage. Resolution 16/18, as shown in its drafting documents, is inspired by the OIC's Secretary General:

> Pakistan (on behalf of the Organization of the Islamic Conference): draft resolution
>
> 16/ … Combating intolerance, negative stereotyping and stigmatization of, and discrimination, incitement to violence, and violence against persons based on religion or belief[2]
>
> *Notes* the speech given by Secretary-General of the Organization of the Islamic Conference, Ekmeleddin Ihsanoglu, at the fifteenth session of the Human Rights Council, and draws on his call on States to take the following actions to foster a domestic environment of religious tolerance, peace and respect …[3]

In turn, UN Resolution 16/18 is the implementation of the OIC's Ten-Year Program of Action, announced at the 2005 OIC Summit (composed of heads of state), as declared by the OIC in Section VII (3), "Combating Islamophobia":

> Endeavour to have the United Nations adopt an interna-
> tional resolution to counter Islamophobia, and call upon all
> States to enact laws to counter it, including deterrent pun-
> ishments.[4]

To fully appreciate the OIC effort in international forums regarding Resolution 16/18 and related activities, it is important to remain focused on the relationship between relevant parts of the Cairo Declaration when templated against
the UN's 1966 *International Covenant on Civil and Political Rights* (ICCPR). The
tactic is the repurposing of laws through the veiled redefinition of terms within
those laws (and treaties) without a public awareness that such an activity occurred,
often accomplished through the disarming use of facially neutral language in the
service of narratives that intend biased outcomes. The targeted term in this instance is "incitement," as used in Article 20 (2) of the ICCPR.

At heart, this strategy is classical Alinskiism of the same kind as Captain
Kirby's use of the term "core values." The OIC is not, however, the lead player
in the effort to repurpose the definition of incitement in international forums.
Rather, the lead role for this initiative appears to be left-leaning entities like the
Center for Media and Communications Studies, Central European University,
and non-governmental organizations (NGOs) like *Article 19*.[5] Central European
University was founded by George Soros[6] to undertake his Open Societies Mission.[7] *Article 19* is an NGO funded by various European ministries and by Open
Society Foundations,[8] also a George Soros entity.[9] As this discussion progresses,
the reader will see how the OIC's Ten-Year Programme of Action pivots on the
repurposed meaning of the term "incitement."

A principle mechanism for this repurposing is a UN activity called the "Rabat
Plan of Action."[10] To be more precise, it's called the

> Rabat Plan of Action on the Prohibition of Advocacy of Na-
> tional, Racial or Religious Hatred that Constitutes Incite-
> ment to Discrimination, Hostility or Violence: Conclusions
> and Recommendations Emanating from the Four Regional
> Expert Workshops Organised [sic] by OHCHR, in 2011,
> and adopted by experts in Rabat, Morocco on 5 October
> 2012.

A footnote in the document title makes it clear that the Rabat Plan of Action concerns incitement as the term is used in Article 20 (2) of the *International
Covenant*:

> [Footnote] 1. Article 20 of the International Covenant on
> Civil and Political Rights reads that "Any advocacy of na-
> tional, racial or religious hatred that constitutes incitement
> to discrimination, hostility or violence shall be prohibited by

law". Throughout the text this will be referenced as "incitement to hatred".[11]

Certainly the successful redefinition of "incitement" as used in the International Covenant on Civil and Political Rights (ICCPR) would lead to a repurposed application of Article 20 (2) that was neither anticipated nor agreed to by either the drafters or signatories when ratified. Just as with "Islamophobia," "incitement" is a key term that the OIC seeks to control. The OIC uses "incitement" in the language of the Cairo Declaration, in UN Resolution 16/18, and even to justify "Days of Rage" events.

Through Rabat, the OIC targets Articles 19 and 20 of the ICCPR as the breach point for the Islamophobia initiative. For example, in 2012, OIC Secretary General Ihsanoglu referred to the ICCPR when making clear that 16/18 fulfills the Ten-Year Programme requirement to flow its policy through the United Nations. His comments take direct aim at the First Amendment:

> At this moment we have the Resolution 16/18 which was issued last year at the UN which **forms a legal groundwork for criminalizing such actions that could lead to violence** ... there is in the International Agreement for Civil and Political Rights (Year 1966 Paragraph 18), a provision that would allow us to put limits on the **misuse of the freedom of speech** including **misuse of freedom of press, freedom of thought,** the misuse of these freedoms towards others, in a sense that it would encourage to violence and to hatred based on religious belief.[12]

An observation on the parallels between the ICCPR and the Cairo Declaration should be addressed before moving on. Starting with how Article 22(a) of the Cairo Declaration ("Everyone shall have the right to express his opinion freely **in such manner as would not be contrary to the principles of the Shari'ah**") mimics Article 19(2) of the ICCPR ("Everyone shall have the right to freedom of expression"), the close fit between Article 22 of the Cairo Declaration and the relevant language of Articles 19 and 20 of the ICCPR should not go unrecognized:

> <u>**Article 19**</u> [ICCPR] (2) **Everyone shall have the right to freedom of expression**; this right shall include freedom to seek, receive and impart information and ideas of all kinds, regardless of frontiers, either orally, in writing or in print, in the form of art, or through any other media of his choice. (3) The exercise of the rights provided for in paragraph 2 of this article carries with it special duties and responsibilities. It may therefore be subject to certain restrictions, but these shall only be such as are provided by law and are necessary:

(a) For respect of the rights or reputations of others; (b) For the protection of national security or of public order (ordre public), or of public health or morals.

Article 20 [ICCPR] (2) Any advocacy of national, racial or religious hatred that constitutes incitement to discrimination, hostility or violence shall be prohibited by law. [13]

Article 22 [Cairo Declaration]: (a) Everyone shall have the right to express his opinion freely in such manner as would not be contrary to the principles of the Shari'ah. (1) Everyone shall have the right to advocate what is right, and propagate what is good, and warn against what is wrong and evil according to the norms of Islamic Shari'ah. ... (c) Information is a vital necessity to society. It may not be exploited or misused in such a way as may violate sanctities and the dignity of Prophets, undermine moral and ethical Values or disintegrate, corrupt or harm society or weaken its faith. (d) It is not permitted to excite nationalistic or doctrinal hatred or to do anything that may be an incitement to any form or racial discrimination.[14]

Note that Article 22 of the Cairo Declaration is grounded in the Qur'an by allusion in Article 22(a)(1) to Qur'an Verse 3:110 ("Ye are the best of peoples, evolved for mankind, enjoining what is right, forbidding what is wrong, and believing in Allah. If only the People of the Book had faith, it were best for them: among them are some who have faith, but most of them are perverted transgressors."). As the objectives of the Ten-Year Programme of Action transition from the shariah language of the Cairo Declaration to the esoteric language of international diplomacy, note that the Islamophobia narrative becomes facially neutral. Camouflaging shariah requirements in facially neutral language is purposeful. In the January 2013 Brookings Doha Center paper "A Rights Agenda for the Islamic World? – The Organization of Islamic Cooperation's Evolving Human Rights Framework," the transition was acknowledged—albeit in facially neutral terms:

In the two decades from the Cairo Declaration in 1990 to the establishment of the Independent Permanent Commission on Human Rights in 2011, the OIC has gradually shed the language of sharia. The Cairo Declaration referred to sharia as its only source, the Covenant on the Rights of the Child mentioned it within the context of Islamic values (2005), and the IPHRC and its statute (2011) abandoned references to sharia altogether. This shift is indicative of the OIC's increasing willingness to discuss rights within the context of international human rights rather than exclusively within that of Islamic law and tradition.[15]

This creates the necessity of extending the Articles 24/25 Rule to work product undertaken in international forums where there are indicators that OIC activities like the Ten-Year Programme of Action are directly or indirectly involved. If analysis of facially neutral work product shows that it conforms to "Islamophobia" objectives when the Article 24/25 Rule is applied, then that is how the activity must be interpreted. Prepare to be surprised.

Article 20 Section 2 of the ICCPR refers to the act of purposefully inciting people to violence by speech to an audience interested in and capable of undertaking that action. An example would be a racist speech at a Ku Klux Klan rally calling for attacks on African Americans to a likeminded crowd where there is a reasonable expectation that such an action will be undertaken. Similarly, Article 20(2)'s "incitement to discrimination, hostility or violence" is supposed to apply when a speaker exhorts a crowd with language like, "Let's kill Muslims," and a crowd of like-minded individuals is disposed to carry out the order. It should be noted that in the pre-Civil Rights Jim Crow era, such incitement sometimes came from members who were also state or local leaders. This was a serious problem and a national disgrace. Under the conventional understanding of Article 20 Section 2, when the OIC and/or the Muslim Brotherhood calls for "Days of Rage" or "holy rage" where non-Muslims are targeted, attacked, and sometimes killed, it is they who actually fall under the understood meaning of "religious hatred that constitutes incitement to discrimination, hostility or violence."

It is in this context that the OIC's "test of consequences" narrative is used to turn the meaning of incitement in Article 20 Section 2 on its head by converting it to a legal standard designed to facilitate the "shut up before I hit you again" standard associated with the battered wife syndrome. The OIC's *Fourth Observatory Report on Islamophobia,* released in June 2011, calls for:

> d. Ensuring swift and effective implementation of the new approach signified by the consensual adoption of **HRC Resolution 16/18**, entitled "combating intolerance, negative stereotyping and stigmatization of, and discrimination, incitement to violence, and violence against persons based on religion or belief," by, inter alia, **removing the gaps in implementation and interpretation of international legal instruments and criminalizing acts of incitement** to hatred and violence on religious grounds with a view to curbing the double standards and racial profiling that continue to feed religious strife detrimental to peace, security and stability.
>
> e. Constructively engaging to bridge divergent views on **the**

limits to the right to freedom of opinion and expression, in a structured multilateral framework, and in the light of events like the burning of Quran geared towards filling the **'interpretation void'** with regard to the interface between articles 19 (3) and 20 of the ICCPR based on **emerging approaches like applying the 'test of consequences.'** [16]

Under the OIC's redefinition of incitement, the "test of consequences" allows a third party to use an utterance as a provocation to violence, which then becomes sanctioned precisely because the third party acted out violently. Moreover, what criminalizes the utterance is the third party's decision to respond violently. The "test of consequences" institutionalizes the calculated suppression of protected speech by naked use of force. This is institutionalized terrorism comfortably nested in facially neutral language.

As in the Cartoon Crisis, the OIC, the Muslim Brotherhood, and other elements stoke the inciting event, and Days of Rage violence follows. Whenever someone says anything deemed offensive to Islam, this is the threat. These entities alone set the standard for what will eventually rise to the level of "incitement." Insulting Christians and Jews will not trigger the incitement clause because Christians and Jews are not in the habit of threatening to kill people if someone says something offensive. Hence, because there is no consequence for insulting Christians and Jews, there is no crime. The "test of consequences" seeks to institutionalize a new international legal standard that facilitates unequal treatment—which typologically echoes the Pact of Umar, legitimizes terrorism as a tool of coercion, and institutionalizes shariah standards on non-Muslim populations. [Note: *For a review of the Pact of Umar, see Part II. For a parallel analysis of how interfaith dialogue is manipulated to the same end, see Appendix I, "The Dawah Mission, Interfaith Penetration and Spiritual Warfare." For a reference to the shariah standard, see Reliance of the Traveller, Book O "Justice" Sections o11.0, o11.10, o11.11,[1] and o9.14.[2]*]

---

1 o11.0 "Non-Muslim Subjects of the Islamic State," Book O "Justice," Reliance of the Traveller, o11.10 The agreement is also violated (A: with respect to the offender alone) if the state has stipulated that any of the following things break it, and one of the subjects does so anyway, though if the state has not stipulated that these break the agreement, then they do not; namely, if one of the subject people:

    (2) conceals spies of hostile forces;
    (3) leads a Muslim away from Islam;
    (4) kills a Muslim;
    (5) or mentions something impermissible about Allah, the Prophet (Allah bless him and give him peace), or Islam.

o11.11 When a subject's agreement with the state has been violated, the caliph chooses between the four alternatives mentioned above in connection with prisoners of war (o9.14).

2 o9.14 "The Rules of War, Book O "Justice", Section 9 "Jihad," When a subject's agreement with the state has been violated, the caliph chooses between the four alternatives mentioned above in connection with prisoners of war (see o9.14).

Because Resolution 16/18 applies to non-Muslims, the "test of consequences" does not have universal applicability. Not only that, it places all responsibility for Muslim violence said to be resulting from an insult to Islam on the speaker (even retroactively and in cases in which no violence was intended or threatened).[17] The lack of situational awareness of this aspect of the "test of consequences" shows how unmoored the guardians of our civil and constitutional rights have become. Just beneath the surface of the facially neutral language of "test of consequences" is the threat of coercive violence that serves as the mechanism by which the OIC seeks to subordinate the ICCPR to the Cairo Declaration—and, through it, to Islamic law.

When ratifying the ICCPR, the United States registered its reservations, thus providing a measure of protection from any misconstruction of Article 20 Section 2. The United Nations Treaty Collection Database[18] memorializes America's reservation, making it clear that the Constitution still trumps a treaty—and the Pact of Umar—for now:

> United States of America: United States of America
>
> Reservations: (1) That Article 20 does not authorize or require legislation or other action by the United States that would restrict the right of free speech and association protected by the Constitution and laws of the United States.[19]

Tests and 'Consequences'

In Istanbul on July 15, 2011, then-Secretary of State Hillary Clinton offered America's willing support to OIC Secretary General Ihsanoglu to help facilitate the implementation of the OIC's Ten-Year Programme at the United Nations through the ratification of Resolution 16/18. This event is important because the United States committed its best efforts to a foreign state actor, the OIC, to help ratify a United Nations resolution that is antithetical to the First Amendment. The process of passing and implementing the requirements of Resolution 16/18 is called the Istanbul Process. There is no question that Ihsanoglu is aware of all the interlocking shariah and OIC links leading up to this process. In a keynote speech at the "U.S.–Islamic World Forum" at the Brookings Institution in Qatar in June 2013, Ihsanoglu was clear that Resolution 16/18 concerns the implementation of the Ten-Year Programme of Action, which passed with the cooperation of Secretary Clinton:

> The basic documents of OIC, such as the 10-year program of action and a new charter provided a provisionary roadmap to meet the challenges of the first 21st Century [sic] we are witnessing today in the Muslim world. …

> Perhaps the most significant example of OIC-United States cooperation is in the consensual passage of United Nations' Human Rights Council Resolution 16-18 on combatting religious intolerance.
>
> It is with this in mind that I initiated with the presence and participation of Secretary Clinton the Istanbul process for consensual implementation of this resolution, and this Resolution 16-18 in July 2011. And this process, Istanbul process, the OIC has demonstrated ability to build consensus on the most sensitive of international issues.[20]

While somewhat outside the scope of this book, it should be noted that many esteemed think tanks, including the Brookings Institution, show disturbing signs of deep penetration. Steven Emerson and John Rossomando of the Investigative Project on Terrorism (IPT) recently completed a detailed four-part analysis of the Brookings Institution and its accommodation of the pro-Brotherhood, pro-jihadi foreign-policy agenda of Qatar, one of its major donors.[3]

Following the OIC narrative in an official State Department release, Secretary Clinton said:

> I want to applaud the Organization of Islamic Conference and the European Union for helping pass Resolution 16/18 at the Human Rights Council. I was complimenting the Secretary General on the OIC team in Geneva. I had a great team there as well. So many of you were part of that effort. And together we have begun to **overcome the false divide that pits religious sensitivities against freedom of expression**, and we are pursuing **a new approach based on concrete steps to fight intolerance wherever it occurs**. Under this resolution, the international community is taking a strong stand for freedom of expression and worship, and against discrimination and violence based upon religion or belief.[21]

After praising the OIC for its efforts, Clinton got more specific about the "concrete steps" she favored. The Secretary of State assured the world that America would not "criminalize speech unless there is an **incitement** to imminent violence."

> The resolution calls upon states to protect freedom of religion, to counter offensive expression through education,

---

3   Steven Emerson, John Rossomando, and Dave Yonkman, "IPT Exclusive: Qatar's Insidious Influence on the Brookings Institution," *IPT News*, 28 October 2014, http://www.investigativeproject.org/4630/ipt-exclusive-qatar-insidious-influence-on.

interfaith dialogue, and public debate, and to prohibit discrimination, profiling, and hate crimes, but not to criminalize speech unless there is an **incitement to imminent violence**. We will be looking to all countries to hold themselves
accountable and to join us in reporting to the UN's Office of
the High Commissioner of Human Rights on their progress
in taking these steps.[22]

For Clinton, "all countries" includes the United States. There are several elements of Clinton's key phrase—criminalizing the "incitement to imminent violence"—that put the OIC's Islamophobia campaign in motion. Through this
process, First Amendment rights are subordinated to what foreign governing entities consider appropriate, as determined by the OIC through its Islamophobia
Observatory and as implemented at the UN Human Rights Council and related
international forums.

Because the advance of Resolution 16/18 and the Istanbul Process raises real
First Amendment concerns, the first question is whether a Secretary of State has
the authority to negotiate our First Amendment rights away in talks with the
European Union, the UN Human Rights Council, and the OIC. In her speech in
Istanbul, Clinton committed to spearheading the 16/18 effort:

> For our part, I have asked our Ambassador-at-Large for Re-
> ligious Freedom, Suzan Johnson Cook, to spearhead our im-
> plementation efforts. And to build on the momentum from
> today's meeting, later this year the United States intends to
> invite relevant experts from around the world to the first of
> what we hope will be a series of meetings to discuss best
> practices, exchange ideas, and keep us moving forward be-
> yond the polarizing debates of the past; to build those mus-
> cles of respect and empathy and tolerance that the secretary
> general referenced. It is essential that we advance this new
> consensus and strengthen it, both at the United Nations and
> beyond, in order to avoid a return to the old patterns of di-
> vision.[23]

While it is not clear that the Secretary knows OIC concepts of tolerance and
human rights are based on shariah, she nonetheless committed to the underlying
logic of Resolution 16/18. Secretary Clinton went on to say:

> Under this resolution, the international community is taking
> a strong stand for freedom of expression and worship, and
> against discrimination and violence based upon religion or
> belief.[24]

To get a sense of how the OIC seeks to enforce what Clinton called "a strong stand for freedom of expression," let's revisit Ihsanoglu's response to Geert Wilders' acquittal in 2011. Just days before meeting with Secretary Clinton, the OIC Secretary General made his thoughts known:

> Insults to Islam and to the honored Prophet of Islam, Haz-rat Muhammad (PBUH), has reached a stage that **can no longer be tolerated under any pretext**, including freedom of speech ...[25]

It is in this context that we should understand the *Charlie Hebdo* massacre[26] and Howard Dean's blind assertions that such events have nothing to do with Islam.[27] Ihsanoglu's view of freedom of expression may trouble non-Muslims, but it conforms to authoritative Islamic law on slander. Aware of this or not, Secretary Clinton accepted this view on behalf of all American citizens. She continued:

> **The Human Rights Council has given us a comprehensive framework for addressing this issue on the international level**. But at the same time, we each have to work to do more to promote respect for religious differences in our own coun-tries. In the United States, I will admit, there are people who still feel vulnerable or marginalized as a result of their reli-gious beliefs. And we have seen how the incendiary actions of just a very few people, a handful in a country of nearly 300 million, can create wide ripples of intolerance. We also un-derstand that, for 235 years, freedom of expression has been a universal right at the core of our democracy. So we are focused on **promoting interfaith education** and collabora-tion, enforcing antidiscrimination laws, protecting the rights of all people to worship as they choose, **and to use some old-fashioned techniques of peer pressure and shaming, so that people don't feel that they have the support to do what we abhor**.[28]

Clinton committed to relying on extra-legal methods like "old-fashioned techniques of peer pressure and shaming" not only because her commitment to a foreign power challenges the First Amendment, but also because our treaty com-mitments to human rights still preference U.S. constitutional constructions over international norms of the same.

It is remarkable that the Secretary of State believed she had the authority to broker our "inalienable" constitutional rights in a foreign forum. She seems to have understood the vulnerability of the trajectory she was charting. When Clinton committed to a foreign power "to use some old-fashioned techniques of peer pressure and shaming" against American citizens in order to facilitate a foreign entities' Programme of Action—itself based on a hostile foreign agenda—

she seemed to recognize that she lacked a constitutional basis to undertake such an effort. Hence, the stated need to resort to extra-legal measures that envision bringing the enormous coercive power of the state to bear against its own citizens to silence them. At what point does "peer pressure and shaming" constitute an end-run around constitutional protections? The Secretary's commitment was given to a foreign entity in her capacity as Secretary of State and communicated to the public in an official State Department release. For the OIC and the Muslim Brotherhood, this is how shariah is to be enforced through the Islamophobia paradigm.

The Secretary of State is not alone. When Representative Trent Franks, Chairman of the House Subcommittee on the Constitution, asked then-Assistant Attorney General Tom Perez to affirm that the administration would "never entertain or advance a proposal that criminalizes speech against any religion," Perez refused to answer.[29]

Although both Secretary of State Clinton and OIC Secretary General Ekmeleddin Ihsanoglu[4] have been succeeded by new leadership within their respective organizations, the process of implementing Resolution 16/18 continues incrementally, often using the UN Human Rights Council as its vehicle. For example, in March 2013, the UNHRC passed Resolution A/HRC/22/L,[40] which states that "terrorism, in all its forms and manifestations, cannot and should not be associated with any religion, nationality, civilization or ethnic group."[30] The clear intent of this resolution is to prevent any association of terrorism with Islamic violence, no matter how straightforward the association may be.

This has immediate consequences for the domestic counterterror mission, as it establishes the requirement that any discussion on terrorism be irrelevant with regard to causation. The DHS Office for Civil Rights and Civil Liberties imposed this standard on the law enforcement and intelligence communities in "Countering Violent Extremism (CVE) Training: Do's and Don'ts," rendering both inert:

> Don't use training that equates radical thought, religious expression, freedom to protest, or other constitutionally protected activity, with criminal activity. One can have radical thoughts/ideas, including disliking the U.S. government,

---

4   In an interesting development, since Ihsanoglu left his position as OIC General Secretary, two of Turkey's main secular opposition parties have formally backed his unsuccessful bid for the presidency to challenge Prime Minister Erdogan. The June 2014 decision to back Ihsanoglu "alarmed the secular segment of the society, who [already] accuse Erdogan of forcing Islamic values on the predominantly Muslim country." To deflect such criticism, Ihsanoglu pledged, "I will defend secularism." See "Turkey's Secular Opposition Endorses Devout Muslim for President," *AhramOnline* (AFP wire), 29 June 2014, URL: http://english.ahram.org.eg/NewsContent/2/8/105044/World/Region/Turkeys-secular-opposition-endorses-devout-Muslim-.aspx, accessed 29 June 2014, and Ilhan Tanir, @WashingtonPoint Twitter Feed, 9 July 2014, URL: https://twitter.com/WashingtonPoint/status/486853813693718528, accessed 9 July 2014. **Twitter feed states:** "Opposition parties' Pres candidate has good looking family: I will defend secularism v @reportturk pic.twitter.com/8sJ8tgHXLW"

without being violent; for example, trainers who equate the desire for Shari'a law with criminal activity violate basic tenets of the First Amendment.[31]

What DHS is doing domestically, the State Department is facilitating internationally. In her endorsement of Resolution 16/18, Hillary Clinton embraced a view of free expression that subordinates First Amendment standards to the will of foreign powers. A truth emerges: One cannot defend the Constitution and enforce the Islamophobia narrative at the same time. [*For a detailed example of how concepts like Islamophobia and incitement work themselves into acceptance in international forums, see Appendix 2.*]

This did not start with Secretary Clinton and the Obama administration. While the willingness to participate in the OIC's anti-blasphemy campaign accelerated during the Obama administration, it was President Bush who established America's initial commitment to enforcing Islamic notions of slander. On March 8, 2006, the Pakistani newspaper *Dawn* reported that:

> Since the cartoon crisis, European Union delegates have entered into discussions with Islamic authorities to discuss effecting laws that make insults to Islam a crime.[32]

The United States was also subjected to the same pressure. From a related article, published on March 4, 2006, that spread widely in the Muslim world:

> During a visit to Pakistan, the Karachi News reported President Musharraf raised the issue of drafting such laws with President Bush and received a favorable response.

> President Musharraf ... raised the offensive caricatures issue and **demanded his US counterpart draft law to avoid such incidents in the future**. President Bush, who hopes to boost the US' image among Muslims, condemned the publications of the cartoons and assured full cooperation.[33]

When Sada Cumber, a naturalized American citizen born in Pakistan, was appointed by President Bush as the first U.S. Special Envoy to the OIC, he was asked to comment on an OIC Conference he had attended that touched on the issue of freedom of expression.

> Cumber said that when researching the OIC's 10-year-plan—which calls for building up education, science and technology, the status of women and human rights—"I thought oh my goodness, **I think the Muslim values that they are aspiring here are exactly in sync' with American values.**"[34]

Cumber's comments make sense only to those who either do not accept or do not understand the First Amendment. There at least appears to be a bipartisan cadre committed—even if there is no subjective intent—to subordinating free speech to Islamic law. Now, if President Bush had actually known what he was communicating to Musharraf (and it's hardly clear that he did), he also would have known that he was assuring the Pakistanis of his full cooperation in the undermining of the First Amendment in furtherance of implementing the OIC's Ten-Year Programme of Action. That is the answer the Pakistanis heard—and the question was asked to elicit that response. For the Ten-Year Programme of Action to succeed, awareness is not necessary, only performance.

In 2010, President Obama appointed Rashad Hussain Special Envoy to the OIC.[35] A year prior to Secretary Clinton's commitments to the OIC, Hussain divulged that the United States would henceforth support OIC efforts at the UN to criminalize defamation of religion:[36]

> One of the issues that's coming up now with regard to the OIC is engagement on this issue of defamation of religions and there's a huge European component to that because many of the concerns of the Muslim countries stem from recent events in Europe and the United States is working with OIC member countries on coming up with a resolution that can be both focused on, ah, primarily focused on ensuring that religious freedom is respected all over the world and addresses the defamation concerns in a manner which is consistent with legal and policy principles here in the United States that would hope to avert some of the worst of that.[37]

As we have seen, Hussain's comments were borne out by events.

Dawah Entities and the Infrastructure of Enforcement

There seems to be broad coordination on the implementation of the Islamic free speech standard in the Islamic world. It includes the OIC from outside and above, and the Brotherhood from beneath and within.

In January 2006—only weeks after ratifying the Ten-Year Programme at its summit in Saudi Arabia—OIC Secretary General Ihsanoglu fired off an email to two individuals linked to the Brotherhood in America. One of the recipients was CAIR Executive Director Nihad Awad. Years earlier, in 1993, Awad had been recorded by the FBI at a high-level meeting of Hamas and Brotherhood operatives.[38] At the time, Awad was an officer with the Islamic Association for Palestine[39] and reported to its founder, Hamas political director Mousa Mohammed Abu Marzook. Due to its extensive fundraising and promotion of the Palestinian terror group, the IAP (along with the Holy Land Foundation) was found liable in court in 2004 for Hamas's murder of David Boim in 1996.[40] Awad was then an open supporter of Hamas.[41] When the Justice Department prosecuted the Holy Land Foundation for its links to Hamas and Brotherhood terrorism four years later, in 2008, both CAIR and the IAP were named unindicted co-conspirators. Months after the 1993 Hamas meeting, CAIR emerged as the group's much-needed public relations organ, claiming to represent the civil rights of America's Muslim community. Recall that the Cairo Declaration defines human rights as shariah. From this standpoint, Awad was a perfect partner in the OIC's efforts to advance the Islamophobia meme in this country.

The other recipient of Ihsanoglu's email was John Esposito, Director of the Prince al-Waleed bin Talal Center for Muslim-Christian Understanding at Georgetown University. As an academic, Esposito has appeared as a defense witness in numerous terrorism trials. He was a supporter of Palestinian Islamic Jihad leader Sami al-Arian, whom he lauded as "an extraordinarily bright, articulate scholar and intellectual-activist."[42] Esposito was an expert witness for the defense at the Holy Land Foundation trial in 2008[43] and, more recently, for Khalid Ali Aldawsari, a young Saudi charged with the "purchase [of] chemicals and equipment necessary to make an improvised explosive device (IED)" after having "research[ed] potential US targets," according to the Justice Department.[44]

Esposito also sponsored a conference with the Brotherhood- and Hamas-linked United Association for Studies and Research. Operating from 1989 to 2004, that group—which was also an unindicted co-conspirator in the Holy Land case—boasted at least two officials with consequential ties to the Islamic Movement: its former director, Ahmed Yousef, now a close adviser to Hamas leader Ismail Haniyeh in Gaza,[45] and founding board member Mohamed Akram, author of the Brotherhood's Explanatory Memorandum.[46] Most recently, in January 2015, Georgetown organized and funded Egyptian Muslim Brotherhood members from the outlawed Freedom and Justice Party when they visited the United States to meet with State Department officials.[47]

In the cross-examination during his Holy Land testimony on behalf of the Brotherhood and Hamas defendants, Esposito painted a picture of the Brotherhood as merely a "major social movement," rejecting any links to violent jihad. He went as far as refusing to acknowledge the Brotherhood's well-known motto,[48] "Allah is our objective. The Prophet is our leader. The Qur'an is our law. Jihad is our way. Dying in the way of Allah is our highest hope."[49] The testimony continued:

> *Question:* In your opinion, is there any proof that the Muslim Brotherhood wants to overthrow governments or create an Islamic state through violent jihad?
>
> *Esposito:* The proof actually runs directly against that. If you

look historically at the track record of the Muslim Brotherhood, not only its statements but what it does, in most countries, certainly in Egypt, in Jordan, it participates within government and within society, **usually as a major social movement**. And when able to function in politics, when governments have opened up and allowed free and fair elections, which is not all that common in the Arab world, then they will participate in government.[50]

Ihsanoglu opened his letter to Nihad Awad and John Esposito by proposing a conference on "the phenomenon of Islamophobia in America." The event was to be sponsored by Georgetown University.

I am pleased that after some serious considerations and exchange of ideas which took a while, now we are at a point of (to) concretize our joint desires. The conference, **which will focus mainly on themes relevant to and various aspects of the phenomenon of Islamophobia**, will be the first ever OIC sponsored event in the United States of America and comes at a most appropriate time **when the issue is in the global agenda**.[51]

Just weeks after the passage of the Ten-Year Programme of Action, the issue of Islamophobia was indeed "in the global agenda." Because the OIC represents state action, its efforts carry the color of authority, and its actions should be assessed accordingly. Why would a Jesuit institution like Georgetown University be interested in helping to impose a foreign standard—based on shariah—against American citizens who are predominantly Christian?

I am also pleased to inform you that the OIC General Secretariat will be **contributing USD 325,000** for the organization of this Conference. **The total amount will be transferred to CAIR** as soon (as) informed of the details of the relevant bank account.[52]

Georgetown agreed to take foreign funds passed through a Brotherhood- and Hamas-associated entity. It's part of the pattern: When the OIC wants to reach Muslims in America, it tends to go through the Muslim Brotherhood in America. In Ihsanoglu's words, this "trilateral collaboration"—the OIC, CAIR, and, in this instance, Georgetown—represents a team effort to launch an anti-Islamophobia campaign in the United States.

Outside the borders of this country, American Muslim Brothers have also met with the OIC to coordinate information campaigns in the United States. For example, on July 4, 2007, *Arab News* reported such a meeting in an article titled "Awad, Ihsanoglu Discuss the Future CAIR/OIC Projects":

The executive director of the Council on American-Islamic Relations, Nihad Awad, attended a meeting yesterday with the secretary-general of the Organization of the Islamic Conference (OIC), Professor Ekmeleddin Ihsanoglu, discussing cooperation on future projects. "I'm pleased to meet with Ihsanoglu to discuss the situation of Muslims in the United States and to work on future projects," Awad told *Arab News*.[53]

The story reads like a reporting activity—a tasking to CAIR to report back to the OIC as if an OIC asset in America. Adding credibility to this claim are CAIR's revenue streams. In just one of CAIR's money-laundering ventures,[5] for example, the 2007 tax returns from CAIR, Inc. reveal that 76 percent of its reported contributions came from entities inside OIC jurisdictions, with Saudi Arabia accounting for 63 percent and the United Arab Emirates 37 percent of OIC-based revenue.[54] A look at the OIC's Charter illustrates that there may be something to this. In it, the OIC claims jurisdiction not only over Muslims inside its Member States, but also over all Muslims living in non-Muslim countries—including the United States. Specifically, Chapter 1, Article 1, Objective 16 of the OIC Charter states:

> The objectives of the Organisation of the Islamic Conference shall be: To safeguard the rights, dignity and religious and cultural identity of **Muslim communities and minorities in non-Member States**.[55]

This is a claim of jurisdiction by an entity that presents itself to the world as a state actor with certain governing authority. Not so coincidentally, both the International Muslim Brotherhood and the Muslim Brotherhood in North America state as an objective the establishment of Islamic law and support of "the global Islamic State wherever it is."[56] From the Bylaws of the International Muslim Brotherhood at Chapter 2, Article 2:

> The Muslim Brotherhood is an international Muslim Body, which seeks to establish Allah's law in the land by achieving the spiritual goals of Islam and the true religion ..."

> [Article 2, Section E:] The need to work on establishing the Islamic State ... [d]efend the (Islamic) nation against the

---

5   Litigation documents were used to establish that CAIR constructed numerous shell organizations to launder its revenue streams. Things got so out of hand that, in June 2013, the original CAIR had to changed its name to the Washington Trust Foundation (Yes, WTF). For example, see Charles C. Johnson, "CAIR Collects Millions from Foreign Donors thanks to Non-Profit Shell Game, *The Daily Caller*, September 2013, URL: http://dailycaller.com/2013/09/21/cair-collects-millions-from-foreign-donors-thanks-to-non-profit-shell-game/, accessed September 2013.

internal enemies ...[57]

From the 1991 Explanatory Memorandum, admitted into evidence in the Holy Land trial, the Muslim Brotherhood in America stated as its general strategic goal:

> The general strategic goal of the Group in America ... is the "Enablement of Islam in North America, meaning: establishing an effective and stable Islamic Movement led by the Muslim Brotherhood which adopts Muslims' causes domestically and globally ... presents a civilization alternative, and **supports the global Islamic State wherever it is**."[58]

There is a pedigree to the language used in the Memorandum. Authored by Mohamed Akram in 1991, the Explanatory Memorandum resembles both the 1982 document *Towards a Worldwide Strategy for Islamic Policy* (the "Project"), seized in a raid of Yousef Nada's[59] home in Switzerland, and Khurram Murad's 1981 monograph *Islamic Movement in the West*. Compare with the Projects "Fifth Point and Departure" and *Islamic Movement*'s "Other Objectives":

> **THE FIFTH POINT OF DEPARTURE.** To dedicate ourselves to the establishment of an Islamic state, in parallel with gradual efforts aimed at gaining control of local power centers through institutional action. a- Elements - To channel thought, education and action in order to establish an Islamic power [government] on the earth. To influence centers of power both local and worldwide to the service of Islam.[60]

> **OTHER OBJECTIVES: WORLDWIDE ISLAMIC MOVEMENT.** As a part of the same ultimate objective of an Islamic movement, that is to change the society into an Islamic mould [sic] and make Islam supreme, we need to pursue three more objectives at the three different levels of operation, which relate to the world-wide Islamic movement: 1) Support and reinforce the 'home' movement. 2) Growth of an international Islamic movement. 3) Support of the movements in all other countries, specially Muslim.[61]

On the amicable relationship between the Brotherhood and the OIC, extending at least as far back as the 1980s, the International Institute of Islamic Thought (IIIT) published an approving monograph titled *OIC: The Organization of the Islamic Conference: An Introduction to an Islamic Political Institution*.[62] (Some points of the book are covered in Part IV.) A leading indicator that the 1989 book endorses the OIC as a *bona fide* Islamic institution is that the IIIT called the OIC "an Islamic political institution" in the title. If the OIC, the International Muslim

Brotherhood, and the Muslim Brotherhood in America are actually committed to the mission statements they long planned and put in writing, what would it look like? How would their actions appear? Is it possible they would look just like what we are seeing? It is with this understanding that we read Section H of the *Third OIC Observatory Report on Islamophobia*, which states:

> h) It should be recognized that Muslims have the same basic needs and desires as others, which are material well-being, cultural acceptance and religious freedom, without political or social intimidation. In that vein, **Muslim [sic] should not be marginalized or attempted to be assimilated, but should be accommodated. Accommodation is the best strategy for integration.**[63]

While most would agree with the first part of the statement, it's the second that gives cause for concern. In a sense, the first part baits the hook so that most will simply read past the second. It is certainly stated in disarmingly neutral terms. What does it mean? Is it saying that, according to the OIC, Muslims who come to live in America should not have to accept the laws of the United States, including the Constitution? That they should not have to assimilate by becoming American citizens? That they "should be accommodated"—as in, allowed to live permanently in the United States, not under U.S. law, but rather under shari-ah? It certainly seems to reflect Tariq Ramadan's view, given his comments at the Muslim American Society-Islamic Circle of North America (MAS-ICNA) Conference in Chicago in December 2012, which mirrored the OIC's demand for "co-existing" jurisdictions when stating Mohammed's activities in Medina as the Islamic legal precedent for a Muslim's claim of citizenship in America. Ramadan put it this way:

> So, if we look and we say what is home, remember what the Prophet of Islam did when he arrived in Medina. ... The Muslims when they first arrived in Asia, Africa, the United States of America, Canada, Europe everywhere the first thing that we did as the first institutions that we had were – was building mosques. Meaning two things. We are at home and the center of our presence is "No God but Allah" (in Arabic). So what you said about our identity is – its not because we are at home that we forget the direction. The direction of the *Kiblah* remains *el Kiblah* (meaning) "No God but Allah." And now we are here and as we heard from the Prophet of Islam, one of the characteristics of the privileges that he had is [that] the earth is a mosque. Wherever you go, this is a masjid (a mosque). It means this is a place where you can prostrate. A place where you can pray. Meaning, I

am at home the very moment I say "No God but Allah!" (in Arabic).[64]

Both the Muslim American Society (MAS) and ICNA are known front organizations of the Muslim Brotherhood and committed to the Islamic Movement. When Ramadan's statements are understood in the context of Brotherhood objectives as defined by shariah, there is little doubt that they line up with OIC directives. In November 2014, the United Arab Emirates designated the MAS, along with CAIR, as terrorist organizations.[65]

Buying Media

At the Conference of Information Ministers in September 2006, OIC Secretary General Ihsanoglu urged "Muslim investors to invest in global media institutions in order to help correct misconceptions about Islam."[66] It wasn't an off-the-cuff remark—the story was issued as a press release by the OIC from the Saudi Embassy. For the OIC, "misconceptions about Islam" tends to be synonymous with Islamophobia. It is important to recognize the forum of the press release. At an inter-governmental meeting of information ministers, the head of the OIC announced an information campaign to affect American and Western decision-making by influencing what we think we know.

The call was not limited to the OIC. Within days, *IslamOnline*, the fatwa publishing web-service associated with Qaradawi, also endorsed the initiative.[67] The article noted Ihsanoglu's statement on the strategic necessity of a media acquisition campaign to influence policies through manipulation of the news cycle and associated editorial processes:

> "Muslim investors must invest in the large media institutions of the world, which generally make considerable profits, so that they have the ability to **affect their policies via their administrative boards**," said OIC chief Ekmeleddin Ihsanoglu.[68]

The OIC's comments line up with those of Saudi Prince bin Talal in both the *Arab News* and *Financial Times*:

> We have to be logical and understand that the US administration is subject to US public opinion. ... And to bring the decision-maker on your side, you not only have to be active inside the US Congress or the administration but also inside US society.[69]

> [T]hat's why we focus on the east coast of America. Because that's where the decision-making process is, with all respect

to west coast, north coast, or south coast.[70]

In America, the government cannot abridge your free speech rights to speak out against the government. The question is whether there is a constitutional obligation to protect the free speech rights of Americans from interference by *all* governments. Should non-American state actors be allowed to curb the free speech rights of American citizens in ways that American federal, state, and local governments cannot? As a state actor, should the OIC or its proxies be allowed entre to the U.S. public given its known objectives? Recently, NewsCorp (the *Wall Street Journal* and the Fox News Channel), AOL/Time Warner (CNN and *Time*),[71] Bloomberg,[72] and even Twitter[73] have come under such influence.

The same news agencies that engage in bitter fights with the U.S. government on free speech seem unconcerned when the same issues arise regarding the Middle East. Unafraid of saying something derogatory about America on the War on Terror, news outlets become less willing to challenge openly or confront the Muslim Brotherhood, al-Qaeda, or even Islam.

Reporting that may not be subject to government censorship domestically may be fearful of such censorship from abroad. What board of directors would risk the company's economic interest by accurately reporting stories concerning the War on Terror that are known to upset Muslim sensibilities? While there is no downside to running down the United States or Israel, real consequences are risked by accurately reporting on the true nature of jihad, not to mention the role of the OIC and its Member States. What is the point of vigilance in the protection of our rights against our own government if we leave the back door open for foreign governing entities to undermine those same rights? As it relates to the OIC, we are on notice. As this may seem too theoretical, just ask yourself how many elite news agencies reported they would not publish pictures of the Mohammad cartoons after the *Charlie Hebdo* assassinations?

A 'Test of Consequences' on 9/11

With the support of the Obama administration under then-Secretary of State Hillary Clinton, the OIC was set to advance the Ten-Year Programme through Resolution 16/18. It was looking for the next opportunity to escalate the "test of consequences" to speech that could be qualified as "incitement to imminent violence" under the proposed Rabat standards. This is a manufactured process to "criminalize" whatever speech the Islamic world deems worthy of reacting to violently. The *Innocence of Muslims* YouTube trailer was the first fully coordinated run on establishing this standard.

Before assessing the YouTube event, it should be noted that the Brotherhood regime in Egypt under Morsi had already facilitated activities for September 11, 2012, designed to disrupt the U.S. Embassy in Cairo. In fact, Islamic Movement entities close to the Brotherhood—i.e., Egyptian Islamic Jihad and Gamaa Islamiyya—were already committed to spinning up events to mark the anniversary of 9/11. The demand was to be for the release of former Muslim Brother and Gamaa Islamiyya leader Omar Abdul-Rahman (the "Blind Sheikh") from prison in the U.S.[74]

Things changed on Sunday, September 9, when the YouTube trailer for *Innocence of Muslims* started airing in Egypt in the lead-up to September 11. Already prepared to launch protests on behalf of the Blind Sheikh, an angry mob escalated its wrath against the film. These groups—who were to play the part of the jihadi entities in the choreographed Days of Rage drama—stormed the U.S. Embassy, burned the American flag, and replaced it with the black flag of Islamic jihad.[75] Al-Qaeda leader Ayman al Zawahiri's brother Mohammed was among the rioters.[76]

Earlier in 2012, a Coptic Christian living in southern California used an 8th-century biography of Mohammed, Ibn Ishaq's *Sirat Rasul-Allah*[77] (which Yahiya Emerick recommended to seventh-grade Muslim students in *What Islam is All About*[78]), to make a low-budget film lampooning the life of Mohammed. Nakoula Basseley Nakoula, the film's writer, producer, and director, said he made *Innocence of Muslims* to illustrate the Islamic doctrinal basis of the inspiration for the original attacks of 9/11.[79] That summer, he uploaded the film's trailer to YouTube.

On September 9, the Cairo news outlet *Al-Nas* translated large portions of the trailer into Arabic and aired it (and re-aired it) as part of a heavily editorialized news commentary calibrated to generate a level of rage[80] that would trigger the "test of consequences" – not just in Cairo on September 11 but over much of the Muslim world later that week and beyond. As anticipated, the video clip unleashed a storm of protests across the Muslim world through the rest of September,[81] leading up to the 67th General Assembly Session of the United Nations.

As with the European "Cartoon Crisis," the "outrage" of the Pope's Regensburg Speech, and the manipulated "Qur'an Burning" events in Afghanistan, the activities associated with the YouTube video were part of a choreographed campaign coordinated by the OIC and assisted by its Member States, which included the active support of the Brotherhood both internationally and domestically (in the U.S.). Note the reinforcing narratives:

From OIC and ummah level entities, we had Turkish Prime Minister Erdoğan ask why no Western country recognizes Islamophobia as a crime,[82] followed by the Egyptian government issuing arrest warrants for the "inflammatory video,"[83] followed by the OIC "reviving long-standing attempts to make insults against religions an international criminal offense,"[84] followed by the Egyptian government making those same "demands that the U.N. criminalize contempt of religion,"[85] while a Pakistani minister called for a $100,000 bounty to the "person who kills the maker of the anti-Islam blasphemous film."[86] As part of the ummah-level effort, two national clerics, Saudi Arabia's Grand Mufti Sheikh Abdul Aziz Al-Asheikh and Egypt's Al-Azhar's Grand Imam Ahmed el-Yayyeb, likewise demanded a global ban on insults to Islam. For the Saudi Grand Mufti, this demand came just six months after calling for the destruction of all churches in the Arabian Peninsula.[87]

From Muslim Brotherhood International, *OnIslam* published "Professor" Yusuf Qaradawi's September 13 call to action, issued through the International Union of Muslim Scholars (IUMS) that he founded and runs, condemning the trailer as "a heinous **provocative** act, which fans the embers of bigotry and hatred among peoples" by "**disregarding the feelings** of the Muslims all over the world." Qaradawi then tasked American Muslims "to haul before the court whoever contributed to the production of this film, and to immediately initiate legal prosecution of anyone who insults Islam," noting that "such evil acts cannot be sheltered under the wing of freedom of expression." An indicator of convergence, Qaradawi recognized the leading role of the OIC when he requested that "the Organization of Islamic Cooperation (OIC) undertake legal proceedings against those who insult the entire humanity through defaming the Messenger of mercy to the whole world."[88] Qaradawi's message was reinforced that same day by Egyptian Shaykh bin Bayyah, also associated with IUMS,[89] who said:

> How then, can the vile block the light of the sun, or how can the putrid stream pollute the lucid water of life? Rabid dogs bark at the moon, but yet the caravan proceeds. They are the enemies of peace, the enemies of prosperity, the enemies of humanity.[90]

From Muslim Brotherhood-associated entities in America, the response was likewise predictable; a perfunctory condemnation of "extremists" abroad was used to set up demands for action domestically that ultimately meet the demands of the extremists. The narrative follows a good cop/bad cop formula, where the American public must rely on the good cop's (the Brotherhood's) best efforts in order to avoid the harsh responses of the bad cop "extremists" whom they are willing to condemn. The *quid pro quo* to this arrangement is that we must work with the Brotherhood to curb protected speech and stay the hand of the aggrieved extremists. By establishing this reciprocity, an equivalency is created between the rioting and killing of the "extremists" on the one hand and those engaged in nothing other than protected speech on the other.

One example of this archetype response came from the Islamic Center of America in Dearborn, Michigan. First, the imam established his good cop *bona fides* by "slamming extremists for attacking U.S. embassies and urged Muslims not to react violently to attacks on their prophet." This was immediately followed by his urging the U.S. to do more to stop the people who made the video: "Somehow, they should be stopped, the U.S. response should be much more stronger than verbal condemnation." Establishing reciprocity between the two activities while stating the conditional offer of assistance, the Dearborn imam established equivalency by reiterating that "this is not what Islam preaches, there is no way we can tolerate killing" – *but*, he added, they could not "sit and watch" as the anti-Islam video is promoted.[91]

Another example follows the political adage, "Never let a good crisis go to waste." In September 2014, CAIR took advantage of the ISIS beheadings to double down on the Islamophobia narrative, issuing a press release on behalf of the U.S. Council of Muslim Organizations (USCMO). Under the guise of condemning the ISIS beheading of Steven Sotloff, USCMO actually used the event to "remind the public to avoid spreading Islamophobia by using the actions of ISIS to characterize and demonize all Muslims, globally and here in the United States."[92] The USCMO was formed in March 2014 to represent the voice of eight Brotherhood-associated organizations headed by Secretary General Oussama Jammal.[93] Jammal was the imam of the Bridgeview Mosque in Illinois when it came under intense scrutiny for Palestinian fundraising activities closely associated with Hamas. He also raised funds for the Sami al-Arian defense when Arian was on trial and routinely praised Sayyid Qutb.[94]

Picking up on this Brotherhood narrative and bringing the Days of Rage narrative full circle, Dr. Hamda Al-Majid, former Saudi official for the National Organization for Human Rights, wrote a commentary for the Saudi *Arsharq Alawsat*, the title of which said it all: "Stop Your Fanatics to Curb our Extremism."[95] Application of the Article 24/25 Rule reveals that the Saudi human rights organization would be primarily concerned with shariah. In fact, the Article 24/25 Rule could be applied to every phase of the "YouTube Crisis."

There are persuasive indicators that the YouTube campaign was stage-managed from beginning to end – from the *Al-Nas* broadcast of the editorialized YouTube clip on September 9[96] to Salam al Marayati's comments[97] aimed at keeping the initiative focused on Resolution 16/18 at the 2012 Human Dimension Implementation Meeting of the Organization for Security and Cooperation in Europe (OSCE) on October 2.[98] In his speech to the OSCE, Marayati said:

> Hate speech that intends to degrade, intimidate or incite violence against someone based on religion is harmful. … Human rights protect individuals, not abstract ideas or social norms. Religious symbols do not need governments or international bodies to defend them. The reaction to hatred can lead to other oppressive measures, such as blasphemy laws, inevitably violating human rights of religious minorities and vulnerable segments of societies. The loose and unclear language of these laws provide a context in which governments can restrict freedom of expression, thought, and religion, resulting in devastating consequences for those holding religious views that differ from the majority religion, as well as

for adherents to minority faiths. Much can be done to fight hatred without restricting speech, or prohibiting the "defamation of religion"; governments should condemn hatred and set the example. In the U.S. we do not ban the speech rather we speak out against it and deploy an array of measures to counter intolerance without banning the speech itself. **The international community has also recently rallied around a consensus approach to combating religious intolerance that is embodied in Human Rights Council resolution 16/18,** which sets effective means for dealing with such intolerance.[99]

As the president of the Muslim Public Affairs Council (MPAC), Marayati gave his speech as "**a public member representing the United States on religious freedom.**"[100] Formed out of the Islamic Center of Southern California by prominent Muslim Brotherhood leaders,[101] MPAC is closely associated with the Muslim Brotherhood and, along with ISNA and CAIR, comprises the public presence of the Islamic Movement in America.[102] This is the same Marayati whom, in 1986, then–House Democratic Leader Richard Gephardt denied a leadership position on the National Commission on Terrorism because he claimed that Hezbollah, a designated terrorist group, was legitimate.[103] With Marayati's words, American policy was joined with the Islamic Movement's and the OIC's. Marayati was not the only one to speak in such terms. A run-through of the timeline of events will help paint the full picture.

Upon the airing of the *Al-Nas* story, U.S. Embassy officials immediately distanced themselves from *Innocence of Muslims* by issuing strong condemnations, humble apologies, and denials of responsibility for the film. Twitter messages from the U.S. Embassy in Cairo—sent out before protesters stormed the facility on September 11, 2012—stated that the Embassy "condemns the continuing efforts by misguided individuals to hurt the religious feelings of Muslims" and asserted that "[w]e consistently stand up for Muslims around the world and talk about how Islam is a wonderful religion."[104] While the State Department was working with the OIC to criminalize free speech through its support of Resolution 16/18 and the Istanbul Process, its Cairo Embassy issued the following Orwellian statement on speech:

> The Embassy of the United States in Cairo condemns the continuing efforts by misguided individuals to **hurt the religious feelings of Muslims**—as we condemn efforts to offend believers of all religions. Today, the 11th anniversary of the September 11, 2001 terrorist attacks on the United States; Americans are honoring our patriots and those who serve our nation as the fitting response to the enemies of democracy. Respect for religious beliefs is a cornerstone of

American democracy. We firmly reject the actions by those who **abuse the universal right of free speech** to **hurt the religious beliefs of others**.[105]

Note the adoption of the "hurt feelings" meme. Also, compare this Embassy statement to the OIC's *Final Communique* from the Third Extraordinary Session in December 2005 (which initiated the Ten-Year Programme of Action), which "stressed the responsibility of all governments to ensure full respect of all religions and religious symbols and the inapplicability of using the freedom of expression as a pretext to defame religions."[106] The Cairo Embassy's lead expert on "political Islam," an Egyptian national named Ahmed Alaibah, would later be arrested for participating in armed riots on January 25, 2014. Alaibah, it turns out, met regularly with the Brotherhood's First Deputy of the General Guide when the Brotherhood was still in power.[107]

As planned, events violently escalated on September 11. The next day, Nassir Abdulaziz al-Nasser, President of the UN General Assembly, said he "condemns and deplores in the strongest terms any acts of defamation of religions and religious symbols" and expressed his concern "that such acts amount to incitement to hatred and xenophobia, and could lead to international instability."[108] He encouraged all Member States and stakeholders to:

> [i]ntensify international efforts to enhance dialogue and broaden understanding among civilizations so as to prevent indiscriminate targeting of religions and cultures. While reaffirming the right to freedom of expression, he calls for the observance of obligations in accordance with International Law.[109]

Compare al-Nasser's statement (and the U.S. Embassy Cairo's release and Marayati's statement) to the language used in Section VII, "Combating Islamophobia," where Paragraph 3 of the OIC's Ten-Year Programme of Action states that OIC Member States are to:

> [e]ndeavor to have the United Nations adopt an international resolution to counter Islamophobia and to call upon all states to enact laws to counter it, including deterrent punishment.[110]

Also compare al-Nasser's language (and the Embassy's and Marayati's) to the OIC Secretary General's language from his 2001 Report on "Defamation of Islam" (now redesignated as "Defamation of Religions" by UN Resolution 16/18 to mask its shariah orientation):

> **Contemporary forms of racism, 3)** Contemporary forms of racism are based on discrimination and disparagement on a cultural, rather than biological basis. In this content, the

increasing trend of Islamophobia, as a distinct form of xeno-phobia in non-Muslim societies is very alarming.[111]

Defamation of religions, 5) The World Conference consid-ers that the defamation of an individual's religion provides the basis of, legitimizes and inevitably leads to the manifes-tation of racism, including in their structural forms, such as Islamophobia against the adherents of that religion.[112]

From the OIC to the Brotherhood to international organizations, we begin to see which non-U.S. entities are driving the narrative that now frames our nation-al-security talking points on free expression. As the planned escalations around the YouTube clip happened on the same day as events in Benghazi, Libya, one might wonder whether the State Department extrapolated from the events in Cairo to explain activities in Benghazi. Then, when the facts of Benghazi did not support their explanation, they doubled down. The activities initiated in Cairo did not end there. Just like the 2006 "Cartoon Crisis," calls for follow-on protests and Days of Rage across the Islamic world were realized on September 14, when no fewer than 26 such events occurred around the globe.[113]

As with other Day of Rage campaigns, reporting on the events seemed to reveal an awareness—and yet not a grasp—of the state action behind them, choos-ing instead to buy in to the skillfully constructed Islamophobia narrative. In a story focusing on "violent crowds furious over an anti-Islamic video made in the United States ... leaving 19 people dead and more than 160 injured" in Pakistan, the *New York Times*, in classic "bury the lead" fashion, stated that this happened on "a day of government-sanctioned protests."[114] Because these buried leads tend to be true, the fact that they are simply stated without being flushed out—more seriously developed—has serious repercussions. After all, who should be held pri-marily responsible for the deaths of citizens killed in riots "sanctioned" – incited - by their own government?

The YouTube campaign culminated with the opening of the 67th Session of the UN General Assembly on September 25, 2012. *Al-Jazeera* reported, "anti-blas-phemy law [was] sharply debated at the UN."[115] At the meeting, speakers from the OIC heads of state took to the podium to denounce the YouTube film. Pakistani President Asif Ali Zardari called for the UN to ban hate speech.[116] Then the Pres-ident of Egypt, the Muslim Brotherhood's Mohamed Morsi, angrily condemned the film, saying, "We reject this. We cannot accept it ... **we will not allow anyone to do this** by word or deed."[117] Turkish Foreign Minister Ahmet Davutoglu de-cried "the protection of Islamophobia," which he claimed was "masquerading as the freedom to speak freely."[118] No fewer than 18 OIC Member States remained on-message when approaching the General Assembly dais to comment.[119]

Toward the end of the 67th Session, OIC Secretary General Ihsanoglu called for a global ban on "offending the character of the Prophet Muhammad," adding that such provocations are "a threat to international peace and security."[120] He then repeated the goal of the OIC's Ten-Year Programme, calling for "adopting measures to criminalize incitement to imminent violence based on religion or belief."

Later in November, Ihsanoglu followed up by saying it "is impossible to defend [the film] in any way," the Secretary General made clear that, in the view of the OIC and its Member States, *Innocence of Muslims* was more than distasteful; its creation was criminal:

> We have to see the issue in its entirety; that is, [*Innocence of Muslims*] was produced by a group whose **hearts are filled with hatred for Islam**, and there was no connection with the American government or their film industry, any connection with this event, the group that put the movie on to the internet are a misguided group that hates Islam. Now when the OIC discovered in one way or another that there is a film that denigrates the prophet, and it indeed denigrates. It's a disgusting piece of work. **It is impossible to defend it in any way; the response was violent, and I think that this violent reaction has [confirmed] the work that we began after the Danish cartoons.**[121]

Note that Ihsanoglu acknowledged the OIC's role in the Cartoon Crisis. Also note that the OIC Secretary General, while condemning the satirical film about Mohammed and Islam in strong terms, did not condemn "responses [that were] violent," which led to the deaths of 50 people. The evidence that OIC-inspired leadership drove the YouTube campaign is strong. In the September–December 2012 edition of the *OIC Journal*, the OIC provided a brief after-action of the YouTube event, where each clause of the statement aligned with an element of the information campaign:

> **(The outrage)** "The film 'Innocence of Muslims' insulting Prophet Mohammed caused a strong wave of anger in the Muslim world;"

> **(The incitement)** "The OIC was among the first to condemn the film <u>as an act of incitement</u>;"

> **(That overrules protected speech)** "Strongly condemning the film as an …. irresponsible misuse of the right to freedom of expression;"

> **(Under Article 19 ICCPR)** "The exercise of which [falls] under International Human Rights Law, according to Arti-

cle 19 of the International Covenant on Civil and Political Rights;"

(Aligned with Resolution 16/18) "They reiterated their strong commitment to take further measures ... on the basis of UN Human Rights Council resolution 16/18;"

(Where the two interests are made equivalencies) "Which emphasizes the respect for freedom of expression and for religious beliefs and symbols are two indivisible principles."[122]

Before moving from the United Nations' role in the YouTube event, a few parting observations are in order. First, neither the U.S. government nor the administration deviated from the collective voice of the Muslim world. Second, as Ambassador to the United Nations, Susan Rice was involved with UN Resolution 16/18, an initiative that remained a focal point of UN activities throughout 2012. Third, at the General Assembly on September 25, President Obama gave a speech announcing "the future must not belong to those who slander the Prophet of Islam."[123] Representatives and heads of state from the 57 OIC Member States could not have been more pleased.

The Obama administration made sure that even if there would be no direct punishment for "slander[ing] the prophet of Islam," there would be consequences—perhaps the "peer pressure and shaming" that Secretary Clinton promised. At the funeral for former Navy Seal Tyrone Woods, who died defending the CIA Annex in Benghazi, Clinton allegedly promised swift punishment for those who angered the Muslim world by producing the video. According to Charles Woods, Tyrone Woods's father, Clinton told him that "we're going to arrest ... the man that made the video."[124]

And indeed, just a day after Obama's speech at the UN, Los Angeles County Sheriff's deputies arrested *Innocence* filmmaker Nakoula.[125] Buoyed by the administration's repeated focus on the film as "incitement to imminent violence," the international press descended on the filmmaker's house in southern California. While he was subsequently imprisoned for one year for violating terms of an earlier conviction unrelated to the YouTube clip, it's hard not to recognize that he was actually imprisoned for making *Innocence of Muslims*. The photographs of Nakoula's arrest were broadcast throughout the Muslim world, still frenzied over the Days of Rage, demonstrating actual American compliance with—and submission to—Islamic speech codes.

From the Cartoon Crisis to the YouTube campaign to *Charlie Hebdo*, the pattern will continue to repeat itself as long as it goes unrecognized and unchallenged. With each campaign, the stakes get higher. Less than a week after the *Charlie Hebdo* executions in January 2015, Ufuk Gokcen, Ambassador to the Permanent Observer Mission of the OIC to the UN,[126] said the "*Charlie Hebdo* attack and reactions underline critical importance of renewed commitment to the resolution of 16/18 and the Rabat Plan of Action."[127] Gokcen's comment linked to an article by the legal officer of the Soros-funded *Article 19* that likewise affirmed the interlocking relationship between the OIC-sponsored UN HRC Resolution 16/18 and the left's effort with Rabat.[128]

Both the OIC and *Article 19* statements presuppose *Charlie Hebdo*'s culpability. Had Resolution 16/18 and the Rabat Plan of Action been fully implemented, the cartoons would have already been criminalized and the incident averted. Ambassador Gokcen's comment verifies — and brings current — the ongoing Islamist / Left alliance.[6] As it is, sanctioned protests in support of the *Hebdo* killings popped up in OIC Member States[129] while OIC Secretary General Iyad Madani announced that the "OIC will not hesitate to prosecute the French magazine" if the law allows. In committing to this action, Madani did so on behalf of the "hurt sentiments of Muslims across the world."[130]

In a public demonstration of convergence, the Muslim Brotherhood immediately fell in line with the OIC. On January 20, 2015, Muslim Brotherhood chief jurist Yusuf Qaradawi posted an announcement from his Doha offices, in his capacity as President of the International Union of Muslim Scholars (IUMS), endorsing the OIC position that further ratified the *Charlie Hebdo* executions. Positioning the Brotherhood as the dawah "good cop" to the jihadi "bad cop," Qaradawi called on the continued demonstration against violations of Islamic slander norms in the West:

> The Union demands the Islamic nation to continue to demonstrate rejecting the abuse to the Great Prophet, the Prophet Muhammad - peace be upon him, who demands respect for religions and all the prophets ...[131]

criminalizing Islamic defamation standards through UN Resolution 16/18:

> The Union calls on Islamic countries to submit a global law draft criminalizing defamation of religions and the prophets and the holy sites of all, through a global conference to discuss

---

6 As will be discussed, Carlos the Jackal (Iliac Ramirez Sanchez) spoke of an active alliance between Marxists and Islamists to destroy the United States.[(a)] The Soros-funded NGO Article 19's efforts with regard to the Rabat Plan of Action in the close relationship with the OIC's promotion of UN Resolution 16/18 is one such example. Along these lines, it's hard not to take notice of a similar correlation of interests between Soros[(b)] and CAIR[(c)] concerning the events in Ferguson, Missouri, in 2014. (a) Iliac Ramirez Sanchez (Carlos the Jackal), *Revolutionary Islam,* published in French, 2003; (b) Kelly Riddell, "George Soros Funds Ferguson Protest, Hopes to Spur Civil Action," *Washington Times,* 14 January 2015, URL: http://www.washingtontimes.com/news/2015/jan/14/george-soros-funds-ferguson-protests-hopes-to-spur/, accessed 18 January 2015; (c) "CAIR Calls for National Action on Racism after Ferguson Grand Jury Decision," CAIR Press Release, 25 November 2014, URL: https://www.cair.com/press-center/press-releases/12741-cair-calls-for-national-action-on-racism-after-ferguson-grand-jury.html, accessed 28 November 2014.

clauses in complete freedom.[132]

while demanding the protection of Muslim minority populations from violence while remaining silent on the killing of non-Muslims:

> The Union calls on Western countries to provide full protection to the Muslims living in their country, whether they are citizens or residents or visitors, especially after a series of systematic attacks, they have suffered from after the events of the French newspaper "Charlie Hebdo" and till now.[133]

further reinforcing that peaceful coexistence is premised on subordinating Western speech standards to Islamic law via ratification of Resolution 16/18:

> The Union stresses on the importance of the issuance of the international code of conduct of peaceful coexistence between nations working on the wording of scholars from all over the world and then be circulated to the internationalist saves means [sic] to ensure the achievement of the desired peaceful coexistence.[134]

and warning that there will be no peace until this happens:

> IUMS believe that coexistence between nations and civilizations [is] in great danger, and international peace and social [sic] has been shaken therefore it calls on the United Nations and other international organizations to remedy this threat through a global conference involving representatives of States, institutions of society; to prevent the practices that lead to a breach of the peace and coexistence, because if you can adjust the settings and eliminate terrorism there.[135]

Positioned as the good cop to the al-Qaeda bad cop, the dawah element works in tandem with the jihadi element under the watchful eye of the ummah, i.e., the Muslim Brotherhood, al-Qaeda, and the OIC. As it is clear that both the ummah and the dawah entities condemn defamation of Islam, and that such a violation can bring the death penalty, there should be little surprise that the jihadi element will act and that there would be indicators that these activities are sanctioned. Islamic apostasy law may provide some guidance – an analogy - on how the operation of shariah law sanctions executions brought on by violating Islamic speech laws. From *Reliance of the Traveller*, once there has been a shariah ruling of apostasy, if someone chooses to take direct action, "there is no indemnity for killing an apostate or any expiation, since it is killing someone who deserves to die."[136]

Recalling that Al-Azhar, the Brotherhood, and the OIC are the same entities that certified *Reliance of the Traveller*,[137] there is no reason to think that the classic shariah stance is not shared by today's leading shariah voices. In fact, on January 19, 2015, Al-Azhar, the highest seat of Sunni Islamic learning, endorsed both OIC and Brotherhood positions on the state of Islamic slander law following the *Charlie Hebdo* massacres.[138]

Commenting on David Cameron's statement that people have a right to say what they want concerning religion in a free society, Al-Azhar Under-Secretary Abbas Shouman responded by saying: "Cameron can say what he wants, but we don't accept it; we don't have to explain 'freedom' to him or to anyone else; freedoms don't include offending religion." Describing the cartoon of Mohammed in *Charlie Hebdo* following the January executions as "counter to human values, freedoms, cultural diversity, tolerance and respect to human rights [that] deepens hatred and discrimination between Muslims and others," Dar Al-Ifta, the Al-Azhar entity responsible for issuing fatwas and related shariah edicts, declared the decision to publish such cartoons was "an act unjustifiably provocative to the feelings of a billion and a half Muslims worldwide who love and respect the Prophet."[139] The Islamic world has staked out its position on enforcing Islamic speech standards after *Hebdo* and that is to proceed on enforcement. The OIC, the Brotherhood, and Al-Azhar are converged on a unified position. Islamic extremism? This is as mainstream, strategic, and institutional as it gets.

Activities surrounding *Charlie Hebdo* serve as a classic—and current—example of convergence, and yet nowhere is this reported as the coordinated existential threat that it is. Perhaps this is because it violently contradicts the "extreme" and "lone wolf" narratives that drive the violent extremist narrative. As this is year ten of the OIC's Ten-Year Programme of Action, the West should be bracing for impact. CAIR may have already sent its first shot across the bow in a January 26, 2015, press release with a title that pretty much says it all: "CAIR Open Letter to 2016 Republican Presidential Candidates: Engage Muslim Voters, Reject Islamophobia."[140]

Blindness and its Consequences

To date, the Islamophobia/Days of Rage narrative follows a familiar arc: Calculated acts of retribution follow acts of so-called Islamophobia. With the January 2015 executions of *Charlie Hebdo* staff, events may be transitioning to enforcement. Yet this type of expression is specifically protected by our Constitution. Understood this way, a supra-national campaign to stamp out Islamophobia more closely resembles an intentional assault on free expression from abroad. When media pundits, in response to Days of Rage, call for reconsideration of otherwise protected speech because it's deemed Islamophobic, watch for the "fire in a crowded theater" analogy. Note how seamlessly it fits with the "test of consequences."

The knowledge deficit caused by Islamic speech standards has consequences that extend beyond questions of free expression and take on strategic proportions.

There are geopolitical consequences to activities sanctioned by Islamic law that need to be recognized before they can be countered. For example, the obligatory requirement to wage jihad when non-Muslim forces are in Muslim lands is more than just an al-Qaeda talking point. It is undisputed Islamic law.

Strategies arising out of the Ten-Year Programme of Action are the defeat mechanism by which those hostile to our way of life plan to defeat us. Its successful implementation would constitute a strategic victory because, through the subversion of our First Amendment, the Islamic world gains a measure of control over the content of America's speech and, ultimately, our thoughts as well. It constitutes a serious threat to our national security, not least because it's so little understood.

If OIC policy on Islamophobia is successfully implemented, there will be no real way to recognize it, because no one knows what to look for. It becomes difficult to defend against assaults to the integrity of the U.S. Constitution (both Article VI and the First Amendment) if one is rendered incapable of recognizing the threat. Our blindness to this whithering assault reflects the effectiveness of a campaign of intimidation; decision-makers and analysts fear being labeled "Islamophobes" more than they are committed to their duties to support and defend the Constitution. The success of the Islamophobia campaign owes much to the fact that it rides in the slipstream of postmodern narratives on diversity and multiculturalism. Our decision "not to know" dovetails nicely with the efforts of foreign entities to keep us from understanding.

The OIC acts covertly in broad daylight. So does the Brotherhood. While this may seem like a contradiction, it speaks to a current reality: The OIC executes its mission openly, in English, and yet our national-security decision-makers and analysts make policy as if unaware both of the organization's existence and of the policies it promotes. You can't defend what you don't know against vulnerabilities you can't see. Al-Qaeda knows it, the Muslim Brotherhood knows it, and our Coalition Partners know it, too.

At a time when a dawah entity, the Muslim Brotherhood, seeks to control domestic discourse on issues relating to Islam inside the United States, the dominant ummah entity, the OIC, is making parallel efforts to control the same discourse in international forums. In terms of information operations, Brotherhood and OIC lines of operation run in harmony and interoperate because they converge on a central point—shariah. If OIC / Brotherhood activities were a kinetic operation, we would call it an envelopment.

There is nothing random about where we currently find ourselves. Our lack of strategic awareness speaks to the active measures that sustain a critical information deficit in the face of the obvious. The droids we cannot see — and should be looking for — are right before us.

Catastrophic Failures

Fi Sabilillah

Speculation could potentially heighten backlash against some of our Muslim soldiers and what happened at Fort Hood was a tragedy, but I believe it would be an even greater tragedy if our diversity becomes a casualty here.

General George Casey
Chief of Staff of the U.S. Army
8 November 2009

Tolerance becomes a crime when applied to evil.

Thomas Mann
A Good Soldier (1924)

And I applied my mind to know wisdom and to know madness and folly. I perceived that this also is but a striving after the wind. For in much wisdom is much vexation, and he who increases knowledge increases sorrow.

Ecclesiastes 1:17–18

Many of those tasked with defending the Constitution and the nation's security have become, in effect, enforcers of a hostile information campaign tailored to deprive America of what it needs to know to defend itself against an existential threat. From the start of the War on Terror, much of the information driving analysis and decision-making has been subordinated to what America's organized Islamic community permits non-Muslims to know. This is a profound failure of the most basic duty of intelligence—threat analysis.

If analysts and policymakers tasked with national security duties undertook real threat analysis, that analysis would illuminate the nexus between Islamic law and our enemies threat doctrine in the War on Terror. It would allow for the generation of new tactics and the ability to forecast future events. It would also highlight the Islamic Movement and the Muslim Brotherhood as major subversive threats. Due to this hostile information campaign, however, our national security establishment remains in the dark.

The purpose of this book is to address demonstrable failures in America's national security, foreign policy, and counterterror efforts. The chapters that follow are examinations of several of these—all with tragic real-world body counts that could have been avoided.

Discouraging Thoughts on Oversight

Because most of Part 7 deals with catastrophic failures in the relevant national security and law enforcement divisions of the Bush and Obama administrations, it seems appropriate to start with a brief vignette designed to provide warning that one should not expect any relief from congressional oversight. The story of Ghulam Nabi Fai's sustained influence operation on Capitol Hill serves as an indicator that Congress may likewise be compromised. Running concurrently, the overt effort to suppress requests for Inspector General reports (on Muslim Brotherhood penetration into the organs of government) that played out through the summer of 2012 warns of the effectiveness of that influence. While the two stories are offered together, there is no claim that the stories are related except that the one confirms a climate that makes the other possible.

On June 13, 2012, five Members of Congress co-signed five requests to five Inspector Generals to report on Brotherhood influence within their respective departments. The Representatives were Michele Bachmann, Louie Gohmert, Trent Franks, Lynn Westmoreland, and Thomas Rooney. The requests were to the Inspectors General of the Department of State,[1] Department of Homeland Security (DHS),[2] Department of Defense (DOD),[3] Department of Justice (DOJ),[4] and the Office of the Director of National Intelligence (ODNI).[5] Rather than attack all five Representatives and all five requests, the strategy was to undermine the otherwise normal oversight requests while intimidating the requesting representatives by narrowing the focus on one Representative, Michele Bachmann, and on one IG request (the one to the State Department). The campaign began on July 12, 2012, with a letter from Democratic Congressman Keith Ellison to Rep. Bachmann.[6]

From there, the Republican Speaker of the House, John Boehner, and Republican Chairman of the House Permanent Select Committee on Intelligence, Rep. Mike Rogers, took the lead in an effort to publically quash Rep. Bachmann's request.

Less than a year earlier, a little-covered but consequential D.C. spy case resulted in the conviction of Ghulam Nabi Fai, a Pakistani Inter-Services Intelligence (ISI) operative, in a multi-decade influence campaign on Capitol Hill.[7] As has often been the case with reporting on domestic terrorism–related issues, one had to learn of espionage on Capitol Hill by reading foreign media. In fact, the story was broadly covered in both Pakistan and India. Fai was under investigation for some time, but it wasn't until the explosive reporting of the *Hindustan Times* that the FBI took action.[8]

At the same time that this broad-spectrum foreign influence campaign was going on, and while U.S. troops were engaged in combat activities in Afghanistan and Iraq, congressional oversight was silent on the Secretary of State's agreeing to work with the OIC to subordinate the First Amendment to Islamic slander law through the façade of UN Resolution 16/18.[9] Also at the same time, the Assistant Attorney General refused to commit to the Chairman of the Subcommittee on the Constitution that he would never enforce such a legal standard made necessary by that resolution.[10] Meanwhile, DHS was relying on leading members of known Muslim-Brotherhood front groups, including ISNA President Mohamed Imam Magid, to develop policies on Countering Violent Extremism that are demonstrably in line with the underlying requirements envisioned by the OIC's Ten-Year Programme of Action.[11] Oversight? What oversight?

In a demonstration of bipartisan support, Rep. Dutch Ruppersberger, the ranking Democrat on the Permanent Select Committee on Intelligence (HPSCI, pronounced "hipsi"), shared Rogers's confidence that the U.S. government is capable of monitoring and preventing espionage and influence operations. He noted, "We have to be very concerned about the Muslim Brotherhood," but concluded by saying, "Believe me, we are very good at intelligence."[12] "Very good"? This is the same HPSCI that listened to the Director of National Intelligence (DNI) testify that the Brotherhood "is a largely secular organization".[13]

This brings us back to the ongoing concern relating to Muslim-Brotherhood penetration. Ghulam Nabi Fai, the convicted Pakistani who worked on the Hill, was not only an agent of influence for the Pakistani ISI, he was also the national president of the Muslim Student Association (MSA) and served on the Shura Council of the Islamic Society of North America (ISNA), both leading organizations known to be affiliated with the Muslim Brotherhood.[14] When *USA Today* reported that Rep. Rogers believes that Rep. Bachmann's concerns about Brotherhood infiltration were unfounded,[15] it was unclear what Rogers's claim was based on. And why did he put such effort into an unseemly power play of this kind? Republican Senator John McCain joined in the attack and slammed Bachmann from the Senate Floor.[16]

The attacks from Boehner, Rogers, and McCain were public, unprovoked, and launched without warning. The activities had all the markings of a political execution of a fellow party member. For her part, Bachmann responded to Rep. Ellison's July 12 letter the very next day with a fact-filled, sixteen-page letter, outlining the factual basis for investigating Brotherhood influence in America.[17] Unsurprisingly, the critics brushed it aside and continued the assault. It's hard not to notice that the Republican leaders went after the lone female Representative and Tea Party leader.

While requests to the Inspector General (IG) for reports into any undue Brotherhood influence in the relevant divisions of the government are entirely within the scope of the Article I oversight mission of the requesting representatives, the Brotherhood would surely exert whatever influence it has to stop such an undertaking.

It is the interplay between these two stories that helps explain why Patrick Poole would title his article on the topic "The Biggest DC Spy Scandal You Haven't Heard About." It is obvious that our national security leadership cannot allow itself to take the case of Nabi Fai seriously. He is no longer serving a sentence, has not been deported, and was free to be a guest speaker at ISNA's annual convention in Detroit in September 2014.[18]

As the coordinated attack on Bachmann suggests, the Muslim Brotherhood, through its various interlocking front organizations, influences government policies through information campaigns with a demonstrated ability to swarm and overwhelm at the point of attack. Where they seek to execute, the targeted leadership can be enveloped and then stampeded. Did this happen here? Two things are certain: First, thirteen years into the War on Terror, Article I oversight continues to be the dog that doesn't bark. Second, the message to House Members is that if you look into the Muslim Brotherhood, no prisoners will be taken.

As this suggests, the chronic blindness to terror threats that emanate from the Muslim community can be explained in part by the obsessive needfulness of our counterterror and media elites to form outreach relationships with the very entities that were, or should have been, the objects of serious investigation. It should be noted, however, that the five Representatives concerned about Brotherhood influence were vindicated by an Inspector General report initiated by former Rep. Frank Wolf suggesting how institutionalized these relations have become. In a September 2013 report from the U.S. Department of Justice, Office of the Inspector General, titled "Review of FBI Interactions with the Council on American-Islamic Relations," the finding was:

> In 2008, the FBI developed a policy intended to restrict FBI field offices' non-investigative interactions with CAIR. However, in three of the five incidents we reviewed, we concluded that the policy was not followed.[19]

While this book does not focus specifically on the Brotherhood's deep penetration into the decision-making apparatus of American institutions of governance, one can hardly address the severity of the situation without making reference to it. For an assessment of the depths of Brotherhood penetration, Patrick Poole's *Dangerous Alliances: The Scandal of US Government Muslim Outreach* (Maccabeus Press, 2014) is the most current, detailed, and accurate. As we continue to witness America's participation in what may be the greatest ongoing malfeasance in U.S. national security history—the establishment of the Muslim Brotherhood and al-Qaeda in the Arab world—the true cost of this penetration has yet to be fully realized.

The Disappearing Language

More than a decade into the War on Terror, national security elites succeeded in dismantling the tools necessary to understand and defeat the enemy. Encouraged by postmodern narratives and a media hostile to anti-terror efforts, national security elites launched their own campaign against any speech or thought that accurately depicts the Islamic drivers of Islamic-based terror. Not surprisingly, it has outperformed their success in the War on Terror.

When assessing the war on Islamophobia, it is critical to keep in mind the relationship between what is considered Islamophobia and the Islamic definition of slander (or blasphemy). Many non-Muslim enforcers of what, in practice, amounts to shariah standards on free speech are motivated not by Islamic law, but rather by postmodern narratives heavily influenced by leftist ideological convictions. For left-leaning individuals who carry such convictions, long chains of assumptions about the War on Terror are tied to postmodern narratives relating to economic depravation, colonialism, and issues of racial grievance. For many on the left, Islamophobia fits into the prevailing diversity narrative that includes race, gender, and homophobia. As one moves farther left on this spectrum, reliance on the narrative enforces conformance even when a critical analysis of the doctrinal elements of Islam demonstrates the narrative to be counterfactual. This lines up with the expansive definition of racism promoted by the OIC—a definition, as noted, that turns the actual definition of racism on its head. In this way, the expansive view of racism associated with the postmodern left merges seamlessly with shariah notions of slander.

Postmodern narratives are not the only motivating force. What the Muslim Brotherhood's *Explanatory Memorandum* called "civilization-jihad" has been in place for some time, furthering its campaign of subversion aimed at the American media, the government, and civil society. Of all its targets, none is more high-value than the national security and law enforcement communities. This is because Brotherhood lines of operation that successfully penetrate these sectors would effectively short-circuit threat analysis in the War on Terror by manipulating national security leaders into targeting national security members who don't toe the line. The success of this effort over the past several years has been shocking.

Conformance to OIC requirements in this postmodern paradigm involves implementing Islamic defamation law in the guise of fighting Islamophobia, which does not require an awareness on the part of those implementing it since specific performance[1] is all that is required. Choosing not to discuss the specifically Islamic aspects of the War on Terror (and domestic terrorism) in the national security arena is submission to that Islamic standard. If left unchecked, it will lead to American defeat in the War on Terror. (Who wants to argue that we're winning?)

The goal behind the Brotherhood's portion of the information campaign is to suppress all discussion concerning Islam in the government and public space. It works as a recurring loop: First, government officials or appointees leak allegations of Islamophobic bias in the national security community. A partisan media outlet then amplifies the claim, triggering loud complaints and demands for restitution from Muslim Brotherhood–linked lobby groups. Next, national security leaders in government, citing the lobby's protests, endeavor to squelch the offending materials, programs, or individuals.

I witnessed this campaign first-hand. In the summer of 2011, National Public Radio carried the news that I was scheduled to appear as a lecturer at a counterterrorism event held by the Central Intelligence Agency.[20] My presentation was to be a sampling of some of the material in this book. Within hours of the original article's publication, CAIR demanded that the CIA cancel my appearance, referring to me as an "Islamophobe." NPR dutifully followed up in minutes, publishing another story to emphasize the Brotherhood-linked pressure group's narrative.[21] "It is vitally important that CIA agents carry out their work protecting our nation based on real security threats, not on inaccurate and agenda-driven Islamophobic rhetoric," wrote CAIR National Executive Director Nihad Awad in a letter to then-CIA Director Leon Panetta.[22]

Days later, under great pressure from the Department of Homeland Security—and, it was whispered to me, the White House—the CIA was ordered to stand down and delay the entire three-day counterterror training program. From then on, DHS was to assume subject-matter jurisdiction over what it calls the "Homegrown Radical Extremism" portfolio:

> The conference topic is a critical one for domestic law enforcement, and the sponsors—in partnership with the De-

---

1   *Black's Law Dictionary* defines "performance" as "the fulfillment or accomplishment of a promise, contract, or other obligation according to its terms, relieving such person of all further obligations" and "specific performance" as "the remedy of requiring exact performance of a contract in the specific form in which it was made, according to the precise terms agreed upon." In this book, the term "specific performance" is not used in its strictly legal sense but rather more generally to mean that those tasked with a role are required only to perform that role but not necessarily to know why. For the Brotherhood and the OIC, it is neither necessary nor desired that those performing missions on their behalf understand the roles they play, just that they perform them. (Lenin had a less kind term for those performing in this status.) *Black's Law Dictionary 6th*, West Publishing, St. Paul, 1990, 1137, 1138.

partment of Homeland Security—have decided to delay the conference so it can include insights from, among other sources, the new National Strategy for Counterterrorism in an updated agenda.23

From the perspective of America's Brotherhood-linked groups, the intended outcome of these frenzied campaigns against Islamophobia is to cause a surrender of situational awareness brought on by an induced knowledge deficit. Ordinary Americans get only an occasional glimpse into this deficit and, when they do, react with disgust. The consequence is a steady undermining of confidence in our leadership. To a public that has growing awareness of the Brotherhood, the loss of confidence in America's national security establishment will at some point overwhelm. In my first year as an ROTC cadet, we were taught that delegitimizing the current regime is a principal objective of any insurgency. There's no reason to think this has changed.

As I briefed while still in the Pentagon, this type of information campaign is designed to cascade and reinforce downstream narratives long after they cease to be credible. When a subordinate starts to track events in a factual manner that challenges the conclusory assumptions of seniors, and the leader begins to suspect that the subordinate is correct, the leader may only then begin to grasp the sheer magnitude of his own negligence and, hence, will develop a heightened personal interest in enforcing the "combating Islamophobia" narrative for no other reason than to protect his reputation. This may also hold true for elite media. Of course, choosing not to know the doctrinal drivers that motivate an enemy will *always* benefit the enemy and *always* harm the friendly. Unfortunately, in this war, it also enhances promotability. Fighting a war in "deer in the headlights" mode *must* lead to systemic failure. The enemy knows this. Increasingly, so does the American public.

Purging the Language

The enemy in the War on Terror plans to win the war through subversion in the information battlespace by making it too politically costly to identify the threat. It accomplishes this by manipulating American leadership and media into imposing Islamic defamation standards on the national security and law enforcement communities and on the American public. For example, by directing entities like the DHS's Office of Civil Rights and Civil Liberties to implement punishment for speech that exceeds the circumscribed limits of Islamic law, the government is enforcing a hostile foreign standard against the enumerated constitutional right it exists to protect. These activities parallel those in the international arena where the OIC takes the lead.

The Muslim Public Affairs Council (MPAC) defines its mission as, among other things, "cultivating relationships with opinion- and decision-makers."24 It was formed in Los Angeles by brothers Maher and Hassan Hathout, two immigrants with longstanding ties to the Brotherhood and disciples of Brotherhood founder Hassan al-Banna. MPAC was established in 1986 as the Political Action Committee of the Islamic Center of Southern California, whose key leaders had their origins in the Egyptian Brotherhood. Since then, MPAC has functioned as the political-lobbying arm of the Islamic Movement and is close to, if not an element of, the Brotherhood in America.[25] In 2004 testimony before the 9/11 Commission, the group demanded that the U.S. government purge its language of references to Islam.

> **The problem with the term Islamism:** Terminology is important in defining our goals as well as removing roadblocks into hearts and minds. The 9/11 Commission identifies Islamist terrorism as the threat. The Muslim Public Affairs Council recommends that the US government find other terminology.[26]

MPAC recommends that the "US government find other terminology" because it rejects linkage between Islam and terrorism. In a way, MPAC is correct, because the operative definition of "terrorism" for MPAC comes from shariah – the killing a Muslim without right. Because jihad involves Muslims fighting non-Muslims, it does not meet the Islamic criteria for terrorism. But this definition does not match U.S. statutory definitions of terrorism; those definitions are concerned with the terrorizing and killing of innocent people, including those terrorized and killed under the banner of jihad. American notions of terrorism[2]

---

2   In the interest of due diligence, the specific statutory definition of terrorism as provided by the FBI, 18 U.S.C. § 2331, defines "international terrorism" and "domestic terrorism" for purposes of Chapter 113B of the Code, entitled "Terrorism":
"International terrorism" means activities with the following three characteristics:

* Involve violent acts or acts dangerous to human life that violate federal or state law;
* Appear to be intended (i) to intimidate or coerce a civilian population; (ii) to influence the policy of a government by intimidation or coercion; or (iii) to affect the conduct of a government by mass destruction, assassination, or kidnapping; and
* Occur primarily outside the territorial jurisdiction of the U.S., or transcend national boundaries in terms of the means by which they are accomplished, the persons they appear intended to intimidate or coerce, or the locale in which their perpetrators operate or seek asylum.

"Domestic terrorism" means activities with the following three characteristics:

* Involve acts dangerous to human life that violate federal or state law;
* Appear intended (i) to intimidate or coerce a civilian population; (ii) to influence the policy of a government by intimidation or coercion; or (iii) to affect the conduct of a government by mass destruction, assassination, or kidnapping; and
* Occur primarily within the territorial jurisdiction of the U.S.

18 U.S.C. § 2332b defines the term "federal crime of terrorism" as an offense that:

* Is calculated to influence or affect the conduct of government by intimidation or coercion, or to retaliate against government conduct; and
* Is a violation of one of several listed statutes, including § 930(c) (relating to killing or attempted killing during an attack on a federal facility with a dangerous weapon); and § 1114 (relating to killing or attempted killing of officers and employees of the U.S.).

involve acts dangerous to human life that are intended to coerce a civilian population or influence the policy of a government by intimidation or coercion, or to affect the conduct of a government by mass destruction, assassination, or kidnapping.[27] Hence, if knowledge of Islam and jihad are removed from the analytical framework when analyzing groups like al-Qaeda, one cannot generate a strategic understanding of why the enemy fights and kills us while also building support from Muslims who sincerely believe they are acting out of faith.

Accusations of Islamophobia—corresponding to Islamic notions of slander—are intended to deny the freedom to express a non-conforming opinion or fact about Islam, even when that opinion or fact is accurate. MPAC's testimony before the 9/11 Commission was an overt call to subordinate American national security interests to that standard by replacing its vocabulary.

The attack on the government's vocabulary in the War on Terror is an attack against cognitive function. We use words not only to convey complex ideas to others, but also to understand those ideas ourselves. Constraining the vocabulary we use to understand a thing necessarily constrains—in fact, alters—our understanding of the thing itself. In terms of national security, this can lead to the loss of life or irreparable harm to the war effort.

Another MPAC report, "A Review of U.S. Counterterrorism Policy: American Muslim Critique & Recommendations," published in 2003, targeted the FBI, DHS, the Treasury Department, and the Justice Department for penetration. The group envisioned using its influence to commandeer the training of government entities in order to ensure that they better service "Islamic Movements":

> National Muslim organizations should develop educational materials and other initiatives designed to **educate law enforcement officials**, particularly at the **Departments of Justice**, **Treasury**, and **Homeland Security** about Islamic culture, the proper use and meanings of religious terms (such as jihad), and the histories behind the growth and ideologies of **Islamic movements**.[28]

Recall the understood doctrinal nature of the term "Islamic Movement." MPAC is demanding that national security decision-makers and analysts be barred from mentioning Islam when analyzing terrorism known to originate from self-identified Islamic entities that self-disclose the Islamic basis of their terrorist activity. In its dealings with the Muslim Public Affairs Council, the Department of Homeland Security was targeted by an Islamic Movement entity openly seeking to propagandize them on the nature of "Islamic Movements," which the Explanatory Memorandum clearly states "lies on the shoulders of Muslims and—on top of them—the Muslim Brotherhood in this country"[29] and whose goal is "a kind of grand Jihad in eliminating and destroying the Western civilization from within and 'sabotaging' its miserable house by their hands."[30] Under this Brotherhood paradigm, "their hands" would necessarily be the hands of those who would import this training and impose it on subordinates.

Today, FBI and Homeland Security analysts are sanctioned if they refer to the Islamic Movement by name, even if citing to threat sources that use those same Islamic terms. There is an "Islamic Movement" in America, and it's run by the Muslim Brotherhood. FBI and DHS special agents and analysts, though, are being told they cannot use terms like "Islam." As a consequence, they cannot discuss or analyze things that concern "Islam," such as **Islamic** Jihad," **Islamic** Society of North America (ISNA), the Council on American **Islamic** Relations (CAIR), the **Islamic** Association for Palestine (IAP), the **Islamic** Resistance Movement (aka Hamas, a designated terrorist organization running unimpeded in this country), and, of course, the "**Islamic Movement**" itself. Both Hamas and the Taliban[31] identify themselves with the Islamic Movement. Even the phrase "observant Muslim base" from the Explanatory Memorandum, which could be transliterated as "*Al Qaeda al-Muslamina al-Moltzema,*" is disfavored.

The order not to use terms such as "Islam" is an order not to know or speak of the enemy in the War on Terror in factual terms. It is an order to blind oneself to the motivations of entities that may be ideologically aligned with the enemy. It is an order not to conduct evidence-driven investigations or intelligence analysis. It is an order for national security analysts to pretend they are talking about threats to the country when in fact they are simply speaking to narratives that support sanitized, soft-science models. As will be discussed, the "pretend" language is the narrative associated with Countering Violent Extremism (CVE). As the name implies, CVE is much more concerned with enforcing diversity interests than threat identification.

MPAC's training on the "proper use and meaning of religious terms" is actually a demand that such terms not be used at all. In an obvious way, this puts groups like the Muslim Brotherhood out of the reach of investigators, national security analysts, and even concerned Members of Congress.

The cumulative effect of this campaign to blind our leadership has effectively put Brotherhood-linked groups and individuals above and outside of the law. That such an effort could succeed so easily is disturbing. One suspects that Muslim Brothers must have to work at keeping a straight face when meeting senior government leaders.

In giving direction to the government, MPAC urges the replacement of the word "Islamic" with abstractions like "radicalized" or "violent extremist." These terms have been used to obscure the discussion in unnecessary and irrelevant discourse on how "terrorists and violent extremists vary in ethnicity, race, gender and religion."[32] A survey of all the terrorism perpetrated by every group through millennia, however, in no way addresses the here and now of the War on Terror. Limiting discussions on terrorism to the realm of the academically plausible reduces combatting terrorism to theoretical babble—which is the intended outcome.

In my years giving presentations on the War on Terror both inside and outside of the government, the most well-known feature of my briefings has been a simple chart. It has been reproduced on television, in books, think-tank papers, congressional hearings, and was even enlarged for display on the floor of the House of Representatives. It is a comparison of four key national and homeland security texts written by the U.S. government—the *9/11 Commission Report*[33] (2004), the *FBI Counterterrorism Analytical Lexicon*[34] (2008) from the Bush administration, the *National Intelligence Strategy of the United States*[35] (2009) from the Obama administration, and *Protecting the Force: Lessons from Ft. Hood* (2010).[36]

The chart examines the incidence of basic terms relating to jihadi-based terrorism in the four documents, illustrating a comparison of word usage by American homeland security, law enforcement, and intelligence over time, from 2004 to 2010. When looking closely at the number of times particular words are used, the chart's title, "the Disappearing Language of Terror," becomes significant.

THE DISAPPEARING LANGUAGE OF TERROR

	9/11 Commission Report (2004)	FBI Counterterrorism Analytical Lexicon (2008)	National Intelligence Strategy (2009)	Protecting the Force: Lessons from Ft. Hood (2010)
Violent Extremism	3	29	9	0
Enemy	39	0	0	0
Jihad	126	0	0	0
Muslim	145	0	0	0
Islam	322	0	0	0
Muslim Brotherhood	5	0	0	0
Religious	65	3	1	59
Hamas	4	0	0	0
Hezbollah	2	0	0	0
al-Qaeda	36	0	1	0
Caliph/Kalif	7	0	0	0
Shariah/Shar'ia	2	0	0	0

With the *9/11 Commission Report* serving as the baseline, the chart demonstrates that, since 2004, the analytical lexicons of our law enforcement and national security communities have been sanitized of references to any terminology relating to relevant Islamic terms - including jihad. Since 2008, if the goal of our official lexicons has been to deny the role of threat identification in the intelligence process, it has succeeded. The purging of language had the intended effect of undermining the 9/11 Commission's findings.

In the three subsequent documents from 2008 to 2010, if the term "Muslim" does not appear, it follows that the Muslim Brotherhood will not be mentioned. While jihadist groups from al-Qaeda to the Taliban to the Muslim Brotherhood self-identify as being a part of a common "Islamic Movement," that umbrella entity, along with its stated objectives, is left unrecognized. With a single exception where al-Qaeda was used in 2009 as an example of a Violent Extremist group, other notorious Islamic terrorist groups were left unnamed.[37] The language of knowledge was purged, replaced by narrative enforcing terms that provide the illusion of knowledge where none exists. So damaging was this information on disappearing language when briefed that at one point the FBI erroneously informed the House Judiciary Staff that the *FBI Counterterrorism Analytical Lexicon*[38] did not exist – suggesting that the analysis was contrived.

In 2010, the censorship extended to include official reporting on Nidal Hasan's jihadist murder spree at Fort Hood, Texas. *Protecting the Force: Lessons from Fort Hood* even refused to designate the premeditated terrorist attack with the normally favored euphemism "violent extremism." Everything about Hasan's activities at Fort Hood that day in 2009 was steeped in jihad. As some of Hasan's slides have already shown, and as will be further demonstrated, the U.S. Army Major's warnings to his fellow service members were brazenly obvious and irrefutable to anyone who took his stated threats seriously. The subsequent report's failure to recognize or account for Hasan's expressed jihadi motivations raised serious questions about its integrity.

The Department of Defense designated the Fort Hood attack as an act of "workplace violence."[39] Americans were outraged. It's better to insult the intelligence of the American people and the memories of the fallen, the Pentagon must have reasoned, than to be accused of writing a report that by virtue of being accurate would also be declared Islamophobic. These narratives are designed to enforce diversity interests over national security. General Casey, Chief of Staff of the U.S. Army, made this clear following the Fort Hood shooting:

> What happened at Fort Hood was a tragedy but I believe it would be an even greater tragedy if our diversity becomes a casualty here ... [40]

You may be wondering: How could the military explain Hasan's actions if its official report refused to provide an honest account of him? Simple—just don't mention him in the report. MAJ Hasan was not mentioned in the *Protecting the Force* report.

The U.S. government's requirement to avoid accusations of Islamophobia feeds the need to fabricate arguments of insanity and diminished capacity. The jumble and nonsense of these arguments has the effect of obviating the need to address motive. After all, if someone is unbalanced, what's the point of looking for a motive? It also masks substantive evidence of a hate crime, not to mention premeditated murder. Why would national leaders submit to the whitewash of "workplace violence" or insanity in light of the brazen terror attack on American citizens on U.S. soil? That the government resorts to such pseudoscientific babble helps to explain how "jihadi" dots fail to get connected in otherwise straightforward cases.

'Violent Extremism'

In the *FBI Counterterrorism Analytical Lexicon* of 2008, the term "violent extremism" displaced any valuable description of the characteristics of the enemy in the War on Terror. This absence of precision mirrors the way America now fights wars. The War on Terror has been fought on a series of twenty-minute PowerPoint briefs, "5x8s," and "quadcharts" designed to do little more than get past the next decision or reporting cycle. Because we are now fighting an abstracted enemy—"violent extremists" who are *extreme* precisely because they are *violent*, and *violent* precisely because they are *extreme*—the analytical model does not require real analysis – in fact, it requires no thinking at all.

The FBI seems to be aware of the problems associated with the term "violent extremism," including the regression to a fourth-grade level of thinking it induces when used by analysts and policymakers. Its *Lexicon* defines the concept as follows:

> "Violent extremism" is any ideology that encourages, endorses, condones, justifies, or supports the commission of a violent act or crim [sic] against the United States, its government, citizens, or allies in order to achieve political, social, or economic changes, or against individuals or groups who hold contrary opinions. Violent extremism differs from "radicalism" in that violent extremists explicitly endorse, encourage, or commit acts of violence or provide material support to those who do. "Radicalism" is a much looser term that does not necessarily indicate acceptance or endorsement of violent methods, and is therefore not preferred. "Extremist" should be coupled with "violent" for purposes of clarity. It should be noted that some "extreme" or "radical" activity—such as spreading propaganda—might be constitutionally protected. **An analytical judgment that an individual is a "violent extremist," "extremist," or "radical" is not predication for any investigative action or technique.**[41]

If you attempt to parse the definition of violent extremism, which I did in a presentation to the FBI's Behavior Analysis Unit, you will see that there is no core definition. On closer inspection, the FBI's definition is not randomly wrong, but rather it is precisely incoherent. Indeed, the same *Lexicon* that demands that FBI personnel use the term "violent extremism" also declares it inappropriate for actual use as "predication for any investigative actions."[42]

Given the prominent status of "violent extremism" in such nihilism-inducing narratives, the calculated reduction-to-meaninglessness of the definition should not be attributed to incompetence.

Despite its recognized lack of definition, the "violent extremism" concept was implemented at the bureaucratic level under the Countering Violent Extremism (CVE) label with DHS's Civil Rights and Civil Liberties Division (CRCL) taking lead. Of note, the CRCL Division does not have a threat identification or intelligence mission. It has no qualification or mission scope in either the threat identification role of intelligence personnel or the investigative processes of special agents. To the extent that CRCL is able to impose its lexicon—and, with it, the associated "violent extremism" narrative—on the rest of the U.S. government, it usurps the intelligence mission from entities with statutory responsibility for undertaking threat analysis or criminal investigations.

At the same time that the FBI was adopting "violent extremism" as the replacement term for terrorism, DHS uncritically outsourced its lexicon requirements to third parties and, in so doing, outsourced its understanding of the nature of the threat. At the direction of DHS Secretary Michael Cherthoff, CRCL published "Terminology to Define the Terrorists: Recommendations from American Muslims" in January 2008. The report's recommendations seemed to reflect the embargoing of Islam-related terminology that groups like MPAC had pressed for since 2004.[43]

> Regarding "jihad," **even if it is accurate** to reference the term, it **may not be strategic** because it glamorizes terrorism, imbues terrorists with religious authority they do not have and damages relations with Muslims around the world. [44]

While there is statutory law that requires action to be taken in furtherance of the constitutional requirement to "support and defend" against all enemies—including terrorists—it has been countered by the emergence of a competing postmodern standard that demands the suppression of facts "even if [they are] accurate." This standard was implemented at the bureaucratic level under the name Countering Violent Extremism (CVE).

The CVE standard makes no distinction between al-Qaeda and returning U.S. combat veterans. Through the course of the War on Terror, a bait-and-switch took place: Our strategic orientation switched from a constitutional legal framework to that of a contra-constitutional narrative enforced by bureaucrats. In other words, the constitutional duty to "support and defend" against enemies was replaced by narratives built around soft-science models that generate generic behavioral indicators of violent extremism that may or may not have anything to do with terrorism. While the American public thinks its government is fighting terrorists, that government has long since transitioned to managing the narrative defined by the CVE. We can pretend they are the same, but they're not. To begin with, only one is real.

Countering MPAC's claim, an accurately defined term is always strategically appropriate. Who benefits from imposing imprecise terms on analytical processes? It is always strategically beneficial to our enemies when our analytical processes are degraded. In 2008, the National Counterterrorism Center (NCTC) issued another document that likewise reflected the linguistic aspirations of Brotherhood-linked groups like MPAC. "Words that Work and Words that Don't: A Guide for Counterterrorism Communications" illustrated that the CVE narrative was in full effect. In one sentence, the NCTC described the seriousness with which they undertake their mission:

> When possible, **avoid using terms drawn from Islamic theology** in conversation unless you are prepared to discuss their **varying meaning over the centuries**. *Examples:* Salafi, Wahhabist, **caliphate**, Sufi, **ummah**. Do not use "ummah" to mean "the Muslim world." It is not a sociological term, rather, it is a theological construct not used in everyday life.[45]

What is one to make of this requirement not to use terms "unless you are prepared to discuss their varying meaning over the centuries"? Just try that with words like "democracy" or "virtue." Of course, the material in the first half of this book would be considered off-limits or impermissible knowledge—as would every terrorist communication that references Islamic terminology in its communications. (That would be nearly all of them.) The very fact that the OIC is an inter-governmental political entity that officially states that it represents the ummah[46] makes the NCTC's "Words that Work" claim regarding the status of ummah both dangerously ignorant and laughable. This is a directive aimed at neutralizing the ability of an analyst or decision-maker to make policy and strategy directives in the War on Terror that account for publicly disclosed realities concerning the orientation of demonstrable truths.

Going even further, the NCTC's Guide required analysts and law enforcement personnel to:

> **Never use the terms "jihadist" or "mujahideen" in conversation to describe the terrorists**. A mujahed, a holy warrior, is a positive characterization in the context of a just war. In Arabic, jihad means "striving in the path of God" and is used in many contexts beyond warfare. **Calling our enemies jihadis and their movement a global jihad unintentionally legitimizes their actions**.[47]

Whether or not the current "jihad" against America is a "just war" (thus making our enemies "holy warriors") is an issue of fact, based in part on whether the activities conform to shariah doctrines. As this book makes clear, the word "jihad" is accurately used by both critics of jihad and by the jihadist. By the jihadists' own standard—the only applicable standard when defining their threat doctrine—the jihadist effort is a "just war," and, from their perspective, it does indeed make them "holy warriors," even as they are killing Americans. Today, analysis that meets professional evidentiary standards is deemed inappropriate for use inside national security and law enforcement spaces. At the Department of Defense, its use is dismissed as "inflammatory" and, even more alarmingly, condemned as harming the war effort. As shown in his classic work on ideological subversion, *Abuse of Language, Abuse of Power*, philosopher Josef Pieper was keenly aware of the role that the manipulation of language plays in such activities:

> The common element in all of this is the degeneration of language into an instrument of rape. It does contain violence, albeit in latent form. … This lesson, in a nutshell, says: the abuse of political power is fundamentally connected with the sophistic abuse of the word, indeed, finds in it the fertile soil in which to hide and grow and get ready, so much so that the latent potential of the totalitarian poison can be ascertained, as it were, by observing the symptom of public abuse of language. [48]

As the NCTC Guidelines indicate, strategic blindness is not limited to the Department of Homeland Security. In an interesting turn on the "One Degree of Kevin Bacon," it turns out that one man, Shaarik Zafar, was Senior Policy Advisor in the DHS Office of Civil Rights and Civil Liberties,[49] where he helped author[50] "Terminology to Define the Terrorists,"[51] while also serving as Deputy Chief of the Global Engagement Group at the NCTC,[52] drafters of "Words that Work and Words that Don't." Meanwhile, he also was affiliated with the United States Mission to the OSCE.[53] Currently, Zafar is the U.S. State Department's Special Representative to the Muslim Communities,[54] whatever that means.

The discussion on language helps explains the ideological nature of Assistant Secretary of Defense Paul Stockton's stonewalling of Congressman Dan Lungren in his testimony at a December 7, 2011, Joint Congressional Hearing on Threats to Military Communities.

While asking Stockton about the Army's preparedness prior to Nidal Hasan's bloody rampage at Fort Hood, Lungren's questioning revealed the pervasive effectiveness of the MPAC narrative. In a display of ideological fidelity, Stockton refused to give Lungren obvious answers to straightforward questions:

Rep. Lungren: Secretary Stockton, are we at war with violent

Islamist extremism?

Stockton: No, sir. We are at war with al-Qaida, its affiliates—

Rep. Lungren: OK, I understand that. My question is, is violent Islamist extremism at war with us?

Stockton: No, sir. We are being attacked by al-Qaida and its allies.

Rep. Lungren: Is al-Qaida—can it be described as being an exponent of violent Islamist extremism?

Stockton: They—al-Qaida are murderers with an ideological agenda—

Rep. Lungren: That wasn't my question. My question was, is al-Qaida acting out violent Islamist extremism?

Stockton: Al-Qaida is a violent organization dedicated to overthrowing the values that we intend to advance—

Rep. Lungren: Yes or no?

Stockton: Can I hear the question again? I'll make it as clear as I can. We are not at war with Islam.

Rep. Lungren: I didn't ask that—I did not ask that, sir. I asked whether we're at war with violent Islamist extremism. That's my question.

Stockton: No, we're at war with al-Qaida and its affiliates.[55]

Rep. Lungren: Al-Qaida—how does al-Qaida define itself? Are they dedicated to violent Islamist extremism?

Stockton: Al-Qaida would love to convince Muslims around the world that the United States is at war with Islam.

Rep. Lungren: I didn't say that.

Stockton: That's a prime propaganda tool. I'm not going to aid and abet that effort to advance their propaganda goals.

Rep. Lungren: Is there a difference between Islam and violent Islamist extremism?

Stockton: Sir, with great respect, I don't believe it's helpful to frame our adversary as Islamic with any set of qualifiers that we might add, because we are not at war with Islam.[56]

Unless we orient on the enemy's stated doctrine by undertaking real threat analysis, we cannot generate credible enemy courses of action. When this happens, our warfighting efforts will be reduced to incoherence and we will end up fighting without the ability to articulate why. This is the opportunity cost of following Assistant Secretary of Defense Stockton's requirement not to "frame our adversary as Islamic with any set of qualifiers that we might add."[57] Because it is not true that "we are not at war with [at least some elements within] Islam," Stockton's comment is an example of reality dislocation as policy.

Rep. Lungren: I understand that. I never said we were at war with Islam. One of the questions we're trying to deal with is the radicalization of Islam, is the radicalization of Islamic youth. **And if we can't distinguish between violent Islamist extremism and Islam, then all this stuff about behavioral indicators doesn't mean anything**. Well, let me ask you this question. Is it a behavioral indicator to put on your card that you're a soldier of Allah?[58]

[. . .]

Rep. Lungren: Sir, I would disagree with you that it may not be about political correctness. We are here talking about the fact that we now have to have behavioral indicators. ... If someone gives inflammatory remarks, as did Major Hasan, in an open setting, if he has on his card that he was a soldier of Allah, it seems to me to be beyond common sense to think those are not behavioral indicators. So my question is, if I'm a member of the military today, and I see those two events or those two circumstances, would it be appropriate for me to report those as behavioral indicators?

Stockton: Inflammatory rhetoric of the sort associated with Major Hasan that [sic?] needs to be reported. And our officers are trained up now to report on that behavior.[59]

Stockton's testimony hit the low point when evading one of Lungren's direct questions:

Stockton: I follow the truth wherever it takes me. And I strongly support the programs of the Department of Defense that focus on al Qaeda and behavioral indicators.

The Secretary's statement that he "follows the truth wherever it takes [him]" was in the context of his focus on al-Qaeda and behavioral indicators. Refusal to include Islam in the development of behavioral indicators with regard to "violent Islamist extremism" (jihad) raises questions about the ability to actually generate "behavioral indicators" capable of distinguishing between Islamic extremism *per se* and Islam, thus rendering the process pointless. Stockton's refusal to make such a connection in the face of evidence that such a relationship exists raises questions as to whether he even understands the truth "wherever it takes [him]." He is correct when saying, "al Qaeda are murderers with an ideological agenda," but he then denies what is obviously true: that al-Qaeda's ideology is immediately associated with Islam, regardless of whether its ideological assumptions are valid.

Confronted by these evasive answers, the Congressman's concern was realized. Behavioral indicators are now to be mapped to soft-science models rather than to real-world indicators of "Islamist extremist" intent. This validates Lungren's concern that "if we can't distinguish between violent Islamist extremism and Islam, then all of this stuff about behavioral indicators doesn't mean anything." It doesn't! It never did. It's not supposed to. Since Secretary Stockton's testimony, the public's been on notice that the Department of Defense refuses to make such life-saving distinctions.

Stockton's testimony became the talk of the media, as Americans caught a glimpse of the militancy underlying the strategic blindness of our national security leaders. Representative Lungren's questions concerning "Soldier of Allah" focused on the events of Fort Hood. This blindness renders our national security community dangerously unaware of threats manifesting themselves in plain sight.

In addition to denying the ability to define the enemy, the Civil Rights and Civil Liberties guidelines effectively conformed to CAIR's 2011 demand to bar the DHS from analyzing doctrines of Islamic terrorism. Section 213 of the Department of Homeland Security Reauthorization Act 2011 (S. 1546) established that:

> The Secretary [of Homeland Security] shall designate an official of the Department [of Homeland Security] to coordinate efforts to **counter violent extremism** in the United States, **particularly the ideology that gives rise to Islamist terrorism**. ....[60]

Taking issue with the emphasis on al-Qaeda and other Islamic terrorism that form the basis of the War on Terror, CAIR fired back:

> "The Department of Homeland Security's own statistics show there are a variety of domestic extremist groups threatening the nation and that each deserves serious consideration and consistent attention," said CAIR Government Affairs Coordinator Robert McCaw.[61]

If Islam has nothing to do with the acts of terrorism that groups like al-Qaeda execute, why fear looking into its ideology? If this underlying claim were true, CAIR's assertion would be borne out. On the other hand, if it is *not* true, that finding will also be borne out. Would a proper analysis of al-Qaeda's ideology reveal a close fit with shariah that points to a common set of reference points and objectives? Could it reveal a close fit between core al-Qaeda ideology and that of the Muslim Brotherhood's? These questions should have been asked and answered thirteen years ago – they certainly could have been.

CAIR makes it clear that rather than conduct threat analysis on al-Qaeda's ideology—an ideology that could be rapidly reduced to doctrine—DHS should instead do what the Department's Civil Rights and Civil Liberties Guidelines explicitly mandated. That is, counterterror analysts in the War on Terror must waste time by demonstrating that "terrorists and violent extremists vary in ethnicity, race, gender, and religion." Of course, this is completely irrelevant to the matter at hand, defeating al-Qaeda, and does not address the War on Terror. In fact, it's a strategic diversion of scarce resources. As stipulated in "Countering Violent Extremism Training Guidance & Best Practices":

> §2(a) Review the training program to ensure that it uses examples to demonstrate that terrorists and violent extremists vary in ethnicity, race, gender, and religion.[62]

This demand represents the subordination of national law-enforcement investigatory and national security analytical processes to Muslim Brotherhood demands. It is also an example of the subordination of the constitutional mandate to "support and defend" to Islamic prohibitions on what we are allowed to know. It was accomplished under the guise of Countering Violent Extremism (CVE).

In October 2011, the DHS Civil Rights and Civil Liberties division released government guidelines forbidding reference to Islam in presentations and related work product. In keeping with the OIC's Programme of Action, "Countering Violent Extremism Training Guidance & Best Practices" formalized the CRCL's aggressive campaign to counter Islamophobia.

The same month that Imam Mohamed Magid, President of ISNA, oversaw the CRCL's CVE guidelines, the Fiqh Council of North America (FCNA)—a subordinate element of ISNA charged with day-to-day management of Islamic legal responsibilities—issued a fatwa. It stated that there is *now* "no inherent conflict between the normative values of Islam and the U.S. Constitution and Bill of Rights."[63] The rather convenient timing raises the question: What changed — Islamic law, the Constitution, or enforcement of the Constitution? As explained in the footnote, the issuance of the fatwa reflects that a threshold was met that made the Constitution acceptable in terms of shariah.[3]

---

3   The Illusion of Agreement: Breaking Down a Fatwa
  When reading a fatwa, it should be read as a legal ruling by an authority authorized to promulgate such opinions. "Resolution On Being Faithful Muslims and Loyal Americans," promulgated by the

A review of the CRCL Guidelines reveals an inherent contradiction that can be resolved only by violating the DHS's new policy or by ceasing to pursue fact-based professional analysis. Most glaringly, while its Section 2(c) proscribes the use of "religious language" to describe "criminal activity," the document also states that al-Qaeda's ideology constitutes **the** preeminent threat to America:

Fiqh Council of North America (FCNA) on October 5, 2011, is a good example of a fatwa from a legitimate and credible organization that represents Muslims in America, or at least so says the Muslim Brotherhood. FCNA, as a subordinate element of ISNA—a known Muslim Brotherhood entity and unindicted coconspirator in the Holy Land Foundation trial—is the legal arm of the Muslim Brotherhood in America. The Brotherhood declares Islamic law to be the law of the land, and FCNA confirms this in the fatwa. In fact, the very issuance of such a fatwa is itself a Brotherhood claim of jurisdiction in the United States. Let's parse the language.

The FCNA fatwa does not accept the Constitution; it accepts the normative values in the Constitution that are consistent—or read in a way that makes them consistent—with shariah.

- Like other faith communities in the US and elsewhere, we see no inherent conflict between the normative values of Islam and the US Constitution and Bill of Rights. ...

The basis of the legal ruling is not integration as fellow citizens but *co-existing* (only while "minorities" until able to take power):

- The Qur'an speaks explicitly about the imperative of **just** and peaceful **co-existence** ...

The FCNA states that authority is based on shariah, and that it serves as the basis of law – including the law driving its fatwa:

- The foregoing values and teachings can be amply documented from the two primary sources of Islamic jurisprudence—the Qur'an and authentic Hadith. These values are rooted, not in political correctness or pretense, but on the universally accepted supreme objectives of Islamic Shari'ah, which is to protect religious liberty, life, reason, family and property of all. The Shari'ah, contrary to misrepresentations, is a comprehensive and broad guidance for all aspects of a Muslim's life—spiritual, moral, social and legal. Secular legal systems in Western democracies generally share the same supreme objectives, and are generally compatible with Islamic Shari'ah. ...

FCNA calls for a certain respect for—not acceptance of—the Constitution while they are minorities but only insofar as there is no conflict with shariah. There is no conflict with the fatwa because shariah supremacy was already established in the document. In the event of a conflict of laws, FCNA favors shariah:

- As a body of Islamic scholars, **we the members of FCNA** believe that it is false and misleading to suggest that there is a contradiction between being faithful Muslims committed to God (Allah) and being loyal American citizens. **Islamic teachings require respect of the laws of the land where Muslims live as minorities, including the Constitution and the Bill of Rights, so long as there is no conflict with Muslims' obligation for obedience to God. We do not see any such conflict with the US Constitution and Bill of Rights.** The primacy of obedience to God is a commonly held position of many practicing Jews and Christians as well.*

As a member of the CRCL DHS Advisory Council and the President of ISNA, Imam Mohamed Magid was well aware that the CRCL was to promulgate restrictions on speech in the name of CVE. These guidelines bring free speech requirements in line with Islamic notions of slander, just as the Secretary of State committed to the OIC General Secretary on 15 July, 2011, in furtherance of the OIC Ten-Year Programme. After the CRCL guidelines were issued—when it became the policy of the Obama administration to forswear any links between Islam and terrorism—a Brotherhood-associated imam could endorse that freedom of expression conflicts no longer exist. If the Muslim Brotherhood was a nation state, maybe this would have been recognized more clearly.

* Fataawah—"Resolution on Being Faithful Muslims and Loyal Americans," Fataawah from Fiqh Council of North America (FCNA), 5 October 2011, URL: http://www.icsd.org/2011/10/resolution-on-being-faithful-muslims-and-loyal-americans/

2. [Counterterror and homeland security] Training should be **sensitive to constitutional values**.

(c) Training should support the protection of civil rights and civil liberties as part of national security. **Don't use training that equates religious expression**, protests, or other constitutionally protected activity **with criminal activity**. [64]

While "constitutional values" are referred to, they are not actually enumerated. Of course, 2(c) flies in the face of the same document's identification of al-Qaeda and its ideology as the key threat and principal driver:

> In recent years, the United States has seen a number of individuals in the U.S. become involved in violent extremist activities, with particular activity by American residents and citizens inspired by al Qaeda and its ideology … **but we also know that the threat posed by al Qaeda and its adherents is the preeminent threat we face in the homeland**.[65]

Section 2(c) renders the identification of al-Qaeda's ideology impossible and makes a mockery of evidence-based professional analysis. This is *not* an unintended consequence but rather a desired effect. This is why the Fiqh Council of North America could issue the fatwa declaring "no inherent conflict." It is a fact that terrorist groups like al-Qaeda define themselves in Islamic terms regardless of whether their view of Islam is correct. How does an analyst evaluate al-Qaeda's "ideology" without reference to the relevant vocabulary on which the group relies to communicate and execute not only its ideology but also its doctrine and mission? The answer: He (or she) can't.

When Section 2(c) of the Countering Violent Extremism guidance states, "Don't use training that equates religious expression," etc., it is calling for a purge of our ability to identify and orient on threats that define themselves in specific Islamic terms. Having no qualification or mission scope in either the threat identification role of intelligence personnel or the investigative processes of special agents, the Office of Civil Rights and Civil Liberties at DHS usurped the authority of entities lawfully tasked for that purpose. Returning to *Abuse of Language, Abuse of Power*, this is what Pieper meant when he wrote:

> Plato evidently knew what he was talking about when he declared sophists' accomplished art of flattery to be the deceptive mirage of the political process, that is, the counterfeit usurpation of power, a power that belongs to the legitimate political authority alone. [66]

It didn't take long for the FBI to institutionalize the CRCL narrative. In

March 2012, the Bureau published "The FBI's Guiding Principles: Touchstone Document on Training."[67] With CRCL's novel "constitutional values" becoming the FBI's "core values," the relevant language of the CRCL Guidelines' Section 2 became the Touchstone Document's Section 1:

> 1. Training must conform to constitutional principles and adhere to the FBI's core values.
>
> FBI training must emphasize the protection of civil rights and civil liberties. Training must clearly distinguish between constitutionally protected statements and activities designed to achieve political, social, or other objectives, and violent extremism, which is characterized by the use, threatened use, or advocacy of use of force or violence (when directed at and likely to incite imminent lawless activity) in violation of federal law to further a movement's social or political ideologies. **This distinction includes recognition of the corresponding principle that mere association with organizations that demonstrate both legitimate (advocacy) and illicit (violent extremism) objectives should not automatically result in a determination that the associated individual is acting in furtherance of the organization's illicit objective(s).**[68] [Emphasis added]

As the language in bold suggests, Section 1 of the Touchstone Document expanded on the CRCL Guidelines by rejecting the material support[4] prohibitions of the Patriot Act[69] that were passed by Congress, signed into law by the president, and upheld by the Supreme Court in *Holder v. Humanitarian Law Project* in 2010.[70] Applying this novel standard to the counterdrug mission, by way of analogy, reveals how deleterious it really is. It's like saying, "Just because a person belongs to a known drug cartel doesn't mean he's participating in that cartel's known criminal activities." Under this standard, how long would it take for the counterdrug mission to severely bog down? As senior FBI bureaucrats wrap themselves in the novel postmodern framework they call "core values," they should ponder the role the Constitution is supposed to play in setting real standards. In doing this, they may want to focus on who is supposed to make the laws and who is supposed to enforce them and, then, on what it means to "support and defend … against all enemies foreign and domestic." Are these the same "core values" that Captain Kirby said are a part of the strategy "we're out there executing?"[71]

---

4   **(b) Definitions.**— As used in this section— **(1)** the term "material support or resources" means any property, tangible or intangible, or service, including currency or monetary instruments or financial securities, financial services, lodging, training, expert advice or assistance, safehouses, false documentation or identification, communications equipment, facilities, weapons, lethal substances, explosives, personnel (1 or more individuals who may be or include oneself), and transportation, except medicine or religious materials. [18 U.S. Code Section 2339A(b)(1)– Providing Material Support to Terrorists]

More than a few FBI special agents have felt the consequences of these new core values. In earlier days, it would have been called an ideologically motivated purge of work product and briefing materials. As noted, by being required to expunge the term "Islamic Movement," the FBI cannot track groups like the Taliban, the Muslim Brotherhood, and MPAC—even as those entities own writings communicate intense alignment with the "Islamic Movement."

When narratives like CVE are enforced, war-planning efforts concentrate on fulfilling the mission to eradicate Islamophobia at the expense of the constitutional requirement to "support and defend" against terrorism. All elements of national power are brought to bear against a seemingly meaningless, politically safe, and bureaucratically derived non-entity called "violent extremism." In this paradigm, the only thing that's certain is that violent extremism is to have nothing to do with Islam. Given the guidance from the CRCL's Advisory Council, this should not come as a surprise. The United States has subordinated the information requirements in the War on Terror to what Islam allows us to know, and our national security and law enforcement leadership is enforcing that standard.

There is no change in sight. In August 2014, Mohamed Elibiary noted his close association with the Republican Party and his ongoing contacts within the national security and law enforcement communities to assure his followers on Twitter that the Brotherhood effort had become sufficiently institutionalized as to be past the point of being countered: "With my 22+ yrs @GOP, friends thru out 100s US security/policing agencies & academia; no future presidency will reverse reforms underway." It is worth noting that the "Rabia" symbol indicating support of the Muslim Brotherhood was in his Twitter feed.[72]

Message Tweeted by Mohamed Elibiary

A Matter of Malpractice

Because it refuses to attach any relevant characteristics to the enemy, the Countering Violet Extremism narrative is silent on the consequences inherent in the doctrinal drivers that underlie the War on Terror. Previously, we introduced the Article 24/25 Rule and its Corollary, two analytical principles made necessary by the Cairo Declaration on Human Rights in Islam. As noted, these rules are applicable to any individual or group that embraces or is beholden to Islamic law. This is only common sense; for Muslims who follow Islamic law, shariah's understanding of foundational concepts will typically take precedence over competing Western or non-Islamic constructs, and our analysis should reflect this.

THE ARTICLE 24/25 RULE FOR ANALYSIS. Human Rights are defined as shariah law for the purpose of any analysis involving the OIC, a Member State, or initiatives reasonably arising from either—including all entities claiming Islamic law as the basis of law, including al-Qaeda, the Muslim Brotherhood, or any individual or entity falling under the Islamic Movement.

COROLLARY TO THE ARTICLE 24/25 RULE. Analysis undertaken on subject matter where the Rule should apply and yet is not applied should be considered suspect, because it fails to meet explicitly stated minimum analytical thresholds.

In analysis of the capabilities and work product arising from DHS's Countering Violent Extremism narrative, the consequence of the Article 24/25 Corollary is readily apparent. When analyzing groups that claim to be at war with America because of their professed orientation to shariah, analytical products under the influence of the Corollary will undermine the production of "most likely" and "most dangerous" enemy courses of action in the threat analysis cycle. It will cause the war-planning process to fail resulting in defeat. FBI and CRCL narratives accept a degraded ability to define the threat's most likely and most dangerous courses of action. Because this is true, all narratives that are similarly silent on known and knowable facts concerning the enemy's threat doctrine will not be able—and should not be allowed—to dispute claims of negligence in the event something goes wrong.

So, where are we? Our doctrine on warfighting and intelligence used to require that we orient on the enemy and his doctrine. In this war, however, we have a self-identified enemy who self-identifies the basis of his threat doctrine: We know who he is and why he fights. We know this because he tells us. He says he is a jihadi or a *mujāhid*. He says he fights *jihad fi sabilillah* according to Islamic law in order to implement Islamic law. These are first-order facts that will not be contradicted. Not knowing either these facts or their downstream consequences raises questions of malpractice. Miscommunication of those realities in favor of models borne of pseudorealities serve to disinform the public of the true scope and nature of what is before us.

There is overwhelming evidence that Islamic law serves as the driver of the enemy's threat doctrine. Knowledge of that evidence made it possible to successfully lay down indicators of activities that have, in fact, come to pass precisely as forecasted. Ignoring this evidence cost lives and undermines our national security. And yet an intelligence officer, an FBI or DHS special agent, or a national security decision-maker can be fired for undertaking or even reciting such analysis—even though this is the very type of analysis that our oaths demand of us and that our positions require from us.

How dire are the consequences for intentional ignorance? On October 16, 2014, the Department of Justice Office of Public Affairs announced the conviction of a man in Raleigh, North Carolina, for providing material support for terrorism:

> Akba Jihad Jordan, 22, of Raleigh, North Carolina, pleaded guilty before United States Magistrate Judge Robert B. Jones to conspiracy to provide material support to terrorists. … "Akba Jordan turned his back on his own country and was willing to fight side by side with terrorist groups in Yemen and Syria who wish to do us harm," said John Strong, Special Agent in Charge of the FBI in North Carolina. "American citizens who offer support to terrorist organizations pose a grave threat to our national security and will face serious consequences for their actions."[73]

The press release then accurately identified the activities that the prospective jihadis sought to engage in:

> As set forth in the affidavit supporting the complaint, Brown initiated contact online with an undercover employee of the Federal Bureau of Investigation (FBI). Brown requested assistance in traveling overseas for "fisabilillah"—a phrase commonly utilized by Islamic Extremists to refer to joining extremist groups in violence overseas.[74]

"Fisabilillah" or "fi sabilillah" or "fi sabil Allah" means "in the Cause of Allah." When the phrase is used by itself, the missing term, jihad, is almost always implied—hence, "jihad fi sabilillah" or "jihad in the cause of Allah." The subject index in *Reliance of the Traveller*, under the heading *Fi Sabil Allah*, says: "See Jihad."[75] Examples of fi sabilillah from the Qur'an include:

> **Then fight in Allah's cause** - Thou art held responsible only for thyself — and rouse the believers. It may be that Allah will restrain the fury of the Unbelievers; for Allah is the strongest in might and in punishment. (Qur'an 4:84)

> **Fight in the cause of Allah** those who fight you, but do not transgress limits; for Allah loveth not transgressors. And slay them wherever ye catch them, and turn them out from where

they have Turned you out; for tumult and oppression are worse than slaughter. (Qur'an 2:190-191)

Not equal are those believers who sit (at home) and receive no hurt, and **those who strive and fight in the cause of Allah** with their goods and their persons. Allah hath granted a grade higher to those who strive and fight with their goods and persons than to those who sit (at home). Unto all (in Faith) Hath Allah promised good: But those who strive and fight Hath He distinguished above those who sit (at home) by a special reward. (Qur'an 4:95)

Those who believe, and suffer exile and **strive with might and main, in Allah's cause**, with their goods and their persons, have the highest rank in the sight of Allah: they are the people who will achieve (salvation). (Qur'an 9:20)

Book 56 of *Sahih Al-Bukhari* is titled *The Book of Jihad*[1] – (*Fighting for Allah's Cause*). Both the footnote and the parenthetical content are parts of the title. The footnote defines jihad as "Holy fighting in Allah's Cause" and continues with an explanation that leaves little doubt about the status of jihad:

(1) *Al-Jihad* (Holy fighting) **in Allah's Cause** (with full force of numbers and weaponry), is given the utmost importance in Islam, and is one of its pillars (on which it stands). By *Jihad* Islam is established, Allah's word is made superior. [His Word being (La *ilaha illahllah* which means none has the right to be worshipped but Allah)], and His religion (Islam) is propagated. By abandoning *Jihad*, (may Allah protect us from that). [sic] Islam and Muslims fall into an inferior position, their honour [sic] is lost, their land is stolen, their rule and authority vanish. *Jihad* is an obligatory duty in Islam, on every Muslim, and he who tries to escape from this duty or does not in his innermost heart wish to fulfil [sic] this duty, dies with one of the qualities of a hypocrite.[76]

Located in Volume IV of *Sahih Bukhari*, *The Book of Jihad* contains 154 pages of hadith on the sayings or acts of the Prophet relating to jihad. Here are two passages that refer to "the Cause of Allah":

The Prophet said, "By Him in Whose hands my life is! Were it not for some men amongst the believers who dislike to be left behind me and whom I cannot provide with means of conveyance, I would certainly never remain behind any Sariya' (army-unit) setting out in Allah's Cause. By Him in Whose hands my life is! I would love to be martyred in Allah's Cause and then get resurrected and then get martyred, and then get resurrected again and then get martyred and then get resurrected again and then get martyred. (*Sahih Bukhari*, Volume 4, Book 52, Number 54)[77]

I heard Allah's Apostle saying, "The example of a Mujahid in Allah's Cause—and Allah knows better who really strives in His Cause—is like a person who fasts and prays continuously. Allah guarantees that He will admit the Mujahid in His Cause into Paradise if he is killed, otherwise He will return him to his home safely with rewards and war booty." (*Sahih Bukhari*, Volume 4, Book 52, Number 46)[78]

Sayyid Qutb provides an example of the Muslim Brotherhood's use of the term in his book *Islam and Universal Peace*,[5] where he associates fi sabilillah with jihad in the section titled "STRIVING IN THE CAUSE OF ALLAH (JIHAD),"[79] and then cites the Qur'an:

Those who believe **fight in the Cause of God**, and those who reject faith fight in the cause of Evil ... (Q. IV. 76)[80]

There is little doubt concerning the doctrinal relationship between jihad as warfare and fi sabilillah. Because it is silent on the Islamic nature of the term and on the immediacy of that term's association with jihad, the Justice Department's treatment of fi sabilillah is underinclusive.[6] The term "fi sabilillah" is also used in Qur'an Verse 9:60 to identify a category of the needy who are eligible for Zakat. In *The Noble Qur'an* translation, fi sabilillah is explained in the body of Verse 9:60, while the Yusuf Ali translation includes an explanation in a note:

As-Sadaqat (here it means *Zakat*) are only for the *Fuqara* (poor), and *Al-Masakin* (the poor) and those employed to collect (the funds); and to attract the hearts of those who have been inclined (towards Islam); and to free the captives; and for those in debt; **and for Allah's Cause (i.e. for *Mujahidun* – those fighting in holy battle**, and for the wayfarer (a traveller who is cut off from everything; a duty imposed by Allah. And Allah is All-Knower, All-Wise. (*The Noble Qur'an* translation, Qur'an 9:60)[81]

Alms are for the poor and the needy, and those employed to administer the (funds); for those whose hearts have been

---

5   Published under the ISNA label American Trust Publications (ATP).
6   Underinclusive. Excluding something that should be included. *FindLaw Legal Dictionary*, URL: http://dictionary.findlaw.com/definition/underinclusive.html.

(recently) reconciled (to Truth); for those in bondage and in debt; **in the cause of Allah**; and for the wayfarer: (thus is it) ordained by Allah, and Allah is full of knowledge and wisdom. (Yusuf Ali's *The Meaning of the Holy Qur'an* translation, Qur'an 9:60)

> Yusuf Ali Note 1320. "Zakah or charitable gifts are to be given to the poor and the needy and those who are employed in their service. That is, charitable funds are not to be diverted to other uses, but the genuine expenses of administering charity are properly chargeable to such funds. Who are the needy? Besides the ordinary indigent, there are certain classes of people whose need is great and should be relieved. Those mentioned here are: (4) Those who are struggling and striving in Allah's Cause by teaching or fighting or in duties assigned to them by the righteous Imam, who are thus unable to earn their ordinary living …"[82]

For Yusuf Ali, "struggling and striving in Allah's Cause by teaching and fighting" refers to both the dawah and jihad missions. *Reliance of the Traveller* likewise recognizes that "fi sabilillah" is used in the context of jihad. In Book H "Zakat," in the section titled "Those Fighting for Allah," *Reliance* explains:

> The seventh category is **those fighting for Allah**, meaning **people engaged in Islamic military operations** for which no salary has been allotted in the Army roster (O: but who are volunteers for jihad without remuneration). They are given enough to suffice them for the operation, even if affluent; of weapons, mounts, clothing, and expenses (O: for the duration of the journey, round trip, and the time they spend there, even if prolonged. Though nothing has been mentioned here of the expense involved in supporting such people's families during this period, it seems clear that they should also be given it).[83]

When shariah speaks of "those fighting for Allah" in regard to those eligible to receive Zakat, where Verse 9:60 says "in the Cause of Allah," they mean those "engaged in Islamic military operations"—jihad. When reading marketing materials provided by groups like the Muslim Brotherhood, one should not lose sight of the shariah understanding of Zakat. Remember that *Reliance of the Traveller* was published in America and was approved by the Fiqh Counsel of North America, a subordinate element of ISNA (just like ATP), and the IIIT.

Why does it matter that the Justice Department's explanation of fi sabilillah is underinclusive when saying "a phrase commonly utilized by Islamic Extremists to refer to joining extremist groups in violence overseas?"[84] **Because** fi sabilillah is a doctrinal term of art in Islam that finds specific support in shariah and the Qur'an concerning the waging of jihad and entitles those acting under its authority to expect the active support of the Muslim community. What Justice calls an "Islamic Extremist" Islam identifies as a declared jihadi. Wherever prospective jihadis claim jihad fi sabilillah, in theory there is a community in place that is obligated to support them.

The explanation is also underinclusive because it limits the term's application to those "joining groups in violence overseas." Because there are jihadi organizations that seek to wage jihad fi sabilillah inside the United States, the statement is misleading. In fact, many organizations within the United States that raise funds based on the claim of fi sabilillah are also brought into organizations like the Department of Justice, the FBI, and DHS to serve as consultants.

For example, both CAIR and MPAC raise tax-deductible revenue based on claims that such contributions fulfill Zakat requirements based on fi sabilillah as identified in Qur'an 9:60. A review of CAIR's webpage in 2009 revealed that CAIR sought donations that were designated as "zakat eligible."[85] I first briefed this to national law enforcement and national security personnel in May 2009.[86] As recently as 2015, CAIR continues to rely on the same eligibility statement—"Does CAIR Qualify to Receive Zakat?"[87] In fact, CAIR declares its eligibility based exclusively on the fi sabilillah mission:

> **Yes.** Numerous Muslim scholars have confirmed that Zakat is payable to organizations that exist to serve the Muslim community by protecting their rights. This is because the work done by CAIR (and other such organizations) can be classified as **fi-sabilillah,** which is one of the eight categories of Zakat recipients detailed in the Quran (Chapter 9, Verse 60)[88] [emphasis in the original].

Applying the 24/25 Rule, protecting the rights of the Muslim community should be understood to mean defending shariah. To establish its Zakat eligibility, CAIR relies on the authority of the fatwa of Sheikh Ahmad Kutty, an Islamic scholar at the Islamic Institute of Toronto.[89] Kutty states:

> **"I think it is not only permissible, rather it is also imperative that we do give our zakah to organizations like CAIR and CAIR-CAN,** since they are fulfilling a most timely and essential service for the healthy survival of the community. Supporting such institutions clearly falls under the legitimate objectives of zakah as expounded by authentic scholars and jurists of Islam, both of the past and the present.

The categories of recipients of zakah are stated in the following verse: "Charities are (meant) only for the poor and the needy, and those who are charged with collecting them, and those whose hearts are to be won over, and for the freeing of human beings from bondage, and (for) those who are overburdened with debts, **and (for those who strive) in Allah's cause (fi sabili-llah)**, and (for) the way-farer: (this is) an ordinance from Allah—and Allah is All-Knowing and All-Wise" (At-Tawbah: 60)[90] [emphasis in the original].

CAIR bases its claim of eligibility exclusively on fi sabilillah. As Kutty continues his explanation of CAIR's eligibility, remember that *Sahih Bukhari* said that "*Jihad* is an obligatory duty in Islam, on every Muslim":[91]

A principle of jurisprudence states: if a thing which has been considered as obligatory cannot be fulfilled without fulfilling another, then fulfilling the latter also becomes obligatory. Thus since protecting the rights of Muslims and empowering Muslims cannot be achieved without such institutions, it is imperative that Muslims support and maintain such institutions.[92]

The institution in question is jihad fi sabilillah. Unlike CAIR, MPAC takes a more subtle approach to its appeal for Zakat donations, claiming that "donations to MPAC Foundation are 100% tax deductible and zakat eligible."[93] In its brochure "An Islamic Perspective on Giving Zakat to the MPAC Foundation," MPAC's tactic is to highlight passages that are relevant to donations. Hence, in the section "Reading the Scripture," the brochure identifies Qur'an 9:60 as the authority for Zakat. It lists all seven classes of eligible recipients but highlights only three:

1. Reading the Scripture. The offering given for the sake of God are [meant] only for:

3) those whose hearts are to be won over, and

4) for freeing of people from bondage, and

6) for [every struggle] **in God's cause** ...

[This is] the ordinance from God, and God is all knowing, wise." – Surah At-Taubah 9:60.[94]

MPAC accepts zakat donations for dawah, for litigation defense, and for jihad fi sabilillah. The next section of the MPAC brochure, "Understanding the Message," states that "understanding this verse through the lens of our current time and place, zakat should be used within the following categories" and then lists all seven categories again. But this time only two of the categories are highlighted:

> 3) provide relations initiatives to win the hearts and minds of others and to neutralize the animosity against Islam in the media, entertainment industry, think tanks, and academia …
>
> 6) for every effort **to serve the cause of God** in establishing justice, emanating mercy, and guarding the freedom and dignity of all.[95]

This reflects that MPAC is involved in both dawah and jihad. The third section, "Applying it Today," explains that "MPAC Foundation's work is applicable in the following zakat categories," listing four categories but highlighting only one:

> **The sixth category** as indicated by a majority of jurists is not limited to the issue of physical struggle. The Foundation works to educate all Americans regarding the teachings of Islam, to serve the Muslim American community and promote Islamic values of mercy, justice peace, human dignity, freedom, and equality for all.[96]

Of course, the sixth category of Section 3 refers to number 6 in Section 1 ("for [every struggle] in God's cause") and Section 2 ("for every effort to serve the cause of God in establishing justice, emanating mercy, and guarding the freedom and dignity of all"). MPAC understands that its ultimate role is the facilitation of the fi sabilillah mission and structures its donation materials accordingly. Because MPAC is a part of the Islamic Movement under the control of the Muslim Brotherhood, its fi sabilillah mission extends to a teaching role, touching on aspects of dawah in the preparation stage leading to kinetic jihad. MPAC is an Islamic entity beholden to shariah, so the statement that MPAC seeks to "promote Islamic values of mercy, justice peace, human dignity, freedom, and equality for all"[97] should be understood in light of the 24/25 Rule: MPAC is simply asserting that it seeks to implement Islamic law. From the selective highlighting within the MPAC brochure, it is clear that MPAC defines its role in terms of the dawah and jihad missions—that it emphasizes the fi sabilillah role that *Reliance* states is for "people engaged in Islamic military operations."[98] In the preparation stage, this role may be more heavily weighted toward the non-kinetic aspects of jihad—including subversion.

This brings us back to the DOJ press release. It is underinclusive because it does not recognize the doctrinal nature of fi sabilillah as an Islamic term of art that is immediately associated with jihad. It misinforms because it limits the term's application to overseas violence.[99] The press release disinforms because it associates fi sabilillah with "Islamic Extremists," a term born of a pseudoreality made necessary by bureaucratic demands for behavioral models designed to conceal the truth. In this process, the Department of Justice misses the fact that its two favored outreach partners, CAIR and MPAC, both raise money based on the fi sabilillah mission, which Justice (even with its degraded level of understanding) still understands to be a hostile call for violence. Hidden in plain sight, this is civilization jihad by our own hands. As we continue through Part 7, we will look at the catastrophic failures associated with not understanding the nature of the threat. Among the first of those failures is our national security community's easy communication of Islamic-based terrorism in narratives that separate acts from their doctrinal basis as a matter of policy. Everything misfires from there.

It's really this simple: There is no knowing this enemy without understanding that doctrine. We can lose a war—and our country—for want of facts that could have been known had there not been a policy decision to ignore and misrepresent them.

A national security professional's duty is not to know true Islam; it is to identify and establish a functional threat doctrine regardless of whether that doctrine accurately tracks with "true" Islam. At the threat analysis level, what matters is that we understand and communicate the enemy's doctrines clearly, not that we determine whether he is correct about them. Because Secretary Stockton's behavioral indicators crowd out relevant facts, he cannot "follow the truth wherever it takes" him. If he did, the truth would lead him to violate "the programs of the Department of Defense that focus on … behavioral indicators" that deny that al-Qaeda's actions have anything to do with Islam.[100]

Today, the Muslim Brotherhood dictates who does and does not do threat analysis for the government on War on Terror issues. The Brotherhood also dictates what can and cannot be discussed. This certainly fulfills key elements of any long-term campaign oriented toward jihad fi sabilillah. We ignore these realities at our peril. This is ignorance that kills.

Undue Influence

The group Hizb ut-Tahrir was founded in 1953, and its primary mission is to unify all Muslim states into a caliphate governed by Islamic law. In this way, it is similar to the Muslim Brotherhood and all other groups within the Islamic Movement. As with the Muslim Brotherhood, Hizb ut-Tahrir is concerned with carrying the "dawah of Islam" to the world. Its affiliate in the United States, Hizb ut-Tahrir America, is similarly dedicated to transforming secular societies into Islamic states that follow shariah.[101]

In 1998, the group published *The Islamic State* outlining the agenda of the hoped-for caliphate. Because of the clarity of its message, the book's description of the caliphate's foreign policy is provocative:

> Therefore, the foreign policy of the Islamic State is to convey
> the Islamic Message to the world. This policy is implement-

ed by **a defined method that never changes, which is Jihad**, regardless of who is in authority. Since the Messenger of Allah founded the State until the end of the Islamic State, **this method never changed.** The Messenger of Allah prepared the army soon after founding the Islamic State. He initiated **Jihad in order to remove the material obstacles that stood in the way of the Islamic Da'wah.** The Quraysh was that material obstacle, so he decided to remove it. Then **he went on to destroy the Quraysh's existence, the very existence that stood in the way of the Islamic Da'wah.** He also removed and destroyed other obstacles until Islam engulfed the whole of the Arabian Peninsula. Then **the Islamic State began knocking on the doors of other nations to spread Islam among them.** It found that the existing ruling systems formed a material obstacle in the face of the Da'wah, thus they had to be removed in order to reach the people themselves and invite them to Islam so that they could visualize and feel the justice of Islam, observe the prosperity and decent living under its banner, and **invite the people to a better life without compulsion or coercion.** Jihad continued as a method of spreading Islam, and by the means of Jihad many countries were conquered. By means of Jihad, kingdoms and states were removed and Islam ruled the same people and nations. **Islam was spread and was embraced by hundreds of millions of people after they had been ruled by it.** The method used in implementing that foreign policy was Jihad. It has never changed and never will.[102]

Notice the familiar rhetoric of adherence to Islamic law: (1) the commitment to the practice of jihad as performed by Mohammed in the first generation; (2) that the task of jihad is to remove obstacles in the way of a campaign of dawah; (3) that there is no contradiction between armed jihad and "compulsion or coercion," as per Islamic doctrine; and perhaps most important, (4) that there is an imperative to impose Islamic law on non-Muslims.

Because it is expressly dedicated to the overthrow of non-Islamic governments (including our own) by jihad, Hizb ut-Tahrir is precisely the kind of group American counterterrorism and law enforcement should be scrutinizing, investigating, and possibly even prosecuting.

Instead, in 2007, the Department of Homeland Security set up a recruiting booth next to that group's table at an ISNA convention. The conference was hosted by ISNA, a Brotherhood-associated group, and was co-sponsored by the Justice Department.[103] That's right; at the same time the Justice Department was prosecuting the Holy Land Foundation, it co-sponsored a conference with ISNA, an unindicted co-conspirator in that trial. If you were looking for an anecdote to illustrate the inability of our national security establishment to see our enemies in the War on Terror, you'd be hard pressed to find one more dramatic. You can't make this stuff up!

Side by side: a Homeland Security recruiting booth and a Hizb ut-Tahrir table at a 2007 conference hosted by ISNA and co-sponsored by the Justice Department.

Undue influence on our analytical process becomes more serious at the more senior levels, as there seems to be a high correlation between being a Muslim advisor and having associations with the Muslim Brotherhood or related Islamic Movement entities. For the same reason that members of the Communist Party, the Ku Klux Klan, or the Nazi Party are officially disfavored, so too should those that too closely associate with the Brotherhood.[104] Unfortunately, this is not the case.

In furtherance of its mission to preserve our freedoms, the Department of Homeland Security's CRCL created strategic partnerships with certain "ethnic and religious communities" by establishing an Incident Community Coordination Team.[105] The Department also created a Countering Violent Extremism Working Group to advance the "violent extremism" narrative—to ensure that its principles would be enforced government-wide.

For its members, DHS approached American Muslims, most with links to the Muslim Brotherhood in America. Allowing a Working Group based out of the Civil Rights and Civil Liberties Division to define the vocabulary that drives national security analysis and work product effectively outsourced the very threat analysis that is supposed to drive the intelligence cycle. In outsourcing it to individuals tied to the Islamic Movement, the government short-circuited its ability to understand the War on Terror.

At the Spring 2010 Countering Violent Extremism Working Group sessions of the Homeland Security Advisory Council, Imam Mohamed Magid, Executive Director of the All Dulles Area Muslim Society in northern Virginia,[106] was among the Council members. As noted, Magid is also President of the Islamic Society of North America, one of the nation's leading Brotherhood-associated groups and an unindicted coconspirator in the Holy Land Foundation trial.[107] The Peaceful Families Project, an ISNA partner and collaborating organization, released a biographical sketch of Magid:[108]

> A Sudanese-born American, Imam Magid is the son of the Grand Mufti of Sudan. At the hand of his father and other notable scholars, **he studied and graduated in traditional Islamic disciplines, including Shari'ah** (Islamic Jurisprudence) and Muwatta (**Maliki School of Islamic Law**). Imam Magid views marriage and pre-marital counseling as his passion. He currently resides in Reston, Virginia with his wife and daughters.[109]

It is not clear that Imam Magid is even a naturalized citizen. If not, why would he be given any role in formulating national security policy? Given the increasingly harsh, genocidal calls for the killing of non-Muslims in Southern Sudan by Sudanese politicians and Islamic leaders in Khartoum, Magid's connections to his father, the Grand Mufti of Sudan, as well as to the Muslim Brotherhood in Sudan should be taken into account. After all, if the imam's jurisprudential training reflects the views now current in Sudan, it would be good to know where he stands on such issues.

Mohamed Elibiary
@MohamedElibiary
NatlSec, HmldSec, Intel, Cyber & Homegrown CVE/CT focused Advisor; opinion expressed = PERSONAL ONLY; bio@link, RT NOT Endrsmnt, TX Repub, proud American.♥Egypt
Plano, TX & Washington, D.C.   dhs.gov/homeland-secur

4,538 TWEETS   222 FOLLOWING   916 FOLLOWERS   Follow

We have already encountered Senior Homeland Security Adviser Mohamed Elibiary, another member of DHS's Security Council. In addition to being a member of CAIR's Dallas-Fort Worth, Texas, chapter,[110] Elibiary started his own foundation in 2002, the Freedom and Justice Foundation.[111] ("Freedom and Justice" is a Brotherhood-associated term, having been the name of the Muslim Brotherhood's now-defunct political party in Egypt.) For a period of time, Elibiary was founder, president, and CEO of his foundation[112] as well as a Committee Chairman[113] and Board Member[114] of the CAIR chapter. He claimed to have begun donating money to the Holy Land Foundation in his late teens[115]/[116] and remains supportive of the convicted Brotherhood defendants. Elibiary has been under oversight scrutiny for trying to sell information obtained from classified DHS and FBI systems regarding the status of American citizens.[117] In September 2013, Elibiary posted a picture of himself in front of an American flag, indicating his official status. The photo, as shown above, also included the Rabia symbol indicating solidarity with the Brotherhood in Egypt and commitment to their resistance efforts there. His profile also played up his national security, intelligence, CVE, and counterterrorism credentials.[118]

Another member of DHS's Homeland Security Council was Omar Alomari, the Community Engagement Officer for Ohio Homeland Security (OHS).[119] Alomari has numerous close relations with Brotherhood-associated groups like CAIR, another organization designated as an unindicted coconspirator in the Holy Land trial.[120] At one point, he oversaw the production of the outreach brochure "Agents of Radicalization" that represented groups such as CAIR and ISNA as "organizations we [OHS] are working with." Thousands of these brochures were later destroyed when OHS discovered the misleading material.[121]

The Rabia symbol (above) indicates solidarity with the Muslim Brotherhood. At right, Brotherhood Judge Waleed Sharaby flashed the Rabia sign during a visit in February 2015 to Washington, D.C., where he and other Brotherhood leaders were hosted by the State Department. The next day, 40 people were killed in a terror attack in Sinai.

Still another member of the Homeland Security Council was the Abu Dhabi Gallup Center's Dalia Mogahed, who also served on the DHS Civil Rights and Civil Liberties Advisory Council. In October 2009, she appeared on a television program in London hosted by admitted members of Hizb ut-Tahrir. As we have seen, Hizb ut-Tahrir calls for the destruction of Western democracy and the creation of a global Islamic State under shariah. During the program, Mogahed smiled and left unchallenged the female host's attack on "man-made law" (i.e., democracy), their calls for shariah to be the source of all law, and their claims that women should not "be permitted to hold positions of leadership in government."[122]

In 2013, the watchdog group Judicial Watch released hundreds of pages of documents received in a Freedom of Information request regarding a CRCL-sponsored meeting in January 2010 that also exhibited a substantial overrepresentation of individuals closely associated with the Muslim Brotherhood and related entities.[123]

Later, Congress would explicitly state its position regarding another federal department's collaboration with a well-known Muslim Brotherhood front. In the Fiscal Year 2013 Appropriations Bill for the Department of Justice, Congress "reaffirms the FBI director's longstanding policy prohibiting employees from engaging in any formal non-investigative cooperation" with the Council of American Islamic Relations (CAIR).[124] Given Congress's prohibition on working with CAIR, the substantial overrepresentation of DHS CRCL Advisory Council members and participants with entities designated as unindicted coconspirators in the Holy Land Foundation trial, as was CAIR, is troubling.[125] In September 2013, however, the Justice Department's Office of Inspector General issued a report titled, "Review of FBI Interactions with the Council on American-Islamic Relations." It found that while both Congress and the FBI had issued directives to keep the Brotherhood-linked group at arm's length, "in three of the five incidents we reviewed, we concluded that the policy was not followed."[126]

Representative Wolf, who requested the investigation, was more pointed in his assessment:

> Today, the department's Inspector General ... confirms the blatant disregard of bureau policy as well as multiple enacted Commerce-Justice-Science Appropriations reports with respect to interactions by the FBI with CAIR. ... Specifically, the OIG report found that the former Special Agents-in-Charge (SAC) of the Chicago, Illinois, Los Angeles, California, and New Haven, Connecticut field offices violated the department's policy, despite numerous electronic communications articulating the policy as well as a mandatory meeting held in November 2008 with all SACs and Assistant Directors-in-Charge to communicate the policy in person. ... The OIG report makes clear that the leadership of several field offices knowingly ignored or selectively applied the policy to suit their interests. In one case documented in the report, the SAC of the LA field office wrote an e-mail to

his staff explicitly noting: "Please instruct your folks at this time that they are not to abide by the [October 24, 2008, Electronic Communication from the REDACTED], but that their direction in regards to CAIR will come from the LA Field Office front office." This is unacceptable and insubordinate behavior from a senior leader of the FBI.[127]

Despite Congress's explicit directives, the pattern of individuals and organizations populating meetings, conferences, and advisory boards is unmistakable. Within the CRCL's "diverse" representation of community leaders from the Muslim community, there is a tight core that can reasonably be associated with a common message. Just as there is no diversity of message from the CRCL's Advisory Council, so too is there no fidelity to civil rights and liberties at the CRCL—unless, of course, one accepts the Muslim Brotherhood's definition of human rights. The list of names in just one CRCL email message obtained by Judicial Watch through a Freedom of Information request is revealing in its extensive Brotherhood representation (see below).

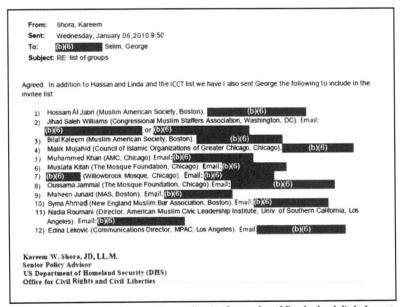

A list of invitees to a CRCL event is revealing in the number of Brotherhood–linked groups represented.

1. **Hossam al-Jabri** was a former Executive Director of the Muslim American Society (MAS) nationally and also former president of its Boston, MA, chapter. Al-Jabri is an immigrant from Egypt who has been a regular speaker at the annual MAS-ICNA Conventions.[128] MAS was founded in 1993 as the U.S. chapter of

the Muslim Brotherhood by self-professed leaders of the Brotherhood, although its leadership has consistently denied the affiliation in order to operate openly but still promote the same ideological goals of the Brotherhood, especially the establishment of Islamic rule under shariah.[129]

2. **Jihad Saleh Williams** (also "J. Saleh Williams") was the Government Affairs Representative at Islamic Relief USA, an offshoot of the UK-based Islamic Relief Worldwide, which provides financial and other assistance to Hamas.[130] From 2007 to 2010, Saleh served as the Program and Outreach Coordinator for the Congressional Muslim Staffers Association,[131] which invited al-Qaeda operative Anwar al-Awlaki to lead the Friday prayers on Capitol Hill some time after the 9/11 attacks.[132] The Class of 1996 University of California Los Angeles Bruin Life/Southern Campus Yearbook lists one "Jihad Saleh" as the business manager of *Al-Talib*, the news publication of the Muslim Student Association (MSA) on the UCLA campus.[133] In July 2012, Saleh joined with panelists from leading Muslim Brotherhood groups—CAIR (Council on American Islamic Relations), ISNA (Islamic Society of North America), and MPAC (Muslim Public Affairs Council)—under the auspices of the Muslim Public Service Network.[134]

3. **M. Bilal Kaleem** is a Dubin Fellow at Harvard Kennedy School's Center for Public Leadership. He currently serves as president of the Muslim American Society of Boston (MAS-Boston),[135] a known Muslim Brotherhood front group.

4. **Imam Dr. Abdul Malik Mujahid** is a former Chairman (2007–2008)[136] of the Council of Islamic Organizations of Greater Chicago (CIOGC),[137] a federation of mosques in the Chicago area. In July 2009, Mujahid (whose name in Arabic means "holy warrior"), spoke on a panel at ISNA's annual convention in Washington, D.C.[138] ISNA is the largest Muslim Brotherhood front group in the United States.[139]

6. **Kifah Mustapha** is a known Hamas operative based on his 1996–2000 employment with the Holy Land Foundation[140] and his position on the Board of Directors of the Islamic Association for Palestine (IAP),[141] a Hamas front organization. Mustapha is an imam and the Associate Director of the Mosque Foundation in Bridgeview, IL. He is also Chairman of the Board for The Quran Institute MAS Chicago.[142] Mustapha was by-name listed by the Department of Justice as unindicted coconspirator in the 2008 Holy Land Foundation Hamas terror funding trial.[143] Appointed the first Muslim chaplain for the Illinois State Police in 2011, Mustapha was disqualified for the post after the FBI's Chicago field office warned that he would never pass an FBI background check.[144] Nevertheless, Mustapha was subsequently admitted to the FBI Citizens Academy program, which likewise required a background check and included a visit to the National Counterterrorism Center and the FBI Academy in Quantico, VA.[145] Mustapha was a featured speaker at the 11th Annual MAS-ICNA Convention

in Chicago, IL, in December 2012.[146]

8. **Osama Jammal** is Vice President of The Mosque Foundation in Bridgeview, IL (the Bridgeview Mosque),[147] where Hamas operative Kifah Mustapha is imam. The Mosque Foundation, long the subject of FBI surveillance, was intensively investigated after the 9/11 attacks for possible involvement in terror financing.[148] The Mosque Foundation website openly solicits *zakat* tax payments, a portion of which must be given to support for jihad, according to Islamic law. Jammal was also a featured speaker at the 11th Annual MAS-ICNA Convention in Chicago, IL, in December 2012.[149]

12. **Edina Lekovic** is the Director of Policy and Programming for the Muslim Public Affairs Council (MPAC). Her MPAC bio states that she is responsible for overseeing strategic initiatives in government, media, and Hollywood engagement as well as leadership development programs. She served from 2004 to 2010 as MPAC's Communications Director.[150] Lekovic participates frequently in national and international conferences and interfaith dialogue events, such as the United Nations program on "Confronting Islamophobia" and the International Conference of Muslim Young Leaders, which served as a precursor to the annual conference of the Organization of Islamic Cooperation (OIC).[151] Headquartered in Southern California, MPAC was established initially in 1986 as the Political Action Committee of the Islamic Center of Southern California, whose key leaders likely had their origins in the Egyptian Muslim Brotherhood. Since that time, MPAC has functioned as the political lobbying arm of the Islamic Movement, if not the U.S. Brotherhood outright.[152] Lekovic was also managing editor of the Muslim Student Association's (MSA) UCLA publication *Al-Talib*. In a 1999 edition of *Al-Talib* titled "Spirit of Jihad," in which Lekovic was the named managing editor, Osama bin Laden was roundly praised for his jihadi leadership in the article "Jihad in America – Maintaining an Islamic Identity in an un-Islamic Environment":

> When we hear someone refer to the great Mujahid (someone who struggles in Allah's cause) Osama bin Laden as a "terrorist," we should defend our brother and refer to him as freedom fighter; someone who has forsaken wealth and power to fight in Allah's cause and speak out against oppressors. We take these stances only to please Allah.[153]

Purging Counterterror Training

While maybe not obvious on first blush, the information requirements driving analysis and decision-making on terrorism have been subordinated to what the Islamic community permits non-Muslims to know—and our leadership has been maneuvered into enforcing it.

The very entities tasked with defending the Constitution have, in effect, been coopted into becoming the chief enforcers of a hostile narrative designed to undermine it. This underlying information campaign is tailored to deprive America of the information requirements it needs to defend itself against named threats.

The subversion campaign enters the Western information domain through the skilled manipulation of postmodern (e.g., diversity and anti-imperialist) narratives. Many progressive reporters' ideological commitments to anti-imperialism or their antipathy toward conservatives make them natural choices for collaboration with Islamist forces. Watching the process long enough, one begins to realize that the groundswell of protest comes from a rather discrete group of players associated with recognized entities that coordinate their activities. As it relates to this book, the relationship is best summed up by Iliac Ramirez Sanchez, aka Carlos the Jackal, in *Revolutionary Islam* (2003):

> "Only a coalition of Marxists and Islamists can destroy the United States."[154]

The hostile information campaign works like this: A progressive news agency puts out a questionable story alleging "Islamophobia." It is closely followed by a demand from a Muslim Brotherhood group. In one example that I am personally familiar with, it was an NPR story followed by a Council on American Islamic Relations (CAIR) demand that a summer 2011 counterterrorism lecture at the CIA be cancelled because of its "Islamophobic" content.[155] (It was Nihad Awad, president and co-founder of CAIR—a group formed out of Hamas—agitating for the CIA training to be cancelled.[156])

Shortly after CAIR's demand came the CIA cancellation notice that emphasized "violations" of policies against "Islamophobia." The announcement disclosed that the new proponent agency for Countering Violent Extremism—the agency that forced the cancellation—would be the Department of Homeland Security's Office of Civil Rights and Civil Liberties. Later, in September 2011, Mohamed Elibiary bragged about the role he had played in my removal:

> For full disclosure, I did not play any role at DOD concerning Coughlin, but did fly up to the Freedom and Justice Foundation office years ago with well-known scholars like Dr. Waleed Bassoon to deeply analyze the arguments in Coughlin's Master's thesis on this topic. I shared that research with some FBI and Homeland Security Intelligence Enterprise allies back then.[157]

Was it in his capacity as President of the Freedom and Justice Foundation that Elibiary believes he played a role in ending my career,[158] or was he acting in his capacity as a member of DHS's CRCL Advisory Council—or was it both? Of course, this raises real questions of due process.

An example of this symbiotic relationship between the Brotherhood and the Left is that of Brotherhood-associated (former) Senior Homeland Security Adviser Mohamed Elibiary and (the now) Washington-based *Guardian* national security reporter Spencer Ackerman. According to Ackerman, Elibiary has long been a favorite Muslim counterterrorism adviser to the national security community, sometimes identified sympathetically as the "FBI's Key Muslim Ally."[159] Already cited numerous times in this book, Elibiary has many affiliations to the Islamic Movement, including associations, ideological declarations, and habitual pro-Brotherhood advocacy on social media.[160] It is not surprising that as a consultant and advisor to the government on terrorism, Elibiary bragged of his efforts to sabotage the prosecution of that same terrorist-funding group. He is also an outspoken critic[161] of one of this country's most effective national security prosecutions based on material support for terrorism.[162]

Also of relevance is Elibiary's endorsement of Sayyid Qutb. Elibiary urged Americans to read the Brotherhood thinker and strategist and "see the potential for a strong spiritual rebirth that's truly ecumenical allowing all faiths practiced in America to enrich us and motivate us to serve God better by serving our fellow man more." He continued, "I'd recommend everyone read Qutb, but read him with an eye to improving America not just to be jealous with malice in our hearts."[163] In June 2014, Elibiary boasted of his pro-Muslim Brotherhood stance regarding events in Egypt.[164] Also disturbing is his support for the "inevitable" establishment of a caliphate in the context of ISIS's (al-Qaeda in Iraq's)[165] murderous rampage through Iraq. In another June 2014 Twitter exchange, Elibiary ridiculed news coverage of ISIS's strict application of shariah[166] in the same news cycle during which ISIS was engaging in mass executions of Muslims.[167] One could see in Elibiary's Twitter comment a confused convergence of a Muslim Brother praising brutal al-Qaeda actions in furtherance of its caliphate even as he supports the proto-Caliphate being established by the OIC[168] as endorsed by the Brotherhood.[169]

Despite everything, Elibiary claims a kind of bipartisan political pedigree; a 2008 Texas delegate for Republican John McCain, he nevertheless is a favorite in the Obama administration. His praise of Qutb and Muslim-Brotherhood affiliations did not disqualify him from serving as an advisor to the Department of Homeland Security and as a member of DHS's Countering Violent Extremism Working Group.[170]

On September 14, 2011, *Wired* published a survey expressing outrage over counterterrorism training material used by the FBI, including my own.[171] Its author, Spencer Ackerman, is a progressive journalist with an established partisan political agenda. His methodology—by his own admission in emails to fellow journalistic provocateurs—includes tarring those with whom he disagrees as "racists." Collaborating with Muslim Brotherhood–associated groups and individuals,

Ackerman did his part to accuse trainers responsible for the material—all focused on published enemy threat doctrine—of "Islamophobia." The excerpts consisted of slides used in training presentations and were wrenched from the contexts of the classroom and the accompanying lectures.

In his assault on threat-focused counterterror training, Ackerman relied, in part, on Elibiary for the information he could provide through his access to DHS archives.[172] In public, Elibiary was vocal in demanding what amounted to the up-ending of counterterror training—and, with that, our national security establishment's understanding of the threat. Of course, he heavily promoted Ackerman's reporting in *Wired*.[173] In fact, Brotherhood media often responded to Ackerman in the same reporting cycle. On October 4, in a letter to then-FBI Director Robert Mueller, no fewer than six known Muslim Brotherhood–associated organizations and the American Civil Liberties Union made demands based on Ackerman's articles. The letter claimed:

> The undersigned civil and human rights groups write to ex-press our deep concern regarding recently-publicized FBI training materials that manifest anti-Muslim bias and fac-tual inaccuracies.[174]

Ackerman later disclosed that his wife worked for the ACLU.[175] In a letter to the White House dated October 19, 2011, elements of the American Muslim Brotherhood demanded that the White House embargo information regarding the nexus between Islam and Islamic-based terrorism—even demanding firings, "re-education" and "purges."[176] The letter was drafted by Farhana Khera, Presi-dent and Executive Director of Muslim Advocates, and directed to John Bren-nan, then-White House Assistant to the President for Homeland Security and Counterterrorism and now the Director of the Central Intelligence Agency. Days later, Brennan responded by agreeing on the necessity for the "White House [to] immediately create an interagency task force to address the problem."[177]

Talks between the administration and the Brotherhood were at a high level, with the FBI Director going so far as to discuss such an undertaking in February 2012[178] against the expressed directives of Congress.[179] More alarming, howev-er, is that the FBI then proceeded to undertake a purging of documents.[180] The Department of Defense followed shortly thereafter with a Soviet-style purge of individuals, disciplinary actions, and re-education.[181] All this in furtherance of Kirby's "core values."

Brennan answered the demand for "purges" and "re-training" by reference to the Obama administration's Countering Violent Extremism (CVE) narrative, stating, "We share your sense of concern over these recent unfortunate incidents and are moving forward to ensure problems are addressed with a keen sense of urgency."[182]

Brennan addressed his commitment to the same Farhana Khera who, in earlier congressional testimony, stood by statements on her Muslim Advocates website warning Muslims in America not to talk to the FBI unless consulting first with a lawyer in circumstances where the contact had nothing to do with the person under investigation.[183] Of course, the lawyers would be Muslim Brotherhood approved, and the concern would be to ensure that Muslims obey published shariah that forbids them from talking to law enforcement,[184] as discussed in Part 3.

By February 2012, the FBI began conducting a classified "purge" of counterterror training materials and lecturers. The lecturers were given no notice and, hence, given no chance to defend their work products—or even to face their accusers.[185] Again, where was the due process? The identities of the subject matter experts brought in to screen the material were withheld, even from Members of Congress and their staff. When confronted, the FBI took the extraordinary step of classifying the names of the subject matter experts. Brotherhood-aligned or -friendly groups suddenly had censorship authority over what the FBI is allowed to know, and American citizens are denied their right to know who was making those decisions. It also meant that the FBI allowed its Special Agents to fall victim to partisan witch-hunts. The sad thing is that FBI leaders did not give their own Special Agents—whose work products were anonymously reviewed—a chance either to defend their work or face their accusers. In true Alinskyist fashion, with a dash of Kafka, the supporting narrative to this activity was that it was done in furtherance of "our core values."[186] Whose core values? Jihad fi sabilillah!

Predictably, this process repeated itself at other government departments, services, and agencies, including the Department of Defense. Based on nothing other than Ackerman's sensationalistic *Wired* article on counterterror training at the FBI, a Joint Staff action was initiated by the Assistant Secretary for Homeland Defense, Jose S. Mayorga. In what appears to have been a coordinated release, on the same early evening that the Joint Chiefs Staff Legislative Affairs Office informed relevant Congressional Committees that the Joint Forces Staff College was being ordered to suspend its training, Ackerman published an "exclusive" taking credit for that action:

> The chairman of the Joint Chiefs of Staff on Tuesday ordered the entire U.S. military to scour its training material to ensure it doesn't contain anti-Islamic content, Danger Room has learned. The order came after the Pentagon suspended a course for senior officers that was found to contain derogatory material about Islam.
>
> The extraordinary order by General Martin Dempsey, the highest-ranking military officer in the U.S. armed forces, was prompted by content in a course titled "Perspectives on Is-

lam and Islamic Radicalism" that was presented as an elective at the Joint Forces Staff College in Norfolk, Virginia. The course instructed captains, commanders, lieutenant colonels and colonels from across all four armed services that "Islam had already declared war on the West," said Lt. Gen. George Flynn, Dempsey's deputy for training and education.[187]

Who would have thought that the Joint Chiefs of Staff could so easily be maneuvered into enforcing a hostile information campaign against its own? In an email to the congressional committees, the Joint Staff Legislative Affairs Office made the following comments with regard to the training material used at the Joint Forces Staff College:

> An initial review reveals that some of the material (1) Included reckless, inflammatory courses of action to deal with Islam; (2) Postulated the idea that all Islam was radical; (3) Characterized all Islam as an ideology instead of a religion; and (4) Appeared to advocate a specific political agenda. Again, these conclusions are based on an initial review and further inquiry is ongoing.[188]

Those seeking to shut down the information presented in briefings to those classes did so in large part because the content could not be honestly countered. I can certainly defend what I briefed. (While the details are not included in this book, there was much that happened at the Joint Forces Staff College that has yet to see the light of day.) The message to Legislative Affairs ended with a call for "intellectual balance." As will be discussed in Part 8, being correct in one's explanation of facts demonstrates intellectual fidelity. "Balance" in the absence of facts, however, cannot be shown to be intellectual at all. Also to be discussed is how "balance" has taken on an Orwellian secondary meaning.

If you are a national security or national law enforcement professional who chooses to conform to the demand to de-professionalize your work product by refusing to analyze the threat according to the relevant evidence (fact-based indicators applied to a doctrinal template), a faux analytical paradigm has been institutionalized that compromises the analytical processes, thereby rendering the quality of the work product permanently degraded. On the bright side, when conforming to MPAC demands, you will also satisfy DHS CRCL Guidelines and thereby be able to present your findings inside the U.S. national security and law enforcement spaces. Yes, you too can make a good living out of briefing the government—if you compromise professional standards (and your principles) by briefing nonsense. National security leaders and elite media have become enslaved by narratives that are simply not reality-based, and they demand that those who play in their space conform to those narratives as the cost of admission. There are career-ending penalties for telling the truth.

Needlessly sanitizing our communications or constraining our analysis out of a heightened sensitivity to accusations of Islamophobia aligns with requirements as stated in the first pact of submission, the Pact of Umar. You remember that Pact; it was discussed in Part 2. Indeed, it is restated in contemporary shariah published for American Muslims today. This continuous understanding, from classical Islamic law to the CRCL's Guidelines (stated in facially neutral terms), should be more clearly understood. It is certainly catching the attention of a growing number of concerned observers. Just look at Syria in February 2014. Raqqa, a Syrian town captured by the Islamic State of Iraq and the Levant (ISIS), gave the Christians of that community three options: convert to Islam, remain Christian but submit to Islam, or "face the sword." The Christians signed the treaty of submission. In return:

> The Christians agreed to a list of conditions: to abstain from renovating churches or monasteries in Raqqa; not to display crosses or religious symbols in public or use loudspeakers in prayer; not to read scripture indoors loud enough for Muslims standing outside to hear; not to undertake subversive actions against Muslims; not to carry out any religious ceremonies outside the church; not to prevent any Christian wishing to convert to Islam from doing so; to respect Islam and Muslims and say nothing offensive about them; to pay the *jizya* tax worth four golden dinars for the rich, two for the average, and one for the poor, twice annually, for each adult Christian; to refrain from drinking alcohol in public; and to dress modestly.[189]

The ISIS pact went on to say, "if they disobey any of the conditions, they are no longer protected and ISIS can treat them in a hostile and warlike fashion."[190] There is no difference between this forced imposition of dhimmitude and the Pact of Umar[191] thirteen hundred years earlier. The language is likewise identical to *Reliance of the Traveller*'s treatment on both the status of dhimmitude[192] and the consequences for violating it.[193]

The CRCL Guidelines' alignment with Islamic speech standards reflects conformance to shariah notions of defamation. Because slander, according to the Islamic understanding, can include true statements, proofs concerning the truth or falsity of claims will not necessarily resolve questions of defamation when such accusations are leveled against national security and law enforcement personnel who argue based on demonstrable truths. Obviously, uncritically enforcing anti-Islamophobia standards brought on by influence campaigns runs the risk of silencing a *bona fide* national security debate. Under the Islamic standard, national security analysts and law enforcement special agents can generate analytical products that are true, valid, and accurate concerning the Islamic nexus to Islamic-based terrorism (jihad) and still be guilty of defamation. It is in this context that the meaning and purpose of the October 2011 fatwa "Resolution On Being Faithful Muslims and Loyal Americans" by the Fiqh Council of North America begins to make sense.[194] When Senior Homeland Security Advisor Mohamed Elibiary said, "Obama removed discriminatory engagement policy towards the Muslim Brotherhood" in the context of the inevitability of the caliphate,[195] perhaps he was referring to the Brotherhood's intimate relationship with CRCL on the suppression of real counterterror efforts.

When U.S. government leaders undertake the suppression of professional work product in the name of combating Islamophobia, they make a mockery of the truth, intimidate investigating officers, decision-makers, and analysts, thereby undermining the counterterrorism effort. Institutionalizing prior restraint[7] as government policy also seriously challenges the First Amendment and runs roughshod over Article VI of the Constitution ("this Constitution ... shall be the supreme law of the land"), to say nothing of putting the nation at risk. When factual analysis is suppressed in the interest of combating Islamophobia, Islamophobia becomes the causative agent for the suppression of relevant facts capable of meeting an evidentiary standard when directed against known terrorists in the War on Terror. It subordinates the oath to "support and defend" to that which Islam permits. This is submission.

Individual Jihad

An understanding of the threat in the War on Terror can be established with demonstrable, repeatable, and relevant facts. If facts can be demonstrated to be relevant, their suppression in furtherance of conforming to "countering Islamophobia" narratives necessarily comes at the cost of excluding those relevant facts from the data used to understand the nature of the threat. In a criminal investigative process, the improper suppression of relevant facts qualifies as "obstruction of justice"[196] or something akin to "suppression of evidence."[197] After all, knowledge is being suppressed that the public would benefit from knowing (obstruction of a professional analytical process / suppression of the relevant facts arising out of those processes). A threat assessment that does not account for relevant facts concerning the nature of the threat is deficient by exactly the margin by which the

---

7   **Prior Restraint**, as explained in *Black's Law Dictionary, 6th Edition*, is "any scheme which gives public officials the power to deny use of a forum in advance of its actual expression. ... Any system of prior restraints of expression bears a heavy presumption against its constitutional validity, and the Government carries a heavy burden of showing justification for imposition of such a restraint. ... Prior restraint on speech and publication are the most serious and least tolerable infringement on First Amendment Rights. ... A prohibited prior restraint is not limited to the suppression of a thing before it is released to the public; rather, an invalid prior restraint is an infringement upon constitutional right to disseminate matters that are ordinarily protected by the First Amendment without there being a judicial determination that the material does not qualify for First Amendment protection." *Black's Law Dictionary 6th*, West Publishing, St. Paul, 1990, 1194.

excluded evidence is relevant.

Everything about al-Qaeda and what its members believe has been knowable and foreseeable for those choosing to orient on facts rather than on narratives designed to entice principals to veer their eyes from those same facts—while compelling others to do likewise. This holds true for the Brotherhood as well. Rather than recognize evolving acts as planned progressions through phases of operation, "radicalization" narratives hold that we conduct outreach with "moderate" Muslims, and when these moderates transition to jihad, they have become "radicalized" into al-Qaeda.

Yet, just about everything that al-Qaeda does that constitutes a threat to the United States can be found in freely available Muslim Brotherhood literature at local mosque-associated bookstores. As part of this "radicalization" narrative, the victim population is held responsible for the perpetrators' decision to act out violently because the victims have induced, by something they said or did, a form of incitement to hostility.

As an indicator of our commitment to successful outreach with our "moderate" friends, we must first alter our lexicons and then suppress our speech so as to keep the moderates "moderate" and appease the "radicals" to keep them from acting. It is a false narrative that generates false options.

Fort Hood

Recalling that individual jihad is a classically recognized form of jihad, one should note that in the first issue (June 2010) of its English language magazine, *Inspire*, al-Qaeda announced a strategic shift to individual jihad in its war against America. Rather than assess al-Qaeda's new threat profile, FBI and DHS chose instead to focus on soft-science profiles under the rubrics of "lone wolf terrorism,"[198] "homegrown terrorism,"[199] and "workplace violence" to explain the rising number of such events that seemingly lack coherent explanations. Of course, the abstracted "lone wolf terrorist" simply masks the real "individual jihadi." Former DHS Secretary Janet Napolitano and former FBI Director Robert Mueller explained the "new" phenomenon by example, referencing the actions of U.S. Army MAJ Nidal Hasan, the Fort Hood shooter.

When Mueller spoke of Hasan's actions, he distinguished al-Qaeda acts of terrorism from those of Hasan: "al-Qaeda and its affiliates are still committed to striking us in the United States [even as] home-grown and lone-wolf extremists pose an equally serious threat."[200] A textbook example of individual jihad, MAJ Hasan's action was characterized by our national security leaders as severable from—and unrelated to—those jihadi acts perpetrated by jihadi groups like al-Qaeda, following Islamic form. Excluding information on jihadi doctrines that motivate such actions guarantees they will recur at escalating levels of violence at a time when al-Qaeda has made it clear that's exactly the form of jihad it intends to promote in the West. The term "lone wolf" exists to obscure individual jihad.

For months before Hasan attacked the military base where he was stationed in 2009, killing over a dozen of his fellow servicemen and civilians after shouting, "Allah Akbar,"[201] he declared himself a jihadi through his briefing. First given in June 2007 to senior military physicians, "The Koranic World View as it Relates to Muslims in the U.S. Military"[202] was supposed to be on a medical topic of Hasan's choice. Instead, it was a lecture about Islam, jihad, and a particular concept of murder in Islamic law.[203] Giving his presentation to fellow officers as part of his medical rounds, Hasan explained his future motivations, all presented in the context of Islamic law, that he tied together through the Islamic doctrine of abrogation. Many of the slides from Hasan's briefing were already shown and discussed earlier in this book. During the course of Hasan's briefing, scores of U.S. military and medial attendees were unaware they were listening to a self-proclaimed "soldier of Allah" announcing his intention to betray the military and the nation that he had sworn to serve by killing his fellow soldiers. Hasan was shot four times by police officers responding to the attack, resulting in paralysis from the chest down.[204] A military jury sentenced Hasan to death in August 2013.[205]

A U.S. Army psychiatrist who completed his internship and residency from 2003 to 2009 at the Walter Reed Medical Center in Bethesda, Maryland, Hasan was also a Muslim whose aggressive dawah effort directed at patients repeatedly drew concern and reprimands from his training supervisors at Walter Reed and from the Uniformed Services University of the Health Sciences.[206] Upon completion of his training, Hasan was transferred to Fort Hood, where he subsequently received orders to deploy to Afghanistan.

The warning signs concerning MAJ Hasan were overt, imminent, and ignored. Trying to make sense of Hasan's actions without reference to the doctrines motivating him rendered the Fort Hood shooting incomprehensible to the national security leaders blinded to the indicators. There was clear warning, because Hasan went out of his way to provide it.

In the years prior to Hasan's attack on Fort Hood, I briefed the national security community on the nexus between abrogation and jihad. As discussed, my presentation explained how abrogation provides the underlying construct that orients some Muslims to jihad. The threat doctrine, based on the rule of abrogation, presents itself to the world through the *Milestones* process. This was among the central points of the "Red Pill Briefings."

U.S. Army MAJ Hasan validated this analysis. In "The Koranic Worldview as it Relates to Muslims in the U.S. Military," he declared his hostility to his fellow officers, announced his status as a jihadi, and stated the reasons and conditions that would prompt him to kill. He specifically grounded his actions in "progressive revelation ... the rule of abrogation,"[207] supported by direct reference to the same Qur'an verses[208] I'd been using since 2004.

After Hasan's attack, FBI agents familiar with my work asked if the Fort Hood terrorist ever attended my briefings. He had not. With uncommon specificity, though, the briefing I'd been giving for years mapped precisely with Hasan's.

How was this possible? I was not briefing my opinion of what Islamic law is or my conjectures about how it motivates its adherents. Rather than relying on sociological or other soft-science constructs, my presentations anticipated MAJ Hasan's because it was based on the same clear reading of Islamic law that Hasan provided in his brief. In other words, my briefings on abrogation and jihad provided actual warning inside the Pentagon because they were factual and threat focused, though ultimately unheeded. In his presentations, Hasan was not taunting his fellow soldiers or doctors; he was giving them notice, just as he felt doctrinally and morally bound to do. There is also the question of proper notice; to be a jihadi, many believe that one must first declare.

Hasan received "uniformly positive evaluations" from the Army for his work as a psychiatrist. One evaluation noted that "the Department Chair of Psychiatry at Walter Reed wrote that Hasan's research on Islamic beliefs regarding military service during the Global War on Terror 'has extraordinary potential to inform national policy and military strategy.'"[209] As I explained in my "Red Pill" briefings, the Department Chair was right: Hasan's research still "has extraordinary potential to inform national policy and military strategy."

If abrogation drove Hasan's analysis, the "killing of a Muslim without right" was the crux of his argument. In Slide 12, "Muslims in the Military," Hasan relied on two verses of the Qur'an to prove that a Muslim U.S. Army officer on deployment in Iraq or Afghanistan—as Hasan himself would have been—would be guilty of a serious breach of shariah because he would be in a position to kill or support the killing of a Muslim without right.[210]

> [4:93] And whoever kills a believer intentionally, his punishment is hell; he shall abide in it, and Allah will send His wrath on him and curse him and prepare for him a painful chastisement.

> [17:33] And do not kill anyone whose killing Allah has forbidden, except for a just cause ...[211]

As we have seen, the killing of a Muslim without right is an explicit Quranic offense that brings eternal damnation. Because this outcome was unacceptable to Hasan, he used his briefing to explain to his fellow officers the conditions under which he would declare jihad and strike out against them.[212]

For the threat-focused, Hasan could not have been any clearer when he said, "it's getting harder and harder for Muslims in the service to morally justify being in a military that seems constantly engaged against fellow Muslims."[213] In his briefing, MAJ Hasan recommended that the Department of Defense allow Muslim soldiers the option of being "released as conscientious objectors," in part to "decrease adverse events."[214] Earlier in his briefing, he provided several examples of "adverse events," including the incident where Hasan Akbar, a Muslim 101st Airborne soldier, killed and injured sixteen fellow troops when he threw grenades and opened fire with his rifle in a camp in Kuwait in 2003.[215] MAJ Hasan also included acts of espionage as an example of adverse events.[216]

Assigned to Fort Hood instead of Iraq or Afghanistan, he did not immediately act upon his threat because the threshold event was not triggered. Hasan's briefing was a clear conditional declaration of jihad, one that was to be acted out against the U.S. military in the expectation of being martyred when the triggering event, actual deployment, occurred.

To understand the immediacy of the threat, an understanding of the Islamic legal drivers as conditioned by abrogation through the Milestones Process is necessary. The murders at Fort Hood reflect the price of choosing not to know.

As was confirmed in his e-mails to Anwar al-Awlaki, part of Hasan's justification for jihad against America and his fellow soldiers concerned his rejection of Judaism and Christianity as religions on the grounds that they were abrogated. In Slide 45 of his briefing, Hasan relies on Bukhari and Muslim for his Islamic understanding of the role of Jesus at the End of Days:

> Al-Bukhari and Muslim said, the messenger of Allah said, quote, by the one in whose hand is my soul, soon the son of Miriam will descend upon you as a just judge. He will break the cross and kill the pigs and abolish the jizyah and money will become abundant till no one will accept it.[217] [Slide 45]

The problem isn't that MAJ Hasan's analysis reflects an extreme interpretation of Islam, but rather that it accurately tracks with undisputed shariah doctrine. For example, his eschatology finds support in the *Reliance of the Traveller*, Book O "Justice," 9 "Jihad," at § o9.8, which corroborates the same End of Days scenario:

> The time and place for which is before the final descent of Jesus (upon whom be peace). After his final coming, nothing but Islam will be accepted from them, for taking the poll tax is only effective until Jesus' descent, which is the divinely revealed law of Muhammad. The coming of Jesus does not entail a separate divinely revealed law, for he will rule by the law of Muhammad. As for the Prophet's saying,
>
> "I am the last, there will be no prophet after me,"
>
> this does not contradict the final coming of Jesus, since he

will not rule according to the Evangel, but as a follower of our Prophet.[218]

Of course, *Reliance* § o9.8 relies on Qur'an Verse 9:29 for its authority. With Slide 45, Hasan explicitly directs his jihad against Jews and Christians. Certainly, it was not lost on him that a high percentage of individuals at Fort Hood would be Christian, in a country that is predominantly Christian. The quoted authoritative hadiths by Bukhari and Muslim that say, "break the cross," refer to Christians; the phrase "kill the pigs" refers to Jews. Hasan's briefing is not novel.

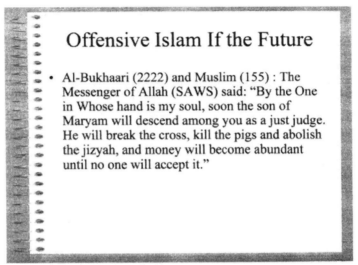

Slide 45 from MAJ Nidal Malik Hasan's presentation, "The Koranic World View as it Relates to Muslims in the U.S. Military."

With all this information, Hasan's prosecutors could not acknowledge the explicitly Islamic basis of his killings. Because it is a fact that he declared the cause-in-fact motive for his actions, we should not forget the obvious: Hasan justified his attack on People of the Book by references to shariah that can be substantiated. Yet the Defense Department, for its part, felt no shame in trying to classify the event as an example of "workplace violence."[219]

In its later review of law enforcement's failure to anticipate Hasan's jihadi outburst, the Webster Commission made no reference to Hasan's presentation, "The Koranic World View," and was therefore silent on its being briefed to U.S. military officers.[220]

MAJ Hasan represents a modern example of individual jihad as classically understood and as called for by al-Qaeda. He addressed his fellow officers and medical staff in dozens of presentations; his language was clear and earnest. He even distributed copies of his slides. Some soldiers who saw his briefing recall being alarmed, but they kept their heads down out of concern for their careers. For them, intervening against Hasan didn't merit earning the label of Islamophobe, which carried with it the threat of career-ending sanctions.

Yet even had Hasan not stated his intentions repeatedly in a public forum, his independent communications with a known jihadi leader in Yemen revealed his intent and should have likewise caused alarm. In 2013, the Webster Commission—charged with reporting on the government's failure to connect the dots that could have prevented the Fort Hood attack in the "Final Report of the William H. Webster Commission on the Federal Bureau of Investigation, Counterterrorism Intelligence, and the Events at Fort Hood, Texas, on November 5, 2009"[221]—concluded that emails between Hasan and a "known radicalizer" probably "deserved scrutiny beyond a simple records check."

> Despite the Army's interest in Hasan's research, his communications with an inspirational and potentially operational <<redacted>> [known radicalizer] under FBI investigation deserved scrutiny beyond a simple records check. As the final sentences of San Diego's lead state: "<<redacted>> **Although the content of these messages was not overtly nefarious**, this type of contact with Aulaqi would be of concern if the writer is actually the [active duty military officer] identified above."[222]

The "known radicalizer" was Anwar al-Awlaki (sometimes spelled "Aulaqi"). Over the course of many months prior to the Fort Hood attack, Hasan had been corresponding with the leader of al-Qaeda in Yemen. In a series of handwritten notes in response to questions from Fox News in late 2012, Hasan wrote:

> [Anwar al-Awlaki] was my teacher, mentor, and friend. I hold him in high esteem for trying to educate Muslims about their duties to our Creator. May All-Mighty Allah accept his martyrdom. We are imperfect Muslims trying to establish the perfect religion of All-Mighty Allah as supreme on the land.[223]

At a time when the U.S. military was directly engaged in combat against al-Qaeda, it is difficult to understand how the FBI could be aware of a U.S. Army officer in direct contact with a person it knows to be an al-Qaeda leader directly operating against the United States and yet feel no compulsion to take immediate action.

The Webster Commission minimized the importance of the contact between Awlaki and Hasan. The Commission—chaired by a former Director of both the FBI and CIA, William Webster—concluded that "the content of these messages [between Hasan and Awlaki] was not overtly nefarious." Yet the correspondence was indeed "nefarious" when understood in the context of the Islamic concepts that both knew defined their communications.

A Look at the letters

Unfortunately for Hasan's victims, the language of jihad was purged from terrorism analysis. Because the operating assumption is that Islam has nothing to do with the communications between a Muslim sideling up to jihad and a self-declared jihadi (and al-Qaeda leader), the FBI missed the overtly nefarious nature of those communications completely. Most of the FBI assessments of Hasan's e-mails with al-Qaeda leader al-Awlaki were, in fact, assessed as "not pertinent" and designated "not a product of interest." A brief look at just a few of Hasan's e-mails, assessed in light of the Islamic concepts that define the messages, will reveal just how troubling these FBI findings were. From the start, for example, MAJ Hasan consistently greeted Awlaki with a phrase suggesting approving support of Awlaki's mission: "*Jazaka 'Allah Khair*" ("May Allah reward you").

Hasan's e-mails in support of Awlaki's efforts were steeped in Quranic references. In an early correspondence in February 2009, Hasan indicated that he "want[ed] to be with those who are the best."[224] This is a reference to Verse 3:110, where the Qur'an describes the difference between those who follow Islamic law by "enjoining what is right [and] forbidding what is wrong." The Qur'an describes these Muslims as the "best of peoples," in stark contrast to what it calls the "perverted transgressors."

> Ye are the best of peoples, evolved for mankind, enjoining what is right, forbidding what is wrong, and believing in Allah. If only the People of the Book had faith, it were best for them: among them are some who have faith, but most of them are perverted transgressors. (Qur'an 3:110)

Of course, the "People of the Book" are Jews and Christians. Several months later, in late May, Hasan elaborated on this point when defending Awlaki from his Muslim detractors who, unlike the al-Qaeda terror master, did not believe in the duty of jihad. He did so by writing that "Allah (SWT) makes it clear that most wont [sic] believe and of those that do; the ones who struggle for his cause are greater in his sight then those who sit back and pray."[225] In this phrase, the Army Major made direct reference to Verses 9:19–20:

> Do ye make the giving of drink to pilgrims, or the maintenance of the Sacred Mosque, equal to (the pious service of) those who believe in Allah and the Last Day, and strive with might and main in the cause of Allah? They are not compa-

rable in the sight of Allah: and Allah guides not those who do wrong. **Those who believe, and suffer exile and strive with might and main, in Allah's cause, with their goods and their persons, have the highest rank in the sight of Allah**: they are the people who will achieve (salvation). (Qur'an 9:19–20)

As these verses make clear that Allah prefers those who fight jihad to otherwise pious Muslims who don't, Hasan indicated his drift towards jihad. Hasan knows that Surah 9 is the "Surah of the Sword"; that Verses 9:19–20 set up Verse 9:29, where Allah commands jihad against the People of the Book; and that, shortly thereafter, the central point of Verses 9:19–20 is escalated and restated in Verses 9:38–39:

> Fight those who believe not in Allah nor the Last Day, nor hold that forbidden which hath been forbidden by Allah and His Messenger, nor acknowledge the religion of Truth, (even if they are) of the People of the Book, until they pay the Jizya with willing submission, and feel themselves subdued. (Qur'an 9:29)

> O ye who believe! what is the matter with you, that, when ye are asked to go forth in the cause of Allah, ye cling heavily to the earth? Do ye prefer the life of this world to the Hereafter? But little is the comfort of this life, as compared with the Hereafter. Unless ye go forth, He will punish you with a grievous penalty, and put others in your place; but Him ye would not harm in the least. For Allah hath power over all things. (Qur'an 9:38–39)

For those who recognize the Quranic subtext of Hasan's messaging, there is little question that he proclaimed both his acceptance of the jihadi mission and of Awlaki's leadership role in it.

> O you who believe! Whoever from among you turns back from his religion (Isli?¢¢m), Alli?¢¢h [sic] will bring a people [like Anwar Al Awlaki] whom He will love and they will love Him; humble towards the believers, stern towards the disbelievers, fighting in the Way of Alli?¢¢h [sic], and never fear of the blame of the blamers. That is the Grace of Alli?¢¢h [sic] which He bestows on whom He wills. And Alli?¢¢h [sic] is AllSufficient [sic] for His creatures' needs, All-Knower.[226]

In this message, Hasan not only paraphrases Verse 5:54, *he places Awlaki in the middle of it.* This is no small thing. In doing this, in his own estimation, Hasan recognized "people like Anwar Al-Awlaki"—i.e., al-Qaeda—as Allah's choice of new leadership. Verse 5:54 states:

> O ye who believe! If any from among you turn back from his Faith, soon will Allah produce a people whom He will love as they will love Him, lowly with the believers, mighty against the rejecters, fighting in the way of Allah, and never afraid of the reproaches of such as find fault. That is the grace of Allah, which He will bestow on whom He pleaseth. And Allah encompasseth all, and He knoweth all things. (Qur'an 5:54)

MAJ Nidal Malik Hasan, a U.S. Army officer, announced his allegiance not just to al-Qaeda but to al-Qaeda as led by Awlaki. He did so in Quranic language that ratified his commitment. Yet this is the content that the FBI designated as "not pertinent" and therefore "not a product of interest."[227]

Just one week later, in a letter praising Awlaki with the greeting "may Allah reward you," Hasan said he was persuaded by the argument on the permissibility of suicide bombing when one has the proper intent. His analogy was to a soldier falling on a grenade to save fellow soldiers:

> For example, he reported a recent incident were an American Soldier jumped on a grenade that was thrown at a group of soldiers. In doing so he saved 7 soldiers but killed himself. He consciously made a decision to kill himself but his intention was to save his comrades and indeed he was successful]. … [sic] So, he says this proves that suicide is permissible in this example because he is a hero. Then he compares this to a soldier who sneaks into an enemy camp during dinner and detonates his suicide vest to prevent an attack that is known to be planned the following day. The suicide bombers intention is to kill numerous soldliers [sic] to prevent the attack to save his fellow people the following day. He is successful [sic]. His intention was to save his people/fellow soldiers and the stategy [sic] was to sacrifice his life. **The logic seems to make sense to me because in the first example he proves that suicide is permissible i.e. most would consider him a hero.**[228]

Hasan's argument on the validity of martyrdom operations is not original; indeed, we have encountered it earlier in this book. According to this view, while suicide is impermissible under Islamic law, martyrdom operations are not considered suicide because of their intent. Years before Hasan, I explained his argument on the validity of martyrdom operations based on intent in my thesis, "To Our

Great Detriment," in July 2007[229] and in an unpublished September 2005 paper, "It's What the Doctrine Says It Is – Rebuttal to 'Islamic Rulings on War,'" which refuted the October 2004 monograph *Islamic Rulings on War* put out by the U.S. Army War College's Strategic Studies Institute.[230]

Hasan could have also reached his conclusion by reading a 2002 back-issue of the *American Muslim*, the Brotherhood-associated Muslim American Society's monthly magazine. In it, Yusuf Qaradawi's colleague Faysal Mawlawi explained that while martyrdom operations are justified, suicide bombing is not. Mawlawi was the Vice President of the European Council for *Fatwa* and Research (ECFR),[231] a Dublin-based Muslim Brotherhood entity[232] that disseminates approved Muslim Brotherhood fatwas. Yusuf Qaradawi was the president of the ECFR.[233] Once Hasan accepted the logic that martyrdom operations were justified according to Islamic law, he raised the issue of collateral damage:

> if (in) the Qur'an it states to fight your enemies as they fight you but don't transgress. So, I would assume that suicide bomber whose aim is to kill enemy soldiers or their helpers but also kill innocents in the process is acceptable.[234]

When he wrote, "fight your enemies as they fight you but don't transgress," the U.S. Army Major underpinned his argument by making reference to Qur'an Verse 2:190. It commands Muslims "to fight in the cause of Allah those who fight you, but do not transgress the limits; for Allah loveth not transgressors." Hasan is aware that Verse 2:190 is followed by - and associated with - Verse 2:191:

> And slay them wherever ye catch them, and turn them out from where they have turned you out; for tumult and oppression are worse than slaughter. (Qur'an 2:191)

Again, the FBI was unconcerned with these communications, stating that this e-mail also was "not pertinent" and "not a product of interest."[235] Around the same time, Hasan dealt with the same issue of martyrdom operations in yet another electronic forum. On a document-sharing website, he published his appraisal on the licit nature of suicide bombing when the shahid acts with the proper intent.

> "If one suicide bomber can kill 100 enemy soldiers because they were caught off guard that would be considered a strategic victory. ... You can call them crazy i [sic] you want but their act was not one of suicide that is despised by Islam. So the scholars main point is that "IT SEEMS AS THOUGH YOUR INTENTION IS THE MAIN ISSUE: and Allah (SWT) knows best.[236]

This, too, went unnoticed, even though the FBI was by that time actively monitoring Hasan. In 2012, the Webster Commission claimed it had undertaken an "independent investigation of all FBI data holdings to assess" what electronic data the FBI had, which included "a second search in support of the criminal investigation and prosecution" and concluded that "contemporaneous searches of FBI data holdings would not have revealed any suggestion of impending wrongdoing by Hasan or any other actionable information about Hasan."[237]

This leaves open the question of what the FBI had at the time it was monitoring MAJ Hasan and later when it undertook a search as part of a criminal investigation. The Webster Report is silent on MAJ Hasan's electronic forum posts both at the time he was being investigated and when he was working up to jihad. That the Report seems to have missed Hasan's forum posting is remarkable, because it was broadly reported as early as the day after the Fort Hood shooting.[238] Also, I personally briefed this to Mr. Webster on December 18, 2009.

In his final email to Awlaki in June 2009, Hasan wrote of the teaching that:

> Allah (SWT) warns us not to take the people of the book as protecting friends (*aulia*) and the lecturer stated that if we ignore Allah (SWT) … we will have no exuse [sic] if we end up in the hell fire.[239]

This is a reference to Verse 5:51:

> O ye who believe! Take not the Jews and the Christians for your friends and protectors: They are but friends and protectors to each other. And he amongst you that turns to them (for friendship) is of them. Verily Allah guideth not a people unjust. (Qur'an 5:51)

As we have seen, Surah 5 controls Islamic rules relating to relations with non-Muslims. In his last communication with Awlaki, therefore, Hasan yet again expressed his intent to separate from his non-Muslim peers—both from the Army and from America more generally. As these e-mails from Hasan to Awlaki indicate, the ability to discern indicators and warnings of a threat is heavily dependent on understanding the intended meaning of the message.

Pointing to the Army's "uniformly positive evaluations" of MAJ Hasan, the FBI "determined that Hasan was not a threat—and believed that no further action was appropriate."[240] The Webster Commission not only concluded that the Army's reporting on Hasan was incomplete and misleading, but also that the FBI never followed up, even if to attend one of Hasan's briefings for due diligence purposes.[241]

By November 10, 2009, the *Washington Post* published MAJ Hasan's presentation, first given to fellow officers and medical staff at Walter Reed in June 2007.[242] It seems that this briefing was MAJ Hasan's "research on Islamic beliefs regarding military service during the Global War on Terror" that the Department Head of Psychiatry said had "extraordinary potential." If true, it is the same presentation that was incorporated into my "Red Pill" brief to demonstrate Hasan's fidelity to the rule of abrogation leading to his commitment to wage jihad against his fellow soldiers and countrymen. The Webster Commission makes no reference to Hasan's "Koranic World View" presentation and was therefore silent on its being briefed to U.S. military officers. This silence is peculiar not only because "Koranic World View" was notoriously discussed since November 2009, but also because I briefed Mr. Webster on that briefing in December 2009.

From the FBI's determination "that Hasan was not a threat—and … that no further action was appropriate" in May 2009[243] to the January 2014 letter the Department of the Army sent to *The Blaze* producers explaining the Army's refusal to grant Purple Hearts to the fallen and injured of Fort Hood, the institutionalized denial of the role jihad played in the Major's decision-making is scandalous. It is simply a lie. To justify its position, the Army relied on the Webster Report:

> Purple Hearts may be awarded to military personnel killed or wounded as a result of an "international terrorist attack;" however, intelligence reports, investigations and studies, such as those by the Webster Commission and Congressional Research Service, all found that Hasan acted as a lone wolf. While there has been no intelligence or findings to date that indicate Hasan was under the direction or control of a foreign element, we stand ready to act accordingly should any evidence to the contrary be presented.[244]

As demonstrated, however, the Webster Report not only documented Hasan's self-declared acceptance of jihadi doctrines and his self-declared affiliation with al-Qaeda, it also documented evidence that Alwaki advised Hasan on the appropriateness of killing of his fellow soldiers and gave his permission to do so:

> [In mid]-2011, an FBI >>**redacted**<< report documented an interview with an FBI subject >>**redacted**<< in which [subject] claimed to have met Aulaqi after the Fort Hood shootings. According to >>**redacted**<< [the subject], Aulaqi told him that Hasan "had contacted him via the Internet and had asked what he could do to help Muslims" and that Aulaqi had "advised Hasan that since he was an American soldier, he should kill other American soldiers." According to >>**redacted**<< [the subject], Aulaqi said he had given Hasan "permission to carry out his attacks at Fort Hood."[245]

Even *Inspire* recognized MAJ Hasan as "a soldier of Allah" when citing his court statement that "I am the Shooter. … The evidence will show I was on the wrong side. The evidence will also show that I then switched sides. The evidence will show we Mujahideen are imperfect soldiers trying to establish a perfect religion in the Land of the Supreme God."[246] With all the factual, doctrinal, circumstantial and inferential evidence that is brought to bear to establish MAJ Hasan's obvious status, in the face of such militant denial, the question worth asking is what will it take to get our national security leaders to abandon their ideologically induced blindness in the face of an American public that increasingly sees it for what it is?

Choosing not to account for the Islamic messaging that defined the intended meaning of Hasan's e-mails to Awlaki suggests that the FBI can convince itself that it undertook a measure of due diligence, pretend to understand the correspondence, and then designate the messages as not pertinent—not a product of interest. But there was no *real* due diligence because there was no *real* understanding of the message, and people are dead because of it. The problem with the FBI's designation, aside from its being untrue, is that those emails provided clear indicators of actual warning that the FBI continues to systematically ignore, as a matter of policy, to this day.

This raises the question of Anwar al-Awlaki. The story of Nidal Hasan's attack on Fort Hood is incomplete without Anwar Awlaki and his long-recognized acceptance of jihad and known ties to terrorism. As he intersected with so many aspects of the Islamic Movement, his name could have been brought up at almost any point in this book. Though Awlaki was both an operational leader of al-Qaeda and one of its lead Internet-savvy English-language propagandists, for years the U.S. government failed to take action against the threat he posed.

The terrorism paradigm relied on by the Webster Report is grounded in the "Violent Radicalization" narrative that drives FBI terrorism assessments. Indeed, Chapter I of the Webster Report is titled "Violent Radicalization."[247] After a brief introduction, Chapter I explains the radicalization model in a section titled "The Process of Violent Radicalization,"[248] which is broken into the "Dynamics of Violent Radicalization,"[249] the "FBI Model,"[250] and the "Lone Actor and Internet Radicalization."[251] The "Violent Radicalization Process" reflects a wholesale swapping out of fact-driven threat analysis with a replacement language in support of narratives that enforce behavioral models that combine pop-psychology with scientism. In so doing, threat analysis and investigatory processes are replaced by behavioral models.

The reality dislocation needed to sustain this pseudoreality is remarkable. As documented, al-Qaeda explicitly states—and has repeatedly published in English—that its preferred operational schema is based on individual jihad, and yet the FBI, not to mention the Webster Report itself, has taken a ball-four on that entire line of operation. This brings us to Josef Pieper's observation on the abuse of language leading to the abuse of power:

> That the existential realm of man could be taken over by
> pseudorealities whose fictitious nature threatens to become
> indiscernible is truly a depressing thought. ... For the gen-
> eral public is being reduced to a state where people are not
> only unable to find out about the truth but also become un-
> able even to search for the truth because they are satisfied
> with deception and trickery that have determined their con-
> victions, satisfied with a fictitious reality created by design
> through the abuse of language. [252]

The strength of the pseudoreality hiding beneath the "Dynamics of Violent Radicalization" model can be measured by its insensitivity to the real-world events that relentlessly pound against it while the world watches. Awlaki turned the "Dynamics of Violent Radicalization" on its head. In an article posthumously published in the Winter 2012 edition of *Inspire*, Awlaki said he was "radicalized" first and then became a "moderate." According to Awlaki, he returned from Afghanistan in 1991 committed to return to jihad. He claimed that the FBI was aware of this at the time and that it affected his college scholarship. It was only when Awlaki realized that the Taliban had already taken control of Afghanistan, making jihad unavailable, that he joined and then led the Muslim Student Association (MSA), a Muslim Brotherhood entity.[253]

By the time Awlaki opened communications with Hasan, the FBI had a long-established history of tracking him. When the FBI met up with Awlaki again in 1999, his story became one of the most public examples of Islamic Movement convergence—or what Shamim Siddiqi called the "methodology of dawah in America." Before America's eyes, Awlaki transitioned from a committed jihadi to one of the Muslim community's most promising "moderate" American Muslim voices as a member of the Brotherhood, and then into the leader of one of the premier international terrorist organizations, al-Qaeda. That is, he transitioned from jihad in one area of the world to the dawah stage in America and then back to the jihad stage, just as described in the Milestones Process. A few short years prior to his death in 2011 by CIA drone strike, Awlaki was an imam at the Dar al-Hijra Islamic Center in suburban Virginia and hailed as a voice of Islamic moderation.[254]

Born in New Mexico but raised in Yemen, Awlaki returned to the United States to attend Colorado State University. While in college, Awlaki spent a summer in Afghanistan training with mujahideen.[255] He was president of the school's chapter of the Muslim Student Association, the first group established by the Brotherhood in North America.[256] After graduation, Awlaki became an imam at the Masjid Ar-Ribat al-Islami mosque in San Diego, and then the vice president of the Charitable Society for Social Welfare. Like the Holy Land Foundation and so many other Islamic "charities," the FBI later identified this group as a "front organization to funnel money to terrorists," notably Hamas.[257]

While law enforcement and homeland security were aware of the al-Qaeda leader's deep ties to the Muslim Brotherhood and Hamas for years, they took no action against him. It was in the run-up to 9/11 that Awlaki again came under FBI scrutiny. In 1999, Awlaki was first identified as a "person of interest" in a request to open a Preliminary Inquiry and Full Investigation owing to his known association with Hamas. The request was first made on June 15, 1999,[258] and then resubmitted on October 28, 1999.[259] The FBI identified Awlaki as a person of interest with the designation "IT-HAMAS" (International Terrorism–Hamas) due to his known associations with Hamas, an FTO designated terrorist organization.[260] (The Foreign Terrorist Organization [FTO] list is the U.S. State Department's list of formally designated foreign terrorist organizations.) Article 2 of the Hamas Covenant states that Hamas is the Muslim Brotherhood.[261] Numerous FBI documents from July 1999 through January 2000 obtained by Judicial Watch through the Freedom of Information Act (FOIA) associated Awlaki with the group.[262]

Months later, as the investigation heated up after September 11, 2001, Awlaki's FBI designation began shifting between IT-HAMAS and IT-UBL (International Terrorism-Usama Bin Laden). Hamas is the branch of the Muslim Brotherhood in Gaza; "UBL" stands for Usama bin Laden's organization, al-Qaeda. In other words, at the time, the FBI was aware that Awlaki was known to be associated as a terrorist under both a Brotherhood and an al-Qaeda designation.[263]

The FBI's first record designating Awlaki as IT-UBL was dated September 27, 2001, and probably owed to the fact that, as the Imam of the Dar al Hijra Islamic Center, he was "spiritual counselor" to two of the terrorists who flew a hijacked plane into the Pentagon on 9/11.[264] As late as October, Awlaki continued to carry the IT-UBL designator while also designated as "not the target of a criminal investigation."[265]

Meanwhile, at the same time the FBI associated Awlaki with al-Qaeda—and two years after opening an investigation because of his association with Hamas—the New York Times hailed him "as a new generation of Muslim leader capable of merging East and West."[266] National Public Radio similarly praised Awlaki as someone who could "bridge the gap between the United States and the worldwide community of Muslims."[267] (Note the "bridge" metaphor.)

It wasn't until February 2002 that the FBI finally designated him as a "terrorist organization member," warning law enforcement to "make no effort to arrest individual" but to "conduct all logical investigation utilization techniques authorized." In that report, Awlaki was identified as a RDCL ISLMC XTMST, or radical Islamic extremist.[268]

Finally, nine months later, in November 2002, an FBI debrief reported that

Awlaki may be transitioning to terrorist activities. This was noted after having identified him a year earlier as belonging to two terrorist organizations and having been in contact with two 9/11 terrorists. His status was then designated as IT-UBL-HAMAS, which indicated his associations with al-Qaeda, Hamas, and the Muslim Brotherhood.[269]

This did not mean Awlaki was in hiding or working too hard to evade law enforcement. In the same period that Awlaki was affirmatively identified as a "terrorist organization member," he visited the Pentagon to meet with senior U.S. military officials to discuss outreach with the Muslim community.[270] He even presided over the Friday prayers in the U.S. Capitol Building,[271] an event featured in the December 2002 PBS documentary *Muhammad: Legacy of a Prophet*.[272] There is no mystery here.

After recognizing his al-Qaeda status in July 2002, the FBI knew that Awlaki was publically listed as a speaker at the 27th Annual ICNA Convention, the first as a joint conference with the Muslim American Society (MAS), along with other prominent Brotherhood speakers and leaders.[273]

On the dual association of "IT-UBL-HAMAS," it's remarkable how the fiction of the prevailing narrative overwrites the facts of the investigation by demanding that investigators position the Muslim Brotherhood as the "moderate" counterweight to the "radical" al-Qaeda when investigations keep putting key leaders in both categories at the same time for essentially the same reason. The information associating Awlaki with Muslim Brotherhood front groups is dispositive.

In September 2001, an FBI report identified Awlaki as the imam of the Dar al-Hijra Islamic Center who attended an ISNA Conference in Chicago, an MSA rally to free Jamil Amin (aka H. Rap Brown) for killing a police officer, and referred individuals to *IslamOnline* and *CAIR.net* as the sources to remain current on events.[274] *IslamOnline* is a web service concerned with issues of Islamic law that is owned and operated by the Brotherhood's chief jurist, Yusuf al-Qaradawi. In referring members to *CAIR.net*, Awlaki further identified Nihad Awad as CAIR's president.

As late as 2006, FBI witness statements noted Awlaki's Muslim Brotherhood status, going so far as to note that a witness had broken contact with Awlaki when learning of his Brotherhood connections.[275] In other words, the FBI's own witnesses associated Awlaki's "radical" nature with his association with the Brotherhood, not al-Qaeda.

As the prevailing narrative focuses on Awlaki being "radicalized" into an al-Qaeda leader, it is appropriate to identify some of his Brotherhood associations that likewise lead up to the FBI designating him a terrorist. In a November 2001 report, the FBI reported on a fundraising event at which Awlaki was associated with the Muslim American Society (MAS),[276] an entity that merged with the

Islamic Circle of North America in 2002.[277] Like ICNA, the MAS is associated with the Muslim Brotherhood. In 2014, the United Arab Emirates designated the MAS, CAIR, and Muslim Brotherhood as terrorist organizations.[278]

The MAS that operates the Islamic Society of Boston Cultural Center[279] also published an article in *The American Muslim* magazine justifying suicide bombings.[280] ICNA was identified in the Explanatory Memorandum as a key player in the Islamic Movement.[281] Other individuals at the fundraising event also identified it as a Muslim Brotherhood function, such as, Dr. Maher Hathout (along with his brother Hassan) who founded the Islamic Center of Southern California out of which the Muslim Public Affairs Council (MPAC) was formed,[282] Suhaib Webb (who has since become the imam at the MAS-operated Islamic Society of Boston Cultural Center),[283] and Hamza Yusef, a leader of the Zaytouna.

Then there is the matter of Awlaki's membership in CAIR. The 2003 Council on American Islamic Relations Membership List for Virginia and Washington, D.C., lists Awlaki as a member on line 1165; his Member Number was 55599.[284] With all of Awlaki's documented Brotherhood connections, if an assessment of Awlaki's affiliation were to be based on the number of his known associations and contacts, a much stronger case could be made that Awlaki was a Muslim Brother.

Awlaki was associated with an Islamic Center in Northern Virginia, and, as explained in Part 3, Islamic Centers are typically associated with the Muslim Brotherhood. Boston Marathon bomber Tamerlan Tsarnaev, who "built a bomb in his mother's kitchen" to detonate at the marathon,[285] was also associated with an Islamic Center, the Islamic Center of Boston, run by Suhaib Webb, a known associate of Awlaki.[286]

The Boston Marathon

On April 15, 2013, two homemade pressure-cooker bombs detonated near the finish line of the Boston Marathon, killing three people and injuring some 264 others.[287] The massive manhunt for the perpetrators—Chechen brothers Tamerlan and Dzhokhar Tsarnaev—culminated four days later, after the pair killed a police officer on the Massachusetts Institute of Technology campus, carjacked an SUV, and exchanged gunfire in several shootouts with police.[288] After the death of his brother, Dzhokhar Tsarnaev was arrested.

The investigation established that the brothers were from a family of Muslim Chechen immigrants whose ethnic roots lay in the Caucasus region of southern Russia.[289] There were numerous Islamic influences in their lives, including family, mosque, Caucasus-based jihadis, and Internet web sites associated with jihadist ideology.

Those influences included their mother, Zubeidat, a devout and committed Muslim who, in 2011, was placed on the Terror Identities Datamart Environment

(TIDE) database along with her older son, Tamerlan.[290]

Russian security officials warned the FBI repeatedly about Tamerlan's deepening dedication to Islamic beliefs as well as his suspicious contacts in the Caucasus.[291] Additionally, the Russians told the FBI that, as early as 2010, Tamerlan was in online contact with an ethnic Russian Canadian citizen named William Plotnikov, who gave Tamerlan's name to Russian security and was later killed in 2012 while fighting against Russian forces in Dagestan.[292] Yet FBI investigators concluded that while the Tsarnaevs were motivated by what they called "extremist" Islamic beliefs, they were not connected to any known terrorist groups.[293]

The method of constructing pressure-cooker bombs like those used in the Boston attack was described in detail in July 2010 in the first publication of al-Qaeda's online magazine, *Inspire*.[294] In that edition, al-Qaeda strategist Abu Mus'ab Al-Suri announced a shift in strategy to emphasize individual jihad.[295]

The name of *Inspire* comes from Qur'an Verse 4:84, which was cited in full on page 33 of the first edition as a header to the section "Build a Bomb in the Kitchen of Your Mom."[296] Where Yusuf Ali uses the word "rouse" in his translation of the Qur'an, Marmaduke Pickthall's translation uses "urge," and the Noble Qur'an uses "incite," Al-Qaeda's translation uses the word "inspire":

> Then fight in Allah's cause—Thou art held responsible only for thyself—and rouse [inspire] the believers. It may be that Allah will restrain the fury of the Unbelievers; for Allah is the strongest in might and in punishment. (Qur'an 4:84)

Because Verse 4:84 promises that "inspired" jihads will be divinely supported by guarantees of an ineffective response, the very ineffectiveness of any given response to a jihadi attack serves to validate that jihad. Hence, our failure to respond effectively to al-Qaeda validates al-Qaeda. With capabilities degraded by the U.S. government-wide purge of training curriculum concerning Islamic-based terrorism, the FBI failed to comprehend—and therefore failed to act on—the critical information provided to them by the Russians. The breakdown in situational awareness enabled the Tsarnaev brothers to carry out the deadly Boston Marathon attack using the target selection criteria provided by Al-Suri in the Winter 2012 edition of *Inspire*.[297] The instructions on bomb making were reprised in a special Spring 2013 edition of *Inspire* titled *Lone Mujahid Pocketbook—A Step to Step Guide on how to become as Successful Lone Mujahid*.[298] In every respect, it can be demonstrated that the Boston bombing was directly out of the al-Qaeda playbook. Al-Qaeda continues to call for similar types of terrorist attacks.

Even with the Russian warnings to U.S. authorities of Tsarnaev's "radicalization"[299] in 2011 and Director Mueller's acknowledgement that he'd been on the FBI's radar two times before that,[300] absent an underlying understanding of jihad doctrines to bring meaning to those activities, the FBI was not able to identify the threat, even as the strategy, tactics, and methods were openly communicated by al-Qaeda and carried out in Boston.

Speaking of what he referred to as yet another failure to "connect the dots" of Islamic terrorism, House Homeland Security Committee Chairman Michael McCaul added that "[m]y fear is that the Boston bombers may have succeeded because our system failed. We can and we must do better."[301] Ahead of any investigation, though, both the Chairman and senior minority member of the House Permanent Select Committee on Intelligence signaled that the FBI would not be held to account for what they could have known leading up to the bombings.[302] Intelligence Committee Chairman Mike Rogers told the press, "I don't think [the FBI special agents] missed anything."[303]

Signaled in advance that there would be little scrutiny of their after-action report by those responsible for oversight, it took the FBI just four months to absolve itself of any responsibility for what they could have known prior to the bombing:

> The F.B.I. has concluded that there was little its agents could have done to prevent the Boston Marathon bombings, according to law enforcement officials, rejecting criticism that it could have better monitored one of the suspects before the attack.[304]

In examining the evidence it had on the Tsarnaev brothers, U.S. law enforcement and counterterror officials dismissed key indicators that would illuminate the pair's clear jihadist orientation. They disregarded, for example, that the brothers had attended the Brotherhood associated Islamic Society of Boston in Cambridge.[305]

In a June 2013 hearing of the House Judiciary Committee, Congressman Louie Gohmert had an intense exchange with then-Director Robert Mueller over the FBI's failure to connect dots and interdict the Tsarnaev brothers prior to their attack. Gohmert asked if Mueller had ever canvassed the Islamic Society of Boston, the mosque the brothers attended. Mueller responded that FBI had done interfaith community "outreach" there. Gohmert then asked if Mueller had been aware that the Islamic Society of Boston was founded by convicted al-Qaeda financier Abdurrahman Alamoudi. Mueller wasn't.

In many respects, Alamoudi's very public path from dawah to jihad is similar to the one Awlaki would take some years later. Surely, al-Qaeda is feeling that 4:84 inspiration.

Abdulrahman Alamoudi

Abdulrahman Alamoudi was a leader of the Muslim Brotherhood in America, helping to found many of its organizations in this country, including his own

American Muslim Council. He was employed by the SAAR Foundation, which was later raided by the FBI; he served as Secretary for the United Association for Studies and Research (UASR); he was acting President of the Muslim Student Association (MSA); and he was a regional representative of the Islamic Society of North America (ISNA).[306] Four of these groups are listed in the Brotherhood's Explanatory Memorandum, and, in 2008 the Justice Department saw fit to designate them unindicted coconspirators in the Holy Land Foundation Hamas funding trial.[307]

Based in the Washington area, Alamoudi was a regular visitor to the White House in both the Clinton and George W. Bush administrations. During this time, he was considered a voice of moderation and represented the State Department abroad as a goodwill ambassador. FBI Director Mueller even addressed one of his organizations.[308] In 1996, Alamoudi prepared the guest list for the first Iftar dinner in the White House at the request of then-First Lady Hillary Clinton.[309] The following month in the *Wall Street Journal*, investigative reporter Steven Emerson chronicled only a sampling of Alamoudi's access to the Clinton administration:

> On November 9, 1995 [Alamoudi] met with President Clinton and Vice President Gore at a meeting with 23 Muslim leaders at the White House. On December 8, National Security Adviser Anthony Lake met at the White House with Alamoudi and several board members of the American Muslim Council. On February 8, 1996, Mrs. Clinton wrote a newspaper column based on talking points provided by Alamoudi.[310]

Owing to these relationships and his near ubiquity in the leadership of the American Muslim community in the 1990s, Alamoudi established the Defense Department's Muslim Chaplain program.[311] In 1993, the Pentagon certified his group, the American Muslim Armed Forces and Veterans Affairs Council (AMAFVAC), to approve Muslim chaplains and imams for the U.S. military.

By 1998 though, even *The New York Post* was reporting on the radicalism of Alamoudi and his American Muslim Council, even as his group—as well as other Brotherhood-associated organizations like CAIR and MPAC—was invited to attend events inaugurating the State Department's Office of International Religious Freedom in Washington.

> The [American Muslim Council] has championed Hamas, which it insists is a "charitable" group with no links to terror. Its leader, Abdulrahman Alamoudi, told a 1996 pro-Hamas convention in Chicago: **"If we are outside this country, we can say, 'Oh, Allah, destroy America.'"** He was the chief fund-raiser for deported Hamas leader Mussa Abu Mar-

zook, and joined CAIR in denouncing the "anti-Muslim" sentences handed down by Federal Judge Kevin Duffy in the [1993] World Trade Center case.[312]

Alamoudi didn't hide his views; they had been in the public record for some time when the Clinton administration invited his groups to Foggy Bottom as honored guests. In 2000, Alamoudi declared his open support for the designated terrorist organizations Hamas and Hezbollah at a rally in Lafayette Park, directly across the street from the White House.

> I have been labeled by the media in New York to be a sup-porter of Hamas. Anybody support Hamas here? Is anybody is a supporter of Hamas here? Anybody is a supporter of Hamas here? Hear that, Bill Clinton, we are all supporters of Hamas, Allahu Akbar. I wish they added that I am also a supporter of Hezbollah. Anybody supports Hezbollah here? Anybody supports Hezbollah here? Takbeer! Takbeer![313]

It seemed that, despite each new red flag, government and social invitations kept coming. In 2002, then-FBI Director Mueller's spokesman described Alam-oudi's AMC as "the most mainstream Muslim group in the United States."[314] The next year, the National Conference of Catholic Bishops similarly recognized the group as "the premier mainstream Muslim group in Washington."[315]

Alamoudi's image was shattered in 2004, however, when he was convicted for involvement in a terrorism-financing scheme. On behalf of Libyan intelligence, he had received money in order to facilitate the assassination of the crown prince of Saudi Arabia by al-Qaeda affiliates.[316] When designating another Islamic group for providing material support to terrorists in 2005, the Treasury Department not-ed that "the September 2003 arrest of Alamoudi was a severe blow to al-Qaeda, as Alamoudi had a close relationship with al-Qaeda and had raised money for al-Qaeda in the United States."[317] In keeping with the radicalization narrative, when speaking of "bad" Alamoudi, he is typically only associated with al-Qaeda and not the Muslim Brotherhood front groups with which he was more closely associated. Had Alamoudi focused instead on continued infiltration and influence operations against the U.S. government—or even more sophisticated kinetic ter-rorist attacks—there is little doubt he would have maintained a good amount of credibility in Washington's halls of power.

As we have seen, the FBI had a long history with Alamoudi. Once he was unmasked as a jihadist and sentenced in 2004, the full extent of his activities in the American Muslim community should have been examined. Law enforcement and DoD counter-intelligence teams should have been under some obligation to investigate his influence on the Muslim Chaplains Program in the U.S. Armed Forces. It's as simple as this: the Muslim Chaplains serving in the U.S. military were handpicked and trained by a Muslim Brotherhood/al-Qaeda operative. Because of AMAFVAC's closeness to Alamoudi, the approving authority for DoD's Muslim Chaplain Program was transferred to another Muslim Brotherhood entity with which Alamoudi was also closely associated, ISNA.[318] This explains why the United States Air Force advertises in *Islamic Horizons*, ISNA's bi-monthly publication operating out of Plainfield, Indiana,[319] for prospecting Muslim Chaplains to serve in the Air Force. Does it bother anyone that the Department of Defense hires only chaplains approved by the Muslim Brotherhood?

Alamoudi played a large role in other organizations such as the Islamic Society of Boston, where the Tsarnaev brothers attended prayer services. The ISB's 1982 Articles of Incorporation designated Alamoudi as both founding president and incorporator.[320]

There are other reasons to examine the Islamic Society of Boston as an incubator for jihadists. For example, Muslim Brotherhood chief jurist Yusuf al-Qaradawi was named one of the mosque's trustees in the 1998, 1999, and 2000 IRS filings.[321] Given his iconic leadership status within the Brotherhood, the Islamic Society had to settle for the sheikh's appearance by video at a 2002 fundraising event because, by then, he had already been barred from entry into the United States.[322] Article III of the Islamic Society of Boston's original 1982 Constitution states that:

> the organization shall be affiliated with the Islamic Society of North America (ISNA), the Muslim Arab Youth Association (MAYA), the North American Islamic Trust (NAIT), and the Muslim Student Association (MSA).[323]

ISNA, NAIT, and the MSA are known Brotherhood-linked organizations. The first two were named as unindicted coconspirators in the Holy Land trial. Despite all of these connections—many of which were publically available years prior to the Boston bombing—neither the FBI nor its director was able to find any evidence that might suggest "radicalization" of the older Tsarnaev, even after warnings from Russian intelligence. If the FBI had been interested in maintaining situational awareness concerning terrorism in Boston, it could have engaged numerous online reports from a local Boston organization, Americans for Peace and Tolerance, known for how seriously it addresses concerns with regard to local Boston area Islamic Centers and Societies.[324]

It is in light of the FBI's ongoing associations with the Muslim Brotherhood, from Alamoudi to Ghulam Nabi Fai, its inaction with regard to Awlaki, and the clear warning of MAJ Hasan that one should understand the suspiciousness of FBI's self-exoneration with regard to the Boston Marathon Bombing:

> But F.B.I. officials have concluded that the agents who conducted the investigation and ultimately told the Russians

that there was no evidence that Mr. Tsarnaev had become radicalized were constrained from conducting a more extensive investigation because of federal laws and Justice Department protocols.[325]

Echoes of this disregard for identified threats could be heard as far back as 1993, when the FBI knew that Hamas was setting up shop in the United States[326] and stood by and watched it grow. It was also in 1993 that the Israeli-Palestinian Peace Accord was signed.[327] Only two years earlier, the Muslim Brotherhood produced its Explanatory Memorandum.[328] Another echo came in 2000 when the Defense Intelligence Agency (DIA) discounted a known al-Qaeda plan to hijack American airliners out of Frankfurt, Germany. From a declassified DIA assessment obtained by *Judicial Watch* in September 2013, we find the DIA concluding that:

> The information was allegedly passed to Western officials (NRI) previously, but was disregarded because nobody believed that Usama bin Laden's organization or the Taliban could carry out such an operation.[329]

The 2000 DIA Report documents the longstanding relationship between the Chechens and al-Qaeda,[330] established long before the 2013 Boston Marathon Bombing. In Boston, the Chechen Tsarnaevs relied on an al-Qaeda's recipe from *Inspire* to build their bombs,[331] and they were members of the Islamic Society of Boston that was founded by Alamoudi,[332] once had Qaradawi on its board of trustees,[333] was operated by MAS,[334] and was run by Imam Suhaib Webb.[335] All this, and yet the Chairman of the HPSCI determined that the FBI could not have foreseen the terror risk.

What does it take? For those familiar with the issue, the findings of both investigations are unsurprising. With the sanitization of any reference to Islam and jihad from national security lexicons—along with the purging of documents and individuals making such associations—Intelligence Committee Chairman Rogers may well be addressing a new reality that he played no small role in creating and enforcing. Everything that made Awlaki and MAJ Hasan threats was knowable ahead of events. This holds true for the Tsarnaevs, as well.

As counterterror analysts know, even if special agents investigating the Boston terrorists had known the right questions to ask concerning jihad, such questions could be asked only at the risk of sanctions. In place of true counterterror threat analysis capable of providing situational awareness and warning, national security and federal law enforcement communities used methodologies that create the illusion of presence through demonstrations of hyperactivity when an event occurs, followed by dramatic after-the-fact vigilance. It is apparent to most Americans that when a self-declared jihadi like Nidal Hasan is in close contact with a known al-Qaeda leader, that fact by itself makes it pertinent to an investigation. It is equally apparent that, when two bombers follow an al-Qaeda bomb manual and attend an Islamic Center founded by an al-Qaeda financier known to promote dawah and jihadi activities, the FBI should be on notice.

The disinformation continues. After the beheading of a woman in Oklahoma by Jah'Keem Yisreal (Alton Nolan), whose Facebook page singled out jihadis for praise,[336] can the FBI really believe its own assessment that the activity is simply a case of workplace violence unrelated to Islam?[337] Does the FBI understand the damage it does to its own reputation by such self-inflicted delegitimization?

We may not have to wait too long to find out. With al-Qaeda publishing periodicals for its individual jihadis in America at a time when its ISIS brand becomes more emboldened, the price for disassociating Islam from acts done explicitly in its name may soon take center stage in the national debate. When asked in November 2014 about identifying Americans traveling to Syria in recruitment from ISIS and related groups, FBI Director James Comey said it was "extremely difficult."[338] While not belittling the difficulties of identifying and tracking individuals engaged in such activities, it cannot be forgotten that these jihadis will return to America as trained committed killers in search of a mission they will most certainly describe as jihad that at some point will most certainly be directed against American citizens. While addressing this needs to be made a priority, as with Awlaki, Hasan, and the Tsarnaev brothers, there is concern that the FBI has already discounted a key source for radicalization and recruitment. As Comey said:

> I actually don't see religious institutions as a central feature of recruitment in the United States. I see it increasingly as an online phenomenon without center, which makes it very difficult for us.[339]

Really? Delegitimizing institutions is a principle objective of any insurgency, and the Muslim Brotherhood says its mission in America is to do so by getting our institutional leaders to delegitimize themselves. What will the American people think if/when a large-scale series of individual jihadi attacks occurs and it turns out that those engaged in the activity were either known or knowable to the FBI before the event?

Given the FBI's chronic refusal to take the necessary steps to understand Islamic-based terrorism, one would think that the bureau would reassess its policy of gagging discussion and analysis of the Islamic drivers that precede terrorist events. On *Meet the Press* in October 2014, former National Counterterrorism Director Michael Leiter acknowledged this shortcoming but effectively limited the range of solutions to that of hiring Muslims:

> "We don't have enough Muslim FBI agents. We don't have enough FBI agents who understand Islam, and we don't have

enough people in government who are doing counterterrorism, who understand 15-to-29-year olds. They're disengaged, and this is also the group which is likely to be most violent. It can't just be Nancy Reagan with, 'Say no to drugs.' You have to do engagement with that demographic."[340]

Given that the FBI sanctions non-Muslims for addressing Islamic drivers of terrorism, the inference is that only Muslims can substantively investigate Islamic-based terrorism. This raises constitutional and discriminatory questions. While not concerned with the hiring of Muslims per se, it is concerning if the FBI is predisposed to hire Muslims associated with the Muslim Brotherhood or the Islamic Movement. This concern is legitimate. Alongside the deep penetration of MPAC and CAIR narratives into the national security and law enforcement spaces has come the perceived need to reach out to Brotherhood-affiliated organizations for support in the counterterror mission. At the same time Justice designated ISNA as an unindicted coconspirator when prosecuting the Holy Land Foundation case, the FBI advertised for recruits in the ISNA periodical *Islamic Horizons*[341] and placed advertisements from ISNA in the FBI's commemorative publication *Federal Bureau of Investigation – 100 Years of Protecting America – 1908-2008.*[342] The Air Force posted recruiting ads in *Islamic Horizons* for its chaplain program as recently as 2013.[343] In this pseudoreality, Leiter's call for hiring Muslims raises enumerable concerns that new hires will be limited to those with Brotherhood or Islamic Movement certifications.

Counterinsurgency in Afghanistan

Returning to President Obama's September 23, 2012, comment on 60 Minutes that "the one organizing principle [in the Islamic world] has been Islam, the one part of society that hasn't been completely controlled by the government,"[344] the author understands that comment to refer to commonly recognized doctrines of Islamic law. A review of the military's Counter Insurgency Strategy (COIN) in consideration of this "one organizing principle" may shed a different light on the status of the War on Terror in Afghanistan.

The military methodology that came to be known as "population-centric counterinsurgency" holds that the local population is always the focus of operations; consequently, it must be protected. The corollary states that the insurgent enemy "cannot be as important or given the same level of emphasis as the population."[345] COIN requires a protracted campaign to "win hearts and minds" by establishing dispersed small outposts among the people in order to protect the civilian population, while pursuing the elimination of insurgent leaders and infrastructure and working to establish a legitimate and accountable host-nation government able to deliver essential human services.[346]

Updated by the U.S. military during operations in Iraq and Afghanistan in the post-9/11 period, COIN doctrine was restated in 2006 by co-authors then-Lt. Gen. David Petraeus and then-Lt. Gen. James Amos in *Field Manual 3-24* (FM 3-24). It was updated and issued again in November 2013 as a joint doctrine under the direction of the Chairman of the Joint Chiefs of Staff.[347] The 2013 version emphasizes discovering the "root causes" of insurgency, developing and disseminating a "narrative" to counter the insurgents' narrative, and urging the host government to undertake reforms to address those "root causes." In its 229 pages, the 2013 version of FM 3-24 mentions Islam just six times; despite the manual's *leit-motif* of "lessons learned," none of those lessons mentions Islamic-based terrorism (jihad) as a possible "root cause" of any insurgency[348] confronting America. Reduction of the need to deploy U.S. troops to battle zones is emphasized, however, as a primary guiding principle of modern COIN as articulated by Secretary of Defense Leon Panetta and cited at the beginning of the 2013 Field Manual:

> In the aftermath of wars in Iraq and Afghanistan, the United States will emphasize nonmilitary means and military-to-military cooperation to address instability and reduce the demand for significant US force commitments to stability operations. US forces will nevertheless be ready to conduct limited counterinsurgency and other stability operations if required, operating alongside coalition forces whenever possible. Accordingly, US forces will retain and continue to refine the lessons learned, expertise, and specialized capabilities that have been developed over the past ten years of counterinsurgency and stability operations in Iraq and Afghanistan.

In a sharply critical essay in *Foreign Affairs*, retired Army Lt. Gen. Karl Eikenberry—who was also the former chief of Combined Forces Command Afghanistan and, later, U.S. Ambassador to Kabul—stated flatly what was obviously true from the beginning, that, "in short, COIN failed in Afghanistan."[349]

Rules of Engagement

The role of COIN in the devolution of American strategic thinking is not just an academic question. If there is truth to the general proposition that those who are unable to articulate a strategy for why they fight are probably executing someone else's, how does one explain the current state of affairs in Afghanistan? If Islamic law really is the "one organizing principle" that is also the one unifying principle, would a review of COIN in light of this "principle" explain the status of America in the War on Terror differently than the prevailing narrative?

As a way of painting a competing view of the current narrative on the status in Afghanistan, and as a proxy for the entire War on Terror, let's look at the Pentagon's strategy in light of COIN, as if Islamic law really is in effect in the Muslim World. A different picture of the same events in Afghanistan may emerge when critical thinking about "the one organizing principle" is not suspended.

The application of COIN to this discussion is relevant because we aligned our efforts through this template with those of the Government of Afghanistan—a declared Islamic Republic, formally committed to standards of governance as defined by Islamic law—by virtue of the Constitution the United States put into effect in that country. The Constitution of Afghanistan opens as follows:

> Article 1 [Islamic Republic]. **Afghanistan is an Islamic Republic**, independent, unitary and indivisible state.

> Article 2 [Religions]. (1) The religion of the state of the Islamic Republic of Afghanistan is **the sacred religion of Islam**.

> Article 3 [Law and Religion]. In Afghanistan, **no law can be contrary to the beliefs and provisions** of the sacred religion of Islam.[350]

If the nation's president, Hamid Karzai, governed according to the constitution we implemented—a constitution with "supremacy clauses" that clearly put Islamic law at the apex—his decision-making and preferences should be understood to have more in common with the Taliban's than with our own. This should remain true as long as both the Taliban and Karzai articulate *bona fide* Islamic reasons for the positions they take.

Additionally, Karzai's governing according to a constitution that specifically subordinates to shariah fulfills the al-Qaeda objective of bringing Afghanistan under Islamic law. It also negates the decade-long expenditure of American blood and treasure to bring real democracy to that country.

What remains of the Afghan Constitution after the supremacy clauses take effect is a chimera, facilitating the illusion that the principles established are in line with Western notions of governance and human rights. As this assessment is controversial, two points should be kept in mind: (1) regardless of how Afghanistan is actually governed, its constitution clearly subordinates itself to Islamic law; and (2) having purged any such knowledge of this organizing principle from our national security analytical processes, our elites are hardly in a position to mount a protest based on what they know they do not know.

Analysis of COIN need not go any deeper than a discussion of how it facilitates our association with the Afghan government. In November 2009, the *Washington Times* published "U.S. Troops Battle both Taliban and their own Rules," a comprehensive discussion of the Rules of Engagement (ROE) in the Afghanistan war as seen through the eyes of the troops actually prosecuting the battles on the ground.

The ROE discussed in the article are a reflection of the COIN strategy and a result of the ISAF (International Security and Assistance Force) Commander's belief that the mission in Afghanistan had been "severely damaged … in the eyes of the Afghan people" because of "an over-reliance on firepower and force protection."

This assessment led General Stanley McChrystal to conclude, "ISAF will have to change its operating culture to pursue a counterinsurgency approach that **puts the Afghan people first**."[351] This entailed ROE that required "accepting some risk in the short term [but would] ultimately save lives in the long term."[352] In other words, putting the Afghan people first meant putting their preferences ahead of the safety of American troops in a long-term effort to save lives. McChrystal made this statement as part of his published guidance. The title of the guidance document states:

> Headquarters, International Security Assistance Force, Kabul, Afghanistan, ISAF Commander's Counterinsurgency Guidance: "Protecting the people is the mission. **The conflict will be won by persuading the population, not destroying the enemy.** ISAF will succeed when GIRoA [Government of the Islamic Republic of Afghanistan] earns the support of the people."[353]

When reading published guidance from a commanding officer, it is important to understand that it has the effect of an order and can bring with it the force of law. The concern is that the stated success criterion, that "ISAF will succeed when GIRoA earns the support of the people," is actually something outside the control of ISAF—and yet the force was being burdened with that mission. A predictable sequence of failures in analysis, policy, and command resulted.

There is something mystifying about this. How can the same national security leadership that formed the "Government of the Islamic Republic of Afghanistan" refer to it in official documents that way (or as the GIRoA), draft its constitution so that everything in it is subordinated to Islamic law, and yet remain unaware that understanding Islamic law would then be critical to understanding the people and institutions they work with in Afghanistan?

It does not seem to have occurred to anyone that ISAF's stated success criteria could be satisfied, as stated, where "GIRoA earns the support of the people" by allowing "the people" of Afghanistan to turn on ISAF forces. Hence, a rather bizarre yet nevertheless real situation was created where so long as the killing of ISAF personnel by GIRoA personnel resulted in the government's gaining support of the people, it could still qualify as a COIN success.

General Petraeus confirmed COIN's orientation in the August 2010 CO-MISAF Counterinsurgency Guidance for the Soldiers, Sailors, Airmen, Marines, and Civilians of NATO ISAF and U.S. Forces—Afghanistan ("COMISAF Guidance"):

> **Secure and serve the population.** The decisive terrain is the human terrain. The people are the center of gravity. Only by providing them security and earning their trust and confidence can the Afghan government and ISAF prevail.[354]

From the COMISAF Guidance, the mission to earn "trust and confidence"—in other words, to be liked—was placed ahead of the national security imperative to defeat the enemy. As the *Washington Times* reported, the troops on the ground continue to be well aware that COIN has the effect of subordinating the U.S. mission to combat terrorism to a "framework to ensure cultural sensitivity in planning and executing operations" that was embedded in the Rules of Engagement.[355]

The troops were also aware that the "cultural sensitivity" driving the planning and execution of operations based on "putting the Afghan people first" required them to conduct themselves according to the Twelve Rules required by President Karzai. As implemented by General McChrystal, these rules were designed "to keep Afghan casualties to a minimum" *by accepting greater U.S. casualties*—or, in other words, "accepting some risk in the short term."[356]

By interviewing U.S. forces engaged in Afghanistan, the *Washington Times* pieced together a few of the Rules of Engagement understood to reflect Karzai's Twelve Rules:

- No night or surprise searches.

- Villagers have to be warned prior to searches.

- Afghan National Army (ANA) or Afghan National Police (ANP) must accompany U.S. units on searches.

- U.S. soldiers may not fire at the enemy unless the enemy is preparing to fire first.

- U.S. forces cannot engage the enemy if civilians are present.

- Troops can fire at an insurgent if they catch him placing an IED, but not if insurgents are walking away from an area where explosives have been laid.[357]

With ROE like this, it should not surprise anyone that U.S. casualties skyrocketed—with over 70 percent of the more than two thousand American deaths in Afghanistan occurring since the COIN strategy was implemented.[358]

As ISAF Guidance made clear, the warfighting mission was subordinated to the subjective desires of the Afghan population, and the arbiter of those preferences was the head of an Islamic Republic whose preferences are constitutionally mandated by the requirements of Islamic law. For this reason, an argument can be made that U.S. warfighting effort was subordinated to what Islamic law permits us to do, by virtue of the constitution we implemented in Afghanistan.

From the beginning, there has been great frustration about the COIN-fueled Rules of Engagement among actual warfighters. On the requirement to be escorted by either the Afghan National Army or its National Police, a U.S. Army company commander from the Stryker Brigade voiced his frustration when saying, "We can't do anything if we don't have the ANA or ANP [Afghan National Army / Afghan National Police]."[359] The requirement to provide warning prior to searches was likewise reflected in the COMISAF Guidance to "consult with elders before pursuing new initiatives and operations."[360]

The troops were well aware of the risk their leaders were willing to accept on their behalf.[361] The frustration wasn't directed toward the enemy they fought but rather toward the restrictions they believed would get them killed.

Why would leaders impose ROE on their warfighters that forswear tactical advantage, including that of surprise? The troops were told, as noted, that such measures were an effort to cut down on civilian casualties so as to win the "hearts and minds" of the population. However, among those in this protected class were fighters known by our soldiers to be hostile but whom they were restricted from engaging. As reported in the *Washington Times* article, "many times, the soldiers said, insurgents have escaped because U.S. forces are enforcing [Karzai's Twelve] Rules. Meanwhile, they say, the toll of U.S. dead and injured is mounting." Among the most distressing aspects of the article is that these two related phenomena— the Rules and the mounting death tolls—are presented as if the two bear no relationship to each other.

The article also reported how the company commander from the Striker Brigade related that since "mid-November [the] unit had lost five soldiers to suicide bombings and improvised explosive devices (IEDs). Many more had been wounded and three of their Stryker vehicles had been destroyed."[362] These casualties should be understood to reflect the "acceptance of some risk in the short term" that necessarily equates to conformance to Karzai's Twelve Rules. The article listed other rules, including that:

> Troops can fire at an insurgent if they catch him placing an IED but not if insurgents are walking away from an area where explosives have been laid.[363]

How can this be understood as anything other than a preference for the safety and security of an actively engaged enemy combatant over the safety and security of our own troops? An insurgent who is allowed to flee an engagement zone is one who is given the opportunity to kill another day.

The fourth Karzai Rule stated, "U.S. soldiers may not fire at the enemy unless the enemy is preparing to fire first." This gives the enemy the initiative (and hence, the first shot). The fifth rule listed further limits on our troops, even if the enemy is observed preparing to fire first, asserting that "U.S. forces cannot engage the enemy if civilians are present." Historically, ROE have held that U.S. service members, in their capacity as American citizens, retain the right of self-preservation, including the right to fire when being fired upon.

What appears to be an extreme example of not firing in the event that civilians may be present concerns the fate of the Seal Team VI team that was shot down in August 2011 in Wardak Province, Afghanistan. All 38 personnel were killed—30 Americans and 8 Afghans. In "SEAL Team VI Family: 'Obama's Rules Are Getting Our Warriors Killed,'" terrorism reporter Patrick Poole detailed the explanation the military gave to family members of those killed in Tangi Valley. Why, for example, was the Taliban team that brought the helicopter down not brought under direct fire? The answer reflected the concern that civilian casualties would upset ISAF's "hearts and minds" effort:

> Amazingly, because of the rules of engagement and the inability to determine whether there were any friendlies in the area, the Taliban team that shot Extortion 17 down was allowed to escape. ... The CENTCOM report indicates that the Task Force Commander declined to strike the Taliban targets with the Apaches or the AC-130 gunship because **they couldn't confirm whether the group of Taliban they were following were carrying weapons.** That shows the counterproductive nature of the rules of engagement, Karen Vaughn [whose son was among the SEALS killed that day] says:

> "When the families from the crash were meeting with the Army's Investigation Team and Naval Officers, a father asked why they didn't use a drone strike to take out the Taliban. A 3-star Admiral responded, 'We are trying to win their hearts and minds.'"[364]

While one would like to hope that, being a civilian, Mrs. Vaughn misunderstood the Admiral, there is the gnawing sense that she didn't. If this account of the fate of the SEAL team is accurate, concern for civilian casualties has been broadened to mean that no firing can occur until there is affirmative confirmation that no civilians are involved. As Afghan combatants are allowed to merge back into the civilian population, there is concern that those ROE held the lives and safety of American service members below that of the rest of the population—including the identified enemy and those known to support them.

Taken in the aggregate, the ROE go beyond "accepting some risk in the short term" to demonstrating a disregard for the lives and safety of the soldiers. When talking to troops who have returned from the fight in Afghanistan—be they special operators, regular infantry, or Marines—it doesn't take long for the conversation to turn to their frustration about ROE that allow the enemy to know everything about them in advance of operations. Surviving families of killed service members tell of their loved ones worrying that it was the constraints under which they fought that would get them killed—not the enemy.

Serious questions have been raised about COIN in its own right. While the strategy has not demonstrated the success it promised, it has resulted in a substantially higher number of service members being killed and coincides with a military-wide morale crisis.[365] Regarding troop morale, over the recent past, the suicide rate exceeds the number killed in combat.[366] Also, there is evidence of a loss of confidence in military leadership as evidenced, for example, by a survey showing that over 90 percent of Army officers polled believed the U.S. Army fails to retain half or more of its best officers. A majority of those polled believed this harms national security and creates a less competent general officer corps.[367] This reflects the mindset of warfighters who believe they are being poorly led.

The question now is whether and how our impression of events in Afghanistan would be influenced if we were to account for the "one organizing principle" our national security leaders embargoed from our analytical processes. As our current decision-making is atypical to historic American norms and practices, one wonders if awareness of Islamic principles would provide some additional or altered understanding of events missing from the current paradigm.

The discussion of Islamic speech law, OIC and Muslim Brotherhood initiatives to enforce it, and the provision of numerous real-world examples of its implementation have progressed to the point at which patterns emerge that are recognizable in some archetypal form. From this observation, a form of typology[368] can be used to help determine whether activities associated with the current COIN strategy can be mapped to recognizable forms.

Modified for this book, such a typology refers to the discernment of activities in prior forms that serve as archetypes of current activities where one can see the footprint (or lack thereof) of a previous form or its resonance (or non-resonance) in other related contemporaneous forms.[369] For example, the archetype form for the OIC's Ten-Year Programme of Action and supporting Islamophobia campaigns is Islamic speech law. The Ten-Year Programme of Action and the Islamophobia campaigns resonate each other. Also, Days of Rage (and the prototypical

Day of Rage, the 2006 Cartoon Crisis) find their archetype in Islamic blasphemy law. Likewise, individual Days of Rage resonate each other.

Having established the peculiar nature of the Afghanistan COIN, the question is whether our understanding of the "one organizing principle" highlights conformance to archetypes that are either friendly or hostile to the mission in Afghanistan—and whether they are friendly or hostile to our constitutional values or to some other players' "core values." Understood from an evidentiary perspective, where a tight fit between observed activities over time can be shown to yield an archetype form, the typology may demonstrate a pattern of behavior that meets evidentiary standards—or at least indicators able to provide warning from an intelligence perspective.

Aside from the Afghan Constitution, there are other influences that affect Afghanistan's orientation to Islam that can be incorporated into this assessment from earlier discussions. For example, Afghanistan is an original Member State of the OIC[370] and is therefore beholden to its commitment to shariah as stated in the Third Islamic Summit Conference in 1981.[371] From its membership in the OIC, Afghanistan is a party to the Cairo Declaration on Human Rights in Islam as well as the 1999 OIC Convention to Combat Terrorism. Through the Cairo Declaration, Afghanistan is committed to define human rights exclusively in terms of Islamic law.[372] From the Convention, Afghanistan is obligated to define terrorism exclusively according to shariah.[373] As already explained, Islamic notions of terrorism are heavily weighted in the Quranic proscriptions against the killing of a Muslim without right.[374] Fort Hood shooter MAJ Hasan explained this to his fellow officers when briefing them about the conditions under which he would strike out in jihad against them.[375]

Because OIC Member States define terrorism according to Islamic law, those unfamiliar with Islamic law are, by definition, unaware of our Middle Eastern Coalition Partners' publicly affirmed positions on terrorism, including those of the governments of Afghanistan and Iraq. This necessarily includes everyone in the national security community who, as a matter of policy, has taken to heart the decision not to know the "one organizing principle." It is established that COIN operates in the service of an Islamic Republic governed by Islamic law. It has also been established that COIN operationally supports President Karzai's Twelve Rules through the Rules of Engagement.

If the Afghan Constitution we implemented really does formally subordinate the laws of the country to Islamic law, then the killing of a Muslim without just cause would be among the worst crimes in Afghanistan—precisely because it is among the worst crimes in Islamic law. How do our national security leaders counter this assessment without claiming something silly like, for example, that the Afghans either do not know or do not believe what Islam requires? Yet our leaders will make such claims precisely because they are unaware.

Since COIN expressly rests the success of our mission in Afghanistan on satisfying the expectations of the Afghan people, shouldn't there be some due diligence review of what those people's preferences are supposed to be—what they ought to be—in light of shariah, which both *de facto* and *de jure* must guide their expectations?[376] Given the COMISAF Counterinsurgency Guidance that troops need to "view [their] actions through the eyes of the Afghans," there is ample evidence that Afghans are in line with their constitution's requirements to conform to Islamic law.[377] This, of course, includes the law that makes jihad obligatory when non-Muslim forces, such as U.S. and ISAF troops, are in Muslim lands.

If the American military constitutes a non-Muslim force in Islamic lands whose actions do not meet the criteria for "just killing," it would explain why U.S. actions are characterized as terrorism by the OIC in thinly veiled language and would trigger the shariah requirement for jihad "by every possible means" "where States are directly or indirectly involved," just as Al-Qaeda stated in its 1998 fatwa.[378]

This is obvious not just from a reading of the law, but also from what is happening on the ground. A review of news stories from a few so-called Green-on-Blue events will demonstrate that these killings are reasonably in line with what one might expect to see if Islamic law is, in fact, the law of the land and the people know it and agree with its dictates.

These deaths did not occur in combat, but when training or working with our armed forces' Afghan counterparts. One father remembers his son telling him just before getting killed: "If I have to stay here until November ... I'm not going to come home."[379]

Green-on-Blue

"Green-on-Blue" is an evasive term used to describe the murder of U.S. or ISAF service members by Afghan partners, often in uniform, in a way that attenuates the reality that our close-working partners are killing our service members. For example, in an *Airforce-Magazine.com* article, Marc V. Schanz reported on the Air Force Office of Special Investigation (AFOSI) report of the largest loss of life by the Air Force in the War on Terror when Afghan Air Force Colonel Ahmed Gul killed nine Americans, eight armed Airmen, and one civilian contractor, on April 27, 2011, at the Kabul International Airport.[380] Gul drew a pistol from under the blouse of his battle dress uniform and shot seven Airmen and one civilian contractor in the air command and control center (ACCC) multiple times (the ninth person was killed outside the ACCC in the hallway). Gul shot the seven uniformed Airmen execution style, most having multiple gunshot wounds but all having at least one round to the back of the head.[381] The civilian contractor was not shot in the head, but died from multiple gunshot wounds to the body.[382]

Since originally writing of these events, I had the good fortune to meet Lt Col Sally Stenton. U.S. Air Force (Ret.). Lt Col Stenton was the Judge Advocate General (JAG) assigned to the 438 Air Expeditionary Wing (AEW) as the Legal Advisor to the Afghan Air Force as well as serving as the 438 AEW Staff Judge Advocate (SJA)—also located at the Kabul International Airport.[8] Lt Col Stenton was a criminal investigator at the Camden County, New Jersey, Prosecutor's Office prior to joining the Air Force Judge Advocate General Corps and the advisor to the Afghan Air Force Criminal Investigation Division (AAF-CID). The AAF-CID undertook the first interviews of the several Afghans present in the ACCC during the massacre. The ACCC is located in the AAF HQ command building. The AAF-CID also assisted in the processing of the crime scene and the collection of evidence. In addition, during her 21-plus-year JAG career, Lt Col Stenton was both a prosecutor and criminal defense counsel. Hence, her observations are particularly relevant not only as a first-hand observer, but also as one uniquely qualified to assess the incident as a forward deployed military officer, an attorney, and a formally trained investigator.

In his article, Schanz noted the official finding that it was difficult to establish motive for any particular attack and said that the over-400-page AFOSI Report of Investigation (ROI) did not pinpoint any cause. Possible motives, the report suggested, may have been mental health issues or debt.[383] But Lt Col Stenton observed that the "part of the AFOSI ROI that addressed motive was debunked in a investigation Congress ordered the Army to conduct (a second AR 15-6 Investigation)." Completed in March 2013, the AR 15-6 Report of Investigation was not released to the *Air Times* until July 2014—a year after submitting a FOIA request. In an August 10, 2014 *Air Force Times* article, the AR 15-6 investigating officer admitted there was "significant evidence that indicates criminal network involvement in the killing of the Americans." For Stenton, this meant that Gul was not "the lone, crazed shooter" that the families and American public were led to believe by the U.S. military.

Schanz went on to report that while "informed officials" noted that most attacks do not come from the Taliban—no more than 25 percent—causation is generally attributed to "battle fatigue or personal grievance felt by an Afghan."[384] Giving voice to the frustration of many forward-deployed servicemembers, Stenton would have none of this: "This is the initial excuse the Afghans almost always put out, where later investigation often show it not to be the case." She continued, "In the April 27, 2011, massacre, it was immediately reported in the Afghan press, which was picked up by the U.S. and international media, that Defense Ministry Spokesman Gen. Zahir Azimi confirmed the incident was triggered by a verbal clash between an Afghan pilot and one of his foreign counterparts."[385]

---

8   The Kabul International Airport has two sides: a civilian side for commercial air traffic and civilian flights, and a military side. The military side is home to the Afghan Air Force (AAF) headquarters and the Kabul Air Wing.

Of particular concern to Lt Col Stenton, General Azimi's comments were published in an online release of *Pajhwok*, an Afghan news outlet, on April 27, 2011, while the base was still on lockdown prior to investigators arriving at the crime scene and before there was a chance to account for all 438 AEW personnel. Yet, at the time of the story's release (12:14 p.m.), the facts in the article were precisely accurate with respect to the headline, the first paragraph, the rank of the shooter, how the shooter was killed, and who killed him.[386] At the time the article was written, the U.S. contingency did not have this information.

Stenton added, "It was later confirmed by the 14 Afghans in the ACCC, who were interspersed with the eight Americans throughout the ACCC during the shooting, that there was no 'verbal clash' or argument before Gul opened fire." The ACCC is located in a large room, approximately 800 square feet, which was furnished with desks, cubicles, file cabinets, tables, computers, and chairs. Gul simply entered the ACCC and, within minutes, and without saying a word, opened fire. Even though the leadership of U.S. Forces-Afghanistan was made aware of this within two days of the massacre, the Commander, Lt Gen Caldwell, did not take action to correct press reports making these claims.[387] It should be noted that it was the same spokesman, Gen Azimi, who spoke of the August 2014 assassination of U.S. Army MAJ General Harold Greene by a "terrorist in an Army uniform" and has spoken to the press after many Green-on-Blue attacks.[388]

Even so, USMC General Allen, the ISAF Commander at the time of the report, "conceded ISAF lacks sufficient data on the attackers to support 'any kind of a definitive conclusion about their motives.'"[389] Does he understand he is speaking foremost to the American people and, among them, the surviving family members who are severely disturbed by such explanations?

Maybe Colonel Gul's killing of nine Americans could be illuminated by an understanding of Islamic law. What else was reported? Schanz noted that, during the rampage, the Afghan Colonel called out to "good Muslims" to stay away or be shot (or words to that effect); that he dipped his fingers in blood and scrawled on a wall, "God is one" and "God, in your name"; that he occasionally voiced "radical sentiments"; and that a relative disclosed that Gul acted out of a desire to "kill Americans."[390] Lt Col Stenton suspects some of this to be conjecture. For example, given the time constraints and his injuries, it's not clear how or when Colonel Gul found the time to write in blood on the walls. "In my opinion, it's more likely it was one of the many Afghans who remained in the building. These uninjured Afghans were in the building for the hour between the massacre and when our first responders were able to enter the building giving any one of them plenty of time to write on the wall in blood."[391]

In an August 2014 phone conversation, the investigating officer told Stenton that while there was no "direct" evidence that the Criminal Patronage Network (CPN), i.e., high-ranking AAF and ANA, was behind the massacre, there was indirect evidence. "I asked what that indirect evidence was and he told me that the CPN used a mullah as a go between to recruit Gul to commit the killings."[392] From a separate account of the event, it was reported that Gul said, "Allah, Allah" as he lay dying;[393] he "attended a mosque that was 'extremely anti-American and pro-Pakistan,'"[394] and "he was upset that foreigners had invaded his country."[395] Stenton also noted that the investigating officer implied that the mullah of that mosque was the same one that was used as a go-between to recruit Gul.[396] This resonates the obligatory requirement of jihad as discussed, though there was no direct evidence of Gul's affiliation with the Taliban. What of the circumstantial evidence? "There is 'significant' circumstantial evidence the CPN recruited Gul to do the killings," said Stenton.[397]

And yet "no definitive conclusions"? There was a definitive conclusion among the troops on the ground (not shared by leadership) that these were insider shootings and, like the killings at the ACCC at the Kabul International Airport, were definitely not the result of cultural insensitivity! One suspects that just about every service member in Afghanistan came to this conclusion within moments of learning of the details. Those in the know and close to the action at the Kabul International Airport believe that the evidence clearly supports the finding that the massacre was the result of a corrupt Afghan military, not of the Taliban. The jihadi narrative was manipulated to get Colonel Gul to act as he did, thus creating a degree of plausible deniability by staging the executions to appear as either a Taliban-inspired or individual act of jihad, or even as the act of an Afghan Serviceman offended by some offensive remark made by a culturally insensitive American, all of which diverted attention from the CPN.[398]

As part of COMISAF Guidance to "view [their] actions through the eyes of the Afghans,"[399] 1,500 people attended Colonel Gul's funeral[400] and he was openly celebrated as a hero. As Lt Col Stenton recalls, "I believe senior Afghan Air Force leaders attended his funeral."

Even though no direct connection between Gul and the Taliban was ever established,[401] if Afghanistan really is beholden to Islamic law, no relationship with "radicalized" Islamic groups is necessary to confirm Gul's decision to strike in furtherance of jihad. This, by itself, could explain why 75 percent of Green-on-Blue attacks are initiated by Afghans with no known "radicalized" affiliations.

The troops on the ground are well aware of the situation. The Stryker Brigade company commander from the *Washington Times* article "Taliban and ROE" also knows the score; his life and those of his troops depend on it. In that article, Imam Sahed, a local imam of the Kashk-E Nokhowd region, acknowledged that U.S. troops were "respectful to his people and provided security."[402] In Kabul, Lt Col Stenton agreed: "Our fallen—as with all of us—were extremely respectful and befriended our counterparts. We advised them, ate with them, got them all the supplies, from paper to planes, that they wanted."[403]

On this point, it should be noted that Colonel Gul likewise "displayed no disrespect, hostility nor arrogance toward his Coalition Forces mentors."[404] Contrary to the Pentagon narrative, this suggests that whatever "personal grievances" the Afghan partners might have, they are generally not directed at the service members who have been targeted for death. MAJ Hasan made similar comments. While there may be "holy rage" in the acts, there is the element of mission, evident in the purposefulness of their actions. Imam Sahed also said, in language that aligns with the obligatory duty of jihad, that the U.S. military:

> need[s] to go. Get out of Afghanistan or it will never be resolved. Between Islam and the infidel there can never be a relationship ... the Americans won't be able to resolve this problem, the longer they stay the more likely there will be another attack like Sept. 11. It's only the Afghan people who will be able to resolve this problem.[405]

It is important to understand the words in the context of the typological form that gives them meaning when spoken by persons known to be beholden to the form. When a form gives clear meaning to a phrase that is otherwise either obscure or lends itself to differing interpretations—especially competing interpretations that our national security leadership would uncritically prefer—then the meaning that derives from the form must prevail in any threat analysis.

When Imam Sahed told the company commander that he had asked his mosque attendees "not to become suicide bombers and to not kill those who want to help us," the commander didn't put much trust in him.[406] He had good reason. The presumption must be that, as an imam, Sahed is well versed in Islamic law. Recalling the bright line that distinguishes suicide killings (the killing of a Muslim without right) from martyrdom operations in the service of jihad, Sahed's precise language was telling: He said "not to become suicide bombers" and "to not kill those who want to help us." This is also in line with MAJ Hasan's understanding of suicide bombing regarding the issue of intent.

We should understand what the imam's comments mean when mapped against shariah standards in order to account for his expressed enmity towards infidels. Sahed did not mean what the company commander may have thought he meant. Sahed was not lying; it is our incomprehension that keeps us from understanding. Sahed was quite clear, and both the Afghans and the Afghan Government understood his meaning; as could the Taliban.

Following Islamic form, Imam Sahed's charge "not to become suicide bombers" could easily mean "you can kill the Americans but you cannot kill the Afghans"—which fully explains Colonel Gul's warning to "good Muslims" to stay clear—while his charge "not to kill those who want to help" could easily be a warning not to impede committed jihadis who take up such a mission and not to *meaningfully* assist in any investigation that follows.

By ensuring that our warfighters do not understand Islamic law, our national security leaders guarantee that they will never understand threats made against their lives, even when stated directly to their faces. Our national security leadership places our troops in threatening situations with rules of engagement that render them helpless in the face of those threats.

To be a jihadi, or at least to cover one's bases, many prospective jihadis believe that they must declare their intent so that, if killed, they become shahids. There are indicators that those engaged in Green-on-Blue killings in Afghanistan show their hand, just as Nidal Hasan did when he briefed his fellow officers. Hasan planned to leave this earth as a shahid. For jihadis in Afghanistan, because they followed the recognized form, both the Afghan people and government recognize their actions. Recall Gul's funeral. By guaranteeing that our service members are unable to recognize direct threats against their lives, we guarantee that the jihadi can make such a declaration and yet still get off the first – and often fatal - shot.

It's not just the soldiers who are aware of this; often the families know as well. Twenty-one-year-old Lance Corporal Gregory Buckley told his father he would not live long enough to return home, owing to the overt hostility of the Afghan trainees he was required to work alongside. His father related the phone conversation where his son and fellow Marines were told they were not welcome in Afghanistan:

> The guy turned around and said to Greg, "We don't want you here. We don't need you here." Greg turned around again and said, "Why would you say that?" Buckley Sr. recalled. The repeated remarks from the trainee [were] too much for Buckley Jr., who reportedly got into a shouting match with the man. His father said he was forced to apologize. His son offered to shake hands, but the trainee wasn't interested …[407]

Buckley was forced to apologize for what ISAF calls a "personal grievance," for the crime of being a U.S. Marine who volunteered to serve his country and stood up for it unapologetically. Two things stand out here, as with the other examples. First, that the Afghan trainee's line of reasoning is in line with Islamic law, the Afghan Constitution, and the OIC's declarations. Second, our troops know they are at risk, even if they are not always aware of precisely how or why.

After Buckley was killed in a Green-on-Blue attack in the summer of 2012, his father wrote an outraged letter to President Obama. "As an American I am horrified and disgusted that your solution to these insider attacks is to ask our soldiers to be more courteous and polite to these murderers."[408] Lt Col Stenton concurred with Mr. Buckley, saying, "Gen Caldwell briefed us two days after the massacre about the need to be more sensitive to the Afghans and their culture. This is when the leadership was still pushing the 'argument between Gul and the advisors in the ACCC' narrative. I remember asking Gen Caldwell about when the Afghans were going to have to be more sensitive to us as military members and partners. That we were not visitors or guests in their country, but a fighting force sent to assist, train, and advise them on their military mission."[409]

Given the evidence, definitive conclusions regarding the motive of attackers against our troops could have been reached at the time. In a separate event, when asked to explain why he killed three Americans, "rogue" Afghan soldier Ghazi Mahmood simply said, "I killed them because they have occupied our country. They are enemies of our religion."[410] There is no sense in which his comment was incorrect. Mahmood made this comment in a Taliban video in which other uniformed Afghans also said that they seek "to kill infidels."[411] How "rogue" are individuals like Mahmood? When asked to clarify such openly communicated behavior, an Army intelligence official explained:

> They're killing us because we're 'infidels' occupying Islamic lands. It's what the Koran and every imam over there is telling them, and no amount of cultural sensitivity is going to stop that or change the fact that we're 'infidels.'[412]

If this is Islamic law, and since Afghanistan is an Islamic Republic (according to the Islamic constitution the U.S. helped put in place), then shouldn't we expect "every imam over there" to be saying this to the people? The Afghans get it, our soldiers get it, the families of the fallen get it; why don't our senior leaders get it? With the exception of those leaders who made the decision not to know "the one organizing principle" that drives the Islamic domain, there really is no mystery here. In the April 2012 "Report on Progress Toward Security and Stability in Afghanistan," the Defense Department attempted to spin the Green-on-Blue attacks any way it could:

> While they are often high-profile, Green-on-Blue incidents are rare, and have resulted in a relatively small number of casualties. … Investigations have determined that a large majority of Green-on-Blue attacks are not attributable to insurgent infiltration of the ANSF, but are due to isolated personal grievances against coalition personnel. There is no indication that these recent attacks are part of a deliberate effort by insurgents, nor were they coordinated with each other.[413]

What about individual jihad? The Pentagon's rationalizations for Green-on-Blue attacks are not just flimsy and insulting; they are irrelevant. Whether the attacks were inspired by the Taliban or freely executed by uniformed Afghan members, those seeking to kill Americans are aware of shariah doctrines that make such actions legal and obligatory. This is the same Islamic legal obligation of which al-Qaeda, the Taliban, the Muslim Brotherhood, the OIC, and the Government of the Islamic Republic of Afghanistan share a common understanding. At least on this point, they are doctrinally converged. The very national security leadership that chooses not to know any of this also calls work products like that found in this book "warped" as they continue to execute the "strategy [they] know [they're] out there executing."[414]

Official explanations have proven to be insufficient and underinclusive to the events discussed. ISAF announced a policy to withhold information on Green-on-Blue killings after witnessing the outrage of survivors' families.[415] They also choose a policy of blaming fallen service members for their own pre-meditated murders/executions. As Lt Col Stenton explained, "this is what senior U.S. military leadership would have preferred the families and American public believed happen with the April 27, 2011, massacre; without reporting the details of the execution style murders, there could be no arguments." She continued, "It seems this is because, if questions become contentious, our fallen then have to be branded as culturally insensitive and therefore responsible for their own murders."[416]

For the Pentagon, the fault lies neither with the COIN strategy nor the murderers, but with the murdered (echoing Battered Wife Syndrome). Such ISAF policy considerations may reflect a sense that professional investigations would expose Islamic legal and doctrinal support for such killings, which would bring COIN under indefensible fire from the American people. There is something else as well. As Lt Col Stenton pointed out, most of these investigations are not professional. AR 15-6 investigations are not conducted by trained law enforcement (LE), or by special agents of the CID, or even by the trained members of the Inspectors General (IG), but rather by randomly appointed officers. The second AR 15-6 investigation into the Kabul International Airport massacre, conducted between January and March 2013, was headed by a communications officer, a Reserve Marine Corps Colonel. The lead "investigator" conducting the interviews in Afghanistan was also a communications officer, this time an Air Force Lt Colonel.

This does not sit well with Stenton as an officer of the court who served as a Staff Judge Advocate and a former police detective. Neither the "investigator" nor the other four members of his "investigation team" had any training in interviewing and/or interrogating in such circumstances. They were also untrained in the forensics associated with a murder scene and unfamiliar with the rules associated with the preservation of evidence and even with what constitutes evidence. In the 15-6 investigative process, when the report is submitted to the appointing authority, it is reviewed by the JAG, who then puts that office's spin on the findings and recommendations. The report reads like a legal brief—not like the findings and recommendations of a professionally investigated and evidence-driven report of investigation.[417]

As General Dempsey, Chairman of the Joint Chiefs of Staff, sees it, "there's a percentage [of attacks] which are cultural affronts."[418] His solution was mandatory Islamic-sensitivity training for the troops, including severe punishment for those who violated the rules. Soldiers were trained that they were being murdered because they "show the bottom of their feet," "share photos of [their] wives or daughters," or blow their noses in the presence of a Muslim.[419] Yet what was the "cultural affront" that justified the killing of 20-year-old Army PFC Dustin Napier, who was murdered during a base volleyball game? It required a reporter to provide that additional detail, as the Pentagon declined to provide any context to the killing.[420]

From whom is this kind of information being withheld? The Afghans are aware of it. The service members are keenly aware of both the unreasonable risk and the official reports that will misrepresent and disparage their fallen comrades. Could it be that it is withheld from the American people—not because they might draw the wrong conclusion, but because they might draw the right one? This is an insult.

Regarding Dempsey's mandate, while no one is arguing for rude or deliberately disrespectful behavior, commanders run the risk of violating the First Amendment when they order American citizens to conform to the religious mandates of a faith. This should not change just because religious conformance is stated in facially neutral terms.

Many of the rules the service members could be punished for violating involve compliance with real Islamic law. This is true regardless of whether those in command are subjectively aware of the situation, especially given their objective duty to know. As one skeptical Army official put it:

> I would like to see a public affairs officer explain to the press
> where showing the bottom of your shoe to a Muslim or shak-
> ing with your left hand was legitimate grounds for murder.[421]

Given the emphasis on conditioning U.S. success on the preferences of the Afghan people, it's legitimate to ask if the Afghans' "hearts and minds" were ever ours to lose. A senior Army intelligence officer provides the best ground truth on that question from both the American and the Afghan perspectives:

> [T]he cultural affronts excuse is a bunch of garbage ... the
> Afghans that know we're doing all this PC cultural sensitivi-
> ty crap are laughing their asses off at our stupidity.[422]

Yet its stupidity that kills. The surviving families of the dead are not laughing. Nor are those with a concern for the state of our national security.

In a way, General Dempsey was correct when he said that "there's a percentage [of Green-on-Blue attacks] which are cultural affronts."[423] In each of the instances discussed, that cultural affront was that U.S. forces in Afghanistan were non-Muslims in Muslim lands. Islamic law mandates that such a non-Muslim military must be fought by "every possible means."[424]

Even *Al-Jazeera* had to stop short of guffawing at the ridiculousness of the generals' rationalizations. In an article whose subtitle says it all for the entire Muslim world ("The Sting of Subjugation: 'Green on Blue' Attacks in Afghanistan:

Afghans are killing Western troops because the U.S. and NATO are in occupation of their country"), it was reported that, while "U.S. commanders insist that the attacks are not the result of Taliban infiltration of Afghan security forces but arise instead from personal grievances and cultural misunderstandings between Afghan trainees and NATO soldiers," the "U.S. generals are fooling themselves if they think correct toilet practices are going to save their troops from the defeat that President Obama has scheduled for them in 2014."[425] *Al-Jazeera* stated the Islamic duty driving Green-on-Blue murders in secular terms:

> Afghans are killing Western troops because the US and NATO are in occupation of their country. The Taliban does not need to "infiltrate" the Afghan National Army or the Afghan National Police. Every Afghan knows they are occupied; every Afghan feels keenly the embarrassed sting of subjugation.[426]

This is the same *Al-Jazeera* that used U.S. Navy Captain Kirby in an information campaign to silence any analysis—like the kind found in this book—that seeks to explain the grave circumstances in which we currently find ourselves. An unsettling aspect of the *Al-Jazeera* article is that it made reference to a historical event in the context of escalating Green-on-Blue violence.[427] There has been chatter recently in the Afghanistan-Pakistan regions about a "Perfect Day," which harkens back to the Sepoy Mutiny of 1857. At the time, British India was composed of India, Pakistan, Bangladesh, and Afghanistan. Muslims and Hindus rose up in mutiny and began killing British subjects.[428] The article identified a similarity between the motivations in the Sepoy Mutiny and those of Green-on-Blue murders, while ISAF leadership was identified with the British leadership at the time of the mutiny:

> Imperial oppressors and occupiers prefer to forget the politics of domination. They like to believe that the "natives" are fundamentally irrational religious bigots. The job of the imperialists is of course to civilize, modernize, develop and enlighten these "natives."[429]

This type of messaging, in the context of escalating violence through independent acts of individual jihad, is similar to the tactics of the 19th-century mutiny, which could, in theory, be synchronized with al-Qaeda's American strategy based on individual jihad. As Afghanistan, the OIC, and the Muslim Brotherhood are beholden to Islamic law, it is worth looking at how that law understands such activities. Because such a scenario is credible, indicators should be developed that would provide warning of future attacks along those lines.

Days of Rage in Afghanistan

In March 2011, an activist pastor burned a Qur'an in Florida, igniting a few Days of Rage in Mazar-i Sharif, Afghanistan. The ensuing violence caught U.S. forces off-guard, and rioters killed several UN employees. Like the earlier Days of Rage, the goal of these riots was to induce a crisis that would disorient American policymakers in both Afghanistan and Washington. The tactic succeeded in prompting the ISAF Commander, then-General David Petraeus, to make a statement questioning—or, at least, making conditional—the First Amendment.

> "This was a surprise," Gen. Petraeus said. The Quran burning in Florida, he added, was "hateful, extremely disrespectful and enormously intolerant."[430]

This statement confirmed that Days of Rage can achieve strategic surprise against a major command engaged in combat activity. Meanwhile, the State Department continues to assist the OIC with the implementation of its Ten-Year Programme of Action, which intends to make defamation of Islam a crime in every jurisdiction – including America. Let's look at one of the lines of operation that the OIC uses to achieve that end, which concerns Afghanistan and involves an inversion of COIN strategy.

Among the tools used by the OIC to intimidate Western leaders and media into compliance is the regular staging of statements of deep offense over localized events deemed insulting to the entire Islamic world, followed by Days of Rage that escalate levels of violence. Major events in this cycle began with the European Cartoon Crisis of 2006 and were repeated with Pope Benedict's Regensburg Speech, the Qur'an-burnings in Afghanistan in 2011 and 2012, the YouTube clip on the life of Mohammed in September 2012, and most recently, with the *Charlie Hebdo* executions and the shootings in Copenhagen.

From the start, the Afghan responses to the Qur'an desecrations in 2011 and 2012 were used as pretexts for the Karzai government to initiate Days of Rage in order to intimidate American senior leaders into issuing apologies. These demands were designed to bring those respondents into *de facto* compliance with the OIC's Ten-Year Programme of Action. Both the OIC and the Government of the Islamic Republic of Afghanistan recognize Islamic law as their "one organizational principle," so it should come as no surprise that they would seek to implement Islamic speech codes—and even to impose them on non-Muslims. Yet it is also true that, as part of their oaths to "support and defend the Constitution", our senior national security leaders have a duty to recognize such open assaults on our First Amendment and respond accordingly. As such, these events are strategic.

The Afghan Days of Rage were intended to have consequences beyond Afghanistan. The April 2011 Days of Rage were intended to intimidate senior national security leaders into associating success in COIN with supporting Islamic legal proscriptions on speech. This was accomplished by getting those leaders to publicly challenge an American citizen's First Amendment rights *inside* the United States. In other words, the Days of Rage in Afghanistan were a part of a sustained attack on the First Amendment in the United States.

What our senior leaders seemed not to grasp is that by buying into the Day of Rage narrative that associates an American's exercise of his First Amendment right inside America with planned Days of Rage calculated to put our troops at risk in Afghanistan, they implicitly accepted the proposition that our troops in Afghanistan are in some sense being held hostage to this campaign by virtue of accepting that proposition.[431]

Recall the discussion on truces in Part 2, with the caveat that the Muslim world also characterizes U.S. forces as a non-Muslim force in Muslim lands. To review, Islamic law does not recognize treaties, but rather truces[432] that can be applied only on a short-term basis.[433] Truces are disfavored in Islamic law because they call for the nonperformance of jihad,[434] so they may be made only because of Muslim weakness or because the other side may convert.[435]

According to this reading of shariah, official friendship with Afghanistan should be understood in the context of a truce that Afghanistan participates in due to its being in a state of weakness. In a legal sense, this remains true even if our partners protested against such an explanation, as they are still formally beholden to this Islamic construct according to the constitution we produced. Truces cannot be undertaken to maintain the status quo but rather to build capability to transition to the offensive: "So do not be fainthearted and call for peace, when it is you who are the uppermost" (Koran 47:35).[436]

Islamic law professor and Pakistani jurist Imran Ahsan Khan Nyazee confirmed this view when he wrote, "the aggressive propagation of Islam and the activity of *jihad* can be suspended with or without necessity in the opinion of some jurists, *but it is only a transitory phase.*"[437] While the Muslim community "may be considered to be passing through a period of truce" given its "present state of weakness," Islamic law provides for the nullification of truces "if tomorrow it were to gain its strength."[438] As noted, there are indicators that the Islamic world understands itself to be undergoing such a transition. It is consistent with:

- Escalating "Green on Blue" murders;

- More openly hostile posture of the Taliban;

- Muslim Brotherhood and al-Qaeda openly seeking control of Arab states with U.S. support;

- Escalating violence of OIC-inspired Days of Rage in which Karzai participates;

- COIN and ROE that put U.S. forces in a submissive posture;

- The rise of ISIS and its declaration of the Caliphate; and

- High profile executions of those that slander Islam, for example, *Charlie Hebdo* and Copenhagen.

If Afghanistan were to follow the template, it should seek out its Islamic form and evolve its relationship with the U.S. along those lines. Typologically speaking, one would expect ISAF to transition from an occupation force to hostages (in some sense), to submitted non-Muslims in a Muslim State, ultimately leaving Afghanistan altogether, possibly as part of a brokered negotiation. This would be mirrored, in turn, by Afghanistan's transition from a weakened occupied state to a liberated and then self-confident Islamic one.

There was a run-up to the March 2011 Qur'an burning event that warrants attention. The pastor of a small nondenominational Christian church in Gainesville, Florida, first came to the public's attention in 2010 when he announced plans for a "Burn a Qur'an Day." The 2010 Qur'an burning day was called off, but not in time to avert a Day of Rage in Afghanistan and Pakistan, complete with scenes of American flag burning, English-language placards, and threats of jihad.

President Obama issued a statement condemning Qur'an burning, terming it a "destructive act," and warned that such an event could put American troops at risk and fan anger against the United States and Americans in the Middle East. He added that Qur'an burning would be a "recruitment bonanza for al-Qaeda."[439] As *Al Jazeera* quoted President Obama:

> I just want [Pastor Jones] to understand that this stunt that he is talking about pulling could greatly endanger our young men and women in uniform who are in Iraq, who are in Afghanistan.[440]

The president also indicated his willingness to prosecute the pastor, expressing annoyance at the lack of legal options available to the U.S. government. As Reuters reported:

> The U.S. leader said the situation was frustrating but there was little that could be done according to the law to confront the minister, other than citing him under local measures against public burning. "My understanding is that he can be cited for public burning," Obama said. **"But that's the extent of the laws that we have available to us."**[441]

As President Obama ran up against the First Amendment, political leaders in the Muslim world, including Pakistani President Asif Ali Zardari, called on U.S. authorities to suspend the pastor's activities. They warned of uncontrollable violent reactions by Muslims. Christians in Iraq were also made fearful of violent reprisals against them and their churches.[442]

British Prime Minister David Cameron, in true OIC-speak, said, "We would strongly oppose any attempt to offend any member of any religious or ethnic group," while Rowan Williams, Archbishop of Canterbury, added that "the threat to desecrate scriptures is deeply deplorable and to be strongly condemned by all people."[443] Then-NATO Afghanistan commander Gen. Petraeus weighed in with concerns about danger to the NATO mission:

> "Images of the burning of a Quran would undoubtedly be used by extremists in Afghanistan—and around the world—to inflame public opinion and incite violence," Petraeus wrote in an e-mail to reporters. … [He] warned that images of Americans burning a Quran would inflame anti-Americanism much like when photos surfaced in 2004 of U.S. service members abusing detainees at Abu Ghraib.

> "Such images could, in fact, be used as were the photos from [Abu Ghraib]. And this would, again, put our troopers and civilians in jeopardy and undermine our efforts to accomplish the critical mission here in Afghanistan," he said.[444]

Petraeus's argument that free expression in America put our troops at risk is deeply troubling. Subordinating the U.S. mission to what will not "inflame" had the effect of subordinating our interests to the agenda expressed by al-Qaeda—the same agenda we went to Afghanistan to defeat.

Rather than being on guard against the implications underlying the Days of Rage, Petraeus legitimized them, stating that such murderous outbursts reflect "understandable passions."[445] America entered the War on Terror because people who had "understandable passions" also believed they had a right to kill Americans because of them. In fact, these "understandable passions" constitute an actual threat to the Constitution and people of the United States. It seems that President Karzai and the OIC correctly calculated that our national security leaders would be so caught up in the moment and in the imperatives of a COIN strategy that recognizes the Afghan people's feelings as the center of gravity that they would lose sight of the equities and freedoms they are there to defend. Yet the ISAF response did succeed at building up the legitimacy of the Islamic Republic in the eyes of the Afghan people.

Though the pastor's Qur'an-burning event did not take place in 2010, at least five people were killed in Afghanistan during that Day of Rage.[446]

The following year, on March 20, 2011, the Florida pastor, together with a small congregation, burned a Qur'an on a grill. This time, thousands of enraged

Afghan Muslims poured into the streets of the northern Afghan city of Mazar-i-Sharif after inflammatory sermons at Friday prayers. They quickly overran the UN compound there, burned down part of it, and murdered at least a dozen people, including seven UN workers.[447]

The violence surprised U.S. forces. Who organized and coordinated these riots? How did a non-English-speaking, nominally literate population in the backwaters of Mazar-i-Sharif, Afghanistan, initiate such a coordinated and targeted campaign based on the actions of an American citizen *inside* the United States that went relatively unreported even in America? The rioters, it turned out, were helped by the Afghan government, which is officially beholden to the Cairo Declaration and the OIC's efforts to curtail free expression that violates Islamic speech laws.

In short order, the head of the Afghan Ulema Council called on American authorities to arrest the pastor. As with all Days of Rage, this undertaking was a stage-managed campaign that showed obvious signs of coordination with the OIC.[448] Karzai also made it clear that the campaign was broadly coordinated inside Afghanistan with, among others, the Taliban.[449] As the *Wall Street Journal* reported at the time:

> Most Afghans learned about the Quran burning in Florida only when Mr. Karzai on March 24 condemned the act as "**a crime against the religion and the entire Muslim nation**," called on the U.S. and the U.N. to bring the perpetrators to justice and demanded "**a satisfactory response to the resentment and anger of over 1.5 billion Muslims around the world**."[450]

An Islamic leader used enabling language to incite and violence ensued. Note the OIC talking points relating to "hurt feelings" and the "1.5 billion Muslims." One would be hard-pressed to find any national or local reporting on the Qur'an burning in the U.S. before Karzai raised these points. When General Petraeus said that "every security force leader's worst nightmare is being confronted by essentially a mob, if you will, especially one that can be influenced by individuals that want to incite violence, who want to try to hijack passions," it's not clear that he understood that he was not talking about the Taliban or al-Qaeda but rather President Karzai and the OIC. The Days of Rage were successful in establishing a nexus between the safety of our soldiers in Afghanistan and placing curbs on the free-speech rights of American citizens inside the United States. An Islamic law student made the association perfectly clear: "We cannot see the difference between that man in Florida and the American soldiers here."[451]

Starting with the Cartoon Crisis in 2006, the calculated manufacture of outrage has been among the principal tactics the OIC used to implement its Ten-Year

Programme. As an OIC Member State, Afghanistan's willingness to resort to Day of Rage tactics needs to be understood in that context. When directed against U.S. personnel, Afghan Days of Rage are hostile acts by state actors seeking to undermine our constitutional principles by getting our leaders to do it for them—"by [our] hands," as the Brotherhood would say. Having taken an oath to support and defend the Constitution, our national security leaders should have recognized the obvious assault on free speech they are under some obligation to recognize, then take appropriate measures to defend against, then counter and finally defeat them. They didn't see it coming and still don't.[452]

Opinion columnist Roger Cohen wrote in the *New York Times* that the Florida pastor "interprets his faith ... as a mission to incite hatred toward Islam."[453] Members of Congress weighed in on CBS's Face the Nation, where Senator Lindsey Graham expressed the desire to hold people accountable. He wasn't referring to the violent Afghan Muslims who had just killed innocent people at the UN compound in Mazar-i-Sharif, but rather to the pastor. He explained, "Free speech is a great idea, but we are in a war."[454] The OIC narrative grabs hold.

The Day of Rage achieved its objective: to shock American officials into challenging the free exercise of an American citizen's enumerated rights inside the United States in furtherance of implementing Islamic legal doctrines of slander. Its orchestrators intimidated and stampeded our national leaders—from Obama to Petraeus to Graham—into associating COIN's success in Afghanistan with the support of Islamic legal proscriptions on protected speech here. What did the OIC get from this Day of Rage? Panic induced performance. The stage was set in Afghanistan for *Hebdo* and Copenhagen.

Yet again, by associating an American's exercise of his constitutional rights with our troops' endangerment in Afghanistan, our leaders implicitly accepted the proposition that our armed forces are, in some sense, hostages.[455] While this hostage mentality complies with Islamic norms requiring submission from non-Muslims, it does not comply with historic U.S. warfighting precedents to engage enemies for the purpose of defeating them. This Day of Rage process will repeat itself as many times as necessary to achieve its objective—and it will come to America. It begs the question: If the legal exercise of free speech by a single American in America is enough to endanger servicemen on the other side of the world—while also suppressing free expression—why are we there, and what are we fighting for?

There are answers to Petraeus's argument that free expression in America puts our troops at risk:

- The armed forces of the United States are constituted for the sole purpose of supporting and defending the Constitution of the United States. The First Amendment is a part of the Constitution.

- Our forces are in Afghanistan precisely because shariah-based rationales are used to kill Americans.

- Subordinating the U.S. mission to what will not "inflame" (our Afghan allies who are, after all, the "center of gravity" in the COIN) has the effect of subordinating our own interests to the Islamic agenda expressed by al-Qaeda.

Our leaders have lost their sense of the mission, and Americans know it. It was not the Taliban or gangs of disconnected Afghan rioters who made demands on their Day of Rage. It was our Coalition Partner:

> Following Sunday's meeting with Gen. Petraeus and the ambassadors, Mr. Karzai requested in a new statement that "the U.S. government, Senate and Congress clearly condemn [Rev. Jones'] dire action and avoid such incidents in the future." **Mr. Karzai issued this demand** even though President Barack Obama has already described the Quran burning as "an act of extreme intolerance and bigotry."[456]

Since Afghanistan is an OIC Member State, its Days of Rage when directed against the United States must be viewed as hostile acts by a state actor. So what is one to think when a senior U.S. military commander apologizes to the very people who deliberately manufactured rage in order to incite the attack and killing of American service members?[457]

Submission and Sensitivity Training

The OIC and its support network have become adept at generating Days of Rage. As our senior national security leaders and decision-makers remain unaware of what drives these events, they fall prey to an action-reaction cycle that keeps America blindfolded while repeatedly falling into the same trap. What would we say of a battlefield commander who walks into the same battlefield ambush over and over again where the ambush itself says, "ambush ahead"? Sometimes, when chronicling these events, I close my eyes and all I can see is Wile E. Coyote.

In February 2012, reports began circulating that members of the U.S. armed forces at Bagram Airbase in Afghanistan assigned to the Parwan Detention Facility had disposed of what they considered "extremist literature" left by Taliban and other detained jihadists. Among the materials incinerated were copies of Qur'ans defiled by the detainees. Soon, thousands of Afghans surrounded the base, chanting anti-American slogans and throwing stones.[458] In the resulting Day of Rage, in true Green-on-Blue fashion, six U.S. servicemen were killed, including two who were murdered by an Afghan soldier inside the Afghan Interior Ministry building. An unnamed officer at the base told Reuters:

> "[The materials] were taken out of the library for good rea-

son but they were being disposed of in a bad way," the official said. "There was a breakdown in judgment in this matter but **there was no breakdown in our respect for Islam**," the official added.[459]

First, here are a few relevant facts concerning the Qur'an burning at the Parwan Detention Facility that are undisputed and yet underreported: The Qur'ans in question had been written in by Parwan detainees, and there was substantive concern that they had been used to send messages.[460] By Islamic standards, writing in a Qur'an is generally impermissible[461] and makes it subject to destruction. The principal manner of destruction of Qur'ans is burning, which has a basis in Islamic law that reaches back to Uthman, the Third Rightly Guided Caliph (644–656 AD).[462] Additionally, it was understood by all parties that there was no malice and no intent to defile on the part of the U.S. service members involved.[463]

In a response to the incident that revealed a level of state-actor coordination, Afghan President Karzai acknowledged that the Qur'an burning was not deliberate, but he nevertheless demanded that the U.S. military personnel involved be punished. In a "detailed session attended by jihadi leaders," he called for restitution in the name of the Islamic world's "pure sentiments":

> Today … we had a detailed session **attended by jihadi leaders, prominent scholars**, speakers of both houses—the lower house and the senate—the esteemed chief justice, vice presidents and other dignitaries and our government. We discussed the matter of the burning of the Holy Koran. **Representing the Afghan nation and their pure sentiments, in fact the Islamic world, once again we call on the US government to bring the perpetrators of the act to justice and put them on trial and punish them.**[464]

The "jihadi leaders" referred to are, of course, the Taliban. Further exposing the coordinated nature of the activity, OIC General Secretary Ekmeleddin Ihsanoglu echoed the Afghan president's demand by emphasizing the Islamic concept of incitement that the OIC seeks to institutionalize through its Day of Rage activities:

> The Secretary General of the Organization of Islamic Cooperation (OIC) today in a statement deplored the burning of copies of the Holy Qur'an at the US base in Bagram, Afghanistan. He said that the incident was **a deplorable act of incitement** and called on the concerned authorities to **take swift and appropriate disciplinary action against those responsible**. The OIC Secretary General said that the act was contrary to the the common efforts of the OIC and

that of the international community including the United States Government, to **combat intolerance, and incitement to hatred** based on religion and belief.[465]

General John Allen quickly took to video:

> I offer my sincere apologies for any offense this may have caused. My apologies to President of the Islamic Republic of Afghanistan and, most importantly, my apologies to the noble people of Afghanistan.[466]

While the offense of burning Qur'ans, for which both Karzai and Ihsanoglu demanded punishment, is not a crime in the United States, in certain circumstances, it can be an offense under Islamic law. As already suggested, COIN directives have the effect of merging the two. For example, the only reference in the September 2010 ISAF COIN Advisory to local Afghan customs and culture was a statement that 99 percent of the country's population was Muslim. From there, the rest of the document concerned itself with instruction on Islam that was, in fact, instruction on shariah:

> Because Muslims believe that the Qur'an records the literal word of God, they treat all copies of the book with extreme veneration. Every complete copy, or even a partial passage, is considered holy. It is considered culturally insensitive for any non-Muslim to touch a copy of the Qur'an.[467]

While it is true that Islamic law states that a Qur'an cannot be sold to non-Muslims, this rule is very selectively enforced.[468] One can easily buy Qur'ans freely at conferences and events sponsored by large Islamic groups in America, at Islamic Society- and Islamic Center-affiliated bookstores, and through Muslim online book vendors. In fact, the Muslim Brotherhood-associated Council on American Islamic Relations (CAIR) routinely gives away copies in translation as a public service. The ISAF COIN Advisory went on to say:

> Additionally, **verbal disrespect for Islam** and/or the Qur'an is considered as inappropriate as physical desecration of the Qur'an. **Insulting the Qur'an is an act of blasphemy.**[469]

The ISAF takes no backseat to *Reliance of the Traveller* or Kamali (author of *Freedom and Expression in Islam*) in its statement and enforcement of Islamic slander law. The ISAF Advisory was promulgating actual Islamic law in the guise of Afghan customs. For example, in his treatise on Islamic speech laws titled *Freedom of Expression in Islam*, Islamic jurist and law professor Hashim Kamali noted that non-Muslims could be held to obey Islamic law on slander.[470] Kamali stated that "throwing the Holy Qur'an on a heap of rubbish" constitutes an act of blasphemy:

> The principal offense of blasphemy in Islam ... is the reviling of God and the Prophet Muhammad, and a contemptuous rejection of their injunctions. ... These include insults to God Most High and the Prophet, irreverent and contemptuous statements that outrage the religious sensibilities of believers, acts such as **throwing the Holy Qur'an on a heap of rubbish**, giving the lie to the fundamentals of law and religion, and so on. These have all been identified as words and acts that at one and the same time amount to **apostasy, disbelief, heresy, and blasphemy**.[471]

Historical military precedence, protocol, decorum, and etiquette suggest that because Islamic law is the law of the land in Afghanistan and we have forces there, a measure of respect is in order. But how far does one go before respect becomes submission to shariah that conflicts with our constitutional principles—not to mention the First Amendment rights of our American citizen soldiers? The COIN Advisory dictates that we go as far as Islamic law requires:

> Muslims believe **they have an inherent duty to stand up against injustices committed against Islam and the Qur'an**. Therefore, they take any perceived disrespect to Islam and/or the Qur'an extremely seriously.[472]

When stating that Muslims "have an inherent duty to stand up against injustices committed against Islam and the Qur'an," the COIN Advisory used Islamic legal form, including the word "duty." Duties exist in law. That duty often includes killing those who disrespect Islam. This is the same underlying theory that drives the Ten-Year Programme of Action, including supporting Days of Rage. In fact, this is the same duty that Al-Qaeda appealed to in its 1998 Fatwa declaring enmity against America and the West,[473] and ISAF legitimized it.

This harsh Islamic legal doctrine was disseminated through the U.S. military command with the recommendation that it be enforced. Though ISAF leadership may not understand that they are conditioning the U.S. military to conform to Islamic legal proscriptions that provide for the death penalty,[474] they are in fact doing so.

The recommendations outlined by the COIN Advisory have the force of law for U.S. personnel under ISAF control. They were recommended, published, and circulated with the intent of being enforced. This should have caused concern, as it necessarily reflects the enforcement of Islamic legal standards against American personnel who are, after all, American citizens. At this point in the Milestones process, *de facto* adherence through strict performance is sufficient. Looking at the first two ISAF recommendations, we can see Islamic law speaking directly to both points:

1　Do NOT handle Qur'ans or other Islamic religious items.

2　Never talk badly about the Qur'an or its contents.[475]

This is the direct imposition of shariah on U.S. forces by senior military leadership. The first point was just covered in the discussion of Kamali's statement on Qur'an burning, save that it should be made explicit that this is Islamic law and there are First Amendment considerations. The second recommendation is of greater concern, not just because there is Islamic law on point but also because ISAF leadership took the OIC's bait to accept that enjoyment of First Amendment rights by American citizens is linked to the safety and security (or lack thereof) of U.S. forces in Afghanistan. Having established the linkage that the enjoyment of the one is associated with harsh sanctions to the other, a hostage mentality becomes institutionalized.

Given General Petraeus's guidance to "view our actions through the eyes of the Afghans,"[476] we find that the population is generally in line with Islamic notions of governance and receptive to the obligatory requirement to fight jihad when non-Muslim forces are in Muslim lands—including U.S. forces in Afghanistan. It should come as no surprise that Afghans are receptive to Islamic blasphemy laws. The fact that the COIN Advisory on Afghan culture (witlessly) focused on shariah indicates that, at some level, even national security leaders sense they are wrong when insisting that the War on Terror has nothing to do with Islam.

Despite no evidence of malice or intent to show disrespect—and despite the fact that no U.S. law was broken—the service members associated with the burning of Qur'ans at Bagram Airbase were punished. No crime was committed, and all agreed, including Karzai, that the requisite *mens rea* did not exist. And yet, at the insistence of a foreign power, American service members were disciplined under the Uniform Code of Military Justice for violating Islamic law.[477] This is shameful.

> They were punished because the leader of an Islamic State demanded punishment, and our leaders, sworn to support and defend the Constitution, complied.[478] It was a strategic information victory in a battle that our side did not even know they we were engaged in. A terrible precedent was set for what should have been an impermissible event: Islamic law was imposed on American personnel, they were punished for violating it, and the leadership gave groveling apologies when it happened. Perhaps this is one of the "core values" that Captain Kirby thinks "we're out there executing".[479]

In the interest of respecting the customs of Afghanistan, our leaders felt it necessary to impose Islamic law on their military personnel, almost all of whom are American citizens and almost none of whom is Muslim. The enmeshing of American policy with that of a foreign government structured on Islamic law is inconsistent with our constitutional values, as well as with the rights and physical security of our deployed soldiers.

At what point does mandating certain practices with regard to Islam constitute an impermissible assault on the sovereign constitutional rights of American personnel to enjoy the free exercise of their beliefs—including the affirmative right not to believe or revere? Compelling conformance to religious beliefs that are not one's own reflects contempt for constitutional principles and a disregard for the rights of Americans. Where does ISAF derive the authority to compel activity abroad—authority that the Constitution specifically denies Congress at home?

Nothing has changed. Now retired, General Allen serves as the Special Presidential Envoy for the Anti-ISIS Coalition. In that capacity in October 2014, he made a few observations:

> "As we seek to expose Da'esh's true nature," Allen told the gathering on Monday, "we must also tell a positive story, one that highlights our respect—our profound respect for Islam's proud traditions, its rich history, and celebration of scholarship and family and community."

"We must work with clerics and scholars and teachers and parents to tell the story of how we celebrate Islam, even as we show that Da'esh perverts it."[480]

Note the outsourcing. We should understand Allen's remarks in the context of the submission narrative that evolved out of Afghanistan while he was there. He is committed to telling "a positive story highlighting *our* profound respect for Islam" and related narratives that outside third parties are to craft for him to communicate to Americans. In the context of Islam, "clerics and scholars" are imams. Will these "clerics and scholars" at least be Americans who are unaffiliated with the Muslim Brotherhood? When a U.S. official expresses his reliance on imams to explain "our" profound respect for Islam, one senses that spreading the dawah message is the price that our Arab anti-ISIS partners charge for the privilege of assisting them in their effort.

Where is the oversight? Indeed, where are the chaplains? Currently, some of our chaplains are receiving bronze stars for training proper Islamic form to our troops. A non-Muslim chaplain received a Bronze Star for issuing this warning during emergency sensitivity training on the proper handling and disposal of Islamic materials: "All that good work, you realize how quickly that work can be undermined."[481] Such training misses the point: the intent of those inciting the Day of Rage was to create a pretext for outrage. In this context, the chaplain's response represents the first fruits of the success of those Days of Rage. Yet even the chaplain knew that, at worst, the Qur'an burnings at Bagram were an accident.[482] Accidents such as this do not upset stable relations unless, of course, someone wants to keep a partner off-balance and reactive. But then are they really partners?

The role of the chaplains is troubling. Outside the purview of this analysis, the Muslim Brotherhood has an entire line of operation specifically directed at neutralizing other religious communities through penetration of the Interfaith Movement. [**Note**: *A brief discussion on this topic is offered in Appendix I, Supporting Lines of Operation – A Look at Interfaith Exploitation.*]

When blasphemy—such as the burning of Qur'ans in early 2012—occurs in Afghanistan, Islamic law is used to encourage violent Days of Rage. According to *Reliance of the Traveller*, relationships between non-Muslims and Muslims are supposed to break down when "something impermissible [is said] about Allah, the Prophet, or Islam."[483] Hence, the COIN Advisory was right, according to Islamic law, to recommend that U.S. personnel not say anything bad about the Qur'an, if the ISAF's only concern is to make its relationships run smoothly by satisfying the feelings of Afghans, a goal that ISAF designated as the mission's center of gravity.

It is through a typological review that one begins to see a correlation between ISAF's position with regard to the Days of Rage and the Islamic law it was manipulated into imposing through top-down advisories. In descending order, two things are true: U.S. forces in Afghanistan are non-Muslim forces in Muslim lands, and most U.S. personnel are not Muslim. While we've seen it before, there is specific Islamic law relating to non-Muslims that falls under the category of "Non-Muslim Subjects of the Islamic State." A look at the relevant law brings this issue to focus:

> o11.1 A formal agreement of protection is made with citizens who are (1) Jews, (2) Christians, (5) and those who adhere to the religion of Abraham or one of the other prophets (upon whom be blessing and peace).

> o11.3 Such an agreement is only valid when the subject people: (a) follow the rules of Islam …

> o11.10 The agreement is also violated with respect to the offender alone if the state has stipulated that any of the following things break it, and one of the subjects does so anyway … (5) or mentions something impermissible about Allah, the Prophet (Allah bless him and give him peace), or Islam.[484]

Since this is *bona fide* Islamic law, it necessarily follows that both the OIC and the Government of Afghanistan would be favourably (and constitutionally) disposed to it. This means they would also be favourably disposed to any proscribed consequences associated with such a violation. The law for non-Muslims in Muslim lands continues:

> o11.11. When a subject's agreement with the state has been violated, the caliph chooses between the four alternatives mentioned above in connection with prisoners of war (see o9.14).[485]

As o11.11 deals with "subjects" and state action (by the caliph), recall that Karzai's actions were the result of a "detailed session **attended by jihadi leaders, prominent scholars,** speakers of both houses—the lower house and the senate—the esteemed chief justice, vice presidents and other dignitaries and our government."[486] As stated, the alternative to obedient submission to the Islamic state is reversion to the status of prisoners of war—a form of hostage. Paragraph o9.14 is concerned with the "Rules of War" in the section of *Reliance of the Traveller* on the law of jihad:

> o9.14 When an adult male is taken captive, the caliph considers the interests of Islam and the Muslims and decides between the prisoner's death, slavery, release without paying anything, or ransoming himself in exchange for money or for a Muslim captive held by the enemy.[487]

When §o9.14 is compared to Kamali's treatment of the same principle by reference to a classical authority, one sees that *Reliance*'s treatment follows classical form: specifically, that under Islamic law, non-Muslim subjects of the Islamic state hold the status of prisoners of war in a state of abeyance.[488] As an Islamic state governed by Islamic law, Afghanistan should be expected to seek to structure its relationships with non-Muslims inside Afghanistan so they comport with those Islamic requirements—in form when possible, in fact when able.

As it relates to U.S. and Coalition forces, if the Afghan government is committed to shariah, and its constitution states that it is, it is not unreasonable to project that its goal should seek to allow Afghanistan to evolve to the preferred Islamic form by manipulating its relationships to that end. Conversely, it is not reasonable for us to think otherwise. With COIN Guidance that made the Afghan people's "hearts and minds" the criteria by which ISAF success is to be measured (alongside Rules of Engagement subordinated to Karzai's Twelve Rules), the Afghan government has the ability to manipulate American leadership with seeming impunity because that leadership remains steadfastly blind to the driving influence of shariah.

A compelling argument can be made that the COIN strategy in Afghanistan has been an ever-growing disaster. From the start, policy was made in the absence of knowable information that would have materially changed our posture. The same goes for the larger War on Terror; the difference between knowing Islamic law and its nexus to the threat doctrine and not knowing it is the difference between winning and losing the war.

With COIN and its attendant ROE, our leaders have been manipulated into compelling the compliance of our forces to Islamic law and holding the constitutional rights of Americans hostage to what the average Afghan is willing to riot over. This is not just submission. It is total defeat.

When viewed from the perspective of the information our national security leaders have embargoed from analysis, the COIN strategy looks like a defeat mechanism imposed on our leadership by Afghanistan, not the other way around. Focused on meeting the demands of the Afghan people—in furtherance of ever-elusive success in the counterinsurgency strategy—ISAF leaders impose Islamic law on service members in Afghanistan and call on American citizens *inside* the United States to suspend the free exercise of their First Amendment rights. Questionable even without reference to Islamic law, the unequal status and danger that COIN and our ROE have placed our troops is truly offensive.

Activities in Afghanistan help establish the action-reaction cycle for future events. Look at the servile apologies, not just in Afghanistan, and not just among our military leaders. The U.S. Embassy in Cairo closed early on September 11, 2012, allowing street riots to overrun our diplomatic station. While the State Department was working with the OIC to criminalize protected speech in America[489] via Resolution 16/18, the Cairo Embassy issued the following statement:

> The Embassy of the United States in Cairo condemns the continuing efforts by misguided individuals to hurt the religious feelings of Muslims - as we condemn efforts to offend believers of all religions. Today, the 11th anniversary of the September 11, 2001 terrorist attacks on the United States; Americans are honoring our patriots and those who serve our nation as the fitting response to the enemies of democracy. Respect for religious beliefs is a cornerstone of American democracy. We firmly reject the actions by those who abuse the universal right of free speech to hurt the religious beliefs of others.[490]

The Embassy released this statement ahead of events. It contained the requisite servile apology evidencing, among other things, that the State Department had *de facto* moved from a First Amendment standard to the shariah standard demanded by the OIC. Understood in light of the Islamic law it refuses to see, COIN served to reverse the momentum of the Afghan war, set the precedent for future events, and has been counterproductive.

The assumption underlying our joint efforts with the Government of Afghanistan is that we share a common understanding of the nature of the problem. *But we don't.* While U.S. forces are supposed to be engaged in Afghanistan to further the constitutional requirement to "support and defend" the United States, the government of Afghanistan is controlled by the requirement to act according to the shariah that we put in their constitution. That law views American forces as inherently hostile and demands their removal by any means. This is true by operation of Afghan law by virtue of the constitution we imposed.

A plain reading of Islamic law would strongly suggest that President Karzai is bound by his country's own constitution to take a hostile view of ISAF, notwithstanding personal feelings. It is not at all clear, in other words, that the underlying assumption of COIN—that Karzai and his government share the same vision—is even reasonable.

U.S. forces must stand-by as their leaders force them into degrading sensitivity training designed to enforce conformance to shariah standards and blame their fallen brethren for their own murders. Yet they also hear COMISAF COIN Guidance tell them not to be "a pawn in someone else's game. Spend time, listen, consult, and drink lots of tea."[491] "Drink lots of tea" is a reference to Greg Mortenson's *Three Cups of Tea*,[492] a book that turned out to be a fabrication.[493] As Mortenson's book was in vogue among senior reading circles at Central Command, its reference in the Guidance is an indicator that much of the COIN has been driven by little more than "feel good about yourself" pop narratives. Talk about being a pawn in someone else's game.

An End-Game Scenario

Regarding possible end-game scenarios for the War on Terror, our national security leaders are so strategically unaware that one can plausibly foresee a scenario that combines the Afghan "Perfect Day" with an American or Western Day of Rage in line with al-Qaeda's push for large-scale acts of individual jihad[494] that rely on car bombings[495] or "building a bomb in your mother's kitchen."[496] Such activities would be designed to escalate to destabilizing levels of violence, resulting in growing calls for the removal of U.S. forces from Afghanistan and the larger Middle East at a time when the American public would be dazed by multiple domestic attacks and outraged because of them. As with the Days of Rage associated with the YouTube film, the activity would be choreographed from beginning to end.

Because the Rage would be based on contrived insults to Islam, those responsible for mismanaging the war will be able to blame domestic terrorism and their retreat from the Middle East on so-called "Islamophobic" elements within the United States. The Islamic world, from al-Qaeda to the Muslim Brotherhood to the OIC, would encourage such a perception because it would facilitate an information campaign to get our leaders to seek passage of legislation to further stifle such speech in the future, enabling enforcement of the Ten-Year Programme of Action through UN Resolution 16/18. As this is the tenth year of the OIC's Ten-Year Programme of Action, there is reason to suspect that related activities will culminate this year. As the *Charlie Hebdo* and Copenhagen attacks suggest, there is more to this than idle speculation. In the Fall 2011 edition of *Inspire*, al-Qaeda signaled its support for such a plan of attack:

> "We will fight for him, we will instigate, we will bomb and we will assassinate, and may our mothers be bereaved of us if we do not rise in his defense."

> Shaykh Anwar Al-Awlaki

> In describing the duty of killing those who insult our Prophet Muhammad[497]

Is ISIS building up to such an event? ISIS is, after all, al-Qaeda in Iraq. Such a scenario is possible, because the scapegoat for the leaders will be the same group that the OIC and Brotherhood are already suppressing. What do the Afghans, the OIC, the Brotherhood, the Islamic Movement, and al-Qaeda see when they look at their American nemesis? An enemy who thinks drinking tea is a strategy. It starts with not recognizing fi sabilillah when it stares you in face.

* * *

There are not enough, if you like, places for those people who want to die as shahid in Iraq, in Afghanistan. There're queues. People, Muslims, are literally queuing up to be part of a struggle and the mujahideen say: "Look, we don't need you, we have too many people already." And this is the big problem for the American-led alliance that there are people being radicalized in their backyard; you don't have to go outside of your country. They can be under the radar, they don't need passports, all they need is access to the Internet. You can sit in Paris and you can download material *and you can make a bomb in your mother's kitchen.*

> Imam Anjem Choudary, London
> Allah Islam, Part 3[498]

VIII

Our Ignorance

There is now the ancient saying corruptio optima pessima, "the best, corrupted, become the worst." Those who have some notion about the worst must also, according to this saying, have a notion about what is best.

Josef Pieper
"Abuse of Language, Abuse of Power"[1]

War is an ugly thing, but not the ugliest of things. The decayed and degraded state of moral and patriotic feeling which thinks that nothing is worth war is much worse. The person who has nothing for which he is willing to fight, nothing which is more important than his own personal safety, is a miserable creature and has no chance of being free unless made and kept so by the exertions of better men than himself.

John Stuart Mill, 1868

Now having an overview of the problem as it stands, it's natural to ask how we got here. Throughout this book, aspects of Islamic law and jihadi doctrine were introduced to explain the nexus between the two and the threat it presents. For those looking deeper into the issue—especially those who reach a level of confidence that these doctrines are both real and ubiquitous—a second, more disturbing question emerges: How was our capacity to recognize such obvious threats completely disabled? This presupposes three realizations: (1) there is something unnatural about this knowledge deficit; (2) this deficit can only partially be explained by the merits of a hostile information campaign; and (3) in order for such a knowledge deficit to be the intended outcome of such a campaign, the threat must have correctly assessed that the reasoning and credulity of our national security and law enforcement communities had been reduced to the assessed pre-condition for such an information campaign to begin.

'To Our Great Detriment'

On December 1, 2005, more than four years after 9/11, General Peter Pace, Chairman of the Joint Chiefs of Staff, gave a speech at America's pre-eminent war college, the National Defense University in Washington, D.C.

> I say you need to get out and read what our enemies have said. Remember Hitler. Remember he wrote *Mein Kampf.* He said in writing exactly what his plan was, and we collectively ignored that to our great detriment. Now, our enemies have said publicly on film, on the Internet their goal is to destroy our way of life. No equivocation on their part. [2]

In referring to *Mein Kampf,* General Pace illustrated what we lose by not taking our enemies seriously. If we had been tasked to read Hitler's book prior to his appointment as Chancellor in 1933, we might have dismissed it as the ravings of a madman. "Why should we read this book? This man will never rise to power. And even if he did, he would never do any of this." But Hitler did take power, and we decided to read his book. Even then, however, we were too caught up in assessing his capabilities to honestly assess the doctrine. "We don't need to study this very deeply. Hitler will never be able to raise an army proficient enough to execute his plans—and certainly, Germans won't allow the Nazis to kill all the Jews." Almost immediately, Hitler started building a capable army and persecuting non-Aryan populations, including Jews. Only after full-scale war, mass murder, and genocide did we undertake a threat-based analysis of what Hitler would do based on his doctrine. But by then it was too late; we were already in a World War.

In urging the national security establishment to "get out and read what our enemies have said," General Pace was telling his audience that *the United States of America is off its doctrine on warfighting.* He told the whole world that we are, in a doctrinal sense, fighting blind.

Soon after General Pace's speech, I spoke to peers on the Joint Staff J-2, the Defense Intelligence Agency element of the Joint Chiefs of Staff. I asked if they'd heard what the Chairman said. It couldn't be more relevant to our mission in the Intelligence Directorate that the Chairman had assessed what he saw as the failure of the entire Intelligence Community in its essential mission. That mission, of course, is to provide indicators and warning of possible threat activity, along with providing a doctrine-based functional understanding of the enemy capable of supporting the production of the enemy's most likely and most dangerous courses of action.

My colleagues' responses were dismissive, and most failed to see how his remarks applied to them. But if it was not directed at the Chairman's own Intelligence Directorate, then whom?

More than a decade into the War on Terror, the nation's intelligence personnel have become disassociated from their essential purpose, bureaucratically churning away. They ask, "How do I get promoted to the next bureaucratic level without being fired for Islamophobia?" That question, properly understood, translates to: "How do I make it to retirement in the Intelligence Community without insulting non-U.S. entities?" The answer to the question is simple: Don't do intelligence.

Clearly, our national security leaders are blind to both our own laws and our own principles on threat development. When General Pace indicated that we have yet to understand the enemy's fighting doctrines, he was saying that the warfighting matrix is broken and, at some level, everyone knows it. To get back to a threat-focused understanding of the enemy, we must first realize that the War on Terror is, primarily, an information war. If we listen to our enemies, that is what they are telling us. Ayman al-Zawahiri himself said that 85 percent of this conflict is information warfare.

The enemy's doctrine tells him not to strike until he has assessed that we are already defeated in our own minds. When such a culminating point is reached, the civilization jihadists can then lightly tap anywhere along the house of cards on which is placed the threat awareness that drives our perceptions in the War on Terror. The entire edifice will come crashing down.

The Doctrinal Template

The deliberate decision-making process that the U.S. military uses to fight its wars is intended to begin with a doctrinal template analysis of the enemy. Until it was disabled in 2009, U.S. doctrine on threat analysis was based on an institutionalized preference for facts as the cornerstone of threat analysis. It was Sun Tzu: Know the enemy, know his doctrine, and know yourself. This doctrine was reflected in its simplest form in an older edition of *Army Field Manual 34-130, Intelligence Preparation of the Battlefield* (FM 34-130, IPB—hereafter the *IPB Manual*).[3] We could call it "classic IPB."

The *IPB Manual* dictated that all threat analysis begins with an evaluation of the enemy's stated threat doctrine based on his doctrine, given his order of battle.[1] This phase of threat analysis is designed to generate a doctrinal template of the enemy based on what he could or would do if able to fully execute his doctrine, **unconstrained** by the environment or by an opposing force.

---

1   **Order of Battle** – Intelligence pertaining to identification, strength, command structure, and disposition of personnel, units, and equipment of any military force. The OB factors form the framework for analyzing military forces and their capabilities, building threat models, and hence, developing COA models. [U.S. Army, Field Manual (FM) 34-130, *Intelligence Preparation of the Battlefield* (Washington, DC: Department of the Army, 08 July 1994), Glossary-8.]

> **Doctrinal template**—A model based on postulated threat doctrine. Doctrinal templates illustrate the disposition and activity of threat forces and assets (HVTs) conducting a particular operation **unconstrained** by the effects of the battlefield environment. They represent the application of threat doctrine under ideal conditions.[4]

At the doctrinal template phase, the enemy is—and only is—what his doctrine says he is. His doctrine accounts for his way of understanding the conflict he sees before him. The downstream product of the doctrinal template, after running through other phases, is the ability to formulate enemy courses of action against which friendly courses of action are to be planned. It is only after the doctrinal template is formed that one considers how the environment and friendly capabilities will constrain the way he achieves his ends.

No Blue in the Red. The language of military planning includes what are known as blue and red models. Blue models represent the strategies and doctrines employed by the United States and its allies; red models refer to the doctrines and strategies of the enemy. By orienting our models entirely on abstractions, we commit the fatal error of confusing our blue expectations with red realities.

A Bayesian model is a statistical tool predicated on the hypothesis that assumed behaviors can, in some way, serve as indicators of possible future behaviors in the absence of facts. Marketers often start with Bayesian models when they field new products, but they realize that the projected numbers are supposed to give way to real numbers once the product is released.

In the realm of national security, when you think blue, you are thinking about how we fight with the assets we bring to the battle—our assets, the blue assets—against a red enemy. Theoretical and behavioral models—anthropological, psycho-social, political, sociological, and economic—are always only projections of blue expectations, as they arise from Western theoretical constructs rather than from real information about the enemy. When enemy motivations are assessed based on blue models, no red is being considered—nothing about his doctrine, no analysis of his understanding of his environment, nothing concerning his equipment, material, or publications. There is no actual discussion of the enemy when threat analysis is based on blue soft-science constructs. When a doctrinal template of a threat is properly produced, however, **there is no blue in the red**.

Through the course of the War on Terror, national security decision-makers and analysts have demonstrated a preference for defining the enemy based strictly in terms of what our blue models allow him to be. It turns out that we always win the war-games when our blue models define the enemy. A major downside of the "peace dividend" at the end of the Cold War was the peacetime military's obsession with undertaking "capabilities-based" training, given there were no peer competitors to the U.S.—or at least that was the assessment. With no "real" enemies, no real threats were used in 1990's war-fighting exercises. The intelligence mission was relegated to constructing "notional" enemies based on blue capabilities—i.e., enemies that were not real, had no ideology, and were based on "capabilities" that blue planners wanted to exercise based on blue requirements.

Model-based war fighting can sustain itself almost indefinitely on the assumption that it serves as a reasonable proxy for fighting a real enemy. All it consists of, however, is mapping blue capabilities to blue expectations based on blue projections. And on and on—until, that is, a real enemy decides to assert himself. Our exclusive reliance on war-fighting processes based on blue modeling has rendered us incapable of knowing real enemies. In the postmodern narrative, there *are* no enemies. Today, Sun-Tzu has little value beyond being a good source for signature block quotes.

Doctrinal-template analysis is not supposed to answer the question, "What will the enemy do?" Rather, it answers the more immediate question of what the end state would be if the enemy's doctrine were allowed to manifest if left unconstrained by the effects of the environment. Imagine hearing this during World War II: "We read *Mein Kampf* and we oriented against it, but we thought that killing the Jews and sending them to concentration camps was a little far-fetched. So we ruled that out when assessing *Mein Kampf*." When we filter the enemy's threat doctrine through our expectations (i.e., through blue expectations), we are no longer engaged in threat analysis.

In the doctrinal-template phase of the threat analysis process, analysis of the enemy is supposed to be unconstrained. Indeed, our warfighting doctrine used the word "unconstrained" three times. The old *IPB Manual* did a very good job of enforcing analytical discipline in the threat analysis process. Unconstrained by what? *By blue thinking*. When constructing a doctrinal template:

> It must be unconstrained by blue methodologies or measuring criteria, as this would have us fight the enemy we want rather than the enemy that exists.
>
> —*In threat development phase, there is NO blue in the red.*

> When constructing the doctrinal template, the enemy is always who he identifies himself to be, and his doctrines are always assessed as true and valid.
>
> —*Only red touches red in this phase.*

> The truth or falsity, validity or invalidity, of a threat doctrine is an issue of fact that begins to come into play only **after** the doctrinal template is established—which begins with the development of the situation template where red's pure

> doctrine is mapped to actual (existing-in-fact) environmental factors.

> Only in the Enemy Course of Action phase does the truth or validity of doctrine manifest itself in actual or predicted enemy behavior.

Blue comes into play only after we have the red—after the intelligence analysts have generated enemy courses of action designed to answer two questions regarding the enemy's course of action: What is the enemy's most likely course of action? What is the enemy's most dangerous course of action?

At the Course of Action phase, blue begins to look at the red and purposefully develop blue courses of action tailored to defeat red COAs by establishing specific lines of operation to counter specifically identified red capabilities. It is in this phase that war-gaming occurs. Blue COA development is part of a deliberate decision-making process that answers every red line of operation with a current or future blue capability. Current or future blue capabilities are expressed in terms of the four elements of national power, called the DIME (Diplomatic, Information, Military, and Economic), or its national security sub-component, PMESII (Political, Military, Economic, Social, Information, and Infrastructure).

How does one apply the concept of a threat-based doctrine to a "thinking" war? To remove all possible ideological overtones, let's analyze an imaginary doctrine we'll call the "Green Cheese Doctrine." The Green Cheese violent extremist announces, "I have a doctrine: the Green Cheese Doctrine. If you join me, you must a) hate Americans, b) want to kill Americans, and c) actually follow through and kill Americans." Then he creates the Green Cheese Party, and people join it. They are of different races and ethnic groups; what unites them is their hatred for and desire to kill Americans.

This Green Cheese Doctrine satisfies all the requirements for being a threat doctrine. If for no other reason than this, national security planners should make the Green Cheese Doctrine the mandatory object of a doctrinal template analysis. At this point, there is no requirement to assess whether the doctrine is right or wrong, stupid or smart, sane or insane. All that matters is that there is a doctrine— the Green Cheese Doctrine—and people affiliate with it and kill us because of it. If these criteria are fulfilled, then all the necessary requirements have been met to make that doctrine the object of a threat analysis.

Someone may object, saying, "This is really about cheddar cheese rather than green cheese; the Green Cheese Party is misrepresenting cheese and taking it out of context." That may be true. But at the doctrinal analysis phase of the assessment, it is also irrelevant. The existence of the Green Cheese Doctrine requires that we perform a threat analysis, beginning with a doctrinal assessment and ending with enemy courses of action. (For military aficionados, enemy courses of action fall under the acronym E-COAs.)

When completed, the doctrinal template must always be assessed as being *true and complete* for all purposes, because, at this level, it is true for those who affiliate with the organization or ideology that is the object of the threat analysis. Failure to do this will compromise our ability to generate enemy courses of action. Wars have been lost because of this.

Only when the doctrinal template of the enemy is completed do we apply it to the actual environment to assess its validity. For example, during the Cold War, we examined the Soviet understanding of how they would array their forces on the battlefield: "They will have a battalion in one position. At exactly x kilometers back from the front line and x kilometers over, there will be a second echelon battalion. Exactly x kilometers back from there will be regimental artillery. And x kilometers behind that will be the reinforcements."

That would be the doctrinal footprint of a Soviet regiment if it fought on a flat surface with no woods, rivers, bridges, or towns. But in real-world conditions, we have to apply that doctrinal template to the specific situation, the real battle-field environment: "There are woods over there, a railroad here, a river over there, and a big hill over yonder. The Soviets can't put their artillery there. But here's an opening in the field; he could put it right there." We would apply the doctrinal template to the actual environment, placing the Soviet forces where they could operate. When the doctrinal template is applied to the environment, the resulting product is called the situation template.

So how could we apply this analytical tool for kinetic operations to the information battle-space in the War on Terror?

Radicals claim that they follow Islamic law, while moderates claim the radicals have hijacked it. Hence, we will use recognized Islamic law—that has currency in both the radical and moderate camps—as the ideological screen when constructing the situation template. The reasoning is simple: As both sides agree that the issue concerns the accurate orientation of shariah, a situation template that filters the enemy's threat doctrine through real Islamic law will either resonate or not resonate with that doctrine.

If the radicals' claims are true, their declarations will pass through the ideological screen, and the conclusion will be that it *is* true that they are fighting jihad fi sabilillah. If that is the case, it points to one set of possible enemy courses of action. If, on the other hand, the radicals claim they are fighting jihad in the cause of Allah but the moderates are right that they do not, then they have indeed misinterpreted shariah, and the ideological screen will filter out the radicals' claims. Of course, such a finding would call for an entirely different set of enemy courses of action. The resulting threat profile would reflect the truth that Secretary Stockton insists he "follows ... wherever it takes [him]."[5] But Stockton was only interested in behavioral indicators—all blue. Unless we orient on the enemy's stated doctrine by undertaking threat analysis, we cannot generate credible enemy courses of action. When this happens, our war-fighting narrative will be reduced to incoherence.

Doctrinal & Situation Templating an Ideology-based Threat Doctrine

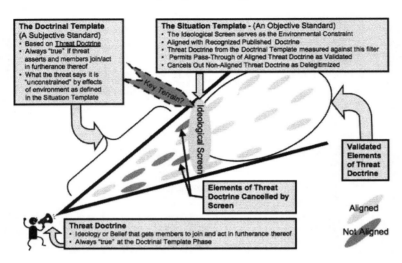

This slide from the author's original brief attempts to demonstrate that classical doctrinal template analysis used for threat identification supports threat identification analysis associated with Islamic-based terrorist threats.

In the War on Terror, it is incumbent on us to incorporate stated jihadi motivations—as the jihadis express them—into our threat doctrine. Unfortunately, when such an analysis is done, it doesn't support the preferred explanation of our senior civilian and military leaders. When they contemplate the actions of the enemy, they ascribe a completely different motivation to him—generally expressed in terms of "violent extremism," usually in furtherance of "underlying causes"—that is invariably based on behavioral models that services blue expectations.

As noted earlier, in order to maintain the "violent extremism" narrative, discourse must be reduced to a fourth-grade level of speaking. "We are fighting violent extremists." Why are they extreme? "Because they resort to violence to achieve their goals." Why are they violent? "Because their extremist views forced them to become violent."

Through this syllogism, any disagreement can be framed in terms of "violent extremism." When a second-grader has a tiff with her friend during recess, everything she does can be understood as "violent extremism." More seriously, anyone who believes in something enough to stand up for it can qualify as a "violent extremist"—including, most especially, those serving in our armed forces and our returning veterans.

In actual usage, it turns out that violent extremism can mean anything you want it to mean, as long as it has nothing to do with jihad. The "violent extremist" narrative is important to analysts in the War on Terror because it fills the need to create value-neutral models. It allows them to pretend they are talking about something when, in fact, they are talking about nothing. Because the Countering Violent Extremism (CVE) narrative reduces analysis to incoherence, it is a nihilist construct.

At a conference in the UK, I asked a senior law enforcement official why he used the term "violent extremism." His reply involved a convoluted discussion using language more appropriate to elementary school children. Someone else followed up by asking him what he called the IRA when it bombs people.

"We call them the IRA."

"What do you call the Jamaican drug lords who commit crimes and kill people?"

"We call them Jamaican drug lords and terrorists."

"Approximately how many people does your government have on a list of 'violent extremists'?"

"Close to two thousand."

"Of those two thousand, what percentage would be people who say they are fighting jihad?"

For a moment, he hesitated. "Hmm. Well ... that's a hard question."

So we asked him to give an estimate. "Well, I would have to say it's pretty close to one hundred percent."

Of course, no one in attendance was surprised by his answer. As the incident made clear, everyone really knows what "violent extremism" conceals; even its most strident advocates know that when they use it, they are obfuscating a reality they'd rather not face. When used in the War on Terror, it is a euphemism for those who wage jihad in the cause of Allah ... and returning veterans (because, as the narrative goes, just like al-Qaeda, they are willing to swear to defend something—the Constitution—which is extreme, and they are willing to fight and die for it, which makes them violent). The equivalency of this last point is not random.[6]

Once the decision not to identify the enemy is made, it becomes impossible to generate a strategy to defeat him. This decision is the desired outcome of a successful information campaign designed to leave decision-makers in a state of strategic unawareness that forces them to react to momentary, tactical events. General Richard Myers, former Chairman of the Joint Chiefs of Staff, discussed the difficulties he experienced in this state of strategic blindness:

> This **lack of** a comprehensive global **strategy** has been a problem since 9/11. Sadly, this broader strategy **never gets the attention** and hard thought **it deserves**, as the importance and **urgency of the moment always trumps** the time needed to develop **a more strategic view**.[7] [emphasis added]

General Myers was right: the War on Terror lacked a strategy because it *never* got the attention it deserved; the urgency of the moment *always* trumped the strategic view. When a serving Chairman of the JCS during the War on Terror makes such a public admission, it means we really did not have a strategy—that we did not know what we were doing or why. That the Chairman seems not to have understood the strategic consequences of his public admission compounds this.

But if we are not fighting the war according to our strategy, then whose strategy and to what end? If there is any possibility that our current, strategically unmoored state is someone else's desired outcome, what strategic advantage would that person have (at our expense)? Certainly, as General Myers made clear, we have yet to understand what we are doing. *But somebody does and is benefitting from it.* This raises a question for Captain Kirby: as you appear on *Al-Jazeera* with known Brotherhood operatives to attack the character of Americans, just what is "the strategy that [you] know we're out there executing"?[8]

Complexity

The typical analyst and decision-maker in the War on Terror has been encouraged to construct abstract models to define the enemy. Invariably, these models are so dense and impermeable that they don't let relevant real-world information through. Many of these abstractions arise out of a bureaucratized exegesis of Complexity Theory, a scientific concept that, when repurposed to serve bureaucratic narratives, is best summed up by the talking point that "the world is so complex, we can't really *know* anything; all we can do is manage the chaos."

In this construct, the only acceptable answer to questions designed to garner a simple understanding of uncomplicated doctrines is that they are "complicated." "It's complicated" has become an officially approved alibi for those who are supposed to be beholden to a professional duty to know. The popularity of complexity theory in bureaucratic decision-making is a signal that something has gone wrong with our national security analytical processes.

First raised in Part 1, consider again what happens when the typical suicide operation occurs: We see the farewell video of the martyr giving his reasons for carrying out the attack. He is calm and very collected. He is a man who made a decision to die for what he believes in, a decision that—given his worldview—can reasonably be described as rational. Any threat doctrine capable of motivating its followers to undertake such action has demonstrated a capacity to inspire intense commitment. Anyone who mocks this commitment or looks down on those able to motivate such a commitment is seriously underestimating the nature of the threat, as well as the strength of its doctrine.

The suicide attack occurs; we watch the carnage on the news. Later, news reports carry images of entire towns celebrating the suicide bomber's becoming a shahid. But this is generally only the first half of the news story. The reporter will then either consult a terrorism expert or a senior U.S. government official who tells the viewer that what he just saw—and what Americans have watched on the news for over a decade—was not real, had nothing to do with Islam, and was too complicated to explain. You've seen this yourself!

I was at the U.S. Army School for Advanced Military Studies arguing exactly this point, and a fellow told me, "In today's complex world, you can't really *know* anything." As he spoke, I noticed a poster on the wall behind him featuring a quote from Sherlock Holmes: "It is a capital mistake to theorize in advance of the facts."[9]

We don't do intelligence anymore. Today, we collect a tremendous amount of raw data. We denature it, break it into data bits, and pour it into a soft-science mold, following the pre-determined path proscribed by the model. The data on which our understanding should have been based now serves only to buttress whichever theory is in vogue.

This process allows us to concentrate on models without having to identify the threat while sounding very scientific, academic, and sophisticated. It is the illusion of knowledge where none exists. A form of scientism, it's the gnostic knowledge of our time thinly wrapped in a veneer of science. Because we don't have to define the actual threat, no one has to worry about being reprimanded because they failed to accurately identify real groups that publish real doctrines that call for the real killing of Americans.

Wrapped in the veneer of science, however, we tell ourselves that only the models' experts are qualified to speak to the issue. We then outsource the analysis supporting national security decision-making to soft-science associate professors who then become the only persons qualified to speak about the enemy. Neither the warfighter nor the planning officer is any longer considered competent to comment on the nature of the threat he engages in combat—except in the most tactical terms. Officers are left echoing the talking points and, when pressed, simply assert that it's "complicated." Our officer corps has participated in its own divestment from the strategic war craft presumed to be its domain.

As previously discussed, the best short work explaining this form of ideological subversion is *Abuse of Language, Abuse of Power* by German philosopher Josef Pieper. Writing in the 1970s, Pieper explained how the Nazis came to be able to abuse power through abuse of the language of discourse:

> It is entirely possible that the true and authentic reality is being drowned out by the countless superficial information bits noisily and breathlessly presented in propaganda fashion. Consequently, **one may be entirely knowledgeable about a thousand details and nevertheless, because of ignorance regarding the core of the matter, remain without basic insight**. This is a phenomenon in itself already quite astonishing and disturbing. Arnold Gehlen labeled it "fundamental ignorance, created by technology and nourished by information."[10]

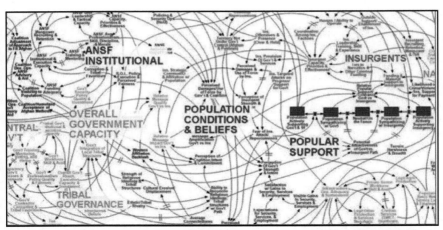

This diagram from the Department of Defense, intended to represent the "complexity" of COIN strategy in Afghanistan, is a vivid example of how the drive for complexity undermines decision-making. In the War on Terror, all soft-science models that drown out the enemy's stated threat doctrine are pseudorealities.

As Pieper later explains, deciding to ignore the essential aspects of the matter makes the information "complicated." Yet this form of complexity emerges from the bureaucratic fiat that knowable things be henceforth treated as unknowable.

If Pieper's pseudoreality sounds uncomfortably familiar, it is because such thinking has become institutionalized. This complexity is not inherent in the nature of the thing itself—in this case, the enemy's threat doctrine—but rather is imposed on it by the requirements of the relevant pseudo-scientific model. When such models are imposed on intelligence analysts who are supposed to be undertaking threat analysis, it precludes them from accounting for what they plainly see by rendering the plainly obvious "too complicated" to comprehend.

An indication of our addiction to soft-science models is the frequency by which they are adopted, embraced, and, ultimately, discarded in favor of a newer pseudo-academic trend. If we tire of seeing the War on Terror through the lens of the anthropological model expressed in terms of the human terrain, for example, we take up the psychological model and discuss "leaderless jihad" or the "self-radicalization process." Analysts, policymakers, and consultants in the national security establishment go to conferences and listen to academics lecture on these models; no one talks about the actual enemy or his threat doctrine. If we can talk about the street-gang dynamics of urban youth in Southern California and pretend this is a proxy for al-Qaeda in some country, at least we are not talking about Islam. We can feel safe, politically correct, and not run afoul of the Islamophobia police.[11]

Enforcing such a standard requires that those seeking a role in the decision-making process first acknowledge that 1 + 1 = 4.725. (The .725 is added to double-down on the illusion of scientific veracity—the veracity being nothing more than the addition of .725 to an already ridiculous number.) Decision-making in the pseudoreality is not about being right; it's about conforming to the model and replacing factual analysis with requirements that conform to narratives, and then weighing the selection criteria for promotion in favor of those willing to enforce narratives over those who analyze facts. The Muslim Brotherhood spotted this vulnerability as far back as 1994, when Ibrahim Ghanem, in *The West in the Eyes of the Egyptian Islamic Movement*, observed:

> The prevailing conception of writers and researchers ... about the Islamic Movement's view of the West and its general perception of it is one that tends to be reductionist, partial, and deformed. This comes from the consolidation of preconceptions and subjective impressions that are being given a scientific colouring.[12]

They've had our number for some time - in all probability, so too have the Russian, Chinese, and Iranians. When I briefed at the more senior war colleges, the topic of "complexity" would often come up in conjunction with the debilitating effects such postmodern rhetoric plays on the decision-making process. I would often hear statements like, "Because there are no facts, there is no truth. Everything is just interpretation."

When I explained the dependence on soft-science models and their self-defeating complexity, I always received silent nods of suppressed recognition, frustration, and anger. I was speaking to something real in the minds of most of the officers in those classes. In one instance, an Army Colonel told me his last war college exercise was based on a complexity model. It was taken for granted that that way of thinking represented the wave of the future. He expressed his comment in terms that made it clear he was not sure he wanted to be a part of that future. Clearly, the ability to conform to postmodern narratives was understood to serve as a discriminator in future career progression.

Over time, this discussion began to surface regularly in the course of my briefings. Books began to show up on my desk concerning various aspects of complexity. Colleagues and students began anonymously sending me examples of this trend, all originating from the same Defense Department Command and Control Research Program (DOD CCRP). For example, I received the following books:

- *Coping with Bounds: Speculation on Nonlinearity in Military Affairs*[13]
- *Complexity Theory and Network Centric Warfare*[14]
- *Complexity, Networking, & Effects-Based Approaches to Operations*[15]
- *Planning: Complex Endeavor*[16]

Needless to say, it is difficult to picture Caesar, Grant, Lee, Patton, Puller, or Eisenhower ever reading—or feeling the need to read—such books when planning actual strategy for real war. Reflecting what seems to be the CCRP motto, the two latter imprints in the listed titles carried the slogan "The Future of Command and Control."[17] In *Coping with Bounds: Speculation in Nonlinearity in Military Affairs*, author Tom Czerwinski opened with a quote from Heinz Pagels, the famous chaos philosopher who was emulated in the movie *Jurassic Park*:

> I am convinced that the nations and people who master the new sciences of complexity will become the economic, cultural and political superpowers of the next century. (Heinz Pagels)[18]

In the last century, politics and policy were unduly influenced by a blind faith in science in the service of the Hegelian march of history. Today, those who do not accept "complexity" in bureaucratic decision-making—a complexity designed to render otherwise knowable events unknowable—are likewise considered out of step with that history. The same mindset that aped the *bona fide* theory of evolution to propagate various social Darwinist programs now drives bureau-academic ideations of complexity. Today, complexity is being used as an ideological tool to immobilize what could otherwise be coherent planning and decision-making. The science of the one should never be confused with the politics of the other.

In his monograph *Complexity Theory and Network Centric Warfare*, James Moffat made it clear that use of the term "complexity theory" is neither scientific nor coherent:

> **Notes to the Reader**. Although I use the term *Complexity Theory* as if it were a coherent body of scientific theory, this area of research is in fact still both young and evolving.[19]

Moffat laid out the "complexity" problem in his foreword:

> For the last couple of decades, attempts have been made to
> develop some general understanding, and ultimately a the-
> ory, of systems that consist of many interacting components
> and many hierarchical layers. It is common to call these sys-
> tems *complex* because it is **impossible to reduce** the overall
> behavior of the system to a set of properties characterizing
> the individual components. Interaction is able to produce
> properties at the collective level that are simply not pres-
> ent when the components are considered individually. As an
> example, one may think of mutuality and collaboration in
> ecology. The function of any ecosystem depends crucially on
> mutual benefits between the different species present. One
> example is the relation between legumes, such as peas and
> beans, and their associated nitrogen-fixing bacteria: the bac-
> teria collects nitrogen for the legume, which in turn produces
> carbohydrates and other organic material for the bacteria.
> Clearly this crucial arrangement cannot be studied by fo-
> cusing on, say, the legume and neglecting the bacteria; the
> ecological function emerges first when the different com-
> ponents are brought together and interaction is taken into
> account.[20]

Applied to threat analysis, as complexity asserts the impossibility of reducing "the overall behavior of the system to a set of properties characterizing the indi- vidual components to a discrete knowable thing," it makes it impossible to analyze the enemy's published doctrine. It's complicated.

As model-based complexity thinking goes, before one can speak to the real- ity of jihad-based terrorism in the War on Terror, one must first understand the concept of terrorism in some abstracted form—preferably in terms of "violent ex- tremism"—so that a model can be extrapolated to apply, first, to all terrorism, and then to the form of terrorism in question. It is through such machinations that al-Qaeda can be understood as an equivalency to returning veterans. For those who invest in this institutionalized pseudoreality, knowing the enemy really does become complicated; in fact, it becomes impossible. Complexity becomes a key enabler of the pseudoreality (or is that the other way around?).

Moffat's foreword demonstrates the irrelevance of complexity theory in the context of decision-making as a warfighting pursuit. Think of the farmer and his legumes in Moffat's example above. At no time does the farmer have to think in terms of "mutuality and collaboration in ecology" or about the "relation between legumes, such as peas and beans, and their associated nitrogen-fixing bacteria" in order to cultivate his garden. If farmers had to think this way before cultivating their gardens, they might never get around to it. In fact, very few people would be surprised if a poll revealed that (1) most farmers don't think this way, and (2) most people who do think this way don't farm. If farmers don't cultivate their crops, we will starve. If we wait for the complexity theorists to cultivate those crops, we will also starve—while listening to them discuss the impossibility of planting a seed until we develop a plan for planting all possible seeds, given the complexity of the ecosystem. In other words, the farmer doesn't have to solve the problems of the universe in order to plant his legumes. Rather, it is sufficient that he knows how to farm in ways that accord with sound farming practices.

And here's the rub: there is neither a necessary nor sufficient reason to have to explain what happens, for example, to the flower in India when the butterfly flaps its wings in Detroit as a precondition to explaining why al-Qaeda follows Islamic law. There is simply the institutionalized mandate that it be so. While national security decision-makers may never be able to explain the complexity underlying either the butterfly in Detroit or the flower in India, the concentration on either of these two issues is a purposefully irrelevant distraction. Complexity theory demands that decision-makers convince themselves through such casuistry that they lack the understanding to explain either the self-identified enemy or his self-identified doctrine. This type of organizational thinking has paralyzed analytical processes and compromised decision-making. Junior officers understand this. Senior leadership does not.

This is what the Brotherhood means when waging a "grand jihad in eliminating and destroying the Western civilization from within and 'sabotaging' its miserable house *by their hands.*"

The process enshrined by the old IPB Manual was formulated to avoid just this type of problem. Classic IPB was designed to be unconstrained by the subjective viewpoints of analysts and decision-makers by requiring that all relevant data be included in the threat analysis. If the Green Cheese Doctrine in the example above demands green cheese, we must include green cheese as a part of the analysis—even if we prefer Swiss cheese, or no cheese at all.

If an entity identifies Islamic law as a basis for its doctrine, then the inclusion of shariah in the threat analysis at the doctrinal template phase becomes mandatory, while its exclusion constitutes both fatal error and professional malpractice.

Because it is an identified element of the threat doctrine, there is no requirement to come to an ultimate determination about whether it constitutes "true Islam" before considering its inclusion, only a factual determination that the enemy states his reliance on it. If the "moderates" are correct that "extremists" have hijacked Islam, a two-tiered solution is in order:

> 1. An education campaign to properly inform the Islamic
>   population of true Islamic requirements.

2. A review of possible "underlying causes" based on an
   actual finding that Islam has been hijacked.

It would be one thing if the national security establishment's "underlying causes" approach to analysis of the enemy in the War on Terror were the product of a deliberate investigation that revealed it to be true. But these soft-science theories can never be the first consideration; they can be introduced only when the cause-in-fact has been ruled out or at least seriously attenuated. This is true because adopting such an approach necessarily entails the invalidation of the enemy and his stated doctrine in his own domain. It would be like fighting the Japanese, Germans, or Soviets only after tossing out their strategic and operational doctrines because we did not approve of them. Adopting "underlying causes" as the principle axis on which to understand the enemy in the War on Terror is a radical departure from fact-based threat analysis that demands an affirmative justification.

Resorting to "underlying causes," we discarded the cause-in-fact—jihad fi sabilillah. This in itself should serve as warning that something has gone profoundly awry in the national security community. Gone are Sun-Tzu, Clausewitz, Jomini, and every intelligence doctrine; gone is everything designed to measure facts and the requirement to know the enemy. In the world of "underlying causes," complexity theory, or whatever pseudoreality is in vogue, it should not be surprising that the classic IPB Manual had to be retired in 2009. Real intelligence does not deal in narratives.

On the other hand, if violent extremists are correct on the role of jihad in shariah, then the presenting cause—jihad in the cause of Allah—remains the cause-in-fact and must, therefore, be assessed as a basis of the threat doctrine for war-planning purposes. Because the cause-in-fact has been validated, there is no basis on which to orient on "underlying causes" as a primary axis. A question in need of a response: If our analysts have read a variety of "underlying causes" onto the enemy's motivations, at what point was the cause-in-fact analyzed and rejected? Properly understood, dismissing the cause-in-fact is such an extreme act that it at least demands that it be the result of a deliberate analytical process. Yet it's not even clear that anyone ever noticed the transition when it happened.

This raises questions regarding the material misrepresentation of known and knowable facts. For professionals in the national security community, the question is not just what they know, but what they should have known. The current approach to national security undermines our national safety and is getting people killed. There is not a theoretical discussion. Pseudorealities can sustain powerful illusions capable of overwriting facts-on-the-ground realities even in the face of life-and-death circumstances.

Nowhere was this more evident than in a recent exchange between former Acting CIA Director Michael Morell and Congresswoman Michele Bachmann in the April 2014 oversight hearings of the House Permanent Select Committee on Intelligence (HPSCI). The exchange concerned the reporting of events around the September 11, 2012, terror attack at the diplomatic annex in Benghazi, Libya. Conceding that the CIA assessment was wrong, the Director nevertheless defended it—but solely on the grounds that it was based on a narrative whose strength was measured by the fact that it penetrated so deeply into the analytical processes that everyone believed it. In fact, this narrative was strong enough to overpower actual warning in the form of real-time reporting of facts on the ground by personnel who had eyes on the activities in which they were directly engaged.

> *Michael Morell*: The narrative that the attack evolved spontaneously from a protest was a narrative that Intelligence Community analysts believed. Not just CIA analysts, Intelligence Community analysts. That turned out to be incorrect but that is what they believed at the time. So there is no politics there whatsoever. That's point number one. ... (*responding to Rep. Bachmann's follow-up question*) Ma'am, if you look at the record what you will see is that the changes I made were fully consistent with what our analysts believed at the time, period.

> *Rep. Michele Bachmann*: The analysts that were part of the bureaucracy, not the individuals who were on the ground who had eyewitness testimony and who as early as September 12th had sent you a cable that it was not a protest, that it was in fact an attack. Those were intentionally ignored.

> *Morell*: So Ma'am, do you believe that we should have accepted the Chief of Station's view without question and it was a protest?

> *Bachmann*: I believe that the totality of the information was obfuscated and that there was an intentional misleading of the public. ... His [the Chief of Station] view was that— we spoke with him yesterday behind closed doors. He was adamant from the very beginning that this was not a spontaneous protest. We heard from him directly yesterday that at no time did he believe it was based upon the video. It isn't just him. It's the RSO, it's the Chief of Base, it's those who came from the Annex, it's the political officers, all of them agreed. You take that versus some press reports and one signal versus—the weight and balance aren't even equal, it isn't even equal. The evidence overwhelmingly pointed to an attack – an attack that was al-Qaeda or jihadist related.[21]

To say that "there is no politics" in the narrative misses the point that narratives *are* political. That everyone believed the narrative only goes to the success of its enforcement over time. It reflects the successful institutionalization of processes calibrated to give narrative enforcement preference over factual analysis. There is a difference between the misreading of facts and the suppression of them. The Intelligence Community's baseline *raison d'etre* is to generate facts that provide warning. Narratives exist to overwrite them. Benghazi was a remote disaster. The faux assessment and decsionmaking surrounding it was not. As the HPSCI testimony revealed, Benghazi provided warning of serious unresolved vulnerabilities that the same type of disaster could happen at higher levels closer to home. When Pieper spoke of how "the existential realm of man could be taken over by pseudorealities whose fictitious nature threatens to become indiscernible from the truth,"[22] he was talking about this.

Our Fashionable 'Pseudorealities'

In fighting the War on Terror, three theoretical models are currently in vogue. The first defines the way we will engage the enemy in anthropological terms—in other words, human terrain teams, i.e., armed anthropological field studies operating in engagement areas. Anthropological explanations to military activities conform to the requirement to explain real-world events in the language of soft-science models, ensuring that rationalizations remain abstract and generic.

The second model is the psycho-social. This model transposes the motivations, dynamics, characteristics, and etiology of America's urban street gangs onto what are called "self-motivating jihadis" and "leaderless jihads." These models are convenient because both "self-motivating" and "leaderless" indicate idiopathic motivations that render analysis into the stated motivations of real actors unnecessary.[23] After all, having asserted either that a terrorist acted as a "lone wolf" or that he is crazy, why should we look any further into his motivations?

The third and most popular "underlying causes" narrative is based on theories of economic deprivation. Underlying this model is the materialist view that, regardless of what an entity claims as its motivations for acting, ultimately the action is simply a response to purely economic realities regarding the lack—or inequitable distribution—of capital and resources, all of which can be resolved by building a road, a school, or a well. It is fashionable because it was used to understand and counter left- and right-wing insurgencies. The benefit of blaming terrorism on economic hardship is identical to that of the preceding models. The drivers become "universal," thereby allowing for a bundle of universal responses that require neither actual knowledge of the group that is deprived nor real knowledge of the culture in which they live.

With "underlying causes," bureaucrats can programmatically generate solutions to economic deprivation as if they really know the problem or the enemy.

From blind reliance on depravation models, winning a population's "hearts and minds" translates into programs of measurables, defined by the dreaded "measures of effectiveness" (MOEs), such as the number of schools built, miles laid for a road, or water facilities installed.

Such "hearts and minds" strategies are premised on strictly materialist solutions that facilitate the illusion that one can prosecute "hearts and minds" campaigns without having to actually know the people, ignoring what's in both their hearts and their minds. This approach allows for concrete measurables (MOEs) that brief well in Washington but often mean very little in the field and are dreaded by soldiers and junior officers.

An abstract understanding of an enemy leads to an abstract understanding of why he fights. Where the analysis of facts is made to yield to the complexities inherent in the model, the enemy can only be said to fight in furtherance of abstract, undefined underlying causes. For the academics that drive these models, the fact that the enemy says he is a jihadi who fights according to Islamic law seems too simple-minded to merit serious analysis.

National security analysts and decision-makers organize themselves around such theories as if they constitute an alternative to strategic assessments based on factual analysis. In fact, however, these theories have converted engagement areas into laboratories designed to prove the legitimacy of behavioral models. While we can win the tactical engagements, we cannot develop strategies to defeat the enemy because we lack the ability to define him. We have lost the ability to aggregate tactical successes into strategic victory. As long as we believe we can fight an enemy based on abstract models, we are not fighting the real enemy. Defeat in such circumstances is a matter of time. This is what Pieper meant when he said, "One may be entirely knowledgeable about a thousand details and nevertheless, because of ignorance regarding the core of the matter, remain without basic insight."[24]

'Balance' and Professional Standards

Through most of the War on Terror, American policymakers fought the enemy based on models of the enemy as Ph.D.s would like him to be rather than as he really is. Associated with the emphasis on complexity theory is the pervasive use inside the national security bureaucracy of postmodern enabling language, such as the terms "balance" and "interpretation." This all serves to enable the pseudoreality.

When briefing senior leaders, I often got the response: "That was a really interesting theory, but it needs 'balance.'" I never understood this comment. If one advocates a position in an appropriate and professional manner, it is someone else's responsibility to provide a competing analysis—assuming, of course, that the competing analysis is presented in an appropriate and professional manner. The demand for balance is no different from asking the plaintiff's attorney to provide a defense for the defendant's counsel, or asking a Democrat to advocate the Republican position (or vice versa) in a speech.

The standard for professional analysis should be based on its ability to validate the enemy's doctrine when mapped against acts undertaken in furtherance of that doctrine. As such, competing analysis must be capable of meeting an articulable burden of proof that is likewise based on professional factual analysis.

Demands for "balance" that allow non-factual arguments to compete with factual ones undermine professionalism. How do you add "balance" to $1 + 1 = 2$? In this example, would someone be allowed to use their "private math" to suggest that $1 + 1 = 9.45$ just to satisfy the request for "balance"? Of course, the decision-maker can magnanimously split the difference by adopting a middle position, $1 + 1 = 4.725$. To ask for balance in such circumstances increases the likelihood of injecting error into the decision-making process. This form of balance comes at the cost of being wrong. It facilitates risk-averse decision-making by those who will not articulate the actual threat. At what point does the demand for balance facilitate something akin to the perpetration of a fraud?

This discussion is not concerned with debates where reasonable people can reasonably disagree on articulable facts but rather on circumstances about which it is not reasonable to disagree. Simply stated, where issues of fact have been properly asserted in a decision-making process[25]—where a burden of proof has been met[26]—demands for "balance" must be constrained by requirements that admit only those "interpretations" capable of meeting a comparable burden.[27] This evidentiary standard should set a minimum threshold—an entry barrier—for competing analysis before it can be allowed into the threat analysis arena. Conversely, all competing arguments capable of meeting such a threshold should never be excluded from that arena.

Postmodern notions of "balance" set a new standard for national security analysis. We have reached the point where anyone who provides a fact-driven threat analysis can be asked to remove citations from briefing materials that establish the underlying authority of the product so as not to "bully" competing analysis that can't. After all, in the postmodern paradigm, what is authority?

Those responsible for providing "balance" to competent analysis often find the analysis too difficult to counter factually. When confronted with the strength of such arguments, assertions are then made that "it's all a matter of interpretation." In the interest of fairness, citations that demonstrate authority are removed. Without references to authority in the work product, two products of very different quality can present the appearance of being equally weighted. The decision-maker is left with the illusion of "balance," which supports the illusion of a safe competing alternative. This situation is not speculative: In the interest "fairness," I was asked to remove references from my briefs so as to not overwhelm.

Lawyers know that what they say is only as good as the authority they use to support their statements. Doctors and other professionals must cite their information in professional journals as well. Even Supreme Court justices have to cite their decisions. Permitting unsourced work product into the decision-making process is itself a decision not to account for the facts. It facilitates a suppression of evidence through dilution. It is a permissive standard that puts assumptions at parity with facts.

Under professional conditions, analytical work product is evaluated based on its ability to reconcile facts to repeatable conclusions to a purpose. When properly used in this context, the call for balance is the call for legitimate competing analytical products to see how they account for the same facts when drawing conclusions or formulating theories. Assuming that competing products meet professional canons on work product, the demand for balance is reasonable; it calls for the full range of professional inputs on a given subject before making a weighted decision.

But we are not talking about that here. When calls for "balance" are used to allow "interpretations" that do not meet factual standards into the analytical mix, the requirement to substantiate an interpretational challenge with relevant evidence is suspended.[28]

Professional analysis should be based on repeatable factual processes, not on mandates for balance. If analytical products offered in the interest of balance lack facts, on what basis is it being allowed to compete with products that do meet that standard? Credible analysis always concerns itself with facts[29] and their relationship to evidence.[30] The postmodern narrative seeks to blur the distinction between facts and assumptions. After all, in a world where there are no facts and there is no truth, everything is a matter of interpretation: "Why should I have to back my interpretation with (what you call) facts? It's true because it's true to me." Or, a la Sheldon Cooper: "All I have to do is postulate one universe in a multiverse where it could be true for me to argue that it is true with regard to my interpretation in this decision-making brief."

To see how postmodern notions of balance facilitate the degradation of analytical processes leading to inferior decision-making, it needs to be understood in relation to its sister term, "interpretation." When the "interpretation" is used to refute professional work product, it is almost never used to mean something like, "I am familiar with the subject matter and, based on my professional (factual) analysis, I think a different interpretation (of facts given a pattern) is valid."

Rather, the term is predominantly used to assert the postmodern standard that, because there is no truth, everything is just interpretation, and each interpretation is as valid as the next. It amounts to simple and dismissive gainsaying. "Well, that's just your interpretation." Used this way, interpretation rejects knowledge as a basis for analysis and, in so doing, subverts the analytical process.

As discussed, the legal standard associated with professionalism is heavily weighted in favor of a reasoned orientation to facts. A postmodern standard renders that orientation irrelevant. In postmodern parlance, because the challenge "it's a matter of interpretation" does not have to suggest a substantive disagreement in order to be offered, its real effect is to degrade decision-making. It pollutes the data-pool used to formulate enemy and friendly courses of action in the decision-making process.

Not only are most of those who conform to this postmodern standard unaware of its dangers, so too are most of those who play an active role in enforcing it. This becomes important when accounting for the Muslim Brotherhood's "by our hand" strategy of civilization-jihad articulated in its 1991 Explanatory Memorandum. The irrational demand for "balance" becomes a term of enforcement associated with postmodern narratives. While peers insist on the primacy of "interpretation," seniors demand "balance." "Balance" is the permissive acceptance of work product from those who believe everything is a matter of "interpretation."

Interpretations that don't account for facts are counterfactual and, hence, suspect. When counterfactual interpretations displace relevant facts in a decision-making formula, they become hostile. "Balance" and "interpretation" invite unprofessional decisions within a professional decision-making regime. Allowing counterfactual interpretations into the stream of thinking that drives the decision-making process de-professionalizes the process and renders all of its decisions suspect.

"Balance" supports fact-deficient narratives that are then allowed to compete on an equal basis with professional analysis. When this happens, the decision-making process is compromised. Has the demand for "balance" in the analytical space come to reflect a downward subversion of professional decision-making? The answer is clear.

Outsourcing our Intelligence

In the classical understanding, key terrain on a battlefield refers to a position that gives the side that holds it a decisive advantage. For example, we are on one side, the enemy is on the other, and in the middle is a hill. That hill is key terrain, because whoever holds it has a decisive advantage. What constitutes key terrain in the information battlespace? *The language of the debate.*

As we have seen, when jihadis talk about what they are going to do, it is almost always in reference to shariah. They call what they do jihad. Those in the Middle East who agree with al-Qaeda call them jihadis. Those who disagree with them call them gangster jihadis.

Yet national security leaders say we cannot use such language. That means we cannot access the canons and doctrines used by either al-Qaeda or Islamic authorities on that topic. When we cannot use an accurate descriptor, we lose the ability to orient on who the enemy is; we lose access to the lexicon that fixes them to their doctrine. Skeptical? Recall the OIC's Ten-Year Programme of Action or the anti-Islamophobia campaigns.

The enemy uses that language to define everything they do and has persuaded our senior leaders and media elites to prevent us from using those same words. Remember, their strategy is the "Civilization-Jihadist Process," which depends on getting us to "sabotage our miserable house by our own hands."

People might ask: "How could our senior leaders be so compromised or co-opted? Surely they wouldn't allow that." And one would like to think most wouldn't—not on purpose.

But submitting to this narrative does not require assent or even the subjective understanding that one has submitted. The frog isn't supposed to know the water in the pot is too hot until it doesn't matter if he does. At a certain point, even if the frog jumps from the hot water, it will be too scalded to survive. We are not supposed to know that we are submitting. We're not supposed to know that we are boiling ... yet. Preposterous? Look at what resulted from the Days of Rage following the Bagram Qur'an burnings.

Think back to the Muslim Brotherhood's strategy in waging war on the United States, their "grand jihad in eliminating and destroying the Western civilization from within." In the subversion of the analytical process that drives threat development and the resulting cluelessness that complexity sustains, we see this happening all around us—"by [our] hands."

Imagine a self-described "moderate" or cultural expert, possibly associated with a Brotherhood-linked group. If he can convince you, an analyst, or a decision-maker of a counterfactual understanding of something related to the enemy's threat doctrine—an understanding that has no basis in fact yet fits with some academic theory—he can walk away once you commit. His work is done. This is how such a conversation might go:

> "You mean, Mr. Moderate, that I can't hope to understand Islam unless I understand classical Arabic?"

> "That's right, Mr. Policy guy."

> "But I can't learn classical Arabic!"

> "That's understandable. But because only those who understand classical Arabic can comprehend the true meaning of Islam, you should not read those English-language publications of approved shariah translations at all, even if we sell them in Islamic bookstores for course instruction for English-speaking Muslims and the books are certified as authentic."

> "You mean all of that stuff written in English that most peo-

ple in the Islamic Center who can't read Arabic are reading? That won't work for me?"

"No, it won't. It's really complicated. No, you have to come to me, and I'll tell you everything you are allowed to know."

"Well thank you, Mr. Moderate. I'm so grateful to you; I know you're fully committed to winning this war."

"Why yes, come to think of it, I'm fully committed to winning!"

Unfortunately, it really is that basic. Once the Brotherhood leads you to a counterfactual understanding of something and you start making policy decisions based on it, then he has accomplished his purpose. You are committed to his cause, regardless of whether you agree with it or even understand what it is. At some future date, you may realize that you were steered wrong, but you will already have been co-opted.

Once co-opted, you will shut down subordinates when they begin to generate competing theories based on factual analysis that compete with your counterfactual assessment. It may be then that you begin to realize you're not prepared to offer a factual or professional response. Years back, you adopted positions based on unsubstantiated assumptions provided by third parties. Now you are beginning to realize you're not sure how to defend your policy positions when challenged by subordinates who are fully prepared to defend theirs. You will shut those dissenting voices down, because your professional reputation depends on it. You will support the Brotherhood's information campaign—civilization jihad by your hand—not because you agree with the Brotherhood, but because years ago someone succeeded at fusing your professional reputation to their narrative.

When national security leaders and decision-makers are confronted with the reality that our enemies' doctrine is firmly rooted in shariah, their reaction is entirely predictable. This raises a topic that has—when briefed inside the government—been quite contentious: the undermining of senior-level situational awareness and decision-making. When briefing audiences of military officers, I would often break the tension with a reference to the *Star Wars* character Obi Wan Kenobi's statement to hapless Imperial Storm Troopers: "These aren't the droids you're looking for."[31] The audience of officers always understood. They always laughed. Because they always agreed. When our moderate friends and cultural experts tell our senior leaders that terrorist actions have nothing to do with Islam, our senior leaders turn to their subordinates and tell them, "This has nothing to do with Islam, case closed, move along to the next point." With such heightened fear of being accused of being Islamophobic, the strategy works. In fact, it is disarming. It goes like this—starting with the "moderate" or cultural expert: "General, why are you listening to this? The issue is complicated and doesn't lend itself to simplistic explanations. This has nothing to do with *my* Islam. This is why your superiors put me on your staff. If you have any questions about Islam, come to me and I'll tell you what you're allowed to know. I am completely committed to victory in this war. That's why I am here ... to help."

This dynamic exposes a two-fold divide. First, between "boots on the ground" officers (usually Army, Marines, and special forces), who generally understand the subject matter being briefed, and other officers who are often not as operational. The second divide, which is much more pronounced, is between senior and junior officers. For those subordinates who actually do analysis based on facts, the order to dismiss Islam as a contributing factor to terrorism is an order to suppress relevant facts that they know are accurate and relevant.

This direct order to ignore facts at some point influences a subordinate's confidence in the leadership. For many, this is deeply sensed if not always expressed. In effect, these men and women are being told they are good enough to fight the war but not good enough to have an opinion on it (professional or otherwise). Polling of West Point graduates indicates a correlation may exist between being given such direction and confidence in their leaders' decision-making.[32] This might help explain the statistics previously examined: 46 percent of Army officers polled think the current military leadership is weak; 82 percent believe the officer development system does a poor job of weeding out weak leaders; 95 percent believe that the military does not retain its best officers; and 78 percent think the exit rate of good young officers is a threat to national security.[33]

In a phenomenon that manifested itself early in the war, Islamic-identity groups, many associated with the Islamic Movement, were allowed to insinuate themselves into the intelligence cycles as the arbiters of what is and is not off limits when undertaking threat analysis of the enemy. A practical result of this is the subordination of the oath to "support and defend" to the requirement not to offend. This is not to argue against the inclusion of properly trained Muslims in the analytical processes, but to argue on behalf of non-Muslims who are also professionally trained and who routinely rely on relevant facts in their analytical products. Regardless, these analysts may be shut down because their work product, however accurate and correct it may be, does not conform to the *de facto* requirement that only Muslims and cultural experts can render an assessment on anything having to do with Islamic-based terrorism.

There are many non-Muslims in the national security space who do not feel such conflict. But this isn't about those who passively accept or are unaware of the implications of the government's requirements to combat Islamophobia above that of doing fact-based analysis in furtherance of "supporting and defending." This is about those who understand the problems they are tasked to analyze, articulate their products in a factual, professional manner, and are summarily silenced.

The problem with the demand that fact-based product be suppressed if its conclusions are inconvenient or "inflammatory" (i.e., they point to an Islamic basis for violence) is that it creates an environment in which responsibility for accurate assessments is constantly being shifted to others. Excuses abound: "Let's leave that to the fifty-pound brains," "That's above my pay grade," "That's not my lane in the road," or (in whispered tones) "I can't be promoted if I'm accused of being a hater." In these responses, one hears the echo of "I was just following orders."

That poll of West Point graduates should have sent shockwaves through the ever-shrinking segment of the country with ties to the military. Inexplicably, the obvious lack of confidence in senior leadership has not been raised by the media or by those responsible for performing their Article I duty of congressional oversight. This is another one of those "dogs that don't bark" issues. Members of Congress appoint the best and brightest to attend West Point. Why isn't some oversight committee asking the large numbers of successful former officers why they left? Remember Gresham's law[34]—the principle that counterfeit or debased currency drives out the valued currency—when considering who is rising to the top if the best and brightest are not staying the course.

There is no reason why properly trained and qualified Muslims or any other Americans should not be a part of the analytical and decision-making processes in this war. But blanket veto power over another's otherwise sound and professionally prepared work product goes too far. Professional standards should be in effect. If an analyst who is Muslim disapproves of a competing analysis that was based on citable facts, he should be required to counter it in a professional manner that meets an established burden of proof. It needs to go beyond the mere assertion that "this is not my Islam." Threat analysis has never been about a Muslim analyst's version of Islam, but rather about the Islam that legitimizes groups like the Muslim Brotherhood and al-Qaeda and drives their threat doctrine, regardless of whether those "versions" of Islam are correct.

If non-Muslim intelligence officers are incapable of conducting threat analysis of the enemy in the War on Terror, then either the doctrine is compromised or their training is incompetent.

Hearsay

As previously noted, in late 2005, more than a year after demobilizing, I was asked to brief principal senior intelligence officers on the Joint Staff. It was then that I first formally voiced my concerns about outsourcing the information requirements driving our decision-making processes. I explicitly stated these concerns at the conclusion to the briefing:

- Can overdependence on third parties to explain non-Western motivations and beliefs lead us to (overly) depend on them for the decisions we make?

- Is there a point where the outsourcing of an under-standing of events leads to the outsourcing of the deci-sion-making associated with those same events?

Whether in tort, contract, or agency, certain duties are non-delegable.[35] These duties include responsibility for the decisions made as well as the reasons for mak-ing them. When senior leaders make warfighting decisions based on the inputs of a subject matter expert (SME), they are outsourcing both their knowledge and the decision-making associated with it. It is the strategy that arises out of this process that Captain Kirby "knows [he's] out there executing."[36]

Among the reasons we are unable to understand the War on Terror is that many of the people who seek to educate us on the topic of Islamic-based ter-rorism have close relationships with the Muslim Brotherhood, either directly or through its various front groups. Publicly available documents, many entered into evidence in the Holy Land trial, demonstrate the Brotherhood's open hostility to the Western world, including the United States. Yet we base our operational and day-to-day understanding of Islam and Islamic "violent extremism" on the coun-sel of individuals linked to "an effective and stable Islamic Movement led by the Muslim Brotherhood which adopts Muslims' causes domestically and globally."[37]

When assessing a threat and given the choice between relying on validated shariah and captured Muslim-Brotherhood strategy documents or on the coun-sel of those same Brothers, our national security establishment has consistently turned to the Brotherhood.

In regard to counsel from individuals with Brotherhood affiliations, it is worth remembering that knowledge derived from third persons does not usually survive a hearsay challenge in many courts of law. And yet, for many in our leadership, it services decision-making in the War on Terror. *Black's Law Dictionary* defines hearsay as "statements (testimony) that are given by a witness who relates not what he or she knows personally, but what others have said, and is therefore dependent on the credibility of someone other than the witness."[38]

When senior decision-makers say they rely on their Subject Matter Experts (SMEs) for their understanding of the enemy, they may be saying that they never undertook reasonable independent due diligence to validate the information that drives their decision-making. If true, this would constitute decision-making based on hearsay, which would mean that the same senior intelligence officers who pro-vide testimony in oversight to Congress might not survive a hearsay challenge when asked to offer that same testimony as a witness in a court of law.[39]

Orientalism, the 'Current Approach,' and Impermissible Knowledge

In my 2007 National Defense Intelligence College masters' thesis, I raised the issue of postmodernism and the influence of Edward Said on our national security leadership and labeled it the "Current Approach." In *Orientalism* (1978), Edward Said took exception to Western scholarship of Arab and Islamic culture, believing it to be a reflection of Western imperialism constructed solely to establish Western intellectual supremacy over the Orient.[40] Because Said believed all scholarship and literature to be political, his own work should be understood as having had a political purpose as well.[41] His objection to Western scholarship did not address the merits of any particular work. Rather, he based his challenge on the fact that such works were produced at all. Hence, the factual accuracy of any specific example of Western scholarship was, to him, of peripheral importance.

For Said, it was not important to progress beyond the "exteriority" of a Western work in order to summarily invalidate the merits of its scholarship.[42] Because the only way for the West to progress beyond its prejudicial ideations of the Arab or Muslim world is to engage in dispassionate discussion, his writing suggests, such a dialogue would have to be arbitrated by cultural experts with ethnic ties—or at least ideological conformance—to narratives that drive the Arab or Muslim advocacy.[43]

Interestingly, if Said's line of reasoning were extended along general lines, two points would emerge: first, that no culture could ever explain another's; and, second, that if Said were held to his own criteria—that members of one culture cannot explain another's—there would be no basis for his writing of *Orientalism* to explain to the West its own "intellectual genealogy ... in a way that has not been done."[44] Said's observations would be invalid based on his own criteria.

The postmodern mindset conditions the national security community to uncritically accept the proposition that all thinking should be kept on the surface of events.[45] While Complexity Theory tells us that we cannot know, Said tells us we ought not look any further, going so far as to mandate how the West should think about the Middle Eastern world. His central claim—that we in the West can never understand the Eastern world—sets up the demand that we turn to cultural experts and "moderate" Muslims to explain to us what we are allowed to know. Furthermore, we cannot look beyond the surface of what is explained to us, even if the due-diligence demands associated with our constitutional duty mandates otherwise. This holds true for the interfaith movement as well. We have been convinced that we cannot know knowable things; we can no longer comprehend events as they actually occur; from the movie *The Matrix*, we have taken the "blue pill"—and so the world really has become "complicated."

Said's influence on national security decision-making is chiefly felt in the uncritical acceptance of these cultural experts. Often, all that is required to halt an inquiry or analysis are the words, "Islam does not stand for this," from a cultural expert. These self-described "moderates" and cultural experts have demonstrated their complete willingness to provide decision-makers and analysts with the information they are permitted to know under the sole condition that it be accepted uncritically and unconditionally. It goes without saying that any intelligence professional with responsibility to do threat-based analysis who agrees with Said's epistemology is unsuitable to undertake the intelligence mission. It certainly puts him in violation of his constitutional oath to "support and defend."

Of course, Said's assault on critical thinking fits seamlessly with Islamic law on blasphemy and slander. The OIC's global campaign to outlaw Islamophobia enters the postmodern narrative at the point of Said's main concept. Said's forbidden knowledge of Islam comes from the postmodern left; prohibitions on slander and blasphemy come from Islamic law. Through Said's narrative, the two ideologies seamlessly intertwine. In both cases, independently and compounded when merged, we are led to artificially limit ourselves in what we allow ourselves to know. Before Said was a Middle Eastern Studies icon, he was a literature professor steeped in postmodern deconstructionism. It's a sobering commentary on the War on Terror that our entire national security apparatus has been brought to its knees by a literature professor. This is the successful execution of Josef Pieper's abuse of language in anticipation of an abuse of power.

Assumptions, Presuppositions, and Fraud

As discussed, our analytical processes have devolved in a manner that puts assumptions at parity with facts. This is wrong. The problem created by the fact that assumptions and narratives can now take precedence over fact-based analysis is illustrated by instructions from an Army writing manual. Below is an excerpt from Chapter 2, "Effective Writing—From Tasking to Final Copy," of the U.S. Army Command and General Staff College manual *Writing and Speaking for Army Leaders* (CGSC *Writing Guide*):

> Reasoning must begin somewhere and must take some things for granted. Assumptions and presuppositions are those things we often take for granted without examining; they are a part of life. They are essential conditions for any course of action to occur. We must clearly identify why our assumptions and presuppositions are essential or not, and reject those that are not essential. The following can help determine if our assumptions and presuppositions are essential.[46]

> If the assumption or presupposition changes and the answer/conclusion changes, then it is essential.

> If the assumption or presupposition changes but the answer or conclusion does not change, then it is not essential.

Because our assumptions influence our reasoning, we must:

Clearly identify our assumptions and check for their probable validity.

Check the consistency of our assumptions.

Reexamine the question at issue when assumptions prove insupportable.

Wittingly or not, assignments associated with the CGSC *Writing Guide* are designed to enforce conformance to the postmodern standard. "Assumptions and presuppositions ... are essential conditions for any course of action to occur." Among the greatest concerns associated with this comment is that very few seem concerned by it. Notice the relative absence of the role of facts in this decision-making paradigm. Uncertainty is often thrust upon us by real-world circumstances, but that does not make it the legitimate *basis* of decision-making analysis. While it may be a necessary circumstance, it is not an "essential condition." In fact, it is the condition we most seek to avoid. From the CGSC *Writing* Guide, it is worth noting that the closest the narrative comes to stating a preference for facts is in the phrase "check for their probable validity." Analyzing to the "probable validity" standard is certainly an easier and safer standard than one that demands actual fact checking. "Probably right" is likewise an easier standard than "assessed to be factually true." One is subjective and the other objective. Only one is professional.

Analysis centered on assumptions and presuppositions puts the analytical center of gravity—the CGSC *Writing Guide*'s "essential condition"—in the non-factual domain. While such a process facilitates the development and easy maintenance of narratives, professional analysis must reconcile facts with circumstances. The *Writing Guide* implements a standard that makes the relationship between facts and assumptions ambiguous. Taught early in the Command and General Staff training cycle, the *Writing Guide* is used as part of a block of instruction that sets the standard for how correspondence is to be written. Once the premise of *The Writing Guide* is internalized, it becomes the first step in getting the officer corps to "drink the Kool-Aid."

Assumptions

The preference for assumption-based decision-making extends beyond CGSC writing requirements. The *Writing Guide* reflects how the *Joint Publication 5-0—Joint Operation Planning* (JP 5-0) manages assumptions. The *Joint Pubs* are fundamental guiding principles for U.S. Military forces. The series outlines "the distilled wisdom" of the military as it pertains to planning, training, and conducting military operations.[47] Versions of JP 5-0 were published in 2006, 2010, and 2011; all of them suggest a consistent preference for analysis in the absence of facts. Starting with the 2006 version of JP 5-0, we find "assumption" defined as:

> An **assumption** provides a supposition about the current situation or future course of events, **assumed to be true in the absence of facts**. Assumptions are necessary to enable the commander to complete an estimate of the situation and select the [course of action]. Assumptions that address gaps in knowledge are critical for the planning process to continue. For planning purposes, subordinate commanders treat assumptions made by higher headquarters as true in the absence of proof to the contrary. However, they should challenge those assumptions if they appear unrealistic. **Assumptions must be continually reviewed to ensure validity.**[48]

The October 2010 version provides a similar definition:

> An **assumption** provides a supposition about the current situation or future course of events, **assumed to be true in the absence of facts**. Planners make assumptions in the absence of facts, which are necessary to continue planning. Assumptions that address gaps in knowledge are critical for the planning process to continue. For planning purposes, subordinate commanders can treat assumptions made by higher headquarters as true in the absence of proof to the contrary. However, they should challenge those assumptions if they appear unrealistic. **Assumptions must be continually reviewed to ensure validity.**[49]

And, finally, the August 2011 version:

> An **assumption** provides a supposition about the current situation or future course of events, **assumed to be true in the absence of facts**. Assumptions that address gaps in knowledge are critical for the planning process to continue. For planning purposes, subordinate commanders can treat assumptions made by higher headquarters as true in the absence of proof to the contrary. However, they should challenge those assumptions if they appear unrealistic. **Assumptions must be continually reviewed to ensure validity.**[50]

The 2011 version of *JP* 5-0 added the term "assumption" to the glossary with a definition that deviates from the one used in the body of the text, replacing the term "absence of facts" with the subjective "absence of positive proof."[51] The three definitions share some common language that requires comment:

> An assumption provides a supposition ... assumed to be true in the absence of facts.

Consistent with the "absence of facts" understanding, *Black's Law Dictionary* defines assumptions as "the act of conceding or taking for granted."[52] Additionally, assumptions provide suppositions that are *conjecture*. As *Black's* explains, supposition is "conjecture based upon possibility or probability that a thing could or may have occurred **without proof that it did occur**,"[53] whereas "conjecture" provides:

> [a] slight degree of credence, arising from evidence too weak or too remote to cause belief. ... An idea or notion founded on a probability **without any demonstration of its truth**. ... In popular use, synonymous with "**guess**."[54]

The term "assumption" is easily the dominant analytical term used in *JP* 5-0. Returning to the *Joint Pub* definition, subordinates are encouraged to "challenge [their superiors'] assumptions if they appear unrealistic. And there is the reminder that assumptions must be continually reviewed to ensure validity." This language is reassuring until one puts it in the context of how the term "assumptions" is used in *JP* 5-0, which raises questions about the actual ability to seriously challenge those assumptions once they are put in motion. In the 2006 version, the issue comes into focus in a graphic titled, "Plan Review Criteria":

> The scope and concept of planned operations can accomplish the assigned mission and comply with the planning guidance provided. Are the assumptions **valid** and do they comply with strategic guidance. **Planning assumptions must be reasonable and consistent with planning guidance**.[55]

Do you see the problem here? *Black's Law Dictionary* defines "valid" as being "founded on truth of fact; capable of being justified; supported, or defended; not weak or defective."[56] Because *JP* 5-0 defines assumptions as operative in the "absence of fact," they cannot also be "founded on truth of fact," can never be "valid," and certainly cannot be "reasonable."

As important, the explanation makes it clear that the only "valid" and "reasonable" assumptions suitable for consideration are those that "comply with strategic guidance" and are "consistent with planning guidance." But assumptions that generate guidance are allowed to take on the status of facts—in the "absence of facts." When assumptions are converted to conclusions, they become conclusory assumptions.[57]

In other words, the only assumptions that can be challenged are those that do not violate the published guidance, even when those assumptions are used to formulate the guidance in the first place. The *Joint Pubs* use the language of certainty to qualify the language of uncertainty.

Why is this important? If our understanding of the enemy in the War on Terror is based on the assumption that the information our "cultural experts" and "moderates" provide us about the enemy and his environment is true and valid, then the war has been fought on the basis of conclusory assumptions founded on hearsay. This is made plausible by postmodern narratives grounded in pseudo-academic constructs. It's Josef Pieper's pseudoreality.

Our Commanders' Presuppositions

It doesn't end here. There is language in the *Joint Pubs'* definition of assumption that is discordant:

> For planning purposes, subordinate commanders treat assumptions made by higher headquarters as true in the absence of proof to the contrary.

As a thought experiment to get a sense for how this statement is perceived, when briefing military officers—majors, lieutenant colonels, and colonels—I would ask, "Do the assumptions of the seniors constitute the facts of the subordinate?"

Almost always, the class would roundly, collectively, and immediately answer in the affirmative. More than once, course instructors and students would validate this point by referring to the exact same reference in *JP* 5-0:

> For planning purposes, subordinate commanders can treat assumptions made by higher headquarters as true in the absence of proof to the contrary. However, they should challenge those assumptions if they appear unrealistic.[58]

While the officers focused on the first part of *JP* 5-0, for completeness of record, the second is also included. Some could argue that the *Joint Pub* does not actually say that "the assumptions of the seniors constitute the facts of the subordinate," and facially it doesn't. But as a practical matter, the *Joint Pub* leads officers to the conclusion that it does, and a year of polling bears that out—almost unanimously. "Assumptions made by higher" is understood to be guidance to "treat assumptions made by higher headquarters as true in the absence of proof to the contrary,"[59] where proof to the contrary can only be admitted if it does not violate the very guidance that was generated in the absence of facts. Challenging assumptions that support guidance is powerfully disfavored. By the time "assumptions from higher headquarters" reach the planners (always subordinate officers), there is already momentum. Also, challenging assumptions from higher headquarters often entails challenging the very seniors who make the assumptions and write subordinate fitness reports. The thought experiment also states: "Treat assumptions ... as true." *Black's* defines "true" as being:

> Conformable to fact; correct; exact; actual; genuine; honest. In one sense, that only is "true" which is conformable to the

actual state of things. In that sense, a statement is "untrue"
which does not express things exactly as they are. But in another and broader sense the word 'true' is often used as a
synonym of ... not "fraudulent."[60]

Given this definition, the *Joint Pub* requires subordinates to treat the "absence
of fact" as being "conformable to fact." Again, this qualifies the language of uncertainty with the language of certainty, blurring a bright line that should never
be blurred.

There is something chilling about the statement "the assumptions of the senior are the facts of the subordinate." When I raised this concern on Capitol Hill,
on more than one occasion, both Members of Congress and their staff would instantly recognize the statement's similarity to the old defense, "I was just following
orders."

The purpose of this analysis of *JP 5-0* is not to play word games. Words are
supposed to mean something, and the *Joint Pubs*, intentionally or not, blur the
distinction between facts and assumptions. These are not academic questions; the
nature and quality of a decision-makers' analysis concerns the national security of
this country, including the lives of the service members who defend it.

Black's definition of "true" lists one of its meanings as "not fraudulent." It defines "fraud" as:

> An intentional perversion of the truth for the purpose of
> inducing another in reliance upon it to part with some valu-
> able thing belonging to him or to surrender a legal right. A
> false representation of a matter of fact, whether by words
> or by conduct, by false or misleading allegations, or **by con-
> cealment of that which should have been disclosed** which
> deceives and is intended to deceive another so that he shall
> act upon it to his legal injury. Anything calculated to deceive,
> whether by a single act or combination, or by **suppression of
> truth**, or suggestion of what is false whether it be by direct
> falsehood or innuendo, by speech or silence, word of mouth,
> or look or gesture.[61]

Black's definition includes some pretty severe language. It might, not unrea-
sonably, lead some to be genuinely offended at even the suggestion of fraud. While
it can certainly be argued that there has been an institutionalized "perversion of
the truth," a "false representation of a matter of fact," a "concealment of that which
should have been disclosed," and a "suppression of truth," with few exceptions,
there is no intention of accusing anyone of having the requisite intent to be accused of fraud, and this book is not going to do so.

Nevertheless, as a reality check as to where we are in the War on Terror, the ongoing suppression of truth is nearly identical in outcome, if not intent. Our national security leadership is ignorant of what it ought to know, people are dying because of it, and the gravity of the situation is being suppressed. Certainly we are suffering from all the consequences of fraud and, irrespective of moral guilt, the public has been deceived as to the true nature of an existential threat. Indeed, the public's confidence has been violated; it has a right to demand that its representatives speak plainly, truthfully, and factually. While I am not willing to accuse anyone of fraud, there is an argument for constructive fraud.[62]/[2]

Given that the *Writing Guide*'s "assumptions and presuppositions" reflect the prevailing standard "for any course of action to occur," shouldn't facts as applied to known doctrines represent the preferred standard? It would certainly be a more professional standard. After defining "conjecture," *Black's* goes on to define a subordinate principle, the Rule of Conjectural Choice, to make it clear that analysis that is the product of conjecture (or assumption or presupposition) can never be used to support a judgment.[63] If assumptions cannot support a judgment, how can they be allowed to support decisions that concern life, national treasure, and national security?

Fraud

Returning to the CGSC *Writing Guide*, we begin to see how the U.S. Army's own educational system is imposing the postmodern narrative on officers being groomed for senior leadership. When assessing an analytical product, the *Guide* sidesteps the issue of fact-checking information:

---

2   NO PRIVATE LANGUAGES - The ongoing manipulation of terms and definitions discussed in *Joint Publication 5-0* speaks to a pervasive issue: the ongoing need to create and recreate terms and glossaries with both novel and shifting definitions. The problem is not with specialized terms that require discrete definitions, but rather with common terms with understood meanings that are nonetheless redefined in ways that deviate from the commonly understood meaning of the terms. Nothing devious is suggested here. The activity in large part can be explained by the creation of commands that exist to write and rewrite policies and doctrines alongside the need of incoming officers to make an impact by rewriting policies and doctrines to demonstrate that they had an impact in furtherance of career progression. But this can lead to the development of a bureaucratic equivalent to Wittgenstein's "private language" as discussed in his *Philosophical Investigations*. If not guarded against, this practice can give rise to yet another form of constructive fraud.

When speaking to the American public or testifying in oversight, the veracity of statements can be held together by the "private" meaning of terms that also have the effect of leading the public—or Members in oversight—to a different understanding of the same statement because the public understanding of what was said is based on common definitions of common terms. The use of "private language" should be disfavored. Those responsible for the production of such language should be held accountable for any confusion or misunderstanding brought about by the ambiguity created. This is simply the application of the ambiguity doctrine* to national security leaders, decision-makers, and analysts for the ambiguity they created in their communications.

Black's Law Dictionary, 9th Edition, West, 2009, 377. *Contra proferentem*. [Latin "against the offeror"] The doctrine that, in interpreting documents, ambiguities are to be construed unfavorably to the drafter. —Also spelled *contra proferentes*. —Also termed *ambiguity doctrine*.

> Clearly identify our assumptions and check for their prob-
> able validity. ... Check the consistency of our assumptions
> [and] reexamine the question at issue when assumptions
> prove insupportable.

Of course, assumptions can be consistently wrong. Wrong assumptions can
also influence an outcome, and relevant facts can register as neutral if the premise
is false. This is basic logic: Where a premise is false, the conclusion is unsound.

Many cadets in the U.S. military system—whether Army, Navy, Air Force,
Marines, or Coast Guard—have experienced that moment when, having committed some unpardonable sin, they are asked to explain themselves to the Professor
of Military Science. They say, "Well, sir, I just assumed ..." Of course, the professor's response is always, "Assumed? Do you know what it means to assume? It
makes an ass of you and me." The wisdom of this admonition remains true when
officers transition to more senior levels. Yet, starting at the Command and General
Staff College level, assumptions have become the standard and facts have become
passé.

As noted, the standard for decision-making analysis should always be the
analysis of facts, where the analytical process has a preference for facts built into
its methodology. Assumptions are to be tolerated in the absence of facts only as
necessary, and only as long as necessary. All three versions of *Joint Pub* 5-0 provide
the same solid definition:

> A fact is a statement of information known to be true (such as
> verified locations of friendly and adversary force dispositions).[64]

The preference for facts has not been a problem when the issue concerns
terrain, environment, force disposition, or even the kinetic side of threat operations. There is a clear preference for facts when understood as tangible things or
activities and are most immediately relevant to tactical and logistical planners. The
problem is with other types of facts—those in the form of non-concrete things
or facts from the world of thought and belief. Perhaps this is because there is an
unstated preference for characterizing nonphysical things as being not real and
hence non-factual, so their status in analysis is programmatically understood to be
an issue of "interpretation."

This leads to the conclusion that *shariah is not real*—and, consequently, cannot
serve as a doctrinal basis for al-Qaeda. Facts in the form of published doctrine
capable of actually explaining al-Qaeda, the Muslim Brotherhood, the Islamic
Movement, the OIC, and even Nidal Hasan at Fort Hood are met with silence
because shariah is not real. You've probably heard it said, "There are a thousand
different interpretations of shariah. It's all a matter of interpretation." It is through
such narratives that facts are affirmatively and systematically suppressed. This is
where our national security analytical framework breaks down. The postmodern

assault on thought targets the decision-making process by polluting its analytical inputs.

This observation generates blowback inside the national security community, even when it's demonstrated to be true. Two consecutively serving Joint Chief Chairmen engaged in the War on Terror publicly acknowledged an absence of threat awareness and the lack of a strategy. With extraordinary candor, General Pace said that "we have collectively ignored" what the enemy says, "to our great detriment."[65] General Myers frankly admitted that the "lack of a comprehensive global strategy has been a problem since 9/11" (i.e., from the very beginning) and that the "broader strategy never gets the attention and hard thought it deserves."[66] While President Obama was roundly criticized in August 2014 for saying that "we don't have a strategy"[67] regarding ISIS, the simple truth is that we've never had a (real) strategy to defeat al-Qaeda. We still don't. In a series of conference calls in late December 2014, the lead for U.S. Special Operations in charge of combating ISIS, MAJ General Michael Nagata, conceded, yet again, that "we do not understand the movement, and until we do, we are not going to defeat it ... we have not defeated the idea. We do not even understand the idea." [68]

The enemy knows he will win this war if he keeps us from identifying him. It is this simple: *you cannot defeat an enemy you refuse to define*, because *you cannot have a strategy to defeat what you will not know*. We have allowed third parties to become our main source of information about the enemy, even where there is evidence that those third parties do not share our objectives. To get past this, we convince ourselves that the events driving the War on Terror are complicated.

As long as we choose not to call him a jihadi and pretend that Islam does not influence his decision-making, we will not be able to defeat the enemy. Eventually, we will be defeated. The enemy knows this. How could he not? From the outside looking in, it's not hard to see we have no strategy.

Points of Failure

In 2006, the authors of the unclassified National Intelligence Estimate (NIE) disclosed what they believed to be the status of the War on Terror:

> We assess that the global jihadist movement is decentral-
> ized, lacks a coherent global strategy, and is becoming more
> diffuse.[69]

How many times have we heard this? Isn't this what we were being told as Jabhat al Nursa (al-Qaeda in Syria) and ISIS (al-Qaeda in Iraq) were cycling up? (Do we need to refer to al-Qaeda by its regional designations—al Nursa and ISIS—to avoid admitting that al-Qaeda was never defeated?) Does anyone really believe that our enemies have no "coherent global strategy"? It's possible that the authors of the report did not believe it themselves. The NIE forces us to pick between two points of failure:

- **Point of failure #1:** The National Intelligence Estimate is wrong; the enemy does have a strategy, but more than a decade into the War on Terror, we have not yet figured this out. In this case, we have a failure of intelligence.

- **Point of failure #2:** The National Intelligence Estimate is correct. The enemy does not have a strategy. In this case the world's most powerful country—the most powerful country in the history of the world—cannot defeat an incoherent enemy.

Both of these points have disastrous implications. We do, however, have stated strategies from multiple dawah and jihadi sources. From the Muslim Brotherhood's 1991 Explanatory Memorandum:

> The *Ikhwan* must understand that their work in America is a kind of grand Jihad in eliminating and destroying the Western civilization from within and "sabotaging" its miserable house by their hands.[70]

And then from the OIC's Ten-Year Programme of Action, as declared in 2005 at the Third Extraordinary Session:

> (To) endeavor to have the United Nations adopt an international resolution to counter Islamophobia and call upon all states to enact laws to counter it including deterrent punishment.[71]

These are hostile strategies. There is no understanding the Days of Rage we've witnessed since the passage of the Ten-Year Programme of Action without understanding their nexus to that Program.

In fact, our current response to these Days of Rage is a real-world manifestation of Pieper's observation on the collapse of coherent decision-making when operating in the pseudoreality. We are "knowledgeable about a thousand details" (regarding these Days of Rage) and yet have remained ignorant "regarding the core of the matter" (the Ten-Year Programme acting in furtherance of enforcing shariah speech law in non-Muslim jurisdictions) because we lack the situational awareness ("remain without basic insight") to understand the design.[72] In a year that opened with *Charlie Hebdo*, this is year ten of the Ten-Year Programme of Action.

Yet even knowing this—even with documents that were entered into evidence in a federal court of law, even with Days of Rage that lead to the intentional killing of Americans, even as we see ISIS roll up whole parts of Iraq—we throw up our hands and say there are no strategies oriented against us. Tens of billions of dollars a year spent on intelligence, and *this* is what we have? There are, indeed, threat strategies that we can access, comprehend, and effectively counter; we just have to make a decision to read them and understand them in the way the threat understands them. After all, this is the mission of our Intelligence Community.

Deliberate decision-making has been replaced by narrative enforcement. We have created an edifice that allows national security decision-makers to sidestep their duty to know—with the simple claim that it's "complicated." One cannot support and defend against all enemies, as the constitutional oath requires, if one is rendered incapable of understanding such basic concepts as "enemy"—a term actually disfavored at one point by U.S. Central Command.[73] Postmodern constructs deny the epistemic basis of concepts like enemy. But not understanding what an enemy is can have the effect of rendering one's oath to the Constitution a nullity, as it is the only thing national security professionals are sworn to "support and defend" against.

Hence, fidelity to decision-making models based on postmodern constructs not only violates professional standards, it may also lead to the violation of the oath to "support and defend" if there is no understanding of the concept of enemy from which to defend against.

"Violent extremist," the euphemism that replaced "enemy," masks this phenomenon. After all, once a person believes that the universe is too complex to understand, he has effectively abandoned his oath, knowingly or not. It is impossible to swear to "support and defend" against what one is convinced he lacks the capacity to know in a worldview that denies concepts like enemy. With the U.S. Army's publication of *The U.S. Army Operating Concept: Win in a Complex World - 2020-2040*[3] in October 2014, the narrative on complexity has become institutionalized.

"Violent Extremist" was instituted as a replacement term for the constitutional term, "enemy"; complexity theory gives us permission not to know what our national security oaths plainly require, and demands for "balance" have flooded the analytical process with counterfeit knowledge. The clear consequence, if not the objective, of the postmodern approach is that thought is rendered meaningless, leaving the community in a nihilist void. In the national security space, the anticipated outcome of such a process is paralysis brought on by an induced form of strategic incomprehension. This was a principle conclusion of my 2007 National Defense Intelligence College thesis:

> The cost of not understanding the enemy has been high and is getting higher every day. It will increasingly be measured by news stories that narrow in on senior leaders' inability to answer basic questions about the nature of the enemy and his

---

3   *The U.S. Army Operating Concept: Win in a Complex World - 2020-2040*, TRADOC Pamphlet 525-3-1, 31 October 2014, URL: http://www.tradoc.army.mil/tpubs/pams/TP525-3-1.pdf.

environment. It will also manifest itself in official responses to terrorist attacks that become progressively less reality-based.[74]

Are we not there? The War on Terror will be won or lost on our ability to
come to grips with precisely the issue of this postmodern rejection of reality. In
many respects, it's the most important issue to be resolved. It's the underlying
cause for our national security paralysis. Once the question of shariah and its
relationship to jihad is resolved, we will have to confront a more fundamental
problem, characterized by the questions: (1) why don't we know this? (2) why is it
suppressed? and (3) who is responsible for suppressing it?

Just beneath the surface of these questions lie the real "underlying causes" of
our national security paralysis that may have little to do with shariah, dawah, or
jihad beyond their setting the conditions for the enemy's success.

It is a fact that the people and entities we fight in the War on Terror openly
define themselves as jihadis who fight according to, and in furtherance of, shariah.

It is a fact that there are publications that reasonably present themselves as
shariah and that, in fact, validate "violent extremist" claims.

It is a fact that we refuse to comprehend this as part of the threat development process.

It is a fact that orienting on the self-identified enemy along with the self-identified basis for his threat doctrine is suppressed inside the national security and
law enforcement spaces.

And, finally, it is a fact that the current analytical preference for analysis based
on the "absence of facts" has effectively been used to suppress facts "known (or
knowable) to be true."

At some point, the institutionalized non-recognition of these facts will bring
about catastrophic failure and certain defeat. Tick-tock.

* * *

"Complexity theory," "balance" and "interpretation," and the limiting of
thought to that which lies on the "surface of events"—all this is influenced by
the postmodern paradigm that denies the role of knowledge as the basis for decsionmaking. Among the better treatments on the postmodern assault on thought
as it relates to the War on Terror is *The Death of the Grown-Up*, by Diana West.
The success of the book rests in part on West's ability to explain complex issues
through a popular history. West explains the phenomena in terms of the infantilization of thinking—how Americans (and the West) have devolved in their
thinking to the point where we think like children, thereby rendering ourselves
incapable of the level of thought required to properly engage the threat on the
plane of ideas. Expressed in terms of the changing relationship between parents
and children, West summarizes this phenomenon by reference to a change in the

response to the question "What do you want to be …?"

In the late 1940s, when parents asked, "What do you want to be when you grow up?" their teenagers would answer, "I want to be 'X' like my parents." Today, parents "want to be cool like their teenage kids." Thinking like adults used to equate to an ability to recognize existential threats for what they are and the will to take measures to defend against them. Today, we are missing this. We don't think on the same level as our enemy—precisely because we think like teenagers. We are outthought in the information domain and hence outmaneuvered in the information battlespace. As West strongly suggests, if we don't up our game, we will lose this war, our way of life, and our country.

The Duty to Know

You can't get second things by putting them first; you can get second things only by putting first things first.

C.S. Lewis,
Time and Tide,
Reprinted in *God in the Dock*, 1942[1]

[Just laws] serve the right end, that of affecting the happiness of those who enjoy them. They, in fact, secure them all good things. But there are two different kinds of good things, the merely human and the divine; the former are consequential on the latter. Hence a city which accepts the greater goods acquires the lesser along with them, but one which refuses them misses both. ... Of divine goods, the first and chiefest is ... wisdom, and next after it sobriety of spirit; a third, resulting from the blending of both of these with valor is righteousness, and valor itself is fourth.

Plato
The Laws 361b-d (360 BC)[2]

This book has described how America's national security establishment has rendered itself incapable of successfully predicting or investigating Islamic-based terror attacks at home and successfully prosecuting the War on Terror abroad. These catastrophic failures are marked by the high cost in American lives. In addition, it has explained how ignorance and disregard of shariah—the basis of the enemy's stated threat doctrine—is the successful result of an in-

---

1 Quoted by the Honorable Joseph E. Schmitz, former Inspector General of the Department of Defense, in The Inspector General Handbook: Fraud, Waste, Abuse, and Other Constitutional "Enemies, Foreign and Domestic," p. 459 (2013). Cited hereafter as Schmitz, IG Handbook.

2 Schmitz, IG Handbook, p. 460 n. 7.

fluence campaign of dawah, as understood by the Muslim Brotherhood and other proponents of the Milestones Process. It has shown how this campaign leverages targeted epistemic vulnerabilities in the national security space that facilitate a misplaced commitment to postmodern notions of "complexity" and "balance," which create the illusion that outsourcing of critical information requirements to academic theorists and self-described "moderates" from suspect organizations is reasonable. Lost is the fact that the person who controls the knowledge necessary to answer such critical information requirements controls the decisions that will be based on them.

Later chapters introduced the reader to the Organization of Islamic Cooperation (OIC), an entity that considers itself the "proto-Caliphate," and its Ten-Year Programme of Action to implement Islamic speech law globally. The program seeks to establish shariah speech laws that dictate what non-Muslims may know or say about the Qur'an, Islam, and its Prophet. By giving precedence to what the OIC, the Brotherhood, and other players in the Islamic Movement consider Islamophobic speech over War on Terror considerations, non-Muslim governments—including our own—are well along the road to *de facto* compliance.

Part 9 will focus on how the abandonment of proper analytic standards in the War on Terror, embodied in our government's campaign to counter Islamophobia, is not only wrong but also dangerously unconstitutional. It represents the actual rejection, by American officials, of their constitutional obligations in favor of what is, in fact, shariah.

This section will also explain how a return to constitutional requirements, professional threat analysis, and the enforcement of basic standards of professional and legal conduct represents a way forward from the induced strategic incomprehension in which we currently find ourselves.

A Matter of the Constitution: Core Values Revisited

As noted in the introduction, U.S. Navy Captain John Kirby, now Admiral Kirby, the Pentagon Spokesperson, distanced the Pentagon from people whose work product on the War on Terror was threat-centered, fact-based, and professional. He did this in November 2012 on an *Al-Jazeera* news program alongside known Muslim Brotherhood operatives. He added that such work product was "warped" and "not in keeping with our core values."

> The concern here is not so much that we would be spinning down and creating a cadre of individuals with these **warped views** but that it's not in keeping, frankly, this material is not in keeping with our **core values** and is not in keeping with **the strategy that we know we're out there executing**.[1]

As this book winds down, I leave it to the reader to decide whose orientation to the threat is warped. But Kirby raised an interesting question: By what criteria are our "core values" measured? Of course, they are supposed to be measured against our "first things"—the Constitution. When senior leaders speak on issues of national security, it is commonplace to hear them express feigned frustration that political correctness gets in the way of their doing their job. The response to such comments is generally one of acceptance evidenced by a lack of resolve. The frustration signals something like surrender. Yet, for those sworn to "support and defend the Constitution against all enemies," doesn't this mean that they put conformance to politically correct standards ahead of their oaths?[2]

The oath demands that all strategy begin with the Constitution—not with the Afghan people and not with vacuous notions of "violent extremism." There cannot be two masters: It's either the Constitution or the postmodern narrative. Already a professor at West Point teaches that the Constitution represents little more than the "nostalgic and romantic ideological aura" of extreme right-wing ideologues.[3] Mohamed Elibiary, Senior Homeland Security Advisor, extended this by merging it with Islamophobia when he stated on Twitter that the "Islamophobia movement promotes right wing self-radicalization and eventual violent extremism and terrorism" that calls for "a counter-radicalization strategy."[4]

Constitutions are among the very few documents that define a nation, govern its people, and stand for its guiding principles. It is through a constitution that the people know why they fight and for whom. You can't defend what you do not understand against an enemy you refuse to comprehend. Constitutions express a nation's "core values." If a nation loses sight of these values, it will be upside-down with Sun Tzu. This holds true for America. Our nation was founded by the Declaration of Independence. It is governed by the Constitution of the United States. These documents established and reflect our core values.

In the War on Terror, the enemy knows why he fights and is willing to sacrifice himself to that end. He believes! He also knows that Americans who don't understand why they fight will eventually stop fighting.

On First Things

Former Inspector General of the Department of Defense Joseph E. Schmitz's "Principle of First and Second Things"[5] influences this discussion on the strategic nature of the oath. As Schmitz explained, when people die, very few put on their tombstones the amount of money they made—even if they made a lot of it. As C.S. Lewis suggested, putting second things first often results in the loss of both. This is the same principle underlying what Josef Pieper referred to when he said, "one may be entirely knowledgeable about a thousand details and nevertheless, because of ignorance regarding the core of the matter, remain without basic insight."[6]

Losing sight of first things is what happened when our national security leaders vested America's success in Afghanistan in the hands of foreign nationals ahead of constitutional considerations that demand otherwise. For declared threats that lack the capacity to defeat a superior adversary through direct military engagement but have time, patience, and a doctrine that serves as an "organizing principle," getting their enemy to fight on terms that foreseeably generate consistently adverse results can become the focus of a strategy.

The decision not to use words like "enemy" in favor of terms like "violent extremist" reflects an enforced ambiguity that delegitimizes the use of national power. The constitutional requirement to swear an oath to the Constitution is the Constitution's way of demanding that it serve as our national first thing. As such, the oath is strategic. As it relates to the War on Terror, this book accepts Schmitz's observation that:

> As a nation, we have lost our understanding of America's founding principles and, as a result, have become increasingly ill prepared to defend the superiority of those principles. This puts us at a distinct disadvantage in being able to identify, understand and confront hostile doctrines—both foreign and domestic—that are in conflict with our own. The result of this combination of confusion and lassitude is that, in the face of Shariah's violent and stealthy jihadist assaults, our peace and prosperity are at risk to the point where the core tenets of our nation—and ultimately its very existence—are in jeopardy.[7]

For America, first things are to be found in this nation's founding documents. Mr. Schmitz continues:

> The authoritative statement of America's founding principles is the Declaration of Independence. The Declaration defines the most fundamental of these in this brief, yet sweepingly comprehensive, passage: "We hold these truths to be self-evident, that all men are created equal, that they are endowed by their Creator with certain unalienable Rights … That to secure these rights, Governments are instituted among Men, deriving their just powers from the consent of the governed."

> In conformity with the Declaration, the U.S. Constitution's Preamble is likewise clear in its purpose: "We the People of the United States, in Order to form a more perfect Union … and secure the Blessings of Liberty to ourselves and our Posterity, do ordain and establish this Constitution …

> "We the people," in ordaining and establishing our Consti-

tution for its stated purposes, consented to the same principles enumerated in our Declaration, in order to secure our natural rights and liberties. In this, "We the People" were acting in our sovereign capacity.[8]

The Constitution was written to require that it be the strategic focal point of all national security planning. The strategic nature of the oath derives from the fact that it constitutes the apex of what is supposed to be "supported and defended" when specifically directed against "enemies, foreign and domestic."[9] It is from this apex that all other considerations flow. It is Pieper's "core of the matter," providing "basic insight" into the "thousand details."

When examined from the perspective of this apex, one begins to see, for example, that the "Violent Extremist" narrative has dire consequences. By seeking to deny the concept of enemy, it undermines the basis of the oath. It casts as "extreme" those who would swear to it and "violently extreme" those who would support and defend it. This corrosive narrative replaces *bona fide* threat analysis with Muslim Brotherhood–approved academic abstractions designed to ambiguate the actual threat.

Still the law of Land—Isn't It?

Campaigns to counter Islamophobia are an assault on constitutionally protected speech and are calculated to control people's understanding of events. In this regard, the expansive definition of Islamophobia is intended to be used as a weapon, as it links criticism of Islam or Muslims with racism and incitement to violence. Within the U.S. government, the Department of Homeland Security's Civil Rights and Civil Liberties (CRCL) division is perhaps the most aggressive in leading the charge, likening disapproval of the Islamic legal system to racism. In this way, the CRCL treatment of Islamophobia merges with the shariah requirements underlying the OIC's initiative. CRCL's 2011 Countering Violent Extremism training requirements stipulate that:

> [t]raining should support the protection of civil rights and civil liberties as part of national security. **Don't use training that equates religious expression**, protests, or other constitutionally protected activity **with criminal activity**.[10]

This raises a series of first-order questions in need of answers. Yes or no— Does the First Amendment:

1 Provide the right to kill in furtherance of foreign law in the name of belief?

2 Allow for the establishment of foreign law as the law of

the land in the United States in furtherance of giving
full effect to that faith?

While they may seem abstract, these questions are raised because a principle
objective of the threat we are facing in the War on Terror is the successful manipulation of the First Amendment. Both the Muslim Brotherhood and the OIC
would answer both questions in the affirmative. In fact, the Constitution's clear
prohibitions on both questions are targets of the countering Islamophobia campaign. For those who have taken the oath to support and defend the Constitution,
however, the answer should be a resounding "no."

Of course, the First Amendment says nothing about a right to kill in furtherance of the establishment of foreign law in the name of belief, as is required under
shariah. Nor does it allow for the establishment of a foreign law as the law of the
land under religious guise. Here's what the First Amendment says:

> Congress shall make no law respecting an establishment of
> religion, or prohibiting the free exercise thereof; or abridging
> the freedom of speech, or of the press; or the right of the
> people peaceably to assemble, and to petition the Govern-
> ment for a redress of grievances.

Not only does the First Amendment not authorize such imposition of foreign
law, but the Constitution prohibits it. Article VI of the Constitution states:

> All Debts contracted and Engagements entered into, before
> the Adoption of this Constitution, shall be as valid against
> the United States under this Constitution, as under the
> Confederation.

> **This Constitution**, and the Laws of the United States which
> shall be made in Pursuance thereof; and all Treaties made,
> or which shall be made, under the Authority of the Unit-
> ed States, **shall be the supreme Law of the Land**; and the
> Judges in every State shall be bound thereby, any Thing in
> the Constitution or Laws of any State to the Contrary not-
> withstanding.

> The Senators and Representatives before mentioned, and the
> Members of the several State Legislatures, and all executive
> and judicial Officers, both of the United States and of the
> several States, shall be bound by Oath or Affirmation, to
> support this Constitution; **but no religious Test shall ever
> be required as a Qualification to any Office or public Trust
> under the United States**.[11]

This raises the next set of first-order questions. Does Article VI:

1 Still apply?

2 Apply to the Muslim Brotherhood in America along with related Islamic Movement organizations that seek to establish shariah law in the land?

As it relates to this discussion, Article VI says three things: (1) the Constitution is the supreme law of the land; (2) public officials shall be bound by oath or affirmation to support the Constitution; and (3) no religious tests shall ever be required as qualification to any office.

When working in the national security space, one hears almost nothing about Article VI of the Constitution from the very people who raise First Amendment questions as a pretext for not analyzing the enemy's stated threat doctrine, as their positions require. Rather, many national security professionals have chosen not to analyze threats because of their own idiosyncratic notions of free speech and religion that often lack any *bona fide* judicial or rule-of-law concern, while their *raison d'être*—giving full effect to the Article VI requirement to "support and defend" the Constitution—is left exposed. While all consideration should be given to the judiciary when upholding our constitutional rights—including, of course, the constitutional rights of Muslims—it is paramount that national security professionals remember that their designated role in the government is, most directly, to "support and defend." They should let judges worry about First Amendment concerns. The Supreme Court will be sure to let them know if they cross the line.

When national security leaders, decision-makers, and analysts say political correctness gets in the way of their doing their job, think about what this means in the context of Article VI. They are acknowledging that fidelity to the postmodern narrative—to political correctness—has taken precedence over their oaths to support and defend the Constitution. For the same reason one cannot do threat-based analysis of the enemy in the War on Terror and conform to Muslim Brotherhood guidelines, one also cannot enforce the National Security Act, not to mention Article VI of the Constitution, and enforce Islamophobia policies. The one denies the other.

The term "Islamophobia" was created by the Muslim Brotherhood in America and evolved under the influence of foreign powers for the purpose of affecting a hostile foreign influence over free speech standards in non-Muslim countries, including the United States. The term is specifically directed against the First Amendment of the Constitution. The intended opportunity cost of conforming to Islamophobia standards is the suspension of one's critical capabilities to the point where they interfere with one's capacity to comply with the oath to "support and defend." If one conforms to Islamophobia standards, one will not undertake real threat analysis. If one does undertake real threat analysis, the Muslim Brotherhood is exposed as a major subversive threat. The Islamophobia narrative exists to blind us to entities like the Muslim Brotherhood in America. Unfortunately, our national security establishment is among those most blinded.

Putting aside the historical requirements of the first section of Article VI (regarding debts), the War on Terror is being fought in a manner that makes a mockery of its remaining three elements.

Yes, Still the Law of the Land

In the second clause of Article VI, we see the basis for the conflict between the Constitution and shariah. It states that the Constitution "shall be the supreme law of the land." As demonstrated, shariah contains its own notions of legal supremacy and aspires to be "the law of the land" as well. For example, recall Abdur Rahman Doi's comment in *Shari'ah: The Islamic Law*:

> In the Shari'ah, there is an explicit emphasis on the fact that Allah is the Lawgiver and the whole Ummah, the nation of Islam, is merely His trustee. **It is because of this principle that the Ummah enjoys a derivative rule-making power** and not an absolute law-creating prerogative.[12]

As revealed law, shariah must rule supreme over man-man law, and its adherents are obligated to supplant secular law, just as Qutb wrote in *Milestones*:

> This religion is really a universal declaration of the freedom of man from servitude to other men and from servitude to his own desires, which is also a form of human servitude; it is a declaration that sovereignty belongs to God alone and that He is the Lord of all the worlds. It means a challenge to all kinds and forms of systems which are based on the concept of the sovereignty of man; in other words, where man has usurped the Divine attribute. Any system in which the final decisions are referred to human beings, and in which the sources of all authority are human, deifies human beings by designating others than God as lords over men. This declaration means that the usurped authority of God be returned to Him and the usurpers be thrown out-those who by themselves devise laws for others to follow, thus elevating themselves to the status of lords and reducing others to the status of slaves. In short, to proclaim the authority and sovereignty of God means to eliminate all human kingship and to announce the rule of the Sustainer of the universe over the entire earth.[13]

> Whenever an Islamic Community exists which is a concrete example of the Divinely-ordained system of life, it has a God-given right to step forward and take control of the political authority so that it may establish the Divine system on earth.[14]

There is no mystery here. Because Islamic law makes unambiguous claims to being the law of the land, to the extent that shariah legal prohibitions are enforced against an American's enumerated rights in contravention of U.S. law—knowingly or not—Article VI is violated.

If Article VI of the Constitution states that the Constitution shall be the supreme law of the land, and if we allow Islamic notions of defamation to control the inputs to our understanding of the nature of that threat, then haven't we *de facto* put our fidelity to combating Islamophobia ahead of our oaths to the Constitution? Because the effort to combat Islamophobia is in the service of an OIC program to import Islamic legal doctrines of defamation into our free speech codes, we are subordinating the Constitution to a foreign legal standard. This is actual submission. The question of whether the national security community has submitted to Islamic law is more serious than you might think.

> Article VI is violated in the first instance ("This Constitution … shall be the supreme Law of the Land") because, under the guise of combating Islamophobia, constitutional requirements have been subordinated to what shariah allows us to know. This is not just because the Pact of Umar, *Tafsir Ibn Kathir*, *Reliance of the Traveller*, and Kamali's *Freedom of Expression in Islam* demonstrate that such law exists in both classical and contemporary forms. It's also because the OIC has an active Ten-Year Programme to impose those same defamation requirements on every jurisdiction in the world. This is what the State Department threw its support behind when agreeing to use its best efforts to secure passage of UN Resolution 16/18. As 2015 is the tenth year of that ten-year program, it should not go unnoticed that *Charlie Hebdo* happened in the first week of the year.

> If it's true that the DHS's Office of Civil Rights and Civil Liberties campaign to fight Islamophobia maps to the OIC language, the CRCL is enforcing a hostile foreign legal standard on the free speech rights of American citizens inside the United States over and against the exercise of their First Amendment rights. To the extent that CRCL's enforcement of such a standard is imposed on government employees and contractors, it forces employees and contractors in national

security and law enforcement spaces to make a choice between fidelity to their oath to the Constitution and keeping their jobs. This is the second way Article VI ("The Senators and Representatives before mentioned, and the Members of the several State Legislatures, and all executive and judicial Officers, both of the United States and of the several States, shall be bound by Oath or Affirmation, to support this Constitution") is violated—by interfering with the taking and keeping of one's oath by enforcing non-compliance to that oath. If the various countering Islamophobia campaigns are aligned with foreign law, both enforcement and compliance of such a standard should be unlawful.

The Strategic Dimension of the Oath

The requirement that one swear an oath to the Constitution is unconditional. When a conflict exists between one's oath and some postmodern construct that cannot be resolved in favor of the Constitution, those beholden to the oath have a duty to resign. Given the strategic nature of the oath, conflicts are impermissible—that's why it's required.

The oath that was mandated by Article VI of the Constitution is found in the United States Code. As the Constitution requires, the oath is incident to entrance into all branches of government: the executive branch (and is required of all officers), the legislative branch (starting with Members of Congress), and the judicial branch (including all judges—local, state, and national).[15] With the exception of the president, anybody seeking to hold a position of responsibility in government is required to take the Title V Oath located at Title V, United States Code, § 3331:

> An individual, except the President, elected or appointed to an office of honor or profit in the civil service or uniformed services, shall take the following oath:
>
> "I, AB, do solemnly swear (or affirm) that I will **support and defend the Constitution of the United States against all enemies, foreign and domestic**; that I will bear true faith and allegiance to the same; that I take this obligation freely, without any mental reservation or purpose of evasion; and that I will well and faithfully discharge the duties of the office on which I am about to enter. So help me God." This section does not affect other oaths required by law.[16]

For those taking it, the Title V Oath is the Constitutional Oath. While it may seem obvious, it must be stressed that neither Article VI of the Constitution nor Title V USC §3331 says anything about "violent extremism." There is no constitutional mandate to combat "violent extremism." There is only a requirement "to support and defend the Constitution against all **enemies**, foreign and domestic."

It is from the legal obligation to support and defend the Constitution from all enemies that the various officers and officials of the Department of Defense derive their duties and their legitimacy. There is no requirement to abstract the nature of the enemy so as to avoid being accused of Islamophobia by the politically correct. One can spend an entire career "countering violent extremism" and yet never spend a moment "supporting and defending against all enemies." This is a real problem: To the extent that our national security and law enforcement organizations have swapped out "enemies" with "violent extremism," those organizations have been dislocated from their constitutional mandate.

This can be true even when al-Qaeda is being successfully engaged in kinetic operations that conform to DHS's Countering Violent Extremism standards. Fidelity to the CVE narrative can cause confusion regarding the difference between killing a declared enemy—which can be justified under the obligation to "support and defend"—and neutralizing "violent extremists," an action for which no constitutional authority exists.

What are "violent extremists"? As DHS made clear, "violent extremists" can include American citizens who take seriously the duty to "support and defend" the Constitution by serving in the nation's armed forces or by otherwise defending it as, for example, with the prosecutors at Justice or the special agents at the FBI and DHS when engaging in disfavored activities. While this last point makes no sense from the perspective of their duty to "support and defend" the Constitution, it does fit the postmodern paradigm that "violent extremism" was manufactured to support, first by facially emulating the role of supporting and defending the Constitution and then by appropriating that mission to the service of postmodern objectives. The very use of the "violent extremism" narrative in government agencies overwrites the statutory missions of those agencies. This is what Pieper was referring to when he spoke of "the deceptive mirage of the political process, that is, the counterfeit usurpation of power, a power that belongs to the legitimate political authority alone."[17] The margin by which current "Countering Violent Extremism" efforts are unmoored from statutory missions or the "support and defend" mandate is the margin that separates constitutional requirements from postmodern preferences.

Religious Tests

The final assault on Article VI ("but no religious test shall ever be required as a qualification to any office or public trust under the United States") has already been covered in the context of our earlier discussion about the "these aren't the droids you're looking for" phenomenon. As noted, early in the war, Islamic-identity groups were made the arbiters of what to include in threat analysis of the enemy in the War on Terror. The immediate result of this has been the subordination of the oath to "support and defend" to the requirement not to offend—or not to "inflame" Islam. When this happens, our national security takes a back seat to the Islamic sensitivities enumerated by members of the Islamic Movement, who have openly declared their goal of destroying America from within. This is submission as prescribed by shariah, implemented in just the way the Muslim Brotherhood and the OIC envisioned. Just look at how often national security leaders are silenced by reference to the overriding requirement not to "inflame" feelings (analogous to the Battered Wife Syndrome.)

The intentional effect of this information campaign is to silence qualified non-Muslim officers, special agents and analysts who understand the problems they are tasked to analyze and articulate their products in a factual, professional manner. They are suppressed, and this is wrong. Article VI of the Constitution states that "no religious test shall ever be required as a qualification to any office or public trust," and yet it has become the *de facto* standard that information and consultation about the War on Terror come only from Muslims.

A Reality-Based Threat Doctrine Analysis

If we are to arrest the damage that our present course of action has inflicted on our national security, we can do so only by returning to proven methods of threat analysis. National security officials have a constitutional obligation to "support and defend against all enemies," but in order to do that, they must first know the enemy. The knowledge that drives our analysis cannot be based on pseudoscientific models or the hearsay of self-declared "moderates," for this is not knowledge at all. Rather, the information requirements that drive work product in national security analysis need to meet professional standards of competency while also conforming to the constitutional mandate.

To accomplish this objective, our analysis of the enemy's stated threat doctrine must meet the classic *IPB Manual*'s requirements of being threat-focused and unconstrained by outside considerations. There can be no blue in the red. Recall the Green Cheese Doctrine discussion from earlier. To qualify as a threat doctrine, all that matters is that there is a doctrine, people affiliate with it, and those people seek to kill Americans because of it. If these requirements are met, then the doctrine must become the object of a serious and professional threat analysis. It's just that simple.

Unless we orient on the enemy's stated doctrine by undertaking threat analysis, we cannot generate credible enemy courses of action. In that case, our warfighting narrative is reduced to incoherence. We end up fighting without knowing why or for whom. In short, we become the weapon for our own defeat.

The Dislocation of Our Faith – in Process

In national or homeland security, those who impose a politically sanitized threat vocabulary from higher up—as DHS began doing in 2008[18]—are ordering their subordinates to violate professional canons, thus undermining their ability to "support and defend." Such an order should be unlawful to issue and unlawful to obey. Subordinates at all levels perceive the lack of professionalism and, consequently, have lost faith in their leadership. Insofar as undermining the analytical process causes a loss of confidence, the leadership is subverting its own command. Call it the downward subversion of the chain of command: the officers won't revolt; they will simply leave the service. And there is evidence the best and the brightest are doing just that.

Recall that Brigadier S.K Malik, in his *Qur'anic Concept of War*, explained how a principal objective in the application of terror in the Islamic concept of war is to dislocate the enemy's faith in preparation for his initiation of the "war of muscle":

> To instill terror into the hearts of the enemy is essential in the ultimate analysis to **dislocate his faith**. An invincible faith is immune to terror. A weak faith offers inroads to terror. … Terror cannot be struck into the hearts of an army by merely cutting its lines of communication or depriving it of its routes to withdraw. It is basically related to the strength or weakness of the human soul. **It can be instilled only if the opponent's faith is destroyed.**[19]

If the West Point survey is an indicator, then the destruction of our officers' faith in their leaders is well underway. The only way we can restore faith is by restoring professional standards that subordinates can recognize and rely on—standards that enable members of our national security apparatus, from policymakers to low-ranking warfighters, to properly orient on the "support and defend" mission against real enemies, foreign and domestic. The strategic nature of the constitutional oath demands that these professional standards be grounded in the Constitution. There can be no conflict.

A Professional Standard

We need to step back and re-examine our evaluation of the true nature of threats posed to America, especially in the War on Terror. We need a back-to-basics approach to threat analysis, one that is based on evidentiary analysis that keeps Sun Tzu's charge to "know the enemy and yourself" at the forefront.

Among the best and most basic doctrines of threat analysis is that contained in classic *IPB Manual*, which used to be taught to newly minted second lieutenants. At the core of the IPB effort is the production of a fact-based, threat-centered doctrinal template that is unconstrained by the effects of the environment—including pop-science fads and issues of political correctness on the blue side. This core "know the enemy" methodology should remain fixed at the front of all threat-analysis production, both tactical and strategic. There must be an institutionalized preference for first-order accuracy based on facts.

So long as such a process is followed with data that is evidentiary and can be validated, the chips should be allowed to fall where they may—regardless of whether they are "inflammatory" and trigger accusations of Islamophobia.[20] In fact, an analysis that is valid and "inflammatory" should defeat one that is invalid and "sensitive" every time.

The term "inflammatory" has emerged in Department of Defense talking points that undermine professional analysis by enforcing the Battered Wife Syndrome narrative. For example, in an email to the congressional committees, the Joint Staff Legislative Affairs Office made the following statement regarding the training material used at the Joint Forces Staff College: "An initial review reveals that some of the material (1) included reckless, inflammatory courses of action to deal with Islam."[21]

Of course, my briefings on abrogation are thought to be "inflammatory" by those who don't want it discussed. But as the explanation of this doctrine demonstrates, especially when understood alongside the *Milestones* process and Major Hasan's decision to kill, it is relevant in the War on Terror. A factual analysis would have revealed this—and, in fact, it did. It was briefed years in advance of the Fort Hood event. While the material may have struck some as inflammatory, it was nonetheless correct and used to provide actual warning in advance of events that did occur.

Unfortunately, because it was deemed "inflammatory" and therefore disfavored by the leadership, we chose to blind ourselves to the analytical processes that drive the enemy's decision-making process. And people are dead because of it.

When Assistant Secretary of Defense Paul Stockton told Rep. Lungren that "inflammatory rhetoric of the sort associated with Major Hasan … needs to be reported—and our officers are trained up now to report on that behavior,"[22] it's reasonably clear this was not the answer Rep. Lungren was looking for. Rather, the representative was raising his concern that Stockton's "behavioral indicators" were supporting "politically correct" narratives that purposefully obscured the nexus between Major Hasan's actions and the jihadi doctrines that inspired them.[23] Lieutenant General George Flynn's statement also highlights how "inflammatory" has become a DoD talking point and shows how the training of our fighting forces has been subordinated to not upsetting our foes:

> "It was inflammatory," Flynn told Danger Room on Tuesday. "We said, 'Wait a second, that's really not what we're talking about.' That is not how we view this problem or the challenges we have in the world today."[24]

The Joint Staff general is correct—"that's really not what we're talking about"—which, of course, is the problem. Would Chesty Puller have suspended threat analysis of the Japanese or the North Koreans had either accused his analytical processes of being "inflammatory"? To whose "core values" does this activity map?[25]

"Inflammatory" is the new DoD term for the analytical threshold that cannot be overstepped. Hence, a competent, accurate, and valid threat analysis can be suppressed simply because it "inflames" someone. Now, all that Muslim Brotherhood front groups need do to suppress meaningful threat analysis is be "inflamed." This has been the underlying objective driving the Days of Rage strategy since the Cartoon Crisis. Subordinating professional work product to what does not inflame should be viewed as an undue command influence that undermines the integrity of the work product in question. And because an accusation of being inflammatory has become a relief-for-cause issue, this is a serious concern. Just ask the officers at the Joint Forces Staff College.[26]

Alongside Sun Tzu's charge to "know the enemy" is the constitutional mandate to support and defend. As national security careers matriculate to professional levels, their policy production, decision-making, and analysis should be held to broadly recognized professional canons that reflect conformance to these twin requirements.

If one undertakes proper threat identification, he will be able to "support and defend" against actual threats that have been properly identified. Conversely, if one "supports and defends" against all enemies, he will have to undertake an effort to know who that enemy actually is by doing real threat analysis. There is a perfect symmetry between the national security requirement and the constitutional mandate; the failure of one necessarily causes a breach of the other.

Professionals in the national security community have a duty to know what the requirements of national security demand that they know. There must be enforceable standards by which national security professionals can be held accountable for not knowing what ought to have been known. This is about instituting professional-competency requirements in the national security space. By way of comparison, a review of the American Bar Association's Model Rules of Professional Conduct Rule 1.1 serves as a good baseline for the duty to be competent:

> Using the *Model Rules of Professional Conduct* as a point of reference, they hold that professionals, in this case attorneys, have a duty to be competent[27] that includes the requirement to inform oneself of the subject matter[28] by taking the necessary time to prepare oneself to a standard of preparedness necessary to provide successful representation.[29]

Embedded in the duty to be competent is the duty to know. Americans have a reasonable expectation that a comparable standard exist in the national security community: A professional in this field has a duty to "inform [himself] of the subject matter by taking the necessary time to prepare [himself] to a standard of preparedness necessary to understand" threats to the United States as they present themselves *in fact*. The duty to know is not the duty to assume. As discussed previously, decision-making based on mere assumptions and presuppositions falls below the competency standard for professionals. Yet this is the current baseline for decision-making in military planning. Analysis based on assumptions and presuppositions is a form of prejudice.[30] From the perspective of the professional standard, it reasonably follows that:

- Assumptions should always yield to facts.
- Statements based on facts are always superior to statements based on assumptions. (Reason always trumps authority.)
- Analysis based on facts is always superior to analysis based on assumptions. (Factual analysis of a threat is always superior to analysis based on assumptions about that same threat.)
- Fact-based models are superior to assumption-based (narrative enforcement) models.
- Behavioral indicators pegged to the fact of the threat are superior to behavioral indicators pegged to narratives in support of soft-science models.
- Theoretical descriptors of a thing should always be subordinated to factual descriptors of the same thing.
- Theoretical descriptors of a thing should never be used in decision-support analysis where factual descriptors exist capable of serving that function.
- Theoretical descriptors should never be used when factual descriptors exist.
- Relevant facts should never be made to compete on an equal basis with assumptions.
- Methodologies that permit competition between relevant facts and assumptions should be suspect for that reason.
- Enforcement of the theoretical in the face of established facts should be considered unlawful when ordered and malpractice when obeyed.

This establishes a preference for the factual and professional that gives rise to questions concerning the relationship between one's professional canons and the oath to "support and defend" when working in the national security realm:

> Does the duty to protect and defend against all enemies create a requirement to know all enemies (or to at least under-

take a reasonable due-diligence effort to do so)?

Does the "*well and faithful*" discharge of a duty call for a standard that requires that the duty be competently discharged?

These questions are easily answered in the affirmative and set up the central question:

> For national security professionals with War on Terror responsibilities, does the decision not to know an enemy violate professional rules of competency in ways that give rise to a failure to meet the constitutional duty to support and defend against all enemies?

As the question indicates, professional canons in the national security space reinforce the oath because they are grounded in the Article VI requirement to "support and defend." Measured in terms of opportunity cost, at what point does the decision to divert all elements of national power to the fiction of "violent extremism" at the expense of the enemy-in-fact constitute a violation of the oath in its own right?

In recognition of the dual duties of competence and knowledge, all parties responsible for policy, decision-making, and analysis should be U.S. citizens beholden to professional canons and to the oaths they have taken. Persons beholden to this standard should be held accountable for being able to answer these basic questions in an evidentiary manner:

- Who is the enemy?
- What is his doctrine?
- What do we know about him?
- How does his doctrine relate to his environment?
- What are his goals?

One could easily add "-in-fact" at the end of each of the above bullets. Along with preferring evidentiary analytical processes, we should measure all truly professional analytical products by the results that would have been known had such processes been followed—regardless of whether they were. This is imperative, and doing so would fix the imbalance caused by deference to soft-science theories driven by malleable models outsourced to third parties. To give this approach some teeth, the old methodology needs to be supported by a new form of accountability, holding policymakers, decision-makers, and analysts accountable for failures of awareness *that would have been avoided had an evidentiary process been used.*

Res Ipsa Loquitur

A standard of accountability for the national security community could emulate a doctrine from civil litigation concerning negligence known as *res ipsa loquitur*.

The doctrine—a Latin term meaning "the thing speaks for itself"—is a rule of evidence that holds that, where an entity has exclusive control and something goes wrong that would not have done so had the responsible person acted properly, the mere fact of something going wrong will give rise to a rebuttable presumption[31] that the alleged wrongdoer was negligent in the performance of his or her duty.[3]

In essence, application of a *res ipsa* schema holds that, given a certain fact pattern, the mere fact that an accident occurred (a terrorist event) and that the act (or, in this case, the policy, decision, or analysis) was under the exclusive control of the alleged wrongdoer (senior analyst, decision-maker or command) raises a rebuttable presumption that the alleged wrongdoer was negligent in the performance of his or her duty. More simply stated, if a terrorist event occurs and the information about it was apparent, tangibly available and under the control of the senior analyst, decision-maker or command, then a rebuttable presumption should arise that the analyst or decision-maker was negligent in the performance of his or her duty because, had the information been competently analyzed by known processes, the event would not have occurred.

This proposed way forward calls for holding all national security leaders and professionals accountable for what they could have known had reasonable due diligence been undertaken to know. The reasoning goes like this: You had access to information that could have been converted to knowledge that would have provided indicators and warning; you could have known it, you had a duty to know it, and yet you made a decision not to know it (or knowingly ignored it); and bad things happened that would not have happened had you known what should have been known and taken appropriate action. Please note that the *res ipsa* schema is focused on analytical processes and should not be onerous. It is a check on analytical processes, not on warfighting decisions. *Such a test would not be used—and would not be appropriate for use—in normal combat situations where the "fog of war" can be unforgiving.*

---

3   From *Black's*, *res ipsa loquitur* is a: "Rebuttable presumption or inference that defendant was negligent, which arises upon proof that instrumentality causing injury was in defendant's exclusive control, and that the accident was one which ordinarily does not happen in absence of negligence. *Res ipsa loquitur* is rule of evidence whereby negligence of alleged wrongdoer may be inferred from mere fact that accident happened provided character of accident and circumstances attending it lead reasonably to belief that in absence of negligence it would not have occurred and that thing which caused injury is shown to have been under management and control of alleged wrongdoer. ... **When a thing which causes injury, without fault of injured person, is shown to be under exclusive control of defendant, and injury is such as in ordinary course of things does not occur if the one having such control used proper care**, it affords reasonable evidence, in absence of an explanation, **that injury arose from defendant's want of care**." *Black's Law Dictionary 6ᵗʰ*, 1305.

As applied here, *res ipsa loquitur* reestablishes the line that should separate professional from unprofessional work product. Excuses about "unintended consequences," for example, should be used only in conjunction with a demonstration of proof that a competent threat analysis would not have foreseen the activity causing things to go wrong. "Unintended consequences" should not be allowed to excuse failures that reflect fidelity to narratives. From the Fort Hood shooting to the Ten-Year Programme of Action to the Boston Marathon Bombing, a *res ipsa* assessment of our threat analysis processes would reveal consistently depressing—but accurate—results.

Recognition must also be given to the downstream effects of replacing factual analysis with soft-science models designed to filter out disfavored facts that would otherwise constitute relevant evidence (or validated indicators capable of providing warning) in favor of narrative enforcement designed to support policy preferences that validate favored models.

While *res ipsa loquitur* is directed toward the negligent activity itself, there is also the matter of communicating the national security picture based on faux narratives that displace cause-in-fact explanations. The narratives arising out of such degraded processes falsely represent what are otherwise knowable matters of fact and, as such, constitute a form of disinformation and even fraud.[32]

What else but "concealment of that which should be known"[33] describes the decisions to suspend threat analysis against groups like al-Qaeda—whose doctrines are self-declared and explicitly based on shariah—and then communicate al-Qaeda activities using CVE narratives that are false and incoherent? Yet, this is exactly what DHS's CRCL does with its 2011 "Countering Violent Extremism (CVE) Training Guidance & Best Practices" manual.[34] Using the "violent extremism" narrative as a replacement for evidence-based work product has the effect of withholding or suppressing evidence by replacing (or prohibiting) explanations that would otherwise inform.[35] "Violent extremism" subordinates facts to ideological considerations. To the extent that its enforcement leads to tragic downstream consequences, neither the Countering Violent Extremism narrative nor the policymakers and analysts who embrace it would survive a *res ipsa* review. The CVE narrative and the priorities behind it constitute one of the "big lies" of this war.

This "violent extremism" narrative was evident in this statement by Assistant Secretary of Defense Paul Stockton:

> Sir, with great respect, I don't believe it's helpful to frame our adversary as Islamic with any set of qualifiers that we might add, because we are not at war with Islam.[36]

Violent extremism is not real—it exists to mask the real. Just because Secretary Stockton closed his eyes doesn't mean that al-Qaeda's jihad doctrines are not there—or that Americans are not being killed because of them. For the national security and law enforcement communities, the priority in the War on Terror has been to subordinate U.S. national security interests to the requirement not to offend Islam—that is, not to be "inflammatory."

The *res ipsa* test should also be applied to subordinate decision-makers and analysts whose specialized training, expertise, and status reasonably qualify them as professionals. Rationales to be disfavored would include the "I was just following orders" defense, often masked in the claim, "I was just following policy" or "I was only complying with the requirement of the model."

Really, when you get down to it, the point is simple: National security professionals should be held to the same professional standards to which non-governmental professionals are held in the conduct of their professional responsibilities.

Call it Obstruction

The *res ipsa* test exposes those who lack the discernment to understand that they do not know what they have a duty to know. But there is also the more serious issue of those who actively suppress relevant facts and doctrines. Underlying the proposed *res ipsa* standard is the operating assumption that those engaged in negligent activity are unaware of their own strategic incomprehension. This assumption is itself debatable. When senior leaders act to undermine or impede competent analysis capable of demonstrating a position's factual basis, that action should be understood to be a form of obstruction. It is of the same nature and kind as that which the legal community recognizes as obstruction of justice, and it should be treated similarly. Obstruction of justice is defined as:

> Interference with the orderly administration of law and justice, as by giving false information to or withholding evidence from a police officer or prosecutor, or by harming or intimidating a witness or juror.[37]

Obstruction of justice is a crime. In circumstances where competent threat analysis is obstructed or analysts are intimidated into suspending such analysis, an enforceable national security standard should be enacted that effectively puts senior leaders on notice of serious consequences similar to those for obstruction of justice in the legal community. What the Joint Staff did to the officers at the Joint Forces Staff College was a disgrace.

In the War on Terror, establishing professional standards—along with the implementation of threat analysis that enables an accurate depiction of the enemy—serves two purposes. First, it will enable the development of accurate Enemy Courses of Action, which we can then use to deploy our national assets effectively. These E-COAs will allow us to shape campaigns capable of transforming tactical victories into much-needed strategic successes (for our side).

As strongly suggested in this discussion, the oath is not a formality. The Article VI requirement to swear an oath to "support and defend" is the Constitution's way of insisting that all strategic planning start with and arise out of the Constitution. Restoring professional canons in intelligence matters as well as in other national security concerns will help us return to the constitutional standard.

Because language is the key terrain in information warfare, understanding the enemy and using accurate descriptors is essential to exposing and countering the enemy's strategy of "civilization-jihad" "by our hand." It enables us to orient on dawah entities like the Muslim Brotherhood and to identify them as among the main drivers of what Brigadier Malik, in *The Quranic Concept of War*, called actions in the "preparation stage," which leads to easy victory in the kinetic phase of operations.

Conclusion

At what point shall we expect the approach of danger? By what means shall we fortify against it? Shall we expect some transatlantic military giant to step the ocean and crush us at a blow? Never! All the armies of Europe, Asia, and Africa combined, with all the treasure of the earth (our own excepted) in their military chest, with a Bonaparte for a commander, could not by force take a drink from the Ohio or make a track on the Blue Ridge in a trial of a thousand years. At what point, then, is the approach of danger to be expected? I answer, if it ever reach us it must spring up amongst us; it cannot come from abroad. If destruction be our lot we must ourselves be its author and finisher. As a nation of freemen we must live through all time, or die by suicide.

Abraham Lincoln
Speech to the Young Men's Lyceum
Springfield, Illinois
January 27, 1838

After 9/11, America's national security leadership pieced together the intelligence and established definitively that the nation had been attacked by al-Qaeda. It realized, along with the public, that we were facing a problem much larger than the clandestine cells that intend to harm us. While many sympathetic statements were issued throughout the Muslim world, disquieting images of celebrations in the region indicated that while Osama bin Laden's forces were comparatively small, they enjoyed some level of support. President George W. Bush's post-attack ultimatum demanding an end to terrorism—including state-sponsored terrorism—was an implicit admission that "draining the swamp" of Islamic terrorism was a tough job. For America to prevail in this new war, it would require an assessment of that "swamp," of exactly how deep it runs and how many and what kind of creatures dwell there.

While the rubble was still burning, self-described "moderate" Muslims urged us to abandon this task. They assured our leadership there was no connection between al-Qaeda and Islam itself. The banner of Islam had been "hijacked by extremists," they claimed. Though these renegades claimed the mantle of mainstream Islam, their beliefs bore little resemblance either to Islam or its history. Accepting this explanation and thereby suspending the intelligence cycle, we should have adopted a two-tiered solution that would involve:

1. An education campaign to properly inform the Islamic population of Islamic requirements.

2. A review of possible underlying causes based on an actual finding that Islam has been hijacked.

Because we failed to do even this, we missed the mark from the beginning. There was never any actual finding that Islam had been hijacked. The claim was merely accepted as true as a conclusory assumption. When it was revealed that many of those who propagated this claim had disturbingly close ties to the Islamic Movement, the tendency was not to investigate their involvement but to suppress those who pointed out such uncomfortable facts.

Where does that leave us? Our doctrine on warfighting and intelligence requires that we orient on the enemy and his doctrine. In this war—unlike in others—we have a self-identified enemy who identifies the basis of his threat doctrine; we know who he is and why he fights. We know this because he tells us. He says he is a jihadi or a mujahid. He says he fights according to Islamic law in order to implement Islamic law. These are facts that cannot be contradicted. Not knowing—or refusing to know—either of these facts or their downstream consequences is malpractice.

There is overwhelming evidence that shariah does in fact serve as the driver of the enemy's threat doctrine. This remains true regardless of whether the enemy's understanding of Islam is accurate. Such evidence makes it possible to successfully lay down indicators of future activities, many of which have, in fact, already come to pass precisely as forecasted. And yet an intelligence officer, an FBI or DHS special agent, or a national security decision-maker can be fired for undertaking or even reciting such analysis. This is the very type of analysis that our oaths demand of us and that our positions require. A national security professional's duty is not to know true Islam; it is to identify and establish a functional threat doctrine, regardless of whether that doctrine accurately tracks with "true" Islam or not. What matters is that we understand the enemy's doctrines, not whether he is correct about them.

Today, individuals with Muslim Brotherhood affiliations dictate who can and cannot work for the government on War on Terror issues. They also dictate what can and cannot be discussed.

As long as they can keep us from understanding the enemy doctrine, they can keep us from winning the war. There is no knowing this enemy without understanding that doctrine, and there is no victory without knowing the enemy. These are facts. We can lose a war—and our country—for want of readily available facts, which are ignored according to policy.

Meanwhile, the main thrust of the enemy's advance continues unabated because our policymakers refuse to this day to recognize it for what it is. The Muslim Brotherhood sits on the board that advises our "Countering Violent Extremism" policy. The United States partners with the Organization of Islamic Cooperation to discuss the implementation of its Islamophobia agenda against U.S. citizens. Our leaders apply government pressure to ordinary U.S. citizens and residents who engage in actions completely within the bounds of First Amendment practices but outside the acceptable boundaries of Islamic law. Our Department of Defense blames our troops when they are murdered by the very partners they have been ordered to help. Our diplomats preemptively apologize for the exercise of American free speech, validating the "Battered Wife Syndrome" brought on by the Days of Rage process. "By our hands," we've de facto instituted real shariah standards on American citizens in contravention of both their constitutional rights and Article VI of the Constitution. We don't have the situational awareness to recognize what is happening right before our eyes. We can turn things around only if the American people hold their elected and appointed officials accountable for having failed to "well and faithfully discharge" their duty to know the enemy so they can then "support and defend" against him. But to do this, the American people must be provided with the same facts that their officials have chosen to ignore.

Time for corrective action is running out. Thirteen years after al-Qaeda's attack on September 11th, we are further from understanding the enemy, further from victory, than we were on September 12th.

The enemy's doctrine tells him he is not supposed to strike us until he judges that we have already been defeated in our own minds. That fact carries with it some troubling connotations regarding just how far along the enemy perceives us to be on the path to defeat. When that point is reached, the civilization jihadists expect they will be able to tap lightly anywhere along the fragile house of cards on which our strategy in the War on Terror was built, and the entire edifice will come down. They may be right.

For those who took the oath to support and defend the Constitution of the United States against all enemies foreign and domestic, all strategic assessments begin and end with the Constitution. The supremacy clause demands that the Constitution come first; it demands that there be no compromises, because there can be no conflicts. This is not complicated. In fact, it's simple. Captain Kirby's claim to the contrary, this is not a "warped view," and it's hardly out of step with "our core values." Rather, it is the very foundation of who we are as a nation.[1]

* * *

> *Neither let us be slandered from our duty by false accusations against us, nor frightened from it by menaces of destruction to the Government nor of dungeons to ourselves. Let us have faith that right makes might, and in that faith, let us, to the end, dare to do our duty as we understand it.*

Abraham Lincoln
Speech at Cooper Institute
New York City
February 27, 1860

1   Josh Rushing, "US Military Under Fire for 'Anti-Islam Class'" (transcript), *Al-Jazeera* TV (Washington Office), 12 May 2012, URL: http://www.aljazeera.com/video/americas/2012/05/20125124178148367.html alternatively released on YouTube URL: http://www.youtube.com/ watch? feature=player_embedded&v=2swVVfZo5eM#!, accessed 20 May 2012.

Appendix One

Interfaith Outreach

Faced with disconcerting episodes of violent fundamentalism, our respect for true followers of Islam should lead us to avoid hateful generalisations, for authentic Islam and the proper reading of the Koran are opposed to every form of violence.

Paragraph 253, *Evangelii Gaudium*

24 November 2013

They have healed the wound of my people lightly, saying, 'Peace, peace,' when there is no peace.

Jeremiah 6:14

The Dawah Mission, Interfaith Penetration, and Spiritual Warfare

As discussed in Part II, *dawah* is more extensive and more closely associated with *jihad* than the prevailing narrative suggests. While the focus of this book is on the role of dawah in undermining national security and civil society, the dawah mission extends into multiple lines of operation directed at multiple subversion efforts, including government, media, education, and religion. As Brigadier S.K. Malik makes clear, the object of jihad is the destruction of the will through, among other things, spiritual warfare as an actual form of warfare. What follows is a discussion of a parallel Muslim Brotherhood penetration operation into the Interfaith Community that supports Brotherhood efforts in the governmental and media sectors.

The Muslim Brotherhood's 1991 *Explanatory Memorandum: On the General*

Strategic Goal for the Group[1] was admitted into a Federal court as evidence that a disorientation strategy exists that aligns with Brigadier Malik's explanation of the preparation stage in the Quranic concept of war. As explained in both the *Explanatory Memorandum* and *Methodology of Dawah*, early Brotherhood lines of operation begin with efforts to penetrate institutions so that downstream efforts can be supported from within. This is what the Brotherhood is referring to when it says it seeks "a kind of grand Jihad in eliminating and destroying the Western civilization from within and 'sabotaging' its miserable house **by their hands** and the hands of the believers."[2]

While penetrating government and civil organizations is important, the interfaith movement constitutes a major supporting line of operation in Brotherhood penetration operations. Through subversion of the interfaith community, the Brotherhood seeks to manipulate other religions in furtherance of dislocating their faith. Regarding the interfaith community, the "hands of the believers" are primarily the Brotherhood and Islamic Movement participants, while "their hands" refers to those non-Muslim clerics (ministers, priests, and rabbis) who help facilitate the mission of "eliminating and destroying Western civilization from within." Because a Quranic basis exists for what the Brotherhood strategy states is its intent, all interfaith activities emanating from or involving known Brotherhood groups should be viewed with this understanding. This, in turn, should give rise to the requirement to review all associated interfaith activities in light of known Brotherhood intent. Basic rules of due diligence demand it.

The Interfaith Community a Principle Target of Muslim Brotherhood Dawah Operations

While *Methodology of Dawah* laid the foundation for the dawah effort in America back in 1988, the International Institute of Islamic Thought (IIIT) addressed interfaith outreach more recently in the 2007 (updated 2011) book *Interfaith Dialogue: A Guide for Muslims*.[3] Because typical discussions of dawah start and end with the "call to Islam," which limits dawah's scope to generic proselytizing, and because *Interfaith Dialogue* offers a window into what really goes on at the "dislocation of faith" phase of dawah, a brief analysis is necessary. Dawah efforts have progressed this far while remaining unrecognized and unchecked.

Owing to the effectiveness of superficial explanations of dawah, the authors of *Interfaith Dialogue* confidently contest claims that their activities in the interfaith domain have anything to do with dawah. Denying the dawah mission, *Interfaith Dialogue* states:

> Other Muslim participants confuse interfaith dialogue with conducting *da'wa* (calling to Islam). Interfaith dialogue should not be considered an opportunity to convert others,

for using such programs this way makes participants defensive and tends to turn them away from dialogue altogether. Genuine interfaith dialogue rests upon the central principle that it is not used for religious conversion.[4]

Interfaith Dialogue is not concerned with minimalist definitions of dawah that limits itself to conversions. As a close reading indicates, from the perspective of penetrating the interfaith community in furtherance of dislocating faith, Brotherhood efforts are nothing but dawah when understood as actions in the preparation stage. In the section of *Methodology of Dawah* titled "Through Contacts with Churches, Synagogues, Colleges and Universities," Shamim Siddiqi identified religious institutions as specific targets of the same form of dawah discussed in the 2007/11 IIIT monograph:

> These are very important public platforms that must be used for the spread of *Dawah* when available, either on the invitation or by offering the services of the *Da'ee* to these institutions for presenting the viewpoint of Islam on various issues of the time.

Note that it's the "*Da'ee*"[1] who engages in such activities. In language that parallels *Interfaith Dialogue*, Siddiqi explained back in 1988:

> The I.M.O.A [Islamic Movement of America—an early designation for the Muslim Brotherhood in America] will open dialogues with dignitaries of the religious institutions, presenting Islam as the common legacy of Judeo-Christian religions and as the only Guidance now available to mankind in its most perfect form for its *Falah* (Deliverance and Salvation). These talks must be held in a **very friendly and non-aggressive atmosphere,** as directed by Allah (SWT) in the Qur'an as to how to talk with people of the scripture – "*And argue not with the people of the Scripture unless it be in a way that is better.*" (Al-Qur'an – 29:46)[5]

As Siddiqi stated, the Brotherhood views the methodologies used in dawah as prescribed by Allah. When assessing the intentions of the Brotherhood's work product, it is important to remember that its manner of communication is generally consistent with Omar Ahmad's requirement to send two messages in the same communication:

---

1 From Siddiqi's *Methodology of Dawah*, a da'ee (Da'ee Ilallah) is "one who calls to the fold of Allah." Tarbiyah is the "training of a da'ee in the art of dawah." Dawah (Dawah Ilallah) is the calling the people to the fold of Allah. Siddiqi, Shamim A. *Methodology of Dawah Illallah in American Perspective.* Brooklyn: The Forum for Islamic Work, New York, 1989, Terminology page.

I believe that our problem is that we stopped working under-
ground. We will recognize the source of any message which
comes out of us. I mean, if a message is publicized, we will
know ... the media person among us will recognize that you
send two messages; **one to the Americans and one to the
Muslims**. If they found out who said that—even four years
later—it will cause a discredit to the Foundation as far as
the Muslims are concerned as they say "Look, he used to tell
us about Islam and that is a cause and stuff while he, at the
same time, is shooting elsewhere."[6] [Emphasis added.]

The meaning of Ahmad's comment is particularly troubling given the Brotherhood and deeper shariah subtext. Omar Ahmad is the founding president of
the Council of American Islamic Relations (CAIR). He made this comment at
a 1993 Hamas meeting held in Philadelphia that led to the formation of CAIR
under the auspices of the Islamic Association for Palestine (IAP), an organization
identified as a Muslim Brotherhood entity in the *Explanatory Memorandum*.[7] The
FBI wiretapped this meeting because Hamas was (and is) a terrorist organization.
The meeting was entered into evidence as "Philly Meeting – 15" in the 2008 Holy
Land Foundation Trial to establish the immediate association of CAIR to Hamas.
This means that the FBI and the Justice Department have known since before
CAIR was formed not only of its association with a terrorist organization but also
that it was given a disinformation mission. So why does the FBI, Justice, DHS,
and DoD still consult an organization known to be (1) formed out of the Palestinian Muslim Brotherhood and (2) created with the intention of disseminating
disinformation? Better yet, why do interfaith partners associate with CAIR?

Because the Brotherhood makes many of their publications available through
normal publishing distribution, they know non-Muslims may actually read their
materials. Omar Ahmad's comment should put all readers on notice that what
they read from Brotherhood-sourced materials may contain a dual meaning: "one
to Americans [i.e., non-Muslims] and one to Muslims."

Interfaith Dialogue: A Guide for Muslims is a Muslim Brotherhood publication. In the Acknowledgements, the authors recognize the role played by known
American Brotherhood entities and those in habitual relations with them, including the Islamic Society of North America (ISNA),[8] the Graduate School of
Islamic Social Science (GSISS), and the IIIT[9]:

"We thank ISNA, especially Dr. Sayyid M. Syeed and Dr.
Louay Safi, and that International Institute for Islamic
Thought (IIIT) for their professional and moral support. ...
The Salam Institute for Peace and Justice and the Center for
Interfaith Studies and Dialogue (CSID)"[10]

The book also identifies ISNA as taking the lead role in interfaith activities,[11] while CAIR is given the social justice and civil rights portfolio.[12] These are recognized Brotherhood entities known to be operating in the United States. *Interfaith Dialogue* was published by IIIT, the *Explanatory Memorandum* identified the IIIT as a Muslim Brotherhood entity,[13] and the IIIT's homepage states it is dedicated "towards the Islamization of knowledge."[14] The IIIT also certified the *Reliance of the Traveller – A Classic Manual of Islamic Sacred Law* as an authoritative translation of shariah under the signature block of Dr. Taha Jabir Al-Alwani, then the president of the IIIT, the Fiqh Council of North America, and a member of the Islamic Fiqh Academy in Jedda[15] The Fiqh Council of North America (the ISNA Fiqh Council [IFC][16] in the *Explanatory Memorandum*) is still a subordinate element of ISNA. The Islamic Fiqh Academy in Jedda is a subordinate element of the Organization of Islamic Cooperation (OIC).[17]

Another indicator that *Interfaith Dialogue* reflects the Muslim Brotherhood mission is the repeated allusion to bridge building. Sayyid Qutb uses this term in *Milestones* to set the limits of dawah interaction with non-Muslims: "the chasm between Islam and *Jahiliyyah* is great, and a bridge is not to be built across it so that the people on the two sides may mix with each other, but only so that the people of Jahiliyyah may come over to Islam."[18] The very use of the bridge building meme serves as a signal to other Brotherhood members that they are operating inside the fold, that the interfaith narrative is designed to set the conditions for bringing people to Islam while also setting the preconditions for the use of force (jihad). Brotherhood commitments to interfaith dialogue should never be understood to extend beyond the parameters set by Qutb.

The relationship of the IIIT to both *Interfaith Dialogue* and *Reliance of the Traveller* requires that we understand *Interfaith Dialogue* strictly in terms of IIIT's commitment to shariah (as stated in *Reliance*) and in conjunction with the Brotherhood objectives to which it is associated. This is **reasonable** because, as the *Explanatory Memorandum* states, the IIIT is committed to the "enablement of Islam in North America, meaning: establishing an effective and a stable Islamic Movement led by the Muslim Brotherhood which adopts Muslims' causes domestically and globally … and supports the global Islamic State wherever it is."[19] It is **not reasonable** to do otherwise.

Applying the 24/25 Rule,[2] where points are made in *Interfaith Dialogue* that lend themselves to competing interpretations, the ones that conform to known

---

2   As developed in Part IV, THE ARTICLE 24/25 RULE FOR ANALYSIS – "the 24/25 Rule" – Human Rights are defined as shariah for the purpose of any analysis involving the OIC, an OIC member state, or initiatives reasonably arising from either — including all entities claiming Islamic law as the basis of law, including al-Qaeda, the Muslim Brotherhood, elements of the Islamic Movement, and the Turkish delegation at the OSCE: When the subject matter of an analysis speaks of "rights and freedoms" or associated defined concepts that arise out of the Cairo Declaration on Human Rights in Islam, those "rights and freedoms" can only be assessed in terms of what Islamic law permits them to mean, where Islamic law is the only criterion by which a determination can be made in the event of any dispute requiring resolution.

IIIT views based on known IIIT positions are the ones to be adopted. This creates a powerful presumption that *Reliance* reflects known IIIT positions whenever shariah from *Reliance* can be accurately aligned with positions advocated by the IIIT in products like *Interfaith Dialogue*. The ability to confirm an issue in question by reference to *Reliance* will generally reflect the Brotherhood view in question. Also in line with the 24/25 Rule, if something in *Interfaith Dialogue* finds an explanation in *Reliance*, then that's what is meant.

A good example is *Interfaith Dialogue*'s treatment of the "Treaty of *Hudaybiyyah*." The key to understanding this narrative is provided early on: "the Prophet provided us with such a model when he signed the Treaty of *Hudaybiyyah* with his Makkan opponents, the very ones who had expelled him and his followers from Makkah."[20] This comment creates the requirement to know the story behind *Hudaybiyyah*, independent of the explanation provided in the book, while remaining aware of Omar Ahmad's two-messages strategy.

The second clue is found in the chapter titled "Treating Non-Muslims in the Light of the Prophet's *Sirah* and Muslim History." As the title indicates, truces are to be understood in "light of the Prophet's *Sirah* and Muslim history." The title also points to the influence of the *Milestones* meme that aligns Brotherhood messaging with Islamic doctrines of progressive revelation. *Interfaith Dialogue* positions *Hudaybiyyah* to establish the claim the Prophet had an overriding interest in maintaining peace, even going so far as entering into treaties that were unpopular and humiliating. *Interfaith Dialogue* states:

> This treaty shows that the Prophet preferred peace even at the cost of annoying some of his close followers. He knew that peaceful living would allow Muslims to dialogue with non-Muslims, move about freely, and build relations with other tribes. This treaty is an excellent example of going the extra mile with others to achieve peace.[21]

Without an awareness of Islamic law, interfaith partners read this observation and think it reflects an ongoing commitment to peace grounded in an explicit preference of the Prophet. Yet a quick reference to *Reliance of the Traveller* makes it clear that this is not the case. The relevant shariah is in the section on jihad concerning truces. *Reliance* shows that Islamic law does not permit treaties but rather recognizes only truces[22] that are made on a short-term basis.[23] Of note, *Interfaith Dialogue* erroneously designates *Hudaybiyyah* as a treaty, not a truce. Further, because truces require the nonperformance of jihad,[24] truces are disfavored, cannot be entered into merely to preserve the status quo, and can only be made in times of Muslim weakness, lack of numbers, or because the other side may convert to Islam.[25]

The seriousness of these conditions is such that *Reliance* grounds them in the Qur'an: "*So do not be fainthearted and call for peace, when it is you who are the upper-*

most. (Koran 47:35)."[26] While both Muslim and non-Muslim participants in the interfaith context read the same section of *Interfaith Dialogue* on peace treaties, the Brotherhood members will have a fundamentally different understanding of what is being communicated. On the meaning of peace,[27] Islamic notions hold that true peace comes with total submission to Islam and world peace when the entire world has submitted (at least to shariah).[28] Of note, the Truce of *Hudaybiyyah* was entered into during a "period of weakness" and was renewed for a second ten-year term. Early in the renewal period, Islam having "regained its strength," the truce was abrogated and Mecca conquered. A cursory review of the *Sirah* and Islamic history reveals this. It is troubling that the Brotherhood bases its expectation of success on a reasoned estimation that its interfaith "partners" either don't know this or don't care enough to find it out.

As this discussion of peace is in the context of interfaith interactions with known Brotherhood entities, it is fair to ask whether non-Muslim "interfaith partners" understand the full meaning of the Brotherhood's position that world peace comes when the entire world has submitted to shariah. A look at Sayyid Qutb's 1951[29] book *Islam and Universal Peace* will help to answer this. Translated and published in 1993 by a prominent American Brotherhood label, American Trust Publications (ATP),[30] *Islam and Universal Peace* explains that, for Qutb, "universal peace must be given with a peace of conscience which can only be achieved through constant contact with the eternal source of power, Allah."[31] It continues:

> Accordingly, Muslims have a responsibility towards humanity. They are to achieve peace on earth, within themselves, at home and in society. It is a peace based on recognizing God's oneness and omnipotence, on instituting justice, equality and liberty; and on achieving social equilibrium and cooperation.[32]

> Islam came to establish justice in its widest sense; socially, legally and internationally, and to apply it to people the world over. Whoever, Muslim or non-Muslim, violates this rule is an antagonist and a transgressor. It is then the duty of Muslims to fight and, if necessary, to use force in order that the Word of God, which is absolute and complete, prevail.[33]

Establishing world peace through the enforcement of shariah. Qutb rhetorically asks, "Then what is the Word of God that justifies war according to Islam?" He answers his question:

> The Word of God is the expression of His Will as specified in the Quranic verse: "... and fight them on until there is no more tumult or oppression." (Q. VIII. 39) God ordains that all religion should belong to Him. This can only be realised

[sic] in one way; through worship, obedience and complete surrender to Him. The divine law must dominate all secular and religious systems. Whoever usurps the right to legislate laws on his own is claiming a share in the Divine powers of organising [sic] the universal system. Such a person would be claiming – implicitly if not explicitly – a share in God's attributions. In other words, he would be taking on himself the right to rule as another god on earth.

In order to propagate the oneness of God on earth and to put an end to the power of those who, by word or deed, challenge His omnipotence, Islam allows Muslims to fight. Such is the only war allowed in Islam.[34]

To Qutb, the ultimate offense is shirk. The form of warfare authorized by Islam to fight for peace is jihad. He makes this clear in the chapter "World Peace" in the section "Striving in the Cause of Allah (Jihad)."[35] In making his case, Qutb clarifies that the goal is not to force conversions to faith but rather to compel subordination to the law, a distinction lost on most non-Muslim interfaith partners who advocate on behalf of the Brotherhood using the Brotherhood's "no compulsion" narrative. Qutb explains:

Islam is not an arbitrary religion, nor has it ever ordered Muslims to force others to adopt it even though it is the final and complete revelation from God. He says:

"Let there be no compulsion in religion: Truth stands out clear from error." (Q. II. 256)

Muslims are first commanded to defend their brothers against deception and materialism. Second, they are ordered to defend the liberty of thought and to invite others to their belief. To this end, they are commanded to eliminate any oppressive force that would suppress the propagation of Islam. Third, they are to establish the sovereignty of God on earth and to repel any aggression against it. Those who claim the right to legislate for people and exclude God's legislation are aggressors and are liable to divine punishment. Fourth, Muslims are required to establish justice in the world and to allow all peoples to enjoy this justice as individuals, as members of a society, as citizens of a nation and as members of the international community. Thus, Muslims are commanded to fight against injustice wherever it may be; whether it be individual, social, national or international.

The struggle to establish the sovereignty of God on earth is called jihad. Jihad is achieved by giving men the chance to emancipate themselves from their oppressors and to restore their human rights granted by God to all mankind. God Says:

> "Those who believe fight in the Cause of God, and those who reject faith fight in the cause of Evil ..." (Q. IV. 76)[36]

When Jewish or Christian "partners" work with Muslim Brothers who declare a complete commitment to peace, are they aware of what is being committed to? The only thing worse than interfaith partners not knowing the Brotherhood's agenda when they engage in outreach with them is that some partners *may* know. As shepherds of their respective flocks, interfaith leaders should take the time to know the equities and interests of all parties. Shepherds who cannot recognize the wolf are not good shepherds.

The analysis used for the explanation of Islamic notions of peace can also be applied to Brotherhood notions of social justice. In 1948, Qutb wrote *Social Justice in Islam*,[37] in which social justice was equated with shariah. As Qutb saw it, Judaism was "suffering an eclipse" that rendered it "an empty and unspiritual sham,"[38] while Christianity had simply "shot its bolt":

> The truth is that all spiritual religions – and Christianity most of all – are opposed equally to European and American materialism; for both of these are of the same nature and are equally at odds with any spiritual philosophy of life. But Christianity, so far as we can see, cannot be reckoned as a real force in opposition to the philosophies of the new materialism; it is an individualist, isolationist, and negative faith. It has no power to make life grow under its influence in any permanent positive way. Christianity has shot its bolt so far as human life is concerned; it has lost its power to keep pace with practical life in succeeding generations, for it came into being only for a limited and temporary period, between Judaism and Islam.[39]

Interfaith Dialogue relies on Dr. Taha Jabir Al-Alwani, who certified *Reliance,* to explain the theory of *dar al-harb* that where a Muslim is able to practice his religion openly in a non-Muslim land, the "land becomes *dar al Islam* by virtue of his settling there."[40] "Settling" is a Brotherhood term of art that is defined in the *Explanatory Memorandum*. In Brotherhood parlance, settling, or the "process of settlement," is a civilization-jihadist process that calls for the destruction of America through a form of jihad based on subversion.[41] Also regarding "settlement," "the role and nature of the work of 'the Islamic Center' in every city" is to "achieve the goal of the process of settlement," which includes "supplying the battalions."[42] Alwani's explanation is also similar to one given by Tariq Ramadan, the grandson of Muslim Brotherhood founder Hasan al-Banna, when he laid out a theory of American citizenship based on Islamic legal principles[43] established by the Prophet Mohammed[44] in a speech at the 2012 MAS-ICNA Conference. (A year earlier at an ICNA event in Dallas, Ramadan reminded attendees that they were in America to colonize, not to be colonized.[3])

Interfaith Dialogue also relies on the Brotherhood's chief jurist, Yusuf al-Qaradawi. This is the same Qaradawi who refused to sit next to Jews at a conference on interfaith dialogue in Doha in 2013,[45] explaining that "after the announcement of the expansion of the conference to be a dialogue of Muslims, Christians, and Jews, I decided not to participate in it so as not to sit with Jews on a single platform";[46] the same Qaradawi who, in 2009, said that Hitler was Allah's punishment for the Jews and that he hopes, before he dies, to go to the Palestinian territories to shoot Jews and then be martyred by them.[47]

Deconstructed Minds: From Squish to Dislocation of Faith

Interfaith Dialogue is consciously sensitive to members of the Muslim community who see risk and potential apostasy associated with interacting with non-Muslims in the interfaith domain. It was also written with an eye toward non-Muslims who might read the book. Hence, *Interfaith Dialogue* addresses the concerns of Muslim skeptics in neutral terms that simply identify the rules interfaith leaders say must govern the interfaith community when engaging in interfaith dialogue.

The IIIT identifies the interfaith movement's non-Muslim members (called "partners") as vulnerable to penetration by virtue of their willingness to abide by self-imposed postmodern regimes, ultimately designed to deconstruct their respective faiths. This becomes clear only when *Interfaith Dialogue* is read in light of the IIIT's mission statement, Muslim Brotherhood doctrines, and the Islamic law that the IIIT certifies. For the Brotherhood, the interfaith venue represents an optimal platform for penetration into the leadership circles of religious organizations. As will be seen, much of the IIIT strategy relies on the interfaith movement's own rules, which enable Brotherhood partners to coopt, neutralize, and undermine their non-Muslim partners in the preparation stage as Islam seeks to transition from weakness to strength.

Temple University's Leonard Swindler and Richard Landau, in *Beliefnet*, provide a sampling of the rules that *Interfaith Dialogue* identifies as governing such

---

3 Tariq Ramadan: "We should all be very careful not to be colonized by something which is coming from this consumerist society. ... It should be us with our understanding of Islam, our principles, colonizing positively the United States of America." - Dr. Tariq Ramadan Speaking at ICNA Fundraising – Dallas Chapter, 28 July 2011, *YouTube* (www.amilimani.com), URL: http://www.youtube.com/watch?v=1WDEfVdsr3M, accessed 22 January 2013, alternate abridged video - "Tariq Ramadan: We Must Colonize the USA with our Religion," posted by *MRCtv*, 17 June 2012, URL: http://www.mrctv.org/videos/tariq-ramadan-we-must-colonize-usa-our-religion, accessed 22 January 2013.

dialogue. On point is Swindler's principle that "dialogue must take place in an atmosphere of mutual trust."[48] This "mutual trust" does not, however, rest on a full understanding of what each side believes, independent of what they disclose. Indeed, this "trust" can take precedence over what one may already know of the other faiths or what one could learn from competent research in the service of due diligence.

Related to the question of whether trust is in any way merited is the question of what distinguishes trust from witlessness. Brotherhood members are aware that shariah says that "when it is possible to achieve such an aim by lying but not by telling the truth," it becomes "obligatory to lie if the goal is obligatory."[49] Does "mutual trust" survive such a disclosure? Should it? The Brotherhood mission is to impose shariah on the world. Before extending such trust, a simple due diligence review of Brotherhood entities engaged in the interfaith process would reveal this to be true. The Brotherhood shows little concern that their outreach partners will come to their senses, possibly because another of Swindler's interfaith principles is that "each dialogue partner has the right to define his or her own religion and belief, [so that] the rest can only describe what it looks like to them from the outside."[50] This rule suggests that persons who undertake a reasonable effort to discharge their duty (to their own faiths) by performing a competent assessment of the "other's" religions could be characterized as lacking the requisite trust by virtue of finding out. Could conformance to this rule help explain why fellow believers are routinely accused of intolerance by interfaith leaders and peers from within their own religious organizations?

Using Swindler's principles to prohibit critical analysis of Islam, the Brotherhood can then leverage yet another principle—"participants entering into dialogue must be willing to reflect upon themselves and their own religion"[51]—to justify withering assaults on the faiths of other interfaith organizations in the name of introspection while remaining consistent to the *Milestones* process. As expressed in *Interfaith Dialogue*, the Brotherhood's ability to manipulate interfaith principles to facilitate a lack of reciprocity establishes a form of constructive subordination structured to lead to actual submission. As such, it facilitates the dhimmification of America's non-Muslim clergy. Just note how often senior rabbis, ministers, and bishops turn on their own members when issues of Islam arise. Clearly the Brotherhood has targeted the interfaith community because its membership exhibits squish characteristics. The interesting question is whether the Brotherhood targeted the interfaith community in order to dislocate their faiths or whether it sees itself as manipulating outreach partners whose faiths have already been dislocated.

How else does one explain the lack of discernment? If postmodern rules governing the interfaith community operate beyond the superficial level, they run the risk of undermining core beliefs associated with any truly believed-in faith. *Interfaith Dialogue*'s authors understand that interfaith partners who actually take such principles to heart are likely to already be compromised in their own faiths. Richard Landau calls for members to "practice fairness when speaking for or about other faith(s)" and to "speak in a way that people of that religion can affirm as accurate."[52] Others, however, including the Brotherhood, recognize that non-Muslim partners who buy into this view are already predisposed to accept the Islamophobia narrative, because they already hold themselves to standards that require uncritical acceptance of outside narratives at the expense of their own beliefs and even of factual analysis (that puts the interfaith paradigm at risk). Self-censorship before speaking, what the American legal system calls "prior restraint,"[4] is established as a self-imposed rule of etiquette that effectively takes precedence over the requirements of one's own faith and of reason.

In the interfaith milieu, violation of these narrative-enforcing rules is, of course, deemed "uncharitable." So long as interfaith discussions concern non-essential topics that don't touch faith, one can tolerate Landau's admonition to "avoid misusing scripture," by which he means that "no one shall attempt to use one's own religion to dismiss another religion as invalid."[53] Because scripture contains the core elements of faith for most religions, however, at some point, actual faith should control, if not override, such interfaith concerns. As a purely logical proposition, to truly believe in one's own faith is to truly disbelieve in others. To argue otherwise is to deny the laws of identity and non-contradiction. It violates reason. The Brotherhood recognizes that its interfaith partners have already imposed relativist notions of "tolerance" (which is actually intolerance) on themselves as a condition of membership. For Brotherhood members engaged in the interfaith process, suppressing otherwise credible faith-based concerns coming from non-Muslims can be as easy as holding their partners to the standards they set for themselves *and then demanding* that they impose those same relativist standards on their co-religionists—at least as regards Islam.

Finally, Landau's rule to "avoid preconditions" because they "usually defeat the purpose of dialogue"[54] allows Brotherhood participants to characterize their partners' existing commitments to faith as just that—a precondition that interfaith rules demand be avoided as an impediment to "dialogue." Every article of faith becomes a precondition that must be sidestepped as the entry cost of dialogue. It is noteworthy how often in interfaith presentations that programmed discussions about "putting our preconceptions aside" serve as the leading edge of an assault on the target audience's faith.

These narratives are used to great effect to hollow out an audience's faith. As

---

4 From *Black's Law 9th*, "The legal doctrine of prior restraint (or formal censorship before publication) is probably the oldest form of press control. Certainly it is one of the most efficient, since one censor, working in the watershed, can create a drought of information and ideas long before they reach the fertile plane of people's minds. In the United States, the doctrine of prior restraint has been firmly opposed by the First Amendment, and by the Supreme Court. But the philosophy behind that doctrine lives zestfully on, and shows no signs of infirmities of age." *Black's Law Dictionary, 9th*, Bryan A. Garner, Editor in Chief, West Publishing (Thomson Reuters), St. Paul, 1314; (citing David G. Clark & Earl R. Hutchinson, Mass Media and the Law 11, 1970)

the discussion on interfaith dialogue proceeds, the postmodern assault on faith will focus on the assault on reason. For example, when a faithful person's adherence to the scriptures of his or her faith are designated a "misuse of scripture" by a fellow member of the same faith who feels the superior pull of interfaith requirements, a self-negating contradiction is being imposed within that faith. Holding back on the expression of a faithfully held scriptural proposition in deference to higher interfaith canons results in one's cooperation in one's own silencing, while holding to one's belief results in being designated as rigid, intolerant, uncharitable, and fundamentalist. One cannot believe in one's faith and in interfaith principles demanding their suppression at the same time without engaging in a logical contradiction that reduces faith to meaninglessness. Interfaith rules are thinly veiled postmodern assaults on reason that succeed by undermining basic principles of logic. It's really just a matter of apples and oranges.[5] The Brotherhood knows a good thing when they see it: The interfaith movement already induces the very dislocation of faith that the Pakistani Brigadier said is a necessary objective in the preparation stage.

---

5 Apples and Oranges explained: The assault on reason can be explained in terms of basic Aristotelian logic. There exist certain laws of thought classically held to form the basis of all logic. Also called logical first principles, they include the *law of identity*, the *law of non-contradiction*, and the *law of the excluded middle*. It's all basic logic; it's all apples and oranges. The *Law of Identity*: If you are an apple, then you are an apple (a = a). The *Law of Non-Contradiction*: If you are an apple, then you are not an orange (a ≠ o). The *Law of the Excluded Middle*: If you are an apple, then you are not not an apple (a ≠ -a).

The *Law of Identity* - holds that an apple is an apple - it is what it is. In other words, that a thing must be identical with itself. As Aristotle observed, in his Metaphysics:

"The fact that a thing is itself is [the only] answer to all such questions as why the man is man, or the musician musical."

The *Law of Non-Contradiction* - holds that an apple cannot be both an apple and not an apple (or an orange) at the same time; that a logically correct proposition cannot affirm and deny the same thing. Aristotle provided several formulations of the law of non-contradiction:

"It is impossible for anyone to believe the same thing to be and not be."

"The same attribute cannot at the same time belong and not belong to the same subject in the same respect."

"The most indisputable of all beliefs is that contradictory statements are not at the same time true."

The *Law of Excluded Middle* - holds that a statement is either true or false, not both and not neither. In Aristotle's words: "It is necessary for the affirmation or the negation to be true or false." (*De Interpretatione*)

The following explanation was assisted by "6. Laws of Thought, Aristotle: Logic," *Internet Encyclopedia of Philosophy (IEP) – A Peer Reviewed Academic Resource*, undated, URL: http://www.iep.utm.edu/aris-log/, accessed 14 June 2013.

Better to Deceive than to Lie

The same section of *Reliance* that spoke of the duty to lie also advises that it is better to deceive:

> But it is more precautionary in all such cases to employ words that give a misleading impression, meaning to intend by one's words something that is literally true, in respect to which one is not lying, while the outward purport of the words deceives the hearer ...[55]

Interfaith Dialogue is concerned with developing narratives to express certain Islamic doctrines that are too harsh to state in plain terms and yet must be communicated. The solution is to develop wordy, facially neutral narratives that are "literally true ... while the outward purport ... deceives the hearer." A good example is the explanation of the "Treaty of *Hudaybiyyah*" discussed above. Another example is when *Interfaith Dialogue* encourages imams not to say, "All non-Muslims go to hell," when a more evasive way of communicating the same thing is more helpful:

> Consider the difference between the following two approaches. On the one hand, one imam mentioned during his Friday sermons that Jews and Christians are bound for hell if they do not accept Islam. On the other hand, another imam said that Islam is Allah's chosen path and that those who believe in Him, the angels, the Biblical prophets, Prophet Muhammad as the seal of the Prophets, all holy scriptures including the Qur'an, the Hereafter, the Resurrection, and in the Day of Judgment – He, in His mercy, will bless such people of heaven. The difference in the approach between these two imams should be clear. Which of these imams more truly represents the spirit of the interfaith dialogue?[56]

Note that the question isn't which statement is more correct, but rather which is more appropriate for the limited purpose of meeting interfaith objectives. As only Islam has all the scriptures (including the Qur'an) and all the prophets (including Mohammed), both statements are true. Only Muslims enter paradise. The IIIT book simply shows how to mask the ultimate message of Islam so that believers will understand it and unbelievers won't. Thus, though the speaker is "not lying," the narrative "deceives the hearers" in a broader audience.

From the skeptic's perspective, the IIIT may believe they are simply facilitating the implosion of a community that already wants to be deceived. Both the Pakistani Brigadier and the Brotherhood understand spiritual warfare to be a major component of dawah. The fact that Brotherhood efforts so easily slide by their interfaith "partners" may lead the Brotherhood to conclude that Siddiqi was right when he said:

> America is a predominantly secular cum permissive society. ... Religion is a personal affair between God and individual. It is limited within the four walls of the church, the synagogue and the temple. It is nowhere visible within the life pattern of the people. ... Churches have become more like social institutions than religious meeting places ... the Judeo-Christian God is powerless.[57]

You can't undermine the already undermined. Interfaith penetration is done in furtherance of the dislocation of faith demanded by Brigadier Malik in the dawah phase. The Brotherhood effort discussed in *Interfaith Dialogue* is a sophisticated, long-term undertaking that enjoys ongoing success. If allowed to continue unchecked, an anticipated secondary effect will be the additional loss of faith when the faithful realize that their current religious leadership (ministers, bishops, and rabbis) has facilitated the Brotherhood narrative that seeks to destroy their faith communities.

Dislocation of Faith: Recognizing It When You See It

A key Brotherhood objective in the interfaith movement is to sustain among its partners a greater commitment to interfaith processes than to their own faiths. Indicators of such a drift should be watched for and recognized. Two examples will demonstrate this.

An Assyrian Catholic woman, Juliana Taimoorazy, was forced to flee Iran with her family. She found safety and a home in Chicago, Illinois. After she gave her testimonial at a Knights of Columbus event, a concerned woman asked her to speak at a Catholic high-school function in Arlington Heights, Illinois. Initially in favor of her speaking, the priest and president of the Catholic high school asked her to rehearse her speech to a small group of parishioners, himself included. Speaking on the persecution of Christians in the Islamic world, Juliana drew on her and her family's life experience reaching back to the Genocide of World War I, better known as the Armenian Genocide, but which was more broadly directed at all Christian minorities and included the physical destruction of the Assyrian nation. Her family history includes a great-grandfather who died in an internment camp, a great-grandmother and two aunts who were kidnapped, another great-uncle who was cut to pieces, and an uncle who was shot by his own Muslim employee for being a Christian. It also includes the serial rape and brutalization of the women in her family—exactly what we are seeing ISIS do to those same populations today. Her familial story extends to mental, emotional, and physical persecutions in the 1980s that finally forced her family to leave. Today, the Christian community, including the Catholic Church, is well aware that upwards of 100,000 Christians a year are killed for being Christian and that most of this is at the hands of those acting in the name of Islam.[58] A simple Google search makes it clear that the persecution of Christians in the Muslim world today is open, violent, systematic, and large-scale. There is nothing about Juliana's testimony that strains credulity. Going through the rehearsal of her testimonial, however, the priest intervened to tell her that Islam is a religion of peace, that he personally believes in the "Five Pillars," and that she could not give her testimonial unless she was prepared to debate with his interfaith partner and peer, the local imam. As the priest explained, to do otherwise would risk poisoning the minds of the Catholic youth.

The priest subordinated the testimonial of a woman's persecution for being Catholic—to be given to fellow Catholics in a Catholic forum—to what he thought would be acceptable to Islam. This reflects the downstream effects of interfaith rules as intended by the Brotherhood. Even given the offense, Juliana accepted the priest's conditions but never heard back from him. Juliana Taimoorazy is currently the director of a non-profit dedicated to raising awareness of the overt persecution of Christians in the Middle East. Who would have thought that a priest would silence such a testimonial? Sadly, a review of the news will indicate that Juliana's experience has become the norm.

Dislocation of faith, strategic disorientation, or simply unaware? Jewish, Muslim, and Christian students posed for this Olive Tree Initiative group photo in the Palestinian Territory (Ramallah) in September 2012. The memorial placard in the background reads, "Martyred Leaders: the Central Committee of the Fateh Movement." Senior Fateh official Hasan Zamlot (center) met with students from the University of California, Irvine, and UCLA. Pictured at the far right is OTI "tour guide" George Rishmawi, co-founder of the International Solidarity Movement.[59]

The Olive Tree Initiative (OTI) is a university-sanctioned program that sends students to Israel and the West Bank to meet with members of organizations associated with terrorism under the pretext of "dialogue and holistic education." It is structured, however, to neutralize Jewish affinity to Israel, Judaism, and Jewish heritage. It has programs spread throughout Europe and the United States. The program is lauded by the Council on American Islamic Relations (CAIR) and works closely with the Muslim Student Association (MSA), both known affiliate organizations of the Muslim Brotherhood. OTI directs a narrative at American college students who lack the ability to recognize that these activities are calculated to undermine affinity to Israel as part of a larger isolation effort, including BDS. While the outreach effort is also directed at Muslims and Christians, the target audience is unquestionably Jewish students. The immediate objective is to establish a pro-Palestinian counter cadre within the Jewish community, inculcated with hostility to Israel and designed to transition to an entrenched form of anti-Semitism. This is done through heavily choreographed travel to the territories under the control of the Palestinian Authority. Nothing so effectively demonstrates the strategic disorientation this program generates than a group of young students cheerfully posing for a picture in a room in Ramallah, the Palestinian Territory, with a memorial placard on the wall in the background dedicated to the "Martyred Leaders; the Central Committee of the *Fateh* Movement."

It's 'Feed My Sheep,' Not 'Feed My Sheep to the Wolves'— The Walk of Shame

Interfaith Dialogue culminates with Chapter V, "The Abrahamic Faiths: A Case Study of Rochester's Experience."[60] This "experience" concerns the efforts of the Center for Interfaith Studies and Dialogue (CISD) at Nazareth College in Rochester, New York. (Nazareth is one of the few colleges formally delisted as a Catholic institution.[61]) *Interfaith Dialogue* identifies CISD as a "leader" in the interfaith effort supported by the IIIT.[62] The main author of *Interfaith Dialogue*, Muhammad Shafiq, holds the IIIT Chair in Interfaith Studies and Dialogue at CISD, which is endowed by the IIIT.[63] "Rochester's Experience" refers to the successful IIIT penetration of the interfaith community, which *Interfaith Dialogue* seeks to have emulated as part of a larger Muslim Brotherhood effort. For those outside the Brotherhood orbit, however, being praised as a positive case study in *Interfaith Dialogue* is being designated a Brotherhood dupe.

These case studies include Temple B'rith Kodesh joining with the Islamic Center of Rochester to celebrate the *adnan* with Muslims praying in congregation,[64] Rev. Gordon Webster of the Presbyterian Church helping to stand up the Commission on Christian-Muslim Relations (CCMR),[65] and the Diocese of Arlington, Virginia, ratifying the Catholic-Muslim Dialogue (CMD).[66]

Each is an example of an entity exhibiting an overly pliable response to a Brotherhood initiative. The problem isn't that Jewish and Christian entities work with Muslims, but that they work with the Muslim Brotherhood. For the Brotherhood, interfaith "bridge building" goes only one way; its immediate objective is "eliminating and destroying Western civilization from within and 'sabotaging' [America's] miserable house by their hands"[67] in furtherance of "establishing Allah's law in the land, ... establishing the Islamic State, ... and defending the [Islamic] nation against internal enemies."[68] If the IIIT is acting in furtherance of its known objectives through such interfaith initiatives, then those working with the Brotherhood under this interfaith regime are helping, "by their hands," to eliminate Western civilization and, indeed, their own faiths (by facilitating the undermining of faith within the respective faith communities).

Other IIIT representatives support more strategic efforts. At a series of interfaith meetings in Washington, D.C., for example, alongside Muhammad Shafiq were Jamal Barzinji, Abubaker al Shingieti, and Iqbal Unus.[69] Jamal Barzinji is the founder of the IIIT and has extensive Muslim Brotherhood associations. He is also a member of CAIR and was associated with the Amana Trust, the American Muslim Council, CSID, IIFTIHAR, Mar-Jac Investments, Mena Investments, Reston Investments, the SAAR Foundation, and the SAFA Trust.[70] Barzinji's home was raided during the Green Quest operation by the U.S. government.[71]

We will look at two of these individuals, beginning with Abubaker Shingieti, whose Brotherhood *bona fides* are established. He is regional director for the IIIT,[72] an active member of the Association of Muslim Social Scientists (AMSS),[73] and was the editor of *Islamic Horizons*, the official monthly magazine of ISNA.[74] The *Explanatory Memorandum* self-identifies the IIIT, AMSS, and ISNA as Muslim Brotherhood entities.[75] Shingieti is president of American Muslims for Constructive Engagement (AMCE), the consolidated Brotherhood entity charged with managing outreach initiatives associated with the Obama Administration.[76] He is also Vice President for Islamic Programs at the International Center for Religion and Diplomacy (ICRD)[77] and Research Associate at the Center for Muslim-Christian Understanding at the Georgetown University School of Foreign Service.[78] According to his ICRD resume, Shingieti:

> Had a distinguished career in government in the Republic of Sudan. He held Ambassador rank in his capacity as Director of Political Affairs for the Presidency (1995-98) and before that served as Councilor at the Embassy of Sudan in Washington, DC (1990-1993), and Secretary General of the External Information Council in Khartoum (1993-95).[79]

But there is more to Shingieti's role. Borrowing from Patrick Poole's research, Sudan in the 1990s was ruled by the Muslim Brotherhood regime of President Omar al-Bashir, which engaged in a sustained jihad of annihilation against Christians and animists that claimed the lives of close to two million people, forcing another four million to flee. In 2008, the International Criminal Court indicted Bashir for war crimes related to the regime's subsequent genocide in Darfur. In this period, Shingieti served Bashir as a close advisor and top aide, first as a government spokesperson from 1993 to 1995 and then, at the height of the regime's murderous activity, as Director of Public Affairs for the Presidency from 1995 to

1998. From 1992 to 1996, Sudan was the hub of the international terror network that sheltered Bin Laden.[80] The situation has not "normalized" since then. For example, as recently as March 2012, MEMRI published a subtitled video of an *Al Jazeera* broadcast of the Sudanese Governor of South Kordofan, Ahmad Haroun, issuing direct orders to the military to annihilate the non-Muslim population, mainly Christians and animists, in jihad:

> The rest of the mission should be completed with high morale. Allah Akbar. Make it clean. Allah Akbar. Wipe them out, crush them, don't bring them back alive. Eat them uncooked. Allah Akbar. Don't cause us any paperwork. Are you ready people?[81]

There is reason to think that "eat them uncooked" is more that just a metaphor. When news popped in May 2013 that the White House was hosting a Sudanese delegation led by seniors of the National Congress Party, the party Bashir once lead, attention shifted to President Obama's lead Muslim outreach person, Abubaker al-Shingieti, President of AMCE.[82]

There is also Imam Magid, the Executive Director of the ADAMS Center and President of the Islamic Society of North America (ISNA).[83] Magid is also associated with ACME[84] and is a Sudanese citizen. He claims to be the son of the Grand Mufti of Sudan, and it was in Sudan, at the direction of his father and other notable scholars, that "he studied and graduated in traditional Islamic disciplines, including shariah (Islamic Jurisprudence) and *Muwatta* (from the Maliki School of Islamic Law)."[85] Written in the 8th century by Malik ibn Anas,[86] founder of the second of the four doctrinal schools of Islamic law (Maliki),[87] *Muwatta* (*Trodden Path*) is among "the oldest corpus of Sunnite law."[88] As Imam Magid's status as an imam derives at least in part from his mastery of the *Muwatta*, a sampling from that text's treatment of jihad and apostasy might provide some indicators of Magid's own views:

21 Jihad, 21.1 Stimulation of Desires for Jihad

> 2 The Messenger of Allah, may Allah bless him and grant him peace, said, "Allah guarantees either the Garden or a safe return to his home with whatever he has obtained of reward or booty for the one who does *jihad* in His way ...[89]

21 Jihad, 21.14 The Martyrs in the Way of Allah

> 27 The Messenger of Allah, may Allah bless him and grant him peace, said, "By He in whose hand my self is! I would like to fight in the way of Allah and be killed, then be brought to life again and so I can be killed, and then be brought to life again so I could be killed."[90]

33 Yahya related to me from Malik that Yahya ibn Sa'id said, "The Messenger of Allah, may Allah bless him and grant him peace, was sitting by the grave which was being dug at Madina. A man looked into the grave and said, "An awful bed for the believer." The Messenger of Allah, may Allah bless him and grant him peace, said "Evil? What you have said is absolutely wrong." The man said, "I didn't mean that, Messenger of Allah. I meant being killed in the way of Allah." The Messenger of Allah, may Allah bless him and grant him peace, said. *"Being killed in the way of Allah has no like!* There is no place on the earth where I would prefer my grave to be than here [Madina]." He repeated it three times.[91]

36 Judgements [sic], 36.18 Judgement [sic] on the Abandonment of Islam.

15 Yahya related to me ... that the Messenger of Allah, may Allah bless him and grant him peace, said, "If someone changes his religion – then strike off his head!" The meaning of the statement of the Prophet, may Allah bless him and grant him peace, in our opinion – and Allah knows best – is that, "If someone changes his religion – then strike off his head!" refers to those who leave Islam for something else – like heretics and suchlike, about whom that is known. They are killed without being called to repent because their repentance is not recognized. They were concealing their disbelief and making their Islam public, so I do not think that one should call such people to repent and one does not accept their word. As for the person who leaves Islam for something else and divulges it, he is called on to repent. If he does not turn in repentance, he is killed.[92]

Divi et Impera

It should be noted that the Brotherhood has separate courses of action and "useful idiots" to deal with Jews and Christians. For Jews, there is the Commission for Jewish Muslim Understanding (CJMU);[93] for Protestants, the Commission for Christian-Muslim Understanding (CCMR);[94] and for Catholics, the Catholic-Muslim Dialogue (CMD).[95] The Brotherhood's strategy to eliminate Western civilization "by our hands" includes the manipulation of these bilateral relationships to bring non-Muslim groups into conflict with each other while advancing Brotherhood objectives, not the least of which is stirring up internecine strife of the type that brought Mohammed to Medina. We should review circumstances where newfound frictions between Christians and Jews align with newfound bilateral "special relationships"[96] with Brotherhood entities.

There is no question that *Interfaith Dialogue* is a Muslim Brotherhood monograph that reflects the Brotherhood's orientation to the interfaith community. The examples of successful outreach in the book concern those Christian and Jewish entities that lack the discernment to look past friendly presentations of facially neutral narratives that mask hostile intent. Building on Qutb's "bridge building" formula, Muslim Brotherhood chief jurist Qaradawi confirms that the objective of interfaith dialogue is to advance the dawah message (to "invite" to Islam) while turning Christians against Jews:

> Dialogue with the People of the Book on matters of faith is not forbidden, according to the Islamic law. However, nobody should do that unless he is well versed in the rules and teachings of Islam and has knowledge of their beliefs, and **provided he intends to do that for the sake of God.** ... So, God has ordered us to argue with them in ways that are best and most gracious. We see that God laid down the principles of the Islamic preaching in the Koran when He says: '**Invite (all)** to the Way of thy Lord with wisdom and beautiful preaching; and argue with them in ways that are best and most gracious.' [Partial Koranic Verse; Al-Nahl, 16:125] ... When you engage in a dialogue, try to establish common grounds between yourself and the other party and say: 'We all believe in one God, so let us come to common terms.' We do not engage in dialogue with them so that they may be pleased with our religion. ... We only converse with them to find common grounds on which to stand together against atheism, obscenity, and grievances. We converse with them and ask them: 'What is your stance on the cause of Palestine, the issue of Jerusalem, or the issue of Al-Aqsa Mosque?' We try to rally the Christians with us to stand together, especially for the cause of Palestine, since Palestine has both Muslims and Christians.[97]

To get a sense for the effectiveness of this campaign, just visit a major Christian denominated university or college campus with a Muslim Student Association (MSA) presence. Alongside entities obligated to lie are groups that want to be lied to. The Brotherhood has identified both a cadre and forum it believes is vulnerable to reason-deadening narratives that undermine discernment and result in the dislocation of faith.

The New Invincible Ignorance

While Shingieti, Magid, and others may try to explain away such statements, one suspects that most in the interfaith community are hardly aware of their existence, and fewer still are willing to undertake any substantive due-diligence effort to find them out, as this would constitute a breach of Landau's "mutual trust," which they feel a higher calling to respect and to enforce. After all, these are the interfaith "partners" to whom we have pledged "to remain committed to being friends when the world would separate us from one another,"[98] supported by "mutual trust"[99] that only allows discussions of Islam that the Brotherhood affirms "as accurate"[100] even though Brotherhood members are required to lie if the goals are obligatory.[101]

In June 2014, Pope Francis invited the Palestinians and Israelis to the Vatican gardens for a day of prayer along with Muslim, Christian, and Jewish clerics. Although the prayers were to be pre-approved, the Palestinian imam (and al-Azhar graduate) went off script and read three verses of the Qur'an specifically hostile to Jews and Christians and then went into a freeform prayer that menaced the Israeli guests. The three Quranic Verses are 2:284, 285, and 286:

> To Allah belongeth all that is in the heavens and on earth. Whether ye show what is in your minds or conceal it, Allah Calleth you to account for it. He forgiveth whom He pleaseth, and punisheth whom He pleaseth, for Allah hath power over all things. (Qur'an 2:284)

> The Messenger believeth in what hath been revealed to him from his Lord, as do the men of faith. Each one (of them) believeth in Allah, His angels, His books, and His messengers. "We make no distinction (they say) between one and another of His messengers." And they say: "We hear, and we obey: (We seek) Thy forgiveness, our Lord, and to Thee is the end of all journeys." (Qur'an 2:285)

> On no soul doth Allah Place a burden greater than it can bear. It gets every good that it earns, and it suffers every ill that it earns. (Pray:) "Our Lord! Condemn us not if we forget or fall into error; our Lord! Lay not on us a burden Like that which Thou didst lay on those before us; Our Lord! Lay not on us a burden greater than we have strength to bear. Blot out our sins, and grant us forgiveness. Have mercy on us. Thou art our Protector; Help us against those who stand against faith." (Qur'an 2:286)

Some Qur'an translations[6] as well as the tafsirs of both ibn Kathir[7] and al-Jalalayn[8] make it clear that Jews and Christians are the focus of these verses. The tafsirs also explain that the meaning of "believers" is limited to those who believe in Mohammed,[9] that Judaism and Christianity have been abrogated,[10] and that the verses are directed at those who are to be fought as enemies[11] because they deny the Prophethood of Mohammed.[12]

---

6 For example, from *Interpretation of the Meanings of the Noble Qur'an in the English Language* with regard to Qur'an Verse 2:286 : "Allah burdens not a person beyond his scope. He gets reward for that (good) which he has earned, and he is punished for that (evil) which he has earned, "Our Lord! Punish us not if we forget or fall into error, our Lord! Lay not on us a burden like that which You did lay on those before us (Jews and Christians); our Lord! Put not on us a burden greater than we have strength to bear. Pardon us and grant us forgiveness, Have mercy on us. You are our Maula (Patron, Supporter and Protector) and give us victory over the disbelieving people." For example, from *Interpretation of the Meanings of the Noble Qur'an in the English Language*: A Summarized Version of At-Tabari; Al-Qurtubi, and Ibn Kathir with Comments from Sahih Al-Bukhari, trans. and commentary by Dr. Muhammad Taqi-ud-Din Al-Hilali, and Dr. Muhammad Muhsin Khan, Darussalam, Riyadh, Saudi Arabia, 1999.

7 *Tafsir of Ibn Kathir*, vol. 2 with regard to Verse 2:284: "Our Lord! Lay not on us a burden like that which You did lay on those before us (Jews and Christians)," from Al-Hafiz Abu al-Fida' 'Imad Ad-Din Isma'il bin 'Umar bin Kathir Al-Qurashi Al-Busrawi ibn Kathir, *Tafsir of Ibn Kathir*, vol. 2, Trans. Abdul-Malik Mujahid. (Riyadh: Darussalam, 2000), 98.

8 From *Tafsir Al-Jalalayn* with regard to Verse 2:284: "We do not differentiate between any of his Messengers, not believing in some and rejecting some as the Jews and Christians do," Jalalu'd-din Al-Mahalli and Jalalu'd-din As-Suyuti, Tafsir Al-Jalalayn, first published in 1461 a.d., trans. Aisha Bewley, 2007, Dar Al-Taqwa Ltd., London, p. 111.

9 *Tafsir of Ibn Kathir*, vol. 2 with regard to Verse 2:285: "Therefore, each of the believers believe that Allah is the One and Only and the Sustainer, there is no deity worthy of worship except Him. The believers also believe in all Allah's Prophets and Messengers, in the Books that were revealed from heaven to the Messengers and Prophets, who are indeed the servants of Allah. Further, the believers do not differentiate between any of the Prophets, such as, believing in some of them and rejecting others. Rather, all of Allah's Prophets and Messengers are, to the believers, truthful, righteous, and they were each guided to the path of righteousness, even when some of them bring what abrogates the Law of some others by Allah's leave. Later on, the Law of Muhammad, the Final Prophet and Messenger from Allah, abrogated all the laws of the Prophets before him. So the Last Hour will commence while Muhammad's Law remains the only valid Law, and all the while a group of his *Ummah* will always be on the path of truth, apparent and dominant." Al-Hafiz Abu al-Fida' 'Imad Ad-Din Isma'il bin 'Umar bin Kathir Al-Qurashi Al-Busrawi ibn Kathir, *Tafsir of Ibn Kathir*, vol. 2, Trans. Abdul-Malik Mujahid. (Riyadh: Darussalam, 2000), 102.

10 *Tafsir of Ibn Kathir*, vol. 2 with regard to Verse 2:286: "You sent your Prophet Muhammad, the Prophet of mercy, to abrogate these burdens through the Law that you revealed to him." Al-Hafiz Abu al-Fida' 'Imad Ad-Din Isma'il bin 'Umar bin Kathir Al-Qurashi Al-Busrawi ibn Kathir, *Tafsir of Ibn Kathir*, vol. 2, Trans. Abdul-Malik Mujahid. (Riyadh: Darussalam, 2000), 104.

11 *Tafsir Al-Jalalayn* with regard to Verse 2:286 (p 111) "so help us against the people of the unbelievers. Establishing the proof against the unbelievers and enable us to overcome them in fighting. The duty of the Master is to help those He protects against their enemies." Jalalu'd-din Al-Mahalli and Jalalu'd-din As-Suyuti, Tafsir Al-Jalalayn, first published in 1461 a.d., trans. Aisha Bewley, 2007, Dar Al-Taqwa Ltd., London, p. 111.

12 *Tafsir of Ibn Kathir*, vol. 2, states with regard to Verse 2:286: "And give us victory over the disbelieving people" means "those who rejected Your religion, denied Your Oneness, refused the Message of Your Prophet, worshipped other than You and associated others in Your worship. Give us victory and

The event at the Vatican was broadcast in Arabic to the entire Muslim world: the imam insulted Christians and Jews in the presence of the Pope for all to see. It was an intentional act. When going to freeform prayer, the imam turned to thinly veiled hostility directed toward the Israeli guests of the Vatican:

> Oh Allah, you are peace, and peace is from you and you bring us to life by peace. Safeguard countries and their people from war and destruction. Make the downtrodden of this world victorious, oh Lord of worlds. **Make victorious those whose blood has been spilled and those bereaved. And those who have been displaced and threatened upon your Earth, oh Lord of Worlds.** Have mercy on humanity through your grace until **a just and complete peace** will reign which will give every person his rights to life. **Free is your Lord, Lord of glory from what they ascribe to Him**. And peace be unto the Messengers and praise be to the Lord of Worlds. Amen.[102]

Being "free ... from what they ascribe to Him" refers to Christians, and the imam's call for a "complete peace" is to be understood in the context of Islamic notions of peace, as previously discussed. The language of "making victorious those whose blood has been spilled ... against those who have been displaced" highlights the Israeli-Palestinian conflict and aligns it with the same Qur'an verses that Fort Hood shooter Major Hasan used when stating his fidelity to Alwaki (as discussed in Part VII):

> Fight in the cause of Allah those who fight you, but do not transgress limits; for Allah loveth not transgressors.⊠And slay them wherever ye catch them, and turn them out from where they have Turned you out; for tumult and oppression are worse than slaughter; but fight them not at the Sacred Mosque, unless they (first) fight you there; but if they fight you, slay them. Such is the reward of those who suppress faith. But if they cease, Allah is Oft-forgiving, Most Merciful. And fight them on until there is no more Tumult or oppression, and there prevail justice and faith in Allah; but if they cease, Let there be no hostility except to those who practice oppression. (Qur'an 2:190-193)

This is what is known about the Quranic verses and what can be reasonably assessed with regard to the imam's freeform portion of the prayer. Neither is a reach. Before we discuss the Vatican's response to this event, however, it should be noted that the imam's language of enmity came just prior to major hostilities ini-

---

make us prevail above them in this and the hereafter." Al-Hafiz Abu al-Fida' 'Imad Ad-Din Isma'il bin 'Umar bin Kathir Al-Qurashi Al-Busrawi ibn Kathir, *Tafsir of Ibn Kathir*, vol. 2, Trans. Abdul-Malik Mujahid. (Riyadh: Darussalam, 2000), 105.

tiated by Hamas against Israel that initiated just weeks later. News of the imam's insult worked its way into the Western media slowly due to the Vatican's editing of the prayer before posting it. In fact, it took a number of days before the Vatican acknowledged the imam's actions, and then did so only in a German article ("Islamfachmann: Koran-Rezitation bei Friednsgebeten ist Legitim") on *Radio Vatikan.*[103] The effect of this non-disclosure was that the Muslim world was aware of what happened while the Western world was not.

The *Radio Vatikan* article insisted there was no hostility on the part of the imam and that the term infidel, as used by the imam, did not apply to Jews and Christians. The *Radio Vatikan* article relied on Fr. Felix Körner, a Jesuit at the Pontifical Gregorian University in Rome, who said that "this Qur'an passage makes reference to unbelievers against whom we beg God's help, then it is completely clear that what is meant here is not the Jews and also not the Christians, both of whom naturally recognize the oneness of God!"[104] Fr. Körner's assessment is simply wrong. At the very time Körner was making these comments, Christians were being murdered, raped, and dispossessed for refusing to recognize the oneness of God, *tawheed*, as expressed by the imam, which categorically rejects Christian concepts of God. Just a few examples from the Qur'an:

> They do blaspheme who say: "Allah is Christ the son of Mary." But said Christ: "O Children of Israel! worship Allah, my Lord and your Lord." Whoever joins other gods with Allah, - Allah will forbid him the garden, and the Fire will be his abode. There will for the wrong-doers be no one to help. (Qur'an 5:72)

> They do blaspheme who say: Allah is one of three in a Trinity: for there is no god except One Allah. If they desist not from their word (of blasphemy), verily a grievous penalty will befall the blasphemers among them. (Qur'an Verses 5:73)

> Christ the son of Mary was no more than a messenger; many were the messengers that passed away before him. His mother was a woman of truth. They had both to eat their (daily) food. See how Allah doth make His signs clear to them; yet see in what ways they are deluded away from the truth! (Qur'an Verses 5:75)

> And behold! Allah will say: "O Jesus the son of Mary! Didst thou say unto men, worship me and my mother as gods in derogation of Allah'? "He will say: "Glory to Thee! never could I say what I had no right to say. (Qur'an Verse 5:116)

For a believing Muslim, these verses reflect direct divine revelation. For those who understand the effects of abrogation, they are the final word. Providing erroneous, non-responsive narratives, as Fr. Körner did, to substantive inquiries is only part of the problem presented by such interfaith narratives. In what's become a hallmark of the interfaith meme, indefensible non-responses often have embedded within them a condescending judgmentalism that questions the motivations of those raising concerns. No matter how obviously wrong an interfaith position might be—Fr. Körner's, for example—and no matter how patently correct the inquiry, the response narrative typically suggests that those raising their concern are uniformed in ways that suggest masked bigotry. Hence, for Fr. Körner, to disagree is to be "skewed" in one's orientation and "biased" in one's understanding of the subject manner:

> And for that reason there is no misunderstanding here; but if one hears something in a skewed manner, one is going to have a mistaken understanding of it.[105]

> One can always hear with a biased ear … therefore, who hears with a biased ear, can understand everything in a biased way.[106]

Under the Brotherhood-enhanced postmodern narrative, anyone who dislikes threatening Islamic rhetoric, as Fr. Körner suggests, is Islamophobic. Note how Fr. Körner's fidelity to the interfaith meme establishes his fidelity to OIC norms, which, according to an OIC press release, the Vatican accepted when agreeing on "the need for greater efforts to foster respect for religious pluralism and cultural diversity, and to counter the spread of bigotry and prejudice" when it met with the OIC General Secretary in December 2013.[107]

This is the same OIC that helped orchestrate the "Day of Rage" attack on Pope Benedict at Regensburg in 2006 because he violated Islamophobia norms that Körner so zealously enforces (see Part V). The most insulting aspect of Körner's defense of the imam is that he not only sanitized and shielded the incident from the Western audience, but he did so by establishing an equivalency between the imam's actions and Pope Benedict's historically accurate lecture to students, faculty, and staff at Regensburg:

> There is something in connection with the prayers for peace in the Vatican garden, now being debated, which is remarkably reminiscent of the results attendant on the so called Regensburg Address of Pope Benedict XVI in September of 2006. We recall: The Pope conveyed an Islam-critical quotation, the content of which he did not adopt as his own and he expressly identified it as a quotation. However, it filled Muslims with consternation and made them angry. Do you also see a parallel?[108]

"There is a certain parallel insofar as a quotation torn out of context is particularly easily misunderstood. And if one removes from the text only the reference to unbelievers, one can easily use it as a peg upon which to hang something and then say that an infringement has taken place here. On the other hand we have in this case a Koran recitation which pertains to someone who not only quotes, but recites, and who also says: what I am reciting here is also what I believe. And in the same breath he is also saying: We Muslims, as the Koran precisely tells us, recognize the other religions with their prophets. Therefore from the Muslim side, there was by no means any deprecation or exclusion intended or expressed. Rather it was said: We are bringing here a religious idea, one which welcomes and accepts you all, and naturally in a certain Koranic way, tries to set things right again. But there was nothing here which was meant to exclude or rebuff; rather a Koran verse was recited, which is meant to express the highest respect and therefore can also be received as such."[109]

Almost everything Körner said is inaccurate or misleading. The Days of Rage staged against Pope Benedict were not caused by any error on Benedict's part, and those seeking to use it to incite violence to intimidate the Vatican were clear in their purpose and intent: submission. Körner's moral equivalency—born of relativism—between the imam's calculated insult and Pope Benedict's professorial lecture is disturbing. The question isn't whether Körner's response was disinformation; that much is clear. The question is whether he was aware of it. Perhaps Körner is guilty only of giving preference to the bond of "mutual trust" with his Qur'an exegete friend at the Gregorian Institute,[110] which compels him to keep the pledge "to remain committed to being friends when the world would separate us from one another."[111] Because the OIC reported that the Vatican is committed "to support interfaith dialogue initiatives,"[112] it is not unreasonable to template Fr. Körner's response to the Brotherhood's narrative as stated in the IIIT's *Interfaith Dialogue*. It certainly lines up with it. We know what Brotherhood (and OIC) objectives are in the interfaith mission. Does the Vatican? If not, why? If they do know, what does it mean? As it stands, the Vatican suppresses discussion of issues in specific conformance to OIC requirements based on shariah notions of slander in the name of interfaith solidarity.

There are other, smaller-scale examples of the Brotherhood's hostility in the interfaith context, as well. Over Labor Day weekend in 2014, a series of churches were vandalized in Columbus, Indiana. At one church, the term "infidel" was written on an exterior wall alongside a reference to Qur'an Verse 19:88, and at another church, "infidel" was written alongside Verse 3:151.[113] In Verse 19:88, Allah notes that Christians call Jesus the Son of God. Verse 19:88 is to be understood in the context of the following two verses, which states that all of creation screams out at such a blasphemy.[13]

> **They say: "Allah Most Gracious has begotten a son!"** Indeed
> ye have put forth a thing most monstrous! At it the skies are
> ready to burst, the earth to split asunder, and the mountains
> to fall down in utter ruin. ⊠(Qur'an 19:88–90)

Verse 19:88–90 establishes divine recognition of the infidelity of Christians. The other verse, Verse 3:151, establishes that Christians can be made the object of terror and that they are going to hell.

> Soon shall We cast terror into the hearts of the Unbelievers,
> for that they joined companions with Allah, for which He
> had sent no authority: their abode will be the Fire: And evil is
> the home of the wrong-doers! (Qur'an 3:151)

"They joined companions with Allah" is a reference to Christians' associating Jesus and the Holy Spirit with God. As direct divine revelation, Allah will cast terror into the hearts of Christians and send them to hell because of their infidelity. That's what those verses say. That's what they mean.[14] Writing "infidel" alongside Qur'an verses that are specific to Christian infidelity and call for "terror" against them is specifically threatening, specifically directed, and should be taken seriously. This was not the work of a random vandal: When Verse 19:88 is used in tandem with Verse 3:151, a jihadi narrative is established that points to a perpetrator who had subject-matter awareness.

Through events like these, the Brotherhood builds up its investment in the interfaith movement. Father Marcotte, associate pastor at one of the churches, responded to the vandalism by saying, "It's upsetting … because there's just not a whole lot to go on."[114] He noted that it's "bizarre … that they hit two other Chris-

---

13 *Tafsir Ibn Kathir*, vol. 6, 312. On Qur'an Verses 19:88-90, *Tafsir ibn Kathir* explains the meaning of the verses under the heading "The Stern Rejection of Attributing a Son to Allah": [regarding 19:88] After Allah affirms in this noble Surah that 'Isa was a worshipper and servant of Allah and He mentioned his birth from Maryam without a father, He then begins refuting those who claim that He has a son. Holy is He and far Exalted in He above such description. [regarding 19:89-90 – the following verse] – that is, out of their high esteem for Allah that is, out of their high esteem for Allah, when they hear this statement of wickedness coming from the Children of Adam. The reason for this is that these are creatures of Allah and they are established upon His Tawhid and the fact that there is no deity worthy of worship except Him. He has no partners, no peer, no child, no mate and no coequal. Rather, He is the One, Self-Sufficient Master, Whom all creatures are in need of.

14 *Tafsir Ibn Kathir*, vol. 2, 288. On Qur'an Verses 3:151, *Tafsir ibn Kathir* explains the meaning of Verse 3:151 under the heading "The Prohibition of Obeying the Disbelievers; the Cause of Defeat at Uhud": Allah next conveys the good news that He will put fear of the Muslims, and feelings of subordination to the Muslims in the hearts of their disbelieving enemies, because of their Kufr and Shirk. And Allah has prepared torment and punishment for them in the Hereafter. […] I [Muhammad] was given five things that no other Prophet before me was given. I was aided with fear the distance of one month, the earth was made a Masjid and clean place for me, I was allowed war booty, I was given the Intercession, and Prophets used to be sent to their people, but I was sent to all mankind particularly.

tian Churches." He then asked, "Why did they pick the three of us?"[115] Could the institutionalized effects of the interfaith bond of "mutual trust" be obscuring the obvious answer? At a time when so many jihadi organizations openly terrorize large populations because they are not Muslim, Father Marcotte expressed skepticism concerning Islamic motivations: "Is there somebody that really believes that we're all infidels so they felt the need to write it all over our church?" In lockstep with the Brotherhood meme, Marcotte's rhetorical question gestured at the only answer that made sense to him: It was either a prank or, more likely, "someone is trying to incite people against Muslims."[116]

To affirm these motivations, Nassim Khaled, a man identified only as a resident of Columbus who volunteers at the Islamic Center, the use of the verses shows "the ignorance [of] who[ever] actually misquoted or misinterpreted the Quran."[117] Yet there was nothing misquoted and nothing to misinterpret. Khaled insisted that the "important thing to realize is [that] reading the verses alone can make them sound scary," but, "in his eyes, they're actually far from that." Perhaps they are not scary—to him. But we know the verses, and we know what they mean. Could Khaled be leveraging the interfaith rule that "each dialogue partner has the right to define his or her own religion and belief, [so that] the rest can only describe what it looks like to them from the outside"?[118] Early offers of friendly support at lower levels of vandalism are used to introduce partners to the pledge meme "to remain committed to being friends when the world would separate us from one another"[119] so that, as the intensity of such events heats up and accelerates over time, the relationship can be reinforced along lines established by such narratives.

Khaled assured that "we are almost certain that it's someone from outside our community or it's an unstable person," and his interfaith "partners" predictably acquiesced. Reverend Bridgewater responded, "Nobody really thought it was somebody from the Islamic community, we just thought is was probably some kids trying to stir up hate."[120] This is how the postmodern narrative is put in the service of dhimmitude.

Initial low-level vandalism sets up an action/response cycle that establishes the "good cop" image while affirming the interfaith pledge ("to remain committed to being friends when the world would separate us from one another"[121]) that fixes partners in the interfaith meme as tensions escalate. As an isolated incident, this assessment might seem an overreach. But there is a pattern of behavior that makes this action/response activity predictable from incident to incident over time. *Black's Law* 9th defines a pattern as "a mode of behavior or series of acts that are recognizably consistent."[122] In certain legal arguments, establishing a pattern of behavior may serve as evidence in a legal proceeding. Michael Samsel, a certified domestic-violence-perpetrator treatment provider,[123] explains that in abusive relationships, it is the pattern that establishes the coercive behavior:

"Abuse consists of both tactics and patterns. Understanding the patterns is essential to understanding abuse since, apart from more extreme acts, it is *in the pattern* that the coerciveness and control resides."[124]

Black's Law 9th goes on to define coerce as "to compel by force or threat" and coercion as "compulsion by physical force or threat of physical force."[125] Mapping the events in Columbus against Brotherhood objectives in interfaith outreach as laid out in *Interfaith Dialogue* is informative, predictable, and depressing. Whether it's the Vatican gardens or priests, ministers, and rabbis in small-town America, the interfaith narrative has established a grip on some within Christian and Jewish leadership that will throttle believers who stand up to such actions – by our own hand.

The situation is not getting any better. The Brotherhood's history of supporting genocidal murder of Christians and Animists in the Sudan; Boko Haram's murderous attacks on Christians and the forced sexual servitude of Christian girls in Nigeria; the mass killings, dispossessions, and sexual servitude in Syria and Iraq that occur on a daily basis—all the groups responsible for these atrocities accurately cite shariah in furtherance of their objectives in jurisdictions that recognize such claims. Yet Bishop Denis Madden, the Auxiliary of Baltimore and Chairman of the U.S. Conference of Catholic Bishops (USCCB) Committee on Ecumenical and Interreligious Affairs, still feels comfortable relying on a Muslim Brotherhood entity (ISNA) and an Islamic Movement group (MPAC) for his authority when claiming that jihadi activities have nothing to do with Islam:

> Stressing the importance of engaging in dialogue "with the religion many people automatically (and wrongly) blame for this violence," Bishop Madden said in a September 2 blog post that "Muslim leaders in the United States, including the Islamic Society of North America and the Muslim Public Affairs Council, have been resolute in their condemnation of the violence in Iraq and Syria."[126]

While the bishop's statement was directed against the group his Brotherhood "partners" condemned—ISIS in Iraq—it should be remembered that the Brotherhood in Syria has worked with Jabhat al-Nusra[127] and has also engaged in such activities in the Sudan. Given the bishop's reliance on ISNA and MPAC for his understanding of Islam, it is not unreasonable to assume he has taken the interfaith rules to heart. It is possible that the bishop—and, through him, the USCCB—may have accepted the bond of "mutual trust" and committed himself to the "Pledge of Remembrance and Commitment to Peace" "to remain committed to being friends when the world would separate us from one another."[128] No matter what.

So when the bishop was quoted in *Newsweek* to the effect that "Islamophobia in America is on the rise,"[129] he did so with an interest in bringing the institutional weight of the USCCB to bear to counter it. This puts the USCCB in position to enforce the OIC's Ten-Year Programme of Action—as executed by the Brotherhood in America under the rubric of Islamophobia—against its own members. Committing to the interfaith bond of "mutual trust" entails a breach of faith with the faithful—and the sheep are taking notice.

We live in times when the shepherds feed their sheep to the wolves and think it virtuous. We already know what the bishop doesn't know; we know what he thinks he knows; we know he lacks discernment to recognize ravenous wolves; we know he is unaware; and we know he's in charge. So do his Brotherhood partners. As the faithful become aware, the knowledge becomes faith-killing. Recall that Pakistani Brigadier S. K. Malik said the destruction of faith is a primary objective of dawah in the preparatory stage. It also meets the "civilization-jihad by our hands" criteria that the American Muslim Brotherhood set for its strategy of subversion. From the Vatican, to small-town American, to the USCCB, to the entire interfaith apparatus, the Brotherhood knows what it has—and it has a good thing. There is reason to believe that the USCCB's interfaith orientation resonates with the Vatican's. In July 2014, Father John Crossin, the Executive Director of the Secretariat for Ecumenical and Interreligious Affairs of the USCCB, was named to the Pontifical Council for Promoting Christian Unity as consultant to Pope Francis.[130]

This is not unique to Catholics, as this scenario is playing itself out in many Protestant, Evangelical and Jewish communities, as well. For example, William M. Schweitzer, a minister in the Presbyterian Church in America (PCA), undertook a review of the "Insider Movement"[15] and found that members dissipate their faith by "contextualizing" it to the point that it becomes meaningless while never saying anything about Christianity that would antagonize. Reverend Schweitzer's research found that Christian missionaries in the Insider Movement, when evangelizing to the Muslim world, are advised not to argue that Jesus is the Son of God, object to the Muslim "testimony" (*shahada*), object to the Muslim concept of Allah, challenge the inspiration of the Qur'an, or ask Muslims to convert to Christianity.[131] The interfaith leadership of the Christian and Jewish communities has reached the reality dislocation that Josef Pieper spoke of:

> "The sophists", he [Plato] says, "fabricate a fictitious reality."
> That the existential realm of man could be taken over by pseu-
> dorealities whose fictitious nature threatens to become indis-
> cernible is truly a depressing thought. And yet, the Platonic

---

15 In a related article on the Insider Movement in Christianity, Philip Mark offers the following definition: "IM affirms that a Christian ought to retain the identity of his socio/religious background. IM denies that a Christian ought to assume a Christian identity." "Insider Movements Defined...Biblically," Reformation21- Alliance of Confessing Evangelicals, June 2014, URL: http://www.reformation21.org/articles/insider-movements-definedbiblically.php.

nightmare, I hold, possesses an alarming contemporary relevance. For the general public is being reduced to a state where people are not only unable to find out about the truth but also become unable even to search for the truth because they are satisfied with deception and trickery that have determined their convictions, satisfied with a fictitious reality created by design through the abuse of language. This, says Plato, is the worst thing that the sophists are capable of wreaking upon mankind by their corruption of the word.[132]

Not only do interfaith partners want to be lied to, they encourage it while seeking to institutionalize ignorance as a higher moral virtue. In the interfaith community, the Brotherhood can recognize deconstructed minds willing to subordinate articles of faith to interfaith rules. For the Brotherhood, interfaith penetration may simply be a case of the shepherds allowing the wolves to assist in a process that is already underway. The regimes established by these interfaith rules reject reason and deny truth. They also sustain a postmodern form of invincible ignorance that cannot be excused by a "through no fault of their own"[133] defense when challenged. They should not be too easily overlooked or too casually forgiven.

Shafiq includes the "Pledge of Remembrance and Commitment to Peace" that was adopted by the Rochester Interfaith Forum in *Interfaith Dialogue* as the model pledge[134] (that is to be understood exclusively in terms of Sayyid Qutb's explanation of universal peace). In the context of the interfaith movement, the "by our hands" strategy has the Brotherhood imposing the interfaith community's own rules against themselves by simply seeking their enforcement. Even if just to satisfy due-diligence concerns, shouldn't Brotherhood-promoted pledges be assessed for the possibility that they might serve as a mechanism to leverage interfaith loyalties? Measures should be taken to ensure that Brotherhood "partners" aren't (so easily) manipulated into acting against their co-religionists in furtherance of that pledge. What does it mean when faith leaders put such an oath ahead of the canons of their own faith not to mention their own followers? From the perspective of a doctrinally aligned Brotherhood effort, how could such a pledge be leveraged in the aftermath of a terrorist attack like the Boston Marathon Bombing ?

> *We Pledge to Remember* that each has the power to heal and bring us closer together or to sting and further divide us. When we speak or act publicly, **regardless of our feelings of rage or terror or shame,** we will remember that we can choose our response, and be sensitive to not using words that are perceived as hurtful.[135] [Emphasis added.]

Paragraph 253

In November 2013, the Apostolic Exhortation *Evangelii Gaudium* was published by the Vatican. Paragraph 253 reads:

> Faced with disconcerting episodes of violent fundamentalism, our respect for true followers of Islam should lead us to avoid hateful generalisations, for authentic Islam and the proper reading of the Koran are opposed to every form of violence.[136]

While the substance of the paragraph does not concern issues of faith,[137] certain knowledge and competence demands that questions be raised.[138] The troubling aspects of Paragraph 253 are twofold: It is not true that "authentic Islam and the proper reading of the Koran are opposed to every form of violence." Consequently, people who point this out are not engaged in "generalizations" or in "hateful generalizations." Because the Paragraph 253 claim is certainly not true, and no offer of proof is given to substantiate it, it takes on the character of a conclusory assumption whose authority rests solely on the derisive accusation that those who disagree—including those acting in good conscience—are presumptively little more than bigoted, uninformed "haters."

Paragraph 253 indicates that the Vatican is drifting down the path of unconsidered adoption of the OIC's Islamophobia narrative as policy through the uncritical acceptance of interfaith dialogue rules. The USCCB, along with most major Christian and Jewish groups in America, already enjoys its "special" relationship with its Muslim Brotherhood partners. At all levels of communication, the approach to the faithful reflects interfaith preferences that have taken on the characteristics of what the American legal system calls "prior restraint"—because the interfaith narrative is calibrated to forestall and silence all *bona fide* debate.

This effort is in furtherance of imposing shariah speech standards on the sheep—regardless of whether the shepherds are aware of it. For the Brotherhood and the OIC, specific performance suffices. Such are the recognized fruits of *Interfaith Dialogue*: guarantees of "mutual trust"[139] that allow only those discussions of Islam that Muslim partners affirm "as accurate,"[140] underpinned by pledges "to remain committed to being friends when the world would separate us from one another."[141] Whether it's the Vatican working with interfaith partners at al-Azhar, the Saudis, or the OIC, or it's the USCCB working with Muslim Brotherhood front groups like ISNA, IIIT, CAIR, or the MSA's (on Catholic college campuses)—if they scratched just beneath the surface, they would know that their Brotherhood partners openly accept the very doctrines that, under Paragraph 253, they would brand their fellow faithful as "haters" for pointing out.

Because this is an issue that affects our freedom and free will, this section will proceed with extensive footnotes to make concrete the dispositive nature of the Islamic doctrines that Paragraph 253 discounts when asserting its claim. It will likewise revisit issues already covered in other parts of the book and tailor them to this issue. Finally, it will rely on sources that not only make reasonable claims to being authentic expressions of Islam but are recognized as such by Muslims directly involved in interfaith dialogue with the Jewish and Christian communities in the West, including the Church at all levels. The discussion will spiral from a single data point. It is not enough to demonstrate that Paragraph 253 is wrong; it is important also to show that the Vatican's interfaith partners and those of the USCCB know this. As with the earlier discussions on the imam's prayer in the Vatican gardens and the desecration of churches in Columbus, IN, each of the events discussed in this section occurred after *Evangelii Gaudium* was published in 2013.

In August 2014, an Egyptian Mufti defended the authoritative status of Bukhari's hadith, *Sahih Al-Bukhari*, going so far as to claim that to challenge Bukhari's status would be to undermine Muslim society and culture.[142] On the back cover of each of the ten volumes of the English-language translations of *Sahih Al-Bukhari*, scholarly consensus[143] is asserted on the authoritative nature of that collection: "All Muslim scholars are agreed that *Sahih Al-Bukhari* is the most authentic and reliable book after the Book of Allah"[144] (meaning the Qur'an).

Paragraph 253 claims that "authentic Islam and the proper reading of the Koran are opposed to every form of violence." Compare that to *Sahih Al-Bukhari*, Book 56 "The Book of Jihad[(1)] – (Fighting for Allah's Cause)," Volume IV, which contains 154 pages of hadith on the sayings or acts of the Prophet on jihad, defined as "Holy fighting." Lest there be any doubt concerning the status of jihad in *Bukhari*, the book title "The Book of Jihad[(1)]" includes a footnote:

> (1) *Al-Jihad* (Holy fighting) in Allah's Cause (with full force of numbers and weaponry), is given the utmost importance in Islam, and is one of its pillars (on which it stands). By *Jihad* Islam is established, Allah's word is made superior. [His Word being (La *ilaha illahllah* which means none has the right to be worshipped but Allah)], and His religion (Islam) is propagated. By abandoning *Jihad*, (may Allah protect us from that). [sic] Islam and Muslims fall into an inferior position, their honour [sic] is lost, their land is stolen, their rule and authority vanish. *Jihad* is an obligatory duty in Islam, on every Muslim, and he who tries to escape from this duty or does not in his innermost heart wish to fulfil [sic] this duty, dies with one of the qualities of a hypocrite.[145]

The footnote is from *The Translation of the Meanings of Sahih Al-Bukhari*, put out by a reputable Islamic publishing house, Darussalam, in Riyadh, Saudi Arabia, with branches in the United States. Because all Muslims are required to emulate the life of the Prophet, a few samplings from *Sahih Bukhari* will illustrate the problem these hadith pose to Paragraph 253's claim that dissenting voices are dealing in "generalizations" when they protest the assertion that "authentic Islam is opposed to violence":

> Muhammad said, "... I have been made victorious with terror cast in the hearts of the enemy." (*Sahih Bukhari*, Volume 4, Book 52, Number 220)[146]

> Allah's Apostle said, "Know that Paradise is under the shades of swords." (*Sahih Bukhari*, Volume 4, Book 52, Number 73)[147]

> The Prophet said, "Who is ready to kill Ka'b bin Al-Ashraf who has really hurt Allah and His Apostle?" Muhammad bin Maslama said, "O Allah's Apostle! Do you like me to kill him?" He replied in the affirmative. (*Sahih Bukhari*, Volume 4, Book 52, Number 270)[148]

> Allah's Apostle entered Mecca in the year of its Conquest wearing an Arabian helmet on his head and when the Prophet took it off, a person came and said, "Ibn Khatal is holding the covering of the Ka'ba (taking refuge in the Ka'ba)." The Prophet said, "Kill him." (*Sahih Bukhari*, Volume 3, Book 29, Number 72)[149]

> The Prophet said, "By Him in Whose hands my life is! Were it not for some men amongst the believers who dislike to be left behind me and whom I cannot provide with means of conveyance, I would certainly never remain behind any Sariya' (army-unit) setting out in Allah's Cause. By Him in Whose hands my life is! I would love to be martyred in Allah's Cause and then get resurrected and then get martyred, and then get resurrected again and then get martyred and then get resurrected again and then get martyred. (*Sahih Bukhari*, Volume 4, Book 52, Number 54)[150]

> I heard Allah's Apostle saying, "The example of a Mujahid in Allah's Cause – and Allah knows better who really strives in His Cause – is like a person who fasts and prays continuously. Allah guarantees that He will admit the Mujahid in His Cause into Paradise if he is killed, otherwise He will return him to his home safely with rewards and war booty." (*Sahih Bukhari*, Volume 4, Book 52, Number 46)[151]

> A man came to Muhammad and said, "Instruct me as to such

a deed as equals Jihad in reward." He replied, "I do not find such a deed." (*Sahih Bukhari*, Volume 4, Book 52, Number 44)[152]

Given the predation of women and girls over the recent past from groups like Boko Haram, Jabhat al Nusra, and ISIS:

> I entered the Mosque and saw Abu Said Al-Khudri and sat beside him and asked him about Al-Azl (i.e., coitus interruptus). Abu Said said, "We went out with Allah's Apostle for the Ghazwa of Banu Al-Mustaliq and we received captives from among the Arab captives and we desired women and celibacy became hard on us and we loved to do coitus interruptus. So when we intended to do coitus interruptus, we said, 'How can we do coitus interruptus before asking Allah's Apostle who is present among us?' We asked (him) about it and he said, 'It is better for you not to do so, for if any soul (till the Day of Resurrection) is predestined to exist, it will exist." (*Sahih Bukhari*, Volume 5, Book 59, Number 459)[153]

Given the recent violence associated with Hamas and the recent prayer of the imam in the Vatican gardens, it is also worth noting that Article 7 of the Hamas Covenant bases its authority to kill Jews on Bukhari 176:

> Allah's Apostle said, "You (i.e., Muslims) will fight with the Jews till some of them will hide behind stones. The stones will (betray them) saying, 'O 'Abdullah (i.e. slave of Allah)! There is a Jew hiding behind me; so kill him.'" (*Sahih Bukhari*, Volume 4, Book 52, Number 176)[154]

From Article Seven of the Hamas Covenant:

> Hamas Covenant, "Article Seven, "The Universality of the Islamic Resistance Movement" ... Moreover, if the links have been distant from each other and if obstacles, placed by those who are the lackeys of Zionism in the way of the fighters obstructed the continuation of the struggle, the Islamic Resistance Movement aspires to the realisation [sic] of Allah's promise, no matter how long that should take. The Prophet, Allah bless him and grant him salvation, has said:

>> "The Day of Judgment will not come about until the Moslems fight the Jews (kill the Jews), when the Jew will hide behind stones and trees. The stones and trees will say O Moslem, O Abdulla, there is a Jew behind me, come

and kill him. Only the Gharkad tree, (evidently a certain kind of tree) would not do that because it is one of the trees of the Jews." (Related by Bukhari and Moslem).[155]

Two final examples from Bukhari will be assessed in an extended vignette to demonstrate that they are parts of a seamless web of shariah that interrelate with each other, from the hadith itself, to other hadith, to verses of the Qur'an, to the tafsirs that provide doctrinal explanations of them, to current shariah that retains their meaning as the current statement of the law. To establish their validity as part of the "fixed inner sphere" of shariah, it will be shown that these hadith actually drive jihadi activities today. This will be done by demonstrating the reinforcing redundancy of Islamic doctrine of jihad that spirals out from just two hadith. The purpose of this exercise is to show that those contesting the point that Islam is "opposed to every form of violence" are not dealing in generalizations. The first hadith:

> I have been commanded to fight people until they testify that there is no god but Allah and that Muhammad is the Messenger of Allah, and perform the prayer, and pay the zakat. If they say it, they have saved their blood and possessions from me, except for the rights of Islam over them. And their final reckoning is with Allah. (Bukhari Volume 4, Book 52, Number 196—as used in *Reliance of the Traveller*)[156]

Reliance of the Traveller uses Bukhari 196 as the hadith that helps establish the scriptural basis for jihad as "warfare to establish the religion."[157] In his briefing justifying his decision to wage jihad against his fellow service members at Fort Hood, Major Hasan cited Bukhari 196 in the slide "Verse of the Sword – Continued."[158] He used Bukhari 196 alongside slides of Qur'an Verses 9:5[159] and 9:29[160]:

> But when the forbidden months are past, then fight and slay the Pagans wherever ye find them, an seize them, beleaguer them, and lie in wait for them in every stratagem (of war); but if they repent, and establish regular prayers and practice regular charity, then open the way for them: for Allah is Oft-forgiving, Most Merciful. (Qur'an 9:5)

> Fight those who believe not in Allah nor the Last Day, nor hold that forbidden which hath been forbidden by Allah and His Messenger, nor acknowledge the religion of Truth, (even if they are) of the People of the Book, until they pay the Jizya with willing submission, and feel themselves subdued. (Qur'an 9:29)

As will be discussed, Verse 9:29 is also prominent in other treatments of jihad, including in *Reliance of the Traveller* and the *Distinguished Jurist's Primer*.

The second hadith:

> Allah's Apostle said, "By Him in Whose hands my soul is, surely (Jesus,) the son of Mary will soon descend amongst you and will judge mankind justly (as a Just Ruler); he will break the Cross and kill the pigs and there will be no Jizya (i.e., taxation taken from non Muslims). Money will be in abundance so that nobody will accept it, and a single prostration to Allah (in prayer) will be better than the whole world and whatever is in it." Abu Huraira added "If you wish, you can recite (this verse of the Holy Book): 'And there is none Of the people of the Scriptures (Jews and Christians) But must believe in him (i.e., Jesus as an Apostle of Allah and a human being) Before his death. And on the Day of Judgment He will be a witness Against them." (4.159) (*Sahih Bukhari*, Volume 4, Book 55, Number 657)[161]

Hasan also relied on Bukhari 657 to establish the ongoing requirement of jihad in his slide "Offensive Islam in the Future"[162] (against Christians). *Tafsir ibn Kathir* associates Bukhari 657 with Qur'an Verse 3:111 ("They will do you no harm, barring a trifling annoyance; and if they fight against you, they will show you their backs, and they will not be helped"). As part of the tafsir explanation, under a section header that mocks the New Testament ("The Good News that Muslims will Dominate the People of the Book"), Ibn Kathir associates Verse 3:111 with jihadi battles leading to the brutal humiliation and murder of entire Jewish tribes in Arabia and, later, Christian groups in Greater Syria (ash Sham), which the tafsir ties together through Bukhari 657:

> This is what occurred, for at the battle of Khaybar, Allah brought humiliation and disgrace to the Jews. Before that, the Jews in Al-Madinah, the tribes of Qaynuqa`, Nadir and Qurayzah, were also humiliated by Allah. Such was the case with the Christians in the area of Ash-Sham later on, when the Companions defeated them in many battles and took over the leadership of Ash-Sham forever. There shall always be a group of Muslims in Ash-Sham area until `Isa, son of Maryam, descends while they are like this on the truth, apparent and victorious. `Isa will at that time rule according to the Law of Muhammad, break the cross, kill the swine, banish the Jizyah and only accept Islam from the people.[163]

Similar supporting treatment is found in *Reliance of the Traveller* in the section "The Objectives of Jihad," which reflects Bukhari 657 to substantiate the objectives of jihad as the conversion, submission, or defeat of Christians and Jews as established in Qur'an Verse 9:29:

> THE OBJECTIVES OF JIHAD - o9.8 The caliph (o35)
> makes war upon Jews, Christians, and Zoroastrians (N: pro-
> vided he has first invited them to enter Islam in faith and
> practice, and if they will not, then invited to enter the social
> order of Islam by paying the non-Muslim poll tax (jizya, def:
> o11.4) – which is the significance of their paying it, not the
> money itself – while remaining in their ancestral religions)
> (O: and the war continues) until they become Muslims or else
> pay the non-Muslim poll tax (O: in accordance with the word
> of Allah Most High,

> > "Fight those who do not believe in Allah and the Last
> > Day and who forbid not what Allah and His messenger
> > have forbidden – who do not practice the religion of
> > truth, being those who have been given the Book – un-
> > til they pay the poll tax out of hand and are humbled"
> > (Koran 9:29),

> the time and place for which is before the final descent of
> Jesus (upon whom be peace). After his final coming, nothing
> but Islam will be accepted from them, for taking the poll tax is
> only effective until Jesus' descent (upon him and our Prophet
> be peace), which is the divinely revealed law of Muhammad.
> The coming of Jesus does not entail a separate divinely re-
> vealed law, for he will rule by the law of Muhammad. As for
> the Prophet's saying (Allah bless him and give him peace),

> > "I am the last, there will be no prophet after me,"

> this does not contradict the final coming of Jesus (upon whom
> be peace), since he will not rule according to the Evangel, but
> as a follower of our Prophet (Allah bless him and give him
> peace)). [164]

Having shown that Major Hasan supported his use of Bukhari 196 by associating it with Verse 9:29, and seeing that *Reliance* likewise relies on it, we can
further note how *The Interpretation of the Meaning of the Noble Qur'an*'s treatment
of that verse provides a more direct translation that includes an annotation that
associates it with Bukhari 176 (and, through it, a direct link to Article Seven of
the Hamas Covenant, as already discussed):

> Fight against those who (1) believe not in Allah, (2) nor the
> Last Day, (3) nor forbid that which has been forbidden by

Allah and His Messenger (Muhammad), (4) and those who acknowledge not the religion of truth (i.e., Islam) among the people of the Scripture (Jews and Christians), until they pay the Jizyah with willing submission and feel themselves subdued. (Qur'an 9:29)[165]

Annotation (1) b) to Verse 9:29 - Narrated by Abu Hurairah: Allah's Messenger said, 'The Hour will not be established until you fight against the Jews, and the stone behind which a Jew will be hiding will say, 'O Muslim! There is a Jew behind me, so kill him.' (Sahih Al-Bukhari, Hadith No. 2926)[166]

Because a relationship has been established between Bukhari 657, Bukhari 176, and Verse 9:29, it is important to provide a review of Verse 9:29's treatment by Ibn Kathir to establish the sacred, doctrinal, and consensus[167] status that jihad holds in shariah as "warfare against non-Muslims to establish the religion,"[168] which further contradicts the assertion in Paragraph 253 that "authentic Islam and the proper reading of the Koran are opposed to every form of violence."[169] Starting with the section header "The Order to Fight the People of Scriptures until They give the *Jizyah*," ibn Kathir explains that Verse 9:29 is about waging war—jihad—against Jews and Christians as a divine mandate:[170]

The Order to Fight the People of Scriptures until They give the *Jizyah*

Therefore, when People of the Scriptures disbelieved in Muhammad, they had no beneficial faith in any Messenger or what the Messengers brought. Rather, they followed their religions because this conformed with their ideas, lusts and the ways of their forefathers, not because they are Allah's Law and religion. Had they been true believers in their religions, that faith would have directed them to believe in Muhammad, because all Prophets gave the good news of Muhammad's advent and commanded them to obey and follow him. Yet when he was sent, they disbelieved in him, even though he is the mightiest of all Messengers. Therefore, they do not follow the religion of earlier Prophets because these religions came from Allah, but because these suit their desires and lusts. Therefore, their claimed faith in an earlier Prophet will not benefit them because they disbelieved in the master, the mightiest, the last and most perfect of all Prophets.[171]

Ibn Kathir's explanation clearly states that the religions of the People of the Book are abrogated, making them the object of jihad. As explained, it is the insincere nature of their belief (Christians and Jews) that causes their belief to be abrogated. Evidence of their insincerity is that, had they actually believed in their formerly valid religions, true faith would have prompted them to convert to Islam when hearing of it. Hence, the failure to convert is *the* evidence of insincerity that supports the claim of abrogation in the service of jihad as warfare. Ibn Kathir continues,

> This honorable *Ayah* was revealed with the order to fight the People of the Book, after the pagans were defeated, the people entered Allah's religion in large numbers, and the Arabian Peninsula was secured under the Muslims' control. Allah commanded His Messenger to fight the People of the Scriptures, Jews and Christians, on the ninth year of Hijrah, and he prepared his army to fight the Romans and called the people to Jihad announcing his intent and destination. The Messenger sent his intent to various Arab areas around Al-Madinah to gather forces, and he collected an army of thirty thousand. Some people from Al-Madinah and some hypocrites, in and around it, lagged behind, for that year was a year of drought and intense heat. The Messenger of Allah marched, heading towards Ash-Sham to fight the Romans until he reached Tabuk, where he set camp for about twenty days next to its water resources.[172]

Today, Ash Sham is Greater Syria, or the Levant, over which ISIS (or ISIL) claims governing authority. Then, as now, those who remain in abrogated former religions rightfully become the objects of jihad. As stated, the divine revelation was issued for the purpose of calling Muslims to wage jihad against the "Romans," i.e., the Byzantines, a Christian "People of the Book." Hence, for Ibn Kathir, the call to jihad in Verse 9:29 is specifically a call to fight Christians because they are Christian. But Ibn Kathir was not finished. Under the section heading "Paying the *Jizyah* is a Sign of *Kufr* and Disgrace,"[173] *Tafsir Ibn Kathir* explains the meaning of "until they pay the jizya out of hand and are humbled" (or, as translated by *The Noble Qur'an*, "until they pay the *Jizyah* with willing submission and feel themselves subdued"[174]):

Paying the *Jizyah* is a Sign of *Kufr* and Disgrace

(until they pay the Jizyah), if they do not choose to embrace Islam,[175]

(with willing submission), in defeat and subservience,

(and feel themselves subdued.), disgraced, humiliated and belittled. Therefore, Muslims are not allowed to honor the people of Dhimmah or elevate them above Muslims, for they are miserable, disgraced and humiliated. Muslim recorded from Abu Hurayrah that the Prophet said, (Do not initiate the Salam to the Jews and Christians, and if you meet any of them in a road, force them to its narrowest alley.)[176]

At this point, Ibn Kathir incorporates the "Pact of 'Umar" in his treatment of Verse 9:29 in its entirety, thus making the pact a part of the shariah explanation of that verse. As discussed in Part II, the "Pact of 'Umar" dictates the classic shariah terms of submission that 'Umar ibn a-Khattab, the second of the Four Rightly Guided Caliphs (634–644 AD),[177] first imposed on the Christians of Ash-Sham to ensure "their continued humiliation, degradation and disgrace."[178] In its entirety (also under the header "Paying the *Jizyah* is a Sign of *Kufr* and Disgrace"):

(Do not initiate the Salam to the Jews and Christians, and if you meet any of them in a road, force them to its narrowest alley.)

This is why the Leader of the faithful `Umar bin Al-Khattab, may Allah be pleased with him, demanded his well-known conditions be met by the Christians, these conditions that en-sured their continued humiliation, degradation and disgrace. The scholars of Hadith narrated from `Abdur-Rahman bin Ghanm Al-Ash`ari that he said, "I recorded for `Umar bin Al-Khattab, may Allah be pleased with him, the terms of the treaty of peace he conducted with the Christians of Ash-Sh-am: `In the Name of Allah, Most Gracious, Most Merciful. This is a document to the servant of Allah `Umar, the Lead-er of the faithful, from the Christians of such and such city. When you (Muslims) came to us we requested safety for our-selves, children, property and followers of our religion. We made a condition on ourselves that we will neither erect in our areas a monastery, church, or a sanctuary for a monk, nor restore any place of worship that needs restoration nor use any of them for the purpose of enmity against Muslims. We will not prevent any Muslim from resting in our churches whether they come by day or night, and we will open the doors [of our houses of worship] for the wayfarer and passerby. Those Muslims who come as guests, will enjoy boarding and food for three days. We will not allow a spy against Muslims into our churches and homes or hide deceit [or betrayal] against Muslims. We will not teach our children the Qur'an, publi-cize practices of Shirk, invite anyone to Shirk or prevent any of our fellows from embracing Islam, if they choose to do so. We will respect Muslims, move from the places we sit in if they choose to sit in them. We will not imitate their clothing, caps, turbans, sandals, hairstyles, speech, nicknames and title names, or ride on saddles, hang swords on the shoulders, collect weapons of any kind or carry these weapons. We will not encrypt our stamps in Arabic, or sell liquor. We will have the front of our hair cut, wear our customary clothes wherever we are, wear belts around our waist, refrain from erecting crosses on the outside of our churches and demonstrating them and our books in public in Muslim fairways and markets. We will not sound the bells in our churches, except discretely, or raise our voices while reciting our holy books inside our churches in the presence of Muslims, nor raise our voices [with prayer] at our funerals, or light torches in funeral processions in the fairways of Muslims, or their markets. We will not bury our dead next to Muslim dead, or buy servants who were captured by Muslims. We will be guides for Muslims and refrain from breaching their privacy in their homes.' When I gave this document to `Umar, he added to it, `We will not beat any Muslim. These are the conditions that we set against ourselves and followers of our religion in return for safety and protection. If we break any of these promises that we set for your benefit against ourselves, then our Dhimmah (promise of protection) is broken and you are allowed to do with us what you are allowed of people of defiance and rebellion.'"[179]

If this refutation of Paragraph 253 were only about a doctrinally accurate explanation of classical shariah on jihad that, while a part of shariah, was otherwise moribund and inoperative, there would be no reason to undertake this effort outside of academic curiosity. But it is immediately relevant to today's events. For example, in February 2014, when the Syrian town of Raqqa was captured by ISIS, the Christians of that community were given three options: convert to Islam, remain Christian but submit to Islam, or "face the sword." The Christians signed the treaty of submission. In return:

The Christians agreed to a list of conditions: to abstain from renovating churches or monasteries in Raqqa; not to display crosses or religious symbols in public or use loudspeakers in prayer; not to read scripture indoors loud enough for Muslims standing outside to hear; not to undertake subversive actions against Muslims; not to carry out any religious ceremonies outside the church; not to prevent any Christian wishing to convert to Islam from doing so; to respect Islam and Muslims and say nothing offensive about them; to pay the *jizya* tax worth four golden dinars for the rich, two for the average, and one for the poor, twice annually, for each adult Christian; to refrain from drinking alcohol in public; and to dress modestly.[180]

Sound familiar? In consideration for their submission, the Pact of ISIS said, "if they disobey any of the conditions, they are no longer protected and ISIS can treat them in a hostile and warlike fashion."[181] The ISIS claim was repeated again on Twitter in July 2014 when Al-Baghdadi, the head of ISIS, told the Christians of Mosul to "Choose one of these: Islam, the sword, al-Jiziya (tax) or till Saturday to flee."[182] Fourteen hundred years later, this is the same forced imposition of dhimmitude that was imposed on the Christians of Ash Sham under the Pact of Umar[183] and that is recognized as shariah today. Moreover, this language is identical to *Reliance*'s treatment of the status of dhimmitude[184] and the consequences for violating it[185] that was approved by the American Muslim Brotherhood and al-Azhar.

Holding to the Paragraph 253 position that "authentic Islam and the proper reading of the Koran are opposed to every form of violence,"[186] the Vatican nevertheless recognizes ISIS events as something they call jihad by an entity that they recognize claims to be an "Islamic State" imposing submission on non-Muslim parts of the population. In August 2014, the Holy See Press Office released the Bulletin "Declaration of the Pontifical Council for Interreligious Dialogue," stating in part:

> The whole world has witnessed with incredulity what is now called the "Restoration of the Caliphate," which had been abolished on October 29,1923 by Kamal Ataturk, founder of modern Turkey. Opposition to this "restoration" by the majority of religious institutions and Muslim politicians has not prevented the "Islamic State" jihadists from committing and continuing to commit unspeakable criminal acts.
>
> This Pontifical Council, together with all those engaged in interreligious dialogue, followers of all religions, and all men and women of good will, can only unambiguously denounce and condemn these practices which bring shame on humanity:
>
> - the massacre of people on the sole basis of their religious affiliation;
>
> - the despicable practice of beheading, crucifying and hanging bodies in public places;
>
> - the choice imposed on Christians and Yezidis between con-

version to Islam, payment of a tax (*jizya*)[16] or forced exile;

- the forced expulsion of tens of thousands of people, including children, elderly, pregnant women and the sick;

- the abduction of girls and women belonging to the Yezidi and Christian communities as spoils of war (*sabaya*); [See below: "*Sabaya*", *Reliance* on The Spoils of War," and "The Status of Captured Women in the Qur'an"]

- the imposition of the barbaric practice of infibulation[17/18]

- the destruction of places of worship and Christian and Muslim burial places;

- the forced occupation or desecration of churches and monasteries;

- the removal of crucifixes and other Christian religious symbols as well as those of other religious communities;

- the destruction of a priceless Christian religious and cultural heritage; [See below: *Reliance*, o11.0 "Non-Muslim Subjects of the Islamic State"]

- indiscriminate violence aimed at terrorizing people to force them to surrender or flee.[187]

Footnotes are embedded in the Holy See Bulletin to point out that the Vati-

---

16 As discussed, but emphasized here, the jizya is a tax on submitted non-Muslims mandated by Qur'an Verse 9:29 that demands humiliation and submission. The Saudi's, al-Azhar, and the American Muslim Brotherhood, all interfaith partners, agree with this divinely mandated doctrine in shariah. As already stated in this section, *Reliance of the Traveller*, in the Section on jihad titled "The Objectives of Jihad," states the relationship between the Quranic mandate for jizya and shariah.

17 **Infibulation**, extreme female genital mutilation involving complete excision of the clitoris, labia minora, and most of the labia majora followed by stitching to close up most of the vagina. *Merriam-Webster Online Dictionary*, URL: http://www.merriam-webster.com/dictionary/infibulation, accessed 14 September 2014.

18 Recalling that *Reliance of the Traveller* is recognized as *bona fide* shariah by al-Azhar and the American Muslim Brotherhood, both deeply involved in interfaith dialogue with the Church, it is important to point out that what the Vatican calls "infibulation," *Reliance* calls female circumcision and is more commonly known as female genital mutilation. *Reliance* endorses the practice of female genital mutilation in Book E "Purification" in the section titled "Circumcision Is Obligatory." *Reliance* states: "... and for women, removing the prepuce (Ar. Bazr) of the clitoris (N: not the clitoris itself, as some mistakenly assert). (A: Hanbalis hold that circumcision of women is not obligatory but sunna, while Hanafis consider it a mere courtesy to the husband.) [*Reliance of the Traveller*, Book E "Purification" Section e4.3" Circumcision Is Obligatory," 59.] In preparation for briefing this information in April 2009, I asked Dr. Tawfik Hamid, MD - and native Egyptian graduate of the Cairo Medical School - to verify the Arabic language statement in *Reliance*. He took exception to *Reliance*'s translation from the Arabic stating "The exact translation of the part about female circumcision in the text stating '... and for women circumcision is by cutting the clitoris'." Dr. Hamid confirmed his translation with Professor Mohamed Rahoma, Dean of Arabic Language, Egypt.

can is protesting the very shariah it refuses to recognize as Islamic law. To further emphasize the completeness of the point, relevant authoritative Islamic sources for specific points the Pontifical Council denounced are included at the end of this Appendix. On one level, the Vatican recognizes that ISIS is justifying their actions, but then it decries that "no cause, and certainly no religion, can justify such barbarity."[188] As the footnotes inserted into the Holy See Bulletin demonstrate, however, ISIS justifies their actions under first-order current and classical understandings of shariah. The interfaith crowd are participating witnesses to the brutal imposition of a new "Pact of 'Umar" while refusing to discern what they are seeing or the role they are playing when they passively wring their hands as events transpire. As noted, the sources in this analysis are recognized as valid by the same Muslim partners that the interfaith movement, including the Vatican and the USCCB, meets with when conducting outreach.

This should come as no surprise. Remember, *Reliance of the Traveller* is recognized by the American Muslim Brotherhood, including the IIIT (the entity that published *Interfaith Dialogue*), the Fiqh Council of North America (a subordinate element of ISNA), Al-Azhar, and the OIC; the Vatican meets with Al-Azhar regularly on interfaith issues and agreed with the OIC "to support interfaith dialogue initiatives."[189] To the extent that Muslim interfaith partners accept *Reliance* as a valid statement of shariah, they also believe that "when it is possible to achieve [their] aim by lying but not by telling the truth," it becomes "obligatory to lie if the goal is obligatory."[190] Christian and Jewish partners in interfaith dialogue have no excuse for not knowing this.

Reliance of the Traveller is not the only shariah publication that claims broad formal acceptance. *Bidayat al-Mujtahid wa Nihayat al-Muqtasid (The Distinguished Jurist's Primer)*, for example, has 33 pages on the law of jihad.[191] The *Primer* was translated and published under the auspices of the Qatari-based Center for Muslim Contribution to Civilization, presided over by a Board of Trustees. The Chairman is a member of the Qatari royal family. Board members include the Sheikh of Al-Azhar; Professor Yusuf Qaradawi; the Director General of ISESCO; the education ministers from Qatar, Kuwait, and Oman; and the Secretary-General of Muslim World Association (Saudi Arabia).[192] ISESCO—the Islamic Educational, Scientific and Cultural Organization—is a specialized OIC organization,[193] and Qaradawi is the chief jurist of the Muslim Brotherhood. As with *Reliance*, the *Distinguished Jurist's Primer* is accepted by the very Muslims that non-Muslim interfaith partners meet with, including the Vatican and the USCCB, when conducting their interfaith mission. Book X "Jihad," Chapter 1 "The Elements (*Arkan*) of War," *§7 "Why Wage War*," could not be any clearer:

> Why wage war? The Muslim Jurists agreed[194] that the purpose of fighting People of the Book, excluding the (Qurayshite) People of the Book and the Christian Arabs, is one of two things: it is either for their conversion to Islam or the pay-

ment of *jizya*. The payment of *jizya* is because of the words of the Exalted, "Fight against such of those who have been given the Scripture as believe not in Allah or the Last Day, and forbid not that which Allah and His Messenger hath forbidden, and follow not the religion of truth, until they pay the tribute and are brought low".(*Primer* footnote to Verse 9:29)/195

Notice how the *Primer* also relies on Verse 9:29.

Other accessible shariah publications include the 311-page *The Islamic Law of Nations: Shaybani's Siyar*,[196] the 62-page Book XIII "*Siyar* (Relations with Non-Muslims)" in Volume II of *Al-Hidaya: The Guidance*,[197] and Pakistani Brigadier S.K. Malik's *Quranic Concept of War*.[198] It is with this understanding of the Qur'an, hadith, and shariah that one should assess interfaith processes that value dialogue over fidelity. For example, as William Kilpatrick noted in "The Downside of Dialogue"[199] in 2006, the USCCB published the study "Revelation: Catholic & Muslim Perspectives," which concluded:

> Through dialogue and improved cooperation, Muslims and Catholics can develop a just and peaceful society in the spirit of the teachings of the Gospel and the Qur'an. Both Jesus and Muhammad loved and cared for all whom they met, especially the poor and oppressed; their teachings and example call for solidarity with the poor, oppressed, homeless, hungry, and needy in today's world.[200]

The question isn't whether the USCCB statement is disinformation; the question is whether they are aware of it. The USCCB co-sponsored "Revelation" with the Muslim Brotherhood front group ISNA. As demonstrated in the discussion of Verse 9:29 and related shariah, ISNA understands the ultimate relationship between Christians and Muslims exclusively in terms of submission. Because the USCCB cannot reasonably argue that an apple is an orange (i.e., that the Gospel and the Qur'an carry the same message), its statement in "Revelation" reflects an abandonment of reason. To compound the contradiction, the very next verse following 9:29 states that Jews and Christians are accursed by Allah for being Jews and Christians:

> "The Jews call 'Uzair a son of Allah, and the Christians call Christ the son of Allah. That is a saying from their mouth; (in this) they but imitate what the unbelievers of old used to say. Allah's curse be on them: how they are deluded away from the Truth!" (Qur'an Verses 9:30)

At least for the Christians, this creates a conflict with the law of non-contradiction, as you cannot believe in the Truth while at the same time being "deluded away from the Truth":

> Jesus said to him, "I am the Way, and <u>the Truth</u>, and the Life;
> no one comes to the Father, but by me. (John 14:6)

This time it's about apples and not apples; you can have one, you can have the other, you can reject both, but you cannot accept both. Pretending to have it both ways violates basic rules of logic and reason. This contradiction cannot be resolved in faith, and the other side knows it. What does the USCCB think it agreed to, with whom, and for what? Outside the boundaries of the interfaith mirage, the USCCB's "Revelation" is indefensible.

There is dispositive evidence to challenge the Paragraph 253 claim that "authentic Islam and the proper reading of the Koran are opposed to every form of violence"[201] and equally demonstrable indicators that Muslim partners reject the Vatican claim, and yet, instead of stopping to reassess, the Holy See Bulletin announced Vatican commitments to double down on the interfaith process that has brought them to this point:

> Moreover, it is on this basis that, in recent years, dialogue between Christians and Muslims has continued and intensified. The dramatic plight of Christians, Yezidis and other religious communities and ethnic minorities in Iraq requires a clear and courageous stance on the part of religious leaders, especially Muslims, as well as those engaged in interreligious dialogue and all people of good will. All must be unanimous in condemning unequivocally these crimes and in denouncing the use of religion to justify them.

Also apples and oranges, the Holy See Bulletin follows this statement with two questions that are asked as if they naturally go hand in hand when in fact they are oppositional and demand a choice:

> If not, what credibility will religions, their followers and their leaders have? What credibility can the interreligious dialogue that we have patiently pursued over recent years have? [202]

The Holy See Bulletin equates the credibility of a religion with its success in interfaith dialogue, not with the faith of the religions themselves. It's the religions that have the credibility, and it's the overriding commitment to interreligious dialogue that is running that credibility down. This brings us back to the IIIT's *Interfaith Dialogue* pledge "to remain committed to being friends when the world would separate us from one another,"[203] supported by guarantees of "mutual trust"[204] that only allows discussions of Islam that Muslim partners affirm "as accurate."[205] The Holy See Bulletin affirms the blind commitment of Paragraph 253. In contrast, it is suspected that the credibility of the non-Muslim religions would increase if they changed strategy and chose to deal with Islam as it exists in fact and not as their Brotherhood partners would have them perceive it. As it stands,

Paragraph 253 maroons Church credibility in Pieper's pseudoreality; the Holy See Bulletin doubles down on it; and the faithful are either terrorized by one group in the interfaith movement or silenced by the other. This subordination of faith to interfaith requirements drives whispered concerns regarding indifferentism as tens of thousands are persecuted.

Since the Bulletin was published, U.S. Army Major Nidal Hasan wrote a six-page letter to Pope Francis titled "A Warning To Pope Francis, Members Of The Vatican, and Other Religious Leaders Around the World," in which he explains the role of jihad and the mission of the jihadi as it faces the Christian world.[206]

> Jihad[24:] The willingness to fight for All-Mighty Allah can be a test in of itself – [2:216; 3:142; 3:140; 2:216; 3:166]/ Believing fighters (mujahideen) have a greater rank in the eyes of Allah than believers who don't fight – [4:95-96; 9:20]; and are encouraged to inspire the believers – [4:84].[207/19]

The paragraph is laced with Quranic references that seem to validate Hasan's claim that "authentic Islam and the proper reading of the Koran are [**NOT**] opposed to every form of violence," in direct contrast to the claims of Paragraph 253. Furthermore, his reference to "inspiring the believers" while referring to Verse 4:84 aligns his message with al-Qaeda.[208] If the Vatican insists on holding to its claims, shouldn't it have to defend them? On what basis does the Vatican refute

---

19 The associated Qur'an verses are from Yusuf Ali's translation:

Fighting is prescribed for you, and ye dislike it. But it is possible that ye dislike a thing which is good for you, and that ye love a thing that is bad for you. But Allah knoweth, and ye know not. (Qur'an 2:216)

Did ye think that ye would enter Heaven without Allah testing those of you who fought hard (In His Cause) and remained steadfast? (Qur'an 3:142)

If a wound hath touched you, be sure a similar wound hath touched the others. Such days (of varying fortunes) We give to men and men by turns: that Allah may know those that believe, and that He may take to Himself from your ranks Martyr-witnesses (to Truth). And Allah loveth not those that do wrong. (Qur'an 3:140)

What ye suffered on the day the two armies Met, was with the leave of Allah, in order that He might test the believers. (Qur'an 3:166)

Not equal are those believers who sit (at home) and receive no hurt, and those who strive and fight in the cause of Allah with their goods and their persons. Allah hath granted a grade higher to those who strive and fight with their goods and persons than to those who sit (at home). Unto all (in Faith) Hath Allah promised good: But those who strive and fight Hath He distinguished above those who sit (at home) by a special reward. (Qur'an 4:95)

Those who believe, and suffer exile and strive with might and main, in Allah's cause, with their goods and their persons, have the highest rank in the sight of Allah: they are the people who will achieve (salvation). (Qur'an 9:20)

Then fight in Allah's cause - Thou art held responsible only for thyself - and rouse the believers. It may be that Allah will restrain the fury of the Unbelievers; for Allah is the strongest in might and in punishment. (Qur'an 4:84)

Hasan's belief in the doctrinal role of violent jihad as supported by the Qur'an? Hasan's letter demands a substantive response.

Major Hasan sits on death row for the massacre at Fort Hood, Texas. He was considered a devout Muslim before the killings, and there is no reason to think he is any less devout today; he believes in his cause enough to undertake the actions he did and suffer the consequences. The question is whether the Vatican is up to the task of refuting Major Hasan in a manner that answers the call of reason by undertaking a principled response. Can the Vatican refute Hasan in a way that would survive a hearsay challenge? Not if it bases its response on an institutionalized preference for allowing its Muslim dialogue partner the right to define Islam so the Vatican is permitted only to describe what Islam looks like from the outside,[209] and not if the Vatican allows itself to speak of Islam only in a way that its Muslim interfaith partners can affirm as accurate.[210]

A persuasive argument can be made that the cost of "interreligious dialogue … patiently pursued over recent years" can be seen in places like Nigeria, Syria, Iraq, and even Fort Hood, with tragic consequences that resulted not in spite of interfaith efforts, but because of them. The Holy See Bulletin lists the very shariah principles causing so much death and destruction while irrationally choosing not to recognize that they are in fact Islamic law properly understood. This renders the Church, and all other interfaith players, impotent in the face of an existential threat that is killing the helpless. When the Holy See Bulletin condemns activities associated with ISIS, they condemn activities firmly grounded in the Qur'an, authoritative hadith, and shariah as stated in *Reliance of the Traveller*. Denying the nexus of Islam to "partners" who know their own doctrines undermines the Vatican's bargaining position, because those partners know their interfaith peers lack the necessary discernment to stake a viable position by virtue of participating in such a dialogue. The dissociative behavior is remarkable. So long as the Vatican and other interfaith partners remain suspended in this interfaith pseudoreality, their interfaith partners know they will continue to have a free hand.

Further contradicting the Holy See Bulletin's assertion that "no cause, and certainly no religion, can justify such barbarity"[211] is the imam of the prestigious Prophet's Mosque in Medina, Saudi Arabia. In August 2014, the imam endorsed the jihadis, including ISIS, as "mujahideen for Allah":

> All the pure blood that has been shed in Iraq for decades against whom are they waging Jihad? They are waging Jihad against the Christian American presence in Iraq. In Somalia and Afghanistan – is it not jihad? Are they not God-fearing? You (Arab rulers) have been remiss and neglectful, so you should have kept your mouths shut. Under these circumstances, you should have kept silent and feared Allah. Instead of that, they accuse the *mujahideen* of being kharijites. … Why?

Did they rebel against the Emir of the Believers? No, they rebelled against infidels who invaded their countries. We pray for Allah to guide those (critics), so that they stop criticizing the mujahideen. If they do not pray for their success, they should at least stop criticizing them. In general, I consider them to be mujahideen for the sake of Allah, who are driving out the infidels who invaded their lands.[212]

Not just Saudi imams. With Al-Azhar twice declaring—in December 2014 and again in January 2015—that "no believer can be declared an apostate" when referring to ISIS,[213] there may be no basis on which to claim that ISIS's statement of the law is erroneous or that it has ever been (truly) overruled. Even average Arab Muslims comment on the strangely unwarranted fidelity that non-Muslim interfaith partners have to interfaith relationships. Pictures are posted on Twitter of interfaith leaders posing with the same Saudi leadership[214] that allows the storming of immigrants' homes in Khafji because they are celebrating a private Christian service.[215]

This is the one-way bridge Sayyid Qutb was talking about when he spoke of Brotherhood objectives in the interfaith sphere.[216] As the faithful become more aware of what is going on, it will result in the destruction of faith in the preparation stage that Pakistani Brigadier S.K. Malik said was a precondition to transitioning to more kinetic forms of jihad. For Malik, who wrote the *Quranic Concept of War* while serving for the Pakistani Army Chief of Staff, success in Quranic warfare requires spiritual dislocation aimed at the complete destruction of faith:

> [Striking terror in the hearts of an enemy] is basically related to the strength or weakness of the human soul. It can be instilled only if the opponent's faith is destroyed. Psychological dislocation is temporary; spiritual dislocation is permanent. Psychological dislocation can be produced by a physical act but this does not hold good of the spiritual dislocation. To instill terror into the hearts of the enemy, it is essential in the ultimate analysis, to dislocate his Faith. An invincible Faith is immune to terror. A weak Faith offers inroads to terror. (QCW, "The Strategy for War," 60) [217]

The Pakistani Brigadier did not simply jump to this conclusion; he reached it by analyzing concepts of war mandated by the Qur'an. He started with three verses:

"I am with you: give firmness to the Believers: I will **instill terror into the hearts** of the Unbelievers." (Anfal: 12)[218]

Soon shall We **cast terror into the hearts** of the Unbelievers. (Al-i-Imran: 151)[219]

And those of the **people of the Book** who aided them, Allah did take them down from their strongholds and **cast terror into their hearts**, (so that) some ye slew, and some ye made prisoners. And He made you heirs of their lands, their houses, and their goods, and of a land which ye had not frequented (before). And Allah has power over all things. (Ahzab: 26-27)[220]

From these verses, Malik reasoned that "we see that, on all these occasions, when Allah wishes to impose His will upon His enemies, He chooses to do so by **casting terror in their hearts**." Malik then asks and answers his own question by reference to yet another verse of the Qur'an: "But, what strategy does He (Allah) prescribe for the Believers to enforce their decision upon their foes?"[221]

"Let not the Unbelievers think," God commands us directly and pointedly, "that they can get the better of the Godly: they will never frustrate them. Against them make ready your strength to the utmost of your power, including steeds of war, **to strike terror into the hearts of the enemies** of Allah and your enemies, and others besides, whom ye may not know, but whom Allah doth know." (Anfal: 59-60)[222]

"Against them make ready," as noted, is on the Muslim Brotherhood's seal. Malik's chilling statement on the destruction of faith recurs frequently in association with a haunting question: Knowing why they are about to be killed (or raped, or tortured, or dispossessed), and knowing that their killer knows with clarity and certitude why he is about to kill them, what are the faithful to think about Paragraph 253's denial of the bitter reality that is about to befall them? This form of existential denial challenges faith, undermines confidence, compromises credibility, and, as Malik points out, dislocates faith. This is the design.

Outside the boundaries of the interfaith pseudoreality, Paragraph 253 is indefensible. The claim that "authentic Islam and the proper reading of the Koran are opposed to every form of violence"[223] has been shown to be untrue as a matter of interlocking shariah from classic to modern, so it cannot simply be claimed that opposing views are based on "generalizations." Because those opposing Paragraph 253 can counter with dispositive shariah that demonstrates actual fidelity to the relevant doctrines being pursued today, expressing those positions cannot reasonably or fairly be labeled "hateful." An erroneous claim coupled with a judgmental statement against fellow believers who have the temerity to say what can be proven to be true as a matter of current events, history, fact, and published Islamic law puts too high a price on blind fidelity to interfaith dialogue as it currently manifests itself. It violates reason and injures the truth. It also constitutes a form of prior restraint that enforces Islamic speech codes in a manner that is in keeping with the Brotherhood's "by our hand" methodology.

It's all so much Gríma Wormtongue. The opportunity cost of interfaith dialogue can be measured in the deaths of those who have been and will be killed knowing there is no effective voice to speak out and take action against groups like ISIS, al-Nusra, Boko Haram, and the Muslim Brotherhood.

An Essential Postscript: Fiddling While Rome Burns

In November 2014, Pope Francis visited Turkey, where he met with the Ecumenical Patriarch of Constantinople, Bartholomew I, signed a Joint Declaration on the plight of Middle-Eastern Christians, met with Turkish leaders, and called on Muslim leaders to condemn terrorism carried out in the name of Islam.[224] In an interview he gave on the flight back to Rome, he seemed positive. Yet there are indicators that events did not go well. The following assessment of Pope Francis's trip includes many issues raised in this book, including the OIC's Islamophobia campaign and, from Appendix II, Turkey's manipulation of that narrative in the diplomatic sphere.

Pope Francis recalled his exchange with the Grand Mufti of Istanbul, Rahmi Yaran: "When I entered the mosque, I could not say: now I'm a tourist! I saw that marvellous [sic] place; the Mufti explained things very well to me, showing great meekness; he quoted the Quran when he spoke about Mary and John the Baptist."[225]

The part of the Qur'an dealing with John the Baptist and Mary is Surah 19 "Maryam." Early on, Surah 19 parallels the infancy narrative of Christ in the Gospel of Luke. In *The Noble Qur'an* translation, which includes extensive embedded commentary, the verses on John the Baptist and Mary culminate with Jesus's birth, followed by his express denial, as an infant, of his divinity:

> He ['Isa (Jesus)] said: "Verily, I am a slave of Allah, He has given me the Scripture and made me a Prophet.[(3)] (*Noble Qur'an* 19:30)

Footnote (3) warns Christians not to "exceed the limits" by believing Jesus to be one of three in the Trinity.[226] In Verse 19:34:

> Such is 'Isa (Jesus), son of Maryam (Mary). It is a statement of truth, about which they doubt (or dispute). (*Noble Qur'an* 19: 34)

Tafsir Al-Jalalayn explains that the "they" in Verse 19:34 are "the Christians who lie when they say that 'Isa is the son of Allah."[227] Verse 19:35 continues with the revelation that begetting offspring is beneath Allah:

> It befits not the majesty of Allah that he should beget a son [this refers to the slander of Christians against Allah, by say-

ing that 'Isa (Jesus) is the son of Allah]. Glorified and Exalted be He above all they associate with Him. When He decrees a thing, He only says to it: "Be!" and it is.[4] (*Noble Qur'an* 19:35)

Both the *Noble Qur'an*[228] and the Yusuf Ali[229] translations include commentaries reinforcing the point that Allah is above having offspring. Finally, while Verse 19:36 has Jesus telling the faithful to believe Allah alone in the Islamic sense of taweed, Verse 19:37 warns Christians who continue to misrepresent Jesus as the son of Allah that they will burn in hell:

> ['Isa (Jesus) said]: "And verily, Allah is my Lord and your Lord. So worship Him (Alone). That is the Straight Path. (Allah's religion of Islamic Monotheism which He did ordain for all of His Prophets)." (*Tafsir At-Tabari*)

> Then the sects differed [i.e. the Christians about 'Isa (Jesus)], so woe unto the disbelievers [those who gave false witness by saying that 'Isa (Jesus) is the son of Allah] from the Meeting of a great Day (i.e. the Day of Resurrection, when they will be thrown in the blazing fire). (*Noble Qur'an* 19:36-37)

In what may appear to be an attempt to establish common ground, the Mufti relied on the Quranic infancy narratives of the Prophet 'Isa (Jesus). However, those verses are meant to correct the "errors" of Luke's account. When the Mufti spoke to Pope Francis about John the Baptist and Mary, he referred to verses that build up to the miracle of baby 'Isa denying his own divinity, alongside other revelations known to be hostile to Christianity. Hence, the Mufti's recitation takes on the character of an inside joke—a personal public insult—at the pope's expense. This was the second time in 2014 that a prominent imam used a public event with the pope to gratuitously insult him where the Vatican revealed a blindness to those acts. Such treatment was not limited to the Mufti, however.

Meeting with the President of Turkey, Recep Tayyip Erdoğan, Francis said of ISIS that "fanaticism and fundamentalism, as well as irrational fears, which foster misunderstanding and discrimination, need to be countered by the solidarity of all believers." He then called on Middle-Eastern states to take action.[230] President Erdoğan responded by blaming ISIS's beheadings, enslavement of prisoners, and the destruction of religious minorities on the "rise of Islamophobia"[231] in the West, using the OIC Islamophobia meme: "[There is a] very serious and rapid trend of growth in racism, discrimination, and hatred of others, especially Islamophobia in the West."[232] Erdoğan's comments, alongside the surreal nature of the interfaith discussion, were so alarming that even the Turkish media took note. From the *Hurriyet Daily News* (Istanbul):

> The Turkish opera buffa is at its best. For his part, the main

character told the pope, "Let's stop Islamophobia." To play his part, the pope called for a "dialogue that can deepen the understanding and appreciation" between faiths. Thundering applause. And, privately, loud laughter.

Could Mr. Erdoğan have told the Pope that he believes Christians, including the Holy See, want to see Muslim children dead [as he said the day previous]? No. That was not in the script featuring their "interfaith dialogue."

At the start of his visit to Turkey, Pope Francis called for interfaith dialogue to counter fanaticism and fundamentalism. Could he, possibly, have told Mr. Erdoğan that a powerful belief that non-Muslims want to see Muslim children die is pure fanaticism and fundamentalism? No. That was not in the script either.

Missing in the opera buffa script also was Mr. Erdoğan's doctrinal commitment that the Middle East must be a "Muslim-only" (preferably Sunni Muslim-only) land, while the pope pledged to support Middle Eastern Christians. Instead, the usual Kodak-moment exchanges of pleasantry, smiles and words of interfaith dialogue. Facts can be ignored.[233]

Praising Francis for not making "theological" waves, Ibrahim Kalin, the Deputy Secretary-General of the Office of the Turkish Presidency, identified Paragraph 253 as the basis for moving forward: "[In] *The Joy of the Gospel* [*Evangelii Gaudium*], the pope takes an unequivocal position against lumping Islam together with extremism and violence."[234] Hence, what made Francis acceptable to Muslims is his willingness to conform to OIC standards as stated at the Foreign Ministers conferences in 2003 (Tehran) and 2004 (Istanbul):

Islam is innocent of **all forms of terrorism** which involve the murder of innocent people **whose killing is forbidden by Islam**, and rejects any attempts to link Islam and Muslims to terrorism because the latter has no relation whatsoever with religions, civilizations or nationalities.[235/236]

While in Turkey, Francis also signed a Joint Declaration with Bartholomew decrying "the terrible situation of Christians and all those who are suffering in the Middle East."[237] The Declaration accurately states the existential nature of the crisis:

We cannot resign ourselves to a Middle East without Christians, who have professed the name of Jesus there for two thousand years. Many of our brothers and sisters are being persecuted and have been forced violently from their homes.[238]

However, the Declaration then subordinated the disastrous plight of Christians to the vagaries of the interfaith movement process:

> We call on all religious leaders to pursue and to strengthen interreligious dialogue and to make every effort to build a culture of peace and solidarity between persons and between peoples.[239]

Fidelity to the requirements of the interfaith movement causes the messaging to ring false. When denying the Islamic nature of a crisis that is otherwise properly identified, actions become disassociated from known actors. Such is the pull of the interfaith narrative that it compels the denial realities unfolding before ones eyes. For example, when ISIS again demanded the payment of the jizyah, they were making a demand that finds authority in Qur'an Verse 9:29. Choosing to minimize such a divine mandate, Francis understated the severity of the circumstances Christians (and others) in Iraq face:

> I'm going to speak frankly: Christians are being chased from the Middle East. In some cases, as we have seen in Iraq, in the Mosul area, they have to leave or pay a tax that may be unnecessary.[240]

Since Turkey, the dissociation with Islam continues. In the face of the brutal nature of the January 2015 *Charlie Hebdo* executions, all that Pope Francis could muster in his initial response was to speak of "deviant forms of religion ... born of a corrupt heart, a heart incapable of recognizing and doing good, of pursuing peace."[241] The deviant religion he blames, however, is an undefined "'religious fundamentalism' [that] eliminates human beings by perpetrating horrendous killings, eliminates God himself, turning him into a mere ideological pretext."[242] While OIC foreign ministers could live with Pope Francis's response, they must have been ecstatic with what he said later that week regarding *Hebdo*. Analogizing the execution of the cartoonists to someone insulting his mother, Pope Francis said:

> If my good friend Dr. Gasparri says a curse word against my mother, he can expect a punch in the nose. [Throwing a pretend punch.] It's normal. You cannot provoke. You cannot insult the faith of others. You cannot make fun of the faith of others. There are so many people who speak badly about religions or other religions, who make fun of them, who make a game out of the religions of others. They are provocateurs. And what happens to them is what would happen to Dr. Gasparri if he says a curse word against my mother. There is a limit.[243]

With this comment, Pope Francis fell in line with the OIC objective of subordinating free speech to Islamic speech codes. In doing so, he validated the OIC's "Day of Rage" terror campaigns, blamed the *Charlie Hebdo* staff for their own executions (his insistence to the contrary notwithstanding[244]), and convicted Pope Benedict for his comments at Regensburg. For the OIC, this was a breakthrough victory for the Ten-Year Programme of Action. When Pope Francis's comments are compared to OIC Secretary General Madani's when he called for the prosecution of *Charlie Hebdo's* editorial staff (after the executions), the parallel language becomes apparent:

> Freedom of speech must not become a hate speech and must not offend others. No sane person, irrespective of doctrine, religion or faith, accepts his beliefs being ridiculed.[245]

It is past time for the Vatican to familiarize itself with the OIC's Ten-Year Programme of Action and the Islamic speech codes it is designed to enforce—that jihadis did enforce in France and again later, in February 2015, in Copenhagen. It is also worth assessing whether interfaith adherence puts the Vatican on the wrong side of an important civilizational issue. As an operational planning consideration, the Vatican must be assessed as being committed to enforcing Islamic speech standards within the span of its own operations and, as such, an asset of the OIC internationally and the Muslim Brotherhood domestically. The fact that the Vatican may be unaware of this hardly matters.

From an analytical perspective, there are enough indicators that the Vatican has abandoned reason in its approach to Islam and has opted instead to adopt interfaith rules—"to remain committed to being friends when the world would separate us from one another,"[246] supported by guarantees of "mutual trust"[247] that only allows discussions of Islam that Muslim partners affirm "as accurate"[248]—that it warrants being analyzed as if true.

Dawah is 'Stealth Jihad'

Dawah is much more than just the Islamic equivalent to proselytizing, and a competent due-diligence review would reveal this. The duty of dawah is doctrinally associated with the duty of jihad and concerns actions taken in preparation for jihad that enhance the effects of terror when the final call to Islam is made. The Brotherhood is committed to implementing these programs through multi-tiered, multi-pronged, interlaced information campaigns along lines of operation that target the governmental, media, religious, and educational sectors. As the Pakistani Brigadier stated, ideological subversion in the preparation stage—dawah—is the main event. Recalling the theological meaning of grace, there is something profoundly disgraceful in the interfaith sector.

Supporting Shariah in Contrast to the Holy See Bulletin

In August 2014, the Holy See Press Office released the Bulletin "Declaration of the Pontifical Council for Interreligious Dialogue," in which the Pontifical Council "unambiguously denounced and condemned" a list of practices "which bring shame on humanity."[249] This list contains shariah and Quranic principles that directly undermine Paragraph 253's claim that "authentic Islam and the proper reading of the Koran are opposed to every form of violence." What follows are portions of shariah from *Reliance of the Traveller* or tafsir treatment of Quranic verses associated with ISIS practices that the Pontifical Council denounced and that are, in fact, recognized elements of Islamic law.

Sabaya and *Reliance* on 'the Spoils of War'

The Holy See Bulletin uses an obscure term—*sabaya*—to discuss shariah norms on the spoils of war. *Reliance of the Traveller* addresses this in "The Spoils of Battle" at Section o10.0. **In its entirety**, o10.0 "The Spoils of Battle":

> **o10.01** A free male Muslim who has reached puberty and is sane is entitled to the spoils of battle when he has participated in a battle to the end of it. After personal booty (def: o10.2), the collective spoils of the battle are divided into five parts. The first fifth is set aside (dis: o10.3), and the remaining four are distributed, one share to each infantryman and three shares to each cavalryman. From these latter also, a token payment is given at the discretion to women, children, and non-Muslim participants on the Muslim side. A combatant only takes possession of his share of the spoils at the official division. (A: Or he may choose to waive his right to it.)

> **o10.02** As for personal booty, anyone who, despite resistance, kills one of the enemy or effectively incapacitates him, risking his own life thereby, is entitled to whatever he can take from the enemy, meaning as much as he can take away with him in the battle, such as a mount, cloths, weaponry, money, or other.

> **o10.03** As for the first fifth that is taken from the spoils, it is divided in turn into five parts, a share each going to:

>> 1) The Prophet (Allah bless him and give him peace), and after his death, to such Islamic interests as fortifying defenses on the frontiers, salaries for Islamic judg-

es, muezzins, and the like;

2) relatives of the Prophet (Allah bless him and give him peace) for the Bani Hashim and Bani Muttalib clans, each male receiving the share of two females;

3) orphans who are poor;

4) those short of money (def: h8.11);

5) and travellers needing money (h8.18).[250]

The Status of Captured Women in the Qur'an

The Qur'an recognizes that a property right attaches to women captured in jihad in five different verses that include tafsir explanations that affirm the status. At section o9.13, *Reliance of the Traveller* recognizes the status of captured women: "when a child or woman is taken captive, they become slaves by the fact of capture, and the woman's previous marriage is immediately annulled."

There is little doubt that the Quranic "slaves whom their right hand possesses" are "slave-girls … [taken] from the war booty" whom owners do not have to treat equally because they are those "whom Allah has assigned to them," whose marriages are dissolved, and whom "Allah has made … permissible" such that the owners "will not be blamed" for whatever sexual license they take. What follows are selected Qur'an verses that speak directly to the question, along with their relevant tafsir explanations from *Tafsir of Ibn Kathir*, vol. 2, Trans. Abdul-Malik Mujahid. (Riyadh: Darussalam, 2000):

> "Also forbidden are women already married, <u>except those slaves whom your right hands possess</u> …" (*Noble Qur'an* 4:24)

> ### *Tafsir Ibn Kathir*, Volume 2, Forbidding Women Already Married, Except for Female Slaves, 421-422.[251]

> Allah said, "*Also forbidden are women already married, <u>except those whom your right hand possesses</u>.*"

> The *Ayah* means, you are prohibited from marrying women who are already married,

> "*except those whom your right hand possesses*"

> except those whom you acquire through war, for you are allowed such women after making sure they are not pregnant.

> Imam Ahmad recorded that Abu Sa'id Al-Khudri said, "We captured some women from the area of Awtas who were al-

ready married, and we disliked having sexual relations with them because they already had husbands. So we asked the Prophet about this matter, and this *Ayah* was revealed,

"*Also forbidden are women already married, except those whom your right hand possesses.*"

Consequently, we had sexual relations with these women. This is the wording collected by At-Tirmidhi, An-Nasa'I, Ibn Jarir and Muslim in his *Sahih.*

"And if you fear that you shall not be able to deal justly with the orphan girls then marry other women of your choice, two or three, or four; but if you fear that you shall not be able to deal justly with them, then only one or slaves that your right hand possesses." (*Noble Qur'an* 4:3)

Tafsir Ibn Kathir, Volume 2, "Marrying Only One Wife When One Fears He Might not Do Justice to His Wife", 375.[252]

"*But if you fear that you will not be able to deal justly with them, then only one or what your right hand possesses.*"

The *Ayah* commands, if you fear that you will not be able to do justice between your wives by marrying more than one, then marry only one wife, or satisfy yourself with only female captives, for it is not obligatory to treat them equally, rather it is recommended. So if one does so, that is good, and if not, there is no harm on him.

"Prophet! We have made lawful to thee thy wives to whom thou hast paid their dowers, and those whom thy right hand possesses out of the prisoners of war whom Allah has assigned to thee." (*Noble Qur'an* 33:50)

Tafsir Ibn Kathir, Volume 7, 720[253]

"*Those slaves whom your right hand possesses whom Allah has given to you*" means, 'the slave-girls whom you took from the war booty are also permitted to you.'

"And those who guard their chastity (i.e., private parts, from illegal sexual acts) except from their wives or the slaves that their right hands possesses, - for they are free from blame; but whoever seeks beyond that, then those are the transgressors." (*Noble Qur'an* 23:5-7)

Tafsir Ibn Kathir, Volume 6, 631[254]

"And those who guard against their private parts. Except from their wives and their right hand possessions, for then, they are free from blame. But whoever seeks beyond that, then those are the transgressors."

means, those who protect their private parts from unlawful actions and do not do that which Allah has forbidden; fornication and homosexuality, and do not approach anyone except the wives whom Allah has made permissible for them or their right hand possessions from the captives. One who seeks whom Allah has made permissible for him is not to be blamed and there is no sin on him. Allah says;

"they are free from blame. But whoever goes beyond that" – meaning, other than wife or slave girl,

"then those are the transgressors." meaning, aggressors.

"Verily, the torment of the Lord is that before which none can feel secure. And those who guard their chastity (i.e., private parts from illegal sexual acts). Except from their wives or women slaves whom their right hands possesses – for then they are not blameworthy." (*Noble Qur'an* 70: 28-30)

Tafsir Ibn Kathir, Volume 10, 169[255]

"Except for their wives or their right hand possessions" meaning, from their female slaves.

Reliance of the Traveller, o11.0 "Non-Muslim Subjects of the Islamic State," Book O *"Justice," Reliance of the Traveller:*

o11.1 A formal agreement of protection is made with citizens who are:

1) Jews;

2) Christians;

3) Zoroastians;

4) Samarians and Sabians, if their religions do not respectively contradict the fundamental bases of Judaism and Christianity;

5) and those who adhere to the religion of Abraham or one of

6) the other prophets (upon whom be blessings and peace).

o11.2 Such an agreement may not be effected with those who are idol worshippers (dis: o9.9(n:)), or those who do not have a Sacred Book or something that could have been a Book. (A: Something that could have been a Book refers to those like the Zoroastrians, who have remnants resembling an ancient Book. As for the pseudoscriptures of cults that have appeared since Islam (n: such as the Sikhs, Baha'is, Mormons, Qadianis, etc.), they neither are nor could be a Book, since the Koran is the final revelation (dis: w4).)

o11.3 Such an agreement is only valid when the subject peoples:

  a) follow the rules of Islam (A: those mentioned below (o11.5) and those involving public behavior and dress, thought in acts of worship and their private lives, the subject communities have their own laws, judges, and courts, enforcing the rules of their own religion among themselves);

  b) and pay the non-Muslim poll tax (jizya).

The Non-Muslim Poll Tax,

o11.4 The minimum non-Muslim poll tax is one dinar (n: 4.235 grams of gold) per person (A: per year). The maximum is whatever both sides agree upon. It is collected with leniency and politeness, as are all debts, and is not levied on women, children or the insane.

o11.5 Such non-Muslim subjects are obliged to comply with the Islamic rules that pertain to safety and indemnity of life, reputation, and property. In addition they:

  1) are penalized for committing adultery of theft, though not for drunkenness;

  2) are distinguished from Muslims in dress wearing a wide cloth belt (zunnar);

  3) are not greeted with "as-Salamu 'alaykum";

  4) must keep to the side of the street;

  5) may not build higher than or as high as the Muslims' buildings, though if they acquire a tall house, it is not razed;

  6) are forbidden to openly display wine or pork, (A: to ring church bells or display crosses,) recite the Torah or Evangel aloud, or make pubic display of their funerals and feast days;

  7) and are forbidden to build new churches.

o11.6 They are forbidden to reside in the Hijaz, meaning the area and towns around Mecca, Medina, and Yamama, for more than three days (when the caliph allows them to enter there of something they need).

o11.7 A non-Muslim may not enter the Meccan Sacred Precinct (Haram) under any circumstances, or enter any other mosque without permission (A: nor may Muslims enter churches without permission).

o11.8 It is obligatory for the caliph (def: o25) to protect those of them who are in Muslim lands just as he would Muslims, and to seek the release of those of them who are captured.

o11.9 If non-Muslim subjects of the Islamic state refuse to conform to the rules of Islam, or to pay the non-Muslim poll tax, then their agreement with the state has been violated (dis: o11.11)(A: though if only one of them disobeys, it concerns him alone).

o11.10 The agreement is also violated (A: with respect to the offender alone) if the state has stipulated that any of the following things break it, and one of the subjects does so anyway, though if the state has not stipulated that these break the agreement, then they do not; namely, if one of the subject people:

1) commits adultery with a Muslim woman or marries her;

2) conceals spies of hostile forces;

3) leads a Muslim away from Islam;

4) kills a Muslim;

5) or mentions something impermissible about Allah, the Prophet (Allah bless him and give him peace), or Islam.

o11.11 When a subject's agreement with the state has been violated, the caliph chooses between the four alternatives mentioned above in connection with prisoners of war (o9.14).[256]

* * *

THIS REFERENCE TO HUMAN *dignity, which is the foundation and goal of the responsibility to protect, leads us to the theme we are specifically focusing upon this year, which marks the sixtieth anniversary of the Universal Declaration of Human Rights.*

Removing human rights from this context would mean restricting their range and yielding to a relativistic conception, according to which the meaning and interpretation of rights could vary and their universality would be denied in the name of different cultural, political, social and even religious outlooks.

The Declaration was adopted as a "common standard of achievement (Preamble) and cannot be applied piecemeal, according to trends or selective choices that merely run the risk of contradicting the unity of the human person and thus the indivisibility of human rights.

The Universal Declaration, rather, has reinforced the conviction that respect for human rights is principally rooted in unchanging justice, on which the binding force of international proclamation is also based.[257]

Pope Benedict XVI
Address to the United Nations General Assembly,
New York
April 18, 2008

* * *

[THE OIC] ASSERTS that human rights are universal in nature and must be considered in the context of dynamic and evolving process of international norm-setting, bearing in mind the significance of national and regional particularities and various historical, cultural and religious backgrounds.[258]

OIC Conference of Foreign Ministers
Resolution on Slander Campaign ... against Islamic
Sharia under the Slogan of Human Rights Protection
June 14-16, 2004

Appendix Two

Penetrating International Forums: OSCE, Islamophobia, and Incitement

The condition upon which God hath given liberty to man is eternal vigilance; which condition if he break, servitude is at once the consequence of his crime and the punishment of his guilt.

John Philpot Curran
Speech upon the Rigght of Election, 1790
Speeches, Dublin, 1808

Given the consistent treatment, use, and definition of "Islamophobia" by Islamic organizations like the OIC and the Brotherhood, one would think that engaging in a discussion on Islamophobia based on OIC/Brotherhood usage would be reasonably safe, uncontroversial, and fair. But just try. The following example comes from events at the Organization for Security and Cooperation in Europe.

As demonstrated throughout the book, there is an Islamic legal basis underlying Islamophobia campaigns. The OIC's Ten-Year Programme of Action seeks to effect this legal status as an international standard. Turkey, as an OIC Member State, is committed to implementing this initiative and is a party to the Cairo Declaration, which requires that the "24/25 Rule"[1] be applied. The European

---

1   As developed in Part IV, The Article 24/25 Rule for Analysis ("the 24/25 Rule") - Human Rights are defined as shariah for the purpose of any analysis involving the OIC, an OIC member state, or initiatives reasonably arising from either — including all entities claiming Islamic law as the basis of law, including al-Qaeda, the Muslim Brotherhood, elements of the Islamic Movement, and the Turkish delegation at the OSCE: When the subject of an analysis speaks of "rights and freedoms" or associated defined concepts that arise out of the Cairo Declaration on Human Rights in Islam, those "rights and freedoms" can only be assessed in terms of what Islamic law permits them to mean, where

Court of Human Rights has already ruled against Turkey on the implementation of regimes "based on shariah" when ruling that "shariah in a State party to the Convention can hardly be regarded as an association complying with the democratic ideal that underlies the whole of the Convention."[1]

Case Study: The OSCE

Founded in the 1970s, the Organization for Security and Cooperation in Europe (OSCE) has 57 participating States, makes decisions based on consensus that are not legally binding, and takes "a comprehensive approach to security that encompasses politico-military, economic, environmental, and human aspects."[2] The United States is a participating State. At the OSCE Human Development and Implementation Meeting in September 2013 in Warsaw, Poland, one could see the grip the OIC "Islamophobia" narrative has on all discussions regarding Islam.

The focus of this discussion is the role of Turkey's Permanent Diplomatic Mission to the OSCE and that of the Advisor on Combatting Intolerance and Discrimination against Muslims to the OSCE Office for Democratic Institutions and Human Rights (ODIHR). The assessment centers on exchanges from two OSCE Side Events in 2013: "Educational Initiatives and Approaches for Addressing anti-Semitism and Intolerance against Muslims[3] on 24 September and "How Bad Definitions Violate Fundamental OSCE Commitments"[4] on 26 September.

The principle takeaway from the Warsaw meeting was the documentation of relevant parties' refusal to engage in a definitional discussion of Islamophobia, even when the definitions had been formally provided by Turkish diplomats in earlier proceedings. The OSCE Muslim Advisor and the Turkish Delegation insisted that Islamophobia is an undefined term. The defensive posture may have been in anticipation of issues to be raised in the 26 September 2013 Side Event,[5] which was organized to address the consequences of defining "Islamophobia" along the lines provided by the Turkish delegation at a May 2013 OSCE meeting in Tirana, Albania.[6]

At the 24 September Side Event,[7] the issue of Islamophobia was raised in a seeming attempt to preemptively place definitional inquiries out of bounds. For example, initially identifying himself as "not a religious person,"[8] Bashy Quraishy, Secretary General of the European Muslim Initiative for Social Cohesion (EMISCO),[9] asserted that "if Muslims want to call it Islamophobia, it is none of anybody's business to call it something else."[10] While Quraishy's demand was in keeping with Islamic speech standards and OIC norms, it is contrary to public policy concerns that demand terms with legal significance be defined with some specificity. If Is-

---

Islamic law is the only criterion by which a determination can be made in the event of any dispute requiring resolution.

lamophobia were just an *inter se* issue within the Islamic community, Quraishy would have a point. But it's not. The term is meant to be applied to non-Muslims.

As noted, Islamophobia is associated with an OIC initiative to criminalize the speech of non-Muslims in non-Muslim jurisdictions. It is alarming that such a standard could be considered and enforced in a predominantly non-Muslim forum like the OSCE, or that a person could be imprisoned for violating a speech standard that lacks definition. It is hard to miss the irony of a man with the name Quraishy imposing a shariah standard in a forum purporting to be concerned with anti-Semitism given the plight of the Banu Qurayza, a Jewish tribe that unconditionally surrendered to Mohammed. Upon surrendering, all the males were put to death and all the women and children put in bondage.[11] This was memorialized in Qur'an Verse 33:26–27, the same verse that Pakistani Brigadier S.K. Malik relied on to argue in favor of terror in furtherance of the Quranic concept of war. From Brigadier Malik quoting Qur'an Verse 33: 26–27:

> And those of the people of the Book who aided them, Allah did take them down from their strongholds and **cast terror into their hearts**, so that some ye slew, and some ye made prisoners. And He made you heirs of their lands, their houses, and their goods, and of a land which ye had not frequented before. And Allah has power over all things. (Ahzab: 26–27)[12]

The Relevant Language

The relevant Islamophobia definition arises out of one that the Turkish diplomatic mission provided at the OSCE forum in May 2013. A review of the Tirana definition of Islamophobia, along with additional relevant information, shows it is in line with OIC definitions in support of OIC objectives. On May 27, 2013, the Turkish Delegation released a "Statement by Turkey" at Plenary Session 4 of the OSCE High-Level Conference on "Tolerance and Non-Discrimination: Combating Intolerance and Discrimination against Muslims" held in Tirana. In this instance, both the source of the statement and forum in which it was presented are as important as the definition itself:

> The former Personal Representative of the Chairperson-in-Office of the OSCE on Combating Discrimination and Intolerance against Muslims, Ambassador Omür Orhun, who is currently the Advisor and Special Envoy of the Secretary General of the Organization of Islamic Cooperation, has defined Islamophobia as follows:
>
> "Islamophobia is a contemporary form of racism and xeno-

phobia motivated by unfounded fear, mistrust and hatred of Muslims and Islam. Islamophobia is also manifested through intolerance, discrimination, unequal treatment, prejudice, stereotyping, hostility and adverse public discourse. Differentiating from classical racism and xenophobia, Islamophobia is mainly based on stigmatization of a religion and its followers. As such, Islamophobia is an affront to the **human rights** and dignity of Muslims."

We can see clearly from this definition that Islamophobia in fact constitutes a violation of **human rights.** Given the crucial role we attach in the OSCE, as well as within the framework of various international norms and instruments, to upholding and promoting human rights and human dignity, it is our duty to combat all forms of human rights violations, including Islamophobia.[13]

The Tirana definition comes from Turkish Ambassador Orhun, who was at one time assigned to the OSCE mission. In his current capacity as Advisor to the Secretary General of the OIC, Orhun authored "Challenges Facing Muslims in Europe." This document was posted on the OIC's "Permanent Observer Mission to the United Nations in New York" website in March 2011. It provides a brief biography of Orhun:

> **Ambassador Ömür Orhun** served as the Personal Representative of the Organisation for Security and Cooperation in Europe (OSCE) between 2004 and 2008. Presently he is the Adviser of the Secretary General of the OIC on 'Combating Discrimination and Promoting **Human Rights**'. Orhun is also a member of the **Human Rights** Committee of the Turkish UNESCO National Commission.[14]

In the OIC document, Orhun noted the lack of a commonly agreed-upon definition of Islamophobia before providing his own:

> Islamophobia needs but lacks a commonly agreed definition. It has often been defined as "fear or suspicion of Islam, Muslims, and matters pertaining to them". I think that this is a rather narrow definition. I prefer to base my definition on the following concepts:

> "Islamophobia is a contemporary form of racism and xenophobia motivated by unfounded fear, mistrust and hatred of Muslims and Islam. Islamophobia is also manifested through intolerance, discrimination and adverse public discourse

against Muslims and Islam. Differentiating from classical racism and xenophobia, Islamophobia is mainly based on radicalisation [sic] of Islam and its followers."

This definition situates this in a **human rights** context especially in the current post 9/11 period where the social climate facing Muslims especially in the Western countries has deteriorated, meaning that pre-existing prejudices and discriminatory tendencies against Muslims have become strengthened.[15]

The OSCE definition provided at Tirana and the OIC definition provided at the United Nations are similar and patterned after the OIC's "contemporary forms of racism" language found in the "Defamation of Religions" document that was formulated at the 2001 OIC Conference of Foreign Ministers in Bamako, Mali. To review:

3) Contemporary forms of racism are based on discrimination and disparagement on a cultural, rather than biological basis. In this content, the increasing trend of Islamophobia, as a distinct form of xenophobia in non-Muslim societies is very alarming.

4) The Committee for the Elimination of Racial Discrimination and the Commission on **Human Rights** along with its subsidiary bodies and mechanisms, have an important guiding role in the elimination of the contemporary forms of racism. All governments should cooperate fully with the Committee and the Special Rapporteur on the Contemporary Forms of Racism, Racial Discrimination, Xenophobia and Related Intolerance with the view to enabling them to fulfill their mandates and to examine the incidents of contemporary forms of racism, more specifically discrimination based on religion, including against Islam and Muslims.[16]

Regarding "contemporary forms of racism," here are a few observations. First, despite the purported lack of an agreed-upon definition of Islamophobia, there are in fact very concrete definitions explicitly based on OIC constructs. Second, the OIC definition of Islamophobia is based on the agreement of state actors in furtherance of inter-governmental objectives that OIC Member States, including Turkey, explicitly seek to impose on non-Muslim peoples in non-Muslim jurisdictions. Third, each of the three definitions provided explicitly associates Islamophobia with human-rights requirements. Through the Cairo Declaration on Human Rights in Islam, however, OIC Member States, including Turkey, define human rights as shariah. Fourth, as an OIC Member State, Turkey is obligated to understand human rights as shariah. Further confirmation of this point is the fact that Turkey's baseline definition of Islamophobia at the OSCE explicitly relies on a definition that the Turkish Ambassador provided while serving as Adviser to the Secretary General of the OIC on "Combating Discrimination and Promoting Human Rights," and the OIC definition matches the OSCE definition. Fifth, this gives rise to the 24/25 Rule, requiring that Turkish Delegation references to human rights be understood strictly in terms of shariah. Finally, it is not reasonable for non-Muslim delegations at the OSCE to engage in Islamophobia discussion while unaware of these circumstances.

Because there is notice that the Turkish use of the term "human rights" refers to shariah, there is warning that the European Court of Human Rights has already ruled that those rights "clearly diverge from values of the Convention for the Protection of Human Rights and Fundamental Freedoms,"[17] more commonly known as the European Convention on Human Rights.

Recognizing the far-reaching consequences of anti-Islamophobia initiatives, Dr. Harald Fiegl of *Mission Europa* made a formal intervention at the July 2013 OSCE meeting in Vienna, Austria. He called on the OSCE to provide a formal definition of the term "Islamophobia" as a condition of its being used by the OSCE and related international forums.[18] Because the Islamophobia agenda's deep penetration into OSCE processes depends largely on its unconsidered adoption by unaware diplomatic missions and because Dr. Fiegl's request would force specific consideration, Umut Topçuoğlu, Counselor at the Permanent Delegation of Turkey, responded that same day in a speech to the plenary session, deriding Dr. Fiegl and restating an Islamophobia definition:

> My name is Umut Topcuoglu, I am a Counselor at the Permanent Delegation of Turkey to the OSCE and I wanted to make a few remarks concerning the Intervention by the representative of the NGO *Mission Europa,* which were made previously in this Session. The gentleman in question, in a statement where he also referred to my Prime Minister, requested an urgent clarification, if I am not mistaken, of the concept of Islamophobia. Now, from the general tenor of his statement, I did indeed get the impression that he is in urgent need of understanding what Islamophobia means. So, I wanted to share with you the definition of Islamophobia made by a former personal representative of the Chairperson in office of the OSCE on combatting discrimination and intolerance against Muslims, Ambassador Orhun, who is currently the advisor and special envoy of the Secretary General of the Organization of the Islamic Cooperation. And according to him,

> Islamophobia is a contemporary form of racism and xeno-
> phobia motivated by unfounded fear, mistrust and hatred of
> Muslims and Islam. Islamophobia is also manifested through
> intolerance, discrimination, unequal treatment, prejudice,
> stereotyping, hostility and adverse public discourse. Differ-
> entiating from classical racism and xenophobia, Islamopho-
> bia is mainly based on stigmatization or religion and its fol-
> lowers.
>
> And as such, Islamophobia is an affront to **human rights**
> and dignity of Muslims and I hope the representative of the
> NGO *Mission Europa* will be able to benefit from contem-
> plating on this definition of Islamophobia. Thank you.[19]

Turkey's messaging on Islamophobia is clear. There is a consistent, explicit, and officially promulgated definition of Islamophobia that Turkey, and hence
the OIC, is working to implant within non-Muslim governing forums like the
OSCE for the purpose of implementing Islamophobia requirements. In each example where the Turkish delegation formally expressed a definition of Islamophobia, it was associated with Ambassador Orhun and human rights. Because, each
reference to human rights is actually a reference to shariah, those claims should
be understood to be contrary to the "Convention for the Protection of Human
Rights and Fundamental Freedoms" (i.e., the European Convention on Human
Rights)—not to mention the First Amendment of the U.S. Constitution. Dr.
Fiegl's concern was that the Islamophobia narrative would integrate into OSCE
processes under the sanctioned fiction that the term "Islamophobia" has no definition when, in fact, those seeking to promulgate it are specifically aware of its OIC
definition and of the intent behind it.

High Drama at the OSCE Corral

Returning to the 24 September Side Event (where Bashy Quraishy set the
stage by declaring that "if Muslims want to call it Islamophobia, it is none of
anybody's business to call it something else"),[20] it was convened by the ODIHR
Tolerance and Non-Discrimination Department[21] and moderated by Taskin Tankut Soykan, the ODIHR/OSCE Advisor on Combating Intolerance and Discrimination against Muslims.[22] The side event highlighted the booklet *Guidelines
for Educators on Countering Intolerance and Discrimination against Muslims: Addressing Islamophobia through Education*, developed by ODIHR, UNESCO, and
the Council of Europe.[23] In the acknowledgements, *Guidelines for Educators* recognized the OIC, specifically Mr. Ufuk Gökçen, former Adviser to the OIC Secretary General,[24] for its support. The booklet also identified the OIC and the OIC
Observatory as resources.[25]

When challenged to provide a functional definition of Islamophobia, *Guidelines for Educators* author and panel member Robin Richardson started by offering the definition provided by the 2007 Runnymede report: "a world view involving an unfounded dread or hatred of Islam and the subsequent dislike of all Muslims."[26] But Richardson was forced to acknowledged that the definition was deficient, going so far as to concede that "terminology is important and we've got the wrong terminology. ... I'm not ashamed that our language isn't good enough."[27] As the *Third OIC Observatory Report* documents, the OIC relies on the Runnymede Trust to develop its talking points.[28] This is relevant because Mr. Richardson made reference to his past affiliation with the Runnymede Trust.[29] (See Part 5 for more about the Runnymede Trust and Mr. Richardson's part in developing the Islamophobia narrative.)

As the discussion grew contentious, Mr. Richardson suggested that "the word Islamophobia" does not appear in the *Guidelines for Educators*, outside of the title.[30] The term "Islamophobia" is not only in the title, it is used 49 times in the pamphlet. Raising his concern for the complications associated with lexicons and epistemologies, Richardson retreated to an increasingly confused complexity narrative. Even Soykan was drawn into Richardson's confusion, saying, "Even if you look at the issue from an epistemological viewpoint, you can't reach an agreement on this."[31]

Two days later at the 26 September Side Event, Umut Topçuoğlu left both "Muslim" and "Islamophobia" out of *Guidelines for Educator*'s title when referring to it to make a point about Islamophobia:

> Look at the title, you're so fixed on the word Islamophobia, look at the title; *Guidelines for Educators on Countering Intolerance and Discrimination [against Muslims: Addressing Islamophobia ...],* this booklet is about inculcating a culture of tolerance and respect for diversity and unity in youth.[32]

At the September 24 Side Event, the Turkish Delegation could see that the moderator and panel members were losing control of the discussion and intervened. After all, with Richardson admitting that the current definition misses the mark and Soykan acknowledging a lack of agreement on the definition, the illusion of consensus was being put at risk. At this point, the Turkish Delegation retreated from its own definition of Islamophobia. As in Vienna, Turkish Councilor Topçuoğlu again took to the floor to speak:

> I just wanted to clarify one simple point. You, Sir, mentioned that the Turkish delegation provided a definition of Islamophobia which came from the Organization of Islamic Cooperation. Now I'm sure I have really stated this before, the definition of Islamophobia, my delegation provided in some

previous sessions or meetings on tolerance and non-discrimination **was formulated by a retired Turkish ambassador,**
Mr. Ömür Orhun. Now this retired Turkish ambassador was
between the years 2004 and 2008 personal representative of
the chairman in office of the Organization for Security and
Cooperation in Europe on intolerance and discrimination
against Muslims. So we have here, of course, right now he's
special envoy to the chairman, the secretary-general of the
OIC. But the point is that the definition was formulated by
someone who has deep experience in these affairs and who
actually worked within the OSCE in these affairs, **so I think
saying it's an OIC definition is really sort of distorting the
facts.**[33]

According to Topçuoğlu, the Turkish definition is now less than official, and
it is a distortion to say that it tracks with OIC definitions. This strategy is one of
dissociation, where things can be both accepted and denied at the same time. Two
days later, at the 26 September Side Event, Counselor Topçuoğlu said:

One other thing I wanted to mention is I keep hearing "the
official definition brought by the Turkish Delegation, the official definition of the Turkish Delegation," now, the definition you're referring to, I'm not going to repeat myself because
we already talked about this in the session on Wednesday or
Tuesday, I believe. The definition you're referring to, my delegation referred to that definition by Ambassador Orhun in
Tirana,[34] because, from our point of view, it highlights many
aspects of the phenomenon known as Islamophobia which
we think needs to be addressed. Of course there is no official
agreement among the OSCE States, Participating States,
about what the definition of Islamophobia should be. We
wanted to highlight that this definition brings forth certain
aspects which do need to be addressed. **And, as long as you
go on saying "the official definition by Turkey, the official
definition by Turkey," well, I mean, you're doing our ad-
vertising, maybe it'll become the official definition** if you
go on saying it long enough. Thank you.[35]

As it already is the official definition for the OIC, Topçuoğlu meant "official"
for the OSCE. In other words, "this is what 'Islamophobia' means when *we* use
it, but not when *you* use it; when you use it, it's undefined, because you have no
right to discuss it"—just as Bashy Quraishy had warned. Another aspect of dissociation was the repeated insistence that, as Topçuoğlu noted, "there is no official
agreement among OSCE participating States about what the definition of Islamophobia should be."[36] Of course, the concern voiced by Dr. Fiegl—and the topic

of the 26 September Side Event—was precisely that the OSCE is moving toward enforcing anti-Islamophobia even as it engages in the contrived fiction that, because the OSCE hasn't agreed upon the OIC definition of Islamophobia, the term has yet to be defined. This was the line held by Taskin Soykan, the Advisor on Combating Intolerance and Discrimination against Muslims at ODIHR/OSCE.

When explaining that the OIC is structuring Islamophobia to monitor non-Muslims through the OIC Observatory, with the ultimate aim of prosecuting those who run afoul of anti-Islamophobia mandates, Soykan deflected the concern by stating that "you can't reach agreement [at the OSCE] on this," that "there is no suggestion [at the OSCE], no suggested educational approach to attack people," and that "it's not a good approach, pedagogical approach, to even accuse a student of being racist **immediately**." As if that were the point.

When concerns were raised regarding OIC intentions with the Islamophobia agenda (that the OSCE was blindly implementing), Soykan's deflected: "You can talk about this issue with the authorities of OIC, this is not the right place."[37] At the 26 September Side Event, Soykan again held the line, this time speaking in more general terms: "In none of these decisions, OSCE participating States have provided either a definition of racism, or xenophobia or anti Semitism or intolerance and so forth; even discrimination is not defined in our commitments." He then reinforced that "we [the OSCE] are against the criminalization of any expression of opinion."[38] Applying the 24/25 Rule to Soykan's statement, free "expression of opinion" should be understood in terms of Article 22 (a) of the Cairo Declaration, which states that "everyone shall have the right to express his opinion freely in such manner as would not be contrary to the principles of the Shariah."[39]▢

Who is Taskin Soykan?

Given his insistence that the OSCE has no agreed-upon definition of Islamophobia and that there is no intention of bringing deterrent action against those who run afoul of Islamophobia strictures, the question is whether Soykan is aware of OIC intentions underlying the implementation of its Ten-Year Programme of Action to criminalize Islamophobia. The answer is that it is not reasonable to think that he isn't. Given his attendance at Istanbul University, his travel with Turkish Ambassador Orhun,[40] and other indications,[41] Soykan appears to be a Turkish citizen. This is important because, given his Turkish diplomatic roots, it is reasonable to assume that his views are in line with Turkey's on the status of the Cairo Declaration with regard to human rights, not to mention the imperatives associated with the Islamophobia initiative that Turkey is committed to implementing in furtherance of the OIC's Ten-Year Programme of Action. There is also Soykan's interest in the study of dhimmitude. In 1998, Soykan submitted his thesis to Professor Tevfik Ozcan (Istanbul University Faculty of Law, Common Law Section, Department of Philosophy and Sociology of Law) under the working title, "Run up to the Conquest of Istanbul Ottoman Tanzimat."[42] It was accepted in

1999 under the title, "The Legal Status of *Dhimmis* During the Ottoman Empire from the Conquest of Istanbul to the Tanzimat."[43]

When Orhun was the Personal Representative of the Chairman-in-Office of the OSCE on Combating Intolerance and Discrimination against Muslims, Soykan was the Adviser on Combating Intolerance and Discrimination against Muslims at the ODIHR, and the 2007 report titled "Second Semi-Annual Report for 2007 by Ambassador Omur Orhun" twice listed Soykan as travelling with the Ambassador. That report also included Annex I "Abstract for the OIC-Georgetown University ACMCU Roundtable on 'Islamophobia and the Challenge of Pluralism in the 21st Century,'" which specifically calls for the criminalization of Islamophobia in Western countries.[44]

Soykan was a speaker at the 2007 International Islamophobia Conference in Istanbul[45] along with Ghulam Nabi Fai, Tariq Ramadan, Louay Safi, and prominent OIC members, including General Secretary Ekmeleddin Ihsanolu.[46] A key takeaway from that conference was that Islamophobia should be criminalized.[47] Add to this Soykan's involvement in "Alliance of Civilization"[48] activities and his speaking engagements with known Muslim Brotherhood organizations[49/50] and it is clear that he has close OIC contacts and is well aware of its Islamophobia objectives. Still, he insists the OSCE has no definition of Islamophobia and there is no intention to criminalize such offenses. He knows there is a set definition of Islamophobia, Turkey is actively committed to it, and there is intent to criminalize it. Soykan could clarify this for the OSCE. At the same time, it is not reasonable to think OSCE participating States would be unaware of this because it is not reasonable that they would be.

The Bottom Line

It matters little that the OSCE lacks a common definition of Islamophobia *today* or that there is no intent to criminalize Islamophobia offenses *today*. What matters is the OIC's ongoing penetration into organizations like the OSCE and its downstream management of objectives. It is called a "Ten-Year" plan for a reason. How could international organizations like the OSCE and the Council of Europe publish on Islamophobia knowing that the term is undefined in its own forum and seemingly unaware of its known definition (and intent) in other forums? As this OSCE snapshot indicates, international bodies that are predominantly non-Muslim have allowed their forum's discussion of Islam to be dominated by entities that define human rights according to shariah, which doesn't recognize the right of non-Muslims to express unsanctioned comments with regard to Islam. Specifically, through capable Turkish agency, the OIC has established shariah speech norms as the *de facto* standard that (as yet) passively governs OSCE discourse under the guise of Islamophobia, even as this standard violates European human and U.S. constitutional rights.

At a time when a dawah entity, the Muslim Brotherhood, seeks to control domestic discourse on issues relating to Islam inside the United States, an ummah entity (the OIC and its Member States) is making a concerted parallel effort to control the same discourse in international forums. In terms of information operations, Muslim Brotherhood and OIC lines of operation are in harmony, converging on the same agreed-upon doctrines. In the information battlespace, our national security establishment has been enveloped.

An interesting side note: As the anti-Islamophobia effort began to escalate at the OSCE, Mr. Shaarik Zafar became associated with the United States Mission to the OSCE.[51] Mr. Zafar was the Senior Policy Advisor in the Office of Civil Rights & Civil Liberties at the Department of Homeland Security[52] (where he would later help author[53] *Terminology to Define the Terrorists: Recommendations from American Muslims*[54]) and also served as Deputy Chief of the Global Engagement Group at the NCTC.[55] Currently, Mr. Zafar serves as the State Department's Special Representative to Muslim Communities.[56]

Parallel Operations – Details on 'Incitement'

Before we leave the OSCE, there is one other activity worth noting that concerns a Side Event on the "Rabat Plan of Action," a United Nations activity focused on the term "incitement" as used in Article 20 (2) of the 1966 *International Covenant on Civil and Political Rights,*[57] discussed Part 4. Recall that the OIC advocates a form of "incitement" that justifies attacks, similar to the way some husbands justify beating their wives because of something the wives said. Also recall that the United States included a reservation to the *International Covenant* explicitly stating that Article 20 (2) does not restrict any First Amendment rights.[58] The 24 September 2013 Side Event "Understanding and Implementing the Obligation to Prohibit Incitement in the OSCE" was convened by the Center for Media and Communications Studies, Central European University, and ARTICLE 19.[59] Central European University (CEU) was founded by George Soros[60] to undertake his Open Societies Mission.[61] ARTICLE 19 is an NGO funded by various European ministries and Open Society Foundations,[62] a George Soros entity.[63]

The underlying effort is to redefine and repurpose laws through the veiled redefinition of those laws' key statutory terms, while leaving third parties blind to what is happening. This is often accomplished through the disarming use of facially neutral language in the service of narratives that intend biased outcomes. This is similar to the Alinskyist tactic of redefining iconic symbols and terms and covertly repurposing them, bringing an unwitting public along in the process. The side event was about "the legal and non-legal policy implications of the Rabat Plan of Action (RPA)," an "expert workshop" convened under the auspices of the United Nations Office of the High Commissioner on Human Rights (OHCHR) in Rabat, Morocco, in October 2012. The relevant document from the Rabat workshop is the "Rabat Plan of Action on the Prohibition of Advocacy of National, Racial or

Religious Hatred that Constitutes Incitement to Discrimination, Hostility or Violence:[1] Conclusions and Recommendations Emanating from the Four Regional Expert Workshops Organised by OHCHR, in 2011, and Adopted by Experts in Rabat, Morocco on 5 October 2012." The footnote in the document title makes it clear that the Rabat Plan of Action (RPA) concerns incitement as the term is used in Article 20 (2) of the *International Covenant*:

> [Footnote 1 in the title] 1. Article 20 of the International Covenant on Civil and Political Rights reads that "Any advocacy of national, racial or religious hatred that constitutes incitement to discrimination, hostility or violence shall be prohibited by law". Throughout the text this will be referenced as "incitement to hatred".[64]

Certainly the successful redefinition of "incitement" as used in the *International Covenant* could lead to a repurposed application of Article 20 (2) that was neither anticipated nor agreed to by either the drafters or signatories when it was ratified. Like "Islamophobia," "incitement" is a key term that the OIC seeks to control. The OIC uses the term "incitement" in the language of the Cairo Declaration in UN Resolution 16/18 and even to justify "Days of Rage" events. In the Cairo Declaration, for example, the same Article 22 that declares in Section (a) that "everyone shall have the right to express his opinion freely in such manner as would not be contrary to the principles of the Shari'ah" goes on to state in Section (d) that:

> It is not permitted to excite nationalistic or doctrinal hatred or to do anything that may be an **incitement** to any form of racial discrimination.[65]

The OIC integrated incitement into the language of Resolution 16/18 in UN instruments:

> … Combating intolerance, negative stereotyping and stigmatization of, and discrimination, **incitement** to violence, and violence against persons based on religion or belief.[66]

It also uses the term to justify "Days of Rage," for example, in Afghanistan:

> The Secretary General of the Organization of Islamic Cooperation (OIC) today in a statement deplored the burning of copies of the Holy Qur'an at the US base in Bagram, Afghanistan. He said that the incident was a deplorable act of **incitement** and called on the concerned authorities to take swift and appropriate disciplinary action against those responsible.[67]

It should come as no surprise that the OIC influences activities intended to manipulate the language of incitement in international forums, even as Soros-affiliated groups like ARTICLE 19 and CEU have taken lead on the Rabat Plan of Action. In fact, the RPA is transparent about implementing OIC objectives in furtherance of the OIC's Ten-Year Programme of Action and, as such, runs in tandem with—and is structured to support—the Islamophobia effort. For instance, while Section 2 of the RPA preface states that "this activity [is] focused on the relationship between freedom of expression and hate speech, especially in relation to religious issues,"[68] no purely religious institution is identified and only the OIC is mentioned. In fact, the RPA calls for cooperation with the OIC[69] while no Christian, Jewish, Hindu, or Buddhist entity is mentioned.

As important, the "contemporary forms of racism" effort arising out of the OIC's 2001 Foreign Ministers Conference in Bamako, Mali, identified the "Special Rapporteur on Racism, Racial Discrimination, Xenophobia and Related Intolerance" as the point of penetration into international forums. Recall Sections 3 and 4 of the Bamako instrument concerning "contemporary forms of racism":

> 3. **Contemporary forms of racism are based on discrimination and disparagement on a cultural, rather than biological basis.** In this content, the increasing trend of Islamophobia, as a distinct form of xenophobia in non-Muslim societies is very alarming.

> 4. The Committee for the Elimination of Racial Discrimination and the Commission on Human Rights along with its subsidiary bodies and mechanisms, have an important guiding role in the elimination of the **contemporary forms of racism**. All governments should cooperate fully with the Committee and the Special Rapporteur on the **Contemporary Forms of Racism, Racial Discrimination, Xenophobia and Related Intolerance with the view to enabling them to fulfill their mandates and to examine the incidents of contemporary forms of racism**, more specifically discrimination based on religion, including against Islam and Muslims.[70] [Emphasis added.]

Compare the OIC language of intent in 2001 with the 2012 language of Part 4 of the 2012 RPA preface:

> 4. The Rabat expert workshop included the four moderators and those experts having participated in all four workshops, including the Special Rapporteur on Freedom of Opinion and Expression, the Special Rapporteur on Freedom of Religion or Belief, and **the Special Rapporteur on Racism, Racial Discrimination, Xenophobia and Related Intoler-**

ance, a member of the Committee on the Elimination of Racial Discrimination and a representative of the Non-Governmental Organization Article XIX.[71] [Emphasis added.]

On the question of freedom of speech, there is an OIC effort to subordinate non-Muslim speech to shariah speech standards, constrained by notions of incitement. The OIC seeks to institutionalize these speech standards through international forums, using facially neutral language that may not even mention Islam and emanates from left-leaning entities. Through the Rabat Plan of Action and associated OHCHR workshops, the OIC is working to manipulate the meaning of "incitement" to justify violence.

When this concern was raised at the Incitement Side Event, however, the panel members responded that the language of the RPA is "not OIC language, [that the] OIC are far more involved in 16/18."[72] While the concession on 16/18 probably was not intended, it was a substantive admission. A more extensive treatment of the OIC's manipulation of language in international forums is beyond the scope of this appendix, but the topic merits directed treatment, starting with a simple recognition that such activities are purposeful and ongoing.

For a practical example of the close relationship between Resolution 16/18 and the Rabat Plan of Action, one need look no further than the events following the *Charlie Hebdo* assassinations in the first week of January 2015. In statements that presuppose culpability, less than a week after *Charlie Hebdo*, Ufuk Gökçen, Ambassador to the Permanent Observer Mission of the OIC to the UN,[73] said the "*Charlie Hebdo* attack and reactions underline critical importance of renewed commitment to the resolution of 16/18 and the Rabat Plan of Action."[74] Gokcen's comment linked to a supporting article by the legal officer of the Soros-funded ARTICLE 19.[75] Days later, on January 20, 2015, the Muslim Brotherhood fell in line when its chief jurist, Yusuf Qaradawi, posted an announcement in his capacity as President of the International Union of Muslim Scholars (IUMS), endorsing the OIC position that further ratified the *Charlie Hebdo* executions.[76]

Noting such covert attacks on protected speech and recalling the U.S. reservation to Article 20 (2) of the *International Covenant* on First Amendment grounds, it is recommended that Congress take immediate action to affirm this reservation and strengthen the language even further.

The OSCE Stands Indicted – Just Ask the OIC

There is no question that all discussions on Islamophobia and incitement in international forums concern the OIC's effort to implement its Ten-Year Programme of Action, which seeks to implement international shariah speech standards that will ultimately include criminal sanctions. The main OIC Islamophobia effort of record is UN HRC Resolution 16/18. (The word "incitement" is even in 16/18's full title: "Combating Intolerance, Negative Stereotyping and Stigmatization of, and Discrimination, <u>Incitement</u> to violence, and Violence against persons based on Religion or Belief."[77]) For the Turkish component to posture otherwise at international forums is disingenuous. For Western diplomats not to know this is malpractice.

This activity is a direct assault on free speech standards guaranteed by the First Amendment and, to a lesser degree, the European Convention on Human Rights. In the *Sixth OIC Observatory Report on Islamophobia,* released in December 2013, the OIC boasted of its progress in implementing its Islamophobia campaign, lauding the OSCE, the Council of Europe, and UNESCO for publishing *Guidelines for Educators on Countering Intolerance and Discrimination against Muslims.*[78] This is the same *Guidelines for Educators* that sparked the OSCE Muslim Advisor and the Turkish Delegation to insist that Islamophobia is not a defined term, though the *Sixth OIC Observatory Report* identified Turkey as an OIC partner on implementing Islamophobia.[79] In the *Observatory Report,* the term Islamophobia or Islamophobe was used 390 times; UN HCR Resolution 16/18 used the term 30 times and "incitement" 29 times. At one point, the *Observatory Report* noted the OIC's authorship of 16/18:

> The historic consensual adoption of the **OIC sponsored** UN Human Rights Council Resolution 16/18 entitled "Combating Intolerance, Negative Stereotyping and Stigmatization of, and Discrimination, **Incitement** to violence, and Violence against persons based on Religion or Belief" on March 21, 2011 as well in the subsequent sessions of the Council and the UN General Assembly, has effectively broken the myth of the global community's inability to take a unified and determined stand to combat intolerance and hatred based on religion and belief.[80]

Noting that this process, the Istanbul Process, was put in motion in partnership with U.S. Secretary of State Hillary Clinton in July 2011,[81] the *Observatory Report* made it clear that this effort is to result in criminalization:

> The meeting was attended by delegations from over sixty countries and addressed three out of the eight points for action provided by **Resolution 16/18**, namely, "Speaking out against intolerance, including advocacy of religious hatred that constitutes **incitement** to discrimination, hostility or violence"; "Adopting measures to **criminalize incitement** to imminent violence based on religion or belief"; and "Recognizing that the open, constructive and respectful debate of ideas, as well as interfaith and intercultural dialogue at the local, national and international levels, can play a positive role in combating religious hatred, **incitement** and violence".[82]

Western Diplomats Should be on Notice

The OIC General Secretary, in a speech to UN and Western dignitaries at a UN forum in Geneva, in June 2013, said the "effort does not stop at mere passage of [the] resolution," that it "must build further on the consensus building that went into resolution 16/18," an effort that constitutes a "triumph of multilateralism." Ihsanoglu was speaking of the OIC's success in the execution of a process it designed to get Western leaders to negotiate our basic rights away.[83] This speech was memorialized in the *Sixth OIC Observatory Report on Islamophobia* and concerned the necessity of implementing Resolution 16/18.[84] The OIC wants everyone to know what it is doing, and it wants to remind the world that its Western counterparts have already agreed to conform. In that same speech, in the presence of Western dignitaries and diplomatic corps, Ihsanoglu not only called for the criminalization of speech in conjunction with Islamophobia; he made it clear this was already agreed to by the OIC's American and European counterparts:

> Two expert events in the framework of the Istanbul Process were held earlier **in Washington D.C.**, in December 2011 and in the **Wilton Park event in London** in December 2012. Discussions at the third expert meeting focused on implementation of points 5, 6 and 8 of Resolution 16/18, namely, "Speaking out against intolerance, including advocacy of religious hatred that constitutes incitement to discrimination, hostility or violence"; "Adopting measures to **criminalize incitement** to imminent violence based on religion or belief"; and "Recognizing that the open, constructive and respectful debate of ideas, as well as interfaith and intercultural dialogue at the local, national and international levels, can play a positive role in combating religious hatred, incitement and violence".

> The Meeting agreed on a number of key points to combat Islamophobia and other cases of religious intolerance. **It was recognized that action needs to be taken to criminalize incitement to violence**; however, most western states insisted that only cases of imminent violence should be criminalized. For its part, the OIC emphasized the fact that criminalization should extend to acts or speech that denote manifest intolerance and hate so as to ensure the preservation of an environment conducive to mutual understanding, cohabitation and respect in line with the principles of the UN Charter.[85]

Remember, when the OIC speaks, it represents state actors. Western diplomats should be held to the knowing standard that requires that, as professionals, they either know or should know the OIC's unambiguously stated objectives. At some point however, given the rights at stake, language of malpractice should transition to language of malfeasance. Using the facially neutral language of diplomacy, the OIC has manipulated the meaning and use of the term "incitement" to conform to shariah norms in non-Muslim forums. Toward the end of his speech, Ihsanoglu gave the hallmark OIC ultimatum, expressed in facially neutral terms, to either implement the OIC's Islamophobia agenda, assessed within the Islamic legal framework established by the Cairo Declaration, or to risk violence. Recalling that Islam recognizes only Islam as a *bona fide* religion and that the OIC conforms to shariah, Ihsanoglu said the methodology to assess incitement is to conform to shariah norms in a progressive manner following the Milestones process:

> I would like to emphasize here, at the outset, that religions are part of international heritage and have all along accommodated critical thinking as an important pillar of human evolution and progress. For instance in Islam, the concept of 'Ijtihad' forms a dynamic tool of jurisprudence that accommodates dissent and critical thinking. It is duly reflected in the admissibility of the different interpretations. **Such dynamism, I believe, is a precondition to the progressive development of all legal systems.**[86]

As bounded by Sections (a) and (d) of Article 22 of the Cairo Declaration. Compare:

> An open and constructive debate of ideas is indeed useful. It must be upheld as a matter of freedom of opinion and expression. It, however, transforms into a case of **incitement** to discrimination, hostility or violence when the freedom is abused to denigrate symbols and personalities sacred to one or the other religion. ... It is, therefore, essential to draw a line between free speech and hate speech. ... Similarly, we could benefit from an integrated approach with regard to international efforts geared towards combating intolerance, discrimination and **incitement** to hatred.[87]

When compared to the language to Article 22 of the Cairo Declaration:

> (a) "Everyone shall have the right to express his opinion freely in such manner as would not be contrary to the principles of the Shari'ah."[88]

> (d) It is not permitted to excite nationalistic or doctrinal hatred or to do anything that may be an **incitement** to any form of racial discrimination.[89]

In keeping with the "good-cop/bad cop" narrative that's been the hallmark of OIC information campaigns, the OIC leader's speech ended with a threat:

> In a world faced with the menace of terrorism, incitement to hatred, discrimination, and violence, cannot and must not be ignored. We would, otherwise, be faced with the unaffordable risk of the agenda hijacked and set by radicals and non-state actors. We need to act to wrest the initiative away from the street to the table of meaningful and result oriented multilateral discourse. [90]

For the OIC, a policy that permits incitedness facilitates the provocation that justifies attacks on non-Muslims in non-Islamic jurisdictions for expressing views that offend Muslims. To keep such attacks from happening, the OIC insists that otherwise protected speech must be criminalized. Once that speech is criminalized, the right to persecute becomes institutionalized. Understood this way, the OIC Ten-Year Programme of Action, its associated Islamophobia campaigns and "Days of Rage," UN Resolution 16/18, the Istanbul Process, and the Rabat Plan of Action seem to institutionalize an implied threat of violence that hovers over processes and is designed to facilitate submission. In Islamic parlance, the word for this is *dhimmitude*, the same topic covered in the OSCE Muslim Advisor's thesis.[91]

Postscript: OSCE 2014 and the Bifurcation Strategy

Returning to the Human Dimension Implementation Meeting in Warsaw in September 2014, it was apparent that tighter control of side events had become a priority. The September 30 Side Event, "Islamophobia: Fact or Fiction,"[92] was sponsored by the European Muslim Initiative for Social Cohesion (EMISCO) and had a more tightly controlled panel of experts,[93] most of whom read from prepared texts. Though it was promoted as an event that would be opened up for questions and discussion, the panel filibustered to the end of the scheduled time. As reflected by both the interventions in the main assembly and in the side event itself, the central meme was focused on pressuring the OSCE/ODIHR to formally adopt the term "Islamophobia" in its official lexicon. The pamphlet "How to Combat Cyber Hate Crime While Respecting Freedom of Expression: The Challenge of Countering Anti-Muslim Hatred on the Internet"[94] was provided at the side event as a support document.

> "We recommend that OSCE should henceforth: (1) Replace the official term intolerance against Muslims to Islamophobia, which is used and accepted by many intergovernmental organizations like UN, Council of Europe, OIC, and EU."[95]

Sidestepping the fact that it was acknowledged in the 2013 side event that

Islamophobia lacks a coherent definition, the pamphlet relied on an EMISCO effort in 2010 to suggest that there is consensus on the word's meaning:

> **The definition of Islamophobia, EMISCO discussed and agreed in 2010.** "Islamophobia is a form of intolerance and discrimination motivated by fear, distrust and hatred of Islam and its adherents. It is often manifested along with racism, xenophobia, anti-immigrant sentiment, and religious intolerance."[96]

The panel exhibited a heightened sensitivity to definitional questions regarding Islamophobia, stating in various ways that "because everyone knows what it is, it really doesn't need to be defined." For example, from panel member Bülent Şenay, listed as a Turkish professor from Uludag University, in Bursa, Turkey, and OSCE/ODIHR Advisor for Freedom of Religion Advisory Council:[97]

> But we all know, everyone around this table knows that the term Islamophobia is a century old term and yet it's still around and it's even more actual than ever. The concept, yes, is contested but we all know what it means, it's an academic word for those who are interested.[98]

An apparent replacement for Taskin Soykan, Professsor Şenay felt so strongly in favor of the ambiguous definition of "Islamophobia" that he suggested that raising such concerns was itself a form of Islamophobia:

> In my personal opinion, to maintain that the term Islamophobia is not accurate or insist on this debate, has the risk of being Islamophobic itself because what is the purpose of really fighting about the terminology if it may continue to be an academic subject.[99]

The professor's opinion is in keeping with the Pact of Umar; non-Muslims are not to question the terms of submission being imposed on them. Agreeing to hold the panel for discussion after the side event concluded, the Secretary General of EMISCO, Bashy Quraishy, opened the forum to questions and discussion.

When called upon, I used that opportunity to remind the panel that in the previous year's forum there had been agreement that Islamophobia lacked a coherent definition; that it was a term that, if implemented, would be used to prosecute individuals; that it is a miscarriage to prosecute people for violating legal constructs that lack definition; that the Islamophobia standard acts as a form of prior restraint; that the term reflects the efforts of state actors, spearheaded by the OIC on behalf of its Member States (and that this should be recognized in diplomatic forums); and that it was inappropriate to accuse someone of Islamophobia for calling for a reasonably articulable definition of a term that is being developed for specific political and legal ends.[100] The question received defensive responses that emphasized EMISCO's desire to use the multicultural narrative[101] to disassociate their efforts from the larger OIC master plan—the Ten-Year Programme of Action. The strategy is one of bifurcation. From Professor Şenay:

> When you speak about Islamophobia, we're talking about a ground level reality. How can OIC control the public opinion among the Muslims in Europe?[102]

From the General Secretary of EMISCO, Bashy Quraishy:

> We are not here representing the OIC, please, that you have to very clearly understand. EMISCO is not related to the OIC or the OSCE or to any other European organization.[103]

> You see, I don't want anybody to be prosecuted for anything.[104]

Of course, one way that the OIC can try to control opinion in Europe is to make it seem that foreign state action is arising out of localized initiatives camouflaged as multicultural initiatives. What is reasonably clear is that the side event was a part of a larger OIC effort to implement laws to prosecute non-Muslims in non-Muslim jurisdictions who violate anti-Islamophobia norms, and EMISCO knows this.

One way to demonstrate this is by looking at Professor Bülent Şenay. There is more to him than was provided in his introduction. According to his own curricula vitae, he sits on the OSCE Human Rights Advisory Council, is a founding member of the Governing Board of EMISCO, and was the Diplomatic Counselor for Religious and Cultural Affairs at the Turkish Embassy in The Hague from 2008 to 2012.[105] Applying the 24/25 Rule, we know that Professor Şenay, as a Turkish diplomat, defines human rights as shariah. Also, as a Turkish diplomat, he recognizes the status of the OIC. During his tenure as the Turkish Diplomatic Counselor, in 2010, Şenay gave a presentation to a COJEP-sponsored OSCE event, "Undoing Hate Crimes: Combating Islamophobia as Cultural Terrorism," in Astana, Kazakhstan, where he argued that "Islamophobists are cultural terrorists" engaging in "psychological terror" in furtherance of the (Edward) Saidian practice of "otherization," which "should be legally recognized as a strong hate crime."[106]

In September 2013, Professor Şenay oversaw the drafting of a declaration that defined Islamophobia as "a groundless fear and intolerance of Islam and Muslims" that is "detrimental to international peace" such that there "should be recognition of Islamophobia as a hate crime and Islamophobic attitudes as human rights violations."[107] The declaration was written for the "International Conference on Islamophobia: Law & Media" in Istanbul, which was co-sponsored by Turkey's Directorate General of Press and Information and the OIC. At the conference, Turkish President Erdoğan stated that "Islamophobia" is a "kind of racism" that is "a crime against humanity."[108] Dalia Mogahed also attended the conference.[109]

Because both the Turkish government and the OIC formally recognize human rights according to Islamic law, violation of shariah relating to non-Muslims in an Islamic state (as identified in *Reliance of the Traveller* at Part o11), repackaged as Islamophobia, would actually be a human rights violation. The relationship between EMISCO, the Government of Turkey, and the OIC demonstrates that EMISCO has immediate awareness of the intent to secure the prosecution of those who violate Islamic slander laws once anti-Islamophobia legislation is passed. Şenay should be able to answer his own question—"How can the OIC control the public opinion among the Muslims in Europe?"[110]—as he is personally involved in the venture. Regarding General Secretary Quraishy's claim that he doesn't "want anybody to be prosecuted for anything"[111]: his efforts, and EMISCO's, are immediately relevant to that objective, notwithstanding his personal intentions or awareness (in the event that his comments are sincere).

It should not go unnoticed that Şenay's statement in 2013 that failure to take action to suppress Islamophobia is "detrimental to international peace" is a not so thinly veiled threat of violence. There is also the escalation of rhetoric from Şenay's 2010 OSCE presentation ("Undoing Hate Crimes: Combating Islamophobia as Cultural Terrorism"), which he concluded by stating:

> Muslims should actively take part in joint efforts to combat against Islamophobic hate crimes, especially at international level. Therefore I would like to finish by a humble word of advice to Muslim fellows: be not just victims but also actors in your destiny.[112]

This is close to what Şenay said when concluding his 2014 presentation in Warsaw, this time with a hint of incitement:

> One last word of friendly advice to Muslim members of Europe. They have to take part in the joint work conducted by international organizations, European organizations, to combat against Islamophobia and Muslims in Europe should not be the victims of Islamophobia but fight against Islamophobia as actors. Thank you.[113]

The Secretary General of EMISCO immediately endorsed his statement:

> Thank you very much Professor Şenay and for these, first of all your good summary and also your good recommendations, especially the last one that the Muslims have to be proactive and take things in their own hands. I think that is one of the best things.[114]

If Muslims in Europe took to the streets in violent protest in response to these admonitions, wouldn't that satisfy the actual elements of incitement? It is in light of these comments that *Charlie Hebdo* and Copenhagen should be understood. Returning to the September 30 Side Event, Professor Şenay gratuitously ridiculed Western concerns over the brutal rise of ISIS. At the same time that the *New York Times* was reporting on ISIS's open recruitment efforts in Turkey, the Turkish news daily *Aydinlikas* reported that ISIS's de facto foreign minister had announced the opening of a diplomatic mission in Istanbul[115] (that was substantive enough to have caused the largest Turkish opposition party to condemn the action,[116] forcing President Erdoğan to come out and deny it). [117] And yet Şenay still felt comfortable chiding the Western audience by saying, "if I were to present a particular favor, this would be the title, 'A New Cultural ISIS – International Strong Ignorance Syndrome'"[118] as he presented his briefing with the title, "Islamophobia in the 21st Century: International Strong Ignorance Syndrome in Europe (**ISIS**)."[119] In doing so, Şenay was suggesting that the extremism was in the reactions of the West, not in the acts of ISIS.

In an interesting move that could be interpreted as either an escalation or a step back, Şenay gave some ground on the general insistence that Islam has nothing to do with terrorism. Stated in terms of an equivalency narrative, Şenay said:

> Outside Europe, certain militant and violent organizations may practice a form of Islam that you find repellent, but to claim that it has nothing to do with the Muslim Religion or that it's rules are not very much a part of the Islamic tradition is not a serious statement. Nor is it serious to say that Islam is a violent religion.[120]

He then concluded that "the natural outcome of this awareness should be that we abandon our popular dichotomy between the so-called 'moderate' and the so-called 'extreme' religion."[121] Şenay may be right on this point. Regardless, his statements are important and in need of assessment, as they may portend an escalation in the narrative that could be matched by an escalation in associated activity.

There is a bifurcation strategy underlying the OSCE line of operation that separates OSCE efforts from the OIC meta-narrative. Another example: Toward the end of the side event, Ms. Özbil Biyikli, on the Faculty of Islamic Sciences of Brussels, insisted that racism no longer concerns race but rather is an issue of religion:

> As the term racism from a sociological and anthropological perspective, racism is not a skin color anymore ....

> So, today racism is not a skin color as we said, which falls upon the religion and, in the European context, Islamophobia, which creates, in public, hate crime, hate discourses.[122]

For Biyikli, as for the OIC, racism is Islamophobia. In fact, her reasoning is a direct lift from both OIC policy statements and general talking points. From the final communiqué of the Third Extraordinary Session of the Islamic Summit

Conference in 2005, Section II, "In the Political Field," we find:

> The Conference underlined the need to collectively endeav-
> or to reflect the noble Islamic values, counter Islamophobia,
> **defamation of Islam** and its values and desecration of Islamic
> holy sites, and to effectively coordinate with States as well
> as **regional** and **international** institutions and organizations
> to **urge them to criminalize this phenomenon as a form of
> racism.**[123]

From the OIC Secretary General Ekmeleddin Ihsanoglu in 2007:

> As reiterated by the OIC, the international community must
> counter **campaigns of calumny against Islam** and Muslims
> to prevent the spread of Islamophobia which attempts to
> cause a rift between civilizations, a situation that has become
> **a new form of racial discrimination.**[124]

This postscript confirms the ongoing successful penetration of the OIC into international forums such as the OSCE through the skilled manipulation of the postmodern narrative. Even so, one has to wonder how the professional diplomatic staffs can remain so strategically unaware of something so obvious to anyone with open eyes.

About the Author

Stephen C. Coughlin, Esq., is an attorney, decorated intelligence officer and noted specialist on Islamic law, ideology, and associated issues as they relate to terrorism and subversion. Coughlin integrates experience in international law, intelligence, strategic communications, and high-level project management in both the national defense and private sectors to develop unique perspectives, assessments, and training packages relating to the intersection of national security and Islamic law. He emphasizes evidentiary-based analysis.

In September 2001, Coughlin was mobilized from his private sector career and assigned to the Directorate for Intelligence, Joint Chiefs of Staff, Targeting (JCS-J2T). Over time, his responsibilities evolved into intelligence support to information operations and strategiccommunications from a targeting perspective. Other assignments included the Pentagon's National Military Command Center, the National Military Joint Intelligence Center, and the National Security Council's Interagency Perception Management Threat Panel before demobilizing in 2004.

In 2006, Coughlin was sought out "by name" and asked to support the Joint Staff J2 in counterterror threat analysis as a lead consultant. In 2007, he was awarded a Master of Science of Strategic Intelligence from the Joint Military Intelligence College / Defense Intelligence Agency on the threat analysis aspects of Islamic law and related doctrines. As a Major in the United States Army (res.), Coughlin was later assigned to USCENTCOM, where he served in an intelligence and strategic communications / information operations role. He has since retired from the Reserves. Until recently, Coughlin also supported Irregular Warfare Support activities.

Recognized as the Pentagon's leading expert on Islamic law as it relates to national security, Coughlin was in demand as a lecturer at leading senior service staff institutions, including the National Defense University, the Army and Navy War Colleges, Marine Corps HQ-Quantico, the Joint Forces Staff College, as well as at the FBI (the Counterterror and the Behavioral Analysis Units, for example) and associated agencies and private sector groups.

Stephen Coughlin's private sector career focused on international law, competitive intelligence, and the development and provision of open source, classified and proprietary commercial data, and information products and programs at leading information publishing houses.

Coughlin currently serves as a Senior Fellow at the Center for Security Policy and a Lincoln Fellow at the Claremont Institute.

Notes

INTRODUCTION

1 "UAE Publishes List of Terrorist Organizations," *Gulf News*, 15 November 2014, URL: http://gulfnews.com/news/gulf/uae/government/uae-publishes-list-of-terrorist-organisations-1.1412895, accessed 15 November 2014. **The full list as provided by the UAE Cabinet, the complete list of terrorist organizations endorsed by the UAE Government, in line with the Federal Law No.7 for 2014 as issued by President His Highness Shaikh Khalifa Bin Zayed Al Nahyan on August 20, 2014, includes:** 1. Muslim Brotherhood in the UAE, 2. Al Islah Society, 3. Fatah Al Islam in Lebanon, 4. Islamic Association in Italy, 5. UAE Jihad cells, 6. Osbat Al Ansar in Lebanon, 7. Islamic Association in Finland, 8. Al Karama Organisation, 9. Al Qaida in the Islamic Maghreb, 10. Islamic Association in Sweden, 11. The Islamic Association in Sweden, 12. Ummah Parties in the Gulf region, 13. Ansar Al Sharia (Supporters of Sharia Law) in Libya, 14. Islamic Association in Norway, 15. Al Qaida, 16. Ansar Al Sharia in Tunisia, 17. Islamic Relief Organisation in London, 18. Islamic State (Daesh), 19. Mujahideen Youth Movement in Somalia, 20. Cordoba Foundation in Britain, 21. Al Qaida in the Arabian Peninsula, 22. Boko Haram in Nigeria, 23. Islamic Relief Organisation, an affiliate of the International, Organisation of the Muslim Brotherhood, 24. Ansar Al Sharia (Supporters of Sharia Law) in Yemen, 25. Almoravids Battalion in Mali, 26. Pakistan Taliban, 27. Muslim Brotherhood Organisation and group, 28. Ansar Al Deen (Defenders of the Faith) in Mali, 29. Abu Thar Al Ghafari Brigade in Syria, 30. Islamic Group in Egypt, 31. Pakistan's Haqqani network, 32. Al Tawhid Brigade in Syria, 33. Egyptian Ansar Jerusalem, 34. Pakistani Lashkar-e-Taiba a group, 35. Tawhid and Faith Brigade in Syria, 36. Ajnad Misr (Egyptian Jihadist Group), 37. East Turkistan movement in Pakistan, 38. Green Brigade in Syria, 39. Mujahideen Shura Council, 40. Aknaf Bait al Maqdis (Defenders of Jerusalem), 41. The Army of Mohammad in Pakistan, 42. Abu Bakr Al Siddiq Brigade in Syria, 43. Al Houhti Movement in Yemen, 44. The Army of Mohammad in Pakistan and India, 45. Talha bin Obaidullah Brigade in Syria, 46. Saudi Hezbollah Al Hejaz, 47. Indian Mujahideen in India/Kashmir, 48. Hezbollah in GCC countries, 49. Al Sarim Al Battar Brigade, 50. The Caucasus Emirate (Chechen Mujahideen), 51. Abdullah Ibn Mubarak Brigade, 52. Al Qaida Organisation in Iran, 53. Islamic Movement of Uzbekistan, 54. Syrian Martyrs Brigade, 55. Badr Organisation in Iraq, 56. Abu Sayyaf Group (Philippines), 57. Abu Omar Brigade, 58. Asa'ib Ahl Al Haq (League of the Righteous) in Iraq, 59. Council on American. Islamic Relations (CAIR), 60. Ahrar Shammar Brigade in Syria, 61. Hezbollah Brigades in Iraq, 62. Kanvas organization in Belgrade, Serbia, 63. Sariyat Al Jabal Brigade in Syria, 64. Abu Fadl Abbas Brigade Iraq, 65. Muslim American Society (MAS), 66. Al Shahba Brigade in Syria, 67. Al Youm Al Maoud Brigade in Iraq, 68. Association of Muslim Scholars, 69. Al. Qa'qa' Brigade in Syria, 70. Omar Bin Yasser Brigade (Syria), 71. Union of Islamic Organisations of France, 72. Sufian Al Thawri Brigade in Syria, 73. Iraqi Ansar Al Islam Group, 74. Federation of Islamic Organizations in Europe, 75. Ibad Al Rahman Brigade in Syria, 76. Al Nusra Front in Syria, 77. Islamic Association in Britain, 78. Omar Ibn Al Khattab Brigade in Syria, 79. Ahrar Al Sham Movement in Syria, 80. Islamic Society of Germany, 81. Al Shaima Brigade in Syria, 82. Army of Islam in Palestine, 83. Islamic Association in Denmark, 84. Al Haq Brigade in Syria, 85. Abdullah Azzam Brigades, and 86. Islamic Association in Belgium.

2 *Explanatory Memorandum*: On the General Strategic Goal for the Group," Mohamed Akram, May 22, 1991, Government Exhibit 003-0085/3:04-CR-240-G U.S. v. HLF, et al., United States District Court, Northern District of Texas, http://www.txnd.uscourts.gov/judges/hlf2/09-25-08/

Elbarasse%20Search%203.pdf, 15 and 18. **The full Explanatory Memorandum list:** 1 - ISNA = Islamic Society of North America, 2- MSA = Muslim Student Association, 3- MCA = The Muslim Communities Association, 4 – AMSS = The Association of Muslim Scientists, 5 – AMSE = The Association of Muslim Scientists and Engineers, 6 – IMA = Islamic Medical Association, 7 – ITC = Islamic Teaching Center, 8 – NAIT = North American Islamic Trust, 9 – FID = Foundation for International Development, 10 – IHC = Islamic Housing Cooperative, 11 – ICD = Islamic Centers Division, 12 – ATP = American Trust Publications, 13 – AVC = Audio-Visual Center, 14 – IBS = Islamic Book Service, 15 – MBA = Muslim Businessmen Association, 16 – MYNA = Muslim Youth of North America, 17 – IFC = ISNA Fiqh Committee (currently Fiqh Council of North America), 18 – IPAC = ISNA Political Awareness Committee, 19 – IED = Islamic Education Department, 20 – MAYA = Muslim Arab Youth Association, 21 – MISG = Malaysian Islamic Study Group, 22 – IAP = Islamic Association for Palestine (replaced by the Council on American Islamic Relations – CAIR), 23 – UASR = United Association for Palestine, 24 – OLF = Occupied Land Fund, 25 – MIA = Mercey International Association, 26 – ICNA = Islamic Circle of North America, 27 – BMI = Baitul Mal Inc, 28 – IIIT = International Institute of Islamic Thought, 29 – IIC = Islamic Information Center

3   Marilyn Stern, "The Muslim Public Affairs Council: Building Bridges to U.S. Law Enforcement - Community-Oriented Policing," *The Investigative Project on Terrorism*, 20 November 2010, http://www.investigativeproject.org/2345/report-assesses-mpac-counterterrorcommitment, 8.

4   Marilyn Stern, "The Muslim Public Affairs Council: Building Bridges to U.S. Law Enforcement - Community-Oriented Policing," *The Investigative Project on Terrorism*, 20 November 2010, http://www.investigativeproject.org/2345/report-assesses-mpac-counterterrorcommitment, 14.

5   Raymond Ibrahim, "Egypt's Sisi: Islamic 'Thinking' is 'Antagonizing the Entire World,'" *Middle East Forum*, 1 January 2015, URL: http://www.meforum.org/4951/egypt-sisi-islamic-thinking-is-antagonizing, accessed 4 January 2015.

6   Abraham Rabinovich, "Egyptian President Calls for 'Religious Revolution' in Islam," *Washington Free Beacon*, 4 January 2015, URL: http://freebeacon.com/national-security/egyptian-president-calls-for-religious-revolution-in-islam/, accessed 4 January 2015.

7   Raymond Ibrahim, "Egypt's Sisi: Islamic 'Thinking' is 'Antagonizing the Entire World,'" *Middle East Forum*, 1 January 2015, URL: http://www.meforum.org/4951/egypt-sisi-islamic-thinking-is-antagonizing, accessed 4 January 2015.

8   Raymond Ibrahim, "Egypt's Sisi: Islamic 'Thinking' is 'Antagonizing the Entire World,'" *Middle East Forum*, 1 January 2015, URL: http://www.meforum.org/4951/egypt-sisi-islamic-thinking-is-antagonizing, accessed 4 January 2015.

9   "Anti-Semitism On Egypt's Al-Rahma TV," MEMRI Special Dispatch No. 2466, MEMRI, 30 July 2009, URL: http://www.memri.org/report/en/print3534.htm, accessed 5 January 2015. **For Example: "They Composed These Black Protocols Themselves, In Order To Destroy the Inner Power of Our Nation"**

Salama Abd Al-Qawi: "Read, if you will, that black book, in which they included those *Protocols of the Elders of Zion*. They composed these black protocols themselves, in order to destroy the inner power of our nation. They composed these protocols in 1897 in Switzerland, in their black congress, which brought together all the Elders of Zion. They began conspiring to annihilate the Islamic and Arab nation, to plunder its resources, and to destroy its youth. Regretfully, the plots they hatched are being implemented today in detail."

"One of Their Conspiracies ... Was to Gain Control Over the Entire Global Economy ... So They Founded Huge Companies"

"One of their conspiracies, which stemmed from their black hatred, was to gain control over the entire global economy, bringing the world under their thumb. So they founded huge companies, which, like spiders, send their webs all over the world. The main goal of these companies was to erase Islamic identity. [...] "[The Jews] say that God - or rather, god as they define it - divided the week into six days. Two days He allocated for creatures and people. For two days, He sat and played with a whale. For the remaining two days, He sat in the company of Eve, who came to Him in her most splendid beauty and whatever... It's inconceivable that anyone with a grain of reason would say such things. [...] "They say that later, when the Holocaust took place, God was angry. Right. When the Holocaust took place, God was angry, and He stopped playing with the whale, and stopped seeing Eve, who would come to Him in her most splendid beauty. These are the things they believe about God." [...]

"All Carbonated Beverages Are Zionist-American Products ... McDonalds is Jewish-Zionist, Kentucky Fried Chicken ... Little Caesar, Pizza Hut, Domino's Pizza, Burger King ... Starbucks"

"Many basic products, which may be found in many Muslim households, like Ariel, Tide, and Persil laundry detergents, are made by Zionist companies. The Coca Cola and Pepsi companies and all their products - Seven Up, Miranda, Fanta, and all these products, all the carbonated beverages, with very few exceptions that don't bear mention... Almost all carbonated beverages are Zionist-American products. [...] "Some restaurants, I'm sad to say, are teeming with Muslim youth, and their safes are full of the money of Muslims... McDonalds is Jewish-Zionist, Kentucky Fried Chicken is Jewish-Zionist, Little Caesar, Pizza Hut, Domino's Pizza, Burger King... By the way, all these products, which I have mentioned... In addition, there is a new type of coffee these days... All these are pure Zionist products, especially what is known as Starbucks, the well-known coffee. It is Zionist."

10   Ahmad Fouad, "Egyptian Government Introduces Unified Friday Prayer Guidelines, Al-Monitor,14 August 2013, trans, by Rani Geha from original Arabic posting on 7 Feburary 2013, URL: http://www.al-monitor.com/pulse/originals/2014/02/egypt-government-control-unified-mosque-sermons.html#, accessed 5 January 2015. **Reads:** "Regarding the Muslim Brotherhood, *Al-Monitor* tried to communicate with Jamal Abdul Sattar and Sheikh Salama Abdel Qawi, the two Muslim Brotherhood figures who used to be in the Ministry of Religious Endowment."

11   "Abdel Fatth Sisi Rides Roughshod of Sacred Texts – Sheikh Salama Abdul Qawi," *YouTube* Clip from *Mekameleen TV*, 2 January 2015, URL: https://www.youtube.com/watch?v=2jLBRcRkTg0 &feature=youtu.be&list=UUzOTTcBYjarXFeRoSKz9igw, accessed 5 January 2015.

12   Mokhtar Awad, @Mokhtar_Awad, *Twitter*, 4 January 2015, URL: https://twitter.com/Mokhtar_Awad/status/551794917220298752, accessed 4 January 2015. **States:** "Sheikh Salama Abdel Qawi: Sisi is a murtad & what he said is kufr.

13   Ahmed Fouad, "Al-Azhar Refuses to Consider the Islamic State an Apostate," trans. Tyler Huffman, *Al-Monitor*, 12 February 2015, URL: http://www.al-monitor.com/pulse/originals/2015/02/azhar-egypt-radicals-islamic-state-apostates.html, accessed 13 February 2015.

14   Our Team page of Freedom and Justice Foundation, Plano, Texas, webpage, 22 June 2007, URL: https://web.archive.org/web/20081211064713/http://www.freeandjust.org/OurTeam.htm, accessed 26 September 2011. **Note:** Mohamed Elibiary, President, CEO and Co-founder.

15   Mohamed Elibiary, "What Would You Say to America's Leading Islamophobes if Given the Opportunity?" Muslim Matters, 6 February 2008, URL: http://muslimmatters.org/2008/02/06/what-would-you-say-to-america's-leading-islamophobes-if-given-the-opportunity/, accessed 27 June 2014. **States in "About Mohamed Elibiary":** <u>Mohamed Elibiary co-founded the Freedom and Justice Foundation (F&J) in November 2002</u> to promote a Centrist Public Policy environment in Texas by coordinating the state level government and interfaith community relations for the organized Texas Muslim community. In 2005, Mohamed spearheaded the launching of the Texas Islamic Council (T.I.C.) as an F&J program for Muslim congregations, which has quickly grown to become the state's largest Muslim network encompassing 100,000 Texans. As Coordinator of the T.I.C., Mohamed developed working relationships with similar faith-based entities around Texas, including the Texas Conference of Churches, Texas Catholic Conference and the Baptist General Convention of Texas. In 2006, the 16 largest Muslim congregations and civic organizations in the Dallas-Fort Worth area followed this example by creating a collective representative body called the North Texas Islamic

Council (NTIC), and Mohamed was elected to its 7 member executive governing body. Since 2005, Mohamed, as a National Security Policy Analyst, has been advising intelligence and law enforcement agencies (ex. FBI, DHS, NCTC, ODNI, etc.) on various Counterterrorism (CT) issues (ex. Domestic Intelligence, Strategic Intelligence Analysis, Information Sharing and Radicalization).

16   Screen Capture, CAIR DFW webpage dated 12 April 2003, in article by Ryan Mauro, "Senior Homeland Security Advisor Formerly CAIR Official," The Clarion Project, 1 December 2013, URL: http://www.clarionproject.org/analysis/senior-homeland-security-adviser-formerly-cair-official, accessed 19 August 2014. **Note:** screen capture identifies Elibiary as Committee Chairman.

17   Form 990 Documenting Mohamed Elibiary's Status as Board Member on CAIR Dallas-Fort Worth Chapter – FY 2003, IRS Form 990 (2003) copy at *The Clarion Project Archives*, URL: http://www.clarionproject.org/document/990-form-proving-mohamed-Elibiary-worked-cair, accessed 19 August 2014. **Note:** Identifies Elibiary as Board Member.

18   Mohamed Elibiary, Mohamed Elibiary Tweet, @MohamedElibiary Twitter, 16 November 2014, URL: https://twitter.com/MohamedElibiary/status/533768748159995904, accessed 16 November 2014. States: "#PT As was published in media interviews, I've sat thru USG briefings on MB in US & did my own field research. US won't follow UAE bullshit."

19   Mohamed Elibiary, Mohamed Elibiary Tweet, @MohamedElibiary Twitter, 16 November 2014, URL: https://twitter.com/MohamedElibiary/status/533768748159995904, accessed 16 November 2014. States: "#PT As was published in media interviews, I've sat thru USG briefings on MB in US & did my own field research. US won't follow UAE bullshit."

20   *Letter to John Brennan*, Assistant to the President for Homeland Security and Counterterrorism and Deputy National Security Advisor, The White House, signed by, among others, numerous organizations known to be associated with the Muslim Brotherhood, PDF document dated 19 October 2011. **Reads:** "We urge you to create an interagency taskforce, led by the White House, tasked with the following responsibilities: 2. Purge *all* federal government training materials of biased materials; 3. Implement a mandatory re-training program for FBI agents, U.S. Army officers, and all federal, state and local law enforcement who have been subjected to biased training; 4. Ensure that personnel reviews are conducted and all trainers and other government employees who promoted biased trainers and training materials are effectively disciplined; 5. Implement quality control processes to ensure that bigoted trainers and biased materials are not developed or utilized in the future; …"

21   Letter to Farhana Khera from John Brennan, the White House, 3 November 2011.

22   *Letter to John Brennan*, The White House, 19 October 2011.

23   Letter to Farhana Khera from John Brennan, the White House, 3 November 2011.

24   ISNA & Nat. Orgs. Meet With FBI Dir. to Discuss Biased FBI Training Materials," *ISNA Press Release*, ISNA, 14 February 2012, Url: http://counterjihadreport.com/2012/02/14/isna-nat-orgs-meet-with-fbi-dir-to-discuss-biased-fbi-training-materials/.

25   71-022, 112th Congress, *Report House of Representatives,* 1st Session, 112-284: Agriculture, Rural Development, Food and Drug Catastrorration, and Related Agencies Programs for the Fiscal Year Ending September 30, 2012, and for Other Purposes, 14 November 2011- Ordered to be printed, to accompany H.R. 2112, signed 18 November 2011, URL: http://thomas.loc.gov/cgi-bin/cpquery/T? &report=hr284& dbname =112&. **States:** *"Liaison partnerships* - The conferees support the FBI's policy prohibiting any formal non-investigative cooperation with unindicted co-conspirators in terrorism cases. The conferees expect the FBI to insist on full compliance with this policy by FBI field offices and to report to the Committees on Appropriations regarding any violation of the policy."

26   FBI Director Mueller, Testimony, "House Judiciary Committee Holds Hearing on Oversight of the FBI," Congressional Hearings, *CQ Congressional Transcripts*, 9 May 2012. Read: Mueller "So it is not as if we have purged a substantial amount of our training materials."

27   David Alexander, "Military Instructor Suspended over Islam Course," *Reuters*, 20 June 2012,

http://www.reuters.com/article/2012/06/20/us-usa-defense-islam-idUSBRE85J0XJ20120620, accessed 20 June 2012.

28   Secretary of State Hillary Clinton, "Remarks at the Organization of the Islamic Conference (OIC) High-Level Meeting on Combating Religious Intolerance," Given at the Center for Islamic Arts and History, Istanbul, Turkey, *United States Department of State Release*, 15 July 2011, http://www.state.gov/secretary/rm/2011/07/168636.htm, accessed July 21 2011.

29   Paragraph 3, Section VII, "Combating Islamophobia," *The Third Extraordinary Session of the Islamic Summit*, Makka Almukarama, Organization of the Islamic Conference, 7-8 December 2005, URL: http://www.oic-oci.org/ex-summit/english/10-years-plan.htm. Cited hereafter as Third Extraordinary Session, "Section VII, Combating Islamophobia." **Reads**: Endeavor to have the United Nations adopt an international resolution to counter Islamophobia and to call upon all states to enact laws to counter it, including deterrent punishment.

30   Secretary of State Hillary Clinton, "Remarks at the Organization of the Islamic Conference (OIC) High-Level Meeting on Combating Religious Intolerance," Given at the Center for Islamic Arts and History, Istanbul, Turkey, *United States Department of State Release*, 15 July 2011, http://www.state.gov/secretary/rm/2011/07/168636.htm, accessed July 21 2011.

31   "High Ranking DOJ Official Refuses to Affirm 1st Amendment Rights," Representative Trent Franks, *YouTube* published by *Rep Trent Franks*, 26 July 2012, at URL: http://www.youtube.com/watch? v=0wwv9l6W8yc&feature=player_embedded, accessed 27 July 2012. Also at URL: https://www.youtube.com/watch?v=0wwv9l6W8yc.

32   "Remarks by the President to the UN General Assembly," given at the United Nations Headquarters, New York, New York, For Immediate Release, Office of the Press Secretary, The White House, 25 September 2012, URL: http://www.whitehouse.gov/the-press-office/2012/09/25/remarks-president-un-general-assembly, accessed 4 October 2012.

33   Josh Rushing, "US Military Under Fire for 'Anti-Islam Class'" (transcript), *Al-Jazeera* TV (Washington Office), 12 May 2012, URL: http://www.aljazeera.com/video/americas/2012/05/20125124178148367.html, alternatively released on YouTube URL: http://www.youtube.com/ watch? feature=player_embedded&v=2swVVfZo5eM#!, accessed 20 May 2012.

34   *Explanatory Memorandum*: On the General Strategic Goal for the Group," Mohamed Akram, May 22, 1991, Government Exhibit 003-0085/3:04-CR-240-G U.S. v. HLF, et al., United States District Court, Northern District of Texas, http://www.txnd.uscourts.gov/judges/hlf2/09-25-08/Elbarasse%20Search%203.pdf, 24.

35   "Countering Violent Extremism (CVE) Training: Do's and Don'ts," *Office for Civil Rights and Civil Liberties*, DHS, undated.

36   Josh Rushing, "US Military Under Fire for 'Anti-Islam Class'" (transcript), *Al-Jazeera* TV (Washington Office), 12 May 2012, URL: http://www.aljazeera.com/video/americas/2012/05/20125124178148367.html alternatively released on YouTube at URL: http://www.youtube.com/ watch? feature=player_embedded&v=2swVVfZo5eM#!, accessed 20 May 2012.

PART I: THE ONE ORGANIZING PRINCIPLE

1   Kroft, Steven, "Conversations with the Candidates for President of the United State: President Obama," *60 Minutes*, 23 September 2012, URL: http://www.cbsnews.com/video/watch/?id=7422772n&tag =cbsnewsMain ColumnArea.6, accessed 5 October 2012.

2   Organization of The Islamic Conference—About the OIC, URL: http://oic-oci.org/page_detail. asp? p_id=52.

3   Article 6, *Charter of the Organisation of the Islamic Conference*, URL: http://www.oic-oci.org/is11/english/Charter-en.pdf. **Reads:** [Article 6] The Islamic Summit is composed of Kings and Heads of State and Government of Member States and is the supreme authority of the Organisation. It convenes once every three years to deliberate, take policy decisions and provide guidance on all issues pertaining to the realization of the objectives and consider other issues of concern to the Member States and the *Ummah*. [Article 7] The Islamic Summit shall deliberate, take policy decisions and provide guidance on all issues pertaining to the realization of the objectives as provided for in the Charter and consider other issues of concern to the Member States and the *Ummah*.

4   Osama bin Laden, "Al-Qaeda's Declaration in Response to the Saudi Ulema: It's Best You Prostrate Yourselves in Secret," (2002), as cited in Raymond Ibrahim, *The Al Qaeda Reader*, trans. Raymond Ibrahim, Broadway Books: NY, 2007, 33, 51, 54.

5   Osama bin Laden, "To the Muslims of Iraq," 2002 as cited in Raymond Ibrahim, *The Al Qaeda Reader*, trans. Raymond Ibrahim, Broadway Books: NY, 2007, 247.

6   Part I, Chapter II, Objective and Means, Article (2), "Bylaws of the International Muslim Brotherhood," *IkhwanWeb*, URL: http://www.investigativeproject.org/documents/misc/673.pdf, accessed 18 January 2010.

7   Elbarasse Search-3, Explanatory Memorandum: On the General Strategic Goal for the Group," Mohamed Akram, May 22, 1991, Government Exhibit 003-0085/3:04-CR-240-G U.S. v. HLF, et al., United States District Court, Northern District of Texas, URL: http://www.txnd.uscourts.gov/judges/hlf2/09-25-08/Elbarasse%20Search%203.pdf, at 4. Cited hereafter as Mohamed Akram, Explanatory Memorandum.

8   Declaration of OIC Member State heads of state, 3rd Islamic Summit Conference, 1981, as cited in Abdullah Ahsan, *OIC: The Organization of the Islamic Conference, an Introduction to an Islamic Political Institution*, (IIIT, Herndon, VA, 1988), 19.

9   "Countering Violent Extremism (CVE) Training: Do's and Don'ts," *Office for Civil Rights and Civil Liberties*, DHS, undated. **Reads:** "1. Don't use programs that venture too deep into the weeds of religious doctrines and history. While interesting, such details will only be of use to the most specialized law enforcement personnel; these topics are not necessary in order to understand the community." Cited hereafter as DHS CRCL, "CVE Training Do's and Don'ts."

10   David Alexander, "Military Instructor Suspended over Islam Course," *Reuters*, 20 June 2012, URL: http://www.reuters.com/article/2012/06/20/us-usa-defense-islam-idUSBRE85J0XJ20120620, accessed 20 June 2012. **Reads:** "'The elective course's military instructor has been relieved of his instructor duties until his permanent change of station, which was previously planned for 2012,' Lapan said. The inquiry also recommended a review of actions by two civilian employees of the staff college to see if disciplinary action was warranted. A second military officer will receive administrative counseling, Lapan said."

11   Robert Houghwout Jackson, Forward to *Law in the Middle East*, The Middle East Institute, Majid Khadduri and Herbert J. Liebesny, ed., Washington, 1955, vi. Note, Justice Jackson was a United States Attorney General (1940-41), an Associate Justice of the United States Supreme Court (1941-54), and Chief United States Prosecutor at the Nuremburg War Crimes Trial (1945-46).

12   'Abd al-Rahman ibn Muhammad ibn Muhammad Abu Zayd Ibn Khaldun, *The Muqaddimah: An Introduction to History*, trans. Franz Rosenthal, (Princeton: Princeton University Press, 1969), 255. Cited hereafter as Ibn Khaldun, *The Muqaddimah*.

13   Akbar Ahmed, Professor, School of International Services, Ibn Khaldun Chair of Islamic Studies, American University, undated, URL: http://www.american.edu/sis/faculty/akbar.cfm, accessed 1 February 2015.

14   *Sign of the Sword* by Shaykh Abdalqadir al-Murabit, Murabitun Publications, P.O. Box 436, Norwich NR3 ILL. (1984), 41.

15   Asaf A.A. Fyzee, Outlines of Muhammadan Law, 4th ed. (Delhi, India: Oxford University Press, 1974), 19-20. Cited hereafter as Fyzee, *Muhammadan Law*.

16   Mohammad Hashim Kamali, *Principles of Islamic Jurisprudence*, 3d rev. ed., (Cambridge, UK: The Islamic Text Society, 2003), 16. Cited hereafter as Kamali, *Principles of Islamic Jurisprudence*.

17   Imam Muhammad ibn Idris **al-Shafi'i**, *Risala Fi Usal al-Fiqh: Treatise on the Foundations of Islamic Jurisprudence*, trans. Majid Khadduri (Cambridge: Islamic Texts Society, 1987), 75, 76. Cited hereafter as Shafi'i, *The Risala*.

18   Shafi'i, *The Risala*. From Keller, *Reliance of the Traveller*, Book X "Biographical Note," § x324. x.324: Imam Shafi'i is Muhammad ibn Idris ibn Idris ibn al-'Abbas ibn 'Uthlman ibn Shafi'i' ibn al-Sa'ib ibn 'Ubayd ibn 'Abd Yazid ibn Hashim ibn al-Muttalib ibn … al-Shafi'i, descended from the great-grandfather of the Prophet (Allah bless him and give him peace). Born in 150/767 in Gaza, Shafi'i was the Imam of the World, the *mujtahid* of his time, one of the most brilliant and original legal scholars mankind has ever known … The Imam and his legacy are monumental. His *al-Risala* [*The Letter*] was the first work in the history of mankind to investigate the theory and practical bases of jurisprudence. In Koranic exegesis, he was the first to formulate the principles of the science of which verses abrogate others and which are abrogated ('*ilm al-nasikh wa al-mansukh*). … He (al-Shafi'i) paved the way for the enormous importance attached by subsequent generations of Muslims to the study of prophetic hadith, as reflected in the fact that most of the Imams in the field were of his school, including Bukhari, Muslim, Abu Dawud, Tirmidhi, Nasa'i, Ibn Majah, Bayhaqi, al-Hakim, Abu Nu'aym, Ibn Hibban, Daraqutni, Ibn Khuzayma, Ibn Salah, al-'Iraqi, Suyuti, Dhahabi, Ibn Kathir, Nur al-Din Haythami, Mundhiri, Nawawi, Taqi al-Din Subki, and others.

19   Ahmad ibn Naqib al-Misri, 'Umdat al-Salik (*Reliance of the Traveller: A Classic Manual of Islamic Sacred Law*), rev. ed. trans. Nuh Ha Mim Keller (Beltsville, MD: Amana Publications, 1994). A Note Before Proceeding – Why *Reliance of the Traveller*? There are a substantial number of citations to Islamic law in the 1994 edition of the English-language translation of Ahmad ibn Naqib al-Misri's '*Umdat al-Salik (Reliance of the Traveller: A Classic Manual of Islamic Sacred Law*).[1] The source selection is due not to a limitation of sources but rather to *Reliance*'s unique status as a broadly available English-language title with certifications from the preeminent center of Islamic thought, the Muslim Brotherhood in America, and the OIC on behalf of its fifty-seven Member States. Cited hereafter as Keller, *Reliance of the Traveller*.

As such, *Reliance* satisfies all the criteria for being broadly authoritative. The subtitle states that it is "A Classic Manual of Islamic Sacred Law." It "represents one of the finest and most reliable short works in Shafi'i jurisprudence."[2] Additionally, "the authors of the present volume and their positions represent the orthodox Muslim intellectual and spiritual heritage that has been the strength of the Community for over a thousand years, and the means through which Allah has preserved His religion, in its purest and fullest sense, to the present day."[3] *Reliance* claims a doctrinal basis.

That claim is only as strong as the authority that certifies it. The authority of *Reliance* is established by certifications from national authorities in Egypt, Saudi Arabia, Jordan, and Syria. Particularly persuasive is the endorsement of Cairo's al-Azhar University (the most prestigious and authoritative institute of Islamic higher learning) with signature and stamps that serve as a kind of Islamic *imprimatur* and *nihil obstat*:

"... concerning the examination of the English translation of the book *'Umadat al-salik wa 'uddat al-nasik* by Ahmad ibn Naqib in the Shafi'i school of jurisprudence, together with appendices by Islamic scholars on matters of Islamic law, tenets of faith, and personal ethics and character: **we certify that the above-mentioned translation corresponds to the Arabic original and conforms to the practice and faith of the orthodox Sunni Community** (*Ahl al-Sunna wa al-Jama'a*)."[4]

Also persuasive is also the certification in Document 3 from the International Institute of Islamic Thought (IIIT), which states:

1. "There is no doubt that this translation is a valuable and important work, whether as a textbook for teaching Islamic jurisprudence to English-speakers, or as a legal reference for use by scholars, educated laymen, and students in this language.

2. As for the correction of the translation, its accuracy, and its fidelity to the meaning and objects, ... the translation presents the legal questions in a faithful and precise idiom that clearly delivers the complete meaning in a sound English style ... demonstrating the translator's knowledge of Sacred law and ability in jurisprudence as well as his complete command of both the Arabic and the English languages.

3. ... general benefit to both followers of Shafi'i school and others of the Muslim community.

4. ... its aim is to imbue the consciousness of the non-Arab-speaking Muslim with a sound understanding of the Sacred Law."[5]

Dr. Taha Jabir al-'Alwani was the signature authority for Document 3 on behalf of the Islamic Fiqh Academy in Jedda, penned on International Institute of Islamic Thought (IIIT) letterhead. Also in the signature block is his title as president of the Fiqh Council of North America (FCNA).[6] The International Islamic Fiqh Academy in Jedda was "established within the framework of the OIC in accordance with a resolution adopted by the Islamic Conference of Kings and Heads of State and Government of the Islamic Conference of Foreign Ministers."[7] This would seem to indicate that approval by the Islamic Fiqh Academy at Jedda reflects broad approval of *Reliance* across the Islamic world in some official capacity. As the president of both FCNA and IIIT, both known American Muslim Brotherhood entities, al-'Alwani's close senior interconnected relationships are evidence that a relationship exists between those organizations and the OIC. Thus, any time *Reliance* is used to establish a point of Islamic law, the burden-shifting presumption should be that Al-Azhar and the OIC share the same construction of Islamic law as the Muslim Brothers in America and that this reflects the "version" of shariah that is popularly sold and broadly available.

1) Keller, *Reliance of the Traveller*, book cover.

2) Keller, *Reliance of the Traveller*, vii.

3) Keller, *Reliance of the Traveller*, viii.

4) Keller, *Reliance of the Traveller* Documents 4, Certification page, letterhead - Al-Azhar Islamic Research Academy, General Department for Research, Writing and Translation, xx, xxi.

5) Keller, *Reliance of the Traveller*, Document 3, Certification page, IIIT letterhead with Alwani signature block, International Institute of Islamic Thought, xviii-xix.

6) Keller, *Reliance of the Traveller*, Document 3, Certification page, letterhead and signature block, International Institute of Islamic Thought, xviii-xix. **Reads:** Both the IIIT and FCNA are associated with the Muslim Brotherhood in the *Explanatory Memorandum: On the General Strategic Goal for the Group,"* Mohamed Akram, May 22, 1991, Government Exhibit 003-0085/3:04-CR-240-G U.S. v. HLF, et al., United States District Court, Northern District of Texas, http://www.txnd.uscourts.gov/judges/hlf2/09-25-08/Elbarasse%20Search%203.pdf. The FCNA is also a subordinate element of the Islamic Society of North America (ISNA). **Also:** The International Islamic Fiqh Academy (IIFA) is listed as a subsidiary organ of the OIC at "Subsidiary Organs, Organization of the Islamic Cooperation," OIC, URL: http://www.oic-oci.org/page_detail.asp? p_id=64#FIQH, 4 February 2013. It was affiliated to the OIC in

its fourteenth session, held in Duha (Qatar) 5–13 Dhul-Qi`dah1423 A.H., 11–16 January 2003 C.E., as cited in *"Jihad*: Rulings & Regulations," "Living Shari'a/Fatwa Bank," *IslamOnline,* URL: http://www.freerepublic.com/focus/news/2390531/replies?c=7.

7) Organization of the Islamic Conference, Subsidiary Organs, URL http://www.oic-oci.org/page_detail.asp?p_id=64, 6 April 2011.

8) Mohamed Akram, Explanatory Memorandum, 18.

20 Keller, *Reliance of the Traveller*, Book P "Enormities," at § p75.3 "Contending with What the Prophet has Brought," 701.

21 Keller, *Reliance of the Traveller*, Book T "A Pure Heart," at § t3.9 "Counsels and Maxims," 804.

22 'Abdur Rahman I. Doi, *Shari'ah: The Islamic Law.* (Kuala Lampur: A.S. Noordeen, 1984), 26. Cited hereafter as Doi, *Shari'ah: The Islamic Law.*

23 Keller, *Reliance of the Traveller*, Book O "Justice," § o22.0 "The Judge and the Court," o22.1(d(II)) "The Types of Sunna (A: i.e. hadith) include," o22.1(d(II(1))): hadiths (*mutawatir*) related by whole groups of individuals from whole groups, in multiple contiguous channels of transmission leading back to the Prophet himself (Allah bless him and grant him peace), such that the sheer number of separate channels at each stage of transmission is too many for it to be possible for all to have conspired to fabricate the hadith (A: which is thereby obligatory to believe in, and denial of which is unbelief (*kufr*)). **Also:** *Keller, Reliance of the Traveller*, Book W "Notes and Appendices," w47.0 "A Warning against Careless Accusations of Unbelief:" There is scholarly consensus that it is unlawful to charge with unbelief anyone who faces Mecca to pray, unless he denies the Almighty Creator, Majestic and Exalted, commits open polytheism that cannot be explained away by extenuating circumstances, denies Prophethood, or something which is necessarily known as being of the religion, or which is *mutawatir* (def: o22.1(d(II))) (N: whether the latter is of the Koran or hadith), or which there is scholarly consensus upon its being necessarily known as part of the religion.

24 Keller, *Reliance of the Traveller*, Book W, § w48.0 "Weak Hadiths," at w48.1: (A:) *Weak (da'if)* is a term for any hadith with a chain of transmission containing a narrator whose memory was poor, one who was not trustworthy, not identified by name, or for other reasons. But *weak* cannot simply be equated with *false.* Were this the case, mere analysis of the transmitters would be the universal criterion for acceptance or rejection of particular rulings based on hadiths. While scholars do use this measure in upgrading the work of preceding generations of legal authorities, they have not employed it as a simplistic expedient to eliminate every piece of legal information that is connected with a weak hadith, because of various considerations.

25 Keller, *Reliance of the Traveller*, Book P "Enormities," at § p9.5: (n: Having discussed lies and forgeries, we mush strictly distinguish them from the hadith category called *not well authenticated* (*da'if*, lit. weak), so-termed because of such factors as having a channel of transmission containing a narrator whose memory was poor, one who was unreliable, unidentified by name, or for other reasons. Such hadiths legally differ from forgeries in the permissibility of ascribing them to the Prophet (Allah bless him and give him peace) and in other ways discussed below at w48 [above].)

26 Keller, *Reliance of the Traveller*, Book P "Enormities," at § p9.0: Lying About the Prophet (Allah Bless His and Give Him Peace). p9.1 Some scholars hold that lying about the Prophet (Allah bless him and give him peace) is (*kufr*) that puts one beyond the pale of Islam. There is no doubt that a premeditated lie against Allah and His messenger that declares something which is unlawful to be permissible or something permissible to be unlawful is pure unbelief. The question (A: as to when as to whether it is an enormity rather than an outright unbelief) only concerns lies about other than that.

27 Keller, *Reliance of the Traveller*, Book W, § w48.0 "Weak Hadiths," at w48.1: (A:) *Weak (da'if)* is a term for any hadith with a chain of transmission containing a narrator whose memory was poor, one who was not trustworthy, not identified by name, or for other reasons. But *weak* cannot simply be equated with *false.* Were this the case, mere analysis of the transmitters would be the universal criterion

for acceptance or rejection of particular rulings based on hadiths. While scholars do use this measure in upgrading the work of preceding generations of legal authorities, they have not employed it as a simplistic expedient to eliminate every piece of legal information that is connected with a weak hadith, because of various considerations.

28　　Keller, *Reliance of the Traveller*, Book O "Justice," at § o22.1(d(II(1))) "The Judge and the Court."—hadith (mutawatir) related by whole groups of individuals from whole groups, in multiple contiguous channels of transmission leading back to the Prophet himself (Allah bless him and give him peace), such that the sheer number of separate channels at each stage of transmission is too many for it to be possible for all to have conspired to fabricate the hadith which is thereby obligatory to believe in, and denial of which is unbelief (kufr).

29　　Keller, *Reliance of the Traveller*, Book O "Justice," at § o22.1(d(II(2))).

30　　'Doi, *Shari'ah: The Islamic Law*, 54.

31　　From Keller, *Reliance of the Traveller*, Book X "Biographical Notes," § x107: al-Bukhari is Mohammed ibn Isma'il ibn Ibrahim ibn Muhira, Abu 'Abdullah al-Bukhari, born in Bukhara (in present day Uzbekistan) in 194/810 (Islamic/Judeo-Christian times or anno hegirae/anno domini). A Shafi'i scholar who learned Sacred Law in Mecca, Bukhari became the greatest Imam in hadith that the world has ever known. He began his long travels in search of hadith from nearly a thousand sheikhs, gathering some 600,000 prophetic traditions from which he selected the approximately 4,400 (not counting those repeated) that compose the Jami' al-Shaih [Rigorously authenticated collection]. Choosing them for their authenticity, he was the first scholar in Islam to compile a work on this basis, and his book in the foremost of the six great hadith collections.

32　　Doi, *Shari'ah: The Islamic Law*, 54.

33　　Doi, *Shari'ah: The Islamic Law*, 26.

34　　"Mufti: 'We Do Not Accept Insulting Bukhari'," Masrawy, 16 August 2014, URL: https://translate.google.com/translate?hl=en&sl=ar&tl=en&u=http%3A%2F%2Fwww.masrawy.com%2FNews%2FNews_Egypt%2Fdetails2%2F2014%2F8%2F16%2F322779%2Fمفتي-الجمهورية-لا-نقبل-التطاول-على-البخاري, translated from Arabic by Google Translate fromMasrawy, 16 August 2014, URL: http://www.masrawy.com/News/News_Egypt/details2/2014/8/16/322779/مفتي-الجمهورية-ال-نقبل-التطاول-على-البخاري, accessed 31 August 2014.

35　　Ahmed, Dr. Israr, "04-Bayan Ul Quran—Introduction to Ul Quran: Urdu," *Quran Academy*, 18 April 2009. Accessed 24 April 2011 at http://www.quranacademy.org/series/bayan-ul-quran-1998-dr-israr-ahmed/240-240.

36　　Imran Ahsan Khan Nyazee, *Theories of Islamic Law: The Methodology of Ijtihad*, 2d ed., (Kuala Lumpur: The Other Press, 2002), back cover. **Note:** Professor Nyazee is both a credentialed Islamic law professor at the Faculty of Shari'ah and Law, International Islamic University, Islamabad, Pakistan, and, with an LLM from the University of Michigan, has substantive understanding of Western, specifically U.S., jurisprudence. He is also author of *Islamic Jurisprudence* and translator of ibn Rushd's *The Distinguished Jurist's Primer*, and Marghinani's *Al-Hidaya: The Guidance*, all cited in this paper. Cited hereafter as Nyazee, *The Methodology of Ijtihad*.

37　　Al-Marghinani, Burhan al-Din al-Farghani, *Al-Hidaya: The Guidance*, Vol. 1, Trans. Imran Ahsan Khan Nyazee. Bristol, England: Amal Press, 2008, *al-Hidaya*, xix. Cited hereafter as Marghinani, *Al-Hidaya: The Guidance*.

38　　Marghinani, *Al-Hidaya: The Guidance*, xxiv.

39　　Keller, *Reliance of the Traveller*, Book B, at § b7.1: ('Abd al-Wahhab Khallaf:) Scholarly consensus (*ijma*) is the agreement of all the *mujtahids* of the Muslims existing at one particular period after the Prophet's death (Allah bless him and give him peace) about a particular ruling regarding a matter or event.

40   Keller, *Reliance of the Traveller*, Book B "The Validity of Following Qualified Leadership," at Book B "The Validity of Following Qualified Scholarship," at b7.0 "Scholarly Consensus," b7.0, 1, 2, 4.

41   Imran Ahsam Khan Nyazee, *Islamic Jurisprudence*, (Kuala Lumpur: The Other Press, 2003), 187. Cited hereafter as Nyazee, *Islamic Jurisprudence*.

42   Keller, *Reliance of the Traveller*, Book B, at § b7.2.

43   Keller, *Reliance of the Traveller*, Book B "The Validity of Following Qualified Leadership," at § b1.2; from al-Misri, Book O "Justice," at § o22.1(d): Mujtahid as defined: "To possess knowledge (O: of the rulings of Sacred Law, meaning by way of personal legal reasoning (ijtihad) (A: from primary texts), not (*taqlid*) (A: i.e. if he follows qualified scholarship, he must know and agree with how the rulings are derived, not merely report them). Being qualified to perform legal reasoning (*ijtihad*) requires knowledge of the rules and principles of the Koran, the *sunna* (A: in this context meaning the hadith, not the sunna as opposed to the *obligatory*), (N: as well as knowledge of scholarly consensus (*ijma*, def: b7)), and analogy (def: III below), together with knowing the types of each of these. (A: The knowledge of each 'type' below implies familiarity with subtypes and kinds, but the commentator has deemed the mention of the category as a whole sufficient to readers a general idea.)"

At o22.1(d)(III) "He must know the reliability ratings of hadith narrators in strength and weakness. When two primary texts seem to contend, he gives precedence to: (5) those which supercede previous rulings. ... He must likewise know the position of the scholars of Sacred Law regarding their consensus and differences, and not contradict their consensus (A: which is unlawful (dis: b7.2)) with his own reasoning.

44   Keller, *Reliance of the Traveller*, Book B, at § b1.1.

45   Keller, *Reliance of the Traveller*, Book B "The Validity of Following Qualified Scholarship", b2.0 "The Quranic Evidence For Following Scholars, at § b2.1.

46   Albert Hourani, *A History of the Arab Peoples*, (New York: MJF Books, 1991), 68. Cited hereafter as Hourani, *A History of the Arab Peoples*.

47   Keller, *Reliance of the Traveller*, Book B "The Validity of Following Qualified Scholarship," b.7 "Scholarly Consensus (ijma), at b7.6. Reads: (n: In addition to its general interest as a formal legal opinion, the following serves in the present context to clarify why other than the four Sunni schools of jurisprudence do not necessarily play a role in scholarly consensus.)

48   Keller, *Reliance of the Traveller*, Book B, at § b7.3-4: The proof of the legal authority of scholarly consensus is that just as Allah Most Glorious has ordered the believers, in the Koran, to obey Him and His messenger, so too He has ordered them to obey those of authority (*ulu al-amr*) among them saying, *"Oh you who believe, obey Allah and obey the Prophet and those in authority among you"* (Qur'an 4:59), such that when those of authority in legal expertise, the *mujtahids*, agree upon a ruling, it is obligatory in the very words of the Koran to follow them and carry out their judgment. And Allah threatens those who oppose the Messenger and follow other than the believers' way, saying, *"Whoever controverts the Messenger after guidance has become clear to him and follows other than the believers' way, We shall give him over to what he has turned to and roast him in hell, and how evil an outcome"* (Qur'an 4:115)

49   Ahmad Hasan, *The Doctrine of Ijma in Islam: A Study of the Juridical Principle of Consensus*, Kitab Bhavan, New Delhi, 1992, 154-154. Cited hereafter as Hasan, *The Doctrine of Ijma in Islam*.

50   Keller, *Reliance of the Traveller*, Book B, at § b1.2: No age of history is totally lacking people who are competent in *ijtihad* on particular questions which are new, and this is an important aspect of Sacred Law, to provide solutions to new ethical problems by means of sound Islamic legal methodology in applying the Koranic and hadith primary texts. But while in this specific sense the door of *ijtihad* is not and cannot be closed, Islamic scholarship has not accepted anyone's claim to absolute *ijtihad* since Imams Abu Hanifa, Malik, Shafi'i, and Ahmad.

51   Keller, *Reliance of the Traveller*, Book B "The Validity of Following Qualified Scholarship," b.7.0

"Scholarly Consensus (*ijma*), at b7.1 at 23.

52   Keller, *Reliance of the Traveller*, Book O "Justice," § o8.0 "Apostasy from Islam (*RIDDA*)," at §§ o8.7 "Acts that Entail Leaving Islam," at 597-598.

53   Keller, *Reliance of the Traveller*, Book O "Justice," o25.0 "The Caliphate," at § o25.1

54   Jihad against Jews and Crusaders World Islamic Front Statement," *Al-Quds Al-Arabi* (English), 23 February 1998, translation posted on the Federation of American Scientists (FAS), URL: http://www.fas.org/irp/world/para/docs/980223-fatwa.htm, accessed 5 February 2013.

55   Al-Zarqawi Group's Legal Council Issues Statements Condemning Aiding 'Polytheists,' Participating in Writing Iraqi Constitution, FBIS 12 AUG 05 GMP20050812371008.

56   Sheikh Yusuf Qaradhawi, Qatar TV Sermons this Past February 25, 2006, Qaradawi elucidated, MEMRI TV Clip 1052, URL: http://www.memritv. org/Transcript.asp?P1=1052

57   *IslamOnline*.net, 8 January 2011. Accessed online 5 June 2011 at http://www.islamonline.net/ar/ IOLCounsel_C/127840 7253854/1278406720653/-مكحلاو-ةيعورشم لا-.نيملسملا-ريغ-داتق-/ , as translated by *IslamOnline*.net: "Offensive Jihad Is Permissible to Secure Islam's Borders, to Extend God's Religion, and … to Remove Every Religion but Islam from the Arabian Peninsula", *Translating Jihad*, Tuesday, January 11, 2011, http://www.translatingjihad.com/2011/01/ islamonlinenet-offensive-jihad-is.html, accessed 12 January 2011.

58   Muhammad ibn Hasan al-Shaybani, *The Islamic Law of Nations: Shaybani's Siyar (Kitab al-siyar al-kabir)*, trans. Majid Khadduri, (Baltimore: Johns Hopkins Press, 1966), at 16. Cited hereafter as Khadduri, *Shaybani's Siyar*.

59   *The Translation of the Meanings of Sahih Al-Bukhari*, Daussalam Publishers, Riyadh, Saudi Arabia, 1997, back cover. Cited hereafter as Bukhari, *Sahih Al-Bukhari*.

60   *Charter of the Organisation of the Islamic Conference*, URL: http://www.oic-oci.org/is11/english/ Charter-en.pdf.

61   OIC Press Release on "Points of Clarification on the Initiative to Spare the Blood of Muslims in Iraq," 12 October 2006. From e-mail correspondence between Stephen Coughlin (Washington, D.C.) and Andrew P. B. White, Canon (Baghdad), from 18 to 27 October 2006, concerning the 12 October 2006 OIC press release on the planned conference in Mecca, Saudi Arabia, and on the actual Mecca Conference, including the 21 October 2006 "Makkah Al-Mukarramah Declaration on the Iraqi Situation."

62   Keller, *Reliance of the Traveller*, vii.

63   Nyazee, *The Methodology of Ijtihad*, 116.

64   Nyazee, *The Methodology of Ijtihad*, 111.

65   Nyazee, *The Methodology of Ijtihad*, 115-116. "The right of Allah (*haqq Allah*) is owed by the Muslim community to Allah, and is not owed by individuals to the community or to the state. This is the crucial point. The right of Allah is fixed by Allah, once and for all and is not subject to legal or judicial review, that is, it is outside the purview of the law. It can never be altered. … All laws that are related to the right of Allah are part of the fixed sphere of the law. All laws that are not related to the right of Allah, that is, those that are the right of the individual or the right of the *saltanah* and have not been expressly stated in the texts are liable to change. In fact, they should change in each age to adapt to new conditions. This statement needs to be qualified though: Any laws that involve the right of the individual, but have been specifically fixed in the Qur'an or the Sunnah belong to the fixed sphere and are to be considered as rights granted by Allah and as boundaries fixed by Him. … Such rights are to be considered together with other basis and inalienable rights that have been explicitly granted by Allah to individuals. They may not be changed or even suspended temporarily, whatever the emergency. They are outside the pale of legal review."

66   Nyazee, *The Methodology of Ijtihad*, 116-118.

67   Hasan, *The Doctrine of Ijma in Islam*, 10.

68   Keller, *Reliance of the Traveller*, Book W, at § w29.0 (2).

69   Doi, *Shari'ah: The Islamic Law*, 39, citing to 'Abdul Qadir 'Audah, *Islam Between Ignorant Followers and Incapable Scholars* (Kuwait: I.I.F.S.O., 1971), 48: It is the consensus opinion that the interpreters of the Qur'an and Muslim jurists that any Muslim who legislatively innovates, or enacts laws inconsistent with what *Allah* has revealed, enforcing his own laws while renouncing the revealed ones—unless he believes that his innovated or self-imposed laws are a correct interpretation of Allah's revelation— would be *classified* under one of the categories of either *Fasidun, Fasiqun, Zalimun*, and finally *Kafirun*. For example, if a ruler does not apply the Islamic penalty for theft or slander or adultery, preferring the judgments of man-made law, such a ruler would be considered definitely an unbeliever. If a ruler fails to apply *Islamic jurisprudence* for reasons other than disbelief, he is considered a wrongdoer, and if, as a result of neglecting *Islamic jurisprudence* he violates a human right or overlooks a principle justice and equality, he is considered a rebel."

70   Saalih Muhammad al-Uthaymeen, *Bid'ah: The Unique Nature of the Perfection Found in Islaam and the Grave Danger of Innovating into it* (Birmingham (UK): Salafi Publications, 1999), 5. Cited hereafter as al-Uthaymeen. Note: As the publisher is "Salafi Publications," it stands to reason that al-Uthaymeen is a Salafist reflecting a Salafist perspective. Cited hereafter as Uthaymeen, *Bid'ah*.

71   Keller, *Reliance of the Traveller*, Book W, at § w29.2.

72   Uthaymeen, *Bid'ah*, 13.

73   Keller, *Reliance of the Traveller*, Book X "Biographical Notes," at § x178: **Ibn Taymiya** (p75.23) is Ahmad ibn 'Abd al-Halim inb 'Abd al-Salam ibn 'Abdullah, Abu al-'Abbas Taqi al-Din Inb Taymiya Ibn Taymiya al-Harrani, born in Harran, east of Damascus, in 661/1263. A famous Hanbali scholar in Koranic exegesis, hadith, and jurisprudence.

74   For example, in his book *The Fundamentals of Takfir*, 'Anbari often refers to Ibn Taymiya as simply the "Shaykh al-Islam", Khalid bin Muhammad al-'Anbari, *Ruling by Other Than What Allah Revealed: The Fundamentals of Takfir, Al-Qur'an Was-Sunnah* Society of North America, Detroit, MI (printed in Lebanon), 1999, 7, 12, 16. Cited hereafter as 'Anbari, *The Fundamentals of Takfir*.

75   For example, consider Ibn Taymiya's treatment in *Reliance of the Traveller*, Keller, *Reliance of the Traveller*, Book X "Biographical Notes," at § x178. **States:** While few deny the Ibn Taymiya was a copious and eloquent writer and hadith scholar, his career, like that of others, demonstrates that a man may be outstanding in one field and yet suffer from radical deficiencies in another, the most reliable index of which is how a field's Imams regard his work in it. By this measure, indeed, by the standard of all previous Ahl al-Sunna scholars, it is clear that despite a voluminous and influential written legacy, Ibn Taymiya cannot be considered an authority on tenets of faith, a field which he made mistakes profoundly incompatible with the belief of Islam, as also with a number of his legal views that violated the **scholarly consensus** (*ijma*) of Sunni Muslims. It should be remembered that such matters are not the province of personal reasoning (*ijtihad*), whether Ibn Taymiya considered them to be so out of sincere conviction, or whether simply because, as Imam Subki said, **"his learning exceeded his intelligence."** He died in Damascus in 728/1328.

76   Hourani, *A History of the Arab Peoples*, 258, 181. Wahhabis are followers of an Islamic movement founded by Muhammad ibn 'Abd al-Wahhab (1703-92). Wahhab "preached the need for Muslims to return to the teaching of Islam as understood by the followers of Ibn Hanbal: strict obedience to the Qur'an and Hadith as they were interpreted by responsible scholars in each generation, and rejection of all that could be regarded as illegitimate innovations. Among these innovations was the reverence given to the dead, saints as intercessors with Allah, and the special devotions of the Sufi orders. The reformer made an alliance with Muhammad ibn Sa'ud, ruler of a small market town, Dir'iyya, and this lead to the formation of a state which claimed to live under the guidance of the *shari'a* and tried to

bring pastoral tribes all around it under its guidance too." The association between ibn Wahhab and ibn Sa'ud "led to the creation of the Saudi state in central Arabia."

77   Keller, *Reliance of the Traveller*, Book X "Biographical Notes," at § x178. **States:** While few deny the Ibn Taymiya was a copious and eloquent writer and hadith scholar, his career, like that of others, demonstrates that a man may be outstanding in one field and yet suffer from radical deficiencies in another, the most reliable index of which is how a field's Imams regard his work in it. By this measure, indeed, by the standard of all previous Ahl al-Sunna scholars, it is clear that despite a voluminous and influential written legacy, Ibn Taymiya cannot be considered an authority on tenets of faith, a field which he made mistakes profoundly incompatible with the belief of Islam, as also with a number of his legal views that violated the **scholarly consensus (*ijma*)** of Sunni Muslims. It should be remembered that such matters are not the province of personal reasoning (*ijtihad*), whether Ibn Taymiya considered them to be so out of sincere conviction, or whether simply because, as Imam Subki said, **"his learning exceeded his intelligence."** He died in Damascus in 728/1328.

78   Kufr is one of the categories of the unlawful - haram – and the severest. *Reliance of the Traveller* **explains its relationship to haram as follows:** Book C "Kinds of Rulings", at c2.5, The *unlawful* (haram) is what the Lawgiver strictly forbids. Someone who commits an unlawful act deserves punishment, while one who refrains from it out of obedience to the command of Allah is rewarded. Scholars distinguish between three forms levels of the unlawful: 3) and *unbelief* (kufr), sins which put one beyond the pale of Islam (as discussed at o8.7) and necessitate stating the Testification of Faith (Shahada) to reenter it. Keller, *Reliance of the Traveller*, Book C "The Nature of Legal Rulings," c2.0 \"Types of Human Acts", at c2.5, 30, 31.

79   'Anbari, *The Fundamentals of Takfir*, 6, 7.

80   'Anbari, *The Fundamentals of Takfir*, 133, 134.

81   'Anbari, *The Fundamentals of Takfir*, 134.

82   'Anbari, *The Fundamentals of Takfir*, 140.

83   Fyzee, *Muhammadan Law*.

84   Doi, *Shari'ah: The Islamic Law*, 5.

85   Doi, *Shari'ah: The Islamic Law*, 465, 466. **Note:** The Verse citations are as listed in Doi's treatise. A review of the Qur'an, however, indicates that the actual verses are as follows: "... no better than those who rebel," (Qur'an 5:47), "... no better than wrong-doers," (Qur'an 5:45), "... no better than unbelievers," (Qur'an 5:44).

86   Doi, *Shari'ah: The Islamic Law*, 466.

87   Kamali, *Principles of Islamic Jurisprudence*, 8.

88   Kamali, *Principles of Islamic Jurisprudence*, 8.

89   Nyazee, *The Methodology of Ijtihad*, 50.

90   Nyazee, *The Methodology of Ijtihad*, 50.

91   Rauf, Feisal Abdul, *Islam: A Sacred Law: What Every Muslim Should Know about Shariah*, Qiblah Books, 2000, 58. Cited hereafter as Feisal Rauf, *Islam: A Sacred Law*.

92   Dr. Walid bin Idris bin 'Abd-al-'Aziz al-Manisi, "Judicial Work Outside the Lands of Islam— What Is Permitted and What Is Forbidden," *Assembly of Muslim Jurists of America (AMJA)*, November 2007, updated translation under the title "Assembly of Muslim Jurists of America Cautions Muslims Against Participating in American Legal System; Urges Them to "Hate It in Their Hearts" Translating Jihad, 14 March 2012, URL: http://www.translatingjihad.com/2012/03/assembly-of-muslim-jurists-of-america.html. **Note:** Dr. Walid bin Idris bin 'Abd-al-'Aziz al-Manisi, [= Waleed Al-Maneese, = Waleed Idris] Member of the Permanent Fatwa Committee for AMJA; Member of the Faculty of

American Open University; Imam and Speaker at the Dar al-Faruq Islamic Center in Minneapolis [also member of Executive Committee of North American Imam Federation (NAIF)]. Cited hereafter as Manisi, "Judicial Work Outside the Lands of Islam—What Is Permitted and What Is Forbidden," (AMJA).

93   Manisi, "Judicial Work Outside the Lands of Islam—What Is Permitted and What Is Forbidden," (AMJA), 28.

94   Manisi, "Judicial Work Outside the Lands of Islam—What Is Permitted and What Is Forbidden," (AMJA), 37-38.

95   "Assembly of Muslim Jurists of America Cautions Muslims Against Participating in American Legal System; Urges Them to "Hate It in Their Hearts" *Translating Jihad*, 14 March 2012, URL: http://www.translatingjihad.com/2012/03/assembly-of-muslim-jurists-of-america.html

96   AMJA Leadership, URL: http://amjaonline.org/amja-leadership/

97   Emerick, Yahiya. *What Islam is all About: A Student Textbook*, Grades 7 to 12. 5th rev. ed. Lebanon: Noorart, 2004, 381. Cited hereafter as Emerick, *What Islam is All About*.

98   Emerick, *What Islam is All About*, 377.

99   Emerick, *What Islam is All About*, 376.

100   Iraq Constitution, 15 October 2005, URL: http://portal.unesco.org/ci/en/files/20704/11332732681iraqi_constitution_en.pdf/iraqi_constitution_en.pdf

101   Afghanistan Constitution, 04 January 2004, URL: http://www.oefre.unibe.ch/ law/icl/af00000_.html.

102   Syria Constitution, 13 March 1973, URL: http://www.oefre.unibe.ch/law/icl/sy 00000_.html

103   Jordan Constitution, 08 January 1952, URL: http://www.cmfmena.org/countrys/ Constitutions/Jordan_Constitution.htm, accessed 20 March 2005.

104   Saudi Arabia Constitution, March 1992, URL: http://www.afghanembassy.com.pl/cms/uploads/images/Constitution/The%20Constitution.pdf

105   Egypt Constitution, 22 May 1980, URL: http://www.oefre.unibe.ch/law/icl/sy 00000_.html

106   Sorcher, Sara. "Rifts in Muslim Brotherhood Mark Egypt's Political Disarray: The challenge: who does the U.S. talk to?" *National Journal*, 15 July 2011, URL: http://www.kinghussein.gov.jo/constitution_jo.html

PART II: THE RED PILL

1   Martin Van Creveld, The Transformation of War: The Most Radical Reinterpretation of Armed Conflict Since Clausewitz (New York: Free Press, 1991) 211-212.

The full quote: "The problem of subversion is likely to be serious. In the recent past, military establishments, so long as they fought each other, were able to take national loyalties more or less for granted. However, this will be decreasingly the case. Nor, probably, will the establishments of the future be able to control their members in the same way, and to the same extent, as do state-run armed forces with their uniforms, regular pay, extensive welfare systems, and powerful counterintelligence services. Tomorrow's warmaking organizations will not recognize the kind of distinctions that, in the past, allowed governments but not individuals to profit from war. They will probably allow their members more room to satisfy their personal needs directly at the expenses of the enemy. Once satisfying personal needs and making a private profit are considered important and legitimate motives, subversion, treachery and shifting allegiances by individuals and entire units will become as commonplace as they have often been in the past. To quote Philip II, father of Alexander the Great: where an army cannot pass, a donkey laden with gold often will. Such is likely to be the stuff of which future strategy is made.

Judging by the experience of the last two decades, the visions of long-range, computerized, high-tech warfare so dear to the military-industrial complex will never come to pass. Armed conflict will be waged by men on earth, not robots in space. It will have more in common with the struggles of primitive tribes than with large scale conventional war of the kind that the world may have seen."

2   Al-Marghinani, Burhan al-Din al-Farghani, Al-Hidaya: The Guidance, 2 vols. Trans. Imran Ahsan Khan Nyazee. Bristol, England: Amal Press, 2008.

3   Khadduri, Shaybani's Siyar.

4   Ibn Rushd, Abu al-Walid Muhammad ibn Ahmad (aka Averoes). *The Distinguished Jurist's Primer* (*Bidayat al-Mujtahid wa Nihayat al-Muqtsid*). 2 vols. Trans. Imran Ahsan Khan Nyazee. Reading: Garnet Publishing, 2002. Cite hereafter as Ibn Rushd, *Distinguished Jurist's Primer*.

5   Ibn Kathir, Al-Hafiz Abu al-Fida' 'Imad Ad-Din Isma'il bin 'Umar bin Kathir al-Qurashi al-Busrawi, *Tafsir of Ibn Kathir*. 10 vols. Trans. Abdul-Malik Mujahid. Riyadh: Darussalam, 2000. Cited hereafter as Ibn Kathir, *Tafsir Ibn Kathir*.

6   Keller, *Reliance of the Traveller*, Book R "Holding One's Tongue," r14.0 "Explaining the Koran by Personal Opinion," at r14.1.

7   Keller, *Reliance of the Traveller*, Book T "A Pure Heart," t3.0 "Counsels and Maxims," at t3.9.

8   Jalalu'd-din Al-Mahalli and Jalalu'd-din As-Suyuti, *Tafsir Al-Jalalayn*, first published in 1461 a.d., trans. Aisha Bewley, 2007, Dar Al-Taqwa Ltd., London, p. v. Cited hereafter as Jalalu'd-din and Jalalu'd-din, *Tafsir Al-Jalalayn*.

9   Jalalu'd-din and Jalalu'd-din, *Tafsir Al-Jalalayn*, 1369.

10   Keller, *Reliance of the Traveller*, Book R "Holding One's Tongue," r14.0 "Explaining the Koran by Personal Opinion," at r14.3.

11   Jalalu'd-din and Jalalu'd-din, *Tafsir Al-Jalalayn*, v, vi.

12   Ibn Kathir, Tafsir Ibn Kathir.

13   Jalalu'd-din and Jalalu'd-din, *Tafsir Al-Jalalayn*, v, vi.

14   Malik, S. K., Brigadier, Pakistani Army. *The Quranic Concept of War*. First Indian Reprint. New Delhi, India: Himalayan Books, 1986.

15   *The Quranic Concept of War* by Brigadier S.K. Malik, (Lahore, Pakistan: Wajid Al's Ltd., 1979. (with a forward by General Zia-ul-Haq) (This paper relies on the 1986 First Indian Reprint), xi. Cited hereafter as Brigadier S.K. Malik, *Quranic Concept of War*.

16   Emerick, Yahiya. What Islam is all About: A Student Textbook, Grades 7 to 12. 5ᵗʰ rev. ed. Lebanon: Noorart, 2004.

17   Nyazee, The Methodology of Ijtihad.

18   Nyazee, Islamic Jurisprudence, 319.

19   Nyazee, Islamic Jurisprudence, 318.

20   Fyzee, *Muhammadan Law*, 19-20.

21   Jalalu'd-din and Jalalu'd-din, *Tafsir Al-Jalalayn*, back cover, 614, 583, 38.

22   Slide 17, "The Rule of Abrogation," Major Nidal M. Hasan, "The Koranic World View as it Relates to Muslims in the U.S. Military," June 2007, first given to fellow psychiatrist/interns at Walter Reed Army Hospital in Washington, D.C., published by the Washington Post as a PowerPoint in PDF format at URL: http://www.washingtonpost.com/wp-dyn/content/gallery/2009/11/10/GA2009111000920.html, 5 November 2009. Cite hereafter as Major Hasan, "The Koranic World View as it Relates to Muslims in the U.S. Military."

23   Yusuf Ali, Abdullah. Commentary 2140, *The Meaning of the Holy Qur'an*. Beltsville: Amana Publications, 1999, 664. Cited hereafter as Yusuf Ali, *Qur'an*. Note: Unless otherwise stated, all Quranic citations to the Qur'an will be from the Yusuf Ali translation.

24   Warning before Fort Hood – Slide 16, "Koran," Major Hasan, "The Koranic World View as it Relates to Muslims in the U.S. Military."

25   Keller, *Reliance of the Traveller*, Book O "Justice," o22.0 "The Judge and the Court," at o22(I) (9 & 10): The necessary qualifications for being an Islamic judge (*qadi*) are: (I) The types of Koranic Rules include, for example: (9) those (*nasikh*) which supersede previously revealed Koranic verses; (10) and those (*mansukh*) which are superseded by later verses.

26   Slide 35, "Jihad-Rule of Abrogation," Major Hasan, "The Koranic World View as it Relates to Muslims in the U.S. Military."

27   Khadduri, *Shaybani's Siyar*, 299.

28   Marghinani, Al-Hidaya: The Guidance, 388.

29   Ibn Rushd, *Distinguished Jurist's Prime*, vol. 1, at 584.

30   Khadduri, *Shaybani's Siyar*, xiii.

31   Majid Khadduri, *War and Peace*, at 24.

32   War and Peace, 63, 64.

33   Keller, *Reliance of the Traveller*, Book O "Justice," 4.0 "Indemnity," at o4.17.

34   Nyazee, The Methodology of Ijtihad, 252-254.

35   Keller, *Reliance of the Traveller*, Book O "Justice," at o9.0: "Jihad," at o9.16 "Truces." There must be some interest served in making a truce other than mere preservation of the status quo. Allah most high says, "So do not be fainthearted and call for peace, when it is you who are the uppermost" (Qur'an 47:35). Interests that justify making a truce are such things as Muslim weakness because of lack of numbers or material, or the hope of an enemy becoming Muslim, for the Prophet (Allah bless him and give him peace) made a truce in the year Mecca was liberated with Safwan ibn Umayya for four months in hope that he would become Muslim, and he entered Islam before its time was up. If the Muslims are weak, a truce may be made for ten years if necessary, for the Prophet (Allah bless him and grant him Peace) made a truce with Quraysh for that long, as it related by Abu Dawud. It is not permissible to stipulate longer than that, save by means of new truces, each of which does not exceed ten years.

36   Nyazee, The Methodology of Ijtihad, 172.

37   Khadduri, *Shaybani's Siyar*, 54.

38   Keller, *Reliance of the Traveller*, Book O "Justice," at o9.0 "Jihad," at o9.16 "Truces."

39   Keller, *Reliance of the Traveller*, Book O "Justice," at o9.0 "Jihad," at o9.16: "Truces."

(O: As for truces, the author does not mention them. In Sacred Law truce means a peace treaty with those hostile to Islam, involving a cessation of fighting for a specified period, whether for payment or something else. The scriptural basis for them includes such Quranic verses as: "An acquittal from Allah and His Messenger..." (9:1) and "If they incline towards peace, then incline towards it also" (8:61) as well as the truce which the Prophet (Allah bless him and give him peace) made with the Quraysh in the year of Hudaybiya, as related by Bukhari and Muslim.

Truces are permissible, not obligatory. The only one who may effect a truce is the Muslim ruler of a region (or his representative) with a segment of the non-Muslims of the region, or the caliph (o22) (or his representative). When made with other than a *portion* of the non-Muslims, or when made with all of them, or with all in a particular region such as India or Asia Minor, then only the caliph (or his representative) may effect it, for it is a matter of the gravest consequence because it entails the nonperformance of jihad, whether globally or in a given locality, and our interest must be looked after therein, which is why it is best left to the caliph under any circumstances, or to someone he delegates to see to the interests of the various regions.

40   Keller, *Reliance of the Traveller*, Book O "Justice," at o9.0: "Jihad," at o9.16 "Truces." There must be some interest served in making a truce other than mere preservation of the status quo. Allah most high says, "So do not be fainthearted and call for peace, when it is you who are the uppermost" (Qur'an 47:35). Interests that justify making a truce are such things as Muslim weakness because of lack of numbers or material, or the hope of an enemy becoming Muslim, for the Prophet (Allah bless him and give him peace) made a truce in the year Mecca was liberated with Safwan ibn Umayya for four months in hope that he would become Muslim, and he entered Islam before its time was up. If the Muslims are weak, a truce may be made for ten years if necessary, for the Prophet (Allah bless him and grant him Peace) made a truce with Quraysh for that long, as it related by Abu Dawud. It is not permissible to stipulate longer than that, save by means of new truces, each of which does not exceed ten years.

41   Ibn Kathir, *Tafsir Ibn Kathir*, vol. 9, 171-176.

42   Pipes, Daniel, "[Al-Hudaybiya and] Lessons from the Prophet Muhammad's Diplomacy," *Middle East Quarterly*, September 1999, URL; http://www.danielpipes.org/316/al-hudaybiya-and-lessons-from-the-prophet-muhammads

43   "Arafat compares Oslo Accords to Muhammad's Hudaybiyyah peace treaty, which led to defeat of the peace partners," Palestinian Media Watch. Originally recorded May 10, 1994. http://www.palwatch.org/main.aspx?fi=711&fld_id=723&doc_id=486

44   "PA Minister: PA agreements are modeled after Muhammad's Hudaybiyyah Peace Treaty," Palestinian Media Watch, 22 July 2013, URL: http://palwatch.org/main.aspx?fi=157&doc_id=9401

45   *Sahih Bukhari, Volume 4, Book 52 "Fighting for the Cause of Allah," (Jihaad), Number 46*, USC Center for Muslim-Jewish Engagement, URL: http://www.usc.edu/org/cmje/religious-texts/hadith/bukhari/052-sbt.php.

46   *Sahih Muslim*, The Book on Government (*Kitab Al-Imara*) Chapter 41: In Proof of the Martyr's Attaining Paradise, Book 20, Number 4678, USC Center for Muslim-Jewish Engagement, URL: http://www.usc.edu/org/cmje/religious-texts/hadith/muslim/020-smt.php.

47   Keller, *Reliance of the Traveller*, Book O "Justice," at § o9.0 "Jihad."

48   *Black's* defines **statutory construction** as: "That branch of the law dealing with the interpretation of laws enacted by a legislature. A judicial function required when a stature is invoked and different interpretations are in contention." *Black's Law Dictionary 6th* Edition, West Publishing, St. Paul, 1990, 1412. Cited hereinafter as *Black's Law, 6th*.

49   Keller, *Reliance of the Traveller*, Book O "Justice," at § o9.0 "Jihad."

50   Keller, *Reliance of the Traveller*, Book O "Justice," at § o9.0 "Jihad."

51   Keller, *Reliance of the Traveller*, Book O "Justice," at § o9.0 "Jihad."

52   Keller, *Reliance of the Traveller*, Book O "Justice," at § o9.0 "Jihad."

53   Ibn Kathir, *Tafsir Ibn Kathir*, vol. 4, 376.

54   Emerick, *What Islam is All About*, 15. "History books about the Blessed Prophet are called books of *Seerah*. Below are the names of four of the most important history books about the Blessed Prophet: Ibn Ishaq, Ibn Sa'd, Ibn Kathir and Ibn Hisham**."**

55   Abu Fadl, "Greater and 'Lesser' *Jihad*: Refutation of a Common Misconception," trans. Khalil Fadl. Online ed. 27 February 2001. URL: iisca://knowledge/*jihad*/grater and 'lesser' *jihad*/, accessed 14 February 2004. Abu Fadl states the rule of quoting without citation: "Al-Hakim and Ibnu Abi Zur'ah state: "We often write statements … only as an example, and we remove ourselves of responsibility from him."

56   Emerick, What Islam is All About, 164.

57   Ibn Khaldun, *The Muqaddimah*, 255.

58   Ibn Khaldun, *The Muqaddimah*, 183.

59   This endnote provides detailed reference in support of the associated footnote defining fatwa:

a) Keller, *Reliance of the Traveller,* Book B "The Validity of Following Qualified Leadership," at b7.6. **States:** "There is scholarly consensus on it being unlawful to follow rulings from schools other than those of the four Imams, meaning in one's personal works, let alone give court verdicts or formal legal opinion to people from them."

b) Keller, *Reliance of the Traveller,* Book B "The Validity of Following Qualified Leadership," at b7.2. **States:** "nor can *mujtahid*s of a succeeding era make the thing an object of new *ijtihad*, because the ruling on it [*ijma*], verified by scholarly consensus, is an absolute legal ruling which does not admit of being contradicted or annulled."

c) Keller, *Reliance of the Traveller,* Book B "The Validity of Following Qualified Leadership," at b1.2, States: "For the key term *qualified to issue expert legal opinion* (Ar. *Mujtahid*, this ability being *ijtihad*), please turn to book o and read o22.1(d), the qualifications of an Islamic judge (qadi). The difference between the qualifications for the Imam of a school and those of a judge or a mufti is the former's competence in giving opinion is absolute, extending to all subject matter in the Sacred Law, while the competence of the judge or mufti is limited respectively to judging court cases or applying his Imam's *ijtihad* to particular questions."

d) Keller, *Reliance of the Traveller,* Book O "Justice," at § o22.1(d): States: "The necessary qualifications for being an Islamic judge (qadi) are: (d) to possess knowledge of the rulings of Sacred Law, meaning by way of personal legal reasoning (*ijtihad*) from primary texts, not merely by following a particular qualified scholar (*taqlid*), i.e., if he follows qualified scholarship, he must know and agree with how the rulings are being derived, not merely report them). Being qualified to perform legal reasoning (*ijtihad*) requires knowledge of the rules and principles of the Koran, the sunna, in this context meaning the hadith, not the *sunna* as opposed to the *obligatory*, as well as knowledge of scholarly consensus (ijma), and analog, together with knowing the types of each of these. … (I) The types of Koranic rules include, for example: (7) those (nass) which unequivocally decide a particular legal question; (9) those (nasikh) which supersede previously revealed Koranic verses; (10) and those (mansukh) which are superseded by later verses."

60   National Society of Defense—The Seat of the Caliphate, "*A Universal Proclamation to All the People of Islam,*" The Seat of the Caliphate: The Ottoman Empire: Muta'at al Hairayet, 1313/1915, trans. American Agency and Consulate, Cairo, in U.S. State Department document 867.4016/57, 10 March 1915, 1. Compliments Dr. Andrew Bostom. . Cited hereafter as Seat of the Caliphate, 1915

Fatwa.

61   Seat of the Caliphate,1 915 Fatwa, 22.

62   Seat of the Caliphate, 1915 Fatwa, 23.

63   Maulana Muhammad Ali, *A Manual of Hadith*, 2nd ed., (Lahore: Ahmadiyya Anjuman Ishaat Islam, 2001), iii. Cited hereafter as Ali, *A Manual of Hadith*, 2nd.

64   Mohamed Akram, Explanatory Memorandum, 4, 7, 12, 18.

65   Mohamed Akram, Explanatory Memorandum, 4, 12.

66   Mohammad Fadel, "Jihad is Imperative to Muslims," ISNA's *Islamic Horizons*, IPT Archive, December 1986, 20. Cited hereafter as Fadel, "Jihad is Imperative to Muslims."

67   Fadel, "Jihad is Imperative to Muslims," 20.

68   Fadel, "Jihad is Imperative to Muslims," 20.

69   Mohamed Akram, Explanatory Memorandum, 4, 7, 12, 18.

70   Mohamed Akram, Explanatory Memorandum, 10 - 15.

71   Fadel, "Jihad is Imperative to Muslims," 20. **Note:** Fadel states that he is citing his verses from Yusuf Ali's translation of the Qur'an. The Yusuf Ali translations are provided for the readers benefit in the this and the following two endnotes. "Think not of those who are slain in Allah's way as dead. Nay, they live, finding their sustenance in the presence of their Lord; they rejoice in the bounty provided by Allah: And with regard to those left behind, who have not yet joined them (in their bliss), the (Martyrs) glory in the fact that on them is no fear, nor have they (cause to) grieve. They glory in the Grace and the bounty from Allah, and in the fact that Allah suffereth not the reward of the Faithful to be lost (in the least)." (Yusuf Ali, Qur'an 3:169-171)

72   Fadel, "Jihad is Imperative to Muslims," 20. "Not equal are those believers who sit (at home) and receive no hurt, and those who strive and fight in the cause of Allah with their goods and their persons. Allah hath granted a grade higher to those who strive and fight with their goods and persons than to those who sit (at home). Unto all (in Faith) Hath Allah promised good: But those who strive and fight Hath He distinguished above those who sit (at home) by a special reward." (Yusuf Ali, Qur'an 4:95)

73   Fadel, "Jihad is Imperative to Muslims," 20. "Ye are the best of peoples, evolved for mankind, enjoining what is right, forbidding what is wrong, and believing in Allah. If only the People of the Book had faith, it were best for them: among them are some who have faith, but most of them are perverted transgressors. They will do you no harm, barring a trifling annoyance; if they come out to fight you, they will show you their backs, and no help shall they get." (Yusuf Ali, Qur'an 3:110-111)

74   Fadel, "Jihad is Imperative to Muslims," 20.

75   Seat of the Caliphate, 1915 Fatwa, 25-26.

76   Abu Mus'ab al-Suri, "The Jihadi Experiences: The Schools of Jihad," *Inspire Magazine*, Issue 1, Summer 1431/2010, URL: http://azelin.files.wordpress.com/2010/06/aqapinspire-magazine-volume-1-uncorrupted.pdf, 49.

77   Foreign Terrorist Organizations, Bureau of Counterterrorism, U.S. Department of State, URL: http://www.state.gov/j/ct/rls/other/des/123085.htm, accessed 28 June 2014. ISIL (or ISIS) is actually a re=designation of the same group reflecting the groups name change from "al-Qaeda in Iraq" that was registered on the FTO 17 December 2004. Cited hereafter as U.S. State Department, FTO List.

78   Nyazee, *The Methodology of Ijtihad*, back cover. **Note**: Professor Nyazee is both a credentialed expert in Islamic law as a Professor at the Faculty of Shari'ah and Law, International Islamic University, Islamabad, Pakistan and, with an LLM from the University of Michigan, has substantive understanding of Western, specifically U.S. jurisprudence. He is also author of *Islamic Jurisprudence* and translator of ibn Rushd's *The Distinguished Jurist's Primer*, both cited in this paper.

79   Keller, *Reliance of the Traveller*, Book X "Biographical Notes," at § x37. (Imam) Abu Hanifa (b1.2) is Abu Hanifa al-Nu'man ibn Thabit, the Greatest Imam born, born in A.H. 80 in Kufa. He was the Scholar of Iraq and the foremost representative and exemplar of the school of juridical opinion (*ra'y*). The Hanafi school, which he founded, has decided court cases in the majority of Islamic lands for the greater part of Islam's history, including the Abbasid and Ottoman periods, and maintains its preeminence in the Islamic courts today. Abu Hanifa was the first to analyze Islamic jurisprudence, divide it into subjects, distinguish its issues, and determine the range and criteria for analogical reasoning (*qiyas*) therein.

80   Nyazee, The Methodology of Ijtihad, 189.

81   Nyazee, The Methodology of Ijtihad, 250-251.

82   Ibn Rushd, Distinguished Jurist's Primer, vol. 1, 464.

83   Ibn Rushd, Distinguished Jurist's Primer, vol. 2, 483.

84   Nyazee, The Methodology of Ijtihad, 251-252.

85   Nyazee, The Methodology of Ijtihad, 252.

86   El Fadl, Khlaled Abou, *The Place of Tolerance in Islam,* eds. Joshua Cohen and Ian Lague, Boston: Beacon Press, 2002, 8.

87   John Esposito in El Fadl, *The Place of Tolerance in Islam*, 74.

88   Stephen Schwartz, The Two Faces of Islam: Saudi Fundamentalism and its Role in Terrorism (New York: Anchor Books, 2003), xii.

89   Saudi Arabian General Investment Authority (SAGIA), "Legal System," 02 July 2006, URL: http://www.sagia.gov.sa/innerpage.asp?ContentID=573&Lang=en, accessed 02 July 2006.

90   Saudi Arabia Information Resource, "The Teachings of Muhammad bin Abdul Wahhab,"03 July 2006, URL: http://www.saudinf.com /main/b5.htm , accessed 03 July 2006.

91   Keller, *Reliance of the Traveller*, Book X "Biographical Notes," at § x72: **(Imam) Ahmad** (b1.2) is Ahmad ibn Muhammad ibn **Hanbal** ibn Hilal ibn Asad, Abu 'Abdullah al-Shaybani, **Imam of Ahl al-Sunna,** born in 164/780 in Baghdad, where he grew up an orphan. . For sixteen years he traveled in pursuit of the knowledge of hadith, to Kufa, Basra, Mecca, Medina, Yemen, Damascus, Morocco, Algeria, Persia, and Khurasan, memorizing on hundred thousand hadiths, thirty thousand of which he recorded in his *Musnad [Ascribed Traditions]*.

92   Nyazee, The Methodology of Ijtihad, 186.

93   Wael B. Hallaq, "Islamic Legal Theories: An Introduction to Sunni *usul al-fiqh*, Cambridge University Press, Cambridge, UK, 1999, 32.

94   Stephen Schwartz, *The Two Faces of Islam: Saudi Fundamentalism and its Role in Terrorism* (New York: Anchor Books, 2003), i. Note: A convert to Islam, Schwartz, or Suleyman Ahmad, introduces himself in his book as the "Washington bureau chief for the Jewish *Forward*."

95   Nyazee, *The Methodology of Ijtihad*, 318. *Hukm taklifi* defined: The obligation-creating rule. The primary rule of the legal system.

96   Nyazee, The Methodology of Ijtihad, 58,59.

97   Nyazee, *The Methodology of Ijtihad*, 313, 318. *Ahkam* defined: Plural of hukm (rule). *Hukm* defined: Rule, injunction, prescription.

98   Nyazee, The Methodology of Ijtihad, 60.

99   Jansen, Johannes J.G, *The Neglected Duty: The Creed of Sadat's Assassins and Islamic Resurgence in the Middle East*, (New York: MacMillan Publishing Company, 1986), 183.

100   An explanation for why jihad cannot be a "Sixth Pillar of Islam" is that the Pillars, being the

"five main practices," are permanent requirements of Islam whereas jihad, in theory, is to end when the world, having been converted entirely to the *dar al-Islam*, has been claimed for Islam. While the duty of jihad exists, its status is on par with the Five Pillars.

101 Nyazee, The Methodology of Ijtihad, 64.

102 Nyazee, The Methodology of Ijtihad, 64.

103 Nyazee, The Methodology of Ijtihad, 71.

104 Emerick, What Islam is All About, 50-51.

105 Emerick, *What Islam is All About*, 164. The small letters in parenthesis are verses from the Qur'an that Emerick uses to provide authority for the position stated. As this is a lesson on the duty of jihad, this particular reference to the Qur'an is included here (9:38, 39 & 41 with 9:40 excluded due to length). (Note: "lightly or heavily" refers to being armed lightly or heavily):

O ye who believe! What is the matter with you, that when ye are asked to go forth in the cause of Allah, ye cling very heavily to the earth? Do ye prefer the life of this world to the Hereafter? But little is the comfort of this life, as compared with the hereafter. (9:38)

Unless ye go forth, He will punish you with a grievous penalty, and put others in your place; But Him ye would not harm in the least. For Allah hath power over all things. (9:39)

Go ye forth, (whether equipped) lightly or heavily, and strive and struggle, with your goods and your persons, in the Cause of Allah. That is best for you, if ye (but) knew. (9:41)

106 Khadduri, *Shaybani's Siyar*, 54.

107 Nyazee, *The Methodology of Ijtihad*, 123. "All this leads us to the conclusion that there are two spheres of Islamic law (and should be two in the law of crimes also), one fixed, existing as the right of Allah, while the other is flexible and changing."

108 Nyazee, *The Methodology of Ijtihad*, 125, 126. "It also becomes obvious that what is binding upon us is the fixed part of the law. Nothing is binding upon us from the flexible sphere that changes with the times unless we consciously follow a system of precedents. ... Finally, the two spheres tell us that our ijtihad today is to be directed more towards the flexible sphere rather than the fixed sphere. The fixed sphere has been developed to its limits and a rich treasure of opinions exists within the established schools."

109 Nyazee, *The Methodology of Ijtihad*, 287. "*Ijtihad* is not a source of law; the sources in the true sense of the term are the texts of the Qur'an and the *Sunnah*. ... The first restriction that is placed on this activity is: There is no *ijtihad* within an explicit rule in the texts (*la ijtihada ma'al-nass*). This implies that when the rule stated in the texts is so clear that more than one meaning cannot be derived from it, the jurist is prohibited from undertaking *ijtihad* in it."

110 Nyazee, *The Methodology of Ijtihad*, 126. "The only way the law in the flexible sphere can be developed is through reasoning from general principles arising from the fixed part of the law."

111 Nyazee, *The Methodology of Ijtihad*, 289. "Calls for *ijtihad*, therefore, must focus upon the area of the law that falls within the domain of the rulers (i.e. the flexible) and this pertains to the bulk of the law obtaining in countries like Pakistan."

112 Nyazee, *The Methodology of Ijtihad*, 251.

113 Keller, *Reliance of the Traveller*, Book X, "Biographical Note," § x324

114 Shafi'i, *The Risala*.

115 Shafi'i, *The Risala*, 81-84.

116 "A time will come when groups of people will go for Jihad and it will be asked, 'Is there anyone amongst you who has enjoyed the company of the Prophet?' The answer will be 'Yes.' Then they will be given victory by Allah. Then a time will come when it will be asked, 'Is there anyone amongst you who

has enjoyed the company of the companions of the Prophet?' It will be said, 'Yes,' and they will be given the victory by Allah. Then a time will come when it will be said, 'Is there anyone amongst you who has enjoyed the company of the companions of the companions of the Prophet?' It will be said, 'Yes,' and they will be given victory by Allah." (Bukhari 4:146)

117 Shafi'i, *The Risala*, 84.

118 Shafi'i, *The Risala*, 83, 84.

119 Shafi'i, *The Risala*, 85-86.

120 Keller, *Reliance of the Traveller*, Book X "Biographical Note," at § x228.

121 Imam Malik ibn Anas, *Al-Muwatta of Imam Malik ibn Anas: The First Formulation of Islamic Law*, trans. Aisha Abdurrahman Bewley (Kuala Lumpur: Islamic Book Trust, 1997), Malik, ¶21.1.4,173. "Yahya related to me from 'Abdullah ibn 'Abd ar-Rahman ibn Ma'mar al-Ansari that 'Ata' ibn Yasar said that the Messenger of Allah, may Allah bless him and grant him peace, *"Shall I tell you who has the best degree among people? A man who takes the rein of his horse to do jihad in the way of Allah."* Cite hereafter as Malik, *Al-Muwatta*.

122 Malik, *Al-Muwatta*, ¶21.14.33,180. "Yahya related to me from Malik that Yahya ibn Sa'id said, "The Messenger of Allah, may Allah bless him and grant him peace, was sitting by a grave which was being dug at Madina. A man looked into the grave and said, 'An awful bed for the believer.' The Messenger of Allah, may Allah bless him and grant him peace, said, 'Evil? What you have said is absolutely wrong.'"

The man said, 'I didn't mean that, Messenger of Allah. I meant being killed in the way of Allah.' The Messenger of Allah, may Allah bless him and grant him peace, said, "Being killed in the way of Allah has no like! There is no place on earth where I would prefer my grave to be than here (meaning Madina).' He repeated it three times."

123 Malik, *Al-Muwatta*, ¶21.18.42,182, ¶21.19.48,183. Yahya related to me this from Malik from Abu'z-Zinad from al-A'raj from Abu Hurayra that the Messenger of Allah, may Allah bless him and grant him peace, said, "By He in whose hand my self is! I would like to fight in the way of Allah and be killed, then be brought to life again so I could be killed and then be brought back to life again so I could be killed." Abu Hurayra said three times, "I testify to it by Allah!"

Yahya related to me from Malik from Yahya ibn Sa'id that the Messenger of Allah, may Allah bless him and grant him peace, was stimulating people to do *jihad*, mentioning the Garden. One of the Ansar was eating some dates he had in his hand, and said, "Am I so desirous of this world that I should sit until I finish them?" He threw aside what was in his hand and took his sword and fought until he was slain.

124 Malik, Al-Muwatta, Al-Muwatta, xxx

125 Khadduri, *Shaybani's Siyar*, 76-77.

126 Malik, *Al-Muwatta*, ¶21.14.

127 "Muhammad said, 'The person who participates in (holy battles) in Allah's cause and nothing compels him to do so except belief in Allah and His Apostles, will be recompensed by Allah either with a reward, or booty (if he survives) or will be admitted to Paradise (if he is killed in the battle as a martyr). Had I not found it difficult for my followers, then I would not remain behind any sariya [army unit] going for Jihad and I would have loved to be martyred in Allah's cause and then made alive, and then martyred and then made alive and then again martyred in His cause.'" (Bukhari 1:35)

128 Youssef H. Aboul-Enein and Sherifa Zuhur, *Islamic Rulings on Warfare*, Monograph, Strategic Studies Institute (Carlisle: U.S. Army War College, October 2004), 14, 15.

129 Ali, *A Manual of Hadith*, 2nd, 206.

130 Ali, *A Manual of Hadith*, 2nd, 213.

131 Keller, *Reliance of the Traveller*, Book O "Justice," at o9.0: "Jihad," at § o9.8: "The Objectives of Jihad." The caliph (o35) makes war upon Jews, Christians, and Zoroastrians (N: provided he has first invited them to enter Islam in faith and practice, and if they will not, then invited to enter the social order of Islam by paying the non-Muslim poll tax (*jizya*, def: o11.4)—which is the significance of their paying it, not the money itself—while remaining in their ancestral religions) (O: and the war continues) until they become Muslims or else pay the non-Muslim poll tax (O: in accordance with the word of Allah Most High, "Fight those who do not believe in Allah and the Last Day and who forbid not what Allah and His messenger have forbidden—who do not practice the religion of truth, being those who have been given the Book—until they pay the poll tax out of hand and are humbled" (Qur'an 9:29), the time and place for which is before the final descent of Jesus (upon whom be peace). After his final coming, nothing but Islam will be accepted from them, for taking the poll tax is only effective until Jesus' descent (upon him and our Prophet be peace), which is the divinely revealed law of Muhammad. The coming of Jesus does not entail a separate divinely revealed law, for he will rule by the law of Muhammad. As for the Prophet's saying (Allah bless him and give him peace), "I am the last, there will be no prophet after me," this does not contradict the final coming of Jesus (upon whom be peace), since he will not rule according to the Evangel, but as a follower of our Prophet (Allah bless him and give him peace).

132 Majid Khadduri, *War and Peace in the Law of Islam*, (Baltimore: Johns Hopkins, 1955), 64; reprint in (Clark, NJ: Lawbook Exchange, 2006), 64. Cited hereafter as Khadduri, *War and Peace in the Law of Islam*.

133 "A fatwa on "dar al-Islam" as inclusive of Dagestan," International Union for Muslim Scholars (IUMS), 17 November 2012, URL: http://www.iumsonline.net/en/default. asp?ContentID=5447&menuID=48.

134 Biography of Shaykh Abdallah bin Bayyah, The Official Website of His Eminence Shaykh Abdallah bin Bayyah, URL: http://binbayyah.net/english/bio/, accessed 10 October 2013.

135 John Rossomando, "Bin Bayyah is No Moderate," *The Hill's Congress Blog*, 28 August 2013, URL: http://thehill.com/blogs/congress-blog/foreign-policy/319213-no-moderate, accessed 10 October 2013.

136 Biography of Shaykh Abdallah bin Bayyah, The Official Website of His Eminence Shaykh Abdallah bin Bayyah, URL: http://binbayyah.net/english/bio/, accessed 10 October 2013.

137 Khadduri, War and Peace in the Law of Islam, 64.

138 Keller, *Reliance of the Traveller*, Book X "Biographical Notes," at § x257. Muhammad ibn Hasan Shaybani.

139 Khadduri, *Shaybani's Siyar*, 76-77.

140 Ibn Kathir, *Tafsir Ibn Kathir*, vol. 4, 406 - 407.

141 Keller, *Reliance of the Traveller*, Book P "Enormities," p1.0 "Ascribing Associates to Allah Most High (*Shirk*), p1.2, p1.3, 652, 653. **Also later in *Reliance*,** *shirk* is again listed in "Ibn Hajar Hatami's List of Enormities" as the first enormity. (*Reliance*, w52.1(A)(1), 966.) In keeping with the severity of such a crime, *shirk* is also listed as the first "among the things that entail apostasy from Islam" in the section in *Reliance* titled "Acts that Entail Leaving Islam": (1) to prostrate to an idol, whether sarcastically, out of mere contrariness, or in actual conviction, like that of someone who believes the Creator to be something that has originated in time. Like idols in this respect are the sun or moon, and like prostration is bowing to other than Allah, if one intends reverence towards it like the reverence due to Allah."

142 *Reliance of the Traveller*, Book O "Justice," o8.0 "Apostasy from Islam (*Ridda*)," Section o8.1, 595. **In addition,** for example, in his authoritative commentary Ibn Kathir (d. 1373) likewise treats *shirk* as a serious crime. In his treatment of Qur'an Verse 2:191, for example, Ibn Kathir associates *shirk* with *fitnah* and polytheism when stating that certain conditions it is better to kill those in such a state than to leave them in that state. Starting with the relevant part of Qur'an Verse 2:191, Ibn Kathir's

discussion of the meaning of "and *Al-Fitnah* is worse than killing" is explained in the section in *Tafsir Ibn Kathir* under the heading "*Shirk* is Worse than Killing":

And kill them wherever you find them, and turn them from out from where they have turned you out. And *Al-Fitnah* is worse than killing… (Qur'an 2:191)

Shirk is worse than Killing

Since *Jihad* involves killing and shedding the blood of men, Allah indicated that these men are committing disbelief in Allah, associating with Him (in the worship) and hindering from His path, and this is much greater evil and more disastrous than killing. Abu Malik commented about what Allah said:

And Al-Fitnah is worse than killing.

"Meaning what you (disbelievers) are committing is much worse than killing." Abu Al-'Aliyah, Mujahid, Sa'id bin Jubayr, 'Ikrima, Al-Hasan, Qatadah, Ad-Dahhak and Ar-Rabi' bin Anas said that what Allah said:

And Al-Fitnah is worse than killing.

"*Shirk* (polytheism) is worse than killing."*

*Al-Hafiz Abu al-Fida' 'Imad Ad-Din Isma'il bin 'Umar bin Kathir Al-Qurashi Al-Busrawi ibn Kathir, *Tafsir of Ibn Kathir*, vol. 1, Trans. Abdul-Malik Mujahid. (Riyadh, SA: Darussalam, 2000), at 526, 528, 529.

143 Keller, *Reliance of the Traveller*, Book O "Justice," at o11 "Non-Muslim Subjects of the Islamic State (*Ahl Al-Dhimma*)," at o11.5.

144 "Coptic Christian Student Murdered By Classmates for Wearing a Cross" *Assyrian International News Agency*, 30 October 2011 http://www.aina.org/news/20111030133621.htm

145 Sara Sorcher, "Rifts in Muslim Brotherhood Mark Egypt's Political Disarray: The challenge: who does the U.S. talk to?," *National Journal*, 15 July 2011, URL: http://nationaljournal.com/whitehouse/rifts-in-muslim-brotherhood-mark-egypt-s-political-disarray-20110715, accessed 18 July 2011. This was a two-part referendum, based on the Egyptian voting system. When totaling both parts of the referendum roughly 64% of voters voted in favor of the constitution, which included the reference to Shari'a as law of the land. "Egyptian voters back new constitution in referendum," BBC, 25 Dec 2012, URL: http://www.bbc.co.uk/news/world-middle-east-20842487

146 "Do Crosses at Catholic University Violate 'Human Rights' of Muslims?" *FoxNews Radio*, 26 October 2011, http://radio.foxnews.com/toddstarnes/top-stories/muslims-want-catholic-school-to-provide-room-without-crosses.html

147 Keller, Reliance of the Traveller, at o11.10.

148 Ibn Kathir, *Tafsir Ibn Kathir*, vol 4, 407.

149 Ibn Kathir, *Tafsir Ibn Kathir*, vol 2, 243.

150 *Catholic Bible Dictionary*, Scott Hahn, editor, Doubleday, New York, 2009, 326.

151 Ibn Kathir, *Tafsir Ibn Kathir*, vol 2, 243-244.

152 "El-Barahmi: Copts are infidels as stated by the Qur'an, will we apologize for the Qur'an to please them? Allah's curse upon them." Al-Rahma Channel, Cairo (Arabic), 13 October 2011, http://www.light-dark.net/vb/showthread.php?p=8826# post8826

153 Zaid Benjamin, @zaidbenjamin Twitter Feed, 18 July 2014, URL: https://twitter.com/zaidbenjamin/status/490165524232687616, accessed 18 July 2014. Twitter feed states: "Al-Baghdadi to #Mosul Christians: "Choose one of these: Islam, the sword, al-Jiziya (tax) or till Saturday to flee" pic.twitter.com/UoGf8pnYh1."

154 Ibn Kathir, *Tafsir Ibn Kathir*, vol 4, 406 - 407.

155 Keller, *Reliance of the Traveller*, Book O "Justice," at o11.0 "Non-Muslim Subjects of the Islamic State," at § o11.11.

156 Keller, *Reliance of the Traveller*, Book O "Justice," at o11.0 "Non-Muslim Subjects of the Islamic State," at § o11.9.

157 Keller, *Reliance of the Traveller*, Book O "Justice," at o11.0 "Non-Muslim Subjects of the Islamic State," at § o11.10.

158 Keller, *Reliance of the Traveller*, Book O "Justice," at o11.0 "Non-Muslim Subjects of the Islamic State," at § o11.11.

159 Keller, *Reliance of the Traveller*, Book O "Justice," at o9.0 "Jihad," at §§ o9.13-14 "The Rules of War."

160 Ibn Kathir, *Tafsir Ibn Kathir*, vol 4, 406 - 407.

161 Kamali, Mohammad Hashim, *Freedom of Expression in Islam*, Islamic Texts Society, Cambridge, 1997, 236. Cited hereafter as Kamali, Freedom of Expression in Islam.

162 First Grade, *Monotheism and Jurisprudence* (Lesson 8), Education Department of Education, Ministry of Education, Kingdom of Saudi Arabia, (2007-2008), 29, as cited in *2007-2008 Academic Year: Excerpts from Saudi Ministry of Education: Textbooks for Islamic Studies: Arabic with English Translations*, Center for Religious Freedom of Hudson Institute (with the Institute for Gulf Affairs), 2008, at 7, at http://www.freedomhouse.org/sites/default/files/TextbooksArabicExcerpts.pdf. Cited hereafter as First Grade Saudi Texts.

163 First Grade Saudi Texts, 7.

164 Keller, *Reliance of the Traveller*, Book W, at § w4.3.

165 Keller, *Reliance of the Traveller*, Book W, at § w4.4.

166 Keller, *Reliance of the Traveller*, Book W, at § w4.4.

167 Keller, *Reliance of the Traveller*, Book W, at § w4.4.

168 Keller, *Reliance of the Traveller*, Book W, at § w4.4.

169 Keller, *Reliance of the Traveller*, Book W, at § w4.4.

170 Warning before Fort Hood -- Slide 47, "Different Paths to Heaven?," Major Hasan, "The Koranic World View as it Relates to Muslims in the U.S. Military."

171 Bin Bayyah, "Christians in the Hereafter," *Follow the Shaykh*, 19 January 2012, URL: http://binbayyah.net/english/2012/01/19/christians-in-the-hereafter/, accessed 29 June 2013.

172 Bin Bayyah, "Christians in the Hereafter," *Follow the Shaykh*, 19 January 2012, URL: http://binbayyah.net/english/2012/01/19/christians-in-the-hereafter/, accessed 29 June 2013.

173 Zaid Benjamin, @zaidbenjamin Twitter Feed, 18 July 2014, URL: https://twitter.com/zaidbenjamin/status/490165524232687616, accessed 18 July 2014. Twitter feed states: "Al-Baghdadi to #Mosul Christians: "Choose one of these: Islam, the sword, al-Jiziya (tax) or till Saturday to flee" pic.twitter.com/UoGf8pnYh1."

174 Eighth Grade, *Monotheism* (Lesson 14), Education Department of Education, Ministry of Education, Kingdom of Saudi Arabia, (2007-2008), 42, as cited in *2007-2008 Academic Year: Excerpts from Saudi Ministry of Education: Textbooks for Islamic Studies: Arabic with English Translations*, Center for Religious Freedom of Hudson Institute (with the Institute for Gulf Affairs), 2008, at 51, at http://www.freedomhouse.org/sites/default/files/TextbooksArabicExcerpts.pdf, Cited hereafter as Eighth Grade Saudi Texts.

175 Eighth Grade Saudi Texts, 51.

176 Eighth Grade Saudi Texts, 51.

177 Eighth Grade Saudi Texts, 51.

178 Article 7, *The Covenant of the Islamic Resistance Movement* ("Hamas Covenant") 18 August 1988, *The Avalon Project*, Lillian Goldman Law Library, Yale Law School, http://avalon.law.yale.edu/20th_century/hamas.asp. Cited hereafter as Hamas Covenant.

179 Ninth Grade, *Hadith*, Education Department of Education, Ministry of Education, Kingdom of Saudi Arabia, 1426-1427 (2005-2006), 146, as cited in *Excerpts from Saudi Ministry of Education Textbooks for Islamic Studies: Arabic with English Translation*, Center for Religious Freedom of Freedom House with the Institute for Gulf Affairs, 2006, at 55, at http://www.freedomhouse.org/sites/default/files/TextbooksArabicExcerpts.pdf. Cited hereafter as Ninth Grade Saudi School Texts.

180 Ninth Grade Saudi School Texts, 55.

181 Sebnem Arsu, "In Turkey, Pope Francis Advocates Dialogue in Battling 'Fanaticism', The New York Times, 28 November 2014, URL: http://www.nytimes.com/2014/11/29/world/europe/on-trip-to-turkey-pope-francis-calls-for-dialogue-in-battling-isis.html?_r=0, accessed 24 December 2014.

182 Ibn Kathir, *Tafsir Ibn Kathir*, vol 2, 243.

183 Keller, *Reliance of the Traveller*, Book O "Justice," at o9.0: "Jihad," at § o9.8. **Note:** The lead up to this statement is as follows: THE OBJECTIVES OF JIHAD - The caliph makes war upon Jews, Christians, and Zoroastrians provided he has first invited them to enter Islam in faith and practice, and if they will not, then invited to enter the social order of Islam by paying the non-Muslim poll tax (*jizya*, def: o11.4)—which is the significance of their paying it, not the money itself—while remaining in their ancestral religions and the war continues until they become Muslims or else pay the non-Muslim poll tax in accordance with the word of Allah Most High,

"Fight those who do not believe in Allah and the Last Day and who forbid not what Allah and His messenger have forbidden—who do not practice the religion of truth, being those who have been given the Book—until they pay the poll tax out of hand and are humbled" (Qur'an 9:29), [followed by text cited in document]

184 Slide 45, "Offensive Islam is the Future," Major Hasan, "The Koranic World View as it Relates to Muslims in the U.S. Military."

185 The Kelly File, *FoxNews*, 30 January 2015, URL: http://www.foxnews.com/shows/the-kelly-file.html, accessed 31 January 2015.

186 *Catechism of the Catholic Church*, 2nd Ed., *Libreria Editrice Vaticana*, Rome, 1997, 877.

187 *Catholic Bible Dictionary*, Scott Hahn, editor, Doubleday, New York, 2009, 326.

188 Patrick Poole, "Homeland Security Advisor Mohamed Elibiary Goes on Hate-Filled Anti-Christian Rant, Attacks Jindal as 'Bottom Feeder'," PJ Media, 28 January 2015, URL: http://pjmedia.com/tatler/2015/01/28/homeland-security-adviser-mohamed-elibiary-goes-on-hate-filled-anti-christian-rant-attacks-jindal-as-bottom-feeder/, accessed 28 January 2015.

189 Malik, *Al.-Muwatta*, xxx.

190 Bukhari, *Sahih Al-Bukhari*, 4:195

191 Nyazee, The Methodology of Ijtihad, 250-251.

192 Nyazee, The Methodology of Ijtihad, 252-254.

193 Emerick, What Islam is All About, 51.

194 Emerick, What Islam is All About, 162.

195 Keller, *Reliance of the Traveller*, Book A "Sacred Knowledge," § a1.1.

196 Keller, *Reliance of the Traveller*, Book A "Sacred Knowledge," § a1.3.

197 Keller, *Reliance of the Traveller*, Book A "Sacred Knowledge," § a1.4.

198   Keller, *Reliance of the Traveller*, Book A "Sacred Knowledge," § a1.5.

199   Shamim A. Siddiqi, *Methodology of Dawah Ilallah in American Perspective*, (Brooklyn: The Forum for Islamic Works, 1989), Abbreviations/Terminology page, xii. Cited hereafter as Siddiqi, *Methodology of Dawah*.

200   Keller, *Reliance of the Traveller*, Book O "Justice," § o9 "Jihad," §o9.8.

201   Alfred Guillaume, *The Life of Muhammad, A Translation of Ishaq's Sirat Rasul Allah*, Karachi: Oxford University Press, 1955 (reissued in Pakistan, 1967), ¶ 959, p. 645. Cited hereafter as Guillaume, *The Life of Muhammad, A Translation of Ishaq's Sirat Rasul Allah*.

202   Zaid Benjamin, @zaidbenjamin Twitter Feed, 18 July 2014, URL: https://twitter.com/zaidbenjamin/status/490165524232687616, accessed 18 July 2014. Twitter feed states: "Al-Baghdadi to #Mosul Christians: "Choose one of these: Islam, the sword, al-Jiziya (tax) or till Saturday to flee" pic.twitter.com/UoGf8pnYh1."

203   Interpretation of the Meanings of the Noble Qur'an in the English Language: A Summarized Version of At-Tabari; Al-Qurtubi, and Ibn Kathir with Comments from Sahih Al-Bukhari, trans. and commentary by Dr. Muhammad Taqi-ud-Din Al-Hilali, and Dr. Muhammad Muhsin Khan, Darussalam, Riyadh, Saudi Arabia, 1999, Verse 9:5 and associated annotation, 248.

204   Brigadier S.K. Malik, *Quranic Concept of War*, xi. **States:** "This book brings out with simplicity, clarity and precision the Quranic philosophy on the application of military force, within the context of the totality that is JEHAD. The professional soldier in a Muslim army, pursuing the goals of a Muslim state, CANNOT become 'professional' if in all his activities he does not take on 'the colour of Allah.' I have read this book with great interest and believe that it has a useful contribution to make towards this understanding that we jointly seek as citizens of an Islamic State, soldier or civilian."

205   Brigadier S.K. Malik, *Quranic Concept of War*, i. **States:** "Brigadier S.K. Malik has made a valuable contribution to Islamic jurisprudence by representing a comprehensive survey of the Quranic Approach to the Principles of War and Peace. His has been what a scholarly presentation of what may be considered as an "analytic *Re-Statement*" of the Quranic wisdom on the subject of war and peace." (emphasis added)

206   Brigadier S.K. Malik, *Quranic Concept of War*, 58.

207   Brigadier S.K. Malik, *Quranic Concept of War*, 60.

208   Brigadier S.K. Malik, *Quranic Concept of War*, 58.

209   Brigadier S.K. Malik, *Quranic Concept of War*, 57.

210   Brigadier S.K. Malik, *Quranic Concept of War*, 57.

211   Brigadier S.K. Malik, *Quranic Concept of War*, 57.

212   Brigadier S.K. Malik, *Quranic Concept of War*, 57-58.

213   Brigadier S.K. Malik, *Quranic Concept of War*, 57-58.

214   Brigadier S.K. Malik, *Quranic Concept of War*, 60.

215   Brigadier S.K. Malik, *Quranic Concept of War*, 60.

216   Brigadier S.K. Malik, *Quranic Concept of War*, 60

217   Emerson, Steven, "Report on the Roots of Violent Islamist Extremism and Efforts to Counter It: The Muslim Brotherhood," Senate Committee on Homeland Security and Governmental Affairs, July 10, 2008, 8.

218   Sayyid Qutb, Milestones, Salimiah, (Kuwait: International Islamic Federation of Student Organizations. 1978 [written 1966]), 30, 31. Cite hereafter as Qutb, *Milestones*, Salimiah edition.

219   Sayyid Qutb, Milestones (*Ma'alim fi'l-tareeq*), ed by A.B. al-Mehri, Maktabah Booksellers and

Publishers, Birmingham, UK, 2006, 3.

220   Sayyid Qutb, Milestones (*Ma'alim fi'l-tareeq*),ed by A.B. al-Mehri, Maktabah Booksellers and Publishers, Birmingham, UK, 2006, 11.

221   Qutb, *Milestones*, Salimiah edition, 14—15.

222   Fathi Yakan, *Islamic Movement: Problems and Perspective*, trans. Maneh al-Johani, American Trust Publications (ATP), Plainfield, Indiana, 1984, footnote 1, page 2. Cite hereafter as Yakan, *Islamic Movement: Problems and Perspective*.

223   Yakan, *Islamic Movement: Problems and Perspective*, 5.

224   Fathi Yakan, *To be a Muslim*, American Trust Publishing (ATP), Plainfield, IN, 1990, 60. Cited hereafter as Yakan, *To be a Muslim*.

225   Qutb, *Milestones*, Salimiah edition, 80.

226   Qutb, *Milestones*, Salimiah edition, 28-29.

227   Qutb, *Milestones*, Salimiah edition, 28-29 / 139-140.

228   Qutb, *Milestones*, Salimiah edition, 14– 15.

229   Qutb, *Milestones*, Salimiah edition, 34.

230   Qutb, *Milestones*, Salimiah edition, 14—15.

231   Qutb, *Milestones*, Salimiah edition, 247, 248.

232   'Anbari, *The Fundamentals of Takfir*, 137, 138.

233   Interview with Nabil Na'eem, 30 April 2014. Nabil Na'eem was a founding member of Egyptian Islamic Jihad (EIJ) around 1978 along with, among others, his close friend and associate, Ayman al-Zawahiri. Na'eem lead the EIJ from 1988 to 1992. In 2001, EIJ merged with al-Qaeda. Even though the EIJ as essentially listed on the FTO through its al-Qaeda affiliation,* the State Department nevertheless independently listed EIJ on the FTO under Islamic Jihad Union (IJU) in 2005.* Na'eem was imprisoned in 1991 until his release in 2011 during the Egyptian Revolution. Since his release, Na'eem has renounced violence and became a vocal critic of the Muslim Brotherhood during Morsi's tenure. The interview took place in Mr. Na'eem's office on Tahrir Square, Cairo.

*Foreign Terrorist Organizations, Bureau of Counterterrorism, U.S. Department of State, URL: http://www.state.gov/j/ct/rls/other/des/123085.htm.

234   Interview with Nabil Na'eem, 30 April 2014. Nabil Na'eem was a founding member of Egyptian Islamic Jihad (EIJ) around 1978 along with, among others, his close friend and associate, Ayman al-Zawahiri. Na'eem lead the EIJ from 1988 to 1992. In 2001, EIJ merged with al-Qaeda. Even though the EIJ as essentially listed on the FTO through its al-Qaeda affiliation,* the State Department nevertheless independently listed EIJ on the FTO under Islamic Jihad Union (IJU) in 2005.* Na'eem was imprisoned in 1991 until his release in 2011 during the Egyptian Revolution. Since his release, Na'eem has renounced violence and became a vocal critic of the Muslim Brotherhood during Morsi's tenure. The interview took place in Mr. Na'eem's office on Tahrir Square, Cairo.

*Foreign Terrorist Organizations, Bureau of Counterterrorism, U.S. Department of State, URL: http://www.state.gov/j/ct/rls/other/des/123085.htm.

235   Doi, *Shari'ah: The Islamic Law*, 6.

236   Qutb, *Milestones*, Salimiah edition, 16—17.

237   Qutb, *Milestones*, Salimiah edition, 99.

238   Qutb, *Milestones*, Salimiah edition, 28-29 / 139-140.

239   Sheikh Ahmad Gad, Senior Egyptian Muslim Brotherhood member, "Implement Shari'a in Stages" *Ikhwanonline* June 11, 2011, translated by MEMRI as Special Dispatch No. 3969, "Article on

Muslim Brotherhood Website: Implement Shari'a in Phases", 5 July 2011, http://www.memri.org/report/en/0/0/0 /0/0/0/5432.htm, date assessed 8 July 2011.

240   "Sunni Scholar Sheikh Yousuf Al-Qaradhawi: Islamic Law Should Be Implemented Gradually in Egypt; There Should Be No Chopping Off of Hands in the First Five Years," Special Dispatch No. 4463, *MEMRI*, 30 January 2012 from story aired on *Al-Nahar TV* (Egypt), 26 January 2012, at http://www.memri.org/report/en/0/0/0/0/0/0/6043.htm

241   "Muslim Brotherhood General Guide Muhammad Badi': Our Ultimate Goal, Establishing a Global Islamic Caliphate, Can Only Be Achieved Gradually and Without Coercion," *MEMRI* Special Dispatch No. 4486, 10 February 2012, http://www.memri.org/report/en/0/0/0/0/0/0/6075.htm

242   Mohamed Akram, Explanatory Memorandum.

243   Tariq Ramadan, *To Be a European Muslim*, Islamic Foundation: London, 1997, 73.

PART III: THE ISLAMIC MOVEMENT AND ITS AWAKENING

1   Dr. Tariq Ramadan Speaking at ICNA Fundraising – Dallas Chapter, 28 July 2011, (www. amilimani.com), URL: http://www.youtube.com/watch?v=1WDEfVdsr3M, accessed 22 January 2013.(Alternate abridged video - "Tariq Ramadan: We Must Colonize the USA with our Religion," captured by Vladtepesblog.com, posted by MRCtv, 17 June 2012, URL: http://www.therightplanet. com/2012/06/tariq-ramadan-we-must-colonize-the-usa-with-our-religion/, accessed 22 January 2013.)

2   Khadduri, *War and Peace in the Law of Islam*, 64.

3   Tarbiyah Guide, Stage 1, ICNA Chicago Tarbiyah Department, Islamic Circle of North America, Education@ICNAchicago.org (**Note:** Guide pulled from ICNA website). Cited hereafter as Tarbiyah Guide, Stage 1, ICNA Chicago.

4   Qutb, *Milestones*, Salimiah edition, 42, 47.

5   Lewis, Bernard. "The Ottoman Empire and Its Aftermath", *Journal of Contemporary History*, Vol. 15, No. 1 (January, 1980).

6   Kazimi, Nibras. "The Caliphate Attempted" Current Trends in Islamist Ideology, July 1, 2008, URL: http://www.currenttrends.org/research/detail/the-caliphate-attempted

7   Borhany, Shaikh Abbas, PhD. "Brief History of Transfer of the Sacred Head of Husain ibn Ali, From Damascus to Ashkelon to Qahera" *Daily News*, Karachi, Pakistan on January 3, 2009, URL: http://www.durrenajaf.com/upload/51310a3ca52c8.pdf

8   Mitchell, Richard. "The Society of the Muslim Brothers," New York: Oxford University Press (1969).

9   Ibrahim Ghanem, *The West in the Eyes of the Egyptian Islamic Movement – Muslim Brotherhood – Jihad – Islamic Group*, Ummah Press Services, Mohandesseen, Egypt (for subscribers only), 1994, 6. Note: the text in brackets in this citation is original to the source. Cite hereafter as Ghanem, *The West in the Eyes of the Egyptian Islamic Movement – Muslim Brotherhood – Jihad – Islamic Group*.

10   Mitchell, Richard. "The Society of the Muslim Brothers," New York: Oxford University Press (1969).

11   Spage, Ana Belen, "Shaykh Yusuf Al-Qaradawi: Portrait of a leading Islamist cleric," *World Security Network*, 17 March 2008. Accessed 24 April 2011 at http://www.worldsecuritynetwork.com/showArticle3.cfm?article_id=15628&topicID=29

12   Al-Qaradawi, Yusuf. *Islamic Education and Hassan al-Banna*. Beirut: International Islamic Federation of Student Organizations, 1984.

13   MEMRI tape, Qatari broadcast by Qaradawi, MEMRI Tape, 26 February 2006.

14   Tibi, Bassam, "War and Peace in Islam," from *The Ethics of War and Peace: Religious and Secular Perspectives*, ed. Terry Nardin (Princeton, NJ: Princeton University Press, 1996), pp. 128-45, reproduced by Andrew G. Bostom, *The Legacy of Jihad: Islamic Holy War and the Fate of Non-Muslims*, (Amherst, NY: Prometheus Books, 2005), p. 335-336.

15   Jerrold M. Post, *Leaders and their Followers in a Dangerous World: The Psychology of Political Behavior*, (Cornell University Press: Ithica, NY, 2004), 139, citing Amir Tehiri, *Holy Terror*, unknown binding, 1989.

16   Khadduri, *War and Peace in the Law of Islam*, 64.

17   Qaradawi, *Islamic Education and Hassan al-Banna*.

18   Mitchell, Richard. "The Society of the Muslim Brothers," New York: Oxford University Press (1969).

19   "Muslim Brotherhood: Structure and Spread." *Ikhwanweb*, June 13, 2007. http://www.ikhwanweb.com/article.php?id=817

20   Theyabi, Jameel, "The Brotherhood's Power Display," *Dar Al-Hayat*, December 18, 2006, URL: http://english.daralhayat.com/opinion/OPED/12-2006/Article-20061218-95ae9eb8-c0a8-10ed-00b1-7119b3684228/story.html

21   "Muslim Brotherhood: Structure and Spread," *Ikhwanweb*, June 13, 2007. http://www.ikhwanweb.com/article.php?id=817

22   "Egypt's deadly history of political assassinations," *Egypt Independent*, February 7, 2013, URL: http://www.egyptindependent.com/news/fact-box-egypt-s-deadly-history-political-assassinations

23   "Message to the Rebel Ranks," *IkhwanOnline*, 27 January 2015, URL: http://www.ikhwanonline.com/Article.aspx?ArtID=220195&SecID=211, accessed 29 January 2015. Note: The Ikhwanonline declaration went on to quote Banna on the stages before announcing that the Brotherhood in January 2015 should prepare for sustained jihad:

> "'We know that the first stage of power is that of faith and doctrine, followed by unity and commitment, culminating in the power of arms. No clan/group shall be deemed powerful if all aforementioned prerequisites are not satisfied. In the event of a decision to take up arms, failure to meet all prerequisites will ultimately result in the clan/group's destruction/annihilation.' Imam Banna."

> [And then declaring for today's Muslim Brotherhood that] "We are entering a new phase where we summon all our strength and the principles of Jihad, where we prepare ourselves, our spouses, children, and our allies for a prolonged Jihad, seeking the honor of Shihadah (martyrdom)".

24   Rubin, Barry, ed. *The Muslim Brotherhood: The Organization and Policies of a Global Islamist Movement.* Palgrave Macmillan, 2010, 42.

25   Ghanem, *The West in the Eyes of the Egyptian Islamic Movement – Muslim Brotherhood – Jihad – Islamic Group*, 3.

26   Ghanem, *The West in the Eyes of the Egyptian Islamic Movement – Muslim Brotherhood – Jihad – Islamic Group*, 5.

27   Fathi Yakan, *To be a Muslim,* American Trust Publishing (ATP), Plainfield, IN, 1990, 97, 100. Cite hereafter as Yakan, *To be a Muslim.*

28   Yakan, *To be a Muslim*, 84-85.

29   Shaykh Yusuf Al-Qaradawi, *Priorities of the Islamic Movement in the Coming Phase*, Rev. Trans. By S. M. Hasan Al-Banna, Awakening Publications, Swansea, UK, 2000 (originally published 1990), 1, 2.

30   Shaykh Yusuf Al-Qaradawi, *Priorities of the Islamic Movement in the Coming Phase*, Rev. Trans. By S. M. Hasan Al-Banna, Awakening Publications, Swansea, UK, 2000 (originally published 1990), 5. Cite as Qaradawi, *Priorities of the Islamic Movement in the Coming Phase.*

31   Yakan, *To be a Muslim*, 64.

32   Yakan, *To be a Muslim*, 65.

33   Yakan, *To be a Muslim*, 61.

34   Yakan, *To be a Muslim*, 75.

35   Larry A. Posten, "Da'wa in the West," *The Muslims of America*, ed. Yvonne Yazbecr Haddad, Oxford University Press, NY, 1991, 129-130. Relying on Posten, Khurram Murad (1932-1996) came from the Pakistani Jamaat-e-Islami and was a disciple of Mawdudi. "Murad took what were essentially

Eastern ideas and applied them to Western contexts; in so doing he gave a philosophical and strategic coherence to the concept of da'wa in America … **Murad's thinking is becoming increasingly influential in North America; at the 1987 Annual Convention of the Islamic Society of North America he was billed as the keynote speaker,** and his address ended with a ringing challenge to the listeners to both maintain and refine their Islamicity in the midst of a secular environment. If this is done, he stated, America will eventually become a Muslim continent."

36   Khurram Murad, *Islamic Movement in the West: Reflections on Some Issues,* The Islamic Foundation, Leicester, UK (also published by Quran House, Nairobi, Kenya, P.M.B., Kano, Nigeria), 1981, 3. Cited hereafter as Murad, *Islamic Movement in the West: Reflections on Some Issues.*

37   Murad, *Islamic Movement in the West: Reflections on Some Issues,* 3.

38   Murad, *Islamic Movement in the West: Reflections on Some Issues,* 3.

39   Qaradawi, *Priorities of the Islamic Movement in the Coming Phase,* 1.

40   Yakan, *To be a Muslim,* 64-65.

41   Mohamed Akram, Explanatory Memorandum, 18, 32 listed as number 26 (ICNA), 5, 7.

42   Yakan, *To be a Muslim,* 86.

43   Yakan, *To be a Muslim,* 96.

44   Mohamed Akram, Explanatory Memorandum, 4.

45   Ghanem, *The West in the Eyes of the Egyptian Islamic Movement – Muslim Brotherhood – Jihad – Islamic Group,* 10.

46   Ghanem, *The West in the Eyes of the Egyptian Islamic Movement – Muslim Brotherhood – Jihad – Islamic Group,* 10.

47   Toward a Worldwide Strategy for Islamic Policy *(Points of Departure, Elements, Procedures and Missions), 1 December 1982, seized* in November 2001 raid of Muslim Brotherhood leader Yusuf Nada's residence in Campione de Italia, Switerland (Lugano).

48   Fathi Yakan, *Islamic Movement: Problems and Perspective,* trans. Maneh al-Johani, American Trust Publications, Plainfield, Indiana, 1984. Cited hereafter as Yakan, *Islamic Movement: Problems and Perspective.*

49   Yakan, *Islamic Movement: Problems and Perspective,* page 2. "The term [**jahiliyyah**] signifies the pre-Islamic period in Arabia but, by extension, applies to all non-Islamic cultures and influences, including, as here, modern secular society."

50   Yakan, *Islamic Movement: Problems and Perspective,* 5. **For example:** In the past as well as in the present, hardship has been an inherent phenomenon in the **Islamic Movement**. Islam is a call to revolution, revolution against the manifeston (sic) of *jahiliyyah* life in all shapes and forms. It is a revolution against the *jahiliyyah* traditions, and a revolution against *jahiliyyah* laws and legislation.

51   Yakan, *Islamic Movement: Problems and Perspective,* 118. **For example:** "It is also a *jihad* movement because it campaigns for the preparation for *jihad* by all means. That is because truth should have the power to protect itself so that the *da'wah* will be able to face challenges and overcome problems."

52   Yakan, *Islamic Movement: Problems and Perspective,* 74, 105. **For example, at page 74:** "Building the Islamic personality is the first step in preparing for the Islamic government regardless of the methods and tactics of the Movement. The Islamic personality cannot be built and developed unless it is freed from the influence of the *jahiliyyah* society. It should be noted here that what is meant by building the Islamic personality is forming a leading front or a leading organized movement on the level of what is needed for confrontation with the present *jahiliyyah*. The Islamic personality should possess the following main characteristics: *Third*, to consider *jihad*, struggle for Allah's cause to make

Allah's authority supreme on earth, as the main goal of existence. This understanding necessitates an unconditional willingness to sacrifice everything for the sake of this goal." **At page 105:** "Ask yourself how much you are ready to sacrifice for Allah's cause. Many burdens pull you down to the vanities of the world and cover you in dust. Have you ever tried to lessen your burdens and free yourself from their control Fear for your life is a burden which keeps you from *jihad*. You should free yourself from it. Too much concern for your material welfare is a burden which prevents you from devoting your time to your Movement and your Islam. You should get rid of this excessive concern. Devotion to your wife, children, relatives, and tribe are burdens from whose grip you must free yourself. You must in all cases put Islam before other concerns and subject your inclinations to the *shari'ah*, constantly ready to die for Allah's cause. Bukhari and Muslim related that 'Abdullah ibn Abi 'Awf reported that the Prophet said: "Know that Paradise is under the shade of the swords." Muslim related that 'Uqbah ibn 'Amir reported that the Prophet said from the pulpit: "Make ready for them whatever force ... you can. Indeed, force is marksmanship, force is marksmanship, force is marksmanship." Tirmidhi related that Abu Hurairah reported that the Prophet said: "Whoever meets Allah without any mark of *jihad*, meets Allah with a rift."

53   Yakan, *Islamic Movement: Problems and Perspective*, 15. **Note:** Chapter 2 "Hardship in the Life of the Call and the Caller," footnote 8, the first use of the term "jihad" is footnoted to a brief definition of the term as "holy war."

54   Yakan, *Islamic Movement: Problems and Perspective*, 105. **Reads: "Warriors not Philosophers -** Another point worth mentioning in this respect is that the Islamic Movement should be a training camp which produces warriors and heroes rather than being an intellectual institution for spreading Islamic culture and abstract principles. We need awareness, profoundness, and wisdom as much as we need courage, sacrifice, and boldness."

55   Yakan, *Islamic Movement: Problems and Perspective*, 78. **For example:** "The method which the Islamic Movement needs is the same method which produced out of the labyrinth of *jahiliyyah* the best of nations brought forth for mankind. It is the method which has the power to produce in every time and every place a righteous generation which fights for truth and will be victorious until the Day of Judgment. Without this type of person, the Islamic Movement will not be able to confront the *jahiliyyah* reality and achieve victory over it. ... It is the perennial right of Islam that the Islamic Movement's conception and understanding of the nature of the Islamic work be in complete accordance with the spirit of the plan adopted by the first dynamic gathering in the history of lslam (sic). This conception will dictate that the Movement follow the original line which the Prophet followed in confronting the *jahiliyyah* society and establishing the Islamic society. The only results of the difference of modern conception of the nature of the Islamic work and its goals, (sic) are the waste of efforts and exhaustion of resources. Neglect to emulate the first Islamic Movement and a lack of accurate, actual practice of its directions concerning the tactics of individual and collective confrontation have led to a deviation from the main orbit and the important desired goals."

56   Yakan, *Islamic Movement: Problems and Perspective*, 78. **For example:** "Thus the group of the faithful during the Prophet's life continued to advance, offering one martyr after another for the sake of God. Days passed as black as the darkness of night. Other days came with more hardships and ordeals. The procession of truth was on the march along the road of eternity."

57   Yakan, *Islamic Movement: Problems and Perspective*, 21, 22, 118, 119. **For example in recognizing the Muslim Brotherhood leaders:** Following in the footsteps of **al-Banna**, there successively followed processions of martyrs and battalions of combatants who, armed with the Truth, destroyed the thrones of tyrants, shook the castles of the oppressor, and struck terror in the hearts of the nonbelievers ... On the same road also travelled the leader of modern Islamic thought, the author of ***In the Shade of the Qur'an*** and ***Milestones***, the martyr **Sayyed Qutb**. ... It is one constant wish in the hearts of the faithful **"Death in God's cause is our noblest hope."** (21-22)

For example, that the Muslim Brotherhood is the organization that initiated the Movement: "*The*

*Approach of Deep Faith, Accurate Formation, and Continuous Work: The **Muslim Brotherhood**'s Experience.* The **Muslim Brotherhood** is the movement which has spread over the majority of Muslim countries. However, in these countries it is not yet a unified movement in terms of planning and organization. The founder of the movement, the martyr **Imam Hasan Al-Banna**, clarified, right from the beginning, the approach, style, and goal of his movement." (117)

For example, that it is the Muslim Brotherhood that put all the necessary pieces of the movement together in one strategy: "We can see from the above quotations that the **Muslim Brotherhood** movement is distinct from other movements by its comprehensiveness. It is an intellectual movement by virtue of its advocating holding fast to Islamic ideas and rejecting every other idea, legislation, or philosophy (to formulate the Islamic mentality). It is an educational and spiritual movement because it calls for commitment to, and application of, Islamic morals and precepts, and to the purification of the self and to its elevation to the state of piety (to formulate the Islamic personality). It is also a *jihad* movement because it campaigns for the preparation for *jihad* by all means. That is because truth should have the power to protect itself so that the *da'wah* will be able to face challenges and overcome problems. **Imam Al-Banna** alluded to this idea in *To What Do We Call Mankind?*:

> How wise was the man who said: 'Force is the surest way of implementing the right.' How beautiful it is that power and right should march side by side. This struggle to propagate Islam, quite apart from preserving the hallowed precepts of Islam, is another religious duty prescribed by Allah for the Muslims, just as he enjoined upon them fasting, prayer, pilgrimage, *zakat*, doing good and avoiding evil. He required it of them and delegated this task to them. He did not excuse anyone possessing strength and capacity from doing it. It is a Qur'anic verse of warning and a binding order: '**Go forth, light and heavy! Struggle in God's way with your possessions and yourselves.'** (9:41)

The martyred imam emphasized this meaning related to *jihad* in most of his speeches and sermons, because unarmed truth will not achieve anything, and because truth which is not supported by force has no real impact.(118-119)

And, finally, that the Muslim Brotherhood has earned the mantle of leadership through its demonstrated sacrifice of its leaders over time: "*The Islamic Movement, Circumstances of the Area, and Logic of Confrontation.* The movement of the **Muslim Brothers** became a very important movement. It was expected to succeed and to achieve the goal of its existence. Therefore, the powers of destruction everywhere unifed (sic) against it, the forces of imperialism conspired against it, and successive blows befell the **movement**. They began with the martyrdom of its founder, **Imam Hasan Al-Banna**, in 1948. This was followed by the martyrdom of a large number of the leaders and important members of the movement who were considered great men not only in the movement itself, but also in the eyes of the entire world." (119)

58   Hamas Covenant.

59   Roi Kais, "Muslim Brotherhood: Hamas Is Our Role Model," *YnetNews*, December 26, 2011, URL: http://www.ynetnews.com/articles/0,7340,L-4167267,00.html

60   Hamas Covenant, Article 5

61   Muslim Brotherhood Creed. Noreen S. Ahmed-Ullah, Sam Roe and Laurie Cohen, "A rare look at secretive Brotherhood in America; Muslims divided on Brotherhood," *Chicago Tribune*, 19 September 2004,   URL: http://www.chicagotribune.com/news/watchdog/chi-0409190261sep19,0,3008717. story, accessed LexisNexis databases 20 November 2005. See also: Richard P. Mitchell, The Society of Muslim Brothers (New York: Oxford University Press, 1969), 193-194.

62   "Holy Land Foundation Defendants *Guilty* on All Counts," Dallas Morning Star, 24 November 2008.

63   Government's Trial Brief United States of America v. Holy Land Foundation for Relief and Development et. al, United States District Court for The Northern District of Texas, 29 May 2007,

URL: http://online.wsj.com/public/resources/documents/govholyland.pdf, 8-9. Cited hereafter as Government's Trial Brief, U.S. v. HLF.

64   "Islamic Action for Palestine, Internal Memo" October, 1992, entered into evidence in US V. HLF et.al as Government Exhibit, 003-0015 3:04-CR-2404.

65   Government's Trial Brief, U.S. v. HLF, 8-9.

66   Steve McGonigle, "Hamas Leader Denies Leading Double Life in Louisiana," Dallas Morning News, April 28, 1996.

67   Jason Trahan and Tanya Eiserer, "Holy Land Foundation Defendants Guilty on All Counts," Dallas Morning News, November 24, 2008. See also, Matthew Levitt, "Prepared Testimony," "Hearing on 'The Role of Charities and NGOs in Financing of Terrorist Activities," House Banking, Housing and Urban Development Committee, Subcommittee on International Trade and Finance," August 1, 2002.

68   Government's Trial Brief, U.S. v. HLF, 10.

69   Government's Trial Brief, U.S. v. HLF, 11.

70   United States v. Holy Land Foundation for Relief and Development et. al, United States District Court for The Northern District of Texas, Government Exhibit 3:04-CR-240-G, Elbarasse Search 1, 25 September 2008, URL: http://www.txnd.uscourts.gov/judges/hlf2/09-25-08/Elbarasse%20 Search%201.pdf. Cited hereafter as Elbarasse Search 1, U.S. v. HLF. United States v. Holy Land Foundation for Relief and Development et. al, United States District Court for The Northern District of Texas cited hereafter as U.S. v. HLF.

71   U.S. v. HLF, Government Exhibit 3:04-CR-240-G Marzook/IAP 1, 29 September 2008, URL: http://www.txnd.uscourts.gov/judges/hlf2/09-29-08/Marzook%20IAP.pdf.

72   Government's Trial Brief, U.S. v. HLF, 10.

73   U.S. v. HLF, Government Exhibit 3:04-CR-240-G Marzook/IAP 2, 29 September 2008, URL: http://www.txnd.uscourts.gov/judges/hlf2/09-29-08/Marzook%20UASR.pdf.

74   U.S. v. HLF, Government Exhibit 3:04-CR-240-G, Ashqar Wiretap-6, 30 September 2008, URL: http://www.investigativeproject.org/documents/case_docs/1521.pdf, http://www.txnd.uscourts. gov/judges/hlf2/09-30-08/Ashqar%20Wiretap%206.pdf.

75   U.S. v. HLF, Shawn M. McRoberts, RMR, CRR Federal Official Court Reporter, Official Court Transcripts 1, URL: http://www.investigativeproject.org/documents/case_docs/1521.pdf

76   Government's Trial Brief, U.S. v. HLF, entire brief.

77   U.S. v. HLF, Government Exhibit 3:04-CR-240-G, Philly Meeting-1, 29 September 2008, URL: http://www.txnd.uscourts.gov/judges/hlf2/09-29-08/Philly%20Meeting%201.pdf.

78   U.S. v. HLF, Government Exhibit 3:04-CR-240-G, Baker Wiretap-4, 29 September 2008, URL: http://www.txnd.uscourts.gov/judges/hlf2/09-29-08/Baker%20Wiretap%204.pdf.

79   "Shocking Video from Holy Land Foundation Trial," Hannity and Colmes (transcript), August 10, 2007   http://www.foxnews.com/story/2007/08/10/shocking-video-from-holy-land-foundation-trial/

80   Government's Trial Brief, U.S. v. HLF, 17.

81   "Alleged Hamas figure arrested by Md. Police," Baltimore Sun, August 24, 2004.

82   Mohamed Akram, Explanatory Memorandum.

83   Mohamed Akram, Explanatory Memorandum.

84   Memorandum Opinion Order of Jorge A. Solis, United States District Judge, United States

of America vs. Holy Land Foundation, United States District Court for Northern District of Texas, Dallas Division, (Case 3:04-cr-0240-P), 1 July 2009, 15. **Relevant Part Reads:** Government Exhibit 3-85 is titled "An Explanatory Memorandum on the General Strategic Goal for the Group in North America," authored by Mohamed Akram of the Shura Council of the Muslim Brotherhood and dated May 22, 1991. (Gov't Ex. 3-85 (Elbarasse 3) at 21.) The "Explanatory Memorandum" includes a section titled "Understanding the role of the Muslim Brother in North America," which states that the work of the Ikhwan in the United States is "a kind of grand Jihad in eliminating and destroying the Western civilization from within and sabotaging its miserable house by their hands and the hands of the believers so that it is eliminated and God's religion is made victorious over all other religions." (Id.) Also contained in that document is a list of the Muslim Brotherhood's "organizations and the organizations of our friends," which includes ISNA, NAIT, the Occupied Land Fund ("OLF") (HLF's former name), and the United Association for Studies and Research ("UASR"). (Id. at 32.) Government Exhibit 3-64, titled "Preliminary vision for preparing future leadership" and dated December 18, 1988, further ties ISNA to the Muslim Brotherhood by listing it as an "apparatus" of the Brotherhood. (Gov't Ex. 3-64 (Elbarasse 4) at 5.)

85   United States Of America, Plaintiff-Appellee V. Holy Land Foundation For Relief And Development, Et Al, Defendants North American Islamic Trust, No. 09-10875, United States Court Of Appeals For The Fifth Circuit, 20 October 2010, URL: http://docs.justia.com/cases/federal/appellate-courts/ca5/09-10875/09-10875-cr0.wpd-2011-03-16.pdf?1301273939; and United States Of America V. Holy Land Foundation For Relief And Development, Also Known As HLF, Et Al, No. 09-10560, United States Court of Appeals for the Fifth Circuit, 7 December 2011, URL: http://www.ca5.uscourts.gov/opinions/byDate/Dec2011/Dec07/09-10560-CR0.wpd.pdf, accessed 26 January 2014.

86   Memorandum Opinion Order, United States Of America V. Holy Land Foundation For Relief And Development, Crim. No In The United States District Court For The Northern District Of Texas, Dallas Division, 1 July 2009, 16.

87   Memorandum Opinion Order, United States Of America V. Holy Land Foundation For Relief And Development, Crim. No In The United States District Court For The Northern District Of Texas, Dallas Division, 1 July 2009, 7

88   U.S. v. HLF, Shawn M. McRoberts, RMR, CRR Federal Official Court Reporter, Official Court Transcripts 2, URL: http://www.investigativeproject.org/documents/case_docs/1952.pdf.

89   "CAIR Executive Director Placed at HAMAS Meeting," *The Investigative Project on Terrorism*, N.p., 2 August 2007, URL: http://www.investigativeproject.org/282/cair-executive-director-placed-at-hamas-meeting.

90   U.S. v. HLF, Government Exhibit 3:04-CR-240-G, Philly Meeting Summary, 29 September 2008, URL: http://www.txnd.uscourts.gov/judges/hlf2/09-29-08/Philly%20Meeting%20Summary.pdf.

91   U.S. v. HLF, Government Exhibit 3:04-CR-240-G, Philly Meeting-4, 29 September 2008, URL: http://www.txnd.uscourts.gov/judges/hlf2/09-29-08/Philly%20Meeting%204.pdf, 17.

92   U.S. v. HLF, Government Exhibit 3:04-CR-240-G, Philly Meeting-7E, 29 September 2008, URL: http://www.txnd.uscourts.gov/judges/hlf2/09-29-08/Philly%20Meeting%207E.pdf, 4.

93   "CAIR Executive Director Placed at HAMAS Meeting," *The Investigative Project on Terrorism*, N.p., 2 August 2007, URL: http://www.investigativeproject.org/282/cair-executive-director-placed-at-hamas-meeting

94   U.S. v. HLF, Government Exhibit 3:04-CR-240-G, Philly Meeting-7, 29 September 2008, URL: http://www.txnd.uscourts.gov/judges/hlf2/09-29-08/Philly%20Meeting%207.pdf. Cited hereafter as Philly Meeting-7, U.S. v. HLF.

95   Philly Meeting-7, U.S. v. HLF.

96   U.S. v. HLF, Government Exhibit 3:04-CR-240-G, Elbarasse Search-9, 25 September 2008, URL: http://www.txnd.uscourts.gov/judges/hlf2/09-25-08/Elbarasse%20Search%209.pdf.

97   U.S. v. HLF, Government Exhibit 3:04-CR-240-G, Elbarasse Search-7, 25 September 2008, URL: http://www.txnd.uscourts.gov/judges/hlf2/09-25-08/Elbarasse%20Search%207.pdf.

98   U.S. v. HLF, Government Exhibit 3:04-CR-240-G, Elbarasse Search-19, September 2008, URL: http://www.txnd.uscourts.gov/judges/hlf2/09-29-08/Elbarasse%20Search%2019.pdf.

99   US Department of Justice, Office of the Inspector General, Evaluation and Inspection Division: "Review of FBI Interactions with the Council on American-Islamic Relations"; September 2013; 1-20 13-007R, URL: http://www.justice.gov/oig/reports/2013/e0707r.pdf.

100   Elbarasse Search 1, U.S. v. HLF.

101   U.S. v. HLF, Government Exhibit 3:04-CR-240-G, Elbarasse Search-4, 25 September 2008, URL: http://www.txnd.uscourts.gov/judges/hlf2/09-25-08/Elbarasse%20Search%204.pdf.

102   Elbarasse Search 1, U.S. v. HLF.

103   About NAIT, NAIT webpage, URL: http://www.nait.net/NAIT_about_%20us.htm.

104   Memorandum Opinion Order, United States Of America V. Holy Land Foundation For Relief And Development, Crim. No In The United States District Court For The Northern District Of Texas, Dallas Division, 1 July 2009, 14.

105   Affidavit of Dr. Sami Amin Al-Arian, Exhibit C Case 1:08-cr-00131-LMB Document 13-4 Filed 14 July 2008, URL: http://www.investigativeproject.org/documents/misc/152.pdf.

106   Hudson Institute: Center on Islam, Democracy, and the Future of the Muslim World; "Current Trends In Islamist Ideologies" Volume. 17; ISSN: 1940-834X; August 2014, print, URL: http://www.currenttrends.org/doclib/20090411_merley.usbrotherhood.pdf. Cited hereafter as Hudson Institute "Current Trends in Islamic Ideologies."

107   Stanley Boim Complaint Case Doc.; Civil No. 00C-2905; United States District Court for the Northern District of Illinois Eastern Division, Docketed 15 May 2000, *The Investigative Project on Terrorism*, URL: http://www.investigativeproject.org/documents/case_docs/81.pdf. Cited hereafter as Boim Complaint.

108   Levitt, Matthew, "Boim Judgment Upheld: Charity Donations to Terrorist Groups Illegal," Washington Institute For Near East Policy, 3 December 2008, URL: http://www.washingtoninstitute.org/policy-analysis/view/boim-judgment-upheld-charity-donations-to-terrorist-groups-illegal.

109   Hudson Institute "Current Trends in Islamic Ideologies."

110   Boim Complaint.

111   Tifanny Gabbay, "Chicago Man Convicted in Israel of Aiding Hamas Removed From U.S. Terrorist Watch-List," *The Blaze*, 9 November 2012, URL: http://www.theblaze.com/stories/2012/11/09/chicago-man-convicted-in-israel-of-aiding-hamas-removed-from-terrorist-watch-list/

112   "Additional Information on the Islamic Society of North America - Discover the Networks," *Discoverthenetworks.org*, Discover the Networks Organization, n.d., URL: http://www.discoverthenetworks.org/viewSubCategory.asp?id=1938

113   "History of the Fiqh Council," *Fiqhcouncil.org*, Fiqh Council, n.d., URL: http://www.fiqhcouncil.org/node/13.

114   Hudson Institute "Current Trends in Islamic Ideologies" and ISNA Board of Directors http://www.isna.net/board-of-directors.html

115   Hudson Institute "Current Trends in Islamic Ideologies."

116 "The Islamic Movement in Light of International Development and the Gulf Crisis: Studies in Political Awareness and the Islamic Movement," United Association for Studies and Research (UASR) / International Institute of Islamic Thought (IIIT) brochure, Second Conference, held 19-21 July 1991, Herndon, Virginia, editor Ahmed bin Youssef, UASR first printing, December 1991, translated by Investigative Project on Terrorism (IPT), IPT Document Archives.

117 List of "Participant in the Conference," "The Islamic Movement in Light of International Development and the Gulf Crisis: Studies in Political Awareness and the Islamic Movement," United Association for Studies and Research (UASR) / International Institute of Islamic Thought (IIIT) brochure, Second Conference, held 19-21 July 1991, Herndon, Virginia, editor Ahmed bin Youssef, UASR first printing, December 1991, translated by Investigative Project on Terrorism (IPT), IPT Document Archives. **Other names on the list:** Dr. Abd al Majid al Najjar (Tunisia), **Dr, Taha Jaber al Alwani** (Iraq), Dr. Ishaq al-Farhan (Jordan), **Dr. Jamal al Barzinji** (Iraq), Dr. **Sami Al Arian** (Palestine), Dr. Ramadan Abdullah (Palestine), Dr. Hashim al Talib (Iraq), Dr. Tawfeeq al Shawi (Egypt), Dr. Ali Ammar (Lebanon), Dr. Khalil al-Shiqaqi (Palestine), Mr. Mohyi al din Ateyah (Egypt), **Mr. Louay Safi** (Syria), Dr. Mahmoud Zayyid"(Palestine), Mr. Muhammad Fayiz (Tunisia), Mr. Abdul Wahhab Mansur (Egypt), Mr. Taisir al Iyyadi (Tunis8a), Mr. Muhjaj Qahaf (Syria), **Mr. Moussa Abu Marzook** (Palestine), Mr. Ibrahim Hassaballah (Egypt), Mr. Ayyad Hilal (Palestine), Mr. Muhamad Najeeb Yassin (Syria), Mr. Muhammad Abbas (Palestine), Mr. Hamud al Zarihi (Yemen), Mr. Muhammad al Hashimi al Hamidi (Tunis), **Mr. Kamal al Helbawi** (Egypt), **Mr. Muhamad Akram Adluni** (Palestine), Mr. Ali Ramadan (Libya), Mr. Tareq al Aazami (Iraq), Mr. Muhammad al As (Syria), Mr. Munzar Ismail (Sudan), Mr. Salah Hasan (Palestine), Mr. Hajja Abu Judeiri (Sudan), Mr. Faisal al Amin (Libya), Mr. Najib al Ghosh (Lebanon), Mr. Hamud Alimat (Jordan). Mr, Subhi Ghandour (Lebanon), **Mr. Yusuf Talal** (America), Mr. Ayman al Awari (Palestine), Dr. Bashir salih al Rashidi (Kuweit), Dr. Saleh bin Husseib al Ayid (Saudi Arabia), Mr, Zuheir ak Fawat Juma (Morocco), Dr. Akram Khurubi (Palestine), Dr. Ilham al Talib (Iraq), Mrs Wafa Hizzin (Palestine), **Dr. Sayyid Muhammad Said** (Kashmir), Dr. Mani Muhammad al Juhni (Saudi Arabia), Dr. Qutbi al Mahdi (Sudan), Mr. Muhammad al Hilali (Yemen), Mr. Ibrahim Abdel Aziz Suhd (Libya), Mr. Sadeq Abbadi (Iran), Mr. Sami Nasir (Palestine), Mr. Jaafar al Shayyib (Iran), **Mr. Zayyad Hamdan** (Palestine), **Mr. Muhammad Tontanji** (Iraq), Mr. Salae al Sirdari, Mr. Muhammad Hizzin (Palestine), Mr. Muhammad Abdul Rahman (Saudi Arabia), Mr. Hussein Ibrahim, Mr. Murtada Yusuf, Mr. Maysun ak Talib (Iraq), Mrs. Zainab Taha Jabir (Iraq), Dr. Kamal Nimr (Palestine), **Mr. Ahmed Taha al Alwani** (Iraq), Mr. Jamal al Tahir (Tunisia), **Mr. Abdel Rahman al Alamoudi**, Mr. Umar Yahya (Palestine), Mr. Ahmed bin Yusuf (Palestine), Dr. Tariq al Suweidan (Kuwait), Mr. Abdullah Mustafa Mutalliq (Palestine), Mr. Wael Kheiru (Syria), Mr. Ibrahim al Wazir (Yemen), Dr. Hamud al Salwi (Yemen).

118 Patrick Poole's Observations on the List of Participants: Ishaq al-Farhan is the head of the Jordanian MB Islamic Action Front, Ramadan Abdullah (Palestine) may well be Ramadan Abdullah Shallah, the current head of Palestinian Islamic Jihad, on FBI's Most Wanted Terrorist List; Hashim al-Talib (Iraq) is one of the founders of the MSA, founding US Muslim Brotherhood leader; Khalil al-Shiqaqi was the assassinated head of Palestinian Islamic Jihad; Yusuf Talal (Delorenzo) is a IIIT board member; Sayyid Muhammad Said (Saeed) is ISNA's national director of interfaith relations; Mrs. Zainab Taha Jabir (Iraq) is daughter of Taha Jaber al-Alwani, and she's on the board of the FCNA; Tariq Suweidan is a notorious Kuwaiti Muslim Brotherhood leader, close disciple of Qaradawi.

119 "The Islamic Movement in Light of International Development and the Gulf Crisis: Studies in Political Awareness and the Islamic Movement," United Association for Studies and Research (UASR) / International Institute of Islamic Thought (IIIT) brochure, Second Conference, held 19-21 July 1991, Herndon, Virginia, editor Ahmed bin Youssef, UASR first printing, December 1991, translated by Investigative Project on Terrorism (IPT), IPT Document Archives.

120 Document Fragment "D. UASR's Gulf War Conference in June 91," Conference date 19-21 July 1991, PDF copy undated, Investigative Project (IPT) on Terrorism Document Archive.

121 Document Fragment "D. UASR's Gulf War Conference in June 91," Conference date 19-21 July 1991, PDF copy undated, Investigative Project (IPT) on Terrorism Document Archive.

122 Mohamed Akram, Explanatory Memorandum, 5.

123 Mohamed Akram, Explanatory Memorandum, 7.

124 Yakan, *Islamic Movement: Problems and Perspective*, 118.

125 Ghanem, *The West in the Eyes of the Egyptian Islamic Movement – Muslim Brotherhood – Jihad – Islamic Group*, 11-12.

126 Government Exhibit: Philly Meeting—15, 3:04-CR-240-G, U.S. v. HLF, et al., at 2, 3, at http://www.txnd.uscourts.gov/judges/hlf2/09-29-08/Philly%20Meeting%2015.pdf.

127 Coding as explained in Part I (pp. 10-11, 16, 17, 20) along the lines explained by Nyazee, *The Methodology of Ijtihad*, 50, 111, and Marghinani, *Al-Hidaya: The Guidance*, xxiv.

128 "Message to the Rebel Ranks," (trans. Cairo), *IkhwanOnline*, 27 January 2015, URL: http://www.ikhwanonline.com/Article.aspx?ArtID=220195&SecID=211, accessed 29 January 2015.

129 "Message to the Rebel Ranks," (trans. Cairo), *IkhwanOnline*, 27 January 2015, URL: http://www.ikhwanonline.com/Article.aspx?ArtID=220195&SecID=211, accessed 29 January 2015.

130 Jen Psaki, "Daily Press Briefing," *U.S. Department of State*, 29 January 2015, URL: http://www.state.gov/r/pa/prs/dpb/2015/01/236959.htm#EGYPT, 29 January 2015. Note: Georgetown has contested the State Department claim of Georgetown support.

131 Adam Kredo, "Muslim Brotherhood-Aligned Leaders Hosted at State Department, *Washington Free Beacon*, 28 January 2015, URL: http://freebeacon.com/national-security/muslim-brotherhood-leaders-hosted-at-state-department/, accessed 28 January 2015.

132 "Egypt's Sisi Pulls Out of AU Summit after Sinai Attacks," *Al-Jazeera*, 30 January 2015, URL: http://www.aljazeera.com/news/middleeast/2015/01/troops-killed-attacks-egypt-north-sinai-150129230953482.html, accessed 30 January 2015.

133 "Simultaneous Attacks in Egypt's Sinai Peninsula Kill at Least Two Dozen," *New York Times/AP*, 29 January 2015, URL: http://www.nytimes.com/aponline/2015/01/29/world/middleeast/ap-ml-egypt-sinai.html, accessed 30 January 2015.

134 "Statement No. 7, From the Leadership (Command) of the Youth Revolution," *Lovers of Ikhwan*, Facebook Page, 30 January 2015, URL: https://www.facebook.com/LOVERS.OF.IKHWAN/posts/834660719940416 - English translation at URL: https://www.facebook.com/LOVERS.OF.IKHWAN/posts/834660719940416, accessed 31 January 2015.

135 "Egypt Muslim Brotherhood Reiterates Commitment to Non-Violence," *Ikhwanweb*, 30 January 2015, URL: http://www.ikhwanweb.com/article.php?id=31988, accessed 30 January 2015.

136 "Egypt Muslim Brotherhood Reiterates Commitment to Non-Violence," *Ikhwanweb*, 30 January 2015, URL: http://www.ikhwanweb.com/article.php?id=31988, accessed 30 January 2015.

137 William Gawthrop, "Islam's Tools of Penetration," CIFA Working Brief, 19 April 2007, slides 6, 7, 15.

138 No 43, Attachment A, List of Unindicted Co-conspirators and/or Joint Ventures, United States of America vs. Holy Land Foundation, United States District Court for Northern District of Texas, Dallas Division, (Case 3:04-cr-00240, Document 656-2), 29 March 2007, at 8, at http://www.aclu.org/images/asset_upload_file142_36171.pdf. Cited hereafter as Attachment A, U.S. v. HLF.

139 Ibn Kathir, *Tafsir of Ibn Kathir*, vol. 2, 141.

140 Keller, *Reliance of the Traveller*, at § r8.2.

141 Keller, *Reliance of the Traveller*, at § r8.2.

142 Keller, *Reliance of the Traveller*, at §§r7.0, r7.1.

143 Keller, *Reliance of the Traveller*, at §r7.1(1).

144 Former FBI Director Mueller ordered the FBI to cease all dealings and contact with CAIR, possibly and probably because of this type of placard and poster which was posted by San Francisco CAIR. I would hope that all law enforcement officials would follow the lead of the FBI director." Congressman Peter King, "House Homeland Security Committee Holds Hearing on Islamic Radicalization in the United States" (The "King Hearings"), Congressional Hearings, *CQ Congressional Transcripts*, 10 March 2011.

145 Senator John Kyl Questioning Farhana Khera, "Senate Judiciary Subcommittee on Constitution, Civil Rights and Human Rights Holds Hearing on Protecting the Civil Rights of American Muslims" (The "Durban" Hearings"), Congressional Hearings, *CQ Congressional Transcripts*, 29 March 2011. **Reads: Senator KYL**: So, thank you. Let me just refer you to several cases here last year, and then ask you about something on your website. Just last year, U.S. Intelligence agents and our justice system uncovered and prosecuted a number of attempted terrorist attacks that were planned by radical Muslim extremists. A compilation produced by the investigative project on terrorism based on recent Justice Department reports, listed the following incidents on November 27, Mohamed Osman Mohamud was arrested in charge with attempting to explode a car bomb, Portland Oregon. October 27, Faruk Ahmed was arrested for attempting to assist others whom he believed to be members of al-Qaeda in planning multiple bombings in the Metro area here in Washington. October 19th Hosam "Sam" Smadi was sentenced to 24 years in prison for attempting to blow up a skyscraper in Dallas, Texas. October 18th, the Federal court in Manhattan found that James Cromartie and four others were guilty of attempting to detonate the explosives near a synagogue in Bronx. On August 2nd, Russell Defreitas and Abdul Kadir were convicted of a conspiracy to attack John F. Kennedy airport by exploding fuel tanks under the airport. On June 21st, Faisal Shahzad pleaded guilty to attempting to detonate a car bomb in Times Square. He was sentenced for life in prison. On March 18th, David Headley pleaded guilty to the charge that he participated in planning the November 2008 attacks in Mumbai, India, which killed 164 people. Every one of these incidents could have resulted in the deaths of hundreds of people. In fact, the Headley plot, of course, did including six Americans. All of these terrorists were obviously indifferent to whom they killed including women and children. And I think we owe a debt of gratitude to the enforcement agents who identified and stopped the plots before they can be carried out. In—in view of this history, I was curious about your website, the so-called community alert section, which is apparently directed to American Muslims notes, and I quote "The FBI is contacting American Muslims to assist—solicit information and advice about addressing violent extremism. Muslim advocates strongly urges individuals not to speak to law enforcement officials without the presence of a lawyer." And I was stunned that you would issue that kind of instruction to people who would read your site, since obviously, cooperation from Muslim Americans is one of the best way that law enforcement can uncover terrorist plots like the ones that I have described.

And it seems to me that it's the specific obligation of all Americans to assist in preventing these heinous crimes, especially given the participation of Muslims in all of the attempted attacks that I mentioned. I would think that Muslim Americans would feel as a special obligation to help intelligence agencies root this out. Do you think it's wrong to investigate and prosecute the individuals that I mentioned? And do you stand by the Muslim Advocates community alert, instructing Muslim Americans not to cooperate with the FBI and other law enforcement investigating potentials acts of terrorism, or at least not without having a lawyer present?

Ms. Khera: Senator Kyl, you know, I fully understand the threat that we are facing. You know, on September 11th, I was working right here in the Capitol. And I ran from the Capitol with my colleagues as planes—as we thought planes were approaching, so I—I fully understand the threat. Those who engage in criminal act must be stopped and brought to justice. And every

American has a civic duty to report criminal activity to law enforcement. You know, and I might add that Attorney General Holder has actually said that the cooperation of the American Muslim community has been essential to detecting and forwarding terrorist plots. At the same time, every Americans has the right to seek legal advice. And that's a right that's guaranteed to every American. And I think—I know you're lawyer. We're both lawyers, and I think—I think we both know that our legal system is quite complex. And so, encouraging community members to seek legal advice as they interact with law enforcement is something that every American has the right to do.

Senator KYL: So   you   standby   that   statement   on   your   website.

Ms. Khera: I standby all the statements on my website.

146   Keller, *Reliance of the Traveller*, at §§r8.0, r8.1

147   Keller, *Reliance of the Traveller*, §r8 "Lying," r8.1.

148   Keller, *Reliance of the Traveller*, at §r8.2.

149   Keller, *Reliance of the Traveller*, at §r8.2.

150   Keller, *Reliance of the Traveller*, at §r10.3.

151   Seat of the Caliphate, 1915 Fatwa, 23.

152   Kroft, Steven, "Conversations with the Candidates for President of the United State: President Obama," *60 Minutes*, 23 September 2012, URL: http://www.cbsnews.com/video/watch/?id=7422772n&tag =cbsnewsMain ColumnArea.6, accessed 5 October 2012.

153   Johnson, Ian, *A Mosque in Munich: Nazis, the CIA, and the Rise of the Muslim Brotherhood in the West*. Houghton Mifflin Harcourt, 2010.

154   Jamal al-Barzinji, *Islamic Resource Bank.org*. Accessed 26 April 2011 at http://www.islamicresourcebank.org/bios/barziniji%20jamal%20bio.pdf

155   Johnson, Ben, "Troubling Presence at a Funeral," FrontPageMagazine, June 11, 2004. Accessed 26 April 2011 at http://archive.frontpagemag.com/readArticle.aspx?ARTID=12670

156   ACMU Profiles—Louay M. Safi. Louay M. Safi currently serves as Common Word Fellow at the Prince Alwaleed bin Talal Center for Muslim-Christian Understanding, Georgetown University. He also serves as an associate faculty with the Indiana University - Purdue University, Indianapolis, and a non-resident fellow with the Institute for Social Policy and Understanding (ISPU). ACMU Profiles, Edmund A. Walsh School of Foreign Service, Prince al-Waleed bin Talal Center for Muslim-Christian Understanding, Georgetown University, URL: http://www.realcatholictv.com/free/index.php?vidID=ciax-2010-03-07&ssnID=88, accessed 10 August 2011.

157   SAC Chairman Dr. Louay Safi Testimony on Human Rights In Syria: Statement before Tom Lantos Human Rights Commission of the House of Representatives, Washington, D.C., 7/12/2011, URL: http://sacouncil.com/2011/07/13/sac-chairman-dr-louay-safi-testimony-on-human-rights-in-syria/, accessed 24 July 2011.

158   Patrick Poole, "Pentagon Islamic Adviser Reappears as Political Leader for Syrian Muslim Brotherhood-Dominated Group," *Breitbart News*, 25 July 2012, URL: http://www.breitbart.com/Big-Peace/2012/07/25/Pentagon-Islamic-Adviser-Reappears-as-Political-Leader-for-Syrian-Muslim-Brotherhood-Dominated-Group.

159   Liz Sly, "Syria's Muslim Brotherhood is Gaining Influence over Anti-Assad Revolt," *The Washington Post*, 12 May 2012, URL: http://www.washingtonpost.com/world/syrias-muslim-brotherhood-is-gaining-influence-over-anti-assad-revolt/2012/05/12/gIQAtIoJLU_story.html

160   Safi, Louay M., *Peace and the Limits of War: Transcending Classical Conception of Jihad* (Herndon, VA: IIIT, 2001), at 2. Cited hereafter as Safi, *Peace and Limits of War*.

161   Safi, Peace and Limits of War, at 2.

162 "Terminology to Define the Terrorists: Recommendations from American Muslims," The Department of Homeland Security, January 2008. http://www.dhs.gov/terminology-define-terrorists-recommendations-american-muslims

163 "Senate Homeland Security and Governmental Affairs Committee and House Homeland Security Committee Hold Joint Hearing on Threats to Military Communities Inside the Inside the United States," Congressional Hearings, *CQ Congressional Transcripts*, Washington, D.C., 7 December 2011, 34.

164 Safi, Louay M., *Peace and the Limits of War: Transcending Classical Conception of Jihad*. Herndon, VA: IIIT, 2001, 42-43.

165 Mohamed Akram, Explanatory Memorandum, 24.

166 This point is made explicit by the header information associated with Paragraph 17.

167 "History of the Muslim Brotherhood in Egypt," IkhwanWeb, 13 June 2007, URL: http://www.ikhwanweb.com/article.php?id=799.

168 Laith al-Khatib, "The Syrian Muslim Brotherhood's Inflated Revival," Al-Akbar, 27 November 2013, URL: http://english.al-akhbar.com/node/17725.

169 Mohamed Akram, Explanatory Memorandum, 25.

170 Mohamed Akram, Explanatory Memorandum, 24.

171 "Message to the Rebel Ranks," *IkhwanOnline*, 27 January 2015, URL: http://www.ikhwanonline.com/Article.aspx?ArtID=220195&SecID=211, accessed 29 January 2015.

172 Mohamed Akram, Explanatory Memorandum, Paragraph 20, 11, 12.

173 *The Fifth Point of Departure*, Toward a Worldwide Strategy for Islamic Policy *(Points of Departure, Elements, Procedures and Missions), 1 December 1982, seized* in November 2001 raid of Muslim Brotherhood leader Yusuf Nada's residence in Campione de Italia, Switerland (Lugano).

174 *The Ninth Point of Departure*, Toward a Worldwide Strategy for Islamic Policy *(Points of Departure, Elements, Procedures and Missions), 1 December 1982, seized* in November 2001Raid of Muslim Brotherhood leader Yusuf Nada's residence in Campione de Italia, Switzerland (Lugano).

175 *The Seventh Point of Departure*, Toward a Worldwide Strategy for Islamic Policy *(Points of Departure, Elements, Procedures and Missions), 1 December 1982, seized* in November 2001 raid of Muslim Brotherhood leader Yusuf Nada's residence in Campione de Italia, Switzerland (Lugano).

176 Yakan, *To be a Muslim*, 71.

177 Yakan, *To be a Muslim*, 86.

178 *The Eight Point of Departure*, Toward a Worldwide Strategy for Islamic Policy *(Points of Departure, Elements, Procedures and Missions), 1 December 1982, seized* in November 2001 raid of Muslim Brotherhood leader Yusuf Nada's residence in Campione de Italia, Switzerland (Lugano).

179 HAMAS Structure Chart, Exhibit List, USA v. Holy Land Foundation for Relief and Development, 09/23/08 Demonstrative 12, URL: http://www.txnd.uscourts.gov/judges/hlf2/09-23-08/Demonstrative%2012.pdf

180 "About the Author: Shamim A. Siddiqi," URL: http://www.dawahinamericas.com/

181 Sayyid Qutb, *In the Shade of the Qur'an*, Volume VII, Surah 8 (The Martyr [Insha'Allah]), Internet Archive, URL: https://ia600803.us.archive.org/27/items/InTheShadeOfTheQuranSayyidQutb/Volume_7_surah_8.pdf, 21-32.

182 Sayeed Abdul A'la Maududi, "Jihad in Islam." Delivered April 13, 1939. Brirut: Holy Koran Publishing House, URL: http://www.muhammadanism.org/Terrorism/jihah_in_islam/jihad_in_

islam.pdf

183 Sayeed Abdul A'la Maududi, "Jihad in Islam." Delivered April 13, 1939. Brirut: Holy Koran Publishing House, URL: http://www.muhammadanism.org/Terrorism/jihah_in_islam/jihad_in_islam.pdf

184 Sujata Ashwarya Cheema, "Sayyid Qutb's Concept of Jahiliyya as a Metaphor for Modern Society," *Islam and Muslim Societies* (New Delhi), Vol. 2, No. 2, February 2006, pp. 391-410, located online at Academia.edu, URL: http://www.academia.edu/3222569/Sayyid_Qutbs_Concept_of_Jahiliyya_as_Metaphor_for_Modern_Society, accessed 5 October 2014, 2.

185 "About ICNA." Islamic Circle of North America website, URL: http://www.icna.org/about-icna/

186 *ICNA Member's Hand Book*, ICNA Sisters Wing, Tarbiyah Dept, March 2010, URL: http://www.investigativeproject.org/documents/misc/475.pdf. Cited hereafter as *ICNA Member's Hand Book*, ICNA Sisters Wing.

187 Mohamed Akram, Explanatory Memorandum, 4, 8, 12.

188 *ICNA Member's Hand Book*, ICNA Sisters Wing.

189 *ICNA Member's Hand Book*, ICNA Sisters Wing.

190 Islam, Udissa. "Death Penalty for Mueen, Ashraf," Dhaka Tribune, November 2, 2013, URL: http://www.dhakatribune.com/law-amp-rights/2013/nov/03/death-penalty-mueen-ashraf

191 Investigative Project on Terrorism. "ICNA Leader Convicted in 1971 Bangladesh Massacres." November 3, 2013, URL: http://www.investigativeproject.org/4204/icna-leader-convicted-in-1971-bangladesh-massacres

192 Shamim A. Siddiqi, *Methodology of Dawah Ilallah in American Perspective* – Post 9/11 Online Edition, The Forum for Islamic Works, Brooklyn, NY, 1989, URL: http://www.dawahinamericas.com/bookspdf/MethodologyofDawah.pdf, v, vi. Cited hereafter as Siddiqi, *Methodology of Dawah* – Post 9/11 Online Edition.

193 Siddiqi, Shamim. "The Haunting Image of Bin Laden," URL: http://www.dawahinamericas.com/haunting.htm

194 Shamim A. Siddiqi, "Evaluation of Obama's Cairo Speech June 4, 09," Dawah in America portal, 5 June 2009, URL: http://www.dawahinamericas.com/EVALUATION%20OF%20PRESIDENT.htm, accessed 12 January 2010.

195 Siddiqi, *Methodology of Dawah*, xiv.

196 Shamim Siddiqi, *Calling Humanity*, The Forum for Islamic Works, Brooklyn, NY, 2012, URL: http://www.dawahinamericas.com/bookspdf/CallingHumanity.pdf, 245.

197 Siddiqi, *Methodology of Dawah*, 51.

198 Siddiqi, *Methodology of Dawah*, xiv.

199 Siddiqi, *Methodology of Dawah*, 50.

200 Qutb, *Milestones*, Salimiah edition, 28, 29.

201 Siddiqi, *Methodology of Dawah*, 63.

202 Siddiqi, *Methodology of Dawah*, 68.

203 Siddiqi, *Methodology of Dawah*, 46.

204 Qutb, *Milestones*, Salimiah edition, 42, 47.

205 Jenkins, Brian. "Outside Expert's View." From "Homegrown Terrorists in the US and UK: An

Emprirical Examination of the Radicalization Process," Foundation for Defense of Democracies Center for Terrorism Research, April 2009, URL: http://www.defenddemocracy.org/stuff/uploads/ documents/HomegrownTerrorists_USandUK.pdf Posted at DHRA website at http://www.dhra.mil/ perserec/osg/terrorism/radicalization.htm

206 "The Radicalization Process," Unclassified Online Guide to Security Responsibilities. Defense Human Resources Activity, URL: http://www.dhra.mil/perserec/osg/terrorism/radicalization.htm

207 Siddiqi, *Methodology of Dawah*, dedication page.

208 Siddiqi, *Methodology of Dawah*, 116.

209 Kalimah. Shamim Siddiqi, *Looking for the Book of Wisdom*, Islamic Center of North America (ICNA), 1997, URL: http://www.dawahinamericas.com/bookspdf/Book%20of%20Wisdom.pdf, 47.

210 Aqidah. Salafipublications.com, (undated), URL: http://www.thenoblequran.com/sps/sp.cfm?se cID=AQD&loadpage=displaysection.cfm, accessed 23 December 2014.

211 Iman Billah. *The Dawah Program*, Forum for Islamic Work, Brooklyn, NY, 1993, URL: http:// www.dawahinamericas.com/bookspdf/The%20Dawah%20Program.pdf, 53, accessed 23 December 2014.

212 Imaan bil-Akhirah. *Ummah Reflections*, Quarterly Issue No 62, 2012, URL: http://www. ummahreflections.co.za/reflections62.htm or "Belief in the Hereafter," Dr. Waheeduddin Ahmed, "Life, Death and the Hereafter," *Islamic Da'wa Center* Milwaukee, 2009, URL: http://www. dawahcenter.org/?page_id=33, also, regarding Akhirah, Shamim Siddiqi, *Calling Humanity*, The Forum for Islamic Works, Brooklyn, NY, 2012, URL: http://www.dawahinamericas.com/bookspdf/ CallingHumanity.pdf, 244, accessed 23 December 2014.

213 Siddiqi, *Methodology of Dawah*, 71.

214 Mark Schone, "Interrogatio Report of Five American Terror Suspects in Pakistan,"*ABC News*, 11 December 2009, URL: http://abcnews.go.com/Blotter/interrogation-report-american-terror-suspects-pakistan/story?id=9312605, accessed 23 December 2014.

215 "Americans Sentenced in Pakistan for Attempting to Join Terrorist Groups and Fight U.S. Forces," Anti-Discrimination League, 15 December 2010, URL: http://archive.adl.org/main_ terrorism/americans_detained_in_pakistan.html#.U-04U1Zvbnd, accessed 14 August 2014.

216 Al-Qaida / Al-Qaeda (the Base), *Global Security*, URL: http://www.globalsecurity.org/military/ world/para/al-qaida.htm

217 Part I, Chapter II: Objective and Means, Article (2), "Bylaws of the International Muslim Brotherhood," *IkhwanWeb*, URL: http://capro.info/Cults/Islam/Muslim_Brotherhood/Bylaws_of_ the_International_Muslim_Brotherhood.pdf

218 Ayman al-Al-Zawahiri, Knights Under the Prophet's Banner: The Al-Qaeda Manifesto, Asharq al-Awsat, 3 December 2001.

219 "Complete Text of Al-Zawahiri 9 July 2005 Letter to Al Zarqawi," FBIS Document ID EUP20051012374001, accessed on DNI Open Source, 12 October 2005.

220 Abdelmalek Droukdel, "Mali Al-Qaida's Sahara Playbook," *AP*, translated by *AP*, 13 February 2013 (date of translation), URL: http://www.ctc.usma.edu/posts/aqims-playbook-in-mali

221 Paul Cruickshank and Tim Lister, "Zawahiri Messages Underline al Qaeda'a Focus on Syria," CNN, 13 September 2012, URL: http://security.blogs.cnn.com/2012/09/13/zawahiri-messages-underline-al-qaedas-focus-on-syria/.

222 Raymond Ibrahim, *The Al-Qaeda Reader*, (New York: Broadway Books, 2007), p. 116.

223 Ayman al-Zawahiri,"In New Al-Qaeda Clip, Al-Qaeda Leader Ayman Al-Zawahiri Tells Arabs

To 'Take Advantage Of U.S. Weakness To Purge Muslim Lands Of Corrupt Rulers,' Presents 9/11 Hijackers Reading Their Wills, Calls For Kidnapping Citizens Of Countries Fighting The Muslims Zawahiri," MEMRI, September 13, 2012, http://www.memri.org/report/en/print6674.htm

224 Ayman al-Zawahiri, "Sharia and Democracy," from *The Bitter Harvest: The [Muslim] Brotherhood in Sixty Years,* circa 1991, translated and reprinted in *The Al-Qaeda Reader,* ed. and translated by Raymond Ibrahim, (New York: Broadway Books, 2007), p. 128.

225 al-Zawahiri, "Sharia and Democracy," from *The Bitter Harvest: The [Muslim] Brotherhood in Sixty Years,* circa 1991, translated and reprinted in *The Al-Qaeda Reader,* ibid., p. 131.

226 Osama bin Laden, "Moderate Islam is a Prostration to the West," *The Al-Qaeda Reader,* ed. and translated by Raymond Ibrahim, (New York: Broadway Books, 2007), p. 42.

227 Azzam, Sheikh Abdullah, *Join the Caravan.* 2d English ed. London: Azzam Publications, 2001, URL: http://www.islamist watch.org/texts/azzam/caravan/part1.html. Cited hereafter as Azzam, *Join the Caravan.*

228 Abdullah Yusuf Azzam, *New World Encyclopedia* at http://www.newworldencyclopedia.org/entry/Abdullah_Yusuf_Azzam

229 Profile: Ayman al-Zawahiri, BBC News – Middle East, 16 June 2011, URL: http://www.bbc.co.uk/news/world-middle-east-13789286, accessed 27 January 2014.

230 Profile: Ayman al-Zawahiri, BBC News – Middle East, 16 June 2011, URL: http://www.bbc.co.uk/news/world-middle-east-13789286, accessed 27 January 2014.

231 Azzam, *Join the Caravan.*

232 Yusuf Ali, *Qur'an.*

233 Interview with Nabil Na'eem, 30 April 2014. Nabil Na'eem was a founding member of Egyptian Islamic Jihad (EIJ) around 1978 along with, among others, his close friend and associate, Ayman al-Zawahiri. Na'eem lead the EIJ from 1988 to 1992. In 2001, EIJ merged with al-Qaeda. Even though the EIJ as essentially listed on the Foreign Terrorist Organization (FTO) list through its al-Qaeda affiliation,* the State Department nevertheless independently listed EIJ on the FTO under Islamic Jihad Union (IJU) in 2005.* Na'eem was imprisoned from 1991 until his release in 2011 during the Egyptian Revolution. Since his release, Na'eem has renounced violence and became a vocal critic of the Muslim Brotherhood during Morsi's tenure. The interview took place in Mr. Na'eem's office on Tahrir Square, Cairo.

234 Marc Ambinder, "'Brotherhood' Invited to Obama Speech By U.S," *The Atlantic,* 3 June 2009, URL: http://www.theatlantic.com/politics/archive/2009/06/-brotherhood-invited-to-obama-speech-by-us/18693/.

235 "Treaty of Peace and Friendship," Signed at Tripoli November 4, 1796, URL: http://avalon.law.yale.edu/18th_century/bar1796t.asp, accessed 14 August 2014.

236 "Text: Obama's Speech in Cairo," *The New York Times,* 4 June 2009, URL: http://www.nytimes.com/2009/06/04/us/politics/04obama.text.html?pagewanted=all&_r=0.

237 "Avalon Project - The Barbary Treaties 1786-1816 - Treaty of Peace and Friendship, Signed at Tripoli November 4, 1796," *Avalon Project - The Barbary Treaties 1786-1816 - Treaty of Peace and Friendship, Signed at Tripoli November 4, 1796,* Yale Law School, n.d., URL: http://avalon.law.yale.edu/18th_century/bar1796t.asp.

238 Keller, *Reliance of the Traveller,* at o11.10.

239 McCarthy, Andrew C. "National Review Online: Will a Key Anti-terror Tool Fall Victim to Obama's Muslim Outreach?" *NPR.* 10 June 2009, URL: http://www.npr.org/templates/story/story.php?storyId=105190825.

240 "Letter from the Editor," *Inspire Magazine*, Issue 1, Summer 1431/2010, URL: http://azelin.files. wordpress.com/2010/06/aqapinspire-magazine-volume-1-uncorrupted.pdf, 2.

241 Abu Mus'ab al-Suri, "The Jihadi Experiences: The Schools of Jihad," *Inspire Magazine*, Issue 1, Summer 1431/2010, URL: http://azelin.files.wordpress.com/2010/06/aqapinspire-magazine-volume-1-uncorrupted.pdf, 51.

242 Abu Mus'ab al-Suri, "The Jihadi Experiences: The Schools of Jihad," *Inspire Magazine*, 53.

243 Abu Atta, "Don't be Sad – Our Brothers in the Movement f al-Shabab al-Mujahideen," *Inspire Magazine*, Issue 1, Summer 1431/2010, URL: http://azelin.files.wordpress.com/2010/06/aqapinspire-magazine-volume-1-uncorrupted.pdf, 55.

244 Yassin Musharbash, "The Future of Terrorism: What al-Qaida Really Wants, Der Spiegel Online, 08 December 2005, URL: http://www.spiegel.de/international/the-future-of-terrorism-what-al-qaida-really-wants-a-369448.html, accessed 6 November 2012.

245 "MB Chairman: Change and reform require sacrifices," IkhwanWeb, October 5, 2010. Accessed online 5 June 2011 at http://www.ikhwanweb.com/article.php?id=26639&ref=search.php

246 IslamOnline.net, 8 January 2011. Accessed online 5 June 2011 at http://www.islamonline. net/ar/IOLCounsel_C/127840 7253854/1278406720653/-لاتق-ل-ريغ-نيملسملا..-نيمورشملا-ةيعورشملا-واحكم , as translated by IslamOnline.net: "Offensive Jihad Is Permissible to Secure Islam's Borders, to Extend God's Religion, and … to Remove Every Religion but Islam from the Arabian Peninsula", Translating Jihad, Tuesday, January 11, 2011, URL: http://www.translatingjihad.com/2011/01/islamonlinenet-offensive-jihad-is.html, accessed 12 January 2011. Cited hereafter as Translating Jihad from IslamOnline, "Offensive Jihad Is Permissible to Secure Islam's Borders."

247 Jihad from IslamOnline, "Offensive Jihad Is Permissible to Secure Islam's Borders"

248 Jihad from IslamOnline, "Offensive Jihad Is Permissible to Secure Islam's Borders."

249 MB Chairman: Change and reform require sacrifices," IkhwanWeb, October 5, 2010. Accessed online 5 June 2011 at http://www.translatingjihad.com/2011/01/islamonlinenet-offensive-jihad-is. html

250 Dan Robinson, "Obama Tells Mubarak That Transition 'Must Begin Now'," *VOA [Voice of America News]*, 31 January 2011, URL: http://www.voanews.com/content/obama-tells-mubarak-that-transition-must-begin-now-115068399/134370.html.

251 Paul Richter and Peter Nicholas, "U.S. Open to a Role for Islamists in New Egypt Government," *Los Angeles Times*, 31 January 2011, URL: http://articles.latimes.com/2011/jan/31/world/la-fg-us-egypt-20110201.

252 Amir Ahmed, Nic Robertson and Caroline Faraj,"Egypt's Mubarak Resigns after 30-year Rule," *CNN*, 11 February 2011, URL: http://www.cnn.com/2011/WORLD/africa/02/11/egypt. revolution/.

253 Dan Murphy, "Egypt Revolution Unfinished, Qaradawi Tells Tahrir Masses," *The Christian Science Monitor*, 18 February 2011, URL: http://www.csmonitor.com/World/Middle-East/2011/0218/Egypt-revolution-unfinished-Qaradawi-tells-Tahrir-masses.

254 David D. Kirkpatrick, "After Long Exhile, Sunni Cleric Takes Role in Egypt," *New York Times*, 18 February 2011, URL: http://www.nytimes.com/2011/02/19/world/middleeast/19egypt. html?pagewanted=all&_r=0, accessed 27 January 2014.

255 Staff, "Muslim Brotherhood to Establish 'Freedom and Justice Party'," *Egyptindependent.com*, 21 February 2011, URL: http://www.egyptindependent.com/news/muslim-brotherhood-establish-freedom-and-justice-party.

256 Raymond Stock, "The Donkey, the Camel, and the Facebook Scam: How the Muslim

Brotherhood Conquered Egypt and Conned The World," Foreign Policy Research Institute, July 2012.

257　Michael J. Totten, "Hanging with the Muslim Brotherhood," Pajamas Media, 14 July 2011, URL: http://pajamasmedia.com/michaeltotten/2011/07/14/hanging-with-the-muslim-brotherhood/, accessed 18 July 2011.

258　Josh Rogin, "State Department Training Islamic Political Parties in Egypt," *Foreignpolicy.com*, 3 November 2011, URL: http://thecable.foreignpolicy.com/posts/2011/11/03/state_department_training_islamic_political_parties_in_egypt.

259　Richard Spencer, "Muslim Brotherhood Heading for Surprise Victory in First round of Egyptian Election," *The Telegraph*, 25 May 2012, URL: http://www.telegraph.co.uk/news/worldnews/africaandindianocean/egypt/9289123/Muslim-Brotherhood-heading-for-surprise-victory-in-first-round-of-Egyptian-election.html.

260　See, for example David D. Kirkpatrick, "Egypt Elections Expose Divisions in Muslim Brotherhood," *New York Times*, 19 June 2011, URL: http://www.nytimes.com/2011/06/20/world/middleeast/20egypt.html?_r=4&ref=world&pagewanted=all, accessed 22 June 2011; and Sara Sorcher, "Rifts in Muslim Brotherhood Mark Egypt's Political Disarray," *National Journal*, 15 July 2011, URL: http://nationaljournal.com/whitehouse/rifts-in-muslim-brotherhood-mark-egypt-s-political-disarray-20110715, accessed 17 July 2011.

261　Eric Trager, "Reports of the Muslim Brotherhood's Demise Were Greatly Exaggerated," *New Republic*, 28 May 2012, URL: http://www.newrepublic.com/article/world/103654/egypt-election-muslim-brotherhood-morsi.

262　"Top Sunni Cleric says Army Should Kill Kadhafi," *Yahoo! News (AFP)*, 21 February 2011, URL: http://news.yahoo.com/s/afp/20110221/wl_mideast_afp/libyapoliticsunrestfatwa_20110221212046, accessed 27 January 2014; and also "Leading Sunni Scholar Sheik Yousuf Al-Qaradawi Issues Fatwa to Army to Kill Libyan Leader Mu'ammar Al-Qadhafi, MEMRI Clip No. 2819, 21 February 2011, URL: http://www.memri.org/clip_transcript/en/2819.htm

263　David Kirkpatrick, "Allies Open Air Assault on Qaddafi's Forces in Libya." *The New York Times*, 19 March 2011, URL: http://www.nytimes.com/2011/03/20/world/africa/20libya.html?pagewanted=all&_r=0.

264　Paul Cruickshank, "Energized Muslim Brotherhood in Libya Eyes a Prize," *CNN*, 25 March 2011, URL: http://www.cnn.com/2011/WORLD/africa/03/25/libya.islamists/.

265　Praveen Swami, "Libyan Rebel Commander Admits His Fighters Have Al-Qaeda Links," *The Telegraph*, 28 April 2011, URL: http://www.telegraph.co.uk/news/worldnews/africaandindianocean/libya/8407047/Libyan-rebel-commander-admits-his-fighters-have-al-Qaeda-links.html.

266　Jeffrey Kofman and Kevin Dolak, "Moammar Gadhafi Dead: How Rebels Killed the Dictator," *ABC News*, 21 October 2011, URL: http://abcnews.go.com/International/moammar-gadhafi-dead-rebels-killed-dictator/story?id=14784776.

267　Sam Greenhill, "Flying Proudly over the Birthplace of Libya's Revolution, the Flag of Al Qaeda," *Mail Online*, 2 November 2011, URL: http://www.dailymail.co.uk/news/article-2055630/Flying-proudly-birthplace-Libyas-revolution-flag-Al-Qaeda.html.

268　Chris Stephen, "Muslim Brotherhood Fell 'Below Expectations' in Libyan Elections," *The Guardian*, 10 July 2012, URL: http://www.theguardian.com/world/2012/jul/10/muslim-brotherhood-expectations-libyan-election.

269　Tom Henegan, "Libya's Muslim Brotherhood Seen Gaining Influence amid Country's Disarray," *FaithWorld RSS*, *Reuters*, 25 August 2013, URL: http://blogs.reuters.com/faithworld/2013/08/25/libyas-muslim-brotherhood-seen-gaining-influence-amid-countrys-disarray/.

270　"Clinton: Syria's Assad Has Lost Legitimacy to Rule," *Msnbc.com*, 11 July 2011, URL: http://

www.nbcnews.com/id/43711672/.

271   Kenneth R. Timmerman, "Pipes Objects to Fox in the Henhouse," *Daniel Pipes, Middle East Forum*, 19 March 2004, URL: http://www.danielpipes.org/1650/pipes-objects-to-fox-in-the-henhouse.

272   Rachel Ehrenfeld, "The Muslim Brotherhood at Work: Tunisia," *American Center for Democracy*, 27 December 2013, URL: http://acdemocracy.org/the-muslim-brotherhood-at-work-tunisia/.

273   "Tunisia's Islamist Ennahda Party Wins Historic Poll," *BBC News*, 27 October 2011, URL: http://www.bbc.co.uk/news/world-africa-15487647.

274   "A Conversation with Shaykh Rached Ghanouchi," ISNA Net, URL: http://www.isna.net/a-conversation-with-shaykh-rached-ghanouchi.html.

275   Robert Traer, "Human Rights in Islam," *Islamic Studies* 28.2 (1989): 117-29, 12 July 2011, URL: http://tlhrc.house.gov/docs/transcripts/2011_07_12_Syria/SYRIA_TRANSCRIPT_FINAL_29aug11.pdf.

276   About Radwan Zideh, Syria National Council, undated, URL: http://www.syriancouncil.org/en/members/item/356-radwan-ziadeh.html

277   About Loai Safi, Syria National Council, undated, URL: http://www.syriancouncil.org/en/members/item/239-loai-safi.html

278   Liz Sly, "Syria's Muslim Brotherhood Is Gaining Influence over Anti-Assad Revolt," *Washington Post*, 12 May 2012, URL: http://www.washingtonpost.com/world/syrias-muslim-brotherhood-is-gaining-influence-over-anti-assad-revolt/2012/05/12/gIQAtIoJLU_story.html. Cited hereafter as Sly, "Syria's Muslim Brotherhood."

279   "Obama Calls on Assad to Step Down, Imposes New Sanctions," *Fox News*, 18 August 2011, URL: http://www.foxnews.com/politics/2011/08/18/sources-us-call-for-assad-departure-imminent/.

280   "An Arms Pipeline to the Syrian Rebels" - graphic, *The New York Times*, 24 March 2013, URL: http://www.nytimes.com/interactive/2013/03/25/world/middleeast/an-arms-pipeline-to-the-syrian-rebels.html

281   Sly, "Syria's Muslim Brotherhood."

282   Khaled Yacoub Oweis, "Syrian Rebels Elect Islamist-dominated Unified Command," *Reuters*(Amman), 7 December 2012, URL: http://www.reuters.com/article/2012/12/07/us-syria-crisis-rebels-idUSBRE8B60QX20121207.

283   Samia Nakhoul, and Khaled Yacoub Oweis, "Syrian Opposition Urges Review of Al-Nusra Blacklisting," *Reuters*, 12 March 2012, URL: http://www.reuters.com/article/2012/12/12/us-syria-crisis-alkhatib-idUSBRE8BB18A20121212, accessed 28 June 2014.

284   Ruth Sherlock, "Syrian Rebels Defy U.S. and Pledge Allegiance to Jihadi Group," *The Telegraph*, 10 December 2012, URL: http://www.telegraph.co.uk/news/worldnews/middleeast/syria/9735988/Syrian-rebels-defy-US-and-pledge-allegiance-to-jihadi-group.html

285   "US Blacklists Syrian Rebel Group al-Nusra," *Al Jazeera*, 11 December 2012, URL: http://www.aljazeera.com/news/middleeast/2012/12/2012121117048117723.html, accessed 28 June 2014.

286   U.S. State Department, FTO List.

287   U.S. State Department, FTO List

288   Martin Chulov, "Syrian Opposition Selects Ghassan Hitto as Interim Prime Minister," *The Guardian*, 19 March 2013, URL: http://www.theguardian.com/world/2013/mar/19/syrian-opposition-hitto-prime-minister.

289   Robert King, "New Syrian Opposition Leader Educated in Indianapolis," *Indianapolis Star*, 19 March 2013, URL: http://www.indystar.com/article/20130319/NEWS/303190048/New-Syrian-

opposition-leader-educated-Indianapolis?nclick_check=1.

290 American Islamist Selected to Run Syrian Opposition," *Investigative Project on Terrorism*, 21 March 2013, URL: http://www.investigativeproject.org/3951/american-islamist-selected-to-run-syrian.

291 "Top Cleric Qaradawi Calls for Jihad against Hezbollah, Assad in Syria," *Al Arabiya News*, 2 June 2013, URL: http://english.alarabiya.net/en/News/middle-east/2013/06/02/Top-cleric-Qaradawi-calls-for-Jihad-against-Hezbollah-Assad-in-Syria.html.

292 "Official Confirms, Defends White House Meeting with Controversial Muslim Scholar," *Fox News*, 27 June 2013, URL: http://www.foxnews.com/politics/2013/06/27/official-confirms-defends-white-house-meeting-with-controversial-muslim-scholar/.

293 Steven Emerson and John Rossomando, "Exclusive: Banned Cleric's Outspoken Deputy Visits White House," *IPT News*, *Investigative Project on Terrorism*, 26 June 2013, URL: http://www.investigativeproject.org/4055/exclusive-banned-cleric-outspoken-deputy-visits.

294 Sly, Liz Sly, "Islamic Law Comes to Rebel-held Syria," *Washington Post*, 20 March 2013, URL: http://www.washingtonpost.com/world/middle_east/islamic-law-comes-to-rebel-held-syria/2013/03/19/b310532e-90af-11e2-bdea-e32ad90da239_story_2.html.

295 Sara Carter, "Muslim Brotherhood in Syria: Shari'a or Death," *The Blaze*, 4 September 2013, URL: http://www.theblaze.com/stories/2013/09/04/muslim-brotherhood-in-syria-sharia-or-death/.

296 Brenden Bordelon, "McCain Rejects Report Claiming Syrian Rebels Are Largely Jihadis," *The Daily Caller*, 18 September 2013, URL: http://dailycaller.com/2013/09/18/mccain-rejects-report-claiming-syrian-rebels-are-largely-jihadis, also Mark Hosenball, Mark and Phil Stewart, "Kerry Portrait of Syria Rebels at Odds with Intelligence Reports." *Reuters*, 05 March 2013, URL: http://www.reuters.com/article/2013/09/05/us-syria-crisis-usa-rebels-idUSBRE98405L20130905.

PART IV: ORGANIZATION OF THE ISLAMIC CALIPHATE

1 Article 6, *Charter of the Organisation of the Islamic Conference*, URL: http://www.oic-oci.org/is11/english/Charter-en.pdf

2 Organization of The Islamic Conference—About OIC, URL: http://oic-oci.org/page_detail.asp?p_id=52

3 "About the OIC," Organization of The Islamic Conference webpage, URL: http://www.oic-oci.org /page_detail.asp?p_id=52

4 Article 6, *Charter of the Organisation of the Islamic Conference.*

5 Article 6, *Charter of the Organisation of the Islamic Conference*, URL: http://www.oic-oci.org/is11/english/Charter-en.pdf

6 Articles 6 and 7, *Charter of the Organisation of the Islamic Conference*, URL: http://www.oic-oci.org/is11/english/Charter-en.pdf. **Reads: [Article 6]** The Islamic Summit is composed of Kings and Heads of State and Government of Member States and is the supreme authority of the Organisation [sic]. It convenes once every three years to deliberate, take policy decisions and provide guidance on all issues pertaining to the realization of the objectives and consider other issues of concern to the Member States and the *Ummah.* **[Article 7]** The Islamic Summit shall deliberate, take policy decisions and provide guidance on all issues pertaining to the realization of the objectives as provided for in the Charter and consider other issues of concern to the Member States and the *Ummah.*

7 Article 10, Chapter V "Council of Foreign Ministers," Charter of the Organization of the Islamic Conference.

8 Ekmeleddin Ihsanoglu, Secretary General, Organization of the Islamic Conference, *Speech at 35th Session of Council of Foreign Ministers of the OIC*, Kampala, Uganda June 2008, URL: http://www.oic-oci.org/35cfm/english/doc/SPSG-35CFM.pdf

9 Ekmeleddin Ihsanoglu, *Speech at 35th Session of Council of Foreign Ministers of the OIC.*

10 Ye'or, Bat. "The OIC and the Modern Caliphate," The American Thinker. September 26, 2010, URL: http://www.americanthinker.com/2010/09/oic_and_the_modern_caliphate.html

11 Keller, *Reliance of the Traveller*, 638. (Book O "Justice," § o25.0 "The Caliphate.")

12 Keller, *Reliance of the Traveller*, 23. (Book B "The Validity of Following Qualified Scholarship," § b7.0 "Scholarly Consenus [Ijma].")

13 Patrick Goodenough, "OIC Fulfills Function of Caliphate, Embodies 'Islamic Solidarity,' Says OIC Chief," *CNSNews*.com, 10 May 2010, URL: http://www.cnsnews.com/news/article/oic-fulfills-function-caliphate-embodies-islamic-solidarity-says-oic-chief

14 Abdullah Ahsan, *OIC: The Organization of the Islamic Conference, an Introduction to an Islamic Political Institution*, (IIIT, Herndon, VA, 1988), 53-4. Cited hereafter as Ahsan, *OIC: An Introduction.*

15 Ahsan, *OIC: An Introduction*, 53-54.

16 Ahsan, *OIC: An Introduction*, 1.

17 Patrick Goodenough, "OIC Fulfills Function of Caliphate, Embodies 'Islamic Solidarity,' Says OIC Chief," CNSNews.com, 10 May 2010, URL: http://www.cnsnews.com/news/article/oic-fulfills-function-caliphate-embodies-islamic-solidarity-says-oic-chief

18 Twitter / MohamedElibiary: @davereaboi, 13 June 2014, URL: https://twitter.com/mohamedelibiary/status/477510829261066241, accessed 18 June 2014. **Actual Tweet:** "As I've said b4 inevitable that "Caliphate" returns. Choice only whether we support EU like Muslim Union

vision or not." [...] US heading in that direction. Bush created OIC Special Envoy. Obama removed discriminatory engagement policy towards MB, etc."

19   OIC Convention of Combating International Terrorism, OIC Permanent Observer Mission to the United Nations in New York, UN Web address http://www.oicun.org/7/38/ — or OIC web address http://www.oic-oci.org/english/convenion/terrorism_convention.htm

20   Said Raja i-Khorassani, Permanent Delegate to the UN from the Islamic Republic of Iran, 1985, as cited in "Why Do Some Muslims Hold Ayatollah Ruhollah Khomeini As a Hero?"Robert Spencer, 18 November 2004, URL: http://www.servat.unibe.ch/icl/sa00000_.html

21   Declaration of Independence, Preamble. "When in the Course of human events, it becomes necessary ... to assume ... the separate and equal station to which the Laws of Nature and of Nature's God entitled them ... We hold these truths to be self-evident, that all men are created equal, that they are endowed by their Creator with certain unalienable Rights ..."

22   For example, see *Reliance of the Traveller*, Section w8.0 Allah is Exalted above Needing Space or Time (from a4.3), "There is nothing whatsoever like unto Him, and He is the All-being, the All-seeing" (Koran 42:11), and "He did not give birth, nor was He born, and there is none who is His equal," (Koran 112:3-4). Aside from all the proofs from the Koran and sunna, the rational evidence is decisive that Allah Most High is absolutely beyond any resemblance to created things.

23   Keller, *Reliance of the Traveller,* Book W at w8.0 "Allah is Exalted above Needing Space or Time," at §w8.0.

24   *Cairo Declaration on Human Rights in Islam*, United Nations UNESCO portal at http://portal. unesco.org/shs/en/ev.php-URL_ID=4686&URL_DO=DO_TOPIC&URL_SECTION=201.html. Cited hereafter as OIC, *Cairo Declaration.*

25   Legal Affairs, §123, Final Communique of the Twenty-Seventh Session of the Islamic Conference of Foreign Minister (Session of Islam and Globalization), Kuala Lumpur, Malaysia, 27-30 June 2000, URL: http://www.oic-oci.org/english/conf/fm/27/final27.htm

26   "Recommendations," Twenty-Eighth Session of the Islamic Conference of Foreign Ministers, Bamako, URL: http://unispal.un.org/unispal.nsf/9a798adbf322aff38525617b006d88d7/c072a96931 75d07d85256a78004b1af2?OpenDocument

27   Human Rights Library, "Cairo Declaration," URL: http://www1.umn.edu/humanrts/instree/cairodeclaration.html

28   OIC Convention to Combat Terrorism (1999-1420H), formal title "Convention of the Organization of the Islamic Conference on Combating International Terrorism," OIC Permanent Observer Mission to the United Nations in New York, UN Web address http://www.oicun.org/7/38/ — or OIC web address http://www.oic-oci.org/english/convenion/ terrorism_convention.htm

29   OIC Convention to Combat Terrorism (1999-1420H), formal title "Convention of the Organization of the Islamic Conference on Combating International Terrorism," OIC Permanent Observer Mission to the United Nations in New York, UN Web address http://www.oicun.org/7/38/ — or OIC web address http://www.oic-oci.org/english/convenion/ terrorism_convention.htm

30   OIC Convention to Combat Terrorism (1999-1420H), formal title "Convention of the Organization of the Islamic Conference on Combating International Terrorism," OIC Permanent Observer Mission to the United Nations in New York, UN Web address http://www.oicun.org/7/38/ — or OIC web address http://www.oic-oci.org/english/convenion/ terrorism_convention.htm

31   "Indian Clerics Conference Issues World's First Anti-Terror Fatwa," MEMRI Special Dispatch Series No. 1959, 13 June 2008, URL: http://www.memri.org/bin/articles.cgi?Page=archives&Area=sd &ID=SP195908. Cited hereafter as MEMRI Special Dispatch 1959.

32   MEMRI Special Dispatch 1959.

33 See, for example, RESOLUTION NO. 43/23-P: "On Convening of an International Conference under the Auspices of the UN to Define Terrorism and Distinguish it from Peoples' Struggle for National Liberation" or RESOLUTION NO. 44/23-P: "On The Follow-up of the Code of Conduct for Combating International Terrorism," Report and Resolutions on Political, Muslim Minorities & Communities, Legal and Information Affairs, Adopted at the Twenty-Third Islamic Conference of Foreign Ministers (Session of Peace, Solidarity and Tolerance) Conakry, Republic of Guinea, 17-20 Rajab 1416H (9-12 December, 1995), URL: http://www.oic- oci.org/oicnew/english/conf/fm /23/Resolutions23-P.htm

34 RESOLUTION No. 7/30-LEG – "On Convening an International Conference Under the Auspices of the UN to Define Terrorism and Distinguish it from Peoples' Struggle for National Liberation," Resolutions on Legal Affairs Adopted by the Thirtieth Session of the Islamic Conference of Foreign Ministers (Session of Unity and Dignity), Tehran, Islamic Republic of Iran, 27-29 Rabi-ul-Awal, 1424H 28-30 May, 2003, URL: http://www.oic-oci.org/oicnew/english/conf/fm/30/30%20 icfm-leg-e.htm. Cited hereafter as OIC Resolution No. 7/30-LEG – Tehran 2003.

35 RESOLUTION No. 2/31-LEG: "On the Follow-up of the Cairo Declaration on Human Rights in Islam," Resolutions on Legal Affairs Adopted by the Thirty-First Session of the Islamic Conference of Foreign Ministers (Session of the Progress and Global Harmony), Istanbul, Republic of Turkey, 26-28 Rabiul Thani 1425H (14-16 June 2004), URL: http://www.oic-oci.org/oicnew/english/conf/fm/31/31%20icfm-leg- eng.htm. Cited hereafter as OIC Resolution No. 2/31-LEG – Istanbul 2004.

36 RESOLUTION No. 6/30-LEG: "On the OIC Convention on Combating International Terrorism Resolution," Resolutions on Legal Affairs Adopted by the Thirtieth Session of the Islamic Conference of Foreign Ministers (Session of Unity and Dignity), Tehran, Islamic Republic of Iran, 27-29 Rabi-ul-Awal, 1424H 28-30 May, 2003, URL: http://www.oic-oci.org/oicnew/english/conf/fm/30/30%20icfm-leg-e.htm. Cited hereafter as OIC Resolution No. 6/30-LEG – Tehran 2003.

37 RESOLUTION No. 6/31-LEG: "The OIC Convention on Combating International Terrorism," Resolutions on Legal Affairs Adopted by the Thirty-First Session of the Islamic Conference of Foreign Ministers (Session of the Progress and Global Harmony), Istanbul, Republic of Turkey, 26-28 Rabiul Thani 1425H (14-16 June 2004), URL: http://www.oic-oci.org/oicnew/english/conf/fm/31/31%20 icfm-leg-eng.htm. Cited hereafter as OIC Resolution No. 6/31-LEG – Istanbul 2004.

38 Sayyid Qutb, *Islam and Universal Peace*, American Trust Publications (ATP), Plainfield, IN, 1993 (last print 1977), 71. **States**: "Accordingly, Muslims have a responsibility towards humanity. They are to achieve peace on earth, within themselves, at home and in society. It is a peace based on recognizing God's oneness and omnipotence, on instituting justice, equality and liberty; and on achieving social equilibrium and cooperation." Cited hereafter as Qutb, *Islam and Universal Peace*.

39 Qutb, *Islam and Universal Peace*, 10. **States**: "In order to propagate the oneness of God on earth and to put an end to the power of those who, by word or deed, challenge His omnipotence, Islam allows Muslims to fight. Such is the only war allowed in Islam."

40 Slide 12 "Muslims in the Military," Major Hasan, "The Koranic World View as it Relates to Muslims in the U.S. Military.". **In Part Reads:** [17:33] "And do not kill anyone whose killing Allah has forbidden, except for a just cause."

41 Slide 12 "Muslims in the Military," Major Hasan, "The Koranic World View as it Relates to Muslims in the U.S. Military."

42 Ibn Kathir, *Tafsir Ibn Kathir*, vol 2, 542.

43 Ibn Kathir, *Tafsir Ibn Kathir*, vol. 5, 618.

44 Ibn Kathir, *Tafsir Ibn Kathir*, vol. 3, 158.

45 Ibn Kathir, *Tafsir Ibn Kathir*, vol. 3, 159.

46   Keller, *Reliance of the Traveller*, Book O "Justice," at o1.0 "Who is Subject to Retaliation for Injurious Crimes" at §o1.0.

47   Keller, *Reliance of the Traveller*, Book O "Justice," o1.0 "Who is Subject to Retaliation for Injurious Crimes" at §o1.1.

48   Keller, *Reliance of the Traveller*, Book O "Justice," o1.0 "Who is Subject to Retaliation for Injurious Crimes" at §o1.2.

49   OIC Resolution No. 7/30-LEG – Tehran 2003.

50   OIC Resolution No. 2/31-LEG – Istanbul 2004.

51   OIC Resolution No. 7/30-LEG – Tehran 2003.

52   OIC Resolution No. 2/31-LEG – Istanbul 2004.

53   OIC Resolution No. 7/30-LEG – Tehran 2003.

54   OIC Resolution No. 2/31-LEG – Istanbul 2004.

55   OIC Resolution No. 7/30-LEG – Tehran 2003.

56   OIC Resolution No. 2/31-LEG – Istanbul 2004.

57   "Jihad against Jews and Crusaders World Islamic Front Statement," *Al-Quds Al-Arabi* (English), 23 February 1998, translation posted on the Federation of American Scientists (FAS), URL: http://www.fas.org/irp/world/para/docs/980223-fatwa.htm, accessed 5 February 2013. Cited hereafter as "Jihad against Jews and Crusaders World Islamic Front Statement," *Al-Quds Al-Arabi* (FAS).

58   Keller, *Reliance of the Traveller*, Certification page, Al-Azhar, xx. Reads: "We certify that the above-mentioned translation corresponds to the Arabic original and conforms to the practice and faith of the Orthodox Sunni Community (*Ahl al-Sunna wa al-Jama'a*)."

59   Keller, *Reliance of the Traveller*, Certification page, Al-Azhar, xviii. **Document Letter Heading and Signature Block:** The letter heading states that the certification comes from the International Institute of Islamic Thought (IIIT). The signature is from Dr. Taha Jabir al-'Alwani. His signature block states that he is signing in his capacity as the President of the IIIT, as President of the Fiqh Council of North America (FCNA), and as a member of the Islamic Fiqh Academy in Jedda. Both the IIIT and FCNA are associated with the Muslim Brotherhood in the *Explanatory Memorandum: On the General Strategic Goal for the Group*," Mohamed Akram, May 22, 1991, Government Exhibit 003-0085/3:04-CR-240-G U.S. v. HLF, et al., United States District Court, Northern District of Texas, URL: http://www.txnd.uscourts.gov/judges/hlf2/09-25-08/Elbarasse%20Search%203.pdf. The FCNA is also a subordinate element of the Islamic Society of North America (ISNA). The International Islamic Fiqh Academy (IIFA) is listed as a subsidiary organ of the OIC at "Subsidiary Organs, Organization of the Islamic Cooperation," OIC, URL: http://www.oic-oci.org/page_detail. asp? p _id=64#FIQH, 4 Feburary 2013. It was affiliated to the OIC in its fourteenth session, held in Duha (Qatar) 5–13 Dhul-Qi`dah1423 A.H., 11–16 January 2003 C.E, as cited in "*Jihad*: Rulings & Regulations," "Living Shari'a/Fatwa Bank," *IslamOnline*, URL: http://www.freerepublic.com/focus/news/2390531/replies?c=7

60   Keller, *Reliance of the Traveller*, Book O "Justice," at o9.0 "Jihad" at §o9.3 "Obligatory Character of Jihad."

61   Bill Gertz, "Constitutional Religious Clause Prevents Obama Administration from Countering Islamic State Ideology," *The Washington Free Beacon*, 7 October 2014, URL: http://freebeacon.com/national-security/surrender-in-the-war-of-ideas/, accessed 30 December 2014.

62   Josh Rushing, "US Military Under Fire for 'Anti-Islam Class'" (transcript), *Al-Jazeera* TV (Washington Office), 12 May 2012, URL: http://www.aljazeera.com/video/americas/2012/05/20125124178148367.html alternatively released on YouTube URL: http://www.

youtube.com/ watch? feature=player_embedded&v=2swVVfZo5eM#!, accessed 20 May 2012.

63   David Martosko, "EXCLUSIVE: Deputy of banned cleric Yusuf al-Qaradawi who endorses Palestinian suicide bombers had White House meeting with National Security Council staff," Mail (London), 25 June 2013, URL: http://www.dailymail.co.uk/news/article-2348479/EXCLUSIVE-Deputy-banned-suicide-bomb-endorsing-cleric-Yusuf-al-Qaradawi-White-House-meeting-National-Security-Council-staff.html, accessed 24 August 2014.

64   "Senior Muslim Clerics use Arab Satellite Television to Condemn Violence in the Name of Islam," *Arabic Media Issues Report*, 16 October 2007 citing Sheikh Yusuf Al-Qaradawi, *Shari'a and Life*, *Al-JazeeraTV*, 30 September 2007.

65   "This is the Promise of Allah – English Declaration of Khaliphate," *Al Hayat Media Center*, 29 June 2014, URL: https://ia902505.us.archive.org/28/items/poa_25984/EN.pdf (originally located at English Declaration, URL: https://drive.google.com/file/d/0Bwcwh5A29xpwbFktY2JwWUFmUlU/preview?pli=1), accessed 29 June 2014, 7. Cited hereafter as ISIS - "This is the Promise of the Allah."

66   ISIS - "This is the Promise of the Allah," 7. **States:** So let those leaders be ruined. And let that "ummah" they want to unite be ruined - an "ummah" of secularists, democrats, and nationalists … an "ummah" of murji'ah (a sect that excludes deeds from faith), ikhwan (the "Muslim Brotherhood" party), and suriiriyyah (a sect influenced by the ikhwan claiming to be Salafi)."

67   "Qaradawi says 'Jihadist Caliphate' Violates Sharia," *"Al Arabiya News*, 5 July 3014, URL: http://english.alarabiya.net/en/News/middle-east/2014/07/05/Qaradawi-says-jihadist-caliphate-violates-sharia-.html, accessed 31 December 2014.

68   "Prominent Scholars Declare ISIS Caliphate 'Null and Void,'" Middle East Monitor, 5 July 2014, URL: https://www.middleeastmonitor.com/news/middle-east/12567-prominent-scholars-declare-isis-caliphate-null-and-void, accessed 31 December 2014.

69   MEMRI Special Dispatch No. 794, "Reactions to Sheikh Al-Qaradhawi's Fatwa Calling for the Abduction and Killing of American Civilians in Iraq," MEMRI Special Dispatch No.794, 6 October 2004, URL: http://www.memri.org/report/en/0/0/0/0/0/0/1231.htm, accessed 5 May 2007. Cited hereafter as MEMRI Special Dispatch No. 794. "Reaction to Qaradawi Fatwa."

70   MEMRI Special Dispatch No. 794. "Reaction to Qaradawi Fatwa."

71   MEMRI TV Monitor Project, "Mahdi 'Akef, Supreme Guide of the Muslim Brotherhood Warns Egyptian Regime: The People Will Trample You Underfoot," Clip No. 1214, 30 July 2006, URL: http://www.memritv.org/Transcript.asp?P1=1214, accessed 20 May 2007.

72   INTERPOL Wanted Notice for Yousf Al Qaradawi, INTERPOL Red Notice, (undated, 2014), URL: http://www.interpol.int/notice/search/wanted/2014-58772, accessed 5 December 2014.

73   Keller, *Reliance of the Traveller*, Book O "Justice," at o9 "Jihad," at o9.3.

74   "Interview with Mohammed Akef, Supreme Guide, International Muslim Brotherhood," Elaph Publishing (in Arabic), 22 May 2008, URL: www.elaph.com. (Elaph Publishing is a Saudi-owned London-based publishing entity.)

75   The Fiqh Council of North America, About Us, 28 February 2010, URL: http://fiqhcouncil.org/AboutUs /tabid/175/Default.aspx. Cited hereafter as About Us, FCNA.

76   "What it Means to be a Muslim in America," Prince Alwaleed bin Talal Center for Muslim-Christian Understanding, Georgetown University, 19 April 2007, URL: http://events.georgetown.edu/events/index.cfm?Action=View&Calandar ID=106&EventID=49881

77   "Islamic Law has Consistently Condemned Terrorism," Imam Yahya Hendi, Fatwas, issued 25 July 2005, URL: http://www.imamyahyahendi.com/fatwas_terrorism.htm

78   The European Council for Fatwa Research, 22 July 2001, URL: http://www.e- cfr.org/en/ECFR.

pdf, 4. Cited hereafter as ECRF.

79   Sheikh Faysal Mawlawi, "*Fatwa* Questions About Palestine," MAS – *The American Muslim*, Vol. 3, no. 2, June 2002.

80   "Martyr Operations or Terrorism," Ask the Scholar, Fatwa Bank, *IslamOnline*, 27 January 2004, URL: http://islamonline.net/servlet/Satellite?pagename=IslamOnline-English-Ask_Scholar/FatwaE/FatwaE&cid=1119503546498, accessed 22 June 2010 ... NOTE: Cites "Islamic Fiqh Academy affiliated to the OIC in its fourteenth session, held in Duha (Qatar) 5–13 Dhul-Qi`dah1423 A.H., 11–16 January 2003 C.E, as cited in "Jihad: Rulings & Regulations."

81   "Jihad against Jews and Crusaders World Islamic Front Statement," *Al-Quds Al-Arabi* (FAS).

82   Subsidiary Organs, Organization of the Islamic Cooperation, undated, OIC, URL: http://www.oic-oci.org/page_detail.asp? p_id=64#FIQH, 4 February 2013.

83   "Imam of the Prophet's Mosque in Medina, Saudi Arabia, in Support of Jihad against Christian American Presence in the Middle East" [also titled "Sheik Muhammad Al-Suhaybani, Imam of the Prophet's Mosque in Medina, Saudi Arabia"], the Internet 30 August 2014, MEMRI Video Clip #4469, URL: http://www.memritv.org/clip/en/4469.htm, MEMRI transcript of #4469 Video Clip URL: http://www.memritv.org/clip_transcript/en/4469.htm, accessed 4 September 2014.

84   Salam Al-Marayati, MPAC Letter of Senator Lieberman, 16 June 2010.

85   A Review of U.S. Counterterrorism Policy: American Muslim Critique & Recommendations,Muslim Public Affairs Council, September 2003, URL: http://www.mpac.org/publications/counterterrorism-policy- paper/counterterrorism-policy-paper.pdf

86   "Martyr Operations or Terrorism," Ask the Scholar, Fatwa Bank, *IslamOnline*, 27 January 2004, URL: http://islamonline.net/servlet/Satellite?pagename=IslamOnline-English-Ask_Scholar/FatwaE/FatwaE&cid=1119503546498, accessed 22 June 2010 ... NOTE: : : Cites "Islamic Fiqh Academy affiliated to the OIC in its fourteenth session, held in Duha (Qatar) 5–13 Dhul-Qi`dah1423 A.H., 11–16 January 2003 C.E, as cited in "Jihad: Rulings & Regulations."

87   "Universal Declaration of Human Rights," United Nations, URL: http://www.un.org/en/documents/udhr/

88   Keller, *Reliance of the Traveller*, at § r2.2.

89   Keller, *Reliance of the Traveller*, at § r23.

90   *Black's Law Dictionary 9ᵗʰ*, Bryan A. Garner, Editor in Chief, West Publishing (Thomson Reuters), St. Paul, 1514. Cited hereafter as *Black's Law, 9ᵗʰ*.

91   *Black's Law Dictionary 9ᵗʰ*, 999.

92   *Black's Law Dictionary 9ᵗʰ*, 479.

93   Keller, *Reliance of the Traveller*, Book R "Holding One's Tongue," r2.0 "Slander," r2.6.

94   Keller, *Reliance of the Traveller*, at § r3.1.

95   Keller, *Reliance of the Traveller*, at o11.10.

96   Keller, *Reliance of the Traveller*, at § r2.16.

97   Kamali, *Freedom of Expression in Islam*, cover and inside leaf.

98   Kamali, *Freedom of Expression in Islam*, 215.

99   Kamali, *Freedom of Expression in Islam*, 235.

100   Kamali, *Freedom of Expression in Islam*, 214.

101   Kamali, *Freedom of Expression in Islam*, 212-213.

102   Keller, *Reliance of the Traveller*, at § o8.7.

103   Keller, *Reliance of the Traveller*, at § o11.10.

104   Keller, *Reliance of the Traveller*, at § o11.10.

105   Keller, *Reliance of the Traveller*, at § o9.14.

106   Keller, *Reliance of the Traveller*, at § o9.14.

107   Emerick, *What Islam is All About*, 15.

108   ibn Kathir, Al-Hafiz Abu al-Fida' 'Imad Ad-Din Isma'il bin 'Umar bin Kathir al-Qurashi al-Busrawi. *Tafsir of Ibn Kathir*. 10 vols. Trans. Abdul-Malik Mujahid. Riyadh: Darussalam, 2000.

109   Ibn Sa'd'. *Kitab al-Tabaqat al-Kabir*, vol 2. Trans. S. Moinul Haq. India: Islamic Book Service, 1990.

110   Guillaume, *The Life of Muhammad, A Translation of Ishaq's Sirat Rasul Allah*, 1967.

111   Ibn Sa'd', *Cita al-Tabaqat al-Kabir*, vol 2, trans. S. Moinul Haq, (India: Islamic Book Service, 1990), 31.

112   Guillaume, *The Life of Muhammad, A Translation of Ishaq's Sirat Rasul Allah*, 676.

113   Guillaume, *The Life of Muhammad, A Translation of Ishaq's Sirat Rasul Allah*, 676.

114   Lawrence Van Gelder, "Bookstores Bar Magazine with Muhammad Cartoons," *New York Times*, 01 April 2006, URL: http://www.nytimes.com/2006/04/01/arts/01arts.html?_r=0, accessed 17 May 2006.

115   Dan Bilefsky and Maia de la Baume, "Suspects Identified in Attack on French Newspaper, Charlie Bebdo," *New York Times*, 7 January 2015, URL: http://www.nytimes.com/2015/01/08/world/europe/charlie-hebdo-paris-shooting.html?_r=0, accessed 7 January 2015.

116   "Howard Dean on Paris Attack: 'I Stopped Calling these People Muslim Terrorists'," *Real Clear Politics*, 7 January 2015, URL: http://www.realclearpolitics.com/video/2015/01/07/howard_dean_on_paris_attack_i_stopped_calling_these_people_muslim_terrorists.html, accessed 7 January 2015.

117   Bill Gertz, "Constitutional Religious Clause Prevents Obama Administration from Countering Islamic State Ideology," *The Washington Free Beacon*, 7 October 2014, URL: http://freebeacon.com/national-security/surrender-in-the-war-of-ideas/, accessed 30 December 2014.

118   Keller, *Reliance of the Traveller*, Document 3, Certification page, IIIT letterhead with Alwani signature block, International Institute of Islamic Thought, xviii-xix.

119   Keller, *Reliance of the Traveller*, at § r8.2.

120   Government Exhibit: Philly Meeting—15, 3:04-CR-240-G, U.S. v. HLF, et al., at 2, 3, at http://www.txnd.uscourts.gov/judges/hlf2/09-29-08/Philly%20Meeting%2015.pdf.

121   Bill Gertz, "Constitutional Religious Clause Prevents Obama Administration from Countering Islamic State Ideology," *The Washington Free Beacon*, 7 October 2014, URL: http://freebeacon.com/national-security/surrender-in-the-war-of-ideas/, accessed 30 December 2014.

122   Bill Gertz, "Constitutional Religious Clause Prevents Obama Administration from Countering Islamic State Ideology," *The Washington Free Beacon*, 7 October 2014, URL: http://freebeacon.com/national-security/surrender-in-the-war-of-ideas/, accessed 30 December 2014.

123   Bill Gertz, "Constitutional Religious Clause Prevents Obama Administration from Countering Islamic State Ideology," *The Washington Free Beacon*, 7 October 2014, URL: http://freebeacon.com/national-security/surrender-in-the-war-of-ideas/, accessed 30 December 2014.

124   **Rebuttable presumption**, from *Black's Law*, 9th, 1306: "An inference drawn from certain facts that establish a prima facie case , which may be overcome by introduction of contrary evidence."

125 **Prima facie**, from *Black's Law*, 9th, 1310: "At first sight; on first appearance but subject to further evidence or information. ... Sufficient to establish a fact or raise a presumption unless disproved or rebutted."

126 **Prima facie case** from *Black's Law*, 6th, 1189-90: "Such as will prevail until contradicted and overcome by other evidence. ... A case which has proceeded upon sufficient proof to that stage where it will support a finding if evidence is disregarded. ... Courts use concept of "prima facie" ... to mean not only that plaintiff's evidence would reasonably allow conclusion plaintiff seeks, but also that plaintiff's evidence compels such a conclusion if the defendant produces no evidence to rebut it." From *Black's Law*, 9th, 1310: "1) Establish as a legally required rebuttable presumption. 2) A party's production of enough evidence to allow the fact-trier to infer the fact at issue and rule in the party's favor."

127 Rachel Ehrenfeld and Alyssa A. Lappen, "The Egyptian Roots of Hatred," *The Washington Times*, July 6, 2007, URL: http://www.washingtontimes.com/news/2007/jul/6/egyptian-roots-of-hatred

128 *Minhaj A. Qidwai, "Organization of Islamic Conference — Vision for 2050," Extracted 11/10/2003 from* ICSSA.org by Amir Ali, http://www.ilaam.net/Opinions/OICVisionFor2050.html See also "The Oriagnziation of the Islamic Conference (OI), One page summary, OIC Overview and Analysis, OIC document first viewed at OIC website, retrieved 1/14/2014 from Forum for Democratic Global Governance, URL: http://fimforum.org/en/library/OIC_Overview_and_Analysis. pdf#page=1&zoom=auto,0,800

129 Marhsall and Shea, *Silenced: How Apostasy and Blasphemy Codes are Chocking Freedom Worldwide*, Oxford University Press (Oxford: New York, 2011), p. 211. Cited hereafter as Marhsall and Shea, *Silenced: How Apostasy and Blasphemy Codes are Chocking Freedom Worldwide.*

130 Marhsall and Shea, *Silenced: How Apostasy and Blasphemy Codes are Chocking Freedom Worldwide*, 211.

131 General Assembly, 54th session, 4th plenary meeting, Sept. 20, 1999, URL: http://daccess-dds-ny. un.org/doc/UNDOC/GEN/N99/858/23/PDF/N9985823.pdf?OpenElement#page=31&zoom=au to,0,527, p. 34.

132 "Defamation of religions," UN Commission on Human Rights resolution 1999/82, URL: http://ap.ohchr.org/Documents/E/CHR/resolutions/E-CN_4-RES-1999-82.doc. Cited hereafter as "Defamation of religions," UN Commission on Human Rights resolution 1999/82.

133 "Defamation of religions," UN Commission on Human Rights resolution 1999/82.

134 "Defamation of religions," UN Commission on Human Rights resolution 1999/82.

135 Marhsall and Shea, *Silenced: How Apostasy and Blasphemy Codes are Chocking Freedom Worldwide*, Oxford University Press (Oxford: New York, 2011), p. 212.

136 "Combating defamation of religions as a means to promote human rights, social harmony and religious and cultural diversity," Commission on Human Rights resolution 2001/4, URL: www. strasbourgconsortium.org/docs/E-CN_4-RES-2001-4.doc

137 Marhsall and Shea, *Silenced: How Apostasy and Blasphemy Codes are Chocking Freedom* Worldwide, 213.

138 Commission on Human Rights, Report on the Fifty-Eight Session, March 18-April 26, 2002, Economic and Social Council, Official records, 2002, Supplement No. 3, URL: http://www.unhchr.ch/ huridocda/huridoca.nsf/AllSymbols/AFE565E9560973C9C1256C93004A41E0/$File/G0215272. pdf?OpenElement

139 "Combating defamation of religions," United Nations Commission on Human Rights resolution 2003/4, URL: http://www.unhchr.ch/Huridocda/Huridoca.nsf/%28Symbol%29/E. CN.4.RES.2003.4.En?Opendocument

140 "Commission adopts resolutions on combating defamation of religions" United Nations Human Rights Commission, press release, April 13, 2004, URL: http://www.un.org/News/Press/docs/2004/hrcn1082.doc.htm

141 "Commission adopts resolutions on combating defamation of religions" United Nations Human Rights Commission, press release, April 13, 2004, URL: http://www.un.org/News/Press/docs/2004/hrcn1082.doc.htm

142 "Combating defamation of religions," United Nations Human Rights Resolution 2005/3, April 12, 2005, URL: http://ap.ohchr.org/documents/E/CHR/resolutions/E-CN_4-RES-2005-3.doc

PART V: DAYS OF RAGE

1   Anderson, John Ward. "Cartoons of Prophet Met with Outrage," *Washington Post*, January 31, 2009, URL: http://www.washingtonpost.com/wp-dyn/content/article/2006/01/30/AR2006013001316.html

2   Kamali *Freedom of Expression in Islam*, 236.

3   Siddiqi, Shamim A. *Methodology of Dawah Ilallah in American Perspective.* (Brooklyn, New York: Forum for Islamic Work, 1989).

4   "Phobia: Definition," The Mayo Clinic, January 7, 2011, URL: http://www.mayoclinic.org/diseases-conditions/phobias/basics/definition/CON-20023478

5   IPT News, "Moderate Muslims Speak Out on Capitol Hill," October 1, 2010, URL: http://www.investigativeproject.org/2217/moderate-muslim-speak-out-on-capitol-hill

6   Mohamed Akram, Explanatory Memorandum, 18.

7   Third OIC Observatory Report on Islamophobia, OIC Observatory, May 2009 to April 2010, OIC Observatory, 22 May 2010, URL: http://www.oic-oci.org/uploads/file/Islamphobia/2010/en/Islamophobia_rep_May_22_5_2010.pdf.pdf, 7. Cited hereafter as Third OIC Observatory Report on Islamophobia, OIC Observatory, May 2009.

8   Summary "Islamophobia a Challenge for us All," The Runnymede Trust, undated, URL: http://www.runnymedetrust.org/uploads/publications/pdfs/islamophobia.pdf, accessed 5 June 2010.

9   "Islamophobia – A Challenge for Us All," The Runnymede Trust, Runnymede, UK, 1997, (available in PDF) URL: http://www.divshare.com/download/launch/9605806-94b, accessed 19 August 2014, 4. Cited hereafter as "Islamophobia – A Challenge for Us All," The Runnymede Trust, 1997.

10   "Islamophobia – A Challenge for Us All," The Runnymede Trust, 1997, 4.

11   "Islamophobia – A Challenge for Us All," The Runnymede Trust, 1997, 7.

12   "Islamophobia – A Challenge for Us All," The Runnymede Trust, 1997, 4.

13   "Torpedoing 'Islamophobia'," Center for Security Policy, 29 September 2013, transcript of OSCE Human Dimension Implementation Meeting Warsaw, Side Event Convened by the ODIHR Tolerance and Non-Discrimination Department: "Educational Initiatives and Approaches for Addressing anti-Semitism and Intolerance against Muslims," 24 September 2013, URL: http://www.centerforsecuritypolicy.org/2013/09/29/torpedoing-islamophobia

14   OIC International Conference on Terrorism: Dimensions, Threats and Countermeasures—Concluding Observations from the Chair, 15-17 November 2007, Tunis, at 2, URL: http://www.oic-oci.org/english/article/terrorism_conference_concl-en.pdf

15   "Political Field," Final Communiqué of the Third Extraordinary Session of the Islamic Conference "Meeting the Challenges of the 21st Century, Solidarity in Action, Makkah al-Mukarramah, 5-6 Dhul Qa'Adah 1426H (7-8 December 2005), URL: http://english.savefreespeech.org/?p=403.

16   "Contemporary forms of Racism," Twenty-Eighth Session of the Islamic Conference of Foreign Ministers, Bamako.

17   Keller, *Reliance of the Traveller*, at § r3.1.

18   "Defamation of Religions," Reports of the Secretary General on the Legal Affairs Submitted to the Twenty-Eighth Session of the Islamic Conference of Foreign Ministers, Bamako, Republic of Mali, 4-8 Rabi-ul-Thani, 1422H (25-29 June, 2001), URL: http://www.oic-oci.org/oicnew/english/conf/fm/28/28-ICFM-SG-Rep-en/28-ICFM-LEG-D-en.htm. Cited hereafter as Twenty-Eighth Session of the Islamic Conference of Foreign Ministers, Bamako.

19   "Defamation of Religions," Reports of the Secretary General on the Legal Affairs Submitted

to the Twenty-Eighth Session of the Islamic Conference of Foreign Ministers, Bamako, Republic of Mali, 4-8 Rabi-ul-Thani, 1422H (25-29 June, 2001).

20   Ambassador Omur Orhun, "Challenges Facing Muslims in Europe – 2011-03-01," Arches Quarterly, Vol. 4 Edition 8, Spring/Summer 2011, Posted on OIC's Official UN portal "Organization of Isalmic Cooperation – Permanent Observer Mission to the United Nations in New York, 1 March 2011, URL: http://www.oicun.org/74/20120116050228155.html, accessed 29 September 2013.

21   *The Firth Point of Departure,* Toward a Worldwide Strategy for Islamic Policy *(Points of Departure, Elements, Procedures and Missions), 1 December 1982, seized* in November 2001 raid of Muslim Brotherhood leader Yusuf Nada's residence in Campione de Italia, Switerland (Lugano).

22   *The Eight Point of Departure,* Toward a Worldwide Strategy for Islamic Policy *(Points of Departure, Elements, Procedures and Missions), 1 December 1982, seized* in November 2001 raid of Muslim Brotherhood leader Yusuf Nada's residence in Campione de Italia, Switzerland (Lugano).

23   *The Seventh Point of Departure,* Toward a Worldwide Strategy for Islamic Policy *(Points of Departure, Elements, Procedures and Missions), 1 December 1982, seized* in November 2001 raid of Muslim Brotherhood leader Yusuf Nada's residence in Campione de Italia, Switzerland (Lugano).

24   "Torpedoing 'Islamophobia'," Center for Security Policy, 29 September 2013, transcript of OSCE Human Dimension Implementation Meeting Warsaw, Side Event Convened by the ODIHR Tolerance and Non-Discrimination Department: "Educational Initiatives and Approaches for Addressing anti-Semitism and Intolerance against Muslims," 24 September 2013, URL: http://www. centerforsecuritypolicy.org/2013/09/29/torpedoing-islamophobia/, accessed 30 September 2013.

25   Partial Transcript, OSCE Side Event "How Bad Definitions Violate Fundamental OSCE Commitments," International Civil Liberties Alliance (ICLA), English, Opera Room, OSCE Human Dimension Implementation Meeting, Warsaw, Poland, 26 September 2013.

26   Section 2, Article VII, "Combating Islamophobia," The Third Extraordinary Session of the Islamic Summit, Makka Al-Mukarama, Kingdom of Saudi Arabia, *Organization of the Islamic Conference,* 7-8 December 2005, at http://www.oic-oci.org/ex-summit/english/10-years-plan.htm. **Reads**: Affirm the need to counter Islamophobia, through the establishment of an observatory at the OIC General Secretariat to monitor all forms of Islamophobia, issue an annual report thereon, and ensure cooperation with the relevant Governmental and Non-Governmental Organizations (NGOs) in order to counter Islamophobia. Cited hereafter as Article VII, "Combating Islamophobia," The Third Extraordinary Session of the Islamic Summit.

27   Transcript, "Ekmeleddin Ihsanoglu, Secretary General of the Organization of the Islamic Cooperation," *Khaleejia TV,* Jeddah, 10 November 2012 (as captured as "Interview with Leader of OIC 2012, captured by *Vladtepesblog.com,* posted on *MRCtv* 5 January 2013), URL: http://www. mrctv.org/videos/interview-leader-oic-2012, accessed 22 January 2013.

28   "Observatory on Islamophobia Established from our Correspondent," *KhaleejTimesOnline,* 8 May 2006, URL: http://www.khaleejtimes.com/DisplayArticle.asp?xfile=data/middleeast/2006/May/ middleeast_May178.xml&section=middleeast&col=.

29   "Sixth OIC Observatory Report on Islamophobia," *Organization of Islamic Cooperation,* Presented to the 40th Council of Foreign Ministers, Conakry, Guinea," 9-11 December 2013, URL: http://www. oic-oci.org/oicv2/upload/islamophobia/2013/en/islamphobia_report_2013.pdf

30   First OIC Observatory Report on Islamophobia, OIC Observatory, 13 March 2008, URL: http://www.theunity.org/en/index.php?option=com_docman&task=cat_view&gid=41&Itemid=14.

31   Second OIC Observatory Report on Islamophobia, OIC Observatory, 23 May 2009, URL: http://www.oic-un.org/document_report/Islamophobia_rep_May_23_25_2009.pdf.

32   OIC Observatory, Third OIC Observatory Report on Islamophobia, May 2009.

33   Seventh OIC Observatory Report on Islamophobia October 2013 – April 2014, Presented to the 41st Council of Foreign Ministers, Jeddah, Kingdom of Saudi Arabia, 18-19 June 2014, URL:

http://www.oic-oci.org/oicv2/upload/islamophobia/2014/en/reports/islamophoba_7th_report_2014.pdf, accessed 20 August 2014.

34   Seventh OIC Observatory Report on Islamophobia October 2013 – April 2014.

35   Article VII, "Combating Islamophobia," The Third Extraordinary Session of the Islamic Summit.

36   Keller, *Reliance of the Traveller,* Book W "Notes and Appendices" at w4.3 "The Abrogation of Previously Revealed Religions," at 848.

37   Keller, *Reliance of the Traveller,* Book W "Notes and Appendices" at w4.0 "The Finality of the Prophet's Message (from a1.5)," at 846.

38   Keller, *Reliance of the Traveller,* Book W "Notes and Appendices" at w4.1(2) "The Finality of the Prophet's Message," at 846.

39   Keller, *Reliance of the Traveller*, Book O "Justice," o8.0 "Apostasy from Islam," at o8.0 at 595.

40   Keller, *Reliance of the Traveller*, Book O "Justice," § o8.0 "Apostasy from Islam (*RIDDA*)," at §§ o8.0 and o8.1.

41   First Grade, *Monotheism and Jurisprudence* (Lesson 8), Education Department of Education, Ministry of Education, Kingdom of Saudi Arabia, (2007-2008), 29, as cited in *2007-2008 Academic Year: Excerpts from Saudi Ministry of Education: Textbooks for Islamic Studies: Arabic with English Translations*, Center for Religious Freedom of Hudson Institute (with the Institute for Gulf Affairs), 2008, at 7, URL: http://www.hudson.org/files/pdf_upload/Excerpts_from_Saudi_Textbooks_715.pdf. Cited hereafter as *First Grade Saudi Texts.*

42   "Christianity No Longer a Religion, says Turkish Minister," Hurriyet Daily News (Dogan News Agency), Istanbul, 31 December 2012, URL: http://www.hurriyetdailynews.com/Default.aspx?PageID=238&NID=38021&NewsCatID=393, accessed 3 September 2014. States: Christianity has ceased to be a religion but has become a culture of its own, Turkish Environment and Urbanism Minister Erdoğan Bayraktar said at a recent conference hosted by the ruling Justice and Development Party's (AKP) Women's Group. "The biggest three countries in the world are not Muslim countries. China, India – only the U.S. believes in a single God. Spirituality and religious feelings are weakening," Bayraktar said. "There are 2.5 billion Christians in the world," Bayraktar said. "Christianity is no longer a religion. It's a culture now. But that is not what a religion is like. A religion teaches; it is a form of life that gives one peace and happiness. That is what they want to turn [Islam] into as well."

43   Keller, *Reliance of the Traveller,* at § r8.2.

44   Belien, Paul, "The Cartoon Hoax," *The Brussels Journal,* 7 February 2006, URL: http://www.brusselsjournal.com/node/775. **NOTE**: An indicator that this activity was designed to build up was addition of data to ensure the sought-after rage. A group of Danish Muslim imams, frustrated with what they viewed as a lack of response in Denmark, compiled a dossier of images in a deliberate attempt to incite violence during a January 2006 tour of Muslim countries. They took with them not only the original twelve cartoons as published in *Jyllands-Posten*, but added three more that were not part of the original set. The imams included these deliberately because of what they perceived would be most offensive to the Muslim ummah. For example, one of the added cartoons was a faxed image of a man wearing a pig-snout and presented by the imams as depicting Mohammad. In fact, the photo had nothing to do with either the original cartoons or Islam at all; it was merely a photo of a French clown performing at a pig festival.

45   "Q & A: the Muhammad cartoons row," *BBC,* 7 February 2006, URL: http://news.bbc.co.uk/2/hi/4677976.stm

46   Siraj Wahab, "OIC Demands Unqualified Danish Apology," *Arab News* (Saudi Arabia), 29 January 2006, URL: http://archive.arabnews.com/?page=1&section=0&article=77007

47   "OIC Condemns Publication of Cartoon of Prophet Muhammad (PBUH)," IRNA (Iranian Republic News Agency), Tehran, 31 January 2006, URL: http://www.workablepeace.org/Cartoons/oic.pdf

48   "Sacrilegious Cartoons: Nawaz Commends Reaction," *The News* (Karachi), 11 February 2006.

49   Ahmed, Dr. Israr, "04-Bayan Ul Quran—Introduction to Ul Quran: Urdu," *Quran Academy*, 18 April 2009. Accessed 24 April 2011, URL: http://www.quranacademy.org/series/bayan-ul-quran-1998-dr-israr-ahmed/240-240

"Erdoğan Appeals to World Leaders to Calm Down Cartoon Crisis," *Turkish Daily News,"* 12 February 2006, RMD.

50   Turki al-Suheil, "Saudi Arabia Recalls Envoy in Danish Row," *Asharq Alawsat*, 27 January 2006, URL: http://aawsat.com/english/news.asp?section=1&id=3571

51   Ahmad Maher, "Norwegian Muslims Blast Magazine Over Prophet Cartoon," 11 January 2006, URL: http://www.islamonline.net/English/News/2006-01/11/article05.shtml

52   P.K. Abdul-Ghafour, "Imams Back Call for Danish Boycott in Cartoons Row," *Arab News*, 28 January 2006, URL: http://www.aawsat.net/2006/01/article55268061

53   MEMRI Special Dispatch No. 1089, "Sheikh Al-Qaradhawi Responds to Cartoons of Prophet Muhammad: Whoever is Angered and Does Not Rage in Anger is a Jackass—We are Not a Nation of Jackasses," February 9, 2006, URL: http://www.memri.org/report/en/0/0/0/0/0/0/1604.htm, accessed 17 February 2006.

54   Amir Taheri, "Opinion: Response to the Cartoon Controversy: What is Right and What is Wrong," *Asharq Al-Awsat* (London), 10 February 2012.

55   "Scholar Praises 'Holy Rage' Over Cartoons," *Bahrain Tribune*, 11 February 2006. From the U.S. Central Command Regional Media Daily, 11 February 2006.

56   Eulich, Whitney, "Blasphemy riots—6 examples around the world," *Christian Science Monitor,* URL: http://www.csmonitor.com/World/Global-Issues/2012/0912/Blasphemy-riots-6-examples-around-the-world/Danish-cartoons-of-the-prophet-Muhammad

57   Batty, David, "Somali charged with murder attempt on Muhammad cartoonist," *The Guardian*, 2 January 2010, URL: http://www.theguardian.com/world/2010/jan/02/kurt-westergaard-muhammad-cartoon-somali. Cited hereafter as Batty, "Blasphemy Riots."

58   "Al-Qaeda tape urges boycott over cartoons," *ABC News,* March 5, 2006, URL: http://web.archive.org/web/20081009195230/http://www.abc.net.au/news/newsitems/200603/s1584198.htm

59   Powers, Shawn, "The Danish Cartoon Crisis: The Import and Impact of Public Diplomacy," *USC Center on Public Diplomacy*, April 5, 2006, URL: http://www.academia.edu/426018/The_Danish_Cartoon_Crisis_The_Import_and_Impact_of_Public_Diplomacy

60   Transcript, "Ekmeleddin Ihsanoglu, Secretary General of the Organization of the Islamic Cooperation," *Khaleejia TV*, Jeddah, 10 November 2012 (as captured as "Interview with Leader of OIC 2012, captured by *Vladtepesblog.com*, posted on *MRCtv* 5 January 2013), URL: http://www.mrctv.org/videos/interview-leader-oic-2012, accessed 22 January 2013.

61   Article 20, §2, *International Covenant on Civil and Political Rights*, Adopted and opened for signature, ratification and accession by General Assembly resolution 2200A (XXI) of 16 December 1966 entry into force 23 March 1976, in accordance with Article 49, Office of the United Nations High Commissioner for Human Rights, United Nations Treaty Collection, URL: http://www.ohchr.org/en/professionalinterest/pages/ccpr.aspx, accessed 16 July 2011. Article 20, §2 states: "Any advocacy of national, racial or religious hatred that constitutes incitement to discrimination, hostility or violence shall be prohibited by law."

62   Batty, "Blasphemy Riots."

63   "Afghans protest over Danish cartoon," *CNN*, March 8, 2008, URL: http://www.cnn.com/2008/WORLD/asiapcf/03/08/afghan.protest/index.html?_s=pm:world

64   Dan Bilefsky and Maia de la Baume, "Suspects Identified in Attack on French Newspaper,

Charlie Bebdo," *New York Times*, 7 January 2015, URL: http://www.nytimes.com/2015/01/08/world/europe/charlie-hebdo-paris-shooting.html?_r=0, accessed 7 January 2015.

65   Cohen, Patricia, "Yale Press Bans Images of Muhammad in New Book," *New York Times*, August 13, 2009, URL: http://www.nytimes.com/2009/08/13/books/13book.html?_r=2&pagewanted=print

66   *Arab News*, 9 December 2005.

67   "Condemning Europe," *Pakistan Observer* (Islamabad), 11 February 2006.

68   "Thousands Protest against Cartoons in Interior Sindh," *The News* (Karachi), 11 February 2006.

69   Mike Lee, "Day of Rage: Anger Not Jihad Muslim Leaders Worldwide Call for Day of Rage Over Popes Comments, Do They Mean Violence?," *ABC News*, 18 September 2006, URL: http://www.freerepublic.com/focus/f-news/1703725/posts.

70   Dana Kennedy, "Islamic Leader to Pope on Blasphemy: Mind Your Own Business," *AOL News*, 11 January 2011, URL: http://www.aolnews.com/2011/01/11/islamic-leader-to-pope-benedict-on-blasphemy-mind-your-own-busi/

71   The "x" signifies a number between 2 and 5. There are 1.2 or 1.3 or 1.4 or 1.5 billion Muslims, depending on the article.

72   "Muslim World League Condemns Norwegian Magazine." *Arab News* (Saudi Arabia). 13 January 2006. From the U.S. Central Command "Regional Media Daily."

73   Siraj Wahab, "OIC Demands Unqualified Danish Apology," *Arab News* (Saudi Arabia), 29 January 2006, URL: http://archive.arabnews.com/?page=1&section=0&article=77007.

74   "Thousands Protest against Cartoons in Interior Sindh," *The News* (Karachi), 11 February 2006.

75   Sixth OIC Observatory Report on Islamophobia - October 2012 - September 2013 (Presented to the 40th Council of Foreign Ministers, Conakry, Republic of Guinea), OIC Observatory, OIC, 9-11 December 2013, URL: http://www.oic-oci.org/oicv2/upload/islamophobia/2013/en/islamphobia_report_2013.pdf, accessed 12 December 2013, 84. Cited hereafter as Sixth OIC Observatory Report on Islamophobia - October 2012 - September 2013.

76   Sixth OIC Observatory Report on Islamophobia - October 2012 - September 2013, 89.

77   "Papal Address at University of Regensburg." Vatican translation. September 12, 2006, URL: http://www.vatican.va/holy_father/benedict_xvi/speeches/2006/september/documents/hf_ben-xvi_spe_20060912_university-regensburg_en.html

78   *Ibid.*

79   Mike Lee, "'Day of Rage': Anger Not Jihad—Muslim Leaders Worldwide Call for 'Day of Rage' Over Pope's Comments, Do They Mean Violence?" ABC News, online ed., 18 September 2006, URL: <http://www.freerepublic.com/focus/f-news/1703725/posts>, accessed 22 September 2006.

80   Pope Benedict XVI infuriates Muslim world slandering Prophet Muhammad and Islam, Pravda, 31 September 2006, URL: http://english.pravda.ru/world/europe/15-09-2006/84464-pope_benedict-0.

81   Suzan Fraser, "Muslims Assail Pope's Remarks on Islam," Associated Press, Ankara, 15 Sep 2006, URL: http://www.levitt.com/news/2006/09/16/muslims-assail-popes-remarks-on-islam/

82   Popham, Peter, "Pope's apology fails to placate Muslims as violence goes on," *The Independent*, 18 September 2006, URL: http://www.independent.co.uk/news/world/europe/popes-apology-fails-to-placate-muslims-as-violence-goes-on-416467.html

83   "Tauran: Christians under Attack," Talk to Al-Jazeera, *Al-Jazeera*, 17 March 2012, URL: http://www.aljazeera.com/programmes/talktojazeera/2012/03/201231705416701698.html, accessed March 2012.

84   "Pope 'deeply sorry' for comments on Islam," *NBC News*, 17 September 2006, URL: http://www.

nbcnews.com/id/14871562/#.UtYIJdJDuSo

85   "Open Letter to His Holiness Pope Benedict VI," URL: http://www.thinkingfaith.org/articles/ACommonWordLetter.pdf

86   Salman Rushdie, "Choice between Light and Dark," *The Observer,* January 22, 1989, 11.

87   Harvey Kushner, *Encyclopedia of Terrorism*, Sage Publications, Thousand Oaks, CA, 2002, 131.

88   "Iran: West to Blame Islam for Forthcoming Terrorism," *Philadelphia Inquirer*, 24 February 1989, p.5A, see also Malaysia's PAS join worldwide protests against Salman Rushdie," AFP, June 21, 2007. Archived at http://archive.is/7KlZe.

89   Malaysia's PAS join worldwide protests against Salman Rushdie," AFP, June 21, 2007. Archived at http://archive.is/7KlZe

90   Kemp, Danny. "Rushdie fatwa looms again amid new protests," AFP. June 23, 2007, URL: http://www.chinapost.com.tw/news/2007/06/23/113131/Rushdie-fatwa.htm. Cited hereafter as Kemp, "Rushdie Fatwa Looms."

91   *Faruqi*, M. H. "*Publishing Sacrilege* is *Not Acceptable,*" *Impact International*, October 28-November 10, 1988: 12-14. Reprinted in *The Rushdie File*, Lisa Appignanesi, Sara Maitland, ed. Syracuse University Press, 1990. P.45 Cited hereafter as *Faruqi,*. "*Publishing Sacrilege* is *Not Acceptable.*"

92   *Faruqi*, "*Publishing Sacrilege* is *Not Acceptable,*" 45.

93   *Faruqi*, "*Publishing Sacrilege* is *Not Acceptable,*" 45.

94   *Faruqi*, "*Publishing Sacrilege* is *Not Acceptable,*" 45.

95   "Iran Rejects Rushdie Death Edict," *SF Gate* (San Francisco)/ Examiner News Servies, 25 September 1998, URL: http://www.sfgate.com/news/article/Iran-rejects-Rushdie-death-edict-3068467.php, accessed 5 September 2014.

96   Malaysia's PAS join worldwide protests against Salman Rushdie," AFP, June 21, 2007. Archived at http://archive.is/7KlZe

97   Kemp, "Rushdie Fatwa Looms."

98   Kemp, "Rushdie Fatwa Looms."

99   Protests spread to Malaysia over knighthood for Salman Rushdie". Reuters, The Associated Press. 20 June 2007, URL: http://www.iht.com/articles/2007/06/20/news/rushdie.php

100   Doward, Jamie. "Rushdie honour breaks UN code, says Pakistan," The Guardian. June 23, 2007, URL: http://www.theguardian.com/uk/2007/jun/24/religion.pakistan

101   "Sir Salman Slammed," Washington Times, online ed., 19 June 2007, URL: http://www.washingtontimes.com/article/20070619/FOREIGN/106190021&SearchID=73284751953045

102   Amit Roy, "Sir Salman Tells Queen He'll Write for Kids," *The Telegraph Calcutta, India*, 26 June 2008, URL: http://telegraphindia.com/1080626/jsp/nation/story_9465193.jsp

103   "Doctor Guilty of Car Bomb Attacks," *BBC*, 16 December 2008. Accessed 24 April 2011, URL: http://news.bbc.co.uk/2/hi/7773410.stm

104   Seat of the Caliphate, 1915 Fatwa, 25-26.

105   Abu Mus'ab al-Suri, "The Jihadi Experiences: The Schools of Jihad," *Inspire Magazine*, Issue 1, Summer 1431/2010, URL: http://azelin.files.wordpress.com/2010/06/aqapinspire-magazine-volume-1-uncorrupted.pdf, 49.

106   Dana Bash and Jeremy Diamond, "Paris Attack Sign of 'Evolving Nature of the Terrorist Threat'," CNN, 7 January 2015, URL: http://www.cnn.com/2015/01/07/politics/jeh-johnson-terror-threat/, accessed 7 January 2015.

107 "Jihad Will Stay in Text Books, Says Minister," Gulf Times (Qatar), 26 July 2006.

108 Conway, Isobel, "Dutch far-right leader shot dead," *The Independent*, May 7, 2004, URL: http://www.independent.co.uk/news/world/europe/dutch-farright-leader-shot-dead-650464.html

109 Simons, Marlese. "Ex-Muslim turns her lens on a taboo", *The New York Times*, September 27, 2004, URL: http://www.nytimes.com/2004/09/27/international/europe/27netherlands.html?_r=0

110 Photo Credit: http://www.answeringmuslims.com/2010_04_01_archive.html

111 Rabinowitz, Beila. "English translation: Letter left on Theo Van Gogh's body by the militant Islamist killer was 'Jihad Manifesto': A call to destroy America and all 'unbelievers'" Militant Islam Monitor, URL: http://www.militantislammonitor.org/article/id/312

112 William C. Mann, "Critics of Islam Finds New Home in U.S.," *Associated Press*, 10 February 2007, URL: http://www.washingtonpost.com/wp-dyn/content/article/2007/02/10/AR2007021000558_pf.html

113 William C. Mann, "Critics of Islam Finds New Home in U.S.," Associated Press, 10 February 2007, URL: http://www.somalicongress.org/article37.html

114 Rabinowitz, Beila. "English translation: Letter left on Theo Van Gogh's body by the militant Islamist killer was 'Jihad Manifesto': A call to destroy America and all 'unbelievers'" Militant Islam Monitor, URL: http://www.militantislammonitor.org/article/id/312

115 Leonard, Tom. "Ayaan Hirsi Ali: the fatwa victim who refuses to keep quiet," *The Telegraph*, July 8, 2010, URL: http://www.telegraph.co.uk/culture/books/7877616/Ayaan-Hirsi-Ali-the-fatwa-victim-who-refuses-to-keep-quiet.html

116 Mock, Vanessa, "Wilders makes shock gains in Dutch elections," *The Independent*, June 11, 2010, URL: http://www.independent.co.uk/news/world/europe/wilders-makes-shock-gains-in-dutch-elections-1997293.html

117 Bawer, Bruce, "Submission in the Netherlands," *The City Journal*, January 22, 2009, URL: http://www.city-journal.org/2009/eon0122bb.html

118 Traynor, Ian, "'I don't hate Muslims. I hate Islam,' says Holland's Rising Political Star," The Guardian, February 17, 2008, URL: http://www.theguardian.com/world/2008/feb/17/netherlands.islam

119 Traynor, Ian, "'I don't hate Muslims. I hate Islam,' says Holland's Rising Political Star."

120 Bawer, Bruce, "Submission in the Netherlands," *The City Journal*, January 22, 2009, URL: http://www.city-journal.org/2009/eon0122bb.html

121 Landen, Thomas, "Dutch Unilever Director Wants Wilders Stopped," *The Brussels Journal*, December 9, 2007, URL: http://www.brusselsjournal.com/node/2751

122 Goldstein, Brooke and Aaron Eitan Meyer, "Death to Free Speech in the Netherlands," *The American Spectator*, January 22, 2009, URL: http://spectator.org/articles/42285/death-free-speech-netherlands

123 "Dutch React to Prosecution of Wilders," Angus Reid Global Monitor. February 3, 2009, URL: http://www.angusreidglobal.com/polls/33884/dutch_react_to_prosecution_of_wilders/

124 "Islam Film Dutch MP to be Charged," *BBC News*, 21 January 2009, URL: http://news.bbc.co.uk/2/hi/europe/7842344.stm, accessed 26 January 2009. States: "'In a democratic system, hate speech is considered so serious that it is in the general interest to... draw a clear line,' the court in Amsterdam said."

125 Dreher, Rod. "Geert Wilders and the Netherlands' shame," Dallas Morning News, January 22, 2009, URL: http://dallasmorningviewsblog.dallasnews.com/2009/01/geert-wilders-a.html/

126 Daniel Foster, "Breaking: Wilders Mistrial; Judges Ordered to Step Down," The Corner,

National Review Online, 22 October 2010, URL: http://www.nationalreview.com/corner/250723/breaking-wilders-mistrial-judges-ordered-step-down-daniel-foster

127 "Fact Sheet: The Trial of Geert Wilders," FORUM Institute for Multicultural Affairs, January 2011, URL: http://www.forum.nl/Portals/International/english-pdf/Factsheet-The-trial-of-Wilders-eng.pdf

128 Mark Steyn, "The Truth Shall Set You Free (Offer Not Applicable in the Netherlands)," The Corner—*National Review Online*, 17 January 2010, URL: http://www.nationalreview.com/node/192951

129 "Dutch MP on Trial for Anti-Islam Campaign, *PressTV*, 20 January 2010, URL: http://www.presstv.ir/detail.aspx?id=116655&sectionid=351020605, The right-wing Dutch lawmaker who has insulted Islam has appeared in the dock to stand trial for inciting hatred and discrimination against Muslims.

130 Lizzie Parry, "Arrested for Quoting Churchill: European Election Candidate Accused of Religions and Racial Harassment after he Repeats Wartime Prime Minister's Words on Islam During Campaign Speech," Mail Online, 28 April 2014, URL: http://www.dailymail.co.uk/news/article-2614834/Arrested-quoting-Winston-Churchill-European-election-candidate-accused-religious-racial-harassment-repeats-wartime-prime-ministers-words-Islam-campaign-speech.html, accessed 3 September 2014.

131 Keller, *Reliance of the Traveller,* Book R "Holding One's Tongue" at r2.0 "Slander," at 730-731.

132 Ekmeleddin Ihsanoglu, *Speech at 35th Session of Council of Foreign Ministers of the OIC.*

133 John W. Miller, "Dutch Politician is Acquitted in Hate-Speech Case," *Wall Street Journal Online*—Europe, 23 June 2011, URL: http://online.wsj.com/article/SB10001424052702304569504576403030202942102.html?KEYWORDS=Geert+Wilders+Acquitted

134 "OIC Blasts Islamophobia in Holland," *PressTV*, 5 July 2011, URL: http://www.presstv.ir/detail/187700.html

135 "Dutch Anti-Islam Lawmaker Geert Wilders under Investigation for Hate Speech," Fox News / AP, 9 October 2014, URL: http://www.foxnews.com/world/2014/10/09/dutch-anti-islam-lawmaker-geert-wilders-under-investigation-for-hate-speech/, accessed 15 October 2014.

136 Ekmeleddin Ihsanoglu, *Speech at 35th Session of Council of Foreign Ministers of the OIC.*

ı

PART VI: BLASPHEMY AND DETERRENT PUNISHMENT IN AMERICA

1   Paragraph 3, Article VII, "Combating Islamophobia," The Third Extraordinary Session of the Islamic Summit.

2   "Racism, Racial Discrimination, Xenophobia and Related form of Intolerance, follow-up and Implementation of the Durban Declaration and Programme of Action Human Rights Council, Agenda Item 9, Sixteenth Session, *Human Rights Commission*, United Nations A/HRC/16/L.38, 21 March 2011, URL: http://ap.ohchr.org/documents/E/HRC/d_res_dec/A_HRC_16_L.38.pdf. Cited hereafter as "Racism, Racial Discrimination, Xenophobia and Related form of Intolerance, follow-up and Implementation of the Durban Declaration and Programme of Action Human Rights Council."

3   "Racism, Racial Discrimination, Xenophobia and Related form of Intolerance, follow-up and Implementation of the Durban Declaration and Programme of Action Human Rights Council."

4   Article VII, "Combating Islamophobia," The Third Extraordinary Session of the Islamic Summit.

5   "Understanding and Implementing the Obligation to Prohibit Incitement in the OSCE," OSCE Side Event, Center for Media and Communications Studies, Central European University (CEU), Article 19, summary of event as posted in "Final Overview of Side Events, OSCE, 23 September – 4 October 2013, Warsaw, Poland, URL: http://www.osce.org/odihr/104902, accessed 13 November 2013. "**Summary:** This event will examine the legal and non-legal policy implications of the Rabat Plan of Action (RPA) for States and non-state actors in the OSCE region.

6   "History", About CEU/History, Central European University, Budapest, Hungary, undated URL: http://www.ceu.hu/about/history, accessed 10 December 2013. **States:** "In 1989, a group of visionary intellectuals—most of them prominent members of the anti-totalitarian democratic opposition—conceptualized an international university that would help facilitate the transition from dictatorship to democracy in Central and Eastern Europe and the former Soviet Union. Among them was George Soros, the Hungarian-American financier and philanthropist, who founded Central European University two years later. Soros championed the project because he understood that open societies can flourish only with people in positions of responsibility who are educated to promote them. His vision was to recruit professors and students from around the world to build a unique institution, one that would train future generations of scholars, professionals, politicians, and civil society leaders to contribute to building open and democratic societies that respect human rights and adhere to the rule of law. Beginning with 100-plus students in 1991, CEU held its first classes in Prague with students from 20 countries, primarily within the region. The University moved to Budapest in 1993."

7   "Open Society Mission", About CEU, Central European University, Budapest, Hungary, undated, URL: http://www.ceu.hu/about/open-society-mission, accessed 10 December 2013.

8   Funders, Article 19, *Article 19* webpage undated, URL: http://www.article19.org/pages/en/funders.html, 16 November 2013. European governmental entities include Department for International Aid (DFID) / UKAID, Dutch Ministry of Foreign Affairs, European Commission, Foreign and Commonwealth Office (FCO), Norwegian Ministry of Foreign Affairs, Swedish International Development Cooperation Agency (SIDA).

9   About Us, Opens Society Foundations, *Open Society Foundations*, webpage undated, URL: http://www.opensocietyfoundations.org/about, 16 November 2013. **States:** "The Open Society Foundations are a family of offices and foundations created by philanthropist George Soros. This directory includes our offices and country and regional foundations located throughout the world."

10   "Rabat Plan of Action on the Prohibition of Advocacy of National, Racial or Religious Hatred that Constitutes Incitement Discrimination, Hostility or Violence:[1] Conclusions and Recommendations Emanating from the Four Regional Rxpert Workshops Organised by OHCHR, in 2011, and adopted

by experts in Rabat, Morocco on 5 October 2012," United Nations High Commissioner on Human Rights (OHCHR), 5 October 2012, URL: http://www.un.org/en/preventgenocide/adviser/pdf/Rabat_draft_outcome.pdf, accessed 21 November 2013.

11   Footnote 1 in Title, "Rabat Plan of Action on the Prohibition of Advocacy of National, Racial or Religious Hatred that Constitutes Incitement to Discrimination, Hostility or Violence:[1] Conclusions and Recommendations Emanating from the Four Regional Rxpert Workshops Organised by OHCHR, in 2011, and adopted by experts in Rabat, Morocco on 5 October 2012," United Nations High Commissioner on Human Rights (OHCHR), 5 October 2012, URL: http://www.un.org/en/preventgenocide/adviser/pdf/Rabat_draft_outcome.pdf, accessed 21 November 2013.

12   Transcript, "Ekmeleddin Ihsanoglu, Secretary General of the Organization of the Islamic Cooperation," *Khaleejia TV*, Jeddah, 10 November 2012 (as captured as "Interview with Leader of OIC 2012, captured by *Vladtepesblog.com*, posted on *MRCtv* 5 January 2013), URL: http://www.mrctv.org/videos/interview-leader-oic-2012, accessed 22 January 2013.

13   Articles 19 and 20, *International Covenant on Civil and Political Rights*, Adopted and opened for signature, ratification and accession by General Assembly resolution 2200A (XXI) of 16 December 1966 entry into force 23 March 1976, in accordance with Article 49, Office of the United Nations High Commissioner for Human Rights, United Nations Treaty Collection, URL: http://www2.ohchr.org/english/law/ccpr.htm#art20, accessed 16 July 2011.

14   Article 22, Annex to Res. No. 49 / 19-P, The Cairo Declaration on Human Rights in Islam, Resolution NO. 49 / 19-P, On the Cairo Declaration on Human Rights in Islam, The Nineteenth Islamic Conference of Foreign Ministers (Session of Peace, Interdependence and Development), Cairo, Arab Republic of Egypt, OIC, 9-14 Muharram 1411H (31 July to 5 August 1990), URL: http://www.oic-oci.org/english/article/human.htm, accessed 22 July 2009.

15   Turan Kayaoğlu, "A Rights Agenda for the Islamic World? – The Organization of Islamic Cooperation's Evolving Human Rights Framework,' Brookings Doha Center Analysis Paper, Number 6, January 2013, URL: http://www.brookings.edu/~/media/Research/Files/Papers/2013/1/08%20oic%20human%20rights%20kayaoglu/Turan%20Kayaoglu%20English.pdf, accessed 30 October 2014, 22.

16   Fourth OIC Observatory Report on Islamophobia – May 2010 to April 2011(Presented to the 38th Council of Foreign Ministers, Astana, Republic of Kazakhstan) OIC Observatory, OIC, 28-30 June 2011, URL: http://www.oic-oci.org/uploads/file/Islamphobia/2011/en/islamphobia_rep_May_2010_to_April_2011_en.pdf, accessed 30 January 2014, 37.

17   Lopez, Clare, "Islamic World Tells Clinton: Defamation of Islam Must be Prevented—in America," *American Thinker*, December 14, 2011, URL: http://www.americanthinker.com/printpage/?url=http://www.americanthinker.com/articles/../2011/12/islamic_world_tells_clinton_defamation_of_islam_must_be_prevented_in_america.html

18   Declarations and Reservations: United States of America, Status, Chapter IV, Human Rights, (4) International Covenant on Civil and Political Rights, United Nations Treaty Collection Databases, United Nations, New York, 16 December 1966, URL: http://treaties.un.org/pages/VeiwDetails.aspx?src=TREATY&mtdsg_no=IV-4&chapter=4&lang=en#EndDec

19   Declarations and Reservations: United States of America, Status, Chapter IV, Human Rights, (4) International Covenant on Civil and Political Rights, United Nations Treaty Collection Databases, United Nations, New York, 16 December 1966, URL: http://treaties.un.org/pages/VeiwDetails.aspx?src=TREATY&mtdsg_no=IV-4&chapter=4&lang=en#EndDec

20   Ekmeleddin Ihsanoglu, Gala Dinner Keynote Speeches, 2013 U.S.-Islamic World Forum, The Brookings Institution – Doha Qatar, 9 June 2013, URL: http://www.brookings.edu/~/media/events/2013/6/09%202013%20us%20islamic%20world%20forum/us%20islamic%20world%20forum%20transcripts%20gala%20dinner.pdf#page=8, accessed 30 October 2014, 9.

21   "Remarks at the Organization of the Islamic Conference (OIC) High-Level Meeting on Combating Religious Intolerance," Hilary Rodham Clinton, Secretary of State, United States Department of State, given at the Center for Islamic Arts and History, Istanbul, Turkey, 15 July 2011, URL: http://www.state.gov/secretary/rm/2011/07/168636.htm

22   "Racism, Racial Discrimination, Xenophobia and Related form of Intolerance, follow-up and Implementation of the Durban Declaration and Programme of Action Human Rights Council."

23   "Racism, Racial Discrimination, Xenophobia and Related form of Intolerance, follow-up and Implementation of the Durban Declaration and Programme of Action Human Rights Council."

24   "Remarks at the Organization of the Islamic Conference (OIC) High-Level Meeting on Combating Religious Intolerance," Hilary Rodham Clinton, Secretary of State, United States Department of State, given at the Center for Islamic Arts and History, Istanbul, Turkey, 15 July 2011, URL: http://www.state.gov/secretary/rm/2011/07/168636.htm

25   "OIC Blasts Islamophobia in Holland," *PressTV*, 5 July 2011, URL: http://www.presstv.ir/detail/187700.html

26   Dan Bilefsky and Maia de la Baume, "Suspects Identified in Attack on French Newspaper, Charlie Bebdo," *New York Times*, 7 January 2015, URL: http://www.nytimes.com/2015/01/08/world/europe/charlie-hebdo-paris-shooting.html?_r=0, accessed 7 January 2015.

27   "Howard Dean on Paris Attack: 'I Stopped Calling these People Muslim Terrorists'," *Real Clear Politics*, 7 January 2015, URL: http://www.realclearpolitics.com/video/2015/01/07/howard_dean_on_paris_attack_i_stopped_calling_these_people_muslim_terrorists.html, accessed 7 January 2015.

28   "Racism, Racial Discrimination, Xenophobia and Related form of Intolerance, follow-up and Implementation of the Durban Declaration and Programme of Action Human Rights Council."

29   "High Ranking DOJ Official Refuses to Affirm 1st Amendment Rights," Representative Trent Franks, 26 July 2012, URL: http://www.youtube.com/watch? v=0wwv9l6W8yc

30   United Nations General Assembly, Human Rights Council, A/HRC/22/L.40, 18 March 2013, URL: http://www.strasbourgconsortium.org/content/blurb/files/A_HRC_22_L40.pdf

31   "Countering Violent Extremism (CVE) Training: Do's and Don'ts," *Office for Civil Rights and Civil Liberties*, DHS, undated.

32   Qudssia Akhlaque, "Spain Backs Initiatives for Action at UN: Blasphemous Cartoons," *Dawn* (Pakistan), 08 March 2006, RMD.

33   "Pakistan urges US to expand cooperation beyond war on terrorism," Kuwait News Agency, 04 March 2006, RMD.

34   US envoy sees more moderate leaders in Muslim World, Yahoo News, 16 March 2008, URL: http://news.yahoo.com/s/afp/ 20080316/pl_afp/oicislamus;_ylt=AjkhH4MBieU4iro11Mn2au87Xs8F

35   U.S. Department of State, Biography of Rashad Hussain. Accessed 27 June 2011, URL: http://www.state.gov/r/pa/ei/biog/140123.htm

36   Webcast Part 1, "Beyond Cairo: Visions of a New Decade in European Islamic Relations," Woodrow Wilson International Center for Scholars, 23 June 2010, URL: http://www.wilsoncenter.org/event/beyond-cairo-visions-new-decade-european-islamic-relations. Note: Rashad Hussain, at the 36:34 to 37:07/

37   Webcast Part 1, "Beyond Cairo: Visions of a New Decade in European Islamic Relations."

38   In the *Holy Land Foundation Case*, the Federal prosecutors submitted 35 different transcripts of a secret Hamas meeting in Philadelphia in 1993 that FBI wiretapped (See Judges – Notable Cases – *USA v. Holy Land Foundation for Relief and Development*, United States District Court, Northern District

of Texas, URL: http://www.txnd.uscourts.gov/judges/hlf2.html). In many of those transcripts a man is identified as "Nihad (LNU)" where LNU means "Last Name Unknown" (see for example "Philly Meeting 2, URL: http://www.txnd.uscourts.gov/judges/hlf2/09-29-08/Philly%20Meeting%202.pdf). The Investigative Project on Terrorism (IPT) assemble the evidence to determine that the "Nihad (LNU)" of the HLF Philly Meeting transcripts is Nihad Awad (see: "CAIR Executive Director Placed at HAMAS Meeting, Investigative Project on Terrorism (IPT) Archive, 2 August 2007, URL: http:// www.investigativeproject.org/282/cair-executive-director-placed-at-hamas-meeting#, accessed 20 August 2014). For example, from an FBI wiretap of a phone conversation on 14 September 1993 (see: Telephone Transcript from FBI Wiretap of Conversation Discussing Mr. Nidah's appearing on Television dated 14 September 1993, Investigative Project on Terrorism (IPT) Archive, undated, URL: http://www.investigativeproject.org/redirect/Telephone_Transcript.pdf), it was determined that "Nihad" was recently on TV. A CNN Crossfire transcript reveals that Nihad Awad, representing the Islamic Association for Palestine (IAP), was on Crossfire on 10 September 1993 (see: CNN Crossfire Transcript #918 for September 10, 1993, Investigative Project on Terrorism (IPT) Archive, 10 September 1993, URL: http://www.investigativeproject.org/redirect/Nihad_on_CNN2.pdf). The 14 September 1993 phone transcript also revealed that the same "Nihad" was quoted in that days edition of the *Dallas Morning News* representing the same Islamic Association for Palestine (IAP), (see: Dallas' Mideast Observers Warn of Conflict Ahead," *Dallas Morning News*, 14 September 1993, 12A, located at the Investigative Project on Terrorism (IPT) Archive, undated, URL: http://www. investigativeproject.org/redirect/Awad_in_DMN.pdf), all accessed 20 August 2014.

39   Dallas' Mideast Observers Warn of Conflict Ahead," *Dallas Morning News*, 14 September 1993, 12A, located at the Investigative Project on Terrorism (IPT) Archive, undated, http://www. investigativeproject.org/redirect/Awad_in_DMN.pdf, accessed 20 August 2014; see also CNN Crossfire Transcript #918 for September 10, 1993, Investigative Project on Terrorism (IPT) Archive, 10 September 1993, URL: http://www.investigativeproject.org/redirect/Nihad_on_CNN2.pdf, accessed 20 August 2014. Note: Identifies Nihad Awad as guest representing Islamic Association for Palestine (IAP) stating: "And in Dallas, Nihad Awad of the Islamic Association for Palestine."

40   Cohen, Laurie, "3 Islamic Fundraisers Held Liable in Terror Death," Chicago Tribune, November 11, 2004, URL: http://articles.chicagotribune.com/2004-11-11/news/0411110231_1_david-boim-magistrate-judge-arlander-keys-joyce-boim

41   CAIR's AWAD: In Support of Hamas Movement," Investigative Project on Terrorism (IPT) Video Archive, 19 October 2011, URL: http://www.investigativeproject.org/223/cairs-awad-in-support-of-the-hamas-movement, accessed 20 August 2014. **Note**: Nihad Awad, Executive Director of CAIR, announces support for Hamas at Barry University, 22 March 1994, saying: "I used to support the PLO, and I used to be the President of the General Union of Palestine Students which is part of the PLO here in the United States, but after I researched the situation inside Palestine and outside, I am in support of the Hamas movement more than the PLO."

42   Esposito letter to U.S. District Judge Leonie Brinkema, July 2, 2008.

43   Testimony of John Esposito, USA v. Holy Land Foundation, 3:04-CR-240-G (ND TX November 4, 2008), URL: http://www.investigativeproject.org/documents/case_docs/770.pdf

44   "Texas Resident Arrested on Charge of Attempted Use of Weapon of Mass Destruction," US Department of Justice press release, Northern District of Texas. February 24, 2011, URL: http://www. justice.gov/usao/txn/PressRel11/aldawsari_compl_pr.html

45   "The Smiling Face of Hamas," Asharq al-Awsat. July 14, 2007, URL: http://www.aawsat. net/2007/07/article55262109

46   "Articles of Incorporation," United Association for Studies and Research. Dated September 18, 1989, URL: http://www.investigativeproject.org/redirect/UASR.pdf

47   Jen Psaki, "Daily Press Briefing," U.S. Department of State, 29 January 2015, URL: http://www.

state.gov/r/pa/prs/dpb/2015/01/236959.htm#EGYPT, accessed 29 January 2015.

48   Transcript, Testimony of John Esposito, *USA v. Holy Land Foundation*, 3:04-CR-240-G (ND TX November 4, 2008), Investigative Project on Terrorism (IPT) Archive, undated, URL: http://www.investigativeproject.org/documents/case_docs/770.pdf, pages 73, 74, accessed 20 August 2014. **Relevant Testimony:** Questioning Professor Esposito is Jim Jacks, Assistant U.S. Attorney for the U.S. District Court for the Northern District of Texas and lead prosecutor in the Holy Land Trial.

Q [ADA Jacks]: Do you consider yourself expert on the Muslim Brotherhood?

A [Professor John Esposito]: I do, and so do many other people.

Q: And what is the motto of the Muslim Brotherhood?

A: Well, you mean in terms of its crest, its crest?

Q: Well, what is the expression that the members of the Muslim Brotherhood refer to as its creed or credo or motto?

A: I don't know. I have referred to it, but it is not a major – I don't think about that regularly. I think about who the Muslim Brotherhood is and what it does.

Q: Well –

A: It is related to – Obviously it is related to, you know, to God, et cetera, but I don't remember the exact words of the motto, no.

Q. But they do have a motto or a creed?

A: Yes. It is listed right under – If you go to the Muslim Brotherhood web page or you go to the office of the Muslim Brotherhood in Cairo, they would have a crest, you know, like – not a crest –

Q: A logo?

A: A logo. And then they would have the motto below the logo. But at this particular point I don't remember the logo.

Q: Is it similar to the Hamas motto?

A: The Hamas motto is similar in terms of its coming from – I am sorry. It is coming from the Muslim Brotherhood. But when you actually look at the teasing out of what Hamas stands for – In other words, if you study its charter, then its charter is at least 50 percent significantly different; let's say any of the charters of the Brotherhood past and present.

Q: My question was just about the Hamas motto and its similarity to the Muslim Brotherhood motto.

A: It would be similar.

Q: And you don't know what the Muslim Brotherhood motto is?

A: I have said that four times. Yes.

Q: Do you know the Hamas motto?

A: I have seen it before, but no, I don't.

Q: Do you consider yourself an expert on Hamas?

A: I said earlier that I am not. I have written on Hamas, but I don't consider myself an expert on Hamas because I haven't spent as much time interviewing Hamas leaders, including the fact that you can't interview Hamas leaders very easily today.

49   Vidino, Lorenzo, "The Muslim Brotherhood's Conquest of Europe," *Middle East Quarterly*, Winter, 2005, URL: http://www.meforum.org/687/the-muslim-brotherhoods-conquest-of-europe

50   Testimony of John Esposito, USA v. Holy Land Foundation, 3:04-CR-240-G (ND TX

November 4, 2008), URL: http://www.investigativeproject.org/documents/case_docs/770.pdf

51   Letter dated 15 January 2006 (faxed date stamp 16 January 2006) from OIC Secretary General Ekmeleddin Ihsanoglu to the Executive Director of CAIR Nihad Awad and the Director for the Georgetown Center for Muslim-Christian Understanding John Esposito, 15 January 2006.

52   Letter dated 15 January 2006 (faxed date stamp 16 January 2006) from OIC Secretary General Ekmeleddin Ihsanoglu to the Executive Director of CAIR Nihad Awad and the Director for the Georgetown Center for Muslim-Christian Understanding John Esposito, 15 January 2006.

53   Maha Akeel, "Awad, Ihsanoglu Discuss Future CAIR-OIC Projects," Arab News, 4 July 2007, URL: http://archive.arabnews.com/?page=1&section=0&article=98157

54   Obtained by AFLC as counsel for CSP during discovery in CAIR v Gaubatz, US D.Ct. DC, Case No. 1:09-cv-02030.

55   Objective 16, Article 1, Chapter 1, "Objectives and Principles," Charter of the Organisation of the Islamic Conference, URL: http://www.oic-oci.org/is11/english/Charter-en.pdf

56   Mohamed Akram, Explanatory Memorandum, 4.

57   "Bylaws of the International Muslim Brotherhood," Ikhwanweb.com, (downloaded) 18 January 2010, URL: http://www.ikhwanweb.com/article.php?id=22687 (**Note:** Ikhwanweb has since pulled the bylaws.)

58   Mohamed Akram, *Explanatory Memorandum*, 18.

59   Patrick Poole, "The Muslim Brotherhood "Project", FrontpageMag.com, 11 May 2006, URL: *www.frontpagemag.com/Articles/ReadArticle.asp?ID=22415*, accessed 14 July 2014. **As Poole explains:** "What Western intelligence authorities know about *The Project* begins with the raid of a luxurious villa in Campione, Switzerland, on November 7, 2001. The target of the raid was Youssef Nada, director of the Al-Taqwa Bank of Lugano, who has had active association with the Muslim Brotherhood for more than 50 years and who admitted to being one of the organization's international leaders. [...] Perhaps coincidentally, Qaradawi was the fourth largest shareholder in the Al-Taqwa Bank of Lugano, the director of which, Youssef Nada, was the individual in whose possession *The Project* was found."

60   *The Firth Point of Departure*, Toward a Worldwide Strategy for Islamic Policy *(Points of Departure, Elements, Procedures and Missions), 1 December 1982, seized* in November 2001 raid of Muslim Brotherhood leader Yusuf Nada's residence in Campione de Italia, Switerland (Lugano).

61   Khurram Murad, *Islamic movement in the West: Reflections on Some Issues*, The Islamic Foundation, Leicester, UK (also published by Quran House, Nairobi, Kenya, P.M.B., Kano, Nigeria), 1981, 11-12.

62   'Abdullah al Ahsan, *OIC: The Organization of the Islamic Conference (An Introduction to an Islamic Political Institution)*, International Institute of Islamic Thought (IIIT), Islamization of Knowledge Series No 7., 1988.

63   *Third OIC Observatory Report on Islamophobia: Intolerance & Discrimination against Muslims*, May 2009 to April 2010, *OIC Observatory*, 22 May 2010, URL: http://www.oic-oci.org/uploads/file/Islamphobia/2010/en/Islamophobia_rep_May_22_5_2010.pdf.pdf, 30.

64   Tariq Ramadan Speech to the 11th MAS-ICNA Annual Convention, Chicago, Illinois, 23 December 2012, from MAS-ICNA 2012: "The New "We" Redefined," MASICNA Channel (YouTube), December 2012, URL: http://www.youtube.com/watch?v=jXDXghymen0, accessed 15 January 2013.

65   "UAE Publishes List of Terrorist Organizations," *Gulf News*, 15 November 2014, URL: http://gulfnews.com/news/gulf/uae/government/uae-publishes-list-of-terrorist-organisations-1.1412895, accessed 15 November 2014. **The full list as provided by the UAE Cabinet, the complete list of terrorist organizations endorsed by the UAE Government, in line with the Federal Law No.7 for**

2014 as issued by President His Highness Shaikh Khalifa Bin Zayed Al Nahyan on August 20, 2014, includes: 1. Muslim Brotherhood in the UAE, 2. Al Islah Society, 3. Fatah Al Islam in Lebanon, 4. Islamic Association in Italy, 5. UAE Jihad cells, 6. Osbat Al Ansar in Lebanon, 7. Islamic Association in Finland, 8. Al Karama Organisation, 9. Al Qaida in the Islamic Maghreb, 10. Islamic Association in Sweden, 11. The Islamic Association in Sweden, 12. Ummah Parties in the Gulf region, 13. Ansar Al Sharia (Supporters of Sharia Law) in Libya, 14. Islamic Association in Norway, 15. Al Qaida, 16. Ansar Al Sharia in Tunisia, 17. Islamic Relief Organisation in London, 18. Islamic State (Daesh), 19. Mujahideen Youth Movement in Somalia, 20. Cordoba Foundation in Britain, 21. Al Qaida in the Arabian Peninsula, 22. Boko Haram in Nigeria, 23. Islamic Relief Organisation, an affiliate of the International, Organisation of the Muslim Brotherhood, 24. Ansar Al Sharia (Supporters of Sharia Law) in Yemen, 25. Almoravids Battalion in Mali, 26. Pakistan Taliban, 27. Muslim Brotherhood Organisation and group, 28. Ansar Al Deen (Defenders of the Faith) in Mali, 29. Abu Thar Al Ghafari Brigade in Syria, 30. Islamic Group in Egypt, 31. Pakistan's Haqqani network, 32. Al Tawhid Brigade in Syria, 33. Egyptian Ansar Jerusalem, 34. Pakistani Lashkar-e-Taiba a group, 35. Tawhid and Faith Brigade in Syria, 36. Ajnad Misr (Egyptian Jihadist Group), 37. East Turkistan movement in Pakistan, 38. Green Brigade in Syria, 39. Mujahideen Shura Council, 40. Aknaf Bait al Maqdis (Defenders of Jerusalem), 41. The Army of Mohammad in Pakistan, 42. Abu Bakr Al Siddiq Brigade in Syria, 43. Al Houthi Movement in Yemen, 44. The Army of Mohammad in Pakistan and India, 45. Talha bin Obaidullah Brigade in Syria, 46. Saudi Hezbollah Al Hejaz, 47. Indian Mujahideen in India/Kashmir, 48. Hezbollah in GCC countries, 49. Al Sarim Al Battar Brigade, 50. The Caucasus Emirate (Chechen Mujahideen), 51. Abdullah Ibn Mubarak Brigade, 52. Al Qaida Organisation in Iran, 53. Islamic Movement of Uzbekistan, 54. Syrian Martyrs Brigade, 55. Badr Organisation in Iraq, 56. Abu Sayyaf Group (Philippines), 57. Abu Omar Brigade, 58. Asa'ib Ahl Al Haq (League of the Righteous) in Iraq, 59. Council on American. Islamic Relations (CAIR), 60. Ahrar Shammar Brigade in Syria, 61. Hezbollah Brigades in Iraq, 62. Kanvas organization in Belgrade, Serbia, 63. Sariyat Al Jabal Brigade in Syria, 64. Abu Fadl Abbas Brigade Iraq, 65. Muslim American Society (MAS), 66. Al Shahba Brigade in Syria, 67. Al Youm Al Maoud Brigade in Iraq, 68. Association of Muslim Scholars, 69. Al. Qa'qa' Brigade in Syria, 70. Omar Bin Yasser Brigade (Syria), 71. Union of Islamic Organisations of France, 72. Sufian Al Thawri Brigade in Syria, 73. Iraqi Ansar Al Islam Group, 74. Federation of Islamic Organizations in Europe, 75. Ibad Al Rahman Brigade in Syria, 76. Al Nusra Front in Syria, 77. Islamic Association in Britain, 78. Omar Ibn Al Khattab Brigade in Syria, 79. Ahrar Al Sham Movement in Syria, 80. Islamic Society of Germany, 81. Al Shaima Brigade in Syria, 82. Army of Islam in Palestine, 83. Islamic Association in Denmark, 84. Al Haq Brigade in Syria, 85. Abdullah Azzam Brigades, and 86. Islamic Association in Belgium.

66   "Conference of OIC Information Ministers opens in Jeddah," Saudi Embassy Release, 13 September 2006, URL: http://www.saudiembassy.net/archive/2006/news/page285.aspx, accessed 19 June 2009.

67   "Muslims Urged to Invest in Global Media," *IslamOnline*, 13 September 2006, URL: www.islamonline.net/servlet/Satellite?c=Article_C&pagename=Zone-English-News/ NWELayout&cid=1159951496482

68   "Muslims Urged to Invest in Global Media," *IslamOnline*, 13 September 2006, URL: http://www.islamonline.net/servlet/Satellite?c=Article_C&pagename=Zone-English-News/ NWELayout&cid=1159951496482

69   Lachlan Carmichael, "Arab Boycott Campaign Worries US Business," *Arab News*, 1 May 2002, URL: http://archive.arabnews.com/?page=9&section=0&article=14848&d=1&m=5&y=2002

70   Simon Kuper, "Lunch with the FT: Royal Subjects," *Financial Times*, 2 December 2005, URL: http://www.ft.com/cms/s/2/9242de9a-6232-11da-8dad-0000779e2340.html

71   Simon Kuper, "Lunch with the FT: Royal Subjects," *Financial Times*, 2 December 2005.

72   "Saudi Prince, Bloomberg, Team-up on New Channel: Saudi billionaire Alwaleed teams up with

Bloomberg on new Arabic satellite news channel," *AP* (*Yahoo Finance*), 13 September 2012, URL: http://finance.yahoo.com/news/Saudi-prince-Bloomberg-team-apf-585264007.html, accessed 23 June 2013.

73   Adam Schreck, "Alwaleed Bin Talal Invests $300 Million in Twitter," *The Huffington Post*, 19 December 2011, URL: http://www.huffingtonpost.com/2011/12/19/alwaleed-bin-talal-twitter_n_1157205.html, accessed 14 June 2013.

74   Joscelyn, Thomas, "Al-Qaeda-linked jihadist helped incite 9/11 Cairo protest," *The Long War Journal*, October 26, 2012. Accessed online 12 January 2014, URL: http://www.longwarjournal.org/archives/2012/10/al_qaeda-linked_jiha.php

75   Joscelyn, Thomas, "Al-Qaeda-linked jihadist helped incite 9/11 Cairo protest," *The Long War Journal*, October 26, 2012.

76   Joscelyn, Thomas, "Zawahiri's Brother at Cairo Embassy Assault," *The Weekly Standard* – The Blog, 12 September 2012, URL: http://www.weeklystandard.com/blogs/zawahiris-brother-cairo-embassy-assault_652217.html, accessed 12 September 2012.

77   Guillaume, A. *The Life of Muhammad: A Translation of Ibn Ishaq's Sirat Rasul Allah*. Karachi: Oxford University Press, 1967.

78   Emerick, *What Islam is All About*, 15.

79   Youssef, Nancy A. and Ismail, Amina, "Anti-U.S. outrage over video began with Christian activist's phone call to a reporter," *McClatchyDC*, September 15, 2012. Accessed online 12 January 2014, URL: http://www.mcclatchydc.com/2012/09/15/168613/anti-us-outrage-over-video-began.html

80   "Expatriate Copts Produce a Movie making Fun of the Prophet Mohammed Hamdy Opened Fire on Them," *Al-Nas* (Cairo)(*El-MokhalesTV* through *YouTube*), 9 September 2012, URL: https://www.youtube.com/watch?v=lnM_NuW0r9M, accessed 2 February 2014.

81   "Fury over Mohammad video simmers on in Muslim world," *Reuters*, 15 September 2012. Accessed online 12 January 2014, URL: http://www.reuters.com/article/2012/09/15/us-film-protests-idUSBRE88D0O320120915

82   Unal, Mustafa, "PM Erdoğan: Islamophobia should be recognized as crime against humanity," Today's Zaman, 16 September 2012, URL: http://www.todayszaman.com/news-292579-pm-erdogan-islamophobia-should-be-recognized-as-crime-against-humanity.html, accessed 17 September 2012.

83   (UNCLASSIFIED) "EGYPT ISSUES ARREST WARRANTS FOR INFLAMMATORY VIDEO," *Federal Bureau of Investigation Executive Secretariat – Operations Center, Afternoon Brief*, 18 September 2012. **States: EGYPT ISSUES ARREST WARRANTS FOR INFLAMMATORY VIDEO,** (U) Egypt's general prosecutor issued arrest warrants and referred to trial seven Egyptian Coptic Christians and American pastor Terry Jones on charges linked to the inflammatory video, media report. The accused, all of whom are believed to be outside Egypt, could face the death penalty if convicted of harming national unity, insulting Islam, and spreading false information. DRL's Office of International Religious Freedom comments President Morsy reportedly directed the Egyptian Embassy in Washington to take legal action in the United States against the individuals. The Egyptian government has been an ardent supporter of anti-defamation resolutions at the UN. *(Ops/Bureau of Democracy, Human Rights, and Labor's Office of International Religious Freedom, AP.)*

84   Evans, Robert, "Islamic States to Reopen Quest for Global Blasphemy Law," *Reuters*, 19 September 2012, URL: http://www.reuters.com/article/2012/09/19/us-protests-religions-blasphemy-idUSBRE88I1EG20120919, accessed 19 September 2012.

85   Marwa Awad, "Egypt Salafi urges U.N. to criminalize contempt of Islam," *Reuters*, 22 September 2012, URL: http://www.reuters.com/article/2012/09/22/us-protests-egypt-idUSBRE88L0B220120922, accessed 22 September 2012.

86   Ema Anis, Asad Kharal, "Federal Minister Announces $100,000 Bounty on the Anti-Islam Filmmaker," *The Express Tribune with the International Herald Tribune*, 22 September 2012, URL: http://tribune.com.pk/story/440855/federal-minister-announces-100000-bounty-on-anti-islam-filmmakers-head/. Accessed 22 September 2012.

87   Goodenough, Patrick, "Leading Sunni Clerics Demand Global Ban on Insults to Islam," *CNSNews*.com, 17 September 2012, URL: http://cnsnews.com/news/article/leading-sunni-clerics-demand-global-ban-insults-islam, accessed 17 September 2012.

88   Shari`ah Staff, "IUMS Calls for Positive Reactions to Prophet Film," *OnIslam*, 13 September 2012, URL: http://www.onislam.net/english/shariah/muhammad/misconceptions/459020-iums-condemns-the-film-insulting-the-prophet.html, accessed 14 September 2012.

89   Biography of Shaykh Abdallah bin Bayyah, The Official Website of His Eminence Shaykh Abdallah bin Bayyah, URL: http://binbayyah.net/english/bio/, accessed 10 October 2013.

90   Shaykh Abdallah bin Bayyah, "Declaration Regarding the Offensive Video to Muslims," The Official Website of His Eminence Shaykh Abdallah bin Bayyah, 13 September 2012, URL: http://binbayyah.net/english/2012/09/13/.

91   Warikoo, Naraj, "Dearborn imam: Violence not what Islam preaches," Detroit Free Press, 15 September 2012, URL: http://www.freep.com/article/20120915/NEWS05/309150151/Dearborn-imam-Violence-not-what-Islam-preaches?odyssey=nav%7Chead, accessed 16 September 2012.

92   "CAIR Muslim Coalition (USCMO) Denounces ISIS for Steven Sotloff's Murder," CAIR Presser on FACEBOOK, 3 September 2014, URL: https://www.facebook.com/CAIRNational/posts/10152382299567695, accessed 4 September 2014.

93   "U.S. Muslim Groups to Launch New Council," Islamic Circle of North America (ICNA) Presser, 10 Marcy 2014, URL: http://www.icna.org/u-s-muslim-groups-to-launch-new-council-with-political-census/, accessed 4 September 2014. Note: the eight groups are "the Mosque Cares (Ministry of Imam W. Deen Mohammed), Muslim American Society (MAS), American Muslims for Palestine (AMP), Council on American-Islamic Relations (CAIR), Islamic Circle of North America (ICNA), Muslim Legal Fund of America (MLFA), Muslim Alliance in North America (MANA), Muslim Ummah of North America (MUNA)."

94   Sam Roe, "Hard-liners Won Battle for Bridgeview Mosque," Chicago Tribune, 8 February 2004, URL: http://www.chicagotribune.com/news/chi-0402080265feb08-story.html#page=1, accessed 4 September 2014.

95   Al-Majid., Dr. Hamad, "Stop Your Fanatics to Curb our Extremism," *Arsharq Alawsat*, 17 September 2012, URL: http://www.asharq-e.com/news.asp?section=2&id=31107, accessed 18 September 2012.

96   "Expatriate Copts Produce a Movie making Fun of the Prophet Mohammed Hamdy Opened Fire on Them,"*Al-Nas* (Cairo)(*El-MokhalesTV* through *YouTube*), 9 September 2012, URL: https://www.youtube.com/watch?v=lnM_NuW0r9M, accessed 2 February 2014.

97   Cited hereafter as Marayati, Representing the United States at the OSCE, October 2012.

98   Salam Al Marayati, Representing the United States on Religious Freedom, "U.S. Public Advocate at OSCE on Religious Freedom," **Session 11: Freedom of thought, conscience, religion or belief** US Policy, Embassy of the United States – Brussels, Belgium, 2 October 2012, URL: http://www.uspolicy.be/headline/us-muslim-advocate-osce-religious-freedom, accessed 3 October 2012. Cited hereafter as Marayati, Representing the United States at the OSCE, October 2012.

99   Cited hereafter as Marayati, Representing the United States at the OSCE, October 2012.

100   Cited hereafter as Marayati, Representing the United States at the OSCE, October 2012.

101   Marilyn Stern, "The Muslim Public Affairs Council: Building Bridges to U.S. Law Enforcement - Community-Oriented Policing," *The Investigative Project on Terrorism*, 20 November 2010, URL: http://www.investigativeproject.org/2345/report-assesses-mpac-counter-terrorcommitment, 8.

102   Marilyn Stern, "The Muslim Public Affairs Council: Building Bridges to U.S. Law Enforcement - Community-Oriented Policing," *The Investigative Project on Terrorism*, 20 November 2010, URL: http://www.investigativeproject.org/2345/report-assesses-mpac-counter-terrorcommitment, 14.

103   Connie Hair, "Muslim Brotherhood Front Group Trains Airport Screeners," *Human Events*, 6 December 2010, URL: http://www.humanevents.com/article.php?id=40395.

104   Picket, Kerry, "U.S. Embassy in Cairo tweets – 'Islam is a wonderful religion,' *Washington* Times, 11 September 2012. Accessed online 12 January 2014, URL: http://www.washingtontimes.com/blog/watercooler/2012/sep/11/picket-us-embassy-cairo-condemns-religious-incitem/

105   "U.S. Embassy Condemns Religious Incitement," Embassy of the United States, Cairo, Egypt, 11 September 2012, URL: http://egypt.usembassy.gov/pr091112.html, accessed 11 September 2012.

106   Section II "In the Political Field," OIC 10-Year Plan.

107   Rabab Fathy, "U.S. Embassy Confirms One of Its Local Employees Detained," *The Cairo Post – A YOUM7 Publication*, 11 February 2014, URL: http://thecairopost.com/news/87667/news/us-embassy-confirms-one-of-its-local-employees-detained, accessed 11 February 2014.

108   President of the 66th Session Nassir Abdulaziz, Al-Nasser, "On Combating Defamation of Religions and Promoting the Culture of Tolerane," General Assembly of the United Nations, United Nations General Assembly Press Release, 12 September 2012, URL: http://www.un.org/en/ga/president/66/news/PRStatements/CultureofTolerance120912.shtml, accessed 11 October 2012.

109   President of the 66th Session Nassir Abdulaziz, Al-Nasser, "On Combating Defamation of Religions and Promoting the Culture of Tolerane."

110   Article VII, "Combating Islamophobia," The Third Extraordinary Session of the Islamic Summit.

111   "Contemporary forms of Racism," Twenty-Eighth Session of the Islamic Conference of Foreign Ministers, Bamako, Republic of Mali, 4-8 Rabi-ul-Thani, 1422H (25-29 June, 2001), URL: http://www.oic-oci.org/oicnew/english/conf/fm/28/28-ICFM-SG-Rep-en/28-ICFM-LEG-D-en.htm.

112   "Defamation of Religions," Reports of the Secretary General on the Legal Affairs Submitted to the Twenty-Eighth Session of the Islamic Conference of Foreign Ministers, Bamako, Republic of Mali, 4-8 Rabi-ul-Thani, 1422H (25-29 June, 2001), URL: http://www.oic-oci.org/oicnew/english/conf/fm/28/28-ICFM-SG-Rep-en/28-ICFM-LEG-D-en.htm. Cited hereafter as "Twenty-Eighth Session of the Islamic Conference of Foreign Ministers, Bamako."

113   (26 Protests) "Muslim Protests – Across the Globe, a 14-Minute YouTube Clip of an Anti-Muslim Movie is Sparking Protest against U.S. Embassies and Institutions," *Google Maps*, 14 September 2012, URL: https://maps.google.com/maps/ms?msid=201645180959880549419.0004c9a894dfb66defab9&msa=0&ie=UTF8&t=m&source=embed&ll=32.10119%2C42.1875&spn=57.886601%2C105.46875&z=3, 14 September 2012.

114   Declan Walsh, "19 Reported Dead as Pakistanis Protest Muhammad Video," New York Times, 21 September 2012, URL: http://www.nytimes.com/2012/09/22/world/asia/protests-in-pakistan-over-anti-islam-film.html?pagewanted=all, 31 January 2014.

115   Anti-Blasphemy Law Sharply Debated at UN, *Al-Jazeera*, 26 September 2012, URL: http://www.aljazeera.com/news/americas/2012/09/2012926112223402623.html, 4 February 2014.

116   President Asif Ali Zardari urges UN to ban hate speech," *News Pakistan*, 26 September 2012. Accessed online 12 January 2014, URL: http://www.newspakistan.pk/2012/09/26/president-asif-ali-zardari-urges-ban-hate-speech/

117 Gearan, Anne, "Egypt's President Morsi tells U.N.: Insults to Muhammad 'Unacceptable,'" *Washington Post*, September 26, 2012. Accessed online 12 January 2014, URL: http://www. washingtonpost.com/world/national-security/egypts-president-morsi-tells-un-insults-to-muhammad-unacceptable/2012/09/26/fef14e46-07f3-11e2-858a-5311df86ab04_story.html

118 Irish, John, "At UN, Muslim world questions Western freedom of speech," *Reuters*, 28 September 2012. Accessed online 12 January 2014, URL: http://www.reuters.com/article/2012/09/29/us-un-assembly-islam-idUSBRE88R1JI20120929

119 For the 18 OIC Countries, see URLs: on 25 September 2012: http://gadebate.un.org/sites/default/files/gastatements/67/NG_en.pdf; on 26 September 2012 – Yemen, http://gadebate.un.org/67/yemen; Kuwait, http://gadebate.un.org/67/kuwait; Niger, http:// gadebate.un.org/67/niger; on 27 September 2012 – Bahrain, http://gadebate.un.org/67/bahrain; Lebanon, http://gadebate.un.org/67/lebanon; Albania, http://gadebate.un.org/67/albania; Brunei Darussalam, http://gadebate.un.org/67/brunei-darussalam; Comoros, http://gadebate.un.org/67/ comoros; Bosnia and Herzegovina (Observer), http://gadebate.un.org/67/bosnia-and-herzegovina; Maldives, http://gadebate.un.org/67/maldives; on 28 September 2012 - Saudi Arabia, http://gadebate. un.org/67/saudi-arabia; United Arab Emirates, http://gadebate.un.org/67/united-arab-emirates; Morocco, http://gadebate.un.org/67/morocco; Azerbaijan, http://gadebate.un.org/67/azerbaijan; and on 1 October 2012 – Oman, http://gadebate.un.org/67/oman; Sierra Leone, http://gadebate. un.org/67/sierra-leone; Djibouti, http://gadebate.un.org/67/djibouti, accessed 28 November 2013.

120 Stringer, David and Diaa Hadid, "Muslim leaders say call for global ban on anti-Islam 'hate speech' is not attack on free speech," *National Post*, September 29, 2012. Accessed online 12 January 2014, URL: http://news.nationalpost.com/2012/09/29/muslim-leaders-say-call-for-global-ban-on-anti-islam-hate-speech-is-not-attack-on-free-speech/

121 Transcript, "Ekmeleddin Ihsanoglu, Secretary General of the Organization of the Islamic Cooperation," *Khaleejia TV*, Jeddah, 10 November 2012 (as captured as "Interview with Leader of OIC 2012, captured by *Vladtepesblog.com*, posted on *MRCtv* 5 January 2013), URL: http://www.mrctv. org/videos/interview-leader-oic-2012, accessed 22 January 2013.

122 "International Condemnation of the anti-Muslim Film and the Violent Reaction Against It," OIC Journal, Issued by the Organization of the Islamic Cooperation (OIC), Issue No. 22, September-December 2012, URL: http://issuu.com/oic-journal/docs/oic_journal_issue_22_english, accessed 3 February 2013, 13.

123 "Remarks by the President to the UN General Assembly," given at the United Nations Headquarters, New York, New York, For Immediate Release, Office of the Press Secretary, The White House, 25 September 2012, URL: http://www.whitehouse.gov/the-press-office/2012/09/25/remarks-president-un-general-assembly, accessed 4 October 2012.

124 "Fallen SEAL's Father: Hillary Told Me 'We're Going to Arrest the Man That Made the Video' At Funeral," *Breitbart/Lars Larson Radio Show*, 25 October 2012. Accessed online 12 January 2014, URL: http://www.breitbart.com/Breitbart-TV/2012/10/25/Fallen-Seals-Father-Hillary-Told-M-Dont-Worry-Were-Going-To-Arrest-The-Man-That-Did-This

125 Wilson, Stan, "Producer of anti-Islam film arrested, ordered held without bail," *CNN*, 28 September 2012. Accessed online 12 January 2014, URL: http://www.cnn.com/2012/09/27/world/ california-anti-islam-filmmaker/

126 United Nations Biography, Ufuk Goksen, Permanent Observer Mission to the United Nations in New York, the United Nations, United Nations webpage, Undated, URL: http://www.oicun.org/ oic_at_un/ambassador/, re-accessed 12 January 2015.

127 Ufuk Gokcen, @iktgokcen, *Twitter*, 15 January 2015, URL: https://twitter.com/iktgokcen/ status/554729195889512448, accessed 12 January 2015. States: "Charlie Hebdo attack&reaction underline critical imp. of renewed commitment to resolution 16/18&Rabat Plan of Action."

128 Andrew Smith, "Charlie Hebdo Attack and Global Reaction Highlights Critical Importance

of Renwed Commitment to the Implementation of Resolution 16/18 and Rabat Plan of Action," Universal Human Rights Group, 12 January 2015, URL: http://universal-rights.org/blogs/119-charlie-hebdo-attack-and-global-reaction-highlights-critical-importance-of-renewed-commitment-to-the-implementation-of-resolution-16-18-and-the-rabat-plan-of-action, accessed 12 January 2015.

129 For example, see Sayed Sarwar Amani, "Afghanistan Rally Hails Charlie Hebdo Attackers as 'Heroes'," *Reuters/Yahoo News Canada*, 11 January 2015, URL: https://ca.news.yahoo.com/afghanistan-rally-hails-charlie-hebdo-attackers-heroes-083446525.html, accessed 12 January 2015 and Mubasher Bukhari, "Anti-Charlie Rally in Pakistan Draws 5,000," *Yahoo News/Reuters*, 18 January 2015, URL: http://news.yahoo.com/anti-charlie-rally-pakistan-draws-5-000-144701875.html;_ylt=AwrSyCTX8btULEcA97XQtDMD, accessed 18 January 2015.

130 "OIC Weighs Legal Action against French Magazine," *Arab News*, Jedda, 18 January 2015, URL: http://www.arabnews.com/featured/news/691261, accessed 18 January 2015.

131 Yusuf Al-Qaradawi, IUMS President, "IUMS Calls for the Islamic Nation to Continue in the Legal Peaceful Demonstrating to Defend the Great Messenger, and Calls for the West to Protect Muslim Communities from Attacks," *IUMS Online*, Doha, Qatar, 20 January 2015, URL: http://iumsonline.org/en/default.asp?menuID=62&contentID=8914, accessed 21 January 2015.

132 Yusuf Al-Qaradawi, IUMS President, "IUMS Calls for the Islamic Nation to Continue in the Legal Peaceful Demonstrating to Defend the Great Messenger, and Calls for the West to Protect Muslim Communities from Attacks," *IUMS Online*, Doha, Qatar, 20 January 2015, URL: http://iumsonline.org/en/default.asp?menuID=62&contentID=8914, accessed 21 January 2015.

133 Yusuf Al-Qaradawi, IUMS President, "IUMS Calls for the Islamic Nation to Continue in the Legal Peaceful Demonstrating to Defend the Great Messenger, and Calls for the West to Protect Muslim Communities from Attacks," *IUMS Online*, Doha, Qatar, 20 January 2015, URL: http://iumsonline.org/en/default.asp?menuID=62&contentID=8914, accessed 21 January 2015.

134 Yusuf Al-Qaradawi, IUMS President, "IUMS Calls for the Islamic Nation to Continue in the Legal Peaceful Demonstrating to Defend the Great Messenger, and Calls for the West to Protect Muslim Communities from Attacks," *IUMS Online*, Doha, Qatar, 20 January 2015, URL: http://iumsonline.org/en/default.asp?menuID=62&contentID=8914, accessed 21 January 2015.

135 Yusuf Al-Qaradawi, IUMS President, "IUMS Calls for the Islamic Nation to Continue in the Legal Peaceful Demonstrating to Defend the Great Messenger, and Calls for the West to Protect Muslim Communities from Attacks," *IUMS Online*, Doha, Qatar, 20 January 2015, URL: http://iumsonline.org/en/default.asp?menuID=62&contentID=8914, accessed 21 January 2015.

136 Keller, *Reliance of the Traveller*, 596. (Book O "Justice," § o8.4 "Apostasy from Islam [Ridda].")

137 Keller, *Reliance of the Traveller*, Book P "Enormities," at § p9.5 There are a substantial number of citations to Islamic law in the 1994 edition of the English-language translation of Ahmad ibn Naqib al-Misri's *'Umdat al-Salik (Reliance of the Traveller: A Classic Manual of Islamic Sacred Law)*.[1] *Reliance* satisfies all the criteria for being broadly authoritative. The subtitle states that it is "A Classic Manual of Islamic Sacred Law." It "represents one of the finest and most reliable short works in Shafi'i jurisprudence."[2] Additionally, "the authors of the present volume and their positions represent the orthodox Muslim intellectual and spiritual heritage that has been the strength of the Community for over a thousand years, and the means through which Allah has preserved His religion, in its purest and fullest sense, to the present day."[3] *Reliance* claims a doctrinal basis. That claim is only as strong as the authority that certifies it. The authority of *Reliance* is established by certifications from national authorities in Egypt, Saudi Arabia, Jordan, and Syria. Particularly persuasive is the endorsement of Cairo's al-Azhar University (the most prestigious and authoritative institute of Islamic higher learning) with signature and stamps that serve as a kind of Islamic *imprimatur* and *nihil obstat*:

> "… concerning the examination of the English translation of the book *'Umadat al-salik wa 'uddat al-nasik* by Ahmad ibn Naqib in the Shafi'i school of jurisprudence, together with appendices by Islamic scholars on matters of Islamic law, tenets of faith, and personal

ethics and character: **we certify that the above-mentioned translation corresponds to the Arabic original and conforms to the practice and faith of the orthodox Sunni Community** (*Ahl al-Sunna wa al-Jama'a*)."[4]

Also persuasive is also the certification in Document 3 from the International Institute of Islamic Thought (IIIT), which states:

1. "There is no doubt that this translation is a valuable and important work, whether as a textbook for teaching Islamic jurisprudence to English-speakers, or as a legal reference for use by scholars, educated laymen, and students in this language.

2. As for the correction of the translation, its accuracy, and its fidelity to the meaning and objects, ... the translation presents the legal questions in a faithful and precise idiom that clearly delivers the complete meaning in a sound English style ... demonstrating the translator's knowledge of Sacred law and ability in jurisprudence as well as his complete command of both the Arabic and the English languages.

3. ... general benefit to both followers of Shafi'i school and others of the Muslim community.

4. ... its aim is to imbue the consciousness of the non-Arab-speaking Muslim with a sound understanding of the Sacred Law."[5]

Dr. Taha Jabir al-'Alwani was the signature authority for Document 3 on behalf of the Islamic Fiqh Academy in Jedda, penned on International Institute of Islamic Thought (IIIT) letterhead. Also in the signature block is his title as president of the Fiqh Council of North America (FCNA).[6] The International Islamic Fiqh Academy in Jedda was "established within the framework of the OIC in accordance with a resolution adopted by the Islamic Conference of Kings and Heads of State and Government of the Islamic Conference of Foreign Ministers."[7] This would seem to indicate that approval by the Islamic Fiqh Academy at Jedda reflects broad approval of *Reliance* across the Islamic world in some official capacity. As the president of both FCNA and IIIT, both known American Muslim Brotherhood entities, al-'Alwani's close senior interconnected relationships are evidence that a relationship exists between those organizations and the OIC. Thus, any time *Reliance* is used to establish a point of Islamic law, the burden-shifting presumption should be that Al-Azhar and the OIC share the same construction of Islamic law as the Muslim Brothers in America and that this reflects the "version" of shariah that is popularly sold and broadly available.

[1] Keller, *Reliance of the Traveller*, book cover.

[2] Keller, *Reliance of the Traveller*, vii.

[3] Keller, *Reliance of the Traveller*, viii.

[4] Keller, *Reliance of the Traveller* Documents 4, Certification page, letterhead - Al-Azhar Islamic Research Academy, General Department for Research, Writing and Translation, xx, xxi.

[5] Keller, *Reliance of the Traveller*, Document 3, Certification page, IIIT letterhead with Alwani signature block, International Institute of Islamic Thought, xviii-xix.

[6] *Reliance*, Document 3, Certification page, letterhead and signature block, International Institute of Islamic Thought, xviii-xix. **Reads:** Both the IIIT and FCNA are associated with the Muslim Brotherhood in the *Explanatory Memorandum: On the General Strategic Goal for the Group*," Mohamed Akram, May 22, 1991, Government Exhibit 003-0085/3:04-CR-240-G U.S. v. HLF, et al., United States District Court, Northern District of Texas, http://www.txnd.uscourts.gov/judges/hlf2/09-25-08/Elbarasse%20Search%203.pdf. The FCNA is also a subordinate element of the Islamic Society of North America (ISNA). **Also:** The International Islamic Fiqh Academy (IIFA) is listed as a subsidiary organ of the OIC at "Subsidiary Organs, Organization of the Islamic Cooperation," OIC, URL: http://

www.oic-oci.org/page_detail.asp? p_id=64#FIQH, 4 February 2013. It was affiliated to the OIC in its fourteenth session, held in Duha (Qatar) 5–13 Dhul-Qi`dah1423 A.H., 11–16 January 2003 C.E, as cited in "*Jihad*: Rulings & Regulations," "Living Shari'a/ Fatwa Bank," *IslamOnline*, at URL: http://www.freerepublic.com/focus/news/2390531/ replies?c=7.

[7] Organization of the Islamic Conference, Subsidiary Organs, at URL http://www.oic-oci.org/page_detail.asp?p_id=64, 6 April 2011.

[8] Mohamed Akram, Explanatory Memorandum, 18.

138 "Al-Azhar Deputy Leader Rejects British PM's Comments on Free Speech," *AhramOnline* (Cairo), 19 January 2015, URL: http://english.ahram.org.eg/News/120718.aspx, accessed 26 January 2015.

139 "Al-Azhar Deputy Leader Rejects British PM's Comments on Free Speech," *AhramOnline* (Cairo), 19 January 2015, URL: http://english.ahram.org.eg/News/120718.aspx, accessed 26 January 2015.

140 "CAIR Open Letter to 2016 Republican Presidential Candidates: Engage Muslim Voters, Reject Islamophobia," CAIR Press Release, 26 January 2015, URL: http://www.cair.com/images/pdf/ Open-Letter-to-2016-Republican-Presidential-Candidates.pdf, accessed 26 January 2015.

PART VII: CATASTROPHIC FAILURES

1   Letter to Ambassador Harold W. Geisel, Inspector General, Department of State from Members of Congress Michele Bachmann, Louie Gohmert, Lynn Westmoreland, Trent Franks and Thomas Rooney, 13 June 2012.

2   Letter to Mr. Charles K. Edward, Acting Inspector General, Department of Homeland Security from Members of Congress Michele Bachmann, Louie Gohmert, Trent Franks, Thomas Rooney and Lynn Westmoreland, 13 June 2012.

3   Letter to Ms. Lynne M. Halbrooks, Acting Inspector General, Department of Defense from Members of Congress Michele Bachmann, Louie Gohmert, Lynn Westmoreland, Trent Franks and Thomas Rooney, 13 June 2012.

4   Letter to Honorable Michael E. Horowitz, Inspector General, Department of Justice from Members of Congress Michele Bachmann, Louie Gohmert, Lynn Westmoreland, Trent Franks and Thomas Rooney, 13 June 2012.

5   Letter to Honorable I. Charles McCullough III, Inspector General, Office of the Director of National Intelligence from Members of Congress Michele Bachmann, Louie Gohmert, Lynn Westmoreland, Trent Franks and Thomas Rooney, 13 June 2012.

6   Congressman Keith Ellison Letter to Representatives Michele Bachmann, Louie Gohmert, Lynn Westmoreland, Trent Franks and Thomas Rooney, 12 July 2012.

7   Patrick Poole, "The Biggest DC Spy Scandal You Haven't Heard About," *CSP*, 16 August 2012, URL: http://www.centerforsecuritypolicy.org/2012/08/16/the-biggest-d-c-spy-scandal-you-havent-heard-about/, accessed 10 March 2013. Cited hereafter as Poole, "The Biggest DC Spy Scandal You Haven't Heard About."

8   Poole, "The Biggest DC Spy Scandal You Haven't Heard About."

9   Secretary of State Hillary Clinton, "Remarks at the Organization of the Islamic Conference (OIC) High-Level Meeting on Combating Religious Intolerance," Given at the Center for Islamic Arts and History, Istanbul, Turkey, *United States Department of State Release*, 15 July 2011, http://www.state.gov/secretary/rm/2011/07/168636.htm, accessed July 21 2011.

10   "High Ranking DOJ Official Refuses to Affirm 1st Amendment Rights," Representative Trent Franks, *YouTube* published by *Rep Trent Franks*, 26 July 2012, http://www.youtube.com/watch?v=0wwv9l6W8yc&feature=player_embedded, accessed 27 July 2012.

11   Countering Violent Extremism (CVE) Working Group, Homeland Security Advisory Council, Department of Homeland Security, Office of Civil Rights and Civil Liberties, Spring 2010, http://www.dhs.gov/xlibrary/assets/hsac_cve _working_group_recommendations.pdf

12   "House Intel Leaders Disavow Bachmann Allegations," *USA Today*—On Politics, 20 July 2012, URL: http://content.usatoday.com/communities/onpolitics/post/2012/07/michele-bachmann-huma-abedin-rogers-ruppersberger/1, accessed 5 March 2013. **Reads:** "Intelligence Committee Chairman Mike Rogers, R-Mich., a former FBI agent, said Bachmann's assertions about the Muslim Brotherhood's infiltration efforts are false. 'That kind of assertion certainly doesn't comport with the Intelligence Committee, and I can say that on the record'." Cited hereafter as "House Intel Leaders Disavow Bachmann Allegations," *USA Today*.

13   "Obama Administration Corrects Clapper's Claim That Muslim Brotherhood Is 'Secular'," *FoxNew.com*, 10 February 2011, URL: http://www.foxnews.com/politics/2011/02/10/administration-corrects-dni-clapper-claim-muslim-brotherhood-secular/, accessed 10 March 2013.

14   Poole, "The Biggest DC Spy Scandal You Haven't Heard About."

15   "House Intel Leaders Disavow Bachmann Allegations," *USA Today*.

16   Amanda Terkel, "John McCain Slams Michele Bachmann's 'Unfounded' Attack on Huma Abedin, Muslim Americans, *Huffington Post*, Politics, 18 July 2013, URL: http://www.huffingtonpost.com/2012/07/18/john-mccain-michele-bachmann-muslim_n_1683277.html, accessed 11 May 2013.

17   Congresswoman Michele Bachmann's Letter in Response to Representative Keith Ellison, 13 July 2012.

18   Niraj Warikoo and Paul Egan, "Muslim Conference in Detroit Stirs Controversy," *USA Today*, 29 August 2014, URL: http://www.usatoday.com/story/news/nation/2014/08/29/muslim-conference-detroit-controversy/14793227/, accessed 30 August 2014. **States:** The convention also features a panel discussion on Kashmir with Ghulam Nabi Fai, a Virginia man who was arrested by the FBI in 2011 and then pleaded guilty to federal charges of conspiracy and violating tax laws. He was sentenced in March 2012 to two years in federal prison after admitting he got millions of dollars from Pakistan's intelligence services.

19   Executive Summary – Review of FBI Interactions with he Council on American-Islamic Relations, September 2013, I-2012-007R, U.S. Department of Justice, Office of the Inspector General (Redacted – For Public Release), 19 September 2013, http://www.justice.gov/oig/reports/2013/e0707r-summary.pdf, accessed 19 September 2013, 4,5. Cited hereafter as Executive Summary – Review of FBI Interactions with CAIR.

20   Dina Temple-Raston, "Terrorism Training Casts Pall Over Muslim Employee," *NPR*, 18 July 2011, http://www.npr.org/2011/07/18/137712352/terrorism-training-casts-pall-over-muslim-employee

21   "CAIR Asks CIA to Drop Islamophobia Trainer: Trainer Exposed by NPR for Smearing Ohio Muslim Scheduled to Lecture at Agency," American Muslim News Briefs, *CAIR* 18 July 2011, http://campaign.r20.constantcontact.com/render?llr=95acjidab&v=001KWNitdH9AKWo1QQ7OeW35d8NWIbnX1hDN0nZsIN3Pb-9IYknGLzFw1H5FHn10IuVqRS6-naoY-yzuxJu0L5bVcLXiAfLrF0tHq0H9Fv0oVw%3D.

22   "CAIR Asks CIA to Drop Islamophobic Trainer," *CAIR Facebook*, 18 July 2011, http://www.facebook.com/notes/cair/cair-asks-cia-to-drop-islamophobic-trainer/10150257307484442?ref=nf

23   (Redacted) E-Mail Cancellation of "Conference on Homegrown Radical Extremism in the United States," August 10-12, 2011, *CIA Sponsoring Entity*, 22 July 2011.

24   "Vision/Mission," Muslim Public Affairs Council (MPAC) website. http://www.mpac.org/about/vision-mission/

25   "MPAC Report Names 25 Individuals Unqualified To Be Islam Experts; MPAC Leaders Fail Their Own Test," *Global Muslim Brotherhood Daily Report*, November 29, 2012. http://globalmbreport.org/?p=7617&print=1.

26   MPAC Testimony Submitted to Congressman Christopher Shays (R-CT), Chairman of the Subcommittee on National Security, Emerging Threats, and International Relations, 24 August 2004, at URL: http://www.mpac.org/programs/government-relations/mpac-executive-director-testifies-before-us-house-committee-on-homeland-security.php .

27   "Definitions of Terrorism in the U.S. Code," What We Investigate, FBI, URL: http://www.fbi.gov/about-us/investigate/terrorism/terrorism-definition, (re)accessed 14 February 2014.

28   A Review of U.S. Counterterrorism Policy: American Muslim Critique & Recommendations, Muslim Public Affairs Council (MPAC), May 2003, 78.

29   Mohamed Akram, Explanatory Memorandum, 5.

30   Mohamed Akram, Explanatory Memorandum, 7.

31   *The Afghan Islamic Emirate Rules and Regulations for Mujahidin Pashto,* Captured Document, Afghanistan AOR, undated. READS: Afghanistan Islamic Emirate Rules and Regulations for Mujahidin Pashto -

"… then the person who committed the crime will not be supported by the Islamic Movement, …"

32   Part 2(a), Countering Violent Extremism (CVE) Training Guidance & Best Practices," Office for Civil Rights and Civil Liberties, DHS, October 2011, http://www.dhs.gov/xlibrary/assets/cve-training-guidance.pdf.

33   *The 9/11 Commission Report*, National Commission on Terrorist Attacks Upon the United States, 22 July 2004, http://www.9-11commission.gov/report/911Report.pdf.

34   *Federal Bureau of Investigation Counterterrorism Analytical Lexicon*, U.S. Department of Justice, Federal Bureau of Investigation, undated but believed to be a 2008 product, at Cryptome at URL: http://cryptome.org/fbi-ct-lexicon.pdf. Cited hereafter as *FBI Counterterrorism Analytical Lexicon*.

35   *National Intelligence Strategy of the United States of America*, Director of National Intelligence, August 2009, http://www.dni.gov/reports/2009_NIS.pdf.

36   Protecting the Force: Lessons from Fort Hood, Report on the DoD Independent Review, Office of the Secretary of Defense, Department of Defense, 15 January 2010, http://www.defense.gov/pubs/pdfs/DOD-ProtectingTheForce-Web_Security_HR_13Jan10.pdf?test=latestnews.

37   National Intelligence Strategy of the United States of America, Director of National Intelligence, August 2009, http://www.dni.gov/reports/2009_NIS.pdf, 6.

38   *FBI Counterterrorism Analytical Lexicon.*

39   Michael Daly, "Nidal Hasan's Murders Termed 'Workplace Violence' by U.S.," *The Daily Beast*, 6 August 2013, URL: http://www.thedailybeast.com/articles/2013/08/06/nidal-hasan-s-murders-termed-workplace-violence-by-u-s.html, accessed 25 January 2015.

40   General Casey comments on Fort Hood on *This Week with George Stepahopoulos, ABCNews*, 8 November 2009.

41   *FBI Counterterrorism Analytical Lexicon*, 3.

42   *FBI Counterterrorism Analytical Lexicon*, 3.

43   Executive Summary of MPAC's 'Counterterrorism Policy Paper,' *Counterproductive Counterterrorism: How Anti-Islamic Rhetoric is Impeding America's Homeland Security*, Muslim Public Affairs Council (MPAC), December 2004, at URL: http://www.civilfreedoms.com/wp-content/uploads/2011/05/Counterproductive-Counterterrorism.pdf .

44   Shaarik Zafar, *Terminology to Define the Terrorists: Recommendations from American Muslims*, Department of Homeland Security, January 2008, at http://www.dhs.gov/xlibrary/assets/dhs_crcl_terminology_08-1-08_accessible.pdf. Cited hereafter as Zafar, *Terminology to Define Terrorist, DHS CRCL*.

45   "Words that Work and Words that Don't: A Guide for Counterterrorism Communication," Counter Communications Center, National Counterterrorism Center, 14 March 2008, from the Investigative Project on Terrorism, at URL: http://www.investigativeproject.org/documents/misc/126.pdf. Cited hereafter as NCTC "Words that Work."

46   Article 6, *Charter of the Organisation of the Islamic Conference*, at URL: http://www.oicoci.org/is11/english/Charter-en.pdf.

47   "Words that Work and Words that Don't: A Guide for Counterterrorism Communication,"

48   Josef Pieper, *Abuse of Language—Abuse of Power*, Ignatius Press, 1992 (trans. Lothar Krauth, Kosel-Verlag, Munich 1974), 32. Cited hereafter as Pieper, *Abuse of Language-Abuse of Power*.

49   "Spotlight on Shaarik Zarar, Sr. Policy Advisor DHS," *PakPac E-Letter*, August 2009, URL: http://pakpac.net/Newsletter%20July09%20onwards/Aug09/VolI/LTR_Aug09_VolI.asp#Religious_Freedom, accessed 23 June 2013.

50   Zafar, *Terminology to Define Terrorist, DHS CRCL*.

51   Zafar, *Terminology to Define Terrorist, DHS CRCL*.

52   Announcement: "First Annual Youth Employment Conference,"*PakPac E-Letter*, July 2010, URL: http://pakpac.net/Newsletter/2010/Jul/LTR_Jul10_volII.asp, accessed 24 June 2013.

53   News Release, "Mr. Shaarik Zafar," United States Mission to the OSCE, Office of Public Affairs, 16 June 2006, URL: http://osce.usmission.gov/media/pdfs/shaarik_zafar.pdf, accessed 10 October 2013.

54   Michelle Boorstein, "State Department Taps Texas Lawyer to Serve as 'America's Ambassador to Muslims'," *Washington Post*, 29 August 2014, URL: http://www.washingtonpost.com/local/zafar-takes-over-as-special-rep...unities/2014/08/29/7d89f0f2-2edd-11e4-bb9b-997ae96fad33_story.html, accessed 30 August 2014. **States:** "State Department's new special representative to Muslim communities. ..."

55   "Senate Homeland Security and Governmental Affairs Committee and House Homeland Security Committee Hold Joint Hearing on Threats to Military Communities Inside the Inside the United States," Congressional Hearings, *CQ Congressional Transcripts*, Washington, D.C., 7 December 2011. Cite hereafter as *CQ Congressional Transcripts*, "Joint Hearing on Threats to Military Communities Inside the United States."

56   *CQ Congressional Transcripts*, "Joint Hearing on Threats to Military Communities Inside the United States."

57   *CQ Congressional Transcripts*, "Joint Hearing on Threats to Military Communities Inside the United States."

58   *CQ Congressional Transcripts*, "Joint Hearing on Threats to Military Communities Inside the United States."

59   *CQ Congressional Transcripts*, "Joint Hearing on Threats to Military Communities Inside the United States."

60   "CAIR Says Bill Unfairly Singles Out U.S. Muslims," *CAIR Release*, 19 September 2011, http://www.cair.com/ArticleDetails.aspx?ArticleID=26885&&name=n&&currPage=1

61   "CAIR Says Bill Unfairly Singles Out U.S. Muslims," *CAIR Release*.

62   §2(a), "Countering Violent Extremism (CVE) Training Guidance & Best Practices," Office for Civil Rights and Civil Liberties, DHS, October 2011, http://www.dhs.gov/xlibrary/assets/cve-training-guidance.pdf. Cite hereafter as DHS CRCL "CVE Training Guidance & Best Practices."

63   Fataawah - "Resolution On Being Faithful Muslims and Loyal Americans," Fataawah from Fiqh Council of North America (FCNA), 5 October 2011, http://www.icsd.org/2011/10/resolution-on-being-faithful-muslims-and-loyal-americans/.

64   DHS CRCL "CVE Training Guidance & Best Practices."

65   DHS CRCL "CVE Training Guidance & Best Practices."

66   Pieper, *Abuse of Language–Abuse of Power*, 29.

67   The FBI's Guiding Principles: Touchstone Document on Training - 2012, Federal Bureau of Investigations, 22 March 2012, URL: http://www.fbi.gov/about-us/training/guiding-principles, originally accessed 23 March 2012.

68   The FBI's Guiding Principles: Touchstone Document on Training - 2012, Federal Bureau of Investigations, 22 March 2012, URL: http://www.fbi.gov/about-us/training/guiding-principles, originally accessed 23 March 2012.

69   18 U.S. Code Section 2339A – Providing Material Support to Terrorists, Legal Information Institute (LLI), Cornell University Law School, undated, URL: http://www.law.cornell.edu/uscode/text/18/2339A, accessed 12 December 2014.

70   Holder v. Humanitarian Law Project, 561 U.S. 1 (2010).

71   Josh Rushing, "US Military Under Fire for 'Anti-Islam Class'" (transcript), *Al-Jazeera* TV (Washington Office), 12 May 2012, URL: http://www.aljazeera.com/video/americas/2012/05/20125124178148367.html, alternatively released on YouTube URL: http://www.youtube.com/ watch? feature=player_embedded&v=2swVVfZo5eM#!, accessed 20 May 2012.

72   Mohamed Elibiary Tweet, Twitter @MohamedElibiary, 13 August 2014, URL: https://twitter.com/MohamedElibiary/status/499590321131782144, accessed 14 August 2014. **States:** With my 22+ yrs @GOP, friends thru out 100s US security/policing agencies & academia; no future presidency will reverse reforms underway.

73   "Raleigh Man Pleads Guilty to Conspiring to Provide Material Support for Terrorism," Department of Justice, Office of Public Affairs presser, 16 October 2016, http://www.justice.gov/opa/pr/raleigh-man-pleads-guilty-conspiring-provide-material-support-terrorism, accessed 16 October 2016. Cite hereafter as DOJ Presser "Raleigh Man Pleads Guilty to Provide Material Support to Terrorism."

74   DOJ Presser "Raleigh Man Pleads Guilty to Provide Material Support to Terrorism."

75   Keller, *Reliance of the Traveller*, Subject Index, 1152. **States:** "*Fi Sabil Allah. See* Jihad." Cited hereafter as Keller, *Reliance of the Traveller*.

76   Bukhari, *Sahih Al-Bukhari*, Vol, 4, 44.

77   Number 54, Book 52 "Expeditions", *Sahih Bukhari*, Volume 4, URL: http://www.sahih-bukhari.com/Pages/Bukhari_4_52.php, accessed 12 September 2014.

78   Number 46, Book 52 "Jihaad", *Sahih Bukhari*, Volume 4, URL: http://www.sahih-bukhari.com/Pages/Bukhari_4_52.php, accessed 12 September 2014.

79   Qutb, Islam and Universal Peace, 72.

80   Qutb, Islam and Universal Peace, 72.

81   Interpretation of the Meanings of the Noble Qur'an in the English Language: A Summarized Version of At-Tabari; Al-Qurtubi, and Ibn Kathir with Comments from Sahih Al-Bukhari, trans. and commentary by Dr. Muhammad Taqi-ud-Din Al-Hilali, and Dr. Muhammad Muhsin Khan, Darussalam, Riyadh, Saudi Arabia, 1999, Verse 9:60, 258. Cited hereafter as Noble Qur'an, Riyadh.

82   Yusuf Ali, *Qur'an*, 456.

83   Keller, *Reliance of the Traveller*, Book H "Zakat," "The Eight Categories of Recipients," at § h8.17 "Those Fighting for Allah".

84   DOJ Presser "Raleigh Man Pleads Guilty to Provide Material Support to Terrorism."

85   "Does CAIR Qualify to Receive Zakat?," CAIR -Council on American-Islamic Relations – webpage, at URL: https://www.cair.com/zakat.html, (first) accessed 15 April 2009, verified 16 February 2015. Cited hereafter as "Does CAIR Qualify to Receive Zakat?," CAIR webpage.

86   Stephen Coughlin, "In Context: Explaining Zakat, SCF Consequences & CAIR," PowerPoint Briefing, 2 May 2009.

87   "Does CAIR Qualify to Receive Zakat?," CAIR webpage.

88   "Does CAIR Qualify to Receive Zakat?," CAIR webpage.

89   "Does CAIR Qualify to Receive Zakat?," CAIR webpage.

90   "Does CAIR Qualify to Receive Zakat?," CAIR webpage.

91   Bukhari, *Sahih Al-Bukhari*, Vol, 4, 44.

92   "Does CAIR Qualify to Receive Zakat?," CAIR webpage.

93   "An Islamic Perspective on Giving Zakat to the MPAC Foundation," Muslim Public Affairs Council flyer, undated, downloaded 18 June 2013. Cited hereafter as MPAC Flyer "An Islamic

Perspective on Giving Zakat to the MPAC Foundation."

94   MPAC Flyer "An Islamic Perspective on Giving Zakat to the MPAC Foundation."

95   MPAC Flyer "An Islamic Perspective on Giving Zakat to the MPAC Foundation."

96   MPAC Flyer "An Islamic Perspective on Giving Zakat to the MPAC Foundation."

97   MPAC Flyer "An Islamic Perspective on Giving Zakat to the MPAC Foundation."

98   Keller, *Reliance of the Traveller*, Book H "Zakat," "The Eight Categories of Recipients," at § h8.17 "Those Fighting for Allah".

99   DOJ Presser "Raleigh Man Pleads Guilty to Provide Material Support to Terrorism."

100   *CQ Congressional Transcripts*, "Joint Hearing on Threats to Military Communities Inside the United States."

101   Taqiuddin An-Nabhani, (Hizb ut-Tahrir), *The Islamic State*, London: Al-Khilafah Publications, 1998, URL: http://www.hizb-ut-tahrir.org/PDF/EN/en_books_pdf/IslamicState.pdf, accessed 23 February 2013.

102   Taqiuddin An-Nabhani, (Hizb ut-Tahrir), *The Islamic State*, 143-144.

103   DHS/Hizb ut-Tahrir picture attribution: "Homeland Security at ISNA Right Next to Hizb ut-Tahrir," Little Green Footballs, 5 September 2007, at http://littlegreenfootballs.com/weblog/?entry=26926_Homeland_Security_at_ISNA_Right_ Next_to_Hizb_Ut-Tahrir&only

104   *Report to Congress on the Department of Homeland Security Office for Civil Rights and Civil Liberties*, Department of Homeland Security, 2007, http://www.dhs.gov/xlibrary/assets/crcl-fy07annualreport.pdf, 1. **Reads:** In accordance with 6 U.S.C. § 345 and 42 U.S.C. § 2000ee-1, the mission of the U.S. Department of Homeland Security (DHS) Office for Civil Rights and Civil Liberties (CRCL) is to assist the dedicated men and women of this Department in securing our country while preserving our freedoms and our way of life.

105   *Report to Congress on the Department of Homeland Security Office for Civil Rights and Civil Liberties*, DHS, 2. **Reads**:   Engagement with American Arab, Muslim, Sikh, South Asian, and Other Ethnic and Religious Communities: CRCL continued to build strategic partnerships between the government and these minority communities. ... In addition, CRCL has established the Incident Community Coordination Team (ICCT) to engage and provide community leaders with timely and relevant information from government agencies in the aftermath of any terrorist act or homeland security incident.

106   "Countering Violent Extremism Workshop (CVE) Working Group Recommendations," U.S. Department of Homeland Security, Homeland Security Advisory Council, 26 May 2010, URL: http://www.dhs.gov/xlibrary/assets/hsac_cve_working_group_recommendations.pdf. Cited hereafter as CVE Working Group Recommendations, DHS.

107   Attachment A, List of Unindicted Co-conspirators and/or Joint Ventures, United States of America vs. Holy Land Foundation, United States District Court for Northern District of Texas, Dallas Division, (Case 3:04-cr-00240, Document 656-2), 29 March 2007, at http://www.scribd.com/doc/49306041/Muslim-Brotherhood-Unindicted-Co-Conspirators. Hereafter cited as Attachment A, List of Unindicted Co-conspirators and/or Joint Ventures.

108   Collaborating   Organizations, *Peaceful   Families   Project*, http://www.peacefulfamilies.org/collaborating.html.

109   Affecting Change as an Imam: Imam Mohamed Magid, *Peaceful Families Project*, http://www.investigativeproject.org/documents/case_docs/423.pdf.

110   Form 990 Documenting Mohamed Elibiary's Status as Board Member on CAIR Dallas-Fort Worth Chapter –FY 2003, IRS Form 990 (2003) copy at *The Clarion Project Archives*, URL: http://www.clarionproject.org/document/990-form-proving-mohamed-elibiary-worked-cair, accessed 19

August 2014. **Note:** Identifies Elibiary as Board Member.

111   Our Team page of Freedom and Justice Foundation, Plano, Texas webpage, 22 June 2007, URL: https://web.archive.org/web/20081211064713/http://www.freeandjust.org/OurTeam.htm, accessed 26 September 2011. **Note:** President, CEO and Co-founder.

112   Muhamed Elibiary, "What Would You Say to America's Leading Islamophobes if Given the Opportunity," Muslim Matters, 6 February 2008, URL: http://muslimmatters.org/2008/02/06/what-would-you-say-to-america's-leading-islamophobes-if-given-the-opportunity/, accessed 27 June 2014. **States in "About Muhamed Elibiary":** Mohamed Elibiary co-founded the Freedom and Justice Foundation (F&J) in November 2002 to promote a Centrist Public Policy environment in Texas by coordinating the state level government and interfaith community relations for the organized Texas Muslim community. In 2005, Mohamed spearheaded the launching of the Texas Islamic Council (T.I.C.) as an F&J program for Muslim congregations, which has quickly grown to become the state's largest Muslim network encompassing 100,000 Texans. As Coordinator of the T.I.C., Mohamed developed working relationships with similar faith-based entities around Texas including the Texas Conference of Churches, Texas Catholic Conference and the Baptist General Convention of Texas. In 2006, the 16 largest Muslim congregations and civic organizations in the Dallas-Fort Worth area followed this example by creating a collective representative body called the North Texas Islamic Council (NTIC) and Mohamed was elected to its 7 member executive governing body. Since 2005, Mohamed, as a National Security Policy Analyst, has been advising intelligence and law enforcement agencies (ex. FBI, DHS, NCTC, ODNI, etc.) on various Counterterrorism (CT) issues (ex. Domestic Intelligence, Strategic Intelligence Analysis, Information Sharing and Radicalization).

113   Screen Capture, CAIR DFW webpage dated 12 April 2003, in article by Ryan Mauro, "Senior Homeland Security Advisor Formerly CAIR Official," The Clarion Project, 1 December 2013, URL: http://www.clarionproject.org/analysis/senior-homeland-security-adviser-formerly-cair-official, accessed 19 August 2014. **Note:** screen capture identifies Elibiary as Committee Chairman.

114   Form 990 Documenting Mohamed Elibiary's Status as Board Member on CAIR Dallas-Fort Worth Chapter –FY 2003, IRS Form 990 (2003) copy at The Clarion Project Archives, URL: http://www.clarionproject.org/document/990-form-proving-mohamed-elibiary-worked-cair, accessed 19 August 2014. **Note:** Identifies Elibiary as Board Member.

115   Muhamed Elibiary, "America Needs to Start a Discussion with the Muslim World," American Muslim Perspective, 31 October 2007, URL: http://www.archives2007.ghazali.net/html/americans_need.html also shared content with *Dallas Morning News* http://www.dallasnews.com/sharedcontent/dws/dn/opinion/viewpoints/stories/DN-elibiary_31edi.ART.State.Edition1.420f259.html#, accessed 19 August 2014. **States**: That man, I would later learn, was Shukri Abu-Baker, the CEO of the Richardson-based Holy Land Foundation. I was very moved by his passion and, at the same time, the plight of 400 Palestinians deported by Israel to a no-man's land between Israel's northern border and Lebanon's southern border. They faced cold conditions, lack of medicine and scorpions. Not only did I sign over my $50 as a donation, but I signed up for a monthly auto-draft that would continue uninterrupted until the foundation was shut down by a presidential executive order in December 2001.

116   Ryan Mauro, "A Window on the Muslim Brotherhood in America – An Annotated Interview with DHS Advisor Mohamed Elibiary, Center for Security Policy Occasional Paper in conjunction with The Clarion Project, 6 October 2013, URL: http://www.centerforsecuritypolicy.org/2013/10/06/a-window-on-the-muslim-brotherhood-in-america-an-annotated-interview-with-dhs-advisor-mohamed-elibiary/, accessed 19 August 2014, 6, 7. **Note: Mauro asks/Elibiary answers: <u>Mauro:</u>** Do you have any connection to the Holy Land Foundation (HLF)? **Elibiary:** My only connection to HLF was as a donor, and I published an op-ed on November 1, 2007 in the *Dallas Morning News*, prior to HLF's conviction, publicly outlining that experience. I disclosed how, as a 16-year old teenager, I was solicited to become a donor, and my journey investigating what happened after the government closed HLF.

117   Patrick Poole, "Breaking: Homeland Security Advisor Allegedly Leaked Intel to Attack Rick Perry,' PJ Media, 26 October 2011, URL: http://pjmedia.com/blog/breaking-homeland-security-

adviser-allegedly-leaked-intel-to-attack-rick-perry/, accessed 27 October 2011.

118 Mohamed Elibiary, Mohamed Elibiary (MohamedElibiary) on Twitter [since changed], 15 September 2013, URL: https://twitter.com/MohamedElibiary, accessed 15 September 2013.

119 Cited hereafter as CVE Working Group Recommendations, DHS., p 27.

120 Attachment A, List of Unindicted Co-conspirators and/or Joint Ventures.

121 National Security Experts File Motion to Dismiss Lawsuit Brought by Islamist with Suspected Ties to Terrorism, Press Release – American Freedom Law Center, 29 May 2013, URL: http://www. americanfreedomlawcenter.org/wp-content/uploads/pressapps/39aa490095832589174688ea2189845 e84ab4502.pdf, accessed 18 August 2014.

122 Andrew Gilligan and Alex Spillius, "Barack Obama adviser says Sharia Law is Misunderstood," *The Telegraph* (London), 8 October 2009, at http://www.telegraph.co.uk/news/worldnews/ barackobama/6274387/Obama-adviser-says -Sharia-Law-is-misunderstood.html

123 *Judicial Watch FOIA* to DHS Regarding January 2010 Meeting: http://www.judicialwatch.org/files/documents/2010/dhs-napolitano-jan-meeting-docs-1.pdf, http://www.judicialwatch.org/files/documents/2010/dhs-napolitano-jan-meeting-docs-2.pdf, http://www.judicialwatch.org/files/documents/2010/dhs-napolitano-jan-meeting-docs-3.pdf

124 "Full House Appropriations Committee Aproves FY 2013 CJS Bill," Congressman Frank Wolf, 10th District of Virginia Presser, 26 April 2012, URL: http://wolf.house.gov/media-center/press-releases/full-house-appropriations-committee-aproves-fy-2013-cjs-bill#.UwGs53kqCao, accessed 4 May 2012.

125 Attachment A, List of Unindicted Co-conspirators and/or Joint Ventures.

126 Executive Summary – Review of FBI Interactions with CAIR, 4, 5.

127 Wolf Statement on IG Report on FBI/CAIR, U.S. House of Representatives: Wolf Calls on FBI to Take Immediate Action Following Release of the IG Report Critical of Bureau's Dealing with CAIR (Report Finds FBI Field Offices Ignored Policy), 10 District of Virginia, 19 September 2013, URL: http://wolf.house.gov/press-releases/wolf-statement-on-ig-report-on-fbicair/, accessed 19 September 2013.

128 YouTube video of Hossam al-Jabri speaking at the December 2010 9th Annual MAS-ICNA Convention: http://www.youtube.com/watch?v=aRng91-Odn8

129 "Muslim American Society, The Investigative Project on Terrorism Dossier," *Investigative Project on Terrorism* (IPT), http://www.investigativeproject.org/documents/misc/44.pdf

130 "Jihad Saleh Williams (A/K/A Jihad F. Saleh)," *The Investigative Project on Terrorism.* http:// www.investigativeproject.org/documents/misc/728.pdf

131 LinkedIn page for Jihad Saleh Williams: http://www.linkedin.com/pub/jihad-saleh-williams/7/ a35/b08

132 Patrick Poole, "Al-Qaeda on Capitol Hill," *Human Events*, URL: http://www.humanevents. com/2010/09/28/alqaeda-on-capitol-hill/, accessed 15 September 2010.

133 Muslim Student Association at UCLA, Bruinwalk webpage, URL: http://www.bruinwalk.com/ groups/ucla-muslim-student-association-msa/, accessed 18 August 2014. Note: Al-Talib Magazine their publication.

134 Muslim Public Service Network (MPSN), http://www.muslimpublicservice.org/node/123

135 University of Southern California, Center for Religion and Civic Culture, American Muslim Civic Leadership Institute, which works in partnership with the Prince Alwaleed Bin Talal Center for Muslim Christian Understanding at Georgetown University. M. Bilal Kaleem bio page: http://crcc. usc.edu/initiatives/amcli/m-bilal-kaleem.html

136 Dr. Abdul Malik Mujahid's editorial, "Anti-Americanism and Public Diplomacy," appeared on page 2 in the November 2007 issue of the *Chicago Crescent*, the CIOGC newsletter. http://www.ciogc. org/images/cc_pdf/NOV-2007.pdf

137 The Council of Islamic Organizations of Greater Chicago (CIOGC) is a Muslim Brotherhood-linked organization whose online website may be found at http://www.ciogc.org/ Ahmed Rehab, CAIR-Chicago's Executive Director, is a featured CIOGC blogger on this homepage as is Dr. Abdul Malik Mujahid.

138 "Illinois Muslim Leaders Make Impact in Washington, DC at ISNA Convention," *CIOGC*, 6 July 2009. http://www.ciogc.org/Go.aspx?link=7654923

139 Mohamed Akram, *Explanatory Memorandum.*

140 Poole, Patrick, "Once Again, FBI's 'Muslim Outreach' Includes Terror-Tied Man," 4 June 2011 - http://pjmedia.com/blog/once-again-fbis-muslim-outreach-welcomes-terror-tied-man/?print=1; see also *US v. Holy Land Foundation, et al.*, 3:04-CR-240-G, "Government Exhibit- HLF Search 2," (N.D. Tx. September 25, 2008).

141 *Boim vs. Quranic Literacy Institute*, 00-C-2905, "Deposition of Kifah Mustapha," (N.D. Ill. March 2, 2004) pg.8.; Islamic Association for Palestine 2000 Chicago Convention Program.

142 Bio Page for the 2012 Guest Speakers for the 11th MAS-ICNA Annual Convention at http://www.investigativeproject.org/documents/case_docs/423.pdf.

143 Attachment A, List of Unindicted Co-conspirators and/or Joint Ventures.

144 "FBI Official: Illinois Imam Wouldn't Pass Background Check," *IPT News*, 27 May 2011, URL: http://www.investigativeproject.org/2914/fbi-official-illinois-imam-wouldnt-pass#, accessed 27 January 2015.

145 Patrick Poole, "Breaking: Homeland Security Advisor Allegedly Leaked Intel to Attack Rick Perry,' PJ Media, 26 October 2011, URL: http://pjmedia.com/blog/breaking-homeland-security-adviser-allegedly-leaked-intel-to-attack-rick-perry/, accessed 27 October 2011.

146 11ᵗʰ Annual MAS-ICNA Convention: http://www.masicna.com/conv2012/Speakers.aspx

147 "The Mosque Foundation's Troubling Record," *The Investigative Project on Terrorism*, http://www.investigativeproject.org/documents/misc/632.pdf

148 Hack, Chris and Allison Hantschel, "U.S. Investigating Mosque Foundation," *Daily Southtown*, September 23, 2003. http://www.religionnewsblog.com/4563/us-investigating-mosque-foundation

149 11ᵗʰ Annual MAS-ICNA Convention: http://www.masicna.com/conv2012/Speakers.aspx

150 Muslim Public Affairs Council (MPAC) Staff and Board, "Edina Lekovic." http://www.mpac.org/about/staff-board/edina-lekovic.php

151 Muslim Public Affairs Council (MPAC) Staff and Board, "Edina Lekovic."

152 "MPAC Report Names 25 Individuals Unqualified To Be Islam Experts; MPAC Leaders Fail Their Own Test," *Global Muslim Brotherhood Daily Report*, November 29, 2012. http://globalmbreport.org/?p=7617&print=1

153 Jihad in America – Maintaining an Islamic Identity in an un-Islamic Environment," "Spirit of Jihad" Edition, *al-Talib – The Muslim Newsmagazine and UCLA*, Edina Lekovic Managing Editor, July 1999, from Investigative Project on Terrorism Archive, URL: http://www.investigativeproject.org/redirect/1999-07_Al-Talib.pdf, accessed 18 August 2014.

154 Iliac Ramirez Sanchez (Carlos the Jackal), *Revolutionary Islam*, published in French, 2003.

155 Dina Temple-Raston, "Terrorism Training Casts Pall Over Muslim Employee," *NPR*, 18 July 2011, http://www.npr.org/2011/07/18/137712352/terrorism-training-casts-pall-over-muslim-employee

156 "CAIR Asks CIA to Drop Islamophobic Trainer," *CAIR Facebook*, 18 July 2011, http://www.

facebook.com/notes/cair/cair-asks-cia-to-drop-islamophobic-trainer/10150257307484442?ref=nf. **Awad States:** "It is vitally important that CIA agents carry out their work protecting our nation based on real security threats, not on inaccurate and agenda-driven Islamophobic rhetoric," wrote CAIR National Executive Director Nihad Awad in a letter to CIA Director Leon Panetta.

157 Mohamed Elibiary, "FBI Training, the Ackerman Expose & American Muslim Community Concerns," *MuslimMatters.org*, 18 September 2011, at http://muslimmatters.org/2011/09/18/fbi-training-the-ackerman-expose-american-muslim-community-concerns/. Elibiary States: I believe as Coughlin's career was ended, so will Gawthrop's and other less infamous full-time analysts inside the National Security enterprise, due to many factors about our country's resilient value system and scientific inquiry appetite that these individuals hardly understand. Cited hereafter as Elibiary, FBI Training, the Ackerman Expose & American Muslim Community Concerns," *MuslimMatters.org*.

158 Elibiary, FBI Training, the Ackerman Expose & American Muslim Community Concerns," *MuslimMatters.org*. **Author's Comment:** For the record, the "FBI and Homeland Security Intelligence Enterprise" never contacted me to defend the positions I took in my thesis and I stand behind it. In almost every instance where reference was made to an Islamic authority, I cited either the authority itself or an Islamic authority with status to offer commentary. As I still retain the source material for most of the authority cited, assertions that I provided an "inaccurate understanding" can be dismissed by simply showing the source of the information itself—for example, like citing the *Catechism of the Catholic Church* to make a point about what Catholics are required to believe.

159 Spencer Ackerman, "FBI's Key Muslim Ally: Bigoted Briefings 'Make My Job Harder," Danger Room *WIRED*, 20 September 2011 at http://www.wired.com/dangerroom/tag/mohammed-elibiary/

160 Sharona Schwartz, "Controversial Homeland Security Adviser Defends Use of Muslim Brotherhood-Associated Icon on His Twitter Profile," The Blaze, 30 September 2013. http://www.theblaze.com/stories/2013/09/30/controversial-adviser-to-department-of-homeland-security-defends-use-of-muslim-brotherhood-associated-icon-on-his-twitter-profile/

161 Mohamed Elibiary, "Mohamed Elibiary: Verdict Misrepresents "Material Support," Dallas News, 24 June 2010, URL: http://www.dallasnews.com/opinion/latest-columns/20100624-Mohamed-Elibiary-Verdict-misinterprets-4772.ece?nclick_check=1, accessed 30 June 2010.

162 Holder v Humanitarian Law Project, 561 U.S. ___(2010), URL: http://www.supremecourt.gov/opinions/09pdf/08-1498.pdf

163 "Sayyid Qutb's Purpose-Driven Life," *DallasNews*, August 28, 2006, http://dallasmorningviewsblog.dallasnews.com/2006/08/sayyid-qutbs-pu.html/.

164 Twitter / MohamedElibiary@MohamedElibiary, 30 June 2014, URL: https://twitter.com/MohamedElibiary/status/483666334123704320, accessed 3 July 2014. **Actual Tweet:** "Year ago I used to have to defend.

165 U.S. State Department, FTO List. ISIL (or ISIS) is actually a re=designation of the same group reflecting the groups name change from "al-Qaeda in Iraq" that was registered on the FTO 17 December 2004.

166 Twitter / MohamedElibiary: @davereaboi, 13 June 2014, URL: https://twitter.com/mohamedelibiary/status/477510829261066241, accessed 18 June 2014. **Actual Tweet:** "CNN just broadcast list of ISIS hudod rules. Reminds me of how we were outraged pre 9/11 by Taliban banning white socks 4 women. […] As I've said b4 inevitable that "Caliphate" returns. Choice only whether we support EU like Muslim Union vision or not."

167 Damien Gayle, "Seconds Before the Slaughter: Global Horror at Images of Iraqi Army Desterters Who were Rounded up at Gunpoint, Herded into Lorries and Shot Dead by Masked ISIS Fanatics," *MailOnline*, 15 June 2014, URL: http://www.dailymail.co.uk/news/article-2658286/Return-Mosul-Days-Iraqs-second-largest-city-fell-feard-Isis-fighters-Iraqis-heading-promise-food-gas-water.html, accessed 15 June 2014.

168 Twitter / MohamedElibiary: @davereaboi, 13 June 2014, URL: https://twitter.com/

mohamedelibiary/status/477510829261066241, accessed 18 June 2014. **Actual Tweet:** "As I've said b4 inevitable that "Caliphate" returns. Choice only whether we support EU like Muslim Union vision or not." ... US heading in that direction. Bush created OIC Special Envoy. Obama removed discriminatory engagement policy towards MB, etc."

169 See for example Ahsan, *OIC: An Introduction.*

170 CVE Working Group Recommendations, DHS.

171 Spencer Ackerman, "FBI Teaches Agents: 'Mainstream' Muslims Are 'Violent, Radical,' Danger Room WIRED, 14 September 2011, http://www.wired.com/dangerroom/2011/09/fbi-muslims-radical/

172 Spencer Ackerman, "FBI's Key Muslim Ally: Bigoted Briefings 'Make My Job Harder,'" Danger Room *WIRED,* 20 September 2011 at http://www.wired.com/dangerroom/tag/mohammed-elibiary/

173 Elibiary, FBI Training, the Ackerman Expose & American Muslim Community Concerns," *MuslimMatters.org.*

174 ACLU Letter to FBI Director Mueller, ACLU, 4 October 2011, http://www.aclu.org/files/assets/sign_on_letter_to_dir_mueller_re_radicalization_report_10.4.11.pdf

175 Spencer Ackerman, "FBI Crime Maps Now 'Pinpoint' Average Muslims," Danger Room *WIRED,* 24 October 2011, http://www.wired.com/dangerroom/2011/10/fbi-geomaps-muslims/. Ackerman states: "The ACLU—where, full disclosure, my wife works."

176 *Letter to John Brennan,* Assistant to the President for Homeland Security and Counterterrorism and Deputy National Security Advisor, The White House, signed by, among others, numerous organizations known to be associated with the Muslim Brotherhood, PDF document dated 19 October 2011.

177 Letter to Farhana Khera from John Brennan, the White House, 3 November 2011.

178 ISNA & Nat. Orgs. Meet With FBI Dir. To Discuss Biased Fbi Training Materials," *Isna Press Release,* Isna, 14 February 2012, Url: http://counterjihadreport.com/2012/02/14/isna-nat-orgs-meet-with-fbi-dir-to-discuss-biased-fbi-training-materials/

179 71-022, 112th Congress, *Report House of Representatives,* 1st Session, 112-284: Agriculture, Rural Development, Food and Drug Administration, and Related Agencies Programs for the Fiscal Year Ending September 30, 2012, and for Other Purposes, 14 November 2011- Ordered to be printed, to accompany H.R. 2112, signed 18 November 2011, URL: http://thomas.loc.gov/cgi-bin/cpquery/T? &report=hr284& dbname =112&. **States:** "*Liaison partnerships*—The conferees support the FBI's policy prohibiting any formal non-investigative cooperation with unindicted co-conspirators in terrorism cases. The conferees expect the FBI to insist on full compliance with this policy by FBI field offices and to report to the Committees on Appropriations regarding any violation of the policy."

180 FBI Director Mueller, Testimony, "House Judiciary Committee Holds Hearing on Oversight of the FBI," Congressional Hearings, *CQ Congressional Transcripts,* 9 May 2012. Read: Mueller "So it is not as if we have purged a substantial amount of our training materials."

181 David Alexander, "Military Instructor Suspended over Islam Course," *Reuters,* 20 June 2012, http://www.reuters.com/article/2012/06/20/us-usa-defense-islam-idUSBRE85J0XJ20120620, accessed 20 June 2012.

182 Letter to Farhana Khera from John Brennan, the White House, 3 November 2011.

183 Senator John Kyl Questioning Farhana Khera, "Senate Judiciary Subcommittee on Constitution, Civil Rights and Human Rights Holds Hearing on Protecting the Civil Rights of American Muslims" (The "Durban" Hearings"), Congressional Hearings, *CQ Congressional Transcripts,* 29 March 2011.

184 Keller, *Reliance of the Traveller,* Book R "Holding One's Tongue," at §§r7.0, r7.1, and r7.1(1)," **Reads:** Giving directions to someone who wants to do wrong. It is not permissible to give directions and the like to someone intending to perpetrate a sin, because it is helping another to commit

disobedience. Giving directions to wrongdoers includes: 1) showing the way to policemen and tyrants when they are going to commit injustice and corruption."

185 Spencer Ackerman, "FBI Purges Hundreds of Terrorism Documents in Islamophobia Probe," Danger Room *WIRED* 15 February 2012 http://www.wired.com/dangerroom/2012/02/hundreds-fbi-documents-muslims/

186 Josh Rushing, "US Military Under Fire for 'Anti-Islam Class'" (transcript), *Al-Jazeera* TV (Washington Office), 12 May 2012, URL: http://www.aljazeera.com/video/americas/2012/05/20125124178148367.html alternatively released on YouTube URL: http://www.youtube.com/ watch? feature=player_embedded&v=2swVVfZo5eM#!, accessed 20 May 2012. Cited hereafter as Rushing, "US Military Under Fire for 'Anti-Islam Class'" (transcript), *Al-Jazeera* TV.

187 Spencer Ackerman, "Exclusive: Senior U.S. General Orders Top-to-Bottom Review of Military's Islam Training," *WIRED*—Danger Room, 24 April 2012, http://www.wired.com/dangerroom/2012/04/military-islam-training/

188 Footnote: Chris Lewis, "Joint Force Staff College Course on Radical Islam," E-Mail to Congressional Committees from the Joint Chiefs of Staff Legislative Affairs, 24 April 2012.

189 Elhanan Miller, "Syrian Christians Sign Treaty of Submission to Islamists," Times of Israel, 27 February 2014, URL: http://www.timesofisrael.com/syrian-christians-sign-treaty-of-submission-to-islamists/#ixzz2uXOQiNMs, accessed 27 February 2014.

190 Elhanan Miller, "Syrian Christians Sign Treaty of Submission to Islamists," Times of Israel.

191 Ibn Kathir, *Tafsir Ibn Kathir*, vol 4, 406 - 407.

192 Keller, *Reliance of the Traveller*, Book O "Justice," at o11 "Non-Muslim Subjects of the Islamic State (*Ahl Al-Dhimma*)," at o11.5.

193 Keller, *Reliance of the Traveller*, Book O "Justice," at o11.0 "Non-Muslim Subjects of the Islamic State," at § o11.11.

194 Fataawah - "Resolution On Being Faithful Muslims and Loyal Americans," Fataawah from Fiqh Council of North America (FCNA), 5 October 2011, http://www.icsd.org/2011/10/resolution-on-being-faithful-muslims-and-loyal-americans/

195 Twitter / MohamedElibiary: @davereaboi, 13 June 2014, URL: https://twitter.com/mohamedelibiary/status/477510829261066241, accessed 18 June 2014. **Actual Tweet:** "As I've said b4 inevitable that "Caliphate" returns. Choice only whether we support EU like Muslim Union vision or not." ... US heading in that direction. Bush created OIC Special Envoy. Obama removed discriminatory engagement policy towards MB, etc."

196 Black's Law, 9th, 1183.

197 *Black's Law 6th*, 1440. **Read:** Suppression of evidence. ... Concept of "suppression" as the term is used in rule that suppression by the prosecution of material evidence favorable to an accused on request violates due process, implies that the government has information in its possession of which the defendant lacks knowledge and which the defendant would benefit from knowing.

198 "Home-grown, solo terrorists as bad as Al-Qaeda: FBI chief," *Breitbart*, 15 April 2010, URL: http://www.breitbart.com/article.php?id=CNG.715a7668fe9975340c7a6290b761a373.01&show_article=1, accessed 20 April 2010.

199 "Napolitano: Internet Monitoring Needed to Fight Homegrown Terrorism," *FOXNews* (*AP*), 18 June 2010, URL: http://www.foxnews.com/politics/2010/06/18/napolitano-internet-monitoring-needed-fight-homegrown-terrorism/?utm_source=feedburner&utm_medium=feed&utm_campaign=Feed%3A+foxnews%2Fpolitics+%28Text+-+Politics%29, accessed 23 June 2010.

200 "Home-grown, solo terrorists as bad as Al-Qaeda: FBI chief," *Breitbart*.

201 McFadden, Robert D., "Army Doctor Held in Ft. Hood Rampage," *New York Times*, November

5, 2009 http://www.nytimes.com/2009/11/06/us/06forthood.html

202 Browne, Pamela and Catherine Herridge, "EXCLUSIVE: Video shows Fort Hood shooter's controversial lecture on Islam," *Fox News*, August 30, 2013. http://www.foxnews.com/us/2013/08/30/fort-hood-killer-warned-before-shooting-possible-adverse-events

203 Priest, Dana, "Fort Hood suspect warned of threats within the ranks," *Washington Post*, November 10, 2014. http://www.washingtonpost.com/wp-dyn/content/article/2009/11/09/AR2009110903618.html?hpid=topnews

204 Riccardi, Nicholas, "Hasan may never walk again: The Ft. Hood shooting suspect's attorney says he's paralyzed from the waist down and in significant pain," Los Angeles Times, November 14, 2009 http://articles.latimes.com/2009/nov/14/nation/na-hasan14

205 "Fort Hood gunman Maj. Nidal Hasan sentence to death," *Fox News*, August 28, 2013. http://www.foxnews.com/us/2013/08/28/fort-hood-gunman-maj-nidal-hasan-sentenced-to-death

206 Hamburger, Tom, "Hasan's supervising doctors questioned his fitness for service," *Los Angeles Times*, November 12, 2009. http://articles.latimes.com/print/2009/nov/12/nation/na-hasan12

207 Slide 16 "Koran," Major Hasan, "The Koranic World View as it Relates to Muslims in the U.S. Military."

208 Slide 17 "Rule of Abrogation," Major Hasan, "The Koranic World View as it Relates to Muslims in the U.S. Military."

209 Final Report of the William H. Webster Commission on The Federal Bureau of Investigation, Counterterrorism Intelligence, and the Events at Fort Hood, Texas, on November 5, 2009, 19 July 2012, URL: http://www.fbi.gov/news/pressrel/press-releases/final-report-of-the-william-h.-webster-commission (as PDF—https://s3.amazonaws.com/s3.documentcloud.org/documents/779134/fort-hood-report.pdfaccessed), accessed 29 August 2013, 56-7. Cited hereafter as Webster Report Events at Fort Hood.

210 Major Hasan, "The Koranic World View as it Relates to Muslims in the U.S. Military."

211 Slide 12, "Muslims in the Military," Major Hasan, "The Koranic World View as it Relates to Muslims in the U.S. Military."

212 In the July 2010 paper "Killing without Right: Islamic Concepts of Terrorism," the killing without right standard is explained.

213 Slide 11, "Fatwa: Muslims in U.S. Military," Major Hasan, "The Koranic World View as it Relates to Muslims in the U.S. Military."

214 Slide 50, "Recommendation," Major Hasan, "The Koranic World View as it Relates to Muslims in the U.S. Military."

215 Browne and Herridge, "EXCLUSIVE: Video shows Fort Hood shooter's controversial lecture on Islam."

216 Slide 13, "Adverse Events," Major Hasan, "The Koranic World View as it Relates to Muslims in the U.S. Military."

217 Slide 45, "Offensive Islam is the Future," Major Hasan, "The Koranic World View as it Relates to Muslims in the U.S. Military."

218 Keller, *Reliance of the Traveller*, Book O "Justice," at o9.0: "Jihad," at § o9.8. **Note:** The lead up to this statement is as follows: THE OBJECTIVES OF JIHAD - The caliph makes war upon Jews, Christians, and Zoroastrians provided he has first invited them to enter Islam in faith and practice, and if they will not, then invited to enter the social order of Islam by paying the non-Muslim poll tax (*jizya*, def: o11.4)—which is the significance of their paying it, not the money itself—while remaining in their ancestral religions and the war continues until they become Muslims or else pay the non-Muslim poll tax in accordance with the word of Allah Most High, "Fight those who do not believe in Allah and the

Last Day and who forbid not what Allah and His messenger have forbidden—who do not practice the religion of truth, being those who have been given the Book—until they pay the poll tax out of hand and are humbled" (Qur'an 9:29), [followed by text cited in document].

219 Michael Daly, "Nidal Hasan's Murders Termed 'Workplace Violence' by U.S.," *The Daily Beast*, 6 August 2013, URL: http://www.thedailybeast.com/articles/2013/08/06/nidal-hasan-s-murders-termed-workplace-violence-by-u-s.html, accessed 25 January 2015.

220 Webster Report Events at Fort Hood, 80.

221 Webster Report Events at Fort Hood.

222 Webster Report Events at Fort Hood, 80.

223 "Handwritten Statements by Maj. Nidal Hasan," *FoxNews*, 18 October 2012 (posted 1August 2013), URL: http://www.foxnews.com/politics/interactive/2013/08/01/statement-by-nidal-hasan/, accessed 24 August 2013.

224 Webster Report Events at Fort Hood, 55.

225 Webster Report Events at Fort Hood, 55.

226 Webster Report Events at Fort Hood, 55.

227 Webster Report Events at Fort Hood, 55.

228 Webster Report Events at Fort Hood, 58.

229 Coughlin, Stephen C, *To Our Great Detriment: Ignoring what Extremists Say about Jihad*, Washington, DC: National Defense Intelligence College, MSSI thesis accepted in July 2007), 150-152.

230 Coughlin, Stephen, It's What the Doctrine Says it is – Rebuttal to "Islamic Rulings on War," unpublished paper, September 2005, 34-35, 82-84.

231 The European Council for Fatwa Research, 22 July 2001, URL: http://www.e-cfr.org/en/ECFR.pdf, 4. Cited hereafter as ECRF.

232 ECRF, 4.

233 ECRF, cover.

234 Webster Report Events at Fort Hood, 58.

235 Webster Report Events at Fort Hood, 58.

236 Nidal Hasan, "NidalHasan scribble," *Scribd*, 20 May 2009 (document appears to have been posted on 20 May 2009), URL: http://www.scribd.com/NidalHasan, originally accessed 8 November 2009.

237 Webster Report Events at Fort Hood, 63.

238 For example, "Fort Hood Shooting: Officials Examine 'Suicide Bomber' Posting," *The Telegraph*, 6 November 2009, URL: http://www.telegraph.co.uk/news/worldnews/northamerica/usa/6512668/Fort-Hood-shooting-officials-examine-suicide-bomber-posting.html, originally accessed 6 November 2009.

239 Webster Report Events at Fort Hood, 61.

240 Webster Report Events at Fort Hood, 56-7.

241 Webster Report Events at Fort Hood, 80.

242 Dana Priest, "Fort Hood Suspect Warned of Threats within the Ranks," Washington Post, 10 November 2009, accessed originally 10 November 2009 updated URL: http://www.washingtonpost.com/wp-dyn/content/article/2009/11/09/AR2009110903618.html.

243 Webster Report Events at Fort Hood, 56-7.

244　E-Mail Correspondence to Blaze Producers from Colonel David H. Patterson, Chief, Media Relations Division, Headquarters, Department of the Army, 30 January 2014, URL: http://www.theblaze.com/wp-content/uploads/2014/02/Army-Letter-January-30.pdf, accessed 16 February 2014.

245　Webster Report Events at Fort Hood, 62.

246　*Inspire Magazine*, Issue 12, Spring 2014/14345, "Shattered: A Story about Change," URL: https://ia600601.us.archive.org/18/items/INSPIRE-12/INS-EH.pdf, accessed 20 March 2014.

247　Webster Report Events at Fort Hood, 6.

248　Webster Report Events at Fort Hood, 7.

249　Webster Report Events at Fort Hood, 7.

250　Webster Report Events at Fort Hood, 8.

251　Webster Report Events at Fort Hood, 9.

252　Pieper, *Abuse of Language-Abuse of Power*, 34.

253　Al-Awlaki, "Spilling the Beans," *Inspire*, Issue 9, Winter 1433/2012, URL: http://azelin.files.wordpress.com/2012/05/inspire-magazine-9.pdf, accessed 16 May 2013, 51.

254　Jennifer Griffin, "Two U.S.-Born Terrorists Killed in CIA-Led Drone Strike," FoxNews, 30 September 2011, URL: http://www.foxnews.com/politics/2011/09/30/us-born-terror-boss-anwar-al-awlaki-killed/, accessed 19 September 2013.

255　Madhani, Aamer. "Cleric al-Awlaki dubbed 'bin Laden of the Internet,'" *USA Today*, August 25, 2010. http://www.usatoday.com/news/nation/2010-08-25-1A_Awlaki25_CV_N.htm

256　Shane, Scott and Souad Mekhennet. "Anwar al-Awlaki: From Condemning Terror to Preaching Jihad," *The New York Times*. May 8, 2010. http://www.nytimes.com/2010/05/09/world/09awlaki.html?_r=1&

257　Shane, Scott and Souad Mekhennet. "Anwar al-Awlaki: From Condemning Terror to Preaching Jihad."

258　Judicial Watch Document Regarding Al-Awlaki, Federal Bureau of Investigation (FBI) document (Obtained by Judicial Watch for FOIA (2 April 2013)), document – DECLASSIFIED - labeled 14969456-1488-04022013, page 62 / 124, 15 June 1999.

259　Judicial Watch Document Regarding Al-Awlaki, Federal Bureau of Investigation (FBI) document (Obtained by Judicial Watch for FOIA (2 April 2013)), document – DECLASSIFIED - labeled 14969456-1488-04022013, page 62 / 124, 28 October 1999.

260　Foreign Terrorists Organization, Bureau of Counterterrorism, *U.S. Department of State*, 27 January 2012, http://www.state.gov/j/ct/rls/other/des/123085.htm. Hamas designated a terrorist organization since 8 October 1997.

261　Article Two, Hamas Covenant. **States**: "The Islamic Resistance Movement is one of the wings of Moslem Brotherhood in Palestine. Moslem Brotherhood Movement is a universal organization which constitutes the largest Islamic movement in modern times. ...

262　Judicial Watch Document Regarding Al-Awlaki, Federal Bureau of Investigation (FBI) document (Obtained by Judicial Watch for FOIA (2 April 2013)), document—DECLASSIFIED— labeled 14969456-1488-04022013, page 81 / 124, 20 July1999.

263　Judicial Watch Document Regarding Al-Awlaki, Federal Bureau of Investigation (FBI) document,(Obtained by Judicial Watch for FOIA (2 April 2013)),document cover DECLASSIFIED— labeled 14969456-1488-04022013, page 5, 25, 39, 42 / 124, 25 September 2001.

264　Judicial Watch Document Regarding Al-Awlaki, Federal Bureau of Investigation (FBI) document (Case ID # 199N-WF-222852) Pending), (Obtained by Judicial Watch for FOIA (2 April 2013)), document – DECLASSIFIED - labeled 14969456-1488-04022013, page 3 / 124, 27 September 2001.

265 Judicial Watch Document Regarding Al-Awlaki, Federal Bureau of Investigation (FBI) document,(Obtained by Judicial Watch for FOIA (2 April 2013)),document cover DECLASSIFIED— labeled 14969456-1488-04022013, page 5, 25, 39, 42 / 124, 25 September 2001.

266 Laurie Goodstein, "A Nation Challenged: The American Muslims; Influential American Muslims Temper their Tone, *New York Times*, 19 October 2001, URL: http://www.nytimes.com/2001/10/19/ us/nation-challenged-american-muslims-influential-american-muslims-temper-their.html, accessed 18 September 2013.

267 Shane, Scott. "Anwar Al-Awlaki: An American Citizen, A CIA Target," National Public Radio. May 18, 2010. http://www.npr.org/templates/story/story.php?storyId=126889383

268 Judicial Watch Document Regarding Al-Awlaki, Federal Bureau of Investigation (FBI) document (Obtained by Judicial Watch for FOIA (2 April 2013)), document—DECLASSIFIED— labeled 14969456-1488-04022013, page 99 / 124, 4 February 2002.

269 Judicial Watch Document Regarding Al-Awlaki, Federal Bureau of Investigation (FBI) document (Case ID # 199N-WF-222852, (Obtained by Judicial Watch for FOIA (2 April 2013)), document—DECLASSIFIED—labeled 14969456-1488-04022013, page 111 / 124, 18 November 2002.

270 Catherine Herridge, "Al Qaeda Leader Dined at the Pentagon Just Months After 9/11," *Fox News*, 20 October 2010, URL: http://www.foxnews.com/us/2010/10/20/alqaeda-terror-leader-dined-pentagon-months/

271 Patrick Poole, "Al-Qaeda on Capitol Hill," *Human Events*, URL: http://www.humanevents.com/2010/09/28/alqaeda-on-capitol-hill/, accessed 15 September 2010.

272 Omar al-Qattan, "Muhammad: Legacy of a Prophet," *PBS* (*KQED*), 18 December 2002, URL: http://www.pbs.org/muhammad/film.shtml, accessed 18 September 2013.

273 ICNA-MAS 1st Annual Conference Flyer – July 2002, Judicial Watch Document Regarding Al-Awlaki, Federal Bureau of Investigation (FBI) document (Obtained by Judicial Watch for FOIA (31 May 2013)), document – flyer - labeled 14969456-1488-04022013, pages 150, 151 / 348, 5-7 July 2002. **Note other speakers**: Imam Siraj Wahhaj, Imam Zaid Shakir, Dr. Mukhtar Maghroui, Dr. Jamal Badawi, Dr. Souheil Ghannouchi, Dr. Imtiaz Ahmad, Dr. Muhammad Yunus, Dr. Zufiqar Ali Shah, Sheikh Mohammed Abdullahi, Mr. Paul Findley, Dr. Munir El-Kasim and special invited guest: Imam of Haram, Sheikh Abdur Rahman As-Sudais.

274 Judicial Watch Document Regarding Al-Awlaki, Federal Bureau of Investigation (FBI) Transcription of Interview at Dar Hijra Mosque, Falls Church, VA, 15 September 2001, (obtained by Judicial Watch via FOIA, 2 January 2013) – DECLASSIFIED – labeled ISB Investigation, 16 November 2001, 90-92/206

275 FBI Witness Transcript – October 2006, Judicial Watch Document Regarding Al-Awlaki, Federal Bureau of Investigation (FBI) document (Obtained by Judicial Watch for FOIA (31 May 2013), document – DECLASSIFIED - labeled 1174529-000, page 257 / 348, 13 October 2006.

276 Judicial Watch Document Regarding Al-Awlaki, Federal Bureau of Investigation (FBI) Transcription of Surveillance at Irvine, California, (File # 265A-NY-280350-302) (obtained by Judicial Watch via FOIA, 2 January 2013) – DECLASSIFIED – labeled ISB Investigation, 16 November 2001, 1-2/206.

277 Mohamed Nimer, *The North American Muslim Resource Guide: Muslim Community Life in the United States and Canada*, Routledge Publishing, NY, 2002, 70.

278 "UAE Publishes List of Terrorist Organizations," *Gulf News*, 15 November 2014, URL: http://gulfnews.com/news/gulf/uae/government/uae-publishes-list-of-terrorist-organisations-1.1412895, accessed 15 November 2014. **The full list as provided by the UAE Cabinet, the complete list of terrorist organizations endorsed by the UAE Government, in line with the Federal Law No.7 for 2014 as issued by President His Highness Shaikh Khalifa Bin Zayed Al Nahyan on August 20,**

2014, includes: 1. Muslim Brotherhood in the UAE, 23. Islamic Relief Organisation, an affiliate of the International, Organisation of the Muslim Brotherhood, 27. Muslim Brotherhood Organisation and group, 59. Council on American. Islamic Relations (CAIR), 65. Muslim American Society (MAS).

279   MAS Boston, Islamic Society of Boston Cultural Center (ISBCC) webpage, URL: http://isbcc. org/mas-boston/, accessed 8 October 2013. **States:** Muslim American Society – Boston Chapter. The Muslim American Society of Boston runs your center (ISBCC)! The Muslim American Society of Boston works to educate, organize, and empower the Muslim community to be active, contributing citizens who are civically engaged, and who are motivated by Islamic values.

280   Sheikh Faysal Mawlawi, "*Fatwa* Questions About Palestine," MAS – *The American Muslim*, Vol. 3, no. 2, June 2002.

281   Mohamed Akram, Explanatory Memorandum, 18, 32 listed as number 26 (ICNA).

282   Marilyn Stern, "The Muslim Public Affairs Council: Building Bridges to U.S. Law Enforcement - Community-Oriented Policing," *The Investigative Project on Terrorism*, 20 November 2010, http:// www.investigativeproject.org/2345/report-assesses-mpac-counterterrorcommitment, 18-19.

283   "About Imam Suhaib Webb," Islamic Society of Boston Cultural Center (ISBCC) webpage, URL: http://isbcc.org/imam-suhaib-webb/, accessed 8 October 2013.

284   Excel Spreadsheet of 2003 CAIR Membership for Virginia and Washington, D.C. (VADC Listing.xls) Membership List – 2003.

285   *Inspire*, **Issue 1**, Summer 1431/2010, URL: http://azelin.files.wordpress.com/2010/06/ aqap-inspire-magazine-volume-1-uncorrupted.pdf, accessed: 16 May 2013, 31; and *Lone Mujahid Pocketbook - A Step to Step Guide on how to become as Successful Lone Mujahid – Collected from Inspire Magazine Issue 1 – 10's OSJ*, OSJ Special, Spring 1434/2013, "Brought to you by … *Inspire*, **Issue 10**, 1434/2013, URL: http://ia601602.us.archive.org/5/items/Al.Mala7m.1/Mujahid1.pdf, accessed: 16 May 2013, 16.

286   Patrick Howley, "Boston Imam Shared Ties with Senior al-Qaeda Operatives," *The Daily Caller*, 27 June 2013, http://dailycaller.com/2013/06/27/dzhokhar-tsarnaevs-imam-shares-ties-with-senior-al-qaeda-operative/, accessed 27 June 2013.

287   Levs, Josh and Plott, Monte, "Boy, 8, one of three killed at Boston Marathon; scores injured," *CNN*, April 18, 2013. Accessed online 12 January 2014 at http://www.cnn.com/2013/04/15/us/boston-marathon-explosions/

288   "Bombing suspect in custody after standoff in Watertown," *The Boston Globe*, April 19, 2013. Accessed online 12 January 2014 at http://www.bostonglobe.com/metro/2013/04/18/mit-police-officer-hit-gunfire-cambridge-police-dispatcher-says/4UeCClOVeLr8PHLvDa99zK/story.html

289   "Tamerlan Tsarnaev and Dzhokhar Tsarnaev were refugees from brutal Chechen conflict," *Washington Post*, April 19, 2014. Accessed online 12 January 2014 at http://www.washingtonpost. com/politics/details-emerge-on-suspected-boston-bombers/2013/04/19/ef2c2566-a8e4-11e2-a8e2-5b98cb59187f_story.html

290   "Mother of bomb suspects eyed in radicalizing son; was on terror database," *Fox News*, April 26, 2013. Accessed online 12 January 2014 at http://www.foxnews.com/us/2013/04/26/father-boston-bombing-suspects-delays-trip-to-us-over-health-problems-ex-wife/

291   Shuster, Simon, "Older Boston Suspect Made Two Trips to Dagestan, Visited Radical Mosque, Officials Say, " *TIME*, April 22, 2013. Accessed online 12 January 2014 at http://world.time. com/2013/04/22/tsarnaev-in-dagestan

292   Tom Parfitt, "Boston Bombs: the Canadian Boxer and the Terror Recruiter Eho 'led Tsarnaev on Path to Jihad'," The Telegraph, 28 April 2013, URL: http://www.telegraph.co.uk/news/worldnews/europe/russia/tom-parfitt/10024185/Boston-bombs-the-Canadian-boxer-and-the-terror-recruiter-who-led-Tsarnaev-on-path-to-jihad.html, accessed 18 August 2014.

293 "Bombing Suspects Are Seen as Self-Taught and Fueled by the Web," *New York Times*, April 23, 2013. Accessed online 12 January 2014 at http://www.nytimes.com/2013/04/24/us/boston-marathon-bombing-developments.html

294 Cooper, Michael, Michael S. Schmidt, and Eric Schmitt. "Boston Suspects Are Seen as Self-Taught and Fueled by Web." *The New York Times*. The New York Times, 23 April 2013, URL: http://www.nytimes.com/2013/04/24/us/boston-marathon-bombing-developments.html?pagewanted=all.

295 Abu Mus'ab al-Suri, "The Jihadi Experiences: The Schools of Jihad," Inspire, Issue 1, Summer 1431/2010, URL: http://azelin.files.wordpress.com/2010/06/aqap-inspire-magazine-volume-1-uncorrupted.pdf, accessed 16 May 2013.

296 *Inspire*, Issue 1, Summer 1431/2010, URL: http://azelin.files.wordpress.com/2010/06/aqap-inspire-magazine-volume-1-uncorrupted.pdf, accessed: 16 May 2013, cover, 33.

297 Abu Mus'ab al-Suri, "The Jihadi Experiences: The Most Important Enemy Targets Aimed at by the Individual Jihad," *Inspire*, Issue 9, Winter 1433/2012, URL: http://azelin.files.wordpress.com/2012/05/inspire-magazine-9.pdf, accessed: 16 May 2013.

298 *Lone Mujahid Pocketbook—A Step to Step Guide on how to become as Successful Lone Mujahid—*Collected from Inspire Magazine Issue 1—10's OSJ, OSJ Special, Spring 1434/2013, "Brought to you by ... *Inspire*, Issue 10, 1434/2013, URL: http://ia601602.us.archive.org/5/items/Al.Mala7m.1/Mujahid1.pdf, accessed: 16 May 2013.

299 "FBI Interviewed Dead Boston Bombing Suspect Years Ago," *CBS News*, 19 April 2013, URL: http://www.cbsnews.com/8301-201_162-57580534/fbi-interviewed-dead-boston-bombing-suspect-years-ago/, 22 April 2013.

300 "FBI Knew Earlier of Boston Bombing Suspect," *Politico*, 15 June 2013, URL: http://www.politico.com/blogs/under-the-radar/2013/06/fbi-knew-earlier-of-boston-bombing-suspect-166313.html, accessed 17 June 2013.

301 Shane, Scott and Schmidt, Michael S., "F.B.I. Did Not Tell Police in Boston of Russian Tip," *New York Times,* May 9, 2013. Accessed online 12 January 2014 at http://www.nytimes.com/2013/05/10/us/boston-police-werent-told-fbi-got-warning-on-tsarnaev.html

302 Ken Dilanian "Boston bombings: FBI is defended on vetting of Tamerlan Tsarnaev," Los Angeles Times, 21 April 2013, URL: http://www.latimes.com/news/nation/nationnow/la-na-nn-boston-bombings-fbi-defended-20130421,0,5330012.story, accessed 22 April 2013.

303 Ken Dilanian "Boston bombings: FBI is defended on vetting of Tamerlan Tsarnaev."

304 Michael Schmidt, "F.B.I. Said to Conclude It Could Not Have Averted Boston Attack," *New York Times*, August 2013, URL: http://www.nytimes.com/2013/08/02/us/fbi-said-to-conclude-it-could-not-have-averted-boston-attack.html?partner=rss&emc=rss&smid=tw-thecaucus&_r=1&, accessed 3 August 2013.

305 Carter, Sara, "For the Record Exposes Radicalized Foundation of the Mosque Attended by the Accused Boston Bomber," The Blaze, 25 September 2013. Accessed online 12 January 2014 at http://www.theblaze.com/stories/2013/09/25/for-the-record-exposes-radicalized-foundation-of-the-mosque-attended-by-the-accused-boston-bombers/

306 "Abdurahman Alamoudi Fact Sheet," *SITE Institute* via *Free Republic*, 29 September 2003, URL: http://www.freerepublic.com/focus/f-news/993757/posts, 6 October 2013.

307 Mohamed Akram, Explanatory Memorandum, 32, listed as numbers 1 (ISNA), 2 (MSA), and 3 (UASR).

308 Lisa Myers, "Muslim Leader with D.C. Ties Indicted," *NBC News*, 24 October 2003, URL: http://www.nbcnews.com/id/3341720/print/1/displaymode/1098, accessed 18 September 2013.

309 Affidavit of Dr. John L. Esposito, Islamic Socieity of Boston v Boston Herald ... The Investigative Project, Inc, Steven Emerson ... Citizens for Peace and Tolerance, Superior Court Department of the

Trial Court, Commonwealth of Massachusetts, (date), URL: http://www.investigativeproject.org/documents/case_docs/1181.pdf, accessed 6 May 2013. 39. "In 1996, when Hilary Clinton decided to host the first ever White House reception to celebrate the end of Ramadan (called the Iftar), Mrs. Clinton asked Mr. Alamoudi to prepare the guest list."

310 Auster, Lawrence. "The Clintons, Abdurahman Alamoudi, and the Myth of "Moderate" Islam." November 6, 2000. Archived at http://www.freerepublic.com/focus/f-news/1007061/posts

311 Team B, "Muslim Brotherhood Penetration of the US Government, A Case Study," *Breitbart*, 27 October 2010, URL: http://www.breitbart.com/Big-Peace/2010/10/27/Muslim-Brotherhood-Penetration-of-the-US-Government--A-Case-Study, accessed 6 October 2013.

312 "Hamas goes to Foggy Bottom," *The New York Post*. September 15, 1998. Archival copy found at http://suhailkhanexposed.com/wp-content/uploads/2011/01/Preview-of-%E2%80%9CArchives-New-York-Post-Online-Edition%E2%80%9D.pdf

313 "Rally at Lafayette Park: Alamoudi," Investigative Project on Terrorism (IPT), 28 October 2000, accessed 7 October 2013.

314 Pipes, Daniel. "[The American Muslim Council:] 'Mainstream' Muslims?" *New York Post*, June 18, 2002. http://www.danielpipes.org/423/the-american-muslim-council-mainstream-muslims

315 Stoll, Ira. "Bye, Alamoudi," *the American Spectator*. October 23, 2003. http://spectator.org/articles/51001/bye-alamoudi

316 "Abdurahman Alamoudi Sentenced to Jail in Terrorism Financing Case," Department of Justice Press Release, 15 October 2004, URL: http://www.investigativeproject.org/documents/case_docs/168.pdf, accessed 6 October 2013.

317 Cline, Meghan, "Treasury Department Tars Alamoudi, Founder of the Islamic Society of Boston," *The New York Sun*. N.p., 9 December 2005, URL: http://www.nysun.com/national/treasury-department-tars-alamoudi-founder-of/24211/

318 Team B, "Muslim Brotherhood Penetration of the US Government, A Case Study," *Breitbart*, 27 October 2010, URL: http://www.breitbart.com/Big-Peace/2010/10/27/Muslim-Brotherhood-Penetration-of-the-US-Government--A-Case-Study, accessed 6 October 2013.

319 USAF Recruiting Advertisement, *Islamic Horizons*, March/April 2013, URL: http://issuu.com/isnacreative/docs/ih_mar-apr_13, 47, accessed 18 September 2013. "*Islamic Horizons* is a bi-monthly publication of the Islamic Society of North America (ISNA), P.O. Box 38, Plainfield, IN 46168-0038."

320 Islamic Society of Boston, Commonwealth of Massachusetts Articles of Organization, 7 October 1982.

321 Report Islamic Society of Boston, Boston, MA, *Investigative Project on Terrorism (IPT)*, URL: http://www.investigativeproject.org/case/531, 6 October 2013. Relying on Form 990s issued by the Islamic Society of Boston for the years 1998, 1999, and 2000, the Investigative Project on Terrorism reported that Yusuf al-Qaradawi was listed on ISB tax filings under "List of Officers, Directors, Trustees, and Key Employees. Qaradawi's trustee status confirmed Affidavit of Dr. John L. Esposito, *Islamic Society of Boston v Boston Herald, The Investigative Project, et al,* Civil Action No. 05-4637-F, Commonwealth of Massachusetts, Superior Court Department of Trial Court, March 2006(?), ¶ 57, page 24.

322 Stephen Kurkjian, "Mosque Lawsuit Dismissal is Sought - Project Dissenters Deny Conspiracy," *Boston Globe*, 29 December 2005 (reprinted in Jewish Russian Telegraph, 30 December 2005), URL: http://www.jrtelegraph.com/2005/12/boston_globe_mo.html, accessed 6 May 2013.

323 Constitution of the Islamic Society of Boston, undated founding document estimated date 1982 (referenced in Massachusetts Articles of Organization dated October 1982) made public through subpoena of Islamic Society of Boston documents in litigation by defendants Steve Emerson and Americans for Peace and Tolerance.

324 See for example, Americans for Peace and Tolerance, "A Moderating Mosque: Islamic Society of Boston Hosts Virulently Anti-Semitic Preacher," http://peaceandtolerance.org/index.php/2012-07-26-13-33-42/a-moderating-mosque. See also, "Islamic Extremism at Northeastern University," http://peaceandtolerance.org/index.php/2012-07-26-13-33-42/islamic-extremism-at-northeastern, "Sudbury to Mumbai,": http://peaceandtolerance.org/index.php/2012-07-26-13-33-42/sudbury-to-mumbai, "The Imam and the Governor,": http://peaceandtolerance.org/index.php/2012-07-26-13-33-42/the-imam-and-the-governor, and "K-12 Mis-Education: School Trip to 'Moderate' Mosque: Inside Video Captures Kids Bowing to Allah,": http://peaceandtolerance.org/index.php/2012-07-26-13-33-03/k-12-mis-education

325 Michael Schmidt, "F.B.I. Said to Conclude It Could Not Have Averted Boston Attack," *New York Times*, August 2013, URL: http://www.nytimes.com/2013/08/02/us/fbi-said-to-conclude-it-could-not-have-averted-boston-attack.html?partner=rss&emc=rss&smid=tw-thecaucus&_r=1&, accessed 3 August 2013.

326 For example, see Government Exhibit: Philly Meeting - 15, 3:04-CR-240-G, U.S. v. HLF, et al., at 2,3, at http://www.txnd.uscourts.gov /judges/hlf2/09-29-08/Philly%20Meeting%2015.pdf

327 "Major Bomb Attacks Since 1993 Peace Accord," *FoxNews/AP*, 2 December 2001, URL: http://www.foxnews.com/story/2001/12/02/major-bomb-attacks-since-13-peace-accord/, accessed 6 October 2013.

328 Mohamed Akram, *Explanatory Memorandum.*

329 Letters Detailing Usama bin Laden and Terrorist's Plans to Hijack an Aircraft Flying Out of Frankfurt, Germany in 2000." Defense Intelligence Agency (DIA) Intelligence Information Report (IRR), 27 September 2001, declassified and provided to Judicial Watch on 29 August 2013 in response to 16 May 2002 Freedom of Information Act (FOIA) request, published 27 September 2013, URL: http://www.judicialwatch.org/document-archive/document-analysis-of-al-qaeda-plot-to-hijack-plane-in-frankfurt-germany/, accessed 27 September 2013, pages annotated 21, 22.

330 Letters Detailing Usama bin Laden and Terrorist's Plans to Hijack an Aircraft Flying Out of Frankfurt, Germany in 2000." Defense Intelligence Agency (DIA) Intelligence Information Report (IRR), 27 September 2001, declassified and provided to Judicial Watch on 29 August 2013 in response to 16 May 2002 Freedom of Information Act (FOIA) request, published 27 September 2013, URL: http://www.judicialwatch.org/document-archive/document-analysis-of-al-qaeda-plot-to-hijack-plane-in-frankfurt-germany/, accessed 27 September 2013, pages annotated 21, 24.

331 *Inspire*, **Issue 1**, Summer 1431/2010, URL: http://azelin.files.wordpress.com/2010/06/aqap-inspire-magazine-volume-1-uncorrupted.pdf, accessed: 16 May 2013, 31; and *Lone Mujahid Pocketbook - A Step to Step Guide on how to become as Successful Lone Mujahid – Collected from Inspire Magazine Issue 1 – 10's OSJ*, OSJ Special, Spring 1434/2013, "Brought to you by … *Inspire*, **Issue 10**, 1434/2013, URL: http://ia601602.us.archive.org/5/items/Al.Mala7m.1/Mujahid1.pdf, accessed: 16 May 2013, 16.

332 Abdulrahman M. Alamoudi listed as sole Founder and President, Islamic Society of Boston, Articles of Organization, Commonwealth of Massachusetts, 6 July 1982 (pdf copy).

333 Report Islamic Society of Boston, Boston, MA, *Investigative Project on Terrorism* (*IPT*), 6 October 2013.

334 MAS Boston, Islamic Society of Boston Cultural Center (ISBCC) webpage, URL: http://isbcc.org/mas-boston/, accessed 8 October 2013.

335 "About Imam Suhaib Webb," Islamic Society of Boston Cultural Center (ISBCC) webpage, URL: http://isbcc.org/imam-suhaib-webb/, accessed 8 October 2013.

336 Jah'Keem Yisreal, Facebook Account of Jah'Keem Yisreal (Alton Nolan), 26 September 2014, URL: https://www.facebook.com/alton.threadgill, accessed 26 September 2014.

337 Abby Ohlheiser, Elahe Izade and Adam Goldman, "Police: Oklahoma Man Beheaded Former

Co-Worker and Attacked Another just after his Firing," *Washington Post*, October 2014, URL: http://www.washingtonpost.com/news/post-nation/wp/2014/09/26/oklahoma-man-beheaded-former-co-worker-and-attacked-another-just-after-his-firing/, accessed 21 October 2014.

338 "FBI Chief: Islamic State Recruits 'Difficult' to ID," New York Law Journal/AP, 4 November 2014, URL: http://www.newyorklawjournal.com/id=1202675409066/FBI-Chief-Islamic-State-Recruits-Difficult-to-ID?slreturn=20141004103319, accessed 4 November 2014.

339 "FBI Chief: Islamic State Recruits 'Difficult' to ID," *New York Law Journal/AP.*

340 Melanie Hunter, "Formet Counterterror Official: 'We Don't Have Enough Muslim FBI Agents'," CNSNews, 27 October 2014, URL: http://cnsnews.com/news/article/melanie-hunter/former-counterterror-official-we-dont-have-enough-muslim-fbi-agents, accessed 27 October 2014.

341 FBI Recruiting Advertisement "FBI Agent Hesham and His Wife", *Islamic Horizons*-ISNA, November/December 2007, 41. For image of advertisement, see image of FBI recruitment advertisement at URL: http://www.investigativeproject.org/documents/misc/96.pdf, see also Steven Emerson, "Looking Under a Rock: FBI and CIA Hit New Low in Recruitment Drive," IPT News, 8 February 2008, URL: http://www.investigativeproject.org/603/looking-under-a-rock-fbi-and-cia-hit-new-low-in-recruitment#, accessed 7 November 2014.

342 Federal Bureau of Investigations – 100 Years of Protecting America – 1908-2008, Fidelity, Bravery, and Integrity, Fair Count Media Group, July 2008, URL: http://issuu.com/faircountmedia/docs/fbi100/14, 102.

343 USAF Recruiting Advertisement, *Islamic Horizons*-ISNA, March/April 2013, URL: http://issuu.com/isnacreative/docs/ih_mar-apr_13, 47, accessed 18 September 2013. "*Islamic Horizons* is a bi-monthly publication of the Islamic Society of North America (ISNA), P.O. Box 38, Plainfield, IN 46168-0038.

344 Kroft, Steven, "Conversations with the Candidates for President of the United State: President Obama," *60 Minutes*, 23 September 2012, URL: http://www.cbsnews.com/video/watch/?id=7422772n&tag =cbsnewsMain ColumnArea.6, accessed 5 October 2012.

345 Gentile, Gian P., "A Strategy of Tactics: Population-centric COIN and the Army," *Strategic Studies Institute, 'Parameters,'"* Autumn 2009. http://strategicstudiesinstitute.army.mil/pubs/parameters/Articles/09autumn/gentile.pdf

346 Eikenberry, Karl, "The Limits of Counterinsurgency Doctrine in Afghanistan," *Foreign Affairs*, September/October 2013. http://www.foreignaffairs.com/articles/139645/karl-w-eikenberry/the-limits-of-counterinsurgency-doctrine-in-afghanistan

347 Joint Publication 3-24, "Counterinsurgency", 22 November 2013. http://www.dtic.mil/doctrine/new_pubs/jp3_24.pdf

348 Joint Publication 3-24, "Counterinsurgency."

349 Karl W. Eikenberry, LtGen USA (Ret), "The Limits of Counterinsurgency Doctrine in Afghanistan – The Other Side of the COIN," September/October 2013 Issue, Foreign Affairs, URL: http://www.foreignaffairs.com/articles/139645/karl-w-eikenberry/the-limits-of-counterinsurgency-doctrine-in-afghanistan, accessed 18 August 2014.

350 Afghanistan Constitution, 04 January 2004, URL: http://www.afghanembassy.com.pl/cms/uploads/images/Constitution/The%20Constitution.pdf , accessed 20 March 2005.

351 Stanley A. McChrystal, Headquarters, International Security Assistance Force, Kabul, Afghanistan, ISAF Commander's Counterinsurgency Guidance: Protecting the people is the mission. The conflict will be won by persuading the population, not destroying the enemy. ISAF will succeed when GIRoA earns the support of the people, undated (2009), URL: http://www.nato.int/isaf/docu/official_texts/counterinsurgency_guidance.pdf, accessed 16 March 2013.

352 "U.S. Troops Battle both Taliban and their own Rules," *Washington Times*, 16 November 2009,

URL: http://www.washingtontimes.com/news/2009/nov/16/us-troops-battle-taliban-afghan-rules/?page=all, accessed 8 January 2013. Cited hereafter as "U.S. Troops Battle both Taliban and their own Rules," *Washington Times.*

353 Stanley A. McChrystal, Headquarters, International Security Assistance Force, Kabul, Afghanistan, ISAF Commander's Counterinsurgency Guidance: Protecting the people is the mission.

354 General David Petraeus, Commander, International Security Assistance Force/United States Forces—Afghanistan, "COMISAF's Counterinsurgency Guidance" For the Soldiers, Sailors, Airmen, Marines, and Civilians of NATO ISAF and US Forces—Afghanistan, 1 August 2010, URL: http://graphics8.nytimes.com/packages/pdf/world/2010/COMISAF-MEMO.pdf, accessed 7 January 2013. Cited hereafter as General Petraeus, "COMISAF's Counterinsurgency Guidance," 1 August 2010.

355 "U.S. Troops Battle both Taliban and their own Rules," *Washington Times.*

356 "U.S. Troops Battle both Taliban and their own Rules," *Washington Times.*

357 "U.S. Troops Battle both Taliban and their own Rules," *Washington Times.*

358 Patrick Burke, "72% of U.S. Causalities in Afghan War under Obama's Watch," *CNSNew.com*, January 11, 2013, URL: http://cnsnews.com/news/article/72-us-casualities-afghan-war-under-obamas-watch, accessed 13 January 2013.

359 "U.S. Troops Battle both Taliban and their own Rules," *Washington Times.*

360 General Petraeus, "COMISAF's Counterinsurgency Guidance," 1 August 2010.

361 Nancy A. Youssef, "Report on Shooting Spree Finds Deep Mistrust between U.S., Afghan Forces," *McClatchy Washington Bureau*, 17 January 2012, URL: http://www.mcclatchydc.com/2012/01/17/v-print/136154/report-on-shooting-spree-finds.html, accessed 8 January 2013. **Reads:** "One U.S. service member at the scene, in his statement about the shooting, said that his initial reaction was simply: 'I knew it'."

362 "U.S. Troops Battle both Taliban and their own Rules," *Washington Times.*

363 "U.S. Troops Battle both Taliban and their own Rules," *Washington Times.*

364 Patrick Poole, "SEAL Team VI Family: 'Obama's Rules Are Getting Our Warriors Killed'," *Breitbart*, 15 October 2012, URL: http://www.breitbart.com/Big-Peace/2012/10/15/Seal-Team-Six-Family-ROE, accessed 15 October 2012.

365 Patrick Burke, "72% of U.S. Causalities in Afghan War under Obama's Watch," *CNSNew.com*, January 11, 2013, URL: http://cnsnews.com/news/article/72-us-casualities-afghan-war-under-obamas-watch, accessed 13 January 2013.

366 Timothy Williams, "Suicides Outpacing War Deaths for Troops, *New York Times*, 8 June 2012, URL: http://www.nytimes.com/2012/06/09/us/suicides-eclipse-war-deaths-for-us-troops.html?_r=0, accessed 8 January 2012. **Reads:** "The suicide rate among the nation's active-duty military personnel has spiked this year, eclipsing the number of troops dying in battle and on pace to set a record annual high since the start of the wars in Iraq and Afghanistan more than a decade ago, the Pentagon said Friday."

367 Tim Kane, *The Entrepreneurial Army: A Survey of West Point Graduates*, The Kaufman Foundation, Kansas City, MO, 4 January 2011, at 17, 18 and 19. *Among the Findings:* The current military personnel system does a good job of retaining the best leaders. (6% non-active duty agree, 5% active duty agree.) Does the current exit rate of the military's best young officers harm national security? (78% agree.)

368 **Typology. Study of or analysis or classification based on types or categories.** *Merriam-Webster Online Dictionary*, URL: **http://www.merriam-webster.com/dictionary/typology, accessed 12 January 2013.**

369 Typology, Glossary, *Catechism of the Catholic Church*, 2nd Edition, *Libreria Editrice Vaticana*, 1997, 902.

370 Member States webpage, Afghanistan listed, The Organization of the Islamic Conference,

http://www.oic-oci.org/member_states.asp, accessed 20 February 2013.

371   Declaration of OIC Member State heads of state, 3rd Islamic Summit Conference, 1981, as cited in Ahsan, *OIC: An Introduction*, 19.

372   Annex to Res. No. 49 / 19-P, The Cairo Declaration on Human Rights in Islam, Resolution NO. 49 / 19-P, On the Cairo Declaration on Human Rights in Islam, The Nineteenth Islamic Conference of Foreign Ministers (Session of Peace, Interdependence and Development), Cairo, Arab Republic of Egypt, OIC, 9-14 Muharram 1411H (31 July to 5 August 1990), http://www.oic-oci.org/english/article/human. htm, accessed 22 July 2009. **Relevant Part Reads:** ARTICLE 24: All the rights and freedoms stipulated in this Declaration are subject to the Islamic Shari'ah. ARTICLE 25: The Islamic Shari'ah is the only source of reference for the explanation or clarification of any of the articles of this Declaration.

373   OIC Convention to Combat Terrorism (1999-1420H), formal title "Convention of the Organization of the Islamic Conference on Combating International Terrorism," OIC Permanent Observer Mission to the United Nations in New York, UN Web address URL: http://www.oicun. org/7/38/ - or OIC web address URL: http://www.oic-oci.org/english/convenion/ terrorism_ convention.htm, accessed 14 June 2009. **Relevant Part Reads:** *Pursuant* to the tenets of the tolerant Islamic Shari'a which reject all forms of violence and terrorism, and in particular specially those based on extremism and call for protection of human rights, which provisions are paralleled by the principles and rules of international law founded on cooperation between peoples for the establishment of peace; *Abiding* by the lofty, moral and religious principles particularly the provisions of the Islamic Shari'a as well as the human heritage of the Islamic Ummah.

374   Ibn Kathir, *Tafsir Ibn Kathir*, vol. 5, Trans. Abdul-Malik Mujahid. (Riyadh: Darussalam, 2000), 618. **Reads:** Allah forbids killing with no legitimate reason. It was reported in the Two *Sahihs* that the Messenger of Allah said: The Blood of a Muslim who bears witness to *la ilaha illallah* and that Muhammad is the Messenger of Allah, is not permissible to be shed except in three cases: a soul for a soul (i.e., in the case of murder), an adulterer who is married, and a person who leaves his religion and deserts the *Jama'ah*.

375   Slide 12, "Muslims in the Military," Major Hasan, "The Koranic World View as it Relates to Muslims in the U.S. Military." **In Part Reads:** [17:33] "And do not kill anyone whose killing Allah has forbidden, except for a just cause."

376   General Petraeus, "COMISAF's Counterinsurgency Guidance," 1 August 2010. **Reads:** "Secure and serve the population. The decisive terrain is the human terrain. The people are the center of gravity. Only by providing them security and earning their trust and confidence can the Afghan government and ISAF prevail."

377   General Petraeus, "COMISAF's Counterinsurgency Guidance," 1 August 2010.

378   "Jihad against Jews and Crusaders World Islamic Front Statement," *Al-Quds Al-Arabi* (FAS).

379   Erik Ortiz, "Long Island Marine, Casualty of 'Green-on-Blue' Killing, Forewarned of Death, Dad Says," *New York Daily News*, 17 September 2012, URL: http://www.nydailynews.com/news/national/ long-island-marine-casualty-green-on-blue-killing-forewarned-death-dad-article-1.1161249, accessed 24 September 2012. **Reads:** "Lance Cpl. Greg Buckley Jr. was tormented by an Afghan trainee who said he'd never go home alive, says family. "'If I have to stay here until November ... I'm not going to come home.'" Buckley Sr. remembers his oldest son saying in a phone call. Buckley Jr., who was stationed in the Helmand Province, was killed in an attack by an Afghan police officer who opened fire in a gymnasium on Aug. 10, according to reports."

380   Marc V. Schanz, "Green on Blue Scourge," *AirForce-Magazine.com*, Vol. 95, No. 11, November 2012, URL: http://web.archive.org/web/20121118071344/http://www.airforce-mag...e.com/MagazineArchive/ Pages/2012/November%202012/1112insider.aspx, accessed 8 January 2012. Cited hereafter as Schanz, "Green on Blue Scourge."

381   Adam Levine. "Airmen killer spoke of hatred of US," CNN, January 17, 2012. http://security. blogs.cnn.com/2012/01/17/airmen-killer-spoke-of-hatred-of-us/, accessed 30 January 2012. See also

Interview of Sally Stenton, Lt Col (Ret) USAF by Patrick Poole and Stephen Coughlin, Runnemede, New Jersey, 17 July 2014. Stenton notes that she got her information from the autopsies report that were part of the AFOSI ROI dated 4 Sep 11

382 Interview of Sally Stenton, Lt Col (Ret) USAF by Patrick Poole and Stephen Coughlin, Runnemede, New Jersey, 17 July 2014. Cited hereafter as Interview of Sally Stenton, Lt Col (Ret) USAF.

383 Adam Levine, "Airmen Killer Spoke of Hatred to US," *CNN* Security Clearance, 17 January 2012, URL: http://security.blogs.cnn.com/2012/01/17/airmen-killer-spoke-of-hatred-of-us/, accessed 7 March 2013. Reads: "While the investigation did not determine a conclusive motive for the killing, the attack appeared to be premeditated." The investigation suggested he had "personal issues that were possibly compounded by alleged financial problems." Citer hereafter as Levine, "Airmen Killer Spoke of Hatred to US."

384 Schanz, "Green on Blue Scourge."

385 "8 NATO-led Troops Killed in Airport Shooting, Pajhwok (Kabul), 1214 hours 27 April 2011, URL: http://www.pajhwok.com/en/2011/04/27/8-nato-led-troops-killed-airport-shooting, accessed 17 July 2014.

386 "8 NATO-led Troops Killed in Airport Shooting, Pajhwok (Kabul), 1214 hours 27 April 2011.

387 Interview of Sally Stenton, Lt Col (Ret) USAF. Stenton states that the statements by Afghans in the ACCC are a part of the AFOSI ROI. See also Tom Vanden Brook, "Taliban Not Only Danger to Troops," *USA Today*, URL: http://usatoday30.usatoday.com/news/world/afghanistan/2011-04-27-afghan-US-troops-attack_n.htm, accessed 17 July 2014.

388 Interview of Sally Stenton, Lt Col (Ret) USAF.

389 Schanz, "Green on Blue Scourge."

390 Schanz, "Green on Blue Scourge."

391 Interview of Sally Stenton, Lt Col (Ret) USAF.

392 Interview of Sally Stenton, Lt Col (Ret) USAF.

393 Diana West, "Where's the Outrage over Murders In Afghanistan?," *TownHall.com*, 20 January 2012, URL: http://townhall.com/columnists/dianawest/2012/01/20/wheres_the_outrage_over_murders_in_afghanistan/page/full/, accessed 9 January 2013.

394 Levine, "Airmen Killer Spoke of Hatred to US."

395 Levine, "Airmen Killer Spoke of Hatred to US."

396 Interview of Sally Stenton, Lt Col (Ret) USAF.

397 Interview of Sally Stenton, Lt Col (Ret) USAF.

398 Interview of Sally Stenton, Lt Col (Ret) USAF.

399 General Petraeus, "COMISAF's Counterinsurgency Guidance," 1 August 2010.

400 Diana West, "Where's the Outrage over Murders In Afghanistan?," *TownHall.com*, 20 January 2012, URL: http://townhall.com/columnists/dianawest/2012/01/20/wheres_the_outrage_over_murders_in_afghanistan/page/full/, accessed 9 January 2013.

401 Schanz, "Green on Blue Scourge."

402 "U.S. Troops Battle both Taliban and their own Rules," *Washington Times*.

403 Interview of Sally Stenton, Lt Col (Ret) USAF.

404 Levine, "Airmen Killer Spoke of Hatred to US."

405 "U.S. Troops Battle both Taliban and their own Rules," *Washington Times*.

406 "U.S. Troops Battle both Taliban and their own Rules," *Washington Times*.

407 Erik Ortiz, "Long Island Marine, Casualty of 'Green-on-Blue' Killing, Forewarned of Death, Dad Says," *New York Daily News*, 17 September 2012, URL: http://www.nydailynews.com/news/national/long-island-marine-casualty-green-on-blue-killing-forewarned-death-dad-article-1.1161249, accessed 24 September 2012.

408 McCloskey, Megan. "Insider outrage: Lance Cpl. Gregory Buckley Jr., 21," *Stars and Stripes*, October 4, 2012. http://www.stripes.com/insider-outrage-lance-cpl-gregory-buckley-jr-21-1.191950

409 Interview of Sally Stenton, Lt Col (Ret) USAF.

410 Paul Sperry, "Blaming Our Troops" *New York Post*, 16 September 2012, URL: http://www.nypost.com/p/news/opinion/opedcolumnists/blaming_our_troops_gsNkgSOnejhkmabM2KA6TI, accessed 24 September 2012. Cited hereafter as Sperry, "Blaming Our Troops."

411 Sperry, "Blaming Our Troops."

412 Sperry, "Blaming Our Troops."

413 "Report on Progress Toward Security and Stability in Afghanistan: US Plan for Sustaining the Afghanistan National Security Forces," Department of Defense, April 2012. http://www.defense.gov/pubs/pdfs/Report_Final_SecDef_04_27_12.pdf

414 Rushing, "US Military Under Fire for 'Anti-Islam Class'" (transcript), *Al-Jazeera* TV.

415 Diana West, "Where's the Outrage over Murders In Afghanistan?," *TownHall.com*, 20 January 2012, URL: http://townhall.com/columnists/dianawest/2012/01/20/wheres_the_outrage_over_murders_in_afghanistan

416 Interview of Sally Stenton, Lt Col (Ret) USAF.

417 Interview of Sally Stenton, Lt Col (Ret) USAF.

418 Sperry, "Blaming Our Troops."

419 Sperry, "Blaming Our Troops."

420 Diana West, "Where's the Outrage over Murders In Afghanistan?," *TownHall.com*, 20 January 2012, URL: http://townhall.com/columnists/dianawest/2012/01/20/wheres_the_outrage_over_murders_in_afghanistan/page/full/, accessed 9 January 2013.

421 Sperry, "Blaming Our Troops."

422 Sperry, "Blaming Our Troops."

423 Sperry, "Blaming Our Troops."

424 Keller, *Reliance of the Traveller*, Book O "Justice," at o9.0 "Jihad," at o9.3 "Obligatory Character of Jihad."

425 Tarak Barkawi, "The Sting of Subjugation: 'Green on Blue' Attacks in Afghanistan: Afghans are killing Western troops because the US and NATO are in occupation of their country," *AlJazeera*, 13 September 2012, URL: http://www.aljazeera.com/indepth/opinion/2012/09/2012910101359505641.html, accessed 7 January 2013. Cited hereafter as Barkawi, "The Sting of Subjugation: 'Green on Blue' Attacks," *Aljazeera*.

426 Barkawi, "The Sting of Subjugation: 'Green on Blue' Attacks," *Aljazeera*.

427 Barkawi, "The Sting of Subjugation: 'Green on Blue' Attacks," *Aljazeera*.

428 Dave Grossman, LTC, USA (ret), "The 'Perfect Day," *The Rhino Den*, 26 September 2012, URL: http://rhinoden.rangerup.com/the-perfect-day-by-ltc-dave-grossman-usa-ret/? utm_source=RangerUp.com&utm_campaign=a29aeb8c3f-20120102_RU_PerfectDay9_30_2012&utm_medium=email, accessed 14 October 2012.

429 Barkawi, "The Sting of Subjugation: 'Green on Blue' Attacks," *Aljazeera.*

430 Yaroslav Tromfimov, "Petraeus Says Quran Burning Endangers War Effort," *Wall Street Journal*, 4 April 2011, http://online.wsj.com/article/SB10001424052748703806304576240643831942006. html. Cited hereafter as Tromfimov, "Petraeus Says Quran Burning Endangers War Effort."

431 Tromfimov, "Petraeus Says Quran Burning Endangers War Effort." **Reads:** Following Sunday's meeting with Gen. Petraeus and the ambassadors, Mr. Karzai requested in a new statement that "the U.S. government, Senate and Congress clearly condemn [Rev. Jones'] dire action and avoid such incidents in the future." Mr. Karzai issued this demand even though President Barack Obama has already described the Quran burning as "an act of extreme intolerance and bigotry"—adding that "to attack and kill innocent people in response is outrageous, and an affront to human decency and dignity."

432 Keller, *Reliance of the Traveller*, Book O "Justice," at o9.0 "Jihad," at o9.16: "Truces." **Reads:** "In Sacred Law truce means a peace treaty with those hostile to Islam, involving a cessation of fighting for a specified period …"

433 Keller, *Reliance of the Traveller*, Book O "Justice," at o9.0 "Jihad," at o9.16: "Truces." **Reads:** "*If the Muslims are weak, a truce may be made for ten years if necessary*, for the Prophet (Allah bless him and grant him Peace) made a truce with Quraysh for that long, as it related by Abu Dawud. It is not permissible to stipulate longer than that, save by means of new truces, each of which does not exceed ten years."

434 Keller, *Reliance of the Traveller*, Book O "Justice," at o9.0 "Jihad," at o9.16: "Truces." **Reads:** "When made with other than a *portion* of the non-Muslims, or when made with all of them, or with all in a particular region such as India or Asia Minor, then only the caliph (or his representative) may effect it, for it is a matter of the gravest consequence because it entails the nonperformance of jihad, whether globally or in a given locality …"

435 Keller, *Reliance of the Traveller*, Book O "Justice," at o9.0 "Jihad," at o9.16: "Truces." **Reads:** "Interests that justify making a truce are such things as Muslim weakness because of lack of numbers or material, or the hope of an enemy becoming Muslim …"

436 Keller, *Reliance of the Traveller*, Book O "Justice," at o9.0 "Jihad," at o9.16: "Truces." **Reads:** "There must be some interest served in making a truce other than mere preservation of the status quo."

437 Nyazee, *The Methodology of Ijtihad*, 252-254.

438 Nyazee, *The Methodology of Ijtihad*, 252-254.

439 Healy, Jack and Steven Erlanger, "Planned Koran Burning Drew International Scorn," *New York Times*, September 9, 2010. Accessed online 13 January 2014 at http://www.nytimes.com/2010/09/10/world/10react.html?pagewanted=all

440 Hill, Evan. "Quran Row Feeds Media Frenzy," Al Jazeera English, September 10, 2010. http://www.aljazeera.com/indepth/features/2010/09/2010910123534220284.html

441 "Obama Says Planned Koran Burning is Boosting Qaeda," Reuters Canada, September 9, 2010. http://ca.reuters.com/article/topNews/idCATRE68820G20100909?sp=true

442 "Obama Says Planned Koran Burning is Boosting Qaeda."

443 "Obama Says Planned Koran Burning is Boosting Qaeda."

444 Neuman, Scott. "Petraeus: Burning Quran Endangers Americans," National Public Radio, September 7, 2010. http://www.npr.org/templates/story/story.php?storyId=129701795

445 Tromfimov, "Petraeus Says Quran Burning Endangers War Effort."

446 Nordland, Rod, "2 Afghans Are Killed in Protests over Koran," *New York Times*, September 16, 2010. Accessed online 13 January 2014 at http://www.nytimes.com/2010/09/17/world/asia/17koran.html

447 Tromfimov, "Petraeus Says Quran Burning Endangers War Effort."

448 "OIC Deplores Burning of the Holy Qur'an," *OIC News Release*, 22 February 2012, URL: http://www.oic-oci.org/topic_detail.asp? t_id=6467

449 Jeffrey, Terence P., "Karzai's Response to Obama's Apology: Put U.S. Troops on Trial and Punish Them," CNSNews.com, 26 February 2012, URL: http://cnsnews.com/news/article/karzai-s-response-obama-s-apology-put-us-troops-trial-and-punish-them

450 Tromfimov, "Petraeus Says Quran Burning Endangers War Effort."

451 Tromfimov, "Petraeus Says Quran Burning Endangers War Effort."

452 "U.S. Commander Apologizes for Koran Desecration 2/21," INEWS, YouTube (from 2145 Afghanistan-Korans Allen Rough Cut), Reuters, 21 February 2012, http://www.youtube.com/watch?v=z_SKYwlYMbg&feature=player_embedded#!, accessed 21 April 2012.

453 Cohen, Roger, "Religion Does Its Worst," *New York Times*, April 4, 2011. Accessed online 13 January 2014 at http://www.nytimes.com/2011/04/05/opinion/05iht-edcohen05.html

454 Bowman, Michael, "Violent Reaction," VOA, April 2, 2011. http://www.voanews.com/content/us-legislators-condemn-quran-burning-violent-reaction-119148959/137441.html See also Catapano, Peter, "Freedom to Inflame," *New York Times*, April 8, 2011. http://opinionator.blogs.nytimes.com/2011/04/08/freedom-to-inflame

455 Tromfimov, "Petraeus Says Quran Burning Endangers War Effort."

456 Tromfimov, "Petraeus Says Quran Burning Endangers War Effort."

457 "U.S. Commander Apologizes for Koran Desecration 2/21," INEWS, YouTube (from 2145 Afghanistan-Korans Allen Rough Cut), Reuters, 21 February 2012, http://www.youtube.com/watch?v=z_SKYwlYMbg&feature=player_embedded#!, accessed 21 April 2012.

458 Zwak, Samar. "Afghans Vent Fury over Koran Burning, US Apologizes," Reuters, February 21, 2012. http://www.reuters.com/article/2012/02/21/us-afghanistan-korans-idUSTRE81K09T20120221

459 Zwak, Samar. "Afghans Vent Fury over Koran Burning, US Apologizes."

460 Alissa J. Rubin, "Chain of Avoidable Errors Cited in Koran Burning," *New York Times*, 2 March 2012, URL: http://www.nytimes.com/2012/03/03/world/asia/5-soldiers-are-said-to-face-punishment-in-koran-burning-in-afghanistan.html, accessed 5 March 2012.

461 Shaykh Faraz Rabbani, "Is it Considered Bad Adab to Write Notes (in Pen/Pencil) in Fiqh Books / Quran / Hadith Books, et" SunniPath.com, 2007, URL: http://qa.sunnipath.com/issue_view.asp?HD=1&ID=3334&CATE=141, accessed 17 March 2012. **States:** "However, one should not write within the Qur'an nor highlight it. If one writes in the margin, one should only do so with the utmost caution, lest one's notes be misunderstood as being commentary by another reader."

462 Tim Funish, "Burning Defaced Korans: Islam Approved," PJMedia, 8 March 2012, URL: http://pjmedia.com/blog/burning-defaced-korans-islam-approved/?singlepage=true, accessed 12 March 2012.

463 Alissa J. Rubin, "Chain of Avoidable Errors Cited in Koran Burning," *New York Times*, 2 March 2012, URL: http://www.nytimes.com/2012/03/03/world/asia/5-soldiers-are-said-to-face-punishment-in-koran-burning-in-afghanistan.html, accessed 5 March 2012.

464 Jeffrey, Terence P., "Karzai's Response to Obama's Apology: Put U.S. Troops on Trial and Punish Them," CNSNews.com, 26 February 2012, URL: http://cnsnews.com/news/article/karzai-s-response-obama-s-apology-put-us-troops-trial-and-punish-them

465 "OIC Deplores Burning of the Holy Qur'an," *OIC News Release*, 22 February 2012, URL: http://www.oic-oci.org/topic_detail.asp? t_id=6467

466 "U.S. Commander Apologizes for Koran Desecration 2/21," INEWS, YouTube (from 2145 Afghanistan-Korans Allen Rough Cut), Reuters, 21 February 2012, http://www.reuters.com/

article/2012/02/21/us-afghanistan-korans-idUSTRE81K09T20120221

467   ISAF, *COIN Advisory* #: 20100924-001—"Cultural Sensitivity: Religious Importance of the Qur'an," Counterinsurgency Advisory and Assistance Team (CAAT), 24 September 2010, URL: http://www.isaf.nato.int/images/stories/File/COIN/COIN%20Advisory%2020100924-001%20%28Religious%20Importance%20of%20the%20Quran%29.pdf, accessed 7 January 2013. (Note: CAAT is also designated as "COMISAF Advisory and Assistance Team" in other postings.) Cited hereafter as ISAF, COIN Advisory on "Cultural Sensitivity".

468   Keller, *Reliance of the Traveller*, Book K "Trade," at k1.2(e). **States:** If a Koran is being purchased for someone, it is obligatory that the person be Muslim. (O: The same is true of books of hadith and books containing the words and deeds of the early Muslims.)

469   ISAF, COIN Advisory on "Cultural Sensitivity."

470   Kamali, *Freedom of Expression in Islam*, 235.

471   Kamali, *Freedom of Expression in Islam*, 215.

472   ISAF, COIN Advisory on "Cultural Sensitivity."

473   "Jihad against Jews and Crusaders World Islamic Front Statement," *Al-Quds Al-Arabi* (FAS).

474   Kamali, *Freedom of Expression in Islam*, 212-213. **Reads:** "I begin my presentation here with a general statement that classical Islamic law penalises both blasphemy and apostasy with death—the juristic manuals of *fiqh* across the *madhahib* leave one in little doubt that this is the stand of the law."

475   ISAF, COIN Advisory on "Cultural Sensitivity"

476   General Petraeus, "COMISAF's Counterinsurgency Guidance," 1 August 2010.

477   *Black's Law 6th*, 985. **Mens Rea.** As an element of criminal responsibility: a guilty mind; a guilty or wrongful purpose; a criminal intent. Guilty knowledge and willfulness.

478   Phil Stewart & David Alexander, "US soldiers punished over Quran Burning in Afghanistan," *Christian Science Monitor (Reuters)*, 27 August 2012, URL: http://www.csmonitor.com/World/Latest-News-Wires/2012/0827/US-soldiers-punished-over-Quran-Burning-in-Afghanistan, accessed 8 March 2013. **Reads:** "Afghan President Hamid Karzai earlier this year branded the Marine's actions in the video as 'inhuman,' and he initially called for a public trial for the soldiers over the Quran incident."

479   Rushing, "US Military Under Fire for 'Anti-Islam Class'" (transcript), *Al-Jazeera* TV.

480   Patrick Goodenough, "US Envoy: To Defeat ISIS, We Must Highlight 'Our Profound Respect' for Islam," CNS News, 29 October 2014, URL: http://www.cnsnews.com/news/article/patrick-goodenough/us-envoy-defeat-isis-we-must-highlight-our-profound-respect-islam, accessed 29 October 2014.

481   Andrew McGinn, "Local Chaplain Played Vital Role in War," *Dayton Daily News*, 6 March 2013, URL: http://m.daytondailynews.com/news/news/local/local-chaplain-played-vital-role-in-war/nWhTm/, accessed 10 March 2013.

482   Andrew McGinn, "Local Chaplain Played Vital Role in War."

483   Keller, *Reliance of the Traveller*, Book O "Justice," at o11.0 "Non-Muslim Subjects of the Islamic State," at § o11.10.

484   Keller, *Reliance of the Traveller*, Book O "Justice," at o11.0 "Non-Muslim Subjects of the Islamic State," at §§ o11.1, o11.3, o11.10.

485   Keller, *Reliance of the Traveller*, Book O "Justice," at o11.0 "Non-Muslim Subjects of the Islamic State," at § o11.11.

486   Jeffrey, Terence P., "Karzai's Response to Obama's Apology: Put U.S. Troops on Trial and Punish Them," CNSNews.com, 26 February 2012, URL: http://cnsnews.com/news/article/karzai-s-response-obama-s-apology-put-us-troops-trial-and-punish-them

487   Keller, *Reliance of the Traveller*, Book O "Justice," at o9.0 "Jihad," at §§ o9.14 "The Rules of War."

488   Kamali, *Freedom of Expression in Islam*, 236. **Reads**: "In yet another report, Imam al-Shafi'i is said to have held that the protected status of the *dhimmi* terminates when he commits blasphemy and that, consequently, he becomes an enemy of war (*harbi*), in which case the head of state is within his rights to punish him as such. Imam al-Shafi'i adds that in this matter the head of state has discretionary powers similar to he has with regard to prisoners of war, that is, over whether to kill the offender or ask for ransom, and over whether or not to expropriate his property."

489   "Remarks at the Organization of the Islamic Conference (OIC) High-Level Meeting on Combating Religious Intolerance," Hilary Rodham Clinton, Secretary of State, United States Department of State, given at the Center for Islamic Arts and History, Istanbul, Turkey, 15 July 2011, URL: http://www.state.gov/secretary/rm/2011/07/168636.htm. Cited hereafter as Secretary Clinton Remarks as OIC Conference on Combating Religious Intolerance, 15 July 2011. **Reads**: "I (Secretary of State of Hilary Clinton) want to applaud the Organization of Islamic Conference and the European Union for helping pass Resolution 1618 at the Human Rights Council. I was complimenting the Secretary General on the OIC team in Geneva. I had a great team there as well. So many of you were part of that effort. And together we have begun to overcome the false divide that pits religious sensitivities against freedom of expression, and we are pursuing a new approach based on concrete steps to fight intolerance wherever it occurs. Under this resolution, the international community is taking a strong stand for freedom of expression and worship, and against discrimination and violence based upon religion or belief."

490   "U.S. Embassy Condemns Religious Incitement," Embassy of the United States, Cairo, Egypt, 11 September 2012, URL: http://egypt.usembassy.gov/pr091112.html, accessed 11 September 2012.

491   General Petraeus, "COMISAF's Counterinsurgency Guidance," 1 August 2010.

492   Greg Mortenson & David Oliver Relin, *Three Cups of Tea: One Man's Mission to Promote Peace ... One School at a Time*, Penguin Books: NY, 2006.

493   "Questions over Greg Mortenson's Stories," *60 Minutes*, 15 April 2011, URL: http://www.cbsnews.com/8301-18560_162-20054397.html, accessed 22 January 2013.

494   Abu Musab Al-Suri, "The Jihadi Experiences – The Schools of Jihad," *Inspire*, **Issue 1**, Summer 1431/2010, URL: http://azelin.files.wordpress.com/2010/06/aqap-inspire-magazine-volume-1-uncorrupted.pdf, accessed 16 May 2013, 48.

495   AQ Chef, "Car Bombs Inside America," *Inspire Magazine*, Spring 2014, URL: https://ia600601.us.archive.org/18/items/INSPIRE-12/INS-EH.pdf, accessed 20 March 2014, 64.

496   *Inspire*, Issue 1, Summer 1431/2010, URL: http://azelin.files.wordpress.com/2010/06/aqap-inspire-magazine-volume-1-uncorrupted.pdf, accessed: 16 May 2013, cover, 33.

497   *Inspire Magazine*, Issue 7, Fall 1432/2011, "The Greatest Special Operation of All Time," 7, URL: http://azelin.files.wordpress.com/2011/09/inspire-magazine-7.pdf, accessed 20 April 2014.

498   Part 3, *Allah Islam – Following Europe's Takeover by Islam*, series by Zvi Yehezkeli and David Deryi, producer Yonit Dror, editor Alon Wallfeyler Kahati, Israel Channel 10, Tel Aviv, Israel, broadcast September 2012.

PART VIII: OUR IGNORANCE

1   Pieper, *Abuse of Language-Abuse of Power*, 34.

2   General Peter Pace, USMC, Chairman Joint Chiefs of Staff, keynote speech presented at National Defense University, "Extemporaneous Remarks on Our National Strategy for Victory in Iraq, " Washington, DC, 01 December 2005, URL: <http://www.jcs.mil/chairman/speeches/051201remarks_NationalStrategyVictoryIraq.html>, accessed 02 December 2005. Cited hereafter as Pace, NDU speech.

3   U.S. Army, Field Manual (FM) 34-130, *Intelligence Preparation of the Battlefield* (Washington, DC: Department of the Army, 08 July 1994). Cited hereafter as U.S. Army FM 34-130. **Note:** The manual selected for use in this paper, U.S. Army Field Manual (FM) 34-130 *Intelligence Preparation of the Battlefield* (FM 34-130 IPB Manual), was chosen because it represents a basic, first-generation discussion of IPB that was simple enough in its explanation of threat development to train newly commissioned Second Lieutenants at the U.S. Army's Military Intelligence Officers Basic Course, yet rigorous enough to facilitate execution once the students transitioned to the field.

4   U.S. Army FM 34-130, GL-6.

5   "Senate Homeland Security and Governmental Affairs Committee and House Homeland Security Committee Hold Joint Hearing on Threats to Military Communities Inside the Inside the United States," Congressional Hearings, *CQ Congressional Transcripts*, Washington, D.C., 7 December 2011.

6   For example, from the 2009 DHS Intelligence Assessment: "(U//FOUO) DHS/I&A assesses that the combination of environmental factors that echo the 1990s, including heightened interest in legislation for tighter firearms restrictions and returning military veterans, as well as several new trends, including an uncertain economy and a perceived rising influence of other countries, may be invigorating rightwing extremist activity, specifically the white supremacist and militia movements. To the extent that these factors persist, rightwing extremism is likely to grow in strength." DHS (U//FOUO) Rightwing Extremism: Current Economic and Political Climate Fueling Resurgence in Radicalization and Recruitment," U.S. Department of Homeland Security, Office of Intelligence Analysis Assessment, 7 April 2009, URL: http://www.fas.org/irp/eprint/rightwing.pdf, originally accessed 14 June 2009, 8.

7   General Myers, "Counterterrorism begs for a strategy," *The Washington Times*, 29 October 2009, at http://www.washingtontimes.com/news/2009/oct/29/myers-counterterrorism-begs-for-a-strategy/

8   Rushing, "US Military Under Fire for 'Anti-Islam Class'" (transcript), *Al-Jazeera* TV. 20125124178148367.html alternatively released on YouTube URL: http://www.youtube.com/ watch? feature=player_embedded&v=2swVVfZo5eM#!, accessed 20 May 2012.

9   Posted on bulletin board, School for Advanced Military Studies, Command and General Staff College, Fort Leavenworth, Kansas.

10   Pieper, *Abuse of Language-Abuse of Power*, 33.

11   "'When We Understand that Slide, We'll have Won the War:' US Generals given Baffling PowerPoint Presentation to try to Explain Afghanistan Mess," Mail Foreign Service, *MailOnline* (London), 28 April 2010, URL: www.dailymail.co.uk/news/worldnews/article-1269463/Afghanistan-PowerPoint-slide-Generals-left-baffled-PowerPoint-slide.html, accessed 5 May 2010.

12   Ibrahim Ghanem, *The West in the Eyes of the Egyptian Islamic Movement – Muslim Brotherhood – Jihad – Islamic Group*, Ummah Press Services, Mohandesseen, Egypt (for subscribers only), 1994, 1-2.

13   Tom Czerwinski, *Coping with Bounds: Speculation on Nonlinearity in Military Affairs*, DoD Command and Control Research Program, 1998.

14   James Moffat, *Complexity Theory and Network Centric Warfare*, DoD Command and Control Research Program, 2003.

15   Edward A. Smith, *Complexity, Networking, & Effects-Based Approaches to Operations*, DoD Command and Control Research Program, 2006.

16   David S. Alberts, Richard E. Hayes, *Planning: Complex Endeavors*, DoD Command and Control Research Program, 2007.

17   Edward A. Smith, *Complexity, Networking, & Effects-Based Approaches to Operations*, DoD Command and Control Research Program, 2006, front cover and David S. Alberts, Richard E. Hayes, *Planning: Complex Endeavors*, DoD Command and Control Research Program, 2007, front cover.

18   Tom Czerwinski, *Coping with Bounds: Speculation on Nonlinearity in Military Affairs*, DoD Command and Control Research Program, 1998, pretentious quote page.

19   James Moffat, *Complexity Theory and Network Centric Warfare*, DoD Command and Control Research Program, 2003, Notes to the Reader.

20   James Moffat, *Complexity Theory and Network Centric Warfare*, DoD Command and Control Research Program, 2003, xi, xii.

21   Bachmann Challenges Former Acting CIA Director on Benghazi," *YouTube*, 2 April 2014, URL: http://www.youtube.com/watch?v=AnOnfHRwi5k#t=552, accessed 3 April 2014.

22   Pieper, *Abuse of Language-Abuse of Power*, 34.

23   *Webster's New College Dictionary*, Merriam-Webster: Springfield, MA, 1980) 564. **Definition:** idiopathic 1) peculiar to the individual 2) arising spontaneously or from an obscure or unknown cause.

24   Pieper, *Abuse of Language-Abuse of Power*, 33.

25   *Black's Law Dictionary* 6ᵗʰ, 1190. **Prima facie evidence.** Evidence good and sufficient on its face. Such evidence as, in the judgment of the law, is sufficient to establish a given fact, or the group or chain of facts constituting the party's claim or defense, and which if not rebutted or contradicted, will remain sufficient. Evidence which, if unexplained or uncontradicted, is sufficient to sustain a judgment in favor of the issue which its supports, but which may be contradicted by other evidence ... That quantum of evidence that suffices for proof of a particular fact until the fact is contradicted by other evidence.

26   *Black's Law Dictionary* 6ᵗʰ, 198. **Burden of Proof.** In the law of evidence, the necessity or duty of affirmatively proving a fact or facts in dispute on an issue raised between the parties in a cause. The obligation of a party to establish by evidence a requisite degree of belief concerning a fact in the mind of the trier of fact or the court.

27   *Black's Law Dictionary* 6ᵗʰ, 1377. **Shifting the burden of proof.** Transferring it from one party to the other, or from one side of the case to the other, when he upon whom it rested originally has made out a *prima facie* case or defense by evidence, of such a character that it then becomes incumbent upon the other to rebut by contradictory or defensive evidence.

28   *Black's Law Dictionary* 6ᵗʰ, 1291. **Relevant evidence.** Evidence tending to prove or disprove an alleged fact. Evidence having any tendency to make the existence of any fact that is of consequence to the determination of the action more probable or less probable than it would be without the evidence.

29   *Black's Law Dictionary 6ᵗʰ*, 591. **Fact.** A thing done; an action performed or an incident transpiring; an event or circumstance; an actual occurrence; an actual happening in time or space or an event mental or physical; that which has taken place ... A fact is either a state of things, that is, an existence, or a motion, that is, an event. The quality of being actual; actual existence or occurrence.

30   *Black's Law Dictionary 6ᵗʰ*, 592. **[Facts in]** *Evidence.* A circumstance, event or occurrence as it actually takes or took place; a physical object or appearance, as it usually exists or existed. An actual and absolute reality, as distinguished from mere supposition or opinion ... Truth, as distinguished from fiction or error. "Fact" means reality of events or things the actual occurrence or existence of which is to be determined by evidence.

31   "These Aren't the Droids You're Looking for ...", Star Wars IV, see for example: "*YouTube*, http://www.youtube.com/watch?v=CnjaUoR15dU, 12 January 2011.

32   Tim Kane, *The Entrepreneurial Army: A Survey of West Point Graduates*, The Kaufman Foundation, Kansas City, MO, 4 January 2011.

33   Tim Kane, *The Entrepreneurial Army: A Survey of West Point Graduates*, 17, 18 and 19.

34   Gresham's Law is an economic principle that, "When a government compulsorily overvalues one type of money and undervalues another, the undervalued money will leave the country or disappear from circulation into hoards, while the overvalued money will flood into circulation." Used in this context, it is meant that some officers remain in "circulation" as quality leaders depart the services.

35   *Black's Law Dictionary*, 9ᵗʰ 580. **Nondelegable duty.** (1902) 1. *Contracts.* A duty that cannot be delegated by a contracting party to a third party. If a contracting party purports to delegate the duty, the other party can rightfully refuse to accept performance by the third party. 2. *Torts.* A duty that may be delegated to an independent contractor by a principal, who retains primary (as opposed to vicarious) responsibility if the duty is not properly performed.

36   Rushing, "US Military Under Fire for 'Anti-Islam Class'" (transcript), *Al-Jazeera* TV.

37   Mohamed Akram, Explanatory Memorandum, 4.

38   *Black's Law Dictionary* 9ᵗʰ Edition, West, 2009, 790.

39   *Black's Law Dictionary 6ᵗʰ*, 578. **Expert Witness.** One who by reason of education or specialized experience possesses superior knowledge respecting a subject about which persons having no particular training are incapable of forming an accurate opinion or deducing correct conclusions.

40   Edward W. Said, *Orientalism*, Vintage Publications, (New York: New York, 1979), 19. Cited hereafter as Said, *Orientalism*.

41   Said, *Orientalism*, 133-14.

42   Said, *Orientalism*, 20-21.

43   Said, *Orientalism*, 26-27.

44   Said, *Orientalism*, 24.

45   Said, *Orientalism*, 20-21.

46   Section 6. "Assumptions and Presuppositions," Chapter 2: "Effective Writing -- From Tasking to Final Copy," CGSC Student Text 22-2, *Writing and Speaking for Army Leaders*, U.S. Army Command and General Staff College, Fort Leavenworth, Kansas, August 1998, 2-4.

47   Joint Electronic Library, "Joint Doctrine." http://www.dtic.mil/doctrine/new_pubs/jointpub.htm

48   Joint Publication 5-0, *Joint Operation Planning*, III-26 (page 86), 26 December 2006 at URL: http://www.scribd .com/doc/37553823/Joint-Ops-Planning, accessed 20 May 2011. (Hereafter *Joint Pub 5-0*, 2006 ed.)

49   Joint Publication 5-0, Joint Operation Planning, Revisions—Final Coordination, 25 October 2010, IV-9 (p. 116), PDF first accessed 20 May 2011.

50   Joint Publication 5-0, Joint Operation Planning, 11 August 2011 at URL: http://www.dtic.mil/doctrine /new_pubs/jp5_0.pdf, accessed 30 August 2011, IV-7, 8 (131, 132). (Hereafter JP 5-0 Version 2011.

51   "**Assumption.** A supposition on the current situation or a presupposition on the future course of events, either or both assumed to be true in the absence of positive proof, necessary to enable the commander in the process of planning to complete an estimate of the situation and make a decision on the course of action." (Approved for incorporation into JP 1-02 with JP 5-0 as the source JP.). JP 5-0, Part II—Terms and Definitions, p. GL 5 (249), 11 August 2011 at URL: http://www.dtic.mil/doctrine/new_pubs/jp5_0.pdf, accessed 30 August 2011. GL-5 (249). **Note:** In fairness, the 2011 version of *Joint Pub* 5-0 does appear to have begun scoping the limits of assumption-based analysis.

52 *Black's Law Dictionary* 6th, 123.

53 *Black's Law Dictionary 6th*, 1440.

54 *Black's Law Dictionary* 6th, 302.

55 *Joint Pub 5-0*, 2006 Edition, at III-50 (110).

56 *Black's Law Dictionary 6th*, 1550.

57 "**Conclusory adj**: consisting of or relating to a conclusion or assertion for which no supporting evidence is offered [allegations]," *Merriam-Webster Dictionary of Law*, 1996. **Also**, Expressing a factual inference without stating the underlying facts on which the inference is based < because the plaintiff's allegations lacked any supporting evidence, they were merely conclusory. *Black's Law Dictionary 9th*, 329.

58 Joint Publication 5-0, Joint Operation Planning, 11 August 2011 at URL: http://www.dtic.mil/ doctrine /new_pubs/jp5_0.pdf, accessed 30 August 2011, IV-7, 8 (131, 132). (Hereafter JP 5-0 Version 2011), IV-7.

59 Joint Publication 5-0, Joint Operation Planning, 11 August 2011 at URL: http://www.dtic.mil/ doctrine /new_pubs/jp5_0.pdf, accessed 30 August 2011, IV-7, 8 (131, 132). (Hereafter JP 5-0 Version 2011.

60 *Black's Law Dictionary 6th*, 1508.

61 *Black's Law Dictionary 6th*, 660.

62 *Black's Law Dictionary 6th*, 314. **Constructive fraud.** Exists where conduct, though not actually fraudulent, has all actual consequences and all legal effects of actual fraud. ... Breach of legal or equitable duty which, irrespective of moral guilt, is declared by law to be fraudulent because of its tendency to deceive others or violate confidence.

63 *Black's Law Dictionary* 6th, 302. "Where all theories of causation rest only on conjecture, no jury question is presented."

64 *Joint Pub 5-0* 2006 Edition at III-26 (86), 2010 Edition at IV-9 (116), 2011 Edition at IV-7 (131).

65 General Peter Pace, USMC, Chairman Joint Chiefs of Staff, keynote speech presented at National Defense University, "Extemporaneous Remarks on Our National Strategy for Victory in Iraq, " Washington, DC, 01 December 2005, URL: <http://www.jcs.mil/chairman/speeches/ 051201remarks_NationalStrategyVictoryIraq.html>, accessed 02 December 2005. Cited hereafter as Pace, NDU speech.

66 Myers: "Counterterrorism begs for a strategy," *The Washington Times*, 29 October 2009, at http:// www.washingtontimes.com/news/2009/oct/29/myers-counterterrorism-begs-for-a-strategy/

67 Erik Ortiz, "Should President Obama have said There's No Strategy yet against ISIS," NBC News, August 2014, URL: http://www.nbcnews.com/storyline/iraq-turmoil/should-president-obama-have-said-theres-no-strategy-yet-against-n192096, accessed 30 August 2014. **States: "**During a news conference Thursday, Obama's blunt admission that 'we don't have a strategy yet' landed with a thud — particularly after others in his administration have been ratcheting up calls to eradicate the Islamic State in Iraq and al-Sham, or ISIS, labeling the extremists as a 'valueless evil'."

68 David Martosko, "'We do not Understand the Movement': Top Special Forces General Confessed the US is Clueless about ISIS as FBI Agent Warns about Terror Army's Youth Recruiting," Daily Mail, 29 December 2014, URL: http://www.dailymail.co.uk/news/article-2890266/We-not-understand-movement-Special-Forces-general-confessed-clueless-ISIS-FBI-agent-warns-terror-army-s-youth-recruiting.html, accessed 28 December 2015.

69 Declassified Key Judgments of the National Intelligence Estimate. Trends in Global Terrorism: Implications for the United States, April 2006, at 1, at http://www.dni.gov/press_releases/Declassified _NIE_Key_Judgments.pdf

70   Mohamed Akram, Explanatory Memorandum, 7.

71   OIC, Third Extraordinary Session—10 Year Plan OIC, Third Extraordinary Session—Ten-Year Progamme.

72   Pieper, *Abuse of Language-Abuse of Power*, 33.

73   Stephen Coughlin, "On Lexicography: Questions on USCENTCOM CPG's Proposed Lexicon," Briefing to the Joint Staff SCIG, UNCLASSIFIED, 14 August 2007, slides 9, 10.

74   Stephen Coughlin, *To Our Great Detriment: Ignoring What Extremists say about Jihad*, unclassified Master of Science, Strategic Intelligence Thesis, National Defense Intelligence College, 2007, 221, 222.

PART IX: THE DUTY TO KNOW

1   Josh Rushing, "US Military Under Fire for 'Anti-Islam Class'" (transcript), *Al-Jazeera* TV (Washington Office), 12 May 2012, URL: http://www.aljazeera.com/video/americas/2012/05/20125124178148367.html, alternatively released on YouTube, URL: http://www.youtube.com/ watch? feature=player_embedded&v=2swVVfZo5eM#!, accessed 20 May 2012.

2   Article VI, the Constitution of the United States, The Charters of Freedom, United States Archives, URL: http://www.archives.gov/exhibits/charters/constitution_transcript.html. **States**: "The Senators and Representatives before mentioned, and the Members of the several State Legislatures, and all executive and judicial Officers, both of the United States and of the several States, shall be bound by Oath or Affirmation, to support this Constitution; but no religious Test shall ever be required as a Qualification to any Office or public Trust under the United States."

3   Arie Perliger, "Challengers from the Sidelines: Understanding America's Violent Far-Right," Counter Terrorism Center at West Point, 15 January 2013, URL: http://www.ctc.usma.edu/wp-content/uploads/2013/01/ChallengersFromtheSidelines.pdf, accessed 24 January 2013, 17. **Reads**: "Regarding affinity towards traditional values ... The far right represents a more extreme version of conservatism, as its political vision is usually justified by the aspiration to restore or preserve values and practices that are part of the idealized historical heritage of the nation or ethnic community. In many cases these past-oriented perspectives help to formulate a nostalgic and romantic ideological aura which makes these groups attractive for many who aspire to restore the halcyon days of a clear hierarchy of values and norms."

4   Mohamed Elibiary, Twitter / MohamedElibiary: @alimhaider, 13 November 2013, URL: https://twitter.com/alimhaider/status/400631019973251072, accessed 13 November 2013. **Actual Tweet**: "Islamophobia Movt promotes RtWing self radicalization & eventual Violent Extremism/ terrorism. Needs C-Rad strategy."

5   Quoted by the Honorable Joseph E. Schmitz, former Inspector General of the Department of Defense, in Schmitz, IG HANDBOOK, p. 359, *supra*.

6   Pieper, Josef, *Abuse of Language*, 33.

7   Hon. Joseph E. Schmitz, "Liberty, Tolerance, and Shariah Supremacism," presented orally as Comments to Milwaukee Lawyers Chapter of the Federalist Society, 31 May 2011, 5. Hereafter cited as "Schmitz, Liberty."

8   Schmitz, Liberty, 5-6.

9   5 U.S.C. § 3331 ("... I will support and defend the Constitution of the United States against all enemies, foreign and domestic. ...").

10   "Countering Violent Extremism (CVE) Training Guidance & Best Practices," Office for Civil Rights and Civil Liberties, DHS, October 2011, http://www.dhs.gov/xlibrary/assets/cve-training-guidance.pdf

11   Article VI, the Constitution of the United States, The Charters of Freedom, United States Archives, URL: http://www.archives.gov/exhibits/charters/constitution_transcript.html

12   Doi, *Shari'ah: The Islamic Law*, 5.

13   Qutb, *Milestones*, Salimiah edition, 103.

14   Qutb, *Milestones*, Salimiah edition, 18.

15   5 USC Section 2903 (b), The United States Code, House of Representatives, the United States Congress, 1/7/2011, http://uscode.house.gov/download/pls/05C29.txt

16   5 USC Section 3331, The United States Code, House of Representatives, the United States Congress,   1/7/2011,   http://www.americanbar.org/groups/professional_responsibility/publications/

model_rules_of_professional_conduct/rule_1_1_competence/comment_on_rule_1_1.html

17   *Josef Pieper, Abuse of Language – Abuse of Power*, Ignatius Press, 1992 (trans. Lothar Krauth, Kosel-Verlag, Munich 1974), 29.

18   DHS Office of Civil Rights Civil Liberties, "Terminology to Define Terrorism: Recommendations from American Muslims," January 2008, URL: http://www.dhs.gov/xlibrary/assets/dhs_crcl_terminology_08-1-08_accessible.pdf.

19   Brigadier S.K. Malik, *Quranic Concept of War*, 60.

20   The term "inflammatory" has become the new designated DoD term reflecting the analytical threshold that cannot be overstepped.

21   Footnote: Chris Lewis, "Joint Force Staff College Course on Radical Islam," E-Mail to Congressional Committees from the Joint Chiefs of Staff Legislative Affairs, 24 April 2012.

22   "Senate Homeland Security and Governmental Affairs Committee and House Homeland Security Committee Hold Joint Hearing on Threats to Military Communities Inside the Inside the United States," Congressional Hearings, *CQ Congressional Transcripts*, Washington, D.C., 7 December 2011.

23   "Senate Homeland Security and Governmental Affairs Committee and House Homeland Security Committee Hold Joint Hearing on Threats to Military Communities Inside the Inside the United States," Congressional Hearings, *CQ Congressional Transcripts*, Washington, D.C., 7 December 2011.

24   Spencer Ackerman, "Exclusive: Senior U.S. General Orders Top-to-Bottom Review of Military's Islam Training," *WIRED*—Danger Room, 24 April 2012, URL: http://www.wired.com/dangerroom/2012/04/military-islam-training/

25   Josh Rushing, "US Military Under Fire for 'Anti-Islam Class'" (transcript), *Al-Jazeera* TV (Washington Office), 12 May 2012, URL: http://www.aljazeera.com/video/americas/2012/05/

20125124178148367.html alternatively released on YouTube, URL: http://www.youtube.com/watch?feature=player_embedded&v=2swVVfZo5eM#!, accessed 20 May 2012.

26   Perry Chiaramonte, "Legal Group comes the Aid of Army Instructor Ousted over Muslim Group Complaints," *Fox News*, 5 October 2012, URL: http://www.foxnews.com/us/2012/10/05/rising-career-us-army-officer-matthew-dooley-halted-for-teaching-soldiers-on/, accessed 5 October 2012.

27   Rule 1.1 Competence, *ABA Model Rules of Professional Conduct* (2002), Amended February 5th, 2002, American Bar Association House of Delegates, Philadelphia, Pennsylvania, per Report No. 401, Rule 1.1, URL: http://www.americanbar.org/groups/professional_responsibility/publications/model_rules_of_professional_conduct/rule_1_1_competence/comment_on_rule_1_1.html, accessed 4 June 2007. (Hereafter "Model Rules"). Competence.

28   Model Rules. Rule 1.1(2) Legal Knowledge and Skill, "A lawyer need not necessarily have special training or prior experience to handle legal problems of a type with which the lawyer is unfamiliar. A newly admitted lawyer can be as competent as a practitioner with long experience. … A lawyer can provide adequate representation in a wholly novel field through necessary study." (Emphasis added)

29   Model Rules. Rule 1.1(5). Thoroughness and Preparation. "Competent handling of a particular matter includes inquiry into and analysis of the factual and legal elements of the problem, and use of methods and procedures meeting the standards of competent practitioners. It also includes adequate preparation."

30   *Black's Law Dictionary 6th*, 1179. **Prejudice.** A forejudgment; bias; partiality; preconceived opinion. A leaning towards one side of a cause for some reason other than a conviction of its justice.

31   *Black's Law Dictionary 6th*, West Publishing, St. Paul, 1267. **Rebuttable Presumption**. In the law of evidence, a presumption which may be rebutted by evidence. … A species of legal presumption which holds good until evidence contrary to it is introduced. … It gives particular effect to certain groups of facts in absence of further evidence, and presumption provides prim facie case which shifts

to defendant the burden to go forward with evidence to contradict or rebut fact presumed.

32   *Black's Law Dictionary 6ᵗʰ*, 660.

33   *Black's Law Dictionary 6ᵗʰ*, 660.

34   Part 2, (c), "Countering Violent Extremism (CVE) Training Guidance & Best Practices," Office for Civil Rights and Civil Liberties, DHS, October 2011, URL: http://www.dhs.gov/xlibrary/assets/cve-training-guidance.pdf.

35   *Black's Law Dictionary 9ᵗʰ*, 1578. **Suppression of Evidence.** (18c) 2. The destruction of evidence or the refusal to give evidence at a criminal proceeding.

36   "Senate Homeland Security and Governmental Affairs Committee and House Homeland Security Committee Hold Joint Hearing on Threats to Military Communities Inside the Inside the United States," Congressional Hearings, CQ Congressional Transcripts, Washington, D.C., 7 December 2011.

37   *Black's Law Dictionary*, 9ᵗʰ 1183.

PART XI: APPENDIX ONE

1   *Explanatory Memorandum*: On the General Strategic Goal for the Group," Mohamed Akram, May 22, 1991, Government Exhibit 003-0085/3:04-CR-240-G U.S. v. HLF, et al., United States District Court, Northern District of Texas, URL: http://www.txnd.uscourts.gov/judges/hlf2/09-25-08/Elbarasse%20Search%203.pdf. **Reads:** "The process of settlement is a "Civilization-Jihadist Process" with all the means. The *Ikhwan* [Muslim Brotherhood] must understand that their work in America is a kind of grand Jihad in eliminating and destroying the Western civilization from within and **"sabotaging" its miserable house by their hands and the hands** of the believers so that it is eliminated and Allah's religion is made victorious over all other religions. ... It is a Muslim's destiny to perform Jihad and work wherever he is ..." Cited hereafter as Mohamed Akram, *Explanatory Memorandum*.

2   Mohamed Akram, *Explanatory Memorandum*.

3   Muhammad Shafiq & Mohammed Abu-Nimer, *Interfaith Dialogue: A Guide for Muslims*, International Institute of Islamic Thought (IIIT), Herndon, VA, 2007 (2ⁿᵈ printing 2011, London). Cited hereafter as Shafiq & Nimmer, *Interfaith Dialogue: A Guide for Muslims*, IIIT.

4   Shafiq & Nimmer, *Interfaith Dialogue: A Guide for Muslims*, IIIT, xvi.

5   Siddiqi, Shamin A. *Methodology of Dawah Illallah in American Perspective*. Brooklyn: The Forum for Islamic Work, New York 1989, 136-7.

6   Government Exhibit: Philly Meeting - 15, 3:04-CR-240-G, U.S. v. HLF, et al., at 2,3, at http://www.txnd.uscourts.gov /judges/hlf2/09-29-08/Philly%20Meeting%2015.pdf

7   Mohamed Akram, Explanatory Memorandum, **Listed:** IIIT (22), 32.

8   Mohamed Akram, Explanatory Memorandum, **Listed:** IIIT (28), 1.

9   Mohamed Akram, Explanatory Memorandum, **Listed:** IIIT (28), xx.

10   Shafiq & Nimmer, *Interfaith Dialogue: A Guide for Muslims*, IIIT, vii.

11   Shafiq & Nimmer, *Interfaith Dialogue: A Guide for Muslims*, IIIT, 37.

12   Shafiq & Nimmer, *Interfaith Dialogue: A Guide for Muslims*, IIIT, 42.

13   Mohamed Akram, Explanatory Memorandum, **Listed:** IIIT (28), 32.

14   International Institute of Islamic Thought homepage, URL: http://www.iiit.org/, accessed 2 September 2013.

15   Ahmad ibn Naqib al-Misri, 'Umdat al-Salik (*Reliance of the Traveller: A Classic Manual of Islamic Sacred Law*), rev. ed. trans. Nuh Ha Mim Keller (Beltsville, MD: Amana Publications, 1994), Certification page, Al-Azhar, xviii. Document Letter Heading and Signature Block: The letter heading states that the certification comes from the International Institute of Islamic Thought (IIIT). The signature is from Dr. Taha Jabir al-'Alwani. His signature block states that he is signing in his capacity as the President of the IIIT, as President of the Fiqh Council of North America (FCNA), and as a member of the Islamic Fiqh Academy in Jedda. Both the IIIT and FCNA are associated with the Muslim Brotherhood in the Explanatory Memorandum. The FCNA is also a subordinate element of the Islamic Society of North America (ISNA). The International Islamic Fiqh Academy (IIFA) is listed as a subsidiary organ of the OIC at "Subsidiary Organs, Organization of the Islamic Cooperation," OIC, URL: http://www.oic-oci.org/page_detail.asp? p _id=64#FIQH, 4 Feburary 2013. It was affiliated to the OIC in its fourteenth session, held in Duha (Qatar) 5–13 Dhul-Qi`dah1423 A.H., 11–16 January 2003 C.E, as cited in "Jihad: Rulings & Regulations," "Living Shari'a/Fatwa Bank," IslamOnline, at URL: http://www.freerepublic.com/focus/news/2390531/replies?c=7.

A Note Before Proceeding – Why *Reliance of the Traveller*? There are a substantial number of citations to Islamic law in the 1994 edition of the English-language translation of Ahmad ibn Naqib al-

Misri's *'Umdat al-Salik* (*Reliance of the Traveller: A Classic Manual of Islamic Sacred Law*). The source selection is due not to a limitation of sources but rather to *Reliance*'s unique status as a broadly available English-language title with certifications from the preeminent center of Islamic thought, the Muslim Brotherhood in America, and the OIC on behalf of its fifty-seven Member States. Cited hereafter as Keller, *Reliance of the Traveller.*

16　Mohamed Akram, Explanatory Memorandum, **Listed:** IIIT (17), 32.

17　Keller, *Reliance of the Traveller*, Certification page, Al-Azhar, xviii. Document Letter Heading and Signature Block: The letter heading states that the certification comes from the International Institute of Islamic Thought (IIIT). The signature is from Dr. Taha Jabir al-'Alwani. His signature block states that he is signing in his capacity as the President of the IIIT, as President of the Fiqh Council of North America (FCNA), and as a member of the Islamic Fiqh Academy in Jedda. Both the IIIT and FCNA are associated with the Muslim Brotherhood in the Explanatory Memorandum: On the General Strategic Goal for the Group," Mohamed Akram, May 22, 1991, Government Exhibit 003-0085/3:04-CR-240-G U.S. v. HLF, et al., United States District Court, Northern District of Texas, URL: http://www.txnd.uscourts.gov/judges/hlf2/09-25-08/Elbarasse%20Search%203.pdf. The FCNA is also a subordinate element of the Islamic Society of North America (ISNA). The International Islamic Fiqh Academy (IIFA) is listed as a subsidiary organ of the OIC at "Subsidiary Organs, Organization of the Islamic Cooperation," OIC, URL: http://www.oic-oci.org/page_detail. asp? p _id=64#FIQH, 4 Feburary 2013. It was affiliated to the OIC in its fourteenth session, held in Duha (Qatar) 5–13 Dhul-Qi`dah1423 A.H., 11–16 January 2003 C.E, as cited in "Jihad: Rulings & Regulations," "Living Shari'a/Fatwa Bank," IslamOnline, at URL: http://www.freerepublic.com/focus/news/2390531/replies?c=7.

18　Sayyid Qutb, *Milestones*, Salimiah, (Kuwait: International Islamic Federation of Student Organizations. 1978 [written 1966]), 263.

19　Mohamed Akram, Explanatory Memorandum, 18.

20　Shafiq & Nimmer, *Interfaith Dialogue: A Guide for Muslims*, IIIT, 9.

21　Shafiq & Nimmer, *Interfaith Dialogue: A Guide for Muslims*, IIIT, 93.

22　Keller, *Reliance of the Traveller*, Book O "Justice," at o9.0 "Jihad," at o9.16: "Truces." Reads: "In Sacred Law truce means a peace treaty with those hostile to Islam, involving a cessation of fighting for a specified period …"

23　Keller, *Reliance of the Traveller*, Book O "Justice," at o9.0 "Jihad," at o9.16: "Truces." Reads: "If the Muslims are weak, a truce may be made for ten years if necessary, for the Prophet (Allah bless him and grant him Peace) made a truce with Quraysh for that long, as it related by Abu Dawud. It is not permissible to stipulate longer than that, save by means of new truces, each of which does not exceed ten years."

24　Keller, *Reliance of the Traveller*, Book O "Justice," at o9.0 "Jihad," at o9.16: "Truces." Reads: "When made with other than a portion of the non-Muslims, or when made with all of them, or with all in a particular region such as India or Asia Minor, then only the caliph (or his representative) may effect it, for it is a matter of the gravest consequence because it entails the nonperformance of jihad, whether globally or in a given locality …"

25　Keller, *Reliance of the Traveller*, Book O "Justice," at o9.0 "Jihad," at o9.16: "Truces." Reads: "Interests that justify making a truce are such things as Muslim weakness because of lack of numbers or material, or the hope of an enemy becoming Muslim …"

26　Keller, *Reliance of the Traveller*, Book O "Justice," at o9.0 "Jihad," at o9.16: "Truces." Reads: "There must be some interest served in making a truce other than mere preservation of the status quo.

27　Louay Safi, Module 6 – The Theology of Islam, Dr. Louay Safi, Islamic Society of North America (ISNA), Battle Command Training Center (BCTC), 135th ESC, 20th EN BN & 193rd MP BN, Leader Development and Education for Sustained Peace, 1-3 December 2009, Fort Hood, TX. **Slide 7,** "Islam is an Arabic word derived from the word peace, which also means submitting to a higher will. Islam mean seeking peace by submitting to the Divine Will."

28   Sayyid Qutb, *Islam and Universal Peace*, American Trust Publications (ATP), Plainfield, IN, 1993 (last print 1977), back cover. Cited hereafter as Qutb, *Islam and Universal Peace*.

29   Hisham Sabrin, "Qutb – Between Terror and Tragedy," *IkhwanWeb*, 20 January 2010, URL: http://www.ikhwanweb.com/article.php?id=22709, accessed 7 July 2014 (1951).

30   Qutb, *Islam and Universal Peace*.

31   Qutb, *Islam and Universal Peace*, back cover.

32   Qutb, *Islam and Universal Peace*, 71.

33   Qutb, *Islam and Universal Peace*, 10.

34   Qutb, *Islam and Universal Peace*, 10.

35   Qutb, *Islam and Universal Peace*, 72.

36   Qutb, *Islam and Universal Peace*, 72.

37   Sayyid Qutb, *Social Justice in Islam*, trans. John B. Hardie and Hamid Algar, Islamic Publication International, Oneonta, NY, 2000.

38   Qutb, *Social Justice in Islam*, 20.

39   Qutb, *Social Justice in Islam*, 316-317.

40   Shafiq & Nimmer, *Interfaith Dialogue: A Guide for Muslims*, IIIT, 75.

41   Mohamed Akram, Explanatory Memorandum.

42   Paragraph 17, Mohamed Akram, Explanatory Memorandum, 24.

43   Transcript of Tariq Ramadan Speech Given to the 11th MAS-ICNA Annual Convention, December 2012. **Ramadan stated:** "So, if we look and we say what is home, remember what the Prophet of Islam did when he arrived in Medina. Its … a message when you start building mosques and this is what we are doing. We did this. The Muslims when they first arrived in Asia, Africa, the United States of America, Canada, Europe everywhere the first thing that we did as the first institutions that we had were – was building mosques. Meaning two things. We are at home and the center of our presence is لا اله الا الله - *laelha ala allh* (No God but Allah). So what you said about our identity is – its not because we are at home that we forget the direction. The direction of *el Kiblah* remains *el* Kiblah means (No God but Allah). And now we are here and as we heard from the Prophet of Islam, one of the characteristics of the privileges that he had is the earth is a mosque. Wherever you go, this is a *masjid* (a mosque). It means this is a place where you can prostrate. A place where you can pray. Meaning, I am at home the very moment I say هلاا لاا (No God but Allah). This is home for me. And as long as I'm not oppressed and I'm not attacked the people around me, if they accept the fact and give me freedom on conscience and freedom of worship they are not enemies."

44   *Sahih Muslim* 1062: "The Messenger of Allah (peace be upon him) said: I have been given superiority over the other prophets in six respects: I have been given words which are concise but comprehensive in meaning; I have been helped by terror (in the hearts of enemies): spoils have been made lawful to me; the earth has been made for me clean and a place of worship; I have been sent to all mankind; and the line of prophets is closed with me."

45   "Al Qaradawi Boycotts Qatar Meet Attended by 'Jews', *Gulf News* (Dubai), 23 April 2013, URL: http://gulfnews.com/news/gulf/qatar/al-qaradawi-boycotts-qatar-meet-attended-by-jews-1.1174230, accessed 2 September 2013.

46   "Starting Interfaith Conference in Doha, Qaradawi Boycotts in Protest at the Jewish Audience," *Al-Ahram* (Cairo)(Arabic - Google Translated), 24 April 2013, URL: http://gate.ahram.org.eg/News/337491.aspx, 2 September 2013.

47   "Sheik Yousuf Al-Qaradhawi: Allah Imposed Hitler upon the Jews to Punish Them - "Allah

Willing, the Next Time Will Be at the Hand of the Believers," *MEMRI* Clip No 2005 (aired on Al-Jazeera TV), 28-30 January 2009, URL: http://www.memritv.org/clip_transcript/en/2005.htm, accessed 2 September 2013. From 20 January 2009: "Throughout history, Allah has imposed upon the [Jews] people who would punish them for their corruption. The last punishment was carried out by Hitler. By means of all the things he did to them – even though they exaggerated this issue – he managed to put them in their place. This was divine punishment for them. Allah willing, the next time will be at the hand of the believers." And on 28 January 2009: "To conclude my speech, I'd like to say that the only thing I hope for is that as my life approaches its end, Allah will give me an opportunity to go to the land of Jihad and resistance, even if in a wheelchair. I will shoot Allah's enemies, the Jews, and they will throw a bomb at me, and thus, I will seal my life with martyrdom. Praise be to Allah, Lord of the Worlds. Allah's mercy and blessings upon you."

48   Shafiq & Nimmer, *Interfaith Dialogue: A Guide for Muslims*, IIIT, 31.

49   Keller, *Reliance of the Traveller*, at § r8.2.

50   Shafiq & Nimmer, *Interfaith Dialogue: A Guide for Muslims*, IIIT, 31.

51   Shafiq & Nimmer, *Interfaith Dialogue: A Guide for Muslims*, IIIT, 31.

52   Shafiq & Nimmer, *Interfaith Dialogue: A Guide for Muslims*, IIIT, 31.

53   Shafiq & Nimmer, *Interfaith Dialogue: A Guide for Muslims*, IIIT, 31.

54   Shafiq & Nimmer, *Interfaith Dialogue: A Guide for Muslims*, IIIT, 31.

55   Keller, *Reliance of the Traveller*, at § r8.2.

56   Shafiq & Nimmer, *Interfaith Dialogue: A Guide for Muslims*, IIIT, 70.

57   Siddiqi, Shamim A. *Methodology of Dawah Illallah in American Perspective*. Brooklyn: The Forum for Islamic Work, New York 1989, 117.

58   "105,000 Christian Martyred Yearly, Says European Official," *The Catholic Register/EWTN – Catholic World News Brief*, 6 June 2011, http://www.ewtn.com/vnews/getstory.asp?number=113734, accessed 14 July 2011.

59   Ha-Emet, URL: http://www.ha-emet.com/index.html, accessed 10 October 2013.

60   Shafiq & Nimmer, *Interfaith Dialogue: A Guide for Muslims*, IIIT, 105.

61   "Letters," National Catholic Register, 27 December 2009, URL: http://www.ncregister.com/site/article/letters_01.03.2010/, accessed 10 October 2013.

62   Shafiq & Nimmer, *Interfaith Dialogue: A Guide for Muslims*, IIIT, 21.

63   "IIIT Chair Inaugurated at Nazareth College," IIIT News, 10 January 2012, URL: http://iiit.org/NewsEvents/News/tabid/62/articleType/ArticleView/articleId/244/IIIT-Chair-Inaugurated-at-Nazareth-College.aspx, accessed 10 October 2013.

64   Shafiq & Nimmer, *Interfaith Dialogue: A Guide for Muslims*, IIIT, 110.

65   Shafiq & Nimmer, *Interfaith Dialogue: A Guide for Muslims*, IIIT, 113.

66   Shafiq & Nimmer, *Interfaith Dialogue: A Guide for Muslims*, IIIT, 115.

67   Mohamed Akram, Explanatory Memorandum.

68   Part I, Chapter II, Objective and Means, Article (2), "Bylaws of the International Muslim Brotherhood," *IkhwanWeb*, URL: http://www.investigativeproject.org/documents/misc/673.pdf, accessed 18 January 2010.

69   IIIT Hosts Catholic Muslim Meeting," IIIT News, 25 March 2008, URL: http://www.iiit.org/NewsEvents/News/tabid/62/articleType/ArticleView/articleId/49/IIIT-Hosts-Catholic-Muslim-Meeting.aspx, accessed 10 October 2013.

70   Jamal al-Barzinji, *Islamic Resource Bank.org.* Accessed 26 April 2011 at http://www. islamicresourcebank.org/bios/barziniji%20jamal%20bio.pdf

71   Johnson, Ben, "Troubling Presence at a Funeral," *FrontPageMagazine*, June 11, 2004. Accessed 26 April 2011 at http://archive.frontpagemag.com/readArticle.aspx?ARTID=12670.

72   Abubaker Y. Ahmed Al-Shingieti, PhD, Islam Resource Bank, URL: http://www. islamicresourcebank.org/bios/alshingietiabub.htm, accessed 10 October 2013. Cited hereafter as Shingieti, Islam Resource Bank.

73   Shingieti, Islam Resource Bank.

74   Shingieti, Islam Resource Bank.

75   Mohamed Akram, Explanatory Memorandum, **Listed:** IIIT (17), AMSS (4), ISNA (1), 32.

76   Shingieti, Islam Resource Bank.

77   Shingieti, Islam Resource Bank.

78   Abubaker Y. Ahmed Al-Shigieti, Vice President for Preventive Engagement, International Center for Religion and Diplomacy, undated, URL: http://icrd.org/aa/, accessed 10 October 2013.

79   Abubaker Y. Ahmed Al-Shigieti, Vice President for Preventive Engagement, International Center for Religion and Diplomacy.

80   Patrick Poole, "Genocide Henchman Leading Muslim Outreach to Obama," PJ Media, 22 January 2009, URL: http://pjmedia.com/blog/genocide-henchman-leads-us-muslim-outreach-to-obama/?singlepage=true, 10 October 2013.

81   "Sudanese Governor of South Kordofan Ahmad Haroun, Wanted by ICC for War Crimes, in Pep Talk to Soldiers: 'Crush Them, Don't Bring Them Back Alive, Eat Them Uncooked'," Ahmad Haroun, Governor, South Kordoafan, Sudan, Wanted by the ICC, MEMRI Video Clip # 3388, Broadcast on Al-Jazeera Network (Qatar), 30 March 2012, URL: http://www.memri.org/clip/en/0/0/0/0/0/0/3388.htm, accessed 4 April 2012.

82   Adam Kredo, "White House Criticized by Holocaust Scholars for Hosting Sudanese War Criminals," Washington Post, 7 May 2013, URL: http://www.washingtontimes.com/news/2013/may/7/white-house-criticized-holocaust-scholars-hosting-/?page=all, accessed 10 October 2013.

83   Mohamed Akram, Explanatory Memorandum. **Listed:** ISNA (1).

84   Advisor Council List, ACME: American Muslims for Constructive Engagement, undated, URL: http://amceweb.net/2.html, accessed 15 October 2013.

85   Affecting Change as an Imam: Imam Mohamed Magid, *Peaceful Families Project*, http://www. peacefulfamilies.org/magid.html, accessed 5 March 2012.

86   Keller, *Reliance of the Traveller*, Book X "Biographical Note," at § x228 – **Imam Malik ibn Anas**, Imam Malik is Malik ibn Anas ibn Malik, Abu 'Abdullah al-Asbahi al-Himyari, the *mujtahid* Imam born in Medina in 93/712. The second of the four greatest Imams of Sacred Law, his school has more followers than that of anyone besides Abu Hanifa. He was the author of *al-Muwatta'* [*The Trodden Path*], the greatest hadith collection of its time, nearly every hadith of which was accepted by Bukhari in his Sahih. He died in Medina in 179/795.

87   Imam Malik ibn Anas, *Al-Muwatta of Imam Malik ibn Anas: The First Formulation of Islamic Law,* trans. Aisha Abdurrahman Bewley. (Kuala Lumpur: Islamic Book Trust, 1997). Cite hereafter as Malik, *Al-Muwatta.*

88   Asaf A.A. Fyzee, Outlines of Muhammadan Law, 4th ed. (Delhi, India: Oxford University Press, 1974), 34. Cited hereafter as Fyzee, *Muhammadan Law.*

89   Malik, *Al-Muwatta*, 173.

90   Malik, *Al-Muwatta*, 180.

91   Malik, *Al-Muwatta*, 180-1.

92   Malik, *Al-Muwatta*, 1989, 303.

93   Shafiq & Nimmer, *Interfaith Dialogue: A Guide for Muslims*, IIIT, 133.

94   Shafiq & Nimmer, *Interfaith Dialogue: A Guide for Muslims*, IIIT, 130.

95   Shafiq & Nimmer, *Interfaith Dialogue: A Guide for Muslims*, IIIT, 138.

96   "Catholic Men's Conference Opens Ticket Sale," *The Catholic Free Press*, 8 February 2013, URL: http://www.catholicfreepress.org/local/2013/02/08/catholic-mens-conference-opens-ticket-sales/, accessed 5 March 2013.

97   "Qaradawi on Interfaith Dialogue," *Al-Watan* website in Arabic, 5 June 2009, translated by *Global Muslim Brotherhood Report*, 10 June 2009 also relying on BBC Monitoring Middle East – Political Supplied by *BBC Worldwide Monitoring*, June 6, 2009 Saturday Al-Qaradawi urges rally of Jerusalem Muslims, Christians against Israel Text, *Al-Watan* website on 5 June [Unattributed report: "Stressing that Islamic Law Does Not Forbid Dialogue with the People of the Book on Matters of Faith: Al-Qaradawi: 'We Have to Rally the Muslims and Christians of Jerusalem to Stand up Together Against Zionism'," URL: http://globalmbreport.org/?p=1501, accessed 10 October 2013. **For Completeness of Record:** *Dr Al-Qaradawi was asked:* "Due to the great development of the modern media, there are networks engaged in proselytizing Christianity. Is there any harm in having a dialogue with them to know what they have and probably find a way to convert them to Islam?

He replied by saying: "In the name of God, the Merciful, the Compassionate and peace be upon the Messenger of God. Dialogue with the People of the Book on matters of faith is not forbidden, according to the Islamic law. However, nobody should do that unless he is well versed in the rules and teachings of Islam and has knowledge of their beliefs, and provided he intends to do that for the sake of God and abide by the etiquette of communication by the modern electronic means, asking God to guide their hearts to the right path." Dr Al-Qaradawi added: "We do not converse with the Christians so that they may be pleased with us. We only carry out dialogue with them in order to find common grounds that serve as a basis for further action. We should not take others as our enemies, as God says: 'And dispute ye not with the People of the Book, except with means better (than mere disputation), unless it be with those of them who inflict wrong (and injury): but say, "We believe in the revelation which has come down to us and in that which came down to you; Our Allah and your Allah is one.' [Koranic verse; Al-Ankabut, 29:46] He went on to say: "So, God has ordered us to argue with them in ways that are best and most gracious. We see that God laid down the principles of the Islamic preaching in the Koran when He says: 'Invite (all) to the Way of thy Lord with wisdom and beautiful preaching; and argue with them in ways that are best and most gracious.' [partial Koranic verse; Al-Nahl, 16:125]

He added: "The Koran says: 'And dispute ye not with the People of the Book, except with means better (than mere disputation), unless it be with those of them who inflict wrong (and injury): but say, We believe in the revelation which has come down to us and in that which came down to you; Our Allah and your Allah is one.' [Koranic verse; Al-Ankabut, 29:46] This means we should talk about the points that bind and the common grounds between them and us and not the points of difference. When you engage in a dialogue, try to establish common grounds between yourself and the other party and say: 'We all believe in one God, so let us come to common terms.' Al-Qaradawi said: "We do not engage in dialogue with them so that they may be pleased with our religion. They will not be satisfied with us unless we follow their form of religion. This is a fact. We only converse with them to find common grounds on which to stand together against atheism, obscenity, and grievances. We converse with them and ask them: 'What is your stance on the cause of Palestine, the issue of Jerusalem, or the issue of Al-Aqsa Mosque?' We try to rally the Christians with us to stand together, especially for the cause of Palestine, since Palestine has both Muslims and Christians. We have to rally the Muslims and Christians of Jerusalem to stand up together against Zionism and the Israeli arrogance and tyranny. There is no objection to that."

98   Shafiq & Nimmer, *Interfaith Dialogue: A Guide for Muslims*, IIIT, 143.

99   Shafiq & Nimmer, *Interfaith Dialogue: A Guide for Muslims*, IIIT, 31.

100 Shafiq & Nimmer, *Interfaith Dialogue: A Guide for Muslims*, IIIT, 31.

101 Keller, *Reliance of the Traveller*, at § r8.2.

102 "Imam Goes off Script at Vatican", 15 June 2014, *ICLA Videos/YouTube*, UR: https://www.youtube.com/watch?v=P93PZmp-_m4, accessed 17 June 2014.

103 "Islamfachmann: Koran-Rezitation bei Friedensgebeten ist Legitim," Radio Vatican, 11 June 2014, URL: http://de.radiovaticana.va/articolo.asp?c=806221, accessed 17 June 2014. References to this article from translation "Islam Specialist: Koran Recitation at the Prayer for Peace is Legitimate," translation from German to English by Rembrandt Clancy, posted on *Gates of Vienna*, URL: http://gatesofvienna.net/2014/06/multiculturalism-in-religious-garb/, accessed 17 June 2014.

104 "Islam Specialist: Koran Recitation at the Prayer for Peace is Legitimate," translation from German to English by Rembrandt Clancy, posted on *Gates of Vienna*, URL: http://gatesofvienna.net/2014/06/multiculturalism-in-religious-garb/, accessed 17 June 2014. Cited hereafter as "Islam Specialist: Koran Recitation at the Prayer for Peace is Legitimate."

105 "Islam Specialist: Koran Recitation at the Prayer for Peace is Legitimate."

106 "Islam Specialist: Koran Recitation at the Prayer for Peace is Legitimate."

107 "OIC Secretary General Ihsanoglu Meets with Pope Francis in the Vatican," *OIC Presser*, 13 December 2013, URL: http://www.oicun.org/9/20131213042052911.html, accessed 18 June 2014.

108 "Islam Specialist: Koran Recitation at the Prayer for Peace is Legitimate."

109 "Islam Specialist: Koran Recitation at the Prayer for Peace is Legitimate."

110 "Islam Specialist: Koran Recitation at the Prayer for Peace is Legitimate."

111 Muhammad Shafiq, 143.

112 "OIC Secretary General Ihsanoglu Meets with Pope Francis in the Vatican," *OIC Presser*, 13 December 2013, URL: http://www.oicun.org/9/20131213042052911.html, accessed 18 June 2014.

113 Eric Levy, "Columbus Community Condemns Graffiti Left on Three Local Churches," FOX 59 (Columbus, IN local FOX News), 31 August 2014, URL: http://fox59.com/2014/08/31/columbus-community-condemns-graffiti-left-on-three-local-churches/, accessed 1 September2014.

114 Eric Levy, "Columbus Community Condemns Graffiti Left on Three Local Churches."

115 "3 Columbus Churches Vandalized with Graffiti Overnight," WTHR TV (Indianapolis, IN local NBC), 31 August 2014, ULR: http://www.wthr.com/story/26416131/2014/08/31/3-columbus-churches-vandalized-with-graffiti-overnight, accessed 1 September 2014.

116 "3 Columbus Churches Vandalized with Graffiti Overnight," WTHR TV (Indianapolis, IN local NBC), 31 August 2014, ULR: http://www.wthr.com/story/26416131/2014/08/31/3-columbus-churches-vandalized-with-graffiti-overnight, accessed 1 September 2014.

117 Eric Levy, "Columbus Community Condemns Graffiti Left on Three Local Churches."

118 Shafiq & Nimmer, *Interfaith Dialogue: A Guide for Muslims*, IIIT, 31.

119 Shafiq & Nimmer, *Interfaith Dialogue: A Guide for Muslims*, IIIT, 143.

120 Jessica Chasmar, "'Infidels,' Quran Verses Painted on Christian Churches in Indiana", *Washington Times*, 2 September 2014, URL: http://www.washingtontimes.com/news/2014/sep/2/infidels-quran-verses-painted-christian-churches-i/, accessed 3 September 2014.

121 Shafiq & Nimmer, *Interfaith Dialogue: A Guide for Muslims*, IIIT, 143.

122 *Black's Law Dictionary 9th*, Bryan A. Garner, Editor in Chief, West Publishing (Thomson Reuters), St. Paul, 1242.

123 "About Michael Samsel", Abuse and Relationships," *Abuse and Relationships* webpage, 2008, URL: http://www.abuseandrelationships.org/Content/Contact/author.html, accessed 4 September 2014.

124 Michael Samsel, "Abuse and Relationships – Warning Signs: Abuse," Abuse and Relationships," *Abuse and Relationships* webpage, 2008, URL: http://www.abuseandrelationships.org/Content/Basics/abuse.html, accessed 4 September 2014.

125 *Black's Law Dictionary 9th*, Bryan A. Garner, Editor in Chief, West Publishing (Thomson Reuters), St. Paul, 294.

126 "Prelate Rues Rising Islamophobia in Wake of Islamic State Atrocities," Catholic Culture.org (Catholic World News), 3 September 2014, URL: http://www.catholicculture.org/news/headlines/index.cfm?storyid=22471, accessed 10 September 2014.

127 Patrick Poole, "Fighter with 'Vetted Moderate' Syrian Rebels Tells L.A. Times they Fight Alongside al-Qaeda," *PJ Media Tatler*, 9 September 2014, URL: http://pjmedia.com/tatler/2014/09/09/fighter-with-vetted-moderate-syrian-rebel-group-tells-la-times-his-group-fights-alongside-al-qaeda/, accessed 10 September 2014.

128 Shafiq & Nimmer, *Interfaith Dialogue: A Guide for Muslims*, IIIT, 143.

129 "Prelate Rues Rising Islamophobia in Wake of Islamic State Atrocities," Catholic Culture.org (Catholic World News).

130 Calol Glatz, "Pope Names U.S. Bishops' Top Ecumenical Officer to Advise Vatican Council," Catholic News Service (CNS), 22 July 2014, URL: http://www.catholicnews.com/data/stories/cns/1403026.htm, accessed 14 September 2014. **States:** Among the new members and consultants Pope Francis named to the Pontifical Council for Promoting Christian Unity is Father John W. Crossin, the executive director of the Secretariat for Ecumenical and Interreligious Affairs of the U.S. Conference of Catholic Bishops. … Father Crossin, a member of the Oblates of St. Francis de Sales, holds a doctorate in moral theology and master's degrees in psychology and theology from The Catholic University of America. … The pope named three bishops – two from Latin America and one from Germany – to be new members of the Vatican council and he appointed four laymen, five priests and one Chinese religious sister from Macau as consultants.

131 William M. Schweitzer, "Is the Insider Movement Really that Bad?," Reformation 21 (Alliance of Confessing Evangelical) webpage, June 2014, URL: http://www.reformation21.org/articles/is-the-insider-movement-really-that-bad.php, accessed 14 September 2014.

132 *Josef Pieper, Abuse of Language – Abuse of Power*, Ignatius Press, 1992 (trans. Lothar Krauth, Kosel-Verlag, Munich 1974), 34, 35.

133 Section 16, Dogmatic Constitution of the Church "*Lumen Gentium*" Solemnly Promulgated by His Holiness Pope Paul VI on November 21, 1964, Vatican Archives, 21 November 1964, URL: http://www.vatican.va/archive/hist_councils/ii_vatican_council/documents/vat-ii_const_19641121_lumen-gentium_en.html, accessed 6 March 2013.

134 Shafiq & Nimmer, *Interfaith Dialogue: A Guide for Muslims*, IIIT, 142.

135 Shafiq & Nimmer, *Interfaith Dialogue: A Guide for Muslims*, IIIT, 143.

136 Pope Francis, "Apostolic Exhortation *EVANGELII GAUDIUM* of the Holy Father Francis to the Bishops, Clergy, Consecrated Persons and the Lay Faithful on the Proclamation of the Gospel in Today's World," the Vatican, 24 November 2013, URL: http://www.vatican.va/holy_father/francesco/apost_exhortations/documents/papa-francesco_esortazione-ap_20131124_evangelii-gaudium_en.html, accessed 27 November 2013. Pope Francis, *EVANGELII GAUDIUM*.

137 §1, Canon 212, Title I, The Obligations and Rights of All the Christian Faithful, *Code of Canon Law* (*Codex Iuris Canonici*), *Libreria Editrice Vaticana*, new English translation prepared under the auspices of the Canon Law Society of America Canon Law Society of America Washington, DC, The Vatican webpage, 1983, URL: http://www.vatican.va/archive/ENG1104/__PU.HTM, accessed 12 September 2014. **States:** Can. 212 §1. Conscious of their own responsibility, the Christian faithful

are bound to follow with Christian obedience those things which the sacred pastors, inasmuch as they represent Christ, declare as teachers of the faith or establish as rulers of the Church.

138   §3, Canon 212, Title I, The Obligations and Rights of All the Christian Faithful, *Code of Canon Law* (*Codex Iuris Canonici*), *Libreria Editrice Vaticana*, new English translation prepared under the auspices of the Canon Law Society of America Canon Law Society of America Washington, DC, The Vatican webpage, 1983, URL: http://www.vatican.va/archive/ENG1104/__PU.HTM, accessed 12 September 2014. **States:** Can. 212 §3. According to the knowledge, competence, and prestige which they possess, they have the right and even at times the duty to manifest to the sacred pastors their opinion on matters which pertain to the good of the Church and to make their opinion known to the rest of the Christian faithful, without prejudice to the integrity of faith and morals, with reverence toward their pastors, and attentive to common advantage and the dignity of persons.

139   Shafiq & Nimmer, *Interfaith Dialogue: A Guide for Muslims*, IIIT, 31.

140   Shafiq & Nimmer, *Interfaith Dialogue: A Guide for Muslims*, IIIT, 31.

141   Shafiq & Nimmer, *Interfaith Dialogue: A Guide for Muslims*, IIIT, 143.

142   Mohammad Hakim, "Mufti: 'We Do Not Accept Insulting Bukhari'," Masrawy, 16 August 2014, URL: http://imtranslator.net/translation/arabic/to-english/translation/, translated from Arabic by *IM Translator* from *Masrawy*, 16 August 2014, URL: http://www.masrawy.com, accessed 31 August 2014. **States:** Mufti: don't accept insulting Al-Bukhari Mohammed Hakim wrote: Shawki said Allam, the Egyptian Mufti, the Dar Al-IFTA was founded in 1895 and receive 1500 to request an advisory opinion on Monday, pointing out that there is liquidity in fatwas by greater openness of information and some senators away from Dar Al-IFTA, especially because of the current conditions in Egypt. Allam said during his interview for the program "life today" broadcast on the satellite channel of "life", Saturday, " there is too much to bear Imam Bukhari, companions of the Prophet and that there was no room for raising those issues it is best in cases that do not give rise to confusion and undermine faith in the hearts of the people ". He stressed that Imam Bukhari collection, accurate system and no one came from people with better methodology of systematic in collecting Hadiths of the Prophet of Islam and peace and he has a great balance in Islamic history and the Sunnah and not accept it or violate it disassociates. He continued: " Islam calls for broader thinking and this is Al-Azhar must come to think, in the interest of mankind if freedom of thought will lead to the stability of societies and the firm beliefs, no doubt of Al-Azhar rejects that and defend the principles of the faith.

143   Keller, *Reliance of the Traveller*, Book B "The Validity of Following Qualified Scholarship," b.7.0 "Scholarly Consensus (*ijma*), §b7.2 at 23, 24. **States:** "When the … necessary integrals of consensus exist, the ruling agreed upon is an authoritative part of Sacred Law that is obligatory to obey and not lawful to disobey. Nor can *mujtahids* of a succeeding era make the thing an object of new *ijtihad*, because the ruling on it, verified by scholarly consensus, is an absolute ruling which does not admit of being contravened or annulled."

144   *The Translation of the Meanings of Sahih Al-Bukhari*, Darussalam Publishers, Riyadh, Saudi Arabia, 1997, back cover.

145   *The Translation of the Meanings of Sahih Al-Bukhari*, Darussalam Publishers, Riyadh, Saudi Arabia, 1997, Vol, 4, 44.

146   Number 220, Book 52 "Jihaad", *Sahih Bukhari*, Volume 4, URL: http://www.sahih-bukhari.com/Pages/Bukhari_4_52.php, accessed 12 September 2014.

147   Number 73, Book 52 "Jihaad", *Sahih Bukhari*, Volume 4, URL: http://www.sahih-bukhari.com/Pages/Bukhari_4_52.php, accessed 12 September 2014. Also: I read in it that Allah's Apostle in one of his military expeditions against the enemy, waited till the sun declined and then he got up amongst the people saying, "O people! Do not wish to meet the enemy, and ask Allah for safety, but when you face the enemy, be patient, and remember that Paradise is under the shades of swords." Then he said, "O Allah, the Revealer of the Holy Book, and the Mover of the clouds and the Defeater of the clans, defeat them, and grant us victory over them." (*Sahih Bukhari*, Volume 4, Book 52, Number 266), URL: http://www.sahih-bukhari.com/Pages/Bukhari_4_52.php.

148   Number 270, Book 52 "Jihaad", *Sahih Bukhari*, Volume 4, URL: http://www.sahih-bukhari.com/Pages/Bukhari_4_52.php, accessed 12 September 2014.

149   Number 72, Book 29 "Jihaad", *Sahih Bukhari*, Volume 3, URL: http://www.sahih-bukhari.com/Pages/Bukhari_3_29.php, accessed 12 September 2014. Also: Allah's Apostle sent us in a mission (i.e. am army-unit) and said, "If you find so-and-so and so-and-so, burn both of them with fire." When we intended to depart, Allah's Apostle said, "I have ordered you to burn so-and-so and so-and-so, and it is none but Allah Who punishes with fire, so, if you find them, kill them." (*Sahih Bukhari*, Volume 4, Book 52, Number 259) URL: http://www.sahih-bukhari.com/Pages/Bukhari_4_52.php.

150   Number 54, Book 52 "Expeditions", *Sahih Bukhari*, Volume 4, URL: http://www.sahih-bukhari.com/Pages/Bukhari_4_52.php, accessed 12 September 2014.

151   Number 46, Book 52 "Jihaad", *Sahih Bukhari*, Volume 4, URL: http://www.sahih-bukhari.com/Pages/Bukhari_4_52.php, accessed 12 September 2014.

152   Number 44, Book 52 "Jihaad", *Sahih Bukhari*, Volume 4, URL: http://www.sahih-bukhari.com/Pages/Bukhari_4_52.php, accessed 12 September 2014. Also: Muhammad said, "A single endeavor of fighting in Allah's cause in the forenoon or in the afternoon is better than the world and whatever is in it. (*Sahih Bukhari*, Volume 4, Book 52, Number 50), URL: http://www.sahih-bukhari.com/Pages/Bukhari_4_52.php.

"Our Prophet told us about the message of our Lord that "... whoever amongst us is killed will go to Paradise." Umar asked the Prophet, "Is it not true that our men who are killed will go to Paradise and theirs (i.e. those of the pagan's) will go to the hell fire?" The Prophet said, "Yes." (*Sahih Bukhari*, Volume 4, Book 52, Number 72), URL: http://www.sahih-bukhari.com/Pages/Bukhari_4_52.php.

Allah's Apostle said, " He who pre pares a Ghazi going in Allah's Cause is given a reward equal to that of) a Ghazi; and he who looks after properly the dependents of a Ghazi going in Allah's Cause is (given a reward equal to that of) Ghazi." (*Sahih Bukhari*, Volume 4, Book 52, Number 96), URL: http://www.sahih-bukhari.com/Pages/Bukhari_4_52.php.

153   Number 459, Book 59 "Expeditions", *Sahih Bukhari*, Volume 5, URL: http://www.sahih-bukhari.com/Pages/Bukhari_5_59.php, accessed 12 September 2014.

154   Number 72, Book 29 "Jihaad", *Sahih Bukhari*, Volume 3, URL: http://www.sahih-bukhari.com/Pages/Bukhari_4_52.php, accessed 12 September 2014. Note: these citations to *Sahih Bukhari* are taken from an online source so readers can verify them. They are also in the ten volume hardcopy set *The Translation of the Meaning of Sahih Al-Bukhari Arabic-English*. Hadith 72 for example, finds two references at Hadith 2925 & 2926, *The Translation of the Meanings of Sahih Al-Bukhari*, Daussalam Publishers, Riyadh, Saudi Arabia, 1997, Vol, 4, 113. **Hadith 2925 states:** Narrated 'Abdullah bin 'Umar: Allah's Messenger said, "You (Muslims) will fight against the Jews till some of them will hide behind stones. The stones will (betray them) saying, 'O Abdullah (i.e., slave of Allah)! There is a Jew hiding behind me; so kill him'." **Hadith 2926 states:** Narrated by Abu Hurairah: Allah's Messenger said, "The Hour will not be established until you fight against the Jews, and the stones behind which a Jew will be hiding, 'O Muslim! There is a Jew hiding behind me, so kill him'."

Al-Bara bin Azib said, "Allah's Apostle sent a group of Ansari men to kill Abu-Rafi'. One of them set out and entered their (i.e. the enemies') fort. That man said, 'I hid myself ... and came upon Abu Rafi' and said, "O Abu Rafi'." When he replied me, I proceeded towards the voice and hit him. He shouted and I came out to come back, pretending to be a helper. I said, "O Abu Rafi'," changing the tone of my voice ... I asked him, "What happened to you?" He said, "I don't know who came to me and hit me." Then I drove my sword into his belly and pushed it forcibly till it touched the bone. Then I came out, filled with puzzlement and went towards a ladder of theirs in order to get down but I fell down and sprained my foot. I came to my companions and said, "I will not leave till I hear the wailing of the women." So, I did not leave till I heard the women bewailing Abu Rafi', the merchant of Hijaz. Then I got up, feeling no ailment, and we proceeded till we came upon the Prophet and informed him.'" (*Sahih Bukhari*, Volume 4, Book 52, Number 264) , URL: http://www.sahih-bukhari.com/Pages/Bukhari_4_52.php.

Anas bin Malik said, "A group of eight men from the tribe of Ukil came to the Prophet [i.e. they became Muslims and began to live in Medina with the Muslims] … Then they killed the shepherd and … became unbelievers after they were Muslims. When the Prophet was informed by a shouter for help, he sent some men in their pursuit, and before the sun rose high, they were brought and he had their hands and feet cut off. Then he ordered for nails which were heated and passed over their eyes, and they were left in the Harra (i.e. rocky land in Medina). They asked for water, and nobody provided them with water till they died." (*Sahih Bukhari*, Volume 4, Book 52, Number 261), URL: http://www.sahih-bukhari.com/Pages/Bukhari_4_52.php.

155   *The Covenant of the Islamic Resistance Movement* ("Hamas Covenant") 18 August 1988, *The Avalon Project*, Lillian Goldman Law Library, Yale Law School, http://avalon.law.yale.edu/20th_century/hamas.asp. **States:** "Article Seven, The Universality of the Islamic Resistance Movement [...] Moreover, if the links have been distant from each other and if obstacles, placed by those who are the lackeys of Zionism in the way of the fighters obstructed the continuation of the struggle, the Islamic Resistance Movement aspires to the realisation of Allah's promise, no matter how long that should take. The Prophet, Allah bless him and grant him salvation, has said: "The Day of Judgment will not come about until the Moslems fight the Jews (kill the Jews), when the Jew will hide behind stones and trees. The stones and trees will say O Moslem, O Abdulla, there is a Jew behind me, come and kill him. Only the Gharkad tree, (evidently a certain kind of tree) would not do that because it is one of the trees of the Jews." (Related by Bukhari and Moslem).

156   Book 52 "Jihaad", *Sahih Bukhari*, Volume 4, URL: http://www.sahih-bukhari.com/Pages/Bukhari_4_52.php, accessed 12 September 2014.

157   Keller, *Reliance of the Traveller*, Book O "Justice," at o9.0 "Jihad." at o9.0.

158   Slide 43 "Verse of the Sword – Cont" (Bukhari), Major Nidal M. Hasan, "The Koranic World View as it Relates to Muslims in the U.S. Military," June 2007, first given to fellow psychiatrist/interns at Walter Reed Army Hospital in Washington, D.C., published by the Washington Post as a PowerPoint in PDF format at URL: http://www.washingtonpost.com/wp-dyn/content/gallery/2009/11/10/GA2009111000920.html, 5 November 2009.

159   Slide 43, "Verse of the Sword – Cont" (Bukhari), Major Nidal M. Hasan, "The Koranic World View as it Relates to Muslims in the U.S. Military," June 2007, first given to fellow psychiatrist/interns at Walter Reed Army Hospital in Washington, D.C., published by the Washington Post as a PowerPoint in PDF format at URL: http://www.washingtonpost.com/wp-dyn/content/gallery/2009/11/10/GA2009111000920.html, 5 November 2009.

160   Slide 44, "Offensive Jihad Cont" (Verse 9:29), Major Nidal M. Hasan, "The Koranic World View as it Relates to Muslims in the U.S. Military," June 2007, first given to fellow psychiatrist/interns at Walter Reed Army Hospital in Washington, D.C., published by the Washington Post as a PowerPoint in PDF format at URL: http://www.washingtonpost.com/wp-dyn/content/gallery/2009/11/10/GA2009111000920.html, 5 November 2009.

161   Number 657, Book 55 "Expeditions", *Sahih Bukhari*, Volume 4, URL: http://www.sahih-bukhari.com/Pages/Bukhari_4_55.php, accessed 12 September 2014. Also: Allah's Apostle said, "By Him in Whose hands my soul is, son of Mary (Jesus) will shortly descend amongst you people (Muslims) as a just ruler and will break the Cross and kill the pig and abolish the Jizya (a tax taken from the non-Muslims, who are in the protection, of the Muslim government). Then there will be abundance of money and no-body will accept charitable gifts. (*Sahih Bukhari*, Volume 3, Book 34, Number 425), URL: http://www.sahih-bukhari.com/Pages/Bukhari_3_34.php.

162   Slide 45 "Offensive Islam is the Future," Major Nidal M. Hasan, "The Koranic World View as it Relates to Muslims in the U.S. Military," June 2007, first given to fellow psychiatrist/interns at Walter Reed Army Hospital in Washington, D.C., published by the Washington Post as a PowerPoint in PDF format at URL: http://www.washingtonpost.com/wp-dyn/content/gallery/2009/11/10/GA2009111000920.html, 5 November 2009.

163   *Tafsir Ibn Kathir*, vol 2, 243.

164 Keller, *Reliance of the Traveller*, Book O "Justice," at o9.0 "Jihad." at o9.8 "The Objectives of Jihad."

165 *Interpretation of the Meanings of the Noble Qur'an in the English Language: A Summarized Version of At-Tabari; Al-Qurtubi, and Ibn Kathir with Comments from Sahih Al-Bukhari*, trans. and commentary by Dr. Muhammad Taqi-ud-Din Al-Hilali, and Dr. Muhammad Muhsin Khan, Darussalam, Riyadh, Saudi Arabia, 1999, Verse 9:29, 252.

166 *Interpretation of the Meanings of the Noble Qur'an in the English Language: A Summarized Version of At-Tabari; Al-Qurtubi, and Ibn Kathir with Comments from Sahih Al-Bukhari*, trans. and commentary by Dr. Muhammad Taqi-ud-Din Al-Hilali, and Dr. Muhammad Muhsin Khan, Darussalam, Riyadh, Saudi Arabia, 1999, Verse 9:29 associated annotation, 252.

167 Keller, *Reliance of the Traveller*, Book B "The Validity of Following Qualified Scholarship," b.7.0 "Scholarly Consensus (*ijma*), §b7.2 at 23, 24. **States:** "When the ... necessary integrals of consensus exist, the ruling agreed upon is an authoritative part of Sacred Law that is obligatory to obey and not lawful to disobey. Nor can *mujtahids* of a succeeding era make the thing an object of new *ijtihad*, because the ruling on it, verified by scholarly consensus, is an absolute ruling which does not admit of being contravened or annulled."

168 Al-Misri, Book O "Justice," at § o9.0 "Jihad."

169 Pope Francis, *EVANGELII GAUDIUM*.

170 Al-Hafiz Abu al-Fida' 'Imad Ad-Din Isma'il bin 'Umar bin Kathir Al-Qurashi Al-Busrawi ibn Kathir, *Tafsir of Ibn Kathir*, vol. 4, Trans. Abdul-Malik Mujahid. (Riyadh: Darussalam, 2000), 404-407. Cited hereafter as Tafsir ibn Kathir #.

171 *Tafsir ibn Kathir*, vol 4, 404-405.

172 *Tafsir ibn Kathir*, vol 4, 404-405.

173 *Tafsir ibn Kathir*, vol 4, 405.

174 *Interpretation of the Meanings of the Noble Qur'an in the English Language: A Summarized Version of At-Tabari; Al-Qurtubi, and Ibn Kathir with Comments from Sahih Al-Bukhari*, trans. and commentary by Dr. Muhammad Taqi-ud-Din Al-Hilali, and Dr. Muhammad Muhsin Khan, Darussalam, Riyadh, Saudi Arabia, 1999, Verse 9:29, 252.

175 **EXPLANATION:** The language in parentheses is the sacred language, and the unparenned text is the meaning as explained by ibn Kathir. Hence, the line:

(until they pay the Jizyah), if they do not choose to embrace Islam, should be read as: The phrase "until they pay the Jizyah" means "if they do not choose to embrace Islam ..."

176 *Tafsir ibn Kathir*, vol 4, 406.

177 Keller, *Reliance of the Traveller*, Book X "Biographical Notes," at x351 "'Umar", 1104, 1105. **States:** "'Umar is 'Umar ibn a-Khattab ibn Nufayl, Abu Hafs al-Qurashi al-'Adawi (Allah be Pleased with Him), born forty years before the Hijra (A.D. 584) in Mecca(1104-1105). He was one of the greatest companions of the Prophet (Allah bless him and give him peace), as renowned for his tremendous personal courage and steadfastness as for his fairness in giving judgements. (sic) ... He fought in all the battles of the Prophet (Allah bless him and give him peace) and was sworn fealty to as the second caliph of Islam on the day of Abu Bakr's death. ... Stabbed by a slave while performing the dawn prayer, he died three nights later in 23/644."

178 *Tafsir ibn Kathir*, vol 4, 406.

179 *Tafsir ibn Kathir*, vol 4, 406 - 407.

180 Elhanan Miller, "Syrian Christians Sign Treaty of Submission to Islamists," Times of Israel, 27 February 2014, URL: http://www.timesofisrael.com/syrian-christians-sign-treaty-of-submission-to-islamists/#ixzz2uXOQiNMs, accessed 27 February 2014.

181 Elhanan Miller, "Syrian Christians Sign Treaty of Submission to Islamists," Times of Israel, 27

February 2014, URL: http://www.timesofisrael.com/syrian-christians-sign-treaty-of-submission-to-islamists/#ixzz2uXOQiNMs, accessed 27 February 2014.

182 Zaid Benjamin, @zaidbenjamin Twitter Feed, 18 July 2014, URL: https://twitter.com/zaidbenjamin/status/490165524232687616, accessed 18 July 2014. **Twitter feed states:** "Al-Baghdadi to #Mosul Christians: "Choose one of these: Islam, the sword, al-Jiziya (tax) or till Saturday to flee" ☒pic.twitter.com/UoGf8pnYh1."

183 *Tafsir ibn Kathir*, vol 4, 406 - 407.

184 Keller, *Reliance of the Traveller*, Book O "Justice," at o11 "Non-Muslim Subjects of the Islamic State (*Ahl Al-Dhimma*)," at o11.5.

185 Keller, *Reliance of the Traveller*, Book O "Justice," at o11.0 "Non-Muslim Subjects of the Islamic State," at § o11.11.

186 Pope Francis, *EVANGELII GAUDIUM.*

187 "Declaration of the Pontifical Council for Interreligious Dialogue," Bulletin Holy See Press Office [B0567, 12 August 2014, URL: http://press.vatican.va/content/salastampa/fr/bollettino/pubblico/2014/08/12/0567/01287.html#Traduzione%20in%20lingua%20inglese, accessed 17 August 2014.

188 "Declaration of the Pontifical Council for Interreligious Dialogue," Bulletin Holy See Press Office [B0567, 12 August 2014, URL: http://press.vatican.va/content/salastampa/fr/bollettino/pubblico/2014/08/12/0567/01287.html#Traduzione%20in%20lingua%20inglese, accessed 17 August 2014.

189 "OIC Secretary General Ihsanoglu Meets with Pope Francis in the Vatican," *OIC Presser*, 13 December 2013, URL: http://www.oicun.org/9/20131213042052911.html, accessed 18 June 2014.

190 Keller, *Reliance of the Traveller*, at § r8.2

191 al-Walid Muhammad ibn Ahmad ibn Muhammad ibn Rushd, *Bidayat al-Mujtahid wa Nihayat al-Muqtasid (The Distinguished Jurist's Primer)*, vol. 1, trans. and ed. Imran Ashan Khan Nyazee, (Reading: Garnet Publishing Ltd, 2002), 454 - 487. **Note:** *Bidayat al-Mujtahid wa Nihayat al-Muqtasid (The Distinguished Jurist's Primer)* was written in the 12th century by Maliki judge (*qadi*) and Imam of the Great Mosque of Cordova -- Abu al-Walid Muhammad ibn Ahmad ibn Rushd – better known in the West as under the *nom de plum* Averoes (xxviii).

192 Al-Walid Muhammad ibn Ahmad ibn Muhammad ibn Rushd, *Bidayat al-Mujtahid wa Nihayat al-Muqtasid (The Distinguished Jurist's Primer)*, vol. 1, trans. and ed. Imran Ashan Khan Nyazee, (Reading: Garnet Publishing Ltd, 2002), v. **Note:** The translation of ibn Rushd's treatise was peer reviewed and published with the approval of the Chairman of the Board of Trustees of the Center for Muslim Contribution to Civilization, Sheikh Muhammad bin Hamad al-Thani or the Qatari Royal Family. Also on the Board of Directors are Sheikh al-Azhar, the Director-General of the Islamic Educational, Scientific and Cultural Organization (ISESCO), Director-General of the Arab League Educational, Cultural and Scientific Organization (ALECSO), the Ministers of Education for the States of Qatar, Kuwait, and Oman, the Secretary-General of the Muslim World Association, Saudi Arabia, **AND** Professor **Yusuf al-Qaradawi**, Director, Sira and Sunna Research Centre, University of Qatar (v).

193 Specialized OIC Entities, Specialized, Organization of Cooperation, URL: http://www.oic-oci.org/oicv2/page/?p_id=65&p_ref=34&lan=en, accessed 18 September 2014. **States:** "**DEFINITION**These are established within the framework of the Organization of Islamic Cooperation (OIC) in accordance with the decisions of the Islamic Summit or Council of Foreign Ministers. Membership to these organs is optional and open to OIC Member States. Their budgets are independent of the budget of the Secretariat General and those of the subsidiary organs and are approved by their respective legislative bodies as stipulated in their Statutes." **Islamic Educational, Scientific and Cultural Organization (ISESCO)** is one of these entities. '**DEFINITION** - ISESCO is a specialize international organization operating in the fields of Education, Science, Culture and

Communication, within the framework of the Organization of Islamic Cooperation."

194 Keller, *Reliance of the Traveller*, Book B "The Validity of Following Qualified Scholarship," b.7.0 "Scholarly Consensus (*ijma*), §b7.2 at 23, 24. **States:** "When the ... necessary integrals of consensus exist, the ruling agreed upon is an authoritative part of Sacred Law that is obligatory to obey and not lawful to disobey. Nor can *mujtahids* of a succeeding era make the thing an object of new *ijtihad*, because the ruling on it, verified by scholarly consensus, is an absolute ruling which does not admit of being contravened or annulled."

195 Al-Walid Muhammad ibn Ahmad ibn Muhammad ibn Rushd, *Bidayat al-Mujtahid wa Nihayat al-Muqtasid (The Distinguished Jurist's Primer)*, vol. 1, trans. and ed. Imran Ashan Khan Nyazee, (Reading: Garnet Publishing Ltd, 2002), Book X, Chapter 1 "The Elements (Arkan) of War", § 7 "Why Wage War," 464. **Note:** *Bidayat al-Mujtahid wa Nihayat al-Muqtasid (The Distinguished Jurist's Primer)* was written in the 12th century by Maliki judge (*qadi*) and Imam of the Great Mosque of Cordova -- Abu al-Walid Muhammad ibn Ahmad ibn Rushd – better known in the West as under the *nom de plum* Averoes (xxviii).

196 Muhammad ibn Hasan al-Shaybani, *The Islamic Law of Nations: Shaybani's Siyar (Kitab al-siyar al-kabir)*, trans. Majid Khadduri, (Baltimore: Johns Hopkins Press, 1966). **Note:** *Shaybani's Siyar* is the classic Islamic treatise is the oldest, extant text of Islamic law on warfare available to us today in Professor Majid Khadduri's translation. Meaning "the conduct of the state in its relationship to other communities,"[39] the term "*siyar*," as used in Shaybani's *Siyar*, reflects Abu Hanifa's view to foreign policy* as al-Shaybani transcribed them and may be regarded as the first systematic treatment on Islamic "law among nations."[40-41] In fact, al-Shaybani's *Siyar* is the first major Muslim work "devoted exclusively to Islamic law dealing with relations with non-Muslims."** *Siyars* "describe the conduct of the Muslim community in its relations with unbelievers from the territory of war (*dar al harb*) as well as with those whom the Muslim state enters into treaties."[40] It is a body of law that "Muslims declared to be binding upon themselves, regardless of whether non-Muslims accept it."[41] As the seminal work on Islamic law among nations, Majid Khadduri counts it as still being good law to this day.[16-17] * Fyzee, *Muhammadan Law*, 34. ** Rudolph Peters, *Jihad in Classical and Modern Islam: A Reader*, (Princeton: Markus Wiener Publishers, 1996), 137.

197 Al-Marghinani, Burhan al-Din al-Farghani, *Al-Hidaya: The Guidance*, Vol 2, trans. Imran Ahsan Khan Nyazee (Bristol, England: Amal Press, 2008), 285-347. Note: *Al-Hidayah by al-Marghinani,* was published in the 12ᵗʰ Century and reflects classic Hanafi Islamic law.

198 *The Quranic Concept of War* by Brigadier S.K. Malik, (Lahore, Pakistan: Wajid Al's Ltd., 1979. (with a forward by General Zia-ul-Haq) (This paper relies on the 1986 First Indian Reprint). **Note:** *The Quranic Concept of War*, written in 1979 by Pakistani Brigadier General S. K. Malik was praised by the country's President, Zia ul Haq, then serving as the Army Chief of Staff. Significantly, Haq declared the book to be Pakistani war doctrine (xi).

199 William Kilpatrick, "The Downside of Dialogue," Crisis Magazine, 25 October 2014, URL: http://www.crisismagazine.com/2014/downside-dialogue, accessed 26 October 2014

200 Revelation: Catholic & Muslim Perspectives, prepared by the Midwest Dialogue of Catholics and Muslims Co-Sponsored by the Islamic Society of North America and the United State Conference of Catholic Bishops, USCCB, Washington, DC. 2006, URL: http://www.usccb.org/beliefs-and-teachings/ecumenical-and-interreligious/interreligious/islam/upload/Revelation-Catholic-and-Muslim-Perspectives.pdf, accessed 26 September 2014, 49.

201 Pope Francis, *EVANGELII GAUDIUM.*

202 "Declaration of the Pontifical Council for Interreligious Dialogue," Bulletin Holy See Press Office [B0567, 12 August 2014, URL: http://press.vatican.va/content/salastampa/fr/bollettino/pubblico/2014/08/12/0567/01287.html#Traduzione%20in%20lingua%20inglese, accessed 17 August 2014.

203 Shafiq & Nimmer, *Interfaith Dialogue: A Guide for Muslims*, IIIT, 143.

204 Shafiq & Nimmer, *Interfaith Dialogue: A Guide for Muslims*, IIIT, 31.

205 Shafiq & Nimmer, *Interfaith Dialogue: A Guide for Muslims*, IIIT, 31.

206 Catherine Herridge, "Fort Hood Shooter Sends Letter to Pope Francis Espousing 'Jihad'," *Fox News*, 10 October 2014, URL: http://www.foxnews.com/politics/2014/10/09/fort-hood-shooter-sends-letter-to-pope-francis-espousing-jihad/, accessed 10 October 2014.

207 "Excerpt from Fort Hood Shooter's Letter to Pope Francis; *Fox News*, undated, URL: http://www.foxnews.com/politics/interactive/2014/10/09/excerpt-from-fort-hood-shooter-letter-to-pope-francis/, accessed 10 October 2014.

208 *Inspire*, Issue 1, Summer 1431/2010, URL: http://azelin.files.wordpress.com/2010/06/aqap-inspire-magazine-volume-1-uncorrupted.pdf, accessed: 16 May 2013, cover, 33.

209 Shafiq & Nimmer, *Interfaith Dialogue: A Guide for Muslims*, IIIT, 31.

210 Shafiq & Nimmer, *Interfaith Dialogue: A Guide for Muslims*, IIIT, 31.

211 "Declaration of the Pontifical Council for Interreligious Dialogue," Bulletin Holy See Press Office [B0567, 12 August 2014, URL: http://press.vatican.va/content/salastampa/fr/bollettino/pubblico/2014/08/12/0567/01287.html#Traduzione%20in%20lingua%20inglese, accessed 17 August 2014.

212 "Imam of the Prophet's Mosque in Medina, Saudi Arabia, in Support of Jihad against Christian American Presence in the Middle East" [also titled "Sheik Muhammad Al-Suhaybani, Imam of the Prophet's Mosque in Medina, Saudi Arabia"], the Internet 30 August 2014, MEMRI Video Clip #4469, URL: http://www.memritv.org/clip/en/4469.htm, MEMRI transcript of #4469 Video Clip at URL: http://www.memritv.org/clip_transcript/en/4469.htm, accessed 4 September 2014.

213 Ahmed Fouad, "Al-Azhar Refuses to Consider the Islamic State an Apostate," trans. Tyler Huffman, *Al-Monitor*, 12 February 2015, URL: http://www.al-monitor.com/pulse/originals/2015/02/azhar-egypt-radicals-islamic-state-apostates.html, accessed 13 February 2015.

214 Promoter@979510, *Twitter*, 5 September 2014, URL: https://twitter.com/979510/status/508136757859065856, accessed 6 September 2014, **Twitter states via Google Translate:** "Country resides interfaith dialogue and prevents any practice contrary to this!

215 See also Twitter messages on Saudi authority raids on immigrant church in in Kafhgi, Saudi Arabia at iContent@iContent_AR, Twitter, 5 September 2014, URL: https://twitter.com/iContent_AR/status/507959241630420992, accessed 6 September 2014 and Hashtaq Arabs@TheArabHash, 5 September 2014, URL: https://twitter.com/TheArabHash/status/507956243848503298, accessed 6 September 2014. **Note:** Both indicate Arab reporting on Saudi raid of Christian service in private home.

216 Sayyid Qutb, *Milestones*, Salimiah, (Kuwait: International Islamic Federation of Student Organizations. 1978 [written 1966]), 263. States: "The chasm between Islam and Jahiliyyah is great, and a bridge is not to be built across it so that the people on the two sides may mix with each other, but only so that the people of Jahiliyyah may come over to Islam."

217 Pakistani Brigadier S.K. Malik, *QCW*, 60.

218 Pakistani Brigadier S.K. Malik, *QCW*, 57.

219 Pakistani Brigadier S.K. Malik, *QCW*, 57.

220 Pakistani Brigadier S.K. Malik, *QCW*, 57.

221 Pakistani Brigadier S.K. Malik, *QCW*, 57-58.

222 Pakistani Brigadier S.K. Malik, *QCW*, 57-58.

223 Pope Francis, *EVANGELII GAUDIUM*.

224 "Pope Francis: Muslim Leaders should Condemn Terrorism," BBC News, 30 November 2014,

URL: http://www.bbc.com/news/world-europe-30265996, accessed 30 November 2014.

225 Andrea Tornielli, "In the Mosque I Prayed to the Lord for these Wars to Stop!", *Vatican Insider* (*La Stampa*), 30 November 2014, URL: http://vaticaninsider.lastampa.it/en/the-vatican/detail/articolo/francesco-turchia-37828/, accessed 24 December 2014.

226 From *The Noble Qur'an*, 402, 147. [3] (V.19:30) See the footnote No. 2 of (V.4:171) - O people of the Scripture (Christians)! Do not exceed the limits in your religion, nor say of Allah aught but the truth. The Messiah 'Isa (Jesus), son of Maryam (Mary), was (no more than) a Messenger of Allah and his Word, ("Be!" – and he was) which He bestowed on Maryam (Mary) and a spirit (*Ruh*)[1] created by Him; so believe in Allah and His Messengers. Say not: "Three (trinity)!" Cease! (it is) better for you. For Allah is (the only) One *Ilah* (God), glory is to Him (Far Exalted is He) above having a son. To Him belongs all that is in the heavens and all that is on the earth. And Allah is All-Sufficient as a Disposer of affairs.[2] (*Noble Qur'an* 4:171)

> (2) (V.4:171) Narrated 'Ubadah: The Prophet said, "If anyone testifies that *La ilaha Illallah* (none has the right to be worshipped but Allah Alone) Who has no partners, and that Muhammad is His slave and His Messenger, and that Jesus is Allah's slave and His Messenger and His Word ("Be!" – and he was) which He bestowed on Mary and a spirit (*Ruh*) created by Him, and that Paradise is the truth, and Hell is the truth – Allah will admit him into Paradise with the deeds which he had done even if those deeds were few." … [*Sahih Al-Bukhari*, 4/3435 (O.P.644)].

227 *Tafsir Al-Jalalayn*, 652.

228 [4] (V.19:35) See the footnote of (V.2:116), 402 then to page 39. "And they (Jews, Christians and pagans) say: Allah has begotten a son (children or offspring).[1] Glory be to Him Exalted is He above all they associate with Him). Nay, to Him belongs all that is in the heavens and on the earth, and all surrender in obedience in worship to Him." (*Noble Qur'an* 2:116)

> [1] (V.2:116) "They (Jews, Christians and pagans) say: Allah has begotten a son (children, offspring). Glory be to Him …Nay…" -Narrated by Ibn 'Abbas: The Prophet said, "Allah said, 'The son of Adam tells lies against Me though he has no right to do so, and he abuses Me though he has no right to do so. As for his telling lies against Me, he claims that I cannot re-create him as I created him before; and as for his abusing Me: it is his statement that I have a son (or offspring). No! Glorified is Me! I am far from taking a wife or a son (or offspring).'" [Sahih Al-Bukhari, 6/4482 (O.P.9)].

229 Comment No. 2487, Yusuf Ali, *The Holy Qur'an*, 751. "Begetting a son is a physical act depending on the needs of men's animal nature. Allah Most High is independent of all needs, and it is derogatory to Him to attribute such an act to Him. It is merely a relic of pagan and anthropomorphic materialist superstitions."

230 Sebnem Arsu, "In Turkey, Pope Francis Advocates Dialogue in Battling 'Fanaticism', The New York Times, 28 November 2014, URL: http://www.nytimes.com/2014/11/29/world/europe/on-trip-to-turkey-pope-francis-calls-for-dialogue-in-battling-isis.html?_r=0, accessed 24 December 2014.

231 Nick Squires, "Pope Francis Fails to Find Common Ground in Turkey (+ video), *The Christian Science Monitor*, 30 November 20124, URL: http://www.csmonitor.com/World/Middle-East/2014/1130/Pope-Francis-fails-to-find-common-ground-in-Turkey-video, accessed 1 December 2014.

232 Nick Squires, "Pope Francis Fails to Find Common Ground in Turkey (+ video), *The Christian Science Monitor*, 30 November 20124, URL: http://www.csmonitor.com/World/Middle-East/2014/1130/Pope-Francis-fails-to-find-common-ground-in-Turkey-video, accessed 1 December 2014.

233 Burak Bekdil, "Turkish Opera Buffa (Now at its Best)," Hurriyet Daily News (Istanbul), 3 December 2014, URL: http://www.hurriyetdailynews.com/turkish-opera-buffa-now-at-its-best.aspx?pageID=449&nID=75118&NewsCatID=398, accessed 24 December 2014.

234 "Pope's Visit to Turkey Positive for Interfaith Dialogue," *Today's Zaman* (Istanbul), 6 December 2014, URL: http://www.todayszaman.com/national_popes-visit-to-turkey-positive-for-interfaith-dialogue_366248.html, accessed 24 December 2014.

235 OIC Resolution No. 7/30-LEG – Tehran 2003.

236 OIC Resolution No. 2/31-LEG – Istanbul 2004.

237 "Text of Joint Declaration Signed by Pope and Ecumenical Patriarch," *Zenit*, 30 November 2014, URL: http://www.zenit.org/en/articles/text-of-joint-declaration-signed-by-pope-and-ecumenical-patriarch, accessed 1 December 2014.

238 "Text of Joint Declaration Signed by Pope and Ecumenical Patriarch," *Zenit*, 30 November 2014, URL: http://www.zenit.org/en/articles/text-of-joint-declaration-signed-by-pope-and-ecumenical-patriarch, accessed 1 December 2014.

239 "Text of Joint Declaration Signed by Pope and Ecumenical Patriarch," *Zenit*, 30 November 2014, URL: http://www.zenit.org/en/articles/text-of-joint-declaration-signed-by-pope-and-ecumenical-patriarch, accessed 1 December 2014.

240 Andrea Tornielli, "In the Mosque I Prayed to the Lord for these Wars to Stop!", *Vatican Insider* (*La Stampa*), 30 November 2014, URL: http://vaticaninsider.lastampa.it/en/the-vatican/detail/articolo/francesco-turchia-37828/, accessed 24 December 2014.

241 Thomas D. Williams, "Pope Denounces Jihad as 'Deviant Forms of Religion'," *Breitbart*, 12 January 2015, URL: http://www.breitbart.com/national-security/2015/01/12/pope-denounces-slavery-to-deviant-forms-of-religion/?utm_source=e_breitbart_com&utm_medium=email&utm_content=Breitbart+News+Roundup%2C+January+12%2C+2014&utm_campaign=20150112_m123954948_Breitbart+News+Roundup%2C+January+12%2C+2014&utm_term=More, accessed 12 January 2015.

242 Thomas D. Williams, "Pope Denounces Jihad as 'Deviant Forms of Religion'," *Breitbart*, 12 January 2015, URL: http://www.breitbart.com/national-security/2015/01/12/pope-denounces-slavery-to-deviant-forms-of-religion/?utm_source=e_breitbart_com&utm_medium=email&utm_content=Breitbart+News+Roundup%2C+January+12%2C+2014&utm_campaign=20150112_m123954948_Breitbart+News+Roundup%2C+January+12%2C+2014&utm_term=More, accessed 12 January 2015.

243 Nick Squire, "," The Telegraph (London), 15 January 2015, URL: http://www.telegraph.co.uk/news/worldnews/the-pope/11347931/Pope-Francis-You-cannot-make-fun-of-the-faith-of-others.html, accessed 15 January 2015.

244 Nick Squire, "," The Telegraph (London), 15 January 2015, URL: http://www.telegraph.co.uk/news/worldnews/the-pope/11347931/Pope-Francis-You-cannot-make-fun-of-the-faith-of-others.html, accessed 15 January 2015.

245 "OIC Weighs Legal Action against French Magazine," *Arab News*, Jedda, 18 January 2015, URL: http://www.arabnews.com/featured/news/691261, accessed 18 January 2015.

246 Shafiq & Nimmer, *Interfaith Dialogue: A Guide for Muslims*, IIIT, 143.

247 Shafiq & Nimmer, *Interfaith Dialogue: A Guide for Muslims*, IIIT, 31.

248 Shafiq & Nimmer, *Interfaith Dialogue: A Guide for Muslims*, IIIT, 31.

249 "Declaration of the Pontifical Council for Interreligious Dialogue," Bulletin Holy See Press Office [B0567, 12 August 2014, URL: http://press.vatican.va/content/salastampa/fr/bollettino/pubblico/2014/08/12/0567/01287.html#Traduzione%20in%20lingua%20inglese, accessed 17 August 2014.

250 Keller, *Reliance of the Traveller*, Book O "Justice," o10.0 "The Spoils of Battle," at o10.0 to o10.03.

251 Ibn Kathir, Al-Hafiz Abu al-Fida' 'Imad Ad-Din Isma'il bin 'Umar bin Kathir al-Qurashi al-Busrawi, *Tafsir of Ibn Kathir*, Vol. 2. Trans. Abdul-Malik Mujahid. Riyadh: Darussalam, 2000, 421-

422.

252 *Tafsir Ibn Kathir*, Vol. 2, "Marrying Only One Wife When One Fears He Might not Do Justice to His Wife", 375.

253 *Tafsir Ibn Kathir*, Vol. 7, 720.

254 *Tafsir Ibn Kathir*, Vol. 6, 631.

255 *Tafsir Ibn Kathir*, Vol. 10, 169.

256 Keller, *Reliance of the Traveller*, Book O "Justice," o11.0 "Non-Muslim Subjects of the Islamic State," at o11.0 to o11.11.

257 "Apostolic Journey to the United States of America and Visit to the United Nations Organization Headquarters: Meeting with the Members of the General Assembly of the United Nations Organization: Address of His Holiness Benedict XVI," New York, 18 April 2008, URL: http://www.vatican.va/holy_father/benedict_xvi/speeches/2008/april/documents/hf_ben-xvi_spe_20080418_un-visit_en.html, accessed 21 Jan 2009.

258 Resolution No. 4/31-LEG, On Slander Campaigns waged by certain Governmental and Non-Governmental Organizations (NGOs) Against a Number of OIC Member States and the Islamic Sharia under the Slogan of Human Rights Protection, Resolutions on Legal Affairs Adopted by the Thirty-First Session of the Islamic Conference of Foreign ministers (Session of Progress and Global Harmony) Istanbul, Republic of Turkey, 26-28 Rabiul Thani 1425h (14-16 June 2004), URL: http://www.oic-oci.org/english/conf/fm/31/31%20icfm-leg-eng.htm#RESOLUTION%A0%20No.%20 4/31-LEG, accessed 2010.

PART XII: APPENDIX TWO

1   European Court of Human Rights, Grand Chamber, Case of Refah Partisi (The Welfare Party) as Others v. Turkey, Judgment, Strasbourg, 13 February 2003, URL: http://www.bailii.org/eu/cases/ECHR/2003/87.html, accessed 30 September 2013.

2   OSCE – "Who We Are", undated, URL: http://www.osce.org/who, accessed 23 November 2013.

3   "Torpedoing 'Islamophobia'," Center for Security Policy, 29 September 2013, transcript of OSCE Human Dimension Implementation Meeting Warsaw, Side Event Convened by the ODIHR Tolerance and Non-Discrimination Department: "Educational Initiatives and Approaches for Addressing anti-Semitism and Intolerance against Muslims," 24 September 2013, URL: http://www.centerforsecuritypolicy.org/2013/09/29/torpedoing-islamophobia/, accessed 30 September 2013. Cited hereafter as "Torpedoing 'Islamophobia'," CSP.

4   OSCE Side Event, "How Bad Definitions Violate Fundamental OSCE Commitments," OSCE Human Dimension Implementation Meeting, Warsaw, Poland, 26 September 2013, Final Overview of Side Events as Submitted by the Organizers Human Dimension Implementation Meeting, 23 September – 4 October 2013, Warsaw, Poland, URL: https://www.osce.org/odihr/104902#page=5, accessed 1 October 2013, 13. Cited Hereafter as OSCE Side Event, "How Bad Definitions Violate Fundamental OSCE Commitments."

5   OSCE Side Event, "How Bad Definitions Violate Fundamental OSCE Commitments."

6   Turkish Delegation, OSCE, STATEMENT BY TURKEY (Plenary Session 4 of the OSCE High-Level Conference on Tolerance and Non-Discrimination: Combating Intolerance an Discrimination against Muslims, Tirana, 22-23 May 2013), 27 May 2013, URL: http://www.osce.org/cio/101935, accessed 29 September 2013.

7   "Torpedoing 'Islamophobia'," CSP.

8   "Torpedoing 'Islamophobia'," CSP.

9   About us page, EMISCO (European Muslim Initiative for Social Cohesion), undated, URL: http://www.emisco.eu/about-us/, accessed 23 November 2013.

10   "Torpedoing 'Islamophobia'," CSP.

11   al-Shaybani, Muhammad ibn al-Hasan. *The Islamic Law of Nations: Shaybani's Siyar (Kitab alsiyar al-kabir)*. Trans. Majid Khadduri. Baltimore: Johns Hopkins University Press, 1966, 86-7. **Reads**: "I heard the Apostle of Allah in the campaign against the Banu Qurayza saying: "He of the enemy who has reached puberty should be killed, but he who has not should be spared." [...] The Apostle of Allah prohibited the killing of women. [...] The Apostle of Allah said: 'You may kill the adults of the unbelievers, but spare their minors – the youth'." **See also** the section "Raid on the B. Qurayza," of Ibn Ishaq's sacralized biography of Muhammad in Alfred Guillaume, "The Raid on B. Qurayza," *The Life of Muhammad, A Translation of Ishaq's Sirat Rasul Allah*, Karachi: Oxford University Press, 1955 (reissued in Pakistan, 1967), ¶ 959, p. 461-9.

12   *The Quranic Concept of War* by Brigadier S.K. Malik, (Lahore, Pakistan: Wajid Al's Ltd., 1979. (with a forward by General Zia-ul-Haq) (This paper relies on the 1986 First Indian Reprint). Cited hereafter as S.K. Malik, 57.

13   Turkish Delegation, OSCE, STATEMENT BY TURKEY (Plenary Session 4 of the OSCE High-Level Conference on Tolerance and Non-Discrimination: Combating Intolerance an Discrimination against Muslims, Tirana, 22-23 May 2013), 27 May 2013, URL: http://www.osce.org/cio/101935, accessed 29 September 2013.

14   Ambassador Omur Orhun, "Challenges Facing Muslims in Europe – 2011-03-01," Arches Quarterly, Vol. 4 Edition 8, Spring/Summer 2011, Posted on OIC's Official UN portal "Organization

of Isalmic Cooperation – Permanent Observer Mission to the United Nations in New York, 1 March 2011, URL: http://www.oicun.org/74/20120116050228155.html, accessed 29 September 2013.

15   Ambassador Omur Orhun, "Challenges Facing Muslims in Europe – 2011-03-01."

16   "Defamation of Religions," Reports of the Secretary General on the Legal Affairs Submitted to the Twenty-Eighth Session of the Islamic Conference of Foreign Ministers, Bamako, Republic of Mali, 4-8 Rabi-ul-Thani, 1422H (25-29 June, 2001) at http://www.oic-oci.org/oicnew/english/conf/fm/28/28-ICFM-SG-Rep-en/28-ICFM-LEG-D-en.htm. Cited hereafter as Twenty-Eighth Session of the Islamic Conference of Foreign Ministers, Bamako.

17   European Court of Human Rights, Grand Chamber, Case of Refah Partisi (The Welfare Party) as Others v. Turkey, Judgment, Strasbourg, 13 February 2003, URL: http://www.bailii.org/eu/cases/ECHR/2003/87.html, accessed 30 September 2013.

18   Dr. Harald Fiegl, "Please Define 'Islamophobia' by Dr. Harald Fiegl, *Mission Europa*, posted on YouTube, 15 July 2013, URL: http://www.youtube.com/watch?v=MMg5zTFxZlc#t=64, accessed 1 October 2013.

19   "Turkish Government Representative Mr. Umut Topcuoglu quotes the Definition of "Islamophobia" Provided by the Organization of Islamic Cooperation, OIC Effectively Making that the OSCE Definition as Well," OSCE Supplementary Human Dimension Meeting, Vienna, Austria, 11 July 2013, posted to *YouTube* 16 July 2013, URL: http://www.youtube.com/watch?v=nk8uxyK8L5U, accessed 29 September 2013.

20   "Torpedoing 'Islamophobia'," CSP.

21   OSCE Side Event "Educational Initiatives and Approaches for Adding Anti-Semitism and Intolerance against Muslims," OSCE Human Dimension Implementation Meeting, Warsaw, Poland, 24 September 2013, Final Overview of Side Events as Submitted by the Organizers Human Dimension Implementation Meeting, 23 September – 4 October 2013, Warsaw, Poland, URL: https://www.osce.org/odihr/104902#page=5, 1 October 2013, 6.

22   "Torpedoing 'Islamophobia'," CSP.

23   OSCE Side Event "Educational Initiatives and Approaches for Adding Anti-Semitism and Intolerance against Muslims," OSCE Human Dimension Implementation Meeting, 6.

24   Guidelines for Educators on Countering Intolerance and Discrimination against Muslims: Addressing Islamophobia through Education, Organization for Security and Cooperation in Europe (OSCE) – Office for Democratic Institutions and Human Rigths, 28 October 2011, URL: http://www.osce.org/odihr/84495, accessed 29 September 2013, 10.

25   Guidelines for Educators on Countering Intolerance and Discrimination against Muslims: Addressing Islamophobia through Education, 49.

26   Third OIC Observatory Report on Islamophobia (Intolerance & Discrimination against Muslims), OIC Observatory, 23 May 2009 – April 2010, 22 May 2010, URL: http://www.oic-oci.org/uploads/file/Islamphobia/2010/en/Islamophobia_rep_May_22_5_2010.pdf.pdf, 7, accessed 23 June 2010.

27   "Torpedoing 'Islamophobia'," CSP.

28   Third OIC Observatory Report on Islamophobia (Intolerance & Discrimination against Muslims), OIC Observatory.

29   "Torpedoing 'Islamophobia'," CSP.

30   "Torpedoing 'Islamophobia'," CSP.

31   "Torpedoing 'Islamophobia'," CSP.

32   Partial Transcript, OSCE Side Event "How Bad Definitions Violate Fundamental OSCE Commitments," International Civil Liberties Alliance (ICLA), English, Opera Room, OSCE

Human Dimension Implementation Meeting, Warsaw, Poland, 26 September 2013.

33 "Torpedoing 'Islamophobia'," CSP.

34 OSCE Side Event, "How Bad Definitions Violate Fundamental OSCE Commitments."

35 Partial Transcript, OSCE Side Event "How Bad Definitions Violate Fundamental OSCE Commitments," International Civil Liberties Alliance (ICLA), English, Opera Room, OSCE Human Dimension Implementation Meeting, Warsaw, Poland, 26 September 2013. Cited hereafter as Partial Transcript, OSCE Side Event "How Bad Definitions Violate Fundamental OSCE Commitments."

36 Partial Transcript, OSCE Side Event "How Bad Definitions Violate Fundamental OSCE Commitments."

37 "Torpedoing 'Islamophobia'," CSP.

38 Partial Transcript, OSCE Side Event "How Bad Definitions Violate Fundamental OSCE Commitments."

39 Annex to Res. No. 49 / 19-P, The Cairo Declaration on Human Rights in Islam, Resolution NO. 49 / 19-P, On the Cairo Declaration on Human Rights in Islam, The Nineteenth Islamic Conference of Foreign Ministers (Session of Peace, Interdependence and Development), Cairo, Arab Republic of Egypt, OIC, 9-14 Muharram 1411H (31 July to 5 August 1990), URL: http://www.oic-oci.org/english/article/human.htm, accessed 22 July 2009.

40 Ambassador Omur Orhun, "Second Semi-Annual Report for 2007 by Ambassador Omur Orhun – Personal Representative of the Chairman-in-Office of the OSCE on Combating Intolerance and Discrimination against Muslims, 24 November 2007, Ankara, URL: http://www.osce.org/what/tolerance/31016, accessed 6 October 2013, 4, 5.

41 Second Alliance of Civilizations Forum, Istanbul, Turkey, 6-7 April 2009, URL: http://www.unaoc.org/docs/AoC_Istanbul-09web.pdf, accessed 18 November 2013, 116.

42 Management of Thesis Completed, Prof. Dr. Mehmet Tevfik Ozcan, Istanbul University, Faculty of Law, Common Law Section, Department of Philosophy and Sociology of Law, 19 April 2012, URL: http://www.google.com/l?sa=t&rct=j&q=&esrc=s&source=web&cd=3&cad=rja&ved=0CDsQFjAC&url=http%3A%2F%2Fistanbuluniversitesi.hukukfakultesi.gen.tr%2Fakademisyenler%2Fmehmet-tevfik-ozcan.doc&ei=o4SKUp3zA-musAT7jYDgBw&usg=AFQjCNFbLnD5J983Wz11hjp7VEI4k1_GwQ&bvm=bv.56643336,d.cWc, accessed 18 November 2013, 4.

43 Master's Degrees, Istanbul University, "Master List of Graduates" (Yüksek Lisans - İstanbul Üniversitesi, YÜKSEK LİSANS MEZUNLARI LİSTESİURL), College of Liberal Arts, Istanbul University, 28 April 2005, URL: http://www.google.com/url?sa=t&rct=j&q=&esrc=s&source=web&cd=1&cad=rja&ved=0CCsQFjAA&url=http%3A%2F%2Fsbe.istanbul.edu.tr%2Fdoc%2Fmezunlarimiz-yuksek-lisans.xls&ei=YXGKUr63ENW-4APMkoCoAQ&usg=AFQjCNFPM1zD2C1rnODApEj69mJofbknHA&bvm=bv.56643336,d.dmg, assessed 4 October 2013.

44 Ambassador Omur Orhun, Annex I "Abstract for the OIC-Georgetown University ACMCU Roundtable on 'Islamophobia and the Challenge of Pluralism in the 21ˢᵗ Century', Washington, DC, 7 September 2007, of "Second Semi-Annual Report for 2007 by Ambassador Omur Orhun – Personal Representative of the Chairman-in-Office of the OSCE on Combating Intolerance and Discrimination against Muslims, 24 November 2007, Ankara, URL: http://www.osce.org/what/tolerance/31016, accessed 6 October 2013, 8. **Reads: 8. What to do? Remedies: (not an exhaustive list);** d) Creation of self- regulatory media bodies to deal with manifestations of discrimination and racism should also be encouraged; e) Western countries must be asked to enact adequate legislation and must also be asked to implement this legislation and their relevant international commitments effectively. (Muslim countries should do the same on their part.); f) Hate crimes must be defined broadly and the information deficit must be addressed. Clear criteria for reporting and registering of hate crimes must be established and reporting of hate crimes must be encouraged. Additionally, hate crimes must be prosecuted in a timely manner and efficiently. Law enforcement officials should be trained.

45 "International Conference on Islamophobia," Islamic Human Rights Commission, 8 December 2007, URL: http://www.ihrc.org.uk/events/5239-International-Conference-on-Islamophobia, accessed 18 November 2013. **States:** A two day conference being held in Istanbul with speakers from all around the world. Organised by The Union of NGOs in the Islamic World (U N I W). IHRC Chairman Massoud Shadjareh will also be addressing the conference. TO VIEW THE OFFICIAL CONFERENCE WEBSITE NAVIGATE TO THE LINK PROVIDED AT THE BOTTOM OF THIS PAGE: SPEAKERS INCLUDE: AHMAD AZAM ABDURRAHMAN / Malaysia (President, Global Peace Mission), Ahmed Bakcan, Dr. / France (Paris Vii University, Social And Human Sciences), Ahmed Muhammed Al Sharkawe / Kingdom Of Saudi Arabia (Participant Professor, Al Azhar & Qassim University, Islamic Studies), Ahmed Von Denffer / Germany (President, Muslime Helfen Institute), Ali Elghatit, Prof. Dr. / Egypt (Deputy President, Egyptian Society Of International Law), Ali Kurt, Lawyer / Turkey (Deputy Secretary General Of Uniw, Representative Of Turkey), ANAS SHEIKH ALI, Dr. / England (Chairman, Forum Against Islamophobia And Racism (CAIR)), Anis Ahmad, Prof. Dr. / Pakistan (Vice Chancellor, Riphah International University), Anwar Ibrahim / Malaysia (Ex-Prime Minister), Bernard Godard / France (Vice President, Religions Office Of The Ministry Of Interior), Erik C. Nisbet, Dr. / USA (Lecturer, Department Of Communication, Cornell University), Fatma Benli, Lawyer / Turkey (President, Women Rights Society Against Discrimination, (Akder)), Fehmi Koru / Turkey (Journalist, Columnist, Yeni Şafak Newspaper), Fethi Güngör, Doç. Dr. / Turkey (Lecturer, Department Of Sociology, Sakarya University), GHULAM-NABI FAI / USA (Executive Director, Kashmiri American Council (KAC)), Hasan Abou Taleb / Egypt (Assstant Director, Ahram Center For Political And Strategic Studies), Haytham Manna, Dr. / France (Arab Commission For Human Rights), Iqbal Sacranie / England (Ex-General Secretary, Muslim Council Of Britain (MCB)), IQBAL UNUS, Dr. / USA (Director, The Fairfax Institute (IIIT)), İbrahim Kalin, Dr. / Turkey (Politics, Economics And Society Researches (SETA)), JOHN ESPOSITO, Prof. Dr. / USA (Religion & International Affairs & Affairs & Islamic Studies, Georgetown University), KAREN ARMSTRONG / England (Writer-Lecturer), LORD NAZIM AHMED / England (Member Of The House Of The Lords), LOUAY M. SAFI, Dr./ USA (Executive Director, ISNA Leadership Development Center), M. Fahmy Howeidy / Egypt (Deputy Editor In Chief, Al-Ahram Newspaper), Manal Abolhasan, Dr. / Egypt (Lecturer, Al-Azhar University), Massoud Shadjareh / England (Chair, Islamic Human Right Commission (IHRC)), Mehmet Görmez, Prof. Dr./ Turkey (Deputy Of Religious Affairs), Merve Safa Kavakçi, Dr. / USA (Lecturer & Writer, International Relations, George Washington University), Mohammad Rayyan, Dr. / Jordan (Shariah, Jordan University), Mojtaba Amiri Vahid / Iran (Deputy Of Oic Mission To Un-Geneva Office), Moncef Marzouki, Dr. / France (Tunisian Intellectual, Writer), Mubarak El-Mutawwa, Lawyer. / Kuwait (Uniw Deputy Secretary General), Mümtazer Türköne, Prof. Dr. / Turkey (Lecturer, Gazi University), Nader Hashemi, Prof. Dr. / USA (Political Science, Northwestern University), NORMAN G. FINKELSTEIN, Prof. Dr. / USA (Political Science, (Formerly) DePaul University), Numan Kurtulmuş, Prof. Dr. / Turkey (Lecturer, Politician), Olsi Jazexhi / Albania (Muslim Forum Of Albania), ÖMÜR ORHUN / Turkey (Personal Representative, On Combating Intolerance And Discrimination Against Muslims, OSCE), Özcan Hidir , Asst. Prof /Netherland (Islamic University Of Rotterdam), Saied Reza Ameli, Prof. Dr. / Iran (Media Studies, University Of Tehran), Salah Abd-El Mutaal, Prof. Dr. / Egypt (Department Of Sociology, Cairo University), Samy Debah / France (President, Association Of Anti-Islamophobia), Shahid Malik / England (House Of Commons, MP For Dewsbury), Sulayman Nyang, Prof. Dr. / USA (African Studies, Howard University), Susana Mangana, Prof. Dr. / Uruguay (Arabic & Islamic Studies, The Catholic University), TARIQ SAID RAMADAN, Prof. Dr. / Switzerland (Academic, Theologian), TAŞKIN TANKUT SOYKAN / Poland (Adviser, OSCE ODIHR), Vincent Geisser / France (President, Study And Information Center On The International Migrants (CIEMI)), WILLIAM BAKER / USA (Founder & President, Christians And Muslims For Peace (CAMP)), Yasin Aktay, Prof. Dr. / Turkey (Lecturer, Department Od Sociology, Selçuk University), Yusuf Kaplan, Doç. Dr. / Turkey (Lecturer, Science And Art Academy), Yusuf Suiçmez, Dr. / Turkish Republic Of Northern Cyprus (Lecturer, Near East University), **ADVISORY BOARD** - Lawyer Ali KURT, TURKEY • Mubarak El-Mutawwa, KUWAIT• Prof. Dr. Salah Abd El MOTAAL, EGYPT • **DR. GHULAM NABI FAI, USA** • Ahmad Azam ABDURRAHMAN, MALAYSIA • Prof. Dr. Anis AHMAD, PAKISTAN • Asst. Prof. Ali Murat YEL, TURKEY • Dr. İbrahim KALIN, TURKEY • Ömer KORKMAZ, TURKEY •

Şemsettin TÜRKKAN, TURKEY, **ORGANIZATION COMMITTEE** - Mustafa ÖZKAYA • A. Cihangir İŞBİLİR • Besim PEROLLİ • İlker TARAVAR • Şengül YİĞİT • Hüseyin CEYHAN • Murat YAŞA • Metin MUTANOĞLU • Turan KIŞLAKÇI.

46   S. Ghulam Nabi, "Islam is compatible with Western ideals of freedom and democracy: Dr. Fai," speech at Istanbul, Turkey, December 12, 2007, *Kashmiri American Council* Report, Washington, D.C., 12 November 2009, URL: http://csonet.org/ngocommittee/content/documents/ans_31-May-2010_7731_11074.pdf, accessed 8 October 2013, 118. **States**: "Those who spoke during the two day conference included: Prof. **DR. EKMELEDDIN IHSANOLU**, the Secretary-General of the Organization of Islamic Conference (OIC); Sardar Abdul Qayyum Khan, former President, Azad Kashmir; the Jewish academic Prof. **DR. NORMAN FINKELSTEIN** famous for his book the Holocaust, Dr. Vincent Geisser, France; **MS. KAREN ARMSTRONG**, England; Prof. Dr. Susana Mangana, Uruguay; Prof. **WILLIAM BAKER**, USA; Mr. Necmi Sadikoglu, Turkey; Dr. Bernard Goddard, France; Eric K. Nisbet, Turkey; **DR. TARIQ SAID RAMADAN**, Switzerland; Prof. Norman Finkelstein, USA; Mr. M. Fahmy Howeidy, Egypt; Lord Nazir Ahmed, England; Mr. Anwar Ibrahim, the Former Deputy Prime Minister of Malaysia; Mr. Ahmed Von Denffer, Germany; **DR. M. LOUAY SAFI**, USA; Prof. Dr. Anis Ahmad, Pakistan; **DR. IQBAL UNUS, USA**; Dr. Ahmet Bakcan, Turkey; Mr. Shahid Malik, M.P., England; Dr. Merve Safa Kavak; USA; Dr. Salah Abdel Mutaal, Egypt; Dr. Olsi Jazexhi, Albania; Mr. Ahmed Azam, Malysia; Mr. Mubarak El-Mutawwa, Kuwait; Dr. Sulayman Nyang, USA; Dr. Mohammad Rayan, Jordan; **DR. TASKIN SOYKAN**, Poland; Dr. brahim Kaln, Turkey; Prof. Dr. Numan Kurtulmu; Prof. Dr. Mümtazer Türköne, Prof. Dr. Ömer Faruk Harman, Prof. Dr. Mehmet Görmez, Mr. Ali Kurt, Turkey; Prof. Dr. Yasin Aktay, Fatma Benli from Turkey and many more.

47   "Islamophobia Should be Considered a Crime," Union of NGOs of the Islamic World (UNIW) citing Haber7.com (Turkish), 9 December 2007, URL: http://www.theunity.org/en/index.php?option=com_content&view=article&id=206:islamophobia-should-be-considered-crime&catid=9:press&Itemid=8, accessed 18 November 2013.

48   For example, Report of OSCE-ODIHR Roundtable: Addressing Intolerance and Discrimination against Muslims: Youth and Education," OSCE – ODIHR, Vienna, Austria, 17 December 2008, URL: http://www.osce.org/odihr/39017, 2013, and the Second Alliance of Civilizations Forum, Istanbul, Turkey, 6-7 April 2009, URL: http://www.unaoc.org/docs/AoC_Istanbul-09web.pdf, both accessed 18 November 2013.

49   For example, at the Muslim Youth: Challenges, Opportunities and Expectations, Organized by the Association of Muslim Social Scientists (AMSS UK), The Department of Theology and Religious Studies, The University of Chester, 20-22 March 2009, URL: http://www.amssuk.com/docs/pdf/AMSSUK%20Chester%202009%20Conference%20Briefing.pdf, accessed 3 October 2013.

50   Explanatory Memorandum: On the General Strategic Goal for the Group," Mohamed Akram, May 22, 1991, Government Exhibit 003-0085/3:04-CR-240-G U.S. v. HLF, et al., United States District Court, Northern District of Texas, http://www.txnd.uscourts.gov/judges/hlf2/09-25-08/Elbarasse%20Search%203.pdf, AMSS listed as No. 4.

51   News Release, "Mr. Shaarik Zafar," United States Mission to the OSCE, Office of Public Affairs, 16 June 2006, URL: http://osce.usmission.gov/media/pdfs/shaarik_zafar.pdf, accessed 10 October 2013.

52   "Spotlight on Shaarik Zarar, Sr. Policy Advisor DHS," *PakPac E-Letter*, August 2009, URL: http://pakpac.net/Newsletter%20July09%20onwards/Aug09/VolI/LTR_Aug09_VolI.asp#Religious_Freedom, accessed 23 June 2013.

53   Shaarik Zafar, "Terminology to Define the Terrorists: Recommendations from American Muslims," Office for Civil Rights and Civil Liberties, Department of Homeland Security (DHS CRCL), January 2008, URL: http://www.dhs.gov/xlibrary/assets/dhs_crcl_terminology_08-1-08_accessible.pdf, accessed 23 June 2013.

54   Shaarik Zafar, "Terminology to Define the Terrorists: Recommendations from American Muslims," Office for Civil Rights and Civil Liberties, Department of Homeland Security (DHS

CRCL), January 2008, URL: http://www.dhs.gov/xlibrary/assets/dhs_crcl_terminology_08-1-08_accessible.pdf, accessed 23 June 2013.

55   Announcement: "First Annual Youth Employment Conference,"*PakPac E-Letter*, July 2010, URL: http://pakpac.net/Newsletter/2010/Jul/LTR_Jul10_volII.asp, accessed 24 June 2013.

56   Michelle Boorstein, "State Department Taps Texas Lawyer to Serve as 'America's Ambassador to Muslims',"*Washington Post*, 29 August 2014, URL: http://www.washingtonpost.com/local/zafar-takes-over-as-special-rep...unities/2014/08/29/7d89f0f2-2edd-11e4-bb9b-997ae96fad33_story. html, accessed 30 August 2014. **States:** "State Department's new special representative to Muslim communities. ...."

57   Article 2, Section 2, "International Covenant on Civil and Political Rights," *Office of the United Nations High Commissioner for Human Rights, United Nations* (Adopted and Opened for Signature, Ratification and Accession by General Assembly Resolution 2200A (XXI)), 16 December 1966 (entry into force 23 March 1976 in accordance with Article 49), at http://www2.ohchr.org/english/law/ccpr. htm#art20.

58   Declarations and Reservations: United States of America, Status, Chapter IV, Human Rights, (4) International Covenant on Civil and Political Rights, United Nations Treaty Collection Databases, United Nations, New York, 16 December 1966, http://treaties.un.org/pages/VeiwDetails. aspx?src=TREATY&mtdsg_no=IV-4&chapter=4&lang=en#EndDec.

59   "Understanding and Implementing the Obligation to Prohibit Incitement in the OSCE,"OSCE Side Event, Center for Media and Communications Studies, Central European University (CEU), Article 19, summary of event as printed in "Final Overview of Side Events, OSCE, 23 September – 4 October 2013, Warsaw, Poland, URL: http://www.osce.org/odihr/104902, accessed 13 November 2013. "**Summary:** This event will examine the legal and non-legal policy implications of the Rabat Plan of Action (RPA) for States and non-state actors in the OSCE region.

60   "History", About CEU/History, Central European University, Budapest, Hungary, undated URL: http://www.ceu.hu/about/history, accessed 10 December 2013. **States:** "In 1989, a group of visionary intellectuals—most of them prominent members of the anti-totalitarian democratic opposition—conceptualized an international university that would help facilitate the transition from dictatorship to democracy in Central and Eastern Europe and the former Soviet Union. Among them was George Soros, the Hungarian-American financier and philanthropist, who founded Central European University two years later. Soros championed the project because he understood that open societies can flourish only with people in positions of responsibility who are educated to promote them. His vision was to recruit professors and students from around the world to build a unique institution, one that would train future generations of scholars, professionals, politicians, and civil society leaders to contribute to building open and democratic societies that respect human rights and adhere to the rule of law. Beginning with 100-plus students in 1991, CEU held its first classes in Prague with students from 20 countries, primarily within the region. The University moved to Budapest in 1993."

61   "Open Society Mission", About CEU, Central European University, Budapest, Hungary, undated, URL: http://www.ceu.hu/about/open-society-mission, accessed 10 December 2013.

62   Funders, Article 19, *Article 19* webpage undated, URL: http://www.article19.org/pages/en/funders.html, 16 November 2013. European governmental entities include Department for International Aid (DFID) / UKAID, Dutch Ministry of Foreign Affairs, European Commission, Foreign and Commonwealth Office (FCO), Norwegian Ministry of Foreign Affairs, Swedish International Development Cooperation Agency (SIDA).

63   About Us, Opens Society Foundations, *Open Society Foundations*, webpage undated, URL: http://www.opensocietyfoundations.org/about, 16 November 2013. **States:** "The Open Society Foundations are a family of offices and foundations created by philanthropist George Soros. This directory includes our offices and country and regional foundations located throughout the world."

64   Footnote 1 in Title, "Rabat Plan of Action on the Prohibition of Advocacy of National, Racial or

Religious Hatred that Constitutes Incitement to Discrimination, Hostility or Violence:[1] Conclusions and Recommendations Emanating from the Four Regional Rxpert Workshops Organised by OHCHR, in 2011, and adopted by experts in Rabat, Morocco on 5 October 2012," United Nations High Commissioner on Human Rights (OHCHR), 5 October 2012, URL: http://www.un.org/en/preventgenocide/adviser/pdf/Rabat_draft_outcome.pdf, accessed 21 November 2013. Main document cited hereafter as OHCHR, "Rabat Plan of Action."

65   Annex to Res. No. 49 / 19-P, The Cairo Declaration on Human Rights in Islam, Resolution NO. 49 / 19-P, On the Cairo Declaration on Human Rights in Islam, The Nineteenth Islamic Conference of Foreign Ministers (Session of Peace, Interdependence and Development), Cairo, Arab Republic of Egypt, OIC, 9-14 Muharram 1411H (31 July to 5 August 1990), URL: http://www.oic-oci.org/english/article/human.htm, accessed 22 July 2009.

66   "Racism, Racial Discrimination, Xenophobia and Related form of Intolerance, follow-up and Implementation of the Durban Declaration and Programme of Action Human Rights Council, Agenda Item 9, Sixteenth Session, *Human Rights Commission*, United Nations A/HRC/16/L.38, 21 March 2011, http://ap.ohchr.org/documents/E/HRC/d_res_dec/A_HRC_16_L.38.pdf.

67   "OIC Deplores Burning of the Holy Qur'an," *OIC News Release*, 22 February 2012, URL: http://www.oic-oci.org/topic_detail.asp? t_id=6467, accessed 27 February 2012.

68   OHCHR, "Rabat Plan of Action,", 1.

69   OHCHR, "Rabat Plan of Action,", 9.

70   "Contemporary forms of Racism," Twenty-Eighth Session of the Islamic Conference of Foreign Ministers, Bamako, Republic of Mali, 4-8 Rabi-ul-Thani, 1422H (25-29 June, 2001) at http://www.oic-oci.org/oicnew/english/conf/fm/28/28-ICFM-SG-Rep-en/28-ICFM-LEG-D-en.htm.

71   Preface, Section 4, OHCHR, "Rabat Plan of Action,", 1-2.

72   Partial Transcript (1:27:40 to 1:38:40), OSCE Side Event "Understanding and implementing the obligation to prohibit incitement in the OSCE," Conveners: Center for Media and Communications Studies (CMCS), Central European University (CEU) and *Article 19*, OSCE Conference Side Event, Warsaw, Poland, 24 September 2013, Transcript created 16 November 2013.

73   United Nations Biography, Ufuk Gökçen, Permanent Observer Mission to the United Nations in New York, the United Nations, United Nations webpage, Undated, URL: http://www.oicun.org/oic_at_un/ambassador/, re-accessed 12 January 2015.

74   Ufuk Gökçen, @iktgokcen, *Twitter*, 15 January 2015, URL: https://twitter.com/iktgokcen/status/554729195889512448, accessed 12 January 2015. States: "Charlie Hebdo attack&reaction underline critical imp. of renewed commitment to resolution 16/18&Rabat Plan of Action."

75   Andrew Smith, "Charlie Hebdo Attack and Global Reaction Highlights Critical Importance of Renwed Commitment to the Implementation of Resolution 16/18 and Rabat Plan of Action," Universal Human Rights Group, 12 January 2015, URL: http://universal-rights.org/blogs/119-charlie-hebdo-attack-and-global-reaction-highlights-critical-importance-of-renewed-commitment-to-the-implementation-of-resolution-16-18-and-the-rabat-plan-of-action, accessed 12 January 2015.

76   Yusuf Al-Qaradawi, IUMS President, "IUMS Calls for the Islamic Nation to Continue in the Legal Peaceful Demonstrating to Defend the Great Messenger, and Calls for the West to Protect Muslim Communities from Attacks," *IUMS Online*, Doha, Qatar, 20 January 2015, URL: http://iumsonline.org/en/default.asp?menuID=62&contentID=8914, accessed 21 January 2015.

77   Sixth OIC Observatory Report on Islamophobia - October 2012 - September 2013 (Presented to the 40th Council of Foreign Ministers, Conakry, Republic of Guinea), OIC Observatory, OIC, 9-11 December 2013, URL: http://www.oic-oci.org/oicv2/upload/islamphobia/2013/en/islamphobia_report_2013.pdf, accessed 12 December 2013, 2. Cited hereafter as Sixth OIC Observatory Report on Islamophobia.

78   Sixth OIC Observatory Report on Islamophobia, 4, 29.

79   Sixth OIC Observatory Report on Islamophobia, 5, 31.

80   Sixth OIC Observatory Report on Islamophobia, 2.

81   Sixth OIC Observatory Report on Islamophobia, 31.

82   Sixth OIC Observatory Report on Islamophobia, 5.

83   Sixth OIC Observatory Report on Islamophobia, 87, 88.

84   Sixth OIC Observatory Report on Islamophobia, 87.

85   Sixth OIC Observatory Report on Islamophobia, 31.

86   Sixth OIC Observatory Report on Islamophobia, 90.

87   Sixth OIC Observatory Report on Islamophobia, 90.

88   Annex to Res. No. 49 / 19-P, The Cairo Declaration on Human Rights in Islam, Resolution NO. 49 / 19-P, On the Cairo Declaration on Human Rights in Islam, The Nineteenth Islamic Conference of Foreign Ministers (Session of Peace, Interdependence and Development), Cairo, Arab Republic of Egypt, OIC, 9-14 Muharram 1411H (31 July to 5 August 1990), URL: http://www.oic-oci.org/english/article/human.htm, accessed 22 July 2009.

89   Annex to Res. No. 49 / 19-P, The Cairo Declaration on Human Rights in Islam, Resolution NO. 49 / 19-P, On the Cairo Declaration on Human Rights in Islam.

90   Sixth OIC Observatory Report on Islamophobia, 90.

91   Master's Degrees, Istanbul University, "Master List of Graduates" (Yüksek Lisans - İstanbul Üniversitesi, YÜKSEK LİSANS MEZUNLARI LİSTESİURL), College of Liberal Arts, Istanbul University, 28 April 2005, URL: http://www.google.com/url?sa=t&rct=j&q=&esrc= s&source=web&cd=1&cad=rja&ved=0CCsQFjAA&url=http%3A%2F%2Fsbe.istanbul.edu. tr%2Fdoc%2Fmezunlarimiz-yuksek-lisans.xls&ei=YXGKUr63ENW-4APMkoCoAQ&usg=AFQj CNFPM1zD2C1rnODApEj69mJofbknHA&bvm=bv.56643336,d.dmg, assessed 4 October 2013.

92   "Overview of Side Events as Submitted by the Organizers," Human Dimension Implementation Meeting, OSCE, Warsaw, Poland, 22 September – 3 October 2014, URL: http://www.osce.org/ odihr/123499?download=true, accessed 4 October 2014, 29.

93   EMISCO Flyer, "EMISCO Side-Event Islamophobia – Fact or Fiction," EMISCO, undated, URL: https://www.facebook.com/129883293733752/photos/gm.1506011836303891/74543934 5511474/?type=1&theater, accessed 4 October 2014. Attendees: Bashy Quraishy, Moderator; Talip Küçükcan, OSCE Representative on Discrimination and Intolerance against Muslims; Dr. Sabine Schiffer, Institute for Media Responsibility – IMV; Ayse Elkiliç, Lawyer and Vice President of ThinkOut; Julie Pascoet, Policy Officer – ENAR; Murat Gümüş, Vice-Secretary General of IGMG; Özbil Biyikli, Faculty of Islamic Sciences of Brussels; Bülent Şenay, OSCE/ODIHR Advisor for Freedom of Religion Advisory Council.

94   Bashy Quarishy, "How to Combat Cyber Hate Crime While Respecting Freedom of Expression: The Challenge of Countering Anti-Muslim Hatred on the Internet," EMISCO (European Muslim Initiative for Social Cohesion) in conjunction with *IEME* and *Thinkout*, 3 July 2014.

95   Bashy Quarishy, "How to Combat Cyber Hate Crime While Respecting Freedom of Expression: The Challenge of Countering Anti-Muslim Hatred on the Internet," 18.

96   Bashy Quarishy, "How to Combat Cyber Hate Crime While Respecting Freedom of Expression: The Challenge of Countering Anti-Muslim Hatred on the Internet," 20.

97   Dr. Bülent Şenay, From PowerPoint Presentation, given at EMISCO Side Event, Human Dimension Implementation Meeting, OSCE/ODIHR, Warsaw, Poland, 30 October 2014.

98   Dr. Bülent Şenay, Partial transcript, EMISCO Side Event, Human Dimension Implementation Meeting, OSCE/ODIHR, Warsaw, Poland, 30 October 2014. Statements from EMISCO Side Event

cited hereafter as Partial transcript, EMISCO Side Event, 30 October 2014.

99	Dr. Bülent Şenay, Partial transcript, EMISCO Side Event, 30 October 2014.

100	Stephen Coughlin, Partial transcript, EMISCO Side Event, 30 October 2014.

101	Bashy Quraishy, Partial transcript, EMISCO Side Event, 30 October 2014. **For an example of the multicultural narrative, Quraishy's response to my question:** "Let me answer you please. I have a Muslim background and when I ask to be recognized as a part of European societies, I live here, I'm a [Danish] citizen, and I look around in every European country we have a law against anti-Semitism. In some countries we have a law against holocaust deniers. We have laws against homophobia, we have laws against almost everything which is unspeakable and should be having laws against. Now, what I'm asking as a [citizen with a] Muslim background, shouldn't that protection also be available to the Muslim communities. If I am not given a job because I have a Muslim name, if I am demonized in media because I have a Muslim background, if I am not given an apartment, if I apply for an apartment and they say no because of a Muslim name, and I can give you a long list, there is a long list of hate crimes, I come from Denmark, the secret police in that country [] the acts of hate crimes in Denmark in 2011, 2012 officer Danish report says Muslim are the [blookh] – the biggest victims of hate crimes the most. Not the Jews, not the … folk, not the LGBT person - but Muslim. Now when we have these statistics from all European countries by the European police secret services and NGOs, how can we close our eyes to that?"

102	Dr. Bülent Şenay, Partial transcript, EMISCO Side Event, 30 October 2014.

103	Bashy Quraishy, Partial transcript, EMISCO Side Event, 30 October 2014.

104	Bashy Quraishy, Partial transcript, EMISCO Side Event, 30 October 2014.

105	Curriculum Vitae – Dr. Bülent Şenay, Professor in History of Religion and Culture Faculty of Theology Uludag Universtiy, Bursa, Turkey, undated, URL: http://www.google.com/url?sa=t&rct=j&q=&esrc=s&source=web&cd=5&cad=rja&uact=8&ved=0CC0QFjAE&url=http%3A%2F%2Fwww.academia.edu%2Fattachments%2F30869381%2Fdownload_file&ei=AtQtVNy7DObbsATil4G4Cg&usg=AFQjCNFqfikbCxTr626b4xLfJlmNEYpo-g&bvm=bv.76802529,d.cWc, accessed 2 October 2014.

106	Bülent Şenay, "Undoing Hate Crimes: Combating Islamophobia as Cultural Terrorism," OSCE COJEP – Astana, Kazakhistan, 27 November 2010, URL: http://www.osce.org/home/73783?download=true, accessed 4 October 2014, 4 - 6.

107	Andrew Harrod and Sam Nunberg, "International 'Islamophobia' Conference Promotes Sharia Agenda," The Legal Project, 28 September 2013, URL: http://www.legal-project.org/4191/international-islamophobia-conference-promotes, accessed 4 October 2014.

108	Andrew Harrod and Sam Nunberg, "International 'Islamophobia' Conference Promotes Sharia Agenda," The Legal Project.

109	Andrew Harrod and Sam Nunberg, "International 'Islamophobia' Conference Promotes Sharia Agenda," The Legal Project.

110	Dr. Bülent Şenay, Partial transcript, EMISCO Side Event, 30 October 2014.

111	Bashy Quraishy, Partial transcript, EMISCO Side Event, 30 October 2014.

112	Bülent Şenay, "Undoing Hate Crimes: Combating Islamophobia as Cultural Terrorism," OSCE COJEP – Astana, Kazakhistan, 27 November 2010, URL: http://www.osce.org/home/73783?download=true, accessed 4 October 2014, 6.

113	Dr. Bülent Şenay, Partial transcript, EMISCO Side Event, 30 October 2014.

114	Bashy Quraishy, Partial transcript, EMISCO Side Event, 30 October 2014.

115	"IS Announces it Intends to Open a Consulate in Istanbul, Leaving Erdogan's Press Officiados Stammering, An Nahar (The Morning or The Day), Lebanon, 1 October 2014, URL: http://en.annahar.

com/article/176253-is-announces-it-intends-to-open-a-consululate-in-istanbul-leaving-erdogens-press, accessed 2 October 2014.

116 "ISIS to Open its First Consulate in Istanbul," *AWDNews,* Dubai, 29 September 2014, URL: http://awdnews.com/top-news/9885-isis-to-open-its-first-consulate-in-istanbul.html, accessed 30 October 2014.

117 "ISIS Opens Diplomatic Consulate in Istanbul, Turkey's President Denies," *Iraqi News,* X October 2014, URL, http://www.iraqinews.com/arab-world-news/isis-opens-diplomatic-consulate-istanbul-turkeys-president-denies/, accessed 2 October 2014.

118 Dr. Bülent Şenay, Partial transcript, EMISCO Side Event, 30 October 2014.

119 Dr. Bülent Şenay, From PowerPoint Presentation, EMISCO Side Event, Human Dimension Implementation Meeting, OSCE/ODIHR, Warsaw, Poland, 30 October 2014.

120 Dr. Bülent Şenay, Partial transcript, EMISCO Side Event, 30 October 2014.

121 Dr. Bülent Şenay, Partial transcript, EMISCO Side Event, 30 October 2014.

122 Ms. Özbil Biyikli, Partial transcript, EMISCO Side Event, 30 October 2014.

123 "Political Field," Final Communiqué of the Third Extraordinary Session of the Islamic Conference "Meeting the Challenges of the 21st Century, Solidarity in Action, Makkah al-Mukarramah, 5-6 Dhul Qa'Adah 1426H (7-8 December 2005), URL: http://english.savefreespeech.org/?p=403.

124 OIC International Conference on Terrorism: Dimensions, Threats and Countermeasures—Concluding Observations from the Chair, 15-17 November 2007, Tunis, at 2, at URL: http://www.oic-oci.org/english/article/terrorism_conference_concl-en.pdf.

Index

A

Abbas Shouman, *38, 117, 124, 332, 601, 607, 613, 631, 639, 674, 734*
Abd Al-Azim Al-Muta'ani, *241*
Abd al-Mu'ti Bayyoumi, *241*
Abd Al-Sabour Shahin, *241*
Abdallah bin Mahfudh ibn Bayyah, *110, 121, 217, 323, 624, 626, 676*
Abdel Fattah al-Sisi, *18*
Abdel Moeti Baoumi, *284*
Abdelhaleem Ashqar, *166*
Abdelmalek Droukdel, *203, 645*
Abdelrahman Odeh, *164*
Abdul Aziz Al-Asheikh, *322*
Abdul Malik Mujahid, *374, 690*
Abdulilah M. al-Khatib, *259*
Abdulla, *124, 546, 729*
Abdullah Azzam, *207-208, 285, 546, 601, 606, 610, 613, 617, 621, 623, 634, 639, 646, 651, 673-674, 723, 728*
Abdulqader, Mufid, *164, 166*
Abdur Rahman Doi, *38-39, 52, 56-57, 141, 492, 609-610, 613-614, 629, 716*
Abdur-Rahman Muhammad, *268*
Abduraham Almoudi, *172*
Abdurrahman Alamoudi, *173, 401-405, 639, 699-701*
Abel, *233-234*
Abi Busir, *94*
Abi Rafi, *94*
abolish the jizyah, *127, 386*
Abrahamic Faiths, *527*
abrogate, *45, 71, 102, 136, 228, 277, 533, 607*
abrogated, *35, 44, 71, 74-76, 90, 102, 120-121, 123-124, 210, 277-278, 386, 517, 533, 550-551, 607*

abrogating, *35, 70-71, 74-76, 90*
Abrogation, *14, 16, 20-21, 44-45, 66-67, 69-76, 78, 104, 108, 119-120, 122, 136-139, 143, 150, 200, 204, 209, 213, 277-278, 292, 384-386, 394, 498, 536, 551, 617, 662, 694*
absence of facts, *380, 446, 473-476, 479, 483*
Abu al-Walid Muhammad ibn Ahmad Ibn Rushd, *731-732*
Abu Bakr, *132, 601, 674, 730*
Abu Dawud, *39, 51-52, 81, 102, 607, 617-618, 707, 720*
Abu Dhabi, *371*
Abu Ghraib, *429*
Abu Hamid Muhammad al-Ghazali, *95, 178, 688*
Abu Hanifa, *80, 99, 611, 621, 723, 732*
Abu Huraira, *83, 548*
Abu Hurrairah 'Abdur Rahman bin Sakhar Dasi, *38*
Abu Mus'ab Al-Suri, *400, 620, 647, 665, 699*
Abu Musab al-Zarqawi, *47, 149, 203, 213, 612, 645*
Abu Said Al-Khudri, *546*
Abu Salama, *103*
Abu Sayyaf, *18, 601, 674*
Abubaker al Shingieti, *528-529, 532, 723*
academia, *183, 250, 358, 366, 644, 663, 686, 745*
Ackerman, Spencer, *377-379, 691-693, 717*
ACLU, *378, 640, 692*
ACMCU, *585, 739*
action-reaction cycle, *432, 440*
ADAMS Center, *529*
Adel-Hakim Al-Hadisi, *215*
adulterer, *233, 235, 704*
adultery, *79, 234, 237, 572-573,*

613

Afghan, *46, 409-413, 415-422, 424-426, 429-434, 436, 439-441, 487, 663, 683, 703-704, 709*

Afghan Air Force, *416-419*

Afghan Air Force Criminal Investigation Division, *417*

Afghan National Army, *411-412, 418, 425, 631*

Afghan National Police (ANP), *411-412, 425*

Afghanistan, *27, 61-63, 99, 193, 204, 207, 215, 223, 233, 246, 266, 290, 322, 337, 384-386, 396, 407-416, 418-442, 454, 488, 560, 587, 615, 679, 683, 702-703, 705-706, 708-709, 711*

AFOSI Report of Investigation, *417*

Africa, *81, 119, 150-151, 282, 288, 319, 507, 647-649, 721*

African, *89, 306, 740*

agent, *23, 170, 337, 360, 382, 508, 682, 702, 714*

Agents, *15, 20-21, 23, 28, 340, 344, 348, 356, 358, 371-372, 379, 381, 385, 401, 404-406, 423, 495-496, 604, 641, 691-692, 702*

Agents of Radicalization, *371*

ahkam, *57, 99, 621*

Ahmad Haroun, *529, 723*

Ahmad ibn Muhammad ibn Hanbal, *621*

Ahmad ibn Naqib al-Misri, *37, 67, 84, 607, 611, 679, 719-720, 730*

Ahmad Kutty, *364-365*

Ahmad Zaki Hammad, *172*

Ahmed Alaibah, *326*

Ahmed Gul, *416-421*

Ahmed Minni, *201*

Ahmed Yousef, *315*

Ahmet Davutoglu, *327*

AhramOnline, *312, 681*

air command and control center (ACCC), *416-419, 421, 705*

Air Expeditionary Wing (AEW), *417-418*

Air Force Office of Special Investigation (AFOSI), *416-417, 705*

Airmen, *411, 416, 703-705*

airport, *292, 416-417, 419, 423, 641, 677, 705*

Akba Jihad Jordan, *360*

Akhirah, *199, 645*

AKP (Turkish Justice and Development Party), *288, 662*

Akram, *18, 24, 155, 162, 168, 173-174, 315, 318, 601, 605-606, 608-609, 620, 630, 633, 636-637, 639-640, 643-644, 654, 660, 673, 680-681, 683, 690, 698-699, 701, 713, 715, 719-723, 741*

Al Aqsa, *166*

Al Qaeda al-Muslamina al-Moltzema, *344*

Al-Akhbar, *186, 643*

al-Arian, Sami, *173, 315, 324, 639*

Al-Azhar University, *152, 213, 284, 607, 679, 740*

Al-Azl (i.e., coitus interruptus), *546*

Al-Baghdadi, *117, 123, 554, 625-626, 628, 731*

Al-Bara bin Azib, *94, 728*

Al-Hafiz Abu al-Fida' 'Imad Ad-Din Isma'il bin 'Umar bin Kathir Al-Qurashi Al-Busrawi ibn Kathir, *533-534, 625, 730*

Al-Hidayah by al-Marghinani, *40, 67, 90, 557, 610, 616-617, 640, 732*

Al-Marghinani, Burhan al-Din al-Farghani, *610, 616, 732*

Al-Masjid Al-Haram, *87*

Al-Mughni, *47, 237*

Al-Muwatta of Imam Malik ibn Anas, *623, 723*

al-Nusrah Front, *217*

al-Qaeda [also al-Qaida], *12-14,*

Index

16-18, 24, 26, 28, 32, 47, 57, 61,
63, 65-67, 76-77, 95, 97, 100,
102, 121, 136, 139, 143, 149-151,
172, 185, 194, 202-205, 207,
209, 211-213, 215-217, 229-230,
237-238, 240, 242, 245-247,
256, 258, 264, 281, 283, 293,
321-322, 331, 333, 339,
343-346, 348, 351-356, 359,
367, 374, 377, 383, 387-389,
391, 394-398, 400-401,
403-406, 409, 416, 422, 425,
427-430, 432, 435, 441-442,
451, 455, 457-458, 460, 465,
469, 479-480, 495, 503,
507-509, 515, 559, 575, 601,
606, 620, 629, 641, 645-648,
663, 674-675, 689, 691, 693,
697-698, 701, 707, 726
al-Qaeda and Associated
  Movements (AQAM), 202
al-Sarakhsi, 99
Al-Tabari, 288
Al-Talib, 374-375, 639, 689-690
Al-Uthaymeen, 52, 613
Al-Zawahiri Letter to Abu Musab
  al-Zarqawi, 149
Alaq, 36
Alawsat, 324, 663, 676
Albania, 576, 678, 740-741
Alexander the Great, 65, 616
Alexandria, Virginia, 201
Ali al-Hudaify, 281
Ali Bardakoglu, 287
Alinskiism, 303
Alinskyist, 23, 379, 586
All Dulles Area Muslim Society,
  370
Allah's sovereignty, 137, 139-140
Allahu Akbar, 20, 256, 403
Allen, John, 418, 434, 437
Almoudi, 172, 216
Alomari, Omar, 371
Aman Hassan Yemer, 201
Amana Trust, 183, 528
AMC, 403

American Muslim Armed Forces
  and Veterans Affairs Council
  (AMAFVAC), 402, 404
American Muslims for
  Constructive Engagement
  (AMCE), 528-529, 723
American Trust Publications
  (ATP), 137, 162, 362-363, 517,
  602, 629, 632-633, 653, 721
Amin, 398, 638-639
Amos, James, 408
Amoudi, 174
Amsterdam, 295, 298, 666
Andalus [now Spain], 68
Andalusia [Spain], 204
Andalusian, 96
Anglo-Saxon, 128
Anjem Choudary, 442
Ankara, 125, 664, 739
Annandale, Virginia, 167
anti-American, 419, 432
anti-Americanism, 429, 690
anti-blasphemy, 313, 327, 677
anti-imperialist, 376
anti-Islamophobia, 316, 381, 465,
  580, 584, 586, 595-596, 740
anti-Muslim, 294, 378, 403, 593,
  678, 744
anti-Semitism, 269, 527, 576-577,
  602, 660-661, 737-738, 745
Anwar Al-Awlaki, 374, 386,
  388-389, 391, 395, 442, 696-697
AOL/Time Warner, 321
Apaches, 413
apes and pigs, 124
apes and swine, 124
apes are Jews, 124
apostasy, 19, 39, 45, 54, 112-113,
  144, 234, 250-253, 278, 331,
  435, 520, 529, 612, 624, 658,
  662, 679, 709
apostate, 19, 26, 288, 331, 561,
  603, 733
Apostolic Exhortation Evangelii
  Gaudium, 543, 726
appellate court, 168

Index

Apples and Oranges, *523, 558*
Appropriations Bill, *372*
Aqidah, *199, 645*
Aqsa, *166, 238, 531, 724*
Arab League, *207, 220, 283, 731*
Arab nation, *204, 602*
Arab News, *279, 281, 284-285,
316-317, 320, 662-664, 673-674,
679, 735*
Arab Spring, *47, 209, 211, 215-216*
Arabian Peninsula, *151, 196-197,
205, 212, 214, 323, 368, 551,
601, 612, 647, 674*
Arabic, *32, 36, 58, 60, 62, 67-68,
70, 81, 115, 170, 173, 176-177,
213, 215, 280, 319-320, 322,
349, 374, 466-467, 534, 553,
555, 603, 608, 610, 625-627,
654-655, 662, 674, 679-680,
720-721, 724, 727-728, 740*
Arafat, Yasser, *81-82, 618*
Archbishop of Canterbury, *429*
Aristotelian, *523*
Aristotle, *523*
Arlington Heights, Illinois, *525*
Arlington, Virginia, *527*
Armed anthropological field
studies, *461*
armed forces, *379, 402-403, 416,
431-432, 451, 495, 616*
Armenian genocide, *95, 525*
Army Field Manual 34-130,
Intelligence Preparation of the
Battlefield (FM 34-130, IPB)
[IPB], *445, 447, 458-459,
496-497, 711*
ARTICLE 19, *248, 303-304, 328,
330, 586, 588-589, 668, 742-743*
Article 20 [ICCPR], *305*
Article 20 Section 2, *306, 308*
Article 22 [Cairo Declaration], *305*
Articles 19 and 20 of the ICCPR,
304
Articles 24/25 Rule, *306*
Articles of Incorporation, *404, 671*
as-Salamu 'alaykum, *113, 572*

Asaf A.A. Fyzee, *35, 55, 607, 723*
Ascribing Associates to Allah, *112,
624*
Asharq Al-Awsat, *280, 645, 663,
671*
Ashrafuzzaman Khan, *193*
Asif Ali Zardari, *327, 428, 677*
Asma, *253-254*
Assad, *216-217, 642, 648-650*
Assembly of Muslim Jurists of
America (AMJA), *58-60, 614-615*
Association (Group) of Legal
Specialists in Shari'a Law in
America, *60*
Association of Muslim Scholars
(IAMS or IUMS), *18, 110, 217,
240, 323, 330-331, 589, 624,
676, 679, 743*
Association of Muslim Social
Scientists (AMSS), *528, 602,
723, 741*
assumed to be true in the absence
of facts, *474*
assumptions and presuppositions,
226, 472-473, 478, 500, 713
Assyrian Catholic, *525*
Assyrian nation, *525*
Astana, Kazakhstan, *595*
asymmetrical warfare, *15*
atheism, *531, 724*
atheists, *281*
Aulaqi [also Awlaki], *388, 394*
Australia, *224*
Austria, *580, 738, 741*
Averroës, *68*
Awad, Nihad, *169-170, 314-317,
340, 376, 398, 603, 671, 673,
675, 691*
Ayaan Hirsi Ali, *294, 666*
Ayatollah, *225, 288, 652*
Ayatollah Ruhollah Khomeini,
225, 288-289, 652
Aydinlikas, *597*
Azhar, *18-19, 47, 152, 207-208,
213, 238, 241, 284, 322,
331-332, 532, 543, 554-556, 561,*

Index

603, 607-608, 654, 679-681,
719-720, 727, 731, 733, 740
Azimi, Gen. Zahir, 417

B

Bachmann, Congresswoman
Michele, 336-338, 459-460,
682-683, 712
Bacon, Kevin, 350
bad cop, 323, 330-331, 593
Baghdadi, 117, 123, 554, 625-626,
628, 731
Bagram Airbase, 432-433,
436-437, 466, 587
Bahrain, 279, 282, 663, 678
balance, 16, 51, 61, 206, 219, 240,
380, 437, 460, 462-465,
482-483, 486, 727
Baltimore, 540, 612, 624, 636,
732, 737
Bamako, Mali, 227, 271-272, 579,
588, 652, 660-661, 677, 738, 743
Bandar al Ayban, 280
Bangladesh, 192-193, 425, 644
Bani Hashim, 569
Bani Muttalib, 569
Banu Al-Mustaliq, 546
Banu Khatma, 254
Banu Qurayza, 577, 737
Baqara, 244
Barbary wars, 210, 646
Barnes and Noble Standard, 33-34
Bartholomew, 563, 565
Bassem Osman, 172
Bassoon, Waleed, 376
Batil, 195-196
battalion, 186, 449, 601, 674
Battalions, 186-187, 520, 634
Battered Wife Syndrome, 285,
306, 423, 496, 498, 509
Bayesian model, 446
BDS, 527
Bedouins, 111, 134

Behavioral Analysis Units, 600
behavioral indicator, 352
behavioral indicators, 348,
352-353, 367, 449, 498, 500
Belgium, 261, 601, 674, 676
Beliefnet, 520
Benghazi, 215, 267, 327, 329,
460-461, 712
Bethesda, Maryland, 384
Bewley, Aisha, 533, 616
Bey of Morocco, 210
Bible, 34, 38, 625, 627
bid'a, 52-54, 140-141
Bidah: The Unique Nature of the
Perfection Found in Islaam and
the Grave Danger of Innovating
It, 52
Bidayat al-Mujtahid wa Nihayat
al-Muqtasid (The Distinguished
Jurist's Primer), 556, 731-732
bigotry, 323, 432, 536, 707
Bil-Akhirah, 199, 645
Bill of Rights, 354-355
billion Muslims, 279, 284-287,
291, 430, 664
bin Laden, Osama, 26, 46, 65, 194,
204, 206-207, 237, 242,
245-247, 375, 397, 405, 507,
529, 606, 616, 644, 646, 696,
701
binding, 35-37, 70, 84, 100, 103,
574, 576, 622, 631, 635, 732
Bingham, Beth, 256
bint Marwan, 254
biological basis, 271-272, 326, 579,
588
biology, 272
Biyikli, Ozbil, 597, 744, 746
blasphemy, 35, 47, 75, 119, 248,
250-253, 257, 259, 263, 265,
267-268, 279, 283, 285-286,
290, 297, 301, 303, 305, 307,
309, 311, 313, 315, 317, 319, 321,
323-325, 327, 329, 331, 333,
339, 415, 434-436, 438, 472,
535, 538, 658, 663-664, 668,

Index

675, 677, 709-710
Blaze, The, *394, 638, 650, 691, 699*
Bloomberg, *321, 674*
Boehner, John, *336*
Boim, David, *172, 315, 638, 671, 690*
Boko Haram, *18, 540, 546, 563, 601, 674*
Bolshevik, *142, 191*
Bolshevism, *190*
Boston Marathon, *95, 399-401, 404-405, 503, 542, 698*
Boston Marathon bomber, *399*
Boston Marathon Bombing, *400, 404-405, 503, 542, 699*
Brandeis University, *283*
Brennan, John, *21, 378-379, 604, 692*
Brian Jenkins, *197, 644*
Bridgeview Mosque, *324, 374-375, 676*
Britain, *269, 289, 291, 601, 674, 740*
British, *94, 155, 215, 269, 291-292, 296, 425, 429, 681*
British High Commissioner, *291*
Brohi, *133*
Brookings Doha Center, *305, 669*
Brookings Institution, *308-309, 669*
Brothers, *17, 92, 94, 151-152, 165, 170, 177, 187, 190, 192, 205, 210-211, 215, 316, 342, 344, 399-401, 404, 406, 470, 518-519, 566, 608, 631-632, 635, 647, 680*
Brussels, *597, 662, 666, 676, 744*
Buckley, Lance Corporal Gregory, *421, 704, 706*
Buddhist, *588*
Bulent Senay, *744-746*
burden of proof, *61, 78, 108, 125, 463, 469, 712*
burden-shifting, *608, 680*
Burns, Lara, *170*
Bursa, Turkey, *594, 745*

Bylaws, *317, 606, 645, 673, 722*
Byzantine Emperor Manuel II Paleologus, *287*

C

Cain, *233-234*
Cairo, *117, 141, 151, 163, 209-211, 224, 226-229, 239, 241, 248, 268, 276, 284, 297, 303-305, 308, 315, 321-322, 325-327, 358, 415, 430, 440, 515, 555, 575, 579, 584, 587, 592, 607, 619, 625, 629, 640, 644, 646, 652-653, 669-670, 672, 675-677, 679, 681, 704, 710, 721, 739-740, 743-744*
Cairo Declaration on Human Rights in Islam, *226-227, 358, 415, 515, 575, 579, 652-653, 669, 704, 739, 743-744*
Cairo Embassy, *325-326, 440, 675*
Cairo University, *209, 211, 740*
Caldwell, Lt Gen, *418, 421*
California, *322, 325, 329, 342, 372, 374-375, 399, 455, 526, 678, 689, 697*
caliph, *81, 118, 132, 151, 253, 307, 345, 433, 439, 549, 573, 618, 624, 627, 694, 707, 720, 730*
caliphate, *16, 27, 30, 46, 54, 89-90, 92-93, 144, 146, 150-151, 153, 182, 193, 203, 212-213, 219, 221, 223-225, 227-229, 231, 233, 235, 237, 239-241, 243, 245, 247, 249, 251, 253, 255, 257, 259, 261, 349, 367, 377, 382, 428, 486, 554, 612, 619-620, 630-631, 642, 651, 655, 665, 691-693*
calumny, *271, 598*
Cameron, David, *332, 429*
Canada, *224, 319, 679, 697, 707, 721*

Index

capitalism, *158, 220*
Capitol Hill, *214, 336-337, 374,*
477, 660, 689, 697
Caprioli, Ettore, *290*
captured women, *555, 569*
Cartoon Crisis
  cartoon, *256, 263-264, 266,*
  279, 281, 283-285, 287, 290,
  307, 313, 322, 327-329, 332,
  415, 426, 430, 499, 662-663
  cartoonists, *256, 283, 566*
Casey, George, *335*
cast terror, *134-135, 538, 561-562,*
577
Cat Stevens [now Yusuf Islam],
289
categorization, *141*
Catholic canon, *228*
Catholic University of America,
114, 726
Catholic-Muslim Dialogue, *527,*
530
Catholicism, *200*
Caucasus, *204, 399-400, 601, 674*
cause-in-fact, *459, 503*
censorship, *279, 321, 346, 379, 522*
Center for Interfaith Studies and
  Dialogue (CSID), *183, 216, 514,*
  527-528
Center for Media and
  Communications Studies, *303,*
  586, 668, 742-743
Center for Security Policy (CSP),
  10, 15, 600, 660-661, 673, 682,
  688, 737-739
Center for the Study of Islam and
  Democracy, *216*
Center of gravity, *411, 429, 432,*
  438, 473, 704
Central Command, *413, 441, 482,*
  663-664
Central European University, *303,*
  586, 588, 668, 742-743
chain of transmission, *39, 609*
Challenges Facing Muslims in
  Europe, *273, 578, 661, 737-738*

Chaplain, *243, 374, 402, 404, 407,*
  437, 709
chaplains, *402-404, 437-438*
Charlie Hebdo, *256, 266, 283,*
  293, 311, 321, 329-332, 426,
  428, 431, 441, 481, 493,
  566-567, 589, 596, 657, 664,
  670, 678-679, 743
Charter of the Organisation of the
  Islamic Conference, *606, 612, 651,*
  673, 684
chastity, *570-571*
Chaudhry, Umer Farooq, *201*
Chechen, *399, 405, 601, 674, 698*
Chechnya, *150*
Cherthoff, Michael, *348*
Chesapeake Bay Bridge, *167*
Chicago, *167, 172, 319, 372,*
  374-375, 398, 402, 525, 631,
  635, 638, 671, 673, 676, 690
Children, *61, 69, 111-112, 115, 177,*
  214, 233, 253-254, 293, 451,
  483, 535, 538, 552, 555, 565,
  568, 572, 577, 632, 634, 641, 734
Chinese, *455, 726*
Christ, *39, 110, 535, 557, 563, 727*
Christian, *34, 63, 73, 96, 114-115,*
  120, 122, 126, 128, 183, 194,
  225, 246, 251, 270, 277, 285,
  315-316, 322, 381, 387, 428, 513,
  519, 525-528, 530-532, 535,
  538, 540-541, 543-544, 548,
  551, 553-556, 559-561, 588, 610,
  625, 642, 647, 656, 663, 673,
  675, 689, 709, 722, 725-727,
  733-734
Christian community, *525*
christianists, *128*
Christianity, *34, 119, 121-123, 128,*
  194-195, 222, 277-278, 386, 519,
  533, 541, 564, 571, 662, 724
Christians, *66-67, 73, 76-77, 95,*
  111, 113-114, 116-118, 120-121,
  123-128, 130, 132, 225-226, 237,
  246, 269, 281, 307, 355, 381,
  387, 389, 393, 429, 438, 520,

524-535, 537-538, 540,
548-554, 557-558, 563-566, 571,
624-628, 662, 664, 675,
693-694, 724, 730-731, 734, 740
church, 32, 111, 113, 119, 239, 381,
428, 525, 527, 537, 539, 541,
544, 552-553, 555, 559-560,
572, 627, 691, 697, 703,
726-727, 733
Churchill, Winston, 296, 667
CIA, 21, 329, 340, 376, 388, 396,
459-460, 642, 683, 690-691,
696-697, 702, 712
CID, 417, 423
circumcision, 555
citizenship, 319, 520
civil liberties, 23, 130, 312, 341,
348, 350, 353-354, 356-357,
370-371, 376, 378, 489, 493,
586, 605-606, 661, 670, 682,
684-685, 687, 716-718, 738-739,
741
civil rights, 23, 306, 312, 315, 341,
348, 350, 353-354, 356-357,
370-371, 373, 376, 489, 493,
515, 586, 605-606, 641, 670,
682, 684-685, 687, 692,
716-718, 741
civil society, 339, 511, 668, 742
civilization-jihad, 12, 339, 465,
505, 541
civilizational, 23, 175, 567
Clausewitz, 459, 616
cleaving from the mainstream, 31,
76
Clinton, Bill, 403
Clinton, Hilary, 216, 308-314, 321,
329, 402-403, 590, 605, 648,
669-670, 678, 682, 700, 710
clitoris, 555
clutches, 140
CNN, 215, 321, 645, 647-648, 663,
665, 671, 678, 691, 698, 704-705
Coalition Forces, 215, 408, 419,
439
code, 40-41, 50, 57, 159, 169, 257,

272, 331, 342, 357, 436, 494,
653, 665, 683, 685, 716, 726-727
coercion, 146, 260, 307, 342-343,
368, 540, 630
coerciveness, 540
cognitive dissonance, 292
coitus interruptus, 546
COJEP, 595, 745
Cold War, 446, 449
colonialism, 188, 204, 339
Columbus, 525, 537, 539-540,
544, 725
combat defamation of Islam, 297
combat Islamophobia, 263, 468, 493,
591
combating defamation of religions,
261, 273, 658-659, 677
combating intolerance, 302, 306,
577, 581, 584-585, 587,
589-590, 592, 737, 739-740
combating Islamophobia, 276, 278,
302, 326, 341, 382, 493,
595-596, 605, 661-662, 668,
677, 745
combating religious hatred,
590-591
combating religious intolerance,
325, 605, 670, 682, 710
Comey, 406
Comey, James, 406
COMISAF, 411-412, 416, 419, 441,
703-705, 709-710
COMISAF Counterinsurgency
Guidance, 411, 416
COMISAF Guidance, 411-412, 419
Command and General Staff
College, 472, 479, 711, 713
commentator, 232, 282, 611
Commission for Christian-Muslim
Understanding, 530
Commission for Jewish Muslim
Understanding, 530
Commssion on Christian-Muslim
Relations (CCMR), 527, 530
compact of submission, 115, 250
competent analysis, 228, 231, 463,

504
competent threat analysis, *12, 88,*
108, 184, 503-504
competing analysis, *23, 462-463,*
469
competing interpretations, *51,*
420, 515
complexity, *452, 454-459, 462,*
466, 471, 482-483, 486, 582, 712
Conclusions and
Recommendations Emanating
from the Four Regional Expert
Workshops Organised by
OHCHR, *587*
conclusory assumption, *226, 508,*
543
Congress, *14-15, 21, 24, 146, 151,*
169, 179, 214, 296, 320, 336,
344, 357, 372-373, 378-379, 417,
431-432, 437, 469-470, 477,
490, 494, 529, 589, 602, 604,
624, 682, 687, 692, 707, 716
Congressional Committees,
379-380, 498, 693, 717
Congressional Hearings, *345, 604,*
641, 643, 685, 692, 711, 717-718
Congressional Muslim Staffers
Association, *374*
Connecticut, *372*
Conquest, *545, 584-585, 672*
conscientious objectors, *386*
Constantinople, *287, 563*
constitution, *16, 22, 47, 55, 61-62,*
114, 164, 192, 195, 224, 228,
239, 248, 264, 280, 308,
312-313, 319, 332-333, 335, 337,
354-355, 357, 375, 382, 404,
409-410, 412, 415-416, 421-422,
426-427, 429, 431, 436-437,
439, 441, 451, 482, 486-497,
505, 509, 581, 612, 615, 625,
641, 692, 700, 702, 716, 726
constitutional, *22, 28, 55, 63, 239,*
256, 258, 308, 311-312, 321, 341,
348, 354, 356-358, 382, 407,
415, 431, 435, 437, 440, 471-472,

482, 485-486, 488, 491,
493-497, 499, 501, 505, 509,
585, 654, 657
constitutionally protected, *23,*
276, 312, 347, 356-357, 489
Constitutions, *46, 61-63, 228, 487,*
615
constructive fraud, *478, 714*
Constructively, *306*
Contemporary Forms of Racism,
271-272, 326, 579, 588, 660,
677, 743
continuous process of warfare, *79,*
91, 110
Convention for the Protection of
Human Rights and Fundamental
Freedoms, *580-581*
convergence, *26, 209, 217, 246,*
264-265, 267, 323, 330, 332,
377, 396
conversion, *96, 134, 195, 513, 548,*
556
converting, *200-201, 306*
Cook, Suzan Johnson, *310*
Cooper, Sheldon, *464*
Copenhagen, *426, 428, 431, 441,*
567, 596
Coptic, *63, 113-114, 117, 322, 625,*
675
Copts, *114, 117, 121, 625, 675-676*
Cordoban, *68*
core values, *22-23, 200, 303,*
357-358, 378-379, 415, 436,
486-487, 499, 510
correlation of forces, *142*
corruptio optima pessima, 443
corruption, *162, 179, 206, 245,*
247, 542, 693, 722
Coughlin, Stephen, *10, 376,*
599-600, 612, 686, 691, 695,
705, 715, 745
Council of Europe, *581, 590, 593*
Council of Islamic Organizations of
Greater Chicago (CIOGC), *374,*
690

Council on American Islamic
  Relations, *18-19, 168-171, 175,
  180, 183, 185, 217, 258, 294,
  314-317, 320, 324-325, 330,
  332, 338, 340, 344, 353-354,
  364-365, 367, 370-374, 376,
  398-399, 402-403, 407, 434,
  514-515, 527-528, 543, 601-602,
  604, 637, 641, 671, 673-674,
  676, 681, 683, 685-691, 698, 740*
Counter Insurgency (COIN),
  *407-412, 414-416, 423, 426,
  428-429, 431-432, 434-436,
  438-441, 454, 702, 709*
Counter Insurgency Strategy, *407*
counterdrug mission, *357*
counterfactual, *31, 61, 339,
  465-467*
countering Islamophobia, *382,
  490, 494*
Countering Violent Extremism, *21,
  312, 337, 344, 348-349,
  354-356, 358-359, 369-371,
  376-378, 451, 489, 495, 503,
  509, 605-606, 670, 682,
  684-685, 687, 689, 692, 716, 718*
Countering Violent Extremism
  Training Guidance & Best
  Practices, *354*
counterinsurgency, *407-408,
  410-411, 416, 440, 702-705,
  709-710*
counterterror, *17, 19, 23, 46, 184,
  258, 312, 336, 338, 340, 354,
  356, 375, 378-379, 382, 401,
  405, 407, 599-600, 702*
counterterror analysis, *17, 23*
counterterrorism, *15, 21, 23, 229,
  239, 247, 257, 340-341, 343,
  345-347, 349, 368, 371, 374,
  376-378, 382, 388, 406-407,
  604, 620, 629, 656, 683-684,
  688, 692, 694, 696, 711, 714*
countless superficial information
  bits, *454*
course of action, *173, 209, 448,*

472-474, 478, 496, 713
Courses of Action (COAs), *29, 63,
  144, 184, 229, 352, 359, 380,
  444-446, 448-450, 465, 496,
  498, 504, 530*
covenant, *84, 103, 116-117, 124,
  163, 283, 303-305, 329, 397,
  546, 549, 586-587, 589, 627,
  635, 663, 669, 696, 729, 742*
Criminal Patronage Network,
  418-419
criminalization, *301, 584-585,
  590-591*
cross, *126-127, 191, 315, 386-387,
  491, 548, 625, 729*
Crown Prince of Saudi Arabia, *403*
crucifix, *114*
crucifixion, *233, 240*
Crusaders, *46, 66, 76, 202, 612,
  654, 656, 704, 709*
Crusades, *288*
culminating point, *194-195, 445*
cultural experts, *13, 54, 62, 67, 70,
  77, 257, 467-468, 471, 475*
culturally insensitive, *419, 423,
  434*
Cumber, Sada, *313*
Curran, John Philpot, *575*
Czerwinski, Tom, *456, 711-712*

D

Da'ee Ilallah, *513*
Dagestan, *400, 624, 698*
Daher, Mimi, *285*
Dallas, *19, 149, 370, 520, 603-604,
  631, 635-638, 640-641, 666,
  671, 687-688, 691*
Damascus, *207, 283, 613-614, 621,
  631*
Danes, *285*
Danger Room, *379, 498, 691-693,
  717*

Index

Dangerous Alliances: The Scandal of US Government Muslim Outreach, *339*

Danish, *255, 263, 266, 279, 282-283, 295, 299, 328, 662-664, 745*

dar al-Hijrah Mosque, *32*

Dar Al-Ifta, *332, 727*

Darfur, *95, 528*

Darussalam, *68, 116, 533-534, 544, 569, 616, 625, 628, 657, 678, 686, 704, 727, 730, 735*

database, *400, 698*

dawa (dawah), *26-27, 90, 92, 98, 106, 117, 127-136, 153-155, 157, 164, 185, 187-190, 192-204, 209, 212, 223, 256, 264-265, 282, 287, 307, 314, 330-331, 333, 363, 365-368, 384, 396, 401, 406, 437, 481, 483, 486, 505, 511-513, 515, 524-525, 531, 541, 567, 586, 628, 644-645, 660, 719, 722*

Dawah Ilallah, *131, 194, 198, 513, 628, 644, 660*

Day of Resurrection, *199, 546, 564*

Day(s) of Rage, *15, 264-267, 269, 271, 273, 275, 277, 279, 281-289, 291, 293, 295, 297, 299, 302, 304, 306-307, 322, 324, 327, 329, 332, 414-415, 426-433, 435, 437-438, 441, 466, 481, 499, 509, 536-537, 567, 587, 593, 660, 664*

Dean, Howard, *256, 311, 657, 670*

Dearborn, Michigan, *323, 676*

death, *38, 79, 118-119, 164, 194, 252-254, 265, 279, 288, 290, 292, 294-295, 331, 384, 396, 399, 412, 420, 435, 439, 459, 483, 548, 560, 568, 577, 610, 634, 644-645, 650, 665-666, 671, 675, 694, 704, 706, 709, 730*

deceit, *112, 181, 552*

deception, *178-179, 182, 185, 396, 518, 542*

deceptive mirage, *356, 495*

decision support, *209, 258*

Decisionmakers, *13, 15-16, 21, 23, 28, 32, 41, 51, 67, 75-76, 92, 128, 182, 198, 200, 220, 238, 254, 293, 333, 341, 343, 382, 432, 446, 452, 458, 462, 467, 470-471, 477-478, 482, 491, 501, 504*

decisionmaking, *11, 13-14, 25, 29, 34, 61, 63, 108, 137, 173, 182, 184, 195, 239, 320, 335, 339, 375, 394, 409, 414, 445, 448, 452-458, 463-465, 467-471, 473, 479-482, 498-501*

Declaration of Jihad against Jews and Crusaders World Islamic Front, *46*

Declaration of the Pontifical Council for Interreligious Dialogue, *554, 568, 731-733, 735*

deconstructionism, *268, 472*

defamation of Islam, *118-119, 252, 265, 271, 275, 278, 297, 326, 331, 426, 598, 669*

defamation of religions, *259-261, 266, 272-273, 301, 314, 326-327, 330, 579, 658-660, 677, 738*

Defense Department Command and Control Research Program, *456, 711-712*

Defense Human Resources Activity (DHRA), *197-198, 645*

Defense Intelligence Agency (DIA), *405, 444, 599, 701*

deference, *62, 501, 523*

delegate, *225, 229, 377, 652, 713*

delegated, *57, 91, 635, 713*

delegitimization, *406*

deliberate decisionmaking process, *445, 448*

democracy, *56, 205, 211, 216, 311, 325-326, 349, 372, 409, 440, 638, 646, 649, 668, 675, 741-742*

Democrat, *337, 462*

democratic, *53, 55, 57, 61, 100,*

140, 151, 211, 256, 295, 325, 336,
576, 658, 666, 668, 738, 742
demoralization, 134-135
demoralized, 134-135, 202
Dempsey, Martin, 379-380,
423-424
denial, 158, 178, 272, 394-395,
562-563, 566, 609-610
Denmark, 279-280, 283-284, 601,
662, 674, 745
denouncing, 403, 558
Deobandis, 98
Department Chair of Psychiatry at
Walter Reed, 385
Department of Defense (DoD),
20-21, 69, 185, 336, 346, 350,
352-353, 367, 376, 378-379,
386, 403-404, 454, 456, 485,
487, 495, 498-499, 509, 514,
682, 684, 706, 711-712, 716-717
Department of Homeland Security
(DHS), 19, 23, 185, 250,
312-313, 336-337, 340-341,
343-344, 348, 350, 353-356,
359-360, 364, 368-372,
376-378, 380, 383, 489, 493,
495, 497, 503, 508, 514,
604-606, 643, 670, 682,
684-685, 687-689, 692, 711,
716-718, 741-742
Department of Justice (DOJ), 336,
338, 360, 364, 366-367, 372,
374, 605, 638, 670-671,
682-684, 686-687, 700
Der Spiegel, 213, 647
designated terrorist, 164, 171, 325,
344, 397, 403
destruction of faith, 135, 541,
561-562
Dexter Standard, 34
dhimma compact, 118
Dhimmah, 116-117, 551, 553
dhimmi, 118-119, 251, 253, 267,
710
dhimmi compact, 253
dhimmification, 521

Dhimmis, 109, 252, 585
DHS Office of Civil Rights and
Civil Liberties (CRCL), 23, 341,
348, 350, 354-359, 369-370,
372-373, 376, 380-382, 489,
493, 503, 606, 682, 684-685,
687, 741-742
Diène, Doudou, 261
diety, 199
Diocese of Arlington, Virginia, 527
Diplomatic, Information, Military,
and Economic (DIME), 448
Director of National Intelligence
(DNI), 336-337, 645, 682, 684,
714
disbelief, 17, 20, 132, 158, 250-251,
435, 530, 613, 625
Discovery Channel, 33
disinformation, 108, 171, 406, 503,
514, 537, 557
dislocating the faith, 185
dislocation of faith, 133, 175, 512,
520, 523, 525-526, 531
disobedience, 53, 82, 179, 693
dissociation, 29, 566, 583
Distinguished Jurist's Primer, The,
68, 547, 556, 610, 616, 620,
731-732
Divi et Impera, 530
divine, 35, 39-40, 49, 70, 76-77,
100, 103, 125, 138, 143, 158, 197,
205, 241, 485, 492-493, 518,
535, 538, 550-551, 566, 721-722
divinely revealed, 126, 386, 549,
624
doctrinal template, 182, 184, 380,
445-450, 458, 498
Doctrine of Abrogation, 14, 20, 67,
70, 78, 104, 108, 139, 143, 150,
384
Doekle Terpstra, 295
Doha, 305, 330, 520, 669, 679,
721, 743
Domestic terrorism, 185, 337, 340,
342, 441
domestically and globally, 27, 269,

318, 470, 515
dominance, 126, 182
domination, 80, 425
downward subversion, 465, 497
Dubin Fellow, 374
due diligence, 63, 128, 207, 229,
   259, 342, 393, 395, 416, 470,
   502, 512, 521
Duffy, Kevin, 403
Dutch Public Prosecution, 296
duty to be competent, 499-500

E

Ecclesiastes, 335
economic deprivation, 30, 293, 461
Ecumenical Patriarch, 563, 735
Egypt, 17, 20, 27, 39, 62-63, 66,
   78, 110, 113, 116, 121, 137,
   141-142, 144-145, 150-151, 153,
   155, 162, 173, 177, 209, 214, 216,
   226, 241, 251, 290, 316,
   321-322, 327, 370-371, 373, 377,
   555, 601-603, 607, 615, 625,
   630-632, 639-640, 643,
   647-648, 669, 671, 674-675, 677,
   679, 704, 710-711, 727, 733,
   739-741, 743-744
Egyptian Islamic Jihad (EIJ), 141,
   203, 208, 321, 629, 646
Eikenberry, Karl, 408
Eisenhower, 456
El Fadl, 98, 601, 619, 621, 674
Elashi, Ghassan, 164-165
Elbarasse, Ismail, 167, 175
Elibiary, Mohamed, 19, 128, 224,
   358, 370-371, 376-378, 382,
   487, 603-604, 627, 686-689,
   691-692, 716
Ellison, Congressman Keith, 336,
   682-683
embargo, 21-22, 27, 378
Embassy of Sudan, 528

Embassy of the United States in
   Cairo, 325, 440
Emerick, Yahiya, 60, 69, 130, 253,
   322
Emerson, Steven, 309, 402, 650,
   699, 702
end-state, 76, 108, 138, 150
Enemy courses of action (E-COAs),
   184, 229, 352, 359, 446,
   448-450, 496, 504
enforcement, 14, 65, 153, 162,
   178-179, 182, 203, 220, 256-257,
   265, 275, 283, 312, 314, 332,
   336, 339-341, 343, 345,
   349-350, 354, 358, 364, 368,
   379-381, 387, 397-398, 401,
   403, 405, 407, 423, 434-435,
   441, 444, 451, 461, 465,
   482-483, 486, 493-495, 500,
   503, 517, 542, 602, 604, 606,
   641-642, 676-677, 688, 698, 739
enforcers, 335, 339, 376
England, 289, 292, 610, 616, 732,
   740-741
English, 16, 23, 32-33, 60-61, 81,
   94-95, 113, 154, 163, 176-177,
   186, 192, 195, 212, 240, 255,
   273, 277, 312, 333, 383, 395,
   428, 430, 466, 533, 544,
   605-608, 612, 624, 626-628,
   632, 640, 643, 646, 650-656,
   660-664, 666-667, 669,
   673-674, 676-677, 679-681, 684,
   686, 704, 707, 719-720,
   725-728, 730, 736, 738-739,
   742-744, 746
enjoining what is right, forbidding
   what is wrong, 130, 305, 389,
   620
enmity, 112, 210, 287, 420, 435,
   534, 552
Ennahda Party, 216, 649
Enormities, 112, 234-235, 609,
   624, 679
enslaved, 26, 206, 380
enslavement, 564

Index

envelopment, *333*
Erdogan, Recep Tayyip, *280, 322,*
 564-565, 595, 597, 662-663, 675
espionage, *337, 386*
Esposito, John, *315-316, 621,*
 671-673, 740
Essam El-Erian, *215*
establishment, *22, 98, 153-154,*
 157, 182, 187, 193, 217, 223, 230,
 305, 317-318, 336, 339, 341,
 369, 374, 377-378, 444, 455,
 459, 470, 485, 489-490, 492,
 586, 661, 704
ethnic, *261, 277, 312, 369,*
 399-400, 429, 448, 471, 558,
 687, 716
ethnicity, *344, 354*
etiquette, *58, 435, 522, 724*
European Convention on Human
 Rights, *580-581, 590*
European Council for Fatwa and
 Research (ECFR), *244, 281, 392,*
 655, 695
European Court of Human Rights,
 580, 737-738
European Muslim Initiative for
 Social Cohesion (EMISCO), *576,*
 593-596, 737, 744-746
European Union, *260, 302,*
 309-310, 313, 710
Evangel, *113, 121, 126, 387, 549,*
 572, 624
Evangelical, *541, 726*
Evangelicals, *128, 541*
evangelistic, *128*
every stratagem of war, *87, 122*
evidence, *12, 34, 43-44, 58, 61,*
 69-70, 99, 155, 161, 163-164,
 166-168, 171-172, 175, 178, 184,
 189-190, 214, 217, 224, 226,
 259, 261, 318, 328, 344, 346,
 353, 356, 359-360, 380,
 382-383, 394-395, 401,
 404-405, 414, 416-419,
 422-423, 436, 460, 464, 470,
 475, 480-481, 497, 502-504,

 508, 512, 514, 539, 551, 558,
 608, 611, 636, 652, 657-658,
 671, 680, 693, 712, 714, 717-718
exegesis, *102, 452, 607, 613*
existential threat, *332, 335, 478,*
 560
Explanatory Memorandum: On the
 General Strategic Goal for the
 Group, *18, 24, 27, 146-147, 155,*
 161-162, 167-169, 172-175,
 186-187, 192, 269, 315, 318, 339,
 343-344, 399, 402, 405, 465,
 481, 511-512, 514-515, 519, 528,
 601-602, 605-606, 608-609,
 620, 630, 633, 636-637, 640,
 643-644, 654, 660, 673,
 680-681, 683, 690, 698-699,
 701, 713, 715, 719-723, 741
Extortion 17, *413*
Extraordinary Session, *271, 301,*
 326, 481, 597, 605, 660-662,
 668, 677, 715, 746
extraterritorial, *302*

F

Facebook, *177, 406, 640, 647, 676,*
 683, 690-691, 701, 744
facially neutral, *129, 237, 247-248,*
 258, 303, 305-308, 381, 424,
 524, 531, 586, 589, 592
factual analysis, *15, 22-23, 33,*
 382, 455, 461-463, 467, 498,
 500, 503, 522
fainthearted, *80, 427, 516, 617-618*
faith, *34, 43, 53, 89-90, 119-121,*
 128, 130, 132-135, 137, 139, 144,
 156, 158-160, 162, 175, 177-178,
 182, 185, 187, 191, 195, 199-200,
 205-206, 208, 210, 215, 238,
 245, 250-251, 285, 287, 305,
 343, 355, 361-362, 389, 391,
 424, 431, 456, 490, 494, 497,
 510, 512-513, 518-523, 525-526,

528, 531-532, 534, 541-543,
549-551, 558-559, 561-562,
566-567, 601, 603, 608,
613-614, 620, 624, 627, 632,
635, 654-655, 674, 679, 688,
694, 724, 727, 735
Faith, Reason, and the University:
Memories and Reflections, 287
faithful, 84, 109, 111, 176, 178, 279,
354-355, 382, 501, 523, 525,
541, 543, 552, 559, 561-562,
564, 608, 620, 634, 680, 685,
693, 726-727
Falls Church, 32, 119, 697
falsity, 249, 381, 447
fanatic, 98
fanaticism, 125, 240, 242,
564-565, 627, 734
Farsi, 67
Fataawah, 355, 685, 693
fatawa [plural of fatwa], 90
Fateh Movement, 526-527
Fathi Yakan, 137, 155, 162, 174,
188, 629, 632-633
fatwa, 43, 46-47, 58, 90-95, 110,
163, 182, 213, 230-231, 237-238,
243-246, 281-282, 288-289,
292-293, 320, 354-356, 364,
382, 392, 416, 435, 609, 612,
614, 619-620, 624, 642, 648,
652, 654-656, 665-666, 681,
694-695, 698, 719-720
Fatwa Questions about Palestine,
244, 656, 698
Faysal Mawlawi, 244-245, 392,
656, 698
Fazalur Rehman, 291
FBI, 20-21, 23, 167, 170-171, 175,
179-180, 214, 314, 337-338,
342-348, 356-360, 364,
371-379, 383, 385, 388-389,
391-398, 400-407, 495, 508,
514, 600, 604, 638-639, 641,
670-671, 682-685, 688-694,
696-697, 699, 701-702, 714
FBI Citizens Academy, 374

federal crime of terrorism, 342
Feisal Abdul Rauf, 58
female genital mutilation, 555; see
also infibulation
Female Slaves, 569, 571
Ferguson, Missouri, 330
Fi Sabil Allah, 360, 686
fi sabili-llah (also fi sabilillah),
335, 359-360, 362-367, 379,
442, 449, 459
Fiegl, Harald, 580, 738
filmmaker, 266, 295, 329, 675, 678
filter, 447, 449, 503
Final Communique from the Third
Extraordinary Session, 326
final descent of Jesus, 126, 386,
549, 624
Finality of the Prophet's Message,
277, 662
finance, 57, 164, 167, 183, 210,
239, 636, 674
financing, 164, 172, 183, 375, 403,
636, 700
fiqh, 36, 172, 207, 216, 242-243,
245-247, 252, 354-356, 363,
382, 515, 556, 602, 607-608,
621, 638, 654-656, 680, 685,
693, 708-709, 719-720
Fiqh Council of North America
(FCNA), 172, 216, 242-243,
354-356, 382, 515, 556, 602,
608, 639, 654-655, 680, 685,
693, 719-720
firebombs, 288
fisabilillah, 360
Fitna, 295, 297, 299
Five Pillars, 100, 105, 526, 622
Fixed and Flexible Spheres, 49
fixed inner sphere, 50, 102, 270,
547
flattery, 356
flexible sphere, 45, 49, 622
Florida, 266, 286, 426, 428-431
Flynn, George, 380, 498
Foggy Bottom, 403, 700

Index

Forbidding Women Already Married, 569
Foreign Terrorist Organization (FTO), 124, 217, 397, 620, 629, 646, 649, 691
foreseeability, 14
Fortuyn, Pim, 294
Frankfurt, 405, 701
Franks, Trent, 312, 336, 605, 670, 682
Free Syrian Army, 18
Freedom and Justice Foundation, 370, 376, 603, 688
Freedom and Justice Party, 215, 315, 647
freedom of expression, 248, 250-251, 253, 256-257, 267, 280, 283, 297, 299, 304, 309-311, 313, 323-324, 326, 328-329, 355, 434, 493, 588, 593, 626, 656, 660, 709-710, 744
Freedom of Information Act (FOIA), 397, 417, 689, 696-697, 701
freedom of opinion, 248, 307, 588, 592
freedom of religion, 260, 309, 588, 594, 744
freedom of speech, 248, 298, 304, 311, 490, 567, 589, 678
Friday prayers, 76, 282, 374, 398, 430
fundamental transformation, 161
fundamentalism, 98, 125, 269, 511, 543, 564-566, 621

G

Gaffney, Frank, 10
Gallup, 371
Gamaa Islamiyya, 322
Gawthrop, William, 178, 640, 691
Gaza, 167, 315, 397, 607
Gehlen, Arnold, 454

gender, 339, 344, 354
general strategic goal, 18, 27, 155, 161, 174, 318, 601, 605-606, 608, 637, 654, 680, 719-720, 741
Genesis, 225-226, 233-234
genetic coding, 50
Geneva, 260, 286, 309, 591, 710, 740
genocide, 95, 444, 525, 528, 723
George Soros, 303, 330, 586, 588-589, 668, 742
Georgetown, 177, 183, 216, 243, 315-316, 528, 585, 640, 642, 655, 673, 689, 739-740
Gephardt, Richard, 325
Germany, 283, 287, 405, 601, 674, 701, 726, 740-741
Ghanem, Ibrahim, 155, 162, 455, 631-633, 640, 711
Ghannouchi, Rached, 216
Gharkad tree, 124-125, 547, 729
Ghazi, 422, 728
ghiba, 248
Ghulam Nabi Fai, 336-337, 404, 585, 683, 740-741
Gibbs, Robert, 214
gnostic, 453
Gnosticism, 15, 198
Gohmert, Congressman Louie, 336, 401, 682
Gokcen, Ufuk, 581, 589, 743
good cop, 265, 323, 330-331, 539
Good Soldier, A, 335
GOP, 358, 686
Gore, Vice President Al, 402
gospel, 84, 103, 128, 557, 563, 565, 726
Gospels, 39, 116, 128
governing authority, 221, 317, 551
Government of the Islamic Republic of Afghanistan (GIRoA), 410, 422, 426, 702
Graduate School of Islamic Social Science (GSISS), 514
Graham, Senator Lindsey, 431

Grand Imam Ahmed el-Yayyeb, 322
Green Cheese Doctrine, *448, 458, 496*
Green Quest, *183, 528*
Green Quest operation, *183, 528*
Green-on-Blue attacks, *418-419, 422, 424, 427, 704-707*
Greene, Harold, *418*
Gregorian University in Rome, *535*
Gríma Wormtongue, *563*
Ground Zero Mosque, *58*
Guidelines for Educators on Countering Intolerance and Discrimination against Muslims: Addressing Islamophobia through Education, *270, 581, 738*
Guillaume, Alfred, *132, 253, 628, 657, 675, 737*
Gulf Emirates, *193*

H

hadith, *35-41, 44, 48-52, 68, 83, 85-86, 88, 92, 94-95, 98-99, 102-104, 107, 111, 120-121, 123-125, 127-129, 178, 182, 235, 270, 277-278, 355, 361, 544-545, 547-548, 550, 552, 557, 560, 607, 609-611, 613-614, 618-621, 623, 627, 708-709, 723, 728*
Hague, *295, 595*
Hair, Connie, *10, 677*
hajj, *99, 105*
Haken al-Mutairi, *287*
Hakim, *101, 215, 607, 619, 727*
halacha, *228*
Halalco Supermarket, *32*
Hamas, *16, 18, 26, 82, 124-125, 163-169, 171-172, 175-176, 189, 203, 258, 314-316, 324, 344-345, 374-376, 397-398, 402-403, 405, 514, 535, 546,*
549, 627, 635-638, 643, 670-672, 696, 700, 729
Hamas conference, *169*
Hamda Al-Majid, *324*
Hampshire, *296*
Hamza Yusef, *399*
Hanbal, *45, 98, 613, 621*
Hanbalism, *53*
haqq Allah, *99, 612*
Haqqani Network, *18, 601, 674*
harbi, *78-79, 119, 181, 267, 710*
harmonized, *224*
Haroun, *529, 723*
Hasan Zamlot, *526*
Hasan, MAJ Nidal Malik, *14, 20-21, 72, 74, 127, 183, 232, 346, 350, 383, 387, 391, 395, 405, 421, 479, 559, 684, 694-695*
Hashir Faruqi, *289*
Hassan al-Banna, *147, 149, 151-153, 155, 160, 175, 186, 342, 631*
Hassan al-Hudaybi, *155*
hate, *59, 67, 77, 136, 266-267, 275, 295, 298, 310, 324, 327, 346, 448, 539, 567, 588, 591-593, 595-597, 614-615, 627, 666-667, 677-678, 739, 744-745*
Hate Crimes, *310, 595-596, 739, 745*
hate speech, *67, 77, 266, 295, 324, 327, 567, 588, 592, 666-667, 677-678*
hateful, *426, 511, 543, 562*
Hathout, Hassan and Maher, *342, 399*
hatred, *59, 204, 260, 271, 273, 283, 286-287, 295, 303-306, 323-326, 328, 332, 431, 434, 448, 564, 578, 581-582, 587, 590-594, 602, 658, 663, 667-669, 704-705, 743-744*
hearsay, *61, 469-470, 476, 496, 560*
hell, *43, 76, 112, 120-122, 126, 232, 244, 277, 385, 393, 524, 538,*

Index

564, 611, 728, 734
Hellfire, *159*
heresy, *52, 250-251, 435*
Herndon, *173, 183, 606, 639,*
642-643, 651, 719
Hezbollah, *217, 325, 345, 403,*
601, 650, 674
High Commissioner on Human
Rights, *586, 669, 743*
hijra, *212, 396-398, 697, 730*
Hijrah, *32, 551*
History of the Arab Peoples, A,
611, 613
Hitler [Adolf], *288, 444, 520,*
721-722
Hitoshi Igarashi, *290*
Hitto, Ghassan, *217, 649*
Hizb ut-Tahrir, *367-369, 372, 687*
Hodaiby, *155*
Hojatoleslam, *282*
Hojatoleslam Ahmad Khatami,
282, 288
Holder [Eric], *357, 642, 685, 691*
Holder v. Humanitarian Law
Project, *357, 685*
Holland, *294, 666-667, 670*
Holmes, Sherlock, *453*
Holy Land Foundation (HLF),
164-169, 171-172, 175, 189, 210,
314-315, 355, 368, 370-372, 374,
396, 402, 407, 514, 601,
605-606, 608, 635-638, 640,
643, 654, 657, 670-672, 680,
687-688, 690, 701, 719-720, 741
Holy See Bulletin, *554-556,*
558-560, 568, 711, 731-733, 735
Holy See Press Office, *554, 568,*
731-733, 735
holy war, *20, 29, 89, 109, 122, 130,*
162, 183-184, 631, 634
homicide detectives, *34*
homophobia, *268, 339, 745*
homosexual, *268, 294*
homosexuality, *571*
Hooper, Ibrahim, *294*
Hossam al-Jabri, *373, 689*

Hourani, Albert, *43, 611, 613*
House of Representatives., *345*
House Permanent Select
Committee on Intelligence
(HPSCI), *336-337, 401, 405,*
460-461
How Bad Definitions Violate
Fundamental OSCE
Commitments, *576, 661, 737-739*
hudna (ten-year truce), *81*
hudud, *99*
hukm (rule), *42, 99-101, 621*
Human Dimension
Implementation, *324, 593,*
660-661, 737-739, 744, 746
Human Events, *652, 677, 689, 697*
human rights, *14-15, 48, 114, 183,*
216, 224-231, 239, 248, 258,
260-261, 268, 272-273, 276,
283, 302, 305-306, 309-313,
315, 324-325, 328-329, 332,
358-359, 373, 378, 409, 415,
515, 519, 574-576, 578-581,
584-586, 588, 590, 595-596,
625, 641-642, 649, 652-653,
656, 658-659, 663, 668-670,
675, 678, 692, 704, 710,
736-740, 742-744
human terrain, *411, 455, 461, 704*
hurt feelings, *253, 284-285, 290,*
295, 326, 430
Hussain, Rashad, *314, 670*
HVTs, *446*

I

Iblis [the Devil], *53*
Ibn Khaldun Chair of Islamic
Studies at American University,
29
Ibrahim, Raymond, *602, 606,*
645-646
ICNA Conventions, *373*
ideations, *15, 173, 456, 471*

Index

idolaters, *85, 87, 196*
Iftar, *402, 700*
Ihsanoglu, Ekmeleddin, *222-223,*
271, 275, 279-280, 283, 286,
297-299, 302, 304, 308,
311-312, 314-317, 320, 327-328,
433-434, 585, 591-592, 598,
651, 661, 663, 667, 669, 673,
678, 725, 731, 741
IIFTIHAR, *183, 528*
IIIT Chair in Interfaith Studies and
Dialogue at CISD, *527*
ijma, *35-36, 41-46, 48, 51, 54, 90,*
214, 278, 610-614, 619, 651, 727,
730, 732
ijtihad, *42-43, 45, 50, 57, 69, 79,*
95-96, 101-102, 129, 592,
610-614, 617, 619-622, 627, 640,
707, 727, 730, 732
Ikhwan, *151, 165, 174, 177, 187,*
215, 481, 637, 640, 655, 719
Ikhwanonline, *144-145, 155, 176,*
187, 629, 632, 640, 643
Ikhwanweb, *154, 163, 177, 186,*
606, 632, 640, 643, 645, 647,
673, 721-722
Iliac Ramirez Sanchez ("Carlos the
Jackal"), *330, 376, 690*
Illinois, *11, 324, 372, 374, 507,*
525, 638, 673, 690
Imam Billah, *199*
Imam Bin-Qadamah, *47, 237*
Imam Yasir al-Bahrani, *117*
iman, *99, 157, 199, 645*
immigrant, *192, 294, 373, 594, 733*
improvised explosive device (IED),
315, 411-412, 602
Imran Ahsan Khan Nyazee, *40-42,*
49-50, 57, 63, 69-70, 79-81, 88,
95-96, 101-102, 104, 107, 129,
138, 176, 427, 610-614, 616-617,
620-622, 627, 640, 707, 731-732
incitement to discrimination, *283,*
303, 305-306, 587, 590-592,
663, 669, 743
incitement to violence, *302, 306,*
489, 587, 590-591
Independent Permanent
Commission on Human Rights,
48, 305
India, *32, 94, 99, 190, 224, 230,*
260, 288, 290, 337, 425, 458,
601, 607, 616, 618, 641, 657,
662, 665, 674, 707, 720, 723
Indiana, *171, 404, 537, 629, 633,*
642, 725
indifferentism, *559*
individual jihad, *90, 93, 95, 293,*
382-384, 387, 395, 400, 422,
425, 699
Indonesia, *32, 99, 150, 251, 282*
infantilization, *483*
infibulation, *555*; see also female
genital mutilation
infidel, *59-60, 78, 94, 136, 150,*
206, 420, 535, 537-538
Influence Operations, *182, 337,*
403
information battlespace, *202, 341,*
465, 484, 586
information campaign, *28, 76-77,*
263, 269, 299, 320, 328, 336,
340-341, 376, 380, 425, 441,
443-444, 452, 467, 496
information deficit, *333, 739*
information operations, *91, 264,*
333, 586, 599
information warfare, *445, 505*
Innocence of Muslims, *266, 286,*
321-322, 325, 328-329
innovation, *52, 54, 140-141*
Inspector, *336, 338, 372, 485, 487,*
638, 682-683, 716
Inspector General (IG), *338*
Inspectors General, *336, 423*
Institute for Multicultural Affairs,
296, 667
intelligence analysis, *12, 63, 229,*
344, 604, 688, 711
Intelligence Community, *15, 67,*
214, 444-445, 460-461, 482
intelligence cycle, *370, 508*

Index

Intelligence Preparation of the
Battlefield, *445, 711*
inter-governmental organization,
220, 283
interfaith community, *401,*
511-513, 520-521, 527, 531-532,
542, 603, 688
interfaith dialogue, *82, 135, 288,*
301, 307, 310, 375, 512-517,
519-521, 523-525, 527, 531, 537,
540, 542-544, 555-556, 558,
562, 565, 719-722, 724-727,
732-733, 735
interfaith outreach, *82, 512-513,*
515, 517, 519, 521, 523, 525, 527,
529, 531, 533, 535, 537, 539-541,
543, 545, 547, 549, 551, 553,
555, 557, 559, 561, 563, 565,
567, 569, 571, 573
interfaith pseudoreality, *560, 562*
intergovernmental, *221, 272, 593*
International Association of
Muslim Scholars, *281*
International Center for Religion
and Diplomacy (ICRD), *528, 723*
International Covenant on Civil
and Political Rights (ICCPR),
283, 303-308, 328-329,
586-587, 663, 669, 742
International Institute of Islamic
Thought (IIIT), *18, 173, 183,*
216, 223, 268-269, 318, 363,
512-516, 520, 524, 527-528, 537,
543, 556, 558, 602, 606, 608,
639, 642-643, 651, 654, 657,
673, 680, 719-727, 732-733, 735,
740
International Security and
Assistance Force (ISAF),
410-413, 416, 418, 421, 423,
425-426, 428-429, 434-441,
702-704, 709
International terrorism, *230, 237,*
342, 397, 652-653, 704
International Union of Muslim
Scholars, *110, 217, 240, 323,*

330, 589
Interpol, *241, 655*
interpretation, *29, 33, 35, 41, 43,*
47, 51, 68, 88, 108, 136, 184,
230, 238, 246, 306-307, 386,
455, 462-465, 479, 483, 533,
549, 574, 613, 618, 628, 686, 730
Interpretation of the Meanings of
the Noble Qur'an in the English
Language, *132, 533, 628, 686,*
730
Interpretations, *41, 44, 51, 54, 78,*
108, 132, 136, 184, 239, 420,
463-465, 479, 515, 592, 618
Intifada, *165-166*
Investigative Project on Terrorism
(IPT), *173, 309, 602, 620,*
637-641, 644, 650, 660,
671-672, 676-677, 684,
689-690, 698, 700-702
invitation, *26, 107, 128-129, 131,*
513
Iran, *61, 225, 229, 288, 525, 601,*
639, 652-653, 665, 674, 740
Iranian, *62, 226, 282, 289, 296,*
298, 662
Iraq, *27, 47-48, 61, 63, 95, 99, 110,*
114, 116, 132, 149-151, 173, 197,
203, 215, 217, 223, 233, 241,
246, 258, 290, 337, 377, 381,
385-386, 407-408, 415,
428-429, 442, 480-481, 540,
558, 560, 566, 601, 606, 612,
615, 620-621, 639, 655, 674,
691, 703, 711, 714
Iraqi Constitution, *47, 612*
IRS, *404, 604, 687-688*
Isa [Muslim prophet], *121, 126,*
538, 548, 563-564, 734
Ishaq, *87, 132, 253-254, 322, 619,*
628, 639, 657, 675, 737
ISIL [also ISIS], *128, 239, 258,*
551, 620, 691
Islam
anti-Islam, *193, 230, 322, 324,*
510, 605, 654, 667, 675,

677-678, 686, 693, 706, 709,
   711, 713, 716-717
anti-Islamic, 327, 379, 684
call to Islam, 26, 128, 131-132,
   134, 146, 196, 512, 567
call to jihad, 102, 551
call to prayer, 129, 251
dar al-harb, 78-80, 109-110,
   136, 143, 150, 153, 181, 268,
   519
dar al-Islam, 56, 78-80,
   109-110, 136, 153, 622, 624
defensive jihad, 47-48, 214
dhimmitude, 113-114, 210, 267,
   381, 539, 554, 584, 593
Hanafi School, 40, 44-45, 49,
   67, 74, 84, 90, 95, 97, 99,
   101-102, 104-105, 107, 151,
   621, 732
Hanbali School, 44, 49, 53, 74,
   90, 97-99, 151, 613
House of Islam, 78
Islamic community, 28, 33-34,
   40, 42, 46, 60, 71, 97, 130,
   143, 157, 161, 169, 195, 197,
   220, 223, 254, 268, 273, 335,
   375, 493, 539, 577
Islamic culture, 343, 471, 634
Islamic doctrine, 46, 50, 67,
   113, 131, 138, 143, 190, 200,
   275, 294-296, 301, 368, 384,
   547
Islamic identity, 170, 182, 297,
   375, 690
Islamic Jihad, 17, 141, 172, 183,
   203, 208, 315, 321-322, 344,
   629, 639, 646
Islamic Jurisprudence, 36-37,
   47-48, 54, 57, 62, 70, 74, 79,
   98, 102, 107, 126, 207, 268,
   270, 355, 370, 529, 607-608,
   610-611, 613-614, 617,
   620-621, 628, 680
Islamic Law, 12-16, 20-21,
   26-31, 33-46, 48-52, 54-58,
   60-61, 63, 66-70, 73-75,

78-89, 91, 94-102, 104, 106,
   108-111, 113-116, 118,
   120-122, 124, 130, 136, 138,
   141, 143, 145, 151-152, 176,
   179-181, 184-185, 191-196,
   201-204, 208-211, 217,
   223-224, 226, 228-231,
   235-236, 238, 242-245,
   247-250, 252, 258, 263-265,
   267-268, 270-271, 275-279,
   282-283, 288, 292-294,
   296-297, 299, 301-302, 306,
   308, 311, 314, 317, 331, 333,
   336, 339, 341, 354-355, 359,
   366-368, 370, 375, 381,
   384-385, 389, 391-392, 398,
   407-410, 412, 415-416,
   418-422, 424-427, 430,
   433-436, 438-441, 443, 449,
   458, 462, 472, 492-493,
   508-509, 515-516, 520, 529,
   531, 556-557, 560, 562, 568,
   575, 596, 599-600, 607-610,
   612-614, 620, 622-623,
   629-630, 650, 655, 679-680,
   709, 716, 719, 723-724, 732,
   737
Islamic Movement, 16, 27, 67,
   136-137, 143-144, 150-151,
   153, 155-163, 165, 167-169,
   171, 173-175, 177, 179,
   181-193, 195-201, 203, 205,
   207, 209-211, 213-215, 217,
   220, 223, 229-230, 232, 238,
   246, 264-265, 267, 315, 318,
   320-321, 325, 336, 342-344,
   346, 358-359, 366-367,
   369-370, 375, 377, 395-396,
   399, 407, 442, 455, 468,
   470, 479, 486, 491, 496, 508,
   512-513, 515, 540, 575, 601,
   613, 629, 631-635, 639-640,
   673-674, 683, 696, 711
Islamic nation, 240, 282, 330,
   679, 743
Islamic Rulings on War, 392,

695
Islamic State, 27, 56, 109, 118,
  146, 187, 193, 197, 213, 217,
  268-269, 307, 315, 317-318,
  367-368, 372, 381, 436,
  438-439, 515, 528, 554-555,
  571, 573, 596, 601, 603,
  625-626, 628, 654, 657, 674,
  687, 693, 702, 709, 714, 726,
  731, 733, 736
Islamic terrorism, 14, 66, 235,
  353, 401, 508
Islamism, 154, 161, 216, 342
Islamist, 173, 183-184, 192,
  201, 215-216, 268, 273, 330,
  342, 351-353, 376, 628,
  631-632, 638, 646, 649-650,
  666, 689
Islamist extremism, 184,
  351-353, 628
Islamist extremist, 353
Islamization of Knowledge,
  515, 673
jihad, 11-12, 14, 16-17, 20-21,
  23, 26, 29-30, 40-41, 46-48,
  54-55, 60, 66, 74-81, 83-110,
  118, 126-130, 132-136, 141,
  143, 147, 150, 152-155,
  157-159, 161-162, 164-165,
  168, 172-174, 176-177,
  181-189, 191, 195, 198,
  200-203, 208-209, 212, 214,
  217, 232, 236-238, 241-242,
  244-246, 258, 264-265, 270,
  279, 293, 307, 315, 321-322,
  333, 339, 342-346, 348-350,
  353, 359-368, 374-375, 379,
  382-387, 389-390, 393-396,
  400-401, 405-406, 408,
  415-416, 419-420, 422, 425,
  427-428, 436, 439, 449, 451,
  455, 457-459, 465-467, 481,
  483, 503, 505, 511-512,
  515-516, 518-519, 528-529,
  541, 544, 546-551, 553-556,
  559-561, 567, 569, 601, 609,

612, 614-615, 617-629,
  631-635, 637, 639-640,
  642-644, 646-647, 650,
  654-656, 664-666, 674, 681,
  686, 689-690, 694-696,
  698-699, 704, 706-707,
  709-711, 715, 719-720, 722,
  727-730, 732-733, 735
Jihad cells, 601, 674
jihadi, 19-20, 26-27, 31-32, 53,
  67, 69, 75, 77, 91, 93, 97-98,
  102-103, 136, 139, 144, 155,
  163, 184, 192, 202, 208-209,
  212, 223, 242, 258, 264-265,
  281, 288, 292-293, 309, 322,
  330-331, 345-347, 359, 364,
  375, 383-385, 387-390, 394,
  396, 400, 405-406, 419, 421,
  433, 439, 443, 450, 462,
  480-481, 498, 508, 538-540,
  547-548, 559, 620, 647, 649,
  665, 699, 710
Jihadis, 15, 29-30, 33, 43,
  53-55, 97, 102, 106, 134, 184,
  215-217, 236, 240, 242, 256,
  264, 349, 360, 364, 399,
  406, 420-421, 450, 461, 465,
  483, 560, 567, 650
jihadist, 43, 143, 150, 161, 174,
  193, 203, 209, 232, 346,
  349-350, 399, 401, 403, 460,
  466, 480, 488, 519, 601, 655,
  674-675, 719
Jihads, 75, 86, 93, 400, 461
Maliki School, 44, 49, 68, 74,
  89-90, 97, 106-107, 151, 370,
  529, 731-732
Shafi'i School, 102, 608,
  679-680
Three Duties of Islam, 130
Two Faces of Islam, The,
  98-99, 621
What Islam Is All About, 60,
  69, 88, 101, 130, 253, 255,
  615, 617, 619, 622, 627, 657,
  675

Index

Islamfachmann: Koran-Rezitation bei Friednsgebeten ist Legitim, *535*

Islamic Association for Palestine (IAP), *165-166, 168-172, 314-315, 344, 374, 514, 602, 636, 671, 690*

Islamic Center, *18, 186-187, 323, 325, 342, 375, 396-399, 406, 434, 467, 519, 527, 539, 615, 645*

Islamic Center of Boston, *399*

Islamic Centers, *150, 172, 186, 399, 404, 602*

Islamic Circle of North America (ICNA), *149-150, 190, 192-193, 201, 319-320, 373-375, 398-399, 520, 602, 631, 633, 644-645, 673, 676, 689-690, 697-698, 721*

Islamic Conference of Foreign Ministers in Bamako, *227*

Islamic Educational, Scientific and Cultural Organization, *556, 731*

Islamic Extremist, *364, 397*

Islamic Fiqh Academy, *245-246, 515, 608, 654, 656, 680, 719-720*

Islamic Movement: Problems and Perspective, *137, 629, 633-634, 640*

Islamic Society of Boston, *399, 401, 404-405, 698, 700-701*

Islamic Society of Boston Cultural Center, *399, 698, 701*

Islamic Society of North America (ISNA), *18, 92, 137, 162, 168, 171-172, 175, 183, 192, 216, 242, 325, 337-338, 344, 354-355, 362-363, 368-371, 374, 398, 402, 404, 407, 514-515, 528-529, 540, 543, 556-557, 602, 604, 608, 620, 633, 637-639, 649, 654, 680, 687, 690, 692, 699-700, 702, 719-720, 723, 732, 740*

Islamiyya, *322*

Islamization, *190, 515, 673*

IslamOnline, *47, 163, 213, 245,* *280, 320, 398, 609, 612, 647, 654, 656, 663, 674, 681, 719-720*

Islamophobia, *14, 250, 257, 259-261, 263-264, 267-276, 278-279, 282, 286, 296, 298, 302-306, 310, 312-313, 315-316, 319-320, 322, 324, 326-327, 332-333, 339-341, 343, 346, 354, 358, 375-376, 378, 381-382, 414, 445, 455, 465, 468, 472, 481, 486-487, 489-495, 498, 509, 522, 536, 540-541, 543, 563-565, 575-598, 605, 660-662, 664, 667-670, 673, 675, 677, 681, 683, 693, 716, 726, 737-741, 743-745*

Ismail Faruqi, *183, 289-290, 665*

Ismail Haniyeh, *163, 315*

Ismailia, *151*

Israel, *81-82, 165-167, 172, 213-214, 233-234, 321, 526-527, 535, 638, 688, 693, 710, 724, 730*

Israeli, *81, 405, 532, 534, 724*

issue of fact, *29, 31, 350, 447, 478*

Istanbul, *231-232, 236, 308-310, 325, 563-565, 584-585, 590-591, 593, 595, 605, 653-654, 662, 670, 682, 710, 734-736, 739-741, 744-746*

It's What the Doctrine Says It Is - Rebuttal to 'Islamic Rulings on War, *392*

Iyad Madani, *330*

J

Jabhat al-Nusra, *18, 217, 480, 540, 546*

Jackson, Robert, *28*

Jah'Keem Yisreal, *406, 701*; see also Nolan, Alton

Jahili, *140*

Jahiliyah [also jahiliyya, jahiliyyah], *100, 137-142, 161-162, 191, 198, 205, 220, 515, 633-634, 644, 733*

Jaish-e-Mohammed (JEM), *201*

Jalalu'd-din Al-Mahalli and Jalalu'd-din As-Suyuti, *533, 616*

Jamaat-e-Islami, *159, 190-193, 632*

Jamal Badawi, *172, 697*

Jamal Barzinji, *173-174, 183, 216, 528, 639, 642, 723*

Jamal Hamami, *166*

Jamiat-e-Ulema-e-Islam, *285*

Jamil Amin (aka H. Rap Brown), *398*

Javed Ashraf Qazi, *293*

Jazaka 'Allah Khair" ("May Allah reward you"), *389*

Jazeera, *22-23, 152, 239, 241, 281-282, 288, 327, 424-425, 428, 452, 486, 510, 529, 640, 649, 664, 677, 693, 706-707, 709, 711, 713, 717, 722-723*

Jedda, *515, 608, 654, 679-680, 719-720, 735*

Jeddah, *259, 275-276, 661, 663, 669, 674, 678*

Jeremiah, *511*

Jericho, *166*

Jerusalem, *81, 259, 285, 531, 601, 674, 724*

Jesuit, *316, 535*

Jesus, *39, 121, 124, 126-127, 156, 251, 386, 535, 537-538, 541, 548-549, 557-558, 563-565, 624, 729, 734*

Jew, *120, 122, 124-125, 251, 277, 546, 550, 728-729*

Jewish, *188, 194, 202, 228, 234, 519, 526-527, 530-532, 540-541, 543-544, 548, 556, 577, 588, 603, 618, 621, 700, 721, 741*

Jewish community, *527*

Jewry, *120*

Jihad Saleh Williams, *374, 689*

Jim Crow, *306*

jizyah [also jizya and Jiziya] (poll tax), *96, 103, 109, 111, 117, 122-123, 126-127, 132, 196-197, 206, 381, 386, 390, 547-555, 557, 566, 572, 624-628, 694, 729-731*

John the Baptist, *563-564*

Johns Hopkins, *78, 101, 612, 624, 732, 737*

Johns Hopkins University, *78, 101, 737*

Johnson, Ian, *183*

Johnson, Jeh, *293*

Joint Chiefs of Staff (JCS), *11, 263, 379-380, 408, 423, 444, 452, 599, 693, 711, 714, 717*

Joint Congressional Hearing on Threats to Military Communities, *350*

Joint Declaration on the plight of Middle-Eastern Christians, *563*

Joint Forces Staff College, *379-380, 498-499, 504, 600*

Joint Staff, *13, 15, 239, 379-380, 444, 469, 498-499, 504, 599, 715*

Jomini, *459*

Jones, Terry, *428, 432, 675, 707*

Jordan, *62-63, 216, 316, 360, 607, 615, 639, 679, 740-741*

Judaism, *119, 121-123, 128, 194-195, 200, 222, 277-278, 386, 519, 526, 533, 571*

Judeo, *73, 225, 513, 525, 610*

Judge Advocate General (JAG), *417, 423*

Judicial Watch, *372-373, 397, 405, 689, 696-697, 701*

juma, *60, 639*

Jyllands-Posten, *263, 279, 662*

K

Kabul, *408, 410, 416-417, 419, 423, 702-703, 705*

Kalimah ["the words"], *199, 645*
Kalin, Ibrahim, *565, 740*
Kamal al Helbawi, *173, 639*
Karachi, *284, 286, 313, 628, 631,*
    663-664, 675, 737
Karzai's Twelve Rules, *411-412,*
    415, 439
Karzai, Hamid, *409, 411-413, 415,*
    426-427, 429-430, 432-434,
    436, 439, 441, 707-709
Kashmir, *173, 204, 601, 639, 674,*
    683, 741
Kathir, *68-69, 87, 89, 109, 111,*
    113, 115-117, 121, 126, 178,
    232-234, 253, 493, 533-534,
    538, 548, 550-552, 569-571,
    607, 616, 618-619, 624-628,
    640, 653, 657, 686, 693, 704,
    729-731, 735-736
Kazakhstan, *595, 669*
Kazimi, Nibras, *151*
Keller, Nuh Ha Mim, *49, 67, 90,*
    607-614, 616-619, 621-628,
    640-642, 646, 651-652,
    654-657, 660, 662, 667,
    679-680, 686-687, 692-694,
    706-707, 709-710, 719-720,
    722-723, 725, 727, 729-732,
    735-736
key terrain, *465, 505*
Khadorri College, *207*
Khaibar, *94*
Khaldun, *29, 89, 607, 619*
Khalid Ali Aldawsari, *315*
Khalid bin Muhammad al-'Anbari,*
    53, 140, 613-614, 629
Khaliphate, *240, 655*
Khan, Waqar Hussain, *201*
kharijites, *246, 560*
Khartoum, *370, 528*
Khaybar, *106-107, 126, 129, 548*
Khera, Farhana, *21, 378-379, 604,*
    641-642, 692
khilafah, *157, 193, 687*
Khorassani, *225-226, 652*
Kifah Mustapha, *374-375, 690*

kifaya, *106*
Kiffer, David, *13*
Killing without Right, *230,*
    233-237, 241-244, 246-247,
    258, 694
Kilpatrick, William, *557, 732*
King Abdul-Aziz University, *207*
King Hearings, *641*
Kirby, John, *22-23, 128, 239, 303,*
    357, 378, 425, 436, 452, 470,
    486-487, 509
Kitab Al-Tabaqat Al-Kabir, *253,*
    612, 657, 732, 737
Klausen, Jytte, *283*
Knights Under the Prophet's
    Banner, *203, 645*
Kodesh, *527*
Koran, *35-38, 45, 56, 68, 73, 112,*
    131, 144, 146, 226, 235, 256, 277,
    289, 295, 422, 427, 433, 511,
    517, 531, 535, 537, 543-544,
    549-550, 554, 558-559, 562,
    568, 572, 609, 611, 616-617, 619,
    643-644, 652, 694, 707-709,
    724-725
koranic, *20, 35, 43, 72, 102, 112,*
    232, 384, 387, 394, 531, 537,
    607, 611, 613, 617, 619, 626-627,
    653, 694, 704, 724, 729
Korner, Felix, *535*
Ku Klux Klan, *55, 306, 369*
kufar, *59-60*
kufr, *19, 53, 111, 277-278, 538,*
    551-552, 603, 609-610, 614
Kuwait, *119, 287-288, 290, 386,*
    556, 613, 628, 639, 670, 678,
    720, 731, 733, 740-741
Kyl, John, *641, 692*

L

La ilaha illahllah [also La ilaha
    illallah], *133, 199, 233, 361, 544,*
    704, 734

Lafayette Park, *403, 700*
Lake, Anthony, *402*
Landau, Richard, *520, 522, 532*
Lashkar-e-Taiba, *18, 601, 674*
Leiter, Michael, *406*
Lekovic, Edina, *375, 690*
Lenin, *142, 263, 340*
Leninism, *142*
Lewis, C.S., *485, 487*
lexicon, *128, 182, 345, 347-348,
    465, 593, 684, 715*
liberty, *11, 248, 355, 488, 517-518,
    575, 653, 716*
Libya, *215-216, 327, 460, 601, 639,
    648, 674*
Libyan, *215, 403, 648*
Libyan Islamic Fighting Group
    (LIFG), *215*
Lieberman, Joseph, *246-247, 656*
Life of Muhammad: A Translation
    of Ibn Ishaq's Sirat Rasul Allah,
    675
Lincoln, Abraham, *11, 24, 507, 510*
lines of communication, *135, 497*
lines of operation, *175, 264, 266,
    333, 339, 426, 438, 448,
    511-512, 567, 586*
liwaa, *186*
London, *269, 280, 289-290, 292,
    372, 442, 533, 591, 601, 616,
    630, 646, 655, 663, 674, 687,
    689, 711, 719, 735*
Lone Mujahid Pocketbook: A Step
    to Step Guide on how to become
    as Successful Lone Mujahid,
    400, 699
lone wolf, *293, 332, 383-384, 394,
    461*
lone wolf terrorism, *383*
Los Angeles, *329, 342, 372, 374,
    647, 694, 699*
Lugano, Switzerland, *183, 187,
    274, 633, 643, 661, 673*
Lungren, Congressman Dan,
    350-353, 498
lying, *33, 71, 99, 178-182, 194,*
    248, 279, 420, 521, 524, 556,
    609, 642

M

M'juma Fuqaha Shariah Amrikia,
    60
M. Bilal Kaleem, *374, 689*
Madden, Denis, *540*
Madina, *110, 530, 623*
Madinah, *126, 197, 548, 551*
Maghreb, *151, 203, 205, 601, 674*
Mahmoud al-Habbash, *82*
Mahmud, *155*
Mahmud Fahmi al-Nuqrashi, *155*
Maimonides, *25*
Majid Khadduri, *48, 67, 78-80,
    90, 101, 109-110, 136, 153, 202,
    606-607, 612, 616-618,
    622-624, 631, 732, 737*
Makkah, *49, 212, 516, 612, 660,
    746*
Makkan, *185, 212, 516*
Malaysia, *57, 150, 250-251, 290,
    652, 665, 740-741*
Malaysian, *56, 141, 602*
Mali, *203, 227, 271, 579, 588, 601,
    645, 660-661, 674, 677, 738, 743*
Malik ibn Anas, *84, 106-107, 128,
    529, 623, 723*
Mann, Thomas, *335, 666*
mansukh, *35, 70-71, 74, 102, 607,
    617, 619*
Mar-Jac Investments, *183, 528*
Marghinani, *67, 90, 610, 616-617,
    640, 732*
martyr, *30, 155, 187, 244-245,
    452, 559, 618, 623, 634-635,
    643, 656*
martyrdom, *83-84, 106-107,
    176-177, 244-246, 388, 391-392,
    420, 632, 635, 722*
martyred, *362, 386, 520, 526-527,
    545, 623, 635, 722*

Index

Martyrs, *106, 159, 243, 294, 529, 601, 620, 634, 674*

Marxists, *330, 376*

Maryam, *126, 538, 548, 563, 734*

Marzook, Mousa Abu, *165-167, 169, 172-173, 314, 636, 639*

MAS-Boston, *374, 698, 701*

masjid, *87, 319, 396, 538, 721*

Masjid Ar-Ribat al-Islami mosque, *396*

materialism, *27, 156, 161, 175, 220, 518-519*

Matrix, The, *14, 66, 471*

matter of fact, *33, 252, 296, 477*

Maulana Muhammad Ali, *92, 107, 620*

Mayo Clinic, *268, 660*

Mayorga, *379*

Mayorga, Jose S., *379*

Mazar-i Sharif, *426*

McCain, Senator John, *337, 377, 650, 683*

McCarthy, Andrew, *210*

McCaul, Michael, *401*

McChrystal, General Stanley A., *410-411, 702-703*

Measures of Effectiveness (MOEs), *462*

Mecca, *48, 81-82, 94, 238, 288, 301, 517, 545, 573, 609-610, 612, 617-618, 621, 730*

Mecca Declaration, *48*

Meccan, *74, 199-200, 212, 573*

Medina, *74, 85, 186, 246, 254, 281, 319, 530, 560, 573, 621, 656, 721, 723, 729, 733*

Medinan, *74, 200-201, 212, 214*

Mein Kampf, *444, 447*

MEMRI, *529, 602, 612, 629-631, 646, 648, 652, 655-656, 663, 722-723, 733*

Mena Investments, *183, 528*

Methodology of Dawah Ilallah in American Perspective, *131, 193-199, 396, 512-513, 628, 644-645, 660, 719, 722*

Methodology of Ijtihad, The, *57, 69, 95-96, 610, 612-614, 617, 620-622, 627, 640, 707*

Michigan, *40, 323, 610, 620*

Milestones, *14, 65, 136-140, 142-147, 150, 155, 157-158, 160, 162, 174, 176, 185, 189-191, 195-201, 203-204, 209-210, 212-214, 384, 386, 396, 435, 486, 492, 498, 515-516, 521, 592, 628-629, 631, 634, 644, 716, 720, 733*

Milestones Process, *136-137, 139, 142-144, 147, 150, 155, 157-158, 160, 162, 174, 176, 185, 189, 195, 198-201, 203-204, 209, 213-214, 384, 386, 396, 435, 486, 498, 521, 592*

Minister of Religious Affairs, *82*

Minneapolis, *58, 60, 615*

Minya, *114*

Miriam, *127, 386*

mirror-imaging, *128*

Mishnah Sanhedrin, *233-234*

Mission Europa, *580-581, 738*

Model Rules of Professional Conduct, *499, 717*

modernist, *158, 160*

Moffat, James, *456-457, 712*

Mogadishu, *288*

Mogahed, *371-372, 595*

Mogahed, Dalia, *371, 595*

Mohamed El-Mezain, *164*

Mohamed Magid, *337, 354-355, 370, 529, 532, 687, 723*

Mohamed Rahoma, *555*

Mohammad Fadel, *92, 620*

Mohammad Hamdan, *280*

Mohammad Hashim Kamali, *36-37, 56-57, 119, 250-252, 254, 256-257, 267, 434, 436, 439, 493, 607, 614, 626, 656, 660, 709-710*

Mohammed Ijaz ul-Haq, *291-292*

Mohammed Mahdi Akef, *241-242, 655*

Mohammed Sa'id Buti, *43*

monotheism, *132, 288, 564, 626, 662*

Morell, Michael, *459-460*

Mormons, *572*

Moroccan, *295*

Morocco, *210, 288, 303, 586-587, 621, 639, 669, 678, 743*

Morsi, Mohamed, *19, 321, 327, 629, 646, 648, 677-678*

Mortenson, Greg, *441, 710*

Moses, *34, 121*

Moslem, *124, 163, 546-547, 696, 729*

mosque, *32, 58, 119, 154, 183, 197, 201, 238, 246, 281, 319, 324, 374-375, 383, 389, 396, 399, 401, 404, 419-420, 531, 534, 546, 560, 563, 573, 642, 656, 676, 690, 697-701, 721, 724, 731-735*

MSNBC, *256, 648*

Mubarak, Hosni, *62, 211, 214, 601, 647, 674, 740-741*

Mueller, Robert, *378, 383, 400-403, 604, 641, 692*

muezzin, *251*

Mufti, *39, 47, 285, 322-323, 370, 529, 544, 563-564, 610, 619, 727*

Muhajideen, *294*

Muhammad 'Abd al-Salam Faraj, *100-101, 105, 647*

Muhammad Abdul Rahman, *639*

Muhammad Abu Zayd Ibn Khaldun, *607*

Muhammad al-Darawardi, *103*

Muhammad Badi, *145, 213, 246, 630*

Muhammad bin Abdul Wahhab, *53, 98, 621*

Muhammad bin Ishaq, *87*

Muhammad Hamid, *225*

Muhammad ibn Hasan al-Shaybani, *612, 732*

Muhammad ibn Idris al-Shafi'i, *37, 607*

Muhammad Muhsin Khan, *533, 628, 686, 730*

Muhammad Qutb, *141*

Muhammad Salah, *172*

Muhammad Shafiq, *527-528, 719, 725*

Muhammad Taqi-ud-Din Al-Hilali, *533, 628, 686, 730*

Muhammad Tontanji, *173, 639*

Muhammadan [also Muhammadun], *55, 70, 199, 607, 614, 617, 723, 732*

Muhsin, *533, 628, 686, 730*

mujahada, *84-86*

mujahed, *203, 349*

mujahedeen [also mujahideen, mujahidun], *184, 204, 207-208, 246, 349, 362, 395-396, 442, 559-561, 601, 647, 674*

mujahid, *83, 87, 117, 204, 242, 362, 374-375, 400, 508, 533-534, 545, 569, 616, 625, 657, 690, 698-699, 701, 704, 730, 735*

mujtahid, *37, 43, 99, 102, 556, 607, 611, 616, 619, 723, 731-732*

mullah, *194, 419*

multiculturalism, *294, 301, 333, 725*

Muqaddimah, *29, 607, 619*

Murad, Khurram, *159, 190, 318, 632-633, 673*

Musharraf, *313-314*

Mushrikin [also Mushrikun], *87, 132*

Mushriks, *121*

Muslim Advocates, *21, 378-379, 641*

Muslim American Society (MAS), *18, 217, 244, 319-320, 373-375, 392, 398-399, 405, 520, 601, 656, 673-674, 676, 689-690, 697-698, 701, 721*

Muslim American Society of Boston, *374, 698*

Index

Muslim Arab Youth Association
(MAYA), *404, 602*
Muslim Brotherhood, *12-24,
26-28, 47, 60, 63, 65-67, 70, 77,
91-93, 98, 100, 110, 113-114, 121,
128, 131, 137-139, 141-147,
149-155, 159, 161-169, 171-177,
179, 182-190, 192, 195, 200-201,
203-205, 207, 209-217,
223-224, 228-230, 234, 236,
238-246, 258, 264-265,
268-270, 274, 280-282, 285,
287, 289, 293-294, 306-307,
309, 312, 314-327, 330-333,
336-346, 349, 354-355,
358-359, 362-363, 366-379,
382-383, 392, 396-399,
401-407, 414, 422, 425, 427,
431, 434, 437-438, 441-442,
452, 455, 458, 465-467,
469-470, 479, 481, 486,
489-492, 496, 499, 505, 509,
511-528, 530-532, 536-543,
554-558, 561-563, 567, 575,
585-586, 589, 601, 603-604,
606-608, 615, 625, 628-635,
637, 639-640, 642-643,
645-650, 654-655, 661, 672-674,
677, 680, 682-683, 687-688,
690-692, 696, 698, 700, 711,
719-720, 722, 724*
Muslim Community, *29, 33, 61,
67, 79-80, 89, 95-97, 100-101,
105, 110, 129, 136, 138, 142, 182,
185, 199, 226, 231, 235,
244-245, 252, 267, 287,
289-290, 315, 338, 364, 373,
396, 398, 402-403, 427, 520,
603, 608, 612, 642, 680, 688,
691-692, 697-698, 732*
Muslim Public Affairs Council
(MPAC), *18, 246-247, 325,
341-344, 348-350, 358,
364-367, 374-375, 380, 399,
402, 407, 540, 602, 656,
676-677, 683-684, 686-687,*
690, 698
Muslim Student Association
(MSA), *18, 172, 201, 337,
374-375, 396, 398, 402, 404,
527, 531, 543, 602, 639, 677,
689, 699*
Muslim World League, *285, 664*
Mussolini, *288*
Mustafa, *47, 150, 213-214, 639,
675, 741*
Mustafa Kemal Atatürk, *150*
Mustaliq, *546*
Mutairi, *287*
mutawatir, *36, 39-40, 49, 88,
609-610*
mutual trust, *521, 532, 537,
539-541, 543, 558, 567*
Muwatta, *107, 128, 370, 529, 623,
627, 723-724*
Muwatta (Trodden Path), *529*
Muzzamil Siddiqi, *172*
Myers, Lisa, *699*
Myers, Richard, *452, 480, 711, 714*

N

nafs, *84, 86*
Nakoula, Basseley, *322*
nasikh, *35, 70-71, 74, 102, 607,
617, 619*
Nassim Khaled, *539*
Nassir Abdulaziz al-Nasser, *326,
677*
National Commission on
Terrorism, *325*
National Conference of Catholic
Bishops, *403*
National Counterterrorism Center,
349, 374, 684
National Counterterrorism Center
and the FBI Academy, *374*
National Intelligence Estimate
(NIE), *480*

Index

National Intelligence Strategy of the United States, *684*

National Military Command Center, *599*

National Military Joint Intelligence Center, *599*

National Public Radio, *340, 376, 397, 646, 683, 690, 697, 707*

National security apparatus, *63, 228, 472, 497*

national security community, *61, 65, 108, 226, 257-258, 293, 340, 353, 367, 377, 384, 415, 459, 471, 480, 493, 499-500, 502*

Navy, *11, 22, 329, 425, 479, 486, 600*

Neglected Duty, *100-101, 621*

negligence, *230, 257, 341, 359, 502*

negligent, *82, 238, 502-504*

Netherlands, *293-296, 298, 666-667*

Nevvichim, Moreh, *25*

New Delhi, *230-231, 611, 616, 644*

New Testament, *34, 39, 116, 121, 548*

NewsCorp, *321*

Nigeria, *114, 116, 197, 540, 560, 601, 633, 673-674*

nihilist, *451, 482*

nihilist void, *482*

Nitze School of Advanced International Studies, *101*

no compulsion, *69, 75, 388, 518*

no deity, *119, 533, 538*

no other sovereign or authority, *57, 63*

Noble Qur'an, *132, 362, 400, 533, 549, 551, 563-564, 569-571, 628, 686, 730, 734*

Nokhowd, *419*

Nolan, Alton, *406, 701*; see also Jah'Keem Yisreal

non-governmental organizations (NGOs), *265, 303, 330, 580-581, 586, 636, 661, 736, 740-741, 745*

Non-Muslim Subjects of the Islamic State, *109, 118, 268, 307, 438-439, 555, 571, 573, 625-626, 693, 709, 731, 736*

Norfolk, Virginia, *380*

North Carolina, *360*

Norwegian, *290, 663-664, 668, 742*

nuclear, *136*

nullification, *427*

nunsikh, *71*

Nuremberg, *28*

Nygaard, *290*

O

Oath, *55, 151, 191, 200, 382, 431, 468, 472, 482, 487-491, 494, 496-497, 500-501, 504-505, 509, 542, 716*

Obama, Barack, *25, 432, 689, 707*

Obi Wan Kenobi, *467*

Observatory Reports on Islamophobia, *276*

Odeh, *164*

Office for Democratic Institutions and Human Rights, *576*

Office of the Director of National Intelligence (ODNI), *336, 604, 682, 688*

Ohio Homeland Security, *371*

Oklahoma, *406, 701-702*

Old Testament, *24*

Olive Tree Initiative (OTI), *526-527*

Omar Abdel-Rahman, *207*

Omar al-Bashir, *528*

On Political War, *219*

Open Societies Mission, *303, 586*

Open Society Foundations, *303, 586, 668, 742*

Organization for Security and Co-operation in Europe (OSCE), *270, 273-275, 324, 350, 515,*

575-581, 583-586, 589-590, 593-598, 660-661, 668, 676, 685, 737-746
Organization of Islamic Cooperation (OIC)
OIC Charter, 48, 221, 317
OIC Convention to Combat Terrorism, 415, 652, 704
OIC Islamic Summits, 221
OIC Special Envoy, 224, 652, 692-693
Organization of the Islamic Conference on Combating International Terrorism, 230, 652, 704
Organization of the Islamic Conference, 220, 317, 605, 670, 682, 710
Orhun, Omur, 585, 661, 737-739
Oslo Accords, 81-82, 166, 618
otherization, 595
Ottoman, 90, 92, 95, 150, 293, 584-585, 619, 621, 631
Oussama Jammal [also Osama Jammal], 324, 375
outrage, 20, 250, 263-265, 279, 284, 289, 322, 328, 377, 423, 430, 435, 437, 660, 675, 705-706
outsourcing, 13, 239, 259, 370, 437, 465, 469-470, 486
Ozcan, Tevfik, 584, 739

P

Pact of Umar, 111, 113, 115, 117, 126, 307-308, 381, 493, 594
pagans, 87, 238, 547, 551, 734
Pagels, Heinz, 456
painful chastisement, 232, 385
Pajhwok, 418, 705
Pakistan, 32, 61, 99, 119, 133, 150, 190, 192-193, 201-202, 229, 251, 260-261, 284-286, 288, 290-293, 302, 313, 327, 337,

419, 425, 428, 601, 610, 616, 620, 622, 628, 631, 645, 664-665, 670, 674, 677, 679, 683, 732, 737, 740-741
Pakistani Army, 133, 561, 616
Pakistani Brigadier S.K. Malik, 20, 32, 38, 45, 69, 72, 84, 106-107, 128-129, 133-136, 174-175, 182, 202, 374, 387, 391, 497, 505, 511-512, 525, 529-530, 533-534, 541, 557, 561-562, 569, 577, 611, 616, 623, 625, 627-628, 657, 690, 704, 717, 723-724, 729-730, 732-733, 735, 737, 740-741
Pakistani Inter-Services Intelligence (ISI), 337
Palestine, 155, 163, 165-173, 175, 204, 244, 344, 374, 514, 531, 601-602, 636, 639, 656, 671, 674, 676, 690, 696, 698, 724
Palestine Committees, 165
Palestinian Liberation Organization (PLO), 81-82, 166, 671
Pan-Arabism, 220
Pan-Islamic Movement, 220
Panetta, Leon, 340, 408, 691
Paragraph 253, 511, 543-545, 550, 553-554, 558-559, 562, 565, 568
Paris, 256, 293, 442, 657, 664-665, 670, 740
Parwan Detention Facility, 432-433
Pasha, Peter Galy, 94
PBS, 398, 697
peaceful coexistence, 331
Penguin Books, 710
Pentagon, 13-15, 20, 22, 66, 128, 135-136, 197-198, 202, 236, 341, 346, 379, 385, 397-398, 402, 420, 422-424, 486, 599-600, 642, 697, 703
people of defiance, 118-119, 553
Perez, Tom, 22, 312
Perfection, 52, 613

Index

persecution, *121, 125, 128, 178,
    525-526*
Petraeus, David, *408, 426, 703*
Philadelphia, *166-167, 169-171,
    175, 183, 514, 665, 670, 717*
Philly Meeting, *514, 636-637, 640,
    657, 671, 701, 719*
Pickthall, Marmaduke, *400*
Pieper, Josef, *275, 350, 356, 395,
    443, 454, 461-462, 472, 476,
    481, 487, 489, 495, 541, 559,
    684-685, 696, 711-712, 715-717,
    726*
Piozada, Syed Sharifuddin, *290*
Pipes, Daniel, *216, 649*
Plainfield, Indiana, *171, 404, 629,
    632-633, 653, 700, 702, 721*
Plato, *356, 485, 541-542*
Pledge of Remembrance and
    Commitment to Peace, *540, 542*
Plotnikov, William, *400*
Points of Clarification on the
    Initiative to Spare the Blood of
    Muslims in Iraq, *48, 612*
Poland, *151, 576, 661, 668,
    737-744, 746*
political correctness, *12, 16, 270,
    352, 355, 487, 491, 498*
political warfare, *90, 219*
Political, Military, Economic,
    Social, Information, and
    Infrastructure (PMESII), *448*
polytheism, *123, 132, 609, 624-625*
Polytheists, *47, 103-104, 106, 612*
Pontifical Gregorian University,
    535
Poole, Patrick, *10, 17, 338-339,
    413, 528, 627, 639, 642, 673,
    682, 688-690, 697, 703, 705,
    723, 726*
Pope Benedict XVI, *264, 266, 285,
    287-288, 426, 536-537, 567,
    574, 664-665, 736*
Pope Francis, *125, 532, 541, 559,
    563-567, 627, 725-726, 730-734*

Population-centric
    counterinsurgency, *407*
Post, Emily, *58*
postmodernism, *158, 268, 470*
prejudice, *500, 536, 578, 581, 717,
    727*
prejudicial, *125, 471*
preparatory stage, *133, 541*
Presbyterian Church in America
    (PCA), *541*
President Bush, *17, 224, 259,
    313-314, 336, 345, 402, 507,
    652, 692-693*
PressTV, *296, 667, 670*
pressure-cooker bombs, *399-400*
priest, *525-526, 694-695*
prima facie, *69, 657-658, 712*
prima facie evidence, *69, 712*
Prince al-Waleed bin Talal, *183,
    315, 320, 642, 655, 675, 689*
Prince al-Waleed bin Talal Center
    for Muslim-Christian
    Understanding, *315*
Principles of Islamic
    Jurisprudence, *36, 57, 207, 607,
    614*
prisoner, *118-119, 253, 439*
process of settlement, *174,
    186-187, 519, 719*
professional standard, *478, 497,
    500*
professional standards, *16, 380,
    462, 469, 482, 496-497, 504*
Prophet Mohammed, *69, 81, 255,
    263, 279-280, 282-283, 328,
    675-676*
proselytizing, *128, 512, 567, 724*
pseudo-analysis, *269*
pseudo-scientific, *454*
Pseudorealities, *359, 396, 454,
    459, 461, 541*
pseudoreality, *366, 395-396, 407,
    454-455, 457, 459, 462, 476,
    481, 559-560, 562*
pseudoscientific, *347, 496*
psychological warfare, *134, 219*

Puller, Chesty, *499*
Pure Punishment, *99*
Pure Worship, *99-100*
Putin, *23-24*

Q

Qaddafi, Muammar, *215*
qadi [judge], *68, 89, 96, 99, 617, 619, 731-732*
Qatari, *556, 631, 731*
QCW, *561, 733*
qiyas, *44-45, 98, 621*
Qom, *288*
quadcharts, *347*
qualified scholarship (taqlid), *43, 611, 619, 651, 727, 730, 732*
Quantico, *374, 600*
Queen Elizabeth II, *290*
Qur'an, *20-21, 34-41, 43-45, 48-51, 53, 56, 60, 62, 66-78, 80, 83-84, 86-93, 97-98, 101-105, 109, 112, 115-117, 119-124, 127, 130, 132-133, 136-139, 141, 143-144, 146, 152-153, 156-159, 161, 164, 178, 191, 196-198, 200, 205, 208, 212, 232-233, 236, 243-244, 250-251, 266, 270, 276-278, 289, 294, 296, 305, 315, 322, 355, 360-365, 384-385, 387, 389-393, 400, 426, 428-430, 433-438, 466, 486, 513, 516, 524, 532-535, 537-538, 541, 544, 547-552, 555, 557, 559-564, 566, 569-571, 577, 587, 611-614, 617-618, 620, 622, 624-625, 627-628, 634, 643, 646, 686, 695, 708-709, 730, 734, 743*
Qur'an burning, *266, 322, 428, 430, 433, 436*
Quraishy, Bashy, *576, 581, 583, 594-595, 744-745*
Quranic Concept of War, The, *69,*
133, 505, 512, 561, 577, 616, 732, 737
Quranic Literacy Institute of Chicago (QLI), *172*
Quraysh, *81, 368, 617-618, 707, 720*
Qurayshite, *96, 556*
Qurayzah, *126, 548*
Qurtubi, *47, 238, 533, 628, 686, 730*
Qutb, *14, 16, 65-66, 137-146, 150-151, 155, 162, 190-191, 196-198, 203, 205, 207, 324, 362, 377, 492, 515, 517-519, 531, 542, 561, 628-629, 631, 634, 643-644, 653, 686, 691, 716, 720-721, 733*

R

Rabat, *303-304, 321, 330, 586-589, 593, 668-669, 678-679, 742-743*
Rabat Plan of Action, *303, 330, 586-589, 593, 668-669, 678, 742-743*
rabbis, *135, 512, 521, 525, 540*
Rabia symbol, *358, 371*
racism, *261, 271-273, 275, 326-327, 330, 339, 489, 564, 577-579, 581, 584, 588, 594-595, 597-598, 660, 668, 670, 677, 739-740, 743*
radicalization, *197-198, 202, 273, 352, 371, 383, 395-396, 400, 403-404, 406, 455, 487, 604, 641, 645, 688, 711, 716*
radicalized, *57, 77, 102, 198, 344, 383, 396, 398, 405, 419, 442, 699*
radicals, *30-31, 77-78, 383, 449, 593, 603, 733*
Radio Vatikan, *535*
Radwan Ziadeh, *216*

Rafeeq Jaber, *169*
Rahma, *117, 602, 625*
Rahman, *38, 52, 56, 87, 103, 111,*
    173, 205, 207, 268, 322, 492,
    552, 601, 607, 609, 623, 639,
    674, 697
Rahmi Yaran, *563*
Raleigh, North Carolina, *360*
Ramadan, Tariq , *147, 149,*
    319-320, 520, 585, 630-631,
    639, 673, 700, 721, 740-741
Ramallah, *526-527*
RAND Corporation, *197*
ransom, *119, 267, 710*
ransoming, *118, 253, 439*
Raqqa, Syria, *381, 553*
Reauthorization Act, *353*
Red Pill, *14, 20, 66-67, 69, 71, 73,*
    75, 77, 79, 81, 83, 85, 87, 89, 91,
    93, 95, 97, 99, 101, 103, 105,
    107, 109, 111, 113, 115, 117, 119,
    121, 123, 125, 127, 129, 131, 133,
    135, 137, 139, 141, 143, 145, 147,
    384-385, 394, 616
Red Pill Briefings, *384*
Reeves, Keanu, *14*
Regensburg, *264, 266, 285,*
    287-288, 322, 426, 536, 567, 664
Regensburg speech, *266, 322, 426*
relevant evidence, *380, 464, 503,*
    712
relevant facts, *22, 257, 367, 382,*
    433, 465, 468, 479, 500, 504
Report of Investigation (ROI), *417,*
    423, 635, 705
reporting cycle, *347, 378*
Republican, *128, 332, 336-338,*
    358, 377, 681
res ipsa loquitur, *502-504*
res ipsa schema, *502*
res ipsa test, *504*
Reservations, *308, 669, 742*
Restatement, *80, 133, 136, 225*
Reston Investments, *183, 528*
Reuters, *217, 428, 432, 522,*
    604-606, 648-650, 656, 665,

675, 678-679, 692, 707-709,
    725-726
Reverend Bridgewater, *539*
Review of US Counterterrorism
    Policy: American Muslim
    Critique & Recommendations,
    247
Ribat, *396*
Rice, Susan, *329*
Richardson, Robin, *270, 274, 582*
Riddell, Kelly, *330*
rightwing extremism, *711*
rigorously authenticated, *120, 277,*
    610
Risala, the, *37, 105, 607, 622-623*
Rishmawi, George, *526*
Riyadh, Saudi Arabia, *533-534,*
    544, 569, 612, 616, 625, 628,
    657, 686, 704, 727-728, 730, 735
Rochester Interfaith Forum in
    Interfaith Dialogue, *542*
Rochester, New York, *527, 542*
Rome, *535, 563, 627*
Rooney, Thomas, *336, 682*
Roosevelt, Eleanor, *224*
Rossomando, John, *309, 624, 650*
ROTC cadet, *341*
Rule of Conjectural Choice, *478*
Rules of Engagement (ROE),
    408-415, 419, 421, 428,
    439-440, 635, 676, 703
Rules of War, *184, 307, 439, 626,*
    710
Run up to the Conquest of Istanbul
    Ottoman Tanzimat, *584*
Runnymede, *269-271, 273-275,*
    582, 660
Ruppersberger, Rep. Dutch, *337,*
    682
Rushdie, Salmon , *251*
Rushing, Josh, *510, 605, 654, 686,*
    693, 716-717

Index

S

S. Moinul Haq, *253, 657*

Sa'id Raja'i-Khorassani, *225*

SAAR Foundation, *183, 402, 528*

sabaya, *555, 568*

Sadaqat, *362*

Sadat, Anwar, *100, 621*

SAFA Trust, *183, 528*

Safi, Louay, *173, 182, 216, 514, 585, 639, 642, 720, 741*

Sahed, *419-420*

sahih, *39-40, 48, 83, 85, 88, 94, 104, 120, 125, 277, 361-362, 365, 533, 544-546, 548, 550, 570, 612, 618, 627-628, 686, 721, 723, 727-730, 734*

Sahih Al-Bukhari, *39, 48, 83, 85-86, 94, 102, 104-105, 107, 124-125, 127, 129, 178, 181, 361-362, 365, 386-387, 533, 544-550, 607, 610, 612, 618, 623, 627-628, 634, 679, 686, 723, 727-730, 734*

Sahih Muslim, *83, 277, 618, 721*

Sahih Sittah, *39*

Said, Edward, *268, 470-471*

Saidian, *595*

Salafi, *31, 52, 98, 139, 152, 213, 217, 282, 349, 613, 655, 675*

Salafist, *207, 613*

Salam Al-Marayati, *246, 324-326, 656, 676*

Salama Abdel Qawi, *603*

Salih bin 'Abd-al-'Aziz al-Shaykh, *59*

Salih Zaydan, *241*

Samsel, Michael, *539, 726*

San Diego, *388, 396*

Sarakhsi, *99*

Satanic Verses, The, *251, 287-290*

Saudi Arabia, *48, 62-63, 98, 119, 123, 125, 141, 150, 207, 215-216, 229, 246, 259, 275-276, 278, 314, 317, 322, 403, 533, 544,*

556, 560, 607, 612, 615, 621, 626-628, 639, 656, 661-664, 678-679, 686, 727-728, 730-731, 733, 740

Saudi Arabian, *124, 621*

Saudi Embassy, *320, 674*

Sayeed Abdul A'la Maududi, *190-192, 643-644*

Sayyaf, *18, 601, 674*

Sayyid Qutb, *14, 16, 65, 137-138, 141-142, 203, 324, 362, 377, 515, 517, 542, 561, 628-629, 643-644, 653, 691, 720-721, 733*

Schanz, Marc V., *416-418, 704-705*

Schmitz, Joseph E., *485, 487-488, 716*

scholarly consensus, *35-36, 41-46, 48, 51-54, 85, 87-88, 90, 96, 102, 130-131, 180, 214, 223, 270, 297, 609-614, 619, 727, 730, 732*

Schwartz, Stephen [aka Suleyman Ahmad], *98-99, 621, 691*

Schweitzer, William M., *541, 726*

scientism, *15, 270, 395, 453*

scripture, *96, 234, 243, 365, 381, 513, 522-523, 550, 553, 557, 563, 734*

Scriptures, *125-126, 196, 429, 523-524, 548, 550-551*

secret apparatus, *154-155*

secret cells, *154-155*

secular, *137, 194, 202, 204, 209, 214, 312, 337, 355, 367, 425, 492, 518, 525, 631, 633, 682*

secularism, *156, 160, 204, 312*

sefaria, *234*

Sepoy Mutiny, *425*

September 11, *11, 194, 202, 321-322, 325-326, 397, 440, 460*

servitude, *109, 156, 492, 540, 575*

settlement, *147, 174, 186-187, 519, 719*

sexual servitude, *540*

Shafi'i, *37, 44-45, 49, 84, 95, 97, 102-107, 119, 151, 234-235, 267, 281, 607-608, 610-611, 622-623,*

Index

679-680, 710
shahada, 215, 541, 614
Shahadah, 199
shaheed, 244, 246
shahid, 30, 392, 421, 442, 453,
    740-741
Shahidah, 177
Shamim Siddiqi, 131, 190-192,
    199, 396, 513, 644-645
shariah [also sharia], 14, 16, 18-19,
    26-29, 31-33, 37, 40-41, 44-46,
    48-49, 51, 54-56, 58, 60-63,
    66-67, 70, 75, 79, 84, 86, 88, 91,
    95-96, 98-100, 102, 108-109,
    112, 114, 117, 121, 125, 131,
    136-137, 141, 150, 152, 154, 157,
    176-177, 182-184, 194-195,
    203-205, 207-208, 212, 217,
    220, 223-224, 226-232,
    237-240, 242, 244-251,
    255-258, 265, 267-268, 270-271,
    273-274, 276-278, 288, 290,
    292, 294, 297, 299, 301-302,
    305, 307-308, 310, 312, 315-316,
    319-320, 324, 326, 331-333,
    339, 342, 345, 350, 354-355,
    359, 363-364, 366-367, 372,
    374, 379, 381, 385-387, 409,
    415-416, 420, 422, 427, 431,
    434-436, 439-441, 449,
    458-459, 465-467, 470, 479,
    481, 483, 485-486, 488-493,
    496, 503, 508-509, 514-517, 519,
    521, 529, 537, 540, 543, 547,
    550, 552-557, 560, 562, 568,
    574-577, 579-581, 584-585, 589,
    592, 595-596, 601, 608, 614,
    646, 650, 655, 674, 676, 680,
    689, 716, 736, 740, 745
shariah-compliant, 239
Shariyah, 193
Shaybani, 67, 78-80, 110, 557, 612,
    616-618, 621-624, 732, 737
Shaybani's Siyar, 67, 78, 110, 557,
    612, 616-618, 622-624, 732, 737
shaykh, 32, 47, 59, 110, 156, 159,

238, 323, 442, 607, 613, 624,
    626, 631-632, 649, 676, 708
Shaykh Abdalqadir al-Murabit,
    607
Sheik Muhammad al-Suhaybani,
    246, 656, 733
Sheikh Mansur Al-Rifa'i Ubeid, 241
Shia, 49, 151, 220, 282
Shifting the burden of proof, 712
Shukri Abu-Baker, 164, 688
Shura Council, 154, 161, 165,
    172-174, 337, 601, 637, 674
Siddiqi, 131, 172, 190-202, 396,
    513, 524, 628, 643-645, 660,
    719, 722
Side Events, 576, 593, 668,
    737-738, 742, 744
signpost along the road, 138
Sinai, 177, 371, 640
Sirah, 516-517
Sirat Rasul Allah, 132, 628, 657,
    675, 737
Sirte, 215
Sister Samah, 166, 169, 176
Six Canonical Collections, 39
slander, 22, 115, 118, 248-250,
    252-257, 259, 263-265,
    267-268, 271-273, 275, 283-284,
    290, 292, 294, 296-297, 299,
    301, 311, 313, 329-330, 332, 337,
    339, 343, 355, 381, 428, 431,
    434, 472, 537, 563, 574, 596,
    613, 656, 667, 736
slave, 51, 117, 546, 563, 569-571,
    728, 730, 734
slavery, 118, 253, 439, 735
Smith, Paul A., Jr., 219
soft-science, 21, 222, 344, 348,
    353, 383, 385, 446, 453-455,
    459, 461, 500-501, 503
soft-science theories, 459, 501
soldier of Allah, 20, 352-353, 384,
    394
Solis, Jorge, 168, 172, 636
Somalia, 246, 288, 560, 601, 674
Sotloff, Steven, 324, 676

Index

South Kordofan, *529, 723*
sovereignty belongs to God alone, *492*
sovereignty of God, *492, 518-519*
Soviet, *21, 142, 378, 449, 668, 742*
Soviet Union, *142, 668, 742*
Soykan, Taskin, *581-582, 584-585, 594, 740-741*
special agent, *23, 360, 508*
Special Agents, *15, 21, 23, 28, 344, 348, 356, 358, 372, 379, 381, 401, 405, 423, 495-496*
Special Operations Command, *263*
Speech at Cooper Institute, *510*
Speech at Edwardsville, Illinois, *11*
Speech upon the Rigght of Election, *575*
spiritual counselor, *397*
spiritual warfare, *84, 86, 135, 307, 511, 524*
Spoils of War, The, *555, 568*
spousal abuse, *279*
Springfield, Illinois, *507*
Staff Judge Advocate (SJA), *258, 417*
state actor, *136, 224, 275-276, 282, 308, 317, 321, 432*
state of abeyance, *118, 253, 439*
State terrorism, *231, 236-237*
Status of Captured Women in the Qur'an, The, *555, 569*
Stenton, Lt Col Sally, *417-419, 421, 423, 705-706*
Stern, Marilyn, *602, 676-677, 698*
stigmatization, *302, 306, 578, 581, 587, 590*
Stockton, Paul, *185, 207, 350-353, 367, 449, 498, 503*
strategic blindness, *350, 353, 452*
strategic communications, *66, 91, 128, 264, 599*
strategic disorientation, *526-527*
strategic incomprehension, *108, 482, 486, 504*
strategic nature of the oath, *487, 489, 494*

strategic unawareness, *452*
strategic victory, *333, 392, 462*
Stryker Brigade, *412, 419*
Stuart Mill, John, *443*
subversion, *12, 14, 60, 65, 134-135, 175, 182, 202, 219, 333, 339, 341, 350, 366, 376, 454, 465-466, 497, 511-512, 519, 541, 567, 599, 616*
subversive, *155, 336, 381, 492, 553*
subvert, *17, 28, 92, 109, 299*
subverting, *175, 189, 497*
Sudan, *114, 229, 370, 528-529, 540, 639, 723*
Sudanese, *370, 529, 723*
Sufi, *95, 152, 154, 349, 613*
suicide bomber, *30, 246, 392, 453, 695*
suicide bombing, *244-245, 391-392, 420*
Sulha Dania, *81*
Sun Tzu, *12, 184, 445, 487, 497, 499*
sunna, *36-37, 39, 49, 83, 121, 152, 159, 180, 226, 555, 609, 611, 613-614, 619, 621, 652, 654, 680, 731*
sunnah, *38, 44-45, 50-52, 54, 60, 80, 97, 141, 157, 612-613, 622, 727*
support and defend, *15-16, 55, 239, 258-259, 333, 348, 354, 357-358, 382, 426, 431, 436, 440, 468, 472, 482, 487, 489-491, 494-497, 499-501, 505, 509, 716*
Supreme Committee for Islamic Affairs, *241*
Surah of the sword, *122, 152, 390*
Surahs, *72-74, 77*
Swindler, Leonard, *520*
Switzerland, *183, 187, 274, 286, 318, 602, 643, 661, 673, 740-741*
synagogue, *525, 641*
Syria, *62-63, 114, 116, 132, 173, 183, 186, 197, 209, 216-217, 258,*

360, 381, 406, 480, 540, 548,
  551, 560, 601, 607, 615, 639,
  642, 645, 648-650, 674, 679
Syrian American Committee, 183
Syrian Muslim Brotherhood, 217,
  642-643
Syrian National Council, 183, 216
Syrian rebels, 216-217, 649-650,
  726

T

tafsir, 68-69, 71, 87, 111, 115, 137,
  178, 253, 493, 533-534, 538,
  548, 551, 563-564, 568-571,
  616-619, 624-627, 640, 653,
  657, 693, 704, 729-731, 734-736
Tafsir Al-Jalalayn, 68-69, 71, 533,
  563, 616-617, 734
Tafsir At-Tabari, 564
Tafsir Ibn Kathir, 68, 115, 253,
  493, 538, 548, 551, 569-571,
  616, 618-619, 624-627, 653,
  693, 704, 729-731, 736
Tafsir of Ibn Kathir, 69, 533-534,
  569, 616, 625, 640, 657, 730, 735
Taha Jaber al Alwani, 173-174,
  216, 515, 519-520, 608, 639,
  654, 657, 680, 719-720
Tahrir Square, 214-215, 629, 646
Taimoorazy, Juliana, 525-526
takfirism, 53, 100, 140-141, 144,
  240
talebearer, 249
talebearing, 248-249, 257, 268,
  272, 297
Taliban, 13, 16, 95, 193-194, 291,
  293, 346, 358, 396, 405, 409,
  413, 417, 419-420, 422, 425,
  427, 430, 432-433, 601, 674,
  691, 702-703, 705-706
Tangi Valley, 413
Tanzimat, 584-585
taqiyya, 178

taqlid, 43, 611, 619
tarabiya, 200
Tarbiyah Guide, 150, 631
Tawfik Hamid, 555
tawheed, 199, 535
Tayfour, Farouq, 217
Taymiya, 53, 613-614
Taymiyan, 53, 97
Tehran, 231-232, 236, 565,
  653-654, 662, 735, 740
Temple B'rith Kodesh, 527
Ten Commandments, 34
Ten Year Programme of Action,
  130, 275, 298
Ten-Year plan, 585
terminology, 40, 78, 86, 144, 166,
  185, 246-247, 268, 270, 342,
  345, 348-350, 513, 582, 586,
  594, 628, 643, 684, 717, 741
Terminology to Define the
  Terrorists: Recommendations
  from American Muslims, 185,
  348, 643, 684
Terms of Inclusion and Exclusion,
  86
Terror Identities Datamart
  Environment, 399
terror in the hearts, 561, 634
Test of Consequences, 306-308,
  321-322, 332
Texas, 20, 149, 217, 346, 370, 377,
  388, 560, 601, 603, 605-606,
  608, 635-638, 640-641, 654,
  670-672, 680, 685, 687-688,
  694, 719-720, 741-742
Thatcher, Margaret, 290
The 9/11 Commission Report, 65,
  342-343, 345, 684
The 11th Annual MAS-ICNA
  Convention, 374-375, 690
The 24/25 Rule, 229-231, 236,
  258, 273, 275-278, 297, 306,
  324, 358-359, 364, 366,
  515-516, 575, 580, 584, 595
The 27th Annual ICNA
  Convention, 398

The 438 Air Expeditionary Wing
  (AEW), *417*
The best, corrupted, become the
  worst, *443*
The Biggest DC Spy Scandal You
  Haven't Heard About, *338, 682*
The FBI's Guiding Principles:
  Touchstone Document on
  Training, *357, 685*
The Islamic Movement in Light of
  International Developments and
  the Gulf Crisis, *173*
The Order to Fight the People of
  Scriptures until They give the
  Jizyah, *550*
The West in the Eyes of the
  Egyptian Islamic Movement,
  155, 455, 631-633, 640, 711
threat analysis, *12-13, 16, 24, 30,
  41, 46, 63, 75, 84, 88, 91,
  107-108, 181, 184, 222, 239,
  336, 339, 348, 352, 354, 359,
  367, 370, 395, 405, 420,
  445-450, 455, 457-459, 463,
  468-469, 486, 489, 492,
  496-497, 499, 503-504, 599*
Threat Doctrine, *12, 29-30, 33, 46,
  55, 63, 69, 75, 78, 83, 88, 109,
  137, 144, 173, 184, 209, 239,
  336, 350, 359, 367, 378, 384,
  439, 445-450, 453-455,
  458-459, 466, 469, 483, 485,
  491, 496, 508*
Three Cups of Tea, *441, 710*
Three Parallel Lines, *154*
Tirana, Albania, *576*
Tirmidhi, *39, 570, 607, 634*
Tom Lantos Human Rights
  Commission of the House of
  Representatives, *183, 642*
Tontanji, *173, 639*
Topcuoglu, Umut, *274, 580, 582,
  738*
Toronto, *364*
Towards a Worldwide Strategy for
  Islamic Policy, *318*

Treasury, *343, 403, 700*
Treaty of Hudaybiyyah, *81-82,
  516-517, 524, 618*
Treaty of Tripoli, *210*
Triple Entente, *94*
Trodden Path, *529, 723*
Trotskyism, *190*
Truces, *79-81, 101, 427, 516,
  617-618, 707, 720*
Tsarnaev brothers, *400-401,
  404-406, 698*
Tsarnaev, Dzhokhar, *399, 698*
Tsarnaev, Tamerlan, *399, 698-699*
tumult or oppression, *238, 517,
  534*
Tunisia, *216, 601, 639, 649, 674*
Turkey, *99, 216, 223, 274-275,
  280, 287, 312, 554, 563-566,
  575-577, 579-581, 583-585, 590,
  594-597, 605, 627, 653, 670,
  682, 710, 734-741, 745-746*
Turkish ambassador, *273-274,
  578, 580, 583-584*
Turkish delegation, *274, 515,
  575-577, 580-583, 590, 737*
Turkish diplomatic mission, *577*
Turkish diplomats, *576*
Turkish Embassy, *595*
Twin Towers, *12*
typology, *414-415, 703*

U

U.S. Army, *232, 335, 346,
  383-385, 388, 391-392, 412,
  414, 418, 445, 453, 472, 478,
  559, 604, 623, 711, 713*
U.S. Army Command and General
  Staff College (CGSC), *472-473,
  478, 713*
U.S. Conference of Catholic
  Bishops (USCCB), *285, 287,
  540-541, 543-544, 556-558, 726,
  732*

Index

U.S. Council of Muslim Organizations (USCMO), *324, 676*

U.S. Embassy, *321-322, 325-326, 440, 677, 710*

U.S. Embassy in Cairo, *321, 325-326, 440, 677*

U.S. Forces, *237, 411-413, 418, 424, 426-428, 430, 436, 438, 440-441, 645*

U.S. State Department's Special Representative to the Muslim Communities, *350*

UBL [al-Qaeda], *397-398*

UK Action Committee on Islamic Affairs, *289*

Umar bin Al-Khattab, *111, 203, 552*

Umdat al-Salik, *37, 67, 607, 679, 719-720*

umma, *18-19, 26, 36, 42, 46, 223, 287*

ummah, *26-27, 49, 56, 136, 141-142, 149, 156-157, 193, 199, 202, 209, 212, 220-224, 230, 236, 240, 245, 247, 264-265, 268, 274, 278, 281-282, 287, 292, 295, 302, 322, 331, 333, 349, 492, 533, 586, 601, 606, 631, 645, 651, 655, 662, 674, 676, 704, 711*

UN Charter, *280, 591*

UN Human Rights Commission, *261, 302*

UN Human Rights Council, *310, 312, 329, 590*

unbelief, *39, 112, 137, 234, 277-278, 609-610, 614*

unbelief (kufr), *277-278, 609-610, 614*

unbeliever, *59, 613*

unbelievers, *56, 71, 103-104, 122, 126, 134-135, 360, 400, 524, 533, 535, 537-538, 557, 559, 561-562, 614, 666, 729, 732, 737*

unconstrained, *12, 445-447, 458, 496, 498*

Uncreated Word of Allah, *34, 133*

UNESCO, *578, 581, 590, 615, 652*

UNHRC, *312*

Uniformed Services University of the Health Sciences, *384*

Unindicted co-conspirator, *172, 178, 315, 369*

United Arab Emirates (UAE), *18-19, 24, 317, 320, 399, 601, 604, 673-674, 678, 697-698*

United Association for Studies and Research (UASR), *165-166, 168-169, 171, 173-174, 315, 402, 602, 637, 639-640, 671, 699*

United Nations Office of the High Commissioner on Human Rights (OHCHR), *303, 586-587, 589, 658-659, 663, 668-669, 742-743*

United States Army, *11, 599*

Universal Declaration of Human Rights, *224-225, 228, 248, 260, 574, 656*

unprofessional, *63, 465, 503*

unqualified apology, *279-280, 284, 286*

unrecoverable error, *62*

Unus, Iqbal, *528, 740-741*

USC, *495, 618, 663, 689, 716*

USCENTCOM, *599, 715*

Usool ul-Fiqh, *207*

usurpation, *356, 495*

usurped, *356, 492*

usurpers, *492*

usurps, *348, 518*

Utbiyya, *32*

Uthman, *240, 433*

Uzair, *557*

V

Van Creveld, Martin, *65, 616*

van Gogh, Theo, *294, 296, 666*

van Roessel, Birgit, *296*

Vatican, *23, 125, 222, 288, 532,*

534-537, 540-541, 543-544, 546,
554-556, 558-560, 564, 567,
664, 725-727, 731-736
Vaughn, Karen, 413
Verse of the sword, 122-123, 547,
729
Vienna, 580, 582, 725, 738, 741
violent extremism, 21, 207, 247,
312, 337, 344-348, 353-354,
356-359, 369-370, 376-378,
450-451, 457, 470, 487, 489,
495, 501, 503, 509, 605-606,
641, 670, 682, 684-685, 687,
716, 718
violent extremist, 150, 207, 332,
344, 346-347, 356, 448, 451,
482-483, 488-489
Virginia, 32, 119, 167, 173, 183,
201, 370, 380, 396, 399, 527,
639, 683, 689, 698
vocabulary, 145, 182, 191, 343,
356, 370, 497

W

Wahhab, 53, 98, 212, 610,
613-614, 621, 639
Wahhabi, 97-98, 141, 240
Wahhabism, 53, 97-98, 212
Wahhabist, 349
Walid bin Idris bin 'Abd Al-'Aziz
Al-Manisi, 58-60, 614-615
Walter Reed National Medical
Center, 20, 236, 384-385, 393,
617, 729
War Crimes, 193, 528, 606, 723
war of will, 134
War on Terror, 12-18, 25-31,
33-34, 46, 65-66, 69, 75, 77, 128,
134, 182-184, 190, 193, 195, 197,
200, 220, 246, 258-259, 280,
321, 335-336, 338-341, 343-345,
347-349, 353-354, 358, 367,
369-370, 382, 385, 394,

407-408, 416, 429, 436, 439,
441, 445-446, 449-452,
454-455, 457, 459, 461-462,
469-470, 472, 475, 477,
480-483, 485-488, 490-492,
496-498, 501, 503-504, 509
Wardak Province, 413
warfare against non-Muslims to
establish the religion, 40, 108,
550
Warsaw, 270, 274, 576, 593, 596,
660-661, 668, 737-739, 742-744,
746
Watt, W. Montgomery, 80, 97
Webb, Suhaib, 399, 405, 698, 701
Webster Commission, 387-388,
393-394, 694
Webster, Gordon, 527
West, Diana, 483, 705-706
Westergaard, Kurt, 283
Western civilization, 161, 168, 174,
187, 343, 458, 466, 481, 512,
527-528, 530, 637, 719
Westmoreland, Lynn, 336, 682
Wiktorowicz, Quintan, 239
Wilders, Geert, 266, 293-296,
298-299, 311, 666-667
Wile E. Coyote, 432
Williams, Rowan [Archbishop of
Canterbury], 429
Wilton Park, 591
Wolf, Rep. Frank, 338, 689
Woods, Tyrone, 329

Y

Yasir al-Bahrani, 117
Yaum al-Ghadab, 287
Ye'or, Bat, 222
Yemen, 360, 388, 396, 601, 621,
639, 674, 678
Yezidi, 555
Yonkman, Dave, 309
Yusuf al-Qaradawi, 18, 47, 110,

Index

*145, 152-153, 156-157, 159-160,
162-163, 183, 213-215, 217,
239-242, 244, 246-247,
281-282, 285, 287, 289, 320,
323, 330, 392, 398, 404-405,
520, 531, 556, 589, 612,
631-633, 639, 647-648, 650,
655, 673, 679, 700, 721, 724,
731, 743*
Yusuf Ali, *72, 93, 276, 362-363,
400, 559, 617, 620, 646, 686,
734*
Yusuf Islam [formerly Cat
Stevens], *289*
Yusuf Nada, *162, 187, 633, 643,
661, 673*

Z

Zafar, Shaarik, *350, 586, 684-685,
741*
zakat, *85, 103, 105, 132, 210,
362-366, 375, 547, 635, 686-687*
Zamzam, Ramy, *201*
Zawahiri, Ayman [also Eaman],
*66-67, 76-77, 141, 149, 151,
202-205, 207, 283, 322, 445,
645-646, 675*
Zayyad Hamdan, *173, 639*
Zia ul Haq, *69, 732*
Ziadeh, *216, 649*
Zionism, *546, 724, 729*
Zionists, *66, 76*
Zoroastrians, *132, 549, 572, 624,
627, 694*

Printed in Poland
by Amazon Fulfillment
Poland Sp. z o.o., Wrocław

22596924R10443